iG

A guide to IFRS

iGAAP 2016

A guide to IFRS reporting

VOLUME A
PART 1

Deloitte.

Published by Wolters Kluwer (UK) Ltd
145 London Road
Kingston upon Thames KT2 6SR
United Kingdom
Telephone +44 (0)844 561 8166
Facsimile +44 (0)208 247 2638
Email: cch@wolterskluwer.co.uk
Website: www.cch.co.uk

ISBN 978-1-78540-230-2

British Library Cataloguing-in-Publication Data

A catalogue record for this book is available from the British Library

Typeset by Innodata Inc., India.

Printed and bound by CPI Group (UK) Ltd, Croydon, CR0 4YY

Foreword

It is a pleasure once again to introduce *iGAAP*, Deloitte's guide to International Financial Reporting Standards. A significant enhancement in the content this year is the introduction of Volume D, an online volume containing disclosure examples drawn from a wide sample of IFRS reporters globally.

Although no major IFRSs have been issued since the release of our last edition, the past year has seen significant activity in many areas of financial reporting. In particular, many companies have started to prepare for the transition to two recently-completed Standards, IFRS 9 *Financial Instruments* and IFRS 15 *Revenue from Contracts with Customers*. Following an amendment to IFRS 15, both Standards are now effective from 1 January 2018 – which sounds a long way off but will be upon us before we know it. Both Standards are important and both will present significant implementation challenges.

Revenue is one of the most significant measures used by investors and the implementation of IFRS 15 will be a major exercise for many. IFRS 15 should result in a consistent measure of revenue irrespective of industry or jurisdiction. It provides more guidance than previous Standards and requires an appropriate use of professional judgement. A joint IASB/FASB Transition Resource Group (TRG), bringing together preparers, auditors, standard-setters and others, has been working to identify, evaluate and resolve implementation issues so as to ease transition and ensure consistent application.

Financial services entities are keenly focused on the implementation of IFRS 9, but this Standard should not be overlooked by others. The rules on impairment apply to all financial assets, including trade accounts and investments. IFRS 9 allows for the consideration of a broader range of information in determining credit loss estimates, and requires recognition of lifetime expected credit losses for those loans that have experienced a significant increase in credit risk. Here, too, the IASB has established the Impairment Transition Resource Group (ITG), whose remit is similar to the TRG established for IFRS 15.

Both IFRS 9 and IFRS 15 will require management and audit committees to consider the transition to the new Standards holistically, because both will require changes to information systems, business processes, compensation and other contractual arrangements. IFRS 15 provides for either a fully retrospective or a modified retrospective transition, and that choice will require careful evaluation. The transition to IFRS 9 will also need careful planning, particularly in deciding whether to continue to apply IAS 39 to hedging relationships. Presentation and disclosure in the financial statements will also be critical for both IFRSs.

Foreword

Looking forward, two significant projects are nearing completion: *Leases* and *Insurance Contracts*. For the leases Standard, much hinges on the definition of a lease, which is still being refined as we go to press. All leases, as defined and subject to the short-term lease exception, will be on-balance sheet, with the accounting being similar to IAS 17's finance lease requirements. Lessor accounting will not change significantly from that in IAS 17.

Having made significant progress, the IASB expects to issue the insurance Standard late in 2016. The interaction between this IFRS and IFRS 9, in particular how to manage the gap between the effective dates of the two Standards, is a current concern. The IASB has recently issued proposals to mitigate this issue (including a possible deferral of the effective date of IFRS 9 for particular entities), with any amendment to IFRS 9 expected in mid-2016.

In financial reporting more generally, the IASB's Disclosure Initiative continues to bear fruit, with a draft Practice Statement on Materiality released in October 2015 and a major discussion paper on the Principles of Disclosure expected in early 2016.

Our aim in writing iGAAP is to provide you with a clear, practical guide to applying IFRSs, helping you get to grips with the issues and complexities that arise. The interpretative guidance provided draws on the wealth of experience of IFRS specialists and clients from around the globe. Our thanks to them for their generous and valuable input.

Veronica Poole

Global IFRS Leader
Deloitte

Principal authors

Veronica Poole

Veronica is a Senior Accounting Technical Partner at Deloitte. She is the UK National Head of Accounting and Corporate Reporting and the firm's Global IFRS Leader. Veronica is a member of the UK Accounting Council, the Financial Reporting Advisory Board to HM Treasury, CBI Companies Committee and the Hundred Group Financial Reporting Committee. She also chairs the Financial Reporting Faculty Advisory Board at the ICAEW.

Andrew Spooner

Andrew is the lead partner on IFRS financial instruments globally across Deloitte. He is a partner of the UK firm advising UK and multinational clients, with particular focus on financial services. Andrew is also a member of the European Securities and Markets Authority's Consultative Working Group for the Corporate Reporting Standing Committee, the Technical Expert Group of the European Financial Reporting Advisory Group and the Financial Reporting Faculty Board of the ICAEW.

Phil Barden

Phil is a partner in Deloitte's UK IFRS Centre of Excellence, assisting UK and multinational clients on a wide range of financial reporting issues. He is a member of the IASB/FASB Joint Transition Resource Group for Revenue Recognition and leads Deloitte's global Expert Advisory Panel on revenue recognition. Phil chairs the Financial Reporting Editorial Board of the ICAEW, and is a member of the Institute's Financial Reporting Committee.

Kush Patel

Kush is a partner in Deloitte's UK IFRS Centre of Excellence and specialises in the accounting for financial instruments. He advises financial and non-financial corporates on complex transactions and emerging accounting issues. He is a member of the ICAEW Financial Instruments Working Group and Deloitte's global Expert Advisory Panel on financial instruments.

Ken Rigelsford

Ken is the Director responsible for UK statutory reporting in Deloitte's UK technical department. He has been closely involved in the development of the new UK GAAP and is a member of the FRC's UK GAAP Technical Advisory Group. Ken is a member of the Financial Reporting, Business Law and Company Law Committees of the ICAEW. He chairs the Distributable Profits Working Party (a joint working party of the ICAEW and the ICAS) and is regarded as one of the leading experts in this field.

Norma Hall

Norma Hall is the team leader of the author team. She is a Director in Deloitte's IFRS Global Office and Editor of the firm's International Accounting Manual. She was formerly a partner in Deloitte's Hong Kong office, with extensive experience of the application of IFRSs to commercial transactions.

Amy Haworth

Amy Haworth is the team leader for UK GAAP volumes. She is a member of the UK IFRS Centre of Excellence and of Deloitte's global Expert Advisory Panel on revenue recognition.

Contributors

The authors would like to express their thanks to Deloitte's Global IFRS Leadership Team and the members of the UK technical department, with particular appreciation to the following for their contributions.

Kristin Bauer (USA)

Hanna Ben Fekih (France)

Jens Berger (Germany)

Mark Bolton (USA)

Robert Carroll (UK)

Evangelina Chatzitsakou (UK)

Chris Chiriatti (USA)

Elizabeth Chrispin (UK)

Brandon Coleman (USA)

Svetlana Cox (UK)

Anna Crawford (Australia)

Mark Crowley (USA)

Chris Cryderman (USA)

Kerry Danyluk (Canada)

Eric Dard (France)

Trevor Derwin (South Africa)

Shivanthi Edwards (USA)

Trevor Farber (USA)

Colin Fleming (UK)

Candy Fong (China)

Adrian Geisel (Germany)

Claudio Giaimo (Argentina)

Richard Gillin (UK)

Tracey Gordon (UK)

Clair Grindley (Canada)

Markus Hahn (UK)

Karen Higgins (Canada)

Tom Hopkins (UK)

Shinya Iwasaki (Japan)

Ryszarda Kingston (UK)

Tim Kolber (USA)

Frank Kroesch (USA)

Nadine Kusche (UK)

Christine Lallouette (France)

An Lam (Canada)

Elise Lambert (USA)

Sarah McWhirter (UK)

Miguel Millan (Mexico)

Jane Miller (Chile)

Jo Mithen (UK)

Robert Morris (USA)

Anthony Mosco (USA)

Rogerio Mota (Brazil)

Shan Nemeth (USA)

Magnus Orrell (USA)

Martine Pelletier (France)

Disna Perera (UK)

Sean Prince (USA)

Linda Riedel (UK)

Laurence Rivat (France)

Estela Rodenstein (UK)

James Rogers (UK)

Helen Shaw (UK)

Melissa Sim (Australia)

Amanda Swaffield (UK)

Nura Taef (Canada)

Stephen Taylor (China)

Alan Texeira (UK)

Jeffrey Thomas (USA)

Vicki Tibbitts (UK)

Robert Uhl (USA)

Maryse Vendette (Canada)

Henri Venter (Australia)

Debra Wan (Australia)

Peter Westaway (UK)

Kenichi Yoshimura (Japan)

Glossary of terms and abbreviations

AC	Acquiring company
AFS	Available-for-sale
ARC	The Accounting Regulatory Committee which advises the European Commission on endorsement of IFRSs
ASC	Accounting Standards Codification, issued by the FASB
CGU	Cash-generating unit
Commission	European Commission
CU	Currency Unit
EBT	Employee benefit trust
EC	European Commission
ED	Exposure draft
EEA	European Economic Area (i.e. the EU plus Norway, Iceland and Liechtenstein)
EFRAG	The European Financial Reporting Advisory Group, a private sector body which makes recommendations to the European Commission's Accounting Regulatory Committee
EIR	Effective interest rate
EPS	Earnings per share
ESOP	Employee share ownership plan
ESMA	European Securities and Markets Authority
EU	European Union
FASB	Financial Accounting Standards Board (USA)
FIFO	First in, first out
FTSE 100	Financial Times Stock Exchange top 100 companies (share index)
FVTOCI	Fair value through other comprehensive income
FVTPL	Fair value through profit or loss
GAAP	Generally accepted accounting practice
HTM	Held-to-maturity
IAS	International Accounting Standard
IASB	International Accounting Standards Board
IASC	International Accounting Standards Committee, predecessor to the IASB

IFRIC	The former International Financial Reporting Interpretations Committee of the IASB, now renamed the IFRS Interpretations Committee (also refers to individual interpretations issued by the Committee)
IFRS	International Financial Reporting Standard
IIRC	International Integrated Reporting Council
IIRF	International Integrated Reporting Framework issued by the IIRC
Individual financial statements	See the guidance at **2.2.2** in **chapter A4**
IOSCO	International Organization of Securities Commissions
IRR	Internal rate of return
JFSA	Financial Services Agency of Japan
JV	Joint venture
LIBOR	London Inter-Bank Offer Rate
LIFO	Last in, first out
LTIP	Long-term incentive plan
MFR	Minimum funding requirement
MOU	Memorandum of Understanding
NCI	Non-controlling interest
NRV	Net realisable value
OCI	Other comprehensive income
ROI	Return on investment
RPI	Retail price index
SAC	Standards Advisory Council
SAYE	Save as you earn
SEC	Securities and Exchange Commission (USA)
Separate financial statements	See the definition and explanations in **section 3** of **chapter A29**
SIC	Standing Interpretations Committee, predecessor to IFRIC (also refers to individual interpretations issued by SIC)
SME(s)	Small and medium-sized entity(ies)
SPE	Special purpose entity
TC	Target company
TRG	IASB/FASB Joint Transition Resource Group for Revenue Recognition
TSR	Total shareholder return
VAT	Value added tax
WEEE	Waste electrical and electronic equipment
WE&EE Directive	The European Union's Directive on Waste Electrical and Electronic Equipment

Table of Contents

Volume A, Part 1

Volume A, Part 2

Introduction

1 Scope and objectives of this manual

The objective of this manual is to introduce and explain the financial reporting requirements under International Financial Reporting Standards (IFRSs). As explained in **section 3**, IFRSs are defined to include the numbered IFRSs issued by the International Accounting Standards Board (IASB), International Accounting Standards (IASs) originally issued by its predecessor body (as amended) and approved Interpretations of those Standards. The expression is used in this broad sense in this manual unless the context requires otherwise.

2 Structure of this manual

The structure of this manual is as follows:

- **chapter A1** provides background information on the IASB and on the application of IFRSs globally;

- **chapters A2** to **A42** and **appendices A1** to **A3** deal with the framework and Standards issued by the IASB and Interpretations of those Standards, and **appendix A4** deals with the International Financial Reporting Standard for Small and Medium-sized Entities (IFRS for SMEs);

- **Volume B** deals with accounting for financial instruments for entities that have adopted IFRS 9 *Financial Instruments*. It covers IAS 32 *Financial Instruments: Presentation*, IFRS 7 *Financial Instruments: Disclosures*, IFRS 13 *Fair Value Measurement* and IFRS 9; and

- **Volume C** deals with accounting for financial instruments for entities that have not yet adopted IFRS 9. It covers IAS 32, IAS 39 *Financial Instruments: Recognition and Measurement*, IFRS 13 and IFRS 7.

Transition requirements are discussed for Standards that have become effective for periods beginning after 1 January 2014. In addition, when IFRS 1 *First-time Adoption of International Financial Reporting Standards* requires compliance with the transition requirements in Standards, the relevant requirements are explained.

The format of the manual has been devised to give guidance on reporting and accounting matters as clearly as possible. Text is highlighted differently to reflect whether it represents official or interpretative material. Accordingly:

- requirements drawn from official IASB material are shown in unshaded text; and

> - interpretative material supplementing the IASB guidance is highlighted by grey shading.

Except when the context requires otherwise, interpretative examples follow the convention often adopted by the IASB of referring to years as 20X1, 20X2 etc. rather than specifying real calendar years. In such examples, although 20X3 follows 20X2, no further significance attaches to the final digit. Thus, subject to context, 20X1 might represent 2015 or any other relevant year.

3 References and abbreviations used

International Financial Reporting Standards are defined in IAS 1 *Presentation of Financial Statements* as Standards and Interpretations adopted by the IASB. They comprise:

- International Financial Reporting Standards;
- International Accounting Standards;
- IFRIC Interpretations; and
- SIC Interpretations.

These are referred to collectively in this manual as 'IFRSs'.

References to International Financial Reporting Standards, International Accounting Standards, IFRIC Interpretations and SIC Interpretations are indicated as follows:

IFRS 2:19	Paragraph 19 of IFRS 2
IFRIC 1:2	Paragraph 2 of IFRIC Interpretation 1
SIC-27:3	Paragraph 3 of SIC Interpretation 27

Unless otherwise stated, all references to 'IFRS 9' are to IFRS 9 as issued in 2014.

References to material accompanying International Financial Reporting Standards, International Accounting Standards, IFRIC Interpretations and SIC Interpretations are indicated as follows:

IAS 39:AG4	Paragraph AG4 of the application guidance to IAS 39
IFRS 2:B18	Paragraph B18 of Appendix B to IFRS 2
IFRIC 13:BC21	Paragraph BC21 of the Basis for Conclusions on IFRIC 13

IFRS 4:IG3	Paragraph IG3 of the guidance on implementing IFRS 4
IAS 32:IE32	Paragraph IE32 of the illustrative examples accompanying IAS 32
CF:OB10	Paragraph OB10 of the *Conceptual Framework for Financial Reporting*
MC:13	Paragraph 13 of the IFRS Practice Statement *Management Commentary*

References to the *International Integrated Reporting Framework* published by the International Integrated Reporting Council are indicated as follows.

| IIRF:1.19 | Paragraph 19 of section 1 of the *International Integrated Reporting Framework* |

A glossary of abbreviations used in the text is presented at the front of this manual.

4 Contents of this edition

This manual deals comprehensively with those Standards issued by the IASB up to 1 September 2015 that apply for periods beginning in 2014 and later.

5 Specialised industries

This manual does not deal with all of the requirements and issues that will affect entities in specialised industries, particularly banking and insurance. In particular, although **Volumes B** and **C** provide an overview of the requirements of IAS 32 *Financial Instruments: Presentation*, IAS 39 *Financial Instruments: Recognition and Measurement*, IFRS 7 *Financial Instruments: Disclosures* and IFRS 9 *Financial Instruments*, they do not address some of the more complex issues (particularly in the area of hedging) that may affect banks and similar financial institutions.

The specialised issues facing insurance companies are beyond the scope of this manual but the requirements of IFRS 4 *Insurance Contracts* are discussed in **chapter A39**. Those requirements are of wider application, because they specify how all entities should determine whether certain arrangements are within the scope of IFRS 4 or of other Standards such as IAS 39 or IFRS 9.

A1 About International Financial Reporting Standards

Contents

Contents

1 Introduction

This chapter provides a brief introduction to the IFRS reporting regime.

2 History

2.1 IASC (1973 – 2000)

The International Accounting Standards Committee (IASC) was established in 1973, through an agreement made by professional accountancy bodies from Australia, Canada, France, Germany, Japan, Mexico, the Netherlands, the United Kingdom and Ireland, and the United States of America. Its goal was to develop, in the public interest, accounting standards that would be accepted all over the world to improve financial reporting. By 2000, sponsorship of the IASC had grown to include all of the professional accountancy bodies that were members of the International Federation of Accountants (IFAC) – 152 organisations from 112 countries. However, even after nearly 30 years of effort, few countries had actually adopted the IASC's standards even for listed companies.

Until 2001, accounting standards were set by a part-time, volunteer IASC Board that, in its later years, had 13 country members and three additional organisational members. The individuals came from a wide range of backgrounds – accounting practice, business (particularly multinational businesses), financial analysis, accounting education and national accounting standard-setting. The Board also had a number of observer members (including representatives of the International Organization of Securities Commissions (IOSCO), the US Financial Accounting Standards Board and the European Commission) who participated in the debate but did not vote.

From 1997, the IASC also had an interpretative body, the Standing Interpretations Committee (SIC), formed for the purpose of developing interpretations of International Accounting Standards (IASs) for final approval by the IASC.

2.2 IASB

In 1997, the IASC concluded that, to continue to perform its role effectively, it should find a way to bring about convergence between national accounting standards and practices and to develop high quality global accounting standards. To achieve that objective, the organisation was restructured, replacing the part-time IASC with a full-time International Accounting Standards Board (IASB), with strengthened due process, greater resources, complete technical independence and other structural changes.

The IASC Foundation constitution took effect on 1 July 2000. On 1 April 2001, the IASB assumed accounting standard-setting responsibilities. On 1 July 2010, the IASC Foundation was re-named the IFRS Foundation.

3   IASB structure

3.1   IASB structure – general

The standard-setting body within the IFRS Foundation is the IASB (the Board), which has sole responsibility for establishing International Financial Reporting Standards (IFRSs). Other components of the structure are the Trustees of the IFRS Foundation, a Monitoring Board of capital market regulatory authorities that oversees the Foundation, the IFRS Interpretations Committee (the Interpretations Committee) the IFRS Advisory Council (the Advisory Council) and the Accounting Standards Advisory Forum (the ASAF).

The overall structure is illustrated below.

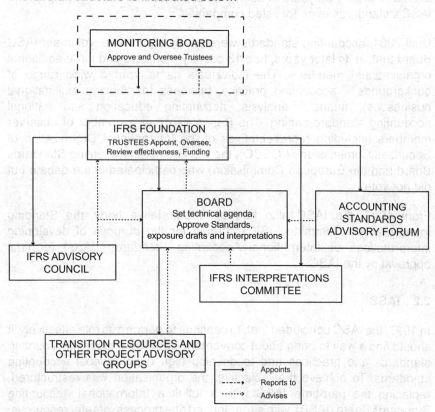

3.2   Monitoring Board

The Monitoring Board provides a mechanism for formal interaction between capital markets authorities responsible for the form and content of financial reporting and the IFRS Foundation. In particular, it assures public accountability of the IFRS Foundation through a formal reporting line from the IFRS Foundation Trustees to the Monitoring Board.

The responsibilities of the Monitoring Board include:

- participating in the process for appointing Trustees and approving the appointment of Trustees according to the guidelines set out in the IFRS Foundation constitution;

- reviewing the adequacy and appropriateness of Trustee arrangements for financing the IASB;

- reviewing the Trustees' oversight of the IASB's standard-setting process, in particular with respect to its due process arrangements;

- conferring with the Trustees regarding their responsibilities, particularly in relation to the regulatory, legal and policy developments that are pertinent to the IFRS Foundation's oversight of the IASB; and

- referring matters of broad public interest related to financial reporting to the IASB through the IFRS Foundation.

As at 1 September 2015, the members of the Monitoring Board are representatives of both the Board and the Growth and Emerging Markets Committee of the International Organization of Securities Commissions (IOSCO), the European Commission (EC), the Financial Services Agency of Japan (JFSA), the US Securities and Exchange Commission (SEC), the Brazilian Securities Commission (CVM), and the Financial Services Commission of Korea (FSC). The Basel Committee on Banking Supervision participates in the Monitoring Board as an observer.

The Monitoring Board may appoint up to a further two members. Prospective members must be a capital markets authority responsible for setting the form and content of financial reporting in its jurisdiction, and meet specified requirements about the use of IFRSs in that jurisdiction and continuing participation in the IFRS Foundation's funding arrangements.

The membership of the Monitoring Board is reviewed every three years based on the agreed membership criteria, with the next review expected in 2016.

3.3 IFRS Foundation

The governance of the IFRS Foundation and oversight of the IASB rests with 22 Trustees. Their geographical mix is: six Trustees from the Asia/ Oceania region; six from Europe; six from North America; and four from any area (subject to maintaining overall geographical balance). The IFRS Foundation's constitution requires an appropriate balance of professional backgrounds, including auditors, preparers, users, academics, and other officials serving the public interest.

Between 2008 and 2012, the Trustees undertook a series of reviews of the structure, constitution and governance of the IFRS Foundation. Changes were made with a view to strengthening all aspects of the IFRS Foundation's institutional structures to ensure that it acts as a truly global accounting standard setter, independent yet accountable to public authorities (via the Monitoring Board). The latest review of the organisational structure and effectiveness was initiated in July 2015.

3.4   International Accounting Standards Board

The IASB is the body responsible for setting and maintaining IFRSs.

The Board has up to 16 members (of whom up to three may serve 'part-time' although, at the time of writing, all members serve on a full-time basis). The Board's principal responsibilities are to:

*   develop, issue and maintain IFRSs in accordance with its established due process; and

*   approve Interpretations developed by the IFRS Interpretations Committee.

The key qualification for Board membership is professional competence and practical experience. The group is required to represent the best available combination of technical expertise and diversity of international business and market experience. To achieve a balance of perspectives and experience, Board members are required to have an appropriate mix of recent practical experience among auditors, preparers, users and academics.

The Board is required to be internationally diverse: there will normally be four members from the Asia/Oceania region; four from Europe; four from North America; one each from Africa and South America; and two appointed from any area (subject to maintaining overall geographical balance). As at 1 September 2015, there are 14 members. The IFRS Foundation does not intend to fill the vacancies on the Board until the strategic and operating review initiated in 2015 is completed.

3.5   IFRS Advisory Council

The Advisory Council is the formal advisory body to the IASB and the IFRS Foundation Trustees, and it provides a forum for a wide range of representatives from user groups, preparers, financial analysts, academics, auditors, regulators, professional accounting bodies and investor groups that are affected by and interested in the IASB's work. The Advisory Council provides advice on a wide range of issues, including:

*   input on the IASB's technical agenda;

*   project priorities;

- issues related to the application and implementation of IFRSs that arise on projects; and
- possible benefits and costs of particular proposals.

3.6 IFRS Interpretations Committee

The IFRS Interpretations Committee is the interpretive body of the IASB.

The Interpretations Committee (previously referred to as the 'IFRIC') has 14 voting members appointed by the Trustees for terms of three years. Like the IASB, the Interpretations Committee comprises the best available combination of technical expertise and diversity of international business and market experience, but with the added requirement that members be experienced in the practical application of IFRSs and analysis of financial statements prepared in accordance with IFRSs. The Interpretations Committee's responsibilities are:

- to assist the IASB in improving financial reporting through timely identification, discussion and resolution of financial reporting issues in accordance with established due process, and to undertake other tasks at the request of the Board (including responsibility for the Annual Improvements process); and
- to report to the Board and obtain Board approval for final Interpretations.

These responsibilities are reflected in a range of possible actions available to the Interpretations Committee to respond to issues referred to it:

- enhancing mandatory requirements (new or revised requirements within IFRSs); and
- providing non-mandatory guidance.

The mandatory requirements can include:

- IFRIC Interpretations; and
- amendments to Standards through:
  - the Annual Improvements process; or
  - proposals to the IASB for targeted, narrow-scope amendments that are beyond the scope of the Annual Improvements process. These might include proposals for additional application guidance.

Non-mandatory solutions that the Interpretations Committee can use to address issues include:

- proposals for additional illustrative examples;
- explanations via 'agenda decisions'; and
- referral to the IFRS Education Initiative.

3.7   Accounting Standards Advisory Forum

The Accounting Standards Advisory Forum (ASAF) is a group of national standard-setters and regional bodies involved with accounting standard-setting.

The ASAF was established in 2013 and it provides a forum in which members can contribute constructively towards achieving the IASB's goal of developing globally accepted high quality accounting standards. In particular, the ASAF:

- supports the IFRS Foundation in its strategic objectives, and contributes towards the development, in the public interest, of a single set of high quality understandable, enforceable and globally accepted financial reporting standards;

- formalises and streamlines the IASB's collective engagement with the global community of national standard-setters and regional bodies as it develops IFRSs;

- ensures that a broad range of national and regional input on major technical issues related to the IASB's standard-setting activities is discussed and considered; and

- facilitates effective technical discussions on standard-setting issues and other issues that have major implications for the IASB's work with representatives at a high level of professional capability and with a good knowledge of their jurisdictions/regions.

The ASAF comprises twelve non-voting members, represented by twelve individuals, plus either the IASB Chair or Vice-Chair, who acts as the Chair of the ASAF. The twelve members are from the following geographical regions: one member from Africa; three members from the Americas (North and South); three members from the Asia-Oceania region; three members from Europe (including non-EU); and two members appointed from any area of the world at large (subject to maintaining an overall geographical balance).

4   Use of IFRSs around the world

4.1   Use of IFRSs around the world – general

Sections 4.2 to **4.5** provide a brief review of IFRS application on a regional basis. IFRSs are used by listed entities in over 120 countries, and by unlisted entities in over 90 countries. The IFRS Foundation has compiled detailed information on the use of IFRSs around the world. Information on nearly 140 countries is available at *www.ifrs.org*. In addition, a detailed country-by-country list of the status of adoption of IFRSs for most countries is available at *www.iasplus.com*.

Each jurisdiction has its own mechanism for incorporating IFRSs into its financial reporting system.

4.2   Use of IFRSs in Europe

4.2.1   *Use of IFRSs in Europe – general*

Since 2005, European Union (EU) and European Economic Area (EEA) companies listed on a regulated market have been required to follow IFRSs in their consolidated financial statements. The IFRS requirement applies not only in the 28 EU countries but also in the three EEA countries. Most large companies in Switzerland (not an EU or EEA member) already used IFRSs prior to 2005.

For the purpose of filings by non-EU companies listed on an EU-regulated market, the European Commission (EC) has designated the GAAPs of the United States, Japan, China, South Korea and India to be equivalent to IFRSs as adopted by the EU. Companies from other countries must use either IFRSs as adopted by the EU or IFRSs as adopted by the IASB.

EU Member States may also extend the IFRS requirement to non-listed companies and to separate (i.e. 'company-only') financial statements. Nearly all Member States permit some or all non-listed companies to use IFRSs in their consolidated statements and the majority permit it in separate financial statements.

4.2.2   *Endorsement of IFRSs for use in Europe*

IFRSs must be individually endorsed for use in Europe. The endorsement process involves the following steps:

- the EU translates the IFRSs into all European languages;
- the private-sector European Financial Reporting Advisory Group (EFRAG) gives its endorsement advice to the EC, having followed its own due process for such advice;
- the EC's Accounting Regulatory Committee makes an endorsement recommendation; and
- the EC submits the endorsement proposal to the European Parliament and to the 28-member Council of the EU. Both must not oppose (or, in specified circumstances, approve) endorsement within three months, otherwise the proposal is sent back to the EC for further consideration.

The process allows for amending the IASB version of IFRSs. Currently, only one such amendment ('carve-out') exists, which allows the use of fair value hedge accounting for interest rate hedges of banks' core deposits on a portfolio basis.

In 2014, various reforms were implemented to reflect the recommendations of the Maystadt Review of the governance of EU bodies in the field of financial reporting and accounting. However, the fundamental nature of the endorsement procedures was retained.

4.3 Use of IFRSs in the Americas

4.3.1 Use of IFRSs in the United States

4.3.1.1 IFRS-US GAAP convergence

Since 2002, the IASB and the US Financial Accounting Standards Board (FASB) have been working together to achieve convergence of IFRSs and US GAAP. As part of the Norwalk agreement, the boards issued a Memorandum of Understanding (MOU) formalising their commitment to:

- making their existing financial reporting standards fully compatible as soon as practicable; and

- co-ordinating their future work programmes to ensure that, once achieved, compatibility is maintained.

In September 2008, an updated MOU was published, which set out priorities and milestones to be achieved on major joint projects. IFRS 15 *Revenue from Contracts with Customers*, and the equivalent US Accounting Standards Codification Update ASC606c, were issued in May 2014. This is likely to be last jointly-developed Standard under the MOU.

4.3.1.2 SEC recognition of IFRSs

Of the approximately 12,000 companies whose securities are registered with the US Securities and Exchange Commission (SEC), about 950 are non-US companies. Prior to November 2007, if these foreign private issuers submitted IFRS or local GAAP financial statements rather than US GAAP, a reconciliation of net income and net assets to US GAAP was required.

Since November 2007, the SEC has permitted foreign private issuers to submit financial statements using IFRSs as issued by the IASB without having to include a reconciliation to US GAAP.

4.3.1.3 Recent regulatory developments

The SEC has explored whether and, if so, how to incorporate IFRSs into the financial reporting system for US domestic issuers. The SEC issued several consultation documents, and, in July 2012, issued a final staff report *Work Plan for the Consideration of Incorporating International Financial Reporting Standards into the Financial Reporting System for U.S. Issuers*. The report did not include a recommendation to the Commission. At the time of writing, the SEC has not signalled when it might make a policy decision about whether (and, if so, when and how) IFRSs should be incorporated into the US financial reporting system.

4.3.2   Use of IFRSs in Canada

Canada adopted IFRSs for most 'publicly accountable enterprises' for financial years beginning on or after 1 January 2011.

Publicly accountable enterprises are entities, other than not-for-profit organisations, that have issued, or are in the process of issuing, debt or equity instruments that are, or will be, outstanding and traded in a public market or hold assets in a fiduciary capacity for a broad group of outsiders as one of their primary businesses.

Mandatory adoption of IFRSs was deferred for entities with rate-regulated activities until 1 January 2015, pending the development of IFRS 14. Not-for-profit entities, public sector entities, pension plans and segregated accounts of life insurance enterprises are not required to adopt IFRSs.

4.3.3   Use of IFRSs elsewhere in the Americas

Nearly all countries in South America require or permit IFRSs as the basis for preparing financial statements (or are in the process of introducing such requirements).

- Argentina has adopted IFRSs for all companies (except banks and insurance companies which continue to apply domestic requirements). In March 2014, the Argentinian Central Bank announced that it will converge the accounting standards for banks with IFRSs and that the new standards will apply from 2018.

- Colombia has adopted IFRSs for publicly traded entities and public interest entities effective from 2015.

- Mexico has adopted IFRSs for all listed entities other than banks and insurance companies which apply Mexican Financial Reporting Standards (MFRSs). A convergence project is underway to eliminate differences between MFRSs and IFRSs.

- Venezuela does not use IFRSs as issued by the IASB. It has adopted the 2008 version of IFRSs with a modification to require price-level adjusted financial statements when the rate of inflation is 10 per cent or more, even if the hyperinflation indication of 100 per cent over three years in IAS 29 *Financial Reporting in Hyperinflationary Economies* is not met.

- IFRSs are already required in a number of other Latin American and Caribbean countries.

4.4   Use of IFRSs in Asia-Pacific

4.4.1   Use of IFRSs in Japan

Listed companies in Japan may use Japanese GAAP, US GAAP or IFRSs in their consolidated financial statements. The number of IFRS reporters, and the relative importance of IFRSs in capital markets, have been increasing in Japan and this trend is expected to continue.

The Financial Services Agency (Japan) operates a process called 'designation' to endorse IFRSs for use in Japan. At the time of writing (July 2015), all IFRSs issued by the IASB up to June 2015 (including IFRIC Interpretations) have been designated for use in Japan.

The IFRS Foundation has an office in Tokyo for enhanced liaison in the Asia-Oceania region. The Tokyo office represents the Foundation's commitment to deepen co-operation across the Asia-Oceania region and allows for expanded opportunities for direct and timely contact for the Foundation and its stakeholders in the region.

4.4.2   Use of IFRSs elsewhere in Asia-Pacific

Other Asia-Pacific jurisdictions are taking a variety of approaches toward convergence of GAAP for domestic companies with IFRSs. For example:

- Australia follows IFRSs as issued by the IASB, without modification, for for-profit companies;

- Hong Kong listed companies use either HKFRSs (identical to IFRSs) or IFRSs as issued by the IASB. Chinese companies listed on the Hong Kong Stock Exchange use either IFRSs as issued by the IASB, HKFRSs or Chinese Accounting Standards;

- Korea uses IFRSs as issued by the IASB for all listed companies and all financial institutions, regardless of whether their securities are traded publicly;

- New Zealand has adopted IFRS equivalent standards for all for-profit entities that have public accountability and for all large for-profit public sector entities. In addition, these entities are required to follow three New Zealand-specific standards that provide specific jurisdictional guidance;

- Sri Lanka has taken the approach that their national standards are virtually word-for-word IFRSs;

- the Philippines and Singapore have adopted most IFRSs word-for-word, but have made some modifications. In May 2014, the Singapore Accounting Standards Council (ASC) announced that it will introduce a new financial reporting framework that is identical to IFRSs for Singapore listed companies for annual periods beginning on or after 1 January 2018;

- India has adopted a roadmap to adopt converged standards (Ind AS) with effect from 1 April 2016 (for large companies) and for all companies from 1 April 2017. For the moment, banks, insurers and non-bank finance companies are exempt from the roadmap;

- by 1 January 2017, all companies in Malaysia will be using standards identical to IFRSs as issued by the IASB;

- Pakistan has adopted some but not all IFRSs; and

- IFRSs are looked to in developing national GAAP to varying degrees in China, Indonesia, Thailand and Vietnam, but significant differences exist in some jurisdictions.

4.5   Use of IFRSs in other parts of the world

Many countries in the rest of the world are either already requiring or permitting IFRSs or are in the process of moving to IFRSs. Listed companies in Nigeria, Kenya and South Africa must use IFRSs, and many of the former Soviet Union countries have adopted (in part or comprehensively) IFRSs as their primary accounting framework. For a detailed country-by-country list of the status of adoption of IFRSs, see *www.iasplus.com*.

5   IFRS for Small and Medium-sized Entities

The IFRS for Small and Medium-sized Entities (SMEs) was issued by the IASB in 2009 and revised in May 2015. It is a self-contained Standard tailored for the needs and capabilities of smaller businesses. Many of the principles in full IFRSs for recognising and measuring assets, liabilities, income and expenses have been simplified; topics not relevant to SMEs have been omitted; and the number of required disclosures has been significantly reduced. To lessen the reporting burden for SMEs further, revisions to the IFRS for SMEs will be limited to once every three years.

The IFRS for SMEs is separate from full IFRSs and is therefore available for any jurisdiction to adopt whether or not it has adopted full IFRSs. It is also for each jurisdiction to determine which entities should use the Standard.

See **appendix A4** for an overview of the IFRS for SMEs.

A2 Conceptual framework for financial reporting

Contents

1   Introduction

1.1   Project to develop an improved conceptual framework

For several years, the IASB and the FASB worked together on a joint project to develop an improved and converged conceptual framework for IFRSs and US GAAP. This project was being carried out in phases with the objective that, as each phase was finalised, the relevant paragraphs in the *Framework for the Preparation and Presentation of Financial Statements* (the IASB's predecessor framework) would be replaced.

The boards completed the first phase of their project in September 2010, when they issued two chapters of the *Conceptual Framework for Financial Reporting* (the Conceptual Framework) – Chapter 1 *The objective of general purpose financial reporting* and Chapter 3 *Qualitative characteristics of useful financial information*. After that first phase was complete, the IASB deferred further work on the joint project until after other more urgent convergence projects were finalised. In 2012, the project was reactivated as an IASB-only project, with an exposure draft issued in May 2015 (see **section 9**).

This chapter follows the text of the *Conceptual Framework for Financial Reporting* in the IASB's 2014 Bound Volume. It incorporates the two chapters of the Conceptual Framework completed in September 2010, with the remaining text (**sections 6** to **8**) carried forward from the predecessor framework.

The Conceptual Framework sets out the concepts underlying the preparation and presentation of financial statements for external users. A comprehensive discussion of each of the topics covered in the Conceptual Framework is beyond the scope of this text; the remainder of this chapter therefore provides a very brief summary of the matters discussed therein.

1.2   Terminology

When the IASB revised IAS 1 *Presentation of Financial Statements* in 2007, it did not amend the terminology used in the *Framework for the Preparation and Presentation of Financial Statements*, and this pre-2007 terminology is carried forward to the Conceptual Framework. Accordingly, the Conceptual Framework still refers, for example, to the 'balance sheet' rather than to the 'statement of financial position'.

2   Purpose and status of the Conceptual Framework

The purpose of the Conceptual Framework is:

- to assist the IASB in the development of future IFRSs and in its review of existing IFRSs;

- to assist the IASB in promoting harmonisation of regulations, accounting standards and procedures relating to the presentation of financial statements by providing a basis for reducing the number of alternative accounting treatments permitted by IFRSs;

- to assist national standard-setting bodies in developing national standards;

- to assist preparers of financial statements in applying IFRSs and in dealing with topics that have yet to form the subject of an IFRS;

- to assist auditors in forming an opinion as to whether financial statements comply with IFRSs;

- to assist users of financial statements in interpreting the information contained in financial statements prepared in conformity with IFRSs; and

- to provide those who are interested in the work of the IASB with information about its approach to the formulation of IFRSs.

The Conceptual Framework is not itself an International Financial Reporting Standard and, therefore, it does not define standards for particular recognition, measurement, presentation or disclosure issues. There may be conflicts between the Conceptual Framework and individual Standards or Interpretations, which are being addressed by the IASB over time. When such a conflict arises, the Standard or Interpretation takes precedence. This is a key point in that it clarifies that the principles of the Conceptual Framework cannot be used to justify a treatment that contravenes an extant IFRS.

In the absence of a Standard or an Interpretation that specifically applies to a transaction or event, IAS 8 *Accounting Policies, Changes in Accounting Estimates and Errors* requires that management should use its judgement in developing and applying an accounting policy that results in information that is relevant and reliable. In making that judgement, IAS 8:11 requires management to consider first the requirements and guidance in Standards and Interpretations dealing with similar and related issues, and second the definitions, recognition criteria and measurement concepts for assets, liabilities, income and expenses in the Conceptual Framework (see **section 3.1** of **chapter A5**).

3   Scope

The Conceptual Framework deals specifically with:

- the objective of general purpose financial reporting (see **section 4**);

- the qualitative characteristics of useful financial information (see **section 5**);

- the definition, recognition and measurement of the elements from which financial statements are constructed (see **sections 6** and **7**); and

- concepts of capital and capital maintenance (see **section 8**).

> The Conceptual Framework is not directly relevant for entities applying the *IFRS for SMEs*, which includes a section setting out its underlying concepts and pervasive principles (see **appendix A4**).

4   The objective of general purpose financial reporting

4.1   The objective of general purpose financial reporting

Chapter 1 of the Conceptual Framework addresses the objective of general purpose financial reporting (hereafter, just 'financial reporting') – which is considered to be the foundation of the Conceptual Framework from which the other aspects flow logically.

The objective of financial reporting is identified as being "to provide financial information about the reporting entity that is useful to existing and potential investors, lenders and other creditors in making decisions about providing resources to the entity. Those decisions involve buying, selling or holding equity and debt instruments, and providing or settling loans and other forms of credit". [CF:OB2]

The primary users of general purpose financial reports are identified as existing and potential investors, lenders and other creditors who cannot require the entity to provide information directly to them and who, consequently, rely on general purpose financial reports for much (but not all) of the financial information they need. [CF:OB5] Other parties (e.g. regulators and members of the public) may make use of general purpose financial reports but the information included therein is not primarily directed to such parties. [CF:OB10]

The needs of all of the primary users are not the same – and the Conceptual Framework establishes the principle that, in developing IFRSs, the IASB "will seek to provide the information set that will meet the needs of the maximum number of primary users". [CF:OB8]

Information is considered to be 'useful' if it helps the primary users of general purpose financial reports to assess the prospects for future net cash inflows to an entity; such an assessment enables the primary users to estimate the return that they can expect from transacting with the entity. [CF:OB3]

To assess an entity's prospects for future net cash inflows, the primary users need information regarding (1) the resources of the entity and claims against the entity, and (2) how efficiently and effectively the entity's management has discharged its responsibilities. [CF:OB4]

The responsibilities referred to in CF:OB4 are generally referred to as management's 'stewardship' responsibilities. Examples of such responsibilities include protecting the entity's resources from unfavourable effects of economic factors such as price and technological changes and ensuring that the entity complies with applicable laws, regulations and contractual provisions.

This subject sparked considerable debate during the development of Chapter 1 of the Conceptual Framework. While 'stewardship' is not a separate objective of financial reporting in the final chapter as some had requested, the IASB has acknowledged that evaluating past performance of an entity is as important as predicting future cash flows. As part of its May 2015 proposals for revisions to the Conceptual Framework (see **section 9**), the Board proposes to reintroduce the term 'stewardship' and to provide expanded guidance on this topic.

4.2   Information about the resources of the entity and claims against the entity

General purpose financial reports provide information about:

[CF:OB12 & OB15]

- the financial position of an entity (i.e. information about its economic resources and claims against it);
- the financial performance of an entity; and
- the effects of other events and transactions that affect the entity's economic resources and claims against it (e.g. issuing debt or equity securities).

Although the Conceptual Framework refers to financial performance, it does not define it. However, it appears clear that financial performance does not reflect all changes in the financial position of an entity in that it excludes changes that relate to contributions from and distributions to equity participants (see the discussion in **section 7**).

Information about the nature and amounts of an entity's economic resources and claims against it is useful for assessing its financial strengths and weaknesses, such as the liquidity of the entity and its financing needs. Information about priorities and payment requirements of existing claims helps users to predict how future cash flows will be distributed among those with a claim against the entity. [CF:OB13]

Information about the performance of an entity helps users to understand the return that the entity has produced from its economic resources (which is an indication of how well management has discharged its stewardship responsibilities). Information regarding the performance of an entity is prepared using the accrual basis of accounting (i.e. focusing on the effects of events and transactions when they occur and not necessarily when cash is received or paid), which is considered to provide a better basis for assessing the entity's past and future performance than information solely about cash receipt and payments. [CF:OB16 & 17]

Information about an entity's cash flows during a period is also considered to be useful in the assessment of the entity's ability to generate future net cash inflows; it helps users to understand an entity's operations, evaluate its financing and investing activities, assess its liquidity or solvency, and interpret other information about financial performance. [CF:OB20]

Finally, information regarding changes in the entity's resources and claims against it for reasons other than financial performance (e.g. the issue of additional ownership shares) is needed to provide users of general purpose financial reports with a complete understanding of why the entity's economic resources and claims against it have changed and the implications of those changes for its future financial performance. [CF:OB21]

5 Qualitative characteristics of useful financial information

5.1 Qualitative characteristics of useful financial information – general

Chapter 3 of the Conceptual Framework considers the qualitative characteristics of decision-useful financial information, and constraints on the information that can be provided by financial reporting, so as to identify the types of information that are likely to be most useful to the primary users of general purpose financial reports.

The Conceptual Framework states that if financial information is to be useful, it must be relevant and faithfully represent what it purports to represent; these are the two fundamental qualitative characteristics of useful financial information – 'relevance' and 'faithful representation'. [CF:QC4 & 5] Information must be both relevant and faithfully represented if it is to be useful. Neither a faithful representation of an irrelevant event or transaction, nor an unfaithful representation of a relevant event or transaction, helps users make good decisions. [CF:QC17]

The usefulness of financial information is considered to be enhanced if it is comparable, verifiable, timely and understandable. [CF:QC4] 'Comparability', 'verifiability', 'timeliness' and 'understandability' are therefore described as enhancing qualitative characteristics. [CF:QC19]

The Conceptual Framework notes that such enhancement should be maximised to the extent possible. However, these qualitative characteristics cannot make information useful if the information is irrelevant or not faithfully represented. [CF:QC33]

Notably, the Conceptual Framework does not include any discussion of 'substance over form' or 'prudence'. These omissions are discussed in the Basis for Conclusions on the Conceptual Framework.

The Board determined that 'substance over form' should not be presented as a separate component of faithful representation because it would be redundant. Faithful representation means that financial information presents the substance of events and transactions rather than merely their legal form. Representing a legal form that differs from the economic substance of the underlying economic event or transaction could not result in a faithful representation. [CF:BC3.26] Therefore, although not specifically referred to in the Conceptual Framework, the concept of 'substance over form' continues to be relevant (see **3.3** in **chapter A4** for further discussion).

No reference is made to prudence or conservatism as an aspect of faithful representation because the Board considered that including either would be inconsistent with neutrality. The Board concluded that, even with the prohibitions against deliberate misstatement that appear elsewhere, an admonition to be prudent would be likely to lead to a bias.

As part of its May 2015 proposals for revisions to the Conceptual Framework (see **section 9**), the IASB proposes to reintroduce guidance on both of these concepts.

5.2   Fundamental qualitative characteristics

5.2.1   Relevance

Financial information is relevant when it is "capable of making a difference in the decisions made by users". [CF:QC6] Information is capable of making a difference in a decision-making process if it has predictive value (i.e. it can be used as an input to predict future outcomes), confirmatory value (i.e. it provides feedback about previous evaluations), or both.

In determining whether information is relevant to the needs of users, preparers of financial information need to take account of the nature and materiality of the information. Information is considered to be material if omitting it or misstating it could influence the decisions of users taken on the basis of the financial information. Because materiality is an entity-specific characteristic to be determined in the context of an individual entity's financial report, the IASB has concluded that it cannot specify a uniform quantitative threshold for materiality or predetermine what could be material in a particular situation. [CF:QC11]

5.2.2 Faithful representation

Relevant financial information must also be faithfully represented to be useful. A faithful representation is one that is "complete, neutral, and free from error" to the extent possible.

[CF:QC12 - QC15]

- A depiction is 'complete' if it includes all of the information that a user needs to understand what is being reported, including all necessary descriptions and explanations.

- A depiction is 'neutral' if it is without bias in the selection or presentation of financial information (i.e. it is not slanted, weighted, emphasised, de-emphasised or otherwise manipulated to increase the probability that financial information will be received favourably or unfavourably by users).

- A depiction is 'free from error' if there are no errors or omissions in the information provided and the process used to produce the reported information has been selected and applied with no errors in the process. In this context, free from error does not mean perfectly accurate in all respects.

5.3 Enhancing qualitative characteristics

5.3.1 Enhancing qualitative characteristics – general

Comparability, verifiability, timeliness and understandability are qualitative characteristics that enhance the usefulness of information that is relevant and faithfully represented. The enhancing qualitative characteristics may also help determine which of two ways should be used to depict an event or transaction if both are considered equally relevant and faithfully represented. [CF:QC19]

5.3.2 Comparability

Information about an entity is considered to be more useful if it can be compared with similar information about other entities and with similar information about the same entity for another period or another date. Comparability is the qualitative characteristic that enables users to identify and understand similarities in, and differences among, items. [CF:QC20 & 21]

Using the same methods for the same items, either from period to period within an entity or in a single period across entities (i.e. consistency), helps to achieve comparability. [CF:QC22]. Although an economic event or transaction can sometimes be faithfully represented in multiple ways, permitting alternative accounting methods for the same economic phenomenon diminishes comparability. [CF:QC25]

5.3.3   Verifiability

Verifiability means that different knowledgeable and independent observers could reach consensus, although not necessarily complete agreement, that a particular depiction is a faithful representation. Quantified information need not be a single point estimate to be verifiable – a range of possible amounts and the related probabilities can also be verified. Verifiability helps assure users that information faithfully represents the events or transactions it purports to represent. [CF:QC26]

Verification can be direct or indirect. Direct verification means verifying an amount or other representation through direct observation (e.g. by counting cash). Indirect verification means checking the inputs to a model, formula or other technique and recalculating the outputs using the same methodology. [CF:QC27]

It may not be possible to verify some explanations and forward-looking financial information until a future period, if at all. To help users decide whether they want to use that information, it would normally be necessary to disclose the underlying assumptions, the methods of compiling the information, and other factors and circumstances that support the information. [CF:QC28]

5.3.4   Timeliness

Timeliness means having information available to decision-makers in time to be capable of influencing their decisions. Generally, the older the information is the less useful it is. However, some information may continue to be timely long after the end of a reporting period because, for example, some users may need to identify and assess trends. [CF:QC29]

5.3.5   Understandability

Classifying, characterising and presenting information clearly and concisely makes it understandable. [CF:QC30]

The Conceptual Framework allows a preparer to assume that users have a reasonable knowledge of business and economic activities, and that users review and analyse the information diligently. Complex financial information should not be excluded from financial reports in order to make those financial reports easier to understand, because the resulting information would be incomplete and, therefore, potentially misleading. [CF:QC31 & 32]

5.4   The cost constraint on financial reporting

The Conceptual Framework acknowledges that cost is a pervasive constraint on the information that can be provided by financial reporting. Reporting financial information imposes costs, and it is important that those costs are justified by the benefits of reporting that information. [CF:QC35]

Costs are incurred by providers of financial information in collecting, processing, verifying and disseminating financial information; users of financial information also incur costs when analysing and interpreting the information provided. If needed information is not provided, users incur additional costs to obtain that information elsewhere or to estimate it. [CF:QC36]

In applying the cost constraint when developing IFRSs, the IASB assesses whether the benefits of reporting particular information are likely to justify the costs incurred to provide and use that information. The Board seeks to consider costs and benefits in relation to financial reporting generally and not just in relation to individual reporting entities. That does not mean that assessments of costs and benefits always justify the same reporting requirements for all entities. Differences may be appropriate because of different sizes of entities, different ways of raising capital (publicly or privately), different users' needs, or other factors. [CF:QC38 & 39]

6　Assumptions underlying the preparation of financial statements

Chapter 4 of the Conceptual Framework identifies 'going concern' as one assumption underlying the preparation of financial statements. This assumption (together with a number of other general features of financial statements introduced in IAS 1 *Presentation of Financial Statements*) is discussed in **chapter A4**.

7　The elements of financial statements

7.1　Assets

7.1.1　Definition

The Conceptual Framework defines an asset as a resource controlled by the entity as a result of past events and from which future economic benefits are expected to flow to the entity. [CF:4.4(a)]

The future economic benefit embodied in an asset is the potential to contribute, directly or indirectly, to the flow of cash and cash equivalents. [CF:4.8] Such benefits may flow to the entity in a number of ways – for example, by use in the production process, by exchange for other assets, as settlement of a liability, or by distribution to the owners of the entity.

Many assets have physical form – but that is not essential to the existence of an asset. For example, intangible assets such as patents and copyrights are assets if future economic benefits are expected to flow from them to the entity and if they are controlled by the entity. [CF:4.11]

The entity's control over those future economic benefits will most commonly be evidenced by legal ownership, but that is not essential. For example, property held on lease is an asset if the entity controls the benefits that are expected to flow from it. [CF:4.12]

The entity will usually have legal rights over an asset – but not necessarily so. For example, know-how obtained from a development activity may meet the definition of an asset when, by keeping the know-how secret, an entity controls the benefits that are expected to flow from it. [CF:4.12]

The assets of an entity must result from a past transaction or event. Assets are most usually acquired by purchasing or producing them – but this will not always be the case (e.g. when assets may be received by way of government grant or contributions from equity participants). [CF:4.13]

There is a 'close association' between incurring expenditure and generating assets, but the two do not necessarily coincide. An entity may incur expenditure with a view to obtaining future economic benefits, but the expenditure may not result in an item satisfying the definition of an asset. Equally, an item may satisfy the definition of an asset without any expenditure having been incurred (e.g. a donated asset). [CF:4.14]

7.1.2 Recognition

An asset should be recognised in the balance sheet when:

[CF:4.44]

- it is probable that the future economic benefits will flow to the entity; and
- the asset has a cost or value that can be measured reliably.

The assessment of the degree of uncertainty attaching to the flow of future economic benefits is made on the basis of the evidence available when the financial statements are prepared. An asset is not recognised in the balance sheet when expenditure has been incurred from which it is considered improbable that economic benefits will flow to the entity beyond the current accounting period. Instead, such a transaction is dealt with as an expense in the income statement.

7.1.3 Measurement

The determination of the monetary amount at which an asset is to be recognised in the balance sheet involves the selection of a particular basis of measurement.

The most common bases of measurement for assets are:

[CF:4.55]

- historical cost – assets are recorded at the amount of cash or cash equivalents paid or the fair value of the consideration given to acquire them at the time of their acquisition;

- current cost – assets are carried at the amount of cash or cash equivalents that would have to be paid if the same or an equivalent asset was acquired currently;

- realisable value – assets are carried at the amount of cash or cash equivalents that could currently be obtained by selling the asset in an orderly disposal; and

- present value – assets are carried at the present discounted value of the future net cash inflows that the item is expected to generate in the normal course of business.

The Conceptual Framework does not indicate a preference for any of these measurement bases. It points out that the measurement basis most commonly adopted is historical cost – often combined with other bases. For example, inventories are usually carried at the lower of cost and net realisable value. [CF:4.56]

7.2 Liabilities

7.2.1 Definition

The Conceptual Framework defines a liability as a present obligation of the entity arising from past events, the settlement of which is expected to result in an outflow from the entity of resources embodying economic benefits. [CF:4.4(b)]

An essential characteristic of a liability is that the entity has a present obligation. An obligation is a duty or responsibility to act or perform in a certain way. Obligations may be legally enforceable (e.g. as a consequence of a binding contract or a statutory requirement). Obligations also arise, however, from normal business practice, custom and a desire to maintain good business relations or to act in an equitable manner. For example, an entity may decide as a matter of policy to rectify faults in its products when these become apparent after the warranty period has expired, even though it has no legal obligation to do so, with the objective of maintaining its reputation with customers. [CF:4.15]

The Conceptual Framework draws a distinction between a present obligation and a future commitment. A decision by management to acquire an asset or to incur expenditure in the future does not, of itself, create a present obligation. An obligation normally arises only when the goods are delivered or an irrevocable agreement is entered into. [CF:4.16]

The settlement of a liability usually involves the entity giving up resources embodying economic benefits – whether by payment of cash, transfer of other assets, provision of services, replacement of the obligation by another obligation, or conversion of the obligation to equity. [CF:4.17]

7.2.2   Recognition

A liability should be recognised in the balance sheet when:

[CF:4.46]

- it is probable that an outflow of resources embodying economic benefits will result from the settlement of a present obligation; and
- the amount at which the settlement will take place can be measured reliably.

In practice, obligations under contracts that are equally proportionately unperformed (e.g. liabilities for inventories ordered but not yet received) are generally not recognised as liabilities in the financial statements (see **chapter A12** for a discussion of executory contracts).

7.2.3   Measurement

The determination of the monetary amount at which a liability is to be recognised in the balance sheet involves the selection of a particular basis of measurement.

The most common bases of measurement for liabilities are:

[CF:4.55]

- historical cost – liabilities are recorded at the amount of the proceeds received in exchange for the obligation or at the amounts of cash or cash equivalents expected to be paid to satisfy the liability in the normal course of business;
- current cost – liabilities are carried at the undiscounted amount of cash or cash equivalents that would be required to settle the obligation currently;
- settlement value – liabilities are carried at their settlement values, i.e. at the undiscounted amounts of cash or cash equivalents expected to be paid to satisfy the liabilities in the normal course of business; and
- present value – liabilities are carried at the present discounted value of the future net cash outflows that are expected to be required to settle the liabilities in the normal course of business.

The Conceptual Framework does not indicate a preference for any of these measurement bases.

7.3 Equity

The Conceptual Framework defines equity as the residual interest in the assets of the entity after deducting all of its liabilities. [CF:4.4(c)]

Equity may be sub-classified in the balance sheet. For example, in a corporate entity, funds contributed by shareholders, retained earnings and capital reserves may be shown separately. Such classifications can be relevant to the decision-making needs of users of the financial statements when they indicate legal or other restrictions on the ability of the entity to distribute or otherwise apply its equity. They may also reflect the fact that parties with ownership interests in an entity have differing rights in relation to the receipt of dividends and the repayment of capital. [CF:4.20]

7.4 Income

7.4.1 Definition

Income is defined as increases in economic benefits during the accounting period in the form of inflows or enhancements of assets, or decreases of liabilities, that result in increases in equity, other than those relating to contributions from equity participants. [CF:4.25(a)]

Income can be subdivided into:

- revenue – which arises in the course of the ordinary activities of the entity and is referred to by a variety of different names including sales, fees, interest, dividends, royalties and rent; and

- gains – which represent other items that meet the definition of income that may, or may not, arise in the course of the ordinary activities of an entity. They include, for example, gains arising on the disposal of non-current assets, and unrealised gains arising on the revaluation of financial instruments or non-current assets.

7.4.2 Recognition

Income is recognised when an increase in future economic benefits related to an increase in an asset or a decrease in a liability has arisen that can be measured reliably. [CF:4.47] This means that recognition of income occurs simultaneously with the recognition of increases in assets or decreases in liabilities. Generally, such recognition will occur when the movements in assets/liabilities can be measured reliably and have a sufficient degree of certainty.

Specific criteria for the recognition of particular types of revenue are set out in IFRSs (e.g. IFRS 15 *Revenue from Contracts with Customers* (see **chapter A14**) or, for entities that have not yet adopted IFRS 15, IAS 18 *Revenue* (see **appendix A1**)).

7.5   Expenses

7.5.1   Definition

Expenses are defined as decreases in economic benefits during the accounting period in the form of outflows or depletions of assets, or incurrences of liabilities, that result in decreases in equity, other than those relating to distributions to equity participants. [CF:4.25(b)]

7.5.2   Recognition

Expenses are recognised in the income statement when a decrease in future economic benefits related to a decrease in an asset or an increase in a liability has arisen that can be measured reliably. [CF:4.49] This means that recognition of expenses occurs simultaneously with the recognition of decreases in assets or increases in liabilities.

The recognition of expenses in the income statement will be affected by any direct association between the costs incurred and the earning of specific items of income (i.e. matching). However, the application of the matching concept does not allow the recognition of items in the balance sheet that do not meet the definition of assets or liabilities. [CF:4.50]

When economic benefits are expected to arise over several accounting periods, and the association with income can only be broadly or indirectly determined, expenses are recognised in the income statement on the basis of systematic and rational allocation procedures (e.g. depreciation or amortisation of non-current assets). These allocation procedures are intended to recognise expenses in the accounting periods in which the associated economic benefits are consumed or expire. [CF:4.51]

An expense is recognised immediately in the income statement in those cases when the expenditure produces no future economic benefits, or when future economic benefits do not qualify, or cease to qualify, for recognition in the balance sheet as an asset. [CF:4.52]

An expense is also recognised in the income statement when a liability is incurred without the recognition of an asset (e.g. when a liability arises under a product warranty). [CF:4.53]

7.6   Transactions with equity participants

The definitions of both income and expenses set out in **7.4.1** and **7.5.1**, respectively, exclude contributions from and distributions to equity participants. These exclusions are based on the principle that profit or loss of the entity cannot be created simply by transferring resources to or from the owners of the entity.

8 Concepts of capital and capital maintenance

The Conceptual Framework identifies two concepts of capital maintenance:

[CF:4.59]

- financial capital maintenance – under which profit is earned only if the financial (or money) amount of the net assets at the end of the reporting period exceeds the financial (or money) amount of net assets at the beginning of the reporting period, after excluding any distributions to, and contributions from, owners during the period; and

- physical capital maintenance – under which a profit is earned only if the physical productive capacity (or operating capability) of the entity (or the resources or funds needed to achieve that capacity) at the end of the period exceeds the physical productive capacity at the beginning of the period, after excluding any distributions to, and contributions from, owners during the period.

The Conceptual Framework does not indicate a preference for either of these concepts of capital maintenance.

The selection of a concept of capital maintenance (and of the measurement basis to be used) determines the accounting model used in preparation of the financial statements. The Conceptual Framework acknowledges that different accounting models exhibit different degrees of relevance and reliability, and that preparers of financial statements should seek a balance between those characteristics.

9 Future developments

The IASB is working on a comprehensive project to revise the Conceptual Framework. In May 2015, the Board published an exposure draft (ED/2015/3) setting out its proposals for revision.

The ED proposes that the revised Conceptual Framework will be structured as follows.

- Chapters 1 & 2 *The objective of general purpose financial reporting* and *Qualitative characteristics of useful financial information*

  The IASB proposes to introduce guidance on stewardship, primary users, measurement uncertainty, substance over form and prudence.

- Chapter 3 *Financial statements and the reporting entity*

  The IASB describes the role of financial statements and introduces proposals on the definition and boundary of a 'reporting entity'.

- Chapter 4 *The elements of financial statements*

  The IASB proposes clearer definitions of assets and liabilities, and more extensive guidance to support those definitions.

- Chapter 5 *Recognition and derecognition*

  The IASB proposes to clarify that only elements of financial statements can be recognised. To achieve recognition, the IASB sets out three criteria: relevance, faithful representation and the cost/benefit restraint. The IASB further proposes to provide clarification that derecognition requirements aim to represent faithfully the assets and liabilities retained after the derecognition event and the change in the entity's assets and liabilities as a result of that event.

- Chapter 6 *Measurement*

  The IASB proposes to describe different measurement bases and factors to consider when selecting a measurement basis.

- Chapter 7 *Presentation and disclosure*

  The IASB proposes to include high level concepts that describe what information is included in financial statements and how that information should be presented and disclosed, as well as guidance on reporting financial performance (including the use of other comprehensive income).

- Chapter 8 *Concepts of capital and capital maintenance*

  The IASB does not propose any changes to this material.

Comments on the proposals are due by 26 October 2015, and the IASB aims to finalise the revised Conceptual Framework in 2016.

A3 First-time adoption of IFRSs

Contents

1   Introduction

1.1   Overview of IFRS 1

IFRS 1 *First-time Adoption of International Financial Reporting Standards* sets out the procedures that an entity must follow when it adopts IFRSs for the first time as the basis for preparing its general purpose financial statements. The Standard imposes a number of mandatory exceptions and grants a number of optional exemptions from the general requirement to comply with each IFRS effective at the end of the entity's first IFRS reporting period.

First-time adopters engaged in rate-regulated activities need to consider IFRS 14 *Regulatory Deferral Account Balances* in addition to IFRS 1. See **chapter A42** for a detailed discussion of the requirements of IFRS 14, and **7.5.5** for consequential amendments to IFRS 1.

1.2   Application of the IFRS 1 framework

The general principle underlying IFRS 1 is that IFRSs effective at the date of an entity's first IFRS financial statements should be applied retrospectively in the opening IFRS statement of financial position, the comparative period and the first IFRS reporting period. In practical terms, this means that if an entity adopts IFRSs for the year ended 31 December 2015, it must apply all IFRSs effective at that date retrospectively to the 2015 and 2014 reporting periods, and to the opening statement of financial position on 1 January 2014 (assuming that only one year of comparative information is presented).

Effectively, this general principle would result in full retrospective application of IFRSs as if they had been the framework for an entity's accounting since its inception. However, IFRS 1 adapts this general principle of retrospective application by adding a limited number of 'exceptions' and 'exemptions':

- the 'exceptions' to retrospective application are mandatory (see **section 6**); and

- the 'exemptions' are optional – a first-time adopter may choose whether and which exemptions to apply (see **section 7**).

From time to time, the IASB also adds short-term exemptions from IFRSs (see **7.23**).

Careful analysis is required to understand fully the nature and impact of both the exceptions and the exemptions when applying IFRS 1.

An entity is only permitted to apply IFRS 1 in its first IFRS financial statements (a term tightly defined to mean the first annual financial statements in which the entity adopts IFRSs by an explicit and unreserved statement of compliance with IFRSs). The Standard provides specific examples of what might or might not qualify as an entity's first IFRS financial statements (see **4.2**).

The following summarises the steps required in preparing an entity's first IFRS financial statements.

1. An opening IFRS statement of financial position is prepared at the 'date of transition'. This is the starting point for an entity's accounting in accordance with IFRSs. The date of transition is the beginning of the first period for which an entity presents full comparative information under IFRSs in its first IFRS financial statements. For entities that present one year of comparative information in their financial reports, the date of transition is the first day of the comparative period.

2. In its first IFRS financial statements, an entity applies the version of IFRSs effective at the end of its first IFRS reporting period. As a general principle, all IFRSs effective at that date are applied retrospectively, subject to a number of exceptions and exemptions set out in IFRS 1 (discussed in detail in **sections 6** and **7**, respectively). The exceptions and exemptions are very specific, and may not be applied by analogy to other items.

3. The entity recognises all assets and liabilities in accordance with the requirements of IFRSs, and derecognises assets and liabilities that do not qualify for recognition under IFRSs.

4. All adjustments resulting from the application of IFRSs to the opening IFRS statement of financial position are recognised in retained earnings (or, if appropriate, another category of equity) at the date of transition, except for reclassifications between goodwill and intangible assets.

5. With limited exceptions, estimates in accordance with IFRSs at the date of transition must be consistent with estimates made for the same date under previous GAAP.

6. An entity's first IFRS financial statements include at least three statements of financial position (including one at the date of transition, i.e. at the beginning of the comparative period), two statements of profit or loss and other comprehensive income, two statements of cash flows and two statements of changes in equity and related notes. All of these statements must be in compliance with IFRSs.

7. Entities are permitted to present historical summaries of data for periods before the date of transition which do not comply with IFRSs, as long as the information is prominently labelled as not being prepared in accordance with IFRSs. When such information is presented, the entity must also explain the nature of the main

adjustments that would be required to render the information compliant with IFRSs.

8. IFRS 1 requires compliance with all of the presentation and disclosure requirements of other Standards and Interpretations, and imposes additional disclosure requirements specific to the first IFRS financial statements. In particular, a first-time adopter is required to provide reconciliations between amounts reported under previous GAAP and the equivalent measures under IFRSs. These reconciliations must clearly identify the correction of any errors in relation to an entity's previous GAAP financial statements.

1.3 Amendments to IFRS 1 since the last edition of this manual

The following amendments have been made to IFRS 1 since the last edition to this manual:

*   August 2014 – *Equity Method in Separate Financial Statements (Amendments to IAS 27)* amended IFRS 1 to reflect that entities are now permitted to use the equity method to account for investments in subsidiaries, associates and joint ventures in their separate financial statements (see **7.8**); and

*   September 2014 – *Annual Improvements to IFRSs: 2012-2014 Cycle* amended IFRS 1 such that a first-time adopter may apply the transition provisions set out in paragraph 44A of IFRS 7 *Financial Instruments: Disclosures* (see **7.23.4**).

2 Objective of IFRS 1

The objective of IFRS 1 is to ensure that an entity's first-time IFRS financial statements (and interim financial reports for part of the period covered by those financial statements) contain high quality information that:

[IFRS 1:1]

*   is transparent for users and comparable over all periods presented;

*   provides a suitable starting point for accounting under IFRSs; and

*   can be generated at a cost that does not exceed the benefits to users.

3 Definitions

3.1 Date of transition to IFRSs

The date of transition to IFRSs is defined as "[t]he beginning of the earliest period for which an entity presents full comparative information under IFRSs in its first IFRS financial statements". [IFRS 1:Appendix A]

This date is of particular significance because it is the date at which an entity prepares its opening IFRS statement of financial position.

3.2 Deemed cost

Deemed cost is defined as "[a]n amount used as a surrogate for cost or depreciated cost at a given date. Subsequent depreciation or amortisation assumes that the entity had initially recognised the asset or liability at the given date and that its cost was equal to the deemed cost". [IFRS 1:Appendix A]

The use of fair value or a previous revaluation as deemed cost on transition to IFRSs is considered at **7.5**.

3.3 Fair value

Fair value is defined as "[t]he price that would be received to sell an asset or paid to transfer a liability in an orderly transaction between market participants at the measurement date. (See IFRS 13.)" [IFRS 1:Appendix A]

3.4 First IFRS financial statements

The first IFRS financial statements are defined as "[t]he first annual financial statements in which an entity adopts International Financial Reporting Standards (IFRSs), by an explicit and unreserved statement of compliance with IFRSs". [IFRS 1:Appendix A]

The meaning of an 'explicit and unreserved statement of compliance with IFRSs' is considered at **4.2**.

3.5 First IFRS reporting period

The first IFRS reporting period is defined as "[t]he latest reporting period covered by an entity's first IFRS financial statements". [IFRS 1:Appendix A]

3.6 First-time adopter

A first-time adopter is defined as "[a]n entity that presents its first IFRS financial statements". [IFRS 1:Appendix A]

A newly incorporated company presenting its first financial statements under IFRSs is not generally viewed as a 'first-time adopter' for the purposes of IFRS 1 – there are no 'past transactions' to restate. This is also the case when a newly incorporated company establishes a business and subsequently acquires another entity in a transaction that is accounted for using the acquisition method in accordance with

IFRS 3 *Business Combinations*. In this situation, it is irrelevant for the purposes of the consolidated financial statements of the acquiring company whether the acquired entity previously reported under IFRSs and, if so, its date of transition.

However, a newly incorporated company may be a continuation of an existing operating entity. This may be the case, for example, when a business is transferred to the company in a common control transaction or as a result of the acquisition of another company (which becomes a 'legal subsidiary') in circumstances which require reverse-acquisition accounting (i.e. for financial reporting purposes, the 'legal subsidiary' is portrayed as acquiring the newly incorporated 'legal parent'). The position may be different in these cases.

For example, consider the circumstances in which a new parent is added at the top of a group by way of a share-for-share exchange and this is accounted for in the same way as a reverse acquisition in accordance with IFRS 3. If the existing group already reports under IFRSs, the new parent 'inherits' the date of transition of the existing group for the purposes of its consolidated financial statements. The new parent should not apply IFRS 1 because reverse-acquisition accounting assumes the continuity of the 'acquired' business and that business is already applying IFRSs.

In contrast, in the case of a reverse acquisition when the 'continuing entity' (i.e. the financial reporting acquirer) did not previously report under IFRSs, the new parent is a first-time adopter for the purposes of IFRS 1 and the Standard is applied in the usual way.

Similar considerations may apply to a combination of businesses under common control that is accounted for as a continuation of an existing business.

3.7   International Financial Reporting Standards (IFRSs)

International Financial Reporting Standards are defined as "Standards and Interpretations adopted by the International Accounting Standards Board (IASB). They comprise:

[IFRS 1:Appendix A]

- International Financial Reporting Standards;
- International Accounting Standards;
- IFRS Interpretations; and
- SIC Interpretations".

3.8   Opening IFRS statement of financial position

An opening IFRS statement of financial position is defined as "[a]n entity's statement of financial position at the date of transition to IFRSs". [IFRS 1:Appendix A]

3.9   Previous GAAP

Previous GAAP is defined as "[t]he basis of accounting that a first-time adopter used immediately before adopting IFRSs". [IFRS 1:Appendix A]

An entity may have previously prepared two complete sets of financial statements under different GAAPs. For example, a company may have prepared its statutory financial statements under local GAAP and, in addition, prepared a complete set of US GAAP financial statements because it is listed on a US stock exchange.

In such cases, it is for management to determine, in accordance with its regulatory environment, whether to transition from the statutory financial statements (under local GAAP) or from the other set of financial statements it has presented. The determination of which GAAP is 'previous GAAP' is subject to the following:

- an entity cannot have more than one set of IFRS financial statements. Therefore, it must have only one starting point for transition to IFRSs (albeit that it may choose to reconcile between this starting point and another previously used accounting framework);

- under IFRSs, management has a free choice in identifying its previous GAAP. However, such a free choice may be eliminated by the regulatory regime(s) within which the entity operates; and

- the choice of previous GAAP must be a reasonable one (e.g. previous financial statements prepared for a specific purpose with limited circulation would not be an appropriate starting point when compared with the financial statements prepared for circulation to the entity's main user groups).

4   Scope

4.1   Scope – general

An entity should apply IFRS 1 in:

[IFRS 1:2]

- its first IFRS financial statements; and

- each interim financial report, if any, that it presents under IAS 34 *Interim Financial Reporting* for part of the period covered by its first IFRS financial statements.

IFRS 1 does not apply to changes in accounting policies made by an entity that already applies IFRSs. Such changes are subject to the requirements of IAS 8 *Accounting Policies, Changes in Accounting Estimates and Errors* (see **chapter A5**) and specific transition requirements in other IFRSs. [IFRS 1:5]

4.2   Meaning of an entity's first IFRS financial statements

As noted at **3.4**, an entity's first IFRS financial statements are the first annual financial statements in which the entity adopts IFRSs, by an explicit and unreserved statement in those financial statements of compliance with IFRSs. [IFRS 1:3]

IFRS 1 indicates that financial statements under IFRSs are an entity's first IFRS financial statements if, for example, the entity presented its most recent previous financial statements:

[IFRS 1:3(a)]

- in accordance with national requirements that are not consistent with IFRSs in all respects;

- in conformity with IFRSs in all respects, except that the financial statements did not contain an explicit and unreserved statement that they complied with IFRSs;

- containing an explicit statement of compliance with some, but not all, IFRSs;

- in accordance with national requirements inconsistent with IFRSs, using some individual IFRSs to account for items for which national requirements did not exist; or

- in accordance with national requirements, with a reconciliation of some amounts to the amounts determined under IFRSs.

Further examples of situations in which IFRS financial statements would be considered an entity's first IFRS financial statements for the purposes of IFRS 1 include situations in which an entity previously:

[IFRS 1:3(b) - (d)]

- prepared financial statements under IFRSs for internal use only, without making them available to the entity's owners or any other external users;

- prepared a reporting package under IFRSs for consolidation purposes without preparing a complete set of financial statements as defined in IAS 1 *Presentation of Financial Statements*; or

- did not present financial statements for previous periods.

It is not appropriate to apply IFRS 1 when an entity:

[IFRS 1:4]

- stops presenting financial statements in accordance with national requirements, having previously presented them as well as another set of financial statements that contained an explicit and unreserved statement of compliance with IFRSs;

- presented financial statements in the previous year under national requirements and those financial statements contained an explicit and unreserved statement of compliance with IFRSs; or

- presented financial statements in the previous year that contained an explicit and unreserved statement of compliance with IFRSs, even if the auditors qualified their audit report on those financial statements.

Some commentators on the exposure draft (ED) preceding IFRS 1 suggested that the test imposed in the ED was too rigid and that an entity should not be regarded as a first-time adopter if its previous financial statements contained a statement of compliance with IFRSs except for some specified and explicit departures. This argument might be particularly strong if the departures related to disclosure only. The IASB considered this and noted that to implement such an approach, it would be necessary to establish how many departures are needed, and how serious they must be, before an entity would conclude that it had not adopted IFRSs. Therefore, the IASB decided that the Standard should contain a simple test that gives an unambiguous answer. [IFRS 1:BC5]

The following examples illustrate some of the situations described in the previous paragraphs.

Example 4.2A

Compliance with IFRSs claimed in the previous year but subsequently discovered that financial statements were not IFRS-compliant

In 20X1, Company A issued financial statements stating compliance with all IFRSs, and with an unqualified audit opinion. In 20X2, Company A's auditors note that certain disclosure requirements of IAS 1 *Presentation of Financial Statements* were omitted, in error, from the 20X1 financial statements.

For the purposes of its 20X2 financial statements, is Company A within the scope of IFRS 1?

No. In the circumstances described, the 20X1 financial statements were stated to be IFRS-compliant. While Company A should not have claimed unreserved compliance with IFRSs in its 20X1 financial statements, those financial statements have already been considered IFRS-compliant and relied upon as such. Therefore, any errors are accounted for in accordance with IAS 8 *Accounting Policies, Changes in Accounting Estimates and Errors*.

Example 4.2B

Reserved statement of compliance with IFRSs in previous year

An entity included a reserved statement of compliance with IFRSs (i.e. a statement of compliance with some, but not all, IFRSs) in its 20X1 financial statements.

Can the entity be a first-time adopter in 20X2?

Yes. An entity that included a reserved statement of compliance with IFRSs in its most recent previous financial statements is not excluded from the scope of IFRS 1 for the current year. The entity becomes a first-time adopter when its financial statements first contain an explicit and *unreserved* statement of compliance with IFRSs.

The following would not be considered unreserved statements of compliance:

- a statement of compliance with local GAAP that is 'consistent with' or 'similar to' IFRSs; or

- a statement of compliance with IFRSs, except for certain Standards or disclosure requirements.

Example 4.2C

Supplementary IFRS financial statements distributed to external users

In 20X1, Company B prepared and presented its statutory financial statements in accordance with local GAAP. It also prepared a supplementary set of financial statements stating compliance with IFRSs and distributed those supplementary financial statements to a select group of users (financial institutions). In 20X2, Company B intends to prepare its statutory financial statements in accordance with IFRSs.

Will Company B be considered a first-time adopter of IFRSs in 20X2?

No. If financial statements stating compliance with IFRSs have been issued externally, regardless of the extent of distribution, those financial statements prevent the entity from being regarded as a first-time adopter. The same principle would apply if an entity had previously issued a set of IFRS financial statements to the counterparties in a specific commercial transaction.

Example 4.2D

Listing documents as the first IFRS financial statements

Company C prepared and published its financial statements for the year ended 31 December 20X7 under national GAAP. During 20X8, in connection with an Initial Public Offering (IPO), it published listing documents containing IFRS financial information for the three years ended 31 December 20X7. The 20X7 statutory financial statements were not amended or reissued.

During 20X9, Company C published IFRS financial statements for the year ended 31 December 20X8 with one year of comparative information and an unreserved statement of compliance with IFRSs.

What is Company C's date of transition to IFRSs?

If the listing documents contained an unreserved statement of compliance with IFRSs, then those listing documents will be the entity's first IFRS financial statements. Consequently, the date of transition to IFRSs will be the beginning of the earliest comparative period for which full IFRS information was provided (i.e. 1 January 20X5).

If the listing documents did not contain an unreserved statement of compliance with IFRSs (e.g. because certain disclosure requirements were omitted as permitted by the local regulator), they cannot be the entity's first IFRS financial statements. In such circumstances, the entity's first IFRS financial statements are those for the year ended 31 December 20X8 and the date of transition to IFRSs is 1 January 20X7.

4.3   Repeated application of IFRS 1

An entity that has applied IFRS 1 in a previous accounting period, but whose most recent previous annual financial statements did not contain an explicit and unreserved statement of compliance with IFRSs, can choose either:

[IFRS 1:4A]

- to apply IFRS 1 (i.e. the entity is treated as a 'first-time' adopter of IFRSs notwithstanding that it has prepared IFRS financial statements in past years but not the most recent previous year); or

- to apply IFRSs retrospectively in accordance with IAS 8 *Accounting Policies, Changes in Accounting Estimates and Errors* as if the entity had never stopped applying IFRSs.

Whichever option is taken:

- hindsight should not be applied in preparing IFRS financial statements (see IFRS 1:BC6C); and

- additional disclosure requirements apply (see **9.3.2**).

Example 4.3

Repeated application of IFRS 1

Company B issued financial statements in 20X1 and 20X2 with an explicit and unreserved statement of compliance with IFRSs. In 20X3, Company B stated compliance with local GAAP only.

If Company B wishes to prepare IFRS-compliant financial statements in 20X4, on what basis should those financial statements be prepared?

In 20X4, Company B can choose either:

- to apply IFRS 1; or
- to apply IFRSs retrospectively as if it had never stopped applying IFRSs.

If Company B elects not to apply IFRS 1 in 20X4, it will in effect need to recreate the IFRS accounting that would have been required if it had prepared financial statements in accordance with IFRSs in 20X3.

5 Recognition and measurement

5.1 General requirement for retrospective application of IFRSs effective at the end of the first IFRS reporting period

The general principle underlying IFRS 1 is that a first-time adopter should apply the version of each IFRS effective at the end of its first IFRS reporting period retrospectively. Therefore, the first IFRS financial statements are presented as if the entity had always applied IFRSs, subject to the exceptions and exemptions discussed later in this chapter.

5.2 Opening IFRS statement of financial position

A first-time adopter is required to prepare and present an opening IFRS statement of financial position (see **3.8**) at the date of transition to IFRSs (see **3.1**). This is the starting point for its accounting under IFRSs. [IFRS 1:6]

As discussed in **5.3.1**, an entity is required to apply the same accounting policies in its opening IFRS statement of financial position and throughout all periods presented in its first IFRS financial statements. These policies are based on IFRSs effective at the end of the first IFRS reporting period, which is at least two years after the date of transition to IFRSs (i.e. the 'as at' date for the opening IFRS statement of financial position). Therefore, it will not be possible to finalise the opening IFRS statement of financial position until it is known that no new or amended IFRSs will be effective for the entity's first IFRS reporting period. If an entity publishes an opening IFRS statement of financial position before this is known (e.g. if the entity is required by the local regulator to disclose information to the market regarding its opening IFRS position but the IASB is still considering amendments which may be effective for the entity's first IFRS financial statements), the entity should state that the amounts disclosed may need to be revised if there are subsequent pronouncements by the IASB that affect the period(s) presented.

The following timeline summarises these requirements and illustrates key dates for a first-time adopter with a calendar year end that presents comparative information for one year.

IFRS adoption timeline

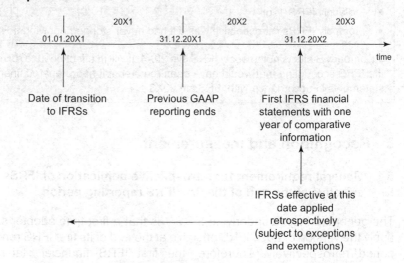

Subject to the exceptions and exemptions discussed in **sections 6** and **7**, respectively, in its opening IFRS statement of financial position an entity should:

[IFRS 1:10]

- recognise all assets and liabilities whose recognition is required by IFRSs;

- not recognise items as assets or liabilities if IFRSs do not permit such recognition;

- reclassify items that it recognised under previous GAAP as one type of asset, liability or component of equity, but are a different asset, liability or component of equity under IFRSs; and

- apply IFRSs in measuring all recognised assets and liabilities.

5.3   Accounting policies

5.3.1   Selection of accounting policies – general

IFRS 1 requires an entity to use the same accounting policies in its opening IFRS statement of financial position and throughout all periods presented in its first IFRS financial statements. Those accounting policies must comply with each IFRS effective at the end of its first IFRS reporting period, subject to exceptions and exemptions that are explained in **sections 6** and **7**, respectively. [IFRS 1:7]

The selection of accounting policies under IFRSs is considered in **section 3** of **chapter A5**. A first-time adopter is not bound by the accounting policy choices it made under previous GAAP, even if the previous GAAP treatment is consistent with IFRSs. In particular, in circumstances in which IFRSs permit an explicit choice, that choice is not constrained by the policy adopted under previous GAAP (e.g. whether to use the revaluation basis for a class of property, plant and equipment). However, in other cases (e.g. when there is no specific guidance in IFRSs), the factors that were relevant in selecting an appropriate policy under previous GAAP should be considered when applying IAS 8 *Accounting Policies, Changes in Accounting Estimates and Errors.*

An entity may not apply different versions of IFRSs that were effective at earlier dates. [IFRS 1:8]

5.3.2   Transition provisions in other IFRSs do not generally apply

The transition provisions in other IFRSs apply to changes in accounting policies made by entities that already use IFRSs. They do not apply to a first-time adopter's transition to IFRSs except in certain specified circumstances that are explained in **sections 6** and **7**. [IFRS 1:9]

For example, an entity with a 31 March year end prepares its first IFRS financial statements at 31 March 20X3. It presents a single year of comparative figures. The entity's date of transition to IFRSs is, therefore, 1 April 20X1.

The entity applies all of those IFRSs that are effective for years beginning on 1 April 20X2 (i.e. those that are effective at the end of its reporting period) and ignores any transition provisions in those IFRSs except when IFRS 1 specifies that they should be applied. Those IFRSs should be applied in preparing the opening statement of financial position at 1 April 20X1, the comparative statement of financial position at 31 March 20X2, and the statement of financial position at 31 March 20X3 in accordance with IFRSs. The entity is permitted, but not required, to apply any new IFRSs that have been issued but are not mandatory, provided that the IFRSs in question permit early adoption (see **5.3.3**).

5.3.3   Application of new IFRSs that are not yet effective

A first-time adopter may apply a new IFRS that is not yet mandatory if the IFRS permits early adoption. [IFRS 1:8]

In December 2013, the Basis of Conclusions on IFRS 1 was amended by *Improvements to IFRSs: 2011-2013 Cycle* to emphasise that a first-time adopter has a choice between applying an existing and currently effective IFRS and applying a new or revised IFRS that is not yet mandatorily effective, provided that the new or revised IFRS permits early application. An entity is required to apply the same version of the IFRS throughout the periods covered by its first IFRS financial statements. Consequently, if a first-time adopter chooses to apply a new IFRS in advance of its effective date, that new IFRS should be applied throughout all the periods presented in the entity's first IFRS financial statements on a retrospective basis, unless IFRS 1 provides an exemption or an exception that permits or requires otherwise. [IFRS 1:BC11A]

5.3.4   New or amended IFRSs effective for the first IFRS reporting period issued after an interim financial report has been published

If an entity publishes an interim financial report during its first IFRS reporting period, it cannot be certain that there will be no subsequent changes to IFRSs that are effective for its first IFRS reporting period. In the event of such changes, the entity should revise its opening statement of financial position to comply with the new requirements and explain that it has done so in any subsequent interim financial report or its first annual financial statements under IFRSs. It is advisable for entities to include a statement in their interim financial reports to highlight the fact that the IFRS accounting policies may be subject to change.

5.3.5   Accounting policy changes after an entity has published an interim financial report in the year of adoption of IFRSs

IAS 8 *Accounting Policies, Changes in Accounting Estimates and Errors* does not apply to the changes in accounting policies that an entity makes when it adopts IFRSs or to changes in those policies until after it presents its first IFRS financial statements. Therefore, IAS 8's requirements regarding changes in accounting policies do not apply in an entity's first IFRS financial statements. [IFRS 1:27]

Consequently, when an entity has prepared an interim financial report under IFRSs during its first IFRS reporting period, it is acceptable for the entity to change the IFRS 1 elections and/or accounting policy choices reflected in that interim financial report in later reporting periods, leading up to and including its first annual financial statements. An entity's choices only need to be fixed by the time it prepares its first annual financial statements in accordance with IFRSs. The requirements of IAS 8 (both as regards justification for a change in accounting policy and disclosure) do not apply to any changes in accounting policies until after an entity presents its first IFRS financial statements (i.e. the first annual financial statements in which it adopts IFRSs).

If during the period covered by its first IFRS financial statements an entity changes its accounting policies or its use of the IFRS 1 exemptions, the effect of those changes should be explained and disclosed in the reconciliations required under IFRS 1, if appropriate (see **9.3.3**).

5.3.6   *Adjustments arising on the restatement of the opening statement of financial position*

The adjustments arising on the restatement of the opening statement of financial position from previous GAAP to IFRSs should be recognised as an adjustment to retained earnings or, if appropriate, another category of equity, at the date of transition to IFRSs. [IFRS 1:11]

The adjustments are usually recognised in retained earnings except when another IFRS requires a separate component of equity to be recognised. For example, when an entity applies the revaluation model in IAS 16, the difference between fair value and depreciated cost at the date of transition is credited to a revaluation reserve. Similarly, a separate reserve is recognised in relation to derivatives classified as cash flow hedges. However, there is nothing to prevent a separate reserve being recognised within retained earnings in other circumstances. This may be appropriate, for example, if the reserve is not distributable or is subject to other legal restrictions.

6   Exceptions to retrospective application of other IFRSs

6.1   List of mandatory exceptions to retrospective application of other IFRSs

IFRS 1 prohibits retrospective application of some aspects of other IFRSs relating to:

[IFRS 1:13 and IFRS 1:B1]

- estimates (see **6.2**);

- derecognition of financial assets and financial liabilities (see **6.3**);

- hedge accounting (see **6.4**);

- non-controlling interests (see **6.5**);

- classification and measurement of financial assets (see **6.6**);

- impairment of financial assets (see **6.7**);

- embedded derivatives (see **6.8**); and

- government loans (see **6.9**).

> The exceptions relating to classification and measurement, and impairment, of financial assets, and embedded derivatives apply only to entities that adopt IFRS 9 *Financial Instruments* in their first IFRS financial statements.

6.2   Estimates

6.2.1   General requirement for estimates to be consistent with those under previous GAAP

IFRS 1 requires estimates under IFRSs at the date of transition to IFRSs to be consistent with estimates made for the same date under previous GAAP, after adjustments to reflect any difference in accounting policies, unless there is objective evidence that those estimates were in error. [IFRS 1:14]

> Therefore, accounting estimates required under IFRSs that were made under previous GAAP may not be adjusted on transition except to reflect differences in accounting policies or unless there is objective evidence that the estimates were in error. The primary objective of this exception is to prevent entities using the benefit of hindsight to adjust estimates based on circumstances and information that were not known when the amounts were originally estimated under previous GAAP.

When restating the opening statement of financial position to IFRSs, an entity may have information about estimates it made under previous GAAP that was not available at the time when those estimates were made. This information is treated as non-adjusting (i.e. the amounts recognised are not adjusted). IFRS 1 gives the following example to illustrate this requirement.

Example 6.2.1

Consistency of estimates with previous GAAP

[IFRS 1:15]

Assume that an entity's date of transition to IFRSs is 1 January 20X4 and new information on 15 July 20X4 requires the revision of an estimate made in accordance with previous GAAP at 31 December 20X3. The entity shall not reflect that new information in its opening IFRS statement of financial position (unless the estimates need adjustment for any differences in accounting policies or there is objective evidence that the estimates were in error). Instead, the entity shall reflect the new information in profit or loss (or, if appropriate, other comprehensive income) for the year ended 31 December 20X4.

It may be necessary to make estimates under IFRSs at the date of transition to IFRSs that were not required at that date under previous GAAP. Those estimates should reflect conditions that existed at the date of transition to IFRSs. In particular, estimates of market prices, interest rates or foreign exchange rates should reflect market conditions at the date of transition to IFRSs. [IFRS 1:16]

The implementation guidance accompanying IFRS 1 explains that this exception does not override the requirements in other IFRSs to base classifications or measurements on circumstances existing at a particular date. Examples given are:

[IFRS 1:IG4]

- the distinction between finance leases and operating leases in IAS 17 *Leases*;

- the restrictions in IAS 38 *Intangible Assets* that prohibit capitalisation of expenditure on an internally generated intangible asset if the asset did not qualify for recognition when the expenditure was incurred; and

- the distinction between financial liabilities and equity instruments in IAS 32 *Financial Instruments: Presentation*.

The use of actuarial assumptions when applying IAS 19 *Employee Benefits* for the first time is considered at **8.10**.

6.2.2 Correction of an error that occurred prior to the date of transition to IFRSs

If, when preparing its first IFRS financial statements, an entity discovers an error in an estimate made under previous GAAP, the effect of the correction of the error should be adjusted against retained earnings in the opening statement of financial position.

Such corrections should be disclosed separately in the reconciliations required under IFRS 1:24(a) and (b) (see **9.3.3**). This disclosure should be on a gross basis; presentation of net errors is not acceptable.

6.2.3 Estimates made at the end of the comparative period

The principle also applies to comparative information presented in an entity's first IFRS financial statements. [IFRS 1:17] Therefore, estimates made at the end of the comparative period (in **example 6.2.1**, at 31 December 20X4) should follow the same rules as the opening IFRS statement of financial position as regards the use of hindsight.

6.3   Derecognition of financial assets and financial liabilities

6.3.1   Derecognition requirements generally to be applied prospectively

A first-time adopter is required by IFRS 1:B2 to apply the derecognition rules in IFRS 9 (or, if the entity has not adopted IFRS 9, IAS 39) prospectively from the date of transition to IFRSs unless it elects to apply those derecognition rules retrospectively from a date of its choosing in accordance with IFRS 1:B3 (see **6.3.2**). Therefore, if a first-time adopter derecognised financial assets or financial liabilities under its previous GAAP in a securitisation, transfer or other derecognition transaction that occurred before the date of transition to IFRSs (or an earlier date of the entity's choosing in accordance with IFRS 1:B3), it does not recognise those assets or liabilities at the date of transition (even if they would not have qualified for derecognition under IFRS 9 or IAS 39), unless they qualify for recognition as a result of a later transaction or event.

In applying this exception, it is important to note the following points.

*   A first-time adopter must recognise any financial interest retained as a result of a derecognition transaction prior to the date of transition to IFRSs that still exists at the date of transition to IFRSs (e.g. any derivatives and other interests, such as servicing rights or servicing liabilities).

*   The exemptions from retrospective application of the derecognition requirements do not extend to consolidation. A first-time adopter must consolidate all entities, including structured entities, that it controls at the date of transition to IFRSs, even if those entities existed before the date of transition to IFRSs or hold financial assets or financial liabilities that were derecognised under previous GAAP. [IFRS 1:IG26] Therefore, although a group may have derecognised financial assets under its previous GAAP before the date of transition to IFRSs (or before a different date of its choosing in accordance with IFRS 1:B3 – see **6.3.2**) by transferring the assets to an unconsolidated transferee, if the transferee is consolidated into the group's statement of financial position under IFRS 10 *Consolidated Financial Statements*, and the transferee did not derecognise the transferred assets under previous GAAP, then the IFRS 9 (or IAS 39) derecognition requirements will be applied to the new group, including the transferred assets, as defined by IFRSs.

6.3.2   Option to apply derecognition rules retrospectively from a chosen date

Notwithstanding the requirement to apply the rules on derecognition prospectively from the date of transition to IFRSs, an entity may choose to apply them retrospectively from a date of the entity's choosing, provided that the information needed to apply IFRS 9 (or, if the entity has not adopted IFRS 9, IAS 39) to the financial assets and financial liabilities derecognised as a result of past transactions was obtained at the time of initially accounting for those transactions. [IFRS 1:B3]

For a more detailed discussion of the application of these derecognition rules on first-time adoption, see **chapter B12** or, for entities that have not adopted IFRS 9, **chapter C13**.

6.4 Hedge accounting

6.4.1 General prohibition on retrospective application of hedge accounting requirements

IFRS 1 prohibits retrospective application of IFRS 9 (or, for entities that have not yet adopted IFRS 9, IAS 39) in respect of hedge accounting. [IFRS 1:B4 - B6] This is consistent with the general hedging requirements in IFRS 9 (IAS 39) under which hedge accounting is only ever available prospectively if the hedge relationship is appropriately designated, documented and satisfies all other hedge accounting criteria.

At the date of transition to IFRSs, an entity is required to measure all derivatives at fair value and eliminate all deferred gains and losses arising on derivatives that were reported under previous GAAP as assets or liabilities in the statement of financial position in respect of hedge relationships under previous GAAP because these do not qualify for recognition as assets and liabilities under IFRSs. [IFRS 1:B4]

If, before the date of transition to IFRSs, a transaction had been designated as a hedge of a type that qualifies for hedge accounting under IFRS 9 (or, for entities that have not yet adopted IFRS 9, IAS 39) but the hedge does not meet all the specific conditions for hedge accounting in IFRS 9 (IAS 39), the requirements of IFRS 9:6.5.6 and 6.5.7 (IAS 39:91 and IAS 39:101) should be applied to discontinue hedge accounting. Transactions entered into before the date of transition to IFRSs should not be retrospectively designated as hedges. [IFRS 1:B6]

The designation and documentation of a hedge relationship must be completed on or before the date of transition to IFRSs if the hedge relationship is to qualify for hedge accounting from that date. Hedge accounting can be applied prospectively only from the date that the hedge relationship is fully designated and documented. [IFRS 1:IG60]

6.4.2 First-time adopters applying IFRS 9 not permitted to use the hedge accounting requirements in IAS 39

The transition requirements in IFRS 9:7.2.21 (see **3.3** in **chapter B12**) permit entities that already apply IFRSs and that are applying IFRS 9 for the first time to continue to use the hedge accounting requirements in IAS 39. However, a first-time adopter applying IFRS 9 in its first IFRS financial statements is not permitted to apply IFRS 9:7.2.21.

The transition provisions in IFRSs apply to changes in accounting policies made by entities that already use IFRSs. They do not apply to a first-time adopter's transition to IFRSs except in the circumstances specified in IFRS 1 (see **sections 6** and **7**), which does not provide any exception equivalent to the requirements of IFRS 9:7.2.21. It is worth noting that if a first-time adopter of IFRSs wishes to apply the hedge accounting requirements of IAS 39, instead of those in IFRS 9, this can be achieved if the first-time adopter's date of transition to IFRSs is prior to the effective date of IFRS 9. The first-time adopter could in that case adopt IAS 39 in full in its first IFRS financial statements and then adopt IFRS 9, applying IFRS 9's transition provisions, in a subsequent period (either at or before IFRS 9's effective date). However, this approach is unlikely to be attractive to most first-time adopters because it may be burdensome to adopt IAS 39 in full and transition to IFRS 9 at a later date.

6.4.3 Re-designation or discontinuation of hedge relationships of a type that does not comply with IFRS requirements

6.4.3.1 Re-designation or discontinuation of hedge relationships of a type that does not comply with IFRS 9

When a first-time adopter applying IFRS 9 has a hedge relationship of a type that does not qualify for hedge accounting under IFRS 9, the entity should not reflect that hedge relationship in its opening IFRS statement of financial position. However, if an entity designated a net position as a hedged item under its previous GAAP, it may designate an individual line item within that net position as a hedged item in accordance with IFRSs, or a net position that meets the requirements in IFRS 9:6.6.1, provided that it does so no later than the date of transition to IFRSs and provided that all other hedge accounting criteria are met. [IFRS 1:B5]

6.4.3.2 Re-designation or discontinuation of hedge relationships of a type that does not comply with IAS 39

When a first-time adopter applying IAS 39 has a hedge relationship of a type that does not qualify for hedge accounting under IAS 39, the entity should not reflect that hedge relationship in its opening IFRS statement of financial position. However, if an entity designated a net position as a hedged item under its previous GAAP, it may designate an individual item within that net position as a hedged item in accordance with IFRSs, provided that it does so no later than the date of transition to IFRSs and provided that all other hedge accounting criteria are met. [IFRS 1:B5]

6.4.4 Hedge relationships that continue to qualify under IFRS 9 (or IAS 39)

For a hedge relationship to continue to qualify as a hedge relationship at the date of transition to IFRSs, it must meet all of the hedge accounting criteria in IFRS 9 or IAS 39 (see **volume B** and **volume C**, respectively, for detailed requirements). In particular, the designation and documentation of a hedge relationship must be completed on or before the date of transition to IFRSs if the hedge relationship is to qualify for hedge accounting from that date. Hedge accounting can be applied prospectively only from the date that the hedge relationship is fully designated and documented.

For a first-time adopter of IFRSs, this may be a significant change from previous GAAP which may not have required such rigorous hedge designation and documentation. Hedge accounting under IFRS 9 (or IAS 39), and consequently on first-time adoption of IFRSs, can only be applied prospectively from the date that the hedge relationship is fully designated and documented, subject to all other hedge accounting requirements of IFRS 9 (or IAS 39) being met.

For a more detailed discussion of the application of hedge accounting requirements on first-time adoption, see **chapter B12** or, for entities that have not adopted IFRS 9, **chapter C13**.

6.5 Non-controlling interests

A first-time adopter should apply the following requirements of IFRS 10 *Consolidated Financial Statements* prospectively from the date of transition to IFRSs:

[IFRS 1:B7]

- the requirement in IFRS 10:B94 that total comprehensive income be attributed to the owners of the parent and to the non-controlling interests even if this results in the non-controlling interests having a deficit balance;

- the requirements in IFRS 10:23 and B96 regarding the accounting for changes in the parent's ownership interest in a subsidiary that do not result in a loss of control; and

- the requirements in IFRS 10:B97 to B99 regarding the accounting for a loss of control over a subsidiary, and the related requirements in paragraph 8A of IFRS 5 *Non-current Assets Held for Sale and Discontinued Operations*.

However, if a first-time adopter elects to apply IFRS 3 *Business Combinations* retrospectively to past business combinations, it must also apply IFRS 10 from the same date (see **7.2**). [IFRS 1:C1]

6.6   Classification and measurement of financial assets (entities applying IFRS 9)

A first-time adopter applying IFRS 9 is required to assess whether a financial asset meets the amortised cost criteria in IFRS 9:4.1.2 or the fair value through other comprehensive income criteria in IFRS 9:4.1.2A on the basis of the facts and circumstances that exist at the date of transition to IFRSs. [IFRS 1:B8]

> The criteria for qualification for amortised cost and fair value through other comprehensive income measurement under IFRS 9 are discussed in detail in **chapter B2**. In summary, in relation to amortised cost measurement, IFRS 9:4.1.2 requires an entity to assess whether the objective of its business model is to manage financial assets so as to collect the contractual cash flows. In relation to measurement at fair value through other comprehensive income, IFRS 9:4.1.2A requires an entity to assess whether the business model is achieved by both collecting contractual cash flows and selling financial assets. The requirement in IFRS 1:B8 for first-time adopters to make this assessment on the basis of facts and circumstances at the date of transition is consistent with the general transition requirement for continuing IFRS reporters in IFRS 9:7.2.1 (which requires that the assessment be carried out at the date of initial application of the Standard). IFRS 9:BC7.18 explains that the IASB believes that it would be "difficult, and perhaps impossible," to make the assessment on the basis of circumstances when the financial asset first qualified for recognition as a financial asset.
>
> Once the classification of a financial asset has been determined on the basis described in IFRS 1:B8, that classification is applied retrospectively irrespective of the entity's business model in prior reporting periods.

If it is impracticable to assess a modified time value of money element in accordance with IFRS 9:B4.1.9B to B4.1.9D on the basis of the facts and circumstances that exist at the date of transition to IFRSs, a first-time adopter is required to assess the contractual cash flow characteristics of that financial asset on the basis of the facts and circumstances that existed at the date of transition to IFRSs without taking into account the requirements related to the modification of the time value of money element in IFRS 9:B4.1.9B to B4.1.9D. (In this case, the entity is also required to apply paragraph 42R of IFRS 7 but references to 'paragraph 7.2.4 of IFRS 9' should be read to mean IFRS1:B8A and references to 'initial recognition of the financial asset' should be read to mean 'at the date of transition to IFRSs'.) [IFRS 1:B8A]

If it is impracticable to assess whether the fair value of a prepayment feature is insignificant in accordance with IFRS 9:B4.1.12(c) on the basis of the facts and circumstances that exist at the date of transition to IFRSs, a first-time adopter is required to assess the contractual cash flow characteristics of that financial asset on the basis of the facts and circumstances that existed at the date of transition to IFRSs without taking into account the exception for prepayment features in IFRS 9:B4.1.12. (In this case, the entity is also required to apply paragraph 42S of IFRS 7 but references to 'paragraph 7.2.5 of IFRS 9' should be read to mean IFRS 1:D8B and references to 'initial recognition of the financial asset' should be read to mean 'at the date of transition to IFRSs'.) [IFRS 1:B8B]

If it is 'impracticable' (as defined in IAS 8 *Accounting Policies, Changes in Accounting Estimates and Errors* – see **chapter A5**) for an entity to apply retrospectively the effective interest method in IFRS 9, the fair value of the financial asset or the financial liability at the date of transition to IFRSs should be the new gross carrying amount of that financial asset or the new amortised cost of that financial liability at the date of transition to IFRSs. [IFRS 1:8C]

For a more detailed discussion of the application of IFRS 9's classification and measurement requirements on first-time adoption, see **chapter B12**.

6.7 Impairment of financial assets (entities applying IFRS 9)

The requirements regarding impairment of financial assets for first-time adopters are the same as the IFRS 9 transition requirements for continuing IFRS reporters.

IFRS 1:B8D requires that the impairment requirements in section 5.5 of IFRS 9 are applied retrospectively subject to IFRS 9:7.2.15 (on whether to restate comparative information) and IFRS 9:7.2.18 to 7.2.20.

At the date of transition to IFRSs, a first-time adopter is required to use reasonable and supportable information that is available without undue cost or effort to determine the credit risk at the date that financial instruments were initially recognised (or, for loan commitments and financial guarantee contracts, the date that the entity became a party to the irrevocable commitment in accordance with IFRS 9:5.5.6) and compare that to the credit risk at the date of transition to IFRSs. [IFRS 1:B8E]

When determining whether there has been a significant increase in credit risk since initial recognition, a first-time adopter is permitted to apply:

[IFRS 1:B8F]

(a) the requirements in IFRS 9:5.5.10 and IFRS 9:B5.5.22 to B5.5.24 in assuming the credit risk on the financial instrument is 'low'; and

(b) the rebuttable presumption in IFRS 9:5.5.11 for contractual payments that are more than 30 days past due if the entity will apply the impairment requirements by identifying significant increases in credit risk since initial recognition for those financial instruments on the basis of past due information.

If, at the date of date of transition to IFRSs, determining whether there has been a significant increase in credit risk since initial recognition would require undue cost or effort, a first-time adopter should recognise a loss allowance at an amount equal to lifetime expected credit losses at each reporting date until that financial instrument is derecognised (unless that financial instrument is low credit risk at a reporting date, in which case IFRS 1:B8F(a) (see above) applies). [IFRS 1:B8G]

6.8   Embedded derivatives (entities applying IFRS 9)

A first-time adopter applying IFRS 9 is required to assess whether an embedded derivative should be separated from the host contract and accounted for as a derivative on the basis of the conditions that existed at the later of the date it first became a party to the contract and the date a reassessment is required by IFRS 9:B4.3.11. [IFRS 1:B9]

IFRS 9's requirements regarding the accounting for embedded derivatives are discussed in detail in **chapter B5**. In summary, IFRS 9 requires separate accounting for embedded derivatives not closely related to the host contract when the entire contract is not one measured at fair value through profit or loss and it is not a financial asset in the scope of IFRS 9. That assessment is generally made when the entity first becomes a party to a contract, and is revisited only when there has been a 'substantial modification' to the contract (see **section 3** of **chapter B5**). IFRS 1:B9 requires that a first-time adopter should make its assessment as to whether an embedded derivative is to be separated on the basis of conditions that existed at the later of the date it first became party to the contract and the date (if any) when the contract is substantially modified.

Once a first-time adopter has determined that an embedded derivative should be separated, the initial carrying amounts of the embedded derivative and the host contract should be determined based on the circumstances at the date the whole instrument satisfied the recognition criteria of IFRS 9. [IFRS 1:IG55]

If the entity cannot determine the initial carrying amounts of the embedded derivative and the host contract reliably, it treats the entire combined contract as a financial instrument as at fair value through profit or loss (see **section 12** of **chapter B5**). [IFRS 1:IG55]

6.9 Government loans

6.9.1 Government loans received to be classified as either a financial liability or as equity

A first-time adopter is required to classify all government loans received as either a financial liability or as an equity instrument in accordance with the requirements of IAS 32 *Financial Instruments: Presentation*. [IFRS 1:B10]

6.9.2 Requirements regarding government loans generally to be applied prospectively to government loans existing at the date of transition

Except as permitted in IFRS 1:B11 (see **6.9.3**), first-time adopters should apply the requirements in IFRS 9 (or, for first-time adopters that have not adopted IFRS 9, IAS 39) and IAS 20 *Accounting for Government Grants and Disclosure of Government Assistance* prospectively to government loans existing at the date of transition to IFRSs. When these requirements are applied prospectively:

[IFRS 1:B10]

- the first-time adopter should not recognise the corresponding benefit of the government loan at a below-market interest rate as a government grant;

- if the first-time adopter did not, under its previous GAAP, recognise and measure a government loan at a below-market rate of interest on a basis consistent with IFRSs, the previous GAAP carrying amount of the loan at the date of transition is used as the carrying amount of the loan in the opening IFRS statement of financial position; and

- IFRS 9 (or IAS 39) is applied in measuring the loan after the date of transition. For this purpose, the entity should calculate the effective interest rate on the loan by comparing the carrying amount of the loan at the date of transition to IFRSs with the amount and timing of expected repayments. [IFRS 1:IG66]

The following example, which is reproduced from the guidance accompanying IFRS 1, illustrates the application of these requirements for a first-time adopter.

Example 6.9.2

Government loan at a below-market rate of interest at the date of transition to IFRSs

[IFRS 1:IG66, Example 12]

To encourage entities to expand their operations in a specified development zone where it is difficult for entities to obtain financing for their projects, the

---

government provides loans at a below-market rate of interest to fund the purchase of manufacturing equipment.

Entity S's date of transition is 1 January 20X2.

In accordance with the development scheme, in 20X0 Entity S receives a loan at a below-market rate of interest from the government for CU100,000. Under its previous GAAP, Entity S accounted for the loan as equity and the carrying amount under previous GAAP was CU100,000 at the date of transition to IFRSs. The amount repayable will be CU103,030 on 1 January 20X5.

No other payment is required under the terms of the loan and there are no further performance conditions attached to the loan. The information needed to measure the fair value of the loan was not obtained at the time of initially accounting for the loan.

The loan meets the definition of a financial liability in accordance with IAS 32. Entity S therefore reclassifies the government loan as a liability. It also uses the previous GAAP carrying amount of the loan at the date of transition to IFRSs as the carrying amount of the loan in the opening IFRS statement of financial position. Entity S therefore reclassifies the amount of CU100,000 from equity to liability in the opening IFRS statement of financial position. In order to measure the loan after the date of transition to IFRSs, the effective interest rate starting 1 January 20X2 is calculated as below:

$= (103,030 / 100,000)^{-3} - 1$

$= 0.01$

The carrying amounts of the loan are as follows:

Date	Carrying amount CU	Interest expense CU	Interest payable CU
1 January 20X2	100,000		
31 December 20X2	101,000	1,000	1,000
31 December 20X3	102,010	1,010	2,010
31 December 20X4	103,030	1,020	3,030

6.9.3 Option on a loan-by-loan basis to apply requirements re government loans retrospectively

Not with standing the requirement under IFRS 1:B10 to apply the relevant requirements of IFRSs prospectively to government loans existing at the date of transition to IFRSs, an entity may choose to apply them retrospectively to any government loan originated before its date of transition to IFRSs, provided that the information needed to do so was obtained at the time of initially accounting for that loan. [IFRS 1:B11]

Consequently, if the information needed to apply IFRS 9 (or IAS 39) was obtained at the time of initially accounting for the loan, an entity can choose to apply the relevant requirements retrospectively; this option is available on a loan-by-loan basis.

6.9.4 Application of the optional exemption relating to designation of previously recognised financial instrument

The requirements and guidance in IFRS 1:B10 and B11 (see **6.9.1** to **6.9.3**) do not preclude an entity from being able to use the exemptions described in IFRS 1:D19 to D19D (see **7.11**) relating to the designation of previously recognised financial instruments at fair value through profit or loss. [IFRS 1:B12]

7 Optional exemptions from retrospective application of other IFRSs

7.1 Optional exemptions – general

7.1.1 List of optional exemptions from retrospective application of other IFRSs

Retrospective application of IFRSs can require significant resources and could, in some circumstances, be impracticable. The IASB decided that the costs of applying IFRSs retrospectively may exceed the benefits in certain instances. IFRS 1 therefore provides a number of optional exemptions from the general principle of full retrospective application. The exemptions described in **7.2** to **7.22** are those that have continuing relevance for annual periods beginning after 1 January 2014.

A first-time adopter may elect to use one or more of the following exemptions:

[IFRS 1:18, IFRS 1:Appendices C & D]

- business combinations (see **7.2**);
- share-based payment transactions (see **7.3**);
- insurance contracts (see **7.4**);
- deemed cost (see **7.5**);
- leases (see **7.6**);
- cumulative translation differences (see **7.7**);
- investments in subsidiaries, associates and joint ventures (see **7.8**);

- assets and liabilities of subsidiaries, associates and joint ventures (see **7.9**);

- compound financial instruments (see **7.10**);

- designation of previously recognised financial instruments (see **7.11**);

- fair value measurement of financial assets or financial liabilities at initial recognition (see **7.12**);

- decommissioning liabilities included in the cost of property, plant and equipment (see **7.13**);

- financial assets or intangible assets accounted for in accordance with IFRIC 12 *Service Concession Arrangements* (see **7.14**);

- borrowing costs (see **7.15**);

- for entities that have not adopted IFRS 15 *Revenue from Contracts with Customers*, transfers of assets from customers (see **7.16**);

- extinguishing financial liabilities with equity instruments (see **7.17**);

- severe hyperinflation (see **7.18**);

- joint arrangements (see **7.19**);

- stripping costs in the production phase of a surface mine (see **7.20**);

- designation of contracts to buy or sell a non-financial item (see **7.21**); and

- for entities that have adopted IFRS 15, revenue (see **7.22**).

Appendix E to IFRS 1 sets out another category of 'short-term exemptions' which are applicable to users for a short time and which will be deleted once they become out of date (discussed in detail in **7.23**).

Unlike the mandatory exceptions discussed in **section 6**, because the exemptions listed above are optional, entities may choose not to take advantage of them and instead to apply their IFRS accounting policies in these areas retrospectively, provided that the effects of retrospective application can be reliably estimated.

7.1.2   More than one optional exemption affecting an account balance

If more than one optional exemption affects an account balance, more than one exemption may be applied. Each optional exemption is applied independently. There is no requirement to use a particular optional exemption as the result of choosing another exemption.

For example, an entity might not restate a business combination prior to the date of transition so that the deemed cost of property, plant and equipment acquired in that business combination is the carrying amount under previous GAAP immediately after the business combination. The entity can override this deemed cost with a later deemed cost, such as fair value at the date of transition.

7.1.3   Optional exemptions not be applied by analogy to other items

IFRS 1 states that the exemptions should not be applied by analogy to other items. [IFRS 1:D1]

For example, a first-time adopter cannot use fair value or the previous GAAP carrying amount of an item as deemed cost except as specifically set out in the exemption (see **7.5**). The Standard specifies limited circumstances in which retrospective restatement in accordance with IFRSs does not apply. Unless the amount is immaterial, in all other circumstances IFRSs should be applied retrospectively.

7.2   Business combinations

7.2.1   Scope of the exemption for business combinations

7.2.1.1   Exemption applies to business combinations to which IFRS 3 applies

Rather than apply IFRS 3 *Business Combinations* retrospectively to business combinations prior to the date of transition to IFRSs, as an optional exemption first-time adopters are permitted to apply the requirements of Appendix C to IFRS 1. [IFRS 1:C1]

The exemption available under IFRS 1:C1 only applies to business combinations to which IFRS 3 applies. The exemption does not apply, for example, to an investment entity's acquisition of a subsidiary to which, under paragraph 31 of IFRS 10 *Consolidated Financial Statements*, IFRS 3 should not be applied (see **13.3.2** of **chapter A24**).

7.2.1.2   Definition of a business combination for the exemption

The determination as to whether a transaction qualifies for the business combination exemption depends on whether that combination meets the definition of a business combination under IFRSs. If the transaction meets the definition, regardless of whether it met the definition under the entity's previous GAAP, use of the exemption for business combinations is permitted for that transaction.

If a subsidiary was not previously consolidated (e.g. because the parent did not regard the entity as a subsidiary under previous GAAP), the requirements of IFRS 1:C4(j) regarding subsidiaries not previously consolidated should be applied (see **7.2.13**).

7.2.1.3   IFRS 3 to be applied all business combinations on or after the date of transition

For first-time adopters, irrespective of any exemptions applied, all business combinations on or after the date of transition to IFRSs should be accounted for in accordance with IFRS 3.

Therefore, if an entity is preparing its first IFRS financial statements for the year ended 31 December 20X2, and its date of transition is 1 January 20X1, all business combinations on or after 1 January 20X1 are required to be accounted for in accordance with IFRS 3. If a business combination occurred in the comparative accounting period (20X1) and it was reported in the entity's previous GAAP financial statements for that period, the amounts previously reported will need to be restated if the application of IFRS 3 has a material effect.

7.2.1.4   Option for full retrospective application of IFRS 3 to business combinations before the date of transition

Entities that wish to apply IFRS 3 retrospectively to all business combinations prior to the date of transition to IFRSs may do so.

Any entity intending to opt for full retrospective application should ensure that it has the information needed to apply the acquisition method retrospectively in accordance with IFRS 3, which in particular includes:

- calculation of the cost of the business combination;

- identification of assets acquired (including any intangible assets), and liabilities assumed;

- measurement of fair value at the date of acquisition of assets acquired and liabilities assumed; and

- impairment test of goodwill each year subsequent to the date of acquisition.

Example 7.2.1.4

Full retrospective application of IFRS 3 – which version of IFRS 3?

Entity A is adopting IFRSs for the first time with a transition date of 1 January 2014 and its first IFRS financial statements will be prepared for the accounting period ended 31 December 2015. Entity A elects not to take the optional exemption in IFRS 1 and instead will apply IFRS 3 retrospectively to all past business combinations. Entity A has been involved in several business combinations dating back to 1990.

Which version of IFRS 3 should be applied to Entity A's business combinations before the effective date of IFRS 3 (as revised in 2008)?

If retrospective application of IFRS 3 is selected, IFRS 1 requires consistent application of the version of IFRS 3 that is adopted for the entity's first IFRS reporting period. Therefore, in the circumstances described, because IFRS 3 (as revised in 2008) is to be applied in the first IFRS reporting period, it must be applied retrospectively to all past business combinations (i.e. the previous version of IFRS 3 (issued in 2004) should *not* be applied to any of the entity's previous business combinations).

7.2.2 Key effects of using the business combinations exemption

The most significant features of the accounting under Appendix C to IFRS 1 (discussed in detail in **7.2.3** to **7.2.16**) are as follows:

- the classification of former business combinations (acquisition or uniting of interests) under previous GAAP is maintained;

- there is no remeasurement of original 'fair values' determined at the time of the business combination (date of acquisition); and

- the carrying amount of goodwill recognised under previous GAAP is not adjusted, other than in specific instances.

It is important to understand that, although business combinations that occurred before the date of transition to IFRSs do not have to be 'restated' when the entity takes this optional exemption, this does not mean that all amounts recognised under previous GAAP relating to such business combinations can simply be carried forward under IFRSs. Adjustments may be required to the assets and liabilities recognised in such business combinations.

The decision to apply the business combinations exemption on first-time adoption, and the date from which the exemption is applied (see **7.2.3**), can have a substantial impact on an entity's first IFRS financial statements. The following table summarises the key differences between using the exemption and restating business combinations to conform with the requirements of IFRS 3.

Subject	Optional exemption in IFRS 1 applied	IFRS 3 applied retrospectively
Classification (see **7.2.6**)	Keep the previous classification (acquisition/ pooling of interests/ reverse acquisition).	Identify the acquirer and the acquiree under IFRS 3

Subject	Optional exemption in IFRS 1 applied	IFRS 3 applied retrospectively
Recognition (see **7.2.7** and **7.2.8**)	Identify assets and liabilities at the date of transition to IFRSs and: • recognise assets and liabilities in compliance with IFRSs (except for some financial assets and financial liabilities derecognised under previous GAAP and some assets and liabilities that were not recognised in the acquirer's statement of financial position under previous GAAP), which means that both recognition criteria – reliable measurement and probability – must be met for all assets and liabilities; and • exclude assets and liabilities not complying with IFRSs.	Identify assets and liabilities at the date of acquisition and: • recognise assets and liabilities in accordance with IFRS 3; and • exclude assets and liabilities not complying with IFRSs.
Measurement (see **7.2.9** to **7.2.11**)	**IFRS measurement basis other than cost:** these assets and liabilities are measured on that basis at the date of transition, e.g. fair value. **Cost-based measured assets and liabilities:** these assets and liabilities are measured at the carrying amount under previous GAAP immediately after the business combination less subsequent accumulated depreciation under IFRSs. **Assets and liabilities not recognised under previous GAAP:** these assets and liabilities are measured as if the acquiree had adopted IFRSs.	All identifiable assets and liabilities are measured in accordance with IFRS 3 (most at fair value at the date of acquisition).
Measurement of goodwill (see **7.2.12**)	Keep the carrying amount of goodwill at the date of transition, except adjust for: • recognition/non-recognition of intangible assets at the date of transition; and • impairment of goodwill. Goodwill deducted from equity under previous GAAP remains deducted from equity at the date of transition.	Goodwill is determined at the date of acquisition in accordance with IFRS 3. This is likely to result in adjustments to the carrying amount of any goodwill recognised under previous GAAP, including reversals of goodwill previously deducted from equity. Reverse previous goodwill amortisation.

Subject	Optional exemption in IFRS 1 applied	IFRS 3 applied retrospectively
Subsidiaries not previously consolidated (see 7.2.13)	Recognise and measure assets and liabilities at the date of transition as if the subsidiary always has applied IFRSs. Determine goodwill at the date of transition as the difference between: • the parent's interest in those adjusted carrying amounts; and • the cost of the investment in the subsidiary.	Apply the general rules as stated above.

7.2.3   *Timing the use of the exemption*

A first-time adopter may elect not to apply IFRS 3 retrospectively to business combinations that occurred before the date of transition to IFRSs. [IFRS 1:C1] In such circumstances, IFRS 3 is applied prospectively for business combinations on or after the date of transition.

However, the entity may elect to restate business combinations from any date prior to the date of transition. If any business combination is restated, then all later business combinations must also be restated. [IFRS 1:C1]

If business combinations prior to the date of transition are restated, they must be restated to conform with the requirements of the version of IFRS 3 that is being applied in the first-time adopter's first IFRS reporting period.

Therefore, if Entity B, with a first IFRS reporting period ending on 31 December 2015, elects to apply IFRS 3 for all business combinations occurring on or after 1 January 2005, IFRS 3 (as revised in 2008) is applied to all restated combinations. This is the case even though, for entities already applying IFRSs, the general transition provisions of IFRS 3 (as revised in 2008) do not permit that version of the Standard to be applied before 30 June 2007. Equally, Entity B must apply IFRS 10 *Consolidated Financial Statements* from 1 January 2005.

These requirements are illustrated in the following diagram.

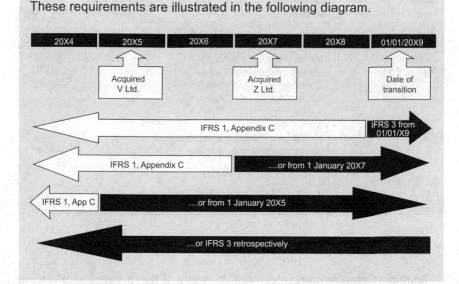

Example 7.2.3

Timing the use of the exemption for business combinations

Company A is adopting IFRSs for the year ended 31 December 20X5. Company A's date of transition is 1 January 20X4. Company A purchased Company B on 31 October 20X3, Company C on 15 March 20X4, Company D on 17 July 20X4 and Company E on 15 February 20X5.

The business combinations involving Company C and Company D must be restated in accordance with IFRS 3 because all business combinations on or after the date of transition (1 January 20X4) must be accounted for in accordance with the accounting requirements in force at the end of the entity's first IFRS reporting period (31 December 20X5). Similarly, the purchase of Company E will be accounted for in accordance with IFRS 3 when the purchase occurs because it is subsequent to the date of transition to IFRSs.

The purchase of Company B may also be restated if Company A elects to restate all business combinations from 31 October 20X3. If Company A does not restate the purchase of Company B, the requirements of Appendix C to IFRS 1 must be applied to the transaction in the first financial statements prepared in accordance with IFRSs.

7.2.4   Past acquisitions of investments in associates, interests in joint ventures and interests in joint operations

The exemption for past business combinations also applies to past acquisitions of investments in associates, interests in joint ventures, and interests in joint operations in which the activity of the joint operation constitutes a business as defined in IFRS 3. The selected date from which business combinations are restated in accordance with IFRS 3 (see **7.2.3**) applies equally for acquisitions of investments in associates, interests in joint ventures, and interests in joint operations in which the activity of the joint operation constitutes a business. [IFRS 1:C5]

If an entity decides to restate an acquisition of a subsidiary at a date prior to the date of transition, restatement is also required of all acquisitions on or after that date of subsidiaries, associates, joint ventures and joint operations in which the activity of the joint operation constitutes a business. In such circumstances, a first-time adopter also applies IAS 28 *Investments in Associates and Joint Ventures* and IFRS 11 *Joint Arrangements* retrospectively to acquisitions of investments in associates, interests in joint ventures and interests in joint operations in which the activity of the joint operation constitutes a business from the same date.

Equally, if an entity chooses to restate an acquisition of an associate at a date prior to the date of transition to IFRSs, all acquisitions of subsidiaries, other associates, joint ventures and interests in joint operations in which the activity of the joint operation constitutes a business on or after that date must also be restated.

In May 2014, the IASB issued *Accounting for Acquisitions of Interests in Joint Operations (Amendments to IFRS 11)*. The amendments to IFRS 11 specify that the acquirer of an interest in a joint operation in which the activity of the joint operation constitutes a business, as defined in IFRS 3, is required to apply the principles of business combinations accounting except for those principles that conflict with the guidance in IFRS 11. Consequential amendments to IFRS 1:C5 also extend the requirements of that paragraph to acquisitions of interests in relevant joint operations.

The application of IFRS 1:C5 to acquisitions of interests in joint operations is effective for annual periods beginning on or after 1 January 2016. If a first-time adopter applies the related amendments to IFRS 11 in a period beginning before 1 January 2016, it should apply the amendments to IFRS 1:C5 at the same time. [IFRS 1:39W]

Example 7.2.4

The effect of a restatement of a business combination on the acquisition of other interests

Company D is adopting IFRSs with a date of transition of 1 January 20X5. It chooses to restate acquisitions of subsidiaries starting from 1 January 20X2. As a result, restatement is also required of all acquisitions on or after that date of associates, joint ventures and joint operations in which the activity of the joint operation constitutes a business.

7.2.5 Step acquisitions

For a step acquisition (i.e. the acquisition of another entity in stages), the timing of the exemption is determined by reference to the date of acquisition of the subsidiary, i.e. the date on which the acquirer obtains control.

Example 7.2.5

Step acquisition completed prior to the date of transition

Company C acquired Company T in stages, beginning with a 10 per cent share purchase on 30 June 20X5, 30 per cent on 31 December 20X5, and 20 per cent on 31 December 20X6. Company C obtained control of Company T on 31 December 20X6, which is its 'acquisition date' as defined in IFRS 3.

Company C is a first-time adopter with 1 January 20X7 as its date of transition to IFRSs and it has elected to restate all business combinations after 1 January 20X6 in accordance with IFRS 3.

In this example, the date of acquisition of Company T is 31 December 20X6 and, consequently, the business combination should be restated. Because the election to restate past business combinations is determined by reference to the date of acquisition of a subsidiary, the steps that occurred prior to 1 January 20X6 do not affect the date from which all business combinations are required to be restated. Therefore, in this example, restatement in accordance with IFRS 3 is not required for any other business combination prior to 1 January 20X6.

7.2.6 Classification of past business combinations

Under previous GAAP, a business combination may have been classified differently than IFRSs would require for the same business combination. For example, under previous GAAP an acquisition may have been classified as:

- a uniting of interests (also known as a 'pooling of interests'), which is not permitted for business combinations within the scope of IFRS 3; or

- an acquisition following the legal form, which would have been classified as a reverse acquisition under IFRS 3.

If an entity elects to apply the optional exemption for business combinations, the classification under previous GAAP is retained. [IFRS 1:C4(a)] If the entity instead elects to apply IFRS 3 retrospectively, the classification is changed retrospectively to comply with IFRS 3.

7.2.7 Recognition of assets and liabilities

When IFRS 3 is not applied retrospectively to a past business combination, Appendix C to IFRS 1 requires that all of the assets acquired and liabilities assumed in that business combination that qualify for recognition under IFRSs should be recognised at the date of transition, other than:

- some financial assets and financial liabilities derecognised under previous GAAP (see **6.3**); and

- assets, including goodwill, and liabilities that were not recognised in the acquirer's consolidated statement of financial position under previous GAAP and also would not qualify for recognition under IFRSs in the separate statement of financial position of the acquiree (see **7.2.11** and **7.2.12**).

Therefore, even though IFRS 3 is not being applied retrospectively, application of Appendix C may result in the recognition of some assets and liabilities that were not recognised under previous GAAP (see **7.2.11**) and in the derecognition of some assets and liabilities that were recognised under previous GAAP (see **7.2.8**).

Note that the recognition criteria to be applied under Appendix C to IFRS 1 are those that generally apply to the specific asset or liability under consideration in accordance with relevant IFRSs rather than the recognition criteria set out in IFRS 3. In a limited number of cases, this can give rise to a different result than if IFRS 3 were applied to that business combination. For example, under Appendix C, the recognition requirements of IAS 37 *Provisions, Contingent Liabilities and Contingent Assets* are applied to contingent liabilities acquired in a business combination, with the result that some contingent liabilities that would have been recognised if IFRS 3 were applied for the same business combination may not be recognised (for further discussion, see **7.2.11**).

Any adjustments arising under Appendix C as a result of the recognition of assets acquired and liabilities assumed in a past business combination that were not recognised under previous GAAP should be made against retained earnings (or another appropriate category of equity), other than when the adjustment relates to an intangible asset that was previously subsumed within goodwill (see **7.2.12**). [IFRS 1:C4(b)]

Adjustments to deferred tax arising from the application of Appendix C to business combinations that occurred before the date of transition to IFRSs are considered at **7.2.16**.

7.2.8 Assets and liabilities that should not be recognised

When Appendix C is applied to a past business combination, assets acquired and liabilities assumed in that business combination that do not qualify for recognition under IFRSs, but that were recognised under previous GAAP, are required to be derecognised. The resulting adjustments should be accounted for as follows.

[IFRS 1:C4(c)]

- The first-time adopter may have classified a past business combination as an acquisition and recognised as an intangible asset an item that does not qualify for recognition as an asset under IAS 38 *Intangible Assets*. Such an item (and any related deferred tax and non-controlling interest) should be reclassified as part of goodwill unless the entity deducted goodwill directly from equity under previous GAAP (see **7.2.12**).

- All other adjustments resulting from the derecognition of assets and liabilities arising from a past business combination that were recognised under previous GAAP should be made against retained earnings. Such changes include reclassifications from and to intangible assets if goodwill was not recognised under previous GAAP as an asset. This may arise if, under previous GAAP, goodwill was deducted directly from equity or the business combination was not treated as an acquisition.

> Example 3 in the implementation guidance accompanying IFRS 1 illustrates the application of these requirements to a provision for restructuring costs which had been recognised under local GAAP but which would not be recognised under IFRSs.

7.2.9   Assets and liabilities subsequently measured on a basis other than historical cost

When IFRSs require subsequent measurement of an asset or a liability on a basis that is not based on original cost (e.g. fair value), that asset or liability should be measured on that basis in the opening IFRS statement of financial position even if it was acquired or assumed in a past business combination.

> Therefore, when applying Appendix C for items that are required by IFRSs to be measured at fair value on an ongoing basis, the carrying amount established in the business combination under previous GAAP is effectively ignored and the IFRS carrying amount at the date of transition is established as its fair value at that date.

Any adjustment to the carrying amount of an asset or liability under this section is made against retained earnings (or, if appropriate, another category of equity) rather than goodwill. [IFRS 1:C4(d)]

7.2.10   Previous GAAP carrying amount to be treated as deemed cost

For assets and liabilities acquired in a past business combination and recognised under previous GAAP, other than those covered by **7.2.9** and other than goodwill (see **7.2.12**), Appendix C requires that their IFRS carrying amounts should be determined by reference to their carrying amounts established in the business combination under previous GAAP.

Immediately after the business combination, the carrying amounts under previous GAAP of assets and liabilities assumed in that business combination are treated as their deemed cost under IFRSs at that date. If IFRSs require a cost-based measurement of those assets and liabilities at a later date, that deemed cost should be the basis for cost-based depreciation or amortisation from the date of the business combination. [IFRS 1:C4(e)]

It is therefore unnecessary to adjust such amounts even if they are calculated on a basis that would not have been acceptable under IFRS 3. For example, if previous GAAP required the assets and liabilities of an acquiree to be measured at the date of acquisition at the acquiree's book value instead of at fair value, those book values would be treated as the deemed cost of those assets and liabilities at the date of acquisition for subsequent accounting under IFRSs.

Note that the deemed cost is established at the date of acquisition of the acquiree; adjustments may be required to reflect depreciation or amortisation between that date and the date of transition to IFRSs.

The principle established in IFRS 1:C4(e) will generally apply to intangible assets acquired in a business combination and recognised under previous GAAP in the same way as other categories of assets and liabilities. However, an exception arises when the carrying amount recognised for the intangible asset under previous GAAP was zero. In such circumstances, the intangible asset should not be recognised in the opening IFRS statement of financial position unless it would qualify under IAS 38 (applying the criteria discussed at **8.8**) for recognition in the separate statement of financial position of the acquiree at the date of transition to IFRSs. If those recognition criteria are met, the asset is measured on the basis that IAS 38 would require in the separate statement of financial position of the acquiree. The resulting adjustment affects goodwill. [IFRS 1:IG49]

The effect of IFRS 1:IG49 is that intangible assets that were recognised in a past business combination under previous GAAP, but at a 'nil' carrying amount, will be dealt with under Appendix C in the same manner as if the intangible asset had not been recognised under previous GAAP (see **7.2.11**).

If there is any indication that the assets and liabilities arising from a past business combination that were recognised under previous GAAP are impaired, they should be tested for impairment based on conditions that existed at the date of transition to IFRSs in accordance with IAS 36 *Impairment of Assets*. [IFRS 1:IG Example 2]

7.2.11 Assets and liabilities not recognised under previous GAAP

If an asset acquired or a liability assumed in a past business combination was not recognised under previous GAAP, it does not have a deemed cost of zero in the opening IFRS statement of financial position. Instead, Appendix C to IFRS 1 requires that the asset or liability be recognised and measured in the consolidated statement of financial position on the basis that IFRSs would require in the separate statement of financial position of the acquiree.

For example, if a finance lease acquired in a business combination was not capitalised under previous GAAP, and the entity has elected not to restate past business combinations in accordance with IFRS 3, Appendix C requires that the lease should be capitalised in the IFRS consolidated statement of financial position because IAS 17 *Leases* would require the acquiree to do so in its own separate IFRS statement of financial position. [IFRS 1:C4(f)]

Example 7.2.11A

Finance lease acquired in a business combination not capitalised under previous GAAP

Parent Company A's date of transition to IFRSs is 1 January 20X5. Parent Company A acquired Subsidiary B on 15 January 20X3 and, under previous GAAP, did not capitalise Subsidiary B's finance leases entered into prior to 15 January 20X3. If Subsidiary B prepared separate financial statements under IFRSs, it would recognise finance lease obligations of CU750 and leased assets of CU625 at 1 January 20X5. On transition to IFRSs, Parent Company A has elected not to restate past business combinations in accordance with IFRS 3.

When applying Appendix C to IFRS 1 on transition to IFRSs, in its consolidated opening IFRS statement of financial position, Parent Company A is required to recognise Subsidiary B's finance lease obligations at CU750 and leased assets at CU625, and the net resulting adjustment of CU125 in retained earnings at that date.

Similarly, if the acquirer had not, under its previous GAAP, recognised a contingent liability assumed in a business combination that still exists at the date of transition to IFRSs, the acquirer should recognise that contingent liability at that date unless IAS 37 *Provisions, Contingent Liabilities and Contingent Assets* would prohibit its recognition in the financial statements of the acquiree. [IFRS 1:C4(f)]

This additional example of a contingent liability was added to IFRS 1:C4(f) when IFRS 3 was revised in 2008. Its application is unclear, because IAS 37:27 prohibits the 'recognition' of all contingent liabilities within its scope. Therefore, it appears that a contingent liability assumed in a past business combination not restated under IFRS 3 will be recognised under IFRS 1:C4(f) only when it is outside the scope of IAS 37 because it is covered by another Standard, in accordance with IAS 37:1(c).

If an asset acquired or a liability assumed in a past business combination was subsumed in goodwill under previous GAAP but would have been recognised separately under IFRS 3, that asset or liability remains in goodwill unless IFRSs would require its recognition in the separate financial statements of the acquiree. [IFRS 1:C4(f)]

Under this principle, when Appendix C to IFRS 1 is applied, intangible assets of the acquiree arising from a past business combination that were not separately recognised under previous GAAP are only recognised in the opening IFRS consolidated statement of financial position if they would have satisfied the criteria for recognition under IAS 38 in the statement of financial position of the acquiree. The criteria for recognition of such assets in the statement of financial position of the acquiree are the same as those explained in IFRS 1:IG46 and IFRS 1:IG48 (in the context of intangible assets arising other than in a business combination). Accordingly, unless they satisfied the criteria for recognition under IAS 38 at an earlier date (including an assessment and documentation at that date regarding the probability of future economic benefits as well as a reliable system of accumulating the costs – see **8.8**), intangible assets generated internally by the acquiree will not be recognised at the date of transition. Conversely, intangible assets acquired by the acquiree externally will be recognised in most cases because the transaction and invoice are usually sufficient documentation and evidence of future economic benefits at that date.

In contrast, if the past business combination were restated in accordance with IFRS 3, all intangible assets acquired in the business combination would be recognised at the date of acquisition.

Example 7.2.11B

Deferred tax asset acquired in a past business combination

Company K acquired Company B on 1 January 20X4. Company K adopts IFRSs in 20X7 (date of transition is 1 January 20X6). Upon transition to IFRSs, Company K chooses not to restate this business combination in accordance with IFRS 3.

Company B has a tax loss that will expire if it is not used before 31 December 20X8. At the date of acquisition, Company K assessed that the tax loss carried forward in Company B could not be used before its expiry date. Consequently, Company K did not recognise the related deferred tax asset at the date of acquisition. The nominal value of the unused tax loss remains unchanged at the date of transition.

At the date of transition to IFRSs, Company K assesses that a portion of the unrecognised tax asset would probably be used before it expires at the end of 20X8.

A deferred tax asset should be recognised at the date of transition to IFRSs. IFRS 1 does not include any exceptions to the general principle for deferred tax assets. Therefore, a deferred tax asset is recognised in the opening IFRS statement of financial position for the amount the entity expects will be used at the date of transition to IFRSs. The resulting adjustment is recognised in retained earnings because this is not one of the permitted adjustments to goodwill under IFRS 1:C4(g) (see **7.2.12**).

Example 7.2.11C

Asset acquired in a business combination but not recognised under previous GAAP for which recognition is required under IFRSs

Company D acquired Company Z and accounted for the transaction under previous GAAP three years prior to Company D's date of transition to IFRSs. Upon transition to IFRSs, Company D chooses not to restate this business combination in accordance with IFRS 3.

Two years prior to being acquired by Company D, Company Z purchased a licence for CU100 with a remaining useful life of 20 years. As part of its acquisition of Company Z, Company D obtained that licence with a remaining life of 18 years. Under previous GAAP, Company D did not (and was not required to) recognise the licence separately from goodwill.

Goodwill was amortised over 20 years under previous GAAP. The intangible asset does not meet the criteria for use of the revaluation model in IAS 38. The licence is not tax deductible.

How should the licence be accounted for in the opening statement of financial position at the date of transition to IFRSs?

For business combinations that occurred before the date of transition to IFRSs and that are not restated in accordance with IFRS 3, under IFRS 1:C4(b)(ii) assets and liabilities are *not* recognised if they (1) were not recognised separately in the acquirer's consolidated statement of financial position, and (2) would not qualify for recognition under IFRSs in the separate statement of financial position of the acquiree.

In the circumstances described, although the licence was not recognised separately in Company D's consolidated statement of financial position, it would qualify for recognition in Company Z's statement of financial position under IFRSs; consequently, it fails the second condition in IFRS 1:C4(b)(ii). The licence should be recognised separately in Company D's consolidated financial statements under the requirements of IFRS 1:C4(f). At the date of transition to IFRSs, Company D should recognise the following adjustments:

- recognition of the intangible asset at its restated IFRS carrying amount of CU100 less accumulated amortisation of CU25 [(100/20) × 5]; and
- adjustment of goodwill by the same amount (under IFRS 1:C4(g)(i), this is one of the limited circumstances in which the carrying amount of goodwill under previous GAAP is adjusted).

Although the amount recognised on restatement of the intangible asset's amortisation may differ from the amortisation that was recognised for the equivalent portion of goodwill recognised under previous GAAP, the previous amortisation of goodwill is not adjusted because that is not permitted under IFRS 1:C4(h)(ii); therefore, the restated goodwill is not necessarily what it would have been if the intangible asset had always been recognised separately.

If the amount to be recognised for the intangible asset exceeds the carrying amount of goodwill under previous GAAP, once goodwill has been reduced to zero the excess should be recognised as an adjustment to retained earnings.

Example 7.2.11D

Costs of development projects not recognised under previous GAAP

Parent Company C acquired Subsidiary D on 1 January 20X2. Parent Company C adopts IFRSs in 20X6 with a date of transition of 1 January 20X5. Upon transition to IFRSs, Parent Company C chooses not to restate this business combination in accordance with IFRS 3.

Under previous GAAP, all development costs were expensed as incurred. Had Subsidiary D applied IFRSs, development costs of CU20 related to a project completed at 31 December 20X1 would have been recognised as an internally generated intangible asset. The useful life of the intangible asset is 5 years. The fair value is assessed to be CU18 at 1 January 20X2 and CU10 at the date of transition (i.e. 1 January 20X5). No active market exists for this type of intangible asset.

The following journal entry is required at the date of transition in accordance with IFRS 1:C4(f).

		CU	CU
Dr	Development costs	20	
Cr	Accumulated amortisation [CU20 × 3/5]		12
Cr	Goodwill [CU20 – CU12]		8

Recognition of the development cost asset.

Because the development costs were not recognised under previous GAAP, the acquirer (Parent Company C) recognises and measures the development costs in its consolidated IFRS statement of financial position on the basis that IFRSs would require in the statement of financial position of the acquiree (Subsidiary D). At the date of transition, this amount is CU8 (CU20 amortised over 3 out of 5 years). Goodwill is adjusted accordingly because the asset was previously subsumed within goodwill.

The option in IFRS 1 to measure intangible assets at fair value is not available in this case because no active market exists for these types of intangible assets.

Example 7.2.11E

Measurement of an asset acquired in a business combination but not recognised under previous GAAP for which recognition is required under IFRSs

Company A purchases a licence to operate a business in a particular jurisdiction for CU10 and recognises an intangible asset. Company A is subsequently acquired by Company B. Under its local GAAP, Company B does not recognise the licence as an intangible asset separately from goodwill.

Company B is subsequently acquired by Company C. Company C determines that the fair value of the licence at the date of acquisition of Company B is CU50 and recognises it as an intangible asset separately from goodwill.

Company C is subsequently acquired by Company D, but Company D does not recognise the licence as an intangible asset separately from goodwill.

The licence is therefore reported separately in the individual financial statements of Company A and in the consolidated financial statements of Company C.

Company D subsequently adopts IFRSs and chooses not to restate its acquisition of Company C in accordance with IFRS 3.

At what amount should the licence be recognised upon first-time adoption of IFRSs?

This example is similar to that discussed in **example 7.2.11C**. Although the intangible asset was not recognised in Company D's consolidated financial statements under previous GAAP, the second condition in IFRS 1:C4(b)(ii) is not met and, therefore, the licence should be recognised separately in Company D's consolidated financial statements under IFRSs.

However, this example raises an additional question because there are two alternatives available on which to base the measurement of the intangible asset in Company D's consolidated financial statements (the original cost of CU10 recognised by Company A and the fair value of CU50 recognised by Company C when it acquired Company B). IFRS 1 does not provide guidance as to which of these measures should be used. In many cases, the measurement would be based on the most reliable information. If both measurements were determined to be reliable, then the most recent fair value (CU50) would be the most relevant measurement and should be used. The amount recognised (and the equivalent adjustment to goodwill) will be adjusted for amortisation of the intangible asset in accordance with IFRSs from the date of the measurement to the date of transition to IFRSs.

7.2.12   Adjustments to goodwill

7.2.12.1   Limited circumstances in which goodwill may be adjusted

As a general principle, under the optional exemption for business combinations, the carrying amount of goodwill in the opening IFRS statement of financial position is its carrying amount under previous GAAP at the date of transition to IFRSs, adjusted only for the following items:

[IFRS 1:C4(g)]

- goodwill is increased when it is necessary to reclassify an item that was recognised as an intangible asset under previous GAAP (see **7.2.8**);

- goodwill is decreased (and, if applicable, deferred tax and non-controlling interests adjusted) when it is necessary to recognise an intangible asset that was subsumed within recognised goodwill under previous GAAP (see **7.2.11**); and

- regardless of whether there is any indication that goodwill may be impaired, IAS 36 should be applied in testing goodwill for impairment at the date of transition to IFRSs and in recognising any resulting impairment loss in retained earnings (or, if required by IAS 36, in revaluation surplus). The impairment test is based on conditions at the date of transition to IFRSs.

> Goodwill should not be subject to amortisation even if it includes a subsumed intangible asset with a finite life. All goodwill should be tested for impairment at the date of transition to IFRSs.

No other adjustments to goodwill are permitted at the date of transition to IFRSs. IFRS 1 highlights the following examples for which goodwill is not adjusted:

[IFRS 1:C4(h)]

- to exclude in-process research and development acquired in that business combination (unless the related intangible asset would qualify for recognition under IAS 38 in the separate statement of financial position of the acquiree);

- to adjust previous amortisation of goodwill; or

- to reverse adjustments to goodwill that IFRS 3 would not permit, but that were made under previous GAAP because of adjustments to assets and liabilities between the date of the business combination and the date of transition to IFRSs.

> Although there is no explicit prohibition in IFRS 1 on the reversal of a past impairment of goodwill, this is similar to a reversal of past amortisation which is explicitly prohibited by IFRS 1:C4(h)(ii). Also, the list of permitted adjustments to goodwill under IFRS 1:C4(g) refers only to "any resulting impairment loss" and does not envisage a profit arising from the impairment review of goodwill at the date of transition.

7.2.12.2 Goodwill no longer amortised from the date of transition

From the date of transition, goodwill is no longer amortised. As a result, IFRS 1 requires that goodwill be tested for impairment at the date of transition, in accordance with IAS 36, irrespective of whether there is any indication that goodwill may be impaired. The effect of any impairment loss identified is deducted from equity in the opening IFRS statement of financial position.

When goodwill has been amortised under previous GAAP, the carrying amount of accumulated amortisation at the date of transition is adjusted against the original cost of goodwill. The net amount is carried forward as the new carrying amount under IFRSs.

7.2.12.3 Requirement to reverse amortisation recognised under previous GAAP after the date of application of IFRS 3

Example 7.2.12.3

Requirement to reverse amortisation recognised under previous GAAP after the date of application of IFRS 3

Entity M is adopting IFRSs for the first time in its financial statements for the year ended 31 December 20X5; its date of transition is 1 January 20X4.

If Entity M uses the optional exemption under IFRS 1 not to apply IFRS 3 to business combinations before its date of transition, the carrying amount of goodwill under previous GAAP at 1 January 20X4 is the starting point for accounting for goodwill under IFRSs. No amortisation is recognised after that date.

Goodwill is required to be tested for impairment at 1 January 20X4 under IAS 36. Any impairment loss identified is recognised in retained earnings at 1 January 20X4.

However, if Entity M elects to apply IFRS 3 for all business combinations after an earlier date (say, 1 January 20X2), Entity M is also required to reverse the goodwill amortisation recognised under previous GAAP in 20X2 and 20X3 related to those business combinations for which the date of acquisition is on or after 1 January 20X2. Goodwill arising from business combinations with a date of acquisition before 1 January 20X2 will continue to be amortised until the date of transition.

If IFRS 3 is applied from 1 January 20X2, goodwill is tested annually for impairment as from 1 January 20X2 and any impairment loss in the period from 1 January 20X2 to 31 December 20X3 is recognised in retained earnings at 1 January 20X4.

7.2.12.4 Goodwill previously deducted from equity

If, under previous GAAP, goodwill was recognised as a deduction from equity and the entity has elected not to restate past business combinations in accordance with IFRS 3:

[IFRS 1:C4(i)]

- that goodwill is not recognised in the opening IFRS statement of financial position;

- that goodwill should not be reclassified to profit or loss if the subsidiary is disposed of or if the investment in the subsidiary becomes impaired; and

- adjustments resulting from the subsequent resolution of a contingency affecting the purchase consideration should be recognised in retained earnings.

7.2.12.5 'Negative goodwill'

If, under previous GAAP, an entity recognised any 'negative goodwill' in its statement of financial position, and the entity has elected not to restate past business combinations in accordance with IFRS 3, any 'negative goodwill' recognised under previous GAAP is derecognised with a corresponding adjustment to retained earnings at the date of transition.

7.2.12.6 Reassessment of provisional fair values after the date of transition

---

Example 7.2.12.6

Reassessment of provisional fair values after the date of transition

Under its previous GAAP, Entity A used provisional fair values at the time of a business combination occurring shortly prior to its date of transition to IFRSs.

How should Entity A measure goodwill in its first IFRS financial statements?

When IFRS 3 is not applied retrospectively to a business combination prior to the date of transition to IFRSs, the carrying amount of goodwill in the opening IFRS statement of financial position is its carrying amount under previous GAAP at the date of transition, adjusted only for three items specified in paragraph C4(g) of IFRS 1 (see **7.2.12.1**). If the business combination was in the period immediately prior to the date of transition, it is possible that adjustments would have been made in the next period, under previous GAAP, to the amount of goodwill because of a reassessment of provisional fair values. It may at first appear that IFRS 1 has the effect of prohibiting the adjustment of goodwill and that the amount would therefore have to remain as originally stated under previous GAAP at the date of transition. This is not so.

Under IFRS 3, adjustments to provisional fair values and goodwill may be made in the period subsequent to the business combination. The period during which such an adjustment is permitted is limited to twelve months from the date of acquisition, which may differ from the period during which such adjustments are permitted under previous GAAP. Under IFRS 3, the adjustment is reflected through a retrospective restatement of the previous period as if the initial accounting had been completed from the date of acquisition but previous GAAP may require the adjustment to be made as a current year adjustment to goodwill.

It is possible to adjust goodwill recognised in the opening IFRS statement of financial position if such an adjustment would be permitted by IFRS 3. The restriction on adjustments to goodwill in IFRS 1 applies only to the amount initially recognised and does not preclude subsequent adjustments as permitted or required by other IFRSs. The amount may be adjusted for the reassessment of fair values on the basis that IFRS 3 requires retrospective restatement for this. In other words, the provisional goodwill figure under previous GAAP is treated as the opening provisional goodwill figure under IFRSs.

7.2.13   Subsidiaries not consolidated under previous GAAP

7.2.13.1   Subsidiaries acquired in a past business combination and not consolidated under previous GAAP

Under previous GAAP, an entity may not have consolidated a subsidiary acquired in a past business combination because, for example, it did not regard the investment as a subsidiary, or because the subsidiary was exempted from consolidation under previous GAAP, or because the entity did not prepare consolidated financial statements under previous GAAP.

If a subsidiary has not previously been consolidated, and the acquirer has elected not to restate past business combinations in accordance with IFRS 3, at the date of transition the parent identifies the assets and liabilities of the subsidiary and adjusts the carrying amounts to the amounts that IFRSs would require in the subsidiary's separate financial statements.

The deemed cost of the goodwill relating to the previously unconsolidated subsidiary at the date of transition is calculated as the difference at the date of transition between:

[IFRS 1:C4(j)]

- the parent's interest in the adjusted carrying amounts of the net assets of the subsidiary; and

- the cost in the parent's separate financial statements of its investment in the subsidiary.

The practical effect of this requirement is to avoid the need to consider (and adjust for) the fair value of the assets and liabilities of the acquired entity either at its acquisition date or at the date of transition to IFRSs.

The procedures for determining goodwill for a subsidiary that was not previously consolidated could lead to the recognition of a significant amount of goodwill if the subsidiary has, subsequent to the date of acquisition, reduced the carrying amount of net assets either by distribution of pre-acquisition reserves or by incurring significant losses. In all cases, goodwill recognised is tested for impairment at the date of transition.

If, on the other hand, the subsidiary has generated a significant amount of profit subsequent to acquisition, goodwill could be very limited. 'Negative goodwill' at the date of transition is recognised directly in retained earnings.

Example 7.2.13.1A

Determining goodwill for a subsidiary not consolidated under previous GAAP

Parent Company T's date of transition to IFRSs is 1 January 20X9. Under its previous GAAP, Parent Company T did not consolidate its 75 per cent share of Subsidiary U, acquired in a business combination on 15 July 20X6. On 1 January 20X9:

- the cost of Parent Company T's investment in Subsidiary U is CU540 (based on the amount paid at the date of acquisition); and

- under IFRSs, Subsidiary U would measure its assets at CU1,500 and its liabilities at CU900. On this basis, the net assets of Subsidiary U under IFRSs at the date of transition are CU600.

On transition to IFRSs, Parent Company T has elected not to restate past business combinations in accordance with IFRS 3; nevertheless, it is required to consolidate Subsidiary U. The consolidated opening IFRS statement of financial position at 1 January 20X9 includes:

- the assets and liabilities of Subsidiary U at CU1,500 and CU900, respectively;

- non-controlling interests of CU150 (25 per cent of [CU1,500 – CU900]);

- goodwill of CU90 (cost of CU540 less 75 per cent of [CU1,500 – CU900]); and

- the elimination of the investment in Subsidiary U of CU540 (if the investment in Subsidiary U was recognised under previous GAAP at an amount other than its original cost, an additional entry would be recognised in retained earnings).

Parent Company T tests goodwill for impairment under IAS 36 based on conditions that existed at the date of transition and recognises any resulting impairment loss in retained earnings.

Example 7.2.13.1B

Measuring the assets of a subsidiary not consolidated under previous GAAP

Company A acquired a building in 20X1 at a cost of CU1 million. Under local GAAP, Company A did not depreciate the building. Company T subsequently acquired Company A on 1 January 20X5. Under local GAAP, Company T did not consolidate Company A. Company T will adopt IFRSs for its 31 December 20X9 annual financial statements with 1 January 20X8 as its date of transition.

Company T has elected not to restate past business combinations in accordance with IFRS 3.

As a consequence of adopting IFRSs, Company T must consolidate Company A and consider whether it should depreciate the building.

In Company T's consolidated IFRS financial statements, how should the building be measured?

Because the asset belongs to a subsidiary that was not previously consolidated, it is subject to the requirements of IFRS 1:C4(j) and, in its consolidated financial statements, Company T is required to adjust the carrying amount of the building to the amount that IFRSs would require in Company A's statement of financial position.

The building should therefore be recognised either at:

- depreciated cost (measured at the date of the original purchase with subsequent depreciation); or
- the fair value of the asset at the date of transition.

Company T will consolidate Company A in its opening IFRS statement of financial position as required by IFRS 1:C4(j). The deemed cost of the goodwill is equal to the difference at the date of transition (i.e. 1 January 20X8) between Company T's interest in the adjusted carrying amounts of the assets and liabilities of Company A and the cost in Company T's separate financial statements of its investment in Company A.

Example 7.2.13.1C

Use of deemed cost to establish goodwill for subsidiaries not previously consolidated

Parent Company T's date of transition to IFRSs is 1 January 20X9. Under its previous GAAP, Parent Company T did not consolidate its 75 per cent share of Subsidiary U, acquired in a business combination on 15 July 20X6. Parent Company T has elected not to restate past business combinations in accordance with IFRS 3.

On transition, Parent Company T elects to recognise its investment in Subsidiary U at 'deemed cost', as permitted by IFRS 1:D15 (see **7.8**).

When applying IFRS 1:C4(j), how should Parent Company T measure goodwill in respect of Subsidiary U?

IFRS 1:C4(j) requires a first-time adopter to calculate the deemed cost of goodwill on transition as the difference between its interest in the adjusted carrying amounts of a subsidiary's assets and liabilities and the cost of its investment in the subsidiary in its own separate financial statements.

IFRS 1:D15 provides first-time adopters who elect under IAS 27 *Separate Financial Statements* to recognise investments in subsidiaries (or associates or joint ventures) at cost with options for establishing the 'cost' on first-time adoption in an entity's separate financial statements. In line with IAS 27, one of the allowed alternatives is the use of 'deemed cost' (either the fair value of the investment at the date of transition or the previous GAAP carrying amount at that date).

When the cost of an investment is measured using deemed cost, the same measurement is used to determine the amount of goodwill for the purposes of IFRS 1:C4(j), irrespective of whether the first-time adopter has actually prepared separate financial statements.

It is possible that the use of deemed cost will result in a larger amount being recognised as goodwill, for example, if the fair value of the investment in a subsidiary is higher than its cost under IAS 27.

As noted at **7.2.4**, the requirements on restatement of business combinations in IFRS 1 apply to associates and joint ventures as well as to subsidiaries. A consequence of this is that if an associate (or a joint venture) was not accounted for using the equity method under previous GAAP but would have to be accounted for using the equity method under IFRSs, the approach adopted should be consistent with the approach prescribed by IFRS 1:C4(j) for subsidiaries not consolidated. This is illustrated in the following example.

Example 7.2.13.1D

Restatement of investment in associate measured at cost under previous GAAP

Company F acquired 20 per cent of Company A (and obtained significant influence over it) prior to Company F's date of transition to IFRSs. Under local GAAP, Company F accounted for its investment in Company A at cost in its consolidated financial statements. Company F has elected not to restate past business combinations in accordance with IFRS 3.

IAS 28 requires associates to be accounted for using the equity method in the consolidated financial statements (with certain limited exceptions). IFRS 1 provides guidance on investments in subsidiaries, including subsidiaries not previously consolidated, and consistently notes that this guidance should also be applied to investments in associates and joint ventures. Therefore, the guidance in IFRS 1:C4(j) should be applied.

As a result, Company F should adjust the carrying amounts of the associate's assets and liabilities to the amounts that IFRSs would require in the associate's statement of financial position, as of the date of transition. Company F's share of the net assets of the associate so adjusted is included in Company F's consolidated opening IFRS statement of financial position, with the difference between this amount and the cost of the investment in the associate to be considered deemed cost of goodwill. Goodwill relating to an associate is included in the carrying amount of the investment, without subsequent amortisation.

7.2.13.2   Subsidiaries not previously consolidated – general guidance

IFRS 1 provides guidance relating to subsidiaries that were not consolidated prior to the adoption of IFRSs in more than one section of the Standard. IFRS 1:C4(j) (discussed at **7.2.13.1**) only addresses subsidiaries that were not consolidated under previous GAAP in the context of business combinations before the date of transition to IFRSs. IFRS 1:IG27 (discussed below) addresses the issue of subsidiaries not previously consolidated more generally, referring to both those acquired in a business combination and those that were not acquired in business combinations. IFRS 1:IG27 refers to adjustment "for the effects of the business combination in which it acquired the subsidiary" but these words do not appear in IFRS 1:C4(j). This could be seen as conflicting guidance. However, because the purpose of the exemption in IFRS 1:C4(j) is to avoid the need to work out fair value adjustments that were not calculated under previous GAAP (see **7.2.13.1**), the words in IFRS 1:IG27 should not be read as requiring such acquisition-date fair value adjustments to be made, but only as requiring normal consolidation elimination entries.

A first-time adopter consolidates all subsidiaries that it controls, unless IFRS 10 *Consolidated Financial Statements* requires otherwise. [IFRS 1:IG26]

This would apply to a subsidiary that was not consolidated under previous GAAP because it was acquired exclusively with a view to its subsequent disposal, for example as part of a business combination. As explained in **section 5** of **chapter A20**, in such circumstances, the disposal group (i.e. the subsidiary) will be classified as held for sale, in accordance with IFRS 5 *Non-current Assets Held for Sale and Discontinued Operations*, if certain conditions are met. However, a subsidiary that is classified as held for sale in accordance with IFRS 5 is still consolidated under IFRS 10; it is just that IFRS 5 requires the amounts for such a subsidiary to be measured and presented in a particular way. If such a subsidiary was not consolidated under previous GAAP, it should be consolidated in accordance with the requirements set out below and IFRS 5.

If a first-time adopter did not consolidate a subsidiary under previous GAAP then, in its consolidated financial statements, it measures the subsidiary's assets and liabilities at the same carrying amounts as in the IFRS financial statements of the subsidiary, after adjusting for consolidation procedures and for the effects of the business combination in which it acquired the subsidiary. If the subsidiary has not adopted IFRSs in its financial statements, the carrying amounts required are those that IFRSs would require in those separate financial statements. [IFRS 1:IG27]

If the parent acquired the subsidiary in a business combination before the date of transition to IFRSs, the parent recognises goodwill as explained in **7.2.13.1**. If the parent did not acquire the subsidiary in a business combination because it created the subsidiary, the parent does not recognise goodwill. [IFRS 1:IG27]

> However, for a subsidiary that was not acquired in a business combination, a difference may still arise between the carrying amounts of the assets and liabilities and the cost of investment (e.g. because of accumulated profits of the subsidiary). IFRS 1:IG27(c) states that the parent does not recognise goodwill in this case but does not specify an alternative treatment for the difference. It should be taken to retained earnings or some other appropriate category of equity (e.g. if the entity maintains a specific reserve for IFRS 1 adjustments).

7.2.14   Effect of restatements on non-controlling interests and deferred tax

When a first-time adopter takes the exemption from full retrospective application of IFRS 3, the measurement of non-controlling interests (NCI) and deferred tax follows from the measurement of other assets and liabilities. Therefore, even if an entity decides to avail itself of the business combination exemption and not restate prior business combinations, some adjustments to non-controlling interests and deferred tax may still be required. [IFRS 1:C4(k)]

Example 7.2.14

Change in measurement of non-controlling interests on first-time adoption

Entity G adopts IFRSs in 20X9 with a date of transition of 1 January 20X8. Entity G acquired an 80 per cent interest in Entity H on 30 June 20X6 and has decided not to restate the business combination in accordance with IFRS 3.

Under previous GAAP, Entity G measured identifiable assets and liabilities acquired in a business combination at:

- the acquirer's interest obtained in the exchange transaction; plus
- the NCI's portion of the pre-acquisition carrying amounts.

Entity G's policy for measuring non-controlling interests under previous GAAP is not acceptable under IFRS 3, which requires that assets and liabilities acquired in a business combination be measured at their values at the date of acquisition. Under IFRS 3, there is a choice between measuring components of non-controlling interests that are present ownership interests at fair value or at the non-controlling interest's proportionate share of the fair value of the net identifiable assets acquired.

Although the manner in which the NCI in Entity H was calculated under previous GAAP is not supportable under IFRSs, Entity G is not required to adjust the amount attributed to NCI at the date of transition. Entity G has chosen not to restate business combinations that occurred before the date of transition to IFRSs in accordance with IFRS 3; therefore, it need not adjust NCI to conform to the measurement basis under IFRS 3.

However, the requirements of IFRS 1:Appendix C may require some assets acquired, or liabilities assumed, in a business combination to be measured at amounts different from the carrying amounts immediately after the business combination under previous GAAP. In such circumstances, because the measurement of NCI follows the measurement of the other assets and liabilities, NCI will be adjusted for the effects of the differences.

7.2.15 Translation of goodwill and fair value adjustments arising in a business combination

Under paragraph 47 of IAS 21 *The Effects of Changes in Foreign Exchange Rates* (see **5.6.1** in **chapter A19**), any goodwill arising on the acquisition of a foreign operation and any fair value adjustments to the carrying amounts of assets and liabilities arising on the acquisition of that foreign operation should be treated as assets and liabilities of the foreign operation. They are therefore expressed in the functional currency of the foreign operation and retranslated at the closing rate at the end of the reporting period. An entity may, under previous GAAP, have treated such goodwill and fair value adjustments as assets and liabilities of the entity rather than as assets and liabilities of the foreign operation. If so, the requirements of IAS 21:47 may be applied prospectively to all acquisitions occurring after the date of transition to IFRSs. [IFRS 1:IG21A]

If this election is used, the fair value adjustments and goodwill arising in business combinations prior to the date of transition to IFRSs should be treated as assets and liabilities of the entity rather than assets and liabilities of the acquiree. Such goodwill and fair value adjustments are either already expressed in the entity's functional currency or are non-monetary foreign currency items, which are reported using the exchange rate applied under previous GAAP. [IFRS 1:C2]

Alternatively, IAS 21 may be applied retrospectively to goodwill and fair value adjustments arising in either:

[IFRS 1:C3]

- all business combinations that occurred before the date of transition to IFRSs; or

- all business combinations that the entity elects to restate to comply with IFRS 3 (see **7.2.3**).

Example 7.2.15

Treating goodwill relating to a foreign subsidiary as an asset of the acquirer

Entity A has previously recognised goodwill relating to a foreign subsidiary arising in a business combination that occurred before the date of transition to IFRSs. Under previous GAAP, Entity A treated goodwill as its own asset and recognised goodwill in its functional currency based on the exchange rate at the date of acquisition.

On transition to IFRSs, Entity A is not required to restate the financial statements retrospectively to treat goodwill as an asset of the acquiree since the acquisition date and translate goodwill at the closing rate at the end of each reporting period.

Entity A can use the exemption in IFRS 1:C2 to avoid applying IAS 21 retrospectively to goodwill arising in business combinations that occurred before the date of transition.

When an entity does not apply IAS 21 retrospectively to goodwill, there are no further translation adjustments to the goodwill balance. Instead of treating goodwill as an asset of the acquiree and translating it at the end of each reporting period at the closing rate, Entity A treats the goodwill balance as its own asset and recognises goodwill in its functional currency at the exchange rate at the date of acquisition (in this case, the rate that was used under previous GAAP).

The exemption applies to goodwill that is deemed to be an asset of the acquirer at the date of transition. However, the exemption is not available for business combinations that occur after the date of transition. Therefore, for all acquisitions after the date of transition, IAS 21 must be fully complied with and goodwill must be treated as an asset of the acquiree (IFRS 1:IG21A).

Although IFRS 1 is not completely clear, it is generally accepted that the exemption in respect of fair value adjustments and goodwill may be applied independently to fair value adjustments and to goodwill. In particular, if fair value adjustments were previously treated as foreign currency assets and liabilities, that treatment can be continued even if goodwill was denominated in the reporting entity's functional currency and the exemption from restatement is applied to this goodwill.

It is possible that under previous GAAP an entity was permitted to choose on an acquisition-by-acquisition basis whether to translate goodwill balances at each reporting date or leave them at the historical rate. It is possible to read IFRS 1:C2 as requiring all existing goodwill to be treated consistently as an asset of the entity when the exemption is used. This would mean that any amounts that had in fact been treated as foreign currency amounts would have to be restated to local currency denominated amounts based on the exchange rate at the date of the acquisition. However, given that the purpose of this exemption is to 'grandfather' the treatment under previous GAAP, it is regarded as acceptable to apply it only to those assets and liabilities that were not retranslated under previous GAAP. Those that were retranslated under previous GAAP would continue to be retranslated in accordance with IAS 21.

In practice, the decision as to whether to apply IAS 21 retrospectively should not be taken in isolation, but in the light of all other factors affecting the transition to IFRSs. The choices made will have consequences in later reporting periods. For example, if goodwill is left denominated in the reporting entity's functional currency, there is a greater risk that it may become impaired in the future, merely as a result of adverse currency movements.

7.2.16   Deferred tax on pre-transition business combinations

7.2.16.1   Deferred tax on pre-transition business combinations – general

On initial adoption of IFRSs, a number of amendments to deferred tax balances may need to be made. Such adjustments will be recognised directly in equity if the entity has elected not to restate its past business combinations in accordance with IFRS 3. If any past business combinations are restated in accordance with IFRS 3, the goodwill figure should be adjusted to take account of the deferred tax balances that would have been recognised at the date of the business combination if IFRS 3 had been applied.

Example 7.2.16.1

Deferred tax on pre-transition business combinations

Parent P is preparing its consolidated financial statements in accordance with IFRSs for the first time. Prior to its date of transition, it acquired Subsidiary S which, at the date of acquisition, owned items of property, plant and equipment that do not attract any tax relief. Parent P has chosen not to restate business combinations prior to the date of transition to IFRSs in accordance with IFRS 3.

When determining the temporary differences related to assets and liabilities of Subsidiary S at the date of transition, Parent P applies the general requirements of IAS 12. The initial recognition exception in IAS 12 *Income Taxes* (see **4.4.2** in **chapter A13**) does not apply because the assets were acquired and the liabilities assumed in a business combination. Accordingly, deferred tax assets and deferred tax liabilities are recognised in respect of the temporary differences identified. Because Parent P has elected not to restate the acquisition of Subsidiary S in accordance with IFRS 3, the effect of the recognition of the deferred tax assets and liabilities at the date of transition is recognised in retained earnings or another reserve used by Parent P for its IFRS 1 adjustments.

7.2.16.2   Recognition of previously unrecognised deferred tax assets

At the date of transition, a first-time adopter that has elected not to restate past business combinations in accordance with IFRS 3 will need to determine whether any tax loss carryforwards or other deferred tax assets not recognised at the date of acquisition of subsidiaries meet the recognition criteria under IAS 12. If so, they should be recognised at the date of transition.

When a deferred tax asset is recognised on transition that was not previously recognised in a past business combination, the resulting adjustment will be made in retained earnings or another reserve used by the entity for its IFRS 1 adjustments. The carrying amount of goodwill should not be adjusted because the recognition of previously unrecognised deferred tax assets is not one of the permitted adjustments to goodwill specifically identified in IFRS 1:C4 (see **7.2.12.1**). (But this does not preclude the adjustment of goodwill if the date of transition falls during the 'measurement period', as discussed in example **7.2.12.6**.)

The realisation of previously unrecognised deferred tax assets after the date of transition is accounted for in accordance with the general requirements of IFRS 3 and IAS 12:68 (IFRS 1 does not allow any ongoing exemptions from these requirements). Therefore, when an entity that has not restated a past business combination subsequently realises an unrecognised deferred tax asset that did not satisfy the recognition criteria at the date of transition, the impact will typically be recognised in profit or loss, and not as an adjustment to goodwill. The only exception to this will be when acquired deferred tax benefits are recognised within the 'measurement period' (generally 12 months after the date of the acquisition) that result from new information about facts and circumstances that existed at the acquisition date. These will be adjusted against goodwill.

Although the adjustment of goodwill for acquired deferred tax benefits recognised within the measurement period is not one of the adjustments to goodwill permitted under IFRS 1:C4(g) (see **7.2.12.1**), it is consistent with the treatment adopted for other adjustments to 'provisional' values (see **7.2.12.6**).

Example 7.2.16.2

Recognition of previously unrecognised deferred tax asset

Entity B presents its first IFRS financial statements for the year ended 31 December 20X5 with a date of transition of 1 January 20X4. In preparing those financial statements, Entity B chooses not to restate business combinations prior to the date of transition in accordance with IFRS 3.

Entity B had previously acquired Entity C during 20X2 in a business combination in which CU300 of goodwill was recognised under previous GAAP, but CU500 of deferred tax assets arising from loss carryforwards were not recognised. The loss carryforwards expire on 31 December 20X6. Under Entity B's previous GAAP, goodwill amortisation was prohibited and the carrying amount of goodwill at the date of transition is CU300.

At the date of transition, Entity B assesses future profitability and determines that CU100 of the deferred tax benefit can be recovered by the end of 20X6. The following journal entry is recorded.

		CU	CU
Dr	Deferred tax asset	100	
Cr	Retained earnings		100

Recognition of the deferred tax asset.

During the year ended 31 December 20X6, Entity B's profitability is even higher than expected and, consequently, all of the tax loss carryforwards are utilised before they expire.

Entity B will account for the realisation of the deferred tax assets after the date of transition in accordance with IAS 12:68. Because the realisation occurs after the measurement period (i.e. more than 12 months after the date of the original acquisition of Entity C), it cannot be adjusted against goodwill.

7.2.16.3 Deferred tax asset relating to goodwill previously written off directly to equity

A deferred tax asset may arise when goodwill has been written off directly to equity but attracts tax relief on an amortisation basis. Subject to the usual recoverability criteria, a deferred tax asset should be recognised, at the date of transition, based on the difference between the carrying amount (i.e. nil) and the tax base (i.e. the amount of future tax deductions). The adjustment is made against retained earnings (or another appropriate category of equity); the carrying amount of any other goodwill may not be adjusted because the recognition of previously unrecognised deferred tax assets is not one of the permitted adjustments to goodwill specifically identified in IFRS 1:C4.

Example 7.2.16.3

Deferred tax asset relating to goodwill previously written off directly to equity

Company D operates in a jurisdiction in which, under previous GAAP, goodwill was written off directly to equity immediately following a business combination. The local tax law allows a deduction of 1/20 of the purchased goodwill in each of the 20 years following an acquisition. Company D acquired a business two years before the date of transition to IFRSs, and all related goodwill was written off directly to equity at that time. At the date of transition, Company D is still entitled to claim 18/20 of the amount of purchased goodwill as a deduction over the next 18 years. Company D has elected not to restate past business combinations prior to the date of transition in accordance with IFRS 3.

At the date of transition to IFRSs, should a deferred tax asset be recognised in respect of the goodwill previously written off directly to equity?

Yes, subject to IAS 12's general recognition criteria for deferred tax assets. Company D should recognise a deferred tax asset in respect of the deductible temporary difference between the carrying amount of the goodwill (nil) and its tax base. The adjustment is made against retained earnings (or another appropriate category of equity). As the deferred tax asset is subsequently reduced when tax deductions are received, the effect of the reduction in the deferred tax asset will be recognised in profit or loss for the period.

7.3 Share-based payment transactions

7.3.1 First-time adopters generally apply the transition provisions of IFRS 2

IFRS 2 *Share-based Payment* contains various transition provisions. The IASB decided that, in general, first-time adopters should be treated in the same way as entities already applying IFRSs in this regard. The exemptions set out in **7.3.2** and **7.3.3** reflect that principle.

7.3.2 Equity-settled transactions

7.3.2.1 Exemptions from retrospective application
IFRS 1 includes two exemptions for equity-settled transactions.

[IFRS 1:D2]

- First-time adopters are not required to apply IFRS 2 to equity-settled share-based payments granted on or before 7 November 2002.

- First-time adopters are not required to apply IFRS 2 to share-based payments granted after 7 November 2002 that vested before the date of transition to IFRSs.

Although entities are not required to apply IFRS 2 in the circumstances described, they are encouraged to do so. [IFRS 1:D2]

Under IFRS 1:D2, first-time adopters are also not required to apply IFRS 2 to share-based payments granted after 7 November 2002 that vested before 1 January 2005 (if the date of transition is earlier than 1 January 2005), but this is likely to be of limited relevance now.

The practical effect of the second exemption is that equity instruments that vested before the date of transition can be ignored. This is logical because, if IFRS 2 were applied to such instruments, no expense would be recognised in the statement of comprehensive income either in the first IFRS reporting period or in the comparative period. Equity instruments granted on or before 7 November 2002 can also be ignored, even if they have not vested at the date of transition, but this is likely to be of limited relevance now.

For share-based payment arrangements to which IFRS 2 must be applied, an entity may have recognised an expense for that share-based payment arrangement under previous GAAP. No adjustment will be necessary if previous GAAP is fully converged with IFRS 2. In other cases, the previous GAAP expense will often be calculated on a basis that is inconsistent with IFRS 2. Any such expense should generally be reversed and replaced with an expense in accordance with IFRS 2.

If a first-time adopter elects to apply IFRS 2 to the equity instruments referred to in IFRS 1:D2, it may do so only if the entity has disclosed publicly the fair value of those equity instruments, determined at the measurement date, as defined in IFRS 2. [IFRS 1:D2]

The effect of this requirement is to prohibit full retrospective application of IFRS 2 by many entities because they will not have disclosed publicly the fair value of the equity instruments granted in previous years. IFRS 1 does not elaborate on what is meant by 'disclosed publicly' but it appears that the IASB had in mind disclosure in the financial statements for the year in which the instruments were granted.

Example 7.3.2.1A

Transition to IFRS 2 for first-time adopter

Company L is a first-time adopter of IFRSs with a reporting date of 31 December 20X5 and a date of transition of 1 January 20X4 (which is after 7 November 2002). Company L has historically granted share-based payments to its employees. Some, but not all, of those grants have vested by 1 January 20X4.

Company L is required to apply IFRS 2 to all share-based payment transactions granted after 7 November 2002 that have not vested at 1 January 20X4. For share-based payment transactions granted before 7 November 2002, or granted after 7 November 2002 but vested before 1 January 20X4, Company L is not required to apply IFRS 2, but may choose to do so if the fair value of those share-based payments was previously disclosed publicly. The fair value must have been determined at the grant date, in accordance with IFRS 2.

Considerable judgement will be required to determine the appropriate valuation of share-based payment transactions retrospectively if valuations were not previously obtained. IFRS 1 provides some guidance in relation to estimates and restrictions on the use of hindsight, which is useful in the context of the measurement of fair value for equity-settled transactions.

Selective application of the IFRS 1 exemption for share-based payments is not acceptable. Electing to apply IFRS 2 to equity instruments covered by the exemption is an accounting policy choice that should be applied consistently to the extent possible. IFRS 1:D2 does not suggest that the exemption may be applied only to specific transactions or arrangements. If an entity has previously published fair values for all equity-settled share-based payments, and it elects to apply IFRS 2 to equity-settled share-based payment arrangements falling within the scope of the exemption, it must apply IFRS 2 to all such arrangements.

However, if the entity disclosed the fair value for some but not all of the equity-settled share-based payment arrangements falling within the scope of the exemption, it may apply IFRS 2 retrospectively only to those instruments for which the fair value had been disclosed.

Example 7.3.2.1B

Measurement of equity-settled share-based payments on first-time adoption

Company M is adopting IFRSs for the first time with a date of transition of 1 January 20X4 and a reporting date of 31 December 20X5. Company M issued share options on 30 June 20X3 (which was after 7 November 2002) that vest after four years (i.e. on 30 June 20X7). The transaction is classified as equity-settled. Under Company M's previous GAAP, Company M did not estimate (or disclose) the fair value of the share options determined as at 30 June 20X3 in accordance with IFRS 2.

Company M is required to apply IFRS 2 to the June 20X3 grant of share options. Because estimates of fair value were not required under previous GAAP, in accordance with IFRS 1:16 the measurement should reflect conditions at the date of transition to IFRSs. Company M should use information available at 1 January 20X4 to determine expected volatility, expected dividends, and the expected life of the options under the equity-settled transaction. However, some inputs to the valuation model will be based purely on contractual or historical fact, in which case that contractual or historical information should be used. Therefore, the share price, exercise price and risk-free rate should be based on information available at grant date – in this case, 30 June 20X3.

For all grants of equity instruments to which IFRS 2 has not been applied (e.g. equity instruments granted on or before 7 November 2002), a first-time adopter should nevertheless disclose the information required by paragraphs 44 and 45 of IFRS 2 (see **chapter A16**). [IFRS 1:D2]

7.3.2.2   Modifications to terms and conditions

If a first-time adopter modifies the terms or conditions of a grant of equity instruments to which IFRS 2 has not been applied, paragraphs 26 to 29 of IFRS 2 (see **chapter A16**) need not be applied if the modifications occurred before the date of transition to IFRSs. [IFRS 1:D2]

Paragraphs 26 to 29 of IFRS 2 deal with modifications to the terms and conditions on which equity instruments were granted, including cancellations and settlements. When a modification is beneficial to the employee, these paragraphs sometimes require additional share-based payment expense to be recognised; and in some other circumstances, they can require accelerated recognition of future share-based payment expense. However, a first-time adopter can ignore these paragraphs if IFRS 2 has not been applied to the share-based payment in question, provided that the modification occurred before the date of transition to IFRSs.

7.3.3   Cash-settled transactions

A first-time adopter is encouraged, but not required, to apply IFRS 2 to liabilities arising from share-based payment transactions that were:

[IFRS 1:D3]

- settled before the date of transition to IFRSs; or

- settled before 1 January 2005.

For liabilities to which IFRS 2 is applied, a first-time adopter is not required to restate comparative information to the extent that the information relates to a period or date that is earlier than 7 November 2002. [IFRS 1:D3]

This exemption is now of limited relevance. The date of transition to IFRSs will invariably be later than 1 January 2005 so the practical effect is that liabilities can be ignored if they were settled before the date of transition to IFRSs. Such liabilities would have no effect on the financial statements even if an exemption did not exist.

Example 7.3.3

Measurement of cash-settled share-based payments on first-time adoption

Company N is adopting IFRSs for the first time with a date of transition of 1 January 20X4 and a reporting date of 31 December 20X5. Company N issued share options on 30 November 20X3 that do not vest until 30 November 20X6. The share options will be settled in cash. The vesting conditions are related to continued employment only. In accordance with IFRS 1, Company N is required to apply IFRS 2 to the November 20X3 grant of share options because the liability is not settled before the date of transition. Under previous GAAP, Company N had neither disclosed nor estimated fair value determined as at 30 November 20X3 in accordance with IFRS 2; however, it recognised and measured the liability in its previous GAAP financial statements at the difference between the exercise price and the current share price at 31 December 20X3.

At the date of transition (1 January 20X4) and at each reporting date until it is settled, Company N measures the liability at its fair value, by applying an option pricing model, taking into account the terms and conditions on which the share options were granted, and the extent to which the employees have rendered service to date. The fair value of the cash-settled share-based payments includes both intrinsic value and time value. Time value in this context is defined as "... the value of the right to participate in future increases in the share price, if any, that may occur between the valuation date and the settlement date". The exclusion of the time value would lead to an inadequate measure of the liability.

The amount recognised under previous GAAP at 31 December 20X3, which was based on the difference between the exercise price and the current share price at 31 December 20X3, cannot be used as an approximation to fair value of the options under IFRS 2 at 1 January 20X4.

Similar to equity-settled transactions, judgement is required to determine the fair value in accordance with IFRS 2 of cash-settled-based payment transactions.

7.4   Insurance contracts

The transition provisions in IFRS 4 *Insurance Contracts* allow entities already applying IFRSs when they adopt that Standard to continue to use their existing accounting policies for liabilities arising from insurance contracts as long as the existing policies meet certain minimum requirements as set out in IFRS 4. IFRS 4 also requires disclosures that identify and explain the amounts in an insurer's financial statements arising from insurance contracts. IFRS 4 is discussed in detail in **chapter A39**.

The IASB recognised that it could be quite onerous for first-time adopters to apply the requirements of IFRS 4 retrospectively. Therefore, IFRS 1 provides an optional exemption whereby an insurer may elect upon first-time adoption to apply the transition provisions of IFRS 4. [IFRS 1:D4]

The transition provisions in paragraphs 41 to 45 of IFRS 4 require an insurer to apply IFRS 4 prospectively for reporting periods beginning on or after 1 January 2005, with earlier application permitted. Therefore, the relief provided in IFRS 1:D4 allows a first-time adopter to apply the requirements of IFRS 4 prospectively from 1 January 2005 rather than applying the requirements of the Standard as if they had always been in place.

While this may have represented significant relief for entities that adopted IFRSs in 2005, its benefit for later adopters is primarily in restricting the period of retrospective application (i.e. from 2005 to the date of transition).

One specific area of relief that continues to benefit first-time adopters is in the application of IFRS 4:39(c)(iii) (see **5.2** in **chapter A39**), under which first-time adopters are not required to disclose information about claims development that occurred earlier than five years before the end of the first financial year in which they apply IFRS 4. If it is impracticable when an entity first applies IFRS 4 to prepare information about claims development that occurred before the beginning of the earliest period for which the entity presents full comparative information that complies with IFRS 4, that fact is required to be disclosed. [IFRS 4:44]

When an insurer changes its accounting policies for insurance liabilities, it is permitted, but not required, to reclassify some or all of its financial assets as measured at fair value under IFRS 9 *Financial Instruments*. (Correspondingly, an insurer applying IAS 39 *Financial Instruments: Recognition and Measurement* is permitted, but not required, to reclassify some or all of its financial assets as 'at fair value through profit or loss'.) This reclassification is permitted:

[IFRS 4:45]

- if an insurer changes accounting policies when it first applies IFRS 4 (e.g. on first-time adoption); and

- if it makes a subsequent policy change permitted by IFRS 4:22 (see **4.4.1** in **chapter A39**), in which case the reclassification is a change in accounting policy and IAS 8 *Accounting Policies, Changes in Accounting Estimates and Errors* applies.

7.5   Deemed cost

7.5.1   Deemed cost exemptions – general

In drafting IFRS 1, the IASB acknowledged that the costs of requiring entities to reconstruct cost information or other transactional data for property, plant and equipment and other long-term assets could be particularly onerous when entities might not have retained the necessary historical information. The IASB also noted that reconstructed data might be less relevant to users, and less reliable, than current fair value data. As a result, IFRS 1 includes optional exemptions that relieve first-time adopters from the requirement to recreate cost information for property, plant and equipment, investment property and (to a much more limited extent) intangible assets. When the exemptions are applied, deemed cost is the basis for subsequent depreciation and impairment tests. Deemed cost is defined by IFRS 1 as 'the amount used as a surrogate for cost or depreciated cost at a given date' (see **3.2**).

There are four types of 'deemed cost' exemption under IFRS 1:

- IFRS 1:D5 to D7 allow fair value at the date of transition or previous GAAP revaluations to be taken as the deemed cost for specified categories of assets (detailed conditions discussed in **7.5.2**);

- IFRS 1:D8 allows 'event-driven' fair values to be taken as the deemed cost at the date of that measurement (detailed conditions discussed in **7.5.3**);

- IFRS 1:D8A deals specifically with oil and gas assets (see **7.5.4**); and

- IFRS 1:D8B deals with assets used in operations subject to rate regulation (see **7.5.5**).

When an asset is initially recognised under IFRSs on a deemed cost basis, subsequent depreciation is based on that deemed cost and starts from the date for which the fair value measurement or revaluation was established. [IFRS 1:IG9]

7.5.2   *Fair value or revaluation as deemed cost*

7.5.2.1   *Scope*

This exemption applies to:

[IFRS 1:D5 - D7]

- property, plant and equipment;

- investment property, if an entity elects to use the cost model in IAS 40 *Investment Property*; and

- intangible assets that meet:

  - the recognition criteria in IAS 38 *Intangible Assets* (including reliable measurement of original cost); and

  - the criteria in IAS 38 for revaluation (including the existence of an active market).

The exemption may be used selectively within the classes of assets described. IFRS 1:BC45 confirms that "the IFRS does not restrict the use of fair value as deemed cost to entire classes of assets". However, indications of impairment cannot be ignored for those assets that are not restated.

The ability to apply this exemption to intangible assets is likely to be of limited relevance given that IAS 38's restrictive criteria for use of the revaluation basis must be met.

The exemption cannot be applied to other classes of assets by analogy. [IFRS 1:D7] The exemption is available regardless of the IFRS accounting policy selected by the entity for ongoing reporting purposes.

IFRS 1:D5 provides the option to measure assets at deemed cost without specifying if the assets have been acquired, self-constructed or held under finance leases. Therefore, the exemption can also be applied to assets held under finance leases and capitalised in the financial statements. A first-time adopter may measure these items at fair value at the date of transition. However, the related finance lease liability is not measured at fair value; rather it is measured at the net present value of the lease payments in accordance with IAS 17 *Leases*.

The exemption in IFRS 1:D5 is not limited to property, plant and equipment within the scope of IAS 16. Consequently, an entity may elect to measure items of property, plant and equipment that are outside the scope of IAS 16 (e.g. certain mineral rights and reserves) at a deemed cost in accordance with IFRS 1:D5 (see also **7.5.4**). Whether mineral rights and reserves are property, plant and equipment or intangible assets is considered in **section 2** of **chapter A7**. Property, plant and equipment used in exploration activities are within the scope of IAS 16.

7.5.2.2   Details of the exemption

IFRS 1:D5 permits any asset in the designated categories to be measured at the date of transition to IFRSs at its fair value and that fair value to be used as the asset's deemed cost at that date. When this election is made, the disclosures required by IFRS 1:30 should be made in the entity's first IFRS financial statements (see **9.3.5**).

A first-time adopter may also elect to use a previous GAAP revaluation of any asset in the designated categories at, or before, the date of transition to IFRSs as deemed cost at the date of revaluation. This is, however, permitted only if the revaluation was, at the date of the revaluation, broadly comparable to:

[IFRS 1:D6]

- fair value; or
- cost or depreciated cost under IFRSs, adjusted to reflect, for example, changes in a general or specific price index.

The reference to the revaluation being 'broadly comparable' is explained in IFRS 1:BC47 as allowing a first-time adopter "to establish a deemed cost using a measurement that is already available and is a reasonable starting point for a cost-based measurement".

A previous GAAP valuation at a percentage of fair value (e.g. 80%) is not broadly comparable to fair value. IFRS 1:BC47 notes that it may not always be clear whether a previous revaluation was intended to be a measure of fair value. For the amount to be used as deemed cost, the measurement must represent a valid estimate of fair value. A percentage of fair value is not broadly comparable to fair value and, therefore, cannot be used as the asset's deemed cost.

However, a revaluation in accordance with previous GAAP that results in a carrying amount that is similar to fair value, such as the application of a price index to a previous carrying amount, may be considered broadly comparable.

In accordance with IFRS 1:D6, the previous GAAP revaluation must be "at, or before, the date of transition to IFRSs" and this would exclude a valuation carried out at the end of the last reporting period under previous GAAP. For example, if the end of the first IFRS reporting period is 31 December 20X8 and the date of transition to IFRSs is 1 January 20X7, a valuation carried out at 31 December 20X7 under previous GAAP would not comply with IFRS 1:D6. However, it might be possible instead to use the measurement at 31 December 20X7 under the exemption in IFRS 1:D8(b) (see **7.5.3**).

Example 7.5.2.2

Accounting for previously recognised revaluation uplift

Under previous GAAP, Company G measured property, plant and equipment at a revalued amount that was broadly consistent with fair value and accumulated the difference between depreciated cost and the revalued amount within equity. Company G has elected to use the revalued amount as deemed cost under IFRS 1.

How should the revaluation uplift recognised under previous GAAP be accounted for at the date of transition to IFRSs?

IFRS 1:11 requires that the adjustments arising from first-time adoption be recognised in retained earnings or, if appropriate, another category of equity. The Standard does not specifically address the accounting for revaluation uplifts recognised under previous GAAP. The adjustment could be recognised as a separate component of equity but that is not required under IFRS 1.

If a previous GAAP revaluation is used as deemed cost under IFRS 1:D6, any revaluation uplift accumulated in equity under previous GAAP does not form part of the revaluation surplus under IFRSs. Therefore, an impairment loss arising after the transition to IFRSs cannot be offset against the amount accumulated in equity under previous GAAP but instead should be recognised in profit or loss.

7.5.3   Event-driven fair value used as deemed cost

A first-time adopter may have established a deemed cost under previous GAAP for some or all of its assets and liabilities by measuring them at their fair value at one particular date because of an event such as a privatisation or initial public offering (IPO). IFRS 1 allows the following exemptions in respect of such event-driven fair values.

- If the measurement date is *at or before* the date of transition to IFRSs, the entity may use the event-driven fair value measurement as deemed cost for IFRSs at the date of that measurement. [IFRS 1:D8(a)]

- If the measurement date is *after* the date of transition to IFRSs, but during the period covered by the first IFRS financial statements, the event-driven fair value measurement may be used as deemed cost when the event occurs. In such circumstances, the entity should recognise the resulting adjustments directly in retained earnings (or, if appropriate, another category of equity) at the measurement date. At the date of transition to IFRSs, the entity should either establish the deemed cost by applying the criteria in paragraphs D5 to D7 or measure assets and liabilities in accordance with the other requirements in IFRS 1. [IFRS 1:D8(b)]

> The exemptions under IFRS 1:D8(a) and (b) can be applied broadly and are not limited to fair value measurements arising from privatisations and IPOs. The use of the expression 'an event such as' implies that these are examples of two such events, not a limitation on what events would qualify.

The scope of these exemptions differs from the exemption available under IFRS 1:D5 and D6, as illustrated in the following example.

Example 7.5.3A

Scope and applicability of the deemed cost exemption in IFRS 1:D8(a)

An entity plans to adopt IFRSs with a date of transition of 1 January 20X5. In November 20X4, the entity experiences financial difficulties and it is forced to file for protection from its creditors.

The entity undertakes a financial reorganisation under which there is a substantial realignment of the equity and non-equity interests in the entity. Under local GAAP, this leads to a comprehensive revaluation of the entity's assets and liabilities (including debt, intangible assets etc.) to fair value. These fair values are recognised in the entity's annual financial statements at 31 December 20X4 prepared under local GAAP.

For the purposes of the exemption in IFRS 1:D8(a), is the entity permitted to use the values established for the purposes of the financial reorganisation for all categories of assets and liabilities?

Yes. Unlike the exemptions available under IFRS 1:D5 and D6, application of the exemption under IFRS 1:D8(a) is not restricted to property, plant and equipment, investment property and some intangible assets. The entity is permitted to use the IFRS 1:D8(a) exemption for any of its assets and liabilities provided that the conditions in that paragraph are met. Those conditions are:

- that the value established at the date of the reorganisation was the fair value; and
- that the value established at the date of the reorganisation was recognised in the entity's financial statements under previous GAAP (see below).

The application of the exemption under IFRS 1:D8(a) to intangible assets is not restricted to intangible assets meeting the revaluation criteria under IAS 38 (see IFRS 1:IG50).

If the entity elects to use the exemption under IFRS 1:D8(a), is it required to use all of the fair value measurements established for the purposes of the reorganisation or is it permitted to apply the exemption only to selected assets and liabilities?

The exemption may be applied to individual assets and liabilities (i.e. the entity is permitted to use the exemption selectively).

IFRS 1:D8(a) is not explicit in this regard. IFRS 1:BC45 clarifies that the exemption available under IFRS 1:D5 can be applied selectively – but it does not address the other deemed cost exemptions. However, in the absence of specific mention, it is reasonable to assume that the entity may choose to use only some of the fair value measurements established at the date of the reorganisation as deemed cost at the date of those measurements.

If a first-time adopter wishes to apply the IFRS 1:D8(a) exemption, it is necessary that the assets and liabilities have been recognised and measured at the event-driven fair value measurements in the first-time adopter's previous GAAP financial statements. It is not sufficient to have publicly disclosed the fair value (e.g. in the notes to the financial statements).

This is supported by IFRS 1:BC95 which states that, if this exemption is taken, it does not lead to a restatement on transition to IFRSs because the exemption applies "only if the measurement was already used in previous GAAP financial statements".

IFRS 1:D8(b) allows a first-time adopter to use an event-driven fair value as deemed cost at the measurement date for measurement events that occurred after the date of transition to IFRSs, provided that the measurement date is during the period covered by the entity's first IFRS financial statements. Notably, when IFRS 1:D8(b) was added to IFRS 1, no changes were made to IFRS 1:BC95. Therefore, at first glance, it could be taken that IFRS 1:BC95 refers equally to the exemption in IFRS 1:D8(b) and, consequently, that IFRS 1:D8(b) can only be applied if the event-driven fair measurements have been recognised in the entity's financial statements under previous GAAP. However, because the IFRS 1:D8(b) exemption relates to event-driven fair value measurements after the date of transition, in the majority of cases these values will not have been recognised in previous GAAP financial statements and such a requirement would be counter-intuitive. If IFRS 1:BC95 were taken to apply to IFRS 1:D8(b), in practice the exemption could only be used in relation to event-driven fair values in the comparative period that were used in the previous GAAP financial statements for the comparative period. It seems clear that the IASB did not intend to restrict the application of the relief in this manner. Accordingly, unlike the IFRS 1:D8(a) exemption, it is reasonable to assume that the event-driven fair value measurement is not required to have been recognised in the entity's previous GAAP financial statements.

Example 7.5.3B

Event-driven fair value established after the date of transition to IFRSs

Entity D is adopting IFRSs for the first time in its financial statements for the year ended 31 December 20X9. Its date of transition is 1 January 20X8. At 31 March 20X9, in producing financial information for an initial public offering (IPO), Entity D establishes fair values for property, plant and equipment.

The following information is relevant.

Fair value of assets established at 31 December 20X2 (recognised under previous GAAP)	CU750
Fair value of assets at 31 December 20X2 less accumulated depreciation and impairment to 1 January 20X8 (determined in accordance with IFRSs)	CU400
Fair value of assets at 31 December 20X2 less accumulated depreciation and impairment to 31 March 20X9 (determined in accordance with IFRSs)	CU300
Fair value of assets at 31 March 20X9	CU1,200

Under IFRS 1:D8(b), the fair value at 31 March 20X9 may be used as the deemed cost of the assets at that date for the purposes of the entity's first IFRS financial statements.

However, Entity D would still need to establish the carrying amount of the assets at the date of transition (1 January 20X8), and account for the assets under IFRSs from the date of transition to 31 March 20X9. For this purpose, Entity D has the usual options to establish the carrying amount of the assets by applying IAS 16 retrospectively or by reference to a deemed cost in accordance with IFRS 1:D5 to D7.

For example, using the exemption available under IFRS 1:D6, Entity D could use the fair value at 31 December 20X2 recognised under previous GAAP as the deemed cost at that date and establish the carrying amount at 1 January 20X8 by adjusting the 31 December 20X2 fair value for subsequent depreciation and impairment. When this option is taken, in the first IFRS financial statements, depreciation recognised from 1 January 20X8 to 31 March 20X9 will be based on the deemed cost at 31 December 20X2 (CU750).

If the fair value at 31 March 20X9 is used as deemed cost for the assets at that date, the difference of CU900 between the carrying amount at 31 March 20X9 (CU300) and the fair value of the assets at 31 March 20X9 (CU1,200) is recognised in retained earnings or another category of equity (e.g. a reserve used for IFRS 1 adjustments). This is not considered to be a revaluation of the property, plant and equipment for the purposes of IAS 16 (and does not result in a requirement for subsequent regular revaluations). Subsequent depreciation (after 31 March 20X9) is based on the uplifted value. No adjustment is made to the depreciation recognised under IFRSs for the period from 1 January 20X8 to 31 March 20X9.

7.5.4 Oil and gas assets

Under some local GAAPs, exploration and development costs for oil and gas properties in the development or production phases are accounted for in cost centres that include all properties in a large geographical area (known as the 'full cost' method).

IFRS 1 permits a first-time adopter that has previously used this basis of accounting to elect to measure the related oil and gas assets at the date of transition to IFRSs on the following basis:

[IFRS 1:D8A]

- exploration and evaluation assets – at amounts determined under the entity's previous GAAP; and

- oil and gas assets in the development or production phases – at the amount determined for the cost centre under the entity's previous GAAP. This amount should be allocated to the cost centre's underlying assets pro rata using reserve volumes or reserve values as of that date.

For the purposes of this exemption, the term 'oil and gas assets' is limited to those assets used in the exploration, evaluation, development or production of oil and gas. [IFRS 1:D8A]

Entities electing to use the exemption are required to test both exploration and evaluation assets and assets in the development and production phases for impairment at the date of transition to IFRSs. The exploration and evaluation assets are tested in accordance with IFRS 6 *Exploration for and Evaluation of Mineral Resources*, and development and production assets are tested in accordance with IAS 36 *Impairment of Assets*. [IFRS 1:D8A]

Any identified impairment losses must be recognised at the date of transition. [IFRS 1:D8A]

7.5.5 Assets used in operations subject to rate regulation

The exemption applies for entities that:

[IFRS 1:D8B]

- hold items of property, plant and equipment that are used, or were previously used, in operations subject to rate regulation; and

- have included in the carrying amount of such items amounts that were determined under previous GAAP but do not qualify for capitalisation under IFRSs.

For this purpose, operations are subject to rate regulation if they are governed by a framework for establishing the prices that can be charged to customers for goods or services and that framework is subject to oversight and/or approval by a rate regulator (as defined in IFRS 14 *Regulatory Deferral Accounts*). [IFRS 1:D8B]

When a first-time adopter falls within the scope of this paragraph, it may elect to use the previous GAAP carrying amount of such an item at the date of transition to IFRSs as deemed cost. If an entity applies this exemption to an item, it need not apply it to all items. [IFRS 1:D8B]

When this option is taken, at the date of transition to IFRSs, the entity is required to test for impairment in accordance with IAS 36 each item to which the exemption is applied. [IFRS 1:D8B]

Subsequent depreciation or amortisation is based on the deemed cost and starts from the date of transition to IFRSs. [IFRS 1:IG51]

7.6 Leases

7.6.1 Determining whether an arrangement contains a lease

7.6.1.1 Transition provisions of IFRIC 4

A first-time adopter may apply the transition provisions of IFRIC 4 *Determining whether an Arrangement contains a Lease*. Therefore, a first-time adopter may determine whether an arrangement existing at the date of transition to IFRSs contains a lease on the basis of the facts and circumstances existing at that date. [IFRS 1:D9]

IFRIC 4 specifies criteria for determining, at the inception of an arrangement, whether the arrangement contains a lease. It also specifies when an arrangement should be reassessed subsequently. IFRS 1 provides an exemption from these requirements. Instead of determining retrospectively whether an arrangement contained a lease at the inception of the arrangement and subsequently reassessing that arrangement as required in the periods prior to transition to IFRSs, entities may determine whether arrangements in existence on the date of transition contain leases by applying paragraphs 6 to 9 of IFRIC 4 to those arrangements on the basis of the facts and circumstances existing at that date (see **2.7.3** of **chapter A17**). [IFRS 1:IG204 - IG205]

7.6.1.2 *Assessment under previous GAAP made at a date other than that required under IFRIC 4*

An additional exemption is available for a first-time adopter that, under its previous GAAP, made an assessment as to whether an arrangement contained a lease at a date other than that required under IFRIC 4. In such circumstances, the first-time adopter is not required to reassess its previous determination if that previous determination made under its previous GAAP would have given the same outcome under IAS 17 *Leases* and IFRIC 4. [IFRS 1:D9A]

Example 7.6.1.2

Exemption from reassessment as to whether an arrangement contains a lease

Entity R is adopting IFRSs with a date of transition of 1 January 20X5. With effect from 1 January 20X3, Entity R's previous GAAP was amended to include guidance relating to whether an arrangement contains a lease. At the time the previous GAAP requirement became effective, Entity R assessed that it had only one arrangement which contained a lease. The arrangement was entered into on 30 June 20X2 and remains in existence at the date of transition to IFRSs. Other arrangements, which were determined not to contain a lease, are also ongoing at the date of transition to IFRSs.

Entity R has determined that the assessment as to whether the arrangement contained a lease under previous GAAP resulted in the same outcome as would have been arrived at under IAS 17 and IFRIC 4.

Therefore, under IFRS 1:D9A, upon adoption of IFRSs, Entity R is not required to reassess whether existing arrangements contain a lease. Instead, Entity R can rely on the assessment made under previous GAAP because that assessment resulted in the same outcome as would have been arrived at under IAS 17 and IFRIC 4.

Note that for the arrangement that was determined to contain a lease, IAS 17 must be applied retrospectively because IFRS 1 does not provide any exemptions in that regard.

7.6.2 *Other aspects of lease accounting*

Apart from the two exemptions described in **7.6.1** for first-time adopters applying IFRIC 4, no special exemptions for leases are available to a first-time adopter under IFRS 1. Accordingly, a first-time adopter is required to apply IAS 17 in full in its first IFRS financial statements, both in respect of the current period and any comparative periods.

A first-time adopter may, therefore, be required to recognise an asset (e.g. property, plant and equipment) on transition to IFRSs that it had not recognised under previous GAAP. This asset might be recognised by the first-time adopter in its role as the lessee under a finance lease (it may have treated the lease as an operating lease under previous GAAP) or as the lessor under an operating lease (it may have treated the lease as a finance lease under previous GAAP). In the former case, in the absence of other exemptions, the first-time adopter would be required to determine (1) the fair value of the asset at the inception of the lease (or the present value of the minimum lease payments, if lower) depreciated to the date of transition to IFRSs, and (2) the finance lease liability amortised at the rate implicit in the lease (or, if appropriate, the lessee's incremental borrowing rate). It may be difficult, and even impracticable, to determine the fair value of the leased asset at the inception of the lease; however, the entity might be able to elect to measure the asset capitalised under a finance lease at fair value at the date of transition to IFRSs in accordance with the optional exemption in IFRS 1 (see **7.5.2**).

At the date of transition to IFRSs, leases should be classified as operating leases or finance leases (by both the lessee and the lessor) on the basis of circumstances existing at the inception of the leases (see IAS 17:13). The lessee and lessor may agree to amend the terms of the lease in a manner that would have resulted in a different classification had the amended terms been in effect at the inception of the lease. If so, the revised agreement is considered as a new agreement over its term, but changes in estimates (e.g. of the economic life or residual value of the leased property) or changes in circumstances (e.g. default by the lessee) do not give rise to a new lease classification. [IFRS 1:IG14]

When IAS 17 was revised in 1997, the net cash investment method for recognising finance income of lessors was eliminated. The transition provisions of IAS 17 permit finance lessors to eliminate this method prospectively. However, this transitional relief is not available to a first-time adopter when preparing its opening IFRS statement of financial position (see **5.3.2**). Therefore, a finance lessor measures finance lease receivables in its opening IFRS statement of financial position as if the net cash investment method had never been permitted. [IFRS 1:IG15]

SIC-15 *Operating Leases – Incentives* (see **7.2.3** of **chapter A17**) applies to lease terms beginning on or after 1 January 1999. However, a first-time adopter must apply SIC-15 to all leases, irrespective of whether they started before or after that date. [IFRS 1:IG16]

7.7 Cumulative translation differences

7.7.1 Option to reset cumulative translation differences to zero at the date of transition to IFRSs

Under IAS 21 *The Effects of Changes in Foreign Exchange Rates*, some translation differences are initially recognised in other comprehensive income and accumulated in a separate component of equity. On disposal of a foreign operation, IAS 21 requires an entity to reclassify the cumulative translation difference for that foreign operation (including, if applicable, gains and losses on related hedges) to profit or loss as part of the gain or loss on disposal. [IFRS 1:D12]

> Retrospective application of IAS 21 could be very onerous for a first-time adopter because it would require an entity retrospectively to determine the translation differences arising on the translation of the financial statements of a foreign operation in accordance with IFRSs from the date on which the operation was formed or acquired. Often, this information will not be readily available. IFRS 1 provides an optional exemption relating to the treatment of cumulative translation differences upon first-time adoption.

A first-time adopter need not comply with these requirements for cumulative translation differences that existed at the date of transition to IFRSs. If this exemption is applied, the cumulative translation differences for all foreign operations are deemed to be zero at the date of transition to IFRSs. The gain or loss on a subsequent disposal of any foreign operation will include only foreign exchange differences that arose after the date of transition. [IFRS 1:D13]

> If the election is used to reset all cumulative translation differences for all foreign operations to zero at the date of transition to IFRSs, this treatment applies to translation differences that arise as a result of first-time adoption of IFRSs. The election applies once all adjustments for first-time adoption have been recognised at the date of transition. If the election is used, the balance of cumulative translation differences in the opening IFRS statement of financial position will be zero.

7.7.2 Reassessment of functional currency on transition to IFRSs

The following example illustrates the application of the exemption when an entity is required to change its functional currency on transition to IFRSs to comply with IAS 21.

Example 7.7.2

Reassessment of functional currency on transition to IFRSs

Under previous GAAP, an entity had Sterling as its functional currency. At the date of transition to IFRSs, when the requirements of IAS 21 are applied, it is determined that the entity's functional currency is US dollars. The entity chooses not to use the exemption available in IFRS 1:D13 but instead applies IAS 21 retrospectively.

The Foreign Currency Translation Reserve (FCTR) should be recalculated from the date the functional currency (under IAS 21) is considered to be US dollars.

If the functional currency of the entity is determined always to have been US dollars, the FCTR at the date of transition will represent the effect of the movements in exchange rates since the acquisition of each asset and liability (including those disposed of before transition to IFRSs). The FCTR should be calculated based on the underlying measurement of assets and liabilities in the functional currency of the entity.

IFRS 1:D5 and D6 permit deemed cost to be used for certain assets. When this exemption is used, the FCTR will not be calculated from the date of acquisition, but from the date at which the deemed cost amount is determined for the assets to which deemed cost has been applied.

If it is determined that the functional currency changed from Sterling to US dollars at some point prior to the date of transition (ignoring the use of any deemed cost exemption), the FCTR is only calculated from the date of change because, under IAS 21:35, translation procedures are only applied prospectively.

Irrespective of whether the exemption in IFRS 1:D13 is used, balances in the financial statements must be recognised in the entity's functional currency following the IAS 21 requirements.

7.7.3   Application of exemption when parent becomes a first-time adopter later than its subsidiary

Example 7.7.3

Application of exemption when parent becomes a first-time adopter later than its subsidiary

Parent P is adopting IFRSs for the first time with a date of transition of 1 January 20X4. In its first IFRS consolidated financial statements, Parent P proposes to use the exemption in IFRS 1:D13 to reset the cumulative translation differences for its foreign operations to zero at 1 January 20X4.

Subsidiary S is a subsidiary of Parent P and a foreign operation of Parent P as defined in IAS 21:8. Subsidiary S adopted IFRSs with a date of transition of 1 January 20X1. Subsidiary S is itself a parent and it has interests in a number of subsidiaries (together forming the 'Subsidiary S sub-group') that are foreign operations of Subsidiary S as defined in IAS 21:8.

IFRS 1:D17 requires that when a parent becomes a first-time adopter later than its subsidiary, the parent should, in its consolidated financial statements, measure the assets and liabilities of the subsidiary at the same carrying amounts as in the financial statements of the subsidiary, after adjusting for consolidation and for the effects of the business combination in which the entity acquired the subsidiary (see **7.9.2**).

Given the requirements of IFRS 1:D17, when considering whether to use the exemption in IFRS 1:D13 in the first IFRS consolidated financial statements for the larger group, is Parent P constrained by whether Subsidiary S elected to use that exemption in the first IFRS consolidated financial statements for the Subsidiary S sub-group?

No. The application of the exemption under IFRS 1:D13 is not affected by the requirements of IFRS 1:D17 because IFRS 1:D17 refers only to the measurement of assets and liabilities whereas IFRS 1:D13 is concerned with the classification of items within equity.

Irrespective of Subsidiary S's approach at its earlier date of transition, Parent P has a choice as to whether to use the exemption in IFRS 1:D13 in the first IFRS consolidated financial statements for the larger group. IFRS 1:D13 explicitly requires that when the exemption is applied, it should be applied to the cumulative translation differences for all of the foreign operations of the first-time adopter. Therefore, if it elects to use the exemption under IFRS 1:D13, Parent P should reset all of the cumulative translation differences for its group (including those relating to the Subsidiary S sub-group) to zero at 1 January 20X4.

7.8 Investments in subsidiaries, associates and joint ventures

7.8.1 Options for measurement of investments in separate financial statements

When an entity prepares separate financial statements, IAS 27 requires it to account for its investments in subsidiaries, associates and joint ventures either:

[IFRS 1:D14]

- at cost (see **7.8.2**);

- in accordance with IFRS 9 *Financial Instruments* (or, if IFRS 9 is not adopted, IAS 39 *Financial Instruments: Recognition and Measurement*); or

- for entities that have adopted the August 2015 amendments to IAS 27, using the equity method as described in IAS 28 (see **7.8.3**).

This choice between measurement at cost, in accordance with IFRS 9 (or IAS 39), or using the equity method, must be made consistently for all investments in the same category. [IAS 27:10]

7.8.2 Investments in subsidiaries, associates and joint ventures measured at cost

If a first-time adopter chooses to measure its investments in subsidiaries, associates or joint ventures at cost in its separate financial statements (see **7.8.1**), for the purposes of its opening IFRS statement of financial position, IFRS 1 requires that 'cost' to be either:

[IFRS 1:D15]

* cost determined in accordance with IAS 27; or
* a deemed cost, determined as either:
  * fair value at the entity's date of transition to IFRSs for its separate financial statements; or
  * the previous GAAP carrying amount at the entity's date of transition to IFRSs for its separate financial statements.

> The exemption available under IFRS 1:D15 permits a first-time adopter to use a deemed cost based on either fair value or previous GAAP carrying amount for its investments in subsidiaries, associates or joint ventures. This exemption is intended to address concerns that it may be difficult, or even impossible, and costly to determine cost in accordance with IAS 27. The alternative available under IAS 27:10 of accounting for such investments at fair value in accordance with IFRS 9 (or, if IFRS 9 is not adopted, IAS 39) on an ongoing basis will often be unattractive because of the cost of obtaining annual valuations.

A first-time adopter may choose either method for the determination of deemed cost (i.e. based on either fair value or previous GAAP carrying amount) to measure its investment in each subsidiary, joint venture or associate that it elects to measure using deemed cost. [IFRS 1:D15]

> That is to say, first-time adopters are permitted to choose which cost measurement basis to use for each investment on an individual basis. Some could be measured at cost in accordance with IAS 27 and others at deemed cost. For those measured at deemed cost, the choice between fair value and previous GAAP carrying amount may also be made on an investment-by-investment basis.

If an entity uses this exemption, it must make the disclosures described at **9.3.10**.

7.8.3 Investments in subsidiaries, associates and joint ventures accounted for using the equity method

If a first-time adopter chooses to account for its investments in subsidiaries, associates or joint ventures using the equity method in its separate financial statements (see **7.8.1**), it should apply the exemption for past business combinations set out in Appendix C of IFRS 1 (see **7.2**) to the acquisition of the investment. [IFRS 1:D15A]

When the equity method is used by a first-time adopter, IFRS 1 also prescribes as follows:

[IFRS 1:D15A]

- when the entity becomes a first-time adopter for its separate financial statements earlier than for its consolidated financial statements, but later than its parent, it should apply the requirements of IFRS 1:D16 (see **7.9.1**) in its separate financial statements; and

- when the entity becomes a first-time adopter for its separate financial statements earlier than for its consolidated financial statements, but later than its subsidiary, it should apply the requirements of IFRS 1:D17 (see **7.9.2**) in its separate financial statements.

The option for first-time adopters to use the equity method was added as a consequential amendment to IFRS 1 arising from *Equity Method in Separate Financial Statements (Amendments to IAS 27)* issued in August 2014. The amendments are effective for periods beginning on or after 1 January 2016, with earlier adoption permitted.

7.9 Assets and liabilities of subsidiaries, associates and joint ventures

7.9.1 Subsidiary becomes a first-time adopter later than its parent

7.9.1.1 Choice of measurement bases in subsidiary's financial statements

If a subsidiary becomes a first-time adopter later than its parent, IFRS 1 permits a choice between two measurement bases in the subsidiary's financial statements. Note that this choice is not available to a subsidiary of an investment entity which is required to be measured at fair value through profit or loss under the *Investment Entities* amendments (see **section 13** of **chapter A24**). [IFRS 1:D16]

The subsidiary may measure its assets and liabilities at either:

[IFRS 1:D16]

(a) the carrying amount that would be included in the parent's consolidated financial statements, based on the parent's date of transition to IFRSs, if no adjustments were made for consolidation procedures and for the effects of the business combination in which the parent acquired the subsidiary; or

(b) the carrying amounts required by IFRS 1 based on the subsidiary's date of transition to IFRSs.

The carrying amounts under these alternatives could differ when the exemptions in IFRS 1 result in measurement that depends on the date of transition to IFRSs. They could also differ when the accounting policies used in the subsidiary's financial statements differ from those in the consolidated financial statements. [IFRS 1:D16]

> The purpose of this exemption is to avoid the need to keep two parallel sets of records which the IASB accepted would be burdensome and not beneficial to users. [IFRS 1:BC60]
>
> When the option to use the parent's date of transition to IFRSs is applied, the amounts recognised by the subsidiary are 'based on' the parent's date of transition. However, the amounts recognised by the subsidiary at its date of transition will not generally be the same amounts recognised as at the parent's date of transition because of the need to account for subsequent depreciation etc. up to the subsidiary's date of transition to IFRSs.

Example 8 in the implementation guidance accompanying IFRS 1 provides an illustration of this choice. The example notes that when the assets and liabilities are measured based on the subsidiary's (later) date of transition to IFRSs, this does not change the carrying amount of the assets and liabilities in the consolidated financial statements. [IFRS 1:IG29]

A similar election is available to an associate or a joint venture that becomes a first-time adopter later than an entity that has significant influence or joint control over it. [IFRS 1:D16]

Paragraphs D16 (discussed in this section) and D17 (discussed at **7.9.2**) of IFRS 1 do not override the following requirements:

[IFRS 1:IG30]

- to apply Appendix C to IFRS 1 (on business combinations – see **7.2**) to assets acquired and liabilities assumed in a business combination that occurred before the acquirer's date of transition to IFRSs. But the acquirer should apply paragraph D17 to new assets acquired and liabilities assumed by the acquiree after that business combination and still held at the acquirer's date of transition to IFRSs;

- to apply the rest of IFRS 1 in measuring all assets and liabilities for which paragraphs D16 and D17 are not relevant; and

- to give all disclosures required by IFRS 1 as at the first-time adopter's own date of transition to IFRSs (see **section 9**).

IFRS 1:D16 applies if a subsidiary becomes a first-time adopter later than its parent (e.g. if the subsidiary previously prepared a reporting package under IFRSs for consolidation purposes but did not present a full set of financial statements under IFRSs). The implementation guidance accompanying

IFRS 1 notes that this may be relevant not only when a subsidiary's reporting package complies fully with the recognition and measurement requirements of IFRSs, but also when it is adjusted centrally for matters such as a review of events after the reporting period and central allocation of pension costs. The implementation guidance accompanying IFRS 1 explains that such adjustments to an unpublished reporting package are not the correction of errors for the purposes of the disclosure requirements of paragraph 26 of the Standard (see **9.3.3**). However, paragraph D16 does not permit a subsidiary to ignore misstatements that are immaterial to the consolidated financial statements but are material to the subsidiary's own financial statements. [IFRS 1:IG31]

> For example, if a subsidiary adopts IFRSs in its December 20X4 financial statements, its date of transition to IFRSs will be 1 January 20X3. Rather than applying IFRS 1 as at that date, the subsidiary can elect to use the assets and liabilities recorded in the group reporting package as at 31 December 20X2 as adjusted for any relevant central adjustments made to bring the reporting package into full compliance with the recognition and measurement requirements of IFRSs. However, if there was an error in the reporting package that was material to the subsidiary's financial statements (but ignored as immaterial to the consolidated financial statements) then the amounts would have to be adjusted to comply with IFRSs.

7.9.1.2 Subsidiary becomes a first-time adopter later than its parent – use of fair value as deemed cost exemption

Example 7.9.1.2

Subsidiary becomes a first-time adopter later than its parent – use of fair value as deemed cost exemption

Parent B's date of transition to IFRSs was 1 January 20X1. On 1 January 20X4, Parent B acquired Subsidiary M, which reports under local GAAP. For the purposes of its consolidated financial statements, Parent B measured the identifiable assets and liabilities of Subsidiary M at fair value at the acquisition date in accordance with the requirements of IFRS 3 *Business Combinations.*

Subsidiary M intends to adopt IFRSs in its financial statements for the year ended 31 December 20X8. Subsidiary M would like to reflect its property, plant and equipment on a fair value basis in its opening IFRS statement of financial position but without incurring the expense of commissioning additional valuations. Subsidiary M would like to use the January 20X4 valuations obtained by Parent B as the basis for an uplifted carrying amount in its first IFRS financial statements, rolling forward to reflect depreciation from 1 January 20X4 to the date of transition to IFRSs.

In the circumstances described, Subsidiary M is not permitted to apply the exemption available under IFRS 1:D16(a). The exemption set out in IFRS 1:D16 refers to circumstances in which a subsidiary becomes a first-time adopter later than its parent. The effect of the exemption is to allow the subsidiary to 'adopt' the parent's earlier date of transition as its own. This approach would not be appropriate in the circumstances described because Subsidiary M was not a subsidiary of Parent B at Parent B's date of transition to IFRSs. Consequently, Parent B's consolidated financial statements at Parent B's date of transition to IFRSs did not include the assets and liabilities of Subsidiary M.

Other IFRS 1 exemptions that allow previous valuations as the basis for an uplifted carrying amount in an entity's first IFRS financial statements are:

- IFRS 1:D6, which allows a previous GAAP revaluation of an item of property, plant and equipment before the date of transition to IFRSs to be taken as the deemed cost of the asset at the date of the revaluation (see **7.5.2**); and

- IFRS 1:D8(a), which allows event-driven fair values on or before the date of transition to be taken as the deemed cost at the date of that measurement (see **7.5.3**).

However, neither of these exemptions is available to Subsidiary M because both exemptions require that the amounts arising from the previous valuation to be taken as deemed cost have been recognised in the entity's previous GAAP financial statements. In the circumstances described, although the fair values at 1 January 20X4 have been incorporated into Parent B's consolidated financial statements since that date, they have not been recognised in Subsidiary M's local GAAP financial statements.

One option that is available to Subsidiary M is to elect as its date of transition to IFRSs the date at which Parent B obtained the valuations (i.e. 1 January 20X4). This would allow Subsidiary M to take advantage of the exemption under IFRS 1:D5 which permits an entity to use fair value at the date of transition as the deemed cost of an item of property, plant and equipment at that date (see **7.5.2**). However, if Subsidiary M were to elect 1 January 20X4 as its date of transition to IFRSs, it would be required to present:

- an opening statement of financial position under IFRSs at 1 January 20X4 prepared in accordance with the requirements of IFRS 1; and

- comparative information for the 20X4, 20X5, 20X6 and 20X7 reporting periods prepared in accordance with IFRSs effective at 31 December 20X8 (subject to the general exceptions and exemptions in IFRS 1).

7.9.2   Parent becomes a first-time adopter later than its subsidiary

If a parent becomes a first-time adopter later than its subsidiary, the parent should, in its consolidated financial statements, measure the assets and liabilities of the subsidiary at the same carrying amount as in the financial statements of the subsidiary, after adjusting for consolidation adjustments and for the effects of the business combination in which the parent acquired the subsidiary. The same approach applies in the case of associates and joint ventures. [IFRS 1:D17]

Note that this exemption does not permit a non-investment entity parent to apply the exception to consolidation used by any investment entity subsidiary following adoption of the *Investment Entities* amendments (see **section 13** of **chapter A24**). [IFRS 1:D17]

Although IFRS 1:D17 appears in an appendix to IFRS 1 dealing with optional exemptions, it is written as a requirement. The reason for this is unclear but the material was presumably included here to contrast with the situation when a subsidiary becomes a first-time adopter later than its parent. The Basis for Conclusions section of IFRS 1 devotes five paragraphs (BC59 to BC63) to explaining the reason for the exemption in the latter case. It then briefly adds "however, if a parent adopts IFRSs later than a subsidiary, the parent cannot, in its consolidated financial statements, elect to change IFRS measurements that the subsidiary has already used in its financial statements, except to adjust for consolidation procedures and for the effects of the business combination in which the parent acquired the subsidiary". This is a statement of fact rather than an explanation of the reason for the requirement.

The requirement for consistency with the financial statements of the subsidiary is subject to adjusting for "consolidation and equity accounting adjustments and for the effects of the business combination in which the entity acquired the subsidiary". These include, for example, accounting policy alignments and adjustments to eliminate profits on intragroup transactions. If the subsidiary was acquired in a business combination, the amounts may be determined after taking into account the IFRS 1 exemptions for business combinations (see **7.2**). However, these exemptions apply only to assets and liabilities that existed at the date of the business combination. It may, therefore, be necessary to analyse the assets and liabilities of the acquired entity between those that existed at its date of acquisition and those that arose subsequently.

Example 9 in the implementation guidance accompanying IFRS 1 provides an illustration of this requirement. [IFRS 1:IG29]

As explained at **7.9.1.1**, IFRS 1:D17 does not override certain other requirements of IFRS 1 as specified by IFRS 1:IG30.

7.9.3 *Parent becomes a first-time adopter for its separate financial statements earlier or later than for its consolidated financial statements*

If a parent becomes a first-time adopter for its separate financial statements earlier or later than for its consolidated financial statements, it should measure its assets and liabilities at the same amounts in both financial statements, except for consolidation adjustments. [IFRS 1:D17]

This might be relevant to a parent that is required to adopt IFRSs for its consolidated financial statements by local laws or regulations, but the requirement does not apply to separate financial statements. The parent may continue to prepare its separate financial statements under previous GAAP for a number of years and then decide to move to IFRSs.

It may not be immediately obvious how a parent could be a first-time adopter for its separate financial statements earlier than for its consolidated financial statements. Separate financial statements alone would not comply with IFRS 10 *Consolidated Financial Statements* when that Standard would require consolidated financial statements to be presented. However, the situation might arise if the parent was entitled to the exemption from preparation of consolidated financial statements in IFRS 10 (i.e. because a higher parent prepares IFRS consolidated financial statements) but subsequently ceased to be entitled to the exemption or chose not to use it.

When a parent adopts IFRSs for its separate financial statements at a later date than for its consolidated financial statements, it is required by IFRS 1:D17 to measure its assets and liabilities at the amounts used in the consolidated financial statements, subject to any consolidation adjustments. This is different from the position for a subsidiary adopting IFRSs at a later date than its parent which has a choice (see **7.9.1.1**) between using its own date of transition or that used for the consolidated financial statements of the group. In practice, it is likely that most entities will find it more convenient to use the amounts used in the IFRS-compliant consolidated financial statements and, therefore, will not be disadvantaged by this requirement.

7.9.4   *Subsidiary adopting IFRSs at the same time as its parent*

IFRS 1 does not specifically address circumstances in which a parent and a subsidiary are adopting IFRSs at the same date. However, considering the underlying objective of IFRS 1:D16 (i.e. to avoid the need to keep two parallel sets of records which the IASB accepted would be burdensome and not beneficial to users – see IFRS 1:BC60), it would appear reasonable to apply IFRS 1:D16 in such circumstances (see **7.9.1.1** for details).

Application of this exemption when a parent and a subsidiary are adopting IFRSs at the same date might be helpful when the parent and the subsidiary have previously applied different GAAPs and, consequently, the accounting policies used in the subsidiary's financial statements differed from those in the consolidated financial statements. For example, if borrowing costs were capitalised under the subsidiary's, but not the parent's, previous GAAP this difference could be eliminated by excluding capitalised borrowing costs from the carrying amount of property, plant and equipment in its opening IFRS statement of financial position – an adjustment that would not otherwise be permitted by IFRS 1:D23(a) (see **7.15**).

As explained in **example 7.9.5**, in the consolidated financial statements of a first-time adopter, the exemptions in IFRS 1 must be applied consistently to all subsidiaries, associates and joint ventures except when the exemption permits otherwise (e.g. the election for deemed cost of property, plant and equipment may be applied on an individual asset basis). This is, however, subject to the requirements described at **7.9.2** if the subsidiary, associate or joint venture becomes a first-time adopter before the investor.

7.9.5 Consistent application of IFRS 1 exemptions to subsidiaries, associates and joint ventures

Example 7.9.5

Consistent application of IFRS 1 exemptions to subsidiaries, associates and joint ventures

Investor I Limited is adopting IFRSs with a date of transition of 1 January 20X5. It has a number of subsidiaries, associates and joint ventures, both domestic and overseas, none of which applies IFRSs.

In I Limited's opening IFRS consolidated statement of financial position at 1 January 20X5, the IFRS 1 exemptions selected by the investor (which represent accounting policy choices) should be applied consistently to all of I Limited's subsidiaries, associates and joint ventures unless otherwise provided for in the specific exemption. This follows the general principle in paragraph 13 of IAS 8 *Accounting Policies, Changes in Accounting Estimates and Errors* that accounting policies should be applied consistently for similar transactions and events unless an IFRS specifically requires or permits otherwise, and the requirements of IFRS 10 and IAS 28 for consistent application of accounting policies among group entities, associates and joint ventures.

Accordingly, I Limited should apply all of the exemptions in Appendix D of IFRS 1 consistently among its subsidiaries, associates and joint ventures in its consolidated financial statements except for the following, which make specific provision for selective application:

- fair value or revaluation as deemed cost (IFRS 1:D5 to D8) – the Standard provides that the deemed cost elections can be applied on an individual asset basis. Therefore, the application of the elections can vary among the various entities and within individual entities; and

- financial assets or intangible assets accounted for in accordance with IFRIC 12 *Service Concession Arrangements* (IFRS 1:D22) – the exemption permits the first-time adopter to apply the transition provisions of IFRIC 12. Because the transition provisions of IFRIC 12 provide relief from retrospective application of the Interpretation for any particular service arrangements for which retrospective application is impracticable, the election can vary for different arrangements in the various entities and within individual entities.

IFRS 1:D16 and D17 (see **7.9.1.1** and **7.9.2**) set out specific rules for the measurement of assets and liabilities of subsidiaries, associates and joint ventures when the parent (investor) and the subsidiary, associate or joint venture adopt IFRSs at different dates. See **7.9.4** for a discussion of the accounting required when a parent (investor) and its subsidiary, associate or joint venture adopt IFRSs at the same date.

With respect to the accounting for investments in subsidiaries, associates and joint ventures in I Limited's separate financial statements, IFRS 1:D14 and D15 set out the allowed alternative accounting treatments (see **7.8**). If I Limited chooses to measure such investments in accordance with IFRS 9 (or, if IFRS 9 is not adopted, IAS 39), or using the equity method, on an ongoing basis, it must apply that policy consistently for all investments in the same category. However, if I Limited chooses to measure its investments at cost, it is permitted to choose which 'cost' measure to use for each investment on an individual basis. Some may be measured at cost in accordance with IAS 27 *Separate Financial Statements* and others at deemed cost. For those measured at deemed cost, the choice between fair value and previous GAAP carrying amount may also be made on an investment-by-investment basis.

7.10   Compound financial instruments

IAS 32 *Financial Instruments: Presentation* requires an entity to split a compound financial instrument at inception into separate liability and equity components (see **chapter B3** or **chapter C3** for a detailed description of this requirement).

IFRS 1:D18 provides some relief for first-time adopters when applying IAS 32 for the first time. To the extent that the liability component of a compound instrument is no longer outstanding at the date of transition to IFRSs, retrospective application of IAS 32's requirement to split the instrument is not required. [IFRS 1:D18]

This exemption is justified on the basis of expediency. The only effect of retrospective application of IAS 32 in the circumstances described would be the separation of two components of equity for compound instruments that have matured: one portion would include the cumulative interest accrued on the liability component during its life using the effective interest method (which would normally reside in retained earnings) and the second portion would include the original equity component that would have been separated on initial recognition of the instrument.

See **section 2.7** of **chapter B12** (entities applying IFRS 9) and **section 2.7** of **chapter C13** (entities applying IAS 39) for examples of the application of IAS 32 at the date of transition to IFRSs.

7.11 Designation of previously recognised financial instruments

7.11.1 Entities applying IFRS 9

IFRS 1 allows a number of optional exemptions in relation to the designation of previously recognised financial instruments for first-time adopters applying IFRS 9:

- a first-time adopter is permitted to designate a financial liability that meets the amortised cost criteria at the date of transition to IFRSs as at fair value through profit or loss (FVTPL) if it meets the criteria in IFRS 9:4.2.2 (see **7.1.2** of **chapter B3**) at that date; [IFRS 1:D19]

- a first-time adopter is permitted to designate a financial asset that meets the amortised cost criteria or the fair value through other comprehensive income criteria at the date of transition to IFRSs as at FVTPL if the criteria in IFRS 9:4.1.5 (see **5.2.1** of **chapter B2**) are met on the basis of the facts and circumstances that exist at the date of transition to IFRSs; [IFRS 1:D19A]

- a first-time adopter is permitted to designate an investment in an equity instrument as at fair value through other comprehensive income at the date of transition to IFRSs if the criteria in IFRS 9:5.7.5 (see **5.3** of **chapter B2**) are met on the basis of the facts and circumstances that exist at the date of transition to IFRSs; [IFRS 1:D19B] and

- when determining whether the presentation of changes in the fair value of a financial liability attributable to changes in credit risk in other comprehensive income would create or enlarge an accounting mismatch in profit or loss (see **7.1.2.5** of **chapter B3**), a first-time adopter is required to make that determination based on the facts and circumstances that exist at the date of transition to IFRSs. [IFRS 1:D19C]

Although IFRS 1:D19C appears in an appendix to IFRS 1 dealing with optional exemptions, it is written as a requirement. IFRS 1:D19C specifies that the determination to be made in the specific circumstances 'shall' be made on the basis of facts and circumstances at the date of transition to IFRSs rather than that it 'may' be made on that basis (as is the case for the exemptions in IFRS 1:D19A and 19B).

When the exemptions in IFRS 1:D19 and D19A are applied, specific disclosure requirements are triggered (see **9.3.4.1**).

7.11.2 Entities applying IAS 39

IAS 39 permits any financial asset, other than an asset that meets the definition of held for trading, to be designated on initial recognition as available for sale (AFS). It also permits financial assets and financial liabilities to be designated as at fair value through profit or loss (FVTPL) provided that they meet specified criteria (see **chapters C2** and **C3** for a detailed description of these requirements). Entities are generally only permitted to make these designations when the financial instrument is first recognised.

IFRS 1 allows two optional exemptions in relation to the designation of previously recognised financial instruments for first-time adopters applying IAS 39:

[IFRS 1:D19]

- a first-time adopter is permitted to designate any financial asset, other than an asset that meets the definition of held for trading, as an AFS financial asset at the date of transition to IFRSs; and

- a first-time adopter is permitted to designate, at the date of transition to IFRSs, any financial asset or financial liability as at FVTPL if it meets the criteria for designation as at FVTPL in IAS 39:9 and 11A.

When the exemptions in IFRS 1:D19 are applied, the designation is made at the date of transition as if the entity had never made a choice under previous GAAP, and this is so even if previous GAAP was identical to IAS 39. When the exemption in IFRS 1:D19 is applied, specific disclosure requirements are triggered (see **9.3.4.2**).

7.12 Fair value measurement of financial assets or financial liabilities at initial recognition

IFRS 9 (or, if IFRS 9 is not adopted, IAS 39) requires that all financial assets and financial liabilities should be initially recognised at fair value; the only exception, for entities that adopt IFRS 15 *Revenue from Contracts with Customers*, is trade receivables that do not have a significant financing component. When determining the carrying amount of financial assets and financial liabilities at the date of transition to IFRSs, a first-time adopter must consider the guidance on measuring fair value in IFRS 13 *Fair Value Measurement*. This applies even if the financial asset or financial liability is not subsequently measured at fair value, because fair value at initial recognition will be the basis for the opening carrying amount at the date of transition to IFRSs.

IFRS 9 and IAS 39 limit up-front gain/loss recognition unless the fair value of the instrument is evidenced by comparison with other observable current market transactions in the same instrument (i.e. without modification or repackaging) or based on a valuation technique whose variables include only data from observable markets. This is often referred to as 'day 1 P&L' and is discussed in more depth at **7.1** in **chapter B7** (for entities applying IFRS 9) and **7.1** in **chapter C7** (for entities applying IAS 39).

IFRS 1:D20 permits that the day 1 P&L guidance contained in IFRS 9:B5.1.2A need not be applied to transactions entered into before the date of transition to IFRSs.

7.13 Decommissioning liabilities included in the cost of property, plant and equipment

7.13.1 Exemption from applying the requirements of IFRIC 1 retrospectively

IFRIC 1 *Changes in Existing Decommissioning, Restoration and Similar Liabilities* (discussed at **4.4** in **chapter A7**) requires specified changes in a decommissioning, restoration or similar liability to be added to or deducted from the cost of the asset to which it relates; the adjusted depreciable amount of the asset is then depreciated prospectively over its remaining useful life. The exemption available under IFRS 1:D21 permits a first-time adopter to elect not to comply with the requirements of IFRIC 1 for changes in such liabilities that occurred before the date of transition to IFRSs. If this option is selected, the first-time adopter includes in the depreciated cost of the asset at the date of transition to IFRSs an amount calculated by the following steps:

[IFRS 1:D21]

* measuring its decommissioning liability as at the date of transition to IFRSs in accordance with IAS 37 *Provisions, Contingent Liabilities and Contingent Assets*;

* to the extent that the liability is within the scope of IFRIC 1, estimating the amount that would have been included in the cost of the related asset when the liability first arose by discounting the liability to that date using its best estimate of the historical risk-adjusted discount rate(s) that would have applied for that liability over the intervening period; and

* calculating the accumulated depreciation on that amount, as at the date of transition to IFRSs, on the basis of the current estimate of the useful life of the asset, using the depreciation policy adopted by the entity under IFRSs.

Example 7.13.1 illustrates the application of this exemption. Note that, when discounting the liability to calculate the adjustment to the cost of the asset, it is necessary to take into account changes in the relevant discount rate between the date the asset was first recognised and the date of transition to IFRSs.

If a first-time adopter does not take the option available under IFRS 1:D21, IFRIC 1 should be applied retrospectively at the date of transition to IFRSs. If IFRIC 1 is applied retrospectively, in order to determine the portion of the decommissioning obligation to be included in the cost of the related asset, the first-time adopter will need to:

- determine the amount that would have been required to settle the obligation at the date the asset was acquired;

- construct a reliable historical record of any changes in the obligation between the date of the acquisition of the asset and the date of transition to IFRSs; and

- allocate those changes in accordance with IFRIC 1.

Whichever alternative is taken, if the deemed cost exemption (see **7.5**) is used for the related asset, care is needed to ensure that the adjustment of the carrying amount related to the decommissioning liability is not counted twice. The valuation of the asset would be the gross amount without any adjustment for the costs of decommissioning. Any adjustment arising from recognition of the decommissioning liability is taken to retained earnings and is not added to the carrying amount of the asset.

Example 7.13.1

Decommissioning obligation not recognised under previous GAAP

Company A is adopting IFRSs with a 1 January 20X4 date of transition. Ten years before that date, Company A paid CU100,000 for an asset with a 40-year useful life. Company A has an obligation to decommission this asset at the end of its useful life, but it was not required to recognise that obligation under its previous GAAP.

Company A elects to take the exemption from retrospective application of IFRIC 1.

As a first step, Company A measures the decommissioning obligation at the date of transition in accordance with IAS 37 by estimating the present value of the expenditures expected to be required to settle the obligation in 30 years. Assume that Company A estimates this present value as CU25,000.

Next, Company A estimates the amount that would have been included in the cost of the asset when the liability first arose (in this example, when the asset was acquired) by discounting CU25,000 to the date on which the asset was acquired 10 years previously. The discount rate used will be Company A's best estimate of the historical risk-adjusted discount rate(s) that would have applied for that liability over the intervening period. Company A estimates this rate to be 5 per cent and that the rate has not changed since the date on which the asset was acquired. Consequently, Company A's estimate of the decommissioning obligation that would have been included in the cost of the asset when it was acquired is CU15,348 ($CU25,000/1.05^{10}$).

Finally, Company A calculates the accumulated depreciation on that amount, as at the date of transition to IFRSs, on the basis of the current estimate of the useful life of the asset, as CU3,837 ($CU15,348 \div 40 \times 10$).

As a result of these calculations, Company A records the following journal entries in its opening statement of financial position as at 1 January 20X4.

		CU	CU
Dr	Cost of asset (the decommissioning portion of the asset)	15,348	
Dr	Retained earnings (the effect of the change)	13,489	
Cr	Provisions (the decommissioning obligation)		25,000
Cr	Accumulated depreciation (from the date of purchase to 31 Dec 20X3)		3,837

Recognition of the decommissioning obligation and the resultant adjustment to cost of asset.

When discounting the liability to calculate the adjustment to the cost of the asset, it is necessary to take into account changes in the relevant discount rate between the date the asset was first recognised and the date of transition to IFRSs. For example if, in the circumstances described in **example 7.13.1**, instead of a single rate of 5 per cent, Company A estimated that the historical risk-adjusted discount rate that would have applied for the first five years of owning the asset is 5 per cent and the rate that would have applied in the second five years of owning the asset is 7 per cent, the estimated decommissioning obligation that would have been included in the cost of the asset when it was acquired is CU13,966 [CU25,000/$(1.05^5 \times 1.07^5)$].

The implementation guidance accompanying IFRS 1 includes another example illustrating the use of this exemption (IG Example 201).

7.13.2   Oil and gas assets

If an entity elects to use the deemed cost exemption (see **7.5.4**) for oil and gas assets in the development or production phases, the entity is required to:

[IFRS 1:D21A]

- measure decommissioning, restoration and similar liabilities as at the date of transition to IFRSs in accordance with IAS 37; and

- recognise directly in retained earnings any difference between that amount and the carrying amount of those liabilities at the date of transition to IFRSs determined under the entity's previous GAAP.

This treatment differs from the general exemption in IFRS 1:D21 which requires entities to measure the liability as at the date of transition to IFRSs in accordance with IAS 37 and then discount this to estimate the amount that would have been included in the cost of the related asset when the liability first arose, and to calculate accumulated depreciation on the latter amount to the date of transition.

7.14   Financial assets or intangible assets accounted for in accordance with IFRIC 12 *Service Concession Arrangements*

A first-time adopter may apply the transition provisions in IFRIC 12. [IFRS 1:D22]

The transition provisions in IFRIC 12 require that the Interpretation should be applied retrospectively, in accordance with IAS 8. However, if it is not practicable for an operator to apply the Interpretation retrospectively at the start of the earliest period presented, the entity should:

[IFRIC 12:30]

- recognise financial assets and intangible assets that existed at the start of the earliest period presented;

- use the previous carrying amounts of those financial and intangible assets (however previously classified) as their carrying amounts as at that date; and

- test financial and intangible assets recognised at that date for impairment, unless this is not practicable, in which case the amounts should be tested for impairment as at the start of the current period.

Therefore, if it is not practicable for a first-time adopter to apply IFRIC 12 retrospectively, the rules set out in IFRIC 12:30 should be applied. The 'start of the earliest period presented' in an entity's first IFRS financial statements is the date of transition to IFRSs.

7.15   Borrowing costs

IAS 23 *Borrowing Costs* prescribes the accounting treatment for borrowing costs and requires that borrowing costs directly attributable to the acquisition, construction or production of a qualifying asset form part of the cost of that asset. All other borrowing costs are expensed as incurred.

IFRS 1 permits a first-time adopter to choose either:

[IFRS 1:D23]

- to apply the requirements of IAS 23 retrospectively; or

- to apply the requirements of IAS 23 from the date of transition to IFRSs or from an earlier designated date, as permitted by IAS 23:28 (see **3.5.1.2** in **chapter A18**).

Note that the decision to take the exemption under IFRS 1:D23 is an accounting policy choice which should be applied consistently for all borrowing costs. The entity is permitted to apply IAS 23 retrospectively at the date of transition to IFRSs but, if it chooses to do so, it must apply that Standard consistently to all qualifying assets.

When a first-time adopter takes the option not to apply the requirements of IAS 23 retrospectively, from the date on which the first-time adopter begins to apply IAS 23 (date of transition to IFRSs or earlier designated date), the entity:

- should not restate any borrowing cost component that was capitalised under previous GAAP and that was included in the carrying amount of assets at that date; and

- should account for borrowing costs incurred on or after that date in accordance with IAS 23, including those borrowing costs incurred on or after that date on qualifying assets already under construction.

However, if the entity establishes a deemed cost for an asset, the entity should not capitalise borrowing costs incurred before the date of the measurement that established the deemed cost. [IFRS 1:IG23]

Example 7.15

Application of borrowing costs exemption

Entity A's date of transition is 1 January 20X7 with its first IFRS financial statements to be prepared as at 31 December 20X8. It has the following assets in respect of which borrowing costs were either not capitalised under previous GAAP or were capitalised using a different methodology from that required by IAS 23.

- Asset 1 – construction commenced 1 January 20X4 and completed 30 June 20X6.

- Asset 2 – construction commenced 1 July 20X6 and not yet completed.

- Asset 3 – construction commenced 1 July 20X7 and completed 31 March 20X8.

In its first IFRS financial statements, Entity A wishes to use the optional exemption from retrospective application of IAS 23 and to apply IAS 23 from its date of transition.

All of these assets meet the definition of 'qualifying assets' under IAS 23 and the 'construction commenced' and 'construction completed' dates noted in each case are the appropriate dates for commencement and cessation of capitalisation of borrowing costs under IAS 23.

Application of the optional exemption in IFRS 1:D23

Asset 1   The construction of Asset 1 began and ended before the date of transition. Entity A does not restate the borrowing costs capitalised in respect of Asset 1 (which may be zero if borrowing costs were not capitalised under previous GAAP).

Asset 2   The construction of Asset 2 began before the date of transition and has extended beyond the end of the first IFRS reporting period.

Any borrowing costs incurred in respect of Asset 2 before 1 January 20X7 are not restated. Any borrowing costs incurred in respect of Asset 2 on or after 1 January 20X7 are accounted for in accordance with IAS 23.

Asset 3   The construction of Asset 3 began after the date of transition; therefore, the requirements of IAS 23 must be applied. Any difference between the borrowing costs capitalised under previous GAAP (which may be zero) and the amount calculated under IAS 23 should be shown in the reconciliation of reported profit or loss for the comparative period in Entity A's first IFRS financial statements.

7.16   Transfers of assets from customers

The exemption in this section refers to IFRIC 18 *Transfers of Assets from Customers* which is superseded by IFRS 15 *Revenue from Contracts with Customers*. Therefore, for first-time adopters that apply IFRS 15, the exemption is no longer relevant.

IFRIC 18 *Transfers of Assets from Customers* addresses the accounting by recipients for transfers of property, plant and equipment from 'customers'; the requirements of IFRIC 18 are discussed in detail at **2.4** of **appendix A1**.

In finalising IFRIC 18, the IFRIC (now the IFRS Interpretations Committee) noted that applying a change in accounting policy to comply with the requirements of IFRIC 18 retrospectively would require entities to establish a carrying amount for assets that had been transferred in the past. That carrying amount would be based on historical fair values which may or may not be based on an observable price or observable inputs. Therefore, the IFRIC concluded that retrospective application could be impracticable and that the Interpretation should require prospective application to transfers received after its effective date.

To provide first-time adopters with the same relief, an exemption was also added to IFRS 1 under which first-time adopters may also apply the transition provisions set out in IFRIC 18:22.

Therefore, IFRS 1 permits a first-time adopter to choose either:

[IFRS 1:D24]

- to apply the requirements of IFRIC 18 retrospectively; or

- to apply the transition provisions of IFRIC 18. When a first-time adopter chooses this option, references to 1 July 2009 are interpreted as 1 July 2009 or the date of transition to IFRSs, whichever is later.

An entity is not, therefore, required to apply IFRIC 18 to transfers of assets that occurred before its date of transition to IFRSs.

A first-time adopter may also designate any date before the date of transition to IFRSs and apply IFRIC 18 to all transfers of assets from customers on or after that date. [IFRS 1:D24]

7.17 Extinguishing financial liabilities with equity instruments

IFRIC 19 *Extinguishing Financial Liabilities with Equity Instruments* addresses the accounting for entities that issue equity instruments in order to extinguish all or part of a financial liability (often referred to as 'debt for equity swaps'). The requirements of IFRIC 19 are discussed in **4.2** in **chapter B8** (for entities applying IFRS 9) and **4.2** in **chapter C8** (for entities applying IAS 39).

The transition provisions of IFRIC 19 require that an entity should apply any change in accounting policy arising from the application of the Interpretation from the beginning of the earliest comparative period presented.

In finalising IFRIC 19, the IFRIC (now the IFRS Interpretations Committee) concluded that it was preferable to require entities that could apply the Interpretation retrospectively to do so, rather than requiring all entities to apply it prospectively to future transactions; the Committee made specific reference to IAS 8's guidance on circumstances in which retrospective application might be impracticable. To simplify transition, the IFRIC also concluded that it should require retrospective application only from the beginning of the earliest comparative period presented because application to earlier periods would result only in a reclassification of amounts within equity. [IFRIC 19:BC33]

IFRS 1 permits first-time adopters to apply the transition provisions in IFRIC 19. [IFRS 1:D25]

First-time adopters therefore have a choice between full retrospective application of IFRIC 19 and application of the transition provisions of IFRIC 19. The option selected will have no impact on amounts reported for the first IFRS reporting period and for the comparative period, but full retrospective application could result in some additional reclassifications within equity.

7.18   Severe hyperinflation

This exemption (detailed below) provides relief for first-time adopters that experienced severe hyperinflation prior to the date of transition to IFRSs; such entities are not required to reconstruct historical values for the assets and liabilities held prior to the entity's emergence from severe hyperinflation. It is an optional exemption and therefore, in theory, the entity could instead opt to apply IFRS 1 in full when the entity resumes presenting IFRS financial statements after a period of severe hyperinflation. However, it is likely that such an approach would be impracticable.

If an entity has a functional currency that was, or is, the currency of a hyperinflationary economy, it is required to determine whether it was subject to severe hyperinflation before the date of transition to IFRSs. This applies to entities that are adopting IFRSs for the first time, as well as to entities that have previously applied IFRSs. [IFRS 1:D26]

The currency of a hyperinflationary economy is subject to 'severe hyperinflation' if it has both of the following characteristics:

[IFRS 1:D27]

- a reliable price index is not available to all entities with transactions and balances in the currency; and

- exchangeability between the currency and a relatively stable foreign currency does not exist.

The 'functional currency normalisation date' is the date when either or both of these characteristics no longer exist and, consequently, the currency is no longer subject to severe hyperinflation, or when the entity's functional currency changes to a currency that is not subject to severe hyperinflation. [IFRS 1:D28]

When an entity's date of transition to IFRSs is on or after the functional currency normalisation date, the entity may elect to measure all assets and liabilities held before the functional currency normalisation date at fair value on the date of transition to IFRSs and use that fair value as the deemed cost of those assets and liabilities in the opening IFRS statement of financial position. [IFRS 1:D29]

The exemption allowing use of fair value as deemed cost should be applied only to those assets and liabilities that are held before the functional currency normalisation date, and not to other assets and liabilities held by the entity at the date of transition to IFRSs.

Further, when a parent entity's functional currency has been subject to severe hyperinflation, but its subsidiary's functional currency has not, the subsidiary would not be able to apply this exemption.

Any adjustments arising from this election are recognised directly in equity at the date of transition to IFRSs and must be accompanied by an explanation of how, and why, the entity had, and then ceased to have, a functional currency that was subject to severe hyperinflation (see **9.3.8**).

When the functional currency normalisation date falls within a 12-month comparative period, the comparative period may be less than 12 months, provided that a complete set of financial statements (as required by paragraph 10 of IAS 1) is provided for that shorter comparative period. [IFRS 1:D30]

7.19 Joint arrangements

IFRS 11 *Joint Arrangements* includes detailed transition provisions for entities that already use IFRSs. Full retrospective application is not required; specific rules are applied to establish the 'opening position' (i.e. at the beginning of the immediately preceding period) for the two circumstances when adoption of IFRS 11 results in a change in accounting model, i.e. when an entity is required to change:

- from proportionate consolidation to the equity method for 'joint ventures'; and

- from the equity method to accounting for asset and liabilities arising from interests in 'joint operations'.

IFRS 1 permits first-time adopters to apply the transition provisions in IFRS 11, subject to two exceptions (see below).

[IFRS 1:D31]

- A first-time adopter that does not apply IFRS 11 retrospectively in full is required to apply the transition provisions of IFRS 11 at the date of transition to IFRSs (i.e. at the beginning of the earliest IFRS period presented). [IFRS 1:D31(a)]

- A first-time adopter that does not apply IFRS 11 retrospectively in full, and that is required to change its accounting method for joint ventures from proportionate consolidation to the equity method, is required to test the investment for impairment in accordance with IAS 36 *Impairment of Assets* as at the date of transition to IFRSs, regardless of whether there is any indication that the investment may be impaired. Any resulting impairment should be recognised as an adjustment to retained earnings at the date of transition to IFRSs. [IFRS 1:D31(b)]

First-time adopters therefore have a choice between (1) full retrospective application of IFRS 11, and (2) application of the transition provisions of that Standard subject to the two exceptions set out above.

The exception in IFRS 1:D31(b) imposes a more stringent requirement for impairment testing on first-time adopters than applies for entities already applying IFRSs; the Board has opted for consistency with the requirement for first-time adopters to apply IAS 36 in testing goodwill for impairment at the date of transition to IFRSs regardless of whether there is any indication that the goodwill may be impaired. [IFRS 1:BC63L]

7.20   Stripping costs in the production phase of a surface mine

IFRIC 20 *Stripping Costs in the Production of a Surface Mine* addresses the accounting for waste removal costs that are incurred in surface mining activity during the production phase of a mine (production stripping costs). The requirements of IFRIC 20 are discussed in **section 10** of **chapter A7**.

The transition provisions of IFRIC 20 require that an entity should apply the requirements of the Interpretation to production stripping costs incurred on or after the beginning of the earliest period presented. [IFRIC 20:A1 & A2]

When IFRIC 20 is first applied, as at the beginning of the earliest period presented, any predecessor stripping asset (i.e. any previously recognised asset balance that resulted from stripping activity undertaken during the production phase) is required to be reclassified as a part of an existing asset to which the stripping activity relates, and depreciated or amortised over the remaining expected useful life of the identified component of the ore body to which the predecessor stripping asset relates.

When there is no identifiable component of the ore body to which the predecessor stripping asset relates, it should be recognised in opening retained earnings at the beginning of the earliest period presented.

IFRS 1 permits first-time adopters to apply the transition provisions in IFRIC 20.

First-time adopters therefore have a choice between full retrospective application of IFRIC 20 and application of the transition provisions of IFRIC 20.

7.21   Designation of contracts to buy or sell a non-financial item

IFRS 9 (or, for first-time adopters that do not adopt IFRS 9, IAS 39) permits some contracts to buy or sell a non-financial item to be designated at inception as measured at fair value through profit or loss (see IFRS 9:2.5 or IAS 39:5A). Despite this requirement, an entity is permitted to designate, at the date of transition to IFRSs, contracts that already exist on that date as measured at fair value through profit or loss but only if they meet the requirements of IFRS 9:2.5 (or IAS 39:5A) at that date and the entity designates all similar contracts. [IFRS 1:D33]

7.22 Revenue (entities that have adopted IFRS 15)

A first-time adopter is permitted to apply the transition provisions in paragraph C5 of IFRS 15 *Revenue from Contracts with Customers*. For first-time adopters, references to the 'date of initial application' should be interpreted as the beginning of the first IFRS reporting period. If a first-time adopter decides to apply these transition provisions, it is also required to apply paragraph C6 of IFRS 15. [IFRS 1:D34]

A first-time adopter is not required to restate contracts that were completed before the earliest period presented. A completed contract is a contract for which the entity has transferred all of the goods or services identified in accordance with previous GAAP. [IFRS 1:D35]

This exemption applies for first-time adopters that apply IFRS 15 *Revenue from Contracts with Customers*. The detailed transition provisions for IFRS 15 are described in **15.2** of **chapter A14**. The specific requirements in IFRS 15:C5 referred to in IFRS 1:D34 allow that when an entity opts to use a fully retrospective approach when IFRS 15 is first applied, it is permitted to use one or more of the following practical expedients:

[IFRS 15:C5]

- for completed contracts, the entity is not required to restate contracts that begin and end within the same annual reporting period;

- for completed contracts that have variable consideration, the entity may use the transaction price at the date the contract was completed rather than estimating variable consideration amounts for the comparative reporting periods; and

- the disclosure requirements of IFRS 15:120 (see **section 14** of **chapter A14**) need not be applied for reporting periods presented before the date of initial application.

IFRS 15:C6 requires that an entity should apply any of the practical expedients described in IFRS 15:C5 consistently to all contracts within all reporting periods presented. The entity should also disclose the following information:

- the expedients that have been used; and

- to the extent reasonably possible, a qualitative assessment of the estimated effect of applying each of those expedients.

7.23   Short-term exemptions

7.23.1   Short-term exemptions – general

Appendix E to IFRS 1 includes short-term exemptions from IFRSs available to first-time adopters. The exemptions described in **7.23.2** to **7.23.4** are those that have continuing relevance for annual periods beginning on or after 1 January 2014.

7.23.2   Exemption from requirement to present comparative information in accordance with IFRS 9

If an entity is a first-time adopter in an annual period beginning before 1 January 2019 and applies the completed version of IFRS 9 (issued in 2014), the comparative information in the entity's first IFRS financial statements need not comply with IFRS 7 *Financial Instruments: Disclosures* or IFRS 9, to the extent that the disclosures required by IFRS 7 relate to items within the scope of IFRS 9. For such entities, references to the 'date of transition to IFRSs' should be taken to mean, in the case of IFRS 9 and IFRS 7 only, the beginning of the first IFRS reporting period. [IFRS 1:E1]

Therefore, in effect, an entity that adopts IFRSs for an annual period beginning before 1 January 2019 and that chooses to apply IFRS 9 has a choice regarding whether to apply IFRS 9 (and the related disclosures in IFRS 7) to the comparative period(s) in the first year of adoption of IFRSs.

If a first-time adopter of IFRSs chooses not to present comparative information in accordance with IFRS 9 (and the related disclosures in IFRS 7), the entity is required to:

[IFRS 1:E2]

- apply the recognition and measurement requirements of its previous GAAP in place of the requirements of IFRS 9 to comparative information about financial instruments within the scope of IFRS 9;

- disclose that fact, together with the basis used to prepare the comparative information;

- treat any adjustment between the statement of financial position at the comparative period's reporting date (i.e. the statement of financial position that includes comparative information under previous GAAP) and the statement of financial position at the start of the first IFRS reporting period (i.e. the first period that includes information that complies with IFRS 9 and IFRS 7) as arising from a change in accounting policy and provide the disclosures required by paragraphs 28(a) to (e) and 28(f)(i) of IAS 8 *Accounting Policies, Changes in Accounting Estimates and Errors*. IAS 8:28(f)(i) applies only to amounts presented in the statement of financial position at the comparative period's reporting date; and

- apply paragraph 17(c) of IAS 1 *Presentation of Financial Statements* to provide additional disclosures when compliance with the specific requirements in IFRSs is insufficient to enable users to understand the impact of particular transactions, other events and conditions on the entity's financial position and financial performance.

7.23.3 Investment entities

A first-time adopter that is a parent is required to assess whether it is an investment entity, as defined in IFRS 10 *Consolidated Financial Statements*, on the basis of the facts and circumstances that exist at the date of transition to IFRSs. [IFRS 1:E6]

A first-time adopter meeting the definition of an investment entity that prepares its first IFRS financial statements for an annual period ending on or before 31 December 2014 may apply the transition provisions in IFRS 10:C3C to C3D and paragraphs 18C to 18G of IAS 27 *Separate Financial Statements*. The references in those paragraphs to the annual period that immediately precedes the date of initial application should be read as the earliest annual period presented in the investment entity's first IFRS financial statements.

IFRS 10 was amended in October 2012 to introduce an exception to its general consolidation requirements when the reporting entity is an 'investment entity' as defined (see **section 13** of **chapter A24** for detailed discussion).

The October 2012 amendments to IFRS 10 are effective for annual periods beginning on or after 1 January 2014, with earlier application permitted. First-time adopters with a first IFRS reporting period ending on or before 31 December 2014 are permitted to apply some of IFRS 10's transition provisions on the basis of practicability. However, this relief is temporary because the Board believes that it not necessary for first-time adopters who have sufficient time to adopt the requirements.

7.23.4 Financial instruments disclosures

The *Annual Improvements to IFRSs: 2012-2014 Cycle* amended IFRS 7 *Financial Instruments: Disclosures* to add guidance to assist an entity to assess whether or not they have continuing involvement in a transferred financial asset. An entity is permitted not to apply the amendments for any period presented that begins before the annual period for which the entity first applies those amendments (see **4.1.6** in **chapter B11**, or for entities that have not yet adopted IFRS 9, **4.1.5** in **chapter C12**). This transition relief is extended to first-time adopters of IFRSs.

8   Other guidance for first-time adopters

8.1   Other implementation guidance accompanying IFRS 1 – general

The implementation guidance accompanying IFRS 1 does not form part of the Standard but it is nevertheless indicative of the way in which the IASB believes the IFRS should be implemented. It explains how the requirements of IFRS 1 interact with the requirements of some other IFRSs (those most likely to involve questions specific to first-time adopters). In addition, it provides an illustration of the reconciliations required under IFRS 1 (as described in **section 9**).

Sections 8.2 to **8.10** deal with specific components of financial statements not dealt with in other sections for which IFRS 1, or its implementation guidance, has specific requirements or guidance. Not all of the issues covered by the implementation guidance accompanying IFRS 1 are addressed.

8.2   IAS 12 *Income Taxes*

There are no exceptions or exemptions in IFRS 1 regarding the accounting for income taxes. An entity applies IAS 12 to temporary differences between the carrying amount of the assets and liabilities in its opening IFRS statement of financial position and their tax bases. Therefore, deferred tax is recognised in respect of adjustments to the carrying amounts of assets and liabilities recognised at the date of transition. However, if a first-time adopter recognised deferred tax under previous GAAP based on an accounting policy that is compliant with its IFRS accounting policy, it does not adjust its deferred tax estimate unless there is objective evidence that the estimate was in error.

The calculation of the deferred tax liability or asset at the date of transition, as well as the assessment of whether it is probable that a tax asset will be recovered, is based on facts, circumstances and probabilities that existed when the financial statements under previous GAAP were prepared for the same date, and should not take into account subsequent information available when the opening IFRS statement of financial position is actually prepared.

When calculating the deferred tax liability or asset to be included in its opening IFRS statement of financial position, a first-time adopter compares the carrying amounts of all assets and liabilities recognised in the opening IFRS statement of financial position (having made all the necessary adjustments and revaluations according to IFRS 1) with the tax bases of those assets and liabilities. [IFRS 1:IG5]

IAS 12 provides an exception (referred to as the 'initial recognition exception') from the requirement to recognise deferred tax arising on the initial recognition of an asset or a liability in a transaction that is not a business combination and that, at the time of the transaction, affects neither accounting profit nor taxable profit. The requirement in IFRS 1:IG5 to recognise deferred taxes on transition to IFRSs does not override the initial recognition exception in IAS 12. In restating deferred taxes under IAS 12, an entity considers whether each temporary difference arose in circumstances covered by the initial recognition exception (i.e. as though IAS 12 had been applied at the date of the transaction). When the temporary difference did arise in such circumstances, the requirements of paragraphs 15 and 24 of IAS 12 still apply and no deferred tax is recognised. In all other cases, the requirements of IFRS 1 to recognise deferred tax should be applied.

Under IAS 12, the measurement of current and deferred tax reflects tax rates and tax laws that have been enacted or substantively enacted by the end of the reporting period. The effects of changes in tax rates and tax laws are accounted for when those changes are enacted or substantively enacted. [IFRS 1:IG6]

The following examples illustrate the application of these requirements. Further examples dealing with deferred tax on pre-transition business combinations are provided at **7.2.16**.

Example 8.2A

Deferred tax when valuation used as deemed cost

Entity G is adopting IFRSs for the first time. Entity G has previously purchased land for CU100. Under its previous GAAP, Entity G revalued the land to CU120, but did not recognise any deferred tax in respect of this revaluation. Entity G decides to obtain a valuation of the land at the date of transition to IFRSs and uses this value (CU150) as the deemed cost in accordance with IFRS 1:D5.

Part of the purchase price (CU10) is not allowable as a deduction by the local taxation authorities and, accordingly, the asset has a tax base at the date of purchase and the date of transition of CU90. The tax rate in the local jurisdiction is 30 per cent.

The initial recognition exception applies to the expenditure of CU10 that is not allowable. There is no temporary difference between the remainder of the initial cost and the tax base (both CU90). Therefore, on the date of transition, Entity G will recognise a deferred tax liability of CU15 [(CU150 − CU100) x 30%] being the deferred tax in respect of the difference between deemed cost and initial cost.

Example 8.2B

Deferred tax on intangible asset not recognised under previous GAAP

Under previous GAAP, Entity X incurred development expenditure, which it recognised immediately as an expense. The expenditure did not affect taxable profit at the time of the transaction – only 80 per cent is deductible over a period of five years.

On transition to IFRSs, Entity X recognises an intangible asset relating to the development expenditure.

Should Entity X recognise a deferred tax liability at the date of transition to IFRSs for the entire temporary difference between the carrying amount of the intangible asset in the opening IFRS statement of financial position and its tax base?

No. Under IFRSs, the intangible asset would have been recognised from the outset. Although a temporary difference (for 20 per cent of the expenditure) would have arisen initially, the transaction (restated to comply with IFRSs) would not have affected either accounting profit or taxable profit at that date; therefore, the initial recognition exception in IAS 12 would have applied. As discussed in **example 8.2A**, in circumstances covered by the initial recognition exception (i.e. as though IAS 12 had been applied at the date of the transaction), no deferred tax is recognised.

Entity X may, however, be required to account for any temporary differences that would have subsequently arisen (i.e. between the initial transaction date and the date of transition to IFRSs) as a result of differences between accounting amortisation under IFRSs and the tax write-off period.

Example 8.2C

Deferred tax asset not recognised under previous GAAP

Company X is a first-time adopter in 20X4. Under previous GAAP, deferred taxes were recognised based on timing differences. In 20X1, by means of an internal group reorganisation that had no effect for financial reporting purposes, Company X generated an asset for tax purposes that will be deductible in its tax return over three years. This asset is not recognised for financial reporting purposes under previous GAAP, and does not meet any asset recognition criteria under IFRSs. Therefore, the asset is not recognised on first-time adoption.

In its first IFRS consolidated financial statements, Company X should recognise a deferred tax asset at the date of transition to IFRSs for the net carrying amount of the tax asset that arose in 20X1. A temporary difference exists and a deferred tax asset should be recognised in the group's consolidated financial statements. The initial credit is an adjustment on first-time adoption of IFRSs and so will be recognised in retained earnings (or another appropriate reserve). Subsequent changes in the amount of the deferred tax asset will be recognised in profit or loss.

Paragraphs 9 and 17 of IAS 12 provide examples of one type of temporary difference (i.e. 'timing differences'). However, IAS 12 is, overall, driven by a 'balance sheet' approach, irrespective of whether an expense or income has previously been recognised, such that the comparison should follow an analysis of the tax consequences on settlement (i.e. deferred tax is recognised on the difference between the tax base and the carrying amount for accounting purposes). If a tax base exists for tax purposes and no asset or liability exists for accounting purposes, the carrying amount of the asset or liability should be deemed to be zero for the purposes of identifying temporary differences.

Example 8.2D

Deferred tax on share options not accounted for retrospectively on first-time adoption

Company A granted share options to employees prior to 7 November 2002 (i.e. before the mandatory application of IFRS 2 *Share-based Payment*). The options vest in 2006 subject to non-market vesting conditions. Company A did not recognise the transaction prior to 7 November 2002, and did not make a retrospective adjustment for the transaction on first-time adoption of IFRSs. On transition to IFRSs in 2005, there is consequently no expense recognised in profit or loss in respect of these options (the entity has not applied IFRS 2 to these options under the requirements of IFRS 2:54/IFRS 1:D2 – see **7.3.2.1**). However, on vesting, Company A will receive a tax deduction based on the intrinsic value at the date of exercise.

Does a temporary difference exist at the date of transition when there has been no accounting recognition of the share-option grant (i.e. no recognition of an asset or liability and no expense)?

Yes, there is a temporary difference. The principle of IAS 12:68A to 68C is to require deferred tax to be recognised on all temporary differences relating to share options. Therefore, when there is no remuneration expense recognised in the financial statements, but there is a future tax deduction, deferred tax on the entire temporary difference, equal to the expected tax deduction, is required to be recognised in equity at the date of transition.

8.3   IAS 16 *Property, Plant and Equipment*

8.3.1   *Depreciation methods and rates*

If an entity's depreciation methods and rates under previous GAAP are acceptable under IFRSs, it accounts for any change in estimated useful life or depreciation pattern prospectively from when it makes that change in estimate. This is consistent with the requirements of IFRS 1 on changes of estimates and with paragraph 61 of IAS 16. [IFRS 1:IG7]

Depreciation methods and rates under previous GAAP may differ from those that would be acceptable under IFRSs. For example, they may have been adopted solely for tax purposes and they may not reflect a reasonable estimate of the asset's useful life. In such cases, when the effect is material, the accumulated depreciation is adjusted retrospectively in the opening IFRS statement of financial position so that it complies with IFRSs. [IFRS 1:IG7]

IAS 16 requires each part of an item of property, plant and equipment with a cost that is significant in relation to the total cost of the item to be depreciated separately. But IAS 16 does not prescribe the unit of measure for recognition of an asset (i.e. what constitutes an item of property, plant and equipment). Thus, judgement is required in applying the recognition criteria to an entity's specific circumstances. [IFRS 1:IG12]

8.3.2   Assets measured under IAS 16's revaluation model

The use of fair value or previous revaluations as deemed cost on first-time adoption of IFRSs is considered at **7.5**.

If the revaluation model in IAS 16 is used for some or all classes of property, plant and equipment, the cumulative revaluation surplus is presented as a separate component of equity. The revaluation surplus at the date of transition to IFRSs should be based on a comparison of the carrying amount of the asset at that date with its cost or deemed cost. If the deemed cost is the fair value at the date of transition to IFRSs, the disclosures required by IFRS 1:30 should be made (see **9.3.5**). [IFRS 1:IG10]

If revaluations under previous GAAP did not satisfy the criteria in IFRS 1:D6 or D8, the revalued assets should be measured in the opening IFRS statement of financial position on one of the following bases:

[IFRS 1:IG11]

- cost (or deemed cost) less any accumulated depreciation and any accumulated impairment losses under the cost model in IAS 16;

- deemed cost, being the fair value at the date of transition to IFRSs; or

- revalued amount, if the entity adopts the revaluation model in IAS 16 as its accounting policy under IFRSs for all assets in the same class.

8.3.3   Asset exchanges

Example 8.3.3

Asset exchanges

IAS 16 requires that an entity measure an item of property, plant and equipment acquired in exchange for a non-monetary asset or assets, or a combination of monetary and non-monetary assets, at fair value unless the exchange transaction lacks commercial substance.

Entity A, adopting IFRSs for the first-time in the current accounting period, acquired an asset via an asset exchange in a prior accounting period and recognised that asset at fair value in accordance with previous GAAP. If IAS 16 had been applied at the date of the asset exchange, the transaction would have been considered to lack commercial substance and the asset would have been recognised at the carrying amount of the asset given in exchange.

Should Entity A adjust accumulated depreciation in its opening IFRS statement of financial position retrospectively to comply with IAS 16?

Under previous GAAP, the acquired asset was recognised at fair value, but IAS 16 would have required it to be recognised at the carrying amount of the asset given up. IFRS 1 does not allow any exemption from retrospective application of the requirements of IAS 16 regarding asset exchanges. Therefore, in theory, restatement is required under IFRS 1. However, provided that the asset was measured at fair value at the date of the transaction, IFRS 1:D6 applies (see **7.5**). Therefore, for the purposes of transition to IFRSs, Entity A may take the fair value at the date of the exchange transaction as the deemed cost of the asset at that date.

8.3.4 Separate recognition of land and building components of property

Example 8.3.4

Separate recognition of land and building components of property

Under local GAAP, an entity did not separately recognise the land and building components of a property asset, which was depreciated as a whole.

On first-time adoption of IFRSs, how should this asset be recognised in the opening IFRS statement of financial position?

At the date of transition, the first-time adopter should recognise the land and building components of the property asset separately. Each component should be measured using either:

- original cost less subsequent depreciation calculated using depreciation methods and rates acceptable under IFRSs; or
- one of the deemed cost measures available under IFRS 1:D5 to D8 (see **7.5**).

8.4 Revenue (IFRS 15 and IAS 18)

8.4.1 IFRS 15 Revenue from Contracts with Customers

The wording of IFRS 1:IG17 has been amended for entities that adopt IFRS 15 (effective for annual periods beginning on or before 1 January 2018, with earlier application permitted). The requirements for entities that have not yet adopted IFRS 15 are set out at **8.4.2**.

143

Amounts may have been received that do not yet qualify for recognition as revenue under IFRS 15 (e.g. the proceeds of a sale that does not qualify for revenue recognition). An entity should recognise a liability in its opening IFRS statement of financial position and measure the liability at the amount received, adjusted (if appropriate) for a significant financing component in accordance with IFRS 15. [IFRS 1:IG17]

8.4.2 IAS 18 Revenue

Amounts may have been received that do not yet qualify for recognition as revenue under IAS 18 (e.g. the proceeds of a sale that does not qualify for revenue recognition). An entity should recognise the amount received as a liability in its opening IFRS statement of financial position and measure the liability at the amount received. [IFRS 1:IG17]

8.5 IAS 29 *Financial Reporting in Hyperinflationary Economies*

The requirements of IAS 21 *The Effects of Changes in Foreign Exchange Rates* should be applied to determine an entity's functional currency and presentation currency. IAS 29 should be applied to any periods during which the economy of the functional or presentation currency was hyperinflationary. [IFRS 1:IG32]

An entity may elect to use the fair value of an item of property, plant and equipment at the date of transition to IFRSs as its deemed cost at that date. In such circumstances, it should make the disclosures required by IFRS 1:30 (see **9.3.5**). [IFRS 1:IG33]

If the entity elects to use the exemptions in IFRS 1:D5 to D8 (i.e. fair value or revaluation as deemed cost – see **7.5**), it should apply IAS 29 to periods after the date for which the revalued amount or fair value was determined. [IFRS 1:IG34]

Example 8.5

Restatement of share capital for first-time adopters in hyperinflationary economies

Country A's economy was hyperinflationary until 31 December 20X1. An entity operating in Country A with CU as its functional currency is a first-time adopter of IFRSs with a transition date of 1 January 20X9. The entity was established and its share capital was contributed by shareholders before 31 December 20X1. The entity applies the IFRS 1:D5 fair value as deemed cost exemption for property, plant and equipment, and does not have any other non-monetary assets or liabilities acquired or originated prior to 31 December 20X1.

The entity should inflate the historical cost amount of its share capital in its first IFRS financial statements. Unless there is a specific exemption, IFRS 1 requires full retrospective application of the Standards effective at the end of the reporting period of the entity's first IFRS financial statements. Therefore, IAS 29

---

should be applied for the period during which the CU was a hyperinflationary currency. Components of equity, such as share capital, should therefore be restated in accordance with IAS 29:24 from the transaction date to the end of the period of hyperinflation.

In the circumstances described, the entity should restate its share capital from the transaction date to 31 December 20X1. There is no exemption from restatement of the share capital, or any other component of equity except retained earnings (which are derived as a balancing figure based on the other amounts in the restated statement of financial position).

8.6 IAS 36 *Impairment of Assets*

A first-time adopter is required to apply IAS 36 at the date of transition. At that date, the first-time adopter:

- performs an impairment test on goodwill and intangible assets with indefinite useful lives regardless of whether an indication of impairment exists;

- determines whether there are any indications that other assets, groups of assets or cash-generating units are impaired at the date of transition;

- performs an impairment test on assets, groups of assets or cash-generating units for which indications of impairment have been identified;

- recognises any impairment losses in retained earnings; and

- reverses any impairment losses that no longer exist at that date except for previously recognised impairment losses on goodwill.

The estimates used at the date of transition to IFRSs to determine whether an impairment loss is recognised (and to measure any such impairment loss) should be consistent with estimates made for the same date under previous GAAP, after making adjustments to reflect differences in accounting policies. This applies unless there is objective evidence that those assumptions were in error. The impact of any later revisions to those estimates should be reported as an event of the period in which the revisions are made. [IFRS 1:IG40]

A first-time adopter recognises any impairment losses arising on transition to IFRSs as a result of changes in accounting policies in retained earnings at the date of transition. If a first-time adopter made a valid IFRS-compliant estimate of an impairment loss under previous GAAP at the date of transition, it does not recognise any additional impairment losses nor reverse any previously recognised impairment losses. Subsequent impairment losses or reversals of impairment losses, including reversals of losses recognised prior to transition, are recognised in profit or loss in accordance with IAS 36.

In assessing the need to recognise an impairment loss and in measuring any such impairment loss at the date of transition to IFRSs, it may be necessary to make estimates that were not necessary under previous GAAP. Such estimates and assumptions should not reflect conditions that arose after the date of transition to IFRSs. [IFRS 1:IG41]

The transition provisions of IAS 36 do not apply to the opening IFRS statement of financial position. [IFRS 1:IG42]

IAS 36 requires the reversal of impairment losses in some circumstances. If the opening IFRS statement of financial position reflects impairment losses, any later reversal of those losses should be reflected in profit or loss except when IAS 36 requires them to be treated as a revaluation. This applies to both impairment losses recognised under previous GAAP and to additional impairment losses recognised on transition to IFRSs. [IFRS 1:IG43]

Example 8.6

Reversal of an impairment loss recognised under previous GAAP in respect of an equity-method investment

Entity F prepared its first IFRS financial statements for the year ending 31 December 20X2; its date of transition to IFRSs was 1 January 20X1. It holds an investment in Entity G which, under IFRSs, is accounted for using the equity method under IAS 28. Under its previous GAAP, Entity F accounted for its investment in Entity G using a similar, but not identical, method of accounting.

Under its previous GAAP, Entity F had recognised an impairment loss in respect of its investment in Entity G.

On the date of transition to IFRSs, Entity F applied the exemption in IFRS 1:C5 (see **7.2.4**) for equity-method investees acquired before that date. Consequently, IAS 28 was applied to those investments only from the date of transition. In addition, at the date of transition, Entity F applied IFRS 1:IG39 and concluded that no additional impairment loss or reversal of the impairment loss was required to be recognised.

Entity F is preparing its financial statements for the year ended 31 December 20X4. No impairment losses have been recognised since the date of transition. Entity F determines that the recoverable amount of its investment in Entity G has increased above its carrying amount and that the criteria for a reversal of an impairment loss under IAS 36 are met.

Should Entity F recognise the reversal of the impairment loss that arose prior to the date of transition to IFRSs?

Yes. The reversal should be recognised in accordance with IFRS 1:IG43, which applies to both impairment losses recognised under previous GAAP and to

---

additional impairment losses recognised at the date of transition to IFRSs. Irrespective of how the original impairment loss was recognised under previous GAAP, the reversal should be reflected in profit or loss.

The amount of the reversal is not affected by whether any goodwill is included in the carrying amount of the investment in Entity G; the investment is treated as a whole and the goodwill is not treated separately. Consequently, there is no prohibition against restoring the carrying amount of the investment to its pre-impairment value in appropriate circumstances (see **4.4.19.4** in **chapter A26** for entities that have adopted IFRS 9, or **4.4.20.4** in **chapter A26** for entities that have not yet adopted IFRS 9).

8.7   IAS 37 *Provisions, Contingent Liabilities and Contingent Assets*

There are no exceptions or exemptions in IFRS 1 relating to provisions. Therefore, the general principle in IFRS 1 of retrospective application of the IFRSs effective at the reporting date applies to provisions, except that a first-time adopter may apply the transition provisions of IFRIC 1 *Changes in Existing Decommissioning, Restoration and Similar Liabilities* (see **7.13.1**).

Therefore, at the date of transition, the first-time adopter analyses any provisions recognised under previous GAAP and assesses whether they meet the recognition criteria under IAS 37. If provisions recognised under previous GAAP do not meet these criteria (e.g. because the entity does not have a present obligation), they are removed from the opening IFRS statement of financial position with a corresponding adjustment to retained earnings at the date of transition.

Likewise, if the first-time adopter has incurred liabilities that meet the recognition criteria for provisions, but for which no provision had been recognised under previous GAAP, a provision is recognised in the opening IFRS statement of financial position measured in accordance with IAS 37 at the date of transition, with a corresponding adjustment to retained earnings.

The best estimate of a provision recognised under previous GAAP made on a basis similar to that required under IAS 37 is not adjusted at the date of transition. However, if a provision recognised under previous GAAP was estimated on a basis that is not similar to that required under IAS 37, the best estimate at the date of transition is determined in accordance with IAS 37 based on circumstances existing at the date of transition.

The estimates used to determine whether a provision is recognised, and to measure any such provision at the date of transition to IFRSs, should be consistent with estimates made for the same date under previous GAAP, after making adjustments to reflect differences in accounting policies. This applies unless there is objective evidence that those assumptions were in error. The impact of any later revisions to those estimates should be reported as an event of the period in which the revisions are made. [IFRS 1:IG40]

In assessing the need to recognise a provision, and in measuring any such provision at the date of transition to IFRSs, it may be necessary to make estimates that were not necessary under previous GAAP. Such estimates and assumptions should not reflect conditions that arose after the date of transition to IFRSs. [IFRS 1:IG41]

The transition provisions of IAS 37 do not apply to the opening IFRS statement of financial position. [IFRS 1:IG42]

8.8   IAS 38 *Intangible Assets*

8.8.1   *Intangible assets – general requirements*

The opening IFRS statement of financial position should:

[IFRS 1:IG44]

- exclude all intangible assets and other intangible items that do not meet the criteria for recognition in IAS 38 at the date of transition to IFRSs; and

- include all intangible assets that meet the recognition criteria in IAS 38 at the date of transition to IFRSs except as described below.

The exception in the second case is for intangible assets acquired in a business combination that were not recognised in the acquirer's consolidated statement of financial position under previous GAAP and also would not qualify for recognition under IAS 38 in the separate statement of financial position of the acquiree (see **7.2**). [IFRS 1:IG44]

The criteria in IAS 38 require an entity to recognise an intangible asset if, and only if:

- it is probable that the future economic benefits that are attributable to the asset will flow to the entity; and

- the cost of the asset can be measured reliably.

8.8.2   *Internally generated intangible assets*

IAS 38 supplements its general recognition criteria with further, more specific criteria for internally generated intangibles. [IFRS 1:IG45] Under IAS 38, the costs of creating internally generated intangible assets are capitalised prospectively from the date when the recognition criteria are met. IAS 38 does not permit the use of hindsight to conclude retrospectively that the recognition criteria were met. Consequently, even if it is possible to conclude retrospectively that a future inflow of economic benefits is probable and the costs can be reconstructed reliably, IAS 38 does not permit the capitalisation of costs incurred before the date when the entity both:

[IFRS 1:IG46]

- concludes, based on an assessment made and documented at the date of that conclusion, that it is probable that future economic benefits from the asset will flow to the entity; and

- has a reliable system for accumulating the costs of internally generated intangible assets when, or shortly after, they are incurred.

If an internally generated intangible asset qualifies for recognition at the date of transition to IFRSs, the asset should be recognised in the opening IFRS statement of financial position even if the related expenditure had been recognised as an expense under previous GAAP. If the asset does not qualify for recognition under IAS 38 until a later date, its cost is the sum of the expenditure incurred from that date. [IFRS 1:IG47]

Example 8.8.2

Capitalisation of costs incurred prior to the date of transition on internally generated intangible assets

Company A adopts IFRSs with a date of transition of 1 January 20X4. At that date, certain internal development projects were determined to be in the development phase in accordance with IAS 38.

Is Company A required to recognise an asset for the development costs that would have been recognised under IAS 38 had Company A reported under IFRSs prior to the date of transition?

It depends. If Company A can reliably measure the development costs incurred, then recognition of the asset is required. However, IFRS 1 recognises that in many cases when prior cost data was not reliably segregated between research and development, the measurement of the development costs may not be reliable and should not be required. If measurement can be determined reliably from the date the recognition criteria were met, then restatement of the asset would be as if IAS 38 had always been applied; that is, only costs incurred during the development phase should be capitalised in the opening IFRS statement of financial position at 1 January 20X4.

The guidance in IFRS 1:IG46 prohibits recognition of an asset for development costs incurred before the date on which the entity concluded, based on an assessment made and documented at the date of that conclusion, that it was probable that future economic benefits from the asset would flow to the entity. In most cases when an entity had a policy of writing off development costs as incurred under previous GAAP, no such assessment would have been made at the time. No asset would therefore be recognised for development costs in the opening IFRS statement of financial position. But, in some cases, development costs may have been recorded and controlled through a system that involved such an assessment being made for commercial rather than financial reporting

---

purposes. Such an assessment might, depending on the facts, constitute an appropriate basis for recognising an asset for development costs on transition to IFRSs.

8.8.3   Intangible assets acquired separately

The criteria described in **8.8.1** for recognition of intangible assets under IAS 38 also apply to intangible assets acquired separately. Documentation prepared at the time to support the decision to acquire an asset will usually contain an assessment of the future economic benefits. Also, the cost of separately acquired intangible assets can usually be measured reliably. [IFRS 1:IG48]

8.8.4   Amortisation methods and rates

If the amortisation methods and rates used under previous GAAP would be acceptable under IFRSs, the accumulated amortisation should not be restated in the opening IFRS statement of financial position. Any change in estimated useful life or amortisation pattern should be accounted for prospectively from the period when the change of estimate is made. But in some cases the amortisation methods and rates under previous GAAP might not be acceptable under IFRSs (e.g. because they were adopted solely for tax purposes and do not reflect a reasonable estimate of the asset's useful life). In such cases, when the effect is material, the accumulated amortisation in the opening IFRS statement of financial position should be adjusted retrospectively so that it complies with IFRSs. [IFRS 1:IG51]

Example 8.8.4A

Indefinite-life intangible asset amortised under previous GAAP

A first-time adopter has an intangible asset. Under previous GAAP, the intangible asset was being amortised over 20 years. Previous GAAP required that all intangible assets be amortised and did not have the concept of indefinite-life intangible assets. On first-time adoption of IFRSs, the asset is determined to have an indefinite useful life.

The entity should treat the change of classification to indefinite life as a change in accounting policy. As discussed in IFRS 1:IG51, the entity's previous amortisation method under previous GAAP is not acceptable under IFRSs. Therefore, the change from finite to indefinite life is a change in accounting policy that should be accounted for retrospectively in accordance with IFRS 1.

The transition provisions in IAS 38:130 (which state that a change in useful life from a finite to an indefinite useful life should be accounted for as a change in accounting estimate) do not apply to first-time adopters of IFRSs. The entity must retrospectively restate the intangible as an indefinite-life asset, subject to mandatory annual impairment tests.

Example 8.8.4B

Restatement of an intangible asset as a result of prior impairments

Company N acquired Company U on 1 January 20X2. As part of the accounting for the business combination, CU100 was allocated to purchased in-process research and development (IPR&D) projects. In accordance with local accounting standards, this amount was expensed immediately in the entity's consolidated statement of comprehensive income.

Company N adopts IFRSs with a 1 January 20X4 date of transition, at which date the IPR&D projects are still in progress.

Should the amount allocated to IPR&D and expensed immediately subsequent to the acquisition of Company U under previous GAAP be recognised at the date of transition under IFRSs?

Yes. IFRS 1 requires the use of IFRS-compliant accounting policies in the opening IFRS statement of financial position and throughout the periods presented in the first IFRS financial statements. IFRS 1:IG51 requires that if an entity's amortisation methods and rates under previous GAAP differ from those that would be acceptable under IFRSs, and those differences have a material effect on the financial statements, the entity should retrospectively adjust the accumulated amortisation in its opening IFRS statement of financial position so that it complies with IFRSs.

The immediate impairment or write-off of IPR&D is not in accordance with IFRSs and, therefore, should be reversed in the opening IFRS statement of financial position. Amortisation should be appropriately recognised in accordance with IAS 38. The IPR&D should be tested at least annually for impairment until the asset to be developed is in the location and condition for it to be capable of operating in the manner intended by management, at which time amortisation should commence (assuming the developed asset has a finite useful life).

Because the write-off of IPR&D occurred outside of the business combination, the exemption from the general rules in Appendix C to IFRS 1 for a business combination does not apply.

This requirement also applies to other impairment losses and reversals recognised in prior periods for assets with continuing useful lives at the date of transition.

8.9 IAS 40 *Investment Property*

If the fair value model in IAS 40 is adopted, investment property should be measured at fair value at the date of transition to IFRSs. The transition requirements in IAS 40 do not apply. [IFRS 1:IG61]

If the cost model in IAS 40 is adopted, the requirements of IFRS 1 and related implementation guidance accompanying IFRS 1 for property, plant and equipment should be applied (see **8.3**). [IFRS 1:IG62]

8.10 IAS 19 *Employee Benefits*

The actuarial assumptions used for defined benefit retirement benefit plans at the date of transition to IFRSs should be consistent with the actuarial assumptions made for the same date under previous GAAP (after adjustments to reflect any differences in accounting policies) unless there is objective evidence that those assumptions were in error. The impact of any later revisions to those assumptions is an actuarial gain or loss of the period in which the entity makes the revisions. [IFRS 1:IG19]

It may be necessary to make actuarial assumptions at the date of transition to IFRSs that were not necessary under previous GAAP. Any such assumptions should not reflect conditions that arose after the date of transition to IFRSs. In particular, discount rates and the fair value of plan assets at the date of transition to IFRSs reflect market conditions at that date. Similarly, actuarial assumptions at the date of transition to IFRSs about future employee turnover rates should not reflect a significant increase in estimated employee turnover rates as a result of a curtailment of the pension plan that occurred after the date of transition to IFRSs. [IFRS 1:IG20]

An entity's first IFRS financial statements will usually reflect measurements of employee benefit obligations at three dates (the end of the reporting period, the date of the comparative statement of financial position and the date of transition to IFRSs). IAS 19 encourages the involvement of a qualified actuary in the measurement of all material post-employment benefit obligations. However, the implementation guidance accompanying IFRS 1 notes that, to minimise cost, an entity may request a qualified actuary to carry out a detailed actuarial valuation at one or two dates and roll the valuation(s) forward or back to other dates. Any such roll forward or roll back should reflect any material transactions and other material events (including changes in market prices and interest rates) between those dates. [IFRS 1:IG21]

9 Presentation and disclosure

9.1 Presentation and disclosure – general

IFRS 1 does not provide exemptions from the presentation and disclosure requirements of other IFRSs. It imposes additional requirements on first-time adopters. There is an exception to this general rule which concerns non-IFRS comparative information and historical summaries as described at **9.2.2**. [IFRS 1:20]

Example 9.1

Disclosure of key management personnel compensation for share-based payments when exemption regarding options granted prior to 7 November 2002 has been applied

Under an entity's executive share option plan, key management personnel received options that were granted prior to 7 November 2002 and that have not yet vested. The entity has elected to apply the exemption in IFRS 1:D2 to these options and, accordingly, has not recognised an expense in relation to them.

Is it appropriate for the entity to apply the exemption in IFRS 1 in determining the amount of key management personnel compensation to be disclosed?

Yes. IAS 24 *Related Party Disclosures* requires disclosure of key management personnel compensation, which is defined as including all employee benefits (as defined in IAS 19), including employee benefits to which IFRS 2 *Share-based Payment* applies (see **5.2** of **chapter A23**).

IAS 24 does not provide guidance on the measurement of amounts to be disclosed for compensation. Reference should therefore be made to the measurement guidance contained in other Standards (such as IAS 19 and IFRS 2) in order to determine the measurement of compensation to be disclosed. Accordingly, when the exemption in IFRS 1 has been applied so that amounts for options granted prior to 7 November 2002 have not been recognised as an expense, the amount disclosed as share-based payment compensation would similarly not include amounts relating to those options.

Entities should consider whether additional disclosures should be provided with respect to the unrecognised share-based payments.

9.2 Comparative information

9.2.1 Requirements for presentation of comparative information

An entity's first IFRS financial statements are required to include at least three statements of financial position, two statements of profit or loss and other comprehensive income, two separate statements of profit or loss (if presented), two statements of cash flows and two statements of changes in equity and related notes, including comparative information for all statements presented. [IFRS 1:21]

A first-time adopter is therefore required to present notes supporting its opening IFRS statement of financial position. This differs from the position for an entity already applying IFRSs that is required to present a third statement of financial position in specified circumstances (see **2.10.4** of **chapter A4**); such an entity need not present related notes for that additional statement of financial position. The Basis for Conclusions on IFRS 1 makes clear the IASB's view regarding notes supporting an opening IFRS statement of financial position by stating that "the requirements for comparative information for a first-time adopter should be different from the requirements for comparative information for an existing preparer. The Board noted that a first-time adopter should not be exempted from presenting three statements of financial position and related notes because it might not have presented this information previously on a basis consistent with IFRSs" (see IFRS 1:BC89B).

9.2.2   Historical summaries and previous GAAP comparatives

Some entities present historical summaries of selected data for periods before the first period for which they present full comparative information under IFRSs. IFRS 1 does not require such summaries to comply with the recognition and measurement requirements of IFRSs. Also, some entities present comparative information under previous GAAP as well as the comparative information required by IAS 1. In any financial statements containing historical summaries or comparative information under previous GAAP, an entity should:

[IFRS 1:22]

- label the previous GAAP information prominently as not being prepared under IFRSs; and

- disclose the nature of the main adjustments that would make it comply with IFRSs. The adjustments need not be quantified.

A first-time adopter is permitted to provide additional comparative information that is presented in accordance with previous GAAP to help users of the financial statements understand the effects of the transition to IFRSs. Note that this is an exception to the general principle in IAS 1 which, for entities already applying IFRSs, requires that all additional comparative information be prepared in accordance with IFRSs (see **2.10.3** in **chapter A4**).

9.3   Explanation of transition to IFRSs

9.3.1   General requirement to explain the effect of transition from previous GAAP

Entities are required to explain how the transition from previous GAAP to IFRSs affected their reported financial position, financial performance and cash flows. [IFRS 1:23] The disclosures required to meet this objective are discussed in the **9.3.2** to **9.3.10**.

9.3.2 Repeated application of IFRS 1

An entity that has applied IFRSs in a previous reporting period, but whose most recent previous annual financial statements did not contain an explicit and unreserved statement of compliance with IFRSs (see **4.3**), is required to disclose:

[IFRS 1:23A]

- the reason it stopped applying IFRSs; and

- the reason it is resuming the application of IFRSs.

If, as is permitted under IFRS 1:4A, an entity elects not to apply IFRS 1 when it resumes application of IFRSs, the entity is required to explain the reasons for electing to apply IFRSs as if it had never stopped applying IFRSs. [IFRS 1:23B]

The Standard states specifically that, if an entity elects not to apply IFRS 1 when it resumes application of IFRSs, it is required to provide the disclosures required under IFRS 1:23A and 23B (see above) as well as those required under IAS 8 *Accounting Policies, Changes in Accounting Estimates and Errors*. [IFRS 1:4B]

9.3.3 Reconciliations

An entity's first IFRS financial statements should include:

[IFRS 1:24]

- reconciliations of its equity reported under previous GAAP to its equity under IFRSs as at:

  - the date of transition to IFRSs; and

  - the end of the latest period presented in the entity's most recent annual financial statements under previous GAAP;

- a reconciliation to total comprehensive income under IFRSs for the latest period in the entity's most recent annual financial statements. The starting point for that reconciliation is total comprehensive income under previous GAAP for the same period or, if the entity did not report such a total, profit or loss under previous GAAP; and

- if the entity recognised or reversed any impairment losses for the first time in preparing its opening IFRS statement of financial position, the disclosures that IAS 36 *Impairment of Assets* would have required if the entity had recognised those impairment losses or reversals in the period beginning with the date of transition to IFRSs.

As explained in IFRS 1:BC94, the rationale for the last of these requirements is that there is inevitably subjectivity about impairment losses. The disclosure is intended to provide transparency about impairment losses recognised on transition to IFRSs. These losses might otherwise receive less attention than impairment losses recognised in earlier or later periods.

IFRS 1 requires the above reconciliations to be included in the financial statements. This contrasts with the requirements for an interim report in accordance with IAS 34 *Interim Financial Reporting* (see **9.3.9**) when a cross reference to another published document is sufficient.

The reconciliations described above should give sufficient detail to enable users to understand the material adjustments to the statement of financial position and statement of comprehensive income. If a statement of cash flows was presented under previous GAAP, an explanation should be provided of the material adjustments to the statement of cash flows. [IFRS 1:25]

Example 11 in the implementation guidance accompanying IFRS 1 shows one way of satisfying these requirements.

An entity may become aware of errors made under previous GAAP. The reconciliations required by paragraphs 24(a) and (b) of IFRS 1 (i.e. the reconciliations of equity and profit or loss and/or total comprehensive income) should distinguish the correction of errors from changes in accounting policies. [IFRS 1:26]

If, during the period covered by its first IFRS financial statements, an entity changes its accounting policies or its use of the exemptions contained in IFRS 1, it is required to explain the changes between its first IFRS interim financial report and its first IFRS financial statements, in accordance with IFRS 1:23, and to update the reconciliations required by IFRS 1:24(a) and (b) (see **5.3.5**). [IFRS 1:27A]

If an entity did not present financial statements for previous periods, its first IFRS financial statements should disclose that fact. [IFRS 1:28]

9.3.4   Designation of financial assets or financial liabilities

9.3.4.1   Entities applying IFRS 9

As discussed in **7.11.1**, an entity that has adopted IFRS 9 *Financial Instruments* is permitted to designate a previously recognised financial asset as a financial asset measured at fair value through profit or loss in accordance with IFRS 1:D19A.

The entity is required to disclose the fair value of financial assets so designated at the date of designation and their classification and carrying amount in the previous financial statements. [IFRS 1:29]

An entity that has adopted IFRS 9 is also permitted to designate a previously recognised financial liability as a financial liability at fair value through profit or loss in accordance with IFRS 1:D19.

The entity is required to disclose the fair value of financial liabilities so designated at the date of designation and their classification and carrying amount in the previous financial statements. [IFRS 1:29A]

9.3.4.2 Entities applying IAS 39

As discussed in **7.11.2**, an entity that applies IAS 39 *Financial Instruments: Recognition and Measurement* is permitted to designate a previously recognised financial asset or financial liability as a financial asset or financial liability at fair value through profit or loss or a financial asset as available for sale in accordance with IFRS 1:D19.

When such a designation is made, the entity is required to disclose the fair value of financial assets or financial liabilities designated into each category at the date of designation and their classification and carrying amount in the previous financial statements. [IFRS 1:29]

9.3.5 Use of fair value as deemed cost

If fair value is used in the opening IFRS statement of financial position as deemed cost for an item of property, plant and equipment, an investment property or an intangible asset (see **7.5**), the first IFRS financial statements should disclose, for each item in the opening IFRS statement of financial position:

[IFRS 1:30]

- the aggregate of those fair values; and
- the aggregate adjustment to the carrying amounts reported under previous GAAP.

These disclosure requirements apply when fair value at the date of transition is used as deemed cost in accordance with IFRS 1:D5 or IFRS 1:D7. They do not apply when a first-time adopter uses a previous GAAP revaluation in accordance with IFRS 1:D6 or IFRS 1:D8.

9.3.6 Use of deemed cost for oil and gas assets

If an entity uses the exemption in IFRS 1:D8A(b) for oil and gas assets (see **7.5.4**), that fact and the basis on which carrying amounts were determined under previous GAAP are required to be disclosed. [IFRS 1:31A]

9.3.7 Use of deemed cost for operations subject to rate regulation

If an entity uses the exemption in IFRS 1:D8B for operations subject to rate regulation (see **7.5.5**), that fact and the basis on which carrying amounts were determined under previous GAAP are required to be disclosed. [IFRS 1:31B]

9.3.8 Use of deemed cost after severe hyperinflation

If an entity elects to measure assets and liabilities at fair value and to use that fair value as the deemed cost in its opening IFRS statement of financial position because of severe hyperinflation (see **7.18**), the entity's first IFRS financial statements are required to include an explanation of how, and why, the entity had, and then ceased to have, a functional currency that is subject to severe hyperinflation' (as defined in IFRS 1:D27). [IFRS 1:31C]

9.3.9 Interim financial reports

When an interim financial report is presented under IAS 34 for part of the period covered by the first IFRS financial statements, the following additional requirements apply in addition to those in IAS 34.

Each such interim financial report should, if the entity presented an interim financial report for the comparable period of the immediately preceding financial year, include:

[IFRS 1:32]

- a reconciliation of its equity under previous GAAP at the end of that comparable interim period to its equity under IFRSs at that date;

- a reconciliation to its total comprehensive income under IFRSs for the comparable interim period (current and year to date). The starting point for that reconciliation is total comprehensive income under previous GAAP for that period or, if the entity did not report such a total, profit or loss under previous GAAP.

In addition, the first interim financial report under IAS 34 for part of the period covered by the first IFRS financial statements should include the reconciliations and other information described at **9.3.3**. Alternatively, a cross-reference to another published document that includes these reconciliations may be provided. [IFRS 1:32]

If an entity changes its accounting policies or its use of the exemptions contained in IFRS 1, it is required to explain those changes in every interim financial report for part of the period covered by an entity's first IFRS financial statements and update the reconciliations required to be presented in interim financial reports. [IFRS 1:32(c)]

IAS 34 requires minimum disclosures that are based on the assumption that users of the interim financial report also have access to the most recent annual financial statements. But IAS 34 also requires disclosure of "any events or transactions that are material to an understanding of the current interim period". Therefore, if a first-time adopter did not, in its most recent annual financial statements under previous GAAP, disclose information material to an understanding of the current interim period, the interim report should disclose that information or include a cross-reference to another published document that includes it. [IFRS 1:33]

> IAS 34:6 allows condensed financial statements and footnotes to avoid repetition of information previously reported. IAS 34:6 also states that "the interim financial report is intended to provide an update on the latest complete set of annual financial statements".
>
> When no previous IFRS annual financial statements have been prepared, the first interim financial report under IFRSs will need to include additional information to assist users in understanding the financial statements.
>
> For example, although condensed interim financial reports are generally only required to describe changes in accounting policies since the annual financial statements, an entity's first interim report under IFRSs should generally include a full description of the accounting policies adopted under IFRSs unless these had already been published in another document to which reference could be made. It would also be appropriate to include expanded notes disclosures on individual areas when information was not provided in the previous GAAP financial statements.

IAS 34 applies if an entity is required, or elects, to prepare an interim financial report in accordance with IFRSs. Therefore neither IAS 34 nor IFRS 1 requires an entity to present interim financial reports that comply with IAS 34. Neither do they require an entity to prepare a new version of interim financial reports presented under previous GAAP. [IFRS 1:IG37]

However, if an interim financial report is prepared under IAS 34 for part of the period covered by an entity's first IFRS financial statements, the comparative information presented should be restated so that it complies with IFRSs. [IFRS 1:IG37]

IFRS 1 should be applied in each interim financial report that is presented under IAS 34 for part of the period covered by the first IFRS financial statements. In particular, the requirements for reconciliations described above apply. [IFRS 1:IG38]

9.3.10   Use of deemed cost for investments in subsidiaries, associates and joint ventures

If an entity uses a deemed cost in its opening IFRS statement of financial position for an investment in a subsidiary, associate or joint venture in its separate financial statements (see **7.8.2**), it is required to disclose:

[IFRS 1:31]

- the aggregate deemed cost of those investments for which deemed cost is their previous GAAP carrying amount;

- the aggregate deemed cost of those investments for which deemed cost is fair value; and

- the aggregate adjustment to the carrying amounts reported under previous GAAP.

10   Future developments

The IASB is working on a number of new Standards which, when finalised, are likely to result in consequential amendments to IFRS 1 regarding the application of the requirements of those Standards for first-time adopters.

A4 Presentation of financial statements

Contents

1 Introduction

1.1 Overview of IAS 1

IAS 1 *Presentation of Financial Statements* sets out the overall requirements for financial statements, including how they should be structured, general requirements for their content, and overriding concepts such as going concern, the accrual basis of accounting and the current/non-current distinction. The Standard requires a complete set of financial statements to comprise a statement of financial position, a statement of profit or loss and other comprehensive income, a statement of changes in equity, a statement of cash flows and notes.

The implementation guidance accompanying IAS 1 sets out an illustrative structure for financial statements.

1.2 Amendments to IAS 1 since the last edition of this manual

IAS 1 was most recently amended in December 2014 by *Disclosure Initiative (Amendments to IAS 1)*. The amendments provide clarification on the following:

- application of the requirements on materiality and aggregation (see **2.7.2**);

- aggregation and disaggregation of the line items required to be presented in the statement of financial position (see **4.4.2**) and statement(s) of profit or loss and other comprehensive income (see **5.1.2**), and additional guidance on the presentation of subtotals in these statements;

- the presentation of an entity's share of other comprehensive income (OCI) of associates and joint ventures accounted for using the equity method (see **5.3.2.1**); and

- presentation of the notes to the financial statements (see **7.1.2**).

Although stated to be effective for annual periods beginning on or after 1 January 2016 (with earlier application permitted), the December 2014 amendments are considered to clarify existing requirements in IAS 1 and an entity is not required to disclose the fact that it has applied the amendments (regardless of whether the amendments have been applied in advance of their effective date). Also, when the December 2014 amendments are adopted, entities need not provide the information required to be disclosed under paragraphs 28 to 30 of IAS 8 *Accounting Policies, Changes in Accounting Estimates and Errors* regarding the effect of adopting a new IFRS (see **section 3.4** of **chapter A5**); these requirements would generally require an entity to provide details of the effect of adopting a new IFRS or voluntarily adopting a new accounting policy. [IAS 1:139P]

The underlying objective of the December 2014 amendments is to encourage entities to apply professional judgement in determining what information to disclose in their financial statements. This emphasis can be seen in the amendments regarding the application of materiality and the determination of the order of the financial statements.

It is unusual that entities are not required to disclose the effect of adopting these amendments. The IASB has taken this approach because application of the amendments does not affect recognition and measurement and should not result in the reassessment of judgements about presentation and disclosure made in periods prior to the application of the amendments. However, if an entity decides to change its accounting policies as a result of applying the amendments, it would be required to follow the requirements in IAS 8 in relation to those accounting policy changes. [IAS 1:BC105D - BC105F]

Throughout this chapter, significant effects of the December 2014 amendments are highlighted. However, because the amendments are considered to be clarifications rather than new requirements, not all of the changes to the text of IAS 1 are described in detail.

2 General requirements

2.1 Objective

The objective of IAS 1 is to prescribe the basis for presentation of general purpose financial statements so as to ensure comparability both with an entity's financial statements of previous periods and with the financial statements of other entities. [IAS 1:1]

2.2 Scope

2.2.1 Scope – general

IAS 1 is required to be applied in preparing and presenting general purpose financial statements in accordance with IFRSs. [IAS 1:2] The impact of the Standard is, therefore, pervasive and it affects every set of financial statements prepared under IFRSs.

Other IFRSs set out the recognition, measurement and disclosure requirements for specific transactions and other events. [IAS 1:3]

General purpose financial statements are defined in IAS 1 as "those intended to meet the needs of users who are not in a position to require an entity to prepare reports tailored to their particular information needs". References to 'financial statements' in IAS 1 should be taken as references to general purpose financial statements. [IAS 1:7]

2.2.2   Application to individual, consolidated and separate financial statements

IAS 1 applies equally to all entities, including those that present consolidated financial statements in accordance with IFRS 10 *Consolidated Financial Statements* and those that present separate financial statements in accordance with IAS 27 *Separate Financial Statements*. [IAS 1:4]

The requirements of IFRSs apply equally to the financial statements of an individual entity and to consolidated financial statements for a group of entities. IFRSs contemplate three types of financial statements:

- 'individual' financial statements prepared by an entity that has no subsidiaries (which will, subject to any exemptions, incorporate the results of any associates or joint ventures using equity method accounting in accordance with IAS 28 *Investments in Associates and Joint Ventures*);

- 'consolidated' financial statements for a parent with consolidated subsidiaries, prepared in accordance with IFRS 10; and

- 'separate' financial statements in which the entity can elect (subject to the requirements of IAS 27 *Separate Financial Statements* – see **chapter A29**) to account for its investments in subsidiaries, joint ventures and associates either (1) at cost, (2) in accordance with IFRS 9 *Financial Instruments* (or, for entities that have not yet adopted IFRS 9, IAS 39 *Financial Instruments: Recognition and Measurement*), or (3) using the equity method in accordance with IAS 28. (For entities that have not yet adopted the August 2014 amendments to IAS 27 (see **1.2** in **chapter A29**), the option of accounting for investments in separate financial statements using the equity method is not available.)

Separate financial statements may be presented:

- in addition to consolidated financial statements or to the individual financial statements of an investor that does not have investments in subsidiaries but does have investments in associates or joint ventures which it is required to account for using the equity method; or

- as the only financial statements of an entity with subsidiaries and/ or joint ventures or associates that is exempted by IFRS 10 and/or IAS 28 from consolidation and/or application of the equity method; or

- as the only financial statements of an investment entity (as defined in IFRS 10 – see **section 13** of **chapter A24**) that is required to measure all of its subsidiaries at fair value through profit or loss.

IAS 1 does not preclude the presentation of consolidated financial statements complying with IFRSs and financial statements of the parent under national GAAP within the same document. In such circumstances, the basis of preparation for each should be clearly disclosed. In practice, the two sets of financial statements should generally be presented as separate sections of the document so as to avoid mixing information prepared under different GAAPs on the same page (e.g. columnar layouts mixing parent-only and consolidated information prepared under different GAAPs should be avoided). This would not preclude cross-references between the two sections of the document to avoid repetition of information that is the same on both bases.

2.2.3   Scope – interim financial reports

IAS 1 does not apply to the structure and content of condensed interim financial statements prepared in accordance with IAS 34 *Interim Financial Reporting*. But paragraphs 15 to 35 of IAS 1 apply to such interim reports. [IAS 1:4]

Paragraphs 15 to 35 of IAS 1 are those dealing with fair presentation and compliance with IFRSs (see **section 3**), going concern (see **section 2.5**), accruals accounting (see **section 2.6**), materiality and aggregation (see **section 2.7**) and offsetting (see **2.8**).

2.2.4   Terminology to be adapted as appropriate to the circumstances

IAS 1 uses terminology that is suitable for profit-oriented entities, including public sector business entities. The Standard notes that entities with not-for-profit activities in the private sector or public sector seeking to apply it may need to amend the descriptions used for particular line items in the financial statements and for the financial statements themselves. [IAS 1:5]

Similarly, entities that do not have equity as defined in IAS 32 *Financial Instruments: Presentation* (e.g. some mutual funds) and entities whose share capital is not equity (e.g. some co-operatives) may need to adapt the presentation in the financial statements of members' or unit holders' interests (see **section 2.1.2** of **chapter B3** or, for entities that have not yet adopted IFRS 9, **section 2.1.2** of **chapter C3**). [IAS 1:6]

Note also that entities are not required to use the titles for financial statements as listed in IAS 1 (see **2.4.1**).

2.3   Purpose of financial statements

Financial statements are a structured representation of the financial position and financial performance of an entity. The objective of financial statements is to provide information about the financial position, financial performance and cash flows of an entity that is useful to a wide range of users in making economic decisions. Financial statements also show the results of management's stewardship of the resources entrusted to it. IAS 1 explains that to meet this objective, financial statements provide information about an entity's:

[IAS 1:9]

- assets;

- liabilities;

- equity;

- income and expenses, including gains and losses;

- contributions by and distributions to owners in their capacity as owners; and

- cash flows.

This information, together with other information in the notes, assists users of financial statements in predicting the entity's future cash flows, including their timing and certainty. [IAS 1:9]

2.4 Complete set of financial statements

2.4.1 Statements required to be presented

IAS 1 specifies that a complete set of financial statements comprises:

[IAS 1:10]

- a statement of financial position as at the end of the period (see **section 4**);

- a statement of profit or loss and other comprehensive income for the period (see **section 5**);

- a statement of changes in equity for the period (see **section 6**);

- a statement of cash flows for the period (see **chapter A21**);

- notes, comprising significant accounting policies and other explanatory information (see **section 7**);

- comparative information in respect of the preceding period as specified in IAS 1:38 and IAS 1:38A (see **section 2.10**); and

- a statement of financial position as at the beginning of the preceding period when an entity applies an accounting policy retrospectively or makes a retrospective restatement of items in its financial statements, or when it reclassifies items in its financial statements (see **section 2.10.4**).

Note that entities are not required to use the titles for financial statements as listed in IAS 1. IAS 1:10 specifically permits the use of other titles for the statements. Therefore, for example, it is acceptable to use the term 'balance sheet' to describe the statement of financial position. Equally, it is acceptable to use the title 'statement of comprehensive income' instead of 'statement of profit or loss and other comprehensive income'.

2.4.2   Choice of presentation for statement of profit or loss and other comprehensive income

An entity may either:

[IAS 1:10A]

* present a single statement of profit or loss and other comprehensive income, with profit or loss and other comprehensive income presented in two sections; or

* present the profit or loss section in a separate statement of profit or loss.

When a single statement is presented, the 'profit or loss' and 'other comprehensive income' sections are required to be presented together, with the profit or loss section presented first followed directly by the other comprehensive income section. [IAS 1:10A]

When a separate statement of profit or loss is presented, the separate statement of profit or loss should immediately precede the statement presenting comprehensive income, which should begin with profit or loss. [IAS 1:10A]

This requirement would not prevent the statements being presented on separate pages, although the statement of comprehensive income should be on the page immediately following the statement of profit or loss and given equal prominence.

2.4.3   Requirement to present all of the financial statements with equal prominence

In a complete set of financial statements, all of the financial statements should be presented with equal prominence. [IAS 1:11]

IAS 1:BC22 explains that the reason for the requirement in IAS 1:11 is that "the financial performance of an entity can be assessed only after all aspects of the financial statements are taken into account and understood in their entirety". In practice, the most significant effects of this requirement are that:

* when an entity elects to present the components of profit or loss in a separate statement as permitted by IAS 1:10A (see **2.4.2**), that

statement and the statement of comprehensive income should be presented with equal prominence; and

- the statement of changes in equity, which presents contributions from and distributions to owners, should be presented with equal prominence as the other statements.

2.4.4 Management commentary presented outside of the financial statements

IAS 1 notes that many entities present, outside of the financial statements, a review by management that describes and explains the main features of the entity's financial performance and financial position together with the principal uncertainties that it faces (generally referred to in international accounting literature as Management Commentary (MC)). Many entities also present, outside the financial statements, other statements, such as environmental reports and corporate governance statements. Reports and statements presented outside the financial statements are outside the scope of IFRSs. [IAS 1:13 - 14]

Information presented in the MC, or other supplementary statements, may repeat information in the financial statements. All information required under IFRSs should be presented in the notes or elsewhere in the financial statements. Omission of a disclosure in the financial statements because it is included in the MC, or a similar statement, is not permitted. However, a disclosure may be included by way of cross-reference if allowed by specific Standards (e.g. IFRS 7:B6 – see **section 5** of **chapter B11** or, for entities that have not yet adopted IFRS 9, **section 5** of **chapter C12**).

The IASB has issued a non-mandatory Practice Statement titled *Management Commentary* (see **chapter A33**). Guidance on the developing area of integrated reporting has been made available in the form of the *International Integrated Reporting Framework* (see **chapter A34**).

2.5 Going concern

2.5.1 Management's assessment of the entity's ability to continue as a going concern

IAS 1 requires management to make an assessment of the entity's ability to continue as a going concern when preparing financial statements. Financial statements should be prepared on a going concern basis unless management intends either to liquidate the entity or to cease trading, or has no realistic alternative but to do so. [IAS 1:25]

The assessment as to whether the going concern basis is appropriate takes into account events after the end of the reporting period. Financial statements are not prepared on a going concern basis if management determines after the end of the reporting period either that it intends to liquidate the entity or to cease trading, or that it has no realistic alternative but to do so (see **section 6** of **chapter A22**). [IAS 10:14]

2.5.2   Departure from going concern basis only in exceptional circumstances

It is important to note that when an entity prepares financial statements on a going concern basis, this does not imply an absolute level of confidence that the entity will be able to continue as a going concern. Even when an entity is in severe financial difficulties, IAS 1:25 *requires* the going concern basis to be used unless management either intends to liquidate the entity or to cease trading, or has no realistic alternative but to do so.

Accordingly, an entity will depart from the going concern basis only when it is, in effect, clear that it is *not* a going concern. When there is significant uncertainty over whether an entity can continue in operational existence, IAS 1 requires the going concern basis to be used and appropriate disclosures to be made (see **2.5.4**).

When there are doubts about an entity's ability to continue trading, the fact that the going concern basis must be used does not eliminate the need to consider whether any assets should be written down to their recoverable amounts and whether provision is required for any unavoidable costs under onerous contracts.

Example 2.5.2

Recognition of impairment when directors are considering ceasing to trade

The directors of an entity are considering whether to cease trading. At the date of preparation of the financial statements, the directors have not yet reached a decision. There is a reasonable possibility that the entity will continue to trade and, therefore, the financial statements are being prepared on a going concern basis.

Should the fact that the directors are considering ceasing to trade be regarded as an indicator of impairment?

It is usually appropriate to regard the fact that the directors are considering ceasing to trade as an indicator of impairment. The directors of an entity do not usually consider ceasing to trade if the entity is expected to be profitable. The fact that the directors are considering ceasing to trade may call into question the ability of the entity to continue to trade profitably and, therefore, whether the carrying amounts of assets are recoverable.

2.5.3 Period to be covered by management's going concern assessment

In assessing whether the going concern assumption is appropriate, management takes into account all available information about the future. IAS 1 states that the information should cover at least twelve months from the end of the reporting period but not be limited to that period. The degree of consideration depends on the facts in each case. When an entity has a history of profitable operations and ready access to financial resources, a conclusion that the going concern basis of accounting is appropriate may be reached without detailed analysis. In other cases, management may need to consider a wide range of factors relating to current and expected profitability, debt repayment schedules and potential sources of replacement financing before it can satisfy itself that the going concern basis is appropriate. [IAS 1:26]

2.5.4 Disclosure required of material uncertainties regarding the entity's ability to continue as a going concern

When management is aware, in making its assessment, of material uncertainties related to events or conditions that may cast significant doubt upon the entity's ability to continue as a going concern, those uncertainties should be disclosed. [IAS 1:25]

IAS 1 does not explain what it means for an entity to 'continue as a going concern', so it is appropriate to look to the IASB's *Conceptual Framework for Financial Reporting*. Paragraph 4.1 of the Conceptual Framework explains that financial statements "are normally prepared on the assumption that an entity is a going concern and will continue in operation for the foreseeable future. Hence, it is assumed that the entity has neither the intention nor the need to liquidate or curtail materially the scale of its operations; …".

2.5.5 Departure from the going concern basis

2.5.5.1 Disclosures required when financial statements are not prepared on a going concern basis

If financial statements are not prepared on a going concern basis, the financial statements should disclose that fact, together with the basis on which the financial statements are prepared and the reason why the entity is not regarded as a going concern. [IAS 1:25]

Before considering further the appropriate basis of preparation for the financial statements of an entity that will cease or that has ceased trading, it is worth considering whether statutory financial statements will be required at all. This will depend on the legal and regulatory requirements in the relevant jurisdiction.

2.5.5.2   Recognition of impairment

It is always appropriate to consider the need to recognise impairment losses when an entity is planning to cease or has already ceased trading. This assessment will require a comparison of the carrying amount of an asset (or, when appropriate, a cash-generating unit) with the higher of its value in use and fair value less costs of disposal. The question arises as to whether, in such circumstances, it is possible to assess impairment by reference to a value in use calculation.

In theory, it is possible to assess impairment of assets by reference to a value in use calculation even when the financial statements are prepared on a basis other than that of a going concern. However, in practice, often the cash flows forecast to arise from the continuing use of such assets are not significant because the expectation is that the assets will be sold or abandoned in the near future. In such circumstances, the amounts arrived at using a value in use calculation will not be materially different from the fair value less costs of disposal.

2.5.5.3   Using a basis other than that of a going concern for preparing financial statements

Even if an entity has ceased trading, if the entity wishes to state compliance with IFRSs then its financial statements should be prepared on a basis that is consistent with IFRSs but amended to reflect the fact that the going concern assumption is not appropriate. Among other things, such a basis requires writing assets down to their recoverable amounts. It also requires recognising a liability for contractual commitments that may have become onerous as a consequence of the decision to cease trading.

Although it is neither defined nor mentioned within IFRSs, some jurisdictions have a concept of financial statements prepared on a 'break-up' basis. Under this basis it is argued that the objective of the financial statements changes from reporting financial performance to (1) considering whether the assets of the entity are sufficient to meet its liabilities, and (2) quantifying the amount of any surplus that may, in due course, be available for distribution to the shareholders. Using this break-up basis, a liability would be recognised for losses arising subsequent to the end of the reporting period and for the costs of winding up the business, irrespective of whether an irrevocable decision to terminate the business had been made at the end of the reporting period. Assets would also be restated to their actual or estimated sale proceeds, even if this was different to their market value at the end of the reporting period. In effect, on a break-up basis, the accruals concept ceases to be of importance and the financial statements become a forecast of future realisation rather than a reflection of transactions and other events that have occurred in the reporting period.

The preparation of financial statements on this basis does not properly reflect the principles of IFRSs and is not considered appropriate under IFRSs except perhaps in very rare circumstances. This is because, under IFRSs, the financial statements should reflect the transactions and other events that have occurred in the reporting period and the circumstances existing at the end of the reporting period. For example, if the assets include quoted securities, it is difficult to see why these should be measured at above or below their market value even if they are sold for a higher or lower amount after the end of the reporting period. The gain or loss on disposal in the subsequent period reflects the decision to hold the securities rather than to sell them at the end of the reporting period. For similar reasons, it would not be appropriate to recognise provisions for future losses or liabilities for which there was no present legal or constructive obligation at the end of the reporting period.

When financial statements are being prepared under IFRSs but on a basis other than that of a going concern, another issue to consider is whether non-current assets and long-term liabilities should be reclassified as current assets and current liabilities. As discussed at **3.1.1** in **chapter A20**, assets classified as non-current in accordance with IAS 1 should not be reclassified as current assets unless and until they meet the 'held for sale' criteria in IFRS 5 *Non-current Assets Held for Sale and Discontinued Operations*. It is possible that the held for sale criteria may be met for some non-current assets but not others, e.g. if the entity is actively marketing some of the assets but not others.

Long-term liabilities should be reclassified as current liabilities if they meet the criteria in IAS 1 to be presented as current liabilities (see **4.3**). Reclassification may be required, for example, because of breaches of borrowing covenants or similar factors in existence at the end of the reporting period that accelerate the repayment requirements, with the result that the entity no longer has an unconditional right to defer settlement of the liability for at least twelve months after the end of the reporting period.

2.5.5.4 *Entities becoming dormant*

IAS 1 and IAS 10 *Events after the Reporting Period* require a departure from the going concern basis in specified circumstances. In particular, an entity should not prepare its financial statements on a going concern basis if:

- at the end of the reporting period, management intends to liquidate the entity or to cease trading (or has no realistic alternative but to do so); or

- management determines after the reporting period that it intends to liquidate the entity or to cease trading (or has no realistic alternative but to do so).

Accordingly, when an entity ceases to trade during the year, or management has determined, either at the reporting date or after the reporting period, that it intends to liquidate the entity, any subsequent financial statements should also be prepared on a basis other than that of a going concern. However, there is no guidance in either IAS 1 or IAS 10 regarding the appropriate basis of preparation for the financial statements of an entity that has ceased to trade during the year but which management intends to keep in existence (e.g. as a dormant company).

Financial statements prepared on a going concern basis would be extremely unlikely to give a true and fair view when the entity had already ceased trading before the end of the reporting period. In fact, when an entity has ceased trading during the year, use of the going concern basis is likely to be very misleading to users of the financial statements who might reasonably assume that this basis implies that trading will continue in future periods. In the financial reporting period in which an entity ceases to trade it is, therefore, appropriate to prepare the financial statements on a basis other than that of a going concern in order to give sufficient emphasis to the effects of cessation of trading.

The question also arises as to what is an appropriate basis of preparation for such entities to use in later reporting periods when the entity is no longer trading but continues to exist (e.g. as a dormant company). Neither IAS 1 nor IAS 10 provides guidance for such circumstances. To provide clarity to users of the financial statements, and to avoid the risk of giving a misleading impression regarding the trading status of the entity, one possible approach would be for the financial statements to be prepared on a basis other than that of a going concern until such time as the only amounts reported in the current and prior year statements of comprehensive income and financial position relate to the entity's ongoing existence (i.e. any effects of ceasing to trade have been 'washed through'). Thereafter, the financial statements will no longer include any items relating to the trade that has ceased and, therefore, references to such cessation may be confusing. Instead, the financial statements should be prepared on a going concern basis, in accordance with IAS 1:25. This approach is illustrated in **example 2.5.5.4**.

Example 2.5.5.4

Departure from going concern basis

Company X has a December year end. It ceases trading during 20X1, and finishes disposing of its assets during 20X2. By the 20X2 year end, the only items in the statement of financial position are intragroup receivables and

---

payables, which are not expected to be settled in the foreseeable future. The directors intend to keep Company X in existence for the foreseeable future.

If the directors choose to apply the possible approach suggested above, the financial statements for each of the 20X1, 20X2, 20X3 and 20X4 reporting periods would be prepared on the following bases.

20X1	A basis other than that of a going concern
20X2	A basis other than that of a going concern (because both the 20X2 and 20X1 statements of comprehensive income include effects of ceasing to trade, i.e. the disposal of the assets of Company X)
20X3	A basis other than that of a going concern (because the 20X2 statement of comprehensive income includes effects of ceasing to trade)
20X4	Going concern basis as explained above (all effects of ceasing to trade have been 'washed through' and there is no impact on either the 20X4 or 20X3 statements of comprehensive income)

Other approaches may also be acceptable.

2.5.5.5 Entities established as dormant

Example 2.5.5.5

Entity established as dormant

Company X is set up as a dormant company. It has never traded and the directors do not intend that it will trade in the future. The directors intend to keep Company X in existence as a dormant company for the foreseeable future.

On what basis should the financial statements of Company X be prepared?

The financial statements should be prepared on a going concern basis. The criteria to depart from the going concern basis in accordance with IAS 1:25 have not been met because the directors do not intend either to liquidate the entity or to cease trading.

2.6 Accruals basis of accounting

IAS 1 requires financial statements, except for cash flow information, to be prepared using the accruals basis of accounting. Under this basis, items are recognised as assets, liabilities, equity, income and expenses when they satisfy the definitions and recognition criteria for those elements in the IASB's *Conceptual Framework for Financial Reporting*. [IAS 1:27 - 28]

2.7   Materiality and aggregation

2.7.1   Materiality – general principle

IAS 1 defines 'material' as follows.

[IAS 1:7]

> "Omissions or misstatements of items are material if they could, individually or collectively, influence the economic decisions that users make on the basis of the financial statements. Materiality depends on the size and nature of the omission or misstatement judged in the surrounding circumstances. The size or nature of the item, or a combination of both, could be the determining factor."

Assessing whether an omission or misstatement could influence the economic decisions of users, and so be material, requires consideration of the characteristics of those users. The IASB's *Conceptual Framework for Financial Reporting* states that financial reports are prepared for "users who have a reasonable knowledge of business and economic activities and who review and analyse the information diligently". The assessment, therefore, needs to take into account how users with such attributes could reasonably be expected to be influenced in making economic decisions. [IAS 1:7]

2.7.2   Material items to be presented separately

The text in this section reflects the December 2014 amendments to IAS 1 as described at **1.2**. The amendments expand the previous guidance in IAS 1 to emphasise that an entity should not obscure useful information by aggregating or disaggregating information (e.g. by aggregating material items with different characteristics or obscuring useful information with immaterial information). In addition, the amendments clarify that the materiality guidance applies to the financial statements as a whole, including the primary statements and the notes, and that disclosures are only required if the information is material. The materiality guidance also applies to specific disclosure requirements set out in a Standard, even if those disclosures are required "as a minimum" by that Standard.

Each material class of similar items is required to be presented separately in the financial statements. Items of a dissimilar nature or function should be presented separately unless they are immaterial. [IAS 1:29]

Financial statements result from processing large numbers of transactions or other events that are aggregated into classes according to their nature or function. The final stage in this process is the presentation of condensed and classified data which form line items in the financial statements. If a line item is not individually material, it is aggregated with other items either in those statements or in the notes. An item that is not sufficiently material to warrant separate presentation in those statements may warrant separate presentation in the notes. [IAS 1:30]

Specifically:

[IAS 1:30A & 31]

- entities are required to decide, taking into consideration all relevant facts and circumstances, how they aggregate information in the financial statements, including the notes;

- an entity should not reduce the understandability of its financial statements by obscuring material information with immaterial information, or by aggregating material items that have different natures or functions;

- entities need not provide a specific disclosure required by an IFRS (including disclosures required in the notes) if the information resulting from that disclosure is immaterial. This is the case even if the IFRS lists specific requirements or describes them as 'minimum' requirements; and

- entities should consider whether additional disclosures are necessary when compliance with the specific requirements in IFRSs is insufficient to enable users of financial statements to understand the impact of particular transactions, other events and conditions on their finanical position and financial performance.

2.8 Offsetting

Assets and liabilities, and income and expenses, are not offset unless required or permitted by an IFRS. [IAS 1:32] This basic principle is supplemented by some further guidance in IAS 1, as described in the remainder of this section. IAS 32 *Financial Instruments: Presentation* sets out more detailed requirements regarding the offset of financial assets and financial liabilities (see **section 6** of **chapter B11** or, for entities that have not yet adopted IFRS 9, **section 6** of **chapter C12**).

It is important that assets and liabilities, and income and expenses, are reported separately. Offsetting in the statements of comprehensive income or financial position, except when this reflects the substance of the transactions or other events, detracts from the ability of users both to understand the transactions (or other events or conditions) that have occurred and to assess the entity's future cash flows. Measuring assets net of valuation allowances (e.g. inventories or receivables) is not regarded as offsetting for the purposes of applying IAS 1. [IAS 1:33]

Example 2.8

Presentation of withholding tax on revenue from investments

Company A pays dividends to Company B. Company B receives a net amount because Company A is required to deduct withholding tax on dividends and to pay the amount deducted to the tax authorities on Company B's behalf.

It is not acceptable for Company B to present its dividend revenue net of the tax withheld. Withholding tax is generally taken to mean tax on dividends (or other income) that has been deducted by the payer of the income (Company A) and is paid over to the tax authorities on behalf of the recipient of the dividends (Company B), so that the recipient receives the net amount. When the withholding tax is tax actually suffered by Company B, it is appropriate to recognise the incoming dividends at an amount that is gross of the withholding tax and to present the tax withheld as part of the tax expense. Therefore, dividends from investments should be presented on a gross basis.

IAS 1:82(d) requires a specific line item for tax expense to be presented in the statement of comprehensive income (see **5.1**). It follows that this line item should include all tax expenses, including withholding taxes suffered.

IFRS 15 *Revenue from Contracts with Customers* (see **chapter A14**) requires an entity to measure revenue from contracts with customers at the amount of consideration to which the entity expects to be entitled in exchange for transferring promised goods or services. For example, the amount of revenue recognised reflects any trade discounts and volume rebates allowed to the customer. Other transactions may be undertaken that do not generate revenue but are incidental to the main revenue-generating activities. The results of such transactions are presented by netting any income and related expenses arising from the same transaction when this reflects the substance of the transactions or other events. For example:

[IAS 1:34]

- gains and losses on disposal of non-current assets, including investments and operating assets, are reported by deducting from the amount of consideration on disposal the carrying amount and related selling expenses; and

- expenditure related to a provision that is recognised in accordance with IAS 37 *Provisions, Contingent Liabilities and Contingent Assets* and reimbursed under a contractual arrangement with a third party (e.g. a supplier's warranty agreement) may be netted against the related reimbursement.

IAS 1:34 was amended in May 2014 by consequential amendments arising from IFRS 15. The amendments replace the terminology of IAS 18 *Revenue* but, in the context of IAS 1:34, do not have any substantive effect.

Also, gains and losses arising from a group of similar transactions are reported on a net basis. For example, foreign exchange gains and losses, and gains and losses arising on financial instruments held for trading, are presented net although they should be reported separately if material. [IAS 1:35]

2.9 Frequency of reporting

2.9.1 Requirement to present financial statements at least 'annually'

IAS 1:36 states that a complete set of financial statements, including comparative information, should be presented at least 'annually'. However, as evidenced by the disclosure requirements of IAS 1:36 (see **2.9.2**), the Standard clearly envisages that the financial statements may cover a period longer or shorter than twelve months.

IFRSs do not provide a definition for an 'annual' reporting period. However, they do provide a definition for an interim period – it is a "financial reporting period shorter than a full financial year" (see IAS 34:4). Therefore, the key feature that distinguishes annual financial statements from interim financial statements is that the former cover a full *financial* year.

The circumstances in which a financial year can be longer or shorter than 12 months will generally be specified by local laws or regulations. Most commonly, a longer or shorter period will be permitted when there is a formal change in reporting date, or when an entity is presenting first-year or cessation financial statements.

Frequently, the transition provisions of new Standards and amendments to Standards refer to application for 'annual periods beginning on or after' a specified date. The reference to 'annual' periods in this context (which is intended to create a distinction from interim periods) is consistent with the reference to reporting 'annually' in IAS 1:36; an annual period for this purpose might therefore be a period of more or less than 12 months.

For practical reasons, some entities prefer to report on a 52/53 week basis (e.g. always to the last Saturday in the month). IAS 1 does not preclude this practice. [IAS 1:37]

2.9.2 Disclosures required when the end of the reporting period is changed

When the end of the reporting period is changed and the financial statements are presented for a period that is longer or shorter than one year, IAS 1 requires the following to be disclosed:

[IAS 1:36]

- the period covered by the financial statements;
- the reason for using a longer or shorter period; and
- the fact that the amounts presented in the financial statements are not entirely comparable.

2.10 Comparative information

2.10.1 Comparative information – general requirements

Except when IFRSs permit or require otherwise, comparative information in respect of the preceding period should be presented for all amounts reported in the financial statements. [IAS 1:38]

An entity is required to present the following statements, as a minimum, together with related notes:

[IAS 1:38A]

- two statements of financial position;
- two statements of profit or loss and other comprehensive income;
- two separate statements of profit or loss (if presented);
- two statements of cash flows; and
- two statements of changes in equity.

2.10.2 Comparative information for narrative and descriptive information

Comparative information is included for narrative and descriptive information if it is relevant to understanding the current period's financial statements. [IAS 1:38]

Narrative information provided in the financial statements for the preceding period(s) may continue, in some cases, to be relevant in the current period. IAS 1 gives the example of a legal dispute, the outcome of which was uncertain at the end of the preceding period and is yet to be resolved. Users of the financial statements may benefit from the disclosure of information that the uncertainty existed at the end of the preceding period and from the disclosure of information about the steps that have been taken during the current period to resolve the uncertainty. [IAS 1:38B]

> The example given in IAS 1:38B is not particularly helpful because it suggests that the uncertainty has yet to be resolved and, therefore, it is clear that some disclosure would be required in the current year. A better example might be when the legal claim had been settled in

the current year. In this case, it is likely that some disclosure would be judged relevant to an understanding of the current period's financial statements but the level of detail provided might be less than in the previous year given that the uncertainties have been resolved.

2.10.3 Additional comparative information

An entity may present comparative information in addition to the minimum required under IAS 1:38A (see **2.10.1**). [IAS 1:38C]

Such additional information might include, for example:

[IAS 1:BC32E]

- additional information that is presented voluntarily; and

- additional comparative information that is required by law or other regulations.

If additional comparative information is presented:

[IAS 1:38C]

- the information must be prepared in accordance with IFRSs;

- the information may consist of one or more statements referred to in IAS 1:10 (see **2.4.1**), but need not comprise a complete set of financial statements; and

- related note information should be presented for the additional statements.

IAS 1 cites as an example an entity that presents a third statement of profit or loss and other comprehensive income (i.e. it presents the statement for the current period, the preceding period and one additional comparative period). In such circumstances, the entity is not required to present a third statement of financial position, a third statement of cash flows or a third statement of changes in equity. However, the entity is required to present supporting notes for the additional statement of profit or loss and other comprehensive income. [IAS 1:38D]

2.10.4 Third statement of financial position required in specified circumstances

2.10.4.1 Circumstances when a third statement of financial position is required to be presented

In specified circumstances, an entity is required to present a third statement of financial position as at the beginning of the preceding period in addition to the minimum comparative financial statements listed in IAS 1:38A (see **2.10.1**). This requirement applies when:

[IAS 1:40A]

- an entity applies an accounting policy retrospectively, makes a retrospective restatement of items in its financial statements or reclassifies items in its financial statements; and

- the retrospective application, retrospective restatement or the reclassification has a material effect on the information in the statement of financial position at the beginning of the preceding period.

Regardless of whether a third statement of financial position is required, an entity should provide the disclosures required under IAS 8 *Accounting Policies, Changes in Accounting Estimates and Errors* regarding the impact of changes in accounting policies and other restatements (see **chapter A5**). IAS 1:41 sets out specific requirements when an entity has reclassified comparative amounts (see **2.10.5.2**).

2.10.4.2 Dates at which statements of financial position are required to be presented

In the circumstances described in IAS 1:40A (see **2.10.4.1**), an entity is required to present statements of financial position as at:

[IAS 1:40B]

- the end of the current period;

- the end of the preceding period; and

- the beginning of the preceding period.

When presented, the date of the third statement of financial position is always at the beginning of the preceding period, regardless of whether the financial statements present comparative information for earlier periods. [IAS 1:40D]

2.10.4.3 What is meant by a 'reclassification' in the context of the requirement for a third statement of financial position?

It appears that the phrase 'reclassifies items in its financial statements' in IAS 1:40A (see **2.10.4.1**) is intended to capture the types of 'reclassification' described in IAS 1:41 (see **section 2.10.5**). In stating that the third statement of financial position is only required if it is materially affected by the reclassification, IAS 1:40A is clear that the following prospective event-driven reclassifications, for example, are not captured, because they do not affect the third statement of financial position:

- reclassification of an asset or a liability from non-current to current under IAS 1 because of the passage of time;

- for entities applying IAS 39 *Financial Instruments: Recognition and Measurement*, reclassification of a financial asset from the held-to-maturity to the available-for-sale category and vice versa;

- for entities applying IAS 39, reclassification of cumulative gains or losses on an available-for-sale financial asset from equity to profit or loss as a reclassification adjustment on impairment or disposal of the asset;

- classification of an operation as discontinued with reclassification of the comparative period statement of comprehensive income; and

- reclassification of a property from inventories to investment property on commencement of an operating lease to another party.

2.10.4.4 Application of the requirement for a third statement of financial position to regulatory filings

Example 2.10.4.4

Application of the requirement for a third statement of financial position to regulatory filings

Entity A with a calendar year end prepares its financial statements in accordance with IFRSs. Entity A's securities are listed on a regulated exchange which requires two statements of financial position and three statements of comprehensive income and cash flows to be presented in the financial statements.

Scenario 1

In its 20X8 financial statements, Entity A has not applied an accounting policy retrospectively or made a retrospective restatement or reclassification requiring the presentation of a third statement of financial position at the beginning of the preceding period (i.e. as at 1 January 20X7) under IAS 1:40A.

As required by its regulator, Entity A presents statements of comprehensive income and cash flows for each of the years ending 31 December 20X8, 20X7 and 20X6.

Entity A is not required to present three statements of financial position. The third statements of comprehensive income and cash flows presented in respect of the earliest comparative period are supplementary information for regulatory purposes only. As clarified in IAS 1:38C (see **2.10.3**), Entity A is only required under IAS 1:38 and 38A to present one year of comparative information for its 20X8 statement of financial position.

Scenario 2

In its 20X9 financial statements, Entity A makes a retrospective restatement that materially affects the statement of financial position at 1 January 20X8.

As a result, IAS 1:40A requires the presentation of an additional statement of financial position at the beginning of the preceding period (i.e. at 1 January 20X8). For regulatory purposes, Entity A also presents the third statements of comprehensive income and cash flows for the year ending 31 December 20X7.

Entity A is not required to present a fourth statement of financial position at 1 January 20X7. As clarified by IAS 1:40D (see **2.10.4.2**), the additional statement of financial position is only required at the beginning of the preceding period (in this example, 20X8), not at the beginning of the earliest period presented (in this example, 20X7). It is acceptable for Entity A to present four statements of financial position if it chooses to do so, but this is not required.

2.10.4.5   Note disclosures required to support a third statement of financial position

When an entity is required to present an additional statement of financial position as at the beginning of the preceding period in accordance with IAS 1:40A, it need not present notes supporting that opening statement of financial position. [IAS 1:40C]

However, in the circumstances when an additional statement of position is required to be presented, the entity is required to disclose the information required by IAS 1:41 to 44 (see **section 2.10.5**) and also to comply with the relevant disclosure requirements of IAS 8 *Accounting Policies, Changes in Accounting Estimates and Errors* (see **chapter A5**). [IAS 1:40C]

2.10.5   Reclassification of comparative amounts

2.10.5.1   Requirement to reclassify comparative amounts

If the presentation or classification of items in the financial statements is amended, comparative amounts are reclassified unless this is impracticable. [IAS 1:41]

2.10.5.2   Disclosures required when comparative amounts are reclassified

When comparative amounts are reclassified, the following information is required to be disclosed (including as at the beginning of the preceding period):

[IAS 1:41]

• the nature of the reclassification;

• the amount of each item or class of items that is reclassified; and

• the reason for the reclassification.

2.10.5.3 When is it 'impracticable' to reclassify comparative amounts?

Applying a requirement is impracticable for this purpose "when the entity cannot apply it after making every reasonable effort to do so". [IAS 1:7]

Enhancing the inter-period comparability of information assists users in making economic decisions, especially by allowing the assessment of trends in financial information for predictive purposes. But in some circumstances it is impracticable to reclassify comparative information to achieve comparability. For example, data may not have been collected in the prior period in a way that allows reclassification and it may be impracticable to recreate the information. [IAS 1:43]

It is not appropriate to conclude that restatement is impracticable merely because of the cost or effort involved. When revising IAS 1 in 2003, the IASB considered replacing the exemption from restating comparative amounts on the basis of 'impracticability' with one based on 'undue cost or effort'. However, based on comments received on the exposure draft, the IASB decided that an exemption based on management's assessment of undue cost or effort was too subjective to be applied consistently by different entities. The IASB decided that balancing costs and benefits was a task for the Board when it sets accounting requirements rather than for entities when they apply those requirements. Therefore, although IAS 1 does not explicitly state that undue cost or effort does not alone make restatement impracticable, this is the clear intention of the Board and is consistent with the definition of 'impracticable' in IAS 1:7. [IAS 1:BC34 - BC36]

2.10.5.4 Is it necessary to label reclassified comparative amounts as 'restated'?

When comparative amounts have been restated in accordance with IAS 1:41, there is no explicit requirement for columns of comparative information to be headed up (e.g. as 'represented', 'restated' or 'adjusted'), although the inclusion of such headings is common practice. Whether the comparative information should be headed up in this way depends on the significance of the change (e.g. its impact on either the entity's results or equity). In each case, it is a matter of judgement and consideration of any local regulatory requirements.

Irrespective of whether comparative information is headed up as discussed above, entities are required to provide the disclosures regarding reclassified comparative amounts set out in IAS 1:41 (see **2.10.5.2**).

2.10.5.5   Disclosures required when it is impracticable to reclassify comparative amounts

When it is impracticable to reclassify comparative amounts, disclosure is required of:

[IAS 1:42]

* the reason for not reclassifying the amounts; and
* the nature of the adjustments that would have been made if the amounts had been reclassified.

2.10.5.6   IAS 8 requirements for adjusting comparative amounts

IAS 8 sets out adjustments to comparative information required when an entity changes an accounting policy or corrects an error (see **chapter A5**). [IAS 1:44]

> The reference to the more specific requirements of IAS 8 within IAS 1 appears to envisage that it is possible to have a 'reclassification' that is not a change in accounting policy. No examples are provided in IAS 1.

2.11   Consistency of presentation

The presentation and classification of items in the financial statements should be retained from one period to the next unless:

[IAS 1:45]

* it is apparent, following a significant change in the nature of the entity's operations (e.g. a major acquisition or disposal) or a review of its financial statements, that another presentation or classification would be more appropriate having regard to the criteria for selection and application of accounting policies in IAS 8 *Accounting Policies, Changes in Accounting Estimates and Errors* (see **section 3.1** of **chapter A5**); or
* an IFRS requires a change in presentation.

The presentation of the financial statements is changed only if the changed presentation provides information that is reliable and is more relevant to users of the financial statements and the revised structure is likely to continue, so that comparability is not impaired. When making such a change of presentation, the comparative information is reclassified in accordance with IAS 1:41 and 42 (see **section 2.10.5**). [IAS 1:46]

2.12   General requirements regarding disclosure and presentation

IAS 1 requires particular disclosures in the statement of financial position, the statement(s) presenting profit or loss and other comprehensive income, and the statement of changes in equity. It also requires disclosure of other line items either in those statements or in the notes. Presentation and disclosure requirements for the statement of cash flows are contained in IAS 7 (see **chapter A21**). [IAS 1:47]

IAS 1 sometimes uses the term 'disclosure' in a broad sense, encompassing items presented in the financial statements. Disclosures are also required by other IFRSs. Unless specified to the contrary in IAS 1 or another IFRS, such disclosures may be made in the financial statements. [IAS 1:48]

The intention of this paragraph in IAS 1 (as revised in 2007) is not very clear from its wording. However, the equivalent paragraph in the previous version of the Standard made the point much more clearly that, unless specified otherwise, disclosures may be made either on the face of statements such as the statement of profit or loss and the statement of financial position, or in the notes.

IAS 1 does not prescribe a fixed format for the presentation of the statement of comprehensive income, the statement of financial position and the statement of changes in equity. It does, however, set out line items that should be presented in those statements (see **section 5**, **4.4** and **section 6**, respectively). In addition, it establishes further items that may be presented either in those financial statements or in the notes (see **5.4** and **4.5**).

The illustrative financial statements accompanying IAS 1 include examples of ways in which the requirements for the statement of profit or loss and other comprehensive income, the statement of financial position and the statement of changes in equity might be presented in the primary financial statements. These are illustrative only and the order of presentation and the descriptions used for line items should be changed when necessary to achieve a fair presentation in an entity's particular circumstances.

2.13 Identification of the financial statements

2.13.1 *Financial statements to be distinguished from other information*

The financial statements should be identified clearly and distinguished from other information in the same published document. [IAS 1:49] IFRSs apply only to financial statements. They do not necessarily apply to other information provided in an annual report, a regulatory filing or other document. Therefore, it is important that users can distinguish information that is prepared using IFRSs from other information that may be useful to users but is not subject to those requirements. [IAS 1:50]

Information given outside of the financial statements may be subject to separate regulatory requirements. For example, there may be a requirement for such information to be consistent with the financial statements.

2.13.2 Information required to describe financial statements

IAS 1 requires that each financial statement and the notes should be identified clearly. In addition, the following information is required to be 'displayed prominently' and repeated when it is necessary for the information presented to be understandable:

[IAS 1:51]

- the name of the reporting entity or other means of identification;

- any change in that information from the end of the preceding reporting period;

- whether the financial statements are of an individual entity or a group of entities;

- the date of the end of the reporting period or the period covered by the set of financial statements or notes;

- the presentation currency, as defined in IAS 21 *The Effects of Changes in Foreign Exchange Rates*; and

- the level of rounding used in presenting amounts in the financial statements (see **2.13.3**).

IAS 1 explains that these requirements are normally met by presenting appropriate headings for pages, statements, notes, columns and the like. Judgement is required in determining the best way of presenting such information. For example, when the financial statements are presented electronically, separate pages are not always used. The items listed above are then presented to ensure a proper understanding of the information. [IAS 1:52]

2.13.3 Amounts may be rounded to enhance understandability

Financial statements may be made more understandable by presenting information in thousands or millions of units of the presentation currency. This is acceptable as long as the level of rounding is disclosed and material information is not omitted. [IAS 1:53]

Different levels of rounding may be appropriate for different disclosures. For example, while it may be appropriate to disclose line items in the statements of financial position and comprehensive income in millions of units of the presentation currency for a very large group, a greater level of detail is likely to be necessary for disclosure of management remuneration and some other related party transactions. In all cases, the level of rounding should be disclosed and care should be exercised to ensure that no material disclosures are omitted.

3 Fair presentation and compliance with IFRSs

3.1 Requirement for fair presentation

Financial statements should present fairly the financial position, financial performance and cash flows of an entity. Fair presentation requires the faithful representation of the effects of transactions, other events and conditions in accordance with the definitions and recognition criteria set out in the Conceptual Framework. The application of IFRSs, with additional disclosure when necessary, is presumed to result in financial statements that achieve a fair presentation. [IAS 1:15]

3.2 Compliance with IFRSs

3.2.1 Financial statements to include an explicit and unreserved statement of compliance with IFRSs

IAS 1 requires an entity whose financial statements comply with IFRSs to make an explicit and unreserved statement of such compliance in the notes. Financial statements should not be described as complying with IFRSs unless they comply with all of the requirements of IFRSs. [IAS 1:16]

An entity cannot claim compliance with IFRSs if it states that it complies with IFRSs 'except for' one or more Standards. Compliance with IFRSs is clearly defined in IAS 1:16 which, taken together with the requirements of paragraphs 11 and 12 of IAS 8 *Accounting Policies, Changes in Accounting Estimates and Errors*, means that financial statements must:

- comply with relevant IASs and IFRSs;

- comply with all relevant IFRICs and SICs; and

- in the absence of specific guidance in IFRSs:

    - apply by analogy other IFRSs;

    - apply the IASB's *Conceptual Framework for Financial Reporting*; or

    - apply pronouncements of national standard-setters to the extent that these are consistent with other IFRSs, other SICs, other IFRICs and the IASB's *Conceptual Framework for Financial Reporting*.

Financial statements should not be described as complying with IFRSs unless they comply with all the applicable requirements.

3.2.2   Departures from IFRSs necessary to comply with national law

Financial statements should not be described as complying with IFRSs when they involve departures from IFRSs that are necessary to comply with national law. For example, consider an entity that is incorporated in a country where legislation does not permit unrealised gains to be reported in profit or loss. The entity prepares its financial statements in compliance with IFRSs including measuring derivatives at fair value; however, to comply with the national laws, fair value gains on those derivatives are taken directly to equity and are not recognised in profit or loss until the derivatives are derecognised. The entity cannot claim compliance with IFRSs. The fact that an entity is prevented by legislation from complying with IFRSs does not change the requirement in IFRSs.

3.3   Substance over form

Prior to the September 2010 release of sections of the IASB's *Conceptual Framework for Financial Reporting* (see **chapter A2**), the Board's predecessor framework (the *Framework for the Preparation and Presentation of Financial Statements*) stated that "[i]n order to ensure a faithful representation, transactions and other events should be accounted for and presented in accordance with their substance and economic reality, and not merely their legal form". This reference to 'substance over form' has been omitted from the *Conceptual Framework for Financial Reporting* because the Board determined that 'substance over form' should not be presented as a separate component of faithful representation because it would be redundant (see **5.1** in **chapter A2**). However, as part of its May 2015 proposals for revisions to the Conceptual Framework (see **section 9** of **chapter A2**), the IASB proposes to reintroduce guidance on this topic.

For the vast majority of routine transactions, substance and form will be the same, and the application of the principle of substance over form will not alter the established method of accounting. However, there will be transactions for which the substance and the legal form differ, or for which the substance is not readily apparent. In practice, common features of such transactions often include:

- the deliberate separation of legal title and the underlying benefits (e.g. leases, consignment inventories, factored debts and the use of structured or special purpose entities);

- options granted for which the exercise of the option can be considered a virtual certainty (e.g. sale with put and call options to repurchase); and

- a series of transactions designed so that the commercial effect can only be appreciated when the series is taken as a whole (e.g. securitisations, project financing and circular finance structures).

The key to accounting in accordance with the principle of substance over form is to obtain a full understanding of the rationale behind the transaction as a whole, including the role of each of the parties, and the commercial logic for their involvement. This requires:

- a realistic appreciation of why the transaction exists and why each party is involved. In determining the substance of a transaction, all of its aspects and implications should be identified and greater weight given to those more likely to have a commercial effect in practice;

- placing the transaction in context. A group or series of transactions that achieves or is designed to achieve an overall commercial effect should be viewed as a whole;

- an assessment of what has been achieved by the transaction. To determine the substance of a transaction, it is necessary to establish whether it has given rise to new assets or liabilities for the reporting entity or whether it has changed the entity's existing assets or liabilities;

- identification of the risk-takers. Evidence that an entity has rights or other access to benefits (and hence has an asset) is provided if the entity is exposed to the risks inherent in the benefits, taking into account the likelihood of those risks having a commercial effect in practice. Similarly, evidence that an entity has an obligation to transfer benefits (and hence has a liability) is given if there is some circumstance in which the entity is unable to avoid, legally or commercially, an outflow of benefits; and

- a realistic appraisal of conditional events. When a transaction incorporates one or more options, guarantees or conditional provisions, their commercial effect should be assessed in the context of all of the aspects and implications of the transaction, in order to determine what assets and liabilities exist.

In practice, the following analysis will assist in understanding the commercial effects of the transaction:

- obtain all relevant documentation and agreements, including side letters, which affect the likely course of events. Documents should always be in final form and include monetary details when relevant;

- identify the role played by each party to the transaction (in particular, the equity participants to a transaction) and the reason for their involvement. It is reasonable to suppose that a financial institution will limit its interest to that of financier – any assertion to the contrary should be supported by clear evidence. If a transaction appears to lack logic from the point of view of one or more participants, then it is likely that either all of the relevant parts of the transaction have not been identified, or that the commercial effect of some aspect of the transaction has been incorrectly assessed;

- assess the likely course of action (including options) – place greater emphasis on the probable course of events and, accordingly, little or no emphasis on unlikely events. The consequences of liquidation of one of the parties should only be considered when this is a likely event; and

- test the transaction's responsiveness, and the return for each participant, in the event of marginal changes in variables, such as interest rates, asset values and the timing of events. This provides useful insight into the role of the parties involved (e.g. whether a participant obtains a risk-taker's return or a financier's return).

3.4   Fair presentation generally achieved by compliance with IFRSs

In virtually all circumstances, a fair presentation is achieved by compliance with applicable IFRSs. A fair presentation also requires an entity:

[IAS 1:17]

- to select and apply accounting policies in accordance with IAS 8 *Accounting Policies, Changes in Accounting Estimates and Errors*, which sets out a hierarchy of authoritative guidance that management considers in the absence of an IFRS that specifically applies to the item (see **chapter A5**);

- to present information, including accounting policies, in a manner that provides relevant, reliable, comparable and understandable information; and

- to provide additional disclosures when compliance with the specific requirements in IFRSs is insufficient to enable users to understand the impact of particular transactions, other events or conditions on the entity's financial position or financial performance.

Inappropriate accounting policies are not rectified either by disclosure of the accounting policies used or by notes or explanatory material. [IAS 1:18]

3.5 Required departures from IFRSs

3.5.1 Departure from IFRSs required when compliance would be misleading

In extremely rare circumstances, management may conclude that compliance with a requirement in an IFRS would be so misleading that it would conflict with the objective of financial statements set out in the IASB's *Conceptual Framework for Financial Reporting*. In such circumstances, IAS 1 requires the entity to depart from that requirement "if the relevant regulatory framework requires, or otherwise does not prohibit, such a departure". [IAS 1:19]

IAS 1 explains that an item of information would conflict with the objective of financial statements when it does not represent faithfully the transactions, other events and conditions that it either purports to represent or could reasonably be expected to represent and, consequently, it would be likely to influence economic decisions made by users of financial statements. When assessing whether complying with a specific requirement of an IFRS would be so misleading that it would conflict with the objective of financial statements set out in the Conceptual Framework, management should consider:

[IAS 1:24]

- why the objective of financial statements is not achieved in the particular circumstances; and

- how the entity's circumstances differ from those of other entities that comply with the requirement. If other entities in similar circumstances comply with the requirement, there is a rebuttable presumption that the entity's compliance with the requirement would not be so misleading that it would conflict with the objective of financial statements set out in the Conceptual Framework.

3.5.2 Disclosures required when a departure is made from IFRSs

When a departure is made from a requirement of an IFRS in the circumstances described in **3.5.1**, the following disclosures are required:

[IAS 1:20]

- a statement that management has concluded that the financial statements present fairly the entity's financial position, financial performance and cash flows;

- a statement that the entity has complied with applicable IFRSs, except that it has departed from a particular requirement to achieve a fair presentation;

- the title of the IFRS from which there has been a departure;

- the nature of the departure, including the treatment that the IFRS would require;

- the reason why that treatment would be so misleading in the circumstances that it would conflict with the objective of financial statements set out in the Conceptual Framework;

- the treatment adopted; and

- for each period presented, the financial effect of the departure on each item in the financial statements that would have been reported in complying with the requirement.

3.5.3   Disclosures required when there was a departure in a prior period

IAS 1 also requires disclosures to be made when there was a departure from a requirement of a Standard or an Interpretation in a prior period that affects the amounts recognised in the financial statements for the current period. In such cases, the disclosures listed in **3.5.2** should be made excluding the first two items. [IAS 1:21 - 22]

3.6   Compliance with IFRSs misleading but regulatory framework prohibits departure from IFRSs

IAS 1 specifies additional disclosures that apply in those extremely rare circumstances in which management concludes that compliance with a requirement in a Standard or an Interpretation would be so misleading that it would conflict with the objective of financial statements set out in the Conceptual Framework but the relevant regulatory framework prohibits departure from the requirement. In such circumstances, the entity should, to the extent possible, reduce the perceived misleading aspects of compliance by disclosing:

[IAS 1:23]

- the title of the IFRS in question;

- the nature of the requirement;

- the reason why management has concluded that complying with that requirement is so misleading in the circumstances that it conflicts with the objectives of financial statements set out in the Conceptual Framework; and

- for each period presented, the adjustments to each item in the financial statements that management has concluded would be necessary to achieve a fair presentation.

IAS 1:BC28 explains that departing from a requirement in a Standard or an Interpretation when considered necessary to achieve a fair presentation would conflict with the regulatory framework in some jurisdictions. But the departure would be required (and not just permitted) by IAS 1 when the relevant conditions are met. Arguably, this is no more of a departure from a Standard than when an exemption is given in specified circumstances. However, the IASB acknowledged these concerns and drafted IAS 1 to enable entities to comply with the requirements of the Standard when the relevant regulatory framework prohibits departures from accounting standards, while retaining the principle that entities should, to the extent possible, ensure that financial statements provide a fair presentation.

4 Statement of financial position

4.1 Presentation of assets and liabilities

4.1.1 *General requirement to distinguish between current and non-current assets and liabilities*

Current and non-current assets, and current and non-current liabilities, are generally presented as separate classifications in the statement of financial position. This is subject to an exception when a presentation based on liquidity provides information that is reliable and is more relevant (see **4.1.2**). [IAS 1:60]

The definitions of 'current assets' and 'current liabilities' are set out in **4.2.1** and **4.3.1**, respectively.

4.1.2 *Presentation of assets and liabilities based on liquidity when appropriate*

For some entities (e.g. financial institutions), a presentation of assets and liabilities in increasing or decreasing order of liquidity provides information that is reliable and is more relevant than a current/non-current presentation. This is because the entity does not supply goods or services within a clearly identifiable operating cycle (see **4.1.4**). [IAS 1:63]

4.1.3 *Disclosure required of amount expected to be recovered or settled after more than twelve months*

Whichever method of presentation is adopted (i.e. current/non-current or liquidity – see **4.1.1** and **4.1.2**, respectively), for each asset and liability line item that combines amounts expected to be recovered or settled:

[IAS 1:61]

- no more than twelve months after the reporting period; and
- more than twelve months after the reporting period,

the amount expected to be recovered or settled after more than twelve months should be disclosed.

> This disclosure may be given in the notes and does not have to be in the statement of financial position itself.

4.1.4   Consideration of an entity's operating cycle – general

When an entity supplies goods or services within a clearly identifiable operating cycle, separate classification of current and non-current assets and liabilities provides useful information by distinguishing the net assets that are continually circulating as working capital from those used in the entity's long term operations. It also highlights assets that are expected to be realised within the current operating cycle and liabilities that are due for settlement within that same period. [IAS 1:62]

The operating cycle of an entity is the time between the acquisition of assets for processing and their realisation in cash or cash equivalents. When an entity's normal operating cycle is not clearly identifiable, its duration is assumed to be twelve months. [IAS 1:68]

4.1.5   Mixed basis of presentation permitted

IAS 1 permits an entity to present some assets and liabilities using a current/non-current classification (see **4.1.1**) and others in order of liquidity (see **4.1.2**) when this provides information that is reliable and more relevant. [IAS 1:64]

> IAS 1 states that such a mixed basis may be appropriate "when an entity has diverse operations". In practice, it is likely to be a combination of financial and non-financial operations, rather than just 'diversity', that would make such an approach necessary.

4.1.6   Information to be disclosed about the expected realisation dates of assets and liabilities

Information about the expected realisation dates of assets and liabilities is useful in assessing liquidity and solvency. IFRS 7 *Financial Instruments: Disclosures* (see **chapter B11** or, for entities that have not yet adopted IFRS 9, **chapter C12**) requires disclosure of the maturity dates of financial assets and financial liabilities. Financial assets include trade and other receivables. Financial liabilities include trade and other payables. Information about the expected date of recovery of non-monetary assets such as inventories and the expected date of settlement for liabilities such as provisions is also useful, whether assets and liabilities are classified as current or as non-current. For example, the amount of inventories that is expected to be recovered more than twelve months after the reporting period should be disclosed. [IAS 1:65]

4.1.7 Presentation of employee benefits

4.1.7.1 No requirement to distinguish between current and non-current portions of post-employment benefits

When an entity uses a current/non-current distinction to present the statement of financial position (i.e. rather than a liquidity presentation), it is not required to analyse assets and liabilities arising from post-employment benefits accounted for under IAS 19 *Employee Benefits* between current and non-current, either in the statement of financial position or in the notes.

IAS 19:133 states that the Standard does not specify whether an entity should distinguish current and non-current portions of assets and liabilities arising from post-employment benefits. IAS 19:BC200 states that the IASC (the IASB's predecessor) decided not to specify whether an entity should distinguish between the current and non-current portions of such assets and liabilities because such a distinction may sometimes be arbitrary.

Although IAS 1 has not been modified to reflect this exemption, the more specific references of IAS 19 apply. Similarly, IAS 1:61 (see **4.1.3**) is not considered to require separate disclosure of the portions of the employment benefit assets and liabilities that are expected to be recovered or settled before and after twelve months from the end of the reporting period because the concepts of 'recovery' and 'settlement' for such assets and liabilities are unclear.

IAS 19 requires the disclosure of the employer's best estimate of contributions expected to be paid to defined benefit plans during the annual period beginning after the reporting period, as soon as that information can reasonably be determined (see IAS 19:147(b)).

4.1.7.2 Requirement to distinguish between current and non-current portions of other employee benefits

The exemption in IAS 19:133 discussed in **4.1.7.1** applies only to post-employment benefits. There is no exemption from the requirements in IAS 1 for short-term and other long-term employee benefit liabilities such as annual leave, long-term disability leave and long-service leave. In respect of such benefits:

- to the extent that employees are entitled to take their annual/long-service leave in the next twelve months, whether they are expected to take it or not, the liability should be presented as a 'current' liability. The entity does not have an unconditional right to defer settlement of the liability for at least twelve months after the end of the reporting period;

- to the extent that employees are not entitled to take a portion of their annual/long-service leave during the next twelve months because, for example, additional years of service must first be rendered (i.e. the leave has not yet vested), and the employer is not expected to allow such leave to be taken early, that portion should be presented as a 'non-current' liability; and

- employees do not have an unconditional right to long-term disability benefits. Those rights arise when employees fall ill. IAS 19:157 requires the measurement for long-term disability benefits to reflect the probability of payment/right arising. Consistent with this is a split between 'current' and 'non-current' based on the expected payment profile at the end of the reporting period.

4.1.7.3   Classification of employee benefits – relationship to current/non-current distinction

The definitions of short-term and 'other long-term' employee benefits set out in IAS 19:8 are as follows (emphasis added).

- *Short-term employee benefits* are "employee benefits (other than termination benefits) that are expected to be settled wholly before twelve months after the end of the annual reporting period in which the employees render the related service".

- *Other long-term employee benefits* are "all employee benefits other than short-term employee benefits, post-employment benefits and termination benefits".

Therefore, the focus in IAS 19 is on the timing of the *expected* settlement, rather than on when the benefits are *due to be settled*. Classification on this basis is different from the basis for presentation as current and non-current under IAS 1 (see **section 4.3**). This difference will not have any effect when a benefit cannot be carried forward beyond twelve months from the end of the annual period in which it is earned (both the 'expected' and the 'due' settlement dates are within twelve months). It will have an effect when employees are entitled to carry forward a benefit beyond twelve months from the end of the annual period in which it is earned (e.g. in some cases, unused holiday entitlement) and some employees are expected to do so, but the employees are also entitled to immediate settlement (e.g. if they were to leave the entity's employment). Under IAS 19, such a benefit is classified as an other long-term employee benefit even though, under IAS 1, it is presented entirely as a current liability.

4.1.8   Presentation of derivatives

The presentation of derivatives in the statement of financial position is considered generally in **section 5** of **chapter B4** (or, for entities that have not yet adopted IFRS 9, **section 5** of **chapter C4**). Guidance on the presentation of embedded derivatives is set out in **section 13** of **chapter B5** (or, for entities that have not yet adopted IFRS 9, **section 13** of **chapter C5**).

4.1.9   Presentation of deferred tax assets and liabilities

When current and non-current assets and current and non-current liabilities are presented as separate classifications in the statement of financial position, deferred tax should not be classified as a current asset or a current liability. [IAS 1:56]

> Given that IAS 1 does not require deferred tax assets or liabilities to be analysed as current, it follows that an entity is not required to disclose under IAS 1:61 (see **4.1.3**) the amount of deferred tax assets (liabilities) that are expected to be recovered (settled) within twelve months after the reporting period. Such a disclosure requirement would negate the relief provided in IAS 1:56 (although such information may be presented if the entity wishes to do so).

4.2   Current assets

4.2.1   Current asset – definition

An asset is classified as a current asset when it satisfies any of the following criteria:

[IAS 1:66]

- it is expected to be realised in the entity's normal operating cycle;

- it is intended for sale or consumption in the entity's normal operating cycle;

- it is held primarily for the purpose of trading;

- it is expected to be realised within twelve months of the reporting period; or

- it is cash or a cash equivalent (as defined in IAS 7 *Statement of Cash Flows* – see **chapter A21**) unless it is restricted from being exchanged or used to settle a liability for at least twelve months after the reporting period.

4.2.2   Consideration of an entity's operating cycle – current assets

Current assets include assets (e.g. inventories and trade receivables) that are sold, consumed or realised as part of the normal operating cycle even when they are not expected to be realised within twelve months after the reporting period. Current assets also include assets primarily held for the purpose of trading (examples include some financial assets that meet the definition of held for trading in IFRS 9 or, for entities that have not yet adopted IFRS 9, IAS 39) and the current portion of non-current financial assets. [IAS 1:68]

Current assets include some, but not necessarily all, financial assets classified as held for trading in accordance with IFRS 9 (or, for entities that have not yet adopted IFRS 9, IAS 39). Further detail in the context of derivatives is given in **section 5** of **chapter B4** (or, for entities that have not yet adopted IFRS 9, **section 5** of **chapter C4**).

4.2.3   Entity holds assets related to different operating cycles

The IFRIC (now the IFRS Interpretations Committee) was asked to consider whether the 'normal operating cycle' criterion in IAS 1:66 (see **4.2.1**) applies only if an entity has a predominant operating cycle. This is particularly relevant to the inventories of conglomerates which, on a narrow reading of the wording, might always have to refer to the twelve-month criteria, rather than the operating-cycle criterion. As reported in the June 2005 *IFRIC Update*, the Committee decided not to consider the question further because, in its view, it was clear that the wording should be read in both the singular and the plural and that it is the nature of the asset in relation to the operating cycle that is relevant for classification. Furthermore, if an entity holds assets (e.g. inventories) related to different operating cycles, and it is material to readers' understanding of an entity's financial position, further information should be disclosed under the general requirements of IAS 1:57 (see **4.4.1**).

4.2.4   Assets classified as non-current

All assets other than those that meet the definition of a current asset in **4.2.1** are classified as non-current. [IAS 1:66]

IAS 1 uses the term 'non-current' to include tangible, intangible and financial assets of a long-term nature. It does not prohibit the use of alternative descriptions provided that the meaning is clear. [IAS 1:67]

4.3   Current liabilities

4.3.1   *Current liability – definition*

A liability is classified as a current liability when it satisfies any of the following criteria:

[IAS 1:69]

- it is expected to be settled in the entity's normal operating cycle;
- it is held primarily for the purposes of trading;
- it is due to be settled within twelve months after the reporting period; or
- the entity does not have an unconditional right to defer settlement of the liability for at least twelve months after the reporting period. Terms of a liability that could, at the option of the counterparty, result in its settlement by the issue of equity instruments do not affect its classification.

In February 2015, the IASB issued an exposure draft which proposes to clarify these criteria (see **section 8**).

4.3.2   *Consideration of an entity's operating cycle – current liabilities*

Some current liabilities, such as trade payables and some accruals for employee and other operating costs, are part of the working capital used in the entity's normal operating cycle. Such items are classified as current liabilities even if they are due to be settled more than twelve months after the reporting period. The same normal operating cycle applies to the classification of an entity's assets and liabilities. When the normal operating cycle is not clearly identifiable, its duration is assumed to be twelve months. [IAS 1:70]

Other current liabilities are not settled as part of the normal operating cycle but are due for settlement within twelve months after the reporting period or held primarily for the purpose of trading (examples include some financial liabilities classified as held for trading in accordance with IFRS 9 or, for entities that have not yet adopted IFRS 9, IAS 39), bank overdrafts, the current portion of non-current financial liabilities, dividends payable, income taxes and other non-trade payables). Financial liabilities that provide financing on a long-term basis (i.e. not working capital used in the normal operating cycle) and that are not due for settlement within twelve months after the reporting period are non-current liabilities. This is subject to an exception when the entity breaches an undertaking under a long-term loan arrangement (see **4.3.8**). [IAS 1:71]

Current liabilities include some, but not necessarily all, financial liabilities classified as held for trading in accordance with IFRS 9 (or, for entities that have not yet adopted IFRS 9, IAS 39). Further detail in the context of derivatives is given in **section 5** of **chapter B4** (or, for entities that have not yet adopted IFRS 9, **section 5** of **chapter C4**).

4.3.3 Refinancing agreed after the reporting period

Financial liabilities are classified as current when they are due to be settled within twelve months after the reporting period even if:

[IAS 1:72]

- the original term was for a period longer than twelve months; and

- an agreement to refinance, or to reschedule payments, on a long-term basis is completed after the reporting period and before the financial statements are authorised for issue.

Therefore, a refinancing after the reporting period should not to be taken into account in assessing whether a liability should be classified as current or non-current. As explained in IAS 1:BC44, the IASB concluded that the reporting of an entity's liquidity and solvency at the end of a reporting period should reflect contractual arrangements in force on that date. A refinancing after the reporting period is a non-adjusting event in accordance with IAS 10 *Events after the Reporting Period* and should not affect the presentation of the entity's statement of financial position.

4.3.4 Entity has the ability to refinance or roll over an obligation for at least twelve months after the reporting period

If an entity expects, and has the discretion, to refinance or roll over an obligation for at least twelve months after the reporting period under an existing loan facility, it classifies the obligation as non-current. This is so even if it would otherwise be due within a shorter period. But when refinancing or rolling over the obligation is not at the discretion of the entity (e.g. there is no arrangement for refinancing), the potential to refinance is not considered (and the obligation is therefore classified as current) (see **example 4.3.7.4**). [IAS 1:73]

4.3.5 Non-adjusting events after the reporting period

For loans classified as current liabilities, IAS 1 states that if the following events occur between the end of the reporting period and the date the financial statements are authorised for issue, those events are disclosed as non-adjusting events in accordance with IAS 10 *Events after the Reporting Period*:

[IAS 1:76]

- refinancing on a long-term basis;

- rectification of a breach of a long-term loan arrangement; and

- the granting by the lender of a period of grace to rectify a breach of a long-term loan arrangement ending at least twelve months after the reporting period.

4.3.6 Liabilities classified as non-current

All liabilities other than those that meet the definition of a current liability in **4.3.1** are classified as non-current. [IAS 1:69]

4.3.7 Current/non-current liabilities – examples

4.3.7.1 Classification of refundable deposits

Example 4.3.7.1

Classification of refundable deposits

A primary school requires a deposit to be paid upon enrolment into the school. Should the student leave the school, this deposit is refundable with one school-term's notice (four months). The majority of students enrol into just one primary school and, having completed the seven-year study period, receive the deposit back at the end of that seven-year period.

Despite the historical evidence that indicates that the majority of the deposits are only repaid after the seven-year period, the deposits are repayable on four months' notice. IAS 1:69 states that a liability should be classified as current when the entity does not have an unconditional right to defer settlement of the liability for at least twelve months after the reporting period. Therefore, the deposits should be classified as current liabilities.

It may be appropriate to disclose why the amounts are presented as current liabilities.

4.3.7.2 Classification of a callable term loan

Example 4.3.7.2

Classification of a callable term loan

Entity A borrows funds from Bank B for which repayment is scheduled over five years. However, Bank B retains a right (either by means of a specific clause in the loan agreement or by inclusion of a cross-reference to the bank's general terms of business) to call for repayment at any time without cause.

Should the loan be classified as current or non-current by Entity A?

The loan should be classified as current if the right to call for repayment at any time without cause is enforceable. IAS 1:69 (see **4.3.1**) requires that a liability should be classified as current if the borrowing entity "does not have an

---

> unconditional right [at the reporting date] to defer settlement of the liability for at least twelve months after the reporting period".
>
> This conclusion was confirmed by the IFRS Interpretations Committee in the November 2010 *IFRIC Update*.

4.3.7.3   Classification of non-derivative financial liabilities

The following example considers the situation in which the amortised cost of a liability at the end of the reporting period exceeds its principal amount (e.g. due to accrued unpaid interest).

Example 4.3.7.3

Classification of non-derivative financial liabilities

An entity issues a 6 per cent CU100 million bond at par on 30 June 20X0. The bond is repayable at par 10 years after issuance on 30 June 20Y0. Interest of CU6 million is paid annually. There are no issue costs. The liability is measured at amortised cost using an effective interest rate of 6 per cent. For illustrative purposes only, it is assumed the amortised cost of the bond is CU103 million at 31 December 20X0.

How should the entity disclose the carrying amount of the bond in its statement of financial position at 31 December 20X0? Specifically, how is the presentation of the bond in the financial statements affected by IAS 1:71 which refers to the inclusion of the 'current portion of non-current financial liabilities' in current liabilities?

Two methods of classification are acceptable under IFRSs. An entity should adopt one of the following methods as an accounting policy choice and should apply it consistently in accordance with paragraph 13 of IAS 8 *Accounting Policies, Changes in Accounting Estimates and Errors*.

One approach is to present the entire amortised cost carrying amount of CU103 million in non-current liabilities. IAS 1:71 (see **4.3.2**) supports this classification because:

- the liability is not expected to be settled in the entity's normal operating cycle;
- the liability is not held primarily for the purpose of trading;
- the liability is not due until 20Y0 (i.e. the principal is not expected to be settled within twelve months of the end of the reporting period); and
- the entity has the unconditional right to defer settlement of the liability for at least twelve months after the reporting period.

Under this approach, interest on the bond is viewed as servicing of the liability instead of its settlement. Therefore, the amount of interest to be paid within twelve months of the end of the reporting period does not constitute the 'current portion of non-current financial liabilities' described in IAS 1:71. The current portion of the bond would be the portion of its principal amount repayable within twelve months of the reporting period.

The alternative method is to present CU3 million (i.e. the difference between the amortised cost carrying amount and the par value repayable on maturity) separately as a current liability. This current liability represents interest accrued at the year end. The remaining carrying amount of CU100 million would be classified as a non-current liability.

4.3.7.4 Classification of a short-term loan with a conditional rollover option

Example 4.3.7.4

Classification of a short-term loan with a conditional rollover option

Entity A has a variable rate loan from Bank B that is due for repayment six months after the end of the reporting period. Entity A may roll over the loan on the same terms for another 12 months from the due date, provided that it passes a specified financial test at that date. Entity A has concluded that the extension option is not a separable embedded derivative.

Should the loan be classified as current or non-current?

It depends on the nature of the conditions attached to the extension option. In circumstances in which the conditions are substantive (which would normally be the case for any financial condition), or management does not expect to extend, the loan should be classified as current.

However, if (1) the conditions are entirely within Entity A's control or totally perfunctory, and (2) management expects to exercise its option, the substance of the option is that the rollover is at Entity A's discretion. The loan would therefore be classified as non-current in accordance with the requirements of IAS 1:73 (see **4.3.4**).

With respect to (1) above, when assessing whether the conditions are within the control of Entity A, the following factors should be considered:

- the defined conditions are customary for these types of financing arrangements;
- the assessment as to whether Entity A has met the conditions (i.e. the result of the 'test') is objectively determinable (e.g. it is not a subjective acceleration clause);
- the conditions are related to Entity A and its operations (e.g. there are no broad economic conditions or lender conditions); and
- it is reasonable to assume, based on facts and circumstances that exist at the end of the reporting period, that meeting the conditions at the rollover date is reasonably possible.

4.3.8 Breaches of covenants

When a provision of a long-term loan arrangement is breached on or before the end of the reporting period with the effect that the liability becomes payable on demand, the liability is classified as current. This is so, even if the lender has agreed, after the reporting period and before authorisation of the financial statements for issue, not to demand payment as a consequence of the breach. The liability is classified as current because, at the end of the reporting period, the entity does not have an unconditional right to defer settlement for at least twelve months after that date. [IAS 1:74]

The liability is classified as non-current if the lender agreed before the end of the reporting period to provide a period of grace (i.e. a period within which the entity can rectify the breach and during which the lender cannot demand immediate repayment) ending at least twelve months after the reporting period. [IAS 1:75]

Example 4.3.8

Overdraft facility with 'lock-box' arrangement

Company A has a 5-year, CU50 million overdraft facility with Bank B that includes a 'lock-box' account arrangement. Under the terms of the lock-box arrangement, Company A's customers are required to remit payments directly to a designated lock-box account, and the amounts received are applied to reduce the debt outstanding under the overdraft facility. At the end of each day, because Company A may request additional borrowings under the facility (Company A is permitted to withdraw an amount equal to the daily cash receipts), the outstanding balance due under the facility could remain unchanged.

Company A uses the overdraft facility as a source of long-term financing and has maintained a minimum balance of CU20 million. Neither Company A nor Bank B expects the balance to be below CU20 million in the next 12 months. Total cash receipts exceed the overdraft facility in any given year.

Should Company A's overdraft be presented as a current or a non-current liability?

The overdraft facility should be presented as a current liability. IAS 1:69 requires an entity to classify a liability as current if it expects to settle the liability in its normal operating cycle. Because the customer remittances represent current working capital of Company A that is being used to settle its obligation, the obligation is considered a short-term obligation of the borrower.

In many situations, entities maintain a minimum balance payable to a trading partner. Similar to the accounting for trade payables, the balance is classified based on the terms of the underlying arrangements or invoices payable – consequently, they are generally classified as current liabilities.

4.3.9 Expected voluntary repayment of a loan not due to be settled within twelve months after the reporting period

Example 4.3.9

Expected voluntary repayment of a loan not due to be settled within twelve months after the reporting period

On 1 January 20X1, Entity X borrows funds from a third-party bank for long-term financing purposes. The loan is due for repayment in 20X5. The loan is classified as a non-current liability in Entity X's financial statements for the year ended 31 December 20X1.

At 31 December 20X2, Entity X has not breached any provisions of the loan agreement and does not expect to do so in the foreseeable future. However, at that date, Entity X intends to enter into a refinancing arrangement that will involve voluntary repayment of the loan and taking out a new loan with a different lender. Entity X has notified the bank of its intentions, but has not entered into an irrevocable commitment to repay within 12 months.

In January 20X3 (before the 31 December 20X2 financial statements are authorised for issue), the refinancing is completed as planned and the loan repaid.

How should Entity X classify the loan in its financial statements at 31 December 20X2?

Entity X should classify the loan as a non-current liability. As at 31 December 20X2, the loan is still due to be settled in 20X5 (i.e. more than twelve months after the reporting period) and Entity X has not given up its unconditional right to defer settlement.

The voluntary repayment after the reporting period is a non-adjusting event which, if material, should be disclosed (including, potentially, the impact on liquidity) in accordance with paragraph 21 of IAS 10 *Events after the Reporting Period* (see **chapter A22**).

4.4 Information to be presented in the statement of financial position

4.4.1 Line items to be presented in the statement of financial position

IAS 1 uses the expression 'in the statement of financial position' rather than 'on the face of the statement of financial position'. However, it is clearly the intention that these items are shown on the face of the statement itself. Disclosure in the notes would not be adequate to comply with the Standard in this regard.

IAS 1:54 has been amended by the December 2014 amendments (as described in **1.2**). Consistent with the clarifications relating to materiality discussed in **2.7.2**, the amendments delete the words 'as a minimum' to address the possible misconception that these line items are required to be presented regardless of their materiality. The amendments clarify that entities can aggregate line items specified in IAS 1:54 if those line items are immaterial.

The statement of financial position should include line items that present the following amounts:

[IAS 1:54]

(a) property, plant and equipment;

(b) investment property;

(c) intangible assets;

(d) financial assets (other than investments accounted for using the equity method, trade and other receivables and cash and cash equivalents, which are presented separately);

(e) investments accounted for using the equity method;

(f) biological assets within the scope of IAS 41 *Agriculture*;

(g) inventories;

(h) trade and other receivables;

(i) cash and cash equivalents;

(j) the total of assets classified as held for sale and assets included in disposal groups classified as held for sale in accordance with IFRS 5 *Non-current Assets Held for Sale and Discontinued Operations* (see **chapter A20**);

(k) trade and other payables;

(l) provisions;

(m) financial liabilities (other than trade and other payables, and provisions, which are presented separately);

(n) liabilities and assets for current tax, as defined in IAS 12;

(o) deferred tax liabilities and deferred tax assets, as defined in IAS 12;

(p) liabilities included in disposal groups classified as held for sale in accordance with IFRS 5 (see **chapter A20**);

(q) non-controlling interests, presented within equity; and

(r) issued capital and reserves attributable to owners of the parent.

IAS 1:54(f) was amended in June 2014 by *Agriculture: Bearer Plants (Amendments to IAS 16 and IAS 41)* to clarify that biological assets required to be presented separately in the statement of financial position are those that fall within the scope of IAS 41 *Agriculture*. Following the June 2014 amendments, bearer plants related to agricultural activity are brought within the scope of IAS 16 *Property, Plant and Equipment* rather than IAS 41 (see **section 2.6** in **chapter A7**). Consequently, for entities that have adopted the June 2014 amendments, such assets are presented in the statement of financial position as part of property, plant and equipment rather than within the 'biological assets' line item.

IAS 1 does not prescribe the order or the format in which items are to be presented. The Standard merely provides a list of items that are sufficiently different in nature or function to warrant separate presentation in the statement of financial position. In addition:

[IAS 1:57]

- line items are included when the size, nature or function of an item or aggregation of similar items is such that separate presentation is relevant to an understanding of the entity's financial position; and

- the descriptions used and the ordering of items or aggregation of similar items may be amended according to the nature of the entity and its transactions, to provide information that is relevant to an understanding of the entity's financial position. For example, a financial institution may amend the above descriptions to provide information that is relevant to the operations of a financial institution.

4.4.2 Presentation of additional line items, headings and subtotals

Additional line items, headings and subtotals are presented in the statement of financial position when such presentation is relevant to an understanding of the entity's financial position. For this purpose, the line items listed in IAS 1:54 (see **4.4.1**) may be disaggregated. [IAS 1:55]

IAS 1:55 has been expanded by the December 2014 amendments (as described in **1.2**) to clarify that the requirements of IAS 1:54 (see **4.4.1**) and 1:55 may be fulfilled by disaggregating the line items specified in IAS 1:54.

The judgement as to whether additional items are presented separately is based on an assessment of:

[IAS 1:58]

- the nature and liquidity of the assets;

- the function of the assets within the entity; and

- the amounts, nature and timing of liabilities.

The use of different measurement bases for different classes of assets suggests that their nature or function differs and, therefore, that they should be presented as separate line items. For example, different classes of property, plant and equipment can be carried at cost or revalued amounts in accordance with IAS 16 *Property, Plant and Equipment*. [IAS 1:59]

When an entity presents additional subtotals in the statement of financial position, in accordance with IAS 1:55, those subtotals should:

[IAS 1:55A and IAS 1:BC38G]

- be comprised of line items made up of amounts recognised and measured in accordance with IFRSs;

- be presented and labelled in a manner that makes the line items that constitute the subtotal understandable. For example, if an entity presents a commonly reported subtotal, but excludes items that would normally be considered as part of that subtotal, the label should reflect what has been excluded;

- be consistent from period to period; and

- not be displayed with more prominence than the subtotals and totals required in IFRSs for the statement of financial position.

IAS 1:55A was added by the December 2014 amendments (as described in **1.2**) to address concerns that subtotals presented in addition to those specified in IFRSs could be misleading or be given undue prominence.

4.4.3   Cash and cash equivalents

The separate line item in the statement of financial position for 'cash and cash equivalents' does not necessarily correspond to 'cash and cash equivalents' as defined in IAS 7 *Statement of Cash Flows*. IAS 7:45 acknowledges this fact by requiring a reconciliation of the amount of cash and cash equivalents in the statement of cash flows with the equivalent line item reported in the statement of financial position.

IAS 7:8 states that bank overdrafts repayable on demand may be classified as a component of cash and cash equivalents for the purposes of the statement of cash flows when they form an integral part of an entity's cash management. IAS 7:8 notes that a characteristic of such banking arrangements is that the balance often fluctuates from being positive to overdrawn.

Even when such overdrafts are classified as a component of cash and cash equivalents under IAS 7, it will not generally be appropriate for them to be netted against cash and cash equivalent assets for the purposes of presenting the 'cash and cash equivalents' line item in the statement of financial position. Such overdrafts should be netted against positive cash balances only when the more restrictive offset criteria in paragraph 42 of IAS 32 *Financial Instruments: Presentation* are met (see **section 6** of **chapter B11** or, for entities that have not yet adopted IFRS 9, **section 6** of **chapter C12**).

When the amounts presented for cash and cash equivalents in the statements of financial position and cash flows are different, entities may wish to consider using different descriptions so as to avoid confusion; for example, the amount presented in the statement of financial position could be described as 'cash and bank balances'. IAS 1:57 permits the use of alternative descriptions in this manner. However, even when different descriptions are used in the two statements, the requirement to present a reconciliation under IAS 7:45 applies.

4.5 Information to be presented either in the statement of financial position or in the notes

4.5.1 General requirement to present further sub-classifications of line items

Further sub-classifications of the line items presented should be disclosed either in the statement of financial position or in the notes, classified in a manner that is appropriate to the entity's operations. [IAS 1:77]

The details provided depend on the requirements of IFRSs and on the size, nature and function of the amounts involved. The factors set out in IAS 1:58 (see **4.4.2**) are also used to decide on the basis of sub-classifications. IAS 1 gives the following examples:

[IAS 1:78]

- items of property, plant and equipment are disaggregated into classes in accordance with IAS 16 *Property, Plant and Equipment*;

- receivables are disaggregated into amounts receivable from trade customers, receivables from related parties, prepayments and other amounts;

- inventories are sub-classified, in accordance with IAS 2 *Inventories*, into classifications such as merchandise, production supplies, materials, work in progress and finished goods;

- provisions are disaggregated into provisions for employee benefits and other items; and

- equity capital and reserves are disaggregated into various classes, such as paid-in capital, share premium and reserves.

4.5.2   Share capital and reserves

4.5.2.1   Presentation when 'legal' share capital is classified as liabilities

IAS 1 requires several disclosures about share capital and reserves. These are described at **4.5.2.4** and **4.5.2.5**.

In straightforward cases, these disclosures will be made in respect of the amounts included in the statement of financial position caption 'issued capital and reserves attributable to owners of the parent'. However, this will not always be the case, because amounts that are legally share capital will sometimes be presented, in whole or in part, as liabilities in the statement of financial position in accordance with IAS 32 *Financial Instruments: Presentation*.

There are a number of ways in which the requirements of IAS 1 can be met. For example, it is generally acceptable to present a single line item on the face of the statement of financial position for 'issued share capital and reserves attributable to owners of the parent'. When this approach is taken, the amount presented on the face of the statement of financial position is the 'net' amount (i.e. excluding amounts that are legally share capital but presented as financial liabilities). Further details (e.g. analysing legal share capital between amounts classified as equity and liabilities) can be shown in the notes. This approach may not be appropriate in some jurisdictions; regulatory requirements or general practice may be such that entities present greater detail on the face of the statement of financial position (e.g. share capital, share premium and specified reserves).

When an expanded analysis of equity items is shown on the face of the statement of financial position (either because this is a regulatory requirement or because the entity wishes to present more detail on the face of the statement of financial position), the question arises as to which line items should be reduced by the amounts presented as liabilities.

When the amounts presented as liabilities represent the proceeds of issue of a class (or classes) of shares, the most common approach is that the amounts presented as 'share capital' and 'share premium' on the face of the statement of financial position exclude those amounts (i.e. they relate to equity shares only). Alternatively, the gross amounts for 'share capital' and 'share premium' may be presented on the face of the statement of financial position, with amounts classified as liabilities shown as a separate deduction. In such circumstances, the supplementary disclosures required by IAS 1 regarding share capital (see **4.5.2.4**) can be presented separately in the relevant notes for the 'equity' and 'liability' classes of shares. Alternatively, details about all classes of share capital may be presented in a single note, but distinguishing separately those classes and amounts that have been presented as liabilities.

The position is more complicated when a class of shares (e.g. redeemable convertible preference shares) is accounted for as a compound financial instrument with both equity and liability components. There are several possibilities for presentation in such circumstances, including:

- the share capital and share premium could be shown on the face of the statement of financial position at their 'legal' amounts, with a separate negative reserve equal to the liability recognised; or

- the share capital and share premium could be shown on the face of the statement of financial position as those amounts that relate to equity shares, with a separate line item such as 'equity component of preference shares'; or

- the deduction for the liability might be made first from the share premium and then from share capital; or

- the deduction for the liability might be made from share capital and share premium in proportion to the allocation of the original proceeds of issue between those captions.

All of these are acceptable provided that adequate explanation is provided and that all of IAS 1's disclosure requirements are met. The key point is that the total amount presented as equity is unaffected by these choices.

4.5.2.2 Analysis of reserves

There are some specific instances when IFRSs require a separate component of equity to be maintained. For example, IAS 21 *The Effects of Changes in Foreign Exchange Rates* requires specified exchange differences to be accumulated in a separate component of equity and IAS 16 requires a surplus on revaluation of an asset to be recognised in other comprehensive income and accumulated in equity under the heading of revaluation surplus. Subject to these (and other) specific requirements, there is some flexibility about which items are accounted for as separate components within equity.

See **4.5.2.5** for a discussion of the disclosure requirements regarding reserves within equity.

4.5.2.3 Meaning of 'retained earnings'

When IFRSs require amounts to be accumulated in equity, in the absence of specific requirements in IFRSs (see **4.5.2.2**), and subject to local regulatory requirements, it is generally acceptable for these amounts to be included within retained earnings.

For example, the credit to equity required by IFRS 2 *Share-based Payment* for equity-settled share-based payments may either be credited to a separate reserve or to retained earnings. This issue is considered further at **5.1.5** in **chapter A16**.

4.5.2.4   Disclosures about share capital

For each class of share capital, the following should be disclosed, either in the statement of financial position or in the notes:

[IAS 1:79(a)]

- the number of shares authorised;
- the number of shares issued and fully paid;
- the number of shares issued but not fully paid;
- the par value per share, or the fact that the shares have no par value;
- a reconciliation of the number of shares outstanding at the beginning and at the end of the period;
- the rights, preferences and restrictions attaching to that class including restrictions on distributions of dividends and the repayment of capital;
- shares in the entity held by the entity or by its subsidiaries or associates; and
- shares reserved for issue under options and contracts for the sale of shares, including the terms and amounts.

In accordance with IAS 32, all or part of the amounts recognised for shares in the statement of financial position may be classified as liabilities. The above disclosure requirements apply irrespective of whether the shares are classified as equity or debt or a combination of the two (see also **4.5.2.1**).

It is unclear whether the requirement to disclose 'shares in the entity held by the entity or by its subsidiaries or associates' refers to the number of shares held or the amount of the deduction from equity in respect of such holdings. In the context of the other disclosures required by this paragraph of IAS 1, the text appears to refer to the number of shares. This would be appropriate for all of the types of holding referred to in IAS 1:79(a), including shares held by associates of the entity which are not deducted from equity as is required for shares held by the entity and its subsidiaries under paragraph 33 of IAS 32 *Financial Instruments: Presentation*.

However, IAS 32:34 states that "[t]he amount of treasury shares held is disclosed separately either in the statement of financial position or in the notes, in accordance with IAS 1". This text refers to the 'amount' of treasury shares rather than their number, but it appears to be a reminder of the disclosure requirement in IAS 1 rather than an additional requirement.

Because of the uncertainty regarding this disclosure requirement, it is recommended that both of the following be disclosed: (1) the number of shares held by the entity and by its subsidiaries and associates, and (2) when relevant, the amount of any deduction from equity in respect of treasury shares.

Some entities such as partnerships or trusts do not have share capital. In such cases, information equivalent to that described above for share capital should be disclosed, showing changes during the period in each category of equity interest and the rights, preferences and restrictions attaching to each category of equity interest. [IAS 1:80]

If an entity has reclassified:

- a puttable instrument classified as an equity instrument, or

- an instrument that imposes on the entity an obligation to deliver to another party a pro rata share of the net assets of the entity only on liquidation and is classified as an equity instrument,

between financial liabilities and equity, the amount reclassified into and out of each category (financial liabilities or equity), and the timing and reason for that reclassification, should be disclosed. [IAS 1:80A]

The terms used in the two bullet points above have the meaning specified in IAS 32 (see **2.1.2** and **2.1.3** in **chapter B3** or, for entities that have not yet adopted IFRS 9, **2.1.2** and **2.1.3** in **chapter C3**).

4.5.2.5   *Disclosures about reserves*

Entities are required to provide a description of the nature and purpose of each reserve within equity, either in the statement of financial position or in the notes. [IAS 1:79(b)]

While IAS 1 requires financial statements to include additional information as to the nature and purpose of each reserve, it does not provide any further clarification regarding what information is needed.

By allowing this information to be disclosed in the statement of financial position, the IASB has indicated that the required information might be sufficiently disclosed by a precise wording of the name of the reserve. Thus, for reserves that are commonly encountered (revaluation reserves on property, plant and equipment, share premium account, translation reserves in respect of foreign operations etc.), no further explanation is necessary for investors to understand the nature and purpose of the reserves.

However, if, for example, the entity wishes to designate special reserves within equity that are not familiar to users of financial statements, supplementary information should be provided regarding the purpose of the reserve, and how it will be utilised.

5   Statement of profit or loss and other comprehensive income

5.1   General requirements regarding the presentation of profit or loss and other comprehensive income

5.1.1   Option to present a single statement or two statements

As discussed in **2.4.2**, an entity may either:

[IAS 1:10A]

- present a single statement of profit or loss and other comprehensive income, with profit or loss and other comprehensive income presented in two sections (a 'one-statement' approach); or

- present the profit or loss section in a separate statement of profit or loss (a 'two-statement' approach).

Whichever approach is adopted to the presentation of the statement of profit or loss and other comprehensive income, the objective is to arrive at an amount for 'total comprehensive income', which is defined as "the change in equity during a period resulting from transactions and other events, other than those changes resulting from transactions with owners in their capacity as owners. Total comprehensive income comprises all components of 'profit or loss' and 'other comprehensive income'". [IAS 1:7]

5.1.2   Presentation of additional line items, headings and subtotals

Sections **5.2** and **5.3** set out items required to be disclosed in profit or loss and in other comprehensive income. Additional line items, headings and subtotals should be presented in the statement(s) presenting profit or loss and other comprehensive income when such a presentation is relevant to an understanding of the entity's financial performance. For this purpose, the line items listed in IAS 1:82 (see **5.2.1**) may be disaggregated. [IAS 1:85]

IAS 1:85 has been expanded by the December 2014 amendments to IAS 1 (as described in **1.2**) to clarify that the requirements of IAS 1:82 (see **5.2.1**) and 1:85 may be fulfilled by disaggregating the line items specified in IAS 1:82.

When an entity presents additional subtotals in accordance with IAS 1:85, those subtotals should:

[IAS 1:85A and IAS 1:BC38G]

- be comprised of line items made up of amounts recognised and measured in accordance with IFRSs;
- be presented and labelled in a manner that makes the line items that constitute the subtotal understandable. For example, if an entity presents a commonly reported subtotal, but excludes items that would normally be considered as part of that subtotal, the label should reflect what has been excluded;
- be consistent from period to period; and
- not be displayed with more prominence than the subtotals and totals required in IFRSs for the statement(s) presenting profit or loss and other comprehensive income.

IAS 1:85A was added by the December 2014 amendments (as described in **1.2**) to address concerns that subtotals presented in addition to those specified in IFRSs could be misleading or be given undue prominence.

Entities are required to present the line items in the statements(s) presenting profit or loss and other comprehensive income that reconcile any subtotals presented in accordance with IAS 1:85 with the subtotals or totals required in IFRSs for such statement(s). [IAS 1:85B]

IAS 1:85B was added by the December 2014 amendments (as described in **1.2**). The purpose of this requirement is to help users of financial statements understand the relationship between the subtotals presented in accordance with IAS 1:85 and the specific totals and subtotals required under IFRSs. Although this requirement is already implicit in existing IFRS requirements (because all recognised items of income and expense are required to be included in the statement(s) of profit or loss and other comprehensive income totals and, consequently, any intervening line items and subtotals necessarily reconcile), the Board decide to make this requirement more explicit. [IAS 1:BC58B]

5.1.3 Adaptations of formats

Disclosing the components of financial performance assists users in understanding the financial performance achieved and in making projections of future financial performance. To explain the elements of financial performance, it may be necessary to:

[IAS 1:86]

- include additional line items in the statement(s) presenting profit or loss and other comprehensive income;

- amend the descriptions used; and/or

- amend the ordering of items.

Although IAS 1 uses the terms 'profit or loss', 'other comprehensive income' and 'total comprehensive income', other terms may be used to describe the totals as long as the meaning is clear. For example, the term 'net income' may be used to describe profit or loss. [IAS 1:8]

Factors to be considered include materiality and the nature and function of the items of income and expense. For example, a financial institution may amend the descriptions of line items to provide information that is relevant to the operations of such an institution. However, income and expense items should not be offset unless the criteria in IAS 1 are met (see **2.8**). [IAS 1:86]

5.1.4   Subtotals and totals required to be presented

The statement of profit or loss and other comprehensive income (statement of comprehensive income) is required to present, in addition to the profit or loss and other comprehensive income sections:

[IAS 1:81A]

- profit or loss;

- total other comprehensive income; and

- comprehensive income for the period, being the total of profit or loss and other comprehensive income.

If an entity presents a separate statement of profit or loss, it should not present the profit or loss section in the statement presenting comprehensive income. [IAS 1:81A]

The 'one-statement' and 'two-statements' approaches to the presentation of profit or loss and other comprehensive income are described at **5.1.1**. If a one-statement approach is adopted, the single statement presents separate sections for (1) profit or loss, and (2) other comprehensive income, with totals shown for each and the aggregate of the two presented as a final total. If a two-statement approach is adopted, the separate statement of profit or loss is presented to arrive at a total for profit or loss; this total is then the starting point for the second statement which presents items of other comprehensive income, a total for other comprehensive income, and a total for comprehensive income (the aggregate of profit or loss and other comprehensive income). Both of these approaches are illustrated in the illustrative financial statements accompanying IAS 1.

5.1.5 Allocation of profit or loss and other comprehensive income

The following items are required to be presented as allocation of profit or loss and other comprehensive income for the period:

[IAS 1:81B]

- profit or loss for the period attributable to:

  - non-controlling interests; and

  - owners of the parent; and

- comprehensive income for the period attributable to:

  - non-controlling interests; and

  - owners of the parent.

If an entity presents profit or loss in a separate statement, the allocation of the profit or loss for the period should be presented in that separate statement. [IAS 1:81B]

The reference to presentation 'as allocation of profit or loss' means that these items are not items of income or expense. This presentation is consistent with IFRS 10 *Consolidated Financial Statements*, which requires non-controlling interests to be presented within equity because they do not meet the definition of a liability in the IASB's *Conceptual Framework for Financial Reporting* (see IAS 1:BC59).

The illustrative financial statements accompanying IAS 1 show how these requirements can be met. A presentation that shows the profit for the period as a subtotal, and then deducts non-controlling interests to arrive at the profit attributable to the equity holders of the parent, would not be regarded as meeting the requirements of IAS 1.

5.1.6 Columnar presentation in the statement of comprehensive income

There is nothing in IAS 1 to prevent the presentation of additional information in the statement of comprehensive income provided that it is not misleading. Such additional information is sometimes presented using a columnar layout, where the total column gives the amounts required by IAS 1 and the additional columns provide an analysis of some or all of those amounts. For example, separate columns might be used to present the results of two operating segments in the statement of comprehensive income. They may also be used to segregate certain types of income or expense such as those required to be disclosed separately under IAS 1:97 (see **5.4.1**).

For entities that have adopted the December 2014 amendments, any columnar presentation will need to comply with the requirements of IAS 1:85A and 85B (see **5.1.2**). In particular, to avoid the risk that the additional information may be misleading when this approach is used, the description of the columns should be unambiguous and as factual as possible. The descriptions should be clear enough to be understood by a general reader of the financial statements without further explanation. The use of terms such as 'core performance', 'underlying performance' and 'special items' should be avoided because they may be ambiguous or, in the extreme, misleading. When necessary, a clear definition should be provided for those items included in a separate column.

Entities should also consider the requirements of local regulators, particularly as regards the inclusion and labelling of non-GAAP measures in financial statements.

5.2   Profit or loss

5.2.1   *Line items to be presented in profit or loss*

In addition to items required by other IFRSs, the profit or loss section or the statement of profit or loss is required to present the following line items:

[IAS 1:82]

- revenue;

- finance costs;

- share of the profit or loss of associates and joint ventures accounted for using the equity method;

- tax expense; and

- a single amount for the total of discontinued operations (see **6.3.1.1** in **chapter A20**).

Entities applying IFRS 9 *Financial Instruments* are also required to disclose:

- interest revenue calculated using the effective interest method separately from other revenue; [IAS 1:82(a)]

- gains and losses arising from the derecognition of financial assets measured at amortised cost; [IAS 1:82(aa)]

- impairment losses (including reversals of impairment losses or impairment gains) determined in accordance with section 5.5 of IFRS 9; [IAS 1:82(ba)]

- if a financial asset is reclassified out of the amortised cost measurement category so that it is measured at fair value through profit or loss, any gain or loss arising from a difference between the previous amortised cost of the financial asset and its fair value at the reclassification date (as defined in IFRS 9); [IAS 1:82(ca)] and

- if a financial asset is reclassified out of the fair value through other comprehensive income measurement category so that it is measured at fair value through profit or loss, any cumulative gain or loss previously recognised in other comprehensive income that is reclassified to profit or loss. [IAS 1:82(cb)]

5.2.2 Income and expenses to be recognised in profit or loss unless an IFRS requires or permits otherwise

All items of income or expense recognised in a period are recognised in profit or loss unless an IFRS requires or permits otherwise. [IAS 1:88]

Some IFRSs specify circumstances in which particular items are recognised outside profit or loss. IAS 8 *Accounting Policies, Changes in Accounting Estimates and Errors* deals with two such circumstances – the correction of errors and changes in accounting policies (see **chapter A5**). Other IFRSs require or permit components of other comprehensive income that meet the definition of income or expense in the *Conceptual Framework for Financial Reporting* to be excluded from profit or loss (see **5.3.1**). [IAS 1:89]

5.2.3 Prohibition on 'extraordinary items'

IAS 1 states that items of income and expense should not be presented as 'extraordinary items' in the statement(s) presenting profit or loss and other comprehensive income, or in the notes. [IAS 1:87]

This may appear to be a slightly odd requirement in that IAS 1 does not define what is meant by 'extraordinary items' or say how such items might be presented if they were not prohibited. To understand the requirements of IAS 1:87, it is necessary to be aware that a previous version of IAS 8 included a definition of extraordinary items as "income and expenses that arise from events or transactions that are clearly distinct from the ordinary activities of the enterprise and, therefore, are not expected to recur frequently or regularly". It required such items to be disclosed on the face of the income statement separately from the profit or loss on ordinary activities (normally as a single net-of-tax number after profit from ordinary activities and before net profit). As part of the revisions of IAS 1 and IAS 8 in 2003, the IASB decided to prohibit the presentation of extraordinary items because they result from the normal business risks faced by an entity and do not warrant presentation in a separate component of the income statement. The reasons are more fully set out in IAS 1:BC60 to BC64.

5.2.4   Presentation of specific items of income and expense

5.2.4.1   Net finance costs

At its October 2004 meeting, the IFRIC (now the IFRS Interpretations Committee) discussed a potential agenda topic regarding whether it is acceptable to present a line item for 'net finance costs' in profit or loss without presenting separately the finance revenue and finance costs comprising the net amount. The Committee noted that, at that time, IAS 1(2003):81 required line items for revenue and finance costs to be presented on the face of the income statement (correspondingly, IAS 1:82 now requires line items for revenue and finance costs to be presented on the face of the statement of comprehensive income). The Committee therefore agreed that:

- taken together with the requirements of IAS 1:32 (prohibition on netting of income and expenses unless required or permitted by a Standard or an Interpretation – see **2.8**), this precludes the presentation of 'net finance costs' (or a similar term) in the income statement (now the statement of comprehensive income) without showing the finance revenue and finance costs comprising the net amount; but

- this does not preclude the presentation of finance revenue followed immediately by finance costs and a subtotal (e.g. 'net finance costs') in the income statement (now the statement of comprehensive income), as illustrated below.

	20X1	20X0
	CU'000	CU'000
Operating profit	126,342	49,774
Investment revenues	3,501	717
Finance costs	(36,187)	(32,165)
Net finance costs	(32,686)	(31,448)
Share of profit of associates	12,763	983
Other gains and losses	(563)	(44)
Profit before tax	105,856	19,265

The above conclusion was set out in the October 2004 edition of *IFRIC Update*.

5.2.4.2   Presentation of negative interest

Under some economic conditions, the overall effective interest rate on some financial assets may be negative. For example, during an economic downturn, strong demand for 'safe harbour' assets can increase their prices sufficiently to result in negative yields. Another example of this phenomenon arises in jurisdictions where, as a matter of monetary policy, negative central bank interest rates are set, resulting in the origination of financial assets with negative interest rates.

Negative interest arising on financial assets should be presented in the statement of comprehensive income within an appropriate expense classification rather than as interest revenue. Negative interest does not meet the definition of revenue in Appendix A of IFRS 15 *Revenue from Contracts with Customers* because it does not represent an increase in economic benefits.

Entities should consider whether negative interest is required to be presented as a separate line item in accordance with IAS 1:85 (i.e. when such separate presentation is relevant to an understanding of the entity's financial performance – see **5.1.2**). If this approach is adopted, and the negative interest is presented in a separate, suitably titled, line item, presentation of a subtotal including this item (e.g. 'net interest income/expense') in the statement of comprehensive income is not precluded (see **5.2.4.1**).

When a separate line item is not presented, entities should develop an accounting policy on the appropriate classification for a negative interest expense in accordance with IAS 8 *Accounting Policies, Changes in Accounting Estimates and Errors* (e.g. to present negative interest on financial assets in the same line as interest expense in the statement of comprehensive income). If the amount is material, entities will also need to consider whether separate presentation is required in the notes to the financial statements in accordance with IAS 1:97 (see **5.4.1**).

This conclusion is consistent with the views expressed by the IFRS Interpretations Committee (see January 2015 *IFRIC Update*) who considered this issue in the context of IAS 18 *Revenue* (the predecessor to IFRS 15).

5.2.4.3   *Investment income as revenue*

IAS 1:82 requires the disclosure of revenue in the statement of comprehensive income but IAS 1:85 requires the presentation of additional line items when necessary to explain the financial performance of the entity.

Paragraphs 4:29 and 4:30 of the *Conceptual Framework for Financial Reporting* distinguish 'revenue' from 'gains'. Investment income may include elements of both investment revenue (e.g. interest and dividends received) and other 'gains' (such as profits on sale of investments and gains on remeasurement to fair value).

Unless investment is one of the principal activities of the entity, in most circumstances it will be necessary to present investment revenue as a separate line item to explain the entity's financial performance.

Other gains and losses that do not meet the definition of revenue might be separately presented in the statement of comprehensive income, or they might be presented in a more general 'other gains and losses' line item, according to their materiality.

5.2.4.4   Results of operating activities

Entities may choose to present a subtotal for 'profit from operations' in the statement(s) of profit or loss and comprehensive income. Although this is not one of the line items listed in IAS 1:82 (see **5.2.1**), IAS 1:85 permits the presentation of additional subtotals when such presentation is relevant to an understanding of the entity's financial performance. Entities that have adopted the December 2014 amendments to IAS 1 will also need to have regard to the requirements in IAS 1:85A and 85B (see **5.1.2**).

IAS 1 does not require the results of operating activities to be disclosed as a line item on the face of the statement of comprehensive income; the IASB omitted this requirement on the basis that the term is not defined and that it is inappropriate to require disclosure of an undefined item.

However, the IASB recognises that an entity may elect to disclose the results of operating activities, or a similar line item, even though the term is not defined. IAS 1:BC56 notes that, in such cases, it is necessary to ensure the amount presented is representative of activities that would normally be considered as 'operating'. In the IASB's view, it would be misleading and would impair the comparability of financial statements if items of an operating nature were excluded from the results of operating activities, even if that had been industry practice. For example, it would be inappropriate to exclude items clearly related to operations (e.g. inventory write-downs and restructuring or relocation expenses) because they occur irregularly or infrequently or are unusual in amount. Similarly, it would be inappropriate to exclude items on the grounds that they do not involve cash flows, such as depreciation and amortisation expenses.

A line item 'profit from operations' is often presented after all income and expenses other than finance costs and income from associates and joint ventures. Investment income would usually be shown below profit from operations (unless the entity is a financial institution or similar entity). Based on the IASB's views expressed in IAS 1:BC56, it would not be appropriate to exclude items such as restructuring costs. There does, however, appear to be flexibility to disclose the results of associates and joint ventures either within or below profit from operations (see **5.2.4.5**).

Entities should also have regard to the requirements of local regulators, particularly as regards the inclusion and labelling of non-GAAP measures in the financial statements.

5.2.4.5 Results of associates and joint ventures accounted for using the equity method

The share of the profit or loss of associates and joint ventures accounted for using the equity method is one of the line items required to be presented in profit or loss.

This item should be presented on an after-tax basis. The separate statement of profit or loss shown in the illustrative financial statements accompanying IAS 1 notes that "[t]his means the share of associates' profit attributable to owners of the associates, ie it is after tax and non-controlling interests in the associates". The same principle applies for the share of profits or losses of joint ventures accounted for using the equity method (not shown in the illustrative financial statements accompanying IAS 1).

The investor's share of the profit or loss of an individual associate or a joint venture accounted for using the equity method should be presented within a single line item in the profit or loss section of the statement of comprehensive income (or, when relevant, the separate statement of profit or loss) and should not be separated over different line items (revenue, expenses etc.).

However, the investor is permitted to present its share of the profits or losses of associates or joint ventures accounted for using the equity method over different line items in the profit or loss section of the statement of comprehensive income (or, when relevant, the separate statement of profit or loss). IAS 1:85 permits the line items to be disclosed under IAS 1:82 to be disaggregated if this is relevant to an understanding of the entity's performance (see **5.1.2**). When an entity chooses to disaggregate the profits or losses of different associates and joint ventures over different line items, it is not necessary to present a total for such items.

For example, an entity might choose to show separately the profits or losses for associates and for joint ventures. Disaggregation on this basis would ensure compliance with the requirement under paragraph B16 of IFRS 12 *Disclosure of Interests in Other Entities* to disclose the investor's share of the profits or losses of associates separately from its share of the profits or losses of joint ventures.

Equally, an entity might present its share of the profits or losses of different associates and joint ventures in different line items if such presentation would be considered relevant to an understanding of the financial statements. For example, an entity might present its share of the profits or losses of some of its associates or joint ventures as part of profit from operations, when such a subtotal is presented (see **5.2.4.4**). Such a presentation might be useful for any of an entity's associates or joint ventures that are considered to be part of its operations.

Given that the results of equity-method investments are presented on an after-tax basis (see above), the question arises as to whether these amounts are required to be presented above the tax expense line in profit or loss. In the list of items in IAS 1:82 (see **5.2.1**), the share of profits or losses of investments accounted for using the equity method appears above tax expense. In the statement of comprehensive income shown in the illustrative financial statements accompanying IAS 1, the item is presented before the tax expense but after all other expenses (including finance costs). However, there is no requirement in the Standard that the items listed in IAS 1:82 must appear in any particular order. Therefore, it would be acceptable to present the share of profits or losses of investments accounted for using the equity method below the tax expense line (although, under IAS 1:88, it must always be presented before the 'profit for the period').

5.2.4.6 Tax-based structuring income

Example 5.2.4.6

Tax-based structuring income

Bank A undertakes to lend money to Company B. Under its general lending rates, Bank A would charge 12 per cent interest to a customer with Company B's credit profile. However, Bank A structures the loan so that it receives a favourable tax deduction and recovers half of the interest that it would have charged Company B from this deduction. Consequently, it charges Company B interest at 6 per cent and requires Company B to agree that if the tax deduction does not arise, or it is less than anticipated, Company B will pay the difference to Bank A as an increased interest charge.

Is it acceptable for Bank A to recognise interest income of 12 per cent in respect of its loan to Bank B and increase its tax expense accordingly?

No. The substance of the transaction is that Bank A has originated a loan that bears interest at 6 per cent. Tax and interest are separate items; they should be accounted for separately and presented in the tax line and the interest line, respectively, of the statement of comprehensive income.

5.2.4.7 Exchange gains and losses

Paragraph 52(a) of IAS 21 *The Effects of Changes in Foreign Exchange Rates* requires an entity to disclose the amount of exchange differences recognised in profit or loss, except for those arising on financial instruments measured at fair value through profit or loss in accordance with IFRS 9 *Financial Instruments* (or, for entities that have not yet adopted IFRS 9, IAS 39 *Financial Instruments: Recognition and Measurement*).

IAS 21 is silent regarding the appropriate classification in profit or loss of foreign exchange gains and losses. Foreign exchange gains and losses should be classified based on the nature of the transactions or events which give rise to those foreign exchange gains or losses. For example, it may be appropriate to recognise foreign exchange gains and losses on operational items (trade receivables, payables etc.) within income from operations, and foreign exchange gains and losses on issued debt as part of finance costs (but not within interest payable).

Classification of foreign exchange gains or losses in profit or loss is a matter of accounting policy which must be disclosed and applied consistently year-on-year. In addition, when the impact of foreign exchange gains or losses is material, in accordance with IAS 1:97 (see **5.4.1**), their nature and amount should be disclosed separately, either in the statement of comprehensive income or in the notes. Therefore, for example, when an entity classifies foreign exchange gains or losses on operating items within income from operations, and the impact of these is material, the entity may elect to present foreign exchange gains and losses on operating items as a separate line item within income from operations.

5.2.4.8 Fair value gains and losses on derivatives that are economic hedges

The presentation of gains and losses on derivatives that are economic hedges when hedge accounting is not applied is discussed at **5.2.2** in **chapter B4** (or, for entities that have not yet adopted IFRS 9, **5.2.2** in **chapter C4**).

5.2.4.9 Release of provisions

A provision should be used only for expenditures for which the provision was originally recognised. [IAS 37:61] This means that when an entity finally settles the liability, the payment should be recorded against the provision.

However, the amount of cash paid does not always equal the amounts of provisions at the date of the payment, as illustrated in the following example.

Example 5.2.4.9

Amount of cash payment differs from provision amount

Company A recognised a restructuring provision under IAS 37 in 20X1 and the amount was included in 'other expenses'. In 20X2, the expenditure was paid in cash and the amount paid was different from the amount recognised as a provision in the previous year. The difference between the two amounts will be recognised in 20X2, either as an additional expense or as a gain due to the release of the provision, in the same line item in which the related restructuring expense was recorded in 20X1 (i.e. it should be included in 'other expenses').

Section 6 of chapter A12 addresses changes in provisions.

5.3   Other comprehensive income

5.3.1   *Components of other comprehensive income*

Other comprehensive income (OCI) comprises items of income and expense (including reclassification adjustments) that are not recognised in profit or loss as required or permitted by IFRSs and includes:

[IAS 1:7]

- changes in revaluation surplus (see IAS 16 *Property, Plant and Equipment* and IAS 38 *Intangible Assets*);

- remeasurements of defined benefit plans (see IAS 19 *Employee Benefits*);

- gains and losses arising from translating the financial statements of a foreign operation (see IAS 21 *The Effects of Changes in Foreign Exchange Rates*);

- for entities that have adopted IFRS 9 *Financial Instruments:*

  - gains and losses from investments in equity instruments designated at fair value through other comprehensive income in accordance with IFRS 9:5.7.5;

  - gains and losses on financial assets measured at fair value through other comprehensive income in accordance with IFRS 9:4.1.2A;

  - the effective portion of gains and losses on hedging instruments in a cash flow hedge and the gains and losses on hedging instruments that hedge investments in equity instruments measured at fair value through other comprehensive income in accordance with IFRS 9:5.7.5 (see IFRS 9:5.7.7);

  - for particular liabilities designated as at fair value through profit or loss, the amount of the change in fair value that is attributable to changes in the liability's credit risk (see IFRS 9:5.7.7);

  - changes in the value of the time value of options when the intrinsic value and the time value of an option contract are separated and only the changes in the intrinsic value are designated as the hedging instrument; and

  - changes in the value of the forward elements of forward contracts when the forward element and the spot element of a forward contract are separated and only the changes in the spot element are designated as the hedging instrument, and changes in the value of the foreign currency basis spread of a financial instrument when it is excluded from the designation of that financial instrument as the hedging instrument; and

- for entities that have not yet adopted IFRS 9:

  - gains and losses on remeasuring available-for-sale financial assets; and

  - the effective portion of gains and losses on hedging instruments in a cash flow hedge.

The credit recognised in equity for equity-settled share-based payments in accordance with IFRS 2 *Share-based Payment* should not be included in OCI. This is because it arises from a transaction with owners in their capacity as such. The net credit represents either the proceeds of the grant of an equity instrument or, when a subsidiary recognises an expense for a grant of its parent's equity instruments, a capital contribution from the parent.

5.3.2 Presentation of items of other comprehensive income

5.3.2.1 General requirements for presentation of items of other comprehensive income

The other comprehensive income section of the statement of comprehensive income is required to present line items for amounts for the period of:

[IAS 1:82A]

(a) items of other comprehensive income (excluding amounts required to be disclosed under IAS 1:82A(b)), classified by nature and grouped into those that, in accordance with other IFRSs:

   (i) will not be reclassified subsequently to profit or loss; and

   (ii) will be reclassified subsequently to profit or loss when specific conditions are met; and

(b) the share of other comprehensive income of associates and joint ventures accounted for using the equity method, separated into the share of items that, in accordance with other IFRSs:

   (i) will not be reclassified subsequently to profit or loss; and

   (ii) will be reclassified subsequently to profit or loss when specific conditions are met.

IAS 1:82A has been reworded as part of the December 2014 amendments (as described in **1.2**). The amendments clarify that entities should present their share of items of OCI arising from associates and joint ventures accounted for using the equity method separately from the rest of OCI. The illustrative financial statements in the implementation guidance accompanying IAS 1 have been amended accordingly.

Note that there is nothing to prevent disaggregation to show the OCI of associates separately from the OCI of joint ventures, or to present the OCI of different associates and joint ventures in different line items, if such presentation would be considered relevant to an understanding of the financial statements (see **5.2.4.5**).

5.3.2.2   Income tax relating to items of other comprehensive income

The amount of income tax relating to each item of OCI, including reclassification adjustments, should be disclosed either in the statement of profit or loss and other comprehensive income or in the notes. [IAS 1:90]

As explained in IAS 1:IN14, the purpose of this requirement is to provide users with tax information relating to the items of OCI because they often have tax rates different to those applied to profit or loss.

The items of OCI may be presented either:

[IAS 1:91]

- net of related tax effects; or
- before related tax effects with one amount shown for the aggregate amount of income tax relating to those items.

This permits a choice of presentation in the statement of comprehensive income. As explained in IAS 1:BC65, there are advantages to each method of presentation and the IASB decided to permit either to be used. However, when the income tax effects are aggregated into a single item on the face of the statement of comprehensive income, it is still necessary to disclose in the notes the amount of tax attributable to each item of OCI as required by IAS 1:90.

If the latter approach is taken (i.e. items of OCI are presented gross with a single amount shown for the aggregate amount of income tax), the amount of tax is required to be allocated between the items that might be reclassified subsequently to profit or loss and those that will not be reclassified subsequently to profit or loss. [IAS 1:91]

The disclosure requirements of IAS 1:90 and 91 do not apply to the tax of an associate or a joint venture that is already reflected in the investor's share of other comprehensive income of the associate or joint venture. However, if the investor itself is liable for tax in respect of its share of other comprehensive income of the associate or joint venture, then IAS 1:90 and 91 would apply to this tax. [IAS 1:BC54L]

5.3.2.3   Reclassification adjustments

Reclassification adjustments are amounts reclassified to profit or loss in the current period that were recognised in OCI in the current or previous periods. [IAS 1:7]

Other IFRSs specify whether and when amounts previously recognised in OCI should be reclassified to profit or loss. Such reclassifications are referred to in IAS 1 as 'reclassification adjustments'. A reclassification adjustment is included with the related component of OCI in the period that the adjustment is reclassified to profit or loss. [IAS 1:93]

The amounts that are reclassified may have been recognised in OCI as unrealised gains in the current or previous periods. Those unrealised gains must be deducted from OCI in the period in which the realised gains are reclassified to profit or loss to avoid including them twice in total comprehensive income. [IAS 1:93]

Reclassification adjustments arise, for example:

[IAS 1:95]

- on disposal of a foreign operation; and

- for entities that have adopted IFRS 9 *Financial Instruments*, when some hedged forecast cash flows affect profit or loss.

Reclassification adjustments do not arise on changes in revaluation surplus recognised in accordance with IAS 16 *Property, Plant and Equipment* or IAS 38 *Intangible Assets*. They also do not arise on remeasurements of defined benefit plans recognised in accordance with IAS 19 *Employee Benefits*. These components are recognised in OCI and are not reclassified to profit or loss in subsequent periods. Changes in revaluation surplus may be transferred to retained earnings in subsequent periods as the asset is used or when it is derecognised. [IAS 1:96]

For entities that have adopted IFRS 9, reclassification adjustments do not arise if a cash flow hedge or the accounting for the time value of an option (or the forward element of a forward contract or the foreign currency basis spread of a financial instrument) result in amounts that are removed from the cash flow hedge reserve or a separate component of equity, respectively, and included directly in the initial cost or other carrying amount of an asset or a liability. These amounts are directly transferred to assets or liabilities. [IAS 1:96]

IAS 1 requires reclassification adjustments relating to components of OCI to be disclosed. [IAS 1:92] Such reclassification adjustments may be presented in the statement(s) of profit or loss and other comprehensive income or in the notes. When reclassification adjustments are presented in the notes, the items of OCI are stated after any related reclassification adjustments. [IAS 1:94]

5.3.3 Entity has no items of other comprehensive income in the current or prior periods

When an entity has no items of OCI to recognise in either the current or the comparative reporting period, the question arises as to how the statement of comprehensive income should be presented. In the absence of explicit guidance in IAS 1, the following treatments, among others, are acceptable (subject to regulatory/jurisdictional requirements):

- presentation of a statement of profit or loss ending with 'profit for the year', followed by a narrative statement to the effect that there were no items of comprehensive income in the current or prior year other than the profit for the year and, accordingly, no statement of comprehensive income is presented; or

- presentation of a single statement of comprehensive income ending with a total line for 'profit for the year and total comprehensive income'.

5.4 Information to be presented either in the statement of profit or loss and other comprehensive income or in the notes

5.4.1 Separate disclosure required of material items of income and expense

IAS 1 requires that, when items of income and expense are material, their nature and amount should be disclosed separately. [IAS 1:97] The Standard lists the following items as examples of circumstances that would give rise to separate disclosure:

[IAS 1:98]

- write-downs of inventories to net realisable value, and reversals of such write-downs;

- write-downs of property, plant and equipment to recoverable amount, and reversals of such write-downs;

- restructuring of activities and reversals of any provisions for such costs;

- disposals of items of property, plant and equipment;

- disposals of investments;

- discontinued operations;

- litigation settlements; and

- other reversals of provisions.

5.4.2 Analysis of expenses by nature or by function

5.4.2.1 Requirement to present analysis of expenses either by nature or by function

An analysis of expenses recognised in profit or loss should be provided using a classification based on either the nature of the expenses (e.g. depreciation, employee costs etc.) or their function within the entity (e.g. cost of sales, administrative expenses etc.). The choice of classification method should be based on whichever provides information that is reliable and more relevant. [IAS 1:99] IAS 1 encourages, but does not require, this analysis to be presented in the statement(s) presenting profit or loss and other comprehensive income. [IAS 1:100]

IAS 1 explains that there are two forms of analysis whereby expenses are sub-classified to highlight components of financial performance that may differ in terms of their frequency, potential for gain or loss and predictability; these are analysis by nature and analysis by function. [IAS 1:101]

5.4.2.2 Analysis by nature of expense

The first method of analysis is by the nature of expenses (e.g. depreciation, purchases of materials, transport costs, employee benefits and advertising costs). This method is simple to apply because no allocation of expenses to functional classifications is necessary. IAS 1 gives the following example of a classification using the nature of expense method. [IAS 1:102]

Example 5.4.2.2

Analysis by nature of expense

[IAS 1:102]

Revenue		X
Other income		X
Changes in inventories of finished goods and work in progress	X	
Raw materials and consumables used	X	
Employee benefits expense	X	
Depreciation and amortisation expense	X	
Other expenses	X	
Total expenses		(X)
Profit before tax		X

5.4.2.3 Analysis by function of expense

The second method of analysis is by function (e.g. cost of sales, distribution costs and administrative expenses). At a minimum, cost of sales must be disclosed separately from other expenses when expenses are analysed by their function. This method can provide more relevant information to users than classification by nature. But allocating costs to functions may require arbitrary allocations and involve considerable judgement. IAS 1 gives the following example of a classification using the function of expense method. [IAS 1:103]

Example 5.4.2.3

Analysis by function of expense

[IAS 1:103]

Revenue	X
Cost of sales	(X)
Gross profit	X
Other income	X
Distribution costs	(X)
Administrative expenses	(X)
Other expenses	(X)
Profit before tax	X

When an entity chooses to classify expenses by function, it is also required to disclose additional information on the nature of the expenses, including:

[IAS 1:104]

- depreciation and amortisation expense; and

- employee benefits expense (as defined in IAS 19 *Employee Benefits*).

5.4.2.4   Choice between analysis of expenses by nature or by function

The choice between the two methods of analysis depends on historical and industry factors and the nature of the entity. Both methods provide an indication of those costs that might vary, directly or indirectly, with the level of sales or production. IAS 1 requires management to select the more relevant and reliable presentation because each method has merit for different types of entities. However, additional disclosure about the nature of the expenses is required when the primary analysis is by function because information on the nature of expenses is useful in predicting future cash flows. [IAS 1:105]

5.4.2.5   Inappropriate to present an analysis of expenses on a 'mixed' basis

Ad hoc mixing of classifications of expenses by nature and function should be avoided. For example, it is not appropriate for an entity to classify expenses on a functional basis but exclude certain 'unusual' expenses from the functional classification to which they relate and present those items separately by nature. Examples are inventory write-downs, employee termination benefits and impairments.

This also applies in the consolidated financial statements of groups when some of the subsidiaries report their expenses by function and other subsidiaries report expenses by nature in their own IFRS financial statements. Management should select one method of presentation for expenses in the consolidated statement of comprehensive income (i.e. either by function or by nature). The financial statements of those subsidiaries using the other basis should be adjusted for the purposes of consolidation.

6   Statement of changes in equity

6.1   Information to be included in the statement of changes in equity

Changes in an entity's equity between the beginning and end of the reporting period reflect the increase or decrease in its net assets during the period. Except for changes resulting from transactions with owners in their capacity as owners (e.g. equity contributions and distributions), the overall change in equity during a period represents the total amount of income and expense, including gains and losses, generated by the entity's activities during that period. [IAS 1:109]

IAS 1 requires the presentation of a statement of changes in equity to include the following information:

[IAS 1:106]

- total comprehensive income for the period, showing separately the total amounts attributable to owners of the parent and to non-controlling interests;

- for each component of equity, the effects of retrospective application or retrospective restatement recognised in accordance with IAS 8 *Accounting Policies, Changes in Accounting Estimates and Errors*; and

- for each component of equity, a reconciliation between the carrying amount at the beginning and the end of the period and, as a minimum, separately disclosing changes resulting from:

  - profit or loss;

  - other comprehensive income; and

  - transactions with owners in their capacity as owners, showing separately contributions by and distributions to owners and changes in ownership interests in subsidiaries that do not result in a loss of control.

The statement of changes in equity is required to present a reconciliation for each component of equity. It is not, therefore, acceptable to present a simple statement showing only the movements in total equity, with details of movements on individual components of equity provided in the notes. In fact, there is no explicit requirement in the Standard to provide totals, across all components of equity, for each type of movement. However, this is likely to be helpful in practice. For example, it will eliminate the effects of amounts transferred between different components of equity which have no effect on total equity.

The statement of changes in equity set out in the illustrative financial statements accompanying IAS 1 adopts a columnar layout with a column for each component of equity and a total column. This format is not prescribed by the Standard but is commonly adopted in practice.

For the purpose of IAS 1:106, components of equity include, for example, each class of contributed equity, the accumulated balance of each class of OCI and retained earnings. [IAS 1:108]

6.2 Adjustments for changes in accounting policies and correction of errors.

IAS 1:106(b) requires disclosure in the statement of changes in equity of the total adjustment to each component of equity resulting, separately, from changes in accounting policies and from correction of errors. These adjustments are disclosed for each prior period and the beginning of the period. [IAS 1:110]

IAS 8 *Accounting Policies, Changes in Accounting Estimates and Errors* requires that changes in accounting policies be applied retrospectively, to the extent practicable, except when the transition provisions in another IFRS require otherwise. IAS 8 also requires that restatements to correct errors be made retrospectively, to the extent practicable. The effects of such retrospective adjustments and retrospective restatements are not changes in equity in the period, but they are included in the statement of changes in equity because they provide a reconciliation between the previous period's closing balance and the opening balance in the statement of changes in equity. [IAS 1:BC74]

6.3 Dividends

6.3.1 General disclosure requirements for dividends recognised as distributions to owners during the period

IAS 1 requires the amount of dividends recognised as distributions to owners during the period, and the related amount of dividends per share, to be presented either in the statement of changes in equity or in the notes. [IAS 1:107]

It is necessary to show dividends, at least in aggregate, in the statement of changes in equity because they are one of the owner changes in equity. However, details of individual dividends and the amounts per share will typically be shown in the notes, combined with the disclosures about dividends proposed or declared after the reporting period required by IAS 1:137(a) (see **7.4.2**).

The presentation of dividends in the statement of comprehensive income is not permitted. IAS 1:BC75 explains that this is because dividends are distributions to owners in their capacity as owners and the statement of changes in equity presents all owner changes in equity.

6.3.2 *IFRIC 17* Distributions of Non-cash Assets to Owners

6.3.2.1 Introduction

IFRIC 17 *Distributions of Non-cash Assets to Owners* addresses the following issues:

- when should the entity recognise the dividend payable?

- how should the entity measure the dividend payable?

- when it settles the dividend payable, how should the entity account for any difference between the carrying amount of the assets distributed and the carrying amount of the dividend payable?

IFRS 5 *Non-current Assets Held for Sale and Discontinued Operations* applies to a non-current asset (or disposal group) that is classified as held for distribution to owners acting in their capacity as owners (see **3.5** and **4.9** in **chapter A20**).

Subject to certain scope exclusions, IFRIC 17 requires distributions of non-cash assets to be accounted for at the fair value of the assets concerned. This will often result in a profit being recognised when the distribution is settled.

6.3.2.2 Scope

IFRIC 17 applies to the following types of non-reciprocal distributions of assets by an entity to its owners acting in their capacity as owners:

[IFRIC 17:3]

- distributions of non-cash assets (e.g. items of property, plant and equipment, businesses, ownership interests in another entity, or disposal groups as defined in IFRS 5); and

- distributions that give owners a choice of receiving either non-cash assets or a cash alternative.

The Interpretation applies only to distributions in which all owners of the same class of equity instruments are treated equally. [IFRIC 17:4]

> IFRIC 17:BC6 explains that distributions when owners of the same class of equity are treated differently may imply that at least some of the owners receiving the distribution gave up something to the entity and/or to the other owners. In other words, such distributions might be more in the nature of exchange transactions.
>
> In practice, such transactions are likely to be rare and will usually be with a controlling shareholder.

The Interpretation does not apply to a distribution of a non-cash asset that is ultimately controlled by the same party or parties before and after the distribution. This exclusion applies to the separate, individual and consolidated financial statements of an entity that makes a distribution. [IFRIC 17:5]

For the purpose of this scope exclusion, a group of individuals is regarded as controlling an entity when, as a result of contractual arrangements, they collectively have the power to govern its financial and operating policies so as to obtain benefits from its activities. This is consistent with the requirement in IFRS 3:B2 for the identification of common control transactions. Therefore, for a distribution to be outside the scope of IFRIC 17 on this basis, a group of individual shareholders receiving the distribution must have, as a result of contractual arrangements, such ultimate collective power over the entity making the distribution. [IFRIC 17:6]

> Therefore, IFRIC 17 applies in the common situation of a demerger of a subsidiary by a listed entity that has no single controlling party. However, it will not apply to intragroup transactions when a subsidiary makes a distribution to its parent. Nor will it apply to distributions by private entities when there is a single controlling shareholder.

Similarly, IFRIC 17 does not apply when an entity distributes some of its ownership interests in a subsidiary but retains control of the subsidiary. The entity making a distribution that results in the entity recognising a non-controlling interest in its subsidiary should account for the distribution in accordance with IFRS 10 *Consolidated Financial Statements*. [IFRIC 17:7]

> For example, if a parent distributes 25 per cent of the shares in its wholly-owned subsidiary to its shareholders but retains control of that subsidiary, the transaction will be outside the scope of IFRIC 17. In accordance with IFRS 10, no profit or loss should be recognised on the transaction. In such circumstances, although there is a reallocation between parent and non-controlling interests, the assets and liabilities of the group do not change.

IFRIC 17 addresses only the accounting by the entity that makes the non-cash distribution. It does not address the accounting by shareholders who receive such a distribution. [IFRIC 17:8]

IFRIC 17 includes some simple examples regarding the application of these scope exclusions which are not reproduced here because they provide no significant interpretational guidance. The first example considers a distribution of available-for-sale securities and contrasts the position when there is not a controlling shareholder (i.e. the distribution is within the scope of IFRIC 17) and when there is a controlling shareholder (i.e. the distribution is not within the scope of IFRIC 17). The second example contrasts the distribution of the whole of a subsidiary by a parent that has no controlling party (i.e. the distribution is within the scope of IFRIC 17) with the distribution of shares in a subsidiary without loss of control by the parent (i.e. the distribution causes a non-controlling interest in the subsidiary to be recognised, and is not within the scope of IFRIC 17). [IFRIC 17:IE1 - IE4]

IFRIC 17 does not include an exemption on the grounds of cost or effort or practicality. The reasons for this are explained in IFRIC 17:BC28 to BC34. IFRIC 17:BC30 states that management would be expected to know the fair value of the asset because management has to ensure that all owners of the entity are informed of the value of the distribution. The IFRIC (now the IFRS Interpretations Committee), therefore, concluded that it would be difficult to argue that the fair value of the asset cannot be determined reliably. It is arguable that when all shareholders are treated in the same way they do not need to know the fair value of the distribution because the value of their total investment will be unaffected. Nevertheless, no scope exclusion is provided for these circumstances.

6.3.2.3 When to recognise a dividend

The liability to pay a dividend is recognised when the dividend is appropriately authorised and no longer at the discretion of the entity, which is the date:

[IFRIC 17:10]

- when declaration of the dividend (e.g. by management or the board of directors) is approved by the relevant authority (e.g. the shareholders) if the jurisdiction requires such approval; or

- when the dividend is declared (e.g. by management or the board of directors) if the jurisdiction does not require further approval.

As explained at **5.3** in **chapter A22**, the principle that a dividend is recognised when it is appropriately authorised and no longer at the discretion of the entity was previously in IAS 10 *Events after the Reporting Period* but has been removed as a consequential amendment of IFRIC 17. The reasons for this are given in IFRIC 17:BC18 to BC20 which explain that the Interpretation did not change the principle as to when to recognise a dividend payable. The principle was moved from IAS 10 into the Interpretation and clarified but without changing the principle. The 'declaration' of a dividend by management does not, therefore, result in a liability when that decision is subject to further approval or when management retains discretion to reverse its decision.

6.3.2.4 Measurement of a dividend payable

A liability to distribute a non-cash asset to owners should be measured at the fair value of the asset to be distributed. [IFRIC 17:11]

If the owners of the entity are given a choice of receiving either a non-cash asset or a cash alternative, the liability for the dividend payable is estimated by considering both the fair value of each alternative and the associated probability of owners selecting each alternative. [IFRIC 17:12]

The carrying amount of the dividend payable is reviewed and adjusted at the end of each reporting period and at the date of settlement. Any changes in the carrying amount are recognised in equity as adjustments to the amount of the distribution. [IFRIC 17:13]

6.3.2.5 Accounting for any difference on settlement

The difference, if any, between the carrying amount of the assets distributed and the carrying amount of the dividend payable is recognised in profit or loss when the dividend is settled. [IFRIC 17:14]

When the fair value of the asset is higher than its carrying amount, the application of IFRIC 17:14 results in the recognition of a profit when the dividend is settled. It will be less usual for a loss to arise. If the fair value of the asset is less than its carrying amount, it will often have been written down for impairment prior to the distribution unless, depending on the nature of the asset, a higher value in use could be justified.

6.3.2.6 Presentation and disclosure

The difference arising on settlement of the dividend described at **6.3.2.5** should be presented as a separate line item in profit or loss. [IFRIC 17:15]

The following information should be disclosed, if applicable:

[IFRIC 17:16]

- the carrying amount of the dividend payable at the beginning and end of the period; and
- the increase or decrease in the carrying amount recognised in the period in accordance with IFRIC 17:13 as a result of a change in the fair value of the assets to be distributed (see **6.3.2.4**).

If, after the end of the reporting period but before the financial statements are authorised for issue, an entity declares a dividend to distribute a non-cash asset, the financial statements should disclose:

[IFRIC 17:17]

- the nature of the asset to be distributed;

- the carrying amount of the asset to be distributed as at the end of the reporting period;

- the estimated fair value of the asset to be distributed as at the end of the reporting period, if different from its carrying amount; and

- the information about the method(s) used to measure that fair value required by IFRS 13:9(b), (d), (g) and (i) and IFRS 13:99 (see **section 11** of **chapter A6**).

6.3.3 Stock or scrip dividends

Companies sometimes issue shares as an alternative to a cash dividend. This is often termed a 'stock dividend', a 'share dividend' or a 'scrip dividend'. Shareholders are usually offered a choice between a cash dividend and a stock dividend alternative. When the dividend is structured such that it is probable that most of the shareholders will decide to take the shares, because the market value of the share alternative is above the cash alternative, the dividend is referred to as an 'enhanced stock dividend'.

Stock dividends may take different legal forms in different jurisdictions. How they affect, for example, distributable reserves and the balance on the share premium reserve will be governed by local legal requirements.

Pure stock dividends (i.e. those without a cash alternative) do not result in a reduction in equity and are not, therefore, strictly 'distributions to owners'. The statement of changes in equity will, therefore, show no net movement for a pure stock dividend.

However, when shareholders have a choice between receiving cash and receiving shares, this will typically involve a distribution to owners. IFRSs do not include any specific guidance on the appropriate accounting in such cases, but the choice of accounting policy may be restricted by local legal or regulatory requirements. One common approach is for the dividend to be shown in the statement of changes in equity, or the note required by IAS 1:137 (see **7.4.2**), at its full 'cash equivalent' amount, irrespective of the extent to which shareholders choose to receive shares rather than cash. When the dividend is presented at its 'gross' or 'full' amount in this manner, there will also be a credit item in the statement of changes in equity to reflect the stock element of the dividend. The notes to the financial statements should provide an explanation of the stock dividend and the policy adopted to account for it. In the absence of clear guidance, other approaches may also be acceptable.

6.4 Capital contributions and deemed distributions

6.4.1 Nature of capital contributions

The term 'capital contribution' is not defined in IFRSs but is generally accepted as meaning a contribution by owners (i.e. a gift made to an entity by an owner which increases the entity's equity without any obligation for the entity to make repayment or to do anything in consideration for receiving it). Capital contributions are most often made by parent entities to their wholly-owned subsidiaries but they may be made in other circumstances. For example, a majority owner might make a capital contribution to an entity in some situations, even though this would result in the benefits being shared with the other owners.

The term 'capital contribution' may be used in some jurisdictions to include arrangements allowing for the contribution to be returned in certain circumstances. The assessment as to whether such a contribution is classified as a liability or as equity is made in accordance with IAS 32 *Financial Instruments: Presentation* (see **chapter B3** or, for entities that have not yet adopted IFRS 9 *Financial Instruments*, **chapter C3**). For the purposes of the analysis below, it is assumed that the contribution is classified as equity in accordance with IAS 32.

Capital contributions are sometimes made for the purpose of improving the financial position of a subsidiary by increasing its net assets without formally increasing its issued share capital (e.g. so as to improve its credit rating). However, in some jurisdictions, capital contributions often serve another purpose which is to eliminate a deficit on distributable profits so that the payment of dividends can be resumed. This may not be achievable by an issue of shares.

Not all non-arm's length transactions between an entity and its owners are in the nature of capital contributions (or distributions). IFRSs do not impose a general requirement to reflect the fair value of such transactions although they require disclosure of related party transactions. Whether a particular transaction should be recognised as a capital contribution is a matter of judgement in the context of the particular facts and circumstances.

6.4.2 Accounting for capital contributions by the recipient

A capital contribution should not be included in profit or loss for the period, nor within other comprehensive income. Instead, it should be presented in the statement of changes in equity (i.e. similar to the proceeds of a share issue). This is because the increase in shareholders' funds is not 'income' as defined in the *Conceptual Framework for Financial Reporting*. The Conceptual Framework defines income as follows.

[CF:4.25(a)]

> "Income is increases in economic benefits during the accounting period in the form of inflows or enhancements of assets or decreases of liabilities that result in increases in equity, other than those relating to contributions from equity participants."

Therefore, income cannot result from 'contributions from equity participants'.

6.4.3 Accounting for capital contributions by the donor

There is no formal financial reporting guidance on the treatment of a capital contribution by the donor (parent) entity, although it is usually capitalised as part of the cost of investment. This is reasonable because, all other things being equal, the net assets of the subsidiary, and therefore its value as an investment, will have increased by the amount of the contribution. However, when the investment is accounted for at cost, it is important to consider whether the investment has suffered an impairment, particularly if the reason for making the contribution is to eliminate the effect of losses made by the subsidiary. An impairment loss should be recognised in respect of the investment, if necessary.

6.4.4 Waiver of intragroup debt

A capital contribution can arise from the waiver of a debt due by a subsidiary to its parent or through the assumption of the subsidiary's liabilities by the parent. A capital contribution can also arise if a subsidiary waives debt due from a fellow subsidiary in the same group. In this case, the waiver of the intragroup debt in one subsidiary is in effect a dividend up to the parent and a subsequent capital contribution from the parent to the fellow subsidiary. While each case should be considered based on the specific facts and circumstances, such transactions should generally be viewed as capital contributions unless there is clearly some other commercial purpose.

The actual amount of debt waived is determined by considering the specific circumstances. For example, in the case of an interest-bearing loan, the amount waived may consist of any principal not yet repaid together with any unpaid interest that has accrued up to the date of waiver. It would not be appropriate to recognise further interest income or expense on such a loan after it has been waived. Accordingly, it is important to establish the date on which the waiver was actually granted, based on a careful assessment of the facts, in order to establish the date on which the capital contribution should be recognised. Separately, the lender should consider whether the loan was already impaired and, if so, recognise any associated impairment loss before accounting for the waiver. (For further discussion of the appropriate accounting entries, see **4.2** and **example 4.2E** in **chapter B8** or, for entities that have not yet adopted IFRS 9, **4.2** and **example 4.2E** in **chapter C8**).

More generally, when a waiver or gift relates to a recent transaction, care should be taken to consider whether the waiver should be accounted for as the reversal of that recent transaction or as a capital contribution. Transactions that are conducted on a non-arms' length basis should be considered on a case-by-case basis to determine whether they result in a capital contribution. It will not usually be appropriate for the borrower to record credits in profit or loss as a result of a waiver of intragroup debt.

6.4.5   Capital contribution made by a parent to a subsidiary as part of a group share-based payment arrangement

When a parent enters into a share-based payment arrangement with employees of its subsidiary and the parent has the obligation to those employees, the subsidiary in its own financial statements measures the services received from its employees in accordance with the requirements of IFRS 2 *Share-based Payment* for equity-settled share-based payment arrangements. A corresponding increase is recognised in equity as a capital contribution from the parent. The accounting by entities within groups for share-based payment arrangements is addressed in **section 8** of **chapter A16**.

There is no requirement within IFRSs to credit the capital contribution to a separate component of equity but this may be affected by local legal and regulatory requirements.

6.4.6   Deemed distribution – interest-free loan from a subsidiary to its parent

Example 6.4.6

Deemed distribution – interest-free loan from a subsidiary to its parent

A subsidiary, Entity S, advances an interest-free loan to its parent, Entity P. The loan is repayable in three years with no option for Entity P to repay the loan in advance of that date or for Entity S to demand early repayment.

Paragraph 5.1.1 of IFRS 9 *Financial Instruments* (or, for entities that have not yet adopted IFRS 9, paragraph 43 of IAS 39 *Financial Instruments: Recognition and Measurement*) requires a financial asset (other than a trade receivable that is determined in accordance with IFRS 15 *Revenue from Contracts with Customers* not to have a significant financing component) to be recognised initially at its fair value. Because Entity S's loan to Entity P is interest-free (and, therefore, not on market terms), the fair value of the loan at initial recognition will be lower than the amount of cash advanced to Entity P.

The difference between the cash advanced to Entity P and the fair value of the loan should be recognised by Entity S as a distribution to Entity P.

The advancement of a loan at a preferential rate of interest is, in substance, a distribution from Entity S to its parent because it reduces the shareholders' funds of Entity S but does not meet the definition of an expense in the *Conceptual Framework for Financial Reporting*. The Conceptual Framework defines expenses as follows.

[CF.4.25(b)]

"Expenses are decreases in economic benefits during the accounting period in the form of outflows or depletions of assets or incurrences of liabilities that result in decreases in equity, other than those relating to distributions to equity participants."

Therefore, an expense cannot result from 'distributions to equity participants'.

A 'deemed distribution' such as this should be presented in the statement of changes in equity (in the same way as any other dividend).

Entity S will recognise interest income in profit or loss using the effective interest method as the discount applied to the cash receivable on maturity of the loan unwinds.

7　The notes

7.1　Structure

7.1.1　Information to be presented in the notes

Notes contain information in addition to that presented in:

[IAS 1:7]

- the statement of financial position;
- the statement(s) of profit or loss and other comprehensive income;
- the statement of changes in equity; and
- the statement of cash flows.

Notes provide narrative descriptions or disaggregations of items presented in those statements and information about items that do not qualify for recognition in those statements. [IAS 1:7]

The notes are required to:

[IAS 1:112]

- present information about the basis of preparation of the financial statements and the specific accounting policies used in accordance with the relevant paragraphs of IAS 1 (see **7.2**);

- disclose the information required by IFRSs that is not presented elsewhere in the financial statements; and

- provide additional information that is not presented elsewhere in the statements but is relevant to an understanding of any of them.

7.1.2 Requirement to present the notes in a systematic manner

The notes should, so far as practicable, be presented in a systematic manner. In determining a systematic manner, an entity should consider the effect on the understandability and comparability of its financial statements. [IAS 1:113]

Examples of systematic ordering or grouping of the notes include:

[IAS 1:114]

- giving prominence to areas of its activities that the entity considers to be most relevant to an understanding of its financial performance and financial position, such as grouping together information about particular operating activities;

- grouping together information about items measured similarly, such as assets measured at fair value;

- following the order of the line items in the statement(s) of profit or loss and other comprehensive income and the statement of financial position, such as:

  - statement of compliance with IFRSs (see **section 3**);

  - significant accounting policies applied (see **7.2**);

  - supporting information for items presented in the financial statements in the order in which each statement and each line item is presented; and

  - other disclosures including (1) contingent liabilities (see **chapter A12**) and unrecognised contractual commitments, and (2) non-financial disclosures, for example an entity's financial risk management objectives and policies (see **chapter B11** or, for entities that have not yet adopted IFRS 9 *Financial Instruments*, **chapter C12**).

IAS 1:113 and 114 have been substantially revised, and IAS 1:115 deleted, as a result of the December 2014 amendments (see **1.2**). These changes are intended to address a perception that IAS 1 requires a specific order for the notes.

In the IASB's view, there must be a system or reason behind the ordering and grouping of the notes. For example, notes could be ordered by importance to the entity, in the order line items are presented in the financial statements, or a combination of these approaches.

The Board also considers that consistency in the order of the notes for a specific entity from period to period is important, and it does not expect the order of an entity's notes to change frequently. A change in the order of the notes previously determined to be an optimal mix of understandability and comparability should generally result from a specific event or transaction, such as a change in business. [IAS 1:BC76D]

Each item in the statement of financial position, the statement(s) of profit or loss and other comprehensive income, the statement of changes in equity and the statement of cash flows should be cross referenced to any related information in the notes. [IAS 1:113]

7.1.3 Non-current assets held for sale and discontinued operations

IFRS 5 *Non-current Assets Held for Sale and Discontinued Operations* clarifies the extent to which the disclosures required by other Standards apply to non-current assets (or disposal groups) held for sale and discontinued operations. It confirms that disclosures required by other IFRSs do not apply to such assets (or disposal groups) or operations unless those IFRSs require:

[IFRS 5:5B]

- specific disclosures in respect of non-current assets (or disposal groups) classified as held for sale or discontinued operations; or

- disclosures about measurement of assets and liabilities within a disposal group that are not within the scope of the measurement requirements of IFRS 5 and such disclosures are not already provided in the other notes to the financial statements.

IFRS 5 also notes that additional disclosures about non-current assets (or disposal groups) classified as held for sale or discontinued operations may be necessary to comply with the general requirements of IAS 1, particularly IAS 1:15 (see **section 3**) and IAS 1:125 (see **7.3**).

The notes supporting the statement of comprehensive income as required by IAS 1 and other Standards will therefore exclude amounts for any discontinued operations. For example, the analysis of expenses by nature or function (see **5.4.2**) will include only amounts for continuing operations. However, it may be helpful in some cases to use a columnar layout to present amounts for continuing operations, discontinued operations and the combined total. This will enable the total amount to be reconciled with other disclosures such as depreciation disclosed in the note for property, plant and equipment.

(For further discussion related to this topic, see **sections 6.3.1** and **7.1** in **chapter A20**.)

7.2   Disclosure of accounting policies

7.2.1   *General requirement to disclose significant accounting policies*

An entity should disclose its significant accounting policies comprising:

[IAS 1:117]

- the measurement basis (or bases) used in preparing the financial statements; and

- the other accounting policies used that are relevant to an understanding of the financial statements.

Notes providing information about the basis of preparation of the financial statements and specific accounting policies may be presented as a separate section of the financial statements. [IAS 1:116]

That is to say, it is acceptable to present a statement of accounting policies that does not form one of the numbered notes to the financial statements.

The December 2014 amendments (see **1.2**) have also clarified that significant accounting policies do not need to be disclosed in one note, but instead can be included with related information in other notes. [IAS 1:BC76C]

7.2.2   *Measurement bases*

It is important that users of the financial statements are informed about the measurement basis or bases used because the basis will significantly affect their analysis. Examples of measurement bases are historical cost, current cost, net realisable value, fair value and recoverable amount. When more than one measurement basis is used in the financial statements (e.g. when particular classes of assets are revalued), it is sufficient to provide an indication of the categories of assets and liabilities to which each measurement basis is applied. [IAS 1:118]

7.2.3 Selection of accounting policies for disclosure

In deciding whether a particular accounting policy should be disclosed, management considers whether disclosure would assist users in understanding how transactions, other events and conditions are reflected in the reported financial performance and financial position. Each entity considers the nature of its operations and the policies that the users of its financial statements would expect to be disclosed for that type of entity. [IAS 1:119]

Disclosure of particular accounting policies is especially useful to users when those policies are selected from alternatives allowed in IFRSs. For example, an entity would disclose whether it applies the fair value or cost model to its investment property. Some IFRSs that permit a choice of policies contain specific disclosure requirements about those choices. For example, IAS 16 *Property, Plant and Equipment* requires disclosure of the measurement bases used for classes of property, plant and equipment. [IAS 1:119]

IAS 1:119 has been amended, and IAS 1:120 deleted, by the December 2014 amendments (see **1.2**) so as to remove unhelpful examples regarding the identification of significant accounting policies.

An accounting policy may be significant because of the nature of an entity's operations even if amounts for current or prior periods are not material. It is also appropriate to disclose each significant policy that is not specifically required by IFRSs but is selected and applied in accordance with IAS 8 *Accounting Policies, Changes in Accounting Estimates and Errors*. [IAS 1:121]

Although IAS 1 highlights the particular importance of the disclosure of policies if there is a choice under the relevant IFRS, it is clear that significant policies should be disclosed even if there is no choice. This is required by IAS 1 and is useful for users of the financial statements who may not be familiar with all of the requirements of the applicable Standards.

7.2.4 Judgements that management has made

An entity should disclose, along with its significant accounting policies or other notes, the judgements management has made, in the process of applying the entity's accounting policies, that have the most significant effect on the amounts recognised in the financial statements. This requirement excludes judgements involving estimations, which are subject to a separate disclosure requirement (see **7.3**). [IAS 1:122]

In the process of applying the entity's accounting policies, management makes various judgements, apart from those involving estimations, that can significantly affect the amounts recognised in the financial statements. Examples given in IAS 1 include:

[IAS 1:123]

- for entities that have not yet adopted IFRS 9, whether financial assets are held-to-maturity investments;

- when substantially all the significant risks and rewards of ownership of financial assets and lease assets are transferred to other entities;

- whether, in substance, particular sales of goods are financing arrangements and, therefore, do not give rise to revenue; and

- whether the contractual terms of a financial asset give rise on specified dates to cash flows that are solely payments of principal and interest on the principal amount outstanding.

In some instances, similar disclosures are specifically required by other IFRSs. For example, IAS 40 *Investment Property* requires, when classification is difficult, disclosure of the criteria developed to distinguish investment property from owner-occupied property and property held for sale in the ordinary course of business. [IAS 1:124]

Disclosure of the most important judgements helps users of financial statements to understand how accounting policies have been applied and to make comparisons between entities. Accordingly, such disclosures are most useful when they avoid 'boilerplate' and explain clearly the most important judgements made.

7.3 Key sources of estimation uncertainty

When there are uncertainties that have a significant risk of causing material adjustment to the carrying amount of assets and liabilities within the next financial year, the notes should disclose:

[IAS 1:125]

- information about the assumptions concerning the future; and

- other major sources of estimation uncertainty at the end of the reporting period.

In respect of those assets and liabilities, the notes should include details of:

[IAS 1:125]

- their nature; and

- their carrying amount at the end of the reporting period.

The disclosures of particular judgements that management made in the process of applying the entity's accounting policies (see **7.2.4**) do not relate to the disclosures of sources of estimation uncertainty described in this section. [IAS 1:132]

Determining the carrying amount of some assets and liabilities requires estimation of the effects of uncertain future events. For example, in the absence of recently observed market prices, future-oriented estimates are necessary to measure:

- the recoverable amount of classes of property, plant and equipment;
- the effect of technological obsolescence on inventories;
- provisions subject to the future outcome of litigation in progress; and
- long-term employee benefit liabilities such as pension obligations.

These estimates involve assumptions about such items as the risk adjustment to cash flows or discount rates, future changes in salaries and future changes in prices affecting other costs. [IAS 1:126]

The assumptions and other sources of estimation uncertainty to be disclosed relate to the estimates that require management's most difficult, subjective or complex judgements. Those judgements become more subjective and complex as the number of variables and assumptions affecting the possible future resolution increases. The potential for a consequential material adjustment to the carrying amount of assets and liabilities normally increases accordingly. [IAS 1:127]

These disclosures are not required for assets or liabilities that are measured at fair value based on a quoted price in an active market for an identical asset or liability. This is so even if there is a significant risk that their carrying amounts might change materially within the next financial year. This is because these changes would not arise from assumptions or other sources of estimation uncertainty at the end of the reporting period. [IAS 1:128]

These disclosures should be presented in a manner that helps users of the financial statements to understand the judgements management makes about the future and about other key sources of estimation uncertainty. The nature and extent of the information to be disclosed will vary according to the nature of the assumptions and the other circumstances. Examples in IAS 1 of the types of disclosures to be made are:

[IAS 1:129]

- the nature of the assumption or other estimation uncertainty;
- the sensitivity of the carrying amounts to the methods, assumptions and estimates underlying their calculation, including the reasons for the sensitivity;

- the expected resolution of an uncertainty and the range of reasonably possible outcomes within the next financial year in respect of the carrying amounts of the assets and liabilities affected; and

- an explanation of changes made to past assumptions concerning those assets and liabilities, if the uncertainty remains unresolved.

However, the Standard confirms that it is not necessary to disclose budget information or forecasts in making these disclosures. [IAS 1:130]

It may be impracticable to disclose the extent of the possible effects of an assumption or another key source of estimation uncertainty at the end of the reporting period. In this case, the entity discloses that it is reasonably possible, based on existing knowledge, that outcomes within the next financial year that are different from assumptions could require a material adjustment to the carrying amount of the affected asset or liability. In all cases, the nature and the carrying amount of the specific asset or liability (or class of assets or liabilities) is disclosed. [IAS 1:131]

Some other IFRSs include specific requirements for disclosures that would otherwise be required by IAS 1. The following examples are given in IAS 1:

[IAS 1:133]

- IAS 37 *Provisions, Contingent Liabilities and Contingent Assets* requires disclosures, in specified circumstances, of major assumptions concerning future events affecting classes of provisions; and

- IFRS 13 *Fair Value Measurement* requires the disclosure of significant assumptions (including the valuation technique(s) and inputs) the entity uses when measuring the fair values of assets and liabilities that are carried at fair value.

It is noteworthy that IAS 1:BC81 states that the disclosures described in this section would be made "in respect of relatively few assets and liabilities (or classes of them)" because they relate only to the most difficult, subjective or complex judgements.

It is also important to understand that the scope of the disclosure is limited to items that have a significant risk of causing material adjustment to the carrying amount of assets or liabilities "within the next financial year". IAS 1:BC84 explains that the longer the future period to which the disclosures relate, the greater the range of items that would qualify for disclosure and the less specific those disclosures could be made. Therefore, the IASB decided to limit the scope of the requirement in this way, noting that a period longer than the next financial year might obscure the most relevant information with other disclosures.

7.4 Other disclosures

7.4.1 Details about the entity

The following should be disclosed in the financial statements, unless disclosed elsewhere in information published with the financial statements: [IAS 1:138]

- the domicile and legal form of the entity;

- its country of incorporation;

- the address of its registered office (or principal place of business, if different);

- a description of the nature of the entity's operations and its principal activities;

- the name of the parent and the ultimate parent of the group; and

- if the entity is a limited life entity, information about the length of its life.

7.4.2 Dividends proposed or declared but not yet recognised

IAS 1 requires disclosure in the notes of: [IAS 1:137]

- the amount of dividends proposed or declared before the financial statements were authorised for issue but not recognised as a distribution to owners;

- the related amount per share; and

- the amount of any cumulative preference dividends not recognised.

These disclosures are in addition to the disclosure required for the amount of dividends recognised as distributions to owners during the period and the related amount per share (see **6.3**).

7.4.3 SIC-29 Service Concession Arrangements: Disclosures

SIC-29 *Service Concession Arrangements: Disclosures* specifies the disclosures that are required for such arrangements to meet the requirements of IAS 1:112(c) (see **7.1.1**). These paragraphs require disclosures to provide additional information that is not presented in the primary financial statements but is relevant to an understanding of them.

Examples of service concession arrangements given in SIC-29 are water treatment and supply facilities, motorways, car parks, tunnels, bridges, airports and telecommunications networks. SIC-29 also explains that outsourcing the operation of an entity's internal services (e.g. employee restaurant, building maintenance, accounting or IT functions) are not service concession arrangements. [SIC-29:1]

Certain aspects and disclosures relating to some service concession arrangements are addressed in other Standards. For example, IAS 16 would apply to property, plant and equipment used in a service concession arrangement. However, SIC-29 points out that service concession arrangements may involve executory contracts that are not addressed in IFRSs, unless the contracts are onerous, in which case IAS 37 applies. SIC-29, therefore, addresses additional disclosures that are relevant to service concession arrangements. [SIC-29:5]

All aspects of service concession arrangements should be considered in determining the appropriate disclosure in the notes. An operator and a grantor should disclose the following in each period:

[SIC-29:6]

- a description of the arrangement;
- significant terms of the arrangement that may affect the amount, timing and certainty of future cash flows (e.g. the period of the concession, repricing dates and the basis upon which repricing or renegotiation is determined);
- the nature and extent (e.g. quantity, time period or amount as appropriate) of:
  - rights to use specified assets;
  - obligations to provide or rights to expect provision of services;
  - obligations to acquire or build items of property, plant and equipment;
  - obligations to deliver or rights to receive specified assets at the end of the concession period;
  - renewal and termination options; and
  - other rights and obligations (e.g. major overhauls);
- changes in the arrangement occurring during the period; and
- how the service arrangement has been classified.

In addition, an operator discloses the amount of revenue and profits or losses recognised in the period on exchanging construction services for a financial asset or an intangible asset. [SIC-29:6A]

These disclosures are required to be provided individually for each service concession arrangement or in aggregate for each class of service concession arrangements. For this purpose, a class is a grouping of service concession arrangements involving services of a similar nature.

For example, arrangements for water treatment services could be treated as a class. [SIC-29:7]

The accounting for certain infrastructure relating to service concession arrangements is dealt with by IFRIC 12 *Service Concession Arrangements* (see **chapter A35** or, for entities that have not yet adopted IFRS 15 *Revenue from Contracts with Customers*, **appendix A3**).

IFRIC 12 explains how an operator should account for infrastructure that it constructs or acquires from a third party for the purpose of the service arrangement, but which is controlled by the grantor. The scope of SIC-29 is wider than this and includes, for example, arrangements in which the operator controls the infrastructure and also applies to the grantor in service concession arrangements.

7.4.4 Disclosures regarding the management of capital

An entity is required to disclose information that enables users of its financial statements to evaluate the entity's objectives, policies and processes for managing capital. [IAS 1:134]

To comply with this principle, IAS 1 requires an entity to disclose the following:

[IAS 1:135]

- qualitative information about its objectives, policies and processes for managing capital, including but not limited to:
  - a description of what it manages as capital;
  - when an entity is subject to externally imposed capital requirements, the nature of those requirements and how those requirements are incorporated into the management of capital; and
  - how it is meeting its objectives for managing capital;
- summary quantitative data about what it manages as capital. Some entities regard some financial liabilities (e.g. some forms of subordinated debt) as part of capital. Other entities regard capital as excluding some components of equity (e.g. components arising from cash flow hedges);
- any changes in the foregoing from the previous period;
- whether, during the period, it has complied with any externally imposed capital requirements to which it is subject; and
- when the entity has not complied with the externally imposed capital requirements to which it is subject, the consequences of such non-compliance.

IAS 1 requires these disclosures to be based on the information provided internally to the entity's key management personnel.

Loan covenants that affect how an entity manages its capital are conditions of a contract between the entity and the lender and are not 'capital requirements'. Consequently, the requirement of IAS 1:135 to disclose the nature of capital requirements and how those requirements are incorporated into the management of capital does not apply. Only capital requirements imposed by external regulators are required to be disclosed under IAS 1:135.

Although IAS 1:134 and 135 do not provide any further guidance regarding what is meant by 'externally imposed capital requirements', paragraphs BC92 to BC97 of the Basis for Conclusions on IAS 1 effectively narrow the scope of the requirements to "entity-specific requirement[s] imposed on a particular entity by its prudential supervisor or other regulator".

Although disclosure of details regarding loan covenants is not required under IAS 1:135, entities should consider whether such details should nevertheless be disclosed in line with the requirements in IAS 1:17 (see **3.4**) to provide additional information to enable users of the financial statements to understand the impact of particular transactions, other events and conditions on the entity's financial position and financial performance.

An entity may manage capital in a number of ways and be subject to a number of different capital requirements. A conglomerate may include entities that undertake banking activities and insurance activities. Those entities may operate in several jurisdictions. When an aggregate disclosure of capital requirements and how capital is managed would not provide useful information or distorts a financial statement user's understanding of an entity's capital resources, the entity should disclose separate information for each capital requirement to which it is subject. [IAS 1:136]

These disclosures are required for all entities, not just regulated entities.

7.4.5 Puttable financial instruments classified as equity

The following disclosures are required for puttable financial instruments classified as equity instruments:

[IAS 1:136A]

- summary quantitative data about the amount classified as equity;

- the entity's objectives, policies and processes for managing its obligation to repurchase or redeem the instruments when required to do so by the instrument holders, including any change from the previous period;

- the expected cash outflow on redemption or repurchase of that class of financial instruments; and

- information about how the expected cash outflow on redemption or repurchase was determined.

Puttable financial instruments have the same meaning as in IAS 32 *Financial Instruments: Presentation* (see **2.1.2** in **chapter B3** or, for entities that have not yet adopted IFRS 9, **2.1.2** in **chapter C3**). [IAS 1:8A]

7.4.6 Employee benefit expense

Whether management elects to report expenses by their nature or by function (see **5.4.2**), the entity will need to disclose an employee benefit expense. Employee benefits in IAS 1 have the same meaning as employee benefits in IAS 19 (see **chapter A15**). [IAS 1:104 & 105]

7.4.7 Disclosures for joint operations

IFRS 11 *Joint Arrangements* requires a joint operator to recognise its share of the assets, liabilities, revenues and expenses of a joint operation in accordance with the IFRSs applicable to those revenues and expenses. Consequently, line items in the entity's financial statements may include amounts relating to operations that are jointly controlled. Neither IAS 1 nor IFRS 11 provides guidance on whether amounts disclosed in the notes required by IAS 1 should include amounts for such operations.

The supporting notes are generally expected to reconcile with the totals presented in the primary financial statements, so they should include amounts in relation to such operations. In some cases, this may lead to a higher level of disclosure in relation to such amounts than would have been required under the equity method.

This approach should also be used for other note disclosures that are not directly linked to totals that appear in the primary financial statements. For example, this would apply to the disclosure of employee benefits expense required by IAS 1:104. However, because IAS 1 is not explicit in this regard, it is important that the basis used (i.e. included or excluded) is explained in the financial statements if this could have a material effect on the amounts disclosed.

8 Future developments

In February 2015, the IASB issued an exposure draft, ED/2015/1 *Classification of Liabilities (Proposed amendments to IAS 1)*, which proposes to clarify the criteria for classification of a liability as either current or non-current. The amendments, if finalised, would:

- eliminate perceived inconsistencies between the requirements in IAS 1:69(d) (see **4.3.1**) and IAS 1:73 (see **4.3.4**);

- clarify that the classification of liabilities as current or non-current should be based on rights that are in existence at the end of the reporting period;

- make the link clear between the settlement of a liability and the outflow of resources from an entity, and explain that the 'settlement' of a liability for classification purposes may be achieved in different forms (e.g. cash, other assets, services and, in some cases, equity); and

- reorganise the guidance on this topic in IAS 1 so that similar examples are presented together.

The comment period on the exposure draft ended on 10 June 2015 and, at the time of writing, the IASB is considering the appropriate next steps for this project.

A5 Accounting policies, changes in accounting estimates and errors

Contents

1 Introduction

1.1 Overview of IAS 8

IAS 8 *Accounting Policies, Changes in Accounting Estimates and Errors* is applied in selecting and applying accounting policies, accounting for changes in estimates and reflecting corrections of prior period errors.

The Standard requires compliance with any specific IFRS applying to a transaction, event or condition, and provides guidance on developing accounting policies for other items that result in relevant and reliable information. Changes in accounting policies and corrections of errors are generally accounted for retrospectively, whereas changes in accounting estimates are generally accounted for on a prospective basis.

IAS 1 *Presentation of Financial Statements* (see **chapter A4**) sets out the disclosure requirements for accounting policies (excluding changes in accounting policies); IAS 8 deals with the accounting and disclosure requirements regarding changes in accounting policies, changes in accounting estimates and the correction of errors.

1.2 Amendments to IAS 8 since the last edition of this manual

None. IAS 8 was most recently amended in May 2011.

2 Definitions

IAS 8:5 provides the following definitions for terms used in the Standard.

- **Accounting policies** are "the specific principles, bases, conventions, rules and practices applied by an entity in preparing and presenting financial statements".

> This definition is fundamental to the sections of IAS 8 dealing with the selection of accounting policies (see **3.1**) and changes in accounting policies (see **3.2**). In particular, it is necessary to distinguish between changes in accounting policies and changes in accounting estimates.

- A **change in an accounting estimate** is "an adjustment of the carrying amount of an asset or a liability, or the amount of the periodic consumption of an asset, that results from the assessment of the present status of, and expected future benefits and obligations associated with, assets and liabilities. Changes in accounting estimates result from new information or new developments and, accordingly, are not corrections of errors".

  The identification, recognition and disclosure of changes in accounting estimates are considered in **section 4**.

- **International Financial Reporting Standards (IFRSs)** are "Standards and Interpretations adopted by the International Accounting Standards Board (IASB). They comprise:

  (a) International Financial Reporting Standards;

  (b) International Accounting Standards;

  (c) IFRIC Interpretations; and

  (d) SIC Interpretations".

  IFRSs are accompanied by guidance to assist entities applying their requirements. All such guidance states whether it is an integral part of IFRSs. Guidance that is an integral part of IFRSs is mandatory; guidance that is not an integral part of IFRSs does not contain requirements for financial statements. [IAS 8:9]

  > IAS 8:9 is clear that implementation guidance published with an IFRS does not form part of that IFRS and, therefore, is not mandatory.
  >
  > Although such guidance does not contain mandatory requirements, it is nevertheless indicative of the way in which the IASB believes the Standard should be implemented. Departures from such guidance should, therefore, be made only after careful consideration and when they can be demonstrated to be fully justified.
  >
  > Agenda decisions issued by the IFRS Interpretations Committee do not form part of IFRSs. However, these agenda decisions can be considered when selecting a suitable accounting policy for a transaction not specifically addressed by a Standard or an Interpretation (see **3.1.2**).

- Omissions or misstatements are **material** if "they could, individually or collectively, influence the economic decisions that users make on the basis of the financial statements. Materiality depends on the size and nature of the omission or misstatement judged in the surrounding circumstances. The size or nature of the item, or both, could be the determining factor".

  > The concept of materiality is also considered in the IASB's Conceptual Framework (see **2.7** in **chapter A4**). The definition of material omissions or misstatements is relevant to the determination of whether prior period errors are material. This, in turn, determines whether retrospective restatement is required when such errors have arisen in a prior period (see **section 5**).

- **Prior period errors** are "omissions from, and misstatements in, the entity's financial statements for one or more prior periods resulting from a failure to use, or misuse of, reliable information that:

  (a) was available when financial statements for those periods were authorised for issue; and

(b) could reasonably be expected to have been obtained and taken into account in the preparation and presentation of those financial statements.

Such errors include the effects of mathematical mistakes, mistakes in applying accounting policies, oversights or misinterpretation of facts, and fraud".

As explained at **5.2**, IAS 8 requires all material prior period errors to be corrected by retrospective restatement unless this is impracticable.

- **Retrospective application** is "applying a new accounting policy to transactions, other events and conditions as if that policy had always been applied".

- **Retrospective restatement** is "correcting the recognition, measurement and disclosure of amounts of elements of financial statements as if a prior period error had never occurred".

- **Prospective application** of a change in accounting policy and of recognising the effect of a change in an accounting estimate, respectively, are:

  (a) "applying the new accounting policy to transactions, other events and conditions occurring after the date as at which the policy is changed; and

  (b) recognising the effect of the change in the accounting estimate in the current and future periods affected by the change".

- Applying a requirement is **impracticable** "when the entity cannot apply it after making every reasonable effort to do so. For a particular prior period, it is impracticable to apply a change in accounting policy retrospectively or make a retrospective restatement to correct an error if:

  (a) the effects of the retrospective application or retrospective restatement are not determinable;

  (b) the retrospective application or retrospective restatement requires assumptions about what management's intent would have been in that period; or

  (c) the retrospective application or retrospective restatement requires significant estimates of amounts and it is impossible to distinguish objectively information about those estimates that:

    (i) provides evidence of circumstances that existed on the date(s) as at which those amounts are to be recognised, measured or disclosed; and

    (ii) would have been available when the financial statements for that prior period were authorised for issue from other information".

For some types of estimates (e.g. a fair value measurement that uses significant unobservable inputs), it is impracticable to distinguish these types of information. When retrospective application or retrospective restatement would require making a significant estimate for which it is impossible to distinguish these two types of information, it is impracticable to apply the new accounting policy or correct the prior period error retrospectively. [IAS 8:52]

> This definition is relevant to exemptions from the general rule of retrospective application for changes in accounting policies (see **3.2**) and the correction of material prior period errors (see **5.2**). Impracticability in respect of retrospective application and retrospective restatement are considered further in **section 6**.

3   Accounting policies

3.1   Selection of accounting policies

3.1.1   Specific IFRS applies

When an IFRS specifically applies to a transaction, other event or condition, the accounting policy or policies applied to that item are determined by applying the IFRS. [IAS 8:7]

It is not necessary to apply these policies if the effect of applying them is immaterial. But this does not mean that immaterial departures from IFRSs can be made, or left uncorrected, in order to achieve a particular presentation of an entity's financial position, performance or cash flows. [IAS 8:8]

> In practice, an entity will sometimes wish to consider applying the requirements of IFRSs even when the effect is immaterial. This is in part because materiality is subject to judgement based on both quantitative and qualitative factors, but also because items that are not material in the current period may become material in a subsequent period.

3.1.2   No specific IFRS applies

If there is no IFRS that specifically applies to the transaction, event or condition under consideration, judgement is required by management in developing and applying an accounting policy that results in information that is:

[IAS 8:10]

- relevant to the economic decision-making needs of users; and
- reliable, in that the financial statements:

- represent faithfully the financial position, financial performance and cash flows of the entity;

- reflect the economic substance of transactions, other events and conditions, and not merely the legal form;

- are neutral (i.e. free from bias);

- are prudent; and

- are complete in all material respects.

IAS 8:10 continues to refer to the selection of an accounting policy with a view to reporting information that is 'prudent' and has not been amended to reflect the changes made in the IASB's *Conceptual Framework for Financial Reporting* (see **chapter A2**). Specifically, no reference is made in the Conceptual Framework to prudence or conservatism as an aspect of faithful representation because the Board considered that including either would be inconsistent with neutrality. The Board concluded that, even with the prohibitions against deliberate misstatement that appear elsewhere, an admonition to be prudent would be likely to lead to a bias. [CF:BC3.27 - 29]

It seems likely that the Board will process required amendments to IFRSs for consistency with the Conceptual Framework as further progress is made on the Conceptual Framework project. In the meantime, it is useful to refer to the wording in paragraph 37 of the *Framework for the Preparation and Presentation of Financial Statements* (the IASB's predecessor framework): "[p]rudence is the inclusion of a degree of caution in the exercise of the judgements needed in making the estimates required under conditions of uncertainty, such that assets or income are not overstated and liabilities or expenses are not understated. However, the exercise of prudence does not allow ... the creation of hidden reserves or excessive provisions, the deliberate understatement of assets or income, or the deliberate overstatement of liabilities or expenses, because the financial statements would not be neutral and, therefore, not have the quality of reliability".

In practical terms, in forming a judgement about a suitable accounting policy, management should refer to, and consider the applicability of, the following sources in descending order:

[IAS 8:11]

- requirements in IFRSs dealing with similar and related issues; and

- the definitions, recognition criteria and measurement concepts for assets, liabilities, income and expenses in the Conceptual Framework.

Agenda decisions issued by the IFRS Interpretations Committee form an important source of guidance although they do not form part of IFRSs. Relevant agenda decisions should be carefully considered as indicative (but not definitive) guidance when selecting a suitable accounting policy for a transaction not specifically addressed by a Standard or an Interpretation.

In the absence of specifically applicable requirements, when an entity is making reference to and considering the applicability of IFRS requirements for similar and/or related issues, the question arises as to whether it is necessary to apply all aspects of the IFRS to the issues being analogised, or whether it could be appropriate to consider only certain aspects of that IFRS. This issue was considered by the IFRS Interpretations Committee in March 2011. The Committee observed that "when management develops an accounting policy through analogy to an IFRS dealing with similar and related matters, it needs to use its judgement in applying all aspects of the IFRS that are applicable to the particular issue".

Therefore, when analogising to the requirements of an IFRS, an entity is not necessarily bound to apply all of the requirements of that IFRS. Rather, the entity should use its judgement in determining which aspects of that IFRS are applicable to the particular issue and then apply all those aspects of the IFRS that it judges to be applicable.

The most recent pronouncements of other standard-setting bodies that use a similar conceptual framework to develop accounting standards, accounting literature and accepted industry practices may also be considered, provided that they do not conflict with the above sources. [IAS 8:12]

Example 3.1.2

Selection of accounting policy for combinations of entities under common control – requirement to restate comparative information

Entities S1 and S2 are two subsidiaries of holding company H. Following a decision by H to reorganise the legal structure of the group, S1 acquires S2 (i.e. H now holds an indirect interest in S2 in place of the direct interest it held before the reorganisation). The acquisition of S2 by S1 is considered a combination of entities under common control and, under paragraph 2(c) of IFRS 3 *Business Combinations*, is excluded from the scope of that Standard.

This is the first time that S1 has entered into a transaction of this nature and, therefore, it is required to develop a new accounting policy. In the absence of specific IFRS literature on the topic, S1 has applied the requirements of IAS 8:10 to 12 and, in its consolidated financial statements, has chosen to account for the transaction at S2's carrying amounts at the date of the transaction (i.e. as a pooling of interests).

Is S1 obliged to restate the comparative periods in its consolidated financial statements as if S1 had acquired S2 at the beginning of the earliest period presented?

No. Even if S1 has developed its accounting policy by reference to a pronouncement of another standard-setting body that requires restatement of comparatives when the pooling-of-interests method is applied, S1 is not bound to apply all of the requirements of that pronouncement.

However, the decision-usefulness of the restated comparative information should be considered by management when developing its accounting policy and, if the failure to restate comparative information would be detrimental to the users of the financial statements, restatement should be considered. In addition, S1 should consider local regulatory requirements that may require (or prohibit) restatement of comparative periods for such transactions.

3.1.3 Accounting policies to be applied consistently

Accounting policies should be applied consistently for similar transactions, other events and conditions, unless an IFRS specifically requires or permits categorisation of items for which different policies may be appropriate. If this is the case, an appropriate accounting policy should be selected and applied consistently to each category. [IAS 8:13]

IFRS 10 *Consolidated Financial Statements* requires that consolidated financial statements should be prepared using uniform accounting policies for like transactions and other events in similar circumstances. [IFRS 10:19] There is no such requirement for the individual or separate financial statements of a parent and its subsidiaries.

In practice, most subsidiaries will choose to apply accounting policies that are applied by their parent because this will simplify the consolidation process. Also, the factors that determine the most appropriate policy for the group will often also determine that the same policy is the most appropriate for the subsidiary.

3.2 Changes in accounting policies

3.2.1 Circumstances in which a change in accounting policy is permitted

An accounting policy can be changed only if the change:

[IAS 8:14]

- is required by an IFRS; or

- results in the financial statements providing reliable and more relevant information about the effects of transactions, other events or conditions on the entity's financial position, financial performance or cash flows.

It is important that changes in accounting policies are only made if one of the criteria in IAS 8:14 is met; otherwise comparability over time within the financial statements will be lost. [IAS 8:15]

One consequence of the requirements of IAS 8:14 is that if a policy is changed in one year, it is unlikely to be justifiable to change it back to the original policy in a subsequent year. Similarly, it would be difficult to justify the adoption of a policy when it is known that the policy will be changed again in a subsequent year because of a new Standard or an Interpretation in issue but not yet effective at the date of the first change.

Example 3.2.1

Voluntary change in accounting policy for investment property

Entity R has applied IFRSs for a number of years. Prior to its 20X3 reporting period, Entity R's policy was to account for all of its investment property using the cost model, as permitted by IAS 40 *Investment Property*. Most of the other participants in Entity R's business sector apply the alternative model permitted under IAS 40 (i.e. the fair value model). In 20X3, because of this prevalence, Entity R decides to change its accounting policy for all investment property to the fair value model on the basis that this model will provide reliable and more relevant information for the users of its financial statements.

Because this is a voluntary change in accounting policy rather than first-time application of the Standard, the transition provisions in IAS 40:80 to 84 do not apply. Consequently, the new accounting policy should be applied retrospectively for all Entity R's investment property, except to the extent that retrospective application is impracticable. (In this scenario, retrospective application will typically be possible because the necessary fair value information in respect of prior periods will have been obtained and disclosed in accordance with IAS 40:79(e), other than in the exceptional cases described in IAS 40:53 (see **5.2.4** in **chapter A8**). Note that the exception from retrospective application in IAS 8:17 (see **3.2.4**) applies only to assets within the scope of IAS 16 *Property, Plant and Equipment* and IAS 38 *Intangible Assets* and, accordingly, is not available for investment property.)

3.2.2   Application of new accounting policy following a change in circumstances

It should be noted that the application of an accounting policy to a transaction, other event or condition that differs in substance from those previously occurring in an entity does not qualify as a change in accounting policy. Equally, the application of a new accounting policy to a transaction, event or condition that had not previously occurred in an entity (or was previously immaterial) does not qualify as a change in accounting policy. [IAS 8:16]

Example 3.2.2

Change in use of property

Entity N owns an office building that in previous reporting periods has been classified as property, plant and equipment and accounted for under IAS 16 using the cost model. During the current reporting period, Entity N has vacated the property and it has been leased to a third party. Entity N's accounting policy for investment property under IAS 40 is to use the fair value model.

Is the change in the accounting treatment for the office building from the cost model under IAS 16 to the fair value model under IAS 40 a change in accounting policy?

No. The change in accounting treatment has arisen because of a change in circumstances rather than a change in accounting policy. Entity N's policy for each type of property remains unchanged but the office building in question is accounted for as an investment property from the date of change of use. No retrospective restatement should be made in these circumstances.

3.2.3 Application of a new IFRS in advance of its effective date

Example 3.2.3

Application of a new IFRS in advance of its effective date

Company M's reporting period ended on 31 December 20X1 and it has applied IFRSs for several years. On 15 January 20X2, a new Standard is issued by the IASB which is effective for annual periods beginning on or after 1 January 20X3, with earlier application permitted. Company M will not issue its 20X1 financial statements until 1 March 20X2.

Is Company M permitted to apply this new Standard issued after the reporting period, but prior to the issue of financial statements, in its 20X1 financial statements?

Yes. Because the new Standard allows for application in advance of its effective date, Company M has the option to apply the new Standard for periods in respect of which financial statements have not yet been issued. If the new Standard did not allow for application in advance of its effective date, early application would not be permitted.

Company M may not adopt exposure drafts or other guidance that has not been issued in its final form by the date of issue of its financial statements if this would conflict with the requirements of IFRSs in effect at the reporting date.

Early application of an IFRS is not a voluntary change in accounting policy (see **3.2.5**). Therefore, any specific transition provisions in the new Standard should be applied for Company M's 20X1 financial year. If the new Standard does not include any specific transition provisions relating to the change in accounting policy, the change should be applied retrospectively.

> If the entity decides not to apply the Standard in advance of its effective date, the requirements of IAS 8:30 apply (see **3.4.3**).

3.2.4 Initial application of a policy to revalue assets in accordance with IAS 16 or IAS 38

The initial application of a policy to revalue assets in accordance with IAS 16 or IAS 38 is a change in accounting policy to be dealt with as a revaluation in accordance with those Standards rather than in accordance with IAS 8. IAS 8 also states that its requirements in paragraphs 19 to 31 do not apply to such changes in accounting policy. [IAS 8:17 - 18]

Application of the exception in IAS 8:17 is restricted to assets within the scope of IAS 16 and IAS 38; it does not apply, for example, when an entity revalues investment property under IAS 40's fair value model for the first time (see **example 3.2.1**).

There is no further guidance in IAS 16 or IAS 38 as to how the initial application of a policy to revalue assets under those Standards should be recognised or disclosed; however, Example 3 in the implementation guidance accompanying IAS 8 (see **3.3.2**) notes that such a change from the cost model to the revaluation model is required to be accounted for prospectively.

3.2.5 Applying changes in accounting policies

When an entity initially applies an IFRS, the change is accounted for in accordance with the specific transition provisions of that IFRS. If the IFRS does not contain transition provisions, the change is applied retrospectively. [IAS 8:19] Early application of a Standard does not constitute a voluntary change in accounting policy. [IAS 8:20]

If an entity changes an accounting policy voluntarily, the change is applied retrospectively. [IAS 8:19]

As noted in **3.1.2**, in the absence of an IFRS that applies to a specific transaction, other event or condition, the pronouncements of standard-setters using a similar conceptual framework may be considered in selecting an appropriate accounting policy. If, following an amendment of such a pronouncement, an entity chooses to change an accounting policy, this change is accounted for, and disclosed, as a voluntary change in accounting policy in accordance with IAS 8. [IAS 8:21]

In other words, the entity may not apply any transition provisions in the pronouncement of the other standard-setter.

3.3 Retrospective application

3.3.1 Retrospective application – general

Except when the impracticability exception discussed at **3.3.2** applies, if retrospective application of an accounting policy is required by the criteria in **3.2.5**, it is accounted for as follows:

[IAS 8:22]

- the opening balance of each affected component of equity for the earliest prior period presented is adjusted as if the new accounting policy had always been applied; and

- the other comparative amounts disclosed for each prior period presented are adjusted as if the new accounting policy had always been applied.

As explained further at **3.3.2**, an entity applies a new accounting policy retrospectively to comparative information for prior periods as far back as is practicable. The amount of the resulting adjustment relating to periods before those presented in the financial statements is made to the opening balance of each affected component of equity of the earliest period presented. Usually the adjustment is made to retained earnings. However, the adjustment may be made to another component of equity (e.g. to comply with an IFRS). Any other information about prior periods, such as historical summaries of financial data, is also adjusted as far back as practicable. [IAS 8:26]

When it is impracticable to restate the earlier periods of any historical summaries in the financial statements, this should be made clear and the affected periods identified.

Entities are required to present an additional statement of financial position, as at the beginning of the preceding period, when a new accounting policy is applied retrospectively and the retrospective application has a material effect on the statement of financial position at the beginning of the preceding period (see **2.10.4** in **chapter A4**).

3.3.2 Limitations on retrospective application

When retrospective application of a change in accounting policy is required by IAS 8:19, the change is applied retrospectively except to the extent that it is impracticable to determine either the period-specific effects or the cumulative effect of the change. [IAS 8:23] The definition of 'impracticable' is considered in **section 2** and further guidance is provided in **section 6**.

The impracticability exemption applies both to voluntary changes in accounting policies and to those made in accordance with the transition provisions in a new or revised IFRS.

When it is impracticable to determine the period-specific effects of changing an accounting policy on comparative information for one or more prior periods presented, the new accounting policy is applied to the carrying amounts of assets and liabilities as at the beginning of the earliest period for which retrospective application is practicable. This may be the current period. Corresponding adjustments are made to the opening balance of each affected component of equity for that period. [IAS 8:24]

When a new policy is applied retrospectively, it is applied to comparative periods as far back as is practicable. Retrospective application to a prior period is not practicable unless it is practicable to determine the cumulative effect on the amounts in both the opening and closing statements of financial position for that period. [IAS 8:26]

When it is impracticable to determine the cumulative effect, at the beginning of the current period, of applying a new accounting policy to all prior periods, the comparative information is adjusted to apply the new accounting policy prospectively from the earliest date practicable. [IAS 8:25] That is to say, the new policy is applied prospectively from the start of the earliest period practicable. The portion of the cumulative adjustment to assets, liabilities and equity arising before that date is therefore disregarded. Changing an accounting policy is permitted even if it is impracticable to apply the policy prospectively for any prior period. [IAS 8:27]

Example 3.3.2

Prospective application of a change in accounting policy when retrospective application is not practicable

[IAS 8:IG3.1 - IG3.4, Example 3]

During 20X2, Delta Co changed its accounting policy for depreciating property, plant and equipment, so as to apply much more fully a components approach, whilst at the same time adopting the revaluation model.

In years before 20X2, Delta's asset records were not sufficiently detailed to apply a components approach fully. At the end of 20X1, management commissioned an engineering survey, which provided information on the components held and their fair values, useful lives, estimated residual values and depreciable amounts at the beginning of 20X2. However, the survey did not provide a sufficient basis for reliably estimating the cost of those components that had not previously been accounted for separately, and the existing records before the survey did not permit this information to be reconstructed.

Delta's management considered how to account for each of the two aspects of the accounting change. They determined that it was not practicable to account for the change to a fuller components approach retrospectively, or to account for that change prospectively from any earlier date than the start of 20X2. Also, the change from a cost model to a revaluation model is required to be accounted for prospectively. Therefore, management concluded that it should apply Delta's new policy prospectively from the start of 20X2.

Additional information:

Delta's tax rate is 30 per cent.

	CU
Property, plant and equipment at the end of 20X1:	
Cost	25,000
Depreciation	(14,000)
Net book value	11,000
Prospective depreciation expense for 20X2 (old basis)	1,500
Some results of the engineering survey:	
Valuation	17,000
Estimated residual value	3,000
Average remaining asset life (years)	7
Depreciation expense on existing property, plant and equipment for 20X2 (new basis)	2,000

Extract from the notes

From the start of 20X2, Delta changed its accounting policy for depreciating property, plant and equipment, so as to apply much more fully a components approach, whilst at the same time adopting the revaluation model. Management takes the view that this policy provides reliable and more relevant information because it deals more accurately with the components of property, plant and equipment and is based on up-to-date values. The policy has been applied prospectively from the start of 20X2 because it was not practicable to estimate the effects of applying the policy either retrospectively, or prospectively from any earlier date. Accordingly, the adoption of the new policy has no effect on prior years. The effect on the current year is to increase the carrying amount of property, plant and equipment at the start of the year by CU6,000; increase the opening deferred tax provision by CU1,800; create a revaluation surplus at the start of the year of CU4,200; increase depreciation expense by CU500; and reduce tax expense by CU150.

3.3.3 Tax effects of retrospective adjustments

IAS 8 states that the tax effects of corrections of prior period errors and of retrospective adjustments made to apply changes in accounting policies are accounted for and disclosed in accordance with IAS 12 *Income Taxes*. [IAS 8:4] Accounting for the current and deferred tax effects of a transaction or other event should be consistent with the accounting for the transaction or event itself. [IAS 12:57] The implementation guidance accompanying IAS 8 provides an example of a retrospective restatement, which clearly demonstrates that the income tax effect is part of the retrospective adjustment.

Therefore, if an adjustment is recognised against opening retained earnings, the tax effect should also be recognised against opening retained earnings.

As explained at **4.7.1** in **chapter A13**, subsequent movements in the deferred tax balance follow the item to which the deferred tax balance relates. For the purpose of subsequent movements (reversals or remeasurements), a deferred tax balance that was recognised through a retrospective adjustment against retained earnings is, nonetheless, considered to have been established in profit or loss if the retrospective adjustment was made in respect of a transaction that affected profit or loss. For example, an item of property, plant and equipment that is recognised at fair value as its deemed cost at the date of transition to IFRSs in accordance with IFRS 1 *First-time Adoption of International Financial Reporting Standards* may give rise to a deferred tax liability. Although the additional deferred tax liability arising on transition is recognised in opening retained earnings, the reversal of that deferred tax balance relates to depreciation of the item of property, plant and equipment. Consequently, it should be recognised in profit or loss, consistent with the recognition of the depreciation expense.

3.4   Disclosure

3.4.1   *Initial application of an IFRS*

The requirements in this section apply on the initial application of an IFRS. They do not apply on first-time adoption of IFRSs, when the disclosure requirements in IFRS 1 apply instead (see **chapter A3**). However, the disclosures detailed below are required when an entity applies a new Standard in advance of its effective date (which, as noted at **3.2.3**, is not regarded as a voluntary change in policy for the purposes of IAS 8).

If the initial application of an IFRS:

- has an effect on the current period or any prior period; or

- would have such an effect except that it is impracticable to determine the amount of any adjustment; or

- may have an effect on future periods,

the following should be disclosed:

[IAS 8:28]

- the title of the IFRS;

- when applicable, that the change in accounting policy is made in accordance with its transition provisions;

- the nature of the change in accounting policy;

- when applicable, a description of the transition provisions;

- when applicable, the transition provisions that might have an effect on future periods; and

- for the current period and each prior period presented, to the extent practicable, the amount of the adjustment:

  - for each financial statement line item affected; and

  - if IAS 33 *Earning per Share* applies to the entity, for basic and diluted earnings per share;

  - the amount of the adjustment relating to periods before those presented, to the extent practicable; and

  - if retrospective application is impracticable for a particular prior period, or for periods before those presented, the circumstances that led to the existence of that condition and a description of how and from when the change in accounting policy has been applied.

Financial statements of subsequent periods need not repeat these disclosures. [IAS 8:28]

When adopting a new Standard or Interpretation with specific transition provisions, the entity should still follow the disclosure requirements of IAS 8:28 to the extent that the transition provisions do not override those requirements or make them inapplicable. For example, if a new Standard requires prospective application only, the disclosures regarding the amount of the adjustments and line items affected in prior periods will not be relevant.

3.4.2   Voluntary change in accounting policy

Early application of a new IFRS is not a voluntary change in accounting policy for the purposes of IAS 8. [IAS 8:20] Therefore, the requirements at **3.4.1** apply to such changes instead of the requirements in this section.

When a voluntary change in accounting policy:

- has an effect on the current period or any prior period; or

- would have such an effect except that it is impracticable to determine the amount of any adjustment; or

- may have an effect on future periods,

the following should be disclosed:

[IAS 8:29]

- the nature of the change in accounting policy;

- the reasons why applying the new accounting policy provides reliable and more relevant information; and

- for the current period and each prior period presented, to the extent practicable, the amount of the adjustment:

  - for each financial statement line item affected; and

  - if IAS 33 applies to the entity, for basic and diluted earnings per share;

  - the amount of the adjustment relating to periods before those presented, to the extent practicable; and

  - if retrospective application is impracticable for a particular prior period, or for periods before those presented, the circumstances that led to the existence of that condition and a description of how and from when the change in accounting policy has been applied.

Financial statements of subsequent periods need not repeat these disclosures. [IAS 8:29]

3.4.3   IFRSs in issue but not yet effective

When an entity has not applied a new Standard or Interpretation that has been issued but is not yet effective, the following should be disclosed by the entity:

[IAS 8:30]

- this fact; and

- known or reasonably estimable information relevant to assessing the possible impact that application of the new IFRS will have on the entity's financial statements in the period of initial application.

The disclosures required by IAS 8:30 should be made in respect of all IFRSs issued before the date of issue of the financial statements that are not yet effective.

It will be helpful if the relevant note to the financial statements either specifies the date at which the details are given or refers explicitly to them being as at the date of authorisation of the financial statements.

In complying with the general requirement of IAS 8:30, an entity should consider disclosing:

[IAS 8:31]

- the title of the new IFRS;

- the nature of the impending change or changes in accounting policy;

- the date by which application of the IFRS is required;

- the date as at which it plans to apply the IFRS initially; and

- either:

  - a discussion of the impact that initial application of the IFRS is expected to have on the entity's financial statements; or

  - if that impact is not known or reasonably estimable, a statement to that effect.

It is clear from BC31 in the Basis for Conclusions on IAS 8 that the matters listed in IAS 8:31 are not intended to be mandatory disclosure requirements; they are instead matters that an entity 'considers' in applying IAS 8:30.

The question arises as to whether it is necessary for the financial statements to list every new or amended IFRS that has been issued but is not yet effective, even if it is expected to have no material effect on the entity's financial statements. The safest approach is to provide a complete list because this clearly meets the requirements of the Standard and reduces the risk that some new pronouncements might be overlooked.

However, a briefer disclosure may be acceptable in some circumstances; for example, it may be acceptable not to mention a pronouncement that plainly does not affect the entity because of its scope. Another factor to consider is that when a new pronouncement has no material effect, it may be acceptable to adopt it in advance of its effective date (which would have no material effect) and so exclude it from the disclosures required by IAS 8:30.

When a complete list is not provided, it may be wise to include a statement to the effect that the impact of all other IFRSs not yet adopted is not expected to be material.

4　Changes in accounting estimates

4.1　Identification of accounting estimates

The definition of a change in an accounting estimate is set out in **section 2**.

Accounting estimates arise from inherent uncertainties in business activities which mean that many items in financial statements cannot be measured with precision but can only be estimated. Estimates are formed using judgements based on the latest available, reliable information. Common examples of estimates in the financial statements include:

[IAS 8:32]

- allowances for bad debts;

- allowances for inventory obsolescence;

- the fair value of financial assets or financial liabilities;

- the useful lives of, or the expected pattern of consumption of the future economic benefits embodied in, depreciable assets; and

- warranty obligations.

The use of reasonable estimates is essential in the preparation of financial statements. A revision of an estimate may be required if the circumstances on which the estimate was based change, or if new information or experience is gained. The revision of an estimate does not relate to prior periods and is not equivalent to the correction of an error. [IAS 8:34]

It should be noted that a change in the measurement basis applied to an item in the financial statements constitutes a change in accounting policy, not a change in accounting estimate. In circumstances when it is difficult to distinguish between a change in an accounting policy and a change in an accounting estimate, the change is treated as a change in an accounting estimate. [IAS 8:35]

4.2   Recognition of changes in accounting estimates

The effect of a change in an accounting estimate is recognised prospectively by including it in profit or loss in:

[IAS 8:36 - 38]

- the period of the change, if the change affects that period only (e.g. revision of a bad debts estimate); or

- the period of the change and future periods, if the change affects both (e.g. revision of the estimated useful economic life of a depreciable asset).

Example 4.2

Change in estimate of a provision for a lawsuit

Should a change in the estimate of the outcome of a pending lawsuit be recognised in profit or loss in the year of the change?

Yes. Even though the original estimate of the outcome may have been made several years previously, and the case may continue for a number of years, a change in the estimate of the outcome should be recognised in profit or loss in the period (year) of the change.

However, to the extent that a change in an accounting estimate gives rise to changes in assets and liabilities, or relates to an item of equity, it should be recognised by adjusting the carrying amount of the related asset, liability or equity item in the period of the change. [IAS 8:37]

In other words, a change in accounting estimate need not be reported in profit or loss when it is appropriately reflected in the carrying amount of other assets or liabilities, or taken directly to equity, in accordance with the requirements of other IFRSs.

When a change in an accounting estimate is recognised in profit or loss, the change should be recognised in the same line item as the underlying item, except when an IFRS requires a different treatment. For example, if the best estimate of a provision for a legal claim is reduced, the credit in profit or loss should be included within the same expense heading as the original expense was recognised. This ensures that the cumulative expense recognised under that heading is correct.

The disclosure requirements of IAS 8:39 and 40 (see **4.3**) should be complied with. In addition, if the change in accounting estimate causes a material distortion in a particular expense heading, additional disclosure may be required in accordance with paragraph 97 of IAS 1 *Presentation of Financial Statements* (see **5.4.1** in **chapter A4**).

4.3 Disclosure

An entity discloses the nature and amount of a change in an accounting estimate that has an effect in the current period or is expected to have an effect in future periods. The disclosure of the effect on future periods is not required when it is impracticable to estimate that effect. [IAS 8:39]

If the amount of the effect in future periods is not disclosed because estimating it is impracticable, the entity should disclose this fact. [IAS 8:40]

5 Errors

5.1 Material errors

Financial statements do not comply with IFRSs if they contain either:

- material errors; or
- immaterial errors made intentionally in order to achieve a particular presentation of an entity's financial position, financial performance or cash flows.

The definition of 'material' for this purpose is considered in **section 2**.

Errors can occur in respect of the recognition, measurement, presentation or disclosure of elements of the financial statements. [IAS 8:41]

Errors are distinguished from changes in accounting estimates because accounting estimates, by their very nature, are items that may need to be revised as additional information becomes known. For example, the gain or loss recognised on the outcome of a contingency is not the correction of an error. [IAS 8:48]

Although, in principle, the distinction between errors and corrections of estimates is clear, it may sometimes be difficult in practice to establish what information was available, or should have been available, at the time when an estimate was made.

5.2 Correction of errors

If a current period error is discovered before the financial statements are authorised for issue, it is corrected in the current period. However, if a material error remains undetected until a subsequent period, the prior period error is corrected retrospectively in the first set of financial statements authorised for issue after its discovery. [IAS 8:41]

Except when it is impracticable to do so (see below), material prior period errors are corrected by:

[IAS 8:42]

- restating the comparative amounts for the prior period(s) presented in which the error occurred; or

- if the error occurred before the earliest prior period presented, restating the opening balances of assets, liabilities and equity for the earliest prior period presented.

The correction of the prior period error is excluded from profit or loss in the period of discovery. [IAS 8:46]

The tax effects of retrospective adjustments are discussed at **3.3.3**.

IAS 8 does not differentiate between fundamental errors and other material prior period errors; the IASB concluded that the definition of 'fundamental errors' in the previous version of the Standard was difficult to interpret consistently because the main feature of the definition (that the error causes the financial statements of one of more prior periods no longer to be considered to have been reliable) was also a feature of all material prior period errors. [IAS 8:BC12]

IAS 8 refers to the correction of material prior period errors by retrospective restatement but does not say that *only* material errors may be corrected in this way. It is silent on the correction of immaterial errors which is consistent with the fact that IFRSs do not apply to immaterial items. Nevertheless, the explicit reference to 'material' in IAS 8:42

suggests that only material errors should be corrected in this way. This is the way in which the requirement is normally interpreted.

A prior period error is corrected by retrospective restatement, except to the extent that it is impracticable to determine either:

[IAS 8:43]

- the period-specific effects; or
- the cumulative effect of the error.

The definition of 'impracticable' is considered in **section 2** and further guidance is provided in **section 6**.

If it is impracticable to determine the period-specific effects of an error on comparative information for one or more prior periods presented, the opening balances of assets, liabilities and equity are restated for the earliest period for which retrospective restatement is practicable. This may be the current period. [IAS 8:44]

If it is impracticable to determine the cumulative effect on all prior periods of a prior period error at the beginning of the current period, the comparative information is restated to correct the error prospectively from the earliest date practicable. [IAS 8:45] The entity therefore disregards the portion of the cumulative restatement of assets, liabilities and equity arising before that date. [IAS 8:47]

Any information presented about prior periods, including any historical summaries of financial data, is restated as far back as practicable. [IAS 8:46]

When it is impracticable to restate the earlier periods of any historical summaries in the financial statements, this should be made clear and the affected periods identified.

5.3 Disclosure of prior period errors

When a material prior period error is corrected in accordance with IAS 8, the following should be disclosed:

[IAS 8:49]

- the nature of the prior period error; and
- for each prior period presented, to the extent practicable, the amount of the correction:
  - for each financial statement line item affected; and
  - if IAS 33 *Earning per Share* applies to the entity, for basic and diluted earnings per share;

- the amount of the correction at the beginning of the earliest prior period presented; and

- if retrospective restatement is impracticable for a particular prior period, the circumstances that led to the existence of that condition and a description of how and from when the error has been corrected.

Financial statements of subsequent periods need not repeat these disclosures. [IAS 8:49]

Entities are required to present an additional statement of financial position, as at the beginning of the preceding period, when an error is corrected by retrospective restatement and the retrospective restatement has a material effect on the statement of financial position at the beginning of the preceding period (see **2.10.4** in **chapter A4**).

6   Impracticability in respect of retrospective application and retrospective restatement

6.1   Obstacles faced in retrospective application and restatement

6.1.1   Meaning of 'impracticable'

The term 'impracticable' is defined in **section 2**. It may be impracticable to adjust comparative information for one or more prior periods to achieve comparability with the current period. This may be the case because data was not collected in the prior period(s) in a way that allows either retrospective application of a new accounting policy, or retrospective restatement to correct a prior period error, and it may be impracticable to recreate the information. [IAS 8:50]

Restatement is not impracticable just because of the cost or effort involved. When revising IAS 8 in 2003, the IASB considered replacing the exemption from retrospective application or restatements on the basis of 'impracticability' with one based on 'undue cost or effort'. However, based on comments received on the exposure draft, the IASB decided that an exemption based on management's assessment of undue cost or effort was too subjective to be applied consistently by different entities. The IASB decided that balancing costs and benefits was a task for the Board when it sets accounting requirements rather than for entities when they apply those requirements. Therefore, although the Standard does not explicitly state that undue cost or effort alone does not render restatement impracticable, this is the clear intention of the Board and is consistent with the definition in the Standard. [IAS 8:BC24]

6.1.2 Estimates

It is often necessary to make estimates in applying an accounting policy to elements of financial statements recognised or disclosed in respect of transactions, other events or conditions. Estimation is inherently subjective, and estimates may be developed after the reporting period.

Further, developing estimates is potentially more difficult when retrospectively applying an accounting policy or making a retrospective restatement to correct a prior period error, because of the longer period of time that may have passed since the affected transaction, other event or condition occurred. However, the objective of estimates relating to prior periods remains the same as for estimates made in the current period, i.e. for the estimate to reflect the circumstances that existed *when the transaction, other event or condition occurred.* [IAS 8:51]

As explained in **section 2**, it may sometimes be impracticable to distinguish information that:

- provides evidence of circumstances that existed on the date(s) as at which the transaction, other event or condition occurred; and

- would have been available when the financial statements for that period were authorised for issue,

from other information. [IAS 8:52]

Nevertheless, IAS 8 notes that the fact that significant estimates are frequently required when amending comparative information presented for prior periods does not prevent reliable adjustment or correction of the comparative information. [IAS 8:53]

6.2 Use of hindsight

Hindsight should not be used when applying a new accounting policy to, or correcting amounts for, a prior period, either in making assumptions about what management's intentions would have been in a prior period or estimating the amounts recognised, measured or disclosed in a prior period.

IAS 8 cites the example of an entity's calculation of its liability for employees' accumulated sick leave in accordance with IAS 19 *Employee Benefits.* When correcting a prior period error in relation to this calculation, the entity disregards information about an unusually severe influenza season during the next period that became available after the financial statements for the prior period were authorised for issue. [IAS 8:53]

A6　Fair value measurement

Contents

1   Introduction

1.1   Overview of IFRS 13

IFRS 13 defines fair value, provides guidance on *how* fair value should be measured, and establishes consistent requirements for disclosures regarding fair value measurements. The Standard defines fair value on the basis of an 'exit price' notion, which is a market-based, rather than an entity-specific, measurement.

The requirements of IFRS 13 apply whenever an entity is required or permitted to use fair value for measurement or disclosure purposes other than in the limited circumstances listed in IFRS 13:6 and IFRS 13:7 (see **section 2**). Its scope is broad; it covers both financial and non-financial items (e.g. real estate properties, intangible assets, biological assets and agricultural produce). However, IFRS 13 does not mandate *when* fair value measurements should be used; requirements regarding when it is appropriate to measure particular categories of assets, liabilities or an entity's own equity instruments at fair value are dealt with in other IFRSs. For example, whether a financial instrument is required to be measured at fair value at the end of each reporting period depends on the classification and measurement requirements of IFRS 9 *Financial Instruments* (or, for entities that have not yet adopted IFRS 9, IAS 39 *Financial Instruments: Recognition and Measurement*). If IFRS 9 (or IAS 39) requires that the financial instrument be measured at fair value, that fair value is determined in accordance with IFRS 13.

This chapter covers the general principles of IFRS 13, the general requirements applicable to both financial and non-financial items, and the specific requirements regarding the measurement of fair value for non-financial items.

IFRS 13's specific requirements regarding the measurement of financial instruments at fair value, and more detailed application guidance, are set out in **chapter B7** (for entities applying IFRS 9) and **chapter C7** (for entities applying IAS 39).

1.2   Application of the IFRS 13 framework

The table and flow chart below set out a step-by-step approach to applying the basic measurement principles of IFRS 13. The table also provides a high level summary of some of the key concepts underlying IFRS 13 and illustrates the framework for measuring fair value. The summary does not address all of the requirements of the Standard – users should refer to the more detailed discussions later in this chapter and to the text of the Standard for a fuller understanding.

Note that Steps 2 to 4 do not necessarily occur in the order set out in the table and flow chart (i.e. they are inter-related).

#	Step	Explanation
1.	Identify the 'asset' or 'liability' being measured (i.e. the **unit of account**) (see **section 3.2**).	IFRS 13 notes that the asset or liability measured at fair value may be (1) a stand-alone asset or liability (e.g. an investment property), (2) a group of assets or a group of liabilities, or (3) a group of assets and liabilities (e.g. a cash-generating unit). The level at which fair value is measured will depend on the 'unit of account' specified in other IFRSs (typically, the level at which the asset or liability is aggregated or disaggregated for recognition or disclosure purposes). For example: • in accordance with IAS 36 *Impairment of Assets*, an entity may be required to measure fair value less costs of disposal for a cash-generating unit (CGU) when assessing its recoverable amount; and • under IFRS 9 *Financial Instruments* (or, for entities that have not yet adopted IFRS 9, IAS 39 *Financial Instruments: Recognition and Measurement*), the unit of account is generally an individual financial instrument.
2a.	For non-financial assets, determine the asset's **highest and best use** (see **section 4**).	A fair value measurement of a non-financial asset is based on its 'highest and best use'. This concept is not relevant for financial assets, liabilities or an entity's own equity instruments because those items do not have alternative uses as contemplated in IFRS 13. The highest and best use must be determined from the perspective of market participants, even if an entity intends a different use. However, there is a presumption that an entity's current use of a non-financial asset is its highest and best use, unless there is evidence to suggest otherwise. Consequently, IFRS 13 does not require an entity to perform an exhaustive search for other potential uses of a non-financial asset. The highest and best use of an asset might provide maximum value through either (1) its use in combination with other assets or other assets and liabilities, or (2) on a stand-alone basis.

#	Step	Explanation
2b.	For **financial assets and financial liabilities with offsetting market risks or counterparty credit risk**, evaluate the criteria for the fair value exception and establish a policy (see **section 6** of **chapter B7** (for entities applying IFRS 9) and **section 6** of **chapter C7** (for entities applying IAS 39)).	IFRS 13 permits an exception to the general fair value measurement requirements for financial assets and financial liabilities if an entity: • manages the group of assets and liabilities on the basis of its net exposure to market risks or counterparty credit risk; • provides information on that basis to key management personnel; and • measures those assets and liabilities at fair value in the statement of financial position. In summary, the exception permits an entity to measure the fair value of the group of assets and liabilities (i.e. the portfolio) rather than the individual assets and liabilities within the portfolio. Details of the exception, including the detailed criteria for qualification, are set out in IFRS 13:48 to 56 (see **section 6** of **chapter B7** (for entities applying IFRS 9) and **section 6** of **chapter C7** (for entities applying IAS 39)). The application of this exception is an accounting policy choice in accordance with IAS 8 *Accounting Policies, Changes in Accounting Estimates and Errors* and must be applied consistently from period to period for a particular portfolio. This exception does not change the *unit of account* (which continues to be the individual instrument determined under IFRS 9 or IAS 39), but changes the *unit of measurement* from the individual financial instrument to the group (portfolio) of financial instruments.
2c.	For liabilities and an entity's own equity instruments, assume the liabilities or equity instruments are **transferred to market participants at the measurement date** (see **section 5**).	IFRS 13 requires that the fair value of a liability or an entity's own equity instrument be based on an assumed transfer to a market participant even if the entity does not intend to transfer the liability or equity instrument to a third party or it is unable to do so.

#	Step	Explanation
		Under this assumption, the fair value of a liability should be measured on the basis that the liability would remain outstanding and the transferee would be required to fulfil the obligation; it should not be assumed that the liability would be settled or otherwise extinguished. Similarly, the fair value of an entity's own equity instrument should be measured on the basis that the equity instrument would remain outstanding and the transferee would take on the rights and responsibilities associated with the instrument; it should not be assumed that the instrument would be cancelled or otherwise extinguished.
		In addition, the measurement of liabilities and own equity instruments depends on whether identical liabilities or equity instruments are held by other parties as assets.
3.	Identify the market in which to price the asset or liability – i.e. either (1) the **principal market**, or (2) if no principal market exists, the **most advantageous market** (see section 3.3).	The principal market is "[t]he market with the greatest volume and level of activity for the asset or liability". The most advantageous market is "[t]he market that maximises the amount that would be received to sell the asset or minimises the amount that would be paid to transfer the liability…".
		If there is a principal market for the asset or liability, the fair value measurement should reflect the price in that market, even if the price in a different market is potentially more advantageous at the measurement date. In the absence of evidence to the contrary, the market in which an entity would normally enter into a transaction to sell the asset or to transfer the liability is presumed to be the principal (or most advantageous) market. Therefore, an entity is permitted to use the price in the market in which it normally enters into transactions unless there is evidence that the principal (or most advantageous) market and that market are not the same.
		A market cannot be identified as the principal (or most advantageous) market unless the entity has access to that market at the measurement date.

#	Step	Explanation
4.	Develop assumptions that **market participants** in the principal (or most advantageous) market would use when pricing the asset or liability (see **section 3.4**).	'Market participants' are buyers and sellers in the principal (or most advantageous) market for the asset or liability that are (1) independent of each other, (2) knowledgeable, (3) able to enter into a transaction for the asset or liability, and (4) willing to enter into such a transaction. An entity need not identify specific market participants, but should identify characteristics that distinguish market participants generally.
5.	Estimate fair value using appropriate **valuation techniques** and related **inputs** (see **sections 8** and **9**).	When the price for an asset or a liability cannot be observed directly, it must be estimated using a valuation technique. Entities should use valuation techniques that are appropriate in the circumstances and for which sufficient data are available to measure fair value, maximising the use of relevant observable inputs and minimising the use of unobservable inputs. Highest priority should be given to unadjusted quoted prices in active markets for identical assets or liabilities. IFRS 13 refers to three widely used valuation techniques: • the market approach (see **8.4**); • the cost approach (see **8.5**); and • the income approach (see **section 8.6**). Any valuation technique used to measure fair value should be consistent with one or more of these approaches. IFRS 13 does not set out a hierarchy of valuation techniques because particular valuation techniques may be more appropriate in some circumstances than in others. The use of multiple valuation techniques may be appropriate in certain circumstances. In those cases, the results should be evaluated considering the reasonableness of the range of values indicated by those results. A fair value measurement is the point within that range that is most representative of the fair value in the circumstances. Once a valuation technique has been selected, it should be applied consistently. A change in a valuation technique or its application (e.g. a change in its weighting when multiple valuation techniques are used or a change in an adjustment applied to a valuation technique) is only appropriate if the change results in a measurement that is equally or more representative of fair value in the circumstances.

#	Step	Explanation
		An entity should evaluate the factors listed in IFRS 13:B37 (see **9.5**) to determine whether there has been a significant decrease in the volume or level of activity for the asset or liability relative to normal market activity. When such a decrease has occurred, this will affect the entity's selection of techniques and/or inputs and the weight placed on quoted prices.
6.	If the exception in Step 2b applies, **allocate the fair value** calculated in Step 5 (which might include several units of account) **to the individual units of account** that are the subject of the fair value measurement (as determined in Step 1) (see **section 6** of **chapter B7** (for entities applying IFRS 9) and **section 6** of **chapter C7** (for entities applying IAS 39)).	If the fair value calculated in Step 5 is for multiple units of account, the fair value should be allocated to the individual units of account that are the subject of the fair value measurement on a reasonable and consistent basis.
7.	Classify the fair value measurement within the **fair value hierarchy** (see **section 10**) and prepare the disclosures required by IFRS 13 (see **section 11**).	IFRS 13 establishes a fair value hierarchy that categorises into three levels the inputs to valuation techniques used to measure fair value (see **section 10.2**). When several inputs are used to measure the fair value of an asset or a liability, those inputs may be categorised within different levels of the fair value hierarchy (e.g. the valuation may be based on some Level 2 and some Level 3 inputs). In such circumstances, the categorisation of the fair value measurement in its entirety is based on the lowest level input that is significant to the entire measurement. IFRS 13 sets out disclosure requirements in respect of fair value measurements. The disclosures vary depending on whether the assets or liabilities are measured at fair value on a recurring or non-recurring basis. The disclosure requirements set out in IFRS 13 do not apply to fair value measurements on initial recognition.

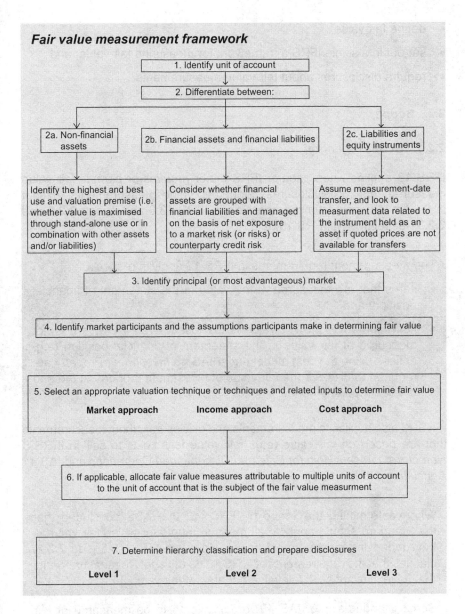

Fair value measurement framework

1. Identify unit of account

2. Differentiate between:

| 2a. Non-financial assets | 2b. Financial assets and financial liabilities | 2c. Liabilities and equity instruments |

| Identify the highest and best use and valuation premise (i.e. whether value is maximised through stand-alone use or in combination with other assets and/or liabilities) | Consider whether financial assets are grouped with financial liabilities and managed on the basis of net exposure to a market risk (or risks) or counterparty credit risk | Assume measurement-date transfer, and look to measurment data related to the instrument held as an asset if quoted prices are not available for transfers |

3. Identify principal (or most advantageous) market

4. Identify market participants and the assumptions participants make in determining fair value

5. Select an appropriate valuation technique or techniques and related inputs to determine fair value

Market approach   **Income approach**   **Cost approach**

6. If applicable, allocate fair value measures attributable to multiple units of account to the unit of account that is the subject of the fair value measurment

7. Determine hierarchy classification and prepare disclosures

Level 1   **Level 2**   **Level 3**

1.3 Amendments to IFRS 13 since the last edition of this manual

None. IFRS 13 was most recently amended in December 2013.

2 Objective and scope

2.1 Objective

The objective of IFRS 13 is to:

[IFRS 13:1]

- define fair value;

- set out in a single IFRS a framework for measuring fair value; and

- require disclosures about fair value measurements.

2.2 Scope

2.2.1 Scope – general

IFRS 13 applies when another IFRS either *requires* or *permits* fair value measurements, or disclosures about fair value measurements, except in the limited circumstances specified in IFRS 13:6 and 7 (see **2.2.2** and **2.2.3**, respectively). [IFRS 13:5]

> The measurement requirements in IFRS 13 apply in respect of:
>
> - items that are measured at fair value in the statement of financial position; and
>
> - items for which the fair value is disclosed, even if the item is not measured at fair value in the statement of financial position (e.g. entities using the cost model under IAS 40 *Investment Property* are required to disclose the fair value of investment property at the end of each reporting period). [IFRS 13:BC25]

IFRS 13 also applies to measurements and disclosures about measurements that are *based on* fair value (e.g. 'fair value less costs to sell' in IFRS 5 *Non-current Assets Held for Sale and Discontinued Operations* and IAS 41 *Agriculture*). [IFRS 13:5]

> When determining the scope of IFRS 13, the IASB concluded that the Standard should apply to all measurements for which fair value is the "underlying measurement basis". However, IFRS 13:6 (see **2.2.2**) clarifies that the requirements of IFRS 13 do not apply to measurements that have similarities to fair value but are not fair value. [IFRS 13:BC24]
>
> Some Standards (e.g. IAS 40) require items to be measured at fair value on an ongoing basis (IFRS 13 refers to this as 'fair value on a recurring basis'); some (e.g. IFRS 5) require fair value only in specified circumstances (IFRS 13 refers to this as 'fair value on a non-recurring basis'); and some (e.g. IFRS 3 *Business Combinations*) require fair value only on initial recognition of an item. IFRS 13 applies in all of these circumstances (subject to the exceptions in IFRS 13:6 and 7 (see **2.2.2** and **2.2.3**, respectively)).

The measurement requirements of IFRS 13 apply equally when an item is measured at fair value at initial recognition and for measurement at fair value subsequent to recognition. [IFRS 13:8]

The discussion in IFRS 13 (and, consequently, throughout this chapter) focuses on assets and liabilities. Note, however, that the Standard also applies when an entity's own equity instruments are measured at fair value. [IFRS 13:4]

Examples of fair value measurements within the scope of IFRS 13 include, but are not limited to:

- identifiable assets and liabilities of an acquiree measured at fair value at the acquisition date under IFRS 3 (but see **2.3.5** regarding the application of IFRS 13's disclosure requirements in such circumstances);

- non-current assets and disposal groups classified as held for sale measured at fair value less costs to sell under IFRS 5;

- property, plant and equipment and intangible assets measured using the revaluation models in IAS 16 *Property, Plant and Equipment* and IAS 38 *Intangible Assets*, respectively;

- measurement by the issuer of the fair value of a compound financial instrument, and the fair value of the liability component of that compound financial instrument, for the purpose of measuring the debt and equity components of the instrument at initial recognition under IAS 32 *Financial Instruments: Presentation*;

- the recoverable amount of an asset or a cash-generating unit determined under IAS 36 when it is based on fair value less costs of disposal (see **2.3.1**);

- financial assets and financial liabilities within the scope of IFRS 9 *Financial Instruments* (or, for entities that have not yet adopted IFRS 9, IAS 39 *Financial Instruments: Recognition and Measurement*) required to be measured at fair value at initial recognition or at subsequent reporting dates;

- investment property measured subsequent to initial recognition using the fair value model under IAS 40 or investment property measured using the cost model under IAS 40 (for which the fair value is disclosed even though the investment property is not measured at fair value in the statement of financial position); and

- biological assets and agricultural produce measured at fair value less costs to sell at initial recognition or at subsequent reporting dates under IAS 41.

2.2.2 Scope exclusions – measurement and disclosure requirements

The measurement and disclosure requirements of IFRS 13 do not apply to the following:

[IFRS 13:6]

- share-based payment transactions within the scope of IFRS 2 *Share-based Payment*;

- leasing transactions within the scope of IAS 17 *Leases*; and

- measurements that have some similarities to fair value but are not fair value (e.g. 'net realisable value' in IAS 2 *Inventories* or 'value in use' in IAS 36 *Impairment of Assets*).

2.2.3   Scope exclusions – disclosure requirements only

The disclosures specified by IFRS 13 are not required for:

[IFRS 13:7]

- plan assets measured at fair value in accordance with IAS 19 *Employee Benefits*;

- retirement benefit plan investments measured at fair value in accordance with IAS 26 *Accounting and Reporting by Retirement Benefit Plans*; and

- assets for which recoverable amount is fair value less costs of disposal in accordance with IAS 36.

2.3   Examples of application of scope requirements and exclusions

2.3.1   Impact of IFRS 13 on impairment testing under IAS 36

In specified circumstances, IAS 36 requires an entity to estimate the recoverable amount of an asset or a cash-generating unit (CGU). The recoverable amount of an asset or a CGU is the higher of its fair value less costs of disposal and its value in use (see **chapter A10** for detailed requirements).

IFRS 13's measurement requirements will affect the impairment testing of assets or CGUs under IAS 36 when an entity is required to estimate the asset's (or the CGU's) fair value less costs of disposal. This will be the case when an entity is required by IAS 36 to estimate the recoverable amount of the asset or CGU, unless it has already been determined that the value in use of the asset or CGU is higher than its carrying amount (see **section 6** of **chapter A10**).

One aspect of the IFRS 13 model that has particular significance in the context of impairment testing is that, when measuring fair value, an entity is required to use the assumptions that market participants would use, even if the entity has no intention of selling the asset (see **section 3.4**). If unobservable inputs (i.e. inputs for which market data are not available) are used, IFRS 13:89 states that "an entity may begin with its own data, but it shall adjust those data if reasonably available information indicates that other market participants would use different data or there is something particular to the entity that is not available to other market participants". Therefore, an entity may need to adjust its internally developed assumptions to reflect the assumptions that market participants would use.

In addition, when measuring the fair value of a non-financial asset, the entity must consider the highest and best use of the asset from the perspective of market participants, even if the entity intends a different use (see **section 4**). However, an entity's current use of a non-financial asset can be presumed to be its highest and best use unless market or other factors suggest that a different use by market participants would maximise the value of the asset (see IFRS 13:29).

Note that, in accordance with IFRS 13:7 (see **2.2.3**), IFRS 13's disclosure requirements do not apply to assets or CGUs for which an entity is required to estimate the fair value less costs of disposal. Instead, an entity should comply with the disclosure requirements in IAS 36.

2.3.2 Application of IFRS 13 to provisions within the scope of IAS 37

Provisions falling within the scope of IAS 37 *Provisions, Contingent Liabilities and Contingent Assets* are not measured at fair value. Such provisions are measured at the entity's best estimate of the expenditure required to settle the present obligation at the end of the reporting period (see **section 4** of **chapter A12**). Consequently, the measurement and disclosure requirements of IFRS 13 do not apply to provisions within the scope of IAS 37.

IAS 37:37 states that the best estimate of the expenditure required to settle a present obligation is "the amount that an entity would rationally pay to settle the obligation at the end of the reporting period or to transfer it to a third party at that time". Although this measure may have some similarities to fair value, it is not fair value or based on fair value and, consequently, in accordance with IFRS 13:6 (see **2.2.2**), IFRS 13 does not apply.

2.3.3 Application of IFRS 13 to the net defined benefit liability (asset) for a defined benefit retirement benefit plan

IFRS 13 does not apply to the net defined benefit liability (asset) reported in the statement of financial position for a defined benefit retirement benefit plan under IAS 19 *Employee Benefits*. However, the measurement requirements of IFRS 13 do apply to plan assets, which is the only component of the net defined benefit liability (asset) that is measured at fair value.

For the other components of the net defined benefit liability (asset) (i.e. those that are not measured at fair value), employers should follow the measurement requirements set out in IAS 19.

Although plan assets are subject to the measurement requirements in IFRS 13, in accordance with IFRS 13:7 (see **2.2.3**), IFRS 13's disclosure requirements do not apply.

2.3.4 Application of IFRS 13 to fair value information disclosed in the financial statements that is not required by IFRSs

An entity may disclose in its financial statements fair value information that is not required to be disclosed by IFRSs. Such 'supplementary' fair value information is generally presented in the notes to the financial statements and it is most commonly presented in one of the following circumstances:

- the disclosure is encouraged (but not required) by an IFRS. For example, IAS 16:79(c) suggests that, when the cost model is being used, a disclosure that might be relevant for users of the financial statements is "the fair value of property, plant and equipment when this is materially different from the carrying amount" ; or

- the disclosure is required by local legislation or by a regulator; or

- the entity wishes to draw attention to particular circumstances (e.g. a significant shift in the fair value of assets measured on a cost basis in the financial statements).

The requirements of IFRS 13 generally apply to such supplementary fair value information. IFRS 13 applies "when another IFRS requires or permits fair value measurements or disclosures about fair value measurements" other than in the limited circumstances listed in IFRS 13:6 and 7 (see **2.2.2** and **2.2.3**, respectively). Therefore, when an entity presents supplementary fair value information that is encouraged by another IFRS (e.g. under IAS 16:79(c) as described above), the fair value measure that is disclosed should comply with the measurement requirements of IFRS 13, and certain of the disclosures required under IFRS 13 as specified in IFRS 13:97 (see **11.5**) should be presented.

Equally, when an entity voluntarily presents information about fair value, a user of the financial statements will generally be entitled to assume, unless otherwise stated, that the term has the same meaning as elsewhere in the financial statements, and the entity should comply with the requirements of IFRS 13 as described in the previous paragraph.

In some circumstances, local legislation or other regulations may require disclosure in the financial statements of an amount described by the relevant authority as 'fair value' but for which the relevant authority specifies a measurement basis that differs from the basis of measurement for fair value under IFRS 13. In such circumstances, while the entity is obliged to comply with the requirements imposed by the relevant authority, the measurement basis used for the specified disclosure, and the fact that the basis differs from that which would be used under IFRSs, should be clearly disclosed.

2.3.5 Application of the disclosure requirements of IFRS 13 to assets and liabilities acquired in a business combination

IFRS 3 generally requires the identifiable assets and liabilities of an acquiree to be measured at fair value at the date of acquisition. As a result, the acquirer is required to apply the measurement requirements of IFRS 13 to these acquisition date fair values.

However, IFRS 13:91 establishes that the disclosure requirements of IFRS 13 apply to assets and liabilities that are measured at fair value on a recurring or non-recurring basis in the statement of financial position *after* initial recognition (see **11.1**). This is supported by IFRS 13:BC184, which clarifies that the disclosure requirements in IFRS 13 apply only to fair value measurements made after initial recognition because other IFRSs address the disclosures required at the time of initial recognition. Consequently, because an acquiree's identifiable assets and liabilities are measured at fair value at the date of acquisition for the purpose of their initial recognition in the consolidated financial statements of the acquirer, the disclosure requirements of IFRS 13 need not be applied to those acquisition-date measurements.

2.3.6 Application of the disclosure requirements of IFRS 13 to assets and liabilities measured at fair value and included within a disposal group classified as held for sale

Under IFRS 5, assets and liabilities excluded from the scope of the measurement requirements of that Standard may nevertheless be included within a disposal group classified as held for sale, and the disposal group as a whole is subject to the measurement requirements and the classification and presentation requirements of IFRS 5 (see **section 2** of **chapter A20** for details).

Items included within a disposal group that are not subject to the measurement requirements of IFRS 5 are measured in accordance with applicable IFRSs; some items (e.g. financial instruments) may be measured at fair value. If assets and liabilities that are measured at fair value on a recurring or non-recurring basis are part of a disposal group classified as held for sale, the question arises as to whether the disclosure requirements of IFRS 13 apply to those assets and liabilities.

The extent to which the disclosure requirements of other IFRSs apply to assets or liabilities included within disposal groups classified as held for sale is addressed in IFRS 5:5B which states that "[d]isclosures in other IFRSs do not apply to [non-current assets held for sale] (or disposal groups) unless those IFRSs require ... disclosures about measurement of assets and liabilities within a disposal group that are not within the scope of the measurement requirement of IFRS 5". Therefore, for assets and liabilities excluded from the scope of the measurement requirements of IFRS 5 that are included within a disposal group classified as held for sale and that are measured at fair value, the effect of IFRS 5:5B is that the disclosure requirements of IFRS 13 apply *to the extent that those disclosure requirements relate to measurement.*

Given that IFRS 13 as a whole is concerned with the measurement of fair value, and with disclosures regarding the measurement of fair value, all of the disclosure requirements of IFRS 13 relate to 'measurement' and, consequently, should be applied.

When determining the classes of assets and liabilities as required by IFRS 13:94 (see **11.3**), and preparing the fair value measurement disclosures, an entity should distinguish assets and liabilities that are part of a disposal group classified as held for sale from its other assets and liabilities. The classes determined in accordance with IFRS 13:94 should be consistent with the major classes of assets and liabilities disclosed separately in accordance with IFRS 5:38 (see **7.3.1** in **chapter A20**).

3 Definition of fair value

3.1 Definition of fair value – general

Fair value is defined as "[t]he price that would be received to sell an asset or paid to transfer a liability in an orderly transaction between market participants at the measurement date". [IFRS 13:Appendix A]

This basis for measuring fair value is commonly referred to as an *exit price* approach because it reflects the price at which a market participant that holds the asset or owes the liability could *exit* that asset or liability by selling the asset or transferring the liability to a third party.

Note that the definition assumes a hypothetical and orderly exchange transaction (i.e. it is not an actual sale or a forced transaction or distress sale). [IFRS 13:BC30]

Fair value as defined above is a market-based measurement (not an entity-specific value). [IFRS 13:2] It is therefore measured using the assumptions that market participants would use when pricing the asset or liability, including assumptions about risk. Consequently, an entity's intention to hold an asset or to settle or otherwise fulfil a liability is not relevant when measuring fair value. [IFRS 13:3]

IFRS 13's definition clarifies that fair value should reflect current market conditions (which reflect the current expectations of market participants about future market conditions, rather than those of the reporting entity). [IFRS 13:BC31]

The extent to which market information is available can vary between different types of assets and liabilities. For some assets and liabilities, observable market transactions or market information may be available. For other assets and liabilities, observable market transactions and market information may not be available. However, the objective under IFRS 13 in both circumstances is the same – to estimate the price at which an orderly transaction to sell the asset or to transfer the liability would take place between market participants at the measurement date under current market conditions. [IFRS 13:2] When a price for an identical asset or liability is not observable, an entity measures fair value using another valuation technique that maximises the use of relevant observable inputs and minimises the use of unobservable inputs. [IFRS 13:3]

A fair value measurement requires an entity to determine all the following:

[IFRS 13:B2]

- the particular asset or liability that is the subject of the measurement (consistently with its unit of account);

- for a non-financial asset, the valuation premise that is appropriate for the measurement (consistently with its highest and best use);

- the principal (or most advantageous) market for the asset or liability; and

- the valuation technique(s) appropriate for the measurement, considering the availability of data with which to develop inputs that represent the assumptions that market participants would use when pricing the asset or liability and the level of the fair value hierarchy within which the inputs are categorised.

Key elements of the definition of fair value are discussed in the following sections, namely:

- the asset or liability that is being measured (see **section 3.2**);

- the market in which the transaction is assumed to occur (see **section 3.3**);

- the market participants that are assumed to enter into the transaction (see **section 3.4**); and

- the 'price' at which the transaction is assumed to occur (see **section 3.5**).

3.2   Identifying the asset or liability

3.2.1   Determining the appropriate unit of account

The asset or liability being measured at fair value may be (1) a stand-alone asset or liability (e.g. an investment property), (2) a group of assets or a group of liabilities, or (3) a group of assets and liabilities (e.g. a cash-generating unit). The level at which fair value is measured will depend on the 'unit of account' (typically, the level at which the asset or liability is aggregated or disaggregated for recognition or disclosure purposes). [IFRS 13:13 and Appendix A]

The unit of account is determined in accordance with the IFRS that requires or permits the fair value measurement, except as provided in IFRS 13. [IFRS 13:14]

IFRS 13 does not generally prescribe the unit of account. The IASB concluded that IFRS 13 should describe *how* to measure fair value, not *what* is being measured at fair value. Other IFRSs specify whether a fair value measurement considers an individual asset or liability or a group of assets or liabilities (i.e. the unit of account). For example:

[IFRS 13:BC47]

- IAS 36 *Impairment of Assets* states that an entity should measure the fair value less costs of disposal for a cash-generating unit when assessing its recoverable amount. Therefore, the cash-generating unit is the unit of account for fair value measurement purposes; and

- under IFRS 9 *Financial Instruments* (or, for entities that have not yet adopted IFRS 9, IAS 39 *Financial Instruments: Recognition and Measurement*), the unit of account is generally an individual financial instrument.

In September 2014, the IASB issued an exposure draft (ED/2014/4) *Measuring Quoted Investments in Subsidiaries, Joint Ventures and Associates at Fair Value*. The ED considers the unit of account for the purposes of measuring the fair value of investments in subsidiaries, joint ventures and associates when the investment is quoted in an active market. The following are examples of circumstances in which:

- an entity chooses to measure such investments at fair value in accordance IFRS 9 (or, for entities that have not yet adopted IFRS 9, IAS 39) in its separate financial statements;

- an acquirer acquires the controlling interest in an investee where the previously-held interest is required to be measured at fair value;

- an investment entity parent measures its investments in subsidiaries (other than subsidiaries that provide investment-related services or activities) at fair value in accordance with IFRS 10; and

- an entity is required to measure the fair value of its investment in a subsidiary, joint venture or associate as part of an impairment assessment in accordance with IAS 36.

In the ED, the IASB proposes that the unit of account for investments in subsidiaries, joint ventures and associates is the investment as a whole, and that the fair value measurement of an investment composed of financial instruments quoted in an active market should be the product of the quoted price of each instrument (P) multiplied by the quantity (Q) of instruments held (i.e. P × Q) without adjustments. This is on the basis that the quoted prices in an active market provide the most reliable evidence of fair value. The comment period for the ED ended in January 2015 and, at the time of writing, the IASB is in the redeliberation phase of the project.

Given the ongoing debate, there are two acceptable approaches to fair valuing interests in subsidiaries, joint ventures and associates when the individual investment is quoted in an active market. The unit of account can be considered the individual investment and, therefore, the interest is fair valued as the quantity multiplied by the price of an individual instrument (i.e. P × Q) or, alternatively, the unit of account can be considered as a whole and thus potentially the P × Q valuation can be adjusted to reflect the premium that would be paid for control, joint control or significant influence over an investee. It should be noted that any such adjustment would be unobservable (i.e. a Level 3 input). If significant, this would result in the entire fair value measurement being categorised as Level 3 and, therefore, additional disclosures stipulated by IFRS 13 with regard to Level 3 fair value measurement (e.g. a description of the valuation process and inputs used and of sensitivity to changes in the unobservable input used) would be required. An entity should select its approach as an accounting policy and apply it consistently in fair valuing interests in subsidiaries, joint ventures and associates when the individual investment is quoted in an active market.

The following examples set out considerations for determining the appropriate unit of account for equity interests held by an entity and how the fair value of those interests should be measured.

Scenario	Unit of account prescribed in the applicable IFRS

Scenario 1

Entity A owns a 16 per cent equity interest in Entity B (160 million ordinary shares). Entity B's ordinary shares are traded in an active market. The share price of each ordinary share at the measurement date is CU0.5. Entity A accounts for the 16 per cent equity interest at fair value at initial recognition and at the end of each reporting period in accordance with IFRS 9 (or, for entities that have not yet adopted IFRS 9, IAS 39).

IFRS 9 (or IAS 39) is the applicable Standard that requires the fair value measurement.

IFRS 13:80 specifically discusses a scenario where an entity holds a position in a single asset or liability (including a position comprising a large number of identical assets or liabilities) and the asset or liability is traded in an active market; in such circumstances, the unit of account is the individual financial instrument (see **10.2.1.1**). The fair value of such a holding of financial instruments is required to be measured within Level 1 as the product of the quoted price (P) for the individual financial instrument and the quantity (Q) held by the entity (i.e. P × Q).

Therefore, in this scenario, the fair value of the 16 per cent equity interest in Entity B is measured as 160 million × CU0.5 = CU80 million.

Scenario 2

Entity C owns a 54 per cent equity interest in Entity D (300 million ordinary shares). Entity D is a subsidiary of Entity C. Entity D's ordinary shares are traded in an active market. The share price of each ordinary share at the measurement date is CU0.5.

In its separate financial statements, Entity C has chosen to account for its investments in subsidiaries in accordance with IFRS 9 (or, for entities that have not yet adopted IFRS 9, IAS 39) at fair value at initial recognition and at the end of each reporting period.

Based on Entity C's accounting policy, IFRS 9 (or IAS 39) is the applicable Standard that requires the fair value measurement in Entity C's separate financial statements.

Entity C's accounting policy for fair valuing interests in subsidiaries, joint ventures and associates is to consider the unit of account as the individual investment. Therefore, the unit of account for Entity C's investment in Entity D is the individual share in Entity D, and the fair value of the 54 per cent equity interest in Entity D is determined as the product of the quoted price (P) for the individual shares and the quantity (Q) held by Entity C (i.e. P × Q = 300 million × CU0.5 = CU150 million).

Note that this question concerns measurement in the separate financial statements of Entity C only. The accounting in the consolidated financial statements is specified in IFRS 10 *Consolidated Financial Statements*.

3.2.2 Determining the characteristics of an asset or a liability to be taken into account

3.2.2.1 Characteristics of an asset or a liability to be taken into account – general

When measuring fair value, the characteristics of an asset or a liability that should be taken into account are those that market participants would consider when pricing that asset or liability at the measurement date. Such characteristics could include, for example:

[IFRS 13:11]

- the condition and location of an asset; and

- restrictions, if any, on the sale or use of an asset.

The effect on the measurement arising from a particular characteristic will differ depending on how that characteristic would be taken into account by market participants. [IFRS 13:12]

3.2.2.2 Restrictions on the sale or use of an asset

Following the principle set out in IFRS 13:11 (see **3.2.2.1**), a legal or contractual restriction on the sale or use of an asset should be incorporated in the asset's fair value measurement if (1) the restriction is a characteristic of the asset, and (2) market participants would take the effect of the restriction into account when pricing the asset.

The following examples, reproduced from the illustrative examples accompanying IFRS 13, illustrate the effect of restrictions on the fair value measurement of an asset. **Example 3.2.2.2A** considers a restriction that is a characteristic of the asset being measured and that would transfer to market participants with the asset; such restrictions should be taken into account when measuring the fair value of the asset. **Example 3.2.2.2B** considers a restriction that is specific to the entity holding the asset and that would not transfer to market participants; such entity-specific restrictions should not be taken into account when measuring the fair value of the asset.

Example 3.2.2.2A

Restriction on the sale of an equity instrument

[IFRS 13:IE28, Example 8]

An entity holds an equity instrument (a financial asset) for which sale is legally or contractually restricted for a specified period. (For example, such a restriction could limit sale to qualifying investors.) The restriction is a characteristic of the instrument and, therefore, would be transferred to market participants. In that case, the fair value of the instrument would be measured on the basis of the quoted price for an otherwise identical unrestricted equity instrument of the same issuer that trades in a public market, adjusted to reflect the effect of the restriction. The adjustment would reflect the amount market participants would demand because of the risk relating to the inability to access a public market for the instrument for the specified period. The adjustment will vary depending on all the following:

(a)   the nature and duration of the restriction;

(b)   the extent to which buyers are limited by the restriction (eg there might be a large number of qualifying investors); and

(c)   qualitative and quantitative factors specific to both the instrument and the issuer.

Example 3.2.2.2B

Restrictions on the use of an asset

[IFRS 13:IE29, Example 9]

A donor contributes land in an otherwise developed residential area to a not-for-profit neighbourhood association. The land is currently used as a playground. The donor specifies that the land must continue to be used by the association as a playground in perpetuity. Upon review of relevant documentation (e.g. legal and other), the association determines that the fiduciary responsibility to meet the donor's restriction would not be transferred to market participants if the association sold the asset, i.e. the donor restriction on the use of the land is specific to the association. Furthermore, the association is not restricted from selling the land. Without the restriction on the use of the land by the association, the land could be used as a site for residential development. In addition, the land is subject to an easement (i.e. a legal right that enables a utility to run power lines across the land). Following is an analysis of the effect on the fair value measurement of the land arising from the restriction and the easement:

(a)   *Donor restriction on use of land.* Because in this situation the donor restriction on the use of the land is specific to the association, the restriction would not be transferred to market participants. Therefore, the fair value of the land would be the higher of its fair value used as a playground (i.e. the fair value of the asset would be maximised through its use by market participants in combination with other assets or with other assets and liabilities) and its fair value as a site for residential development (i.e. the fair value of the asset would be maximised through its use by market participants on a stand-alone basis), regardless of the restriction on the use of the land by the association.

(b) *Easement for utility lines*. Because the easement for utility lines is specific to (i.e. a characteristic of) the land, it would be transferred to market participants with the land. Therefore, the fair value measurement of the land would take into account the effect of the easement, regardless of whether the highest and best use is as a playground or as a site for residential development.

Sometimes it is immediately clear whether a restriction is a characteristic of an asset and would transfer to market participants. In other circumstances, significant judgement may be required to make the assessment and it may be necessary to obtain expert advice.

Consistent with **example 3.2.2.2A**, when a restriction needs to be taken into account when measuring the fair value of the asset, this is achieved by adjusting the fair value of an identical unrestricted asset to reflect the 'compensation' that a market participant would require because of the restriction. The adjustment will vary depending on (1) the nature and duration of the restriction, (2) the extent to which buyers are limited by the restriction, and (3) qualitative and quantitative factors specific to the asset (including factors specific to the issuer of the asset, as appropriate).

When categorising the fair value measurement for the purposes of the fair value hierarchy under IFRS 13:72, an entity will need to evaluate the significance of any adjustment made to reflect a restriction on the sale or use of the asset (see **10.3.3.2** for additional guidance regarding such evaluations).

The following are additional common examples of restrictions on the sale of assets.

Restriction on the sale of securities specified in contractual terms
When a restriction on the sale of securities (e.g. prohibiting sale of the securities to specified groups of investors or only permitting the securities to be sold to specified groups of investors) is embedded in the contractual terms of the securities, the restriction is a characteristic of the securities and would transfer to market participants. Consequently, the fair value measurement of the securities should reflect the asset-specific restriction.

Founders' shares Founder shareholders may be contractually prevented from selling their shares immediately following an initial public offering (IPO). Such a restriction may be outlined in the IPO prospectus. Assuming that the restriction is not embedded in the contractual terms of the shares (and, accordingly, would not transfer to a market participant in a hypothetical sale of the shares), the restriction is specific to the founder shareholders and is not a characteristic of the shares. In such circumstances, the restriction on the sale of the shares would not be taken into account when measuring the fair value of the shares.

Directors' shareholdings Assume that Company A owns ordinary shares issued by Company B and Company A is entitled to appoint a member of its management team to Company B's board of directors. Because Company A appoints a director of Company B, Company A is restricted from selling any of its shares in Company B during the period surrounding Company B's periodic release of earnings. Other market participants that are not directors of Company B or that do not have a right to appoint directors of Company B would not be subject to this restriction. Because the restriction is entity-specific (i.e. it is not a characteristic of the shares) and would not transfer with the shares, Company A should not reflect the effect of the restriction in the fair value measurement of its investment in Company B.

Assets pledged as collateral An entity may enter into a borrowing arrangement that requires assets to be pledged as collateral. The borrowing arrangement may restrict the entity from selling or transferring the assets during the term of the arrangement. Other market participants, however, would not be subject to this restriction. Because the restriction is entity-specific (i.e. it is not a characteristic of the assets) and would not transfer with the assets, it should not be reflected in the fair value measurement of the pledged assets.

3.3   Identifying the market in which to price the asset or liability

3.3.1   *Principal market versus most advantageous market*

IFRS 13 requires an entity to consider the market in which the sale of an asset or the transfer of a liability will take place. The Standard introduces the concepts of a 'principal market' and a 'most advantageous market'. Both terms are important in establishing the market in which the particular asset will be sold or the liability transferred and, consequently, in determining what price will be achieved if the sale or transfer occurs in that market at the measurement date.

For the purposes of measuring fair value, the transaction to sell the asset or transfer the liability is assumed to take place either:

[IFRS 13:16]

- in the 'principal market' for the asset or liability; or
- in the absence of a principal market, in the 'most advantageous market' for the asset or liability.

The principal market is defined as "[t]he market with the greatest volume and level of activity for the asset or liability". [IFRS 13:Appendix A]

The most advantageous market is defined as "[t]he market that maximises the amount that would be received to sell the asset or minimises the amount that would be paid to transfer the liability, after taking into account transaction costs and transport costs". [IFRS 13:Appendix A]

Note that, although transaction costs are not deducted (for an asset) or added (for a liability) when measuring fair value, they are considered when identifying the most advantageous market for an asset or a liability (see **3.5.3**).

The principal market should be identified on the basis of the volume or level of activity for the asset or liability rather than the volume or level of activity of the reporting entity's transactions in a particular market. [IFRS 13:BC52] Therefore, the assessment as to which of two or more accessible markets is the principal market is made from the perspective of market participants rather than the entity.

Equally, in the absence of a principal market, the most advantageous market is identified using the assumptions that market participants would use.

A principal market may not exist, for example, when the volume or level of activity for the asset or liability is the same in two different markets to which the entity has access, or when there is no observable market for the asset or liability. In such circumstances, an entity needs to identify the most advantageous market or develop assumptions from the perspective of a market participant in a hypothetical most advantageous market.

IFRS 13 does not require an entity to conduct an exhaustive search of all possible markets to identify the principal market (or, in the absence of a principal market, the most advantageous market), but an entity is required to take into account all information that is reasonably available. In the absence of evidence to the contrary, the market in which an entity would normally enter into a transaction to sell the asset or to transfer the liability is presumed to be the principal (or most advantageous) market. [IFRS 13:17]

Therefore, an entity is permitted to use the price in the market in which it normally enters into transactions unless there is evidence that the principal market and that market are not the same. [IFRS 13:BC53]

If there is evidence that the market in which an entity would normally transact is not the principal (or most advantageous) market, the principal (or most advantageous) market should be identified by:

- firstly, identifying other markets to which the entity has access; and
- secondly, when relevant, assessing which of two or more accessible markets is the principal (or most advantageous) market.

If there is a principal market for the asset or liability, the fair value measurement should reflect the price in that market, even if the price in a different market is potentially more advantageous at the measurement date. [IFRS 13:18]

3.3.2   Access to the market

To use the price in the principal (or most advantageous) market as the basis for measuring fair value, an entity must have access to that market at the measurement date. Because different entities (and businesses within those entities) with different activities may have access to different markets, the principal (or most advantageous) market for the same asset or liability might be different for different entities (and businesses within those entities). Therefore, the principal (or most advantageous) market should be considered from the perspective of the entity, thereby allowing for differences between and among entities with different activities. [IFRS 13:19]

> Example 7 of the illustrative examples accompanying IFRS 13 (summarised at **7.2**) illustrates a scenario in which two entities measure the same instrument differently because each identifies its principal market on the basis of the market to which it has access.

Although an entity must be able to access the market, the entity does not need to be able to sell the particular asset or transfer the particular liability on the measurement date to be able to measure fair value on the basis of the price in that market. [IFRS 13:20]

> For example, as discussed in **example 3.2.2.2A**, an entity may be restricted from selling a particular asset at the measurement date. Nevertheless, if the entity has access to the principal market at that date, the entity could measure the asset's fair value using observed prices for sales of similar (but unrestricted) assets in that market. If the restriction is a characteristic of the asset (i.e. it would transfer with the asset in a hypothetical sale), an entity should make an adjustment to observed market prices for similar (but unrestricted) assets to reflect the restriction (see **3.2.2.2** for further discussion).

3.3.3   Measuring fair value when no apparent exit market exists

Even when there is no observable market to provide pricing information about the sale of an asset or the transfer of a liability at the measurement date, a fair value measurement should assume that a transaction takes place at that date, considered from the perspective of a market participant that holds the asset or owes the liability. That assumed transaction establishes a basis for estimating the price to sell the asset or to transfer the liability. [IFRS 13:21]

When an observable market for an asset or a liability does not exist, an entity must assume a hypothetical transaction at the measurement date. This is consistent with the fair value objective in IFRS 13 to measure fair value as "the price that would be received to sell an asset or paid to transfer a liability in an orderly transaction between market participants at the measurement date" (see IFRS 13:Appendix A). See **3.4.3** for guidance on how an entity might identify market participants when no apparent exit market exists.

3.3.4 Factors indicating a change in the principal (or most advantageous) market

While it is presumed that the market in which an entity normally transacts is the principal (or most advantageous) market (see **3.3.1**), an entity should reassess the principal (or most advantageous) market for an asset or a liability at each measurement date based on reasonably available information. Factors indicating that there may have been a change in the principal (or most advantageous) market include the following (the list is not exhaustive):

- a significant change in market conditions;

- a decrease in the volume or level of activity relative to other markets;

- the development of a new market (see below);

- a change in the entity's ability to access particular markets (e.g. an entity loses access to a market or gains access to a market to which it did not previously have access); and

- when there is no principal market, a change in value such that the price for the asset or liability in a market previously considered most advantageous is no longer the most advantageous.

Events such as those listed above may indicate that there has been a change in the principal (or most advantageous) market for the asset or liability, or that circumstances have changed such that there is no longer a principal market for the asset or liability (in which case the entity should refer instead to the most advantageous market).

When a market first develops (e.g. for a new form of securities), it may operate primarily as a principal-to-principal or over-the-counter market. However, the volume and level of activity in the exchange market may increase over time. As the volume and level of activity change, and the balance of market activity shifts, an entity should take this into account when reassessing the principal (or most advantageous) market for an asset or a liability.

3.4 Market participants

3.4.1 Definition of market participants

Market participants are defined as "[b]uyers and sellers in the principal (or most advantageous) market for the asset or liability that have all of the following characteristics:

(a) They are independent of each other, i.e. they are not related parties as defined in IAS 24, although the price in a related party transaction may be used as an input to a fair value measurement if the entity has evidence that the transaction was entered into at market terms.

(b) They are knowledgeable, having a reasonable understanding about the asset or liability and the transaction using all available information, including information that might be obtained through due diligence efforts that are usual and customary.

(c) They are able to enter into a transaction for the asset or liability.

(d) They are willing to enter into a transaction for the asset or liability, i.e. they are motivated but not forced or otherwise compelled to do so". [IFRS 13:Appendix A]

3.4.2 Use of assumptions that market participants would use

IFRS 13 requires an entity to use the assumptions that market participants would use when pricing the asset or liability, assuming that market participants act in their economic best interest. [IFRS 13:22]

In developing those assumptions, an entity is not required to identify specific market participants, but is expected to identify characteristics that distinguish market participants generally, considering factors specific to:

[IFRS 13:23]

- the asset or liability;

- the principal (or most advantageous) market for the asset or liability; and

- market participants with whom the entity would enter into a transaction in that market.

Example 3.4.2

Use of assumptions that market participants would use

Entity F uses a discounted cash flow model to measure the fair value of a financial asset. Entity F has obtained information about the assumptions that market participants would use to measure the fair value of the asset. However, Entity F believes that some of those assumptions are not appropriate.

Entity F is not permitted to rely on its own internal data rather than use the assumptions that market participants would use. A fair value measurement is a market-based measurement and not entity-specific. IFRS 13:22 requires that the fair value of an asset or a liability should be measured using the assumptions that market participants would use when pricing the asset or liability, assuming that market participants act in their economic best interest.

When using a discounted cash flow model to measure the fair value of a financial asset, Entity F should incorporate relevant observable inputs whenever available. Any unobservable inputs used in the fair value measure (e.g. estimated future cash flows or risk adjustments incorporated into the discount rate) should be based on management's estimate of assumptions that market participants would use in pricing the asset in a current transaction at the measurement date. If market data from transactions involving comparable assets indicate, for example, that a significant liquidity discount applies at the measurement date to compensate for the difficulty in selling assets under current market conditions, Entity F should incorporate that information in its cash flow model (e.g. through an adjustment to the discount rate) even if management's internal data would not result in such a liquidity adjustment.

3.4.3 Identifying market participants when no apparent exit market exists

IFRS 13:21 requires that, even when there is no observable market to provide pricing information about the sale of an asset or the transfer of a liability at the measurement date, a fair value measurement should assume that a transaction takes place at that date, considered from the perspective of a market participant that holds the asset or owes the liability. That assumed transaction establishes a basis for estimating the price to sell the asset or to transfer the liability (see **3.3.3**).

In such circumstances, the entity is not required to identify specific market participants. Instead, the entity should consider the characteristics of potential market participants who would purchase the asset or accept a transfer of the liability being measured. In addition, the entity should identify the assumptions that such market participants would make in a transaction that maximises the amount received to sell an asset or minimises the amount paid to transfer a liability.

Potential market participants include the following (the list is not exhaustive).

- For non-financial assets, groups of non-financial assets, or groups of non-financial assets and liabilities in a business or cash-generating unit:
  - **strategic buyers**: these buyers have related assets and the asset being measured would enhance the value of the business unit within which the buyer would use the asset. Examples of strategic buyers are direct competitors or others with characteristics similar to those of the entity; and

- **financial buyers**: these buyers do not have related or substitute assets. Examples of financial buyers are financial institutional investors and private equity and venture capital investors.

- For financial instruments: counterparties to a derivative instrument, investors maximising return, investors trying to establish a strategic relationship with an investee, or a range of other participants with a specific objective.

When identifying a potential market participant, care should be taken to ensure that the unit of account from the perspective of the market participant is consistent with the unit of account of the item being measured.

When developing assumptions that market participants would use in such a hypothetical transaction, an entity may start with its own assumptions and make adjustments for factors specific to the asset or liability being measured, including (the list is not exhaustive):

- transportation costs necessary to transfer an asset from its current location to the hypothetical market (if location is a characteristic of the asset);

- conversion costs to transform a non-financial asset from its current condition to its highest and best use from the perspective of potential market participants;

- synergies that are specific to the entity and not available to market participants and thus would not be taken into account in the hypothetical transaction (e.g. cost savings from synergies related to other groups of assets held by the entity);

- growth rates and risk adjustments to reflect market participant assumptions; and

- performance and risk indicators (e.g. delinquencies, defaults, prepayment speeds and interest rates).

Market participant assumptions that are developed when no apparent market exists may be based on unobservable inputs or adjustments. An entity needs to evaluate the significance of these inputs or adjustments when determining the appropriate level in the fair value hierarchy within which the measurement should be categorised (see **10.3.3.2** for additional guidance regarding such evaluations).

3.5 The price at which a transaction is assumed to occur

3.5.1 Characteristics of the price at which a transaction is assumed to occur

The price at which a transaction is assumed to occur in the principal or most advantageous market is the price:

[IFRS 13:24]

- in an 'orderly' transaction (see **3.5.2**); and

- under current market conditions at the measurement date.

The price may be directly observable or estimated using another valuation technique (see **section 8**). [IFRS 13:24]

The price should not be adjusted for 'transaction costs', but it should be adjusted for 'transport costs' in specified circumstances (see **3.5.3**). [IFRS 13:25 & 26]

3.5.2 An 'orderly' transaction

A fair value measurement assumes that the asset or liability is exchanged in an 'orderly' transaction in the principal (or most advantageous) market. An orderly transaction is defined as "[a] transaction that assumes exposure to the market for a period before the measurement date to allow for marketing activities that are usual and customary for transactions involving such assets or liabilities; it is not a forced transaction (e.g. a forced liquidation or distress sale)". [IFRS 13:Appendix A]

Appendix B to the Standard provides additional guidance regarding the identification of orderly transactions (see **9.6**).

3.5.3 Transaction costs and transport costs

Transaction costs are defined as "[t]he costs to sell an asset or transfer a liability in the principal (or most advantageous) market for the asset or liability that are directly attributable to the disposal of the asset or the transfer of the liability and meet both of the following criteria:

(a) They result directly from and are essential to that transaction.

(b) They would not have been incurred by the entity had the decision to sell the asset or transfer the liability not been made (similar to costs to sell, as defined in IFRS 5)". [IFRS 13:Appendix A]

Transaction costs do not include transport costs. [IFRS 13:26] Transport costs are defined as "[t]he costs that would be incurred to transport an asset from its current location to its principal (or most advantageous) market". [IFRS 13:Appendix A]

IFRS 13 specifies that, when measuring fair value, the relevant market price should *not* be reduced (for an asset) or increased (for a liability) for transaction costs. Because such costs are specific to a transaction and will differ depending on how an entity enters into a transaction for an asset or a liability, they are not considered to be a characteristic of the asset or liability. [IFRS 13:25]

The appropriate treatment for transaction costs should be determined in accordance with other relevant IFRSs. [IFRS 13:25]

Note, however, that transaction costs are considered when identifying the most advantageous market for an asset or a liability (see **3.3.1** and **example 3.5.3A**).

In contrast, the price in the principal (or most advantageous) market used to measure the fair value of an asset *is* adjusted for any transport costs (as defined above) *if* location is a characteristic of the asset (which might be the case, for example, for a commodity). [IFRS 13:26]

The appropriate treatments for transaction and transport costs are illustrated in the following example, which is reproduced from the illustrative examples accompanying IFRS 13.

Example 3.5.3A

Level 1 principal (or most advantageous) market

[IFRS 13:IE19 - IE22, Example 6]

An asset is sold in two different active markets at different prices. An entity enters into transactions in both markets and can access the price in those markets for the asset at the measurement date. In Market A, the price that would be received is CU26, transaction costs in that market are CU3 and the costs to transport the asset to that market are CU2 (ie the net amount that would be received is CU21). In Market B, the price that would be received is CU25, transaction costs in that market are CU1 and the costs to transport the asset to that market are CU2 (ie the net amount that would be received in Market B is CU22).

If Market A is the principal market for the asset (ie the market with the greatest volume and level of activity for the asset), the fair value of the asset would be measured using the price that would be received in that market, after taking into account transport costs (CU24).

If neither market is the principal market for the asset, the fair value of the asset would be measured using the price in the most advantageous market. The most advantageous market is the market that maximises the amount that would be received to sell the asset, after taking into account transaction costs and transport costs (ie the net amount that would be received in the respective markets).

Because the entity would maximise the net amount that would be received for the asset in Market B (CU22), the fair value of the asset would be measured using the price in that market (CU25), less transport costs (CU2), resulting in a fair value measurement of CU23. Although transaction costs are taken into account when determining which market is the most advantageous market, the price used to measure the fair value of the asset is not adjusted for those costs (although it is adjusted for transport costs).

IFRS 13 requires entities to reflect characteristics specific to the asset or liability being measured when measuring fair value. Consequently, *if* location is a characteristic of an asset, an entity should adjust the price in the principal (or most advantageous) market for transport costs when measuring the fair value of the asset.

The following two examples illustrate how transport costs may be a subtractive input or an additive input as an adjustment to an observable market price for an asset.

Example 3.5.3B

Transport costs are a subtractive input

Company A has agricultural produce ready for harvesting at Location 1. As required under IAS 41 *Agriculture*, the agricultural produce is measured at fair value less costs to sell at the point of harvest. The fair value less costs to sell at that date will subsequently be used as the cost when applying IAS 2 *Inventories* to the harvested produce.

Company A has identified Location 2 as the principal market for sale of its produce. The quoted price for the produce in Location 2 is CU100 per unit. Company A determines that transport costs of CU5 per unit would be incurred to move the produce from Location 1 to Location 2. Therefore, the fair value of the produce at its current location would be CU95 per unit (i.e. CU100 per unit quoted price at Location 2 less CU5 per unit to transport the produce to the principal market at Location 2). Note that this represents the fair value before deduction of costs to sell in accordance with IAS 41.

Company A's analysis (per unit)

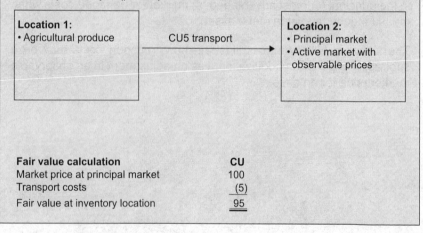

Fair value calculation	CU
Market price at principal market	100
Transport costs	(5)
Fair value at inventory location	95

Example 3.5.3C

Transport costs are an additive input

Company B has agricultural produce ready for harvesting at Location 1. As required under IAS 41, the agricultural produce at the point of harvest is measured at fair value less costs to sell.

Location 1 is a developing retail market for Company B's produce with a relatively low level of activity. Location 1 is the only market to which Company B has access and therefore it is identified as Company B's principal market.

There is also a wholesale market for the agricultural produce at Location 2 which is an active market. Although Company B does not have access to the wholesale market at Location 2, that market provides an observable current price for comparable produce of CU100 per unit. Company B determines that this price represents a more reliable input for the fair value measurement of its produce because of the higher level of activity in the market at Location 2 compared to Location 1.

However, when measuring the fair value of its produce, Company B must apply an adjustment to the prices quoted at Location 2, because they reflect a location other than its principal market. Company B determines that the cost to transport the produce from Location 2 to Location 1 is CU5 per unit. Based on observations in Company B's principal market at Location 1, it can be corroborated that market participants in the principal market would be willing to pay a retail price that is based on the wholesale price in Location 2 plus the cost to transport the produce from Location 2 to Location 1. Accordingly, the fair value of the produce at Location 1 is measured at CU105 per unit (i.e. CU100 per unit at Location 2 plus CU5 per unit to transport the produce to Company B's principal market at Location 1).

Company B's analysis (per unit)

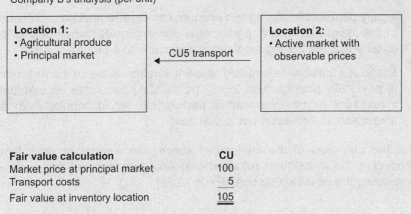

Fair value calculation	CU
Market price at principal market	100
Transport costs	5
Fair value at inventory location	105

4 Measuring the fair value of non-financial assets – highest and best use

4.1 Meaning of 'highest and best use'

A fair value measurement of a non-financial asset is based on its 'highest and best use' (see below). This concept is not relevant for financial assets, liabilities or an entity's own equity instruments because those items do not have alternative uses as contemplated in IFRS 13. [IFRS 13:BC63]

When measuring the fair value of a non-financial asset, an entity is required to take into account a market participant's ability to generate economic benefits by using the asset in its 'highest and best use' or by selling it to another market participant that would use the asset in its highest and best use. [IFRS 13:27]

The highest and best use of a non-financial asset is defined as "[t]he use of a non-financial asset by market participants that would maximise the value of the asset or the group of assets and liabilities (eg a business) within which the asset would be used". [IFRS 13:Appendix A]

The highest and best use takes into account the use of the non-financial asset that is:

[IFRS 13:28]

- physically possible (taking into account the physical characteristics of the asset that market participants would consider when pricing the asset – e.g. the location or size of a property);

- legally permissible (taking into account any legal restrictions on the use of the asset that market participants would consider when pricing the asset – e.g. the zoning regulations applicable to a property); and

- financially feasible (taking into account whether a use of the asset that is physically possible and legally permissible generates an adequate investment return that market participants would require from an investment in that asset put to that use).

For the purposes of the final bullet above, the income or cash flows producing the investment return should take into account the costs of converting the asset to that use. [IFRS 13:28]

4.2 Meaning of 'legally permissible'

In the context of IFRS 13:28, the question arises as to whether the term 'legally permissible' should be taken to refer to a use of the asset that is currently legally permitted, or should be more broadly interpreted to mean a use that may be permitted in the future.

This question is not specifically addressed in the body of IFRS 13, but it is referred to in the Basis for Conclusions, as follows.

> "Some respondents asked for further guidance about whether a use that is legally permissible must be legal at the measurement date, or if, for example, future changes in legislation can be taken into account. The IASB concluded that a use of an asset does not need to be legal at the measurement date, but must not be legally prohibited in the jurisdiction (eg if the government of a particular country has prohibited building or development in a protected area, the highest and best use of the land in that area could not be to develop it for industrial use). The illustrative examples that accompany IFRS 13 show how an asset can be zoned for a particular use at the measurement date, but how a fair value measurement can assume a different zoning if market participants would do so (incorporating the cost to convert the asset and obtain that different zoning permission, including the risk that such permission would not be granted)." [IFRS 13:BC69]

This discussion clarifies that the term 'legally permissible' is not restricted to uses that are legal at the measurement date. For example, in the context of zoning regulations and depending on the rules in the particular jurisdiction, if a property is zoned only for commercial use at the measurement date, but market participants would take a potential change in use into account in pricing the property, the illustrative example set out in IFRS 13:IE7 and 8 (see **example 4.2**) indicates that such a potential change in use should be incorporated in the fair value measurement.

The key to determining whether a particular use should be considered to be legally permissible is set out in IFRS 13:28: "[a] use that is legally permissible takes into account any legal restrictions on the use of the asset that market participants would take into account when pricing the asset (eg the zoning regulations applicable to a property)". In line with the general requirement under IFRS 13:22 to measure fair value using the assumptions that market participants would use, if market participants in pricing an asset would factor in the possibility that current legal restrictions might change in the future, then that potential for future changes in restrictions should be incorporated into the fair value measurement.

Example 4.2

Land

[IFRS 13:IE7 & IE8, Example 2]

An entity acquires land in a business combination. The land is currently developed for industrial use as a site for a factory. The current use of land is presumed to be its highest and best use unless market or other factors suggest

---

a different use. Nearby sites have recently been developed for residential use as sites for high-rise apartment buildings. On the basis of that development and recent zoning and other changes to facilitate that development, the entity determines that the land currently used as a site for a factory could be developed as a site for residential use (ie for high-rise apartment buildings) because market participants would take into account the potential to develop the site for residential use when pricing the land.

The highest and best use of the land would be determined by comparing both of the following:

(a) the value of the land as currently developed for industrial use (ie the land would be used in combination with other assets, such as the factory, or with other assets and liabilities).

(b) the value of the land as a vacant site for residential use, taking into account the costs of demolishing the factory and other costs (including the uncertainty about whether the entity would be able to convert the asset to the alternative use) necessary to convert the land to a vacant site (ie the land is to be used by market participants on a stand-alone basis).

The highest and best use of the land would be determined on the basis of the higher of those values. In situations involving real estate appraisal, the determination of highest and best use might take into account factors relating to the factory operations, including its assets and liabilities.

Example 4.2 deals with a scenario in which land currently used for industrial purposes could be developed as a site for residential use, and illustrates how to determine the highest and best use of the land by comparing the value of the land as currently used with its value as a vacant site for residential use. The example focuses on the determination of the highest and best use of the land – it does not address the implications for the measurement of any buildings on that land. See 4.6 for guidance on the measurement of such buildings.

4.3 Highest and best use to be determined from the perspective of market participants

Highest and best use is determined from the perspective of market participants, even if the entity intends a different use. However, an entity's current use of a non-financial asset is presumed to be its highest and best use unless market or other factors suggest that a different use by market participants would maximise the value of the asset. [IFRS 13:29]

IFRS 13 does not require an entity to perform an exhaustive search for other potential uses of a non-financial asset if there is no evidence to suggest that the current use of an asset is not its highest and best use. The IASB concluded that an entity that seeks to maximise the value of its assets would use those assets at their highest and best use and that it would be necessary for an entity to consider alternative uses of those assets only if there was evidence that the current use of the assets is not their highest and best use (i.e. an alternative use would maximise their fair value). [IFRS 13:BC71]

There may be reasons why an entity intends not to use an acquired non-financial asset actively or according to its highest and best use (e.g. if an entity acquires an intangible asset solely in order to protect its competitive position by preventing others from using the intangible asset). Nevertheless, in such circumstances, the entity is required to measure the fair value of the asset assuming its highest and best use by market participants. [IFRS 13:30]

The requirements of IFRS 13:30, which are illustrated in **example 4.3**, are consistent with guidance already included in IFRS 3 *Business Combinations* regarding assets acquired in a business combination that the acquirer intends not to use or to use in a way that is different from the way other market participants would use them (see also **7.2.3** in **chapter A25**).

Example 4.3

Research and development project

[IFRS 13:IE9, Example 3]

An entity acquires a research and development (R&D) project in a business combination. The entity does not intend to complete the project. If completed, the project would compete with one of its own projects (to provide the next generation of the entity's commercialised technology). Instead, the entity intends to hold (ie lock up) the project to prevent its competitors from obtaining access to the technology. In doing this, the project is expected to provide defensive value, principally by improving the prospects for the entity's own competing technology. To measure the fair value of the project at initial recognition, the highest and best use of the project would be determined on the basis of its use by market participants. For example:

(a) The highest and best use of the R&D project would be to continue development if market participants would continue to develop the project and that use would maximise the value of the group of assets or of assets and liabilities in which the project would be used (ie the asset would be used in combination with other assets or with other assets and liabilities). That might be the case if market participants do not have similar technology, either in development or commercialised. The fair value of the project would be measured on the basis of the price that would be received in a current transaction to sell the project, assuming that the R&D would be used with its complementary assets and the associated liabilities and that those assets and liabilities would be available to market participants.

(b) The highest and best use of the R&D project would be to cease development if, for competitive reasons, market participants would lock up the project and that use would maximise the value of the group of assets or of assets and liabilities in which the project would be used. That might

---

be the case if market participants have technology in a more advanced stage of development that would compete with the project if completed and the project would be expected to improve the prospects for their own competing technology if locked up. The fair value of the project would be measured on the basis of the price that would be received in a current transaction to sell the project, assuming that the R&D would be used (ie locked up) with its complementary assets and the associated liabilities and that those assets and liabilities would be available to market participants.

(c) The highest and best use of the R&D project would be to cease development if market participants would discontinue its development. That might be the case if the project is not expected to provide a market rate of return if completed and would not otherwise provide defensive value if locked up. The fair value of the project would be measured on the basis of the price that would be received in a current transaction to sell the project on its own (which might be zero).

4.4 Highest and best use as a stand-alone asset

If the highest and best use of the asset is on a stand-alone basis, the fair value of the asset is the price that would be received in a current transaction to sell the asset to market participants that would use the asset on a stand-alone basis. [IFRS 13:31(b)]

4.5 Highest and best use as part of a group of assets or in combination with other assets and liabilities

If the highest and best use of the asset is in combination with other assets, or with other assets and liabilities, the fair value of the asset is the price that would be received in a current transaction to sell the asset assuming that the asset would be used with other assets, or with other assets and liabilities, and that those assets and liabilities would be available to market participants. [IFRS 13:31(a)(i)]

Therefore, in such circumstances, the price used would be the price for a sale to a market participant that has, or can obtain, the other assets and liabilities needed to generate cash inflows by using the asset (i.e. its complementary assets and the associated liabilities). [IFRS 13:BC74(a)]

When the highest and best use of a non-financial asset is in combination with other assets and liabilities, the liabilities associated with the asset and with the complementary assets include liabilities that fund working capital, but do not include liabilities used to fund assets other than those within the group of assets. [IFRS 13:31(a)(ii)]

Assumptions about the highest and best use of a non-financial asset should be consistent for all the assets (for which highest and best use is relevant) of the group of assets, or the group of assets and liabilities, within which the asset would be used. [IFRS 13:31(a)(iii)]

> See **4.6** for a discussion illustrating the implications of the requirement to use consistent assumptions about highest and best use for all of the assets in an asset group.

Even when it is considered that the highest and best use of a non-financial asset is in combination with other assets, or with other assets and liabilities, the unit of account for the purposes of the fair value measurement (see **section 3.2**) is the unit of account specified in other IFRSs (which may be an individual asset). Specifically, the fair value measurement assumes that the market participant already holds the complementary assets and the associated liabilities and, therefore, that the non-financial asset is sold by itself. [IFRS 13:32]

> It is assumed that the non-financial asset being measured at fair value is sold on its own (at the unit of account level) even if transactions in the asset are typically the result of sales of the asset as part of a group of assets or a business. Even when an asset is used in combination with other assets, the exit price for the asset is a price for that asset individually because a fair value measurement assumes that a market participant (buyer) of the asset already holds the complementary assets and the associated liabilities. Because the buyer is assumed to hold the other assets (and liabilities) necessary for the asset to function, that buyer would not be willing to pay more for the asset solely because it was sold as part of a group. [IFRS 13:BC77]

When measuring the fair value of a non-financial asset used in combination with other assets, or with other assets and liabilities, the effect of the requirements in IFRS 13:31 and 32 (as described above) depends on the circumstances. The fair value of the asset may be the same whether the asset is used on a stand-alone basis or in combination with other assets or with other assets and liabilities. That might be the case if the asset is a business that market participants would continue to operate. In such circumstances, the business should be valued in its entirety, thus reflecting the synergies that would be available to market participants. [IFRS 13:B3]

The Standard provides the following examples of how an asset's use in combination with other assets, or with other assets and liabilities, might be incorporated into a fair value measurement.

[IFRS 13:B3]

- It might be incorporated through adjustments to the value of the asset used on a stand-alone basis. That might be the case if the asset is a machine and the fair value measurement is determined using an observed price for a similar machine (not installed or otherwise configured for use), adjusted for transport and installation costs so that the fair value measurement reflects the current condition and location of the machine (installed and configured for use).

- It might be incorporated through the market participant assumptions used to measure the fair value of the asset. For example, if the asset is work in progress inventory that is unique, and market participants would convert the inventory into finished goods, the fair value of the inventory would assume that market participants have acquired or would acquire any specialised machinery necessary to convert the inventory into finished goods.

- It might be incorporated into the valuation technique used to measure the fair value of the asset. That might be the case when using the multi-period excess earnings method to measure the fair value of an intangible asset because that valuation technique specifically takes into account the contribution of any complementary assets and the associated liabilities in the group in which such an intangible asset would be used.

- In more limited situations, when an entity uses an asset within a group of assets, the entity might measure the asset at an amount that approximates its fair value when allocating the fair value of the asset group to the individual assets of the group. That might be the case if the valuation involves real property and the fair value of improved property (i.e. an asset group) is allocated to its component assets (such as land and improvements).

The following example, reproduced from the illustrative examples accompanying IFRS 13, describes the measurement of the fair value of an asset that is used as part of a group of assets.

Example 4.5

Asset group

[IFRS 13:IE3 - IE6, Example 1]

An entity acquires assets and assumes liabilities in a business combination. One of the groups of assets acquired comprises Assets A, B and C. Asset C is billing software integral to the business developed by the acquired entity for its own use in conjunction with Assets A and B (ie the related assets). The entity measures the fair value of each of the assets individually, consistently with the specified unit of account for the assets. The entity determines that the highest and best use of the assets is their current use and that each asset would provide maximum value to market participants principally through its use in combination with other assets or with other assets and liabilities (ie its complementary assets and the associated liabilities). There is no evidence to suggest that the current use of the assets is not their highest and best use.

In this situation, the entity would sell the assets in the market in which it initially acquired the assets (ie the entry and exit markets from the perspective of the entity are the same). Market participant buyers with whom the entity would enter into a transaction in that market have characteristics that are generally representative of both strategic buyers (such as competitors) and financial buyers (such as private equity or venture capital firms that do not have complementary investments) and include those buyers that initially bid for the assets. Although market participant buyers might be broadly classified as strategic or financial buyers, in many cases there will be differences among the market participant buyers within each of those groups, reflecting, for example, different uses for an asset and different operating strategies.

As discussed below, differences between the indicated fair values of the individual assets relate principally to the use of the assets by those market participants within different asset groups:

(a) Strategic buyer asset group. The entity determines that strategic buyers have related assets that would enhance the value of the group within which the assets would be used (ie market participant synergies). Those assets include a substitute asset for Asset C (the billing software), which would be used for only a limited transition period and could not be sold on its own at the end of that period. Because strategic buyers have substitute assets, Asset C would not be used for its full remaining economic life. The indicated fair values of Assets A, B and C within the strategic buyer asset group (reflecting the synergies resulting from the use of the assets within that group) are CU360, CU260 and CU30, respectively. The indicated fair value of the assets as a group within the strategic buyer asset group is CU650.

(b) Financial buyer asset group. The entity determines that financial buyers do not have related or substitute assets that would enhance the value of the group within which the assets would be used. Because financial buyers do not have substitute assets, Asset C (ie the billing software) would be used for its full remaining economic life. The indicated fair values of Assets A, B and C within the financial buyer asset group are CU300, CU200 and CU100, respectively. The indicated fair value of the assets as a group within the financial buyer asset group is CU600.

The fair values of Assets A, B and C would be determined on the basis of the use of the assets as a group within the strategic buyer group (CU360, CU260 and CU30). Although the use of the assets within the strategic buyer group does not maximise the fair value of each of the assets individually, it maximises the fair value of the assets as a group (CU650).

4.6 Measurement of an asset accounted for under the revaluation model that would be demolished to achieve highest and best use of real estate

Illustrative Example 2 accompanying IFRS 13 (see **example 4.2**) deals with a scenario in which land currently used for industrial purposes could be developed as a site for residential use, and illustrates how to determine the highest and best use of the land by comparing the value of the land as currently used with its value as a vacant site for residential use. The example focuses on the determination of the highest and best use of the land – it does not address the implications for the measurement of any buildings on that land.

Assume that the facts are as set out in **example 4.2**. Assume also that:

- there is a factory building on the site which is currently used for industrial purposes and which is accounted for under the revaluation model in IAS 16 *Property, Plant and Equipment*; and

- the highest and best use of the land and the factory in combination, taking into account the costs of demolishing the factory and other costs (including the uncertainty about whether the entity would be able to convert the land to an alternative use), is determined to be redevelopment for residential use.

Because the factory building has no value under the highest and best use assumption (which assumes its demolition), it is allocated a fair value of nil. This conclusion is consistent with the requirement of IFRS 13:31(a)(iii) (see **4.5**) to use consistent assumptions about highest and best use for all of the assets in an asset group.

Therefore:

- the full fair value of the asset group (land and factory building) is attributed to the land; and

- assuming that the land is freehold and consequently not depreciated, no depreciation will be recognised in the financial statements.

As noted in IFRS 13:BC72 to BC73, the IASB considered an alternative approach to avoid assigning nil value to a factory in current use but decided instead upon a disclosure solution.

Consequently, in these circumstances, the entity would be required by IFRS 13:93(i) (see **11.4.12**) to disclose the fact that the current use of the land and factory building differs from their highest and best use and why that is the case.

5 Measuring the fair value of liabilities and an entity's own equity instruments

5.1 Measuring the fair value of liabilities and an entity's own equity instruments – general

5.1.1 General principles

Except when indicated otherwise, the guidance in this section regarding liabilities applies equally to financial and non-financial liabilities.

The fair value of a liability or an entity's own equity instrument (e.g. an equity share issued as part of the consideration in a business combination) is measured based on the assumption that the liability or equity instrument is transferred to a market participant at the measurement date. [IFRS 13:34]

For a liability, it is assumed that the liability would remain outstanding and the market participant transferee would be required to fulfil the obligation. It would not be settled with the counterparty or otherwise extinguished on the measurement date. [IFRS 13:34(a)]

IFRS 13 is clear that the fair value of a liability is based on a transfer amount, i.e. the amount the reporting entity would need to pay a third party to take on the obligation, and that obligation remains outstanding and contractually unaltered before and after transfer. Fair value is therefore *not* based on the premise of settling the liability with the counterparty at the measurement date.

For an entity's own equity instrument, it is assumed that the equity instrument would remain outstanding and the market participant transferee would take on the rights and responsibilities associated with the instrument. The instrument would not be cancelled or otherwise extinguished on the measurement date. [IFRS 13:34(b)]

IFRS 13 requires that the fair value measure be based on an assumed transfer to a market participant even if an entity does not intend to transfer its liability or own equity instrument to a third party (e.g. because the entity has advantages relative to the market that make it more beneficial for the entity to fulfil the liability using its own internal resources) or it is unable to do so (e.g. because the counterparty would not permit the liability to be transferred to another party). [IFRS 13:BC81 & 82]

Even when there is no observable market to provide pricing information about the transfer of a liability or an entity's own equity instrument (e.g. because contractual or other legal restrictions prevent the transfer of such items), there might be an observable market for such items if they are held by other parties as assets (see **5.1.2**). [IFRS 13:35]

Consistent with the objective of fair value measurement and the prioritisation in the fair value hierarchy (see **section 10**), when measuring the fair value of a liability or an entity's own equity instrument, the entity should maximise the use of relevant observable inputs and minimise the use of unobservable inputs. [IFRS 13:36]

5.1.2   *Liabilities and equity instruments held by other parties as assets*

When a quoted price for the transfer of an identical or a similar liability or an entity's own equity instrument is not available, and the identical item is held by another party as an asset, an entity is required to measure the fair value of the liability or equity instrument from the perspective of a market participant that holds the identical item as an asset at the measurement date. [IFRS 13:37] This requirement could be relevant, for example, when measuring the fair value of corporate bonds or a call option on an entity's shares. [IFRS 13:35]

> Determining the fair value of a liability or an entity's own equity instrument from the perspective of the counterparty holding the same instrument as an asset reinforces the notion that the fair value ascribed to the contract is the same irrespective of whether the entity is the issuer or the holder. This is based on the theory that fair value is based on a transaction in which the contract is transferred, as opposed to being settled or extinguished with the holder. In all cases, the fair value is based on the premise that the instrument remains outstanding and therefore is a theoretical transfer value.

In the circumstances described above, the appropriate bases for measuring the fair value of the liability or the entity's own equity instrument are listed below, in descending order of preference:

[IFRS 13:38]

(a) using the quoted price in an active market (see below) for the identical item held by another party as an asset, if that price is available;

(b) if that price is not available, using other observable inputs, such as the quoted price in a market that is not active for the identical item held by another party as an asset; and

(c) if the observable prices in (a) and (b) above are not available, using another valuation technique, such as:

    (i) an income approach (e.g. a present value technique that takes into account the future cash flows that a market participant would expect to receive from holding the liability or equity instrument as an asset – see **section 8.6**); or

(ii) a market approach (e.g. using quoted prices for similar liabilities or equity instruments held by other parties as assets – see **8.4**).

An active market is defined as "[a] market in which transactions for the asset or liability take place with sufficient frequency and volume to provide pricing information on an ongoing basis". [IFRS 13:Appendix A]

A quoted price of a liability or an entity's own equity instrument held by another party as an asset should be adjusted only if there are factors specific to the asset that are not applicable to the fair value measurement of the liability or equity instrument. An entity should ensure that the price of the asset does not reflect the effect of a restriction preventing the sale of an asset. [IFRS 13:39]

IFRS 13 provides the following examples of factors that might indicate that the quoted price of the asset should be adjusted.

[IFRS 13:39]

- The quoted price for the asset relates to a similar (but not identical) liability or equity instrument held by another party as an asset. For example, the liability or equity instrument may have a particular characteristic (e.g. the credit quality of the issuer) that is different from that reflected in the fair value of the similar liability or equity instrument held as an asset.

- The unit of account for the asset is not the same as for the liability or equity instrument. For example, for liabilities, in some cases the price for an asset reflects a combined price for a package comprising both the amounts due from the issuer and a third-party credit enhancement. If the unit of account for the liability is not for the combined package, the objective is to measure the fair value of the issuer's liability, not the fair value of the combined package. In such circumstances, the entity would adjust the observed price for the asset to exclude the effect of the third-party credit enhancement.

5.1.3 Liabilities and equity instruments not held by other parties as assets

5.1.3.1 Liabilities and equity instruments not held by other parties as assets – general

When a quoted price for the transfer of an identical or a similar liability or entity's own equity instrument is not available, and the identical item is not held by another party as an asset, the fair value of the liability or equity instrument is required to be measured using a valuation technique from the perspective of a market participant that owes the liability or has issued the claim on equity. [IFRS 13:40]

This requirement could be relevant, for example, for measuring the fair value of a decommissioning liability. [IFRS 13:B31]

For example, when applying a present value technique, an entity might take into account either of the following:

[IFRS 13:41]

- the future cash outflows that a market participant would expect to incur in fulfilling the obligation, including the compensation that a market participant would require for taking on the obligation (see **5.1.3.2**); or

- the amount that a market participant would receive to enter into or issue an identical liability or equity instrument, using the assumptions that market participants would use when pricing the identical item (e.g. having the same credit characteristics) in the principal (or most advantageous) market for issuing a liability or an equity instrument with the same contractual terms.

5.1.3.2   Estimating future cash outflows

IFRS 13's general guidance regarding the use of present value techniques is discussed in detail in **section 8.6**. This section covers the Standard's specific guidance for applying present value techniques to liabilities and an entity's own equity instruments not held by other parties as assets.

When using a present value technique to measure the fair value of a liability that is not held by another party as an asset, an entity should, among other things, estimate the future cash outflows that market participants would expect to incur in fulfilling the obligation. [IFRS 13:B31]

Those future cash outflows should include:

[IFRS 13:B31]

- market participants' expectations about the costs of fulfilling the obligation; and

- the compensation that a market participant would require for taking on the obligation.

The compensation that a market participant would require for taking on the obligation should include the return that a market participant would require for the following:

[IFRS 13:B31]

- undertaking the activity (i.e. the value of fulfilling the obligation – for example by using resources that could be used for other activities); and

- assuming the risk associated with the obligation (i.e. a risk premium that reflects the risk that the actual cash outflows might differ from the expected cash outflows).

The Standard cites as an example a non-financial liability that does not contain a contractual rate of return and for which there is no observable market yield. In some cases, the components of the return that market participants would require will be indistinguishable from one another (e.g. when using the price a third-party contractor would charge on a fixed fee basis). In other cases, an entity needs to estimate those components separately (e.g. when using the price a third-party contractor would charge on a cost plus basis, because the contractor in that case would not bear the risk of future changes in costs). [IFRS 13:B32]

IFRS 13 defines a risk premium (also referred to as a 'risk adjustment') as "[c]ompensation sought by risk-averse market participants for bearing the uncertainty inherent in the cash flows of an asset or a liability". [IFRS 13:Appendix A] A risk premium can be included in the fair value measurement of a liability or an entity's own equity instrument that is not held by another party as an asset in one of the following ways:

[IFRS 13:B33]

- by adjusting the cash flows (i.e. as an increase in the amount of cash outflows); or

- by adjusting the rate used to discount the future cash flows to their present values (i.e. as a reduction in the discount rate).

An entity should ensure that it does not double-count or omit adjustments for risk. For example, if the estimated cash flows are increased to take into account the compensation for assuming the risk associated with the obligation, the discount rate should not be adjusted to reflect that risk. [IFRS 13:B33]

The following example, reproduced from the illustrative examples accompanying IFRS 13, describes the use of the present value technique to measure the fair value of a decommissioning liability.

Example 5.1.3.2

Decommissioning liability

[IFRS 13:IE35 - IE39, Example 11]

On 1 January 20X1 Entity A assumes a decommissioning liability in a business combination. The entity is legally required to dismantle and remove an offshore oil platform at the end of its useful life, which is estimated to be 10 years.

On the basis of IFRS 13:B23 - B30, Entity A uses the expected present value technique to measure the fair value of the decommissioning liability.

If Entity A was contractually allowed to transfer its decommissioning liability to a market participant, Entity A concludes that a market participant would use all the following inputs, probability-weighted as appropriate, when estimating the price it would expect to receive:

(a)   labour costs;

(b)   allocation of overhead costs;

(c)   the compensation that a market participant would require for undertaking the activity and for assuming the risk associated with the obligation to dismantle and remove the asset. Such compensation includes both of the following:

   (i)   profit on labour and overhead costs; and

   (ii)   the risk that the actual cash outflows might differ from those expected, excluding inflation;

(d)   effect of inflation on estimated costs and profits;

(e)   time value of money, represented by the risk-free rate; and

(f)   non-performance risk relating to the risk that Entity A will not fulfil the obligation, including Entity A's own credit risk.

The significant assumptions used by Entity A to measure fair value are as follows:

(a)   Labour costs are developed on the basis of current marketplace wages, adjusted for expectations of future wage increases, required to hire contractors to dismantle and remove offshore oil platforms. Entity A assigns probability assessments to a range of cash flow estimates as follows:

Cash flow estimate (CU)	Probability assessment	Expected cash flows (CU)
100,000	25%	25,000
125,000	50%	62,500
175,000	25%	43,750
		131,250

The probability assessments are developed on the basis of Entity A's experience with fulfilling obligations of this type and its knowledge of the market.

(b)   Entity A estimates allocated overhead and equipment operating costs using the rate it applies to labour costs (80 per cent of expected labour costs). This is consistent with the cost structure of market participants.

(c)   Entity A estimates the compensation that a market participant would require for undertaking the activity and for assuming the risk associated with the obligation to dismantle and remove the asset as follows:

   (i)   A third-party contractor typically adds a mark-up on labour and allocated internal costs to provide a profit margin on the job. The profit margin used (20 per cent) represents Entity A's understanding of the operating profit that contractors in the industry generally earn to dismantle and remove offshore oil platforms. Entity A concludes that this rate is consistent with the rate that a market participant would require as compensation for undertaking the activity.

(ii) A contractor would typically require compensation for the risk that the actual cash outflows might differ from those expected because of the uncertainty inherent in locking in today's price for a project that will not occur for 10 years. Entity A estimates the amount of that premium to be 5 per cent of the expected cash flows, including the effect of inflation.

(d) Entity A assumes a rate of inflation of 4 per cent over the 10-year period on the basis of available market data.

(e) The risk-free rate of interest for a 10-year maturity on 1 January 20X1 is 5 per cent. Entity A adjusts that rate by 3.5 per cent to reflect its risk of non-performance (ie the risk that it will not fulfil the obligation), including its credit risk. Therefore, the discount rate used to compute the present value of the cash flows is 8.5 per cent.

Entity A concludes that its assumptions would be used by market participants. In addition, Entity A does not adjust its fair value measurement for the existence of a restriction preventing it from transferring the liability. As illustrated in the following table, Entity A measures the fair value of its decommissioning liability as CU194,879.

	Expected cash flows (CU) 1 January 20X1
Expected labour costs	131,250
Allocated overhead and equipment costs (0.80 × CU131,250)	105,000
Contractor's profit mark-up [0.20 × (CU131,250 + CU105,000)]	47,250
Expected cash flows before inflation adjustment	283,500
Inflation factor (4% for 10 years)	1.4802
Expected cash flows adjusted for inflation	419,637
Market risk premium (0.05 × CU419,637)	20,982
Expected cash flows adjusted for market risk	440,619
Expected present value using discount rate of 8.5% for 10 years	194,879

5.2 Non-performance risk

5.2.1 Requirement to reflect the effect of non-performance risk

The fair value of a liability should reflect the effect of non-performance risk. [IFRS 13:42]

Non-performance risk is defined as "[t]he risk that an entity will not fulfil an obligation. Non-performance risk includes, but may not be limited to, the entity's own credit risk". [IFRS 13:Appendix A]

Credit risk is defined in IFRS 7 *Financial Instruments: Disclosures* as "[t]he risk that one party to a financial instrument will cause a financial loss for the other party by failing to discharge an obligation". [IFRS 7:Appendix A]

Non-performance risk is assumed to be the same before and after the transfer of the liability. [IFRS 13:42]

The IASB acknowledges in the Basis for Conclusions on IFRS 13 that it is unlikely that non-performance risk is the same before and after the transfer of the financial liability. However, the IASB concluded that such an assumption was necessary when measuring the fair value of a financial liability in order for the transfer concept to apply. If the transferee, acting as a market participant, had a different credit standing to the transferor it would not take on the obligation of the transferor because either (1) in the case of the transferee's credit standing being worse than the transferor's, the counterparty to the obligation would not permit the transfer to take place, or (2) in the case of the transferee's credit standing being better than the transferor's, the transferee would not choose to take on the obligation without renegotiating the terms to reflect the difference in credit standing. Furthermore, if it is assumed that market participants have different credit standings, this would result in fundamentally different valuations depending on the identity of the transferee. It was also noted that those that hold the entity's obligations as assets do consider the effect of an entity's credit risk and other risk factors when pricing those assets and, therefore, this effect should be equally reflected in the fair value of the entity's obligations to those holders of assets. [IFRS 13:BC94]

Example 5.2.1

Impact of guarantee by acquirer on the fair value of an acquiree's loan

Entity A acquires 100 per cent of Entity B from Entity C in a business combination. One of the identifiable liabilities of Entity B is a loan owed to a third party. The loan was originally guaranteed by Entity C as part of the loan terms. However, as a result of the business combination, the terms of the loan are revised so that Entity A becomes the guarantor of the loan (i.e. the guarantee by Entity A becomes part of the revised loan terms).

IFRS 3 *Business Combinations* requires that the third party loan is measured at fair value at the date of acquisition. The measurement requirements of IFRS 13 apply.

There are no quoted prices available for the transfer of an identical or a similar liability.

When measuring the fair value of the loan at the date of acquisition for the purpose of preparing consolidated financial statements, Entity A should take into account the effect of its own guarantee of the loan because the guarantee is part of the loan terms.

As discussed at **5.1.2**, IFRS 13:37 requires that when a quoted price for the transfer of an identical or a similar liability is not available, and the identical item is held by another party as an asset, an entity should measure the fair value of the liability from the perspective of a market participant that holds the identical item as an asset at the measurement date.

In the circumstances described, the loan is guaranteed by Entity A from the date of acquisition. From the perspective of a market participant holding the loan as an asset, the fact that the loan is guaranteed by Entity A would be taken into account when measuring the fair value of the loan receivable because the market participant would expect to recover the loan from Entity A if Entity B defaulted on the loan. Consequently, when measuring the fair value of the loan, a market participant would take into account (1) the credit standing of Entity B, and (2) the guarantee provided by Entity A.

This is also consistent with the requirement in IFRS 13:43 (see below) that an entity should take into account the effect of its own credit risk (credit standing) and any other factors that might influence the likelihood that the obligation will or will not be fulfilled.

The effect of an entity's credit standing and other factors that might influence the likelihood that the obligation will or will not be fulfilled may differ depending on the nature of the liability (e.g. whether it is a financial or a non-financial liability, or whether any credit enhancements are attached). [IFRS 13:43]

To understand non-performance risk, it is necessary to consider the specific terms of the instrument rather than simply looking at the overall credit rating or quality of the entity in its entirety. Looking at the latter will generally obscure the particular credit characteristics of the instrument itself, like credit enhancements, or fail to reflect the relative seniority or subordination of the liability relative to the liabilities of the entity.

The fair value measurement for a liability should reflect the effect of non-performance risk based on the unit of account for financial reporting purposes specified in relevant IFRSs (see also **section 3.2**). The issuer of a liability issued with an inseparable third-party credit enhancement (e.g. a third-party guarantee of debt) that is accounted for separately from the liability should not include the effect of the credit enhancement in the fair value measurement of the liability; in such circumstances, the fair value measurement should reflect the credit standing of the issuer and not that of the third-party guarantor. [IFRS 13:44]

As required under IFRS 13:44, when an entity has in issue a liability with a third-party guarantee, and the liability and the guarantee are accounted for separately under relevant IFRSs, the fair value of the liability should not reflect the effect of the guarantee. In such circumstances, the fair value of the liability from the issuer's perspective will not equal its fair value as a guaranteed liability held by another party as an asset. [IFRS 13:BC98]

5.2.2   Effect of collateral on fair value measurement of liabilities

When an entity has provided collateral in respect of a liability, this will affect the fair value measurement of the liability under IFRS 13. As discussed at **5.2.1**, IFRS 13:42 requires that the fair value of a liability should reflect the effect of non-performance risk, and that non-performance risk is assumed to be the same before and after the transfer of the liability. The definition of non-performance risk in IFRS 13:Appendix A (see **5.2.1**) clarifies that it encompasses an entity's own credit risk (credit standing) and any other factors that might influence the likelihood that the obligation will be fulfilled. One factor specifically mentioned in IFRS 13:43(b) is "the terms of credit enhancements related to the liability, if any".

Collateral is a form of credit enhancement that is contractually linked to a liability (i.e. the terms of the obligation require a lien on the collateral until settlement of the obligation). The fact that an entity has provided collateral typically means that the stated terms of the liability (e.g. the interest rate charged) differ from the terms of an identical liability that is not supported by collateral. The collateral is a characteristic of the liability and, consequently, it should be reflected in the fair value measurement of the collateralised liability.

Example 5.2.2 illustrates how collateral might affect the fair value of a liability on initial recognition.

Example 5.2.2

Effect of collateral on fair value measurement of liabilities

On 1 January 20X1, Company A borrows CU10 million repayable in five years. The fixed interest rate is one-year LIBOR plus 125 basis points. Company A is required to pledge specified property interests as collateral. Management estimates that Company A could have arranged a similar loan with no collateral at a 200 basis point spread to LIBOR. On 1 January 20X1, the one-year LIBOR rate is 1.5 per cent. For simplicity, transaction costs are ignored.

At 1 January 20X1, the fair value of the loan (including any impact from the collateral) is CU10 million. The present value of the loan's contractual cash flows, discounted at Company A's unsecured borrowing rate of 3.5 per cent (i.e. 1.5 per cent LIBOR plus 200 basis points), is CU9.7 million.

This example illustrates that the effect of an issuer's credit standing as well as the effect of credit enhancements should be taken into account in measuring the fair value of the liability. If Company A ignored the reduction in the interest

---

rate attributable to the collateral, it would mistakenly conclude that the fair value of its debt was CU9.7 million rather than CU10 million.

5.2.3 Risks associated with entity's ability to deliver goods or perform services

The definition of non-performance risk in IFRS 13:Appendix A (see **5.2.1**) clarifies that it encompasses an entity's own credit risk (credit standing) and any other factors that might influence the likelihood that the obligation will be fulfilled. Therefore, in addition to an entity's own credit risk, non-performance risk may include the risk associated with the entity's ability to deliver goods or perform services.

For example, consider a contract for the delivery of a commodity (e.g. oil, natural gas, electricity) that is measured as a derivative liability at fair value in accordance with IFRS 9 *Financial Instruments* (or, for entities that have not yet adopted IFRS 9, IAS 39 *Financial Instruments: Recognition and Measurement*). When measuring the fair value of the liability, the entity is required to reflect its own credit risk (i.e. the risk that there will be financial loss for the counterparty because the entity fails to meet its financial obligation). In addition, there is the risk that the entity will not be able to obtain and deliver the commodity to the counterparty (e.g. because of supply issues for the commodity) which is also part of non-performance risk.

Such contracts may contain 'make-whole' or other default clauses to mitigate the risk of non-delivery because the entity would be required to compensate the counterparty for damages incurred if the entity is unable to deliver the commodity. The effect of such clauses will need to be considered in assessing the non-performance risk.

5.2.4 Effect of changes in non-performance risk

Changes in the fair value of collateral or an entity's credit standing should be taken into account in measuring the fair value of a liability on an ongoing basis. This is to ensure that the fair value measurement reflects market participant assumptions at the measurement date.

Examples 5.2.4A and **5.2.4B** illustrate the effect of some of these factors on the fair value of collateralised obligations.

Example 5.2.4A

Effect of a decline in the fair value of collateral

On 1 January 20X1, Company B issues CU100 million of bonds collateralised by a portion of its aircraft fleet. On 30 September 20X3, there has been a substantial decline in the fair value of the aircraft that serve as collateral for the bonds. Assume that Company B's credit standing remains unchanged and all other stated terms of the bonds represent current market conditions for the remaining term of the obligation.

When measuring the fair value of the bonds at 30 September 20X3, Company B must do so from the perspective of a market participant that holds the bonds as an asset (i.e. a bondholder) – see **5.1.1**. A market participant would reflect the reduced level of collateral in the price at which a transfer of the bond would take place.

Company B determines that the hypothetical market participant would be willing to transfer the liability for only CU80 million. In other words, the fair value of the bonds has decreased by CU20 million due to the decline in value of the collateral even though Company B's credit standing remains unchanged.

Example 5.2.4B

Effect of a decline in the borrower's credit standing

The facts are the same as in **example 5.2.4A**, except that, at 30 September 20X3, the fair value of the aircraft pledged as collateral remains unchanged. Instead, the credit standing of Company B has declined from AAA to AA-.

When measuring the fair value of the bonds at 30 September 20X3, Company B is required to consider the effect of the decline in its credit standing but also the fact that the fair value of the collateral has not changed.

Company B observes that the wider credit spread for uncollateralised AA- corporate bonds suggests that the fair value of the bonds has declined by 10 per cent (i.e. to CU90 million). However, because the fair value of the collateral has not changed, the note remains well collateralised. Consequently, the fair value of the note may not have declined by as much as 10 per cent. Company B determines that the increase in non-performance risk arising from the decline in its own credit standing is partially offset by the collateral. Based on credit spreads observed for similar, collateralised bonds, Company B concludes that the fair value of the notes has decreased by CU7 million to CU93 million.

5.2.5   Additional examples

IFRS 13 provides many examples of measuring the fair value of financial liabilities. These examples are included at **section 5.2** of **chapter B7** (for entities applying IFRS 9) and at **section 5.2** of **chapter C7** (for entities applying IAS 39).

5.3 Restriction preventing the transfer of a liability or an entity's own equity instrument

When measuring the fair value of a liability or an entity's own equity instrument, no separate input or adjustment to other inputs should be included to reflect the existence of a restriction that prevents the transfer of the item. The effect of a restriction that prevents the transfer of a liability or an entity's own equity instrument is either implicitly or explicitly included in the other inputs to the fair value measurement. [IFRS 13:45]

For example, at the transaction date for a liability, both the creditor and the obligor accepted the transaction price for the liability with full knowledge that the obligation includes a restriction that prevents its transfer. As a result of the restriction being included in the transaction price, a separate input or an adjustment to an existing input is not required at the transaction date to reflect the effect of the restriction on transfer. Similarly, a separate input or an adjustment to an existing input is not required at subsequent measurement dates to reflect the effect of the restriction on transfer. [IFRS 13:46]

5.4 Financial liability with a demand feature

The fair value of a financial liability with a demand feature (e.g. a demand deposit) is not less than the amount payable on demand, discounted from the first date that the amount could be required to be paid. [IFRS 13:47]

6 Measuring the fair value of financial assets and financial liabilities with offsetting positions in market risks or counterparty credit risk

The application of IFRS 13's requirements under this heading is limited to financial assets and financial liabilities. Consequently, they are not dealt with in this chapter but are discussed separately in **section 6** of **chapter B7** (for entities applying IFRS 9 *Financial Instruments*) and in **section 6** of **chapter C7** (for entities applying IAS 39 *Financial Instruments: Recognition and Measurement*).

7 Fair value measurement at initial recognition

7.1 Potential for difference between the transaction price and fair value at initial recognition

Some IFRSs require or permit assets or liabilities to be recognised initially on the basis of 'fair value'. If the asset has been acquired, or the liability assumed, in a market transaction, it might be assumed that the transaction price (i.e. the price paid to acquire an asset or received to assume a liability) can be taken to be the fair value of the asset or the liability. However, the price paid to acquire an asset, or received to assume a liability, is an *entry* price and, consequently, it is not necessarily the same as the fair value of the asset or liability for IFRS 13 purposes (which is an *exit* price – see **3.1**). The Standard notes that entities do not necessarily sell assets at the prices paid to acquire them; nor do they necessarily transfer liabilities at the prices received to assume them. [IFRS 13:57]

7.2   Indicators that the transaction price differs from fair value at initial recognition

When determining whether the fair value at initial recognition equals the transaction price, an entity should take into account factors specific to the transaction and to the asset and liability. [IFRS 13:59]

IFRS 13:B4 lists a number of factors which may suggest that the transaction price is not the fair value of the asset or liability at initial recognition.

The following table repeats the factors listed in IFRS 13:B4 and provides examples for each. Note that this list of indicators is not exhaustive, and other factors may exist that should be considered in evaluating whether a transaction price represents fair value (see IFRS 13:BC133).

Factor (IFRS 13:B4)	Example
The transaction is between related parties, although the price in a related party transaction may be used as an input into a fair value measurement if the reporting entity has evidence that the transaction was entered into at market terms.	An entity purchases a portfolio of troubled loans from an unconsolidated investee. The parties meet the definition of related parties under IAS 24 *Related Party Disclosures*. The fact that the parties are related may indicate that the transaction price does not reflect fair value. However, this alone would not be determinative. Evidence that the transaction was entered into at market terms may include: • the appointment of third parties to negotiate or measure fair value; or • the terms of the transaction are consistent with available market data for similar transactions between unrelated parties; or • there is no evidence that one of the parties to the transaction is under duress (see the next factor).

The transaction takes place under duress or the seller is forced to accept the price in the transaction (e.g. if the seller is experiencing financial difficulty).

A hedge fund must sell all of its non-marketable assets in response to a spike in redemptions that may lead to a liquidity crisis. A liquidity crisis may be an indicator of financial difficulty.

The factors in IFRS 13:B43 indicating that a transaction is not orderly (see **9.6**) may also indicate that the transaction price does not represent fair value.

The unit of account represented by the transaction price is different from the unit of account for the asset or liability measured at fair value. For example, this might be the case if the asset or liability measured at fair value is only one of the elements in the transaction (e.g. in a business combination), if the transaction includes unstated rights and privileges that are measured separately in accordance with another IFRS, or if the transaction price includes transaction costs.

IFRS 13:14 requires that the unit of account for an asset or a liability should be determined in accordance with the IFRS that requires or permits the fair value measurement, except as provided in IFRS 13 (see **3.2.1**). The following example illustrates a scenario in which the unit of account for the asset is different from the unit of account represented by the transaction price.

On 30 June 20X1, Company A acquires a 3 per cent equity interest (3 million shares) in Company B from an independent third party. Quoted prices in an active market are available for Company B's shares. Company A pays CU100 million for the entire 3 per cent equity interest (the transaction price is determined based on a negotiated arm's length price for the entire 3 per cent equity interest). The quoted price for Company B's shares on 30 June 20X1 is CU36 per share. Company A needs to identify the unit of account in order to measure the fair value of the 3 per cent equity interest on initial recognition.

In identifying the unit of account for fair value measurement purposes, IFRS 9 (or, for entities that have not yet adopted IFRS 9, IAS 39) is the applicable Standard.

IFRS 13:BC47 states, in part, that "[i]n IAS 39 and IFRS 9... the unit of account is generally an individual financial instrument". This guidance is also consistent with the guidance set out in IFRS 13:80 which states that "[i]f an entity holds a position in a single asset ... and the asset ... is traded in an active market, the fair value of the asset ... shall be measured within Level 1 as the product of the quoted price for the individual asset ... and the quantity held by the entity".

Therefore, notwithstanding the fact that Company A paid a transaction price of CU100 million for the entire 3 million shares, the unit of account in this example is each individual share, not the entire 3 per cent equity interest acquired. Specifically, the fair value of the 3 per cent equity interest in Company B is measured as the product of the quoted price for each individual share and the quantity held ('P × Q') (i.e. CU108 million = 3 million shares × CU36 per share).

The market in which the transaction takes place is different from the principal market (or most advantageous market). For example, those markets might be different if the entity is a dealer that enters into transactions with customers in the retail market, but the principal (or most advantageous) market for the exit transaction is with other dealers in the dealer market.

Entity A (a retail counterparty) enters into an interest rate swap in a retail market with Entity B (a dealer) for no initial consideration (i.e. the transaction price is zero). Entity A can access only the retail market. Entity B can access both the retail market (i.e. with retail counterparties) and the dealer market (i.e. with dealer counterparties).

From the perspective of Entity A, the fair value at initial recognition is zero because Entity A does not have access to the dealer market.

From Entity B's perspective, the transaction price of the interest rate swap (i.e. zero) does not represent fair value at initial recognition if prices observed or market participant assumptions in the dealer market (i.e. Entity B's principal market) indicate that fair value is something other than zero.

Note: This final scenario is a summary of Example 7 from the illustrative examples accompanying IFRS 13 (see IFRS 13:IE24 to IE26).

7.3 Recognition of 'day 1 p&l'

In many cases, the transaction price and the fair value will be equal (e.g. when the transaction date is the same as the measurement date and an asset is acquired in the market in which it would be sold). [IFRS 13:58] However, when the amounts are not equal, the asset or liability should be measured at fair value and the difference between the transaction price and fair value (generally referred to as a 'day 1 gain or loss' , 'day 1 profit or loss, or 'day 1 p&l'') is required to be recognised as a gain or loss in profit or loss unless the relevant IFRS specifies otherwise. [IFRS 13:60]

For example, IFRS 9 *Financial Instruments* and IAS 39 *Financial Instruments: Recognition and Measurement* state that an entity cannot recognise a day 1 gain or loss for a financial instrument unless the instrument's fair value is evidenced by a quoted price in an active market for an identical asset or liability or based on a valuation technique that uses only data from observable markets. In contrast, IFRS 3 *Business Combinations* and IAS 41 *Agriculture* require the recognition of day 1 gains or losses even when fair value is measured using unobservable inputs (see IFRS 13:BC135).

When, in accordance with the relevant IFRS, a day 1 gain or loss is not recognised, the asset or liability should be measured at fair value and the day 1 gain or loss deferred and accounted for separately under the relevant Standard (see **7.3** in **chapter B7** for entities applying IFRS 9 and **7.3** in **chapter C7** for entities applying IAS 39).

8   Valuation techniques

8.1   Valuation techniques required to maximise the use of observable inputs

When the price for an asset or a liability cannot be observed directly, it must be estimated using a valuation technique. When used in the context of fair value measurement, 'valuation technique' is a generic term and its application is not limited to complex fair valuation models. For example, valuing an asset or a liability using quoted prices in an active market for identical assets and liabilities is a valuation technique. In other cases, when prices cannot be observed directly and more judgement is required, it will be appropriate to use more complex valuation techniques.

An entity is required to use valuation techniques that are appropriate in the circumstances and for which sufficient data are available to measure fair value, maximising the use of relevant observable inputs and minimising the use of unobservable inputs. [IFRS 13:61]

Observable inputs are defined as "[i]nputs that are developed using market data, such as publicly available information about actual events or transactions, and that reflect the assumptions that market participants would use when pricing the asset or liability". [IFRS 13:Appendix A]

Unobservable inputs are defined as "[i]nputs for which market data are not available and that are developed using the best information available about the assumptions that market participants would use when pricing the asset or liability". [IFRS 13:Appendix A]

8.2   Widely used valuation techniques

IFRS 13 refers to three widely used valuation techniques:

[IFRS 13:62]

- the market approach (see **8.4**);

- the cost approach (sometimes referred to as 'replacement cost') (see **8.5**); and

- the income approach (see **section 8.6**)

Any valuation technique used to measure fair value should be consistent with one or more of the above approaches. [IFRS 13:62]

8.3 Selecting an appropriate valuation technique

IFRS 13 does not set out a hierarchy of valuation techniques; this is because particular valuation techniques may be more appropriate in some circumstances than in others (see IFRS 13:BC142).

Each valuation technique has its own merits and may or may not be suitable for measuring the fair value of a specified item or items in particular circumstances. In practice, different valuation techniques can give rise to different estimates of fair value and, therefore, it is important to select the most appropriate methodology for the particular circumstances.

Choosing a valuation technique requires judgement and involves the selection of a method, formulae and assumptions. The reliability of a fair value measurement derived from a valuation technique is dependent on both the reliability of the valuation technique and the reliability of the inputs used. Consequently, when selecting a valuation technique, it will be important to consider the availability of reliable inputs for that valuation (see **section 9**). In addition to selecting a technique that maximises the use of relevant observable inputs and minimises the use of unobservable inputs, an entity must also ensure that the best possible evidence is used to support unobservable inputs.

In assessing the appropriateness of each valuation technique, an entity should also evaluate all available inputs significant to the valuation technique and compare the technique with other valuation techniques. For example, in a given situation, an entity may conclude that it is appropriate to use a market approach rather than an income approach because the market approach uses superior market information as inputs.

An entity should consider using a valuation specialist, when appropriate.

See **8.7** for a discussion of when it is appropriate to use multiple valuation techniques.

Example 8.3 illustrates how an entity might approach the selection of a valuation technique (or techniques) for unquoted equity securities in specified circumstances.

Example 8.3

Selecting an appropriate valuation technique or techniques for unquoted equity securities

Company A holds equity investments in two entities – Company B and Company C. Company A measures these investments at fair value on a recurring basis.

- Company B is a clothing retailer that operates in the niche market of the baby clothing industry. Quoted prices are not available for Company B's shares. Most of Company B's competitors are either privately held or are subsidiaries of larger publicly traded clothing retailers. Company B is similar to two other organisations, whose shares are thinly traded in an observable market.

- Company C is a retailer that operates in the competitive consumer electronics industry. Although quoted prices are not available for Company C's shares, Company C is comparable to many entities whose shares are actively traded.

Because the prices of Company B's and Company C's shares cannot be observed directly, Company A must measure the fair value of these investments using a valuation technique (or techniques).

Company A is considering a market approach, an income approach or a combination of these two approaches. The market approach and the income approach are common valuation techniques for equity investments that are not publicly traded. Under the market approach, entities use prices and other relevant information generated by market transactions involving identical or comparable securities. Under the income approach, future amounts are converted into a single present amount (e.g. discounted cash flows model). Company A is not considering the cost approach to value its equity securities because it is not considered relevant. (See **8.4** to **8.6** for detailed descriptions of these valuation techniques. See also **8.7** for a discussion of when it is appropriate to use multiple valuation techniques.)

Company A should select the valuation technique (or techniques) that is (are) appropriate in the circumstances and for which sufficient data are available to measure fair value, maximising the use of relevant observable inputs and minimising the use of unobservable inputs.

Investment in Company B

Using a market approach, the fair value measurement of Company A's investment in Company B would involve an analysis of market prices and other relevant information for the two similar organisations that are traded (albeit thinly) in an observable market. It is likely that the observable market data would need to be adjusted to reflect differences between Company B and the two similar organisations that are traded. For example, Company A might consider that market participants would incorporate significant entity-specific adjustments into the valuation of Company B's shares (e.g. adjustments to reflect the relative illiquidity of Company B's shares, profitability, net assets, unrecognised assets such as internally generated intangible assets, and differences in business model between Company B and the two traded organisations). These adjustments would be made using Company A's own assumptions. Consequently, in such circumstances, a market approach would rely on unobservable inputs that are significant to the fair value measurement.

Using an income approach based on discounted cash flows, the fair value measurement of Company A's investment in Company B would also be based on significant entity-specific assumptions in forecasting Company B's future cash flows. As a result, the income approach would also rely on unobservable inputs that are significant to the fair value measurement.

Based on the above information, it is likely that Company A would conclude that both the market approach and the income approach are appropriate techniques for measuring the fair value of its investment in Company B. In making its selection, Company A would consider the reliability of the evidence supporting the inputs used in each of the valuation techniques. Provided that relevant and reliable inputs are available, and there are no other factors indicating that one of the approaches is superior, it would seem appropriate to use a combination of both approaches, even if one approach is used only to corroborate the results of the other.

Investment in Company C

When selecting an appropriate approach to measure the fair value of its investment in Company C, Company A should perform an analysis similar to that outlined for Company B.

Using a market approach, it is more likely that market participants would incorporate fewer unobservable adjustments into the valuation of Company C's shares because of the large number of comparable traded entities and the high trading volume of the shares of those comparable entities. However, Company A should consider whether to make an adjustment for illiquidity to reflect the fact that Company C's shares are unquoted whereas those of comparable entities in the same sector are listed and actively traded.

Using an income approach based on discounted cash flows, the fair value measurement of Company A's investment in Company C would be based on forecasted future cash flows. This forecast would include projections of future profitability and, therefore, would be likely to include entity-specific assumptions that are not observable.

As a result, it is likely that Company A would conclude that it is appropriate to measure the fair value of its investment in Company C using the market approach because it uses more observable inputs (i.e. in terms of the hierarchy described in **section 10**, 'Level 2' inputs vs. 'Level 3' inputs) with a significant effect.

8.4 Market approach

The 'market approach' is defined as "[a] valuation technique that uses prices and other relevant information generated by market transactions involving identical or comparable (ie similar) assets, liabilities or a group of assets and liabilities, such as a business". [IFRS 13:Appendix A]

A quoted price for an identical asset or liability in an active market that the entity can access at the measurement date provides the most reliable evidence of fair value. [IFRS 13:77] Quoted prices for an identical asset or liability are regarded as Level 1 inputs within the fair value hierarchy (see **section 10.2.1**). When a quoted price exists for an identical asset or liability, it should be used without adjustment, except in the circumstances described at **section 10.2.1**. [IFRS 13:77] When a quoted price for an asset or a liability exists in multiple active markets, it will be necessary to identify the market and price which represent fair value for the specific facts and circumstances.

Valuation techniques consistent with the market approach often use market multiples derived from a set of comparable assets or liabilities. A range of multiples may be derived, with a different multiple for each comparable asset or liability. The selection of the appropriate multiple within the range requires the exercise of judgement – with appropriate consideration of the qualitative and quantitative factors specific to the measurement. [IFRS 13:B6]

One valuation technique that is consistent with the market approach is 'matrix pricing'; matrix pricing is a mathematical technique used principally to value some types of financial instruments, such as debt securities, without relying exclusively on quoted prices for the specific securities, but rather relying on the securities' relationship to other benchmark quoted securities. [IFRS 13:B7]

8.5 Cost approach

The 'cost approach' is defined as "[a] valuation technique that reflects the amount that would be required currently to replace the service capacity of an asset (often referred to as current replacement cost)". [IFRS 13:Appendix A] This method is often used to measure the fair value of tangible assets that are used in combination with other assets or with other assets and liabilities. [IFRS 13:B9]

When the cost approach is applied, the fair value of the asset is based on what it would cost a market participant buyer to acquire or construct a substitute asset of comparable utility, adjusted for obsolescence (i.e. its current replacement cost). The approach is based on the rationale that a market participant buyer would not pay more for an asset than the amount for which it could replace the service capacity of that asset. [IFRS 13:B9]

For the purpose of measuring an asset's current replacement cost, obsolescence encompasses (1) physical deterioration, (2) functional (technological) obsolescence, and (3) economic (external) obsolescence; obsolescence is a broader concept than depreciation for financial reporting purposes or tax purposes. [IFRS 13:B9]

The inclusion of the cost approach as an appropriate valuation technique may seem counter-intuitive in the light of IFRS 13's exit price definition of fair value. However, the IASB points out that an entity's cost to replace an asset would equal the amount that a market participant buyer of that asset would pay to acquire it (i.e. the entry price and the exit price would be equal in the same market). Therefore, the cost approach is considered to be consistent with an exit price definition of fair value. [IFRS 13:BC141]

8.6 Income approach

8.6.1 Income approach – general

The 'income approach' is defined as "[v]aluation techniques that convert future amounts (eg cash flows or income and expenses) to a single current (ie discounted) amount. The fair value measurement is determined on the basis of the value indicated by current market expectations about those future amounts". [IFRS 13:Appendix A]

Income approaches that are used for measuring fair value include, for example:

[IFRS 13:B11]

- present value techniques (see below);

- option pricing models, such as the Black-Scholes-Merton formula or a binomial model (i.e. a lattice model), that incorporate present value techniques and reflect both the time value and the intrinsic value of an option; and

- the multi-period excess earnings method, which is used to measure the fair value of some intangible assets.

IFRS 13 describes two types of present value technique:

- the discount rate adjustment technique (see **8.6.4.2**); and

- the expected cash flow (expected present value) technique (see **8.6.4.3**).

IFRS 13 does not specifically require that one of these present value techniques be used. The most appropriate present value technique for the measurement of fair value in a particular scenario will depend on the facts and circumstances specific to the asset or liability being measured (e.g. whether prices for comparable assets or liabilities can be observed in the market) and the availability of sufficient data. [IFRS 13:B12]

8.6.2 Components of a present value measurement

Present value is a tool used to link future amounts (e.g. cash flows or values) to a present amount using a discount rate. A fair value measurement of an asset or a liability using a present value technique captures all of the following elements from the perspective of market participants at the measurement date:

[IFRS 13:B13]

- an estimate of future cash flows for the asset or liability being measured;

- expectations about possible variations in the amount and timing of the cash flows representing the uncertainty inherent in the cash flows;

- the time value of money, represented by the rate on risk-free monetary assets that have maturity dates or durations that coincide with the period covered by the cash flows and pose neither uncertainty in timing nor risk of default to the holder (i.e. a risk-free interest rate);

- the price for bearing the uncertainty inherent in the cash flows (i.e. a risk premium);

- other factors that market participants would take into account in the circumstances; and

- for a liability, the non-performance risk relating to that liability, including the obligor's own credit risk.

When using post-tax cash flows (and a post-tax discount rate) to measure the fair value of a depreciable asset, an entity should include all relevant cash flows. These would include cash inflows resulting from future tax deductions for the asset's depreciation or amortisation expense that a market participant would expect to receive. A market participant would expect to receive the future tax deductions if the depreciation or amortisation is deductible for tax purposes in the jurisdiction in which the transaction is entered into. Judgement will be required to determine which jurisdiction should be considered from a market participant perspective.

This conclusion is consistent with the following guidance in paragraph C35 of IVS 210 *Intangible Assets* issued by the International Valuation Standards Council.

> "In many tax regimes, the amortisation of an *intangible* asset can be treated as an expense in calculating taxable income. This "tax amortisation benefit" can have a positive impact on the value of the asset. When an *income approach* is used, it will be necessary to consider the impact of any available tax benefit to buyers and make an appropriate adjustment to the cash flows."

8.6.3   General principles underlying present value measurement

Present value techniques differ in how they capture the elements listed in **8.6.2**. However, all of the following general principles govern the application of any present value technique used to measure fair value.

[IFRS 13:B14]

- Cash flows and discount rates should reflect assumptions that market participants would use when pricing the asset or liability.

- Cash flows and discount rates should take into account only the factors attributable to the asset or liability being measured.

- To avoid double-counting or omitting the effects of risk factors, discount rates should reflect assumptions that are consistent with those inherent in the cash flows. For example, a discount rate that reflects the uncertainty in expectations about future defaults is appropriate if using contractual cash flows of a loan (i.e. a discount rate adjustment technique). That same rate should not be used if using expected (i.e. probability-weighted) cash flows (i.e. an expected present value technique) because the expected cash flows already reflect assumptions about the uncertainty in future defaults; instead, a discount rate that is commensurate with the risk inherent in the expected cash flows should be used.

- Assumptions about cash flows and discount rates should be internally consistent. For example, nominal cash flows, which include the effect of inflation, should be discounted at a rate that includes the effect of inflation. The nominal risk-free interest rate includes the effect of inflation. Real cash flows, which exclude the effect of inflation, should be discounted at a rate that excludes the effect of inflation. Similarly, after-tax cash flows should be discounted using an after-tax discount rate. Pre-tax cash flows should be discounted at a rate consistent with those cash flows.

> Care should be taken in determining a pre-tax discount rate by adjusting a post-tax rate. Because the tax consequences of cash flows may occur in different periods, the pre-tax rate of return is not always the post-tax rate of return grossed up by the standard rate of tax. See **8.4.2** in **chapter A10** for further guidance on how to adjust a post-tax discount rate to arrive at a pre-tax discount rate.

- Discount rates should be consistent with the underlying economic factors of the currency in which the cash flows are denominated.

8.6.4 Risk and uncertainty

8.6.4.1 Risk and uncertainty – general
A fair value measurement using present value techniques is made under conditions of uncertainty because the cash flows used are estimates rather than known amounts. In many cases, both the amount and timing of the cash flows are uncertain. Even contractually fixed amounts, such as the payments on a loan, are uncertain if there is risk of default. [IFRS 13:B15]

Market participants generally seek compensation (i.e. a risk premium) for bearing the uncertainty inherent in the cash flows of an asset or a liability. A fair value measurement should include a risk premium reflecting the amount that market participants would demand as compensation for the uncertainty inherent in the cash flows. Otherwise, the measurement would not faithfully represent fair value. In some cases, determining the appropriate risk premium may be difficult. However, the degree of difficulty alone is not a sufficient reason to exclude a risk premium. [IFRS 13:B16]

Present value techniques differ in how they adjust for risk and in the type of cash flows they use. For example, the discount rate adjustment technique described in **8.6.4.2** uses contractual, promised or most likely cash flows and a risk-adjusted discount rate. [IFRS 13:B17(a)]

Expected present value techniques incorporate the effects of risk and uncertainty in one of two ways. The calculation either uses risk-adjusted expected cash flows and a risk-free rate to discount them or uses expected cash flows that are not risk-adjusted and a discount rate adjusted to include the risk premium that market participants require (see **8.6.4.3**). That rate is different from the rate used in the discount rate adjustment technique described in **8.6.4.2**. [IFRS 13:B17(b)&(c)]

8.6.4.2 Discount rate adjustment technique

The discount rate adjustment technique uses a single set of cash flows from the range of possible estimated amounts, whether contractual or promised (as is the case for a bond) or most likely cash flows. In all cases, those cash flows are conditional upon the occurrence of specified events (e.g. contractual or promised cash flows for a bond are conditional on the event of no default by the debtor). The discount rate used in the discount rate adjustment technique is derived from observed rates of return for comparable assets or liabilities that are traded in the market. Accordingly, the contractual, promised or most likely cash flows are discounted at an observed or estimated market rate for such conditional cash flows (i.e. a market rate of return). [IFRS 13:B18]

The discount rate adjustment technique requires an analysis of market data for comparable assets or liabilities. Comparability is established by considering the nature of the cash flows (e.g. whether the cash flows are contractual or non-contractual and are likely to respond similarly to changes in economic conditions), as well as other factors (e.g. credit standing, collateral, duration, restrictive covenants and liquidity). Alternatively, if a single comparable asset or liability does not fairly reflect the risk inherent in the cash flows of the asset or liability being measured, it may be possible to derive a discount rate using data for several comparable assets or liabilities in conjunction with the risk-free yield curve (i.e. using a 'build-up'approach). [IFRS 13:B19]

Example 8.6.4.2

Deriving a discount rate using a build-up approach

[Based on IFRS 13:B20 - B21]

Assume that Asset A is a contractual right to receive CU800 in one year (i.e. there is no timing uncertainty). There is an established market for

---

comparable assets, and information about those assets, including price information, is available. Of those comparable assets:

(a) Asset B is a contractual right to receive CU1,200 in one year and has a market price of CU1,083. Thus, the implied annual rate of return (i.e. a one-year market rate of return) is 10.8 per cent [(CU1,200/CU1,083) – 1].

(b) Asset C is a contractual right to receive CU700 in two years and has a market price of CU566. Thus, the implied annual rate of return (i.e. a two-year market rate of return) is 11.2 per cent [(CU700/CU566)^0.5 – 1].

(c) All three assets are comparable with respect to risk (i.e. dispersion of possible pay-offs and credit).

On the basis of the timing of the contractual payments to be received for Asset A relative to the timing for Asset B and Asset C (i.e. one year for Asset B versus two years for Asset C), Asset B is deemed more comparable to Asset A. Using the contractual payment to be received for Asset A (CU800) and the one-year market rate derived from Asset B (10.8 per cent), the fair value of Asset A is CU722 (CU800/1.108).

Alternatively, in the absence of available market information for Asset B, the one-year market rate could be derived from Asset C using the build-up approach. In that case, the two-year market rate indicated by Asset C (11.2 per cent) would be adjusted to a one-year market rate using the term structure of the risk-free yield curve. Additional information and analysis might be required to determine whether the risk premiums for one-year and two-year assets are the same. If it is determined that the risk premiums for one-year and two-year assets are not the same, the two-year market rate of return would be further adjusted for that effect.

When the discount rate adjustment technique is applied to fixed receipts or payments, the adjustment for risk inherent in the cash flows of the asset or liability being measured is included in the discount rate. In some applications of the discount rate adjustment technique to cash flows that are not fixed receipts or payments, an adjustment to the cash flows may be necessary to achieve comparability with the observed asset or liability from which the discount rate is derived. [IFRS 13:B22]

8.6.4.3 Expected present value technique

The expected present value technique uses as a starting point a set of cash flows that represents the probability-weighted average of all possible future cash flows (i.e. the expected cash flows). The resulting estimate is identical to expected value, which, in statistical terms, is the weighted average of a discrete random variable's possible values with the respective probabilities as the weights. All possible cash flows are probability-weighted; consequently, the resulting expected cash flow is not conditional upon the occurrence of any specified event (unlike the cash flows used in the discount rate adjustment technique described in **8.6.4.2**). [IFRS 13:B23]

In making an investment decision, risk-averse market participants would take into account the risk that the actual cash flows may differ from the expected cash flows. Portfolio theory distinguishes between unsystematic (diversifiable) risk, which is the risk specific to a particular asset or liability, and systematic (non-diversifiable) risk, which is the common risk shared by an asset or a liability with the other items in a diversified portfolio. Portfolio theory holds that in a market in equilibrium, market participants will be compensated only for bearing the systematic risk inherent in the cash flows. In markets that are inefficient or out of equilibrium, other forms of return or compensation might be available. [IFRS 13:B24]

IFRS 13 describes two methods for applying the expected present value technique. Both methods are illustrated in **example 8.6.4.3**.

[IFRS 13:B25 & B26]

- Method 1 adjusts the expected cash flows of an asset for systematic (i.e. market) risk by subtracting a cash risk premium (i.e. risk-adjusted expected cash flows). Those risk-adjusted expected cash flows represent a certainty-equivalent cash flow, which is discounted at a risk-free interest rate. A certainty-equivalent cash flow refers to an expected cash flow (as defined), adjusted for risk so that a market participant is indifferent to trading a certain cash flow for an expected cash flow. For example, if a market participant were willing to trade an expected cash flow of CU1,200 for a certain cash flow of CU1,000, the CU1,000 is the certainty equivalent of the CU1,200 (i.e. the CU200 would represent the cash risk premium). In that case, the market participant would be indifferent as to the asset held.

- Method 2 adjusts for systematic (i.e. market) risk by adding a risk premium to the risk-free interest rate. Accordingly, the expected cash flows are discounted at a rate that corresponds to an expected rate associated with probability-weighted cash flows (i.e. an expected rate of return). Models used for pricing risky assets, such as the capital asset pricing model, can be used to estimate the expected rate of return. Because the discount rate used in the discount rate adjustment technique (see **8.6.4.2**) is a rate of return relating to conditional cash flows, it is likely to be higher than the expected rate of return relating to expected or probability-weighted cash flows.

Example 8.6.4.3

Present value techniques: discounting risk-adjusted expected cash flows by the risk-free rate vs. discounting unadjusted expected cash flows by a risk-adjusted discount rate

[Based on IFRS 13:B27 - B30]

Assume that an asset has expected cash flows of CU780 in one year determined on the basis of the possible cash flows and probabilities shown below. The applicable risk-free interest rate for cash flows with a one-year horizon is

---

5 per cent, and the systematic risk premium for an asset with the same risk profile is 3 per cent.

Possible cash flows	Probability	Probability-weighted cash flows
CU500	15%	CU75
CU800	60%	CU480
CU900	25%	CU225
Expected cash flows:		CU780

In this simple illustration, the expected cash flows (CU780) represent the probability-weighted average of the three possible outcomes. In more realistic situations, there could be many possible outcomes. However, to apply the expected present value technique, it is not always necessary to take into account distributions of all possible cash flows using complex models and techniques. Rather, it might be possible to develop a limited number of discrete scenarios and probabilities that capture the array of possible cash flows. For example, an entity might use realised cash flows for some relevant past period, adjusted for changes in circumstances occurring subsequently (e.g. changes in external factors, including economic or market conditions, industry trends and competition as well as changes in internal factors affecting the entity more specifically), taking into account the assumptions of market participants.

In theory, the present value (i.e. the fair value) of the asset's cash flows is the same whether determined by discounting the risk adjusted expected cash flows by the risk-free rate (Method 1) or by discounting the unadjusted expected cash flows by the risk-adjusted discount rate (Method 2).

Using Method 1, the expected cash flows are adjusted for systematic (i.e. market) risk. In the absence of market data directly indicating the amount of the risk adjustment, such adjustment could be derived from an asset pricing model using the concept of certainty equivalents. For example, the risk adjustment (i.e. the cash risk premium of CU22) could be determined using the systematic risk premium of 3 per cent (CU780 − [CU780 × (1.05/1.08)]), which results in risk-adjusted expected cash flows of CU758 (CU780 − CU22). The CU758 is the certainty equivalent of CU780 and is discounted at the risk-free interest rate (5 per cent). The present value (i.e. the fair value) of the asset is CU722 (CU758/1.05).

Using Method 2, the expected cash flows are not adjusted for systematic (i.e. market) risk. Rather, the adjustment for that risk is included in the discount rate. Thus, the expected cash flows are discounted at an expected rate of return of 8 per cent (i.e. the 5 per cent risk-free interest rate plus the 3 per cent systematic risk premium). The present value (i.e. the fair value) of the asset is CU722 (CU780/1.08).

When using an expected present value technique to measure fair value, either Method 1 or Method 2 could be used. The selection of Method 1 or Method 2 will depend on facts and circumstances specific to the asset or liability being measured, the extent to which sufficient data are available, and the judgements applied.

8.7 Use of multiple valuation techniques

In some cases, it is appropriate to use a single valuation technique (e.g. when valuing an asset or a liability using quoted market prices in an active market for identical assets or liabilities). However, in other circumstances, it is appropriate to use multiple valuation techniques. [IFRS 13:63]

When multiple valuation techniques are used to measure fair value, the results (i.e. the fair value measurements) should be evaluated taking into account the reasonableness of the range of values indicated by those results. A fair value measurement is the point within that range that is most representative of the fair value in the circumstances. [IFRS 13:63]

In determining whether it is more appropriate to use a single approach or multiple approaches, an entity should consider the appropriateness (i.e. relevance and applicability) of each valuation technique and the observability of the available inputs that are significant to the valuation technique. If one valuation technique is clearly superior to the other techniques (e.g. because it uses more observable inputs), it may be appropriate to use a single valuation technique. Conversely, if no valuation technique is superior (e.g. because all techniques use unobservable inputs that are significant to the measurement), it may be appropriate to use a combination of valuation techniques provided that reliable and relevant inputs are available.

Examples **8.7A** and **8.7B**, which are reproduced from the illustrative examples accompanying IFRS 13, illustrate the use of multiple valuation techniques.

Example 8.7A

Machine held and used

[IFRS 13:IE11 - IE14, Example 4]

An entity acquires a machine in a business combination. The machine will be held and used in its operations. The machine was originally purchased by the acquired entity from an outside vendor and, before the business combination, was customised by the acquired entity for use in its operations. However, the customisation of the machine was not extensive. The acquiring entity determines that the asset would provide maximum value to market participants through its use in combination with other assets or with other assets and liabilities (as installed or otherwise configured for use). There is no evidence to suggest that the current use of the machine is not its highest and best use. Therefore, the highest and best use of the machine is its current use in combination with other assets or with other assets and liabilities.

The entity determines that sufficient data are available to apply the cost approach and, because the customisation of the machine was not extensive, the market approach. The income approach is not used because the machine does not

---

have a separately identifiable income stream from which to develop reliable estimates of future cash flows. Furthermore, information about short-term and intermediate-term lease rates for similar used machinery that otherwise could be used to project an income stream (ie lease payments over remaining service lives) is not available. The market and cost approaches are applied as follows:

(a) The market approach is applied using quoted prices for similar machines adjusted for differences between the machine (as customised) and the similar machines. The measurement reflects the price that would be received for the machine in its current condition (used) and location (installed and configured for use). The fair value indicated by that approach ranges from CU40,000 to CU48,000.

(b) The cost approach is applied by estimating the amount that would be required currently to construct a substitute (customised) machine of comparable utility. The estimate takes into account the condition of the machine and the environment in which it operates, including physical wear and tear (ie physical deterioration), improvements in technology (ie functional obsolescence), conditions external to the condition of the machine such as a decline in the market demand for similar machines (ie economic obsolescence) and installation costs. The fair value indicated by that approach ranges from CU40,000 to CU52,000.

The entity determines that the higher end of the range indicated by the market approach is most representative of fair value and, therefore, ascribes more weight to the results of the market approach. That determination is made on the basis of the relative subjectivity of the inputs, taking into account the degree of comparability between the machine and the similar machines. In particular:

(a) the inputs used in the market approach (quoted prices for similar machines) require fewer and less subjective adjustments than the inputs used in the cost approach.

(b) the range indicated by the market approach overlaps with, but is narrower than, the range indicated by the cost approach.

(c) there are no known unexplained differences (between the machine and the similar machines) within that range.

Accordingly, the entity determines that the fair value of the machine is CU48,000.

If customisation of the machine was extensive or if there were not sufficient data available to apply the market approach (eg because market data reflect transactions for machines used on a stand-alone basis, such as a scrap value for specialised assets, rather than machines used in combination with other assets or with other assets and liabilities), the entity would apply the cost approach. When an asset is used in combination with other assets or with other assets and liabilities, the cost approach assumes the sale of the machine to a market participant buyer with the complementary assets and the associated liabilities. The price received for the sale of the machine (ie an exit price) would not be more than either of the following:

(a) the cost that a market participant buyer would incur to acquire or construct a substitute machine of comparable utility; or

(b) the economic benefit that a market participant buyer would derive from the use of the machine.

Example 8.7B

Software asset

[IFRS 13:IE15 - IE17, Example 5]

An entity acquires a group of assets. The asset group includes an income-producing software asset internally developed for licensing to customers and its complementary assets (including a related database with which the software asset is used) and the associated liabilities. To allocate the cost of the group to the individual assets acquired, the entity measures the fair value of the software asset. The entity determines that the software asset would provide maximum value to market participants through its use in combination with other assets or with other assets and liabilities (ie its complementary assets and the associated liabilities). There is no evidence to suggest that the current use of the software asset is not its highest and best use. Therefore, the highest and best use of the software asset is its current use. (In this case, the licensing of the software asset, in and of itself, does not indicate that the fair value of the asset would be maximised through its use by market participants on a stand-alone basis.)

The entity determines that, in addition to the income approach, sufficient data might be available to apply the cost approach but not the market approach. Information about market transactions for comparable software assets is not available. The income and cost approaches are applied as follows:

(a)   The income approach is applied using a present value technique. The cash flows used in that technique reflect the income stream expected to result from the software asset (licence fees from customers) over its economic life. The fair value indicated by that approach is CU15 million.

(b)   The cost approach is applied by estimating the amount that currently would be required to construct a substitute software asset of comparable utility (ie taking into account functional and economic obsolescence). The fair value indicated by that approach is CU10 million.

Through its application of the cost approach, the entity determines that market participants would not be able to construct a substitute software asset of comparable utility. Some characteristics of the software asset are unique, having been developed using proprietary information, and cannot be readily replicated. The entity determines that the fair value of the software asset is CU15 million, as indicated by the income approach.

8.8   Calibration of valuation techniques

If the transaction price is fair value at initial recognition and a valuation technique that uses unobservable inputs will be used to measure fair value in subsequent periods, the valuation technique should be calibrated so that at initial recognition the result of the valuation technique equals the transaction price. Calibration ensures that the valuation technique reflects current market conditions, and it helps an entity to determine whether an adjustment to the valuation technique is necessary (e.g. there might be a characteristic of the asset or liability that is not captured by the valuation technique). After initial recognition, when measuring fair value using a valuation technique or techniques that use unobservable inputs, an entity should ensure that those valuation techniques reflect observable market data (e.g. the price for a similar asset or liability) at the measurement date. [IFRS 13:64]

Some IFRSs require or permit assets or liabilities to be recognised initially at fair value. When an asset is acquired or a liability assumed in a market transaction, it cannot be assumed that the price paid to acquire the asset or received to assume the liability (i.e. transaction or entry price) is the same as the fair value of the asset or liability in accordance with IFRS 13 (an exit price) (see **section 7** for further discussion).

IFRS 13:64, as discussed above, deals specifically with circumstances in which:

- a valuation technique that uses unobservable inputs is used to measure the fair value of an asset or a liability in subsequent periods; and

- the transaction price for the asset or liability *is* an appropriate measure of fair value at initial recognition in accordance with IFRS 13.

In such circumstances, IFRS 13:64 requires that the valuation technique should be calibrated (i.e. adjusted) so that, at initial recognition, the result of the valuation technique equals the transaction price.

If the transaction price is fair value at initial recognition, calibration of an entity's pricing model eliminates differences between the transaction price and the model's output (the 'inception difference'). IFRS 13 does not prescribe any specific method for the calibration of pricing models. Therefore, an entity should select the most appropriate method for the particular circumstances. If the transaction price is fair value at initial recognition, calibration of an entity's pricing model eliminates differences between the transaction price and the model's output (the 'inception difference'). IFRS 13 does not prescribe any specific method for the calibration of pricing models. Therefore, an entity should select the most appropriate method for the particular circumstances.

Factors to consider when selecting the calibration method include:

- the valuation technique used;

- the availability of information about market participant assumptions (e.g. relevant observable inputs, estimated timing of when unobservable inputs may become observable);

- the complexity involved (i.e. complexity in different calibration methods, or in the identification of the causes underlying differences

363

between transaction price and fair value estimates based on the entity's pricing model);

- the terms of the instrument; and
- the nature of the entity's portfolio.

In outline, calibration might be approached in the following manner.

- **Step 1** Identify the source of the inception difference.

- **Step 2** Adjust the unobservable inputs or establish valuation adjustments such that the adjusted model result equals the transaction price at inception (i.e. the inception difference is eliminated).

- **Step 3** Changes in fair value measured using the entity's pricing model will be recognised subsequent to initial recognition. The adjustments identified at Step 2 may be reversed or modified when (1) unobservable inputs become observable, or (2) unobservable inputs or valuation adjustments are adjusted to reflect new information (e.g. through subsequent calibration of the model or model inputs to reflect new transaction data).

Step 2 may result in either direct adjustment to model inputs or an adjustment to the model's output (a valuation adjustment).

When calibration is achieved through direct adjustment to model inputs, an entity should consider the impact of such adjustments on the valuation of other instruments in its portfolio (e.g. instruments valued using the same or similar pricing inputs). The calibration may affect the valuation of other instruments because the calibrated inputs may replace or supersede the assumptions previously used for unobservable inputs.

When calibration is achieved through a valuation adjustment, the entity should review the valuation adjustment periodically to ensure that the adjustment reflects any new information and that it is consistent with the exit price notion in IFRS 13.

See **example 8.8** for an illustration of a model calibration approach that may be acceptable when the inception difference can be isolated to a particular unobservable model input.

Example 8.8

Calibration of models or model inputs

Entity X enters into an electricity forward contract to purchase 100 megawatts of electricity (daily) for a 10-year term. The electricity forward contract is within the scope of IFRS 9 *Financial Instruments* (or, for entities that have not yet adopted IFRS 9, IAS 39 *Financial Instruments: Recognition and Measurement*) and is measured at fair value.

No cash is exchanged between the parties at the inception of the forward contract. Using the guidance in IFRS 13:B4 (see **section 7**), Entity X determines that the transaction price equals the exit price (i.e. the fair value of the forward contract equals zero at inception).

Entity X develops its own valuation technique to measure the fair value of the forward contract at subsequent reporting dates. At inception, there are three years of observable forward prices available in the relevant market. Entity X's model uses estimated forward electricity prices beyond three years. At inception, and prior to calibration, the pricing model values the forward contract as an asset of CU1 million. Consequently, Entity X needs to calibrate its model so that the model result at inception equals the transaction price of zero.

In this simple scenario, Entity X might calibrate its model as follows.

- **Step 1** Entity X establishes that the only unobservable input that significantly affects the model value is forward electricity prices. Consequently, Entity X attributes the inception difference of CU1 million (i.e. the difference between the model's result and the fair value of zero) to its estimate of unobservable forward electricity prices for Years 4 to 10 of the contract.

- **Step 2** Entity X adjusts the unobservable forward price points at Years 4 to 10 on the forward price curve such that the model produces a fair value of zero.

  Because Entity X attributed the inception difference solely to the unobservable electricity prices in the relevant market, any calibration adjustment represents a calibration of these unobservable electricity prices to the most recent available information (the forward contract's transaction price). As a result, if Entity X owns a portfolio of contracts whose fair values are estimated using long-dated electricity prices in the same market, the calibration adjustment to the electricity forward prices would most likely also affect the fair value of those other long-dated contracts.

  Similar considerations are also relevant when a calibration results in valuation adjustments to the pricing model's output. In general, calibration adjustments provide updated information about assumptions used by market participants in assessing unobservable inputs or valuation adjustments. Therefore, calibration adjustments may have an effect beyond the recently executed transaction.

- **Step 3** Assuming no other calibration adjustments are made and that observable forward prices remain available for the next three years, the calibration adjustments would be removed as the inputs for Years 4 to 10 become observable. (For example, at the end of Year 1 of the contract, observable forward prices would be available for Years 2 to 4, and unobservable inputs for Years 5 to 10 would be used. As a result, the calibration adjustments for Year 4 should be removed from the valuation as this input has become observable.) All calibration adjustments should be removed once all the unobservable inputs become observable (e.g. in the last 3 years of the contract). In addition, no calibration adjustments should remain in the model in a period in which settlement has occurred.

8.9 Changes in valuation techniques

Once a valuation technique has been selected, it should be applied consistently. A change in a valuation technique or its application (e.g. a change in its weighting when multiple valuation techniques are used or a change in an adjustment applied to a valuation technique) is only appropriate if the change results in a measurement that is equally or more representative of fair value in the circumstances. [IFRS 13:65]

IFRS 13 provides the following examples of events that might appropriately lead to a change in valuation technique:

[IFRS 13:65]

- new markets develop;
- new information becomes available;
- information previously used is no longer available;
- valuation techniques improve; or
- market conditions change.

If a valuation technique does not use unadjusted quoted prices, and in a subsequent period a quoted price in an active market becomes available, the quoted price should be used because IFRS 13:77 states that "a quoted price in an active market provides the most reliable evidence of fair value and shall be used without adjustment to measure fair value whenever available", with limited exceptions.

Depending on the particular circumstances, a change from a valuation technique that uses unadjusted quoted prices to a different valuation technique (such as a discounted cash flow technique) may be appropriate when:

- quoted prices for an identical asset or liability are no longer available; or

- quoted prices are available, but the market is no longer active. Note, however, that prices from relevant observable transactions must be considered in determining fair value even if the market is not active (see **9.5**); or

- the entity no longer has access to the market in which the prices are quoted. The entity must be able to access the market in order to use a quote from that market without adjustment to reflect the lack of access, but the entity does not need to be able to sell the particular asset or transfer the particular liability on the measurement date (see **section 3.3** for further details); or

- quoted prices are no longer based on relevant observable market data and do not reflect assumptions that market participants would make in pricing the asset at the measurement date. As discussed at **9.7**, an entity cannot necessarily assume that a price provided by an external source is representative of fair value at the measurement date.

A decrease in the volume or level of activity in a market does not necessarily mean that the market is no longer active (see **10.2.1.1** for a discussion of active vs. inactive markets) and, consequently, that a change in the valuation technique is warranted.

In selecting another valuation technique, when appropriate, an entity should maximise the use of relevant observable inputs (e.g. quoted prices for a similar asset or liability with adjustments as appropriate) and minimise the use of unobservable inputs.

If there is a change in the valuation technique used or its application, any resulting difference should be accounted for as a change in accounting estimate in accordance with IAS 8 *Accounting Policies, Changes in Accounting Estimates and Errors*; however, the disclosures generally required under IAS 8 regarding a change in accounting estimate are not required for revisions resulting from a change in a valuation technique or its application. [IFRS 13:66]

9 Inputs to valuation techniques

9.1 Definition of inputs

Inputs are defined as "[t]he assumptions that market participants would use when pricing the asset or liability, including assumptions about risk, such as the following:

(a) the risk inherent in a particular valuation technique used to measure fair value (such as a pricing model); and

(b) the risk inherent in the inputs to the valuation technique". [IFRS 13:Appendix A]

Inputs may be observable or unobservable. [IFRS 13:Appendix A] Valuation techniques used to measure fair value are required to maximise the use of relevant observable inputs and minimise the use of unobservable inputs (see **section 8**). [IFRS 13:67]

Valuation inputs that are observable are more reliable than those that are unobservable (sometimes referred to as 'entity-specific' because these inputs are derived by an entity rather than by the 'market').

The inputs used should be consistent with the characteristics of the asset or liability that market participants would take into account in a transaction for the asset or liability (see **section 3.2**). [IFRS 13:69]

9.2   Observable inputs

Examples of markets in which inputs might be observable for some assets and liabilities include the following.

[IFRS 13:68 & B34]

- **Exchange markets** In an exchange market, closing prices are both readily available and generally representative of fair value (e.g. the London Stock Exchange).

- **Dealer markets** In a dealer market, dealers stand ready to trade (either buy or sell for their own account), thereby providing liquidity by using their capital to hold an inventory of the items for which they make a market. Typically, bid and ask prices (representing the price at which the dealer is willing to buy and the price at which the dealer is willing to sell, respectively) are more readily available than closing prices. Over-the-counter markets (for which prices are publicly reported) are dealer markets. Dealer markets also exist for some other assets and liabilities, including some financial instruments, commodities and physical assets (e.g. used equipment).

- **Brokered markets** In a brokered market, brokers attempt to match buyers with sellers but do not stand ready to trade for their own account. Brokers do not use their own capital to hold an inventory of the items for which they make a market. The broker knows the prices bid and asked by the respective parties, but each party is typically unaware of another party's price requirements. Prices of completed transactions are sometimes available. Brokered markets include electronic communication networks, in which buy and sell orders are matched, and commercial and residential real estate markets.

- **Principal-to-principal markets** In a principal-to-principal market, transactions (both originations and re-sales) are negotiated independently with no intermediary. Little information about those transactions may be made available publicly.

9.3   Applying a premium or discount

In some cases, the characteristics of an asset or a liability that market participants would take into account in a transaction for the asset or liability result in the application of an adjustment, such as a premium or discount (e.g. a control premium or non-controlling interest discount). However, a fair value measurement should not incorporate a premium or discount that is inconsistent with the unit of account in the IFRS that requires or permits the fair value measurement (see **section 3.2**). [IFRS 13:69]

Premiums or discounts that reflect size as a characteristic of the entity's holding (specifically, a blockage factor that adjusts the quoted price of an asset or a liability because the market's normal daily trading volume is not sufficient to absorb the quantity held by the entity) are not permitted in a fair value measurement. [IFRS 13:69]

> For example, an investor holding one share that is quoted in an active market may receive a different amount of consideration per share compared to an investor that sells 15 per cent of the total equity shares. The difference between the two holdings is simply the size of the investor's holding, which is typically not a characteristic of the financial asset and thus is not considered in the fair value measurement in this circumstance. For both investors, the fair value measurement of the shares is the price for disposing of a single share multiplied by the quantity held.

In contrast, when measuring the fair value of a controlling interest, it is appropriate to incorporate a control premium because IFRS 13 regards the control premium as a characteristic of the asset or liability. [IFRS 13:69]

In all cases, if there is a quoted market price in an active market for an asset or a liability, the entity should use that price without adjustment when measuring fair value, except as specified in IFRS 13:79 (see **10.2.1.1**). [IFRS 13:69]

9.4 Bid price and ask price inputs

9.4.1 Bid price and ask price inputs – general

If an asset or a liability measured at fair value has a bid price and an ask price (e.g. an input from a dealer market), the price within the bid-ask spread that is most representative of fair value in the circumstances should be used to measure fair value regardless of where the input is categorised within the fair value hierarchy (i.e. Level 1, 2 or 3 – see **section 10**). [IFRS 13:70]

IFRS 13 permits, but does not require, that asset positions may be measured at bid prices and that liability positions may be measured at ask prices. [IFRS 13:70]

IFRS 13 allows an entity to use mid-market pricing or other pricing conventions that are used by market participants as a practical expedient for fair value measurements within a bid-ask spread. [IFRS 13:71]

> An entity does not need to meet any specific qualifying criteria to use mid-market pricing or other pricing conventions as a practical expedient for measuring fair value, provided that the selected pricing convention:

- is used by market participants (e.g. an industry-accepted pricing convention); and

- is consistent with the fair value measurement objective of IFRS 13. For example, it would not be appropriate to use ask prices for recognised assets or bid prices for recognised liabilities because such a pricing approach would be inconsistent with the IFRS 13 objective that fair value is an exit price.

The decision to use a particular pricing convention is an accounting policy choice that should be consistently applied from period to period and for assets or liabilities with similar characteristics and risk. The policy should also be disclosed, if appropriate.

Example 9.4.1

Mid-market prices

Entity X and Entity Y hold the same debt security as an asset. Entity Y, a broker-dealer, is a market-maker in the debt security. Entity X is not. The debt security is traded in an active market by Entity Y (and other broker-dealers) using bid and ask prices.

Even though Entity X would most likely sell the debt security at or close to the bid price, Entity X may select a policy to use the mid-market price as the fair value of the debt security as a practical expedient. However, it would not be appropriate to use the ask price for the debt security because this would be inconsistent with the objective of fair value being an exit price.

Even though Entity Y may be able to exit at a price greater than the bid price, Entity Y may choose as its policy to measure the debt security by using the bid price as a practical expedient.

IFRS 13 also contains detailed guidance for circumstances when an entity may fair value a portfolio of similar items together that have offsetting market risks and in doing so use mid-market prices for the offsetting market risks. This detailed guidance applies to financial assets and financial liabilities and is dealt with in **section 6** of **chapter B7** (or, for entities that have not yet adopted IFRS 9 *Financial Instruments*, in **section 6** of **chapter C7**).

9.4.2   Changes in the use of bid, ask or mid-market pricing or other pricing conventions

When an entity has in the past complied with the requirements of IFRS 13:70 (see **9.4.1**) and measured fair value at the price within the bid-ask spread that is most representative of fair value in the circumstances, it is not generally appropriate for the entity to change its accounting policy to using the practical expedient of mid-market pricing or another pricing convention as permitted by IFRS 13:71.

Once a valuation technique has been selected, it should generally be applied consistently. A change in a valuation technique is only appropriate if the change results in a measurement that is equally or more representative of fair value in the circumstances (see IFRS 13:65).

Having established a policy of measuring fair value at the price within the bid-ask spread that is most representative of fair value in the circumstances, a change to using a practical expedient such as mid-market pricing or another pricing convention would generally be inappropriate because it would not typically result in a measurement that is equally or more representative of fair value.

9.5 Measuring fair value when the volume or level of activity for an asset or a liability has significantly decreased

IFRS 13 notes that the fair value of an asset or a liability might be affected when there has been a significant decrease in the volume or level of activity for that asset or liability in relation to normal market activity for the asset or liability (or similar assets or liabilities). [IFRS 13:B37]

The consequence of a significant decrease in the volume or level of activity could be that a transaction price or a quoted price for that item is not representative of fair value. However, a decrease in the volume or level of activity on its own may not indicate that a transaction price or quoted price does not represent fair value or that a transaction in that market is not orderly. [IFRS 13:B38]

The following are examples of factors that can help determine whether, on the basis of the evidence available, there has been a significant decrease in the volume or level of activity for the asset or liability:

[IFRS 13:B37]

- there are few recent transactions;

- price quotations are not developed using current information;

- price quotations vary substantially either over time or among market-makers (e.g. some brokered markets);

- indices that previously were highly correlated with the fair values of the asset or liability are demonstrably uncorrelated with recent indications of fair value for that asset or liability;

- there is a significant increase in implied liquidity risk premiums, yields or performance indicators (such as delinquency rates or loss severities) for observed transactions or quoted prices when compared with the entity's estimate of expected cash flows, taking into account all available market data about credit and other non-performance risk for the asset or liability;

- there is a wide bid-ask spread or a significant increase in the bid-ask spread;

- there is a significant decline in the activity of, or there is an absence of, a market for new issues (i.e. a primary market) for the asset or liability or similar assets or liabilities; and

- little information is publicly available (e.g. for transactions that take place in a principal-to-principal market).

In assessing whether there has been a significant decrease in the volume or level of activity, an entity should evaluate the significance and relevance of factors such as those listed above. [IFRS 13:B37]

> Note that the presence of one or more of the factors listed in IFRS 13:B37 alone is not sufficient to conclude that a market is not 'active' (see **10.2.1.1** for further discussion).

If it is concluded that there has been a significant decrease in the volume or level of activity for the asset or liability in relation to normal market activity for the asset or liability (or similar assets or liabilities), further analysis of the transactions or quoted prices is needed. If it is determined that a transaction or quoted price does not represent fair value (e.g. there may be transactions that are not orderly), an adjustment to the transactions or quoted prices will be necessary if those prices are to be used as a basis for measuring fair value. The adjustment can be significant to the fair value measurement in its entirety. [IFRS 13:B38]

Adjustments may also be necessary in other circumstances (e.g. when a price for a similar asset requires significant adjustment to make it comparable to the asset being measured, or when the price is 'stale'). [IFRS 13:B38]

IFRS 13 does not prescribe a methodology for making significant adjustments to transactions or quoted prices. Consistent with valuation techniques, as discussed in **section 8**, appropriate risk adjustments should be applied, including a risk premium reflecting the amount that market participants would demand as compensation for the uncertainty inherent in the cash flows of an asset or a liability. Otherwise, the measurement does not faithfully represent fair value. In some cases, determining the appropriate risk adjustment may be difficult. However, the degree of difficulty alone is not a sufficient basis on which to exclude a risk adjustment. The risk adjustment should be reflective of an orderly transaction between market participants at the measurement date under current market conditions. [IFRS 13:B39]

If there has been a significant decrease in the volume or level of activity for the asset or liability, a change in valuation technique or the use of multiple valuation techniques may be appropriate (e.g. the use of a market approach and an income approach – see **8.4** and **section 8.6**, respectively). When weighting indications of fair value resulting from the use of multiple valuation techniques (see **8.7**), an entity should consider the reasonableness of the range of fair value measurements. The objective is to determine the point within the range that is most representative of fair value under current market conditions. A wide range of fair value measurements may be an indication that further analysis is needed. [IFRS 13:B40]

Even when there has been a significant decrease in the volume or level of activity for the asset or liability, the objective of a fair value measurement remains the same. Fair value is the price that would be received to sell an asset or paid to transfer a liability in an orderly transaction (i.e. not a forced liquidation or distress sale) between market participants at the measurement date under current market conditions. [IFRS 13:B41]

Estimating the price at which market participants would be willing to enter into a transaction at the measurement date under current market conditions if there has been a significant decrease in the volume or level of activity for the asset or liability depends on the facts and circumstances at the measurement date and requires judgement. An entity's intention to hold the asset or to settle or otherwise fulfil the liability is not relevant when measuring fair value because fair value is a market-based measurement, not an entity-specific measurement. [IFRS 13:B42]

If an entity is unwilling to transact at a price from an external source (such as a quoted market price or a price provided by a broker, pricing service or potential buyer), the entity's unwillingness to transact at that price is not sufficient evidence for the entity to disregard that price in measuring fair value. If the best information available in the circumstances indicates that market participants would transact at a price from an external source, an entity is not permitted to disregard that price simply because it is not willing to transact at that price.

Examples 9.5A and **9.5B** explore this issue further.

Example 9.5A

Assumptions can be readily derived from current observable market data

Entity A is using a valuation model to measure the fair value of its investment in privately placed corporate debt securities issued by Entity X. No quoted price for identical securities is available. Entity A's valuation model uses assumptions about default rates and discount rates. Default rate assumptions can be readily derived from current observable market data for actively traded credit default swaps on publicly traded bonds of Entity X. When measuring the fair value of its investment, Entity A cannot disregard this market data even if Entity A would not be willing to transact at a price consistent with this market data.

Example 9.5B

Active markets for similar securities

Entity A holds distressed debt securities. Transactions in the securities occur infrequently and there is no active market for the securities, but there are active markets for similar securities. Entity A's own valuation model, which is based on observable Level 2 inputs current at the measurement date, indicates that market participants would be willing to buy and sell the debt for CU30 at the measurement date. Entity A has calibrated the model to the best information available at the measurement date (including transaction prices in similar securities and risk premiums).

At the measurement date, a potential buyer provides an unsolicited bid to buy the securities for CU20. When measuring the fair value of the debt securities, Entity A can neither disregard this bid price simply because it is not willing to transact at that price, nor can it assume that the bid price provides better evidence of fair value than its own model. Although the bid price is the price one potential buyer would be willing to pay for Entity A's asset, it may not necessarily be the price at which market participants (buyers and sellers) would be willing to transact on the measurement date.

Valuation techniques to measure fair value should maximise the use of relevant observable inputs (i.e. Level 1 and Level 2 inputs that do not require significant adjustment) and minimise the use of unobservable inputs (Level 3 inputs). If the bid price is classified as a Level 3 input, it may be appropriate for Entity A to place less weight on the bid price in measuring the fair value of its debt securities given that Entity A's own model is based on Level 2 inputs. However, if Entity A obtains several bid prices and the fair value indicated by the valuation model is not in the range of the bid prices obtained, Entity A may need to consider whether its model is valid and identify the reasons for the discrepancy between the model amount and the bid prices.

IFRS 13 provides an illustrative example of estimating a market rate of return when the volume or level of activity for a financial asset has significantly decreased (see **example 9.5C** in **chapter B7** (for entities applying IFRS 9) and **example 9.5C** in **chapter C7** (for entities applying IAS 39)).

9.6   Identifying transactions that are not orderly

The determination as to whether a transaction is orderly is more difficult if there has been a significant decrease in the volume or level of activity for the asset or liability in relation to normal market activity. In such circumstances, it is not appropriate to conclude that all transactions in that market are not orderly (i.e. forced liquidations or distress sales). [IFRS 13:B43]

IFRS 13 does not require an entity to undertake exhaustive efforts to determine whether a transaction is orderly, although the entity should not ignore information that is reasonably available. However, the Standard does establish a presumption that, when an entity is a party to a transaction, it has sufficient information to conclude whether the transaction is orderly. [IFRS 13:B44]

An entity is expected to evaluate the circumstances to determine whether, on the weight of the evidence available, the transaction is orderly. [IFRS 13:B43]

The Standard identifies the following circumstances that may indicate that a transaction is not orderly:

[IFRS 13:B43]

- there was not adequate exposure to the market for a period before the measurement date to allow for marketing activities that are usual and customary for transactions involving such assets or liabilities under current market conditions;

- there was a usual and customary marketing period, but the seller marketed the asset or liability to a single market participant;

- the seller is in or near bankruptcy or receivership (i.e. the seller is distressed);

- the seller was required to sell to meet regulatory or legal requirements (i.e. the seller was forced); or

- the transaction price is an outlier when compared with other recent transactions for the same or a similar asset or liability.

If a transaction is determined not to be orderly, little if any weight (compared to other indications of fair value) is placed on that transaction price. [IFRS 13:B44(a)]

If a transaction is determined to be orderly, that transaction price is taken into account in estimating fair value. However, the amount of weight placed on that transaction price when compared with other indications of fair value will depend on the facts and circumstances, such as:

[IFRS 13:B44(b)]

- the volume of the transaction;

- the comparability of the transaction to the asset or liability being measured; and

- the proximity of the transaction to the measurement date.

If there is not sufficient information available to conclude whether a transaction is orderly, the transaction price should be taken into account in estimating fair value. However, the transaction price may not represent fair value and, consequently, would not necessarily be the sole or primary basis for measuring fair value or estimating market risk premiums and less weight should be placed on it when compared with other transactions that are known to be orderly. [IFRS 13:B44(c)]

Example 9.6

Determining whether a transaction is orderly

Entity A is acting as an administrator on behalf of the creditors of Entity B, which is subject to bankruptcy proceedings. The administrator's role is to seek to maximise the return to Entity B's creditors. As part of Entity A's responsibilities, it auctions a portfolio of Entity B's financial assets. Entity A promotes the auction to interested parties with the expectation of receiving bids for the financial assets over a specified period.

Even though the financial assets are being sold as part of bankruptcy proceedings, the auction process may be considered to be an orderly transaction provided that all of the necessary conditions are met.

IFRS 13:Appendix A defines an orderly transaction as "[a] transaction that assumes exposure to the market for a period before the measurement date to allow for marketing activities that are usual and customary for transactions involving such assets or liabilities; it is not a forced transaction (eg a forced liquidation or distress sale)".

In the circumstances described, it seems possible that the auction process may be considered to be an orderly transaction because the sale is not immediate and there is sufficient (i.e. usual and customary) time to market the assets to other market participants.

If transactions in assets or liabilities occur between willing buyers and sellers in a manner that is usual and customary for transactions involving such assets or liabilities, these should be considered to be orderly transactions. Persuasive evidence is required to establish that an observable transaction is not an orderly transaction.

See **10.3.4** for the effect of observable transactions in inactive markets on the categorisation of the fair value measurement within the fair value hierarchy.

9.7   Quoted prices provided by third parties

IFRS 13 does not preclude the use of quoted prices provided by third parties, such as pricing services or brokers, if it is determined that the quoted prices provided by those parties are developed in accordance with IFRS 13. [IFRS 13:B45]

However, if there has been a significant decrease in the volume or level of activity for the asset or liability, an entity is required to evaluate whether the quoted prices provided by third parties are developed using current information that reflects orderly transactions or a valuation technique that reflects market participant assumptions (including assumptions about risk). In weighting a quoted price as an input to a fair value measurement, an entity should place less weight (when compared with other indications of fair value that reflect the results of transactions) on quotes that do not reflect the result of transactions. [IFRS 13:B46]

Further, the nature of a quote (e.g. whether the quote is an indicative price or a binding offer) should be taken into account when weighting the available evidence, with more weight given to quotes provided by third parties that represent binding offers. [IFRS 13:B47]

Broker or pricing service quotes are not necessarily determinative of fair value if an active market (as defined in IFRS 13:Appendix A – see **10.2.1.1**) does not exist for the item being measured. In assessing whether a broker or pricing service quote appropriately represents fair value, an entity needs to understand how the broker or pricing service has arrived at the quoted price, and the inputs and other information used.

Quote based on information from an active market

Consistent with IFRS 13:77 (see **10.2.1.1**), when a broker or pricing service quote represents the unadjusted price quoted for an identical asset, liability or equity instrument in an active market to which the entity has access at the measurement date, the entity is required to use the quoted price without adjustment when measuring fair value, subject to limited exceptions as discussed in IFRS 13:79. Such a quote represents a Level 1 input.

If any adjustment is made to the broker or pricing service quote in the circumstances specified in IFRS 13:79, or in the absence of an active market, a broker or pricing service quote does not represent a Level 1 input. However, it may nevertheless be determinative of fair value.

Quote based on valuation technique(s)

If a quote is based on a valuation technique that is used by market participants and uses market-observable or market-corroborated inputs that reflect the assumptions of market participants, it is determinative of fair value if no significant adjustment to the quote is needed. If a significant adjustment is needed, the quote is not determinative of fair value but it could represent a relevant observable input into the entity's fair value measurement.

General considerations

In assessing whether a quote is determinative of fair value, the entity should consider all relevant circumstances, including the following questions (the list is not exhaustive).

- Are there differences between the asset or liability being measured and the item for which a quote is available (e.g. differences in the terms or risk attributes)? Such differences may necessitate adjustments to the price quoted by the broker or pricing service.

- Does the quote reflect currently occurring orderly transactions for the asset or liability being measured? That is, are market participants currently transacting in the asset or liability at the price quoted by the broker or pricing service or does the quote reflect 'stale' information or transactions that are not orderly? IFRS 13:B46 (see above) provides specific guidance for circumstances in which there has been a significant decrease in the volume or level of activity for the asset or liability.

- Is the broker or pricing service using a valuation technique that complies with the fair value measurement principles in IFRS 13? For example, does the valuation technique used by the broker or pricing service (1) reflect market participant assumptions, including assumptions about risk, (2) maximise the use of relevant observable inputs, and (3) minimise the use of unobservable inputs? If the valuation technique does not reflect the assumptions market participants would use in pricing the asset or liability, the price quoted by the broker or pricing service may need adjustment or may not be relevant to the entity's fair value measurement.

- Is the quote provided by the broker or pricing service an indicative price or a binding offer? That is, does the broker or another market participant stand ready to transact at the price quoted by the broker or pricing service? As noted above, IFRS 13:B47 indicates that more weight should be given to quotes based on binding offers. Typically, a quote obtained from a broker or pricing service is an indicative price and not a binding offer (unless the broker is a market-maker).

- Does the quote come from a reputable broker or pricing service that has a substantial presence in the market and the experience and expertise to provide a representationally faithful quote for the asset or liability being measured? An entity may place more weight on a quote from a broker or pricing service that has more experience and expertise related to the asset or liability being measured.

As the number of market transactions decreases, brokers or pricing services may rely more on proprietary models based on their own assumptions to arrive at a quote. The entity should evaluate how the quote has been arrived at and whether it reflects market participant assumptions, including assumptions about risk. This information may be difficult to obtain if quotes are based on proprietary models that brokers or pricing services may not be willing to share. However, even when brokers or pricing services do not wish to share detailed information about their models, it may still be possible to obtain information about the nature of the assumptions and the inputs used in the model. If the quote does not reflect assumptions that market participants would use in pricing the asset or liability, the quote will most likely not be determinative of fair value because adjustments may be required. In such cases, the quote may be an input to the entity's fair value measurement, but other indications of fair value may be equally or more useful when estimating fair value (e.g. a valuation based on the entity's own estimates of the inputs that market participants would use in pricing the asset or liability).

Multiple quotes

An entity may need to perform additional analysis when quotes for an individual asset or liability are obtained from different brokers or pricing services. Multiple quotes within a narrow range constitute stronger evidence of fair value than multiple quotes that are widely dispersed. IFRS 13:B40 states that a wide range of measurements may be an indication that further analysis is needed. The entity should consider the reasonableness of the range of fair value measurements, with the objective of determining the point within the range that is most representative of fair value under current market conditions.

In addition, if an entity's own estimate of fair value is outside the range of broker or pricing service quotes, the entity should understand the reason(s) for such a difference. If the range of quotes provides strong evidence of fair value, the entity may need to make adjustments to its valuation technique to reflect current market information.

10 Fair value hierarchy

10.1 Fair value hierarchy – general

To increase consistency and comparability in fair value measurements and related disclosures, IFRS 13 establishes a fair value hierarchy that categorises into three levels the inputs to valuation techniques used to measure fair value, as follows:

[IFRS 13:72]

- Level 1 inputs comprise unadjusted quoted prices in active markets for identical assets and liabilities that the entity can access at the measurement date (see **section 10.2.1**);

- Level 2 inputs comprise other observable inputs not included within Level 1 of the fair value hierarchy (see **10.2.2**); and

- Level 3 inputs comprise unobservable inputs (including the entity's own data, which are adjusted, if necessary, to reflect the assumptions market participants would use in the circumstances) (see **10.2.3**).

Observable inputs are defined as "[i]nputs that are developed using market data, such as publicly available information about actual events or transactions, and that reflect the assumptions that market participants would use when pricing the asset or liability". [IFRS 13:Appendix A]

Unobservable inputs are defined as "[i]nputs for which market data are not available and that are developed using the best information available about the assumptions that market participants would use when pricing the asset or liability". [IFRS 13:Appendix A]

The fair value hierarchy gives the highest priority to Level 1 inputs and the lowest priority to Level 3 inputs. [IFRS 13:72]

For example, if a fair value measurement for an asset is based on an unadjusted quoted price in an active market for an identical asset that the entity can access at the measurement date, this is categorised within 'Level 1' of the fair value hierarchy. In contrast, a valuation based on unobservable inputs would be categorised within 'Level 3'. [IFRS 13:72]

When an entity approaches the measurement of an asset, or a liability, or an entity's own equity instrument, at fair value, it looks at the available valuation techniques and at the inputs available for those techniques. When selecting the techniques and inputs to be used, the entity is required to maximise the use of observable inputs and minimise the use of unobservable inputs (see **section 8**). Once the selection has been made, each of the inputs is categorised within the fair value hierarchy outlined above; **section 10.2** summarises IFRS 13's requirements regarding the categorisation of inputs.

When an entity has determined the appropriate categorisation of the inputs into a fair value measurement, and has arrived at a measure of fair value using those inputs, it is then necessary to determine the appropriate categorisation of the fair value measurement in its entirety; this topic is discussed in **section 10.3**.

10.2 Categorisation of inputs to valuation techniques within the fair value hierarchy

10.2.1 Level 1 inputs

10.2.1.1 Level 1 inputs – general
Level 1 inputs are quoted prices (unadjusted) in active markets for identical assets or liabilities that the entity can access at the measurement date. [IFRS 13:76 & Appendix A]

A quoted price for an identical asset or liability in an active market provides the most reliable evidence of fair value. Such prices should be used without adjustment to measure fair value whenever available, except in any of the circumstances described in IFRS 13:79 (see below). [IFRS 13:77]

Therefore, when a Level 1 input is available, it must be used without adjustment, except in any of the circumstances described in IFRS 13:79.

An active market is defined as "[a] market in which transactions for the asset or liability take place with sufficient frequency and volume to provide pricing information on an ongoing basis". [IFRS 13:Appendix A]

Determining whether a market is active focuses on the trading activity for the individual asset or liability being measured and not on the general levels of activity in the market in which the asset or liability is traded. For example, a security listed on the FTSE in London or HKEx in Hong Kong could be considered to be traded in an inactive market if the security itself is traded infrequently.

IFRS 13:B37 sets out a list of factors that may indicate that there has been a significant decrease in the volume or level of activity for an asset or a liability relative to normal market activity for that asset or liability (or similar assets or liabilities) (see **9.5**).The presence of one or more of the factors listed in IFRS 13:B37 alone is not sufficient to conclude that a market is not active. An entity should evaluate the relevance and significance of these factors to the individual asset or liability measured at fair value in order to determine whether the market for that asset or liability is inactive. A market is not deemed inactive simply because of insufficient trading volume relative to the size of an entity's position.

The characterisation of a market as 'active' or 'inactive' may change as market conditions change. However, a decline in the volume of transactions for a particular asset or liability does not automatically mean that the market has become inactive. A market would still be considered active as long as the frequency and volume of relevant transactions are sufficient to provide ongoing pricing information.

Further, quoted prices from a market affected by a decline in the volume or level of activity should not be ignored unless the price is associated with a transaction that is not orderly. It is not appropriate to conclude automatically that all transactions occurring in a market exhibiting a significant decline in volume or level of activity are not orderly. IFRS 13:B43 sets out a list of factors that may indicate that a transaction is not orderly (see **9.6**). Very little weight should be given to prices observed for a transaction that is not orderly; more weight may be given to a price observed for an orderly transaction. However, the entity should evaluate carefully whether an adjustment may be needed to that price to ensure the fair value measurement is consistent with the objectives in IFRS 13.

When an asset or a liability could be exchanged in a number of markets (e.g. a financial asset or a financial liability that could be exchanged on a number of exchanges), the entity will need to consider which market is the most relevant for measuring fair value. IFRS 13 states explicitly that the emphasis within Level 1 is on determining both of the following:

[IFRS 13:78]

- the principal market for the asset or liability or, in the absence of a principal market, the most advantageous market for the asset or liability (see **section 3.3**); and

- whether the entity can enter into a transaction for the asset or liability at the price in that market at the measurement date.

When a quoted price in an active market is available, it should not be adjusted except in the circumstances listed below.

[IFRS 13:79]

- When an entity holds a large number of similar (but not identical) assets or liabilities (e.g. debt securities) that are measured at fair value and a quoted price in an active market is available but not readily accessible for each of those assets or liabilities individually (i.e. given the large number of similar assets or liabilities held by the entity, it would be difficult to obtain pricing information for each individual asset or liability at the measurement date). In such circumstances, as a practical expedient, an entity may measure fair value using an alternative pricing method that does not rely exclusively on quoted prices (e.g. matrix pricing – see **8.4**). However, the use of an alternative pricing method results in a fair value measurement categorised within a lower level of the fair value hierarchy.

- When a quoted price in an active market does not represent fair value at the measurement date. That might be the case if, for example, significant events (such as transactions in a principal-to-principal market, trades in a brokered market or announcements) take place after the close of a market but before the measurement date. An entity should establish and consistently apply a policy for identifying those events that might affect fair value measurements. However, if the quoted price is adjusted for new information, the adjustment results in a fair value measurement categorised within a lower level of the fair value hierarchy.

- When measuring the fair value of a liability or an entity's own equity instrument using the quoted price for the identical item traded as an asset in an active market and that price needs to be adjusted for factors specific to the item or the asset (see **5.1.1**). If no adjustment to the quoted price of the asset is required, the result is a fair value measurement categorised within Level 1 of the fair value hierarchy. However, any adjustment to the quoted price of the asset results in a fair value measurement categorised within a lower level of the fair value hierarchy.

If an entity holds a position in a single asset or liability (including a position comprising a large number of identical assets or liabilities, such as a holding of financial instruments) and the asset or liability is traded in an active market, the fair value of the asset or liability should be measured within Level 1 as the product of the quoted price for the individual asset or liability and the quantity held by the entity. That is the case even if a market's normal daily trading volume is not sufficient to absorb the quantity held and placing orders to sell the position in a single transaction might affect the quoted price. [IFRS 13:80]

10.2.1.2   Published net asset values for open-ended investment funds as Level 1 inputs

Some open-ended investments funds not listed on a stock exchange may publish daily quotations of their net asset values (NAVs) at which redemptions or purchases of units occur without any adjustments to the published NAV. The redemptions and unit purchases may take place regularly at the quoted NAVs and there is no secondary market for the units because they are not transferrable (i.e. the sole transactions are issuances and redemptions of the units by the fund). These quoted NAVs may meet the definition of a Level 1 input provided that all of the elements of the definition in IFRS 13:76 (see **10.2.1.1**) are met.

Consequently, the following criteria must be satisfied:

* the price must be quoted in an active market (see **10.2.1.1**);

* the price must be unadjusted;

* the price must be for an asset or a liability that is identical to the asset or liability being measured; and

* the entity must have access to the price at the measurement date.

For the price to be classified as a Level 1 input, it is not required that there be an active market between the holders of the financial instrument and other potential holders that are not the issuer of the financial instrument; it is possible that the financial instrument does not have an active market other than between the holders of the financial instrument and the issuer of the financial instrument.

Careful analysis is required when assessing whether such prices meet the definition of a Level 1 input. In particular, the assessment should include (1) whether quoted prices are readily and regularly available, (2) whether transactions occur regularly, and (3) whether the regularly occurring transactions take place at the quoted (unadjusted price) on an arm's length basis.

10.2.2   Level 2 inputs

Level 2 inputs are inputs other than quoted prices included within Level 1 that are observable for the asset or liability, either directly or indirectly. [IFRS 13:81 & Appendix A]

Level 2 inputs include the following:

[IFRS 13:82]

- quoted prices for similar assets or liabilities in active markets;

- quoted prices for identical or similar assets or liabilities in markets that are not active;

- inputs other than quoted prices that are observable for the asset or liability, for example:

  - interest rates and yield curves observable at commonly quoted intervals;

  - implied volatilities; and

  - credit spreads; and

- inputs that are derived principally from, or corroborated by, observable market data by correlation or other means (market-corroborated inputs).

Under IFRS 13:82 (see above), when an entity measures the fair value of an asset or a liability and no Level 1 inputs are available, it may use quoted prices for 'similar' assets or liabilities in active markets as a Level 2 input. Equally, under IFRS 13:79(a) (see **10.2.1.1**), entities holding a large number of 'similar' assets or liabilities for which a quoted price is not accessible for all of the assets and liabilities being measured, may measure fair value using alternative pricing (e.g. matrix pricing) as a practical expedient.

IFRS 13 does not provide any specific guidance as to what is meant by 'similar' in this context. The identification of a similar asset or liability involves the exercise of judgement and requires both:

- an understanding of the terms and other factors that affect the fair values of the asset or liability being measured and the asset or liability for which the quoted price exists; and

- an identification and assessment of any differences in the terms and other factors that affect the fair values of these assets or liabilities.

Specifically in relation to financial instruments, the IASB Expert Advisory Panel's October 2008 report *Measuring and disclosing the fair value of financial instruments in markets that are no longer active* provides additional material for consideration (see **10.2.2** in **chapter B7** (for entities applying IFRS 9) and **10.2.2** in **chapter C7** (for entities applying IAS 39)).

If the asset or liability has a specified (contractual) term, a Level 2 input must be observable for substantially the full term of the asset or liability. [IFRS 13:82]

Guidance on the meaning of 'substantially the full term' is provided in **example 10.2.2A**.

Example 10.2.2A

Determining how an input is classified when the item being measured has a specified contractual term

Company X enters into a fixed-price six-year agreement to sell 50 megawatts (MW) of on-peak electricity for delivery at location ABC beginning on 1 January 20X1 and continuing through to 31 December 20X6. On 31 March 20X1, Company X is measuring the fair value of the fixed-price agreement. Active market quotes are available for forward contracts to sell electricity at location ABC for two years (31 March 20X1 to 31 March 20X3). Accordingly, Company X will use the two years of observable forward pricing data and develop an expectation for the remaining 3 years and nine months (i.e. 1 April 20X3 to 31 December 20X6) using a model that relies on pricing data and weather patterns from the previous four years. The model also incorporates all relevant physical constraints (capacity of existing power plants and power plants expected to be completed near location ABC, projected supply and demand etc.).

In the circumstances described, the five-year and nine-month forward price curve represents a Level 3, rather than a Level 2, input.

An input for an item with a specified contractual term falls within Level 2 of the hierarchy only if it meets both of the following criteria:

- as required by IFRS 13:82 (see above), the input must be observable for substantially the full term of the asset or liability; and
- the impact of the unobservable period must not be significant to the fair value of the asset or liability. The guidance set out in **10.3.3.2** should be applied when evaluating whether the effect of the unobservable period is significant.

IFRS 13:B35(b) cites as an example an interest rate swap with a term of 10 years and for which the fair value is determined using a swap rate based on a yield curve that is observable at commonly quoted intervals for 9 years. The swap rate input is a Level 2 input provided that any reasonable extrapolation of the yield curve for Year 10 would not be significant to the fair value measurement of the swap in its entirety.

In contrast, in the circumstances described, Company X can observe forward prices for only 24 months of the remaining 69-month term of the agreement (i.e. 35 per cent of the term). Because this does not represent substantially the full term, the first criterion above is not met. An analysis of the second criterion is unnecessary; the forward price curve is considered a Level 3 input. However,

---

if the forward price curve had been observable for substantially the full term, Company X would need to consider the second criterion (i.e. whether the effect of the unobservable term is significant to the fair value of the agreement) to determine whether the forward price curve is a Level 2 or Level 3 input.

Adjustments to Level 2 inputs will vary depending on factors specific to the asset or liability. Those factors include the following:

[IFRS 13:83]

- the condition or location of the asset;

- the extent to which inputs relate to items that are comparable to the asset or liability (including those factors described in IFRS 13:39 – see **5.1.1**); and

- the volume or level of activity in the markets within which the inputs are observed.

An entity should consider whether adjustments to the quoted price for a similar asset or liability are necessary to reflect differences between the terms of the items being compared and other factors that may affect the fair values of those items. For example, the entity may need to make adjustments to reflect differences in the condition, location or risks (including non-performance risk and liquidity risk) of the items being compared.

Under IFRS 13:37, when a quoted price for the transfer of an identical or similar liability is not available and the identical item is held by another party as an asset, the fair value of the liability is measured from the perspective of a market participant that holds the identical item as an asset at the measurement date. The value should only be adjusted for factors specific to the asset that are not applicable to the fair value measurement of the liability. IFRS 13:39 provides a number of examples of such factors (see **5.1.1**).

In addition, if an entity uses a quoted price for a similar item in its valuation technique, the entity may need to make adjustments to reflect differences in risk, including liquidity differences. For example, the item being measured may be in shorter supply (relative to demand) than the similar item for which a quoted price exists. In this situation, a liquidity risk premium exists for the item being measured that should be factored into the fair value measurement as an adjustment to the quoted price of the similar item.

Example 10.2.2B provides an illustration of circumstances in which the quoted price for a similar asset needs to be adjusted to reflect the different characteristics of the asset being measured.

Example 10.2.2B

Using quoted prices for a similar asset or liability

Sales of genetically modified wheat are increasing globally. However, there are no separate markets for genetically modified wheat and wheat that is not genetically modified. Thus, when measuring their agricultural produce at the time of harvest at fair value less costs to sell under IAS 41 *Agriculture*, sellers of genetically modified wheat use quoted prices for wheat that is not genetically modified. Because the quoted price is for a similar asset, that price would generally represent a Level 2 input. However, because genetically modified wheat has different characteristics to the wheat for which a quoted price exists, an adjustment should be made to reflect market participant assumptions about the price that would be received for selling genetically modified wheat. If the adjustment is significant to the entire measurement and based on unobservable data, the entire measurement would be classified as a Level 3 measurement.

An adjustment to a Level 2 input that is significant to the entire measurement might result in a fair value measurement categorised within Level 3 of the fair value hierarchy if the adjustment uses significant unobservable inputs. [IFRS 13:84] See **10.3.3.2** for further discussion.

IFRS 13 provides the following examples of Level 2 inputs for particular assets and liabilities.

[IFRS 13:B35]

- **Receive-fixed, pay-variable interest rate swap based on the London Interbank Offered Rate (LIBOR) swap rate** A Level 2 input would be the LIBOR swap rate if that rate is observable at commonly quoted intervals for substantially the full term of the swap.

- **Receive-fixed, pay-variable interest rate swap based on a yield curve denominated in a foreign currency** A Level 2 input would be the swap rate based on a yield curve denominated in a foreign currency that is observable at commonly quoted intervals for substantially the full term of the swap. That would be the case if the term of the swap is 10 years and that rate is observable at commonly quoted intervals for 9 years, provided that any reasonable extrapolation of the yield curve for Year 10 would not be significant to the fair value measurement of the swap in its entirety (but see **example 10.2.2A** for circumstances when observable data is not available for substantially the full term of the agreement).

- **Receive-fixed, pay-variable interest rate swap based on a specific bank's prime rate** A Level 2 input would be the bank's prime rate derived through extrapolation if the extrapolated values are corroborated by observable market data, e.g. by correlation with an interest rate that is observable over substantially the full term of the swap.

- **Three-year option on exchange-traded shares** A Level 2 input would be the implied volatility for the shares derived through extrapolation to Year 3 if both of the following conditions exist:

  - prices for one-year and two-year options on the shares are observable; and

  - the extrapolated implied volatility of a three-year option is corroborated by observable market data for substantially the full term of the option.

  In that case, the implied volatility could be derived by extrapolating from the implied volatility of the one-year and two-year options on the shares and corroborated by the implied volatility for three-year options on comparable entities' shares, provided that correlation with the one-year and two-year implied volatilities is established.

- **Licensing arrangement** For a licensing arrangement that is acquired in a business combination and was recently negotiated with an unrelated party by the acquired entity (the party to the licensing arrangement), a Level 2 input would be the royalty rate of the contract with the unrelated party at inception of the arrangement.

- **Finished goods inventory at a retail outlet** For finished goods inventory that is acquired in a business combination, a Level 2 input would be either a price to customers in a retail market or a price to retailers in a wholesale market, adjusted for differences between the condition and location of the inventory item and the comparable (i.e. similar) inventory items so that the fair value measurement reflects the price that would be received in a transaction to sell the inventory to another retailer that would complete the requisite selling efforts. Conceptually, the fair value measurement will be the same, whether adjustments are made to a retail price (downward) or to a wholesale price (upward). Generally, the price that requires the least amount of subjective adjustments should be used for the fair value measurement.

- **Building held and used** A Level 2 input would be the price per square metre for the building (a valuation multiple) derived from observable market data, e.g. multiples derived from prices in observed transactions involving comparable (i.e. similar) buildings in similar locations.

- **Cash-generating unit** A Level 2 input would be a valuation multiple (e.g. a multiple of earnings or revenue or a similar performance measure) derived from observable market data, e.g. multiples derived from prices in observed transactions involving comparable (i.e. similar) businesses, taking into account operational, market, financial and non-financial factors.

10.2.3   Level 3 inputs

Level 3 inputs are unobservable inputs for the asset or liability. [IFRS 13:86 & Appendix A]

Unobservable inputs should be used to measure fair value to the extent that relevant observable inputs are not available (e.g. when there is little, if any, market activity for the asset or liability at the measurement date). However, unobservable inputs should reflect the assumptions that market participants would use when pricing the asset or liability, so as to achieve the general fair value measurement objective (i.e. an exit price at the measurement date from the perspective of a market participant that holds the asset or owes the liability). [IFRS 13:87]

Unobservable inputs should reflect, among others, assumptions that market participants would make about risk. Assumptions about risk include the risk inherent in a particular valuation technique used to measure fair value (such as a pricing model) and the risk inherent in the inputs to the valuation technique. A measurement that does not include an adjustment for risk would not represent a fair value measurement if market participants would include one when pricing the asset or liability. For example, it might be necessary to include a risk adjustment when there is significant measurement uncertainty (e.g. when there has been a significant decrease in the volume or level of activity when compared with normal market activity for the asset or liability (or similar assets or liabilities) and the entity has determined that the transaction price or quoted price does not represent fair value – see **9.5** to **9.7**). [IFRS 13:88]

Unobservable inputs should be developed using the best information available in the circumstances, which might include an entity's own data. In developing unobservable inputs, an entity's own data should be adjusted if reasonably available information indicates that other market participants would use different data or there is something particular to the entity that is not available to other market participants (e.g. an entity-specific synergy). IFRS 13 does not require an entity to undertake exhaustive efforts to obtain information about market participant assumptions. However, the entity is required to take into account all information about market participant assumptions that is reasonably available. Unobservable inputs developed in the manner described above are considered market participant assumptions and meet the objective of a fair value measurement. [IFRS 13:89]

IFRS 13 provides the following examples of Level 3 inputs for particular assets and liabilities.

[IFRS 13:B36]

- **Long-dated currency swap** A Level 3 input would be an interest rate in a specified currency that is not observable and cannot be corroborated by observable market data at commonly quoted intervals or otherwise for substantially the full term of the currency swap. The interest rates in a currency swap are the swap rates calculated from the respective countries' yield curves.

- **Three-year option on exchange-traded shares** A Level 3 input would be historical volatility, i.e. the volatility for the shares derived from the shares' historical prices. Historical volatility typically does not represent current market participant expectations about future volatility, even if it is the only information available to price an option.

- **Interest rate swap** A Level 3 input would be an adjustment to a mid-market consensus (non-binding) price for the swap developed using data that are not directly observable and cannot otherwise be corroborated by observable market data.

- **Decommissioning liability assumed in a business combination** A Level 3 input would be a current estimate using the entity's own data of the future cash outflows to be paid to fulfil the obligation (including market participants' expectations about the costs of fulfilling the obligation and the compensation that a market participant would require for taking on the obligation to dismantle the asset) if there is no reasonably available information that indicates that market participants would use different assumptions. That Level 3 input would be used in a present value technique together with other inputs, e.g. a current risk-free interest rate or a credit-adjusted risk-free rate if the effect of the entity's credit standing on the fair value of the liability is reflected in the discount rate rather than in the estimate of future cash outflows.

- **Cash-generating unit** A Level 3 input would be a financial forecast (e.g. of cash flows or profit or loss) developed using the entity's own data if there is no reasonably available information that indicates that market participants would use different assumptions.

10.2.4   Determining the level within the fair value hierarchy when broker or pricing service quotes are used

IFRS 13 allows the use of quoted prices provided by brokers or pricing services if the entity has determined that the quoted prices provided by a broker or pricing service are developed in accordance with IFRS 13. See **9.7** for more detailed guidance regarding when a quoted price provided by a broker or pricing service can be considered to be determinative of fair value.

When quoted prices are provided by a broker or pricing service, and are used by an entity in measuring the fair value of an asset or a liability, the following considerations are relevant for the entity's assessment of the level within the fair value hierarchy in which the quoted prices fall.

Level 1 inputs

Level 1 inputs are unadjusted quoted prices in active markets for identical assets or liabilities. If the quote provided by a broker or pricing service relies solely on unadjusted quoted prices in an active market for an identical instrument that the entity can access at the measurement date, the quoted price should be used to measure the fair value of the asset or liability without adjustment, subject to limited exceptions as discussed in IFRS 13:79 (see **10.3.3.2**).

If an adjustment is necessary in accordance with IFRS 13:79, or if the quoted price originates from a market that is not active, the broker or pricing service quote does not represent a Level 1 input.

Level 2 inputs

Level 2 inputs are inputs other than quoted prices included within Level 1 that are observable for the asset or liability, either directly or indirectly. Observable inputs are defined in IFRS 13:Appendix A as "[i]nputs that are developed using market data, such as publicly available information about actual events or transactions, and that reflect the assumptions that market participants would use when pricing the asset or liability [or own equity instrument]".

If a quote from a broker or pricing service meets any of the following criteria, it represents a Level 2 input.

- The entity can determine that the broker or pricing service quote itself represents a quoted price for similar assets or liabilities in active markets.

- The entity can determine that the quote is based on quoted prices for identical or similar assets or liabilities in markets that are not active, from transactions that are orderly and for which adjustments are based only on information that is (1) observable, or (2) market-corroborated, or (3) unobservable, but insignificant to the measurement.

- The entity can determine that the quote was established using a valuation technique and that the inputs the broker or pricing service used to arrive at the quoted price are observable or market-corroborated and any unobservable inputs do not have a significant effect on the measurement.

- The entity can corroborate the broker or pricing service quote or inputs using prices (1) from orderly transactions in an active market, or (2) from orderly transactions in an inactive market for which any adjustment needed to ensure the price is representative of fair value is insignificant to the measurement.

In some circumstances, adjustments to the Level 2 inputs may be necessary, for example if the quoted price is based on a similar (but not identical) asset or liability. If an adjustment is required, an entity should determine whether the adjustment is significant to the entire measurement and whether it is based on unobservable inputs (see **10.3.3.2**). If this is the case, the entire measurement will be categorised within Level 3.

Level 3 inputs

Level 3 inputs are unobservable inputs for the asset or liability. Broker or pricing service quotes meeting any of the following criteria are categorised in Level 3 of the fair value hierarchy.

- The entity can determine that the quote is based on a Level 1 or Level 2 input but an adjustment is required that is significant to the measurement and based on unobservable inputs.

- The entity can determine that the quote is based on unobservable inputs with a significant effect.

Regardless of whether the entity determines that the broker or pricing service quote is based on observable or unobservable inputs, it is not appropriate for an entity to accept, without further analysis, that the inputs used are appropriate in the circumstances. The entity must gain sufficient understanding of the inputs to be able to conclude that they reflect assumptions market participants would use, including assumptions about risks inherent in a particular valuation technique and the inputs used. Further, an entity must be able to conclude that the inputs used are based on the best information available. Adjustments should be made if reasonably available information, including the entity's own data, indicates that other market participants would use different inputs.

Other considerations

Depending on the asset or liability being measured at fair value, a quote from a broker or pricing service may be the only input, or one of many inputs, into an entity's fair value measurement of that asset or liability. All inputs must be considered before determining the level within the fair value hierarchy for measurement of the asset or liability (see **section 10.3**).

Other factors indicating that a broker or pricing service quote may be given more weight in the fair value measurement include that:

- the quote is binding on the entity making the quote; or

- the quote is available from more than one broker or pricing service.

IFRS Interpretations Committee agenda decision – January 2015

The IFRS Interpretations Committee considered the application of the fair value hierarchy when prices provided by a third party are used. In an agenda decision reported in the January 2015 *IFRIC Update*, the Committee concluded that "the classification of those measurements within the fair value hierarchy will depend on the evaluation of the inputs used by the third party to derive those prices, instead of on the pricing methodology used". Consequently, as discussed above, the inputs used by the broker or pricing service in determining a quotation must be assessed to determine the classification of the asset or liability within the fair value hierarchy.

Disclosure

IFRS 13:IE64(b) in the illustrative examples accompanying IFRS 13 suggests that, in order to comply with the disclosure requirements in IFRS 13:92(d), an entity may disclose "how third-party information such as broker quotes, pricing services, net asset values and relevant market data was taken into account when measuring fair value" as part of the entity's additional information about significant unobservable inputs. Further, IFRS 13:IE65(d) suggests that, in order to comply with the disclosure requirements in IFRS 13:93(g), an entity may disclose how the entity determined that third-party information, such as broker quotes or pricing services, used in the fair value measurement was developed in accordance with IFRS 13 as part of the entity's description of its valuation process for Level 3 fair value measurements. See **section 11** for IFRS 13's disclosure requirements.

10.2.5 Use of historical transaction prices in determining the fair value of real estate properties

Although there may be circumstances when properties are sufficiently similar that the sales price of one is considered as indicative of the value of another, historical prices for sales of similar properties are not always an appropriate measure of fair value.

IFRS 13:61 requires entities to maximise the use of relevant observable data and minimise the use of unobservable data; consequently, an appropriate, publicly available comparable transaction price should be used in preference to, for example, an unobservable estimate of the reversionary yield on a property.

However, evidence of historical market transactions should not be followed without question. Trends in value and the market evidence available (whether for directly comparable transactions or otherwise) should be taken into account and, when appropriate, the valuation should be adjusted for such evidence to reflect the fair value definition. Judgement should also be applied in attaching more or less weight to various sources of evidence.

Market trends and the time elapsed since historical transactions occurred will also dictate whether those transactions are relevant to the valuation of the property concerned. For example, when, at the measurement date, there is evidence that the market has changed significantly since the most recent transaction in similar property, and/or a significant period has passed since that most recent transaction, historical transactions will not necessarily reflect those subsequent market changes. It would not be appropriate to take into account historical transaction prices which are not indicative of market conditions at the measurement date.

In a depressed market, when a significant proportion of sales may be made by vendors such as liquidators or receivers, historical transaction prices may still be relevant in measuring the fair value of investment property. However, care should be exercised to ensure that such transaction prices reflect exchange prices in an orderly transaction (see **example 9.6** for further discussion).

10.3 Categorisation of fair value measurements within the fair value hierarchy

10.3.1 Categorisation of fair value measurements – general

The categorisation of a fair value measurement within the fair value hierarchy is a two-step process. Initially, the entity determines the appropriate categorisation of the inputs to the valuation techniques used in the fair value measurement (see **section 10.2**). Once the valuation techniques have been applied, and the fair value measured, it is then necessary to determine the appropriate categorisation of the fair value measurement in its entirety. This is required in order to arrive at the appropriate analysis of the fair value measurements for disclosure purposes (see **section 11**).

As can be seen from the discussion in **sections 10.3.2** to **10.3.6**, the appropriate categorisation of a fair value measurement is determined by the 'mix' of inputs used. For example, if only Level 1 inputs are used, the fair value measurement will be categorised as a Level 1 measurement (see **10.3.2**). The same principle applies if only Level 2 or only Level 3 inputs are used. Alternatively, the fair value measurement may be derived from several inputs from different categories, in which case it will be necessary to consider the significance of each of those inputs (see **section 10.3.3**).

10.3.2 Categorisation of measurements made using Level 1 inputs

A fair value measurement can only be categorised as a Level 1 measurement when only Level 1 inputs are used, and no adjustments are made.

In any of the circumstances described in IFRS 13:79 (see **10.2.1.1**), a Level 1 input cannot be used without adjustment. IFRS 13:79 outlines the appropriate adjustments for each circumstance. Note that any adjustment to a Level 1 input, regardless of its significance, means that the resulting fair value measurement cannot be categorised as a Level 1 measurement.

Based on the definition in IFRS 13:76 and Appendix 1 (see **10.2.1.1**), for a fair value measurement to be categorised in Level 1 of the fair value hierarchy, the following criteria must be satisfied:

- the only input used must be a price (or prices) quoted in an active market;

- the price must be unadjusted. IFRS 13:79 requires that any adjustment to a fair value measurement (regardless of its significance) that would otherwise meet the Level 1 criteria results in the fair value measurement being categorised as a lower-level measurement;

- the price must be for an asset or a liability that is identical to the asset or liability being measured (see **examples 10.3.2A** to **10.3.2D**); and

- the entity must have access to the price at the measurement date. For example, an entity has access to the price if it has the ability to transact at that price in an exchange market. In addition, an entity has access to the price if there are dealers who stand ready to transact with the entity at that price. However, broker quotes by themselves are not sufficient evidence that the entity has access to the price if the brokers do not stand ready to transact at that price. Any adjustment made to a quoted price in an active market because the entity has limited or no access to that market results in a Level 2 or a Level 3 measurement, depending on the nature of the adjustment. Further, although a quoted price in an active market may be available, such pricing may not be readily accessible for all of the assets and liabilities being measured, if an entity holds a large volume of similar (but not identical) instruments. As a result, the entity may measure fair value using alternative pricing (e.g. matrix pricing) as a practical expedient, which would result in a lower level measurement in the fair value hierarchy.

Example 10.3.2A

Application of Level 1 classification criteria – debt security

Entity P holds a debt security that is traded in a dealer market in which bid and ask prices are available. The market is an active market and it is the principal market for the security. The market is accessible by Entity P. No adjustments have been made to the quoted price.

If the quoted price used to measure the fair value of the debt security is for a debt security identical to that held by Entity P, the measurement of the debt security should be classified within Level 1 of the fair value hierarchy. The fact that a price is derived from a dealer market (rather than an 'exchange' market) does not in itself preclude classification as a Level 1 measurement because such dealer markets may be active and accessible to the entity (see also **10.2.1.1**).

Example 10.3.2B

Application of Level 1 classification criteria – issued debt security with identical instrument traded as an asset

Entity Q has issued an exchange-traded debt security. Entity Q has elected to account for this instrument using the fair value option under IFRS 9 (or, for entities that have not yet adopted IFRS 9, IAS 39). A quoted price for the transfer of an identical or a similar liability is not available; however, an identical instrument is currently trading as an asset in an active market. Entity Q uses the quoted price for the asset as its initial input for the fair value measurement of the issued debt security. Entity Q also evaluates whether the quoted price for the asset requires adjustment for factors, such as third-party credit enhancements, that would not be applicable to the issued debt security. Entity Q determines that no adjustments are required to the quoted price of the asset.

Because the quoted price used to measure the fair value of the issued debt security is for an identical debt security (e.g. the identical ISIN*) traded as an asset, and no adjustments to the quoted price of the instrument are required, the resulting measurement of the issued debt security should be classified as a Level 1 measurement in the fair value hierarchy.

* ISIN refers to the International Securities Identification Number, a 12-character alpha-numerical code that does not contain information characterising financial instruments but serves for uniform identification of a security at trading and settlement.

Example 10.3.2C

Application of Level 1 classification criteria – 'look-alike' forward contract

Entity R holds an over-the-counter (OTC) 'look-alike' forward contract (i.e. it mirrors another contract). The counterparty to this contract is contractually obligated to settle it on the basis of the quoted price for a similar futures contract traded on an active futures exchange. The forward contract meets the definition of a derivative and is therefore measured at fair value.

While the look-alike forward contract mirrors the exchange-traded futures contract, and the value of the look-alike forward contract is intended to approximate the quoted price for the exchange-traded futures contract, the forward and futures contracts are not identical. Even if the parties to the forward contract both have the highest credit quality (resulting in the same level of credit risk as the exchange-traded futures contract), the forward contract is not considered identical because (1) the counterparties are different, and (2) Entity R cannot sell the forward contract on the futures exchange (i.e. the forward contract has different levels of counterparty and liquidity risk when compared to the futures contract). While the quoted price for the futures contract may be a Level 1 input (when the market for it is active), the fair value measurement of the look-alike forward contract can only be classified as Level 2 or Level 3.

Example 10.3.2D

Application of Level 1 classification criteria – interest rate swap

Entity S is a party to an interest rate swap that is transacted on an over-the-counter (OTC) market. The OTC market does not quote prices for interest rate swaps. Entity S would determine the fair value of the swap by using either (1) a discounted cash flow approach based on market-based yield curves, or (2) the price at which a similar swap was exchanged on the OTC market. While similar swaps may have been exchanged on the OTC market, the similar swaps would have different counterparties and would, therefore, not be identical to the swap held by Entity S.

The price at which Entity S would be able to sell the swap would result from a negotiated transaction contemplating the credit standings of the two parties to the swap as well as the terms of the specific swap. Because the swap held by Entity S is not identical to any similar swap for which there may be transactions on the OTC market, the measurement of the swap by Entity S would be classified as a Level 2 or a Level 3 measurement, depending on the inputs that are significant to the measurement.

10.3.3 Determining the level within the fair value hierarchy when several inputs are used

10.3.3.1 Determining the level within the fair value hierarchy – general

When several inputs are used to measure the fair value of an asset or a liability, those inputs may be categorised within different levels of the fair value hierarchy (e.g. the valuation may be based on some Level 2 and some Level 3 inputs). In such circumstances, the categorisation of the fair value measurement in its entirety is based on the lowest level input that is significant to the entire measurement. [IFRS 13:73] See **10.3.3.2** for a discussion of the meaning of the term 'significant'.

Example 10.3.3.1

Classification of fair value measurements within the fair value hierarchy

Entity I holds an investment in equity instruments that are not traded in an active market (e.g. equity instruments issued by a private entity). In accordance with IFRS 9 (or, for entities that have not yet adopted IFRS 9, IAS 39), the investment is measured at fair value subsequent to initial recognition.

How should Entity I classify the fair value measurement of its investment within the fair value hierarchy (i.e. as Level 1, Level 2 or Level 3)?

The examples below illustrate the application of the guidance in IFRS 13 on the classification of measurements within the fair value hierarchy.

Note that, because the equity instruments are not traded in an active market, Level 1 inputs are not available.

Scenario 1 – Fair value is estimated based on recent transactions

If Entity I estimates the fair value of its investment based on recent transactions between independent third parties (e.g. quoted prices in an inactive market, privately negotiated acquisitions or disposals of the equity instruments etc.), these transaction prices would be considered Level 2 inputs if they meet the definition of fair value. This would be the case if the price represents an exit price for the equity instruments at the date of the transaction, the transaction is executed at terms that are consistent with how other market participants would transact, and the transaction is not executed under duress.

Similarly, prices based on recent transactions between Entity I and third parties may be considered Level 2 inputs if they meet the criteria above. For example, Entity I owns a 5 per cent equity investment in Entity X and measures that investment at fair value. Entity I acquires an additional 10 per cent of Entity X. If the transaction price for the additional 10 per cent meets the definition of fair value, Entity I may use that price as a basis for valuing its entire 15 per cent investment at the next reporting date.

In either case, it may be necessary to adjust the recent transaction price to measure the investment appropriately at fair value at the reporting date. For example, the recent transaction price should be adjusted for events or changes in the entity's financial position that have occurred since the date of the transaction that would affect the value of the equity investment in the entity. Unobservable adjustments to a Level 2 input that are significant to the entire measurement would change the categorisation to Level 3.

Scenario 2 – Fair value is determined based on a discounted cash flow technique

IFRS 13:B36 (see **10.2.3**) cites as an example of a Level 3 input "a financial forecast (eg of cash flows or earnings) developed using the entity's own data if there is no reasonably available information that indicates that market participants would use different assumptions". While certain information used in the model may be observable (e.g. interest rate curves), the entity's projected cash flows (which are not observable) would probably be significant to the entire fair value measurement. Therefore, the measurement of the investment would probably be classified as Level 3.

Scenario 3 – Fair value is determined based on a market-based multiple applied to a financial measure

IFRS 13:B35 (see **10.2.2**) cites as an example of a Level 2 input "a valuation multiple (eg a multiple of earnings or revenue or a similar performance measure) derived from observable market data, eg multiples derived from prices in observed transactions involving comparable (that is, similar) businesses, taking into account operational, market, financial, and non-financial factors". The market-derived multiple may thus be considered a Level 2 input. However, the historical financial measure (i.e. earnings or EBITDA) and any adjustments needed to reflect differences between the entity and comparable entities would probably be Level 3 inputs because they are entity-specific and are not considered market-observable data. Therefore, the measurement of the investment would probably be classified within Level 3 of the fair value hierarchy.

For measurements such as 'fair value less costs to sell' that are based on fair value, the adjustments to fair value (e.g. for costs to sell) to arrive at the required measurement are not taken into account when determining the level of the fair value hierarchy within which the measurement is categorised. [IFRS 13:73]

Therefore, for example, if an asset is required to be measured at fair value less costs to sell, and the fair value of the asset can be measured by reference solely to Level 1 inputs, the valuation at fair value less costs to sell is categorised within Level 1, notwithstanding that the adjustment for costs to sell may be based on unobservable inputs.

The availability of relevant inputs and their relative subjectivity might affect the selection of appropriate valuation techniques. However, the fair value hierarchy prioritises the inputs to valuation techniques, not the valuation techniques used to measure fair value. For example, a fair value measurement developed using a present value technique might be categorised within Level 2 or Level 3, depending on the inputs that are significant to the entire measurement and the level of the fair value hierarchy within which those inputs are categorised. [IFRS 13:74]

In other words, the categorisation of the fair value measurement in the fair value hierarchy is based on inputs, not on the valuation technique in which they are used.

If an observable input requires an adjustment using an unobservable input and that adjustment results in a significantly higher or lower fair value measurement, the resulting measurement is a Level 3 measurement. For example, if a market participant would take into account the effect of a restriction on the sale of an asset when estimating the price for the asset, an entity would adjust the quoted price to reflect the effect of that restriction. If that quoted price is a Level 2 input and the adjustment is an unobservable input that is significant to the entire measurement, the measurement would be categorised within Level 3 of the fair value hierarchy. [IFRS 13:75]

10.3.3.2 Determining the 'significance' of an input or an adjustment

The Standard does not expand on what is meant by 'significant' in the context of IFRS 13:73, other than to state that the assessment of the significance of a particular input to the entire measurement requires judgement, taking into account factors specific to the asset or liability. [IFRS 13:73]

To determine the level in which the fair value measurement should be categorised, an entity should aggregate the inputs to the measurement by level and determine the lowest level of inputs that are significant to the fair value measurement in its entirety. For example, a measurement that includes inputs with significant effect from Levels 2 and 3 would be classified in its entirety in Level 3, because Level 3 is the lowest level input with a significant effect.

Entities should establish a methodology for determining whether an input or aggregated inputs are significant to the measurement in its entirety. The methodology should be applied consistently.

In some cases, a qualitative assessment of the inputs used may be sufficient. For example, changes in discount rates generally have a significant effect on fair value measurements determined using a discounted cash flow model.

In other cases, a quantitative analysis of the inputs may be required. One quantitative approach might involve the following steps.

- **Step 1** Select a threshold or percentage of the overall fair value measurement as a benchmark for significance.

- **Step 2** Perform a sensitivity analysis, calculating the percentage change in the fair value measurement arising from reasonably possible changes to each input.

- **Step 3** Compare the percentage change in the fair value measurement for each input calculated under Step 2 to the benchmark selected under Step 1. If the percentage change in the fair value measurement for a particular input exceeds the selected benchmark, that input would be considered significant. If none of the individual Level 3 inputs are considered significant, the combined effect of all the Level 3 inputs should be considered to determine whether they have a significant effect in aggregate on the fair value measurement.

When this approach is used, the benchmark should represent a percentage of the overall measurement and not a percentage of a particular component of the fair value measurement. In addition, the threshold should not represent a percentage of total assets, total liabilities, gains or losses, or other line items in the statement of financial position or the statement of comprehensive income because this would not be specific to the fair value measurement.

Example 10.3.3.2 illustrates this approach.

> **Example 10.3.3.2**
>
> **Determining the significance of an input**
>
> Entity A holds a hybrid instrument which includes an embedded option. Entity A is measuring the instrument at fair value in its entirety. One of the inputs to its valuation model is the volatility of the embedded option for which market data are not available (i.e. it is unobservable and, consequently, a Level 3 input).
>
> Entity A is evaluating whether the unobservable volatility input is significant to the overall fair value measurement for the hybrid instrument. In making its assessment, Entity A considers the significance of the volatility in relation to the hybrid instrument in its entirety and not solely in relation to the embedded option.
>
> Entity A uses a quantitative methodology and selects a threshold or percentage of the overall fair value measurement of the hybrid instrument as a benchmark for significance. Entity A then performs a sensitivity analysis to determine how the volatility input affects the overall fair value of the hybrid instrument within a reasonably possible range of values for the volatility input.
>
> If reasonable changes in the volatility input cause the percentage change in the fair value measurement of the hybrid instrument to exceed the selected threshold, Entity A would conclude that the unobservable volatility input is significant to the measurement in its entirety. In that case, the fair value measurement of the hybrid instrument would represent a Level 3 measurement within the fair value hierarchy.

10.3.4 *Observable transactions in inactive markets*

The level of market activity does not affect the IFRS 13 measurement objective, i.e. fair value is the price in an orderly transaction between market participants at the measurement date under current market conditions.

Observable transactions are relevant inputs to a fair value measurement when they reflect market participants' assumptions in orderly transactions and, thus, are representative of fair value. Relevant observable inputs should be given priority when measuring fair value in accordance with IFRS 13. IFRS 13:67 (see **9.1**) states that "[v]aluation techniques used to measure fair value shall maximise the use of relevant observable inputs and minimise the use of unobservable inputs". Further, IFRS 13:87 (see **10.2.3**) states, in part, that "[u]nobservable inputs [Level 3] shall be used to measure fair value to the extent that relevant observable inputs [Level 1 and 2] are not available...".

However, when the volume and level of activity in a market have significantly decreased and the market is not active, observable transactions may not be representative of fair value because of increased instances of transactions that are not orderly (e.g. forced liquidations or distress sales). Consequently, an entity should perform further analysis of the transactions or quoted prices available to determine whether they represent fair value. In some circumstances, a change in valuation technique or the use of multiple valuation techniques may be appropriate, as discussed below.

Transactions are not orderly

If the observable transactions are not orderly, IFRS 13:B44(a) states that "the entity shall place little, if any, weight (compared with other indications of fair value) on that transaction price" (see **9.6**). If an entity previously used quoted prices to measure fair value, and quoted prices from orderly transactions are no longer available, the entity may need to change its valuation technique or use multiple valuation techniques. If the entity measures fair value by using the price from a transaction that is not orderly, the price should be adjusted to reflect the assumptions that market participants would use in pricing the asset or liability in an orderly transaction. The resulting measurement would generally be classified as a Level 3 measurement.

Transactions are orderly

If the observable transactions are orderly, the entity should consider the transaction price when estimating fair value. However, the entity may also need to adjust the transaction price when measuring fair value to meet the measurement objective. IFRS 13:B44(b) states that the "amount of weight placed on that [orderly] transaction price when compared with other indications of fair value will depend on the facts and circumstances" (see **9.6**).

If an entity determines that it does not need to make any significant adjustment to the transaction price using unobservable inputs to arrive at the fair value of the asset or liability, the transaction price represents a relevant observable input and the measurement would be classified as a Level 2 measurement. However, if the entity determines that it needs to make a significant adjustment to the transaction price using unobservable inputs, the measurement would be classified as a Level 3 measurement.

Insufficient information to determine whether transactions are orderly

If an entity is unable to obtain, without undue cost and effort, sufficient information to determine whether the transaction is orderly, the entity must consider the transaction price in determining fair value; however, the transaction price may not be the 'sole or primary' basis for estimating fair value. In such circumstances, because the transaction price may not reflect the assumptions that market participants would use, a fair value measurement that has this price as its principal input would most likely represent a Level 3 measurement. As above, the use of multiple valuation techniques may be appropriate in this case.

10.3.5 Relationship between the quality of a valuation and its classification in the fair value hierarchy

The classification of a fair value measurement within the hierarchy specified by IFRS 13 is not indicative of the 'quality' of that valuation. The hierarchy differentiates between inputs to a fair value measurement on the basis of their *observability*, not their quality. As stated in IFRS 13:72, the purpose of the hierarchy is to increase the consistency and comparability of fair value measurements, an aim which is achieved by giving priority to more observable inputs. It is clear from IFRS 13:75, however, that if a market participant would take account of a less observable factor then that must be incorporated into a fair value measurement.

In particular, it is important to note that the fact that a fair value measurement incorporates significant unobservable inputs and is, therefore, classified as 'Level 3' does not mean that the fair value measurement is of low quality or is not reliable. IFRS 13:BC173 acknowledges that unobservable inputs by necessity include some degree of subjectivity, but concludes that this is best addressed by requiring enhanced quantitative and qualitative disclosures (e.g. details of valuation techniques and inputs being used and sensitivity analysis as required by IFRS 13:93(d) and IFRS 13:93(h), respectively) for fair value measurements incorporating such inputs. As noted in IFRS 13:BC190, these disclosures give the user information about inputs for which limited or no information is publicly available and, as such, exist to address the lack of *observability* of Level 3 inputs rather than because such inputs are not deemed to be of sufficient quality.

10.3.6 Classification of fair value measurements of real estate properties within the fair value hierarchy

In practice, the majority of fair value measurements for real estate properties are likely to be classified as Level 3 because the underlying valuation techniques use significant unobservable inputs. Less commonly, the appropriate classification of the fair value measurement of a real estate property could be Level 2 if sufficient observable data are available and no significant adjustments to the observable data are required.

Given that no two properties are identical in terms of location, condition, specification and other factors, it would be extremely rare for Level 1 inputs to be available for the valuation of real estate properties.

The following examples illustrate contrasting scenarios.

Example 1

Entity A owns a completed commercial building in Hong Kong which is classified as an investment property in accordance with IAS 40 *Investment Property* and is currently leased out to tenants. Buy-and-sell transactions in the same market for similar properties are infrequent. Consequently, Entity A engages a valuer who uses a valuation technique requiring the estimation of future rental income and yield for the property (e.g. an income capitalisation approach when the fair value of the property is arrived at by discounting (1) the contracted annual rent at a capitalisation rate over the existing contractual lease period, and (2) the current market rent at a reversionary yield over the period beyond the existing contractual lease period).

In such circumstances, the contracted annual rent may be observable, but the capitalisation rate and the reversionary yield are unlikely to be so, particularly when sale and leasing transactions for similar properties in the same market are not frequent. Use of a significant unobservable input (such as the capitalisation rate or reversionary yield) will result in the property being classified as Level 3.

Example 2

Entity B owns a residential apartment unit in Hong Kong that is classified as an investment property in accordance with IAS 40. The fair value of the apartment unit can be measured based on publicly available information regarding the average of recent transaction prices for similar properties (e.g. located in the same or a similar building with similar size and facing), and no significant adjustments are required to be made to the average transaction price.

In such circumstances, it would be appropriate to classify the fair value measurement as Level 2. In contrast, if adjustments are required to the observable data that are (1) based on unobservable data, and (2) significant to the fair value measurement as a whole, the fair value measurement should be classified as Level 3.

In the case of properties under development (e.g. investment properties under construction that are measured at fair value at each reporting date in accordance with IAS 40), the measurement of fair value will generally require the use of valuation methodologies with significant unobservable inputs because buy-and-sell transactions for similar properties under development are infrequent. Consequently, the fair value measurements will generally be classified as Level 3. For example, the residual approach to measuring the fair value of properties under development takes into account the expected completion value of the property, less the expected future development costs, with adjustments for profit and risk. The estimated costs to develop the property and the adjustments for risk are specific to the property and are unobservable inputs.

11 Disclosure

11.1 General

The disclosures required by IFRS 13 in respect of a fair value measurement vary depending on whether the fair value measurement is recognised in the statement of financial position on a recurring or a non-recurring basis or is only disclosed in the notes to the financial statements. See **11.6** for a table summarising the application of IFRS 13's disclosure requirements.

IFRS 13 requires that the entity should disclose information that helps users of its financial statements to assess both of the following:

[IFRS 13:91]

- for assets and liabilities that are measured at fair value on a recurring or non-recurring basis in the statement of financial position after initial recognition, the valuation techniques and inputs used to develop those measurements; and

- for recurring fair value measurements using significant unobservable inputs (Level 3) (see **10.2.3**), the effect of the measurements on profit or loss or other comprehensive income for the period.

See **11.2** for an explanation of what is meant by measurement of fair value on a 'recurring' and a 'non-recurring' basis.

To meet the objectives of IFRS 13:91, the entity is required to consider all the following:

[IFRS 13:92]

- the level of detail necessary to satisfy the disclosure requirements;

- how much emphasis to place on each of the various requirements;

- how much aggregation or disaggregation to undertake; and

- whether users of financial statements need additional information to evaluate the quantitative information disclosed.

To meet the objectives of IFRS 13:91, the Standard sets out minimum disclosure requirements that are aggregated by class of assets and liabilities. If the specific disclosures provided in accordance with IFRS 13 and other

IFRSs are insufficient to meet the objectives described in IFRS 13:91, the entity should disclose whatever additional information is necessary to meet those objectives. [IFRS 13:92]

The quantitative disclosures required under IFRS 13 should be presented in a tabular format unless another format is more appropriate. [IFRS 13:99]

11.2   Scope of disclosure requirements

In line with the general scope of IFRS 13 (see **section 2**), the disclosure requirements of IFRS 13 generally apply whenever assets or liabilities are measured at fair value (or using a measurement based on fair value). The general disclosure requirements of IFRS 13 do not apply to the following:

[IFRS 13:7]

- plan assets measured at fair value in accordance with IAS 19 *Employee Benefits*;

- retirement benefit plan investments measured at fair value in accordance with IAS 26 *Accounting and Reporting by Retirement Benefit Plans*; and

- assets for which recoverable amount is fair value less costs of disposal in accordance with IAS 36 *Impairment of Assets*.

The majority of IFRS 13's disclosure requirements apply only to assets and liabilities measured in the statement of financial position at fair value. Certain of these requirements are specified for assets and liabilities not measured at fair value in the statement of financial position but for which the fair value is disclosed (see **11.5**).

IFRS 13's disclosure requirements do not apply to fair value measurements at initial recognition; the disclosures required when a fair value measurement is used at initial recognition are dealt with in other IFRSs (e.g. IFRS 3 *Business Combinations* regarding the measurement of assets acquired and liabilities assumed in a business combination). [IFRS 13:BC184]

For each disclosure requirement, the Standard is explicit as to whether it applies in respect of 'recurring' fair value measurements, 'non-recurring' fair value measurements, or both.

Recurring fair value measurements are those that other IFRSs require or permit in the statement of financial position at the end of each reporting period (e.g. investment property measured at fair value at the end of each reporting period under IAS 40 *Investment Property*). Non-recurring fair value measurements are those that other IFRSs require or permit in the statement of financial position in particular circumstances (e.g. an asset held for sale measured at fair value less costs to sell under IFRS 5 *Non-current Assets Held for Sale and Discontinued Operations* because it meets the criteria for classification as held for sale and fair value less costs to sell is lower than its carrying amount). [IFRS 13:93(a)]

11.3 Classes of assets and liabilities

For the purposes of IFRS 13's disclosure requirements, assets and liabilities are segregated into 'classes'. Entities are required to determine appropriate classes of assets and liabilities on the basis of:

[IFRS 13:94]

- the nature, characteristics and risks of the asset or liability; and

- the level of the fair value hierarchy within which the fair value measurement is categorised.

The following additional guidance is provided:

[IFRS 13:94]

- a class of assets and liabilities will often require greater disaggregation than the line items presented in the statement of financial position. However, the entity is required to provide information sufficient to permit reconciliation to the line items presented in the statement of financial position;

- if another IFRS specifies the class for an asset or a liability, the entity may use that class for the purpose of providing the disclosures under IFRS 13 if that class meets the requirements set out in IFRS 13:94; and

- the number of classes may need to be greater for fair value measurements classified within Level 3 of the fair value hierarchy because those measurements have a greater degree of uncertainty and subjectivity.

The identification of appropriate classes of assets and liabilities for which disclosures about fair value measurements should be provided requires the exercise of judgement. [IFRS 13:94]

11.4 Financial and non-financial items measured at fair value

11.4.1 Disclosures regarding financial and non-financial items measured at fair value – general

At a minimum, the information set out in **11.4.2** to **11.4.13** is required to be disclosed for each class of assets and liabilities measured at fair value in the statement of financial position after initial recognition (including measurements based on fair value within the scope of IFRS 13, e.g. fair value less costs to sell). [IFRS 13:93]

11.4.2   *Fair value measurements by class of assets or liabilities*

For recurring and non-recurring fair value measurements, an entity is required to disclose the fair value measurement at the end of the reporting period. [IFRS 13:93(a)]

11.4.3   *Reasons underlying non-recurring measurements*

For non-recurring fair value measurements (see **11.2**), an entity is required to disclose the reasons for the measurement. [IFRS 13:93(a)]

11.4.4   *Level within the fair value hierarchy*

For recurring and non-recurring fair value measurements, an entity is required to disclose the level within the fair value hierarchy within which the fair value measurements are categorised in their entirety (i.e. Level 1, 2 or 3). [IFRS 13:93(b)]

> IFRS 13:IE60 provides an illustrative example of the disclosures required by IFRS 13:93(a) and (b) in the case of assets measured at fair value (see **example 4.3.3.3** in **chapter B11** (for entities applying IFRS 9) and **example 4.3.3.3** in **chapter C12** (for entities applying IAS 39)).

11.4.5   *Transfers within the fair value hierarchy*

For assets and liabilities held at the end of the reporting period that are measured at fair value on a recurring basis, an entity is required to disclose:

[IFRS 13:93(c)]

* the amounts of any transfers between Level 1 and Level 2 of the fair value hierarchy;
* the reasons for those transfers; and
* the entity's policy for determining when transfers between levels are deemed to have occurred (see below).

Transfers into each level are required to be disclosed and discussed separately from transfers out of each level. [IFRS 13:93(c)]

An entity is required to disclose and consistently follow its policy for determining when transfers between levels of the fair value hierarchy are deemed to have occurred. The policy must be the same for transfers in and transfers out of the levels. Examples of policies for determining the timing of transfers include the following:

[IFRS 13:95]

- the date of the event or change in circumstances that caused the transfer;

- the beginning of the reporting period; and

- the end of the reporting period.

See **11.4.8** for a discussion as to how an entity should determine the amounts to be reported for transfers between levels of the fair value hierarchy.

11.4.6   Valuation techniques and inputs (Levels 2 and 3)

For recurring and non-recurring fair value measurements categorised within Level 2 and Level 3 of the fair value hierarchy, an entity is required to disclose:

[IFRS 13:93(d)]

- a description of the valuation technique(s) and the inputs used in the fair value measurement; and

- if there has been a change in valuation technique (e.g. changing from a market approach to an income approach or the use of an additional valuation technique), details of the change and the reason(s) for making the change.

The objective of these disclosures is to help users of the financial statements understand not only the valuation techniques and inputs used, but also the judgements made by the entity when measuring fair value.

When developing the disclosures required under IFRS 13 about valuation techniques and the overall valuation process, entities may wish to consider the description of valuation techniques and processes in the IASB Expert Advisory Panel's October 2008 report *Measuring and disclosing the fair value of financial instruments in markets that are no longer active*. This report notes that a description of valuation techniques is important to enable users to understand the subjectivity and the judgements that are a part of measuring fair values. Specifically, for fair value measurements in Level 2 or Level 3 of the fair value hierarchy, the report indicates that information that an entity might consider disclosing about the valuation techniques and inputs used includes:

- whether the entity can choose between various valuation techniques and how it makes that choice;

- a description of the valuation techniques selected and the risks or shortcomings (if any) of those techniques. When a model is used, a description of the model and related inputs, and how the inputs are sourced by the entity;

- if the valuation technique has changed since previous reporting periods, the reason why the entity made the change and a quantification of the impact on the financial statements;

- the methods the entity uses to calibrate models to market prices, and the frequency of calibration;

- a description of the use of broker quotes or pricing services, which may include how many quotes were obtained, how these quotes were verified, what brokers or pricing services the entity used and why, whether quotes are adjusted, whether a quote is binding or non-binding and how the ultimate fair value used was determined;

- when an entity measures fair value by using prices for similar instruments, how the entity adjusts these prices to reflect the characteristics of the instruments subject to the measurement;

- the key drivers of value for each significant Level 2 and Level 3 asset/liability class and the extent to which the inputs used are observable or unobservable;

- an entity's consideration of illiquidity when performing the valuation; and

- a description of how the entity's and counterparty's non-performance risk was taken into consideration in the valuation (e.g. for derivatives or debt instruments).

11.4.7 Quantitative information about significant unobservable inputs (Level 3)

For recurring and non-recurring fair value measurements categorised within Level 3 of the fair value hierarchy, an entity is required to provide quantitative information about the significant unobservable inputs used in the fair value measurement. [IFRS 13:93(d)]

An entity is not required to create quantitative information to comply with this disclosure requirement if quantitative unobservable inputs are not developed by the entity when measuring fair value (e.g. when an entity uses prices from prior transactions or third-party pricing information without adjustment). However, when providing this disclosure, an entity cannot ignore quantitative unobservable inputs that are significant to the fair value measurement and are reasonably available to the entity. [IFRS 13:93(d)]

IFRS 13:IE63 provides an illustrative example of the disclosures required by IFRS 13:93(d) in respect of unobservable inputs for Level 3 valuations.

Having regard to the general requirements of IFRS 13:92 (see **11.1**), an entity might disclose some or all of the following information in order to help users of its financial statements to evaluate the quantitative information disclosed under IFRS 13:93(d):

[IFRS 13:IE64]

- the nature of the item being measured at fair value, including the characteristics of the item being measured that are taken into account in the determination of relevant inputs. For example, for residential mortgage-backed securities, an entity might disclose the following:

  - the types of underlying loans (e.g. prime loans or sub-prime loans);

  - collateral;

  - guarantees or other credit enhancements;

  - seniority level of the tranches of securities;

  - the year of issue;

  - the weighted-average coupon rate of the underlying loans and the securities;

  - the weighted-average maturity of the underlying loans and the securities;

  - the geographical concentration of the underlying loans; and

  - information about the credit ratings of the securities; and

- how third-party information such as broker quotes, pricing services, net asset values and relevant market data was taken into account when measuring fair value.

11.4.8   Reconciliation of fair value measurements (Level 3 recurring)

For recurring fair value measurements categorised within Level 3 of the fair value hierarchy, IFRS 13 requires a reconciliation from the opening to the closing balances. [IFRS 13:93(e)]

The reconciliation should include separate disclosure of changes during the period attributable to the following:

[IFRS 13:93(e)]

- total gains or losses for the period recognised in profit or loss, and the line item(s) in profit or loss in which those gains or losses are recognised;

- total gains or losses for the period recognised in other comprehensive income, and the line item(s) in other comprehensive income in which those gains or losses are recognised;

- purchases, sales, issues and settlements (each of those types of changes disclosed separately); and

- the amounts of any transfers into or out of Level 3 of the fair value hierarchy, the reasons for those transfers, and the entity's policy for determining when transfers between levels are deemed to have occurred (see **11.4.5**).

Transfers into Level 3 are required to be disclosed and discussed separately from transfers out of Level 3. [IFRS 13:93(e)]

The Standard cites the following examples of policies for determining the timing of transfers:

[IFRS 13:95]

- the actual date of the event or change in circumstances that caused the transfer;
- the beginning of the reporting period; and
- the end of the reporting period.

The 'amounts' to be disclosed for transfers between the levels of the fair value hierarchy should be the fair values of the items transferred. However, IFRS 13 is not prescriptive as to the timing of the recognition of the transfers (i.e. the date at which the fair values of the transferred items should be measured).

In addition, IFRS 13:95 requires that:

- an entity should disclose and consistently follow its policy for determining when transfers between levels of the fair value hierarchy are deemed to have occurred; and
- the entity's policy regarding the timing of recognising transfers should be the same for transfers into the levels as that for transfers out of the levels.

Accordingly, it would not be appropriate for an entity to determine the amount of 'transfers in' by using the beginning-of-period fair value and the amount of 'transfers out' by using the end-of-period fair value.

Example 11.4.8

Disclosure of transfers into and out of Level 3

Entity R holds two securities and is preparing its quarterly financial statements for the period ended 30 September.

- Security A was a Level 2 measurement at the beginning of the period (1 July) and transferred into Level 3 on 15 July.
- Security B was a Level 3 measurement at the beginning of the period (1 July) and transferred out of Level 3 into Level 2 on 15 August.

The fair values of Securities A and B at the beginning and end of the period, and at the actual dates of transfer, are set out below.

	Fair value		
	At date of transfer	**At 1 July**	**At 30 September**
	CU	**CU**	**CU**
Security A	125 (15 July)	150	50
Security B	250 (15 August)	150	300

The following table sets out the amounts that would be disclosed by Entity R for transfers into and out of the Level 3 hierarchy using each of the example methods identified in IFRS 13:95. The table also sets out the amount of gain/(loss) included in profit or loss that would be reflected in the reconciliation of fair value changes in Level 3 as required by IFRS 13:93(e).

	Method 1	**Method 2**	**Method 3**
	Fair value at actual date of transfer	**Fair value at beginning of reporting period**	**Fair value at end of reporting period**
Impact on levels	**CU**	**CU**	**CU**
Security A			
Level 2 transfer-out value	(125)	(150)	(50)
Level 3 transfer-in value	125	150	50
Loss reflected in Level 3 reconciliation	(75)	(100)	–
Security B			
Level 2 transfer-in value	250	150	300
Level 3 transfer-out value	(250)	(150)	(300)
Gain reflected in Level 3 reconciliation	100	–	150

IFRS 13:IE61 provides an illustrative example of the reconciliation required to be presented under IFRS 13:93(e) for Level 3 measurements.

In addition, an entity is required to disclose the amount of the total gains or losses recognised in profit or loss in the period (and included in the Level 3 reconciliation) that is attributable to the change in unrealised gains or losses relating to those assets and liabilities held at the end of the reporting period, and the line item(s) in profit or loss in which those unrealised gains or losses are recognised. [IFRS 13:93(f)]

IFRS 13:IE62 provides an illustrative example of information required to be disclosed under IFRS 13:93(f).

11.4.9   Valuation processes (Level 3)

For recurring and non-recurring fair value measurements categorised within Level 3 of the fair value hierarchy, an entity is required to disclose a description of the valuation processes used (including, for example, how an entity decides its valuation policies and procedures and analyses changes in fair value measurements from period to period). [IFRS 13:93(g)]

An entity might disclose the following information in order to comply with IFRS 13:93(g):

[IFRS 13:IE65]

- for the group within the entity that decides the entity's valuation policies and procedures:

  - its description;

  - to whom that group reports; and

  - the internal reporting procedures in place (e.g. whether and, if so, how pricing, risk management or audit committees discuss and assess the fair value measurements);

- the frequency and methods for calibration, back testing and other testing procedures of pricing models;

- the process for analysing changes in fair value measurements from period to period;

- how the entity determined that third-party information, such as broker quotes or pricing services, used in the fair value measurement was developed in accordance with IFRS 13; and

- the methods used to develop and substantiate the unobservable inputs used in a fair value measurement.

For further guidance based on the IASB Expert Advisory Panel's October 2008 report *Measuring and disclosing the fair value of financial instruments in markets that are no longer active*, see **11.4.6**.

11.4.10   Sensitivity to changes in significant unobservable inputs (Level 3 recurring)

For recurring fair value measurements categorised within Level 3 of the fair value hierarchy, an entity is required to provide a narrative description of the sensitivity of the fair value measurement to changes in unobservable inputs if a change in those inputs to a different amount might result in a significantly higher or lower fair value measurement. If there are interrelationships between those inputs and other unobservable inputs used in the fair value measurement, the entity is also required to provide a description of those interrelationships and of how they might magnify or mitigate the effect of changes in the unobservable inputs on the fair value measurement. To comply with that disclosure requirement, the narrative description of the sensitivity to changes in unobservable inputs should include, at a minimum, the unobservable inputs disclosed when complying with IFRS 13:93(d) (see **11.4.7**). [IFRS 13:93(h)(i)]

IFRS 13:IE66 provides an illustrative example of the information required to be disclosed about sensitivity to changes in significant unobservable inputs under IFRS 13:93(h)(i).

11.4.11   Sensitivity to changes in significant unobservable inputs (Level 3 recurring – financial assets and financial liabilities)

For recurring fair value measurements of financial assets and financial liabilities categorised within Level 3 of the fair value hierarchy, if changing one or more of the unobservable inputs to reflect reasonably possible alternative assumptions would change fair value significantly, an entity is required to state that fact and disclose the effect of those changes. [IFRS 13:93(h)(ii)]

The entity is required to disclose how the effect of a change to reflect a reasonably possible alternative assumption was calculated. For that purpose, significance is required to be judged with respect to profit or loss, and total assets or total liabilities, or, when changes in fair value are recognised in other comprehensive income, total equity. [IFRS 13:93(h)(ii)]

11.4.12   Highest and best use of non-financial asset differs from its current use

For recurring and non-recurring fair value measurements, if the highest and best use of a non-financial asset differs from its current use, an entity should disclose that fact and why the non-financial asset is being used in a manner that differs from its highest and best use. [IFRS 13:93(i)]

11.4.13 Liability measured at fair value and issued with an inseparable third-party credit enhancement

For a liability measured at fair value and issued with an inseparable third-party credit enhancement, an issuer is required to disclose the existence of that credit enhancement and whether it is reflected in the fair value measurement of the liability. [IFRS 13:98]

11.5 Financial and non-financial items for which fair value is disclosed

For each class of assets and liabilities not measured at fair value in the statement of financial position but for which the fair value is disclosed, an entity is required to disclose the information required by IFRS 13:93(b), (d) and (i) (see **11.4.4**, **11.4.6** and **11.4.12**). [IFRS 13:97]

However, an entity is not required to provide the quantitative disclosures about significant unobservable inputs used in fair value measurements categorised within Level 3 of the fair value hierarchy required by IFRS 13:93(d). [IFRS 13:97]

For such assets and liabilities, an entity does not need to provide the other disclosures required by IFRS 13. [IFRS 13:97]

11.6 Summary of the application of IFRS 13's disclosure requirements

The disclosures required in respect of a fair value measurement vary depending on whether the fair value measurement is recognised in the statement of financial position on a recurring or a non-recurring basis or is only disclosed in the notes to the financial statements.

The following table summarises the application of the disclosure requirements in IFRS 13. The quantitative disclosures should be presented in a tabular format unless another format is more appropriate.

Required disclosure	Assets and liabilities measured at fair value (FV) in the statement of financial position after the date of initial recognition		FV disclosed in notes only
	Recurring	Non-recurring	
Fair value at the reporting date [IFRS 13:93(a)]	X	X	X
Reason for the fair value measurement [IFRS 13:93(a)]		X	
The level of the fair value measurement in the fair value hierarchy [IFRS 13:93(b)]	X	X	X
For assets and liabilities held at the reporting date, amounts of transfers between Levels 1 and 2 (separately for transfers into and out of each level), the reasons for those transfers, and the entity's policy for determining that a transfer has occurred [IFRS 13:93(c)]	X		
For Level 2 and Level 3 measurements, a description of the valuation techniques and inputs used [IFRS 13:93(d)]	X	X	X

	Assets and liabilities measured at fair value (FV) in the statement of financial position after the date of initial recognition		
Required disclosure	**Recurring**	**Non-recurring**	**FV disclosed in notes only**
For Level 2 and Level 3 measurements for which there has been a change in valuation technique, the nature of that change and reason for it [IFRS 13:93(d)]	X	X	X
For non-financial assets with a highest and best use that differs from its current use, that fact and why the asset is being used in a manner different from its highest and best use [IFRS 13:93(i)]	X	X	X
Information sufficient to permit a reconciliation between the amounts disclosed for classes of assets and liabilities by level of the fair value hierarchy and the line items presented in the statement of financial position [IFRS 13:94]	X	X	Not required by IFRS 13 but may be required by other IFRSs
If an entity chooses as its accounting policy to use the portfolio valuation exception permitted by IFRS 13:48, that fact [IFRS 13:96]	X		

| Required disclosure | Assets and liabilities measured at fair value (FV) in the statement of financial position after the date of initial recognition | | FV disclosed in notes only |
	Recurring	Non-recurring	
For liabilities measured at fair value, the existence of inseparable third-party credit enhancements and whether they are reflected in the fair value measurement of the liabilities [IFRS 13:98]	X	X	
The disclosures below only apply to Level 3 fair value measurements			
Quantitative information about the significant unobservable inputs used in the fair value measurement [IFRS 13:93(d)]	X	X	

	Assets and liabilities measured at fair value (FV) in the statement of financial position after the date of initial recognition		
Required disclosure	**Recurring**	**Non-recurring**	**FV disclosed in notes only**
Reconciliation of movements in fair value from opening to closing balances, showing separately: [IFRS 13:93(e)] • total gains and losses recognised in profit or loss (including the line items in profit or loss);	X		
• total gains and losses recognised in other comprehensive income (including the line items in other comprehensive income);	X		
• purchases, sales, issues, settlements (each disclosed separately); and	X		
• the amounts of transfers into and out of Level 3 separately (including the reasons for those transfers and the entity's policy for determining that a transfer has occurred)	X		

	Assets and liabilities measured at fair value (FV) in the statement of financial position after the date of initial recognition		
Required disclosure	Recurring	Non-recurring	FV disclosed in notes only
Amount of total gains and losses for the period recognised in profit or loss that is attributable to the change in unrealised gains or losses for those assets or liabilities held at the reporting date, and the line items in profit or loss in which those unrealised gains or losses are recognised [IFRS 13:93(f)]	X		
Description of the valuation processes used, including a discussion of how the entity decides on valuation policies and procedures and how it analyses changes in fair value from period to period [IFRS 13:93(g)]	X	X	

	Assets and liabilities measured at fair value (FV) in the statement of financial position after the date of initial recognition		
Required disclosure	Recurring	Non-recurring	FV disclosed in notes only
Narrative description of the sensitivity of the fair value measurement to changes in unobservable inputs if a change in those inputs might result in a significantly different fair value measurement and a description of the interrelationships between those inputs and other unobservable inputs, if any, including how those interrelationships might magnify or mitigate the impact on fair value arising from changes in such inputs. The narrative description of the sensitivity should include, as a minimum, all significant unobservable inputs used in the fair value measurement [IFRS 13:93(h)(i)]	X		

	Assets and liabilities measured at fair value (FV) in the statement of financial position after the date of initial recognition		
Required disclosure	**Recurring**	**Non-recurring**	**FV disclosed in notes only**
For financial assets and liabilities, when a change in one or more of the unobservable inputs to reflect reasonably possible alternative assumptions would change fair value significantly, that fact, the effect of those changes, and how the effect of such a change is calculated [IFRS 13:93(h)(ii)]	X		

12 Future developments

In September 2014, the IASB issued an exposure draft, ED/2014/4 *Measuring Quoted Investments in Subsidiaries, Joint Ventures and Associates at Fair Value (Proposed amendments to IFRS 10, IFRS 12, IAS 27, IAS 28 and IAS 36 and Illustrative Examples for IFRS 13)*. Although no amendments are proposed for the Standard, the proposals are relevant in the context of IFRS 13 because they relate to the unit of account for measurement of fair value (see **3.2.1**). See the 'future developments' sections of the relevant chapters of this manual (dealing with IFRS 10, IFRS 12, IAS 27, IAS 28 and IAS 36) for details of the proposed amendments.

A7 Property, plant and equipment

Contents

1 Introduction

1.1 Overview of IAS 16

IAS 16 *Property, Plant and Equipment* specifies the required accounting treatment for most types of property, plant and equipment, and addresses issues such as the recognition of assets, the determination of their carrying amounts, and the depreciation charges and impairment losses to be recognised in relation to them.

Under IAS 16, property, plant and equipment is initially measured at its cost, subsequently measured using either a cost or a revaluation model, and depreciated so that its depreciable amount is allocated on a systematic basis over its useful life.

1.2 Amendments to IAS 16 since the last edition of this manual

None. IAS 16 was most recently amended in June 2014.

2 Scope

2.1 Scope – general

IAS 16 should be applied when accounting for property, plant and equipment, which the Standard defines as tangible items that:

[IAS 16:6]

- are held for use in the production or supply of goods or services, for rental to others, or for administrative purposes; and

- are expected to be used during more than one period.

IAS 16 is applied except when another Standard requires or permits a different accounting treatment. [IAS 16:2] An example of another Standard requiring a different accounting treatment for property, plant and equipment is IAS 17 *Leases* which prescribes a different approach as regards recognition for assets held under leases.

The Standard excludes the following from its scope:

[IAS 16:3]

- property, plant and equipment classified as held for sale in accordance with IFRS 5 *Non-current Assets Held for Sale and Discontinued Operations* (see **chapter A20**);

- biological assets related to agricultural activity other than bearer plants (addressed by IAS 41 *Agriculture* – see **chapter A38**). IAS 16 applies to bearer plants but it does not apply to the produce on bearer plants; and

Bearer plants related to agricultural activity were brought within the scope of IAS 16 by amendments in June 2014 (see **2.6**).

- mineral rights and mineral reserves such as oil, natural gas and similar non-regenerative resources.

Although biological assets (other than bearer plants) and mineral rights and reserves are excluded from the scope of IAS 16, the Standard does apply to property, plant and equipment used to develop or maintain those assets. [IAS 16:3] Thus, for example, it applies to agricultural land.

The term 'mineral rights' is not defined in IFRSs. In practice, it is often used to refer to both an 'intangible' right to explore or mine and the 'tangible' underlying mineral reserve. The illustrative examples accompanying IFRS 3 *Business Combinations* list 'use rights' such as drilling rights as an example of a contract-based intangible asset that should be recognised separately from goodwill in a business combination. However, it is not always possible to distinguish the intangible right from the tangible element. In accordance with paragraph 4 of IAS 38 *Intangible Assets*, an entity should assess which element is more significant when an asset incorporates both intangible and tangible elements. For that reason, the entity should assess whether the underlying reserve or the right to mine is more significant. If the tangible resource/reserve is the more significant element, the combined mineral rights should be classified as tangible.

Factors to consider in this assessment include:

- whether the rights are granted for extraction of the mineral resource;
- whether the rights include ownership of the land on which the mineral resources are located; and
- whether the rights are granted for exploration only.

Investment property, including property being constructed or developed for future use as investment property, is within the scope of IAS 40 *Investment Property*. When an entity chooses to apply the cost model to investment properties under IAS 40, it should use the cost model as specified in IAS 16.

2.2 Classification of hotel properties

The question is often asked as to whether hotel properties should be classified as property, plant and equipment within the scope of IAS 16 or as investment properties within the scope of IAS 40. The key determinant is whether the owner acts primarily as the hotel operator or as a landlord. If the property owner's primary source of income from the property depends on day-to-day or week-by-week occupancy of hotel rooms and usage of restaurants and other facilities, and the property owner is providing services directly to hotel guests and diners, the hotel is likely to be property held by the entity for use in the production of services, in which case IAS 16 applies. On the other hand, if the owner's primary source of income from the property comes from longer-term leases (months and years rather than days or weeks), the hotel is likely to be an investment property, in which case IAS 40 applies. That is the case even if the property owner provides a relatively insignificant amount of ancillary services such as cleaning. Management should make the determination based on facts and circumstances. It is not a matter of accounting policy choice.

IAS 40 acknowledges that it may be difficult to determine when ancillary services are so significant that a property does not qualify as an investment property. For example, the owner of the hotel may transfer certain responsibilities to a third party under a management contract. The terms of such management contracts vary widely. At one end of the spectrum, the owner's position may, in substance, be that of a passive investor. At the other end of the spectrum, the owner may simply have outsourced certain day-to-day functions, while retaining significant exposure to variations in the cash flows generated by the operations of the hotel. In the latter case, classification as an investment property is not appropriate.

Classification as an investment property may also be acceptable if the direct involvement of the reporting entity in the operation of the property is short-term. For example, following the acquisition of a hotel, if the reporting entity continues to operate it while seeking a suitable third party manager, the operation of the hotel can be seen to be incidental to the underlying objective of investment return.

2.3 Base stock of assets

It is common for restaurants and similar operations to maintain a base stock inventory of items such as silverware and dishes in an unchanging amount. Additions to the stock are recognised in profit or loss. On average, the turnover of the items is likely to exceed one year. These items are tangible assets held for use in the supply of goods and services and are expected to be used for more than one period. They are therefore appropriately classified as property, plant and equipment and should not be included in current assets.

2.4 Property, plant and equipment used in research activities

Property, plant and equipment used in research activities should be accounted for in the same way as other property, plant and equipment under IAS 16. Paragraph 54 of IAS 38 *Intangible Assets*, which requires all expenditure on research to be recognised as an expense when it is incurred, does not require that expenditure on property, plant and equipment used in research activities should be recognised in profit or loss when acquired. However, the depreciation of property, plant and equipment used in research activities constitutes a research expense to which IAS 38 applies.

2.5   Gold bullion held by a central bank

Central banks commonly hold significant gold reserves to support the national currency. Such reserves are not traded and the levels frequently do not change from one year to the next.

The gold bullion should be classified as property, plant and equipment, and accounted for under IAS 16, using either the cost model or the revaluation model. Gold bullion meets the definition of property, plant and equipment in that it is a tangible item, held for use in the supply of services (stabilisation of the exchange rates for the benefit of entities operating in the jurisdiction) and can be expected to be used during more than one period.

IFRS 9:IG B.1 *Definition of a financial instrument: gold bullion* (which is also included in the implementation guidance accompanying IAS 39 *Financial Instruments: Recognition and Measurement*) states that gold bullion "... is a commodity. Although bullion is highly liquid, there is no contractual right to receive cash or another financial asset inherent in bullion". Accordingly, gold bullion is not a financial instrument and is outside the scope of IFRS 9 *Financial Instruments* (or, for entities that have not yet adopted IFRS 9, IAS 39).

In the circumstances described, the gold bullion is not held for sale; it is not in the process of production for sale, nor is it to be consumed in a production process or the rendering of services. Therefore, it does not meet the definition of inventories in paragraph 6 of IAS 2 *Inventories*.

2.6   Bearer plants related to agricultural activity

2.6.1   Bearer plants included within the scope of IAS 16

Although biological assets related to agricultural activity are generally excluded from the scope of IAS 16 (and accounted for in accordance with IAS 41 *Agriculture* – see **chapter A38**), an exception applies for 'bearer plants'. A bearer plant is a living plant that:

[IAS 16:6]

- is used in the production or supply of agricultural produce;

- is expected to bear produce for more than one period; and

- has a remote likelihood of being sold as agricultural produce, except for incidental scrap sales.

The following additional guidance on the identification of bearer plants is included in IAS 41:

- the following are *not* bearer plants (and, consequently, are within the scope of IAS 41 rather than IAS 16):
  [IAS 41:5A]

  - plants cultivated to be harvested as agricultural produce (e.g. trees grown for use as lumber);

  - plants cultivated to produce agricultural produce when there is more than a remote likelihood that the entity will also harvest and sell the plant as agricultural produce, other than as incidental scrap sales (e.g. trees that are cultivated both for their fruit and their lumber); and

  - annual crops (e.g. maize and wheat); and

- when bearer plants are no longer used to bear produce, they might be cut down and sold as scrap (e.g. for use as firewood). Such incidental scrap sales would not prevent a plant from satisfying the definition of a bearer plant. [IAS 41:5B]

Bearer plants were brought into the scope of IAS 16 by *Agriculture: Bearer Plants (Amendments to IAS 16 and IAS 41)* issued in June 2014. Examples of such assets include mature oil palms and rubber trees. The IASB determined that these assets are more appropriately accounted for under IAS 16 because, once mature, they are held by an entity solely to grow produce over their productive life. Under IAS 16, entities have a choice to measure these assets subsequent to initial recognition using either a cost model or a revaluation model. [IAS 16:BC38]

In developing the June 2014 amendments, the IASB specifically considered the case of crops that are perennial plants because their roots remain in the ground to sprout for the next period's crop; an example would be sugar cane if its roots are retained for a second harvest. The Board agreed that, if an entity retains the roots to bear produce for more than one period and the roots are not later sold, the roots would meet the definition of a bearer plant. [IAS 16:BC60]

2.6.2   Livestock used as bearer biological assets

The scope of the June 2014 amendments is limited to bearer *plants*. Livestock held for breeding purposes only, with only a remote likelihood that it will ever be sold, should be accounted for under IAS 41.

In the course of its deliberations on the June 2014 amendments, the IASB considered whether livestock should be treated in the same manner as bearer plants. However, the Board decided to restrict the scope of the amendments to plants because, unlike plants, livestock is not attached to land and there is usually an active market for livestock, meaning that fair value information is more likely to be readily available and easier to apply than cost measurement. [IAS 16:BC52]

2.6.3   Plants with more than one potential use

Plants which have more than one potential use (e.g. trees cultivated both for their lumber and their fruit) are not bearer plants and should be accounted for under IAS 41. [IAS 41:5A(b)] In its Basis for Conclusions on the June 2014 amendments, the IASB clarified that bearer plants within the scope of IAS 16 are those that are *solely* used in the production or supply of agricultural produce. [IAS 16:BC48 - BC50]

If plants are intended to be sold as agricultural produce after they have been used as bearer plants for a period of time, apart from incidental scrap sales, they are not considered to be solely used in the production or supply of agricultural produce and, consequently, should be accounted for under IAS 41, including during the period for which they are used as bearer plants. [IAS 16:BC51]

2.6.4   Bearer plants that are not yet mature

Bearer plants that are not yet mature should be accounted for under IAS 16 provided that it is intended that they will only be used in the production or supply of agricultural produce. In the course of its deliberations on the June 2014 amendments, the IASB determined that, although such plants continue to undergo biological transformation, they should be accounted for under IAS 16 throughout their lives. [IAS 16:BC70 - BC72]

2.6.5   Produce growing on a bearer plant

Consistent with the requirements for other biological assets, produce growing on a bearer plant should be accounted for at fair value less costs to sell under IAS 41 from the date it starts to grow (unless the presumption in IAS 41 that fair value can be measured reliably has been rebutted – see **5.2.5** in **chapter A38**). [IAS 16:BC73 - BC78]

2.6.6 Unit of measure for bearer plants

The IASB considered whether guidance was required regarding the unit of measure for bearer plants (e.g. is it the individual plant or some larger aggregation, such as a field or a planting cycle?). Specific issues arise in this regard because agricultural activity is often a continuous process, meaning that older plants are continuously removed from service and replaced. If bearer plants are accounted for using a cost model, this continuous process needs to be made discrete.

Without providing specific guidance, the Board noted that applying the recognition criteria in IAS 16 to bearer plants will require judgement. This would give an entity flexibility, depending on its circumstances, to decide how to aggregate individual plants for the purpose of determining a measurable unit of bearer plants. [IAS 16:BC80 & BC81]

2.6.7 Effective date and transition provisions for the June 2014 amendments

The June 2014 amendments are effective for annual periods beginning on or after 1 January 2016, with earlier application permitted. If an entity applies the June 2014 amendments for an accounting period beginning before 1 January 2016, that fact is required to be disclosed. [IAS 16:81K]

In general, the June 2014 amendments are required to be applied retrospectively in accordance with IAS 8 *Accounting Policies, Changes in Accounting Estimates and Errors*, with prior year amounts restated to reflect any reclassification of bearer plants. Two exceptions apply, as set out below.

[IAS 16:80B & 80C]

- An entity may elect to measure an item of bearer plants at its fair value at the beginning of the earliest period presented in the first financial statements in which the entity applies the June 2014 amendments and use that fair value as its deemed cost at that date. Any difference between the previous carrying amount and fair value should be recognised in opening retained earnings at the beginning of the earliest period presented.

Therefore, for example, if an entity adopts the June 2014 amendments for its annual financial statements to 31 December 2015, and it presents one year of comparative information in those financial statements, the entity may measure a bearer plant at fair value at 1 January 2014 and that fair value is the deemed cost of the bearer plant at that date. Any difference between the previous carrying amount and the fair value at 1 January 2014 is recognised in retained earnings at that date. The requirements of IAS 16 regarding depreciation, impairment etc. should be applied from 1 January 2014. This relief is aimed primarily at entities that have previously measured bearer plants at fair value less costs to sell in accordance with IAS 41 and for which the reconstruction of historical cost data for those bearer plants might be costly. [IAS 16:BC95]

- When the June 2014 amendments are first applied, an entity need not present the quantitative information required by paragraph 28(f) of IAS 8 for the current period.

IAS 8:28(f) generally requires an entity to disclose, for the current period and for each prior period presented, the amount of any adjustment for each financial statement line item affected when an IFRS is first applied. The IASB concluded that it would be burdensome for entities to present this information for the year in which the June 2014 amendments are first applied because it would require an entity to maintain dual systems in the year of initial application. However, entities are required to provide the disclosures required under IAS 8:28(f) for prior periods presented in the financial statements in the year of application. [IAS 16:BC97]

3 Recognition

3.1 General recognition criteria

The recognition criteria for property, plant and equipment are derived from the general principles for asset recognition reflected in the *Conceptual Framework for Financial Reporting* (see **chapter A2**). An item of property, plant and equipment is to be recognised as an asset if, and only if:

[IAS 16:7]

- it is probable that future economic benefits associated with the asset will flow to the entity; and

- the cost of the asset to the entity can be measured reliably.

3.2 Spare parts, stand-by equipment and servicing equipment

Items such as spare parts, stand-by equipment and servicing equipment should be recognised as property, plant and equipment when they meet the definition of property, plant and equipment. Otherwise, they should be classified as inventories in accordance with IAS 2 *Inventories*. [IAS 16:8]

Example 3.2

Classification of stand-by equipment

An entity has installed two turbines. One will produce energy for the plant, and the other will be used as a back-up in case the first turbine fails, or is otherwise rendered out of service. The probability that the spare turbine will ever be used is very low. The spare turbine is necessary, however, to ensure the continuity of the production process if the first turbine fails. The useful life of the stand-by turbine will equal the life of the plant, which is the same as the useful life of the primary turbine.

IAS 16:8 states that stand-by equipment qualifies as property, plant and equipment when it meets the definition of property, plant and equipment. Although the definition in IAS 16:6 (see **2.1**) requires that the entity should expect to use the turbine during more than one period, it does not state that such use should be regular. Therefore, the spare turbine is classified as property, plant and equipment and should be depreciated from the date it becomes available for use (i.e. when it is in the location and condition necessary for it to be capable of operating in the manner intended by management). (See also **7.6.5** for a discussion of depreciation of stand-by equipment.)

3.3 Items acquired for safety or environmental reasons

The acquisition of property, plant and equipment for safety or environmental reasons, while not directly increasing the future economic benefits of any particular existing item of property, plant and equipment, may be necessary in order for the entity to obtain the future economic benefits from its other assets. Such acquisitions qualify for recognition as assets, in that they enable future economic benefits to be derived from related assets in excess of what could otherwise have been derived. The resulting carrying amount of such an asset and the related assets is reviewed for impairment in accordance with IAS 36 *Impairment of Assets*. [IAS 16:11] IAS 16 cites the following example.

Example 3.3

Items acquired for safety or environmental reasons

[IAS 16:11]

A chemical manufacturer is required to install certain new chemical-handling processes in order to comply with environmental requirements in relation to the production and storage of dangerous chemicals. Related plant enhancements are recognised as an asset because, without them, the entity is unable to manufacture and sell chemicals.

3.4 Aggregation of individually insignificant items

IAS 16 does not prescribe what constitutes a separate item of property, plant and equipment, and allows a degree of judgement according to the entity's circumstances. It does, however, suggest that, for individually insignificant items (such as moulds, tools and dies), it may be appropriate to aggregate the items and to apply the recognition criteria to the aggregate value. [IAS 16:9]

However, IAS 16:43 requires that each part of an item of property, plant and equipment with a cost that is significant in relation to the cost of the item should be depreciated separately. Componentisation is therefore implicitly required under IAS 16:43 for all significant components of property, plant and equipment.

The determination as to whether an item is significant requires a careful assessment of the facts and circumstances. This assessment would include, at a minimum:

- comparison of the cost allocated to the item to the total cost of the aggregated property, plant and equipment; and

- consideration of the potential impact of componentisation on the depreciation expense.

3.5 Subsequent costs

3.5.1 General recognition criteria to be applied to subsequent costs

IAS 16 also deals with the recognition of costs incurred subsequently to add to, replace part of, or service a previously recognised item of property, plant and equipment. The general recognition criteria set out in **3.1** are applied to such expenditure. If the recognition criteria are met, the expenditure should be added to the carrying amount of the property, plant and equipment. If the recognition criteria are not met, the expenditure should be expensed when incurred.

3.5.2 Repairs and maintenance

The costs of the day-to-day servicing, repair or maintenance of an item of property, plant and equipment should not be recognised in the carrying amount of the item. These costs are primarily the cost of labour and other items consumed in the service/repair. They may also include the cost of small parts. [IAS 16:12]

3.5.3 Replacement parts

Costs incurred on a replacement part for property, plant and equipment are recognised in the carrying amount of the affected item of property, plant and equipment when the costs are incurred if the recognition criteria set out in **3.1** are met. [IAS 16:13]

If the cost of the replacement part is recognised in the carrying amount of an asset, the carrying amount of what was replaced should be derecognised (regardless of whether it had been identified as a component and depreciated separately), so that the replacement and the replaced item are not both carried as assets. [IAS 16:13] When it is not practicable to determine the carrying amount of the replaced part, the cost of the replacement may be used as an indication of what the cost of the replaced part was at the time it was acquired or constructed. [IAS 16:70]

Example 3.5.3

Replacement costs

A hotel operator refurbishes its hotels every ten years, on average. The cost of refurbishment is considered a replacement of assets capitalised (i.e. the recognition criteria in IAS 16:7 are met). The replacement indicates, however, that previously recognised assets may now be required to be derecognised, typically giving rise to a loss to the extent that they have not already been depreciated.

3.5.4 Major inspections or overhauls

Major inspections or overhauls may be required at regular intervals over the useful life of an item of property, plant and equipment to allow the continued use of the asset. For example, an entity might acquire a ship that requires a major overhaul, say, once every five years. When each major inspection or overhaul is performed, its cost is recognised in the carrying amount of the item of property, plant and equipment as a replacement if the recognition criteria set out at **3.1** are met. [IAS 16:14]

Any remaining carrying amount of the cost of the previous inspection is derecognised, regardless of whether the previous inspection was separately identified at the time that the asset was acquired or constructed. If the previous inspection was not separately identified, the estimated cost of a similar future inspection may, if necessary, be used as an indication of what the cost of the existing inspection component was when the asset was acquired or constructed. [IAS 16:14]

3.5.5 Substantial modifications

IAS 16 does not distinguish between subsequent expenditure that maintains the existing service potential of an asset ('repairs and maintenance') and subsequent expenditure that enhances that service potential ('improvements'). Instead, all major subsequent expenditure should be capitalised, provided that it is probable that future economic benefits will flow to the entity, and any part of the existing asset that has been replaced should be derecognised, irrespective of whether it has been depreciated separately. However, the costs of the day-to-day servicing of property, plant and equipment are not capitalised, even though they are arguably incurred in the pursuit of future economic benefits, because they are not sufficiently certain to be recognised in the carrying amount of an asset under the general recognition principle. [IAS 16:BC5 - BC12]

Accordingly, when an entity incurs both maintenance costs and substantial modification costs in relation to a specific item of property, plant and equipment, the expenditure should be analysed according to its nature. Any costs of day-to-day servicing should be accounted for in profit or loss, but substantial modification costs should be capitalised as part of the cost of the asset if it is probable that future economic benefits associated with the modification will flow to the entity.

Example 3.5.5

Substantial modification costs

A retail outlet needs to be redecorated each year. Because the expenditure is incurred on a regular basis and is not particularly large, the retailer treats the redecoration as part of the day-to-day servicing of the store and recognises an expense as it is incurred. In the current year, the entity has asked the supplier carrying out the redecoration work to install new partitioning, which is intended to make the outlet more profitable and result in additional future economic benefits.

The redecoration costs should be recognised in profit or loss as an expense under IAS 16:12, while the incremental partitioning costs should be capitalised if they satisfy the recognition criteria set out in IAS 16:7 (i.e. the cost incurred to install new partitioning can be measured reliably and it is probable that future economic benefits associated with the partitioning will flow to the entity). To the extent that the new partitioning replaces existing partitioning, the partitioning being replaced should be derecognised.

3.5.6   Subsequent expenditure on an impaired asset

When an entity incurs capital expenditure on an item of property, plant and equipment in respect of which an impairment loss has previously been recognised, the expenditure should be recognised in accordance with IAS 16 and included in the cost of the asset if the criteria in IAS 16:7 are met (see **3.1**).

In order for those criteria to be met, it must be probable that the future economic benefits associated with the expenditure will flow to the entity. An entity will generally only choose to incur additional expenditure on an impaired asset when it expects that expenditure to generate net future economic benefits. If this is the case, the criteria in IAS 16:7 are likely to be met.

Note that this analysis applies equally to subsequent expenditure on a completed asset and continuing expenditure on an asset in the course of construction.

4 Measurement at recognition

4.1 Measurement at cost

When an item of property, plant and equipment qualifies for recognition as an asset, it should initially be measured at its cost. [IAS 16:15]

Cost is defined as the amount of cash or cash equivalents paid or the fair value of the other consideration given to acquire an asset at the time of its acquisition or construction or, when applicable, the amount attributed to that asset when initially recognised in accordance with the specific requirements of other IFRSs (e.g. IFRS 2 *Share-based Payment*). [IAS 16:6]

4.2 Elements of cost

4.2.1 Cost of an acquired asset

4.2.1.1 Components of cost

In the case of an acquired asset, cost comprises:

[IAS 16:16]

- the purchase price, including import duties and non-refundable purchase taxes, after deducting trade discounts and rebates;

- any directly attributable costs of bringing the asset to the location and condition necessary for it to be capable of operating in the manner intended by management; and

- the initial estimate of the costs of dismantling and removing the item and restoring the site on which it is located, the obligation for which the entity incurred either when the item was acquired, or as a consequence of having used the item during a particular period for purposes other than to produce inventories during that period. (See **4.4** for guidance on how to deal with subsequent changes in the estimate of these costs and **4.2.10** for guidance regarding the cost of obligations that did not exist when the item was acquired.)

It is perhaps worth emphasising that the final element noted above should be included only when, and to the extent that, the entity has an obligation to dismantle and remove the asset, and has therefore recognised a provision in accordance with IAS 37 *Provisions, Contingent Liabilities and Contingent Assets*. For many assets, no such obligation will exist.

Costs cited by IAS 16 as suitable for inclusion in the cost of an item of property, plant and equipment are:

[IAS 16:17]

- costs of employee benefits arising directly from the construction or acquisition of the item of property, plant and equipment;

- costs of site preparation;

- initial delivery and handling costs;

- installation and assembly costs;

- costs of testing whether the asset is functioning properly, after deducting the net proceeds from selling any items produced while bringing the asset to that location and condition (e.g. samples produced when testing equipment) (see **4.2.1.3**); and

- professional fees.

Example 4.2.1.1A

Land clearing costs

A ski slope operator has developed a piece of land into a ski resort; as part of the development, the operator has cut down trees, cleared and graded the land and hills, and constructed ski lifts.

Should the tree cutting, land clearing and grading costs be capitalised as part of the cost of land or as part of the cost of the ski lifts?

The tree cutting, land clearing and grading costs should be capitalised as part of the cost of the land. These costs are expenditures directly attributable to bringing the land to working condition for its intended use and, therefore, are part of the cost of the land, not the ski lifts.

As required under IAS 16:59, when the cost of site dismantlement, removal and restoration is included in the cost of land, that portion of the land asset is depreciated over the period of benefits obtained by incurring those costs.

Example 4.2.1.1B

Compensation for late delivery of an asset

When, under the terms of a contract for the purchase of an asset, a supplier is required to compensate the purchaser because the asset is not delivered on

---

time (e.g. in the form of penalty payments or additional discounts), how should the purchaser account for such compensation?

In the vast majority of cases, such compensation will represent a reduction in the cost of the asset for the purchaser and it should be accounted for accordingly. For example, when compensation is calculated as a percentage of the contract price or based on notional damages suffered by the purchaser (e.g. a fixed rate per day), the compensation represents a penalty imposed on the supplier for the delayed delivery of the asset and it should be accounted for as a reduction in the cost of the asset.

However, in very limited circumstances when the contract specifies that the supplier will reimburse actual costs incurred by the purchaser as a result of the delayed delivery, it may be appropriate to account for those elements as reimbursements of costs under paragraphs 53 and 54 of IAS 37 *Provisions, Contingent Liabilities and Contingent Assets* (see **section 5** of **chapter A12**). Such a treatment may be appropriate if:

- the costs being reimbursed are clearly identifiable and are actual incremental costs incurred by the purchaser as a result of the delay; and

- the compensation is payable whether or not the asset is eventually delivered to the purchaser.

If it is determined that the amounts are appropriately accounted for as reimbursements, they should be recognised in profit or loss when it is virtually certain that they will be received (see IAS 37:53). Under IAS 37:54, they may be offset against the related costs in profit or loss or presented as 'other income'.

4.2.1.2   Costs not suitable for capitalisation

Costs listed in IAS 16 as unsuitable for capitalisation and, therefore, to be expensed are:

[IAS 16:19]

- costs of opening a new facility;

- costs of introducing a new product or service (including costs of advertising and promotional activities);

- costs of conducting business in a new location, or with a new class of customer (including costs of staff training); and

- administration and other general overhead costs.

Example 4.2.1.2

Training cost as a component of the cost of an asset

An entity acquires equipment of a type that its employees have never operated before. During the installation period, the employees receive extensive training on the equipment. The cost to the entity includes the incremental cost of hiring experts to conduct the training, and the directly attributable cost of wages of the employees during the training period. The equipment could not be used by the entity unless its employees received the training.

These training costs do not qualify as a component of the cost of the equipment; they do not fall within the scope of costs directly attributable to bringing the asset to the location and condition necessary for it to be capable of operating in the manner intended by the management. The equipment would be capable of operating in the manner intended by the management without the entity incurring the training cost – even though the employees would not know how to operate the equipment.

In accordance with paragraphs 15 and 69 of IAS 38 *Intangible Assets*, the training costs will typically be recognised as an expense when incurred.

4.2.1.3 Offsetting proceeds from selling output against costs of testing property, plant and equipment

Example 4.2.1.3

Offsetting proceeds from selling output against costs of testing property, plant and equipment

Entity R is constructing a petrochemical complex with several autonomous manufacturing facilities. Construction of some of the facilities has been completed; these have been certified as ready for commercial production by the relevant authority and they have commenced producing chemicals that are sold on the market. Other facilities are still in the commissioning phase and they are not yet ready for production.

IAS 16:16 states that the cost of an item of property, plant and equipment comprises "any costs directly attributable to bringing the asset to the location and condition necessary for it to be capable of operating in the manner intended by management". IAS 16:17 states that costs directly attributable to bringing an asset to the location and condition necessary for it to be capable of operating in the manner intended by management include "costs of testing whether the asset is functioning properly, *after deducting the net proceeds from selling any items produced while bringing the asset to that location and condition (such as samples produced when testing equipment)*" (emphasis added).

In the circumstances described, is it appropriate to offset the proceeds received from selling chemicals produced by the completed manufacturing facilities against the costs of testing the other facilities still in the commissioning phase (i.e. could such proceeds be accounted for as a reduction in the cost of facilities under construction, rather than recognised as revenue in profit or loss)?

IAS 16 does not provide any specific guidance in respect of assets or projects that are completed in parts and the extent to which one part can be considered to be 'in the location and condition necessary for it to be capable of operating in the manner intended by management' while construction of other parts continues. Paragraphs 24 and 25 of IAS 23 *Borrowing Costs* do, however, address this topic in the context of capitalising borrowing costs on qualifying assets, as follows (see **3.5.3.6** in **chapter A18**).

"When an entity completes the construction of a qualifying asset in parts and each part is capable of being used while construction continues on other parts, the entity shall cease capitalising borrowing costs when it completes substantially all the activities necessary to prepare that part for its intended use or sale.

A business park comprising several buildings, each of which can be used individually, is an example of a qualifying asset for which each part is capable of being usable while construction continues on other parts. An example of a qualifying asset that needs to be complete before any part can be used is an industrial plant involving several processes which are carried out in sequence at different parts of the plant within the same site, such as a steel mill."

Applying this principle to the circumstances under consideration, it is likely that the petrochemical complex should be thought of as consisting of a number of parts (the autonomous manufacturing facilities), each of which is capable of operating in the manner intended by management while construction of the other parts continues. Consequently, when an individual facility has been completed and is ready for commercial use, it should be considered to be in the location and condition necessary for it to be capable of operating in the manner intended by management. When that point is reached, proceeds received from the sale of chemicals produced by that facility should be recognised as revenue in profit or loss (subject to meeting the requirements of IFRS 15 *Revenue from Contracts with Customers* (see **chapter A14**) or, for entities that have not yet adopted IFRS 15, IAS 18 *Revenue* (see **appendix A1**)) because those chemicals are produced after the facility is operational and, consequently, proceeds from their sale do not qualify for deduction from the cost of the asset in accordance with IAS 16:17(e).

4.2.2 Cost of a self-constructed asset

4.2.2.1 Components of cost for a self-constructed asset

The cost of a self-constructed asset is determined using the same principles as for an acquired asset, as set out at **section 4.2.1**. IAS 16 states that if an entity makes similar assets for sale in the normal course of business, the cost of the asset is usually the same as the cost of constructing the asset for sale, in accordance with the principles of IAS 2 *Inventories*. [IAS 16:22]

For example, if the entity were a car manufacturer, the costs used to determine the cost of a car for sale under IAS 2 could also be used in determining the cost of a car that will be held as property, plant and equipment.

However, if the entity does not construct similar assets for sale, only those elements of costs described in IAS 16:16 (see **4.2.1.1**) can be incorporated in the cost of a self-constructed asset. Accordingly, costs which can be included are:

- direct materials;
- direct labour costs; and
- unavoidable costs that are directly attributable to the construction activity (i.e. costs that would have been avoided if the asset had not been constructed).

This concept of 'directly attributable' costs is different from the concepts applied in the measurement of costs of conversion in IAS 2. The latter include a systematic allocation of fixed and variable production overheads that are incurred in converting materials into finished goods. Such systematic allocation of fixed overheads is not appropriate under IAS 16, because IAS 16 looks to capitalise only directly attributable costs.

The Standard gives no further guidance on how to determine which costs should be viewed as 'directly attributable'. Costs that are directly incremental as a result of the construction of a specific asset would generally be eligible, if they relate to bringing the asset to working condition. When an entity regularly constructs assets, however, it is possible that some element of apparently 'fixed' costs may also be directly attributable. In such circumstances, an entity should consider which costs would have been avoided if none of those assets had been constructed. For example, a construction company may employ builders who are normally engaged on the construction of properties for sale. If those builders are engaged for part of the year on the construction of a new head office for the entity, their direct employment costs should be capitalised as part of the cost of the new head office.

It is, therefore, likely that some variable production overheads may be incorporated into the cost of a self-constructed asset (depending on whether they could have been avoided absent the self-construction of the asset) but that no fixed production overheads can be incorporated.

4.2.2.2   Administration and overhead costs

Administration and other general overhead costs are not a component of the cost of property, plant and equipment because they cannot be directly attributed to the acquisition of the asset or bringing the asset to its working condition.

4.2.2.3   Costs incurred to demolish existing structures

The costs that may be included in the carrying amount of an asset are limited to those that arise directly from the construction or acquisition of the asset. When, for example, costs are incurred to demolish existing structures in order to build on a site, the cost of demolition may be incremental to the construction cost or it may be associated with derecognition of a previously held asset. It depends on whether the existing structures were previously used in the entity's business, or were acquired as part of the site with the specific intention of demolishing them. In the latter case, the demolition costs are clearly incremental and should be included in the cost of the new asset. In the former case, the cost of the old asset should be written off to profit or loss through accelerated depreciation once the decision to demolish is made; the demolition costs incurred relate to the derecognition of the old asset and should be expensed when incurred.

Example 4.2.2.3

Existing building demolished in order to construct new building

In 20X1, Company E purchased land and buildings for CU100 million (land: CU40 million and building: CU60 million). The building is used by Company E in its business; it is classified as property, plant and equipment and is depreciated over its estimated useful life. In 20X3, Company E demolishes the building and constructs a new building for its own use on the same piece of land. The carrying amount of the old building prior to demolition was CU55 million.

Should the CU55 million be written off to profit or loss or be capitalised as part of the cost of the new building?

The carrying amount of CU55 million should be written off to profit or loss. Under IAS 16, Company E is required to depreciate the building to its residual value over its useful life. The remaining useful life of Company E's building is equivalent to the period from when Company E decided to demolish the building to the demolition date in 20X3. The residual value of the building is zero because the building will be demolished. Therefore, after management's decision to demolish the building, Company E should revise its estimates for both the remaining useful life and the residual value of the building and should adjust the depreciation expense accordingly, resulting in a write-down of the building to zero before demolition.

4.2.2.4 Bearer plants related to agricultural activities

Bearer plants related to agricultural activities are accounted for in the same way as self-constructed items of property, plant and equipment before they are in the location and condition necessary to bear produce. Consequently, references to 'construction' in IAS 16 should be read as covering activities that are necessary to cultivate bearer plants before they are in the location and condition necessary to be capable of producing in the manner intended by management. [IAS 16:22A]

IAS 16:22A was added to the Standard as part of the June 2014 amendments which brought bearer plants within the scope of IAS 16 (see **2.6**).

4.2.2.5 Additional requirements for self-constructed assets

The following principles also apply in relation to self-constructed assets:

[IAS 16:22]

- any internal profits are eliminated in arriving at the cost of an asset;
- the costs of abnormal amounts of wasted material, labour or other resources incurred in the production of the self-constructed asset are excluded from its cost; and
- borrowing costs incurred during the period of production should be included in accordance with IAS 23 *Borrowing Costs* if the self-constructed asset meets the definition of a qualifying asset (see **chapter A18**).

Example 4.2.2.5

Cost of abnormal amounts of waste in producing a self-constructed asset

A power company, Company P, signed a contract with a contractor to construct a power plant. Company P believed that the quality of the construction work was poor and terminated the construction contract. The contractor sued Company P for breach of contract and Company P lost. Company P then paid a lump sum to the contractor as compensation for the breach of contract, and the construction work was resumed thereafter.

Should the lump sum compensation paid to the contractor be recognised immediately as an expense or added to the construction cost of the power plant?

The amount does not fall within the scope of costs that are directly attributable to bringing the asset to the location and condition necessary for it to be capable of operating in the manner intended by management. This cost is similar in nature to the cost of abnormal amounts of wasted material, labour or other resources described in IAS 16:22 and, therefore, should be expensed.

See **3.5.6** for a discussion of the appropriate accounting when an entity continues to incur capital expenditure on an item of property, plant and equipment in respect of which an impairment loss has previously been recognised.

4.2.3 Cost of dismantling, removal and site restoration

Costs incurred by an entity in respect of obligations for dismantling, removing and restoring the site on which an item of property, plant and equipment is located are recognised and measured in accordance with IAS 37 *Provisions, Contingent Liabilities and Contingent Assets*. If the obligations are incurred when the asset is acquired, or during a period when the item is used other than to produce inventories, they are included in the cost of the item of property, plant and equipment, as specified in **4.2.1**. If the obligations are incurred during a period when the entity uses the item of property, plant and equipment to produce inventories, the costs are accounted for under IAS 2 *Inventories*. [IAS 16:18]

The accounting for changes in such obligations is discussed at **4.4** and accounting for the cost of obligations that did not exist when the item was acquired is discussed at **4.2.10**.

4.2.4   Start-up or commissioning period

It is appropriate to recognise directly attributable costs in the carrying amount of an item of property, plant and equipment during a commissioning period in which it is not possible to operate at normal levels because of the need to run machinery, test equipment, or ensure the proper operation of the equipment. This circumstance generally relates to the physical preparation for use. An example would be a printing press if it is necessary to run it for a period in order to achieve full functionality.

The following are examples of costs that are *not* included in the carrying amount of an item of property, plant and equipment:

[IAS 16:20]

- costs incurred while an item capable of operating in the manner intended by management has yet to be brought into use or is operated at less than full capacity;

- initial operating losses, such as those incurred while demand for the item's output builds up; and

- costs of relocating or reorganising part or all of an entity's operations.

See **4.2.1.3** for an example addressing whether proceeds from selling output can be offset against the costs of testing an item of property, plant and equipment.

4.2.5   Incidental operations

Some operations occur in connection with the construction or development of an item of property, plant and equipment, but are not necessary to bring the item to the location and condition necessary for it to be capable of operating in the manner intended by management. These incidental operations may occur before or during the construction or development activities. For example, income may be earned through using a building site as a car park until construction starts. Because these incidental operations are not necessary to bring an item of property, plant and equipment to the location and condition necessary for it to be capable of operating in the manner intended by management, the income and related expenses of incidental operations are recognised in profit or loss, and included in their respective classifications of income and expense. [IAS 16:21]

4.2.6   Reimbursement of part of the cost of an asset

Example 4.2.6

Reimbursement of part of the cost of an asset

Company A enters into a contract with Company B to produce and sell a specific product. Company A needs to transform a major part of its plant to be able to produce that product, and commissions the transformation work from a third party, Company C, unconnected with Company A and Company B. The transformation costs are significant and exclusively for the purpose of this sales contract. As a result, Company A and Company B enter into an agreement under which Company B will reimburse Company A for a portion of the transformation costs. The cash received from Company B can only be used to offset the costs of the transformation for Company A.

Should the reimbursement be deducted from the cost of the transformation?

No. From the perspective of Company A, two transactions are occurring: the purchase of services (transformation costs) from Company C, and the supply of products to Company B. Accordingly, Company A must determine whether the amount receivable from Company B relates to the former or to the latter.

The arrangement between Company A and Company B is within the scope of IFRS 15 *Revenue from Contracts with Customers*. While, in this case, the cash from Company B must be used to acquire transformation services from Company C that will create assets controlled by Company A and to be used exclusively to provide Company B with the supply of a specific product, the amount received as a reimbursement from Company B should be treated as revenue in accordance with IFRS 15, and not as a reduction in the cost of the transformation. This is because Company B's contract is only with Company A and, therefore, the transaction price (as defined in IFRS 15) will include all amounts payable by Company B to Company A.

The following accounting should be applied:

* when Company A receives the reimbursement from Company B, the amount should be deferred and subsequently recognised as revenue in accordance with the requirements of IFRS 15 in relation to the specific contract; and

* the cost of the transformation should be recognised separately, without any offset of the amount received by Company B. as property, plant and equipment, without any offset of the amount received from Company B.

For entities that have not yet adopted IFRS 15, both IAS 18 *Revenue* and the specific requirements of IFRIC 18 *Transfers of Assets from Customers* apply (see **section 2.4** of **appendix A1**). Nevertheless, it would still be necessary for Company A to account for the full amount received from Company B as revenue, and for the amount paid to Company C to be recognised separately as a cost of transformation.

4.2.7 Broker's commission rebate to purchaser of property

Example 4.2.7

Broker's commission rebate to purchaser of property

During negotiations to purchase a property, the purchaser was unwilling to accept the seller's best offer. To induce the purchaser to proceed with the transaction, the broker agreed to rebate a portion of the seller-paid commission to the purchaser.

As far as the purchaser is concerned, only one transaction has occurred – the purchase of property. The commission rebate is not immediate income to the purchaser. The seller's best offer is not the price that the purchaser actually paid. If the purchaser had been required to pay a brokerage commission, that commission would have been part of the cost of the property as a cost necessarily incurred to obtain the asset. In the circumstances described, the commission rebate is similarly a component of the cost of the property.

4.2.8 Utility fees paid to a government

In some jurisdictions, developers of factories, offices, apartment buildings and shopping malls must pay a 'capacity fee' to the government for the privilege of being able to purchase, on an ongoing basis, defined quantities of electricity and other utilities beyond certain minimum quantities that can be purchased without paying the fee. The fee is paid on a one-off basis and covers supply, either on an indefinite basis or at least for a substantial number of years. However, the building owner still pays the market rate to purchase the electricity and other utilities. The capacity fee attaches to the entity that owns the building, and it can be transferred to another building if the capacity allowed by the fee is not fully utilised.

Because a capacity fee is transferable between buildings, it is not part of the cost of the building but should be recognised as a purchased intangible asset in its own right. As such, it is subject to the requirements of IAS 38 *Intangible Assets* relating to amortisation and impairment (see **chapter A9**).

If, instead, a capacity fee were attached to the building and not transferable, it would be recognised as part of the cost of the building and depreciated.

4.2.9 Cessation of capitalisation

Recognition of costs in the carrying amount of an item of property, plant and equipment ceases when the item is in the location and condition necessary for it to be capable of operating in the manner intended by management.

Therefore, costs incurred in using or redeploying an item are not included in the carrying amount of that item. [IAS 16:20]

In the case of a self-constructed asset, or the installation of a major asset, a policy decision should be made and applied consistently as to what event or activity characterises the point at which an asset's physical construction/installation is complete (i.e. when the item is in the location and condition necessary for it to be capable of operating in the manner intended by management), so that all costs incurred after that point are identified and expensed. When a commissioning period is involved, it will similarly be essential to determine in principle the point that characterises reaching the capability of operating at normal levels, and then to ensure that costs incurred after reaching that point are captured and expensed.

When there is delay in achieving final physical completion, costs arising during the period of delay are likely to fall into the category of abnormal costs and so be expensed as incurred. Borrowing costs incurred during such a period of delay will not qualify for capitalisation under IAS 23 *Borrowing Costs*, which requires that capitalisation should cease when active development is suspended (see **chapter A18**).

Regulatory consents (e.g. health and safety clearance) are sometimes required before an asset may be used legally. Cost capitalisation will not necessarily continue until such consents are in place. Management will normally seek to ensure that such consents are in place very close to the time-frame for physical completion and testing, and that they do not delay the commencement of operations. Avoidable delays in obtaining consents which prevent the start of operations should be seen as abnormal and similar in effect to an industrial dispute, with the result that capitalisation should cease (see **example 4.2.9**).

The words 'capable of operating in the manner intended by management' in IAS 16 cannot be used to justify ongoing capitalisation of costs (and postponement of depreciation) once the asset has actually been brought into use just because the asset does not live up to management's original intentions. This may, however, constitute an impairment indicator under IAS 36 *Impairment of Assets*.

Example 4.2.9

Capitalisation of costs incurred between the completion of a building and the date of approval for occupation

On 20 September 20X0, Company A completed the construction of a building intended for use as its administrative headquarters.

By law, the local health and safety authority must approve the offices for occupation before any activity can commence. This approval can be requested only when the building is physically complete, and it takes on average three months to obtain the approval.

The health and safety authority issued the approval for occupation on 20 December 20X0. In the three months from 20 September 20X0, Company A incurred CU10 of building management costs (e.g. utility and security expenses) and interest expenses. (The building is identified as a qualifying asset under IAS 23.)

Should the costs incurred by Company A between 20 September 20X0 (when the building was physically completed) and 20 December 20X0 (when the approval for occupation was issued) be included in the initial cost of the building?

Yes. The management costs incurred are considered "directly attributable to bringing the asset to the location and condition necessary for it to be capable of operating in the manner intended by management" (IAS 16:16(b)). In addition, obtaining the approval for occupation is considered to be an activity "necessary to prepare the qualifying asset for its intended use or sale" (IAS 23:25); therefore, Company A should continue to capitalise borrowing costs until the approval is obtained.

However, any abnormal amounts of wasted resources incurred in obtaining that approval should not be capitalised (IAS 16:22). For example, if the approval for occupation had taken longer than the customary three-month period from the completion of construction, due to avoidable delays caused by Company A failing to provide the required information to the health and safety authority, Company A could include in the original cost of the building only costs incurred during the time usually required to obtain the approval for occupation (in the circumstances under consideration, three months).

If the delays were due to a slow response from the health and safety authority (without cause by Company A), the capitalisation period would be extended.

4.2.10   Rehabilitation liability – change in legislation

Example 4.2.10

Rehabilitation liability – change in legislation

Company X acquired a building in 20X1. Asbestos was used in the construction of the building. During 20X5, legislation is enacted which requires Company X either to remove the asbestos or to vacate the building.

Company X obtains a reliable estimate of the costs of removing the asbestos. In accordance with IAS 37, Company X recognises a provision for the cost of removing the asbestos.

Should Company X capitalise the estimated cost of removing the asbestos from the building?

IAS 16:16 states that the cost of an item of property, plant and equipment should include the initial estimate of the costs of dismantling and removing the item and restoring the site on which it is located, the obligation for which the entity incurred either when the item was acquired, or as a consequence of having used the item during a particular period for purposes other than to produce inventories during that period (see **4.2.1**). IAS 16:BC14 confirms that IAS 16:16 does not specifically address how an entity should account for the "cost of obligations an entity did not face when it acquired the item, such as an obligation triggered by a law change enacted after the asset was acquired".

Company X should therefore assess whether the costs of removing the asbestos meet the general recognition criteria in IAS 16:7. In this scenario:

- the cost of removing the asbestos can be reliably measured; and
- it is probable that economic benefits associated with the asbestos removal will flow to Company X (because the building would otherwise be vacated).

Therefore, Company X should capitalise the estimated cost of removing the asbestos.

The change in legislation is also an indicator of impairment; consequently, when the legislation is enacted, Company X should estimate the recoverable amount of the building.

4.3   Measurement of cost

4.3.1   Measurement of cost – general

The cost of an item of property, plant and equipment (or of an element of an item) is the cash price equivalent (i.e. the amount that the entity would need to pay if it were to purchase the asset by paying cash immediately upon purchase) at the date on which the asset is recognised. [IAS 16:23]

4.3.2   Payments deferred beyond normal credit terms

When payment for an item of property, plant and equipment is deferred beyond normal credit terms, the difference between the cash price equivalent and the total payments is recognised as an interest expense over the period of credit, unless it is capitalised in accordance with the requirements of IAS 23 *Borrowing Costs* (see **chapter A18**). [IAS 16:23]

Example 4.3.2A

Deferred payment terms

On 1 January 20X1, an item of property is offered for sale at CU10 million, with payment terms being three equal instalments of CU3,333,333 over a two year period (payments are made on 1 January 20X1, 31 December 20X1 and 31 December 20X2). The property developer is offering a discount of 5 per cent (i.e. CU500,000) if payment is made in full at the time of completion of the sale and purchase agreement (which corresponds to an implicit interest rate of 5.36 per cent per annum).

A purchaser that takes up the deferred payment terms will recognise the acquisition of the asset as follows.

		CU	CU
Dr	Property, plant and equipment	9,500,000	
Cr	Cash		3,333,333
Cr	Accounts payable		6,166,667

Initial recognition of property.

The following entry will be required at the end of 20X1.

		CU	CU
Dr	Interest expense (5.36% × CU6,166,667)	330,459	
Dr	Accounts payable	3,002,874	
Cr	Cash		3,333,333

Recognition of interest expense and payment of second instalment.

The following entry will be required at the end of 20X2.

		CU	CU
Dr	Interest expense (5.36% × (CU6,166,667 − CU3,002,874))	169,541	
Dr	Accounts payable	3,163,793	
Cr	Cash		3,333,334

Recognition of interest expense and payment of final instalment.

Example 4.3.2B

Payment for an asset deferred beyond 'normal credit terms'

The commercial property market in a particular city is very slow. As an inducement to potential purchasers, a seller of commercial property in that city advertises a property for sale at 'no interest for the first three years after purchase, market rate of interest thereafter'. Other property sellers in the city are making similar offers. A buyer purchases a property on those terms. IAS 16:23 requires imputation of interest if payment for an item of property is deferred beyond 'normal credit terms'.

In this circumstance, does the three-year interest-free period represent normal credit terms?

No. The intention of IAS 16:23 is to ensure that the asset is recognised at its current cash sale price. The 'normal credit terms' requirement is intended to recognise that settlement of cash purchases often takes a few days, weeks, or even months (depending on the industry and national laws), and imputation of interest is not required in those circumstances. Particularly for a large item such as a property, however, the cash sale price would be significantly lower if cash payment is made up-front rather than deferred for three years. If the deferral period is greater than what can be considered normal credit terms, the imputed interest element should be recognised.

Example 4.3.2C

Time value of money on deposit paid for the acquisition of an asset

Company A has two choices regarding payment for an item of property, plant and equipment:

- it can pay the list price of CU10,000 when the asset is delivered in 2 years' time; or
- it can pay CU5,000 as an up-front, non-refundable deposit, and make a final payment of CU3,500 when the asset is delivered.

If Company A chooses to pay the up-front deposit, how should the time value of money associated with the deposit be accounted for?

Because such a substantial deposit is paid up-front, the total amount that Company A is required to pay is reduced; that is, the time value of money associated with the up-front payment is reflected in the total amount payable.

The deposit is non-refundable and, therefore, it is not a financial asset. Nevertheless, the deposit represents not only a payment on account for the asset but also, in effect, provides financing to the supplier. Therefore, it will be appropriate to recognise the implicit financing as part of the cost of the asset by unwinding the time value of money over time, using the discount rate implicit in the original transaction (14 per cent in the above example), as follows.

Year	Carrying amount of deposit b/fwd	Interest income at 14%	Final payment	Carrying amount of deposit/asset c/fwd
1	CU5,000	CU700		CU5,700
2	CU5,700	CU800	CU3,500	CU10,000

Including the time value of money as part of the cost of the asset is consistent with IAS 16:23, as discussed earlier in this section.

4.3.3   Exchanges of assets

When an item of property, plant and equipment is acquired in exchange for a non-monetary asset or assets, or a combination of monetary and non-monetary assets, the cost of that item is measured at fair value (even if the entity cannot immediately derecognise the asset given up) unless:

[IAS 16:24]

- the exchange transaction lacks commercial substance; or
- the fair value of neither the asset received nor the asset given up is reliably measurable.

If the acquired item is not measured at fair value, its cost is measured at the carrying amount of the asset given up.

The entity should determine whether an exchange transaction has commercial substance by considering the extent to which its future cash flows are expected to change as a result of the transaction. An exchange transaction has commercial substance if:

[IAS 16:25]

- either:

  - the configuration (risk, timing and amount) of the cash flows of the asset received differs from the configuration of the cash flows of the asset transferred; *or*

  - the entity-specific value of the portion of the entity's operations affected by the transaction changes as a result of the exchange; *and*

- the difference arising in either of the two circumstances outlined above is significant relative to the fair value of the assets exchanged.

Entity-specific value is the present value of the cash flows an entity expects to arise from the continuing use of an asset and from its disposal at the end of its useful life or expects to incur when settling a liability. [IAS 16:6] For the purpose of assessing commercial substance, post-tax cash flows are used. [IAS 16:25]

Example 4.3.3

Exchange of assets

A ship charterer owns land and buildings which are carried in its statement of financial position at an aggregate carrying amount of CU10 million, but which have a fair value of CU15 million. It exchanges the land and buildings for a ship, which has a fair value of CU18 million, and pays an additional CU3 million cash.

Provided that the transaction has commercial substance, the entity should recognise the ship at a cost of CU18 million (its fair value) and should recognise a profit on disposal of the land and buildings of CU5 million, calculated as follows:

	CU'000
Consideration received	18,000
less:	
– carrying amount of land and building disposed of	(10,000)
– cash paid	(3,000)
	5,000

	CU'000	CU'000
The required journal entry is therefore as follows.		
Dr Property, plant and equipment (ship)	18,000	
Cr Property, plant and equipment (land and buildings)		10,000
Cr Cash		3,000
Cr Profit on exchange of assets (profit or loss)		5,000

The fair value of an asset is reliably measurable if:

[IAS 16:26]

- the variability in the range of reasonable fair value measurements is not significant for that asset; or

- the probabilities of the various estimates within the range can be reasonably assessed and used when measuring fair value.

If an entity is able to measure reliably the fair value of either the asset received or the asset given up, then the fair value of the asset given up is used to measure the cost of the asset received, unless the fair value of the asset received is more clearly evident. [IAS 16:26]

4.3.4 Assets held under finance lease

The cost of assets held under finance leases is determined using the principles set out in IAS 17 *Leases* (see **chapter A17** for details). [IAS 16:27]

4.3.5 Government grants

The carrying amount of an item of property, plant and equipment may be reduced by government grants, in accordance with IAS 20 *Accounting for Government Grants and Disclosure of Government Assistance* (see **chapter A36**). [IAS 16:28]

4.3.6 Assets acquired as part of a business combination

IFRS 3 *Business Combinations* requires that property, plant and equipment of a subsidiary acquired as part of a business combination be measured initially at fair value for the purpose of inclusion in the consolidated financial statements (see **chapter A25** for detailed discussion). This fair value is the cost of the asset for the purpose of subsequent accounting under IAS 16. All other aspects of the accounting treatment for these assets, including depreciation, are determined by reference to the requirements of IAS 16.

The fair value exercise does not amount to a revaluation of the assets concerned. Accordingly, it is not necessary thereafter to comply with the revaluation model prescribed in IAS 16 merely because the assets have been recognised initially at fair value. As discussed in **section 5**, an entity makes an accounting policy choice whether to apply the cost model or the revaluation model to a particular class of assets.

4.4 IFRIC 1 *Changes in Existing Decommissioning, Restoration and Similar Liabilities*

4.4.1 IFRIC 1 – scope

IFRIC 1 *Changes in Existing Decommissioning, Restoration and Similar Liabilities* provides guidance on how to account for the effect of changes in the measurement of existing decommissioning, restoration and similar liabilities. For example, such liabilities may exist for decommissioning a plant, rehabilitating environmental damage in extractive industries, or removing equipment. IFRIC 1 applies to changes in the measurement of any existing decommissioning, restoration or similar liability that is both:

[IFRIC 1:2]

- recognised as part of the cost of an item of property, plant and equipment in accordance with IAS 16; and

- recognised as a liability in accordance with IAS 37.

The guidance below deals with how to account for changes in the measurement of an existing decommissioning, restoration or similar liability that result from changes in the estimated timing or amount of the outflow of resources required to settle the obligation, or a change in the discount rate.

4.4.2 Cost model

If the related asset is measured using the cost model:

[IFRIC 1:5]

- changes in the liability are added to, or deducted from, the cost of the related asset in the current period, except that the amount deducted from the cost of the asset must not exceed its carrying amount. If a decrease in the liability exceeds the carrying amount of the asset, the excess is recognised immediately in profit or loss; and

- if the adjustment results in an addition to the cost of an asset, the entity should consider whether this may indicate that the new carrying amount of the asset may not be fully recoverable. If so, the asset should be tested for impairment in accordance with IAS 36 (see **chapter A10**).

4.4.3 Revaluation model

If the related asset is measured using the revaluation model:

[IFRIC 1:6]

- changes in the liability alter the revaluation surplus or deficit previously recognised on that asset, so that:
  - a decrease in the liability is generally recognised in other comprehensive income and increases the revaluation surplus within equity, but is recognised immediately in profit or loss:
    - to the extent that it reverses a revaluation deficit on the asset that was previously recognised in profit or loss; or
    - to the extent that it exceeds the carrying amount that would have been recognised had the asset been carried under the cost model; and
  - an increase in the liability is recognised in other comprehensive income and reduces the revaluation surplus within equity to the extent of any credit balance relating to that asset, with the balance being recognised in profit or loss;
- a change in the liability is an indication that the asset may have to be revalued in order to ensure that the carrying amount does not differ materially from fair value at the end of the reporting period. Any such revaluation is taken into account in determining the amounts to be recognised in profit or loss or in other comprehensive income. If a revaluation is necessary, all assets of that class are revalued; and
- to comply with IAS 1 (see **5.3.1** in **chapter A4**), the change in the revaluation surplus arising from a change in the liability is separately identified and disclosed as a component of other comprehensive income.

4.4.4 Other requirements

The adjusted depreciable amount of the asset is depreciated over its useful life. Accordingly, once the related asset has reached the end of its useful life, all subsequent changes in the liability are recognised in profit or loss as they occur. This applies under both the cost model and the revaluation model. [IFRIC 1:7]

The periodic unwinding of the discount is recognised in profit or loss as a finance cost as it occurs. Capitalisation under IAS 23 *Borrowing Costs* is not permitted. [IFRIC 1:8]

5 Alternatives for measurement after recognition

5.1 Alternative bases available for measurement after recognition

IAS 16 permits two different bases for the determination of the carrying amount of property, plant and equipment at the end of subsequent reporting periods – a cost model and a revaluation model. Whichever accounting policy is selected, it is required to be applied to entire classes of property, plant and equipment. [IAS 16:29]

5.2 Cost model

When the cost model is selected, after recognition an item of property, plant and equipment is carried at cost less any accumulated depreciation and any accumulated impairment losses. [IAS 16:30]

When the cost model is used, the cost of the asset normally remains unchanged until it is derecognised. The treatment of subsequent costs is considered at **3.5**.

5.3 Revaluation model

When the revaluation model is selected, after recognition as an asset an item of property, plant and equipment whose fair value can be measured reliably is carried at a revalued amount, being its fair value at the date of the revaluation less any subsequent accumulated depreciation and any subsequent accumulated impairment losses. Revaluations are required to be carried out with sufficient regularity to ensure that the carrying amount does not differ materially from that which would be determined using fair value at the end of the reporting period. [IAS 16:31]

6 Revaluation model

6.1 Initial adoption of revaluation basis

When an entity that previously adopted IAS 16's cost model initially adopts a policy to measure property, plant and equipment using the revaluation model, this initial adoption of the valuation basis represents a change in accounting policy. However, paragraph 17 of IAS 8 *Accounting Policies, Changes in Accounting Estimates and Errors* specifies that the change should be dealt with as a revaluation rather than as a prior period adjustment. Consequently, the valuation uplift or write-down occurring on the initial adoption of the revaluation basis is dealt with in other comprehensive income (and accumulated in the revaluation surplus) or in profit or loss, as appropriate, in accordance with the requirements of IAS 16 (see **6.8**). Prior period amounts are not restated.

This is a practical and helpful exemption from the general rules for changes in accounting policies, which means that it will not be necessary to obtain valuations at the end of earlier reporting periods. One side effect of the approach, however, is that the amounts of depreciation included in current and prior year profit or loss may not be comparable, because they are likely to be based on revaluation and on cost, respectively. When the impact is significant, the entity may wish to provide a brief explanation.

6.2 Definition of fair value

Fair value is defined as "the price that would be received to sell an asset or paid to transfer a liability in an orderly transaction between market participants at the measurement date. (See IFRS 13 *Fair Value Measurement*.)" [IAS 16:6]

IAS 16 does not include any detailed guidance on how fair value should be measured; entities measuring property, plant and equipment at fair value should refer to the guidance in IFRS 13 (see **chapter A6**).

6.3 Frequency of revaluations

IAS 16:31 requires that revaluations should be made with sufficient regularity such that the carrying amount does not differ materially from that which would be determined using fair value at the end of the reporting period.

In order to meet this requirement, an entity must estimate the fair value of its revalued items of property, plant and equipment at the end of each reporting period. This does not mean, however, that revaluation adjustments must be made every year, unless the estimate of fair value differs significantly from the carrying amount of the intangible asset.

IAS 16, therefore, does not require annual revaluations. The frequency of revaluations will depend upon fluctuations in the fair values of the items of property, plant and equipment under consideration. Some items of property, plant and equipment (e.g. properties situated in countries with high capital asset inflation rates) may experience significant and volatile movements in fair value, thus necessitating annual revaluations. Such frequent revaluations would be unnecessary for items of property, plant and equipment with only insignificant movements in fair value (e.g. machinery situated in countries with relatively low capital asset inflation rates).

When items of property, plant and equipment have only insignificant changes in fair value, the Standard indicates that it may be necessary to revalue them only every three or five years. [IAS 16:34]

6.4 Accumulated depreciation at the date of revaluation

6.4.1 Alternatives for treatment of accumulated depreciation at the date of revaluation

When an item of property, plant and equipment is revalued, the carrying amount of that asset is adjusted to the revalued amount. At the date of the revaluation, the asset is treated in one of the following ways:

[IAS 16:35]

(a) the gross carrying amount is adjusted in a manner that is consistent with the revaluation of the carrying amount of the asset. For example, the gross carrying amount may be restated by reference to observable market data or it may be restated proportionately to the change in the carrying amount. The accumulated depreciation at the date of the revaluation is adjusted to equal the difference between the gross carrying amount and the carrying amount of the asset after taking into account accumulated impairment losses; or

(b) the accumulated depreciation is eliminated against the gross carrying amount of the asset.

Example 6.4.1 illustrates the alternative methods permitted under the Standard.

Example 6.4.1

Elimination of accumulated depreciation at the date of revaluation

Entity E acquires an asset at 1 January 20X1 for CU100,000. At that date, it is estimated to have a useful life of 20 years. At the beginning of 20X3, the remaining useful life of the asset is re-estimated at 10 years. At the end of 20X5, the asset is revalued (Entity E previously having determined that the fair value of the asset did not differ materially from its carrying amount); its fair value at that date is estimated to be CU84,000 and its gross carrying amount is estimated to be CU150,000 (determined by reference to the fair value of similar assets at the beginning of their useful lives). Its estimated remaining useful life is unchanged.

Both at acquisition and subsequently, the asset is estimated to have a nil residual value.

If Entity E selects the alternative under IAS 16:35(a) to restate the gross carrying amount by reference to the observable market data, the following amounts would be recognised.

End of	Gross carrying amount	Accumulated depreciation	Carrying amount
	CU'000	CU'000	CU'000
20X1	100	(5)	95
20X2	100	(10)	90
20X3	100	(19)[a]	81
20X4	100	(28)	72
20X5 (before revaluation)	100	(37)	63
20X5 (after revaluation)	150	(66)	84
20X6	150	(78)	72
20X7	...		

[a] 2 years depreciation at (100,000 × 5%) plus 1 year depreciation at (90,000 × 10%)

The required journal entry at the date of revaluation would be as follows.

		CU'000	CU'000
Dr	Property, plant and equipment (CU150,000 – CU100,000)	50	
Cr	Accumulated depreciation (balancing figure)		29
Cr	Revaluation gain (other comprehensive income) (CU84,000 – CU63,000)		21

Entity E could equally have chosen to restate the gross carrying amount of the asset proportionately to the change in carrying amount. If it had done so, the gross carrying amount would have been restated to CU133,000 (CU100,000 × 84/63) and the accumulated depreciation would have been calculated at the balancing amount of CU49,000 (CU133,000 – CU84,000) (a proportionate restatement).

Under this approach, the required journal entry at the date of revaluation would be as follows.

		CU'000	CU'000
Dr	Property, plant and equipment	33	
Cr	Accumulated depreciation		12
Cr	Revaluation gain (other comprehensive income)		21

If Entity E selects the alternative under IAS 16:35(b), the accumulated depreciation at the date of revaluation of CU37,000 will be eliminated against the gross carrying amount of the asset, so that the gross carrying amount and the net carrying amount after revaluation are both CU84,000. The required journal entry would be as follows.

		CU'000	CU'000
Cr	Property, plant and equipment		16
Dr	Accumulated depreciation	37	
Cr	Revaluation gain (other comprehensive income)		21

Whichever of the alternatives is selected, the amount recognised as a revaluation gain remains unchanged at CU21,000.

6.4.2 Effective date and transition for December 2013 amendments

IAS 16:35 was amended in December 2013 by *Annual Improvements to IFRSs: 2010-2012 Cycle*. The effect of the amendments is to allow that, when an asset is revalued and the alternative under IAS 16:35(a) is selected, the restatement of accumulated depreciation is not always proportionate to the change in the gross carrying amount of the asset. The amendment was necessary because, in some circumstances when the residual value, the useful life or the depreciation method of the asset has been re-estimated prior to the revaluation, a proportionate restatement is not relevant.

The December 2013 amendments are effective for annual periods beginning on or after 1 July 2014, with earlier application permitted. If the amendments are applied for a period beginning before 1 July 2014, that fact is required to be disclosed. [IAS 16:81H]

The amendments are required to be applied prospectively to all revaluations recognised in annual periods beginning on or after the date of initial application and in the immediately preceding annual period. An entity may also present adjusted comparative information for any earlier periods presented, but it is not required to do so. If an entity presents unadjusted comparative information for any earlier periods, it is required to clearly identify the information that has not been adjusted, state that it has been presented on a different basis and explain that basis. [IAS 16:80A]

Take, for example, an entity that applies the December 2013 amendments for the first time in its annual financial statements for the year ended 31 December 2015 and that presents two years of comparative information. In its 2015 financial statements, the entity is required to:

- apply the revised requirements to all revaluations recognised on or after 1 January 2014; and

- either restate all revaluations recognised between 1 January 2013 and 31 December 2013 or, if it chooses not to do so, clearly identify revaluations that have not been restated and provide an explanation of the basis on which those revaluations are presented.

6.5   Revaluation of assets by class

6.5.1   Revaluation to be made for entire class of assets

When an item of property, plant and equipment is revalued, the entire class of property, plant and equipment to which that asset belongs is required to be revalued. [IAS 16:36] Items within a class of property, plant and equipment are revalued simultaneously to avoid selective revaluation of assets and the reporting of amounts in the financial statements that are a mixture of costs and valuations at different dates. [IAS 16:38] This is intended to prevent the distortions caused by the selective use of revaluation, also referred to as 'cherry-picking', so as to take credit for gains without acknowledging falls in the value of similar assets.

6.5.2   Definition of a 'class' of assets

A class of property, plant and equipment is defined as a grouping of assets of a similar nature and use in an entity's operations. [IAS 16:37] The following examples of separate classes are cited:

- land;
- land and buildings;
- machinery;
- ships;
- aircraft;
- motor vehicles;
- furniture and fixtures;
- office equipment; and
- bearer plants.

Bearer plants were added to the examples in IAS 16:37 as part of the June 2014 amendments which brought bearer plants within the scope of IAS 16 (see **2.6**).

The examples cited as separate classes are not intended to be prescriptive or comprehensive. In practice, it is not uncommon for some of these classes to be combined. For example, when motor vehicles are not significant to an entity, motor vehicles and machinery may be combined in a plant and machinery class. For similar reasons, office equipment may be included in the furniture and fixtures class.

6.5.3 Disclosure of classes

As discussed in **11.2**, detailed disclosures are specified for each class of property, plant and equipment. This should be borne in mind when distinguishing classes, because multiple classes could lead to voluminous disclosures.

6.5.4 Revaluation on a rolling basis

The requirement to revalue entire classes of assets is a potentially onerous requirement because, for some reporting entities, a class of assets could comprise a large number of items. For this reason, IAS 16:38 allows a class of assets to be revalued on a rolling basis, provided that revaluation of the class of assets is completed within a short period of time and that the revaluations are kept up to date.

No further guidance is provided as to how a 'short period' should be interpreted for the purposes of IAS 16:38 although, given the drafting of the Standard, it is presumably less than a financial year. The general approach of IAS 16:38 is, however, to require simultaneous valuations so as to avoid the reporting of amounts that are a mixture of costs and values as at different dates. Accordingly, it would seem appropriate:

- for all such valuations to take place in the same accounting period (and in the same interim period when an entity presents interim financial statements); and

- for the acceptable length of the period to take into account how stable fair values are, so that greater volatility requires a shorter period over which to perform valuations.

6.6 Assets for which fair value cannot be reliably measured

Even when an entity has selected the revaluation model for its property, plant and equipment, only those assets whose fair value can be measured reliably are carried at revalued amounts. [IAS 16:31]

IAS 16 provides no guidance as to the circumstances in which it is appropriate to conclude that the fair value of an item of property, plant and equipment cannot be measured reliably, nor does it address the appropriate accounting for those assets whose fair value cannot be measured reliably.

However, IAS 40 *Investment Property* contains useful guidance on the circumstances in which it is appropriate to conclude that the fair value of an item of property, plant and equipment cannot be measured reliably. Under that Standard, the exception is allowed when, and only when, comparable market transactions are infrequent and alternative reliable estimates of fair value (e.g. based on discounted cash flow projections) are not available. IAS 40 is very restrictive, and allows this exception to be invoked only when an entity first acquires an investment property. IAS 16 is not so explicit, and seems to permit a greater degree of flexibility. It seems, however, that the intention of the IASB is that, when the entity has selected the revaluation model as its accounting policy for a particular class of assets, there should be a rebuttable presumption that all of the assets within that class will be carried at revalued amounts. The 'not reliably measurable' exception should be invoked only in exceptional circumstances. When the entity holds particular types of assets for which it will frequently be difficult to establish fair values (e.g. specialised plant and machinery), then it is preferable to adopt the cost basis for that entire class of assets, so as to avoid the reporting of amounts in the financial statements that are a mixture of costs and valuations at different dates.

When fair value cannot be reliably measured, the only reasonable approach is to account for those assets using IAS 16's cost model. This is consistent with the treatment required by IAS 40 for those investment properties whose fair value is not reliably measurable. To assist users of the financial statements, additional disclosures should be provided in respect of those assets carried at cost less accumulated depreciation and accumulated impairment losses. Again, useful guidance can be found in IAS 40 which requires that such assets be disclosed separately. In addition, entities are required by IAS 40 to disclose:

- a description of the property;
- an explanation of why fair value cannot be determined reliably;
- if possible, the range of estimates within which fair value is highly likely to lie; and
- on disposal of the property:
  - the fact that the entity has disposed of property not carried at fair value;
  - the carrying amount of the property at the time of sale; and
  - the amount of gain or loss recognised.

Although IAS 16 does not require equivalent disclosures, they should be seen as best practice. In addition, some of these disclosures may on occasions be necessary in order to comply with paragraph 97 of IAS 1 *Presentation of Financial Statements*, which requires that when items of income and expense are material, their nature and amount should be separately disclosed.

6.7 Voluntary disclosure of revalued amounts

Entities that adopt the cost model of accounting for their property, plant and equipment may wish to disclose the fair value of their property, plant and equipment in a note to the financial statements, when this is materially different from the carrying amount. Such disclosures are encouraged by IAS 16:79(d). In disclosing such fair values, such entities are not strictly bound by IAS 16's revaluation rules. However, when the amounts disclosed do not represent current fair values, they could mislead users of the financial statements. Therefore, the entity should either disclose the current fair values of the assets concerned, or not disclose revalued amounts at all. Similar considerations apply when an entity engages in 'cherry-picking', by disclosing current values only for those assets whose fair values are significantly above carrying amounts and ignoring those assets whose fair values are significantly below their carrying amounts. Accordingly, when fair values are disclosed voluntarily under IAS 16:79(d), they should normally be disclosed for an entire class of assets.

6.8 Treatment of surplus or deficit arising on revaluation

6.8.1 Revaluation surplus

IAS 16 requires that when an asset's carrying amount is increased as a result of a revaluation, the increase (being the difference between the fair value at the date of revaluation and the carrying amount at that date) should generally be recognised in other comprehensive income and accumulated in equity, under the heading of revaluation surplus. [IAS 16:39]

A revaluation increase should be recognised in profit or loss, however, to the extent that it reverses a revaluation decrease of the same asset previously recognised as an expense. [IAS 16:39]

When a revaluation surplus is recognised, no amendment is made to profit or loss to reverse depreciation previously recognised.

6.8.2 Revaluation deficit

The Standard requires that when an asset's carrying amount is decreased as a result of a revaluation, the decrease should generally be recognised in profit or loss. [IAS 16:40]

A revaluation decrease should be recognised in other comprehensive income, however, to the extent of any credit balance existing in the revaluation surplus in respect of that same asset. The decrease reduces the amount of the revaluation surplus accumulated in equity. [IAS 16:40]

6.8.3   Examples illustrating the treatment of valuation movements

The following examples illustrate the appropriate treatment of valuation movements in a number of circumstances. In each case, the deferred tax implications are ignored.

Example 6.8.3A

Revaluation surplus

An entity purchased a parcel of land on 1 July 20X1 for CU125 million. At 31 December 20X1, the land was valued at CU150 million.

The revaluation surplus of CU25 million is recognised in other comprehensive income and credited to a property revaluation reserve within equity.

Example 6.8.3B

Revaluation surplus reversing previous deficit

An entity purchased a parcel of land on 1 July 20X1 for CU140 million. At 31 December 20X1, the land was valued at CU125 million. At 31 December 20X2, the fair value of the land had increased to CU150 million.

20X1: Revaluation deficit of CU15 million is recognised in profit or loss.

20X2: Revaluation surplus is treated as follows:

- CU15 million is credited to profit or loss (i.e. reversal of the previous deficit).
- CU10 million is recognised in other comprehensive income and credited to the property revaluation reserve within equity.

Example 6.8.3C

Revaluation deficit reversing previous surplus

An entity purchased a parcel of land on 1 July 20X1 for CU60 million. At 31 December 20X1, the land was valued at CU70 million. At 31 December 20X2, the fair value of the land had decreased to CU55 million.

20X1: Revaluation surplus of CU10 million is recognised in other comprehensive income and credited to the property revaluation reserve within equity.

20X2: Revaluation deficit is treated as follows.

- CU10 million is recognised in other comprehensive income and debited to the property revaluation reserve within equity (i.e. reversal of the previous surplus).
- CU5 million is recognised in profit or loss (i.e. excess of deficit over available surplus attributable to the same parcel of land).

Example 6.8.3D

Revaluation surplus reversing previous deficit: effect of depreciation

The cost of a property with a useful life of 20 years is CU10 million. Depreciation each year is CU0.5 million.

At the end of Year 5, the property has a carrying amount of CU7.5 million and a fair value of CU6 million. At that date, the directors move to the revaluation basis of accounting. The deficit on revaluation of CU1.5 million is recognised in profit or loss.

At the end of Years 6 through 9, the directors determine that there is no material difference between the carrying amount of the property and its fair value and, therefore, no valuation adjustments are required. Depreciation of CU2 million (i.e. 5 × CU0.4 million) is recognised in the periods up to the end of Year 10, at which time the property has a carrying amount of CU4 million. During Year 10, however, the value of the property increases sharply to a closing fair value of CU7 million.

Applying the basic principle as stated in IAS 16:39, the portion of the revaluation surplus that is to be credited to profit or loss at the end of Year 10 might appear to be CU1.5 million (i.e. the amount of the deficit previously recognised in profit or loss). In effect, however, part of this revaluation decrease has already been reversed through the recognition of a lower depreciation charge for Years 6 to 10.

Accordingly, the amount of the revaluation surplus that is credited to profit or loss should be reduced by the cumulative reduction in depreciation in Years 6 to 10 as a result of recognising the revaluation deficit (i.e. (CU0.5 million less CU0.4 million) × 5 years). Therefore, the amount of the revaluation surplus credited to profit or loss is CU1 million. The remaining CU2 million of the revaluation surplus is recognised in other comprehensive income and credited to the revaluation reserve within equity. The end result is that the balance on the revaluation reserve (CU2 million) is the excess of the carrying amount (CU7 million) over what it would have been had the property never been revalued (CU5 million).

This treatment is consistent with the treatment prescribed for the reversal of an impairment loss under IAS 36 *Impairment of Assets* (see **chapter A10**).

6.8.4 Utilisation of revaluation reserve

Under IAS 16:41, the revaluation reserve may be transferred directly to retained earnings when the asset is derecognised. The reserve may be transferred on the retirement or disposal of the asset. Part of the reserve may, however, be transferred over the period for which the asset is used by the entity. In such circumstances, the amount of the reserve transferred is the difference between the depreciation charge based on the revalued carrying amount of the asset and the depreciation charge based on the asset's original cost. The transfer from revaluation reserve to retained earnings, whether on disposal or on a systematic basis over the life of the asset, is not made through profit or loss.

The reserve transfers referred to in IAS 16:41 are implied to be at the option of the reporting entity, rather than being mandated by the Standard. There would, therefore, appear to be another alternative – to make no reserve transfer. That option would, however, result in the permanent retention of the portion of the revaluation reserve relating to assets that have been fully depreciated or disposed of.

Any transfer between the revaluation reserve and retained earnings, which should be made on a net of tax basis, will reduce the amount that is available for offset against future revaluation deficits in respect of individual assets.

Example 6.8.4

Transfer from revaluation reserve to retained earnings

The cost of a property with a useful life of 20 years is CU10 million. Depreciation each year is CU0.5 million.

At the end of Year 5, the property has a carrying amount of CU7.5 million and a fair value of CU12 million. The surplus on revaluation of CU4.5 million is credited to the revaluation reserve and the property will be depreciated over its remaining 15-year useful life at the rate of CU0.8 million per annum. Assume that, for the remainder of its useful life, the depreciated carrying amount of the property is not materially different from its fair value. Therefore, no further revaluation adjustments are required.

In Years 6 through 20, depreciation has been increased by CU0.3 million per annum as a result of the revaluation. Therefore, at the end of each of those years, it is acceptable to make a transfer from the revaluation reserve to retained earnings of an amount of CU0.3 million, to reflect the realisation of the revaluation surplus. If such periodic transfers are made, then the revaluation reserve will have been reduced to zero at the point that the property is fully depreciated.

Alternatively, if no annual transfers are made, the reserve may be transferred in its entirety on the retirement or disposal of the asset.

6.9   Deferred tax implications

The revaluation of assets is also likely to have deferred tax implications. For the purposes of the examples in this chapter the deferred tax impact is ignored. Readers should refer to **chapter A13** for a detailed discussion of the deferred tax impact of revaluations.

7 Depreciation

7.1 Requirement to depreciate items of property, plant and equipment

If an item of property, plant and equipment has a limited useful economic life, then its cost or, if applicable, its fair value, is reduced to its estimated residual value by the systematic allocation of depreciation over the asset's useful economic life. [IAS 16:50]

The depreciation charge for each period should be recognised in profit or loss, unless it qualifies to be capitalised in the carrying amount of another asset. [IAS 16:48] For example, the depreciation of plant and machinery used for construction purposes may be included in the cost of a self-constructed property.

Depreciation, as defined in IAS 16:6, is the systematic allocation of the depreciable amount of an asset (i.e. the cost of the asset, or other amount substituted for cost, less its residual value) over its useful life. In order to comply with the requirements of IAS 16 relating to depreciation, it is necessary to identify:

- the parts (components) of each item of property, plant and equipment that are to be depreciated separately;

- the cost or valuation of each separately depreciable component;

- the estimated residual value of each separately depreciable component;

- the length of time during which each separately depreciable component will be commercially useful to the entity; and

- the most appropriate depreciation method for each separately depreciable component.

7.2 Each significant component to be depreciated separately

IAS 16 requires that each part of an item of property, plant and equipment with a cost that is significant in relation to the total cost of the item should be depreciated separately. [IAS 16:43]

When an item of property, plant and equipment is first recognised, the Standard requires that the entity should allocate the amount initially recognised between the item's significant parts (i.e. those separately identifiable components of the item with a cost that is significant to the total cost of the item). Each significant part is required to be depreciated separately. [IAS 16:44]

There may be some significant parts which, although separately identifiable, have the same useful life and which are appropriately depreciated using the same depreciation method. Such items will generally be grouped together for the purposes of calculating the depreciation charge. [IAS 16:45]

Once the individually significant parts have been identified, the remaining parts that are not individually significant are grouped together. Although the entity may have varying expectations as to the useful lives and pattern of consumption of the benefits of these remaining components, because they are not individually significant, IAS 16 allows that they can be depreciated as a group, provided that the depreciation rate and method selected result in a faithful representation of the pattern of consumption of benefits. [IAS 16:46]

A common example of the allocation of the cost of an item of property, plant and equipment is that of an aircraft, as mentioned in IAS 16:44. The airframe, engines and cabin interior of a single plane are likely to have significantly different useful lives. Under IAS 16, these parts are separately identified at the time that the aircraft is acquired, and each is depreciated separately over an appropriate useful life.

This approach of depreciating separate parts of a single item of property, plant and equipment is easily understood in relation to the physical components of a single item, as in the aircraft example discussed. There will, however, also be 'parts' that are less tangible. An entity may purchase an item of property, plant and equipment that is required to undergo major inspections or overhauls at regular intervals over its useful life. For example, an entity might acquire a ship that requires a major overhaul, say, once every five years. Part of the cost of the ship may be allocable to a separate component representing the service potential required to be restored by the periodic overhauls. That separate component is isolated when the asset is acquired, and depreciated over the period to the next overhaul.

The identification of this inherent component at the time of acquisition may not be simple, because it will generally not have been separately invoiced. Therefore, an estimate of the cost will be required. This will generally be based on the current cost of the expected overhaul or inspection (i.e. the estimated cost of those activities if they were performed at the time of the purchase).

As discussed at **3.5**, expenditure incurred subsequently on the major inspection or overhaul is capitalised provided that the recognition criteria set out in IAS 16:7 are met. To the extent that the separate component representing the estimated cost of the inspection or overhaul has not been fully depreciated by the time that the inspection/overhaul expenditure is incurred, it is derecognised and will therefore give rise to a loss.

Example 7.2 illustrates the accounting treatment for major inspection or overhaul costs that qualify for separate recognition.

Example 7.2

Separate depreciation of cost of major overhaul

An entity purchases a ship for CU40 million. This ship will be required to undergo a dry dock overhaul every five years to restore its service potential. At the time of purchase, the service potential that will be required to be restored by the overhaul can be measured based on the cost of the dry docking if it had been performed at the time of the purchase of the ship, say CU4 million.

The following shows the calculation of the depreciation of the ship for Years 1 to 5, using the straight-line method.

	Amount CU'000	Useful life (years)
Purchase price of ship	40,000	
Comprising:		
– the ship, excluding projected overhaul cost	36,000	30
– projected overhaul cost	4,000	5
For Years 1 to 5, depreciation charges per annum are:		
– ship (excluding the service potentialt component)	1,200	
– service potential	800	

By the end of Year 5, the service potential would be fully depreciated. When a dry docking is carried out in Year 6, the expenditure is capitalised to reflect the restoration of service potential, which is then depreciated over the period to the next overhaul in Years 6 to 10.

The process in Years 6 to 10 repeats every five years from Year 11 onwards until Year 30, when both the ship and the cost of dry docking are fully depreciated and a new ship is acquired.

Note that the entity is required to use its best efforts to identify separately components such as the service potential component, as described in **example 7.2**, when the asset is first acquired or constructed. That separate identification, and the subsequent separate depreciation of the service potential component, is not, however, a necessary condition for the capitalisation of the subsequent expenditure on the overhaul as part of the cost of the asset. For example, if the entity described in **example 7.2** had failed to identify the service potential component at the date of acquisition, because it was not considered significant, and had not depreciated it separately during Years 1 to 5, the expenditure on the overhaul in Year 6 would still be capitalised as part of the cost of the asset, provided that the general recognition criteria were met. In this circumstance, the entity would be required to estimate the remaining carrying amount of the service potential component at the date of the first overhaul (which would be approximately CU3.33 million, i.e. CU4 million depreciated for 5 years out of 30), and to derecognise that carrying amount at the same time as the expenditure on the overhaul is capitalised.

IAS 16 gives a further example of circumstances in which cost may need to be allocated to significant parts of an asset. If an entity acquires property, plant and equipment subject to an operating lease in which it is the lessor, it may be appropriate to depreciate separately amounts reflected in the cost of the item that are attributable to favourable or unfavourable lease terms relative to market terms. [IAS 16:44]

Land and buildings acquired in such circumstances might qualify as investment property, in which case this guidance would apply when the cost model within IAS 40 *Investment Property* is adopted (see **5.3.2** in **chapter A8**).

7.3   Residual value

IAS 16 defines residual value as the estimated amount that an entity would currently obtain from disposal of the asset, after deducting the estimated costs of disposal, if the asset were already of the age and in the condition expected at the end of its useful life. [IAS 16:6]

In practice, the residual value of an asset is often insignificant and, therefore, is immaterial in the calculation of the depreciable amount. However, when the residual value is significant, then it will directly affect the depreciation recognised over the life of the asset.

The residual value of an asset is required to be reviewed at least at each financial year end. [IAS 16:51] The revised estimate should be based on market conditions current at the end of the reporting period. If the revised estimate differs significantly from previous estimates of residual value, the effect is accounted for prospectively as a change in estimate, in accordance with the requirements of IAS 8 *Accounting Policies, Changes in Accounting Estimates and Errors*. [IAS 16:51] Effectively, the depreciation recognised over the remaining useful life of the asset is adjusted to take account of the revised estimate of residual value.

If the revised estimate of residual value is equal to or greater than the asset's carrying amount, whether due to inflation or otherwise, then the asset's depreciation charge is zero unless and until its residual value subsequently decreases to an amount below the asset's carrying amount. [IAS 16:54]

The definition of residual value refers to the potential disposal value of the asset if it were already of the age and in the condition expected at the end of its useful life. The amount is therefore quite separate from the current fair value of the asset. If the fair value of the asset exceeds its carrying amount (generally because the entity has adopted the cost model for accounting for its property, plant and equipment), this does not remove the obligation to recognise depreciation. [IAS 16:52]

Further, the definition focuses on the amount that could currently be obtained on disposal of the asset, rather than the amount that is expected to be obtained at the end of the asset's useful life. Therefore, expectations as to future increases or decreases in that disposal value are not taken into account. Thus, an increase in the expected residual value of an asset because of past events will affect the depreciable amount; expectations of future changes in residual value other than the effects of wear and tear will not. [IAS 16:BC29]

7.4 Estimates of useful lives

7.4.1 Definition of useful life

The useful life of an asset is defined as:

[IAS 16:6]

- the period over which an asset is expected to be available for use by an entity; or

- the number of production or similar units expected to be obtained from the asset by an entity.

7.4.2 Commencement of depreciation

Depreciation of an asset commences when it is available for use, i.e. when it is in the location and condition necessary for it to be capable of operating in the manner intended by management. [IAS 16:55] This is the same point in time at which the entity is required to cease capitalising costs within the carrying amount of the asset. (See **4.2.9** for guidance as to when this point in time occurs.)

7.4.3 Cessation of depreciation

Depreciation of an asset ceases at the earlier of:

[IAS 16:55]

- the date that the asset is classified as held for sale (or included in a disposal group that is classified as held for sale) in accordance with IFRS 5 *Non-current Assets Held for Sale and Discontinued Operations* (see **9.1**); and

- the date that the asset is derecognised.

IFRS 5 requires that a non-current asset (or disposal group) be classified as held for sale if its carrying amount will be recovered principally through a sale transaction rather than through continuing use. [IFRS 5:6] For this to be the case, the asset (or disposal group) must be available for immediate sale in its present condition, and its sale must be 'highly probable' (see **chapter A20** for further guidance).

IAS 16 sets out requirements in respect of the derecognition of items of property, plant and equipment – see **section 9**.

Therefore, depreciation of an asset does not cease when an asset becomes idle or is retired from active use unless the asset is fully depreciated. If the depreciation is calculated by reference to the usage of the asset, however, the depreciation recognised may be zero while there is no production. [IAS 16:55] In any case, when an asset becomes idle, or is retired from active use, this may trigger the recognition of an impairment loss which will result in the reduction of the carrying amount of the asset to its estimated recoverable amount.

Example 7.4.3

Depreciation of an asset retired from active use

Company Q uses specialised machinery to manufacture its products and is the only entity in its market that operates this type of machinery.

Company Q plans to increase its production capacity by introducing new specialised machinery with improved technology. As a result, Company Q will discontinue using the specialised machinery currently in use. However, in order to protect its competitive advantage and deny other market participants access to the technology, Company Q will not sell the machinery currently in use, even though it is still in good working condition; instead, the machinery will be retired from active use and 'mothballed' by Company Q for potential further use or sale at a later date.

At the date of retirement, the fair value less costs to sell of the specialised machinery exceeds its carrying amount.

Should Company Q continue to depreciate the machinery when it is retired from active use and, if so, over what period?

Company Q should continue to depreciate the depreciable amount of the machinery on a systematic basis over its estimated useful life. The useful life of the machinery is defined in terms of its expected utility to Company Q (see IAS 16:57). This utility may be either the use of the asset by Company Q or alternatively the retention of a competitive advantage by denying others access to such machinery. However, the useful life of the machinery will be limited to its economic life.

IAS 16:55 specifies that deprecation of an asset should cease only at the earlier of (1) the date the asset is classified as held for sale (or is included in a disposal group classified as held for sale) under IFRS 5, and (2) the date that the asset

---

is derecognised. Neither of these conditions is met in the circumstances under consideration.

IAS 16:55 also states explicitly that "depreciation does not cease when the asset becomes idle or is retired from active use unless the asset is fully depreciated".

Note that the retirement of the asset from active use is likely to be an indicator of impairment under paragraph 12 of IAS 36 *Impairment of Assets*. However, in the circumstances under consideration, because the fair value less costs to sell of the machinery is greater than its carrying amount, no impairment loss will be recognised.

7.4.4 Factors affecting the useful life of an asset

7.4.4.1 Factors affecting the useful life of an asset – general

The consumption of the future economic benefits embodied in an asset occurs principally through usage. Other factors should also be taken into account, however, such as technical obsolescence and wear and tear while an asset remains idle, because they may result in a reduction in the economic benefits expected to be derived from the asset. Consequently, all of the following factors need to be considered in determining the useful life of an asset:

[IAS 16:56]

(a) the expected usage of the asset by the entity. Usage is assessed by reference to the asset's expected capacity or physical output;

(b) the expected physical wear and tear, which depends on operational factors such as the number of shifts for which the asset is to be used and the repair and maintenance programme of the entity, and the care and maintenance of the asset while idle;

(c) technical or commercial obsolescence arising from changes or improvements in production, or from a change in the market demand for the product or service output of the asset. Expected future reductions in the selling price of an item that was produced using an asset could indicate the expectation of technical or commercial obsolescence of the asset which, in turn, might reflect a reduction of the future economic benefits embodied in the asset; and

(d) legal or similar limits on the use of the asset, such as the expiry dates of related leases.

The final sentence of IAS 16:56(c) was added by *Clarification of Acceptable Methods of Depreciation and Amortisation (Amendments to IAS 16 and IAS 38)* issued in May 2014. The May 2014 amendments are required to be applied prospectively for annual periods beginning on or after 1 January 2016, with earlier application permitted. If an entity applies this guidance for a period beginning before 1 January 2016, it is required to disclose that fact. [IAS 16:81J]

> Although the May 2014 amendments are stated to be effective from 2016, the principle that expected reductions in the selling price of an item may be an indicator of obsolescence of the asset which was used to produce it will already be applied by many entities. In the Basis of Conclusions accompanying the amendments, the IASB emphasises that the expectation of technical or commercial obsolescence is relevant for estimating both the pattern of consumption of future economic benefits and the useful life of an asset. [IAS 16:BC33F]

7.4.4.2 Impact of an entity's asset management policy

Because the useful life of an asset is defined in terms of its expected utility to the entity, the asset management policy of the reporting entity should be taken into account when estimating the useful life of an asset. For example, an entity may have a policy of disposing of assets after a specified time or after consumption of a specified proportion of the economic benefits embodied in the assets. In such circumstances, the useful life of an asset may be shorter than its economic life. [IAS 16:57] For example, it is often the case that company cars are disposed of well before the end of their economic life.

7.4.5 Change in estimate of useful life

IAS 16 requires that the estimate of the useful life of an item of property, plant and equipment should be reviewed at least at the end of each financial year. If expectations differ from previous estimates, the change is accounted for as a change in accounting estimate in accordance with IAS 8 *Accounting Policies, Changes in Accounting Estimates and Errors*. [IAS 16:51]

> Estimates of useful lives require adjustment from time to time in the light of changes in experience and knowledge. These changes may reflect the extension of estimated useful lives due to exceptional maintenance expenditure, curtailment of estimated useful lives due to excessive use, or obsolescence not included in the original estimates. When the original estimate of the useful life of an asset is revised, the undepreciated cost (or valuation) should be recognised in profit or loss over the revised remaining useful life, except to the extent that the depreciation expense qualifies for capitalisation into the cost of other assets, such as inventories.

Example 7.4.5

Change in estimate of useful life

An entity purchased an item of plant at a cost of CU1.2 million with an estimated useful life of 10 years.

At the end of Year 3, the asset has a carrying amount of CU840,000. During Year 4, on the basis of experience of similar assets, the item of plant is now estimated to have a remaining useful life of 4 years. The asset is determined not to be impaired. Consequently, the carrying amount of CU840,000 is depreciated over the remaining 4 years at CU210,000 per annum.

Depreciation charges for Years 1 to 7 will be as follows.

	CU'000		CU'000
Year 1	120	Year 5	210
Year 2	120	Year 6	210
Year 3	120	Year 7	210
Year 4	210		

A significant reduction in the estimated useful life of an asset may indicate that the asset has been impaired because the amount that the entity expects to generate from the use of the asset may have been reduced below its carrying amount (see IAS 36:12(f)). In such circumstances, a detailed impairment test should be performed and, if necessary, an impairment loss recognised to reduce the carrying amount of the asset to its recoverable amount (see **chapter A10**). The recoverable amount is then depreciated over the revised estimate of the useful life of the asset.

7.4.6 Fully-depreciated assets

If estimates of the useful lives of items of property, plant and equipment are made realistically, and kept under regular review as required by IAS 16:51, there should be few fully depreciated assets still in use. If fully-depreciated assets are no longer in use, they should either be classified as held for sale in accordance with IFRS 5 or they should be derecognised (see **section 9**).

7.5 Methods of depreciation

7.5.1 Method of depreciation should reflect expected consumption of economic benefits

It is necessary to select a method of applying depreciation that results in the carrying amount of the asset being allocated as fairly as possible to the periods expected to benefit from the use of the asset. The method used should be that which reflects most closely the pattern in which the asset's economic benefits are expected to be consumed by the entity. [IAS 16:60]

7.5.2   Alternative methods of apportioning depreciation

There are several methods of apportioning depreciation over the anticipated useful life of the asset. Those most commonly employed are the straight-line method and the reducing balance (diminishing balance) method. Straight-line depreciation results in a constant charge over the useful life of the asset, because the annual depreciation charge is a fixed percentage of the original cost (or revalued amount). The reducing balance method results in a decreasing charge over the life of the asset, because the annual depreciation charge is a fixed percentage of the opening carrying amount. The straight-line method is the most popular, principally because of its simplicity.

Another useful basis is the unit of production method, which apportions the cost of the asset over its productive life measured in terms of the units produced or machine hours utilised in relation to the total of such units or hours estimated to comprise the productive life of the asset. This method is theoretically superior to the straight-line and reducing balance methods in that it more accurately matches costs with the consumption of economic benefits, if the life of the asset can be measured with some precision in terms of its ultimate total output. This method is commonly used in the oil, gas and other extractive industries, where the life of an asset may be expressed in terms of a quantity of output and production assets have no further value once mineral reserves have been extracted.

More generally, alternative methods of depreciation (e.g. decreasing charge depreciation and the sum-of-digits method, or 'rule of 78') are acceptable under IFRSs only if they reflect the pattern in which the asset's economic benefits are expected to be consumed. As a consequence, a method based on tax allowances granted (e.g. the double declining balance method) is not permitted unless it also reflects the expected consumption pattern of the asset.

7.5.3   Increasing charge depreciation

Entities will often construct items of property, plant and equipment that are expected to generate benefits over many years. Customer demand to use the assets may, however, be expected to start slowly and take a number of years to reach an expected 'normal' level. An example of this might be a cable-television distribution network. In such cases, an entity may wish the depreciation charge for the asset to increase gradually to reflect customers' expected phased-in demand.

The appropriateness of such a policy will depend on how the asset's benefits are being consumed. IAS 16:60 requires that depreciation should reflect the pattern in which the asset's economic benefits are consumed by the entity. Those benefits should be viewed in terms of physical capacity or physical output (using up physical capability, wear and tear, technical obsolescence) and legal limits on the physical use of the asset (such as by a lease).

While an 'increasing charge' or 'sinking fund' method of calculating depreciation is not appropriate under IAS 16, a unit of production method of calculating depreciation is appropriate if it reflects the pattern of benefit consumption. This method is more likely to be justified for a physical asset, reflecting wear and tear, than for an intangible asset (see **chapter A9**).

The depreciation method adopted should be based on the economic depreciation of the asset, rather than the return from the asset (e.g. the annuity method). Therefore, consideration of the time value of money in determining the depreciation method is not appropriate.

7.5.4 Depreciation method based on revenue

It is not appropriate to use a depreciation method based on revenue that is generated by an activity that includes the use of an asset; such revenue generally reflects factors other than the consumption of the economic benefits of the asset (e.g. other inputs and processes, selling activities and changes in sales volumes and prices). [IAS 16:62A]

IAS 16:62A was added by *Clarification of Acceptable Methods of Depreciation and Amortisation (Amendments to IAS 16 and IAS 38)* issued in May 2014. The May 2014 amendments are required to be applied prospectively for annual periods beginning on or after 1 January 2016, with earlier application permitted. If an entity applies these amendments for a period beginning before 1 January 2016, it is required to disclose that fact. [IAS 16:81J]

The May 2014 amendments explicitly prohibit the use of revenue-based depreciation methods (which allocate an asset's depreciable amount based on revenues generated in an accounting period as a proportion of the total revenues expected to be generated over the asset's useful economic life). The IASB has concluded that such methods do not comply with the general requirement under IAS 16:60 (see **7.5.1**) that the depreciation method for an asset should reflect the pattern in which the asset's future economic benefits are expected to be consumed by the entity. [IAS 16:BC33B & BC33E]

The May 2014 amendments are required to be applied prospectively (from 1 January 2016, or an earlier date of application selected by an entity). If adoption of the amendments results in a change in depreciation method, prospective application will have the same effect as the required treatment for all changes in depreciation methods, as described in **7.5.5** – the carrying amount of the asset at the date of change is written off using the new method over its remaining useful life, commencing with the period in which the change takes place. **Example 7.5.5** illustrates this treatment.

7.5.5 Change in depreciation method

IAS 16 requires that the depreciation method applied to an item of property, plant and equipment should be reviewed at least at the end of each financial year. Except when there is a change in the expected pattern of consumption of economic benefits embodied in the asset, the depreciation method adopted should be applied consistently from period to period. If there has been a significant change in the expected pattern of consumption of benefits, the depreciation method is changed to reflect the changed pattern. The change is accounted for as a change in accounting estimate in accordance with IAS 8 *Accounting Policies, Changes in Accounting Estimates and Errors.* [IAS 16:61]

Therefore, a change from one method of recognising depreciation to another does not constitute a change in accounting policy but is accounted for as a change in accounting estimate in accordance with IAS 8. The carrying amount of the asset is written off using the new method over the remaining useful life, commencing with the period in which the change takes place. Separate disclosure of the impact of the change is required if the change has a material effect in the current period or is expected to have a material effect in subsequent periods.

Example 7.5.5

Change in depreciation method

An entity acquired an asset 3 years ago at a cost of CU5 million. The depreciation method adopted for the asset was 10 per cent reducing balance.

At the end of Year 3, the carrying amount of the asset is CU3,645,000. The entity estimates that the remaining useful life of the asset is 8 years and determines to adopt straight-line depreciation from that date so as to reflect better the revised estimated pattern of recovery of economic benefits.

Depreciation charges for years 1 to 11 will be as follows.

	CU'000		CU'000
Year 1	500	Year 7	456
Year 2	450	Year 8	456
Year 3	405	Year 9	455
Year 4	456	Year 10	455
Year 5	456	Year 11	455
Year 6	456		

7.6 Depreciation of particular classes of assets

7.6.1 Freehold land

Freehold land that is not subject to depletion (e.g. by the extraction of minerals) does not have a limited useful life and, therefore, should not be depreciated. In consequence, it is necessary, when freehold property is purchased, to allocate the purchase consideration between the value of the land and that of the buildings. Similarly, any revaluations of freehold property should distinguish between land and buildings.

When the cost of site dismantlement, removal and restoration is included in the cost of land, that portion of the land asset is depreciated over the period of benefits obtained by incurring those costs. In some cases, the land itself may have a limited useful life, in which case it is depreciated in a manner that reflects the benefits to be derived from it. [IAS 16:59]

When the value of freehold land is adversely affected by long-term environmental factors, an impairment loss should be recognised to reflect any decline in its estimated recoverable amount below its carrying amount.

7.6.2 Freehold buildings

Buildings have limited useful economic lives and are no different from other depreciable assets. Although their estimated useful lives are usually significantly longer than other items of property, plant and equipment, they should nevertheless be depreciated in a similar manner, generally using the straight-line method. IAS 16 emphasises that an increase in the value of the land on which a building stands does not affect the determination of the useful life of the building. [IAS 16:58] An exception to the general requirement to depreciate buildings is allowed for those properties that qualify as investment properties and that are accounted for using the fair value model (see **chapter A8** for details).

IAS 16 does not grant an exemption in respect of historic buildings: the fact that they may have been built centuries earlier, and may be expected to last for centuries more, does not exempt them from depreciation. It is possible that the useful life of such a building may be very long. Also, when an entity intends to sell such a building in due course, rather than use it for the remainder of its physical life, it is possible that the residual value may be relatively high. Both of these factors may lead to the depreciation recognised being relatively small. Care should be taken to identify any components (e.g. roofs) that may require replacement at periodic intervals, which need to be depreciated over a shorter period (see **7.2**).

7.6.3   *Plant and machinery, tools and equipment, ships, vehicles etc.*

Depreciation recognised is, in general, computed using the straight-line method, but the reducing balance and unit of production methods are also suitable in appropriate circumstances. Some small assets with very short useful lives, such as loose tools, jigs and patterns may, however, be dealt with more satisfactorily in aggregate, as discussed at **3.4**.

7.6.4   *Leased assets*

Tangible assets that are held under finance leases are required by IAS 17 *Leases* to be depreciated. That Standard requires that the depreciation policy adopted for depreciable leased assets should be consistent with that for similar assets that are owned, and that the depreciation recognised should be calculated in accordance with the principles of IAS 16, as discussed throughout this section. [IAS 17:27]

IAS 17 also stipulates that, if there is reasonable certainty that the lessee will obtain ownership by the end of the lease term, the period of expected use is the useful life of the asset; otherwise, the asset is to be depreciated over the shorter of the lease term and its useful life. [IAS 17:28]

7.6.5   *Stand-by equipment*

The useful life of stand-by equipment should be determined by the useful life of the equipment for which it serves as a back-up. In the example cited at **3.2** (entity has installed two turbines), one turbine produces energy for the plant, and the other is used as a back-up in case the first turbine fails or is otherwise rendered out of service. The stand-by equipment should be depreciated from the date it is made available for use (i.e. when it is in the location and condition necessary for it to be capable of operating in the manner intended by management) over the shorter of the life of the turbine and the life of the plant of which the turbine is part (assuming the turbine cannot be removed and used in another plant). Note that, if the residual value of the stand-by turbine is estimated to be significantly higher than the residual value of the primary turbine (because it is expected to be in better condition at the end of the asset's useful life due to lower usage), this will affect the depreciation charged over that useful life.

7.6.6   *Spare parts*

In contrast to the depreciation of stand-by equipment, the useful life of spare parts classified as property, plant and equipment commences when they are put into use, rather than when they are acquired.

> **Example 7.6.6**
>
> **Depreciation of spare parts classified as property, plant and equipment**
>
> An entity buys five new machines for use in its production facility. Simultaneously, it purchases a spare motor to be used as a replacement if a motor on one of the five machines breaks. The motor will be used in the production of goods and, once brought into service, will be operated during more than one period. It is therefore classified as property, plant and equipment.
>
> The motor does not qualify as stand-by equipment because it will not be ready for use until it is installed. Therefore, the useful life of the motor commences when it is available for use within the machine rather than when it is acquired. It should be depreciated over the period starting when it is brought into service and continuing over the shorter of its useful life and the remaining expected useful life of the asset to which it relates. If the asset to which it relates will be replaced at the end of its useful life and the motor is expected to be used or usable for the replacement asset, a longer depreciation period may be appropriate. During the period before the motor is available for service, any reduction in value should be reflected as an impairment loss under IAS 36 at the time impairment is indicated.

8 Impairment

8.1 General requirements for the identification of an impairment loss

An entity should refer to the requirements of IAS 36 *Impairment of Assets* to determine whether an item of property, plant and equipment is impaired. IAS 36 explains how an entity reviews the carrying amount of its assets, how it determines the recoverable amount of an asset, and when it recognises or reverses an impairment loss (see **chapter A10**). [IAS 16:63]

8.2 Compensation for impairment or loss

When an asset is impaired, lost or given up, any compensation from third parties is included in profit or loss when the compensation becomes receivable. [IAS 16:65]

Examples of such circumstances include:

- reimbursements by insurance companies after the impairment or loss of items of property, plant and equipment (e.g. due to natural disasters, theft etc.);

- indemnities by governments for items of property, plant and equipment that are expropriated (e.g. compulsory purchase of land to be used for public purposes);

- compensation related to the involuntary conversion of items of property, plant and equipment (e.g. relocation of facilities from a designated urban area to a non-urban area in accordance with government land policy); and

- physical replacement in whole or in part of an impaired or lost asset.

IAS 16 emphasises that impairments or losses of items of property, plant and equipment, related claims for or payments of compensation from third parties, and any subsequent purchase or construction of replacement assets are separate economic events and should be accounted for as such. The three economic events should be accounted for separately as follows:

[IAS 16:66]

- in respect of impairment or loss:

  - impairments of items of property, plant and equipment should be recognised in accordance with IAS 36; and

  - derecognition of items of property, plant and equipment retired or disposed of should be determined in accordance with IAS 16;

- compensation from third parties for items of property, plant and equipment that were impaired, lost or given up should be included in determining profit or loss when it becomes receivable; and

- the cost of items of property, plant and equipment restored, purchased or constructed as replacements should be determined in accordance with IAS 16.

9   Derecognition

9.1   Derecognition – general

IAS 16 requires that the carrying amount of an item of property, plant and equipment should be derecognised:

[IAS 16:67]

- on disposal; or

- when no future economic benefits are expected from its use or disposal.

Example 9.1

Disposal of property, plant and equipment

An entity enters into a transaction whereby it sells an item of property, plant and equipment to a third party. It concurrently enters into a contract with the third party to buy all of the actual output of the asset over its remaining useful life at a fixed per-unit price, but in total not less than a minimum payment equal to the

---

value of 90 per cent of the expected output. The minimum payment must be made even if the actual output is below expectation.

Should the entity recognise the sale of the asset by removing it from its statement of financial position?

In this situation, the entity should consider the requirements of IFRIC 4 *Determining Whether an Arrangement Contains a Lease* (see **section 2.7** of **chapter A17**). If it is concluded that the supply arrangement involves a finance lease, the requirements of IAS 17 *Leases* regarding sale and leaseback transactions apply, and the entity will still recognise the asset in its statement of financial position after title has been transferred to the third party.

Except when IAS 17 *Leases* requires otherwise in the circumstances of a sale and leaseback, the gain or loss arising on the derecognition of an item of property, plant and equipment should be included in profit or loss when the amount is derecognised. [IAS 16:68]

On the derecognition of an item of property, plant and equipment, the gain or loss arising is determined as the difference between the net disposal proceeds, if any, and the carrying amount of the item. [IAS 16:71] As discussed at **6.8.4**, when a revalued asset is disposed of, any credit balance on the revaluation reserve attributable to that asset may be transferred directly to retained earnings (though such a transfer is not mandatory) but must not be reflected in profit or loss.

The amount of consideration to be included in the gain or loss arising from the derecognition of an item of property, plant and equipment is determined in accordance with the requirements for determining the transaction price in paragraphs 47 to 72 of IFRS 15 *Revenue from Contracts with Customers* (see **chapter A14**). Subsequent changes to the estimated amount of the consideration included in the gain or loss should be accounted for in accordance with the requirements for changes in the transaction price in IFRS 15 (see **chapter A14**). [IAS 16:72]

The wording of IAS 16:72 was amended in June 2014 as a consequential amendment arising from IFRS 15. For entities that have not yet adopted IFRS 15, IAS 16:72 states that the consideration receivable on disposal of an item of property, plant and equipment is recognised initally at its fair value. If payment is deferred beyond normal credit terms, the consideration received is recognised initially at the cash price equivalent. The difference between the nominal amount of the consideration and the cash price equivalent is recognised as interest income on an effective yield basis, in accordance with IAS 18.

IAS 16 specifically prohibits the classification of gains arising on the derecognition of property, plant and equipment as revenue (other than in the circumstances described in **9.3**). [IAS 16:68] The Standard does, however, specify that the date of disposal of an item of property, plant and equipment is the date the recipient obtains control of that item in accordance with the requirements for determining when a performance obligation is satisfied in IFRS 15 (see **chapter A14**). [IAS 16:69]

The wording of IAS 16:69 was amended in June 2014 as a consequential amendment arising from IFRS 15. For entities that have not yet adopted IFRS 15, IAS 16:69 states that the date of disposal of an item of property, plant and equipment should be determined using the criteria for recognising revenue from the sale of goods, as set out in IAS 18 (see **appendix A1**).

9.2 Application of IFRS 5 to 'in-period' disposals of assets

It is necessary to consider the requirements of IFRS 5 *Non-current Assets Held for Sale and Discontinued Operations* not only for items meeting the criteria for classification as held for sale at the end of the reporting period, but also for all 'in-period' disposals, including assets sold during the reporting period that were not classified as held for sale at the previous reporting date.

The following example illustrates how the requirements of IFRS 5 are applied to an asset that was not classified as held for sale at the previous reporting date.

Example 9.2

Application of IFRS 5 to 'in-period' disposals of assets

Entity R prepares its financial statements to 31 December and it does not prepare interim financial reports. At 31 December 20X1, Entity R carried a property asset in its statement of financial position at its revalued amount of CU2 million in accordance with IAS 16. Depreciation is CU60,000 per year. In April 20X2, management decides to sell the property and it is advertised for sale. By 30 April 20X2, the sale is considered to be highly probable. At that date, the asset's fair value is CU2.6 million and its value in use is CU2.8 million. Costs of disposal of the asset are estimated at CU100,000. On 15 June 20X2, the property is sold for CU2.75 million.

Is Entity R required to apply IFRS 5 to the disposal of the property?

Yes. When the effect is material, the requirements of IFRS 5 should be applied to 'in-period' disposals of assets.

In the circumstances described, the following steps are required.

- Entity R should determine the date at which the IFRS 5 criteria for classification as held for sale are met (assume the date is determined to be 30 April 20X2 in this case).

- Entity R should depreciate the property until the date of reclassification as held for sale. Accordingly, the depreciation charge is CU60,000 × 4/12 = CU20,000.

- The property should be revalued to its fair value at that date of CU2.6 million if the difference between the property's carrying amount at that date and its fair value is material. The revaluation increase should be recognised in other comprehensive income in accordance with IAS 16.

- Entity R should consider whether the property is impaired by comparing its carrying amount (fair value) with its recoverable amount (higher of value in use and fair value less costs of disposal). In the above example, no impairment loss is recognised because value in use of CU2.8 million is higher than fair value less costs of disposal of CU2.5 million. If any impairment loss were identified at this point, it would be accounted for as a revaluation decrease under IAS 16.

- The property should be reclassified as held for sale and remeasured to fair value less costs to sell (CU2.5 million). Because, in this example, the property is already carried at fair value, the requirement to deduct costs to sell results in the immediate recognition of a loss of CU100,000. In accordance with IFRS 5, this write down to fair value less costs to sell should be recognised in profit or loss.

- When the property is disposed of on 15 June 20X2, a profit on disposal of CU150,000 is recognised (net proceeds of CU2.65 million less carrying amount of CU2.5 million). Any remaining revaluation reserve relating to the property is not recognised in profit or loss, but it may be transferred to retained earnings in accordance with IAS 16.

The application of IFRS 5 in the above example affects the amounts reported in profit or loss, because the valuation movement prior to the date of reclassification (CU620,000) is recognised in other comprehensive income and is not subsequently reclassified to profit or loss. In addition to the depreciation expense of CU20,000, a net gain is recognised of CU50,000 in profit or loss which is comprised of the fair value movement after reclassification (CU150,000) less costs of disposal (CU100,000). If IFRS 5 had not been applied, in addition to the depreciation expense of CU27,500 (CU60,000 × 5.5/12), the net gain recognised in profit or loss would have been CU677,500 (net proceeds of CU2.65 million less the carrying amount at 15 June 20X2 of CU1,972,500).

For assets measured under IAS 16's cost model, the application will not affect the net amount reported in profit or loss for the period. However, it will affect the amounts disclosed under IFRS 5:41(c) (see **7.4** in **chapter A20**) and, when disclosed separately, amounts reported for gains or losses arising on the disposal of property, plant and equipment (see **5.4.1** in **chapter A4**).

9.3 Sales of property, plant and equipment held for rental

When an entity, in the course of its ordinary activities, routinely sells items that it has held for rental to others, it transfers those assets to inventories at their carrying amount when they cease to be rented and become held for sale. Sale proceeds from such assets are recognised as revenue in accordance with IFRS 15 *Revenue from Contracts with Customers* (or, for entities that have not yet adopted IFRS 15, IAS 18 *Revenue*). When such assets are transferred to inventories, IFRS 5 does not apply to them. [IAS 16:68A]

10 IFRIC 20 *Stripping Costs in the Production Phase of a Surface Mine*

10.1 IFRIC 20 – scope

IFRIC 20 *Stripping Costs in the Production Phase of a Surface Mine* aims to address diversity in practice in the accounting for costs of removing waste material to gain access to mineral ore deposits ('stripping activity') incurred during the production phase of a surface mine ('production stripping costs'). The Interpretation concludes that costs related to stripping activity should be recognised as an asset if specified criteria are met.

IFRIC 20 applies to waste removal costs that are incurred in surface mining activity during the production phase of a mine. [IFRIC 20:6] It does not apply to waste removal costs during the development phase of the mine, i.e. before production begins; but it acknowledges that such costs are usually capitalised as part of the depreciable cost of building, developing and constructing the mine. [IFRIC 20:2]

Material removed during stripping activity in the production phase of the mine will often be a combination of mineral ore and waste. The ratio of mineral ore to waste can range from uneconomic low grade to profitable high grade. The material removed may result in some useable mineral ore that can be used to produce inventory. In addition, the removal of material may also provide improved access to deeper levels of mineral ore deposits that have a higher ratio of mineral ore to waste. Therefore, stripping activity may result in two benefits: useable mineral ore for the production of inventory and improved access to the mineral ore body that will be mined in future periods. [IFRIC 20:4] IFRIC 20 addresses the accounting for these two benefits.

10.2 Recognition of production stripping costs as an asset

To the extent that the benefit from the stripping activity relates to useable mineral ore for the production of inventory, the costs of the stripping activity should be accounted for in accordance with the principles of IAS 2 *Inventories* (see **chapter A11**). [IFRIC 20:8]

To the extent that the benefit from the stripping activity relates to improved access to the mineral ore body, the costs of the stripping activity should be recognised as a non-current asset (referred to as the 'stripping activity asset'), if, and only if, all of the following criteria are met:

[IFRIC 20:9]

- it is probable that the future economic benefit (improved access to the ore body) associated with the stripping activity will flow to the entity;

- the entity can identify the component of the ore body for which access has been improved; and

- the costs relating to the stripping activity associated with that component can be measured reliably.

> Therefore, a stripping activity asset should only be recognised if the definition of an asset in the *Conceptual Framework for Financial Reporting* is met and the component of the ore body for which access is improved can be specifically identified. Otherwise, the costs of the stripping activity should be expensed as incurred. [IFRIC 20:BC7]

The stripping activity asset should be accounted for as an addition to, or an enhancement of, an existing asset, i.e. it should be accounted for as part of an existing asset. [IFRIC 20:10] IFRIC 20:BC10 states that the stripping activity asset may add to or improve a range of existing assets (e.g. the mine property (land), the mineral deposit itself, an intangible right to extract the ore, or an asset that originated in the mine development phase). Classification of the stripping activity asset as a tangible or an intangible asset will be determined consistent with the nature of the existing asset to which it relates. [IFRIC 20:11]

10.3   Initial measurement of the stripping activity asset

The stripping activity asset should be measured initially at cost, being the accumulated costs directly incurred in performing the stripping activity that improves access to the identified component of the ore body, plus an allocation of directly attributable overhead costs. However, costs associated with incidental operations that take place at the same time as the stripping activity but that are not necessary for the stripping activity to continue as planned should not be included in the cost of the stripping activity asset. [IFRIC 20:12]

In practice, it may be difficult to identify separately the costs associated with any inventory produced (i.e. useable mineral ore for the production of inventory) and the stripping activity asset (i.e. improved access to the specified component of the ore body). When the costs of the stripping activity asset and the inventory produced are not separately identifiable, a relevant production measure should be used as the basis to allocate the production stripping costs between the inventory produced and the stripping activity asset. The production measure should be calculated for the identified component of the ore body and used as a benchmark to identify the extent to which activity has taken place beyond what would otherwise be expected for the inventory production in the period, and that therefore may have created future access benefit (i.e. the stripping activity asset). [IFRIC 20:13 & BC16] Examples of production measures include:

[IFRIC 20:13]

- cost of inventory produced compared with expected cost;
- volume of waste extracted compared with expected volume, for a given volume of ore production; and
- mineral content of the ore extracted compared with expected mineral content to be extracted, for a given quantity of ore produced.

10.4   Subsequent measurement of the stripping activity asset

After initial recognition, the stripping activity asset should be measured at cost or revalued amount, less depreciation or amortisation and less impairment losses in the same way as the existing asset of which it is a part. [IFRIC 20:14]

The stripping activity asset should be depreciated or amortised on a systematic basis over the expected useful life of the identified component of the ore body to which access is improved as a result of the stripping activity. [IFRIC 20:15] The expected useful life of the identified component of the ore body to which the stripping activity asset relates will usually differ from the expected useful life of the mine itself and the related life-of-mine assets, unless the stripping activity improves access to the entire remaining ore body. This might be the case, for example, towards the end of the mine's useful life when the identified component represents the final part of the ore body to be extracted. [IFRIC 20:16]

An entity should use the units of production method of depreciation, unless another method is more appropriate. [IFRIC 20:15]

11   Presentation and disclosure

11.1   Presentation

IAS 1 *Presentation of Financial Statements* requires that, if material, the aggregate carrying amount of the entity's property, plant and equipment should be presented in the statement of financial position. [IAS 1:54(a)]

11.2   Disclosure

11.2.1   General

In respect of each class of property, plant and equipment, an entity is required to disclose:

[IAS 16:73]

- the measurement bases (i.e. cost or valuation) used for determining the gross carrying amount;

- the depreciation methods used;

- the useful lives or the depreciation rates used; and

- the gross carrying amount and the accumulated depreciation (aggregated with accumulated impairment losses) at the beginning and end of the period.

An entity is also required to provide a reconciliation of the carrying amount at the beginning and end of the period, in respect of each class of property, plant and equipment, showing:

[IAS 16:73(e)]

- additions;

- assets classified as held for sale, or included as a disposal group classified as held for sale in accordance with IFRS 5 *Non-current Assets held for Sale and Discontinued Operations*, and other disposals;

- acquisitions through business combinations;

- increases or decreases resulting from revaluations and from impairment losses recognised or reversed in other comprehensive income;

- impairment losses recognised in profit or loss during the period;

- impairment losses reversed in profit or loss during the period;

- depreciation;

- the net exchange differences arising on the translation of the financial statements from the functional currency into a different presentation currency, including the translation of a foreign operation into the presentation currency of the reporting entity; and

- other changes.

The financial statements are also required to disclose:

[IAS 16:74]

- the existence and amounts of restrictions on title, and property, plant and equipment pledged as security for liabilities;

- the amount of expenditures recognised in the carrying amount of an item of property, plant and equipment in the course of its construction;

- the amount of contractual commitments for the acquisition of property, plant and equipment; and

- if not disclosed separately in the statement of comprehensive income, the amount of compensation from third parties for items of property, plant and equipment that were impaired, lost or given up that is included in profit or loss.

Although the drafting is a little unclear in the Standard, it appears that the second bullet above requires disclosure of the cost of assets that are still in the course of construction at the end of the reporting period (i.e. rather than those that were in the course of construction when the costs were incurred). The drafting is also unclear whether it is the costs incurred in the year or the total cumulative costs incurred on such assets which should be disclosed, although the latter interpretation appears more logical.

Disclosures may also be required by IAS 8 *Accounting Policies, Changes in Accounting Estimates and Errors* in respect of changes in accounting estimates for residual values, useful lives, depreciation methods or provisions for dismantling, removing or restoring assets (see **chapter A5**), or by IAS 36 *Impairment of Assets* (see **chapter A10**). [IAS 16:76 & 78]

11.2.2   Items stated at revalued amounts

In respect of items of property, plant and equipment stated at revalued amounts, the entity is required to disclose:

[IAS 16:77]

- the effective date of the revaluation;
- whether an independent valuer was involved;
- for each revalued class of property, plant and equipment, the carrying amount that would have been recognised had the assets been carried under the cost model; and
- the revaluation surplus, indicating the movement for the period and any restrictions on the distribution of the balance to shareholders.

The disclosures required under the final bullet above could be made in the reserves note rather than the property, plant and equipment note.

11.2.3   Additional recommended disclosures

IAS 16:79 also encourages, but does not require, disclosure of the following information:

- the carrying amount of temporarily idle property, plant and equipment;
- the gross carrying amount of any fully depreciated property, plant and equipment that is still in use;

- the carrying amount of property, plant and equipment retired from active use and not classified as held for sale in accordance with IFRS 5; and

- when the cost model is used, the fair value of property, plant and equipment when this is materially different from the carrying amount.

The IFRIC (now called the IFRS Interpretations Committee) was asked to consider to what extent disclosures are required for property, plant and equipment that is temporarily idle and for assets under construction when additional construction has been postponed.

Although the item was not taken onto the IFRIC agenda, the Committee did note that IAS 16:74(b) requires an entity to disclose the amount of expenditures recognised in the carrying amount of an item of property, plant and equipment in the course of its construction. IAS 16:79(a) encourages an entity to disclose the amount of property, plant and equipment that is temporarily idle. Paragraph 112(c) of IAS 1 *Presentation of Financial Statements* requires an entity to provide in the notes to the financial statements information that is not presented elsewhere in the financial statements but is relevant to an understanding of any of the financial statements.

The IFRIC concluded that, in combination, the requirements of IAS 16 and IAS 1 lead to an expectation that, when the amount of idle assets or postponed construction projects becomes significant, such amounts will be separately disclosed.

The conclusions above were set out in the May 2009 edition of *IFRIC Update*.

A8 Investment property

Contents

1 Introduction

1.1 Overview of IAS 40

IAS 40 *Investment Property* applies to the accounting for property (land and/or buildings) held to earn rentals or for capital appreciation (or both). Investment properties are initially measured at cost and, with some exceptions, may subsequently be measured using a cost model or a fair value model. Changes in fair value under the fair value model are recognised in profit or loss.

1.2 Amendments to IAS 40 since the last edition of this manual

None. IAS 40 was most recently amended in June 2014.

2 Scope

2.1 Scope – general

IAS 40 is to be applied in the recognition, measurement and disclosure of 'investment property' (see **2.2**). [IAS 40:2]

The Standard also deals with the measurement in the lessee's financial statements of investment property interests held under a lease accounted for as a finance lease, and with the measurement in a lessor's financial statements of investment property leased out under an operating lease. The more general requirements regarding the classification and measurement of leased investment property are not dealt with in IAS 40 but fall within the general requirements of IAS 17 *Leases*. In particular, the following matters are dealt with in IAS 17 rather than in IAS 40:

[IAS 40:3]

- classification of leases as finance leases or operating leases;

- recognition of lease income from investment property;

- measurement in a lessee's financial statements of property interests held under a lease accounted for as an operating lease (but see **2.4**);

- measurement in a lessor's financial statements of its net investment in a finance lease;

- accounting for sale and leaseback transactions; and

- disclosures regarding finance leases and operating leases.

Also specifically excluded from the scope of IAS 40 are:

[IAS 40:4]

- biological assets related to agricultural activity (see IAS 41 *Agriculture* (**chapter A38**) and IAS 16 *Property, Plant and Equipment* (**chapter A7**)); and

- mineral rights and mineral reserves such as oil, natural gas, and similar non-regenerative resources.

2.2   Distinguishing between investment property and owner-occupied property

IAS 40 acknowledges that judgement is often required to determine whether a property qualifies as an investment property and requires entities to develop criteria to enable them to make that determination in a consistent manner. Disclosure of such criteria is required when classification is difficult (see **9.2.1**). [IAS 40:14]

> IAS 40 was amended by *Annual Improvements to IFRSs: 2011–2013 Cycle* to clarify that the requirements in IAS 40:7 to 14 (see this section and **2.3** to **2.6**) provide guidance for distinguishing between investment property and owner-occupied property and not for determining whether the acquisition of property is a business combination. When an entity acquires property, it is necessary to determine separately whether the transaction is a business combination (using the principles of IFRS 3 *Business Combinations*) and whether the property acquired is investment property (using the principles of IAS 40) (see **3.2**). [IAS 40:14A]

2.3   Investment property – definition

Investment property is defined in IAS 40 as follows.

[IAS 40:5]

> "Investment property is property (land or a building – or part of a building – or both) held (by the owner or by the lessee under a finance lease) to earn rentals or for capital appreciation or both, rather than for:
> (a)   use in the production or supply of goods or services or for administrative purposes; or
> (b)   sale in the ordinary course of business."

Included within this definition are:

[IAS 40:8]

- land held for long-term capital appreciation, and not for short-term sale in the ordinary course of business;

- land held for a currently undetermined future use. If an entity has not decided whether land will be used for owner-occupation or for short-term sale in the ordinary course of business, it should be regarded as held for capital appreciation;

- a building owned or held under a finance lease by an entity and leased out under operating lease(s);

- a vacant building that is being held to be leased out under an operating lease (or leases); and

- property that is being constructed or developed for future use as investment property.

Examples of items that are *not* investment property include:

[IAS 40:9]

- property that is being held for sale in the ordinary course of business, or that is under construction or development for such sale (within the scope of IAS 2 *Inventories* – see **chapter A11**). This means that properties acquired specifically for the purpose of subsequent disposal in the near future, or for development and resale, are excluded from the scope of IAS 40;

- owner-occupied property (within the scope of IAS 16 *Property, Plant and Equipment* – see **chapter A7**), which includes property held for future development and subsequent use as owner-occupied property, property held for future use as owner-occupied property, employee-occupied property (whether or not the employees pay rent at market rates) and owner-occupied property awaiting disposal; and

- property leased to another entity under a finance lease.

For entities that have not yet adopted IFRS 15 *Revenue from Contracts with Customers*, IAS 40:9 also cites property being constructed or developed on behalf of third parties (within the scope of IAS 11 *Construction Contracts*) as an example of an item that is not investment property.

2.4 Property held under an operating lease

A property interest that is held by a lessee under an operating lease may be classified and accounted for as an investment property if, and only if, the property would otherwise meet the definition of an investment property and the lessee uses IAS 40's fair value model (see **5.2**) for the asset recognised. It is important to note that:

[IAS 40:6]

- this is an option (a 'classification alternative'). Entities may elect whether they wish to classify such interests as investment property;

- the classification alternative is available on a property-by-property basis;

- the classification alternative is not available for assets not accounted for using the fair value model;

- once this classification alternative is selected for one property interest held under an operating lease, all property classified as investment property must be accounted for using the fair value model; and

- property interests accounted for under the classification alternative are considered to be part of the entity's investment property for the purposes of IAS 40's disclosure requirements (see **9.2**).

The option allowed under IAS 40:6 to classify selected property interests under operating leases as investment property is intended to facilitate the classification of assets such as land held under long-term operating leases as investment property, provided that the general criteria for such classification are met. This is particularly relevant in jurisdictions such as Hong Kong and the United Kingdom where interests in property are commonly – or, in the former case, exclusively – held under long-term lease arrangements.

In contrast to the option available in relation to property held under an operating lease under IAS 40:6 (see above), IAS 40:8 *requires* that property held under a finance lease be treated as investment property, provided that the property otherwise meets the definition of an investment property. IAS 40:8 also applies to property held under a lease that is classified as a finance lease because the lease payments cannot be allocated reliably between the land and buildings elements (see **section 5.2** of **chapter A17**).

The detailed requirements when property or property interests held under leases are classified as investment property are considered further at **4.3**.

Example 2.4

Classification – lease of an investment property

Company A (as lessee) leases a property which meets the definition of an investment property.

Company A is unable to obtain a reliable allocation between the land element and the buildings elements of the leased property. Therefore, in accordance with IAS 17:16, the entire lease is classified as a finance lease (it is *not* clear that both elements are operating leases, otherwise the entire lease would be classified as an operating lease).

The requirement in IAS 40:6 (also referred to in IAS 17:19) to adopt the fair value model applies when an entity chooses to account for a property interest held under an operating lease as an investment property. Because, in the circumstances described, Company A classifies the entire lease as a finance lease, IAS 40 permits a choice between the cost model and the fair value model. This option is available for finance leases (as determined by IAS 17) irrespective of whether there may be an 'operating lease' component for land which cannot be reliably determined.

2.5 Property held for more than one purpose

In circumstances when property is held partly for capital appreciation and/or rentals, and partly for the production of goods or services or administrative purposes, the two parts are accounted for separately if they could be sold, or leased out under a finance lease, separately. If they could not be sold (or leased out under a finance lease) separately, the property is accounted for as an investment property only if an insignificant portion is held for use in the production or supply of goods or services or for administrative purposes. [IAS 40:10]

IAS 40 does not include any guidance as to what constitutes an 'insignificant' portion for this purpose. This is a deliberate omission – the Basis for Conclusions on IAS 40 explains that quantitative guidance has not been provided because the Board concluded that such guidance could lead to arbitrary distinctions.

2.6 Ancillary services

If an entity provides ancillary services to the occupants of its property, the property is accounted for as investment property provided that the services are an 'insignificant' portion of the arrangement. [IAS 40:11]

Example 2.6A

Services provided by the owner of an office building

The owner of an office building provides cleaning services for the lessees of the building and these services are 'insignificant' in the context of the total arrangement. Therefore, the building is classified and accounted for as an investment property.

As indicated in **example 2.6A**, it would be unusual for cleaning services to be so material that they would prevent a property from being classified as an investment property. A similar conclusion is likely for security and maintenance services (see IAS 40:11). At the other extreme, some entities rent out fully furnished offices including a whole range of services such as IT systems and secretarial services. Such arrangements are in the nature of the rendering of a service rather than property investment and the property would be classified as owner-occupied and accounted for under IAS 16 *Property, Plant and Equipment*. However, there are many instances in between these extremes for which the appropriate classification can only be determined based on a detailed assessment of the arrangements and whether or not the services provided are judged to be 'insignificant'.

Example 2.6B

Hotel property as investment property

A hotel operator owns a significant number of buildings. The hotel operator seeks to maximise revenue by selling room occupancy.

Is it acceptable for the hotel operator to classify these buildings as investment properties?

The property is for use by the hotel operator in the normal course of business and, therefore, is not investment property. IAS 40:12 cites the direct provision of services to hotel guests as services that will generally be considered to be 'significant'. Although the hotel operator may hold the buildings for long-term appreciation, that is not the principal reason for holding them.

The determination as to whether ancillary services are significant (thus excluding the property from the scope of IAS 40) requires the exercise of judgement. The Standard considers the case of hotels and acknowledges the variety of arrangements that may exist. For example, the owner of a hotel property may transfer some responsibilities to third parties under a management contract. The terms of such contracts may vary widely. The owner's role may be restricted to that of a passive investor, in which case the property would be more likely to qualify as investment property. At the other extreme, the contract may simply result in the outsourcing of some day-to-day responsibilities, while the owner retains significant exposure to variations in the cash flows generated by the operation of the hotel. In the latter case, the contract has little effect on the substance of the owner's interest and the property is likely to be classified as owner-managed. [IAS 40:13]

2.7   Property leased to other group members

If an entity owns a property that is leased to, and occupied by, another group member (e.g. a parent or another subsidiary), the property is not recognised as an investment property in the consolidated financial statements because it will be treated as owner-occupied from the perspective of the group. However, from an individual-entity perspective, the property is treated as an investment property if it meets the requirements of IAS 40:5 (see **2.3**). [IAS 40:15]

2.8 Property accepted as loan settlement

Example 2.8

Property accepted as loan settlement

Entity A, a financial institution, provides mortgage loans to individuals and corporate entities to finance the acquisition of properties. The terms of these mortgage loans require the property to be pledged as collateral for the loan. If a counterparty defaults under the terms of a mortgage loan and is no longer entitled to redeem the collateral, Entity A accepts the property as settlement of the loan receivable. The former owner ceases to have any rights over the property or over the income that it generates. The derecognition criteria in IFRS 9 *Financial Instruments* (or, for entities that have not yet adopted IFRS 9, IAS 39 *Financial Instruments: Recognition and Measurement*) are met and Entity A derecognises the loan receivable, and recognises the property as its asset, initially measured at fair value. Under local regulations, Entity A is required to sell the asset within two years.

Should Entity A classify the property as an investment property in accordance with IAS 40 or as inventories in accordance with IAS 2? How should Entity A account for any rentals received during the period for which it holds the asset?

The appropriate classification of the property as investment property or inventories depends on management's intent. If management intends to hold the property to earn rentals or for capital appreciation (or both), the property would meet the definition of an investment property and should be accounted for under IAS 40. In contrast, if the property is being actively marketed for sale, but it is not sold within a short timeframe (e.g. because of seasonal fluctuations in the property market), such activity would indicate that Entity A views the property as a form of settlement of amounts due under the defaulted mortgage loan and that it is an asset acquired and held for sale in the ordinary course of business. In such circumstances, the property should be accounted for as inventories under IAS 2.

Regardless of whether the property is classified as investment property or inventories, any rentals received should be recognised as rental income in profit or loss.

2.9 Group of assets leased under a single operating lease

Example 2.9

Group of assets leased under a single operating lease

IAS 40:5 defines investment property as "property (land or a building – or part of a building – or both) held (by the owner or by the lessee under a finance lease) to earn rentals or for capital appreciation or both".

IAS 40:50 states (see **5.2.1**) that "[i]n determining the carrying amount of investment property under the fair value model, an entity does not double-count assets or liabilities that are recognised as separate assets or liabilities. For example:

505

(a)   equipment such as lifts or air-conditioning is often an integral part of a building and is generally included in the fair value of the investment property, rather than recognised separately as property, plant and equipment.

(b)   if an office is leased on a furnished basis, the fair value of the office generally includes the fair value of the furniture, because the rental income relates to the furnished office. When furniture is included in the fair value of investment property, an entity does not recognise that furniture as a separate asset".

Consider the following example:

- a lessor leases out a farm for the purpose of earning rentals;
- the farm is made up of the following assets: (1) land and agricultural buildings, and (2) agricultural fittings, fixtures and machinery that are an integral part of the agricultural buildings;
- the lease agreement meets the definition of an operating lease for the lessor; and
- the lessor measures investment property after initial recognition at fair value.

The lessor should account for all the assets included in the operating lease agreement as a unique investment property and, as a consequence, measure it using the fair value model.

Although agricultural fittings, fixtures and machinery do not meet the definition of an investment property in their own right, the lessor should follow the requirements in IAS 40:50 to determine the fair value of its investment property, including the other assets that form part of the lease agreement.

In the above example, the lease agreement includes all the assets (i.e. land and agricultural buildings and fittings, fixtures and machinery) that are an integral part of the farm and are necessary for operating the farm. Therefore, the rental income reflects the right to use of the complete set of assets. Consequently, the lessor should recognise investment property comprising all the assets (i.e. the land and agricultural buildings and the agricultural fittings, fixtures and machinery), measured in accordance with IAS 40.

Specific facts and circumstances should be considered by the lessor in each operating lease agreement covering a piece of land or a building, or part of a building, or both together with property, plant and equipment items held to earn rentals, in order to establish which assets covered by the agreement should be regarded as investment property.

3 Recognition

3.1 Recognition – general

Investment property is recognised as an asset when:

[IAS 40:16]

- it is probable that the future economic benefits that are associated with the investment property will flow to the entity; and

- the cost of the investment property can be measured reliably.

This general principle is used to consider whether capitalisation is appropriate both in respect of the costs incurred initially to acquire or construct an investment property, and costs incurred subsequently to add to, replace part of, or service a property (see **3.3**). [IAS 40:17]

3.2 Distinguishing the acquisition of an investment property asset (or assets) from a business combination

When investment property is acquired, it is necessary to consider whether the transaction is the acquisition of an asset or a group of assets, or a business combination in the scope of IFRS 3 *Business Combinations*. If a transaction is identified as a business combination, the investment property acquired as part of that transaction should initially be recognised and measured in accordance with IFRS 3 rather than in accordance with the requirements of IAS 40.

IAS 40:14A (see below) was added to IAS 40 in December 2013 by *Annual Improvements to IFRSs: 2011–2013 Cycle* to provide expanded guidance for when an entity is required to determine whether the acquisition of investment property is the acquisition of an asset or a group of assets, or a business combination.

When an entity acquires investment property:

[IAS 40:14A]

- judgement is required to determine whether the acquisition is the acquisition of an asset or a group of assets, or a business combination in the scope of IFRS 3; and

- this judgement should be based on the guidance in IFRS 3 rather than on the requirements in IAS 40:7 to 14 (see **2.2** to **2.6**).

The Standard notes that the requirements in IAS 40:7 to 14 provide guidance for distinguishing between investment property and owner-occupied property and not for determining whether the acquisition of property is a business combination. When an entity acquires property, it is necessary to determine separately whether the transaction is a business combination (using the principles of IFRS 3) and whether the property acquired is investment property (using the principles of IAS 40). [IAS 40:14A]

The December 2013 amendments are effective for annual periods beginning on or after 1 July 2014, with earlier application permitted. If an entity applies the requirements of IAS 40:14A for an annual period beginning before 1 July 2014, it is required to disclose that fact. [IAS 40:85D]

The requirements of IAS 40:14A are required to be applied prospectively for acquisitions of investment property from the beginning of the first period for which the entity adopts the December 2013 amendments. Acquisitions of investment property in prior periods should not be adjusted. However, an entity may choose to apply the requirements of IAS 40:14A to individual acquisitions of investment property that occurred prior to the beginning of the first annual period occurring on or after the 1 July 2014 (or earlier date of adoption) if, and only if, information needed to apply the amendment to those earlier transactions is available to the entity. [IAS 40:84A]

Therefore, entities should generally apply the requirements of IAS 40:14A prospectively for acquisitions of investment property in annual periods beginning on or after 1 July 2014. Entities may also choose:

- to adopt the amendments for an earlier accounting period and to apply IAS 40:14A to all acquisitions of investment property that occur on or after the first day of that accounting period. For example, an entity may adopt the amendments for an accounting period beginning on or after 1 January 2014 and apply IAS 40:14A to all acquisitions of investment property that occur on or after 1 January 2014; and/or

- to restate individual acquisitions of investment property that occur before the date of initial application (whether 1 July 2014 or an earlier date). Therefore, for example, an entity applying the amendments for the first time in its annual financial statements for the period beginning 1 January 2015 may choose to restate an acquisition of investment property that occurred during its 2014 accounting period (provided that it has the necessary information) without restating all acquisitions that occurred during the 2014 accounting period.

Acquisitions in prior accounting periods can only be restated if the necessary information is available to the entity. The IASB has stipulated prospective application of the December 2013 amendments, and limited the scope for restatement of past acquisitions, because of concerns that such restatements might involve the use of hindsight when determining the fair values, at acquisition date, of the identifiable assets acquired and of the liabilities assumed as part of the business combination transaction. [IAS 40:BC22]

3.3 Subsequent costs

Appropriate application of the recognition principle set out at **3.1** results in: [IAS 40:19]

- the immediate expensing of the costs of the day-to-day servicing of a property (e.g. the costs of labour, consumables and minor parts used for repairs and maintenance); and

- costs incurred to replace parts of the original property being recognised in the investment property if they meet the recognition criteria.

When the costs of replacement parts are capitalised, the carrying amounts of the replaced parts are derecognised. [IAS 40:19]

If the entity has been using the cost model to measure its investment property, but the replaced part was not being depreciated separately, and the carrying amount of the replaced part cannot be determined, the cost of the replacement may be used as an indication of what the cost of the replaced part would have been at acquisition. [IAS 40:68]

When the fair value model is being used, the carrying amount of the investment property may already reflect the deterioration in value of the replaced part. In other cases it may be difficult to discern how much fair value should be reduced for the part being replaced. An alternative to reducing fair value for the replaced part, when it is not practical to do so, is to include the cost of the replacement in the carrying amount of the investment property, and then to reassess the fair value of the property (i.e. in the same way as would be required for additions not involving replacement). [IAS 40:68]

3.4 Investment property in the course of construction

IAS 40 does not deal specifically with the recognition of the cost of a self-constructed investment property. The appropriate accounting for such property is therefore determined in accordance with general principles.

Over the period of construction, the costs of construction will be capitalised as part of the cost of the investment property in accordance with the general principle outlined at **3.1**. Paragraphs 16 to 22 of IAS 16 *Property, Plant and Equipment* (see **section 4.2** of **chapter A7**) provide guidance as to what is appropriately included within such costs.

The capitalisation of borrowing costs is considered in accordance with the general requirements of IAS 23 *Borrowing Costs* (see **chapter A18**). IAS 23:4 provides an optional exemption from the requirement to capitalise borrowing costs for qualifying assets that are measured at fair value (which would include investment property under construction if an entity follows the fair value model for investment property). Therefore, entities can choose, as a matter of accounting policy, whether to capitalise borrowing costs in respect of such assets. When relevant to an understanding of the financial statements, that accounting policy should be disclosed.

If an entity follows the fair value model in accounting for its investment property (see **section 5.2**), provided that the fair value of the property under construction can be measured reliably, the costs capitalised during the course of construction do not affect the carrying amount of the investment property under construction, which is remeasured to fair value at the end of each reporting period. Therefore, any costs capitalised during the reporting period simply reduce the amount recognised in profit or loss for any gain (or increase the amount recognised for any loss) arising on remeasurement to fair value at the end of the reporting period. Although the amount reported in the statement of financial position is not affected, it is important to capitalise construction costs when appropriate, because this may affect the classification of amounts in the statement of comprehensive income (e.g. any gain on remeasurement may be overstated and property expenses overstated by the same amount).

4   Measurement at recognition

4.1   Measurement at recognition – general

An investment property is measured initially at its cost. Transaction costs are included in the initial measurement. [IAS 40:20]

The cost of an investment property includes its purchase price (if purchased) and other directly attributable expenditure (e.g. professional fees for legal services, property transfer taxes and other transaction costs). [IAS 40:21]

Start-up costs are not included unless they are necessary to bring the asset to the condition required for its intended operation. Abnormal costs, and operating losses incurred before the property reaches its required level of occupancy, are excluded from the cost of the investment property. [IAS 40:23]

Example 4.1A

Expenditure to be capitalised as part of the cost of an investment property

Entity R acquires a building for CU95 million in March 20X1 as an investment property. In June 20X1, Entity R refurbishes entirely the building at a cost of CU5 million to bring it to the condition required by the rental market. Entity R will pay an estate agent two months' rent if the agent locates a lessee. In December

---

20X1, Entity R (the lessor) finally rents the property under an operating lease to Entity S (the lessee).

Is it appropriate for Entity R to include the refurbishment costs and the estate agent's fees as part of the initial cost of the investment property?

Yes. When it buys the building, Entity R should recognise the purchase price as the initial cost of the building under IAS 40. The refurbishment costs are necessary to bring the property to a condition suitable for renting out and, therefore, these costs should also be included in the initial cost of the building.

The estate agent's fees are not part of the initial cost of the building but they are considered to be "initial direct costs incurred in negotiating and arranging an operating lease" under IAS 17 *Leases*. They are, therefore, capitalised as part of the leased building in accordance with IAS 17:52. When the cost model is used, the expenditure should be depreciated over the lease term. When the fair value model is used, the costs should be capitalised and will, therefore, result in a smaller revaluation gain (or larger revaluation loss) when the building is next remeasured to fair value.

Example 4.1B

Termination payments by a lessor to a lessee

Company A owns an office building that it leases to Company B. The lease is classified as an operating lease in accordance with IAS 17. Company A would like to convert the office building into a block of flats, believing that this will attract significantly higher rental income. First, however, Company A must terminate the lease contract with Company B.

Company A applies the cost model as its accounting policy for the measurement of its investment property subsequent to initial recognition.

Should Company A capitalise the lease termination costs as part of the cost of converting the office building into a block of flats?

Yes. Paragraph 16(b) of IAS 16 *Property, Plant and Equipment* states that the cost of an item of property, plant and equipment includes "any costs directly attributable to bringing the asset to the location and condition necessary for it to be capable of operating in the manner intended by management". IAS 16:7 requires that the cost of an item of property, plant and equipment be recognised as an asset if "it is probable that future economic benefits associated with the item will flow to the entity" and if "the cost of the item can be measured reliably".

Therefore, if Company A's cost of terminating Company B's operating lease meets the recognition criteria for property, plant and equipment in IAS 16:7, Company A should capitalise this cost because it is a directly attributable cost of enabling operation of the asset in the manner intended by management.

Company A should also consider whether there is an indicator of impairment and whether any further impairment testing should be performed to ensure that the building is not recognised at a carrying amount higher than its recoverable amount as a result of capitalising the lease termination costs.

4.2 Deferred payments

The cost of an investment property for which payment is deferred is the cash price equivalent of the deferred payments. The difference between the cash price equivalent recognised at initial measurement, and the total payments made, is recognised as an interest expense over the period of credit, i.e. the period from the point of receipt of the property until the point of settlement of the related liability. [IAS 40:24]

There is no definition of 'cash price equivalent' in IAS 40. It is presumably intended to equate to the present value of the deferred payment but might also encompass a cash price offered by the vendor as an alternative to the deferred payment terms.

4.3 Property held under lease and classified as investment property

4.3.1 Measurement of investment property held under lease – general

The initial cost of a property interest held under a lease and classified as an investment property is prescribed by IAS 17:20. The property is recognised at the lower of its fair value and the present value of the minimum lease payments. An equivalent amount is recognised as a liability in accordance with the same paragraph. [IAS 40:25]

IAS 40:25 applies to all property interests held under leases (whether operating or finance) and classified as investment property. Therefore, in effect, such interests are recognised as if the underlying lease were a finance lease, even if it would be classified as an operating lease under the general requirements of IAS 17.

When a premium is paid on the lease, it is treated as part of the minimum lease payments for this purpose. It is included within the cost of the asset, but excluded from the liability (because it has already been paid). If a property interest held under a lease is classified as an investment property, the item accounted for at fair value is that interest and not the underlying property. [IAS 40:26]

This means that it is the fair value of the leasehold interest, rather than the fair value of the property, that is recognised in the financial statements. Normally, in a very long lease with only nominal 'ground rent', the difference between these two values is very small. However, IAS 40 allows any property held under an operating lease to be classified as an investment property provided that certain criteria are met (see **2.4**). In some cases, therefore, the difference between the fair value of the leasehold interest and the fair value of the property can be significant. For example, in the case of a short lease at market rent, the market value of the leasehold interest will be small compared to the value of the freehold interest in the property.

4.3.2 Gross value of leasehold interest

As noted at **4.3.1**, a liability should be recognised in the statement of financial position for the present value of the minimum lease payments. If the property is subsequently accounted for under the fair value model, it is important to ensure that the valuation reflected in the statement of financial position is consistent with this. Valuers may value very long leasehold interests on the basis of the freehold interest and then deduct from that value the present value of the ground rent on the head lease and the present value of the estimated residual value at the end of the lease term. But if the liability for the ground rent is recognised separately in the financial statements, it is the gross valuation before any such deduction (but excluding any amount attributable to the residual value) that should be recognised as an asset to avoid double-counting the liability.

4.4 Investment property acquired through exchange of another asset

When an investment property is exchanged for an asset (assets), whether monetary or non-monetary, IAS 40 prescribes the treatment for such an exchange. The cost of the investment property is measured at fair value unless either:

[IAS 40:27]

- the exchange transaction lacks commercial substance; or

- the fair value of neither the asset received nor the asset given up is reliably measurable.

The acquired asset is measured in this way even if an entity cannot derecognise immediately the asset given up. If the acquired asset is not measured at fair value, its cost is measured at the carrying amount of the asset given up. [IAS 40:27]

Whether an exchange transaction has commercial substance is determined by considering the extent to which the future cash flows are expected to change as a result of the transaction. IAS 40 states that a transaction has commercial substance if:

[IAS 40:28]

- the configuration (risk, timing and amount) of the cash flows of the asset received differs from the configuration of the cash flows of the transferred asset; or

- the entity-specific value of the portion of the entity's operations affected by the transaction changes because of the exchange; and

- the difference in either of these is significant relative to the fair value of the assets exchanged.

In determining whether an exchange transaction has commercial substance, the entity-specific value of the portion of the entity's operations affected by the transaction should reflect post-tax cash flows. The Standard notes that the results of these analyses may be clear without having to perform detailed calculations. [IAS 40:28]

In most instances, it will be readily apparent whether a transaction lacks commercial substance. The reference in IAS 40 to the entity-specific value of the portion of the entity's operations affected by the transaction is not explained in detail but clearly is intended to indicate that a transaction will have substance when it has a significant effect on the present value of the entity's future cash flows.

The fair value of the asset is reliably measurable if:

[IAS 40:29]

- the variability in the range of reasonable fair value measurements is not significant for the asset; or

- the probabilities of the various estimates within the range can be reasonably assessed and used when measuring fair value.

If the fair value of either the asset received or the asset given up can be measured reliably, then the fair value of the asset given up is used to measure cost unless the fair value of the asset received is more clearly evident. [IAS 40:29]

5 Measurement after recognition

5.1 Selection of accounting policy for investment property

5.1.1 Selection of accounting policy for investment property - general

In general, IAS 40 (1) allows an entity to choose whether it adopts a fair value model or a cost model for investment property, and (2) requires that, having decided on its policy, an entity should apply that model to all of its investment property. [IAS 40:30]

There are two exceptions to this general principle. These are:

[IAS 40:30]

- when a lessee chooses to classify a property interest held under an operating lease as investment property, the lessee automatically forfeits the choice of model offered by IAS 40 – the fair value model must be used for all investment property (see **2.4**); [IAS 40:6 & 34] and

- when an entity has investment property backing liabilities that pay a return linked directly to the fair value of, or returns from, specified assets including that investment property, the entity is not required to apply the same policy for that property as it does for its other investment property (see **5.1.3**). [IAS 40:32A]

> Note also that one of the criteria for qualification as an investment entity under IFRS 10 *Consolidated Financial Statements* (see **section 13** of **chapter A24** for details) is that an entity should measure and evaluate substantially all of its investments on a fair value basis. Accordingly, in order to meet the investment entity exception in IFRS 10, and measure its investments in subsidiaries (other than subsidiaries that provide investment-related services or activities) at fair value through profit or loss rather than consolidating them, an entity will need to select IAS 40's fair value model for its investment property.

If an entity adopts the cost model, it must still measure the fair value of all of its investment property for disclosure purposes, other than in exceptional circumstances when the fair value cannot be reliably measured (see **5.2.4**).

5.1.2 Change in accounting policy for investment property

Once a policy has been adopted, any change will be considered a voluntary change in accounting policy which, under IAS 8 *Accounting Policies, Changes in Accounting Estimates and Errors*, is permitted only if it will result in financial statements providing reliable and more relevant information. IAS 40 notes that it is highly unlikely that a change from the fair value model to the cost model will result in a more relevant presentation. [IAS 40:31]

5.1.3 Investment property linked to liabilities

When an entity has investment property backing liabilities that pay a return linked directly to the fair value of, or returns from, specified assets including that investment property, the entity may choose a model for all such investment property and independently choose a different model for all other investment property. The choice of policy made by an entity for such property does not affect the entity's choice for the rest of its property, e.g. the entity could choose the fair value model for its investment property linked to liabilities, but choose the cost model for the rest of its investment property. [IAS 40:32A]

> This choice is typically applicable to vehicles that have been set up to own investment property and that are funded by debt instruments

instead of equity instruments (see **2.1.2** in **chapter B3** (or, for entities that have not yet adopted IFRS 9 *Financial Instruments*, **2.1.2** in **chapter C3**) for the classification of puttable instruments).

For an entity that operates an internal property fund that issues notional units whereby some units are held by investors and others are held by the entity, the property held by the fund cannot be held partly at cost and partly at fair value. [IAS 40:32B]

If different models are chosen, sales of investment property between pools of assets are recognised at fair value and the cumulative change in fair value is recognised in profit or loss. [IAS 40:32C]

5.1.4   Investment property classified as held for sale

Investment property accounted for under IAS 40's cost model falls within the scope of IFRS 5 *Non-current Assets Held for Sale and Discontinued Operations*, both as regards measurement and as regards presentation in the statement of financial position. Therefore, from the point at which an investment property accounted for under the cost model meets the criteria for classification as held for sale (or is included within a disposal group meeting the criteria for classification as held for sale), the asset is accounted for under that Standard (see **chapter A20**).

Investment property accounted for under IAS 40's fair value model is excluded from the measurement requirements of IFRS 5, but is otherwise subject to the requirements of that Standard. [IFRS 5:5] Therefore, from the point at which investment property accounted for under the fair value model meets the criteria for classification as held for sale (or is included in a disposal group meeting the criteria for classification as held for sale), the asset is presented as held for sale in the statement of financial position, as required by IFRS 5:38 (see **7.3.1** in **chapter A20**), but it continues to be measured at fair value in accordance with the entity's accounting policy for investment property.

5.2   Fair value model

5.2.1   Fair value model – general

After initial recognition, an entity that chooses the fair value model measures all of its investment property at fair value, except when the requirements of IAS 40:53 apply (inability to determine fair value reliably – see **5.2.4**). [IAS 40:33]

Fair value is defined as "the price that would be received to sell an asset or paid to transfer a liability in an orderly transaction between market participants at the measurement date. (See IFRS 13 *Fair Value Measurement*.)" [IAS 40:5]

When measuring the fair value of investment property, an entity should ensure that the fair value reflects, among other things, rental income from current leases and other assumptions that market participants would use when pricing the investment property under current market conditions. [IAS 40:40]

Assets or liabilities recognised elsewhere in the financial statements (e.g. prepaid or accrued operating lease income) should not be double-counted in determining the carrying amount of investment property under the fair value model. For example, if the lifts and air-conditioning system in a property are considered an integral part of the building, they are generally included in the fair value of the investment property and are not recognised as separate assets. Similarly, if an office is leased on a furnished basis, and the rental income relates to the furnished office, the fair value of the office generally includes the fair value of the furniture, and the furniture is, therefore, not recognised as a separate asset. [IAS 40:50]

These requirements would extend to lease incentives. That is to say that assets/liabilities recognised for lease incentives received/given should not be double-counted in the statement of financial position.

Example 5.2.1

Acquisition of investment property with existing operating lease in place

Entity C acquires an investment property with an operating lease that is not at current market rates.

IAS 40:40 states as follows.

"When measuring the fair value of investment property in accordance with IFRS 13, an entity shall ensure that the fair value reflects, among other things, rental income from current leases and other assumptions that market participants would use when pricing the investment property under current market conditions."

Should the fair value of the off-market lease be included within the carrying amount of the investment property or presented separately (whether as an asset or as a liability)?

IAS 40 does not provide any specific guidance on this area and it appears that Entity C may adopt either presentation as an accounting policy choice. Inclusion within the carrying amount of the investment property is supported by IAS 40:26, which states, in the context of investment property held under a lease, that a premium paid for a lease should be included in the cost of an investment property. This acknowledges the fact that, conceptually, an investment property includes not only land and buildings but other assets (customer relationships, furniture and favourable leases) and liabilities (unfavourable leases) that are interrelated in determining the overall fair value of the property. However, IAS 40 does not require that these elements be presented as a single asset; indeed

IAS 40:50 recognises that items such as furniture and prepaid operating lease income may be presented as separate balances.

If the operating lease element is shown separately, it is important to have regard to the requirements of IAS 40:50 which states that, in measuring the fair value of an investment property, an entity should not "double-count assets or liabilities that are recognised as separate assets or liabilities". Therefore, the fair value of an investment property is adjusted to exclude, among other things, assets or liabilities arising from favourable or unfavourable leases. If it applies a policy of recognising a separate asset or liability for the off-market lease, Entity C should ensure that the combined carrying amount of that balance and the investment property asset does not exceed the fair value of the investment property.

Example 2.9 addresses whether a group of assets leased under a single operating lease (e.g. agricultural machinery leased together with agricultural land and buildings) meets the definition of investment property.

The fair value of an investment property held under a lease reflects expected cash flows (including contingent rent that is expected to become payable). Thus, if a valuation obtained for a property is net of all payments expected to be made, any recognised lease liability must be added back to arrive at the carrying amount of the investment property using the fair value model. [IAS 40:50(d)]

5.2.2 Remeasurement of investment property: transaction costs incurred on acquisition

Example 5.2.2

Remeasurement of investment property: transaction costs incurred on acquisition

Entity A acquires an investment property (in an orderly transaction with a third-party market participant) immediately before the end of its reporting period for CU100 million. It incurs additional costs in the form of legal and other professional fees of CU2 million at the time of initial recognition which are directly attributable to the acquisition of the property. These transaction costs are included in the initial measurement of the investment property in accordance with IAS 40:21 (see **4.1**). Therefore, the investment property is initially recognised at CU102 million.

Entity A measures its investment property using IAS 40's fair value model. At the end of the reporting period, the fair value of the investment property is unchanged from the price paid by Entity A of CU100 million.

How should the difference of CU2 million between the carrying amount of the property and its fair value be accounted for at the end of the reporting period?

Under IFRS 13, the fair value of the investment property should be measured at the reporting date at the amount that would be received at that date from the sale of the property in an orderly transaction in Entity A's principal (or most advantageous) market. If the property were to be sold, costs might be incurred by Entity A (as the seller) or by the purchaser as part of the transaction. However, under IFRS 13:25, transaction costs that would be incurred by Entity A if the property were sold should not be deducted from the fair value of the property. Likewise, costs that would be incurred by a purchaser (e.g. those similar to the legal and other professional fees capitalised by Entity A) would not be received by Entity A on sale of the investment property and, consequently, do not affect the investment property's fair value as defined by IFRS 13.

Accordingly, the property should be measured at the reporting date at CU100 million. The difference between this amount and the carrying amount of CU102 million should be recognised as a fair value adjustment in profit or loss in accordance with IAS 40:35 (see **5.2.6**).

Example 5.2.2 demonstrates that when an investment property is acquired immediately before the end of a reporting period, such that its fair value is unlikely to change between the date of acquisition and the end of the accounting period, it is likely that a downward revaluation will be recognised in profit or loss that is equal and opposite to the capitalised acquisition costs, if any.

5.2.3 Use of independent valuers

Entities are encouraged (but not required) to use, as the basis for measuring fair value, a valuation by an independent valuer "who holds a recognised and relevant professional qualification and has recent experience in the location and category of the investment property being valued". [IAS 40:32]

The IASB decided that an independent valuation should not be required under IAS 40 because of the following considerations:

- the cost-benefit ratio of an independent valuation may be inappropriate for some entities; and

- independent valuers with appropriate expertise are not available in some markets.

Consequently, paragraphs B55 and B56 of the Basis for Conclusions on IAS 40 explain that it is for the preparers of financial statements to decide, in consultation with auditors, whether an entity has sufficient internal resources to determine reliable fair values.

5.2.4 Inability to measure fair value reliably

There is a rebuttable presumption that the fair value of an investment property can be measured reliably on a continuing basis. But in exceptional cases, when an investment property is first acquired (or when an existing property first becomes an investment property after a change of use), there may be clear evidence that the fair value of the property is not reliably measurable on a continuing basis. This arises when, and only when, the market for comparable properties is inactive (e.g. there are few recent transactions, price quotations are not current or observed transaction prices indicate that the seller was forced to sell) and alternative reliable measurements of fair value (e.g. based on discounted cash flows) are not available. [IAS 40:53]

Note that the exception under IAS 40:53 is available only when the investment property is first recognised as such. If an investment property has previously been measured at fair value, it should continue to be measured at fair value until disposal (or until it otherwise ceases to be an investment property, for example because it becomes owner-occupied) even if comparable market transactions become less frequent or market prices become less readily available. [IAS 40:55]

When, in the circumstances described above, it is not possible for an entity that uses the fair value model to measure the fair value of a particular property (other than an investment property under construction) reliably on initial recognition, that particular investment property is measured using the cost model in IAS 16 *Property, Plant and Equipment*. In accounting for the property under IAS 16, the entity is required to assume that the residual value of the property is zero. IAS 16 is then applied until the disposal of the property. [IAS 40:53] Special rules apply for investment properties under construction – see **5.2.5**.

When an entity is compelled, for the reasons set out in IAS 40:53, to measure an investment property using the cost model under IAS 16, it continues to measure all of its other investment property at fair value. [IAS 40:54]

The circumstances described in IAS 40:53 are also relevant to determining the circumstances in which an entity using the cost model would be exempt from disclosing the fair value of investment property (see **9.2.3**).

An economic downturn may increase the volatility of prices in real estate markets and restrict the level of comparator transactions against which to assess value. This may increase uncertainty around reported investment property fair value compared to 'normal' market conditions. For this reason, third party valuers may include valuation uncertainty paragraphs in their reports in order to draw the reader's attention to the financial backdrop against which the valuations have been assessed. Generally, this type of uncertainty paragraph may not caveat the valuation opinion provided, but it may make reference to major upheaval in the financial sector, reduced liquidity in the market place, restricted availability of debt and similar factors, and may state that these factors have caused increased uncertainty in respect of current real estate prices.

There is a rebuttable presumption in IAS 40:53 that the fair value of an investment property can be determined reliably on a continuing basis; there is no exemption in a period of significant valuation uncertainty, even if comparable market transactions become less frequent or market prices become less readily available. It is only in exceptional cases, when there is clear evidence when the entity first acquires an investment property (or when an existing property first becomes an investment property after an evidenced change in use) that fair value is not reliably determinable, that the entity is permitted to measure that investment property at cost, while measuring its other investment properties at fair value. These exceptional cases are expected to be very rare.

5.2.5 Investment property in the course of construction

If an entity determines that the fair value of an investment property under construction is not reliably measurable but expects the fair value to be reliably measurable when construction is complete, the entity measures the investment property under construction at cost until the earlier of the fair value becoming reliably measurable or the completion of construction. [IAS 40:53]

Once the entity is able to measure reliably the fair value of the investment property under construction, that property should be measured at fair value. Once construction is complete, it is presumed that fair value can be measured reliably. If this is not the case, following completion, the property is accounted for using the cost model in accordance with IAS 16, under the general requirements of IAS 40:53 (see **5.2.4**). [IAS 40:53A]

The presumption that the fair value of investment property under construction can be measured reliably can be rebutted only on initial recognition. An entity that has measured such property at fair value may not conclude that the fair value of the completed investment property cannot be determined reliably. [IAS 40:53B]

5.2.6 Changes in fair value

Changes in the fair value of investment property are recognised in profit or loss in the period in which they arise. [IAS 40:35]

5.2.7 Property held under a lease and classified as investment property

When a property held under a lease that is negotiated at market rates is classified as an investment property (i.e. accounted for as a finance lease), the fair value of the interest in the leased property at acquisition, net of all expected lease payments including those relating to recognised liabilities, should be zero. This fair value does not change, regardless of whether the leased asset and liability are recognised at fair value or at the present value of minimum lease payments as per paragraph 20 of IAS 17 *Leases*. This means that there should be no initial gain or loss arising from the remeasurement of a leased asset from cost to fair value unless fair value is measured at different times. This could occur when an election to apply the fair value model is made after initial recognition. [IAS 40:41]

5.2.8   Anticipated liabilities

When an entity expects that the present value of its payments relating to an investment property (excluding payments relating to recognised liabilities) will exceed the present value of the related cash receipts, IAS 37 *Provisions, Contingent Liabilities and Contingent Assets* should be applied to determine whether a liability should be recognised and, if so, how that liability should be measured. [IAS 40:52]

5.3   Cost model

5.3.1   Cost model – general

IAS 40:5 defines cost as "the amount of cash or cash equivalents paid or the fair value of other consideration given to acquire an asset at the time of its acquisition or construction or, where applicable, the amount attributed to that asset when initially recognised in accordance with the specific requirements of other IFRSs …".

> For example, if the consideration for the purchase of a property was an issue of equity shares in the entity, IFRS 2 *Share-based Payment* should be applied to establish the cost of the property.

After initial recognition, an entity that chooses the cost model measures all of its investment property in accordance with IAS 16's requirements for that model, other than investment property classified as held for sale or included in a disposal group classified as held for sale, which is measured in accordance with IFRS 5 (see **5.1.4**). [IAS 40:56]

5.3.2   Component accounting for in-place leases

> If an entity acquires an investment property with operating leases already in place, the amount paid for the property will reflect the effect of those in-place leases (above and below market rentals, direct costs associated with obtaining new tenants etc.). IAS 16:44 states that, in the circumstances described, "it may be appropriate to depreciate separately amounts reflected in the cost [of the property] that are

attributable to favourable or unfavourable lease terms relative to market terms". If, for example, an entity determines, through the exercise of judgement, that the components of cost attributable to favourable or unfavourable lease terms are significant, those components should be depreciated separately. This will result in a higher (if the lease terms are favourable) or lower (if they are unfavourable) total depreciation charge over the period for which the in-place lease terms apply (see **example 5.3.2** for a numerical example).

However, IAS 16 is silent with respect to other amounts related to the value of in-place leases that may be reflected in the cost of the property. Therefore, whether an entity recognises such amounts as separate components for depreciation purposes is an accounting policy choice to be applied consistently for all similar transactions.

Example 5.3.2

Component accounting for in-place leases

Entity A acquires a building for CU200,000. The building has an existing tenant with a remaining lease term of five years. The rentals from that in-place lease are unfavourable when compared with the current market. If Entity A had been able to secure vacant possession, it would have been willing to pay CU240,000 for the building.

Entity A applies the cost model for investment property under IAS 40 (i.e. Entity A measures the property in accordance with IAS 16's cost model). The remaining useful life of the building is estimated to be 20 years, with nil estimated residual value.

Entity A should identify two separate components reflected in the price paid for the building - a 'gross cost' of CU240,000 offset by the component attributable to the unfavourable lease of CU40,000 (which is determined to be significant in relation to the total cost). The former is depreciated over 20 years, the latter over five years. The annual depreciation charges recognised over the life of the building are therefore as follows.

	Years 1 – 5	Years 6 – 20*
Depreciation on 'gross cost'	12,000	12,000
Depreciation on unfavourable lease component	(8,000)	–
Net charge	4,000	12,000

* Assuming no change to the building's useful life or residual value.

In this example, the component approach results in a lower total depreciation charge over the period for which the in-place lease terms apply.

---

6   Transfers

6.1   Transfers to, or from, investment property – general

This section reflects the requirements of IAS 40 at the date of writing. The IASB has tentatively decided to amend the Standard to clarify that the circumstances listed in IAS 40:57 are examples, and not an exhaustive list, of when a transfer into, or out of, investment property is permitted (see **section 10**).

Transfers to, or from, investment property are made when, and only when, there is a change in use evidenced by one of the following:

[IAS 40:57]

* commencement of owner-occupation, for a transfer from investment property to owner-occupied property;

* commencement of development with a view to sale, for a transfer from investment property to inventories;

* end of owner-occupation, for a transfer from owner-occupied property to investment property; or

* commencement of an operating lease to another party, for a transfer from inventories to investment property.

These circumstances are discussed more fully in **6.2** to **6.5**.

Paragraphs 60 to 65 of IAS 40 apply to recognition and measurement issues that arise when the fair value model is used for investment property and transfers are made to or from investment property (see **6.2** to **6.5**). When the cost model is used, transfers between investment property, owner-occupied property and inventories do not change the carrying amount of the property transferred. They do not, therefore, change the cost of the property for measurement or disclosure purposes. [IAS 40:59]

6.2   Transfer from investment property to owner-occupied property

IAS 40 requires an investment property to be transferred to owner-occupied property only when there is a change of use evidenced by commencement of owner-occupation. [IAS 40:57(a)]

When an investment property carried at fair value is transferred to owner-occupied property, the property's deemed cost for subsequent accounting in accordance with IAS 16 *Property, Plant and Equipment* is its fair value at the date of change in use. [IAS 40:60]

6.3 Transfer from investment property to inventories

IAS 40 requires an investment property to be transferred to inventories only when there is a change of use evidenced by commencement of development with a view to sale. [IAS 40:57(b)]

When an investment property carried at fair value is transferred to inventories, the property's deemed cost for subsequent accounting in accordance with IAS 2 *Inventories* is its fair value at the date of change in use. [IAS 40:60]

6.4 Transfer from owner-occupied property to investment property

The end of owner-occupation signals a potential transfer to investment property. If an owner-occupied property becomes an investment property that will be carried at fair value, IAS 16 is applied up to the date of change of use. Any difference at that date between the carrying amount of the property in accordance with IAS 16 and its fair value is treated in the same way as a revaluation in accordance with IAS 16. [IAS 40:61]

This means that any decrease in the carrying amount of the property is recognised in profit or loss, unless the decrease is the reversal of a previous revaluation surplus, in which case the decrease is recognised in other comprehensive income and reduces that revaluation surplus within equity. [IAS 40:62]

Any increase in the carrying amount is recognised in other comprehensive income and increases the revaluation surplus within equity, unless the increase reverses a previous impairment loss on that property in which case the increase is recognised in profit or loss. The amount recognised in profit or loss should not exceed the amount needed to restore the carrying amount to the amount that would have been determined (net of depreciation) had no impairment loss been recognised. [IAS 40:62]

On subsequent disposal of such a property, the revaluation surplus may be transferred to retained earnings, but not through profit or loss. [IAS 40:62]

6.5 Transfer from inventories to investment property

A transfer from inventories to investment property should be made when, and only when, there is a change in use, evidenced by the commencement of an operating lease to another party. For a transfer to investment property, if the property will be carried at fair value, any difference between the fair value and the carrying amount of the property at the date of transfer is recognised in profit or loss. [IAS 40:63] This is consistent with the treatment of sales of inventories. [IAS 40:64]

6.6   Continued classification as investment property

If an entity decides to dispose of an investment property without development, the property continues to be treated as an investment property until its disposal. It is not treated as inventories. [IAS 40:58]

When an entity has decided to dispose of an investment property through sale, the requirements of IFRS 5 *Non-current Assets Held for Sale and Discontinued Operations* need to be considered (see **5.1.4** and **chapter A20**).

Similarly, if redevelopment of an existing investment property commences but the property is intended for future use as an investment property, the property continues to be recognised as an investment property. [IAS 40:58]

When the fair value model is used, expenditure incurred in the redevelopment of an investment property which remains classified as an investment property (e.g. rebuilding costs) should initially be capitalised (see **3.3**). The effect of remeasuring the asset to fair value is that any resulting gain or loss will be taken to profit or loss. Disclosures required by IAS 40:76 distinguish between the cost of additions and fair value movements (see **9.2.2.1**).

Undeveloped land may fall within the definition of investment property in IAS 40 (see **2.3**) although this will depend on the particular circumstances. When such land is subsequently developed for future use as an investment property, the property continues to be recognised as an investment property while the development takes place.

7   Disposals

7.1   Disposals (entities that have adopted IFRS 15)

Consequential amendments have been made to the requirements in this section for entities that have adopted IFRS 15 *Revenue from Contracts with Customers*. For convenience, the requirements for entities that have not yet adopted IFRS 15 are presented separately at **7.2**.

An investment property is derecognised (i.e. removed from the statement of financial position) on disposal or when it is permanently withdrawn from use and no future economic benefits are expected from its disposal. [IAS 40:66]

The disposal of an investment property may occur through sale of the property or through entering into a finance lease. The date of disposal for investment property is the date the recipient obtains control of the investment property in accordance with the requirements for determining when a performance obligation is satisfied in IFRS 15 *Revenue from Contracts with Customers* (see **chapter A14**). IAS 17 *Leases* applies to a disposal effected by entering into a finance lease and to a sale and leaseback (see **chapter A17**). [IAS 40:67]

The gain or loss on the retirement or disposal of an investment property is calculated as the difference between the net disposal proceeds and the carrying amount of the property and is recognised in profit or loss in the period of the retirement or disposal. This is subject to the requirements of IAS 17 in the case of a sale and leaseback transaction. [IAS 40:69]

The amount of consideration to be included in the gain or loss arising from the derecognition of an investment property is determined in accordance with requirements for determining the transaction price in paragraphs 47 to 72 of IFRS 15 (see **section 7** of **chapter A14**). Subsequent changes to the estimated amount of the consideration included in the gain or loss should be accounted for in accordance with the requirements for changes in the transaction price in IFRS 15. [IAS 40:70]

When any liabilities are retained relating to the property after its disposal, IAS 37 *Provisions, Contingent Liabilities and Contingent Assets* or other relevant Standards are applied to those liabilities. [IAS 40:71]

7.2 Disposals (entities that have not yet adopted IFRS 15)

An investment property is derecognised (i.e. removed from the statement of financial position) on disposal or when it is permanently withdrawn from use and no future economic benefits are expected from its disposal. [IAS 40:66]

The disposal of an investment property may occur through sale of the property or through entering into a finance lease. In determining the date of disposal for an investment property, the criteria in IAS 18 *Revenue* for recognising revenue from the sale of goods should be applied and the related guidance in the appendix to IAS 18 should be considered (see **appendix A1**). IAS 17 *Leases* applies to a disposal effected by entering into a finance lease and to a sale and leaseback (see **chapter A17**). [IAS 40:67]

The gain or loss on the retirement or disposal of an investment property is calculated as the difference between the net disposal proceeds and the carrying amount of the property and is recognised in profit or loss in the period of the retirement or disposal. This is subject to the requirements of IAS 17 in the case of a sale and leaseback transaction. [IAS 40:69]

The consideration receivable on the disposal of an investment property is recognised initially at fair value. In particular, if payment is deferred, the consideration is recognised initially at its cash price equivalent. The difference between this amount and the nominal amount is recognised as interest revenue under the effective interest method in accordance with IAS 18. [IAS 40:70]

> There is no definition of 'cash price equivalent' in IAS 40. It is presumably intended to equate to the present value of the deferred payment but might also encompass a cash price offered by the vendor as an alternative to the deferred payment terms.

When any liabilities are retained relating to the property after its disposal, IAS 37 *Provisions, Contingent Liabilities and Contingent Assets* or other relevant Standards are applied to those liabilities. [IAS 40:71]

8   Compensation for impairment of investment property

Impairments or losses of investment property, related claims for or payment of compensation from third parties and any subsequent purchase or construction of replacement assets are separate economic events and are accounted for separately. Therefore:

[IAS 40:73]

- impairments of investment property are recognised in accordance with IAS 36 *Impairment of Assets*;
- retirements or disposals of investment property are recognised as set out in **section 7** in accordance with IAS 40:66 to 71;
- compensation from third parties for investment property that was impaired, lost or given up is recognised in profit or loss when it becomes receivable; and
- the cost of assets restored, purchased or constructed as replacements is determined as set out in **section 4** in accordance with IAS 40:20 to 29.

Example 8

Insurance claim

A building carried as an investment property burns down during the reporting period. A valuation of the building in its damaged state is performed at the end of the reporting period.

Should the value of the property at the end of the reporting period include any amount receivable from insurance?

The amount receivable from insurance should be recognised separately in the statement of financial position if it meets the relevant recognition criteria.

Any valuation of the property recognised as an investment property should not include the insurance receivable.

9 Presentation and disclosure

9.1 Presentation

IAS 1 *Presentation of Financial Statements* requires that, when material, the aggregate carrying amount of the entity's investment property should be presented in the statement of financial position. [IAS 1:54(b)]

9.2 Disclosure

9.2.1 General disclosures

The disclosures required by IAS 40 are made in addition to the disclosures required by IAS 17 *Leases* for leases entered into by lessees and lessors.

An entity is required to disclose:

[IAS 40:75]

- whether it applies the fair value or the cost model;

- whether, and in what circumstances, properties held under operating leases are classified as investment property when the fair value model is used;

- the criteria used to distinguish investment property from owner-occupied property or property held for sale in the normal course of business, when that classification is difficult;

- the extent to which the fair value of investment property (as measured or disclosed in the financial statements) is based on a valuation by an independent valuer who holds a recognised and relevant professional qualification and has recent experience in the location and category of the investment property being valued. If there has been no such valuation, that fact should be disclosed;

- the amounts recognised in profit or loss for:

  - rental income from investment property;

  - direct operating expenses (including repairs and maintenance) arising from investment property that generated rental income during the period;

  - direct operating expenses (including repairs and maintenance) arising from investment property that did not generate rental income during the period; and

- the cumulative change in fair value recognised in profit or loss on a sale of investment property from a pool of assets, in which the cost model is used, into a pool in which the fair value model is used (i.e. on investment property linked to liabilities – see **5.1.3**);

Property investment entities often make service charges to their tenants (e.g. to cover the cost of repairs and maintenance) which are the responsibility of the tenants under the terms of the lease but which are arranged and managed by the lessor. These costs are typically passed on at cost or with a fixed percentage mark-up under the terms of the lease. When the lessor is in substance merely acting as agent for the payment of these costs, the reimbursement will generally not be recognised as revenue. Nevertheless, it would be helpful to disclose the amount of such receipts and related costs in the notes to the financial statements.

- the existence and amounts of restrictions on the realisability of investment property or the remittance of income and proceeds of disposal; and

- contractual obligations to purchase, construct or develop investment property or for repairs, maintenance or enhancements.

In addition, if there has been a material reduction in asset values after the reporting date, whether arising from a specific event or not, disclosure of the non-adjusting event is required in accordance with IAS 10 *Events after the Reporting Period* (see **chapter A22**).

9.2.2   Fair value model

9.2.2.1   Reconciliation of movements in carrying amount

In addition to the general disclosure requirements set out at **9.2.1**, an entity that applies the fair value model is required to present a reconciliation between the carrying amounts of investment property at the beginning and end of the period, showing the following:

[IAS 40:76]

- additions, disclosing separately those additions resulting from acquisitions, those resulting from subsequent expenditure recognised in the carrying amount of an asset and those resulting from acquisitions through business combinations;

- assets classified as held for sale, or included in a disposal group classified as held for sale, in accordance with IFRS 5 *Non-current Assets Held for Sale and Discontinued Operations* and other disposals;

- net gains or losses from fair value adjustments;

- the net exchange differences arising on the translation of the financial statements into a different presentation currency and on translation of a foreign operation into the presentation currency of the entity;

- transfers to and from inventories and owner-occupied property; and

- other changes.

9.2.2.2 Reconciliation of adjustments to valuation of property

When a valuation obtained for investment property is adjusted significantly for the purpose of the financial statements (e.g. to avoid double-counting of assets or liabilities that are recognised as separate assets and liabilities), the entity is required to present a reconciliation between the valuation obtained and the adjusted valuation included in the financial statements, showing separately the aggregate amount of any recognised lease obligations that have been added back, and any other significant adjustments. [IAS 40:77]

9.2.2.3 Details about property exceptionally stated at cost

In the exceptional circumstances referred to at **5.2.3**, when an entity applying the fair value model measures investment property using the cost model in IAS 16 *Property, Plant and Equipment*, the reconciliation described at **9.2.2.1** should disclose amounts relating to that investment property separately from amounts relating to other investment property. In addition, the following should be disclosed:

[IAS 40:78]

- a description of the investment property;

- an explanation of why fair value cannot be measured reliably; and

- if possible, the range of estimates within which fair value is highly likely to lie.

On disposal of such investment property not carried at fair value, the following should be disclosed:

[IAS 40:78]

- the fact that the entity has disposed of investment property not carried at fair value;

- the carrying amount of that investment property at the time of sale; and

- the amount of gain or loss recognised.

9.2.3 Cost model

In addition to the general disclosure requirements set out at **9.2.1**, an entity that applies the cost model is required to disclose:

[IAS 40:79]

- the depreciation methods used;
- the useful lives or the depreciation rates used; and
- the gross carrying amount and the accumulated depreciation (aggregated with accumulated impairment losses) at the beginning and end of the period.

An entity that applies the cost model is also required to provide a reconciliation of the carrying amount of investment property at the beginning and end of the period, showing:

[IAS 40:79(d)]

- additions, disclosing separately those additions resulting from acquisitions and those resulting from subsequent expenditure recognised as an asset;
- additions resulting from acquisitions through business combinations;
- assets classified as held for sale, or included in a disposal group classified as held for sale, in accordance with IFRS 5 and other disposals;
- depreciation;
- the amount of impairment losses recognised, and the amount of impairment losses reversed, during the period in accordance with IAS 36 *Impairment of Assets*;
- the net exchange differences arising on the translation of the financial statements into a different presentation currency, and on translation of a foreign operation into the presentation currency of the entity;
- transfers to and from inventories and owner-occupied property; and
- other changes.

An entity that applies the cost model is also required to disclose the fair value of its investment property. In the exceptional cases described at **5.2.3**, when an entity cannot measure the fair value of the investment property reliably, it should disclose:

- a description of the investment property;
- an explanation of why fair value cannot be measured reliably; and
- if possible, the range of estimates within which fair value is highly likely to lie.

10   Future developments

In May 2015, the IASB discussed recommendations from the IFRS Interpretations Committee regarding when transfers into, and out of, investment property are permitted. It was noted that the current drafting of IAS 40 implies that such transfers are only permitted when the change in use of the property falls within one of the circumstances set out in IAS 40:57 (see **6.1**). As a result of the discussions, the IASB tentatively decided to amend the Standard to clarify that these circumstances are examples, and not an exhaustive list, of when a transfer into, or out of, investment property is permitted. The IASB also tentatively agreed that disclosure of the evidence used to support a change in use for each transfer would not be required. At the time of writing, it is expected that an exposure draft proposing these amendments will be published before the end of 2015.

A9 Intangible assets

Contents

1 Introduction

1.1 Overview of IAS 38

IAS 38 *Intangible Assets* outlines the accounting requirements for intangible assets, which are non-monetary assets without physical substance that are identifiable (either by being separable or arising from contractual or other legal rights). Intangible assets meeting the relevant recognition criteria are initially measured at cost, subsequently measured at cost or using the revaluation model, and amortised on a systematic basis over their useful lives (unless the asset has an indefinite useful life, in which case it is not amortised).

1.2 Amendments to IAS 38 since the last edition of this manual

None. IAS 38 was most recently amended in May 2014.

2 Scope

2.1 Scope – general

IAS 38 applies to all intangible assets, except:

[IAS 38:2 & 3]

- intangible assets that are within the scope of another Standard, for example:
  - intangible assets held by an entity for sale in the ordinary course of business (addressed by IAS 2 *Inventories* and, for entities that have not yet adopted IFRS 15 *Revenue from Contracts with Customers*, IAS 11 *Construction Contracts*);
  - deferred tax assets (addressed by IAS 12 *Income Taxes*);
  - leases within the scope of IAS 17 *Leases*;
  - assets arising from employee benefits (addressed by IAS 19 *Employee Benefits*);
  - goodwill acquired in a business combination (addressed by IFRS 3 *Business Combinations*);
  - deferred acquisition costs, and intangible assets arising from an insurer's contractual rights under insurance contracts within the scope of IFRS 4 *Insurance Contracts*;
  - non-current intangible assets classified as held for sale (or included in a disposal group that is classified as held for sale) in accordance with IFRS 5 *Non-current Assets Held for Sale and Discontinued Operations*; and

- for entities that have adopted IFRS 15, assets arising from contracts with customers that are recognised in accordance with that Standard;

- financial assets, as defined in IAS 32 *Financial Instruments: Presentation*;

- the recognition and measurement of exploration and evaluation assets (addressed by IFRS 6 *Exploration for and Evaluation of Mineral Resources*); and

- expenditure on the development and extraction of minerals, oil, natural gas and similar non-regenerative resources.

2.2   Intangible assets contained in or on a physical substance

When an intangible asset is contained in or on a physical substance (such as computer software on a compact disc or a motion picture on film), management must assess which element is more significant. For example, software that controls machinery would normally be considered an integral part of the machinery and, therefore, would be treated as property, plant and equipment rather than as an intangible asset. The same would normally be true for the operating system for a computer. When the software does not form an integral part of the machinery or computer hardware to which it relates, it is separately accounted for under IAS 38. [IAS 38:4]

Research and development activities may give rise to an asset with physical substance (e.g. a prototype). Because the activities are primarily directed to the development of knowledge, the physical element of the asset is secondary to its intangible component, i.e. the knowledge embodied in it. In such circumstances, the activities are accounted for under IAS 38. [IAS 38:5]

2.3   Leases for intangible assets

A reporting entity may enter into a lease in respect of an intangible asset. The appropriate classification of the lease is determined in accordance with the requirements of IAS 17 *Leases*. When the lease is a finance lease, IAS 17 directs the lessee to IAS 38 for the appropriate accounting treatment after initial recognition. However, certain rights are specifically excluded from the scope of IAS 17 (rights under licensing agreements for items such as motion picture films, video recordings, plays, manuscripts, patents and copyrights) and are accounted for under IAS 38. [IAS 38:6]

2.4   Programme rights

Programme rights meet the definition of an intangible asset (see **section 3**). However, if they are held or developed for sale, or 'consumption' through broadcasting, in the ordinary course of business, they may also meet the definition of inventories (e.g. a right to broadcast a particular programme only once is an asset that will be consumed in the rendering of broadcasting services). Judgement is required in determining whether classification as an intangible asset or as inventories is appropriate. When classified as inventories, programme rights should not be amortised. An entity may be able to demonstrate that a programme right comprises identifiable components (e.g. different transmission rights) which should be accounted for separately.

2.5 Intangible assets used in the extractive and insurance industries

Although certain specialised activities and transactions associated with the extractive and insurance industries are excluded from the scope of IAS 38 (see **2.1**), the Standard does apply to other intangible assets used in such industries (such as computer software) and other expenditure incurred (such as start-up costs).

IFRIC 20 *Stripping Costs in the Production Phase of a Surface Mine* addresses the appropriate treatment for waste removal costs that are incurred in surface mining activity during the production phase of a surface mine (referred to as 'production stripping costs'). If specified criteria are met, the requirements of that Interpretation may result in production stripping costs being accounted for as an addition to, or an enhancement of, existing intangible assets or existing property, plant and equipment – see **section 10** of **chapter A7** for details.

3 Identification of intangible assets

3.1 Intangible asset – definition

An intangible asset is defined as an identifiable non-monetary asset without physical substance. [IAS 38:8]

The key components of this definition are:

* identifiability; and
* asset (the definition of which encompasses control).

3.2 Identifiability

Identifiability is the characteristic that conceptually distinguishes other intangible assets from goodwill. [IAS 38:11] In a business combination, it is often difficult to determine whether an intangible item qualifies for recognition as an intangible asset or whether it is merely part of goodwill. The word 'identifiable' in the definition is intended to help in such situations.

An asset is identifiable if either:

[IAS 38:12]

- it is separable, i.e. it is capable of being separated or divided from the entity and sold, transferred, licensed, rented or exchanged, either individually or together with a related contract, identifiable asset or liability, regardless of whether the entity intends to do so; or

- it arises from contractual or other legal rights, regardless of whether those rights are transferable or separable from the entity or from other rights and obligations.

The IASB has concluded that all assets that are separable, as defined in IAS 38:12, are identifiable. Therefore, any intangible asset that has that characteristic and that is acquired in a business combination should be recognised as an asset separate from goodwill.

However, separability is not the only indication of identifiability. IAS 38 is clear that, while an asset that is separable meets the identifiability criterion, there are other ways to meet that criterion. For example, a legal right, such as a broadcasting licence, may give rise to future benefits that are 'identifiable' under IAS 38, even if they are not separable from the underlying broadcasting business, because it is unlikely that the broadcasting licence could be sold without disposing of the underlying broadcasting business. Therefore, in a business combination, all intangible assets that arise from contractual or other legal rights, whether or not they are separable, should be identified as assets separate from goodwill.

The illustrative examples accompanying IFRS 3 *Business Combinations* provide a number of examples of items acquired in a business combination that meet the definition of an intangible asset. These examples are not exhaustive, but they do illustrate many of the more common items that arise in the circumstances of a business combination, and they provide a very useful framework for the determination as to whether particular items qualify for recognition as intangible assets (see **7.4.2.4** in **chapter A25**).

3.3   Asset (control)

3.3.1   Control – definition

IAS 38 takes its definition of an asset from the *Conceptual Framework for Financial Reporting*, i.e. an asset is defined as a resource controlled by an entity as a result of past events and from which future economic benefits are expected to flow to the entity. [IAS 38:8] In the context of intangible assets, it is sometimes difficult to determine whether an entity can exert control over the expected future economic benefits. Control in this context means that the entity has the power to obtain the economic benefits that the asset will generate and to restrict the access of others to those benefits. [IAS 38:13]

Normally, control of an intangible asset is achieved through legal rights (e.g. a brand name is protected by a trademark, a publishing title by copyright, a licence by contract). Less frequently, an intangible asset may be controlled merely through custody (e.g. a product formula or intellectual property may be controlled simply by keeping it a secret from outsiders).

3.3.2 Assembled workforce

Certain intangible items of value to an entity may not be controlled by it. For example, it is unusual for an entity to have control over its employees – usually employee contracts can be terminated with a short period of notice and without penalty. Therefore, when a business combination is accounted for as an acquisition, the benefit of an assembled workforce is more likely to be treated as goodwill than as an intangible asset, because the workforce cannot normally be controlled (at least in the IAS 38 sense). This is consistent with paragraph 11 of IFRS 3 *Business Combinations* which only permits those identifiable assets acquired that meet the asset definition in the *Conceptual Framework for Financial Reporting* to be recognised at the acquisition date. For similar reasons, specific management or technical talent is unlikely to meet the definition of an intangible asset, unless it is protected by legal rights to use it and to obtain the future economic benefits expected from it, and it also meets the other parts of the definition. [IAS 38:15]

However, occasionally, an entity may be able to demonstrate that it has sufficient control to be able to capitalise an employee contract as an asset. For example, when a football club acquires a new player, the contract negotiated may give the club exclusive rights to use the player for a specified period of time, and the club may also be entitled to sell that contract to a third party.

3.3.3 Customer relationships and similar items

IAS 38 allows that customer relationships and similar items may meet the definition of intangible assets when either:

[IAS 38:16]

- they are protected or otherwise controlled by legal rights; or

- the ability to control the expected benefits flowing from the relationships, and the separability of the customer relationships, have been evidenced by exchange transactions for the same or similar non-contractual customer relationships (other than as part of a business combination).

An established customer base or market share is not usually controlled by the entity. There may be an expectation that customers will continue to buy from the entity but, usually, they are under no obligation to do so. Clearly, when the relationship is protected by a legal right, the entity has control over the future economic benefits. However, such control may also be evidenced when the entity has acquired a non-contractual customer relationship in a separate exchange transaction, or when there have been exchange transactions for similar relationships. Because these exchange transactions also provide evidence that the customer relationships are separable, such customer relationships meet the definition of an intangible asset. [IAS 38:16]

For example, in some industries, such as those providing mobile telephone services, one service provider may purchase subscriber bases of existing customers from another. The price paid for the subscriber bases usually exceeds the value of the existing contracts, the difference representing the expectation that existing subscribers will renew their contracts. The exchange transaction may provide sufficient evidence to enable the entity to recognise this difference as a separable intangible asset in its own right, even if the existing customers are under no obligation to renew their contracts. (However, this should not be confused with the situation when payments are made directly to customers to enter into a contract. Such contracts should be accounted for as consideration payable to a customer in accordance with paragraphs 70 to 72 of IFRS 15.)

Another example of a common scenario when a non-contractual relationship may qualify for recognition as a separate intangible asset is in a business combination when the acquiree has an established programme for customer award points to which the guidance in paragraphs B39 to B43 of IFRS 15 applies (or, for entities that have not yet adopted IFRS 15, IFRIC 13 *Customer Loyalty Programmes*).

The illustrative examples accompanying IFRS 3 address various types of customer-related intangible assets acquired in a business combination and whether they meet the definition of an intangible asset (see **7.4.2.4** in **chapter A25**).

3.3.4 Commissions paid to acquire contracts

Example 3.3.4

Commissions paid to acquire contracts

Company A pays commission to an external party, Company B, which markets its security contracts. When a customer commits to a security contract, the customer agrees to use Company A's security services for a minimum of two years and Company B earns a commission of CU100. If, for any reason, the customer cancels within those two years, it is required to pay in full for the unexpired term of the contract. Company A has a history of enforcing these payments in the event of cancellation.

The commission is paid to acquire an asset (the ability to obtain revenues over a minimum two-year period.) The asset is controlled by Company A as evidenced by the enforcement of cancellation penalties, and it has arisen as a result of past events (the signing of the contract) from which future economic benefits (security contract revenues) are expected to flow.

More specifically, the asset meets the definition of an intangible asset because it is "an identifiable non-monetary asset without physical substance". The amount, which represents a right to receive future revenue from customers, is clearly identifiable; it is non-monetary, because it cannot be readily converted into cash; and it does not have physical substance. [IAS 38:8]

3.3.5   Non-competition agreements

Non-competition agreements (NCAs) are often entered into in conjunction with a business combination and can be structured in a variety of ways. For example, a subsidiary and its parent (the vendor) may enter into an NCA prior to the subsidiary being sold to an unrelated third party. Alternatively, the acquirer may enter into an NCA with the vendor.

It is presumed for the purposes of the following discussion that a reliable valuation of an NCA can be obtained.

Consolidated financial statements

The illustrative examples accompanying IFRS 3 cite non-competition agreements as items that, when acquired in a business combination, meet the definition of an intangible asset because they arise from contractual or other legal rights. While they may not be separable assets, separability is not a necessary condition to satisfy the recognition criteria for intangible assets in IAS 38 (see **3.2**). Because they are contractual rights, NCAs should be recognised separately as intangible assets in the consolidated financial statements.

The value of an NCA will depend on a number of different factors, such as barriers to entry in the market in which the entities operate. For example, the existence of a customer list in the acquired entity alone does not indicate that the NCA is valuable.

When an NCA is recognised as a separate intangible asset, it forms part of the same cash-generating unit (or units) as the underlying assets of the acquired business to which it relates for the purposes of impairment testing in the consolidated financial statements (see **chapter A10**).

Separate financial statements of acquirer

When the NCA is between the subsidiary and the vendor, the acquirer does not have the legal rights arising from the contract. In such circumstances, the acquirer should simply recognise an investment in a subsidiary in its separate financial statements (i.e. it should not recognise a separate intangible asset for the NCA).

When the NCA is between the acquirer and the vendor, the acquirer does have a separately identifiable legal right with respect to the NCA in addition to its investment in the subsidiary. The right has a value in the separate financial statements of the acquirer. Therefore, in these circumstances, the acquirer should recognise a separate intangible asset for the NCA in accordance with IAS 38 in addition to the investment in its subsidiary. If the NCA and the investment are acquired at the same time, which will usually be the case, it will be necessary to consider whether the amounts specified in the acquisition agreement/NCA are the appropriate amounts for inclusion in the financial statements. In some cases, a different allocation of the total amount payable between the two items may be necessary in order to reflect the substance of the transaction.

When an NCA is recognised as a separate intangible asset, the NCA and the investment in the subsidiary will be tested for impairment jointly.

3.3.6   Regulatory assets

The appropriate accounting for rate-regulated activities is the subject of a major IASB project; the Board has issued an interim Standard for first-time adopters of IFRSs (see **chapter A42**), and a more comprehensive project is at the research stage (see **section 14** for details).

An example of a rate-regulated scenario is set out in **example 3.3.6**.

Example 3.3.6

Regulatory assets

Company X, an electricity producer, operates in Country B. Electricity producers in Country B are subject to government regulation of electricity charges. Company X has incurred operating losses in the two years ending 20X0 as a consequence of the regulatory pricing mechanism.

The government of Country B subsequently approves a regulatory agreement allowing the electricity producers to increase their prices in future years to offset losses incurred for the previous two years ending 20X0.

Company X should not recognise an asset and associated revenues at the end of 20X0 for the recovery of past operating losses through invoicing future

---

consumption at higher prices. In order to recover operating losses incurred, electricity producers are required to produce electricity for their clients in the future. Even though it is arguable that electricity producers will recover the operating losses, Company X has not, at the end of 20X0, provided the service for which the customers will be paying and, therefore, the regulatory asset cannot be recognised because it does not qualify for recognition as an asset in accordance with the *Conceptual Framework for Financial Reporting*. Moreover, customers can choose not to purchase electricity from this producer even if electricity is produced. In other words, it is not just a matter of producing electricity for clients in the future but clients purchasing electricity.

Consequently, the authorisation given by the government to increase prices in the future is merely a pricing mechanism that regulates prices for the following periods, and does not give rise to an asset and additional revenue in the current period (i.e. 20X0). The recovery of the operating loss is included in the calculation of the price the regulated entity may charge to its customers and should be recognised only when such revenues are received or receivable.

4 Recognition and initial measurement

4.1 Requirements for recognition and initial measurement

IAS 38 establishes general principles for the recognition and measurement of intangible assets, as set out in **4.2**, and discusses the treatment of subsequent expenditure as set out in **section 4.3**. The Standard then considers in detail the following situations:

- separate acquisition (see **section 4.4**);
- acquisition as part of a business combination (see **section 4.5**);
- acquisition by way of a government grant (see **4.6**);
- exchanges of assets (see **4.7**); and
- internally generated intangible assets (see **section 4.8**).

4.2 Recognition and measurement – general principles

4.2.1 Recognition criteria – general

Provided that an item meets the definition of an intangible asset, as discussed in **section 3**, it should be recognised in the financial statements if, and only if:

[IAS 38:18 & 21]

- it is probable that the expected future economic benefits that are attributable to the asset will flow to the entity (the probability criterion); and
- the cost of the asset can be measured reliably.

While the term 'probable' is not defined in IAS 38, it should be interpreted as 'more likely than not', consistent with the definition in the IASB Glossary of Terms.

These recognition criteria apply both to costs incurred to acquire an intangible asset and those incurred to generate an asset internally. The Standard imposes additional criteria, however, for the recognition of internally generated intangible assets (see **section 4.8**).

When assessing the probability of expected future economic benefits, reasonable and supportable assumptions should be used, representing management's best estimate of the set of economic conditions that will exist over the useful life of the asset. [IAS 38:22]

4.2.2   Measurement at initial recognition – general

Intangible assets are initially recognised at cost. [IAS 38:24] Cost is defined as "the amount of cash or cash equivalents paid or the fair value of other consideration given to acquire an asset at the time of its acquisition or construction, or, when applicable, the amount attributed to that asset when initially recognised in accordance with the specific requirements of other IFRSs, eg IFRS 2 *Share-based Payment*". [IAS 38:8]

Example 4.2.2

Capitalisation of periodic licence fees on purchase of an intangible asset

In 20X0, Entity A, a telecoms operator, is granted a licence from a national authority for a fixed period commencing 1 January 20X2. The purchase of the licence is deemed to be an executed transaction and the definition of and recognition criteria for an intangible asset in IAS 38:8 and IAS 38:21, respectively, are met.

Entity A is required to pay an up-front fee for the licence and, in addition, from 20X2 onwards Entity A will be required to pay a fixed fee on a quarterly basis irrespective of whether the licence is used. The obligation to pay the quarterly licence fees will remain constant over the whole licence period and is non-cancellable.

Entity A is permitted to sell the licence, in which case the buyer would be expected to take on the obligation for the quarterly fees, but permission from the national authority would be required for any such transaction.

Should the quarterly licence fees be accounted for as part of the cost of the intangible asset or as an operating expense on a quarterly basis as they become due?

The quarterly licence fees should be accounted for as part of the cost of the intangible asset when the asset is acquired. The total cost of the licence will

---

be the up-front payment plus the present value of the quarterly fees over the licence period.

The definition of cost (see above) refers to 'the amount of cash or cash equivalents paid or the fair value of other consideration given to acquire an asset at the time of its acquisition'. In the circumstances described, Entity A has incurred an obligation for the quarterly licence fees at the date of acquisition. This obligation is part of the consideration given and meets the definition of a financial liability in accordance with paragraph 11 of IAS 32 *Financial Instruments: Presentation* because it constitutes a contractual obligation to deliver cash that Entity A cannot avoid unconditionally. Any subsequent sale of the licence to a third party would involve both that party and the national authority agreeing to the transfer of that obligation and would result in derecognition of the liability only when Entity A is legally released from primary responsibility for payment (see paragraph B3.3.1 of IFRS 9 *Financial Instruments* or, for entities that have not yet adopted IFRS 9, paragraph AG57 of the application guidance to IAS 39 *Financial Instruments: Recognition and Measurement*).

Consequently, the obligation to make quarterly licence fee payments is reflected when measuring the cost of the intangible asset (as part of the fair value of consideration given) and also gives rise to a financial liability that is initially measured at fair value in accordance with IFRS 9:5.1.1 (or, for entities that have not yet adopted IFRS 9, IAS 39:43).

As discussed in **example 10.3.1**, amortisation of the cost of the licence should commence at the date the licence is available for use (i.e. 1 January 20X2), with the effect of discounting on the quarterly licence fee payments treated as illustrated in **example 4.3.2A** in **chapter A7**).

4.3 Subsequent expenditure

4.3.1 Subsequent expenditure on intangible assets capitalised only rarely

The recognition criteria set out in **4.2** apply equally to those costs incurred to add to, replace part of, or service an intangible asset. [IAS 38:18] Unlike a physical asset, it is not common to add to or replace parts of an intangible asset. Most expenditure incurred on an acquired intangible asset subsequent to its initial recognition, or on an internally generated intangible asset after completion, is incurred to maintain the benefits expected from the asset, and therefore will not meet the recognition criteria set out in **4.2**. Additionally, expenditure incurred on intangible assets can be difficult to differentiate from expenditure related to the business as a whole. Therefore, IAS 38 concludes that only rarely should subsequent expenditure on an intangible asset be recognised in the carrying amount of the asset. [IAS 38:20]

One of the rare circumstances in which subsequent costs may be added to the carrying amount of an intangible asset is in the case of waste removal costs falling within the scope of IFRIC 20 *Stripping Costs in the*

Production Phase of a Surface Mine, provided that specified criteria are met (see **section 10** of **chapter A7** for details).

4.3.2 Prohibition on capitalisation of subsequent expenditure on brands and similar items

Specifically, IAS 38 prohibits the capitalisation of any subsequent expenditure incurred on brands, mastheads, publishing titles, customer lists and items similar in substance (whether externally acquired or internally generated). Because such expenditure cannot be distinguished from expenditure to develop the business as a whole, it is always recognised in profit or loss as incurred. [IAS 38:20]

4.3.3 Additional recognition criteria for subsequent expenditure on in-process research and development

IAS 38 also addresses specifically subsequent expenditure on an in-process research and development project acquired separately or in a business combination that has been recognised as an intangible asset. Such expenditure is subject to the additional recognition criteria established for internally generated intangible assets (see **section 4.8**). [IAS 38:42] Therefore, the expenditure is:

- recognised as an expense when it is incurred if it is research expenditure (see **4.8.4**);

- recognised as an expense when it is incurred if it is development expenditure that does not satisfy the recognition criteria set out in IAS 38:57 (see **4.8.5.1**); and

- added to the carrying amount of the acquired in-process research or development project if it is development expenditure that satisfies the recognition criteria set out in IAS 38:57 (see **4.8.5.1**).

4.3.4 Capitalisation of cost of replacement parts

If the cost of a replacement for part of an intangible asset is capitalised, in accordance with IAS 38:21 (see **4.2**), the carrying amount of the replaced part is derecognised. If it is not practicable to determine the carrying amount of the replaced part, the cost of the replacement may be used as an indication of what the cost of the replaced part was at the time it was acquired or internally generated. [IAS 38:115]

4.4 Separate acquisition

4.4.1 Recognition criteria for intangible assets acquired separately

Assuming that the asset acquired meets IAS 38's definition of an intangible asset (see **section 3**), it should be recognised in the financial statements provided that (1) it is probable that expected future economic benefits will flow to the entity, and (2) the cost of the asset can be measured reliably (see **4.2**).

These conditions are generally met when an asset is acquired separately. The anticipation of future economic benefits, even if there is uncertainty about the timing or the amount, is built into the price paid for the asset. Therefore, the probability criterion is always considered to be satisfied for separately acquired intangible assets. [IAS 38:25]

Cash or other monetary assets expended will establish a reliable measure of the cost of the asset. [IAS 38:26] The only circumstance when it may not be possible to measure the cost of the asset reliably is when the purchase consideration comprises non-monetary assets (see **4.7**).

4.4.2 Measurement of cost for intangible assets acquired separately

4.4.2.1 Elements of cost for intangible assets acquired separately

When an intangible asset is purchased separately, and the consideration given is in the form of cash or other monetary assets, the determination of cost is relatively straight-forward. The cost of the intangible asset comprises:

[IAS 38:27]

- its purchase price, including import duties and non-refundable purchase taxes, after deducting trade discounts and rebates; and

- any directly attributable expenditure on preparing the asset for its intended use.

Examples of directly attributable expenditure are:

[IAS 38:28]

- the salaries, wages and other employment-related costs of personnel directly engaged in bringing the asset to its working condition;

- professional fees arising directly from bringing the asset to its working condition; and

- costs of testing whether the asset is functioning properly.

Examples of expenditure that *does not* form part of the cost of an intangible asset are:

[IAS 38:29]

- costs of introducing a new product or service (including costs of advertising and promotional activities);

- costs of conducting business in a new location or with a new class of customer (including the cost of staff training); and

- administration and general overhead costs.

4.4.2.2 Deferred consideration

If the payment of consideration is deferred beyond normal credit terms, the asset is recognised at the equivalent cash price and the difference between this amount and the amount actually paid is recognised as interest expense (unless capitalised in accordance with IAS 23 *Borrowing Costs*). [IAS 38:32]

> See **4.3.2** in **chapter A7** for further discussion of the application of this principle (in the context of measuring the cost of an item of property, plant and equipment, which is subject to equivalent requirements).

4.4.2.3 Cessation of capitalisation

Recognition of cost in the carrying amount of an intangible asset ceases when the asset is in the condition necessary for it to be capable of operating in the manner intended by management. The following costs are excluded from the carrying amount of an intangible asset:

[IAS 38:30]

- costs incurred in using or redeploying an asset;
- costs incurred while an asset capable of operating in the manner intended by management has yet to be brought into use; and
- initial operating losses, such as those incurred while demand for the asset's output builds up.

4.5 Acquisition as part of a business combination

4.5.1 Recognition criteria for intangible assets acquired as part of a business combination

IFRS 3 *Business Combinations* stipulates that, if an intangible asset is acquired in a business combination, the cost of that intangible asset is its fair value at the acquisition date. The fair value of the asset reflects market participants' expectations at the acquisition date as to the economic benefits that will flow from it, even if there is uncertainty about the timing or the amount of those benefits. Therefore, the probability criterion, as set out in **4.2**, is always considered to be satisfied for intangible assets acquired in a business combination. [IAS 38:33]

The acquirer should recognise an intangible asset acquired in a business combination, separately from goodwill, irrespective of whether the asset was previously recognised by the acquiree. This should include any in-process research and development project of the acquiree if the project meets the definition of an intangible asset, and its fair value can be measured reliably. [IAS 38:34]

4.5.2 Measuring fair value

When an asset acquired in a business combination is separable or arises from contractual or other legal rights, sufficient information always exists to measure reliably the asset's fair value. [IAS 38:33]

See **7.2** for the definition of fair value.

IAS 38:33 was amended as a consequential amendment arising from IFRS 3 (as revised in 2008) so as to be clear that it should always be possible to reach a reliable measure of the fair value of an intangible asset acquired in a business combination. The effect of the amendment was to remove the possibility of arguing for the non-recognition of such intangible assets on the basis that their value cannot be measured reliably.

When the estimates used to measure the fair value of an intangible asset indicate that there is a range of possible outcomes with different probabilities, that uncertainty should be incorporated into the measurement of fair value. [IAS 38:35]

When an intangible asset acquired in a business combination is separable, but only together with a related contract, identifiable asset or liability, the acquirer should recognise the intangible asset separately from goodwill, but together with the related item. [IAS 38:36] Similarly, a group of complementary intangible assets (e.g. a trademark and its related trade name, formulas, recipes and technological expertise) may be combined into a single asset (often described as a 'brand') if the individual assets have similar useful lives. [IAS 38:37]

4.6 Acquisition by way of a government grant

An intangible asset may be granted to an entity free of charge or for nominal consideration by a government. This may be the case for assets such as airport landing rights, broadcasting licences, import licences or quotas, or rights to access other restricted resources.

In these circumstances, an entity may either:

[IAS 38:44]

- recognise both the grant and the intangible asset at fair value; or

- recognise both the grant and the intangible asset at a nominal amount plus any expenditure that is directly attributable to preparing the asset for its intended use.

The alternatives allowed for under IAS 38:44 are consistent with those allowed for non-monetary government grants under IAS 20 *Accounting* for Government Grants and Disclosure of Government Assistance (see **section 5** of **chapter A36**).

4.7   Exchanges of assets

When an intangible asset is acquired in exchange for a non-monetary asset or assets, or a combination of monetary and non-monetary assets, the cost of the asset received is measured at fair value (even if the entity cannot immediately derecognise the asset given up), unless either:

[IAS 38:45]

- the exchange transaction lacks commercial substance; or
- the fair value of neither the asset received nor the asset given up is reliably measurable.

In either of these circumstances, which result in the acquired asset not being measured at fair value, its cost is measured at the carrying amount of the asset given up. [IAS 38:45]

Whether or not a transaction has commercial substance is determined by considering the extent to which the entity's future cash flows are expected to change as a result of the transaction. An exchange transaction is considered to have commercial substance if:

[IAS 38:46]

- the configuration (i.e. risk, timing and amount) of the cash flows of the asset received differs from the configuration of the cash flows of the asset transferred; *or*
- the entity-specific value (reflecting post-tax cash flows) of the portion of the entity's operations affected by the transaction changes as a result of the exchange; *and*
- the difference arising in either of the two circumstances outlined is significant relative to the fair value of the assets exchanged.

As set out in **4.2**, no intangible asset can be recognised unless its cost can be measured reliably. In an exchange transaction that has commercial substance, if an entity is able to measure reliably the fair value of either the asset received or the asset given up, the fair value of the asset given up should be used to measure cost, unless the fair value of the asset received is more clearly evident. Fair value can be measured reliably if either (1) the variability in the range of reasonable fair value measurements is not significant for that asset, or (2) the probabilities of the various estimates within the range can be reasonably assessed and used when measuring fair value. [IAS 38:47]

4.8 Internally generated intangible assets

4.8.1 Additional recognition criteria for internally generated intangible assets – background

Inherently, it is more difficult to assess whether an internally generated intangible asset qualifies for recognition because of problems in identifying whether and when there is an identifiable asset that will generate future economic benefits, and in determining the cost of the asset reliably. Therefore, IAS 38 includes additional recognition criteria for internally generated intangible assets which expand on the general recognition criteria. It is assumed that these additional criteria are met implicitly whenever an entity acquires an intangible asset.

Example 4.8.1

Development costs paid to an external party

Company A pays Company B, an external party, to develop an asset that would meet the requirements of IAS 38 for recognition as an internally generated intangible asset in Company A's financial statements (see **4.8.5.1**). Company B is performing only development work; all the associated research has already been performed, and the costs expensed, by Company A.

Company A should recognise an internally generated intangible asset for these development costs under IAS 38. Whether Company A incurs the costs directly via an internal development function or outsources the development process to an external party does not influence how Company A should account for the asset in its financial statements.

Therefore, because the expenditure meets the requirements for the recognition of an internally generated intangible asset under IAS 38, Company A should recognise the asset as an internally generated intangible asset in its financial statements. If the asset being developed did not meet the requirements for recognition of an internally generated intangible asset under IAS 38, the costs would be considered research expenditures and would be expensed as incurred. Similarly, if Company B was paid by Company A to perform both research and development activities, the research element would be expensed as incurred, but the development element would be capitalised provided that it met the requirements of IAS 38.

4.8.2 Items that should not be recognised as internally generated intangible assets

The Standard prohibits the recognition of internally generated goodwill as an asset. [IAS 38:48]

Some other internally generated items are specifically identified in IAS 38 as not capable of being distinguished from the cost of developing the business as a whole and therefore are prohibited from being capitalised as internally generated intangible assets. These are internally generated:

[IAS 38:63]

- brands;
- mastheads;
- publishing titles;
- customer lists; and
- items similar in substance to any of the above.

Although IAS 38 bans these items from recognition as internally generated assets, when such assets are purchased either individually or as part of a business combination, they may meet the general recognition criteria for intangible assets and, therefore, potentially may be recognised. This difference means that intangible assets such as brands can be recognised as intangible assets if acquired but should be expensed if they are generated internally.

4.8.3 Distinction between research and development

IAS 38 distinguishes between two phases in the generation of an intangible asset internally – the research phase and the development phase. Capitalisation is only permitted during the development phase. The additional recognition criteria are discussed at **4.8.5.1**.

Research is defined as original and planned investigation undertaken with the prospect of gaining new scientific or technical knowledge and understanding. [IAS 38:8]

Development is the application of research findings or other knowledge to a plan or design for the production of new or substantially improved materials, devices, products, processes, systems or services prior to the commencement of commercial production or use. [IAS 38:8]

If it is not possible to distinguish the research phase from the development phase of an internal project to create an intangible asset, the expenditure on that project is treated as relating only to the research phase. [IAS 38:53]

The following examples of research activities given in the Standard illustrate that the main objective of research activities is the discovery of something new:

[IAS 38:56]

- activities aimed at obtaining new knowledge;
- the search for, evaluation and final selection of, applications of research findings or other knowledge;

- the search for alternatives for materials, devices, products, processes, systems or services; and

- the formulation, design, evaluation and final selection of possible alternatives for new or improved materials, devices, products, processes, systems or services.

The following examples of development activities illustrate that the main objective of development activities is to apply research findings for a business purpose:

[IAS 38:59]

- the design, construction and testing of pre-production or pre-use prototypes and models;

- the design of tools, jigs, moulds and dies involving new technology;

- the design, construction and operation of a pilot plant that is not of a scale economically feasible for commercial production; and

- the design, construction and testing of a chosen alternative for new or improved materials, devices, products, processes, systems or services.

4.8.4   Research phase

Research costs are, by their nature, incurred with the intent of gaining new knowledge rather than creating a practical application from which future economic benefits will flow. Therefore, research costs do not meet the criteria for recognition of an internally generated asset. Costs incurred during the research phase are required to be expensed. [IAS 38:54]

Example 4.8.4

Capitalisation of supplies purchased during the research phase

Entity A is developing a new pharmaceutical product, Product X. The project is still at the research phase and the criteria in IAS 38:57 (see **4.8.5.1**) for recognition of an intangible development-phase asset have not yet been met. Consequently, costs of the project are currently expensed when incurred.

To manufacture Product X for the purpose of feasibility testing, Entity A needs to purchase a raw material, Supply Y. It purchases a large volume of Supply Y, sufficient for all planned feasibility testing, so as to take advantage of bulk-buying discounts. If at any point during the feasibility testing process Entity A decides not to proceed with the development of Product X, it will be able to sell the remaining Supply Y in the market.

Should Entity A recognise Supply Y as an asset in its statement of financial position?

Yes. Supply Y should be recognised as a current asset provided that its carrying amount can be recovered by alternative means if the research project

---

is abandoned. Supply Y should be initially recognised at cost, subsequently measured at the lower of cost and recoverable amount, and expensed as it is consumed.

Prior to the decision to proceed with commercial production of Product X, Supply Y does not meet the definition of inventories (see paragraph 6 of IAS 2 *Inventories*); nor does it meet the definition of property, plant and equipment (see paragraph 6 of IAS 16 *Property, Plant and Equipment*). Nevertheless, it does meet the definition of an asset in paragraph 4:4(a) of the Conceptual Framework, i.e. it is "a resource controlled by the entity as a result of past events and from which future economic benefits are expected to flow to the entity". The Framework stipulates that an asset should be recognised when (1) it is probable that the future economic benefits will flow to the entity, and (2) the asset has a cost or a value that can be measured reliable. [CF 4:44]

Note that if Entity A did not have alternative means to recover the carrying amount of Supply Y if the research project is abandoned (whether by re-sale in the market or otherwise), the criteria for recognition as an asset would not be met and the cost should be recognised as an expense upon purchase of Supply Y.

4.8.5   Development phase (additional recognition criteria)

4.8.5.1   Additional recognition criteria for internally generated intangible assets

In limited circumstances, during the development phase of a project, an entity is able to identify an intangible asset and demonstrate that the asset will generate probable future economic benefits. [IAS 38:58] However, criteria in addition to those for externally acquired intangible assets must be met in order to recognise an internally generated intangible asset.

Specifically, an intangible asset arising from development (or from the development phase of an internal project) should be recognised if, and only if, an entity can demonstrate all of the following:

[IAS 38:57]

- the technical feasibility of completing the intangible asset so that it will be available for use or sale;

- its intention to complete the intangible asset and use or sell it;

- its ability to use or sell the intangible asset;

- how the intangible asset will generate probable future economic benefits. Among other things, the entity can demonstrate the existence of a market for the output of the intangible asset or the intangible asset itself or, if it is to be used internally, the usefulness of the intangible asset;

- the availability of adequate technical, financial and other resources to complete the development and to use or sell the intangible asset; and

- its ability to measure the expenditure attributable to the intangible asset during the development phase.

IAS 38 does not provide any guidance in respect of the first criterion as to when technical feasibility is established. Although it is difficult to set one guideline, due to the differing types of internally generated intangible assets, when the asset is the product of 'traditional' research and development activities or software development activities, an appropriate point may be when the entity has completed all the planning, design and testing activities that are necessary to establish that an asset can be produced to meet its design specifications, including functions, features and technical performance requirements.

If regulatory approval is required before the technical feasibility can be established, the entity should consider carefully the process involved and the likelihood of achieving approval. If there is significant uncertainty regarding the approval process or outcome at any time during the development process, it is unlikely that the entity has met the criteria to recognise an internally generated asset. However, if the entity is confident it will obtain approval, and has evidence to support this, it may be more likely that the technical feasibility criterion has been met.

In respect of the fourth criterion, IAS 38 suggests that an entity can demonstrate that the asset will generate future economic benefits by using the principles in IAS 36 *Impairment of Assets* relating to the estimation of future cash flows. [IAS 38:60] As discussed in more detail in **chapter A10**, cash flow projections should be based on reasonable and supportable assumptions that represent management's best estimate of the set of economic conditions that will exist over the useful life of the asset, with greater weight given to external evidence. Such projections should not normally cover a period of more than five years. The cash flows should be discounted using a pre-tax rate that reflects current market assessments of the time value of money and the risks specific to the asset. If the internally generated intangible asset will only produce economic benefits together with other assets (e.g. new computer software that will significantly reduce overhead costs), its cash flows cannot be independently assessed. Therefore, it is included in its cash-generating unit and the unit as a whole is evaluated. (See **chapter A10** for further discussion of cash-generating units.)

The fifth criterion (availability of resources) would normally be met by a business plan that details the planned expenditure on the project and the resources that will be available to fund it. If the project is being financed externally, a lender's indication of its willingness to finance the business plan may be sufficient to demonstrate availability of external finance. [IAS 38:61]

In order to meet the final criterion (ability to measure attributable expenditure), an entity should have a costing system to track costs incurred related to the specific development project. In many cases, this can be a simple system based on the time sheets of the employees involved in the development of the intangible asset but, on more complex projects, the system should also track direct expenses incurred.

In practice, in different industries, the relative lengths of the research and development phases of a project are likely to be significantly different. In some industries (e.g. the pharmaceutical industry), some of the criteria will only be met very late in the process so that, of the total research and development costs incurred, only a small proportion will form part of the cost of an internally generated intangible asset. In other industries, the criteria may be met at a much earlier stage in the process and an intangible asset may be recognised for a higher proportion of the costs incurred. Often, this is influenced by how early, or late, in the overall process it is possible to be confident that the project outcome will be successful.

4.8.5.2 Impairment indicators identified during development phase

If an impairment indicator has been identified in respect of an internally generated intangible asset that is currently being developed for internal use as part of a cash-generating unit (and for which IAS 38's criteria for recognition of an internally generated intangible asset have been met), but no impairment loss has been recognised because the recoverable amount of the cash-generating unit as a whole is greater than its carrying amount, the entity should generally include subsequent expenditure in the cost of the intangible asset.

Usually, an entity will only continue with such a development project if it expects the future benefits from completing the project to exceed the additional costs that will need to be incurred (even though those benefits may not be sufficient also to cover costs already incurred, i.e. 'sunk' costs). When the future benefits are expected to exceed the additional costs, it is appropriate to capitalise the subsequent costs in accordance with the requirements of IAS 38:57. **Example 4.8.5.2** illustrates the approach taken in such circumstances.

If, exceptionally, an entity decides to continue with a development project even though it does not expect the future benefits from completing the project to exceed the additional costs that will need to be incurred, then the entity will need to consider carefully whether the fourth criterion in IAS 38:57 (probability of future economic benefits) is met. If it is not, subsequent expenditure should be recognised as an expense.

Example 4.8.5.2

Subsequent expenditure on an internally generated intangible asset under development for use in a cash-generating unit after impairment indicators are identified

Entity R is developing computer software for use in its business. On 1 January 20X1, the criteria for recognition as an internally generated intangible asset are met and expenditure on the development incurred after that date is included in the cost of the asset. Budgeted total expenditure to completion of the project at the end of 20X3 is CU3 million and the incremental benefits to be derived from the software are expected to be approximately CU5 million.

At 31 December 20X1, the intangible asset is tested for impairment as required by IAS 36:10(a), but no impairment loss is identified.

At 31 May 20X2, the carrying amount of the intangible asset is CU1.5 million. In June 20X2, estimates of the additional costs to complete the project are increased to CU4.5 million (i.e. total project costs of CU6 million). (Note that this is not as a result of operating inefficiencies or error.) A decision is taken to proceed with the project because the expected incremental benefits (CU5 million) are still in excess of the costs not yet incurred (CU4.5 million). However, the directors consider that this is an indication of impairment and that the recoverable amount of the software should be estimated.

The software does not generate independent cash flows, and its fair value less costs of disposal is estimated to be lower than its carrying amount; accordingly, the software asset is tested for impairment as part of its cash-generating unit.

The recoverable amount of the cash-generating unit as a whole is determined to be CU100 million and its carrying amount is CU75 million; therefore, no impairment loss is recognised.

As additional expenditure is incurred on completion of the software development, Entity R should continue to include that expenditure in the cost of the software asset in accordance with IAS 38:57. In addition, although the total costs are significantly in excess of the original budget, and are expected to exceed the incremental benefits that will be generated by the software, no impairment loss is required to be recognised unless the carrying amount of the cash-generating unit as a whole exceeds its recoverable amount.

4.8.6 Cost of an internally generated intangible asset

The requirement that an intangible asset should be initially recognised at its cost applies equally to internally generated intangible assets. Cost includes all costs incurred from the date on which all of the recognition criteria (i.e. those for purchased as well as for internally generated intangible assets) are met. If costs have been expensed prior to the recognition criteria being met, they may not be reinstated upon satisfaction of the criteria. [IAS 38:65 & 71]

Similar to self-constructed items of property, plant and equipment, the cost of an internally generated intangible asset includes all directly attributable costs necessary to create, produce and prepare an asset to be capable of operating in the manner intended by management. These costs may include:

[IAS 38:66]

- expenditure on materials and services used or consumed in generating the intangible asset;

- the salaries, wages and other employment-related costs of personnel directly engaged in generating the asset;

- borrowing costs, in accordance with the requirements of IAS 23 *Borrowing Costs* (see **chapter A18**); and

- any other expenditure that is directly attributable to generating the asset, such as fees to register a legal right and the amortisation of patents and licences that are used to generate the asset.

IAS 38 specifically prohibits the inclusion of the following items in the cost of an internally generated intangible asset:

[IAS 38:67]

- selling, administrative and other general overhead expenditure unless this expenditure can be directly attributed to preparing the asset for use;

- clearly identified inefficiencies and initial operating losses incurred before an asset achieves planned performance; and

- expenditure on training staff to operate the asset.

Example 4.8.6

Evaluating whether overheads are 'directly attributable costs'

Company A is developing a product in premises used solely for the product's development. The criteria in IAS 38 for the recognition of an intangible asset arising from the development activities have been met. Company A expects to continue to use the premises after the product's development is completed.

Is it acceptable for the costs of these premises to be included in the cost of the internally generated development asset?

IAS 38:66 states that "the cost of an internally generated intangible asset comprises all directly attributable costs necessary to create, produce and prepare the asset to be capable of operating in the manner intended by management". Premises costs are more likely to fall under IAS 38:67, which states that selling, administrative and other general overhead costs are not part of the cost of an internally generated intangible asset "unless this expenditure can be directly attributed to preparing the asset for use". Whether such costs can be considered 'directly attributable' is a matter of judgement in the particular

---

circumstances. However, to qualify as directly attributable, it would be expected that the costs would have been avoided had the entity not engaged in the development activities.

Therefore, if the premises are rented, it may be possible to demonstrate that the rental costs are directly attributable costs if they would not have been incurred had the entity not engaged in the development activities. For example, Company A might be able to demonstrate that:

* it did not rent the premises until commencement of the development activities; and

* had it not engaged in the development activities, it would not have rented the premises until a later date for use in other activities.

Alternatively, if the development activities take place in a property owned by Company A, prior to commencing those activities, Company A would need to demonstrate that the costs of the building (or portion of the building) in which the development activities are carried out would have been avoided, such as in one of the following scenarios:

* the building (or portion of the building) is separately identifiable and could have been separately subleased if not used for the development activities; or

* the building (or portion of the building) would have been used to house other activities for which Company A has rented additional premises.

4.8.7 Research and development activities performed under contract for others

When an entity carries out research and development activities for others, the substance of the arrangement dictates the accounting treatment of the research and development expenditure for both entities. If the entity carrying out the research and development activities will control any asset that is developed, it should account for the expenditure on the research and development activities in accordance with IAS 38. If the entity carrying out the research and development activities will not retain control of any asset that is developed, the entity carrying out the activities should account for its activities in accordance with IFRS 15 *Revenue from Contracts with Customers* (see **chapter A14**) or, for entities that have not yet adopted IFRS 15, IAS 18 *Revenue* or IAS 11 *Construction Contracts*, as appropriate (see **appendix A1** and **appendix A2**, respectively). The following factors may indicate that control of any asset developed is retained by the entity carrying out the activities:

* the entity conducting the research and development activities will retain full rights to any intellectual property that is developed;

* the entity conducting the research and development activities will only receive payment from the other entity if the outcome of the

research and development activities is successful (i.e. the outcome meets criteria specified by that other entity);

- the entity conducting the research and development activities is contractually obliged to repay any of the funds provided by the other entity, regardless of the outcome of the research and development activities; or

- even though the contract does not require the entity conducting the research and development activities to repay any of the funds provided by the other entity, repayment could be required at the option of the other entity or the surrounding conditions indicate that repayment is probable.

4.8.8   Web site costs

SIC-32 *Intangible Assets – Web Site Costs* addresses the appropriate accounting treatment for internal expenditure to develop, enhance and maintain a web site incurred by an entity (whether for internal or external access). Specifically, the Interpretation addresses the application of IAS 38 to web site development costs.

The Interpretation does not apply to purchasing, developing and operating the hardware associated with a web site (accounted for under IAS 16 *Property, Plant and Equipment*), nor to expenditure on the development or operation of a web site for sale to another entity (accounted for under IAS 2 *Inventories* and IAS 11 *Construction Contracts*).

SIC-32 identifies the following stages of web site development:

[SIC-32:2 & 3]

- Planning (including undertaking feasibility studies, defining objectives and specifications, evaluating alternatives and selecting preferences);

- Application and Infrastructure Development (including obtaining a domain name, purchasing and developing hardware and operating software, installing developed applications and stress testing);

- Graphical Design (including designing the appearance of web pages);

- Content Development (including creating, purchasing, preparing and uploading information, either textual or graphical in nature, on the web site before the completion of the web site's development. This information may either be stored in separate databases that are integrated into, or accessed from, the web site or coded directly into the web pages); and

- Operating (including maintaining and enhancing the applications, infrastructure, graphical design and content of the web site).

The Interpretation states that:

[SIC-32:7 & 8]

- a web site developed by an entity for its own use (whether for internal or external access) is an internally generated intangible asset that is subject to the requirements of IAS 38;

- future economic benefits, as envisaged by IAS 38's criteria for recognition of internally generated intangible assets, will be generated from a web site only when the web site is capable of generating revenue. For example, the requirement may be satisfied when the web site is capable of generating direct revenues from enabling orders to be placed; and

- if the web site has been developed solely or primarily for promoting or advertising the entity's products and services, the entity will be unable to demonstrate that such a web site will generate future economic benefits, and costs incurred on the development of the web site should be expensed as incurred.

SIC-32 concludes as follows:

[SIC-32:9]

- the nature of each activity for which expenditure is incurred (e.g. training employees and maintaining the web site) and the web site's stage of development or post-development are evaluated to determine the appropriate accounting treatment (additional guidance is provided in the appendix to SIC-32);

- the Planning stage of a web site development is similar to the research phase described at **4.8.4** and, therefore, any expenditure incurred in this stage is recognised as an expense when it is incurred;

- the Application and Infrastructure Development stage, the Graphical Design stage and the Content Development stage are similar in nature to the development phase described at **4.8.5**. Therefore, expenditure incurred in these stages is recognised as an intangible asset if the expenditure can be directly attributed and is necessary to creating, producing or preparing the web site for it to be capable of operating in the manner intended by management. For example, expenditure on purchasing or creating content (other than content that advertises and promotes an entity's own products and services) specifically for a web site, or to enable use of the content (e.g. a fee for acquiring a licence to reproduce) on the web site, is included in the cost of development when this condition is met; and

- expenditure incurred in the Content Development stage, to the extent that content is developed to advertise and promote an entity's own products and services (e.g. digital photographs of products), is recognised as an expense when incurred. For example, when accounting for expenditure on professional services for taking digital photographs of an entity's own products and for enhancing their display, expenditure is recognised as an expense as the professional services are received during the process, not when the digital photographs are displayed on the web site.

In accordance with IAS 38:71 (see **4.8.6**), expenditure on web site development that has previously been recognised as an expense should not be recognised as part of the cost of the web site intangible asset at a later date.

The Operating stage commences once the web site is available for use and, therefore, expenditure to maintain or enhance the web site after development has been completed should be recognised as an expense when it is incurred, unless it meets the criteria discussed at **4.3.1** (criteria for recognising subsequent expenditure as an asset). Similarly, when an entity incurs expenditure on an Internet service provider hosting the entity's web site, the expenditure is recognised as an expense when the services are received.

SIC-32 indicates that the best estimate of a web site's useful life, for the purpose of amortisation, is short. [SIC-32:10]

4.8.9   Accounting for costs related to compliance with REACH

4.8.9.1   REACH regulation – background

The Registration, Evaluation, Authorisation and Restriction of Chemicals (REACH) regulation requires commercial users of chemical substances in the European Union (EU) to perform studies demonstrating the properties of each of the substances they use or sell and to pay a one-time fee to register each of the chemical substances. The registration process (the performance of the studies and the one-time registration fee) is required for all chemical substances already in use and those that will be developed. If the registration process is not followed for a substance, a commercial user cannot market that chemical substance or the products containing the substance.

In addition, the REACH regulation allows studies performed by one commercial user to be sold to other users as a means of sharing costs among users.

In the July 2009 edition of *IFRIC Update*, the IFRIC (now the IFRS Interpretations Committee) declined to provide guidance on the appropriate accounting for the costs of complying with the REACH regulation. The IFRIC noted that IAS 38 includes definitions and recognition criteria for intangible assets that provide guidance to enable entities to account for the costs of complying with the REACH regulation.

The appropriate accounting for the costs of the registration process depends on whether the costs incurred relate to chemical substances (and products made with such substances) already in commercial use when the REACH regulation came into effect or to new substances (and new products made with such substances) developed after the effective date of the REACH regulation.

4.8.9.2 Existing chemical substances and existing products made with chemical substances

The preferred treatment is to recognise the REACH costs relating to existing chemical substances and products in profit or loss as incurred because those costs do not add value to the entity's business but rather enable the entity to continue its operations.

However, because there is no clear guidance on the issue, it would also be acceptable to recognise an intangible asset arising from the costs incurred to comply with the REACH regulation, provided that the recognition criteria of IAS 38 are met. This is because the costs incurred under REACH result in an entity obtaining identifiable rights for the commercial use of a specific substance that are necessary to earn benefits from that substance or the product that embodies the substance.

The accounting policy adopted should be disclosed and applied consistently.

4.8.9.3 New chemical substances and new products made with chemical substances

The REACH costs are necessary for the development of new chemical substances (or new products) and their commercial use. Therefore, if the recognition criteria in IAS 38 are met, an intangible asset should be recognised arising from the costs incurred to comply with the REACH regulation.

4.8.9.4 Income from sale of the studies

In either case, any income received from the sale of the studies should be recognised in profit or loss as 'other income' because it is incidental to the development of the studies.

5 Items to be recognised as an expense

As a general rule, expenditure on an intangible item should be recognised as an expense as incurred unless:

[IAS 38:68]

- it forms part of the cost of an intangible asset that meets the appropriate definition and recognition criteria; or

- the item is acquired in a business combination and does not meet the criteria for separate recognition. In such cases, it forms part of the amount recognised as goodwill at the acquisition date.

IAS 38 states that the following types of expenditure should always be recognised as an expense:

[IAS 38:69]

- research (except to the extent that it relates to an intangible asset acquired in a business combination);

- start-up activities, unless the expenditure qualifies to be included in the cost of an item of property, plant and equipment. Start-up costs may include:

  - establishment costs such as legal and secretarial costs incurred in establishing a legal entity;

  - expenditure to open a new facility or business (i.e. pre-opening costs); and

  - expenditure prior to starting new operations or launching new products or processes (i.e. pre-operating costs);

- training activities;

- advertising and promotional activities (including mail order catalogues); and

- relocating or reorganising part or all of an entity.

More generally, if expenditure does not give rise to an intangible asset:

[IAS 38:69 & 69A]

- for a supply of goods, an expense is recognised when the entity has a right to access those goods. This is when the entity owns the goods or, if they have been constructed by a supplier in accordance with the terms of a supply contract, when the entity could demand delivery of them in return for payment; and

- for a supply of services, an expense is recognised when the entity receives the services. Services are received when they are performed by a supplier in accordance with a contract to deliver them to the entity and not when the entity uses them to deliver another service, for example to deliver an advertisement to customers.

This does not, however, preclude the recognition of a prepayment asset when payment for goods or services has been made in advance of the entity obtaining a right to access those goods, or in advance of receiving those services. [IAS 38:70]

The specific reference to mail order catalogues being part of advertising and promotional activities (and, consequently, always required to be recognised as an expense) is designed to prohibit entities from recognising a prepayment asset for the costs of production of mail order catalogues or advertising, and only recognising those costs as an expense when the catalogues are distributed to the end-customer or when the advertisements are broadcast or published. Once an entity has a right to access, or has taken delivery of, mail order catalogues or advertisements, any associated expenditure is required to be recognised as an expense immediately.

For entities that have adopted IFRS 15 *Revenue from Contracts with Customers*, that Standard contains specific guidance regarding the treatment of both costs to obtain and costs to fulfil a contract (see **section 12** of **chapter A14**).

6   Alternatives for measurement after initial recognition

6.1   Alternatives for measurement after initial recognition – general

IAS 38 sets out two alternatives for subsequent measurement – the cost model and the revaluation model. However, the conditions imposed for use of the revaluation model are strict and this alternative is unlikely to be available in practice other than in very rare cases (see **section 7.1**).

6.2   Cost model

If an intangible asset is accounted for using the cost model, after initial recognition, it is carried in the statement of financial position at its cost (measured as described in **section 4**) less any accumulated amortisation and any accumulated impairment losses. [IAS 38:74]

6.3   Revaluation model

If the revaluation model is adopted, the intangible asset is carried at a revalued amount, which is its fair value at the date of the revaluation less any subsequent accumulated amortisation and any subsequent accumulated impairment losses. [IAS 38:75] The revaluation model is described in **section 7**.

7 Revaluation model

7.1 Assets for which the revaluation model is available

7.1.1 Revaluation model only available for assets traded on an active market

In order to use the revaluation model, the fair value of an intangible asset is required to be measured by reference to an active market. Therefore, only intangible assets that are traded on an active market can be revalued under the Standard.

An active market is defined as "[a] market in which transactions for the asset or liability take place with sufficient frequency and volume to provide pricing information on an ongoing basis". [IFRS 13:Appendix A]

IAS 38 permits no basis for the measurement of fair value other than by reference to an active market. It is quite rare for an active market to exist for intangible assets. Therefore, the revaluation of intangible assets is not expected to be common. Examples of intangible assets for which the revaluation option might be available are freely transferable taxi licenses, fishing licenses or production quotas. [IAS 38:78]

Other intangible assets that are not traded on an active market may be traded in private transactions, with the price for each transaction being specifically negotiated between the individual buyer and seller. In such circumstances, the price paid for one asset may not provide sufficient evidence of the fair value of another. [IAS 38:78]

Example 7.1.1

Revaluation not permitted in the absence of an active market

Over the past two years, a group has developed various items of computer software to be used internally and/or to be sold to prospective buyers. In accordance with IAS 38, the group capitalised the development costs incurred during the development phase and recognised an intangible asset of CU1 million. After the reporting date, the group began discussions with a third party for the sale of the subsidiary that owns the software, or the sale of that subsidiary's assets. The selling price under negotiation is much higher than the carrying amount of the subsidiary's assets (which mainly relate to the internally generated intangible asset and other computer equipment).

The group is not permitted to revalue its internally generated intangible asset because no active market exists. [IAS 38:75] Although the entity has entered into sale negotiations, this is not sufficient to indicate an active market. If an active market, as defined, genuinely existed, the price for which the asset could be sold would be publicly available and would not be a matter for negotiation. Indeed, IAS 38:78 indicates that the fact that there is a sale agreement between an entity and a buyer does not provide evidence of an active market.

7.1.2 Active market cannot exist for specified types of intangible assets

IAS 38 specifically states that, due to their unique nature, an active market cannot exist for any of the following items:

[IAS 38:78]

- brands;
- newspaper mastheads;
- music and film publishing rights; and
- patents or trademarks.

7.1.3 Revaluation not permitted for items that have not previously been recognised as assets

The revaluation model does not permit:

[IAS 38:76]

- the revaluation of intangible assets that have not previously been recognised as assets; or
- the initial recognition of intangible assets at amounts other than their cost.

Therefore if, in developing an asset internally, the criteria for recognition as set out at **4.8.5.1** are not met, and all of the costs are written off as incurred, the asset should not be subsequently measured at fair value. If, however, part of the asset was initially recognised as an asset (e.g. because the recognition criteria were met part way through the project), the whole of that asset is eligible for the revaluation model, if the conditions for revaluation are met. [IAS 38:77]

7.1.4 Intangible assets received by government grant

If the conditions for revaluation are met, IAS 38 states specifically that the revaluation model may be adopted for intangible assets received by way of government grant and recognised at a nominal amount (see **4.6**). [IAS 38:77]

7.2 Basis for revaluation

When an intangible asset is revalued, it is revalued to its fair value. As discussed at **7.1.1**, for the purpose of revaluing intangible assets, such fair values can only be measured by reference to an active market.

Fair value is defined as "the price that would be received to sell an asset or paid to transfer a liability in an orderly transaction between market participants at the measurement date. (See IFRS 13 *Fair Value Measurement*.)" [IAS 38:8]

7.3 Frequency of revaluations

IAS 38 does not set a specific requirement for the frequency of revaluations, but states that they should be carried out with sufficient regularity so that, at the end of each reporting period, the carrying amount of a revalued intangible asset does not differ materially from its fair value. [IAS 38:75]

> In order to meet this requirement, an entity must estimate the fair value of its revalued intangible assets at the end of each reporting period. This does not mean, however, that revaluation adjustments must be made every year, unless the estimate of fair value differs significantly from the carrying amount of the intangible asset.
>
> When permitted, the revaluation of intangible assets should, in practice, be a straightforward matter, because it is a pre-requisite that an active market exists.

The frequency of revaluations depends on the volatility in the active market on which the intangible asset is traded. Some intangible assets may experience significant and volatile movements in fair value, thus necessitating annual revaluation. Such frequent revaluations are unnecessary for intangible assets with only insignificant movements in fair value. [IAS 38:79]

7.4 Scope of revaluations

When an intangible asset is accounted for using the revaluation model, all of the other assets in its class should also be accounted for using the revaluation model, unless there is no active market for those assets. [IAS 38:72] If there is no active market for a particular intangible asset which is included in a revalued class of intangible assets, that asset is carried at its cost less any accumulated amortisation and any accumulated impairment losses. [IAS 38:81]

A class of intangible assets is defined as a grouping of assets of a similar nature and use in the operations of an entity. Examples of separate classes may include:

[IAS 38:119]

- brand names;
- mastheads and publishing titles;
- computer software;
- licences and franchises;

- copyrights, patents and other industrial property rights, service and operating rights;

- recipes, formulae, model designs and prototypes; and

- intangible assets under development.

If the fair value of a revalued intangible asset can no longer be measured by reference to an active market, the intangible asset is carried at its fair value at the date of the last revaluation by reference to the active market less any subsequent accumulated amortisation and any subsequent impairment losses. [IAS 38:82] The disappearance of the active market may be an indicator of impairment which triggers an impairment review under IAS 36 *Impairment of Assets* (see **chapter A10**). If the active market re-emerges, the intangible asset should once again be revalued by reference to the active market. [IAS 38:84]

7.5 Accumulated amortisation at the date of revaluation

7.5.1 *Alternatives for treatment of accumulated amortisation at the date of revaluation*

When an intangible asset is revalued, the carrying amount of that asset is adjusted to the revalued amount. At the date of the revaluation, the asset is treated in one of the following ways:

[IAS 38:80]

(a) the gross carrying amount is adjusted in a manner that is consistent with the revaluation of the carrying amount of the asset. For example, the gross carrying amount may be restated by reference to observable market data or it may be restated proportionately to the change in the carrying amount. The accumulated amortisation at the date of the revaluation is adjusted to equal the difference between the gross carrying amount and the carrying amount of the asset after taking into account accumulated impairment losses; or

(b) the accumulated amortisation is eliminated against the gross carrying amount of the asset.

These treatments are similar to those permitted for accumulated depreciation when an item of property, plant and equipment is revalued. **Example 6.4.1** in **chapter A7** illustrates the alternative methods permitted under both IAS 16 and IAS 38.

7.5.2 *Effective date and transition for December 2013 amendments*

IAS 38:80 was amended in December 2013 by *Annual Improvements to IFRSs: 2010-2012 Cycle*. The effect of the December 2013 amendments is to allow that, when an asset is revalued and the alternative under IAS 38:80(a) is selected, the restatement of accumulated amortisation is not always proportionate to the change in the gross carrying amount of the asset. The amendments were necessary because, in some circumstances when the residual value, the useful life or the amortisation method of the asset has been re-estimated prior to the revaluation, a proportionate restatement is not relevant.

The December 2013 amendments are effective for annual periods beginning on or after 1 July 2014, with earlier application permitted. If the amendments are applied for a period beginning before 1 July 2014, that fact is required to be disclosed. [IAS 38:130H]

The amendments are required to be applied prospectively to all revaluations recognised in annual periods beginning on or after the date of initial application and in the immediately preceding annual period. An entity may also present adjusted comparative information for any earlier periods presented, but it is not required to do so. If an entity presents unadjusted comparative information for any earlier periods, it is required to clearly identify the information that has not been adjusted, state that it has been presented on a different basis and explain that basis. [IAS 38:130I]

Take, for example, an entity that applies the December 2013 amendments for the first time in its annual financial statements for the year ended 31 December 2015 and that presents two years of comparative information. In its 2015 financial statements, the entity is required to:

- apply the revised requirements to all revaluations recognised on or after 1 January 2014; and

- either restate all revaluations recognised between 1 January 2013 and 31 December 2013 or, if it chooses not to do so, clearly identify revaluations that have not been restated and provide an explanation of the basis on which those revaluations are presented.

7.6   Treatment of surplus or deficit arising on revaluation

7.6.1   Revaluation surplus

When a valuation indicates that the fair value of an intangible asset is greater than its carrying amount, the amount of the surplus is generally recognised in other comprehensive income and accumulated in equity as a revaluation surplus. [IAS 38:85]

However, if the increase in the fair value of the asset reverses a previously recognised decrease in the fair value of the same asset, it is recognised in profit or loss to the extent that the previous decrease was recognised in profit or loss. [IAS 38:85]

7.6.2 Revaluation deficit

When a revaluation indicates that the fair value of an intangible asset is less than its carrying amount, the amount of the deficit is generally recognised in profit or loss. [IAS 38:86]

However, if the decrease in the fair value of the intangible asset reverses a previously recognised increase in the fair value of the same asset, it is recognised in other comprehensive income to the extent of any credit balance in the revaluation surplus in respect of that asset. The decrease reduces the amount of revaluation surplus. [IAS 38:86]

The treatment of revaluation surpluses and deficits arising on intangible assets is the same as that for items of property, plant and equipment (see the illustrative examples at **6.8.3** in **chapter A7**).

7.6.3 Realisation of the revaluation surplus

The revaluation surplus may be transferred to retained earnings as the surplus is realised, although such a transfer is not mandatory. Realisation of the entire surplus may occur on the retirement or disposal of the asset. Some realisation of the revaluation surplus may occur, however, through the use of the intangible asset. The amount of the surplus that is realised through use of the asset is calculated as the difference between the amortisation calculated on the historical cost of the asset and the amortisation calculated on the revalued amount. This difference may be transferred from the revaluation surplus to retained earnings in each period. [IAS 38:87]

If an entity chooses to make such periodic transfers, when a revalued intangible asset is fully amortised in the statement of financial position, the related revaluation surplus will have been reduced to zero.

Whether the revaluation surplus is realised on disposal or on a systematic basis over the life of the asset, any transfer from revaluation reserve to retained earnings is not made through profit or loss. [IAS 38:87]

8 Determining the useful life of an intangible asset

8.1 Determining the useful life of an intangible asset – general

The subsequent accounting for an intangible asset is determined on the basis of its useful life. If the useful life of the asset is determined to be finite, the asset is amortised over that useful life. If the useful life of the asset is determined to be indefinite, the asset is not amortised. [IAS 38:89] IAS 38 provides a significant amount of guidance to assist in this determination, which is summarised in **8.2** to **8.6**.

8.2   Finite or indefinite useful life?

Entities are required to assess whether the useful life of an intangible asset is finite or indefinite and, if finite, the length of, or number of production or similar units constituting, that useful life. [IAS 38:88]

An intangible asset should be regarded as having an indefinite useful life when, based on all of the relevant factors, there is no foreseeable limit to the period over which the asset is expected to generate net cash inflows for the entity. [IAS 38:88] Therefore, if management has the intention and the ability to maintain an intangible asset so that there is no foreseeable limit on the period over which the asset is expected to generate net cash inflows for the entity, the asset is regarded as having an indefinite useful life.

> Note that the term 'indefinite' does not mean 'infinite'. [IAS 38:91] There does not need to be an expectation that the cash inflows generated by the asset will go on forever – simply that, at the date of assessment, there is no foreseeable point at which the cash inflows will cease.

If there is a foreseeable limit to the period over which net cash inflows are expected to flow to the entity, the asset is regarded as having a finite life.

> The assessment as to whether an intangible asset has an indefinite useful life is clearly crucial for the purposes of the subsequent accounting treatment for the intangible asset. IAS 38 provides a number of illustrative examples for this determination, which are summarised at **8.5**.

8.3   Factors for consideration in determining useful life

The useful life of an intangible asset is either:

[IAS 38:8]

- the period over which the asset is expected to be available for use by the entity; or

- the number of production or similar units expected to be obtained from the asset by an entity.

Factors to consider in estimating the useful life of an intangible asset include:

[IAS 38:90]

- the expected usage of the asset by the entity and whether the asset could be efficiently managed by another management team;

- typical product life cycles for the asset and public information on estimates of useful lives of similar types of assets that are used in a similar way;

- technical, technological, commercial or other types of obsolescence;

- the stability of the industry in which the asset operates and changes in the market demand for the products or services output from the asset;

- expected actions by competitors or potential competitors;

- the level of maintenance expenditure required to obtain the expected future economic benefits from the asset and the entity's ability and intent to reach such a level;

- the period of control over the asset, and legal or similar limits on the use of the asset, such as the expiry dates of related leases; and

- whether the useful life of the asset is dependent on the useful life of other assets of the entity.

The useful life of an intangible asset reflects only that level of future maintenance expenditure required to maintain the asset at its standard of performance assessed at the time of estimating the asset's useful life, and the entity's ability and intention to reach such a level. A conclusion that the useful life of an intangible asset is indefinite should not depend on planned future expenditure in excess of that required to maintain the asset at that standard of performance. [IAS 38:91]

IAS 38 notes that, given the history of rapid changes in technology, computer software and many other intangible assets are susceptible to technological obsolescence. Therefore, it will often be the case that their useful lives will be short. Expected future reductions in the selling price of an item that was produced using an intangible asset could indicate the expectation of technological or commercial obsolescence of the asset which, in turn, might reflect a reduction of the future economic benefits embodied in the asset. [IAS 38:92]

The final sentence of IAS 38:92 was added by *Clarification of Acceptable Methods of Depreciation and Amortisation (Amendments to IAS 16 and IAS 38)* issued in May 2014. The May 2014 amendments are required to be applied prospectively for annual periods beginning on or after 1 January 2016, with earlier application permitted. If an entity applies this guidance for a period beginning before 1 January 2016, it is required to disclose that fact. [IAS 38:130J]

Although the May 2014 amendments are stated to be effective from 2016, the principle that expected reductions in the selling price of an item may be an indicator of obsolescence of the asset which was used to produce it will already be applied by many entities. In the Basis of Conclusions accompanying the amendments, the IASB emphasises that the expectation of technological or commercial obsolescence is relevant for estimating both the pattern of consumption of future economic benefits and the useful life of an asset. [IAS 38:BC72K]

Uncertainty may lead to estimating the useful life of an intangible asset on a prudent basis; however, it is not appropriate to choose a useful life that is unrealistically short. [IAS 38:93]

8.4   Assets arising from contractual or other legal rights

Control over the future economic benefits from an intangible asset is often achieved through legal rights that have been granted for a finite period. Under most circumstances, the estimated useful life of the intangible asset is the shorter of the period of the legal rights and the period over which economic benefits are expected to be generated. [IAS 38:94]

In some cases, however, the legal rights may be renewable. The question then arises as to whether it is appropriate to assume that the legal rights will be extended. IAS 38:94 stipulates that the useful life of an intangible asset should include the renewal period(s) only if there is evidence to support renewal by the entity without significant cost. The following factors are listed which indicate that an entity would be able to renew the contractual or other legal rights without significant cost:

[IAS 38:96]

- there is evidence (possibly based on past experience) that the legal rights will be renewed. If renewal is contingent upon the consent of a third party, this includes evidence that the third party will give its consent;

- there is evidence that the conditions necessary to obtain the renewal of the legal right (if any) will be satisfied; and

- the cost to the entity of renewal is not significant when compared with the future economic benefits expected to flow to the entity from renewal.

If the cost of renewal is significant when compared with the future economic benefits expected to flow to the entity from renewal, the 'renewal' represents, in substance, the acquisition of a new intangible asset at the renewal date. [IAS 38:96]

The useful life of a reacquired right recognised as an intangible asset in a business combination is the remaining contractual period of the contract in which the right was granted, and does not include renewal periods. [IAS 38:94]

8.5 Examples illustrating the determination of the useful life of an intangible asset

The illustrative examples accompanying IAS 38 provide guidance for the determination of the useful life of an asset in accordance with the Standard. Each example details the specific facts and circumstances surrounding the determination of the asset's useful life. The following table summarises the key determinants for each example. Readers should refer to the text of the Standard, however, to obtain a full understanding of each of the circumstances and of the factors assessed in each scenario.

Asset description	Finite or indefinite life?	Amortisation period
Acquired customer list – anticipated to generate benefits for between 1 and 3 years. [IAS 38 Illustrative examples: Example 1]	Finite. Although the entity may expect to generate further benefits by the addition of new customers to the list, the useful life is determined by reference only to customers on the list at the acquisition date.	Management's best estimate of the useful life – say 18 months.
Acquired patent that expires in 15 years. The entity intends to sell the patent to a committed third party in five years for 60 per cent of its fair value at the date of acquisition. [IAS 38 Illustrative examples: Example 2]	Finite	The period over which the patent is expected to generate cash inflows for the entity, i.e. five years. The residual value should equal the present value of 60 per cent of the fair value at the date of acquisition.
Copyright with remaining legal life of 50 years, but management estimates that net cash inflows will only be generated for 30 years. [IAS 38 Illustrative examples: Example 3]	Finite	30 years

Asset description	Finite or indefinite life?	Amortisation period
Broadcasting licence that expires in five years. Can be renewed indefinitely, at little cost every 10 years, provided that certain conditions are met. Management intends to renew the licence indefinitely, and evidence supports its ability to do so. No third party or obsolescence issues that would indicate a problem with indefinite renewal. [IAS 38 Illustrative examples: Example 4]	Indefinite. Potential to renew indefinitely is taken into account.	N/a
Same licence as previous example but, when licence has three years remaining, licensing authority decides to auction licences at future renewal dates. [IAS 38 Illustrative examples: Example 5]	Finite. No potential to renew the existing arrangement.	Three years
Acquired airline route authority that expires in three years. Renewable indefinitely, at minimal cost, every five years provided that conditions are complied with. Management expects to renew indefinitely, and no indication that they will not be able to do so. [IAS 38 Illustrative examples: Example 6]	Indefinite. Potential to renew indefinitely is taken into account.	N/a

Asset description	Finite or indefinite life?	Amortisation period
Acquired trademark for a market-leading consumer product with a remaining legal life of five years, but renewable every 10 years at little cost. Management intends to renew indefinitely and market indicators support cash inflows for an indefinite period. [IAS 38 Illustrative examples: Example 7]	Indefinite. Potential to renew indefinitely is taken into account.	N/a
Acquired trademark for leading consumer product previously regarded as having an indefinite life. Increased competitor activity indicates reduced future cash inflows for an indefinite period. [IAS 38 Illustrative examples: Example 8]	Indefinite. If, as a result of the reduced future cash inflows, the recoverable amount is less than the carrying amount of the intangible asset, an impairment loss is recognised.	N/a
Trademark acquired in a business combination some years ago, previously considered to have an indefinite life. Management decides to discontinue related product line over the next four years. [IAS 38 Illustrative examples: Example 9]	Finite	Four years

8.6 Subsequent reassessment of useful life

Whether an intangible asset is determined to have a finite useful life, or an indefinite useful life, IAS 38 requires that the initial determination be reviewed at least annually (see **section 9** and **10.3.3**).

The determination of useful life for each intangible asset requires a comprehensive consideration of all pertinent factors surrounding the assets. Subsequent to the initial determination of useful life, entities must establish sufficient procedures to identify and evaluate appropriately those events or circumstances that, if occurring after, or changed from, the initial determination, may affect the remaining useful life. Some events or circumstances will represent both discrete and readily identifiable events to which the entity should respond (e.g. a change in regulation). Other events or circumstances may develop more gradually over time but, nevertheless, must be monitored and given appropriate consideration by the entity (e.g. obsolescence, competition and demand). Given the varying nature of the intangible assets, and each entity's unique background and circumstances, procedures employed by entities to evaluate useful lives of intangible assets are expected to vary.

9   Subsequent accounting for intangible assets with indefinite useful lives

Entities are not permitted to amortise intangible assets that have been assessed as having an indefinite useful life. [IAS 38:107] Rather, in accordance with the requirements of IAS 36 *Impairment of Assets*, such assets are tested for impairment by comparing their recoverable amounts with their carrying amounts once a year, at a minimum. An additional impairment test is required whenever there is an indication that an intangible asset may be impaired. [IAS 38:108] The requirements of IAS 36 are dealt with in detail in **chapter A10**.

If an asset has been assessed as having an indefinite useful life, resulting in the asset not being amortised in accordance with IAS 38:107, that assessment is revisited each period to determine whether events and circumstances continue to support an indefinite useful life for that asset. If not, the change in the indefinite life assessment is accounted for as a change in accounting estimate in accordance with IAS 8 *Accounting Policies, Changes in Accounting Estimates and Errors*. [IAS 38:109]

When the useful life of an intangible asset is reassessed as finite rather than indefinite, this is an indicator that the asset may be impaired. Accordingly, the asset is tested for impairment by comparing its recoverable amount, determined in accordance with IAS 36, with its carrying amount, and recognising any excess of the carrying amount over the recoverable amount as an impairment loss. [IAS 38:110]

Following the annual reassessment of the useful life of an intangible asset previously considered to have an indefinite useful life:

- if the intangible asset still has an indefinite useful life, it should be tested for impairment in accordance with the requirements of IAS 36; and

- if the intangible asset is determined to have a finite useful life, it should be tested for impairment, and should be amortised over its estimated remaining useful life and accounted for in the same manner as other intangible assets that are subject to amortisation, including further impairment testing when indicators of impairment exist.

10   Subsequent accounting for intangible assets with finite useful lives

10.1   Depreciable amount to be amortised over the asset's useful life

The depreciable amount of an intangible asset with a finite useful life is required to be amortised on a systematic basis over its useful life. [IAS 38:97] The depreciable amount of an asset is defined as the cost of the asset, or other amount substituted for cost, less its residual value. [IAS 38:8]

In the majority of cases, amortisation is recognised in profit or loss. If the economic benefits of the intangible asset are used by the entity in the production of other assets, however, the amortisation is added to the cost of the other assets and included in their carrying amount. For example, if a patented production process has been capitalised as an intangible asset, as the relevant inventory items are produced using the patented process, the amortisation of the intangible asset is added to the cost of the inventories. [IAS 38:99]

10.2   Residual value

IAS 38 defines residual value as the estimated amount that an entity would currently obtain from disposal of the asset, after deducting the estimated costs of disposal, if the asset were already of the age and in the condition expected at the end of its useful life. [IAS 38:8]

Under most circumstances, the residual value of an intangible asset with a finite life is zero. A residual value of greater than zero, which implies that the entity expects to dispose of the intangible asset before the end of its useful life, may arise if:

[IAS 38:100]

- there is a commitment by a third party to purchase the asset at the end of its useful life; *or*

- there is an active market for the asset, *and*:

  - residual value can be determined by reference to that market; *and*

- it is probable that such a market will exist at the end of the asset's useful life.

See **7.1.1** for the definition of an active market.

If the residual value is significant, it has a direct impact on the amortisation recognised over the life of the asset.

The residual value of an asset is required to be reviewed at least at each financial year end. The revised estimate should be based on conditions and prices current at the end of the reporting period. When the revised estimate differs significantly from previous estimates of residual value, the effect is accounted for prospectively as a change in estimate, in accordance with the requirements of IAS 8 *Accounting Policies, Changes in Accounting Estimates and Errors*. [IAS 38:102] Effectively, the amortisation recognised over the remaining useful life of the asset is adjusted to take account of the revised estimate of residual value.

When the revised estimate of residual value is equal to or greater than the asset's carrying amount, whether due to inflation or otherwise, then no amortisation is recognised unless and until the asset's residual value subsequently decreases to an amount below the asset's carrying amount. [IAS 38:103]

IAS 38 does not allow a reversal of earlier amortisation in these circumstances.

10.3   Amortisation period

10.3.1   Commencement of amortisation

Amortisation commences from the date the asset is available for use, i.e. when it is in the location and condition necessary for it to be capable of operating in the manner intended by management. [IAS 38:97]

It is important to distinguish the date an asset is available for use from the date on which it is actually brought into use. Amortisation will commence from the former.

Example 10.3.1

Date of commencement of amortisation of an intangible asset

Operators usually are required to purchase a telecom licence prior to the provision of services in a particular location or prior to the provision of certain types of services (e.g. 4G services). Because telecom licences normally are granted for a specified period of time, the cost of the licence has to be amortised

---

over the best estimate of its useful life. The operator is generally required to build and commission its network before it can earn revenues from the use of its licence.

The ability to receive economic benefits from the licence is linked directly to the ability to use the network; therefore, the licence is only available for use when the network is in place. Consequently, amortisation of the licence should commence at the date the network is available for use (i.e. it is in the location and condition necessary for it to be capable of operating in the manner intended by management).

In some countries, the full network may not be operational in the entire targeted areas until a certain date. However, as soon as one area (one connection) is in place and working, the amortisation of the licence should commence. In most instances, the amortisation of the licence should begin before the full commercial launch.

10.3.2 Cessation of amortisation

Amortisation ceases at the earlier of:

[IAS 38:97]

- the date that the asset is classified as held for sale (or included in a disposal group that is classified as held for sale) in accordance with IFRS 5 *Non-current Assets Held for Sale and Discontinued Operations*; and

- the date that the asset is derecognised (see **section 12**).

Amortisation does not cease when an intangible asset is taken out of use, unless the asset is classified as held for sale or is already fully amortised. [IAS 38:117]

The circumstances that cause an intangible asset to be taken out of use could also indicate that it may be impaired, in which case an impairment review may be required in accordance with IAS 36 *Impairment of Assets* (see **chapter A10**).

10.3.3 Review of amortisation period

At least at each financial year end, the amortisation periods for intangible assets with finite lives should be reviewed. If the expected useful life of the asset is different from previous estimates, the amortisation period should be adjusted accordingly. Any such change is accounted for as a change in estimate in accordance with IAS 8, by adjusting current and future periods. [IAS 38:104]

When the annual review of the amortisation period of a previously-amortised intangible asset results in a determination that the asset has an indefinite useful life:

- it should be tested for impairment;

- it should no longer be amortised, but should be accounted for in the same manner as other intangible assets that are not subject to amortisation; and

- previous amortisation of that asset is not reversed.

10.4   Amortisation method – general

10.4.1   Amortisation method should reflect expected consumption of economic benefits

IAS 38 requires that the entity should select an amortisation method that reflects the pattern in which the asset's future economic benefits are expected to be consumed by the entity. [IAS 38:97]

10.4.2   Alternative methods of apportioning amortisation

There are several methods of apportioning amortisation over the anticipated useful life of the asset; those most commonly employed are the straight-line method and the reducing balance (diminishing balance) method. These, and other, methods of depreciation and amortisation are discussed in **section 7.5** of **chapter A7**.

10.4.3   Identification of the predominant limiting factor inherent in an intangible asset

In choosing an appropriate amortisation method, the IASB suggests that an entity could determine the predominant limiting factor that is inherent in the intangible asset. For example, the contract that sets out the entity's rights over its use of an intangible asset might specify the entity's use of the intangible asset as a predetermined period of time, as a number of units produced or as a fixed total amount of revenue to be generated. [IAS 38:98B]

The identification of such a predominant limiting factor could serve as the starting point for the identification of an appropriate amortisation method; however, the underlying requirement is to select a method that is based on the expected pattern of consumption of economic benefits. [IAS 38:98B]

IAS 38:98B was added as part of the May 2014 amendments (see **10.5.1**). The concept of a 'predominant limiting factor' (essentially, the measurement used to determine when the rights embodied in an asset expire) is used in the specification of an exception to IAS 38's general presumption against revenue-based amortisation methods (see **section 10.5**); however, the concept is equally useful in other circumstances as an aid to the identification of the pattern of consumption of the economic benefits of an intangible asset.

10.4.4 Amortisation on a straight-line basis if the expected pattern of economic benefits cannot be determined reliably

In some circumstances, it may not be possible to determine reliably the expected pattern of consumption of future economic benefits. In such circumstances, use of the straight-line method is mandatory. [IAS 38:97]

10.4.5 Change in amortisation method

At least at the end of each financial year, the amortisation methods for intangible assets with finite useful lives should be reviewed. If there has been a change in the expected pattern of consumption of the future economic benefits embodied in an asset, the amortisation method should be changed to reflect the changed pattern. Any such change is accounted for as a change in estimate in accordance with IAS 8, by adjusting current and future periods. [IAS 38:104]

10.5 Amortisation method based on revenue

10.5.1 May 2014 amendments limit the use of revenue-based amortisation methods

Paragraphs 98A to 98C (see **10.5.2** and **10.5.3**) were added to IAS 38 by *Clarification of Acceptable Methods of Depreciation and Amortisation (Amendments to IAS 16 and IAS 38)* issued in May 2014. The May 2014 amendments are required to be applied prospectively for annual periods beginning on or after 1 January 2016, with earlier application permitted. If an entity applies these amendments for a period beginning before 1 January 2016, it is required to disclose that fact. [IAS 38:130J]

The May 2014 amendments address the use of revenue-based amortisation methods, which allocate an asset's amortisable amount based on revenues generated in an accounting period as a proportion of the total revenues expected to be generated over the asset's useful economic life. The amendments establish a rebuttable presumption that the use of revenue-based amortisation methods is inappropriate because such methods generally do not comply with the requirement that the amortisation method for an intangible asset should reflect the pattern in which the asset's future economic benefits are expected to be consumed by the entity (see **10.4.1**). [IAS 38:BC72C - BC72E]

The IASB concluded that the rebuttable presumption can be overcome in two limited circumstances (see **10.5.3**). These exceptions have not been permitted in the equivalent amendments to IAS 16 *Property, Plant and Equipment* (see **7.5.4** in **chapter A7**) because the IASB believe that the circumstances in which a revenue-based amortisation method for intangible assets is acceptable are not likely to arise in respect of items of property, plant and equipment.

If adoption of the amendments results in a change in amortisation method, prospective application will have the same effect as the required treatment for all changes in amortisation methods, as described in **10.4.5** – the carrying amount of the asset at the date of change is amortised using the new method over its remaining useful life, commencing with the period in which the change takes place. **Example 7.5.5** in **chapter A7** illustrates this treatment.

10.5.2   Rebuttable presumption against revenue-based amortisation methods

There is a rebuttable presumption that an amortisation method based on the revenue generated by an activity that includes the use of an intangible asset is inappropriate. [IAS 38:98A]

Such methods are generally considered to be inappropriate because the revenue generated by an activity that includes the use of an intangible asset typically reflects factors that are not directly linked to the consumption of the economic benefits embodied in the intangible asset. For example, revenue is affected by other inputs and processes, selling activities and changes in sales volumes and prices. The price component of revenue may be affected by inflation, which has no bearing upon the way in which an asset is consumed. [IAS 38:98A]

The circumstances in which this rebuttable presumption can be overcome are set out in **10.5.3**.

10.5.3   Rebuttal of the presumption against revenue-based amortisation

IAS 38's general presumption that the use of revenue-based amortisation methods is inappropriate can be overcome only in two specific circumstances:

[IAS 38:98A]

(a) when the intangible asset is expressed as a measure of revenue, as described in IAS 38:98C (see below); or

(b) when it can be demonstrated that revenue and the consumption of the economic benefits of the intangible asset are highly correlated.

When the predominant limiting factor inherent in an intangible asset is a revenue threshold, the revenue to be generated can be an appropriate basis for amortisation, provided that the contract specifies a fixed total amount of revenue to be generated on which amortisation is to be determined. [IAS 38:98C]

The IASB concluded that it may be appropriate to use a revenue-based amortisation method when the right embodied by an intangible asset is expressed as a total amount of revenue to be generated (rather than time, for example), in such a way that the generation of revenue is the measurement used to determine when the right expires. In such circumstances, the pattern of consumption of future economic benefits that is embodied in the intangible asset is defined by reference to the total revenue earned as a proportion of the contractual maximum and, consequently, the amount of revenue generated contractually reflects the consumption of the benefits that are embodied in the asset. [IAS 38:BC72G]

Note, however, that another basis may be more appropriate if it more closely reflects the expected pattern of consumption of economic benefits.

IAS 38 identifies two examples in which the predominant limiting factor inherent in an intangible asset is the achievement of a revenue threshold.

[IAS 38:98C]

- An entity acquires a concession to explore and extract gold from a gold mine and the expiry of the contract is based on a fixed amount of total revenue to be generated from the extraction (e.g. the contract allows the extraction of gold from the mine until total cumulative revenue from the sale of gold reaches CU2 billion) and is not based on time or on the amount of gold extracted.

- A right to operate a toll road is based on a fixed total amount of revenue to be generated from cumulative tolls charged (e.g. the contract allows operation of the toll road until the cumulative amount of tolls generated from operating the road reaches CU100 million).

10.5.4 Intangible asset used in multiple activities to provide multiple revenue streams

In the course of its deliberations on revenue-based amortisation methods, the IASB also analysed situations in which an intangible asset is used in multiple activities to provide multiple revenue streams (e.g. the producer of a motion picture uses the intellectual property embodied in the film to generate cash flows through exhibiting the film in theatres, licensing the rights to characters to manufacturers of toys and other goods, selling DVDs or digital copies of the film and licensing broadcast rights to television broadcasters). It had been suggested (1) that the application of the units of production method in such circumstances is not practicable, because the units of production are not homogenous, and (2) that a revenue-based method of amortisation might be more appropriate because revenue might be considered a common denominator to reflect a suitable proxy of the pattern of consumption of all the benefits received from the multiple activities in which the intellectual property could be used.

The IASB acknowledged that determining an appropriate amortisation method in circumstances when an intangible asset is used in multiple activities and generates multiple cash flow streams in different markets, requires judgement. Although no explicit guidance was developed, the IASB referred to the possibility that an intangible asset could be componentised for amortisation purposes in circumstances in which the asset is used to generate multiple cash flow streams. [IAS 38:BC72H & BC72I]

11 Impairment

The requirements of IAS 36 *Impairment of Assets* are applied to determine whether an intangible asset is impaired and to measure any such impairment loss (see **chapter A10**). Any impairment loss is then recognised in accordance with the requirements of IAS 36.

For intangible assets with indefinite lives, an impairment review is required at least annually (see **section 9**).

12 Derecognition

IAS 38 requires that the carrying amount of an intangible asset should be derecognised:

[IAS 38:112]

- on disposal; or

- when no future economic benefits are expected from its use or disposal.

The gain or loss arising from the derecognition of an intangible asset is to be recognised in profit or loss when the asset is derecognised (unless IAS 17 *Leases* requires otherwise in the circumstances of a sale and leaseback). [IAS 38:113]

IAS 38 specifically prohibits the classification as revenue of gains arising on the derecognition of intangible assets. [IAS 38:103] The Standard does specify, however, that the date of disposal of an intangible asset is the date that the recipient obtains control of the asset in accordance with the requirements for determining when a performance obligation is satisfied in IFRS 15 *Revenue from Contracts with Customers* (see **chapter A14**). For entities that have not yet adopted IFRS 15, the date of disposal should be determined using the criteria for recognising revenue from the sale of goods, as set out in IAS 18 *Revenue* (see **appendix A1**). [IAS 38:114]

The gain or loss arising from the derecognition of an intangible asset is determined as the difference between the net disposal proceeds, if any, and the carrying amount of the item. [IAS 38:113] Therefore, as discussed at **7.6.3**, when a revalued asset is disposed of, any credit balance on the revaluation reserve attributable to that asset may be transferred directly to retained earnings, but should not be reflected in profit or loss. [IAS 38:87]

In the case of a reacquired right in a business combination, if the right is subsequently reissued (i.e. sold) to a third party, the related carrying amount, if any, is used in determining the gain or loss on reissue. [IAS 38:115A]

The amount of consideration to be included in the gain or loss arising from the derecognition of an item of an intangible asset is determined in accordance with the requirements for determining the transaction price in paragraphs 47 to 72 of IFRS 15 *Revenue from Contracts with Customers* (see **chapter A14**). Subsequent changes to the estimated amount of the consideration included in the gain or loss should be accounted for in accordance with the requirements for changes in the transaction price in IFRS 15 (see **chapter A14**). [IAS 38:116]

The wording of IAS 38:116 was amended in June 2014 as a consequential amendment arising from IFRS 15. For entities that have not yet adopted IFRS 15, IAS 38:116 states that the consideration receivable on disposal of an intangible asset is recognised initially at its fair value. If payment is deferred beyond normal credit terms, the consideration received is recognised initially at the cash price equivalent. The difference between the nominal amount of the consideration and the cash price equivalent is recognised as interest income on an effective yield basis, in accordance with IAS 18 *Revenue*.

13 Presentation and disclosure

13.1 Presentation

IAS 1 *Presentation of Financial Statements* requires that, if material, the aggregate carrying amount of the entity's intangible assets should be presented in the statement of financial position (see **chapter A4**). [IAS 1:54(c)]

13.2   Disclosure

13.2.1   *Disclosure – general*

The following disclosures should be made for each class of intangible assets, distinguishing between internally generated intangible assets and other intangible assets:

[IAS 38:118]

- whether the useful lives are indefinite or finite and, if finite, the useful lives or amortisation rates used;

- the amortisation methods used for intangible assets with finite useful lives;

- the gross carrying amount and any accumulated amortisation (aggregated with accumulated impairment losses) at the beginning and end of the period; and

- the line item(s) of the statement of comprehensive income in which any amortisation of intangible assets is included.

An entity is also required to provide a reconciliation of the carrying amount at the beginning and end of the period, in respect of each class of intangible assets, showing:

[IAS 38:118(e)]

- additions, indicating separately those from internal development, those acquired separately, and those acquired through business combinations;

- assets classified as held for sale or included in a disposal group classified as held for sale in accordance with IFRS 5 *Non-current Assets Held for Sale and Discontinued Operations*, and other disposals;

- increases or decreases during the period resulting from revaluations and from impairment losses recognised or reversed in other comprehensive income;

- impairment losses recognised in profit or loss during the period;

- impairment losses reversed in profit or loss during the period;

- any amortisation recognised during the period;

- net exchange differences arising on the translation of the financial statements into the presentation currency, and on the translation of a foreign operation into the presentation currency of the entity; and

- other changes in the carrying amount during the period.

Examples of classes of intangible assets are listed at **7.4**. Those classes are disaggregated (aggregated) into smaller (larger) classes if this results in more relevant information for the users of the financial statements. [IAS 38:119]

13.2.2 Intangible assets having an indefinite useful life

For an intangible asset assessed as having an indefinite useful life, the financial statements should disclose the carrying amount of the asset and the reasons supporting the assessment of an indefinite useful life. In giving these reasons, the entity should describe the factor(s) that played a significant role in determining that the asset has an indefinite useful life. [IAS 38:122(a)] The factors listed at **8.3** should be considered. [IAS 38:123]

13.2.3 Intangible assets that are individually material

For any individual intangible asset that is material to the entity's financial statements, the financial statements should disclose a description of the asset, its carrying amount and its remaining amortisation period. [IAS 38:122(b)]

13.2.4 Intangible assets acquired by way of government grant and initially recognised at fair value

For intangible assets acquired by way of government grant and initially recognised at fair value (see **4.6**), the financial statements should disclose:

[IAS 38:122(c)]

- the fair value initially recognised for those assets;

- their carrying amount; and

- whether they are measured after recognition under the cost model or the revaluation model.

13.2.5 Title restrictions and capital commitments

The financial statements should also disclose:

- the existence and carrying amount of intangible assets whose title is restricted and the carrying amounts of intangible assets pledged as security for liabilities; [IAS 38:122(d)] and

- the amount of contractual commitments for the acquisition of intangible assets. [IAS 38:122(e)]

13.2.6 Changes in estimates

In addition to the disclosure requirements included in IAS 38, if there has been a change in estimate during the period, the disclosure requirements set out in IAS 8 *Accounting Policies, Changes in Accounting Estimates and Errors* apply (see **section 4.3** of **chapter A5**). Changes in estimate related to intangible assets include changes regarding:

- the assessment as to whether the useful life of an intangible asset is finite or indefinite;

- the assessment of an intangible asset's useful life;
- the amortisation method; and
- residual values.

13.2.7   Impairment losses

If an intangible asset has suffered an impairment loss, the disclosure requirements set out in IAS 36 *Impairment of Assets* apply (see **section 11** of **chapter A10**).

13.2.8   Intangible assets carried at revalued amounts

In addition to the disclosures listed in the previous sections, if an entity accounts for any intangible assets at revalued amounts, the following disclosures are required:

[IAS 38:124]

- by class of intangible assets:
  - the effective date of the revaluation;
  - the carrying amount of revalued intangible assets; and
  - the carrying amount that would have been included in the financial statements had the revalued intangible assets been accounted for under the cost model; and
- the amount of the revaluation surplus that relates to intangible assets at the beginning and end of the period, indicating the changes during the period and any restrictions on the distribution of the balance to shareholders.

If necessary, it is acceptable to aggregate the classes of revalued assets into larger classes for disclosure purposes. Classes are not aggregated, however, if this would result in the combination of a class of intangible assets that includes amounts measured under both the cost and revaluation models. [IAS 38:125]

13.2.9   Research and development expenditure

The aggregate amount of research and development expenditure recognised as an expense during the period should be disclosed. [IAS 38:126]

13.2.10   Additional recommended disclosures

The following disclosures are encouraged but not required:

[IAS 38:128]

- a description of any fully amortised intangible asset that is still in use; and

- a brief description of significant intangible assets controlled by the entity but not recognised as assets because they did not meet the recognition criteria in IAS 38 or because they were acquired or generated before the 1998 version of IAS 38 (which prohibited retrospective recognition) became effective.

14   Future developments

The IASB has an ongoing project titled *Rate-regulated Activities* which is concerned with whether IFRSs should require entities with rate-regulated activities (i.e. activities subject to restrictions on prices that can be charged to customers) to recognise assets and liabilities arising from the effects of rate regulation. Some national GAAPs provide specific guidance on this matter, but there is no equivalent guidance in IFRSs.

The IASB reactivated this project following its Agenda Consultation in 2011. A new comprehensive project was initiated in September 2012 and a discussion paper DP/2014/2 *Reporting the Financial Effects of Rate Regulation* was published in September 2014. A second discussion paper is expected, but not before 2016.

In January 2014, the IASB issued IFRS 14 *Regulatory Deferral Accounts*. This is an interim Standard which permits entities adopting IFRSs for the first time to continue to use their local GAAP for rate-regulated activities until the comprehensive project is completed (see **chapter A42**).

A10 Impairment of assets

Contents

1 Introduction

1.1 Overview of IAS 36

IAS 36 *Impairment of Assets* seeks to ensure that an entity's assets are not carried at more than their recoverable amount (i.e. the higher of fair value less costs of disposal and value in use). With the exception of goodwill and certain intangible assets for which an annual impairment test is required, entities are required to conduct impairment tests when there is an indication of impairment of an asset; the test may be conducted for a 'cash-generating unit' when an asset does not generate cash inflows that are largely independent of those from other assets.

1.2 Application of the IAS 36 framework

The principles of IAS 36 apply to a wide range of assets (those assets outside its scope are described in **section 2**). The idea is that, for those assets within its scope, the requirements for the recognition of impairment losses should be specified in a single Standard. Thus, other Standards dealing with such asset categories (e.g. IAS 16 *Property, Plant and Equipment*) simply refer to IAS 36 for the requirements regarding impairment testing.

IAS 36 requires that a review for impairment be carried out if events or changes in circumstances indicate that the carrying amount of an asset may not be recoverable. The review will compare the carrying amount of the asset with its recoverable amount, which is the higher of its value if sold (if known) and its value in use.

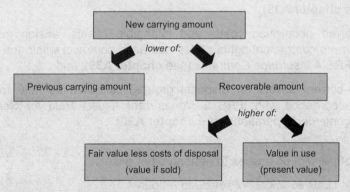

Any shortfall is deemed an impairment loss which, for assets carried at cost, is recognised in profit or loss and, for assets carried at a revalued amount, is treated as a revaluation decrease (which may or may not lead to an expense being recognised in profit or loss).

1.3 Amendments to IAS 36 since the last edition of this manual

None. IAS 36 was most recently amended in June 2014.

2 Scope

IAS 36 applies to all assets except:

[IAS 36:2]

- inventories (dealt with in IAS 2 *Inventories* – see **chapter A11**);

- for entities that have adopted IFRS 15 *Revenue from Contracts with Customers*, contract assets and assets arising from costs to obtain or fulfil a contract that are recognised in accordance with IFRS 15 (see **chapter A14**);

- for entities that have not yet adopted IFRS 15, assets arising from construction contracts (dealt with in IAS 11 *Construction Contracts* – see **appendix A2**);

- deferred tax assets (dealt with in IAS 12 *Income Taxes* – see **chapter A13**);

- assets arising from employee benefits (dealt with in IAS 19 *Employee Benefits* – see **chapter A15**);

- financial assets that are within the scope of IFRS 9 *Financial Instruments* (see **chapter B2** and **chapter B6**) or, for entities that have not yet adopted IFRS 9, IAS 39 *Financial Instruments: Recognition and Measurement* (see **chapter C2** and **chapter C6**);

- investment property that is measured at fair value (dealt with in IAS 40 *Investment Property* – see **chapter A8**);

- biological assets related to agricultural activity within the scope of IAS 41 *Agriculture* that are measured at fair value less costs to sell (see **chapter A38**);

- deferred acquisition costs, and intangible assets, arising from an insurer's contractual rights under insurance contracts within the scope of IFRS 4 *Insurance Contracts* (see **chapter A39**); and

- non-current assets (or disposal groups) classified as held for sale in accordance with IFRS 5 *Non-current Assets Held for Sale and Discontinued Operations* (see **chapter A20**).

Therefore, IAS 36 applies to (among other assets):

- land carried at cost or revalued amounts;

- buildings carried at cost or revalued amounts;

- machinery and equipment carried at cost or revalued amounts;

- investment property carried at cost;

- biological assets carried at cost;

- intangible assets carried at cost or revalued amounts;

- goodwill; and

- investments in subsidiaries, associates and joint ventures (other than those accounted for in accordance with IFRS 9 or, for entities that have not yet adopted IFRS 9, IAS 39).

Note that, although investments in subsidiaries, associates and joint ventures are financial assets, they are included within the scope of IAS 36 unless they are accounted for in accordance with IFRS 9 (or, for entities that have not yet adopted IFRS 9, IAS 39).

IAS 36:2 was amended in June 2014 by *Agriculture: Bearer Plants (Amendments to IAS 16 and IAS 41)*, to clarify that the biological assets excluded from the scope of IAS 36 are those that fall within the amended scope of IAS 41 *Agriculture*. Following the June 2014 amendments, bearer plants related to agricultural activity are brought within the scope of IAS 16 *Property, Plant and Equipment* rather than IAS 41 (see **section 2.6** of **chapter A7**). Consequently, for entities that have adopted the June 2014 amendments, such biological assets are within the scope of IAS 36.

3 Definitions

The terms used in IAS 36 have specific meanings within the context of the Standard. The more important definitions, as set out in IAS 36:6, are reproduced below for reference.

- **Recoverable amount** for an asset or a cash-generating unit is the higher of its fair value less costs of disposal and its value in use.

- **Fair value** is the price that would be received to sell an asset or paid to transfer a liability in an orderly transaction between market participants at the measurement date (see IFRS 13 *Fair Value Measurement* – **chapter A6**).

- **Costs of disposal** are incremental costs directly attributable to the disposal of an asset or cash-generating unit, excluding finance costs and income tax expense.

- **Value in use** is the present value of the future cash flows expected to be derived from an asset or cash-generating unit.

- An **impairment loss** is the amount by which the carrying amount of an asset or a cash-generating unit exceeds its recoverable amount.

- **Carrying amount** is the amount at which an asset is recognised in the statement of financial position after deducting any accumulated depreciation (amortisation) and accumulated impairment losses thereon.

- A **cash-generating unit (CGU)** is the smallest identifiable group of assets that generates cash inflows that are largely independent of the cash inflows from other assets or groups of assets.

- **Corporate assets** are assets other than goodwill that contribute to the future cash flows of both the cash-generating unit under review and other cash-generating units.

4   Requirement for impairment review when there are indications of impairment

4.1   Requirement for impairment review – general

An asset is impaired when its carrying amount exceeds its recoverable amount. [IAS 36:8] At the end of each reporting period, entities are required to assess whether there is any indication that an asset may be impaired. If any such indication exists, the entity is required to estimate the recoverable amount of the asset. [IAS 36:9]

See **4.2** for a discussion of impairment indicators.

Example 4.1

Decline in demand for output

An entity has a machine that was purchased in January 20X1 for CU1 million. It is being depreciated over its estimated useful life of 10 years on a straight-line basis. The carrying amount at 31 December 20X3 is therefore CU700,000.

At 31 December 20X3, the directors become aware that a new technological development means that demand for the output produced by the machine is likely to decline significantly. Consequently, under IAS 36:9, they are required to estimate the asset's recoverable amount.

The following items are required to be tested for impairment at least annually, irrespective of whether there is any indication of impairment:

[IAS 36:10]

- intangible assets with an indefinite useful life;

- intangible assets that are not yet available for use; and

- goodwill acquired in a business combination.

Other than in these three specific circumstances (which are discussed in **section 5**), there is no requirement to make a formal estimate of an asset's recoverable amount if no indication of an impairment loss is present. [IAS 36:8]

4.2 Indications of impairment

4.2.1 Indications of impairment – general

Sections **4.2.2** to **4.2.4** describe a number of indications that an impairment loss may have occurred. In making its assessments as to the possibility of impairment losses having arisen, the entity is required, at a minimum, to consider the indications listed. The lists are not exhaustive, however, and all of the items listed will not apply to every entity. If an impairment indicator that is not on these lists exists at the end of the reporting period, a detailed impairment review is required nonetheless. [IAS 36:13]

4.2.2 Internal sources of information

The following internal sources of information may indicate that an asset is impaired:

[IAS 36:12]

- evidence is available of obsolescence or physical damage of the asset;

- significant changes with an adverse effect on the entity have taken place during the period, or are expected to take place in the near future, in the extent to which, or the manner in which, an asset is used or is expected to be used. These changes include the asset becoming idle, plans to discontinue or restructure the operation to which an asset belongs, plans to dispose of an asset before the previously expected date, and reassessing the useful life of an asset as finite rather than indefinite; or

- evidence is available from internal reporting that indicates that the economic performance of an asset is, or will be, worse than expected.

Such evidence may include:

[IAS 36:14]

- cash flows for acquiring the asset, or subsequent cash needs for operating or maintaining it, that are significantly higher than those originally budgeted; or

- actual net cash flows or operating profit or loss flowing from the asset that are significantly worse than those budgeted; or

- a significant decline in budgeted net cash flows or operating profit, or a significant increase in budgeted loss, flowing from the asset; or

- operating losses or net cash outflows for the asset, when current period figures are aggregated with budgeted figures for the future.

Impairment indicators related to obsolescence or physical damage may be the easiest to identify because they can be observed physically.

Items such as unused factory equipment or equipment that has been damaged by fire are two examples that may indicate impairment.

An impairment indicator may also arise because an asset is to be taken out of use to be sold. If the asset qualifies as held for sale, in accordance with IFRS 5 *Non-current Assets Held for Sale and Discontinued Operations*, it will be measured under the rules of that Standard (see **chapter A20**) and will fall outside the scope of IAS 36. However, immediately before this reclassification, IFRS 5:18 requires the asset to be measured in accordance with other applicable Standards. If the requirements of IAS 36 result in the recognition of an impairment loss before reclassification, that loss should be reported separately as an impairment loss and should not be included as part of the gain or loss disclosed in accordance with IFRS 5:41(c) (see **7.4** in **chapter A20**) or as part of any subsequent gain or loss on disposal disclosed in accordance with paragraph 98(c) of IAS 1 *Presentation of Financial Statements* (see **5.4.1** in **chapter A4**).

4.2.3   External sources of information

The following external sources of information may indicate that an asset is impaired:

[IAS 36:12]

- there are observable indications that the asset's value has declined during the period significantly more than would be expected as a result of the passage of time or normal use;

  Such a decline could be caused by a decrease in the external market value for an asset (e.g. a head office building), or by a decrease in the sales price of items produced by a group of assets, such as the property, plant and equipment making up a factory.

- significant changes with an adverse effect on the entity have taken place during the period, or will take place in the near future, in the technological, market, economic or legal environment in which the entity operates or in the market to which the asset is dedicated;

  For example, if a factory produces a product that is judged harmful to the environment, and the government introduces a ban on the use of such equipment after a phase-out period, the carrying amount of the factory and the associated plant and equipment would need to be assessed for impairment. As another example, the value of a luxury hotel would need to be assessed if occupancy rates are declining as a result of a downturn in the economy.

- the carrying amount of the net assets of the entity is more than its market capitalisation;

> In some cases, the business prospects of the entity may not have changed, but the sector in which the entity operates may be 'out of favour' with market analysts, resulting in a decline in share price. In such circumstances, a write-down may not be required, but a formal review should be carried out. In particular, great care should be taken in determining the appropriate discount rate with which to calculate value in use, to ensure that it is consistent with current market assessments.

- for an investment in a subsidiary, joint venture or associate, the investor recognises a dividend from the investment and evidence is available that:

  - the carrying amount of the investment in the separate financial statements exceeds the carrying amounts in the consolidated financial statements of the investee's net assets, including associated goodwill; or

  - the dividend exceeds the total comprehensive income of the subsidiary, joint venture or associate in the period the dividend is declared; and

> Dividends are recognised in profit or loss, rather than as a reduction of the cost of the associated investment. Accordingly, when a dividend reduces the recoverable amount of an investment to below its carrying amount, the investment is impaired.

- market interest rates or other market rates of return on investments have increased during the period, and those increases are likely to affect the discount rate used in calculating the asset's value in use and decrease the asset's recoverable amount materially.

> If in prior years an asset has been the subject of an impairment test, and there is a change in market interest rates in the current period that will affect the discount rate used in the previous calculation, it is appropriate to revisit the calculation. However, this does not necessarily mean that, once an impairment review has been carried out, it must be revisited each year or whenever market rates move. The review in subsequent periods is required only when the change in rates is likely to affect materially the recoverable amount of the asset.

IAS 36:16 specifically states that no formal review is required when the discount rate used in calculating the asset's value in use is:

- unlikely to be affected by the increase in market interest rates or other market rates of return on investments. For example, increases in short-term interest rates may not have a material effect on the discount rate used for an asset that has a long remaining useful life; or

- likely to be affected by the increase in these market rates, but previous sensitivity analysis of recoverable amount shows that:

  - it is unlikely that there will be a material decrease in the recoverable amount because future cash flows are also likely to increase. For example, in some cases, an entity may be able to demonstrate that it adjusts its revenues to compensate for any increase in market rates; or

  - the decrease in recoverable amount is unlikely to result in a material impairment loss.

If there is an indication that the asset may be impaired, the underlying facts should be kept in mind when performing the annual reviews of the useful life of the asset, the depreciation or amortisation method used and the estimated residual value. These items may need to be adjusted even if no impairment loss is recognised. [IAS 36:17]

4.2.4 Other examples of impairment indicators

4.2.4.1 Directors are considering ceasing to trade

As discussed in **section 2.5** of **chapter A4**, it is usually appropriate to regard the fact that the directors of an entity are considering ceasing to trade as an indication of impairment. The directors of an entity do not usually consider ceasing to trade if the entity is expected to be profitable. The fact that the directors are considering ceasing to trade may call into question the ability of the entity to continue to trade profitably and, therefore, whether the carrying amounts of assets are recoverable.

4.2.4.2 Investment property carried at depreciated cost

It is necessary to exercise careful judgement when identifying impairment indicators for investment property carried at depreciated cost. In addition to the events and circumstances detailed in IAS 36:12 (see **4.2.2** and **4.2.3**), the following conditions may indicate that an investor may be unable to realise the carrying amount of an investment property carried at depreciated cost (list is not exhaustive):

- the investor recently sold a portion of its similar income-generating investment properties and realised losses on the sale transactions;

- income-generating properties have significant vacancy rates or are expected to be vacant in the near future (e.g. because of non-competitive lease terms);

- depressed market conditions are adversely affecting the rental or sale activities of significant properties;

- the investor does not appear to have the ability to recover the current net carrying amount of investment properties from future cash flows due to a decline in rental rates or occupancy rates; or

- the investor is encountering cash flow difficulties, which may require forced sale of some or all of its investment properties.

4.2.4.3 Appraisal or valuation below carrying amount

The existence of an appraisal or other independent valuation information indicating that the fair value less costs of disposal of a held-and-used asset is below its carrying amount does not, in itself, require that an impairment loss be recognised. When the asset's recoverable amount was previously based on value in use, the entity should consider whether the appraisal is an indication of impairment; it is possible that the factors resulting in the lower valuation do not affect the value in use calculations. When the entity does consider the lower valuation to be an indication of impairment, the entity should calculate the value in use of the asset (or, when appropriate, of the CGU to which it belongs – see **section 8.2**). If the recoverable amount of the asset (i.e. the higher of the asset's fair value less costs of disposal and its value in use) is less than its carrying amount, an impairment loss should be recognised.

4.2.4.4 Computer software asset developed (or under development) or purchased for internal use

It is necessary to exercise careful judgement when identifying impairment indicators for recognised computer software assets developed or purchased for internal use. In addition to the events and circumstances detailed in IAS 36:12 (see **4.2.2** and **4.2.3**), the following conditions may indicate that the entity may not be able to recover the amounts recognised as an asset (list is not exhaustive):

- the internal-use computer software is not expected to provide service potential as originally planned;

- a significant change occurs in the extent to which, or the manner in which, the software is used or is expected to be used such that the future benefits expected to be generated are reduced;

- a significant change is made or will be made to the software program such that the future benefits expected to be generated are reduced; or

- the cost of developing or modifying the software significantly exceeded the amount originally budgeted.

Specifically in connection with software currently in development for internal use, indications that the software may no longer be expected to be completed and placed into service include the following:

- no expenditures budgeted or being incurred for the project;

- programming difficulties that cannot be resolved on a timely basis;

- significant cost overruns;

- the costs of internally developed software will significantly exceed the costs of comparable third-party software, and management intends to acquire the third-party software instead of completing the internally developed software;

- technologies are introduced in the marketplace so that management now intends to obtain third-party software instead of completing the internally developed software; or

- the business segment or unit to which the software relates, or relates in part, is unprofitable and has been or will be discontinued.

If events and circumstances indicate that the carrying amount of software recognised as an asset may not be recoverable, the entity will need to determine whether an impairment loss should be recognised (see **8.2.3**)

4.2.4.5 Impairment indicators after the reporting period

If information is received after the reporting period, but before the financial statements are authorised for issue, indicating that an asset is impaired, management should consider whether that information is indicative of impairment that existed at the end of the reporting period. If so, an impairment review should be carried out.

Even if management has already undertaken an impairment review in respect of that asset as at the end of the reporting period, additional information received after the reporting period that is indicative of impairment that existed at the end of the reporting period should lead management to re-perform that impairment review.

If the information received after the reporting period is not indicative of conditions existing at the end of the reporting period, it should not trigger an impairment test (or the re-performance of any impairment test already carried out). Rather, the information should be disclosed as a non-adjusting event after the reporting period when it is of such importance that non-disclosure would affect decisions of users of the financial statements (see **section 7** of **chapter A22** for further discussion of the disclosure requirements for events occurring after the reporting period).

Example 4.2.4.5

Closure announcement after the reporting date

An entity is a manufacturer of aircraft engines. After the reporting date, management decides and announces its intention to close its operations in Country A. Closure of the operation will not be completed within three years. The equipment and fixtures will only have a remaining life of three years, and there is no alternative use for the property.

The decision after the reporting date to close the operations in Country A is an indication of impairment. Any assessment of recoverable amounts should be based on the conditions and commitments existing at the reporting date. In accordance with IAS 10 *Events after the Reporting Period*, if the decision was made after the reporting date then any impairment resulting only from that decision (i.e. that was not already present in the business) is a non-adjusting event after the reporting period, although disclosure may be required. For further guidance on whether an entity was committed to a restructuring at the end of the reporting period, see **section 3.9.3** of **chapter A12**.

Although, in the circumstances described, the decision to close the operations in Country A may have been made after the reporting date, the decision may have resulted from conditions that existed at the reporting date (e.g. poor trading performance). Recognition of an impairment loss may therefore still be required to reflect those conditions that existed at the reporting date.

It will also be necessary to establish revised depreciation rates for the fixtures and equipment based on revised estimates of the useful lives and residual values of the affected assets, and those revised depreciation rates should be applied prospectively.

4.2.4.6 *Events and circumstances indicating that goodwill is impaired*

In addition to testing goodwill for impairment annually, goodwill should be tested for impairment whenever there is an indication that it might be impaired (as for other assets). It is necessary to exercise careful judgement when identifying impairment indicators for goodwill. The following are examples of events and circumstances that might indicate that goodwill is impaired (list is not exhaustive):

- the merger of business information systems does not occur as planned, and the acquirer does not achieve the savings that were expected from operating a merged system;

- industrial agreements do not permit the level of workplace reform that the acquirer had planned, and the employee headcount is higher than that planned at acquisition;

- the acquirer identified at acquisition the feasibility of developing several research projects, and these projects subsequently have been abandoned;

- a regulatory ruling prevents the acquirer from operating in certain markets, and the acquirer will not achieve the level of sales planned at acquisition; or

- a competitor introduces a new product earlier than expected, and the acquirer will not achieve the level of sales planned at acquisition.

4.2.4.7   Asset life shortened by physical damage

Example 4.2.4.7

Asset life shortened by physical damage

An entity has an asset that has been damaged such that the life of the asset has been shortened, but the carrying amount of the asset will still be recovered by the cash flows over the shortened life. The damage to the asset is an indication of impairment in accordance with IAS 36:12 (see **4.2.2**) and, therefore, the asset must be tested for impairment.

Because the carrying amount of the asset will be recovered by the cash flows over the asset's revised useful life, no impairment loss should be recognised. Nevertheless, the useful life of the asset is changed and the depreciation amount should be recalculated prospectively and accounted for as a change in estimate in accordance with the requirements of IAS 8 *Accounting Policies, Changes in Accounting Estimates and Errors*.

4.2.4.8   Competitor enters an existing market

Example 4.2.4.8

Competitor enters an existing market

An entity has several retail outlets in an area where no other significant competition has previously existed. During the current period, a large well-established competitor opens two stores in the region, selling similar products at similar prices.

The entrance into the market of a competitor is an impairment indicator. In determining value in use, revised cash flow forecasts should be prepared and new estimations of assets' recoverable amounts should be calculated, based on the best information available.

4.2.4.9   Increase in sales tax

Example 4.2.4.9

Increase in sales tax

An entity operates a chain of bookshops. Under the local tax regulations, a sales tax payable by purchasers of books is increased in the current period from 5 per cent to 10 per cent.

> The change in tax rates may affect levels of demand for books and is an impairment indicator. Revised cashflow forecasts should be prepared by management, based on the best information available, so as to determine the value in use of the assets.

5 Requirements for annual reviews

5.1 Items required to be tested for impairment at least annually

As noted at **4.1**, irrespective of whether there is any indication of impairment, the following items are required to be tested for impairment at least annually:

[IAS 36:10]

- intangible assets with an indefinite useful life (see **5.2**);

- intangible assets that are not yet available for use (see **5.2**); and

- goodwill acquired in a business combination (see **5.3**).

5.2 Intangible assets required to be tested for impairment at least annually

Intangible assets with an indefinite useful life and intangible assets not yet available for use are tested for impairment by comparing their carrying amounts with their recoverable amounts both:

[IAS 36:10(a)]

- annually; and

- whenever there is an indication, at the end of a reporting period, that the asset may be impaired.

IAS 36 allows that the annual impairment test may be performed at any time during the annual period, provided that it is performed at the same time every year. Different intangible assets may be tested for impairment at different times. [IAS 36:10(a)]

In the case of a newly recognised intangible asset (e.g. an intangible asset with an indefinite useful life purchased in the current period), an impairment test must be carried out before the end of the current annual period. [IAS 36:10(a)]

Although IAS 36 requires an annual review for the specified intangible assets, it does allow that the most recent detailed calculation of an asset's recoverable amount made in a preceding period may be used in the impairment test for that asset in the current period, provided that the following criteria are met:

[IAS 36:24]

- the most recent recoverable amount calculation resulted in an amount that exceeded the asset's carrying amount by a substantial margin;

- based on an analysis of events that have occurred and circumstances that have changed since the most recent recoverable amount calculation, the likelihood that a current recoverable amount determination would be less than the asset's carrying amount is remote; and

- for intangible assets tested for impairment as part of a CGU (see **8.2**), the assets and liabilities making up that unit have not changed significantly since the most recent recoverable amount calculation.

5.3   Goodwill

5.3.1   Cash-generating units to which goodwill has been allocated

Impairment testing for goodwill is always carried out in the context of a CGU or a group of CGUs because goodwill does not generate cash flows independently of other assets. The detailed rules for the allocation of goodwill to CGUs are set out in **8.2.8**.

When goodwill has been allocated to a CGU, or to a group of CGUs (in the circumstances discussed at **8.2.8**), that unit or group of units is tested for impairment both:

[IAS 36:90]

- annually; and

- whenever there is an indication that the unit, or group of units, may be impaired.

The impairment test is carried out by comparing the carrying amount of the unit (or group of units), including the goodwill, with the recoverable amount of the unit(s). If the recoverable amount of the unit(s) exceeds the carrying amount of the unit(s), the unit(s) and the goodwill allocated to the unit(s) are not regarded as impaired. If the carrying amount of the unit, or group of units, exceeds its (their) recoverable amount, the entity recognises an impairment loss in accordance with the requirements set out in **9.2**. [IAS 36:90]

5.3.2   Timing of impairment tests for a cash-generating unit to which goodwill has been allocated

The annual impairment test for a CGU to which goodwill has been allocated may be performed at any time during the annual period, provided that it is performed at the same time every year. Different CGUs may be tested for impairment at different times. [IAS 36:96]

When some or all of the goodwill allocated to a CGU was acquired in a business combination during the current annual period, that CGU must be tested for impairment before the end of the current annual period. [IAS 36:96]

Example 5.3.2

Impairment testing for goodwill acquired in the period

An entity routinely tests goodwill for impairment in the second quarter of its annual reporting period. During the third quarter of 20X0, the entity makes an acquisition in which goodwill arises. The acquired goodwill (determined on a provisional basis) is allocated to CGUs in accordance with the requirements of IAS 36. There is no indication that the acquired or existing goodwill is impaired.

In 20X0, although there is no indication that the acquired goodwill is impaired, and the annual impairment test for goodwill has already been performed, a further impairment test must be conducted before the end of the 20X0 reporting period on each CGU to which the newly acquired goodwill has been allocated.

5.3.3 Individual assets to be tested before cash-generating unit to which goodwill has been allocated

When assets within a CGU to which goodwill has been allocated (such as intangible assets with indefinite lives) are tested for impairment at the same time as the CGU containing the goodwill, the assets should be tested for impairment before the CGU containing the goodwill. Similarly, when CGUs are tested for impairment at the same time as the group of CGUs to which they belong and to which goodwill has been allocated in aggregate, the individual CGUs should be tested for impairment first (see **9.3**). [IAS 36:97]

In addition, at the time of testing a CGU to which goodwill has been allocated, there may be an indication that a specific asset within the CGU is impaired. In such circumstances, the individual asset is tested for impairment first (and any identified impairment loss relating to that asset is recognised) before the CGU is tested for impairment. This requirement is imposed so as to ensure that any losses that can be identified with a specific asset are not 'lost' in the testing of the CGU. Similarly, when goodwill has been allocated to a group of CGUs, and there is an indication that an individual CGU within the group is impaired, the individual CGU is tested for impairment first (and any identified impairment loss relating to the individual CGU recognised) before testing for impairment the group of units to which goodwill has been allocated. [IAS 36:98]

Example 5.3.3A

Asset within cash-generating unit that provides no future benefit

An entity provides worldwide wireless communications to its customers through a network of 10 satellites. The entity has determined appropriately that its satellite business as a whole represents a 'lowest level' for which identifiable cash flows are largely independent of the cash flows of other assets and liabilities. A meteor destroys one satellite. However, the entity can continue to provide worldwide service with the remaining 9 satellites.

Should the entity continue to recognise the satellite that has been destroyed as part of the CGU if the recoverable amount of the CGU exceeds its carrying amount?

No. IAS 36 is not intended to allow an entity to continue to recognise as an asset an item that does not meet the definition of an asset. If no future benefits are expected to be gained from holding or disposing of the satellite, it is likely that the asset should be written off in full in accordance with the derecognition requirements of paragraph 67 of IAS 16 *Property, Plant and Equipment* (see **section 9** of **chapter A7**). In such circumstances, even though the entity continues to have positive cash flows from its satellite communications business, the entity must recognise the loss of a satellite.

Example 5.3.3B

Asset within cash-generating unit that no longer contributes to cash flows

A machine within a CGU has become redundant and is no longer contributing to cash flows. Its carrying amount exceeds its recoverable amount. However, the recoverable amount of the CGU is above its carrying amount.

The entity should recognise an impairment loss for the machine because its carrying amount is above its recoverable amount. The general principle is that impairment should be identified at the individual asset level, if possible. The recoverable amount should be calculated for the smallest CGU to which the asset belongs only when the recoverable amount for the individual asset cannot be identified. The machine is no longer in use and, therefore, no longer belongs to the CGU. The smallest CGU is now the machine itself. The entity is able to determine the future cash inflows arising from using this machine; they are nil. Therefore, the entity should determine the fair value less costs of disposal of the machine (because it is possible the machine has some scrap or resale value), and it should recognise the impairment loss identified.

5.3.4   Rolling forward detailed calculations from a preceding period

Although IAS 36 requires an annual review for CGUs to which goodwill has been allocated, it does allow that the most recent detailed calculation of a unit's recoverable amount made in a preceding period may be used when testing that unit for impairment in the current period, provided that the following criteria are met:

[IAS 36:99]

- the assets and liabilities making up the unit have not changed significantly since the most recent recoverable amount calculation;

- the most recent recoverable amount calculation resulted in an amount that exceeded the unit's carrying amount by a substantial margin; and

- based on an analysis of events that have occurred and circumstances that have changed since the most recent recoverable amount calculation, the likelihood that a current recoverable amount determination would be less than the unit's carrying amount is remote.

5.3.5   Cash-generating units to which it has not been possible to allocate goodwill

As discussed in **8.2.8.1**, it may not be possible to allocate goodwill to an individual CGU to which it relates. In such circumstances, the unit concerned is tested for impairment whenever there is an indicat unit may be impaired by comparing the unit's carrying amount, excluding any goodwill, with its recoverable amount. Any impairment loss is recognised in accordance with the rules set out in **9.2**. [IAS 36:88]

If no goodwill has been allocated to a CGU but the CGU includes an intangible asset that has an indefinite life or that is not yet available for use, it will be necessary to carry out an annual impairment test for that CGU if that asset can be tested for impairment only as part of the CGU. [IAS 36:89] In such circumstances, the rules described at **5.2** apply.

6   Measurement of recoverable amount

6.1   Measurement of recoverable amount – general

An asset or CGU is considered to be impaired when its recoverable amount declines below its carrying amount. Following the identification of any indication of impairment, the entity is required to make a formal estimate of the recoverable amount of the asset or CGU. [IAS 36:8] It is only by making such an estimate that the entity can determine whether an impairment loss has occurred.

The recoverable amount of an asset is the higher of its fair value less costs of disposal and its value in use. IAS 36 measures impairment loss based on an assumption that the entity will choose to recover the carrying amount of the asset in the most beneficial way. Therefore, if the entity could earn more by selling the asset than by continuing to use it, the entity would choose to sell the asset, and *vice versa*.

Example 6.1A

Measurement of recoverable amount

An entity buys a machine for CU7 million on 1 January 20X1. The asset has a seven-year life, with nil residual value. The carrying amount at 31 December 20X3 is CU4 million. The machine generates largely independent cash inflows and, therefore, is tested for impairment as a stand-alone asset.

Due to changes in market conditions, the entity considers that the machine may be impaired. It is determined that the asset could be sold for CU2 million (with costs of disposal of CU200,000). The directors have estimated that the value in use of the asset is CU3.5 million.

First, the fair value less costs of disposal of the asset (CU1.8 million) is compared with the estimated value in use (CU3.5 million). The recoverable amount is the higher of these, i.e. CU3.5 million.

The recoverable amount is then compared with the carrying amount and an impairment loss of CU500,000 is recognised.

Example 6.1B

Recoverable amount based on fair value less costs of disposal

Entity A is reviewing all of its assets for impairment as a result of a fall in the demand for its products. One item of machinery is 10 years old and has a carrying amount of CU80 million and a value in use of CU75 million (calculated on the basis of revised sales estimates). The fair value of the machine is CU82 million.

It is estimated that if the machine were to be disposed of, costs attributable to the disposal would be approximately CU1 million. Management has no intention of selling the machine.

The fair value less costs of disposal of the machine (CU81 million) is higher than its value in use; therefore, the fair value less costs of disposal represents the machine's recoverable amount. The carrying amount is less than the recoverable amount; consequently, no impairment loss should be recognised.

6.2   Circumstances in which it is not necessary to calculate both fair value less costs of disposal and value in use

For the purposes of an impairment review, it is not always necessary to calculate both fair value less costs of disposal and value in use.

- If either the fair value less costs of disposal or the value in use is found to be higher than the carrying amount, the asset is not impaired, and there is no need to calculate the other amount. [IAS 36:19]

- If there is no basis for making a reliable estimate of fair value less costs of disposal, recoverable amount is measured by reference to value in use alone. [IAS 36:20]

- The detailed calculations involved in measuring value in use may be avoided if a simple estimate is sufficient to show either that value in use is higher than the carrying amount (in which case there is no impairment) or that it is lower than fair value less costs of disposal (in which case recoverable amount is the fair value less costs of disposal). [IAS 36:23]

6.3 Circumstances in which recoverable amount is determined in the context of a cash-generating unit

Recoverable amount is determined for an individual asset, unless the asset does not generate cash inflows that are largely independent of those from other assets or groups of assets. If this is the case, recoverable amount is determined for the CGU to which the asset belongs, unless either:

[IAS 36:22]

- the asset's fair value less costs of disposal is higher than its carrying amount; or

- the asset's value in use can be estimated to be close to its fair value less costs of disposal and fair value less costs of disposal can be measured.

For example, a CGU may include an office building whose fair value can be readily determined. If either (1) the fair value less costs of disposal of the office building is higher than its carrying amount, or (2) its value in use can be estimated to be close to its fair value less costs of disposal, the building is first considered by itself for impairment testing. In addition, if an impairment test is required for the CGU of which the building forms part, the building should be included within the carrying amount of the CGU for the purpose of that impairment test. However, any loss identified for the CGU (in excess of any loss already recognised for the building) should be allocated to other assets.

As explained at **9.2**, when allocating an impairment loss to an individual asset within a CGU, the carrying amount of such an asset should not be reduced below its fair value less costs of disposal.

For guidance on the identification of CGUs, see **section 8.2**.

6.4 Impairment testing of goodwill relating to associates and joint ventures

As described at **4.4.10** in **chapter A26**, the entire carrying amount of an investment in an associate or a joint venture accounted for using the equity method, including any goodwill, is tested for impairment as a whole. Impairment losses recognised in respect of such investments may be reversed, as described in **section 10**.

6.5   Impairment testing of assets when financial statements are not prepared on a going concern basis

As discussed in **section 2.5** of **chapter A4**, it is always appropriate to consider the need to recognise impairment losses when an entity is planning to cease or has already ceased trading. This assessment will require a comparison of the carrying amount of an asset (or, when appropriate, CGU) with the higher of its value in use and fair value less costs of disposal. The question arises as to whether, in such circumstances, it is possible to assess impairment by reference to a value-in-use calculation.

In theory, it is possible to assess impairment of assets by reference to a value-in-use calculation even when the financial statements are prepared on a basis other than that of a going concern. However, in practice, often the cash flows forecast to arise from the continuing use of such assets are not significant because the expectation is that the assets will be sold or abandoned in the near future. In such circumstances, the amounts arrived at using a value-in-use calculation will not be materially different from the fair value less costs of disposal.

7   Fair value less costs of disposal

7.1   Fair value and costs of disposal – definitions

Fair value is defined as the price that would be received to sell an asset or paid to transfer a liability in an orderly transaction between market participants at the measurement date. [IAS 36:6] No further guidance is provided on the measurement of fair value – the reader is directed to IFRS 13 *Fair Value Measurement* (see **chapter A6**).

See **2.3.1** in **chapter A6** for a discussion of the extent to which IFRS 13 affects impairment testing under IAS 36.

Costs of disposal are defined as incremental costs directly attributable to the disposal of an asset or a CGU, excluding finance and income tax expense. [IAS 36:6]

7.2   Costs of disposal to be deducted

Costs of disposal to be deducted in arriving at fair value less costs of disposal include:

[IAS 36:28]

- legal costs;

- stamp duty or similar transaction taxes;

- costs of removing the asset; and

- other direct incremental costs to bring the asset into condition for its sale.

Costs such as termination benefits to employees and reorganisation expenses following a disposal are not considered direct, incremental costs of sale and, as such, are not deducted in arriving at fair value less costs of disposal. [IAS 36:28]

Costs of disposal that have been recognised as liabilities should not be deducted in measuring fair value less costs of disposal. [IAS 36:28]

> For example, when an entity already had an obligation to remove an asset at the end of its life, a provision will have been recognised and those costs will already be included in the carrying amount of the asset. Accordingly, in such circumstances, either:
>
> - the costs should not be included as costs of disposal in arriving at fair value less costs of disposal; or
>
> - in some cases (e.g. when the buyer will have to assume the liability), it may be necessary to deduct the carrying amount of the liability from that of the asset in order to determine a carrying amount that can be compared with fair value less costs of disposal, in accordance with IAS 36:29 and IAS 36:78 (see **8.2.7**).

7.3 Fair value less costs of disposal for revalued assets

As discussed in **section 2**, the scope of IAS 36 includes some assets carried at a revalued amount (e.g. property, plant and equipment accounted for under the revaluation model in IAS 16 *Property, Plant and Equipment* – see **chapter A7**).

The only difference between a revalued asset's fair value and its fair value less costs of disposal is the direct incremental costs attributable to the disposal of the asset.

[IAS 36:5]

- If the disposal costs are negligible, the recoverable amount of a revalued asset is, by definition, close to, or greater than, its revalued amount. In this case, after the revaluation requirements have been applied, it is unlikely that the revalued asset is impaired and recoverable amount need not be estimated.

- If the disposal costs are not negligible, the fair value less costs of disposal of the revalued asset is necessarily less than its fair value. Therefore, the revalued asset will be impaired if its value in use is less than its revalued amount. In this case, after the revaluation requirements have been applied, the entity should apply IAS 36 to determine whether the asset may be impaired.

7.4   Contrasting fair value and value in use

Fair value differs from value in use. Fair value reflects the assumptions market participants would use when pricing the asset. In contrast, value in use reflects the effects of factors that may be specific to the entity and not applicable to entities in general. For example, fair value does not reflect any of the following factors to the extent that they would not be generally available to market participants:

[IAS 36:53A]

- additional value derived from the grouping of assets (such as the creation of a portfolio of investment properties in different locations);

- synergies between the asset being measured and other assets;

- legal rights or legal restrictions that are specific only to the current owner of the asset; and

- tax benefits or tax burdens that are specific to the current owner of the asset.

8   Value in use

8.1   Stages in the calculation of value in use

The calculation of value in use can be broken down into four stages:

- identification of cash-generating units (see **8.2**);

> If the recoverable amount of an asset can be individually determined, Stage 1 is omitted.

- estimation of expected future cash flows (see **8.3**);

- determination of an appropriate discount rate (see **8.4**); and

- discounting and aggregating expected cash flows to arrive at value in use (see **8.5**).

8.2   Stage 1: Identification of cash-generating units

8.2.1   Cash-generating unit – definition

A cash-generating unit is defined as the smallest identifiable group of assets that generates cash inflows that are largely independent of the cash inflows from other assets or groups of assets. [IAS 36:6]

8.2.2   Circumstances in which it is necessary to identify the cash-generating unit to which an asset belongs

It is often not possible to estimate the recoverable amount of an individual asset because assets frequently generate cash when working together rather than singly. When this is the case, an entity should determine the recoverable amount of the CGU to which the asset belongs. [IAS 36:66]

IAS 36:67 specifically states that the recoverable amount of an individual asset cannot be determined when both of the following conditions exist:

- the value in use of the asset cannot be estimated to be close to its fair value less costs of disposal (e.g. when the future cash flows from the continuing use of the asset are not negligible); and

- the asset does not generate cash inflows that are largely independent of those from other assets.

When the recoverable amount of an individual asset cannot be determined, its CGU should be identified as the lowest aggregation of assets that generates largely independent cash inflows. [IAS 36:68]

Examples 8.2.2A and **8.2.2B** are reproduced from the Standard.

Example 8.2.2A

Recoverable amount cannot be determined

[IAS 36:67]

A mining entity owns a private railway to support its mining activities. The private railway could be sold only for scrap value and it does not generate cash inflows that are largely independent of the cash inflows from the other assets of the mine.

It is not possible to estimate the recoverable amount of the private railway because its value in use cannot be determined and is probably different from scrap value. Therefore, the entity estimates the recoverable amount of the cash-generating unit to which the private railway belongs, i.e. the mine as a whole.

Example 8.2.2B

Lowest aggregation of assets that generate largely independent cash flows

[IAS 36:68]

A bus company provides services under contract with a municipality that requires minimum service on each of five separate routes. Assets devoted to each route and the cash flows from each route can be identified separately. One of the routes operates at a significant loss.

Because the entity does not have the option to curtail any one bus route, the lowest level of identifiable cash inflows that are largely independent of the cash inflows from other assets or groups of assets is the cash inflows generated by the five routes together. The cash-generating unit for each route is the bus company as a whole.

Example 8.2.2C

Group of interchangeable assets

A national wireless communication provider owns a number of sets of antennae, radio transmitters and receivers (collectively referred to as 'antennae sets') installed on cell towers which together provide the infrastructure for its telecommunications network. If a specific antennae set is damaged or otherwise is not capable of operating, its output can be delivered from a similar antennae set on another cell tower so that services are virtually uninterrupted, and all cash flow streams will remain intact. This interchangeability is a feature deliberately built into the integrated logistical design of the network.

In the circumstances described, the cash flows generated by each individual antennae set are not 'largely independent' as contemplated in the definition for a cash-generating unit; it is not appropriate to attribute specific cash flows to individual antennae sets because the sets are almost instantaneously interchangeable and, as a result, whether an individual antennae set is capable of operating does not affect cash inflows. However, each antennae set is part of a group of assets that make up the entity's national network of towers and antennae. Because the wireless communication provider operates using a national network, the national network infrastructure asset group would be the smallest identifiable asset group that generates cash flows that are largely independent; therefore, the national network infrastructure asset group is a cash-generating unit and it is at that level that the network should be assessed for impairment.

Example 8.2.2D

Identification of cash-generating units for entities operating in multiple locations

If an entity operates from multiple locations that generate cash inflows in the same (or a similar) manner, in what circumstances can several of those locations constitute a single CGU for the purpose of impairment testing?

In line with the definition of a CGU (see **8.2.1**), an individual location will constitute a single CGU when its cash inflows are independent of other locations. In some cases, however, there may be evidence of a significant degree of interdependence between the cash inflows from each location resulting from revenue substitution between those locations and it may be determined that the appropriate CGU comprises a group of two or more locations.

This will be the case when there is evidence of a significant degree of revenue substitution between the locations in the group. In the circumstances under consideration, revenue substitution means a degree of interaction between the cash inflows from different locations of the entity such that a decrease in cash inflows in one location can be demonstrated to be accompanied by an increase in cash inflows from one or more other locations. Such interactions may occur, for example, in the following scenarios:

- a mining or manufacturing operation with multiple, interchangeable facilities providing overall available capacity that is used to fulfil demand for the same product or products; or
- multiple locations providing the same service to a common customer base (e.g. a network of dealerships for a car manufacturer).

IAS 36:68 (see **example 8.2.2B**) also gives an example of multiple locations (bus routes) used to provide goods or services under a single contract and concludes that this would represent a single CGU.

In assessing whether the cash inflows of different locations are interdependent, it is important to consider any barriers to revenue substitution between locations (e.g. distance). Example 1 of the Illustrative Examples accompanying IAS 36 refers to this in the context of a chain of retail stores and states that the fact that all of the stores are in different neighbourhoods suggests that each store would have a different customer base. In such cases, it would be difficult to demonstrate revenue substitution.

It is also important to distinguish between interdependence of cash inflows from different locations operated by an entity and common dependence on an external factor (e.g. commodity prices) or an asset (e.g. a brand). In addition, as discussed in **example 8.2.2E**, interdependence of cash outflows (resulting from, for example, a centralised purchasing function or shared management costs) is not relevant to the identification of CGUs.

Example 8.2.2E

Identification of cash-generating units in the retail industry

Entity A, a retail company, operates three stores that generate largely independent cash inflows. The three stores share expenditures (cash outflows) such as on infrastructure, marketing and human resources.

When Entity A is tested for impairment under IAS 36, should Entity A's CGU be composed of the three stores, on the basis that the net cash flows associated with the stores are interdependent?

No. The definition of a CGU (see **8.2.1**) requires the identification of an asset's CGU on the basis of independent cash inflows generated by the asset, not independent net cash flows (i.e. cash inflows and outflows). Therefore, outflows such as shared infrastructure and marketing expenditures are not considered when identifying a CGU. In the circumstances described, when a store is tested for impairment under IAS 36, the store's CGU is the store itself.

8.2.3 Consideration of whether, and how, an asset will continue to be used

If events and circumstances indicate that the carrying amount of an asset may not be recoverable, the appropriate accounting will depend on whether the entity expects to continue to use the asset and, if so, whether it will be used as part of a CGU.

For example, consider the situation in which events and circumstances indicate that the carrying amount of a computer software asset developed (or under development) or purchased for internal use may not be recoverable (see **4.2.4.4**). The appropriate accounting will depend on whether the entity expects to continue to use the software and, if so, whether it will be used as part of a CGU.

The outcome of events and circumstances of the nature described in **4.2.4.4** may result in a determination, either during development or after development is completed, that the software is no longer expected to be placed into service or that it will be removed from service. In such circumstances, the entity should determine whether the software asset should be derecognised in accordance with paragraph 112 of IAS 38 *Intangible Assets* (see **example 5.3.3A**).

Alternatively, it may be determined that the software will continue to be used.

- If the software generates cash flows independently, the entity should estimate the software's recoverable amount, which will be the higher of its fair value less costs of disposal (based on selling the software) and its value in use (based on the cash flows that it is expected to generate from use, less any associated costs). An impairment loss should be recognised if the software's carrying amount is in excess of recoverable amount.

- If the software does not generate cash flows independently, it should generally be tested for impairment as part of the CGU to which it relates (see IAS 36:66 and 67). In such circumstances, whether it is necessary to recognise an impairment loss will depend on the recoverable amount of the CGU as a whole. If the recoverable amount of the CGU as a whole exceeds its carrying amount, no impairment loss is recognised. This may be the case even though the software will be used less frequently than was originally intended and even though, had they foreseen this, the directors might not have been prepared to incur the costs of the software.

8.2.4 Relevance of internal management reporting to the identification of cash-generating units

Cash inflows are inflows of cash and cash equivalents received from parties outside the reporting entity. In general terms, cash inflows are likely to follow the way in which management monitors and makes decisions about continuing or closing the different lines of business of the entity. [IAS 36:69]

An entity's internal management reporting is relevant to the identification of CGUs insofar as it provides evidence regarding the independence (or interdependence) of cash inflows generated by assets or groups of assets (including, as discussed in **example 8.2.2D**, cash flows generated in different locations in which an entity operates). However, internal management reporting is not a determinative factor in its own right and should not override other evidence that demonstrates that cash inflows from an asset or a group of assets are indeed independent.

As noted in IAS 36:BCZ114, the concept of CGUs is intended to be a matter of fact. The independence (or interdependence) of cash inflows is something which cannot be overridden by the internal management reporting process of an entity. Such reporting may provide insights as to how cash inflows are generated, but must be considered alongside other factors in order to determine the appropriate CGU.

In considering an entity's internal management reporting as part of the process of identifying CGUs, it should be noted that:

- IAS 36:69 refers to "how management monitors the entity's operations". In this context, 'management' may be at any level within the organisation, not necessarily that of the chief operating decision maker (as defined in IFRS 8 *Operating Segments* – see **chapter A30**); and

- consistent with the concept of a CGU being based on largely independent cash *inflows*, the identification of a CGU does not require that management reporting presents a measure of operating profit for an asset or a group of assets (as is the case for the identification of operating segments in IFRS 8). Instead, reporting of a separate measure of revenue may be sufficient to indicate that a CGU exists at that level.

IAS 36:69 also refers to "how management makes decisions about continuing or disposing of the entity's assets and operations" as a factor in the identification of CGUs. Again, this decision-making process may provide insight into economic reality because, for example, a decision to retain or dispose of a manufacturing facility on the basis of the overall capacity needed to make a particular product may indicate a level of interdependence between cash inflows from a number of facilities dedicated to the manufacture of that product.

8.2.5   Active market exists for the output of an asset or a group of assets

If an active market exists for the output produced by an asset or a group of assets, it should be identified as a CGU, even if some or all of the output is used internally. The asset or group of assets forms a separate CGU if the entity could sell this output in an active market. This is because this asset or group of assets *could* generate cash inflows that would be largely independent of the cash flows from other assets or groups of assets. [IAS 36:70 & 71]

In the circumstances described in the previous paragraph, management estimates the expected market price for the output of the unit and uses that estimate not only when determining the value in use of the supplying unit, but also when determining the value in use of the other CGU that is using the output. In other words, market prices rather than internal transfer prices are used when estimating the recoverable amount of a CGU. [IAS 36:70]

Example 8.2.5

Active market for product used internally

An entity manufactures two products – Product 1 and Product 2. Product 1 is manufactured in the entity's factory in Country A, and all of the items produced are transferred to the entity's factory in Country B where they are used in the assembly of Product 2. The entity does not sell Product 1 externally.

If there is an active market for Product 1, the factory in Country A is treated as a separate CGU. The value in use of the factory in Country A is calculated using the market price of the units of Product 1 produced. The estimated value in use of the factory in Country B will be calculated using the market price of the units of Product 1 purchased as the basis for estimating cash outflows for the purchase of subcomponents.

8.2.6 Cash-generating units to be identified consistently from period to period

CGUs should be identified consistently from period to period for the same asset or types of assets, unless a change is justified. [IAS 36:72] When a change is made during a period in which an impairment loss is recognised or reversed, disclosure is required of the current and former ways of aggregating assets and the reasons for changing the way the CGU is identified (see **11.4**).

8.2.7 Allocation of assets and liabilities to CGUs

The allocation of assets and liabilities to a CGU, so as to establish the carrying amount of the CGU, should be determined on a basis consistent with the way the recoverable amount of the CGU is determined. [IAS 36:75]

As a general rule, the carrying amount of a CGU:

[IAS 36:76]

- includes the carrying amount of only those assets that can be attributed directly, or allocated on a reasonable and consistent basis, to the CGU and that will generate the future cash inflows used in determining the CGU's value in use; and

- does not include the carrying amount of any recognised liability, unless the recoverable amount of the CGU cannot be determined without consideration of this liability.

This allocation is consistent with the calculation of fair value less costs of disposal and value in use of a CGU, which both exclude cash flows that relate to assets outside the CGU and liabilities that have already been recognised in the financial statements (see Stage 2 at **8.3**). [IAS 36:76]

There will be some assets that contribute to cash flows, such as goodwill and corporate assets, which cannot be allocated to the CGU on a reasonable and consistent basis. These are discussed in **8.2.8** (goodwill) and **8.2.9** (corporate assets).

In some situations, due to the nature of a particular recognised liability, it may be appropriate to include it in the carrying amount and the recoverable amount of a CGU. This will be the case when a CGU could not be sold without the assumption of the related liability by the buyer. In such circumstances, the fair value less costs of disposal (or the estimated cash flow from ultimate disposal) of the CGU is the price to sell the assets and the liability together, less disposal costs. In order to be consistent and compare like items, the carrying amount of the liability should be deducted in determining both the value in use and carrying amount of the CGU. [IAS 36:78]

Example 8.2.7 is reproduced from the Standard.

Example 8.2.7

Liability included in a cash-generating unit

[IAS 36:78]

A company operates a mine in a country where legislation requires that the owner must restore the site on completion of its mining operations. The cost of restoration includes the replacement of the overburden, which must be removed before mining operations commence. A provision for the costs to replace the overburden was recognised as soon as the overburden was removed. The amount provided was recognised as part of the cost of the mine and is being depreciated over the mine's useful life. The carrying amount of the provision for restoration costs is CU500, which is equal to the present value of the restoration costs.

The entity is testing the mine for impairment. The cash-generating unit for the mine is the mine as a whole. The entity has received various offers to buy the mine at a price of around CU800. This price reflects the fact that the buyer will assume the obligation to restore the overburden. Disposal costs for the mine are negligible. The value in use of the mine is approximately CU1,200, excluding restoration costs. The carrying amount of the mine is CU1,000.

The cash-generating unit's fair value less costs of disposal is CU800. This amount considers restoration costs that have already been provided for. As a consequence, the value in use for the cash-generating unit is determined after consideration of the restoration costs and is estimated to be CU700 (CU1,200 less CU500). The carrying amount of the cash-generating unit is CU500, which is the carrying amount of the mine (CU1,000) less the carrying amount of the provision for restoration costs (CU500). Therefore, the recoverable amount of the cash-generating unit exceeds its carrying amount.

IAS 36:79 states that, for practical purposes, it is sometimes necessary to include assets that are not part of the CGU (e.g. receivables or other financial assets) or liabilities that have already been recognised in the financial statements (e.g. payables, pensions and other provisions) when determining recoverable amount. When this is the case, these items are also included in the carrying amount of the CGU.

Therefore, although best practice is to exclude these items, if they are included they should be included consistently, i.e. both in the carrying amount of the CGU and in the estimation of recoverable amount. To do otherwise would be to compare unlike items.

8.2.8 Allocation of goodwill to cash-generating units

8.2.8.1 Requirement to allocate goodwill to a cash-generating unit (or a group of cash-generating units)

For the purpose of impairment testing, goodwill acquired in a business combination is, from the acquisition date, required to be allocated to each of the acquirer's CGUs, or groups of CGUs, that are expected to benefit from the synergies of the combination, irrespective of whether other assets or liabilities of the acquiree are assigned to those units or groups of units. [IAS 36:80]

Goodwill recognised in a business combination is an asset representing the future economic benefits arising from other assets acquired in a business combination that are not individually identified and separately recognised. Goodwill does not generate cash flows independently of other assets or groups of assets and, therefore, it will always be tested for impairment as part of a CGU or a group of CGUs. [IAS 36:81]

In fact, it may not be possible to allocate goodwill to individual CGUs on a reasonable basis and it will often be the case that goodwill can only be allocated to a group of CGUs. IAS 36 permits such aggregation provided that the CGU or group of CGUs to which goodwill is allocated:

[IAS 36:80]

- represents the lowest level within the entity at which goodwill is monitored for internal management purposes; and

- is not larger than an operating segment, as defined by paragraph 5 of IFRS 8 *Operating Segments*, before aggregation (see **chapter A30**).

The objective of the IASB in setting these conditions is to require entities to allocate goodwill to the lowest possible level without resorting to arbitrary allocations and without, generally, having to develop new or additional reporting systems to perform impairment testing. The Board's approach is that goodwill should be tested for impairment at a level at which information about the operations of the entity and the assets that support them is provided for internal reporting purposes.

In many cases, the goodwill purchased in a business combination enhances the value of all of the acquirer's pre-existing CGUs. Some might argue that, in such circumstances, goodwill should be tested for impairment at the entity level. The Board has rejected this argument and determined that the highest level at which goodwill should be tested for impairment is the operating segment level, before aggregation. If the entity monitors goodwill at a level higher than the operating segment level, it may be necessary to develop additional reporting systems to perform the impairment testing of goodwill mandated by IAS 36.

Example 8.2.8.1A

Level at which goodwill is tested for impairment

Company A has three retail divisions, each of which is classified for reporting purposes as an operating segment under IFRS 8. All three divisions consist of a number of individual stores that operate independently of one another. Goodwill was recognised on the acquisition of each division. Management does not monitor goodwill for internal purposes.

For IAS 36 purposes, goodwill is required to be monitored and assessed for impairment annually for financial reporting purposes. Management currently only monitors goodwill for impairment at an operating segment level. However, management also has the ability to allocate goodwill to each store within each operating segment and to monitor goodwill for impairment at that lower level.

Given that management is capable of monitoring the impairment of goodwill at a lower level than is currently the case, should management perform its goodwill impairment assessment at that lower level?

Management's current practice is appropriate. IAS 36:80 requires goodwill to be assessed for impairment at a level no larger than an operating segment determined under IFRS 8, and which represents the lowest level at which goodwill is monitored for internal management purposes. Company A complies with both requirements and does not need to alter the level at which goodwill is currently assessed for impairment.

Example 8.2.8.1B

Allocation of goodwill by unlisted entities

Group A is an unlisted entity. It is therefore not within the scope of IFRS 8; nor does it choose to apply that Standard voluntarily. Group A acquired a subsidiary some years ago, which resulted in the recognition of goodwill.

Management generally monitors Group A's activities on a country-by-country basis. However, goodwill has not been allocated to individual countries for internal management purposes. If Group A were to apply IFRS 8, each country would represent an operating segment under that Standard.

Should Group A test goodwill for impairment at the reporting entity (group) level, or should it test for impairment at a lower operating segment (individual country) level, i.e. at the level at which management generally monitors activities?

IAS 36:82 clarifies that the objective of the guidance in IAS 36 on allocating goodwill is to ensure that goodwill is tested for impairment "at a level that reflects the way an entity manages its operations and with which the goodwill would naturally be associated".

In specifying the level at which goodwill should be allocated, IAS 36:80(b) requires that the unit or group of units to which goodwill is allocated "not be larger than an operating segment as defined by paragraph 5 of IFRS 8 *Operating Segments*, before aggregation". Note that this requirement does not refer to the level of *reported* operating segments. Therefore, irrespective of whether an entity reports segment information in respect of its operating segments in accordance with IFRS 8, it should assess its goodwill at the operating segment level in accordance with IAS 36:80(b).

In the circumstances described, the internal management reporting system on an individual country basis appears to represent an appropriate operating segment level for Group A. Therefore, goodwill should be tested for impairment at the country level.

Example 8.2.8.1C

Goodwill allocation methodologies

Entity M is a mining conglomerate. Entity M acquires Entity N, which operates a number of mines remotely located from each other, for consideration of CU10 million. For the purpose of accounting for the acquisition under IFRS 3 *Business Combinations*, Entity M measures the fair value of the net identifiable assets of Entity N at CU8 million. Goodwill of CU2 million is therefore recognised at the acquisition date.

IAS 36:80 requires that "[f]or the purpose of impairment testing, goodwill acquired in a business combination shall, from the acquisition date, be allocated to each of the acquirer's CGUs, or groups of CGUs, that is expected to benefit from the synergies of the combination, irrespective of whether other assets or liabilities of the acquiree are assigned to those units or groups of units".

Entity M determines that each independently operating mine is a CGU.

How should Entity M allocate the goodwill arising on the acquisition of Entity N among its CGUs?

Entity M should first identify the CGUs or groups of CGUs throughout the group that are expected to benefit from the synergies of the combination, irrespective of whether other assets and liabilities of Entity N are allocated to those CGUs or groups of CGUs.

The level at which goodwill is required to be allocated to a CGU or group of CGUs is determined by the level at which management monitors goodwill and the operating segments of the entity. When it is necessary to allocate goodwill among individual CGUs or groups of CGUs, because that is the level at which the goodwill is monitored for internal management purposes, the Standard does not specify any particular method of allocation.

In the circumstances described, assume that Entity M has concluded that only the newly acquired CGUs will benefit from the synergies of the combination. Consequently, Entity M needs to identify an appropriate method to allocate the goodwill among the Entity N mines that are expected to benefit from those synergies.

For Entity M, appropriate methods of allocating the goodwill may include:

- in proportion to the relative fair value of the identifiable net assets in each CGU; or

- in proportion to the relative fair values of the CGUs; or

- in proportion to the possible reserves beyond proven and probable (whether or not used in determining the value of the purchased assets) in each CGU; or

- in proportion to proven reserves in each CGU.

None of these allocation methods is prohibited by the Standard. However, other considerations to take into account include that:

- the method used to determine the purchase price may indicate an appropriate allocation methodology, which could include any of those proposed; and

- the allocation methodology used should not be inconsistent with any disclosed factors that support the goodwill figure.

Note that paragraph 21 of IFRS 6 *Exploration for and Evaluation of Mineral Resources* addresses the determination of an accounting policy for allocating exploration and evaluation assets to CGUs or groups of CGUs for the purpose of assessing such assets for impairment (see **5.2** in **chapter A40** for further guidance). However, the allocation of any goodwill arising on the acquisition of a mining entity remains within the scope of IAS 36 rather than IFRS 6.

8.2.8.2   Interaction of goodwill allocation and identification of cash-generating units

Example 8.2.8.2

Interaction of goodwill allocation and identification of cash-generating units

Entity Z operates from multiple locations spread over ten regions. In accordance with IAS 36:80, Entity Z has allocated goodwill at a regional level for the purposes of impairment testing.

Does the allocation of goodwill at a regional level mean that each region is automatically considered a CGU?

No. The identification of CGUs and the allocation of goodwill to those CGUs (or groups of CGUs) are two separate steps in the impairment testing process, with different considerations to be applied at each step.

A CGU is defined as "the smallest identifiable group of assets that generates cash inflows that are largely independent of the cash inflows from other assets or groups of assets" [IAS 36.6]. As discussed in **8.2.4**, the structure of an entity's internal management reporting is only relevant to the identification of CGUs as an indicator of whether an asset or a group of assets generates cash inflows that are largely independent.

Conversely, the allocation of goodwill to CGUs or groups of CGUs is driven by an entity's internal reporting because it depends on:

- the level at which goodwill is monitored for internal management purposes; and

- the level at which operating results are regularly reviewed by the entity's chief operating decision maker to make resource allocation decisions and to monitor performance (because this forms part of the definition of an operating segment in IFRS 8 *Operating Segments*).

The distinction between a CGU and a group of CGUs to which goodwill is allocated is important due to the 'two-step' approach required by IAS 36 (see **9.3**) whereby each individual CGU (excluding any goodwill) for which there is an indication of impairment is tested and any resulting impairment losses are recognised before groups of CGUs including goodwill are tested and any further impairment losses recognised. The effects of this two-step approach are illustrated in **example 9.3**.

8.2.8.3 Completing the initial allocation of goodwill

Ideally, the initial allocation of goodwill recognised in a business combination to CGUs should be completed before the end of the annual period in which the business combination is effected. If this is not possible, the initial allocation should be completed before the end of the first annual period beginning after the acquisition date. [IAS 36:84]

This rule differs from that specified by IFRS 3 *Business Combinations* when the initial accounting for a business combination can be determined only provisionally by the end of the period in which the combination is effected. In such circumstances, IFRS 3 requires the acquirer to:

- account for the combination using the provisional values; and

- recognise any adjustments to those provisional values as a result of completing the initial accounting within the measurement period, which is not to exceed twelve months from the acquisition date.

Therefore, the period allowed to complete the initial allocation of goodwill to CGUs is longer than the period to complete the initial accounting for a business combination. The IASB decided to allow this longer period because the allocation of goodwill will often not be possible until after the initial accounting for the combination is complete.

8.2.8.4 Disposal of a portion of a CGU including goodwill

If goodwill has been allocated to a CGU, or a group of CGUs, and the entity disposes of an operation within that unit or group, the goodwill associated with the operation disposed of should be:

[IAS 36:86]

- included in the carrying amount of the operation when determining the gain or loss on disposal; and

- measured on the basis of the relative values of the operation disposed of and the portion of the CGU retained, unless the entity can demonstrate that some other method better reflects the goodwill associated with the operation disposed of.

In accordance with the requirements set out in the previous sections, the entity will already have allocated goodwill to the CGU, or group of CGUs, at the lowest level at which goodwill is monitored for internal management purposes. It may be that goodwill cannot easily be identified with smaller operations within that unit or group, except in an arbitrary fashion. However, even if this is the case, when such smaller operations are being disposed of, it is appropriate to assume that some amount of goodwill is associated with the operation being disposed of, and to make an allocation of goodwill for that purpose.

The following example is included in IAS 36.

Example 8.2.8.4

Goodwill measured on basis of relative values

[IAS 36:86]

An entity sells for CU100 an operation that was part of a CGU to which goodwill has been allocated. The goodwill allocated to that unit cannot be identified or associated with an asset group at a level lower than that unit, except arbitrarily. The recoverable amount of the portion of the CGU retained is CU300.

Because the goodwill allocated to the CGU cannot be non-arbitrarily identified or associated with an asset group at a level lower than that unit, the goodwill associated with the operation disposed of is measured on the basis of the relative values of the operation disposed of and the portion of the unit retained. Therefore, 25 per cent of the goodwill allocated to the CGU is included in the carrying amount of the operation that is sold.

When goodwill cannot be allocated, except arbitrarily, at a lower level than that at which it is monitored for internal management purposes, the most appropriate method of allocation will generally be based on the relative values of the operation disposed of and the portion of the CGU retained. There may be circumstances when some other method better reflects the amount of goodwill associated with the operation disposed of, and the Standard allows the use of another method of allocation, provided that the superiority of the chosen method can be demonstrated. For example, assume that a CGU is acquired and integrated with a pre-existing CGU that did not include any goodwill.

Assume that, almost immediately after the business combination, the entity disposes of a pre-existing loss-making operation from within the integrated CGU. In such circumstances, it might reasonably be argued that no part of the goodwill has been disposed of and, therefore, no part of its carrying amount should be derecognised by being included in the determination of the gain or loss on disposal.

8.2.8.5 Reorganisation of reporting structure

An entity may reorganise its reporting structure in a way that changes the composition of one or more CGUs to which goodwill has been allocated. In these circumstances, the goodwill should be reallocated to the units affected. Unless the entity can demonstrate that some other method better reflects the goodwill associated with the reorganised units, the reallocation should be performed using a relative value approach similar to that discussed in **8.2.8.4**. [IAS 36:87]

The following example is set out in IAS 36.

Example 8.2.8.5

Reorganisation of reporting structure

[IAS 36:87]

Goodwill had previously been allocated to CGU A. The goodwill allocated to A cannot be identified or associated with an asset group at a level lower than A, except arbitrarily. A is to be divided and integrated into three other CGUs, B, C and D.

Because the goodwill allocated to A cannot be non-arbitrarily identified or associated with an asset group at a level lower than A, it is reallocated to units B, C and D on the basis of the relative values of the three portions of A before those portions are integrated with B, C and D.

8.2.8.6 Goodwill relating to non-wholly-owned subsidiaries

IFRS 3 *Business Combinations* requires goodwill to be measured as at the acquisition date as the excess of (a) over (b) below:

[IAS 36:C1]

(a) the aggregate of:

(i) the consideration transferred measured in accordance with IFRS 3, which generally requires acquisition-date fair value;

(ii) the amount of any non-controlling interest in the acquiree measured in accordance with IFRS 3; and

(iii) in a business combination achieved in stages, the acquisition-date fair value of the acquirer's previously held equity interest in the acquiree.

(b) the net of the acquisition-date amounts of the identifiable assets acquired and liabilities assumed measured in accordance with IFRS 3.

Goodwill acquired in a business combination is allocated to each of the acquirer's CGU's, or groups of CGU's, expected to benefit from the synergies of the combination, irrespective of whether other assets or liabilities of the acquiree are assigned to those units, or groups of units. It is possible that some of the synergies resulting from a business combination will be allocated to a CGU in which the non-controlling interest does not have an interest. [IAS 36:C2]

Example 8.2.8.6A

Allocation of goodwill relating to non-wholly-owned subsidiary

Entity A has an existing wholly-owned subsidiary, Entity B. Subsequently, Entity A acquires 80 per cent of Entity C in a business combination. Synergies arising from that business combination are expected to benefit Entity B.

Accordingly, some of the goodwill acquired in the business combination may be allocated to CGUs within Entity B.

When an entity chooses to measure components of non-controlling interests that are present ownership interests at their proportionate interest in the net identifiable assets of a subsidiary at the acquisition date, rather than at fair value, goodwill attributable to non-controlling interests is included in the recoverable amount of the related CGU but is not recognised in the parent's consolidated financial statements. To deal with this mismatch, for the purpose of impairment testing, the carrying amount of goodwill allocated to the unit is grossed up to include the goodwill attributable to the non-controlling interest. This adjusted carrying amount is then compared with the recoverable amount of the unit to determine whether the CGU is impaired. [IAS 36:C4]

Example 8.2.8.6B

Gross-up of goodwill for impairment testing when components of non-controlling interests that are present ownership interests arising in a business combination are measured at their proportionate interest in the net identifiable assets of the subsidiary

Entity A acquires 80 per cent of Entity B in a business combination. On acquisition, Entity A chooses to measure the components of non-controlling interests (NCI) that are present ownership interests in Entity B at their proportionate interest in the net identifiable assets of Entity B. This results in goodwill of CU20,000, which is allocated in its entirety to Entity B for the purposes of impairment testing under IAS 36.

IAS 36:C4 requires the carrying amount of goodwill to be grossed up to include the goodwill attributable to the NCI. The adjusted carrying amount should then

---

be compared with the recoverable amount of Entity B to determine whether there is impairment.

IAS 36 does not prescribe a method for grossing up goodwill to include the amount attributable to NCI when the components of NCI that are present ownership interests arising in a business combination are measured at the proportionate interest in the net identifiable assets of the subsidiary.

Example 7A in the illustrative examples accompanying IAS 36 demonstrates a mathematical gross-up based on ownership interests. Therefore, in the above example, it would be appropriate to gross up goodwill to CU25,000 (being CU20,000 x 100/80).

However, in the absence of guidance to the contrary, Entity A could gross up goodwill based on the fair value of NCI at the acquisition date (i.e. the amount of goodwill that would have been recognised if NCI had been measured at fair value at the acquisition date), if that information can be determined reliably.

IAS 36:C4 does not apply to situations in which the non-controlling interests arise from transactions or events other than a business combination (e.g. a decrease in ownership in a subsidiary without loss of control) even if the components of non-controlling interests that are present ownership interests are measured at the proportionate share of a subsidiary's net assets.

This is because the purpose of IAS 36:C4 is to ensure consistency (for the purpose of impairment testing) between the goodwill included in the recoverable amount of a CGU and the goodwill included in the carrying amount of that CGU. The cash flows used to determine the recoverable amount of a CGU reflect 100 per cent of its activities; as a result, the recoverable amount includes 100 per cent of the goodwill attributable to the CGU.

When components of non-controlling interests that are present ownership interests arise as a result of a business combination and are measured at the proportionate share of the acquiree's identifiable net assets, the goodwill recognised in the consolidated financial statements reflects only the parent's share of the goodwill. Therefore, there is a potential mismatch for the purpose of impairment testing, which is avoided by IAS 36:C4's requirement to gross up the goodwill included in the carrying amount of the CGU.

However, when a parent initially purchases 100 per cent of the subsidiary, the goodwill recognised in the consolidated financial statements represents 100 per cent of the goodwill of the subsidiary. This remains the case after a disposal of a non-controlling interest in the subsidiary, even when components of non-controlling interests that are present ownership interests recognised subsequent to the acquisition are measured at the proportionate share of the net assets. Therefore, grossing up goodwill for the purpose of impairment testing would not be appropriate.

This is illustrated in **example 8.2.8.6C**.

Example 8.2.8.6C

Application of IAS 36:C4 when components of non-controlling interests that are present ownership interests arise subsequent to a business combination

On 1 January 20X3, Parent P acquires 100 per cent of Subsidiary S for CU1,900. At that date, the fair value of Subsidiary S's net identifiable assets is CU1,500. Parent P recognises goodwill of CU400 in its consolidated financial statements as a result of the business combination.

On 1 July 20X3, Parent P disposes of 20 per cent of its interest in Subsidiary S for CU380. For simplicity, it is assumed that the fair value of Subsidiary S's net identifiable assets on that date is still CU1,500. Parent P recognises non-controlling interests of CU300 (20% × CU1,500) and the difference of CU80 between this amount and the proceeds received is recognised in equity. Because control is retained, there is no adjustment to the carrying amount of goodwill (i.e. goodwill remains at CU400).

At the end of 20X5, Parent P determines that the recoverable amount of Subsidiary S is CU1,000. The carrying amount of the net assets of Subsidiary S, excluding goodwill, is CU1,350.

Because all of the goodwill attributable to Subsidiary S is included in the recoverable amount of Subsidiary S and is also recognised in Parent P's consolidated financial statements, no adjustment is required to gross up goodwill for the purpose of impairment testing. In the circumstances described, an impairment loss of CU750 should be recognised, calculated as follows.

End of 20X5	Goodwill of Subsidiary S	Net identifiable assets	Total
	CU	CU	CU
Carrying amount	400	1,350	1,750
Recoverable amount			1,000
			750

In accordance with IAS 36:104, the impairment loss of CU750 is allocated to the assets in Subsidiary S by first reducing the carrying amount of goodwill (see **9.2**). Therefore, CU400 of the CU750 impairment loss is allocated to the goodwill and the remaining impairment loss of CU350 is recognised by reducing the carrying amounts of Subsidiary S's identifiable assets.

If a subsidiary, or part of a subsidiary, with a non-controlling interest is itself a CGU, the impairment loss is allocated between the parent and the non-controlling interest on the same basis as that on which profit or loss is allocated. [IAS 36:C6]

When non-controlling interests (NCI) are measured at fair value, paragraph B45 of IFRS 3 indicates that the fair values of the parent's interest in an entity and the NCI on a per-share basis may differ (e.g. due to the inclusion of a control premium in fair value of the parent's interest or, conversely, the inclusion of a discount to reflect its lack of control in the fair value of the NCI). In such circumstances, the goodwill attributable to the parent's interest is not necessarily proportional to the goodwill attributable to the NCI.

Despite this fact, in line with the explicit requirement in IAS 36:C6, any impairment loss arising on the goodwill should be allocated to the parent and to the NCI on the same basis as that on which profit or loss is allocated (i.e. in proportion to their respective present ownership interests).

Example 8.2.8.6D provides an illustration of such circumstances.

Example 8.2.8.6D

Allocation of goodwill impairment loss when non-controlling interests are measured at fair value

Entity A acquires 80 per cent of Entity B for CU1,250. Entity B has identifiable net assets with a fair value of CU1,000 and the fair value of the non-controlling interests (NCI) is determined to be CU250.

	Ownership	Share of identifiable net assets	Fair value	Goodwill	Goodwill
	%	CU	CU	CU	%
Parent interest	80	800	1,250	450	90
NCI	20	200	250	50	10
		1,000	1,500	500	

If an impairment loss of CU100 subsequently arises on Entity B's goodwill, it is allocated 80 per cent to Entity A (CU80) and 20 per cent to the NCI (CU20).

Equally, if the impairment loss arising on Entity B's goodwill is CU300, CU60 (i.e. 20 per cent) is allocated to the NCI and CU240 (i.e. 80 per cent) is allocated to Entity A. This is so even though, in this example, the goodwill impairment allocated to the NCI exceeds the goodwill originally included in the NCI.

If a subsidiary, or part of a subsidiary, with a non-controlling interest is part of a larger CGU, goodwill impairment losses are allocated to the parts of the CGU that have a non-controlling interest and the parts that do not.

The impairment losses should be allocated to the parts of the CGU on the basis of:

[IAS 36:C7]

- to the extent that the impairment relates to goodwill in the CGU, the relative carrying values of the goodwill of the parts before the impairment; and

- to the extent that the impairment relates to identifiable assets in the CGU, the relative carrying values of the net identifiable assets of the parts before the impairment. Any such impairment is allocated to the assets of the parts of each unit pro rata on the basis of the carrying amount of each asset in the part.

In those parts that have a non-controlling interest, the impairment loss is allocated between the parent and the non-controlling interest on the same basis as that on which profit or loss is allocated.

If an impairment loss attributable to a non-controlling interest relates to goodwill that is not recognised in the parent's consolidated financial statements, that impairment is not recognised as a goodwill impairment loss. In such cases, only the impairment loss relating to the goodwill that is allocated to the parent is recognised as a goodwill impairment loss. [IAS 36:C8]

Example 8.2.8.6E

Allocation of impairment loss

Entity A has an existing wholly-owned subsidiary, Entity B. Subsequently, Entity A acquires 80 per cent of Entity C in a business combination. Synergies arising from that business combination are expected to benefit Entity B. Accordingly, under IAS 36:C2, some of the goodwill acquired in the business combination is allocated to CGUs within Entity B.

Following the allocation of goodwill, Entity A compares the adjusted carrying amounts of the CGUs with their recoverable amounts. Entity A has chosen to measure the components of non-controlling interests that are present ownership interests at their proportionate interest in the net identifiable assets of Entity C at the acquisition date. Therefore, in accordance with IAS 36:C4, the carrying amount of goodwill allocated to Entity C is grossed up to include the goodwill attributable to the non-controlling interests (see **example 8.2.8.6B**). On the basis of this comparison, Entity C is determined to be impaired.

	Adjusted carrying amount	Recoverable amount	Impairment
	CU	CU	CU
Entity C	29,500	25,000	(4,500)
Entity B	32,500	40,000	–

The impairment of CU4,500 for Entity C relates to goodwill, and is allocated between the parent and the non-controlling interests on the same basis as that on which profit or loss is allocated, i.e. 80 per cent to the parent (CU3,600) and 20 per cent to the non-controlling interests (CU900). But, because the impairment loss attributable to the non-controlling interests relates to goodwill that is not recognised in the parent's consolidated financial statements, that impairment is not recognised as a goodwill impairment loss.

Accordingly, CU3,600 is recognised as a goodwill impairment loss in the consolidated financial statements, being the impairment loss relating to the goodwill that is allocated to the parent (Entity A).

Examples 8.2.8.6F to **8.2.8.6H** reproduce illustrative examples 7A to 7C accompanying IAS 36, which illustrate the impairment testing of a non-wholly-owned CGU.

Example 8.2.8.6F

Non-controlling interests measured initially as a proportionate share of the net identifiable assets

[IAS 36:IE62 - IE68, Example 7A]

In this example, tax effects are ignored.

Background

Parent acquires an 80 per cent ownership interest in Subsidiary for CU2,100 on 1 January 20X3. At that date, Subsidiary's net identifiable assets have a fair value of CU1,500. Parent chooses to measure the non-controlling interests as the proportionate interest of Subsidiary's net identifiable assets of CU300 (20% of CU1,500). Goodwill of CU900 is the difference between the aggregate of the consideration transferred and the amount of the non-controlling interests (CU2,100 + CU300) and the net identifiable assets (CU1,500).

The assets of Subsidiary together are the smallest group of assets that generate cash inflows that are largely independent of the cash inflows from other assets or groups of assets. Therefore Subsidiary is a cash-generating unit. Because other cash-generating units of Parent are expected to benefit from the synergies of the combination, the goodwill of CU500 related to those synergies has been allocated to other cash-generating units within Parent. Because the cash-generating unit comprising Subsidiary includes goodwill within its carrying amount, it must be tested for impairment annually, or more frequently if there is an indication that it may be impaired (see paragraph 90 of IAS 36).

At the end of 20X3, Parent determines that the recoverable amount of cash-generating unit Subsidiary is CU1,000. The carrying amount of the net assets of Subsidiary, excluding goodwill, is CU1,350.

Testing Subsidiary (cash-generating unit) for impairment

Goodwill attributable to non-controlling interests is included in Subsidiary's recoverable amount of CU1,000 but has not been recognised in Parent's consolidated financial statements. Therefore, in accordance with paragraph C4 of Appendix C of IAS 36, the carrying amount of Subsidiary is grossed up to include goodwill attributable to the non-controlling interest, before being compared with the recoverable amount of CU1,000. Goodwill attributable to Parent's 80 per cent interest in Subsidiary at the acquisition date is CU400 after allocating CU500 to other cash-generating units within Parent. Therefore, goodwill attributable to the 20 per cent non-controlling interest in Subsidiary at the acquisition date is CU100.

Schedule 1. Testing Subsidiary for impairment at the end of 20X3

End of 20X3	Goodwill of Subsidiary	Net identifiable assets	Total
	CU	CU	CU
Carrying amount	400	1,350	1,750
Unrecognised non-controlling interests	100	–	100
Adjusted carrying amount	500	1,350	1,850
Recoverable amount			1,000
Impairment loss			850

Allocating the impairment loss

In accordance with paragraph 104 of IAS 36, the impairment loss of CU850 is allocated to the assets in the unit by first reducing the carrying amount of goodwill.

Therefore, CU500 of the CU850 impairment loss for the unit is allocated to the goodwill. In accordance with paragraph C6 of Appendix C of IAS 36, if the partially-owned subsidiary is itself a cash-generating unit, the goodwill impairment loss is allocated to the controlling and non-controlling interests on the same basis as that on which profit or loss is allocated. In this example, profit or loss is allocated on the basis of relative ownership interests. Because the goodwill is recognised only to the extent of Parent's 80 per cent ownership interest in Subsidiary, Parent recognises only 80 per cent of that goodwill impairment loss (i.e. CU400).

The remaining impairment loss of CU350 is recognised by reducing the carrying amounts of Subsidiary's identifiable assets (see Schedule 2).

Schedule 2. Allocation of the impairment loss for Subsidiary at the end of 20X3

End of 20X3	Goodwill	Net identifiable assets	Total
	CU	CU	CU
Carrying amount	400	1,350	1,750
Impairment loss	(400)	(350)	(750)
Carrying amount after impairment loss	–	1,000	1,000

Example 8.2.8.6G

Non-controlling interests measured initially at fair value and the related subsidiary is a stand-alone cash-generating unit

[IAS 36:IE68A - IE68E, Example 7B]

In this example, tax effects are ignored.

Background

Parent acquires an 80 per cent ownership interest in Subsidiary for CU2,100 on 1 January 20X3. At that date, Subsidiary's net identifiable assets have a fair value of CU1,500. Parent chooses to measure the non-controlling interests at fair value, which is CU350. Goodwill of CU950 is the difference between the aggregate of the consideration transferred and the amount of the non-controlling interests (CU2,100 + CU350) and the net identifiable assets (CU1,500).

The assets of Subsidiary together are the smallest group of assets that generate cash inflows that are largely independent of the cash inflows from other assets or groups of assets. Therefore, Subsidiary is a cash-generating unit. Because other cash-generating units of Parent are expected to benefit from the synergies of the combination, the goodwill of CU500 related to those synergies has been allocated to other cash-generating units within Parent. Because Subsidiary includes goodwill within its carrying amount, it must be tested for impairment annually, or more frequently if there is an indication that it might be impaired (see paragraph 90 of IAS 36).

Testing Subsidiary for impairment

At the end of 20X3, Parent determines that the recoverable amount of cash-generating unit Subsidiary is CU1,650. The carrying amount of the net assets of Subsidiary, excluding goodwill, is CU1,350.

Schedule 1. Testing Subsidiary for impairment at the end of 20X3

End of 20X3	Goodwill	Net identifiable assets	Total
	CU	CU	CU
Carrying amount	450	1,350	1,800
Recoverable amount			1,650
Impairment loss			150

Allocating the impairment loss

In accordance with paragraph 104 of IAS 36, the impairment loss of CU150 is allocated to the assets in the unit by first reducing the carrying amount of goodwill. Therefore, the full amount of impairment loss of CU150 for the unit is allocated to the goodwill. In accordance with paragraph C6 of Appendix C of IAS 36, if the partially-owned subsidiary is itself a cash-generating unit, the goodwill impairment loss is allocated to the controlling and non-controlling interests on the same basis as that on which profit or loss is allocated.

Example 8.2.8.6H

Non-controlling interests measured initially at fair value and the related subsidiary is part of a larger cash-generating unit

[IAS 36:IE68F - IE68J, Example 7C]

In this example, tax effects are ignored.

Background

Suppose that, for the business combination described in paragraph IE68A of Example 7B [**example 8.2.8.6G**], the assets of Subsidiary will generate cash inflows together with other assets or groups of assets of Parent. Therefore, rather than Subsidiary being the cash-generating unit for the purposes of impairment testing, Subsidiary becomes part of a larger cash-generating unit, Z. Other cash-generating units of Parent are also expected to benefit from the synergies of the combination. Therefore, goodwill related to those synergies, in the amount of CU500, has been allocated to those other cash-generating units. Z's goodwill related to previous business combinations is CU800.

Because Z includes goodwill within its carrying amount, both from Subsidiary and from previous business combinations, it must be tested for impairment annually, or more frequently if there is an indication that it might be impaired (see paragraph 90 of IAS 36).

Testing Subsidiary for impairment

At the end of 20X3, Parent determines that the recoverable amount of cash-generating unit Z is CU3,300. The carrying amount of the net assets of Z, excluding goodwill, is CU2,250.

Schedule 3. Testing Z for impairment at the end of 20X3

End of 20X3	Goodwill	Net identifiable assets	Total
	CU	CU	CU
Carrying amount	1,250	2,250	3,500
Recoverable amount			3,300
Impairment loss			200

Allocating the impairment loss

In accordance with paragraph 104 of IAS 36, the impairment loss of CU200 is allocated to the assets in the unit by first reducing the carrying amount of goodwill. Therefore, the full amount of impairment loss of CU200 for cash-generating unit Z is allocated to the goodwill. In accordance with paragraph C7 of Appendix C of IAS 36, if the partially-owned subsidiary forms part of a larger cash-generating unit, the goodwill impairment loss would be allocated first to the parts of the cash-generating unit, Z, and then to the controlling and non-controlling interests of the partially owned Subsidiary.

Parent allocates the impairment loss to the parts of the cash-generating unit on the basis of the relative carrying values of the goodwill of the parts before the impairment. In this example Subsidiary is allocated 36 per cent of the impairment (450/1,250). The impairment loss is then allocated to the controlling and non-controlling interests on the same basis as that on which profit or loss is allocated.

8.2.9 Allocation of corporate assets to cash-generating units

Corporate assets are assets other than goodwill that contribute to the future cash flows of both the CGU under review and other CGUs. [IAS 36:6] Such assets may include group or divisional assets such as a headquarters building or a research centre. Key characteristics of corporate assets are that:

[IAS 36:100]

- they do not generate cash inflows independently from other assets or groups of assets; and

- their carrying amount cannot be fully attributed to the CGU under review.

Other examples of corporate assets may include brands and operating licences.

Because corporate assets do not generate separate cash flows, they are tested for impairment in the context of the CGU or group of CGUs to which the asset belongs. If a portion of the carrying amount of a corporate asset:

[IAS 36:102]

- can be allocated on a reasonable and consistent basis to a CGU, the entity compares the carrying amount of the unit (including the allocated portion of the carrying amount of the corporate asset) with its recoverable amount. Any impairment loss is recognised in accordance with **9.2**;

- cannot be allocated on a reasonable and consistent basis to that unit, the entity:

  - compares the carrying amount of the unit, excluding the corporate asset, with its recoverable amount, and recognises any impairment loss in accordance with **9.2**;

  - identifies the smallest group of CGUs that includes the CGU under review and to which a portion of the carrying amount of the corporate asset can be allocated on a reasonable and consistent basis; and

  - compares the carrying amount of that group of CGUs, including the allocated portion of the carrying amount of the corporate asset, with the recoverable amount of the group of units. Any impairment loss is recognised in accordance with **9.2**.

Illustrative example 8 accompanying IAS 36 illustrates the application of the requirements for corporate assets.

8.3 Stage 2: Estimation of expected future cash flows

8.3.1 General approach to present value

Appendix A to IAS 36 (which is an integral part of the Standard) provides some guidance on the use of present value techniques in measuring value in use. In particular, it considers some of the practical difficulties in estimating future cash flows and arriving at an appropriate discount rate for those cash flows. This section provides a brief summary of the guidance in Appendix A to IAS 36 as regards the general approach to present value. The selection of an appropriate discount rate is dealt with in **section 8.4**.

IAS 36 identifies the following elements which, taken together, capture the economic differences between assets:

[IAS 36:A1]

- an estimate of the future cash flows the entity expects to derive from the asset;
- the time value of money, represented by the current market risk-free rate of interest;
- expectations about possible variations in the amount or timing of the future cash flows;
- the price for bearing uncertainty inherent in the asset; and
- other factors, such as illiquidity, that market participants would reflect in pricing the future cash flows that the entity expects to derive from the asset.

When estimating the value in use of an asset, the last three elements described in the previous paragraph can be reflected either:

- as adjustments to the discount rate (called the 'traditional' approach); or
- as adjustments to the future cash flows (called the 'expected cash flow' approach).

The traditional approach involves the use of a single set of estimated cash flows, and a single discount rate. It emphasises the selection of an appropriate discount rate, assuming that a single discount rate can incorporate all the expectations about the future cash flows and appropriate risk premium. However, the traditional approach may not be easy to apply, for example, in the case of non-financial assets when no market for the item or a comparable item exists.

IAS 36 supports the expected cash flow approach as being, in some situations, a more effective measurement tool. This approach uses all expectations about possible cash flows instead of the single most likely cash flow. For example, a cash flow might be CU100, CU200 or CU300, with probabilities of 10 per cent, 60 per cent and 30 per cent, respectively. The expected cash flow is CU220, i.e. (CU100 x 10%) + (CU200 x 60%) + (CU300 x 30%). The expected cash flow approach therefore differs from the traditional approach by focusing on a direct analysis of the cash flows in question and on more explicit statements of the assumptions used in the measurement. It is highly dependent on assigning probabilities to estimates of future cash flows.

Appendix A to IAS 36 provides a more detailed discussion and comparison of the two approaches. Whichever approach the entity adopts to reflect expectations about possible variations in the amount or timing of future cash flows, the objective is to arrive at an estimate that best reflects the expected present value of future cash flows, i.e. the weighted average of all possible outcomes. [IAS 36:A2]

Whichever approach is selected, key principles to be borne in mind are:

[IAS 36:A3]

- consistent assumptions should be used for the estimation of cash flows and the selection of an appropriate discount rate in order to avoid any double-counting or omissions. For example, a discount rate of 12 per cent might be applied to the contractual cash flows of a loan receivable. That rate reflects expectations about future defaults from loans with particular characteristics. That same 12 per cent should not be used to discount expected cash flows because those cash flows already reflect assumptions about future defaults;

- estimated cash flows and discount rates should be free from both bias and factors unrelated to the asset in question. For example, deliberately understating estimated net cash flows to enhance the apparent future profitability of an asset introduces a bias into the measurement; and

- estimated cash flows or discount rates should reflect a range of possible outcomes, rather than a single, most likely, minimum or maximum possible amount.

8.3.2 Use of forecasts/budgets/cash flow projections

8.3.2.1 Estimation of expected future cash flows

When estimating expected future cash flows, the following rules apply.

- Projections of cash flows should be based on reasonable and supportable assumptions that represent management's best estimate of the range of economic conditions that will exist over the remaining useful life of the asset. Greater weight should be given to external evidence. [IAS 36:33(a)] The reasonableness of the assumptions on which current cash flow projections are based should be assessed by examining the causes of differences between past cash flow projections and actual cash flows. The assumptions used should be consistent with past actual outcomes, provided the effects of subsequent events or circumstances that did not exist when those actual cash flows were generated make this appropriate. [IAS 36:34]

- Cash flow projections should be based on the most recent financial budgets/forecasts that have been approved by management. Projections based on these budgets/forecasts should cover a maximum period of five years, unless a longer period can be justified. [IAS 36:33(b)] Detailed budgets/forecasts for a period of greater than five years are generally not available and, if they are available, are less likely to be accurate. If management has produced budgets/forecasts for a period greater than five years, however, and can demonstrate, based on past experience, that its forecasting methods are reliable for such extended periods, it can use forecasts for periods exceeding five years if it is confident that these projections are reliable. [IAS 36:35] This is expected to be very much the exception, not the rule.

- Projections of cash flows beyond the period covered by the most recent budgets/forecasts should be estimated by extrapolating the projections based on the budgets/forecasts using a steady or declining growth rate for subsequent years, unless an increasing rate can be justified based on objective information about patterns over a product or industry lifecycle. This growth rate should not be overly optimistic and should not exceed the long-term average growth rate for the products, industries, or country or countries in which the entity operates, or for the market in which the asset is used, unless a higher rate can be justified. [IAS 36:33(c)] In some cases, it may be appropriate for the growth rate to be zero or negative. [IAS 36:36]

- Projections of cash flows should be consistent with the discount rate assumptions as regards price increases due to general inflation. Thus, if the discount rate includes the effect of price increases due to general inflation, future cash flows are estimated in nominal terms. If the discount rate excludes the effect of price increases due to general inflation, cash flows are estimated in real terms (but including future specific price increases or decreases). [IAS 36:40]

In principle, the guidance in the final bullet above also applies when a currency is hyperinflationary. However, in the case of hyperinflation, frequently there will be difficulties in determining the likely future rate of inflation and the relevant nominal interest rate. Calculating the value in use generally will be easier in real terms.

8.3.2.2 Impact of inflation

As noted at **8.3.2.1**, IAS 36:40 sets out two ways to deal with inflation when estimating future cash flows.

The first method is to forecast cash flows in real terms – i.e. forecast cash flows that are increased or decreased in real terms, to reflect the likely relation between future changes in specific prices and general inflation. These cash flows are then discounted at a real discount rate (i.e. a rate that excludes general inflation).

Alternatively, the forecast cash flows can reflect the estimated increase or decrease in specific prices in nominal terms, but those 'nominal cash flows' then need to be discounted at a nominal rate of interest (i.e. a rate that includes general inflation).

Care will be needed when revenues and costs are expected to change at different rates in the future. This would happen when there are specific factors applicable to the different cash flow streams that will make them vary, other than general price level changes (the general price level change will be the same for all cash flow streams). For example, the regulator may restrict the revenues of a regulated entity, but its costs will be unrestricted. The entity's costs and revenues, therefore, will be subject to different assumptions as to the rates at which they will change. In such circumstances:

- if the first method described above is used, it will be necessary to reflect the different estimated rates of variation of revenues and costs in real terms; and

- if the second method is used, it will be necessary to reflect the different estimated changes to revenues and costs in nominal terms.

Example 8.3.2.2 illustrates the application of these two methods.

Example 8.3.2.2

Taking inflation into account when forecasting cash flows – illustration of alternative methods

Entity A is estimating the value in use of a machine with four years of remaining expected useful life.

The following general information is relevant:

- forecast inflation for the next four years – 3 per cent per year;

- forecast interest (nominal rate) for the next four years – 9 per cent per year; and

- forecast interest (real rate) for the next four years – 5.8252* per cent per year.

The specific revenues and costs of Entity A are expected to increase at the following rates for the next four years.

Year	1	2	3	4
Revenues	3%	2%	2%	1%
Raw material	4%	4%	5%	6%
Labour	3%	3%	3%	3%

* Forecast real rate is calculated as follows.

$$\frac{1 + \text{nominal interest rate}}{1 + \text{inflation rate}} - 1 = \frac{1 + 0.09}{1 + 0.03} - 1 = 0.058252 \text{ or } 5.8252\%$$

Method 1 – real cash flows discounted using real rate of interest

The following are the cash flows expected to be generated by the machine in real terms.

Cash flows forecast in real terms

	Base (Year 0)	Year 1	Year 2	Year 3	Year 4	Total (Years 1 to 4)
Revenues	100,000	100,000	99,029	98,068	96,163	
Raw material	−35,000	−35,340	−35,683	−36,376	−37,435	
Labour	−25,000	−25,000	−25,000	−25,000	−25,000	
Net cash flows	40,000	39,660	38,346	36,692	33,728	**148,426**

When these 'real' cash flows are discounted at the real interest rate, the outcome is as follows.

Cash flows forecast in real terms discounted at the real interest rate (5.8252% per year)

	Year 1	Year 2	Year 3	Year 4	Total (Years 1 to 4)
Revenues	94,495	88,427	82,748	76,675	
Raw material	−33,394	−31,863	−30,693	−29,849	
Labour	−23,624	−22,323	−21,095	−19,933	**Value in use**
Net cash flows	37,477	34,241	30,960	26,893	**129,571**

Method 2 – nominal cash flows discounted using nominal rate of interest

The following are the cash flows expected to be generated by the machine in nominal terms.

Cash flows forecast in nominal terms

	Base (Year 0)	Year 1	Year 2	Year 3	Year 4	Total (Years 1 to 4)
Revenues	100,000	103,000	105,060	107,161	108,233	
Raw material	−35,000	−36,400	−37,856	−39,749	−42,134	
Labour	−25,000	−25,750	−26,522	−27,318	−28,138	
Net cash flows	40,000	40,850	40,682	40,094	37,961	**159,587**

When these nominal cash flows are discounted at the nominal interest rate, the outcome is as follows.

Cash flows forecast in nominal terms discounted at the nominal interest rate (9% per year)

	Year 1	Year 2	Year 3	Year 4	Total (Years 1 to 4)
Revenues	94,495	88,427	82,748	76,675	
Raw material	−33,394	−31,863	−30,693	−29,849	
Labour	−23,624	−22,323	−21,095	−19,933	Value in use
Net cash flows	37,477	34,241	30,960	26,893	**129,571**

8.3.3 Cash flows to be included

Estimates of future cash flows should include:

- projections of cash inflows from the continuing use of the asset; [IAS 36:39(a)]

- projections of cash outflows that are necessarily incurred to generate the cash inflows from continuing use of the asset. This includes cash outflows to prepare the asset for use (if such preparation has not yet been completed), and future overheads that can be directly attributed, or allocated on a reasonable and consistent basis, to the asset (see **example 8.3.3**); [IAS 36:39(b)]

- net cash flows, if any, to be received (or paid) for the disposal of the asset at the end of its useful life. [IAS 36:39(c)] This is the amount that an entity expects to obtain from the disposal of the asset in an arm's length transaction between knowledgeable, willing parties, after deduction of the estimated costs of disposal. [IAS 36:52] In estimating these net cash flows, the same approach is taken as for estimates of fair value less costs of disposal, except that:

  - prices used are those prevailing at the date of the estimate for similar assets that have reached the end of their useful life and that have operated under similar conditions; [IAS 36:53(a)] and

- the prices are adjusted for the effect of both future price increases due to general inflation and specific future price increases/decreases. However, if estimates of future cash flows from the asset's continuing use and the discount rate exclude the effect of general inflation, this effect is also excluded from the estimate of net cash flows on disposal; [IAS 36:53(b)]

- projections of cash outflows for the day-to-day servicing of the asset as well as future overheads that can be attributed directly, or allocated on a reasonable and consistent basis, to the use of the asset; [IAS 36:41] and

- in the same way that corporate assets can be allocated to a CGU's carrying value, the CGU's cash flows should also include an appropriate apportionment of corporate overheads when calculating value in use. However, care should be taken around internal charges for using the asset as explained in **8.3.4**.

Example 8.3.3

Testing an asset under construction for impairment – costs of construction not yet incurred

Company D designs, develops and manufactures components for high speed optical networks. The majority of Company D's customers are building communication infrastructures. In December 20X1, Company D purchased a plot of land in an industrial complex with the intent to build a state-of-the-art production facility for its integrated circuit and module products.

Construction of the new facility began in March 20X2 and is expected to be completed by the end of August 20X2. In June 20X2, a number of Company D's customers announced plans to cut the level of capital expenditures related to their infrastructure development, and Company D received several order cancellations. At 30 June 20X2, due to the significant change in business climate, Company D identified indications of impairment of the new production facility under IAS 36.

Company D should include the remaining costs associated with completing the production facility in its estimates of future cash flows when assessing the asset group for impairment. IAS 36:42 clearly states that when the carrying amount of an asset does not yet include all the cash outflows to be incurred before it is ready for use, the estimate of future cash outflows includes an estimate of any further cash outflow that is expected to be incurred before the asset is ready for use.

8.3.4 *Cash flows to be excluded*

Estimates of future cash flows should exclude:

- cash inflows from assets that generate cash inflows that are largely independent of the cash inflows from the asset under review (e.g. financial assets such as receivables); [IAS 36:43(a)]

- cash outflows that relate to obligations that have already been recognised as liabilities (e.g. payables, pensions or provisions), except in the limited circumstances described at **8.2.7**; [IAS 36:43(b)]

- cash outflows or related cost savings (e.g. reductions in staff costs) or benefits that are expected to arise from a future restructuring to which an entity is not yet committed. [IAS 36:45(a)] The guidance in IAS 37 *Provisions, Contingent Liabilities and Contingent Assets* should be used to determine when an entity is committed to a restructuring (see **chapter A12**). Once an entity is committed to the restructuring, estimates of future cash inflows and cash outflows reflect the cost savings and other benefits from the restructuring based on the most recent financial budgets/forecasts that have been approved by management. [IAS 36:47(a)] An entity's internal forecasts may include the impact of a restructuring before the financial statements. Such forecasts may, therefore, need to be adjusted to comply with the principles of IAS 37;

- estimated future cash flows that are expected to arise from improving or enhancing an asset's performance. [IAS 36:44(b)]

> Estimates of future cash flows do, however, include future cash flows necessary to maintain the level of economic benefits expected to arise from the asset in its current condition, for example overhauls or fault inspections. In practice it may not be easy to distinguish between maintenance and improvements, which are addressed in **example 8.3.4A**.

When a CGU consists of assets with different estimated useful lives, the replacement of assets with shorter lives is considered to be part of the day-to-day servicing of the unit when estimating the future cash flows associated with the unit. Similarly, when a single asset consists of components with different estimated useful lives, the replacement of components with shorter lives is considered to be part of the day-to-day servicing of the asset when estimating the future cash flows generated by the asset; [IAS 36:49]

Example 8.3.4A

Expenditure on maintaining and improving assets

The assets of a CGU comprise a factory and plant and machinery. The factory is expected to last 50 years, but will need a new roof in 30 years, and the machinery needs to be replaced every 10 years. The entity expects to be able to reduce costs per unit of production by extending the factory to double production in a few years, but is not yet committed to such a restructuring.

The replacement expenditure for the 50 years, including the new roof and new machinery, should be included in the cash flows.

> Neither the expenditure to increase the size of the factory nor the additional income and revenue expenditure consequent on that expansion should be included.

- cash inflows or outflows from financing activities. [IAS 36:50(a)] The assumptions underlying the discount rate must be consistent with the estimated future cash flows. Therefore, because the time value of money is considered by discounting the estimated future cash flows, these cash flows exclude cash inflows/outflows from financing activities; [IAS 36:51]

> IAS 36:50(a) prohibits the inclusion of financing cash outflows or inflows in a value in use calculation and does not provide for any exceptions to this rule. Therefore, borrowing costs that will be capitalised as part of the cost of an asset under IAS 23 *Borrowing Costs* are excluded from estimates of future cash flows when testing an asset under development for impairment.

- income tax receipts or payments. [IAS 36:50(b)] As discussed in Stage 3 (see **8.4**), a pre-tax discount rate is used and, therefore, future cash flows are also estimated on a pre-tax basis; [IAS 36:51] and

- when corporate assets have been allocated to a CGU's carrying amount, any internal charges incurred by the CGU for using such assets should not be included in the CGU's expected future cash flows. To do so would be to double-count the impact of the corporate assets and could result in an impairment loss being recognised incorrectly.

Example 8.3.4B

Payments for corporate assets

The present value of the net cash inflows of a CGU is CU220 before charges for the use of corporate assets, and the carrying amount of the assets of the CGU (excluding corporate assets) is CU140. The present value of the cash outflows for the use of the corporate assets is CU50, and the carrying amount of the portion of the corporate assets allocated to the CGU is CU45. The corporate assets can be allocated to the CGU on a reasonable and consistent basis.

In these circumstances, IAS 36:102 requires that the portion of the corporate assets allocated to the CGU should be included in its carrying amount. Therefore, the value in use of CU220 is compared to the CGU's carrying amount of CU185 (CU140 + CU45). The headroom is CU35 and there is no impairment loss.

The entity should *not* factor into the determination of recoverable amount both the portion of the corporate assets and the related outflows; if it does so, it will incorrectly recognise an impairment loss of CU15 (value in use of CU170 (CU220 − CU50) compared to carrying amount of CU185 (CU140 + CU45)).

Illustrative examples 5 and 6 accompanying IAS 36 illustrate, respectively, how future restructurings and improvements or enhancements to asset performance affect a value in use calculation.

8.3.5 Foreign currency cash flows

Future cash flows are estimated in the currency in which they will be generated and then discounted using a discount rate appropriate for that currency. The present value obtained is then translated using the spot exchange rate at the date of the value in use calculation. [IAS 36:54]

If goodwill or intangible assets are being assessed for impairment during the year rather than at the reporting date, the rate used will be the spot rate at the time that the testing is performed.

It is not appropriate to use a forward exchange rate to translate the value in use expressed in a foreign currency. A forward rate reflects the market's adjustment for the differential in interest rates, so using such a rate would double-count the time value of money (in the discount rate and also in the forward rate). [IAS 36:BCZ49]

8.3.6 Impact of leases on the calculation of value in use

Although IAS 36 does not explicitly discuss the treatment of leased assets, applying the principles that do exist would suggest the following approach:

- for a lessee, assets under an operating lease should not be included in a CGU's carrying amount, but the lease payments should be included in the CGU's cash outflows;

- for a lessor, an asset leased out under an operating lease should be included in its CGU's carrying amount, and the cash flows arising from the lease should also be included in the CGU's future cash inflows;

- for a lessee, assets under a finance lease should be included in a CGU's carrying amount, but the lease payments (and the associated finance lease creditor) should be excluded from the cash flows on the grounds that they represent financing activities (see **8.3.4**) and do not affect the economic benefits that can be derived from the assets; and

- for a lessor, receivables under a finance lease are scoped into IFRS 9 *Financial Instruments* (or, for entities that have not yet adopted IFRS 9, IAS 39 *Financial Instruments: Recognition and Measurement*) for the purpose of impairment testing.

When a lessee has operating lease accruals in its statement of financial position, it is important to compare like items. It is usually appropriate to include these balances in the carrying amount of the CGU. But, if they are excluded, it is necessary to adjust the cash outflows accordingly. For example, if a lessee excludes an accrual of CU100 for an operating lease, the future cash outflows of CU100 that will settle this liability should also be excluded.

8.3.7   Impact of cash flow hedges on the calculation of value in use

When an entity has entered into derivative contracts to hedge cash flows related to the purchase and sale of goods within a specific CGU, and the contracts are designated and qualify as cash flow hedges, the entity may either include or exclude the cash flows on the hedging contracts in determining the value in use of the CGU, as long as the carrying amount of the CGU is established in a consistent manner.

IAS 36:68 defines a CGU as "the smallest group of assets that includes the asset and generates cash inflows that are largely independent of the cash inflows from other assets or groups of assets". IAS 36:69 explains that "[i]n identifying whether cash inflows from an asset (or group of assets) are largely independent of the cash inflows from other assets (or groups of assets), an entity considers various factors including how management monitors the entity's operations (such as by product lines, businesses, individual locations, districts or regional areas) or how management makes decisions about continuing or disposing of the entity's assets and operations" (see **8.2**).

Accordingly, the decision to include or exclude the effect of hedging instruments and associated cash flows for the purpose of testing the carrying amount of a CGU for impairment should reflect how management defines its CGUs.

Example 8.3.7

Impact of cash flow hedges on the calculation of value in use

Entity A has entered into derivative contracts to hedge the cash flows related to the purchase and sale of commodities in a specific CGU. These contracts are designated and qualify as cash flow hedges.

Entity A may either include or exclude the cash flows on the hedging contracts in determining the value in use of the CGU, as long as the carrying amount of the CGU is established in a consistent manner.

If Entity A includes the cash flows on the hedging contracts in determining the value in use of the CGU, it must also include the fair value of the hedging contracts in the carrying amount of the CGU. Conversely, if the cash flows on the hedging contracts are excluded, it would be appropriate also to exclude the hedging contracts from the carrying amount of the CGU.

Entity A may define its CGU strictly based on the independence of cash flows (i.e. by including only those assets that may not be operated without other assets). When this approach is taken, Entity A may consider that the CGU could operate without the hedging instruments and that the hedging instruments generate their own independent cash flows. Therefore, it would exclude the hedging instruments and their cash flows in testing the CGU for impairment.

Alternatively, Entity A may define its CGU based on the manner in which it operates the assets. When this approach is taken, Entity A may consider that the CGU should include the hedging contracts if they are acquired specifically for the operations of a specific CGU and have no other business purposes.

Both approaches are acceptable.

8.3.8 Dividend discount models

When calculating the value in use of a CGU in accordance with IAS 36:33, estimated future cash flows expected to arise from dividends calculated using dividend discount models (DDMs) represent an appropriate cash flow projection in some circumstances.

IAS 36:30 to 57 and IAS 36:74 to 79 provide guidance on the principles to be applied in calculating the value in use of a CGU. Calculations using a DDM that values shares at the discounted value of future dividend payments may be appropriate when calculating the value in use of a single asset (e.g. when an entity applies IAS 36 in determining whether an investment is impaired in the separate financial statements of an entity).

Some DDMs focus on future cash flows that are expected to be available for distribution to shareholders rather than future cash flows from dividends. Such a DDM could be used to calculate the value in use of a CGU in consolidated financial statements, if it is consistent with the principles and requirements in IAS 36.

This was confirmed in an agenda decision of the IFRS Interpretations Committee published in the November 2010 *IFRIC Update*.

8.4 Stage 3: Determination of an appropriate discount rate

8.4.1 Characteristics of an appropriate discount rate

IAS 36:55 specifies that the discount rate (or rates) used should be:

- a pre-tax rate (or rates);
- that reflect(s) current market assessments of:
  - the time value of money; and
  - the risks specific to the asset for which the future cash flow estimates have not been adjusted (but not those for which the cash flows have been adjusted).

Effectively, the discount rate used is an estimate of the rate that the market would expect on an equally risky investment. This rate is ideally estimated from either:

[IAS 36:56]

- the rate implicit in current market transactions for similar assets; or
- the weighted average cost of capital (WACC) of a listed entity that has a single asset (or portfolio of assets) similar in terms of service potential and risks to the asset under review.

> In practice, asset-specific rates, such as those suggested in the previous paragraph, will seldom be available due to the unique nature of different transactions and the fact that there are likely to be few listed entities that offer a readily usable comparison because listed entities generally have a wider product/service base, wider markets and potentially lower risk profile. When an asset-specific rate is unavailable, a discount rate must be estimated. Appendix A to IAS 36, which is an integral part of the Standard, provides additional guidance on estimating the discount rate in such circumstances. This guidance is summarised in the following sections.

8.4.2   Estimation of a market rate

The entity may consider one of the following rates as a 'starting point' for its estimation. The rates would then be adjusted as discussed below. The starting-point rates include:

[IAS 36:A17]

- the WACC of the entity determined using techniques such as the Capital Asset Pricing Model;
- the entity's incremental borrowing rate; and
- other market borrowing rates.

This starting-point rate is then adjusted:

[IAS 36:A18]

- to reflect the way that the market would assess the specific risks associated with the asset's estimated cash flows (such as country risk, currency risk and price risk); and

- to exclude risks that are not relevant to the asset's estimated cash flows or for which the estimated cash flows have been adjusted.

If the starting-point rate is post-tax, it must be adjusted to arrive at a pre-tax rate. [IAS 36:A20]

In practice, estimating a suitable pre-tax rate is far from straightforward. The pre-tax discount rate is the rate of return that will, after tax has been deducted, give the post-tax rate of return. However, the pre-tax discount rate is generally not the post-tax rate grossed up by a standard rate of tax - IAS 36:BCZ85 includes an example illustrating this point.

Conceptually, discounting post-tax cash flows at a post-tax discount rate should give the same result as discounting pre-tax cash flows at a pre-tax discount rate, provided that the pre-tax discount rate is the post-tax discount rate adjusted to reflect the specific amount and timing of the future tax cash flows (see IAS 36:BC94).

In the example set out in IAS 36:BCZ85, one of the reasons for the difference between the grossed-up post-tax discount rate and the 'real' pre-tax discount rate is that the tax deductions for the asset do not arise evenly over its life. In practice, in a CGU comprised of a group of assets acquired at different times, it is possible that the overall pattern of tax deduction for assets will be more even and that a simple grossed-up post-tax rate may give a reasonable approximation of the actual pre-tax rate of return.

Example 8.4.2 illustrates the calculation of a pre-tax discount rate.

Example 8.4.2

Calculating a pre-tax discount rate from a post-tax rate – asset is not deductible for tax purposes

At the end of 20X0, an asset has a remaining useful life of 5 years. The asset is not deductible for tax purposes. The tax rate is 20 per cent. The discount rate for the asset can be determined only on a post-tax basis and is estimated to be 10 per cent. Therefore, the pre-tax discount rate grossed-up at the standard rate of tax is 12.5 per cent [10 per cent/(100 per cent – 20 per cent)].

At the end of 20X0, cash flow projections determined on a pre-tax basis are as follows.

	20X1	20X2	20X3	20X4	20X5
(1) Pre-tax cash flows (CF)	500	500	500	500	500

Value in use calculated using post-tax cash flows and post-tax discount rate

	20X1	20X2	20X3	20X4	20X5
(2) Tax CF [(1) × 20 per cent]	100	100	100	100	100
(3) Post-tax CF [(1) – (2)]	400	400	400	400	400
(4) Post-tax CF discounted at 10% to the end of 20X0	364	331	300	273	248
Value in use [Σ(4)] =					1,516

Value in use calculated using pre-tax cash flows and the grossed-up pre-tax discount rate

	20X1	20X2	20X3	20X4	20X5
(5) Pre-tax CF discounted at 12.5% to the end of 20X0	444	395	351	312	278
Value in use [Σ(5)] =					1,780

Calculating the 'real' pre-tax discount rate by iteration

Using iterative computation (i.e. so that the value in use determined using pre-tax cash flows and a pre-tax discount rate equals the value in use determined using post-tax cash flows and a post-tax discount rate), the pre-tax discount rate would be 19.4 per cent.

	20X1	20X2	20X3	20X4	20X5
(6) Pre-tax CF discounted at 19.4% to the end of 20X0	419	351	294	246	206
Value in use [Σ(6)] =					1,516

The 'real' pre-tax discount rate differs from the post-tax discount rate grossed up by the standard rate of tax depending on the tax rate, the post-tax discount rate and the useful life of the asset.

Similar calculations to those outlined above were carried out, but with the asset assumed to have a 10, 15 and 20 years life (and be worth nil at the end of that life).

A post-tax discount rate of 10 per cent in these similar scenarios equated to the following 'real' pre-tax discount rates:

Assumed life	Pre-tax discount rate
10 years	15.5 per cent
15 years	14.2 per cent
20 years	13.5 per cent

The discount rate is independent of the capital structure of the entity and of the way in which the entity financed the purchase of the asset because the future cash flows expected to arise from an asset do not depend on the way in which the entity financed the purchase of the asset. [IAS 36:A19]

Generally, a single discount rate is used to estimate the value in use of an asset. Separate discount rates for different future periods should be used, however, when value in use is sensitive to a difference in risks for different periods or to the term structure of interest rates. [IAS 36:A21]

8.5   Stage 4: Discounting and aggregating expected cash flows to arrive at value in use

The formulae for calculating value in use are derived from the following formulae:

Single cash flow

Present value of a single cash flow occurring in n years = $\dfrac{\text{Cashflow}}{(1 + d)^n}$

Series of equal cash flows

Present value of n annual cash flows = Cashflow $\times \dfrac{1 - (1 + d)^{-n}}{d}$

Perpetuity

Present value of fixed annual cash flow, in perpetuity = $\dfrac{\text{Cashflow}}{d}$

Where d = annual discount rate

In the first (single cash flow) formula, the cash flow is an actual cash flow. The discount rate will therefore be a nominal rate, matching the cash flow by including a compatible estimate of the effect of inflation.

In the second (series) and third (perpetuity) formulae, it is assumed that all cash flows are the same, with the first cash flow occurring at the end of Year 1. When these cash flows will increase due to growth and inflation, this effect can be achieved by using a cash flow for Year 1 and reducing the nominal discount rate by both growth and inflation rates. When the actual cash flow for the previous period is used, it will first be necessary to increase it by the first year's growth and inflation in order to find the cash flow at the end of Year 1. (This adjustment of the discount rate for growth is a substitute for building growth into the cash flows. It should not be confused with a real rate of return that would adjust for inflation only.)

At a discount rate of 10 per cent, perpetuity can be assumed to approximate to 35 years or more, since any amounts beyond that horizon will be immaterial.

Example 8.5A

Assumed steady growth in cash flows to perpetuity

The calculation is based on the perpetuity formula. Cash flow is for Year 1. Thus, when the previous year's actual cash flow is used, it is first necessary to increase it to reflect growth and inflation in Year 1.

$$\text{Value in use} = \frac{CF_0}{d_a}(1+g)(1+i)$$

Where:

CF_0 = actual cash flow for previous period

i = annual inflation rate

g = annual growth rate in cash flows

d_a = nominal pre-tax discount rate adjusted to reflect inflation and growth in cash flows.

Example 8.5B

Cash flows forecast for five years and assumed steady growth thereafter

The calculation is the sum of individual present values for the first 5 years, plus a perpetuity from Year 6 onwards re-expressed from Year 5 back to present value at time 0.

Value in use = Present value of each cash flow for Years 1 to 5

+ Present value of cash flows from Year 6 onwards

$$= \frac{CF_1}{1+d_n} + \frac{CF_2}{(1+d_n)^2} + \frac{CF_3}{(1+d_n)^3} + \frac{CF_4}{(1+d_n)^4} + \frac{CF_5}{(1+d_n)^5} + \frac{CF_5(1+g)(1+i)}{d_a \times (1+d_n)^5}$$

Where:

CF_n = Cash flow in nth year

i = annual inflation rate after Year 5

g = annual growth rate in cash flows after Year 5

d_n = nominal pre-tax discount rate

d_a = nominal pre-tax discount rate adjusted to reflect growth and inflation in cash flows

Note:

The sixth term in the formula above,

$$\frac{CF_5(1 + g)(1 + i)}{d_a \times (1 + d_n)^5}$$

is a compound of two functions.

$$\frac{CF_5(1 + g)(1 + i)}{d_a}$$

is the present value of cash flows from Year 6 onwards expressed as a present value at the beginning of Year 6. Further adjustment to multiply by

$$\frac{1}{(1 + d_n)^5}$$

re-expresses this as a present value at the beginning of Year 1.

Example 8.5C

Cash flows are forecast for 2 years and assumed steady growth thereafter

Assume:

Cash flow for Year 1	CU20 million
Cash flow for Year 2	CU24 million
Assumed steady growth thereafter	2.5 per cent
Inflation	2.5 per cent
Nominal pre-tax discount rate	15 per cent
Adjusted pre-tax discount rate	10 per cent

Value in use =

$$\frac{CU20m}{1.15} + \frac{CU24m}{1.15^2} + \frac{CU24m \times 1.025 \times 1.025}{0.1 \times 1.15^2} = CU226 \text{ million}$$

9   Recognition and measurement of an impairment loss

9.1   Recognition and measurement of an impairment loss – individual asset

If, and only if, the recoverable amount of an asset is less than its carrying amount, the carrying amount of the asset should be reduced to its recoverable amount. That reduction is an impairment loss. [IAS 36:59]

An impairment loss should be recognised in profit or loss immediately unless it relates to an asset carried at a revalued amount. If an asset has been revalued (e.g. an item of property, plant and equipment), the impairment loss is dealt with as a revaluation decrease in accordance with the relevant Standard (in this case, IAS 16 *Property, Plant and Equipment* – see **chapter A7**). [IAS 36:60] Generally, an impairment loss will first result in a decrease in any revaluation surplus related to the asset. This decrease is recognised in other comprehensive income rather than in profit or loss. When no related revaluation surplus exists, or to the extent that the impairment loss is greater than the related revaluation surplus, the excess impairment loss is recognised in profit or loss. [IAS 36:61]

If the impairment loss is greater than the carrying amount of the asset, a liability should be recognised only if it is required by another Standard. [IAS 36:62] A liability will only be recognised in respect of present obligations arising as a result of past events. IAS 37 *Provisions, Contingent Liabilities and Contingent Assets* describes the appropriate recognition criteria (see **chapter A12**). When a provision is required to be recognised, it is measured in accordance with the general requirements of IAS 37.

IAS 16 requires that the estimated useful life, the depreciation method and residual value of an item of property, plant and equipment should be reviewed at the end of each reporting period. After an impairment loss is recognised, these three items are reviewed, and the new carrying amount is depreciated over the asset's remaining useful life. [IAS 36:63] Similar rules for intangible assets are set out in IAS 38 *Intangible Assets*.

Because an impairment loss affects the carrying amount of an asset, it affects the relationship between the asset's carrying amount and its tax base. Therefore, any deferred tax asset or liability is determined by comparing the revised carrying amount of the asset with its tax base (see **chapter A13**). [IAS 36:64]

Example 9.1

Recognition of an impairment loss creates a deferred tax asset

[IAS 36:IE36 & IE37, Example 3B]

An entity has an identifiable asset with a carrying amount of CU1,000. Its recoverable amount is CU650. The tax rate is 30 per cent and the tax base of the asset is CU800. Impairment losses are not deductible for tax purposes. The effect of the impairment loss is as follows:

	Before impairment	Effect of impairment	After impairment
	CU	CU	CU
Carrying amount	1,000	(350)	650
Tax base	800	–	800
Taxable (deductible) temporary difference	200	(350)	(150)
Deferred tax liability (asset) at 30%	60	(105)	(45)

In accordance with IAS 12, the entity recognises the deferred tax asset to the extent that it is probable that taxable profit will be available against which the deductible temporary difference can be utilised.

When an entity incurs capital expenditure on an item of property, plant and equipment in respect of which an impairment loss has previously been recognised, the expenditure should be recognised in accordance with IAS 16 and included in the cost of the asset if the criteria in IAS 16:7 are met (see **3.1** and **3.5.6** in **chapter A7**). For intangible assets, similar considerations apply and the expenditure should be recognised in accordance with IAS 38 and included in the cost of the asset if the criteria in IAS 38:57 are met (see **example 4.8.5.1** in **chapter A9**).

9.2 Recognition and measurement of an impairment loss – cash-generating unit

An impairment loss should be recognised for a CGU (or the smallest group of CGUs to which goodwill or a corporate asset has been allocated) if, and only if, its recoverable amount is less than its carrying amount. The impairment loss should be allocated to reduce the carrying amount of the assets of the unit or group of units in the following order:

[IAS 36:104]

- first, to goodwill allocated to the CGU (group of CGUs); and

- then, to the other assets of the unit or group on a pro rata basis based on the carrying amount of each asset in the unit or group of units.

Example 9.2A

Allocation of impairment loss within a cash-generating unit

Entity C has a soft drinks CGU which contains both goodwill and intangible assets in the form of brands with indefinite lives. Entity C tests the CGU for impairment and determines that an impairment loss has occurred. The directors attribute the impairment loss to the poor performance of a particular brand, B.

> *In the light of the directors' belief that the impairment is attributable to brand B, is it acceptable for Entity C to allocate the impairment loss to the carrying amount of that brand, rather than following the allocation specified in IAS 36:104?*
>
> No. Because it is not practicable to estimate the recoverable amount of each individual asset, the rules set out in IAS 36:104 (see above) result in an arbitrary allocation of any impairment loss between the assets of the unit (including brand B) other than goodwill. These reductions in carrying amounts should be dealt with in the same manner as impairment losses on individual assets as discussed at **9.1**.
>
> Therefore, in the circumstances described, the impairment loss identified must first be allocated to goodwill. Following this, any excess is then available for allocation against the carrying amount of Entity C's other assets (including brand B).

When allocating an impairment loss to individual assets within a CGU, the carrying amount of an individual asset should not be reduced below the highest of:

[IAS 36:105]

- its fair value less costs of disposal (if measurable);

- its value in use (if determinable); and

- zero.

If this results in an amount being allocated to an asset which is less than its pro rata share of the impairment loss, the excess is allocated to the remaining assets within the CGU on a pro rata basis. [IAS 36:105]

If the recoverable amount of an individual asset cannot be determined:

[IAS 36:107]

- an impairment loss is recognised for the asset if its carrying amount is greater than the higher of its fair value less costs of disposal and the results of the allocation procedures described; and

- no impairment loss is recognised for the asset if the related CGU is not impaired. This applies even if the asset's fair value less costs of disposal is less than its carrying amount.

After the allocation procedures have been applied, a liability is recognised for any remaining impairment loss for a CGU if, and only if, that is required by another Standard. [IAS 36:108] A liability will only be recognised in respect of present obligations arising as a result of past events. IAS 37 describes the appropriate recognition criteria (see **chapter A12**). When a provision is required to be recognised, it is measured in accordance with the general requirements of IAS 37.

Example 9.2B

Corporate assets

An entity produces different types of packaging based on paper. The three main types of packaging materials produced for its customers are the following:

- tubes;
- corrugated board; and
- solid board.

Each of the three main types of packaging associated with the business is identified as an operating segment under IFRS 8 *Operating Segments*, and as a CGU under IAS 36. Asset M is partly used for the production of tubes (CGU T) and corrugated board (CGU C).

The following information relates to CGU T.

- Goodwill = zero
- Carrying amount of machinery used exclusively in manufacturing tubes (excluding Asset M) = CU4,500
- Carrying amount of Asset M = CU1,000
- Capacity of Asset M used for the tubes production = 60 per cent
- Recoverable amount of CGU T (including Asset M) = CU4,000

For CGU C, the excess of value in use over the carrying amount is CU2,000.

In accordance with IAS 36, Asset M should be allocated on a reasonable and consistent basis to CGUs T and C. The entity should compare the carrying amount of each CGU, including the portion of the carrying amount of the corporate asset allocated to the CGU, with its recoverable amount. In this case, 60 per cent of Asset M's capacity is used for the production of the tubes; accordingly, it seems reasonable to allocate 60 per cent of the carrying amount of Asset M to CGU T. Therefore, the carrying amount of CGU T is CU5,100 (CU1,000 × 60% + CU4,500) which exceeds its recoverable amount (CU4,000) by CU1,100.

An impairment loss should be recognised and should be allocated to all assets of CGU T (including Asset M) pro rata based on the carrying amount of each asset in the unit:

- to Asset M: CU1,100 × CU600 / CU5,100 = CU129
- to other assets: CU1,100 × CU4,500 / CU5,100 = CU971

However, if the entity were able to determine the fair value less costs of disposal of Asset M, and that number was CU1,000 or more, the impairment loss in respect of CGU T would be allocated on a pro rata basis to the other assets of CGU T in accordance with the requirements of IAS 36:104 and 105.

No impairment loss is recognised in respect of CGU C because the amount of Asset M to be allocated (CU400) is less than the excess of CGU C's value in use over CGU C's carrying amount (CU2,000).

> Even though the difference between the carrying amount and the recoverable amount (CU2,000) of CGU C is higher than the impairment loss of CGU T, an impairment loss should be recognised in CGU T. The entity cannot test for impairment at a higher level to avoid the impairment loss.

9.3 Two-step approach for goodwill allocated to a group of cash-generating units

When goodwill is allocated to a group of CGUs for the purpose of impairment testing but cannot be allocated on a non-arbitrary basis to individual CGUs, the individual CGUs must be tested for impairment before the group of CGUs containing the associated goodwill. [IAS 36:81, 88 and 97 - 98] The allocation of goodwill to CGUs is discussed at **8.2.8**. This two-step approach is illustrated in the following example.

Example 9.3

Two-step approach for goodwill allocated to a group of CGUs

In 20X0, Entity X acquires a business comprising three CGUs, A, B and C. The entire goodwill arising in the business combination is allocated to the three CGUs as a group (this allocation complies with the requirements of IAS 36:80). At the end of 20X5, the carrying amount of the net assets in each CGU and the associated goodwill and the value in use of each CGU is as set out below. Entity X has determined that the fair value less costs of disposal of each of the CGUs and of the business as a whole is less than the value in use of each CGU and of the business, respectively.

Cash-generating unit	A	B	C	Goodwill	Total
	CU	CU	CU	CU	CU
Carrying amount	80	120	140	50	390
Value in use	100	140	120		360

Step 1

Firstly, Entity X assesses each individual CGU for impairment. This first assessment results in an impairment loss of CU20 being recognised in respect of CGU C, thereby reducing its carrying amount from CU140 to CU120, and the total carrying amount of the group of CGUs (including goodwill) from CU390 to CU370.

Cash-generating unit	A	B	C	Goodwill	Total
	CU	CU	CU	CU	CU
Original carrying amount	80	120	140	50	390
Impairment recognised in Step 1	–	–	(20)	–	(20)
Carrying amount following Step 1	80	120	120	50	370
Value in use	100	140	120		360

Step 2

Secondly, the group of CGUs including the associated goodwill is tested for impairment. This second assessment gives rise to an impairment loss of CU10 in respect of the goodwill, reducing its carrying amount from CU50 to CU40. The total carrying amount of the group of CGUs including goodwill is reduced to CU360.

Cash-generating unit	A	B	C	Goodwill	Total
	CU	CU	CU	CU	CU
Carrying amount	80	120	140	50	390
Impairment recognised in Step 1	–	–	(20)	–	(20)
Impairment recognised in Step 2	–	–	–	(10)	(10)
Carrying amount following Step 2	80	120	120	40	360
Value in use	100	140	120		360

10 Reversals of impairment losses

10.1 Reversals of impairment losses – general

An impairment loss on goodwill should not be reversed. This is discussed in **10.5**. [IAS 36:124] Note that, for entities that have not yet adopted IFRS 9 *Financial Instruments*, paragraph 66 of IAS 39 *Financial Instruments: Recognition and Measurement* applies a similar requirement to an unquoted equity instrument that is not carried at fair value because its fair value cannot be reliably measured, and to a derivative asset that is linked to, and must be settled by delivery of, such an unquoted equity instrument (see **5.3** in **chapter C6**).

When an impairment loss was recognised for an asset other than goodwill (or for a CGU) in prior years, an entity is required to assess at the end of each reporting period whether there is any indication that the impairment loss may no longer exist or may have decreased. If such an indication exists, the entity should estimate the recoverable amount of that asset (or CGU). [IAS 36:110]

An impairment loss recognised in a prior period for an asset other than goodwill (or for a CGU) may be reversed if, and only if, there has been a change in the estimates used to determine the recoverable amount of the asset (or CGU) since the last impairment loss was recognised. When this is the case, the carrying amount of the asset (or CGU) is increased to its recoverable amount in accordance with the rules set out in **10.3** (or in **10.4** for a CGU). [IAS 36:114]

Example 10.1A

Determining whether the reversal of an impairment loss is appropriate

An acquired business produces bottled mineral water. Just before the year end, a consumer group tests the water and publicises the fact that it contains high levels of a harmful chemical. Sales of the mineral water plummet.

Situation 1

Assume that there is great uncertainty about the validity of the consumer group's claim, but it is assumed to be valid and that sales of the product will recover only after the problem has been sorted out, and the product has been re-tested and re-marketed. The future cash flows indicate that the recoverable amount of the CGU (which consists mainly of an intangible asset, being the brand of mineral water) is less than its carrying amount, so the CGU/intangible asset is written down by the entity.

However, in the next period, further tests demonstrate that the consumer group had been wrong in its claims and it retracts them publicly. Sales of the mineral water recover very quickly and soon are back to the previous level.

In this specific case, it is clear that an unforeseen change in the estimates of future cash flows used in determining the recoverable amount has resulted in the recognition of the impairment loss, and later in the reversal of that impairment loss. The CGU/intangible asset can be written back up to the value that would have been recognised had the impairment never occurred (refer to **example 10.3A**). This write-up is recognised immediately in profit or loss.

Situation 2

Assume that, by year end, the mineral water company has conducted its own tests and satisfied both itself and independent experts that the consumer group was wrong in its claims. So the entity forecasts that, although there has been a temporary reduction in sales, sales will soon recover when the consumer group retracts the claims.

The temporary reduction in sales has caused a small temporary impairment in the value of the CGU/intangible asset as measured at the end of the reporting period. The CGU/intangible asset is written down by this small amount to its recoverable amount.

In the next period, sales increase back to their previous levels in line with expectations and the value of the CGU/intangible asset recovers to its original level. But, the (small) impairment loss cannot be reversed in the financial statements. Its reversal was foreseen in the original impairment calculations and has occurred simply because of the passing of time; therefore, the reversal does not arise from a change in the estimates used in the original recoverable amount calculation.

A reversal of an impairment loss must reflect an increase in the estimated service potential of an asset (or CGU), either from use or sale. Examples of such changes in estimate include:

[IAS 36:115]

- a change in the basis for recoverable amount (i.e. whether recoverable amount is based on fair value less costs of disposal or value in use);

- if recoverable amount was based on value in use, a change in the amount or timing of estimated future cash flows or in the discount rate; or

- if recoverable amount was based on fair value less costs of disposal, a change in estimate of the components of fair value less costs of disposal.

An increase in the recoverable amount of the asset due to the passage of time does not, however, represent an increase in the estimated service potential of an asset and, therefore, it is not acceptable to recognise a reversal of an impairment loss on this basis. In other words, the value in use of an asset may increase and even become greater than the carrying amount of the asset simply because the present value of future cash inflows increases as they become closer (i.e. 'the discount unwinds'). This does not, however, represent an economic change in the value of the asset. Therefore, a reversal of an impairment loss should not be recognised on this basis. [IAS 36:116]

Example 10.1B

Unwinding of discounted cash flows does not reverse an impairment loss

At the beginning of 20X0, Entity X acquires a machine with an expected useful life of four years for CU1,000. Depreciation is charged on a straight-line basis. At the end of 20X0, there is an indication that the machine may be impaired and consequently its recoverable amount is assessed by Entity X. Entity X determines that the fair value less costs of disposal is lower than the value in use of the machine. The value in use of the machine is determined using estimated future cash flows and a discount rate of 10 per cent as follows.

	20X1	20X2	20X3	Total
	CU	CU	CU	CU
Estimated future cash flows	250	250	300	800
Present value at 20X0	227	207	225	659

The carrying amount of the machine of CU750 is higher than its value in use of CU659. Therefore, Entity X should recognise an impairment loss of CU91 to reduce the machine's carrying amount to its value in use. The revised carrying amount is then depreciated over the remaining useful life of three years. The cash flows and discount rate used in estimating the value in use of the machine do not change in subsequent years. The value in use based on the original estimated future cash flows and discount rate in each of the subsequent years is as follows.

	20X1	20X2	20X3
	CU	CU	CU
Carrying amount at year end	439	220	–
Estimated future cash flows	550	300	–
Value in use at year end	475	273	–

Although the machine's value in use exceeds its carrying amount in 20X1 and 20X2, this increase simply arises from the unwinding of the discount relating to the future cash flows. Consequently, the impairment loss of CU91 should not be reversed.

10.2   Indications of reversals of impairment losses

The indications of the reversal of impairment losses listed in IAS 36:111 are broadly the mirror image of the impairment indicators discussed at **section 4.2**, and are reproduced in the following paragraphs.

The following external sources of information may indicate that an impairment loss previously recognised for an asset other than goodwill (or for a CGU) no longer exists or has decreased:

[IAS 36:111]

- there are observable indications that the asset's (or CGU's) value has increased significantly during the period;

- significant changes with a favourable effect on the entity have taken place during the period, or will take place in the near future, in the technological, market, economic or legal environment in which the entity operates or in the market to which the asset (or CGU) is dedicated; and

- market interest rates or other market rates of return on investments have decreased during the period, and those decreases are likely to affect the discount rate used in calculating the asset's (or CGU's) value in use and increase the asset's (or CGU's) recoverable amount materially.

The following internal sources of information may indicate that an impairment loss previously recognised for an asset other than goodwill (or for a CGU) no longer exists or has decreased:

[IAS 36:111]

- significant changes with a favourable effect on the entity have taken place during the period, or are expected to take place in the near future, in the extent to which, or the manner in which, the asset (or CGU) is used or is expected to be used. These changes include costs incurred during the period to improve or enhance the asset's (or CGU's) performance or restructure the operation to which the asset (or CGU) belongs; and

- evidence is available from internal reporting that indicates that the economic performance of the asset (or CGU) is, or will be, better than expected.

If there is an indication that an impairment loss previously recognised for an asset other than goodwill may no longer exist or may have decreased, this may indicate that the remaining useful life, the depreciation/amortisation method or the residual value may need to be reviewed and adjusted in accordance with the Standard applicable to the asset, even if no impairment loss is reversed for the asset. [IAS 36:113]

10.3 Reversal of impairment loss for an individual asset

The increased carrying amount of an asset other than goodwill due to a reversal of an impairment loss should not exceed the carrying amount that would have been determined (net of amortisation or depreciation) had no impairment loss been recognised for the asset in prior years. [IAS 36:117] Any increase in excess of this amount would be a revaluation and would be accounted for under the appropriate Standard (e.g. IAS 16 *Property, Plant and Equipment* for an item of property, plant and equipment). [IAS 36:118]

Example 10.3A

Reversal of an impairment loss

Entity A holds an intangible asset and accounts for it under the cost model of IAS 38 *Intangible Assets*. The intangible asset cost CU10 million and it is amortised over 10 years. Two years after it is purchased, the intangible asset becomes impaired and it is written down from its carrying amount of CU8 million to its estimated recoverable amount of CU4 million. Its estimated useful life is unchanged (8 years remaining). Two years after the recognition of the impairment loss, with the carrying amount at CU3 million, the recoverable amount of the intangible asset is estimated to be CU7 million, following a change in estimates of the future cash flows arising from this asset.

Because the reversal of the impairment loss arises from a change in the estimates used to determine the recoverable amount, the impairment loss should be reversed. However, the impairment loss can only be reversed to the extent that it does not increase the carrying amount above what it would have been had the impairment loss never been recognised. Had the impairment loss never been recognised, the carrying amount would be CU6 million (CU8 million less two further years depreciation at CU1 million per annum); therefore, only CU3 million of the original CU4 million impairment loss can be reversed.

> **Example 10.3B**
>
> **Limited reversal of impairment loss**
>
> Entity A holds a property and accounts for it under IAS 16's cost model. The cost of the property is CU10 million and its useful life is 20 years. Depreciation each year is, therefore, CU0.5 million.
>
> At the end of Year 5, the property has a carrying amount of CU7.5 million. Due to changes in the economic environment, the directors perform a detailed impairment review and determine that the property's recoverable amount is its value in use, which is CU5 million. Their estimate of the remaining useful life of the asset is 10 years.
>
> Therefore an impairment loss of CU2.5 million is recognised in Year 5. In Years 6 and 7, the property is depreciated by CU0.5 million per year so that its carrying amount at the end of Year 7 is CU4 million.
>
> Due to shortages in the supply of properties, the directors determine that the fair value less costs of disposal of the property at the end of Year 7 is CU8 million. The recoverable amount of the asset has therefore increased to CU8 million.
>
> The reversal of the impairment loss is limited, however, to the amount that would restore the carrying amount to what it would have been had no impairment loss been recognised (i.e. CU7.5 million − (CU7.5 million × 2/10) = CU6 million). Therefore, only CU2 million of the impairment loss is reversed.
>
> If the entity wishes to recognise the market value of the property in its statement of financial position, the remainder of the uplift would be treated as a revaluation movement. (This will only be possible, however, if the entity decides to adopt the revaluation model for all assets in that class.)

A reversal of an impairment loss for an asset other than goodwill is recognised immediately in profit or loss unless the asset is carried at a revalued amount in accordance with another Standard. When an asset is carried at a revalued amount, the reversal is considered a revaluation increase and treated accordingly. [IAS 36:119] Normally, a revaluation increase is recognised in other comprehensive income and increases the revaluation surplus within equity. But to the extent that an impairment loss on the same revalued asset was previously recognised in profit or loss, a reversal of that impairment loss is recognised in profit or loss. [IAS 36:120]

After the reversal of an impairment loss, the depreciation (amortisation) charge for the asset is adjusted in future periods to allocate the asset's revised carrying amount, less its residual value (if any), on a systematic basis over its remaining useful life. [IAS 36:121]

10.4 Reversal of impairment loss for a cash-generating unit

A reversal of an impairment loss for a CGU should be allocated to increase the carrying amount of the assets of the unit, except for goodwill, pro rata based on the carrying amount of each asset in the unit. These increases in carrying amounts should be dealt with as reversals of impairment losses for individual assets in the same manner as discussed at **10.3**. [IAS 36:122]

In allocating a reversal of an impairment loss for a CGU, the carrying amount of an asset should not be increased above the lower of:

[IAS 36:123]

- its recoverable amount (if determinable); and

- the carrying amount that would have been determined (net of amortisation/ depreciation) had no impairment loss been recognised for the asset in prior years. (Any further increase would constitute a revaluation.)

> It follows, therefore, that the reversal of the impairment loss will be allocated only between those assets (excluding goodwill) against which the original loss was allocated, though not necessarily in the same proportions.

If this results in a reversal being allocated to an asset which is less than its pro rata share of the reversal, the amount of the reversal of the impairment loss that would otherwise have been allocated to the asset should be allocated to the other assets of the unit, other than goodwill, on a pro rata basis. [IAS 36:123]

10.5 Reversal of impairment loss for goodwill not permitted

When an impairment loss has previously been recognised for goodwill, that impairment loss should not be reversed in a subsequent period. [IAS 36:124]

> The IASB has concluded that, because any increase in the recoverable amount of goodwill in the periods following the recognition of an impairment loss is likely to be an increase in internally generated goodwill, rather than a reversal of an impairment loss, it is inappropriate to recognise any such increase in recoverable amount (because it would result in the recognition of internally generated goodwill, which is prohibited by IAS 38).

IFRIC Interpretation 10 *Interim Financial Reporting and Impairment* states that an entity should not reverse an impairment loss recognised in a previous interim period in respect of goodwill. For entities that have not yet adopted IFRS 9, a similar requirement applies in respect of investments in equity instruments and financial assets carried at cost. For further discussion of IFRIC 10, see **5.6.16.2** in **chapter A32**.

11 Disclosure

11.1 Amended disclosure requirements issued in May 2013

IAS 36 was amended in May 2013 by *Recoverable Amount Disclosures for Non-Financial Assets*, which provided clarification on a number of the disclosure requirements in the Standard. These amendments are effective for annual periods beginning on or after 1 January 2014, with earlier application permitted.

The amendments made in May 2013 have the following effects:

- to restrict the requirement to disclose the recoverable amount of an asset or a CGU to periods in which an impairment loss has been recognised or reversed. Consequential amendments to IAS 36 in May 2011 arising from IFRS 13 had a broader impact than the IASB had intended; in particular, they introduced a requirement to disclose in every reporting period the recoverable amount of each CGU or group of CGU's to which a significant portion of the overall carrying amount of goodwill (or other intangible assets with indefinite useful lives) had been allocated. The IASB had intended to limit such disclosures to reporting periods in which an impairment loss was recognised or reversed. Amendments to IAS 36:130(e) and IAS 36:134(c) (see **11.4** and **11.7.1**, respectively,) are designed to achieve this objective; and

- to expand and clarify the disclosure requirements applicable when the recoverable amount of an asset or a CGU has been determined on the basis of fair value less costs of disposal (see amendments to IAS 36:130(f) in **11.4**).

Entities are not permitted to apply the May 2013 amendments unless they have also adopted IFRS 13 *Fair Value Measurement*. In the period in which an entity applies the May 2013 amendments for the first time, it should not restate disclosures for comparative period(s) unless it also applies IFRS 13 in those comparative period(s).

11.2 Disclosure – general

For each class of assets (defined as a grouping of assets of similar nature and use in the operations of the entity), the financial statements should disclose the amount of:

[IAS 36:126]

(a) impairment losses recognised in profit or loss during the period and the line item(s) of the statement of comprehensive income in which those impairment losses are included;

(b) reversals of impairment losses recognised in profit or loss during the period and the line item(s) of the statement of comprehensive income in which those impairment losses are reversed;

(c) impairment losses on revalued assets recognised in other comprehensive income during the period; and

(d) reversals of impairment losses on revalued assets recognised in other comprehensive income during the period.

This information may be presented in the reconciliation of the carrying amounts of property, plant and equipment, intangible assets, or elsewhere as appropriate. [IAS 36:128]

Example 11.2

Impairment loss not included within depreciation expense

An entity recognises an impairment loss in respect of certain intangible assets with indefinite useful lives in the fourth quarter of 20X1 in accordance with IAS 36. The entity has certain debt covenants that state that it must maintain a specified multiple of EBITDA (earnings before interest, taxes, depreciation and amortisation).

Impairment losses recognised in accordance with IAS 36 should not be included within depreciation expense. IAS 16 *Property, Plant and Equipment* defines depreciation as the systematic allocation of the depreciable amount of an asset over its useful life. The recognition of an impairment loss is as a result of a valuation exercise, rather than an allocation exercise, and should not be presented in a manner that might encourage the belief that it is part of the regular allocation (i.e. the depreciation expense).

11.3 Entities reporting segment information

Entities that report segment information in accordance with IFRS 8 *Operating Segments* (see **chapter A30**) are required to disclose the following for each reportable segment:

[IAS 36:129]

(a) the amount of impairment losses recognised in profit or loss and in other comprehensive income during the period; and

(b) the amount of reversals of impairment losses recognised in profit or loss and in other comprehensive income during the period.

11.4 Impairment losses recognised or reversed in the period

The following disclosures are required in respect of an individual asset (including goodwill) or a CGU for which an impairment loss has been recognised or reversed during the period:

[IAS 36:130]

(a) the events and circumstances that led to the recognition (reversal) of the loss;

(b) the amount of the loss recognised (reversed);

(c) for an individual asset:

  (i)   the nature of the asset; and

  (ii) for entities that apply IFRS 8, the reportable segment to which the asset belongs (see **chapter A30**);

(d) for a CGU:

  (i)   a description of the CGU (such as whether it is a product line, a plant, a business operation, a geographical area, a reportable segment or other);

  (ii) the amount of the loss recognised or reversed by class of assets and, for entities that apply IFRS 8, by reportable segment; and

  (iii) if the aggregation of assets for identifying the CGU has changed since the previous estimate of the CGU's recoverable amount (if any), the entity should describe the current and former ways of aggregating assets and the reasons for changing the way the CGU is identified;

(e) the recoverable amount of the asset or CGU, and whether the recoverable amount of the asset or CGU is its fair value less costs of disposal or its value in use;

(f) if the recoverable amount is fair value less costs of disposal:

  (i)   the level of the fair value hierarchy (see IFRS 13) within which the fair value measurement of the asset or CGU is categorised in its entirety (without taking into account whether the 'costs of disposal' are observable);

  (ii) for fair value measurements categorised within Level 2 and Level 3 of the fair value hierarchy, a description of the valuation technique(s) used to measure fair value less costs of disposal. If there has been a change in valuation technique, the entity should disclose that change and the reason(s) for making it; and

  (iii) for fair value measurements categorised within Level 2 and Level 3 of the fair value hierarchy, each key assumption on which management has based its determination of fair value less costs of disposal. Key assumptions are those to which the asset's or CGU's recoverable amount is most sensitive. The entity should also disclose the discount rate(s) used in the current measurement and previous measurement if fair value less costs of disposal is measured using a present value technique; and

(g) if recoverable amount is value in use, the discount rate(s) used in the current estimate and previous estimate (if any) of value in use.

11.5 Other impairment losses/reversals material in aggregate to the financial statements

If impairment losses recognised (reversed) during the period, other than those disclosed under **11.4**, are material in aggregate to the financial statements taken as a whole, the entity should disclose a brief description of the following:

[IAS 36:131]

(a) the main classes of assets affected by those impairment losses (reversals); and

(b) the main events and circumstances that led to the recognition (or reversal) of those impairment losses.

11.6   Unallocated goodwill

If any portion of the goodwill acquired in a business combination during the period has not been allocated to a CGU (group of CGUs) at the end of the reporting period (see **8.2.8.3**), the amount of the unallocated goodwill should be disclosed, together with the reasons why that amount remains unallocated. [IAS 36:133]

11.7   Cash-generating units containing goodwill or intangible assets with indefinite useful lives

11.7.1   *Information to be disclosed for cash-generating units to which significant goodwill or indefinite-life intangible assets have been allocated*

The wording below reflects the amendments to IAS 36:134(c) in May 2013 (see also the discussion at **11.1**). Previously, the Standard required disclosure, in every reporting period, of the recoverable amount of each CGU or group of CGU's to which a significant portion of the overall carrying amount of goodwill (or other intangible assets with indefinite useful lives) had been allocated. The IASB had intended to limit such disclosures to reporting periods in which an impairment loss was recognised or reversed. To achieve this effect, the requirement to disclose the recoverable amount of each CGU or group of CGUs has been moved from IAS 36:134(c) to IAS 36:130(f) (see **11.4**)

The following information should be disclosed for each CGU (or group of CGUs) for which the carrying amount of goodwill or intangible assets with indefinite useful lives allocated to that unit (or group of units) is significant in comparison with the entity's total carrying amount of goodwill or intangible assets with indefinite useful lives:

[IAS 36:134]

(a) the carrying amount of goodwill allocated to the unit (or group of units);

(b) the carrying amount of intangible assets with indefinite useful lives allocated to the unit (or group of units);

(c) the basis on which the unit's (or group of units') recoverable amount has been determined (i.e. value in use or fair value less costs of disposal);

(d) if the unit's (or group of units') recoverable amount is based on value in use:

(i) each key assumption on which management has based its cash flow projections for the period covered by the most recent budgets/forecasts. Key assumptions are those to which the unit's (or group of units') recoverable amount is most sensitive;

(ii) a description of management's approach to determining the value(s) assigned to each key assumption, whether those value(s) reflect past experience or, if appropriate, are consistent with external sources of information, and, if not, how and why they differ from past experience or external sources of information;

(iii) the period over which management has projected cash flows based on financial budgets/forecasts approved by management and, when a period greater than five years is used for a CGU (or group of CGUs), an explanation as to why that longer period is justified;

(iv) the growth rate used to extrapolate cash flow projections beyond the period covered by the most recent budgets/forecasts, and the justification for using any growth rate that exceeds the long-term average growth rate for the products, industries, or country or countries in which the entity operates, or for the market to which the unit (or group of units) is dedicated; and

(v) the discount rate(s) applied to the cash flow projections;

(e) if the unit's (or group of units') recoverable amount is based on fair value less costs of disposal, the valuation technique(s) used to measure fair value less costs of disposal. An entity is not required to provide the disclosures required by IFRS 13. If fair value less costs of disposal is not measured using a quoted price for an identical unit (or group of units), the following information should also be disclosed:

(i) each key assumption on which management has based its determination of fair value less costs of disposal. Key assumptions are those to which the unit's (or group of units') recoverable amount is most sensitive;

(ii) a description of management's approach to determining the value (or values) assigned to each key assumption, whether those values reflect past experience or, if appropriate, are consistent with external sources of information, and, if not, how and why they differ from past experience or external sources of information;

(iii) the level of the IFRS 13 fair value hierarchy (see **section 10** of **chapter A6**) within which the fair value measurement is categorised in its entirety (without giving regard to the observability of 'costs of disposal'); and

(iv) if there has been a change in valuation technique, the change and the reason(s) for making it.

In addition, if fair value less costs of disposal is measured using discounted cash flow projections, the following information should also be disclosed:

(v)   the period over which management has projected cash flows;

(vi) the growth rate used to extrapolate cash flow projections; and

(vii) the discount rate(s) applied to the cash flow projections; and

(f)   if a reasonably possible change in a key assumption on which management has based its determination of the unit's (or group of units') recoverable amount would cause the unit's (or group of units') carrying amount to exceed its recoverable amount:

(i)   the amount by which the unit's (or group of units') recoverable amount exceeds its carrying amount;

(ii)   the value assigned to the key assumption; and

(iii) the amount by which the value assigned to the key assumption must change, after incorporating any consequential effects of that change on the other variables used to measure recoverable amount, in order for the unit's (or group of units') recoverable amount to be equal to its carrying amount.

11.7.2   *Information to be disclosed for cash-generating units to which insignificant goodwill or indefinite-life intangible assets have been allocated*

If some or all of the carrying amount of goodwill or intangible assets with indefinite useful lives is allocated across multiple CGUs (or groups of CGUs), and the amount so allocated to each unit (or group of units) is not significant in comparison with the entity's total carrying amount of goodwill or intangible assets with indefinite useful lives, that fact should be disclosed, together with the aggregate carrying amount of goodwill or intangible assets with indefinite useful lives allocated to those units (or groups of units). [IAS 36:135]

In addition to the requirements set out in the previous paragraph, if the recoverable amounts of any such units (or groups of units) are based on the same key assumption(s) and the aggregate carrying amount of goodwill or intangible assets with indefinite useful lives allocated to them is significant in comparison with the entity's total carrying amount of goodwill or intangible assets with indefinite useful lives, the entity should disclose that fact, together with:

[IAS 36:135]

(a)   the aggregate carrying amount of goodwill allocated to those units (or groups of units);

(b)   the aggregate carrying amount of intangible assets with indefinite useful lives allocated to those units (or groups of units);

(c)   a description of each key assumption;

(d)   a description of management's approach to determining the value assigned to each key assumption, whether those value(s) reflect past experience or, if appropriate, are consistent with external sources of information, and, if not, how and why they differ from past experience or external sources of information; and

(e) if a reasonably possible change in the key assumptions would cause the aggregate of the units' (or groups of units') carrying amounts to exceed the aggregate of their recoverable amounts:

(i) the amount by which the aggregate of the units' (or groups of units') recoverable amounts exceeds the aggregate of their carrying amounts;

(ii) the value(s) assigned to the key assumption(s); and

(iii) the amount by which the value(s) assigned to the key assumption(s) must change, after incorporating any consequential effects of that change on the other variables used to measure recoverable amount, in order for the aggregate of the units' (or groups of units') recoverable amounts to be equal to the aggregate of their carrying amounts.

As discussed at **5.2** and **5.3.4**, provided that specified criteria are met, the most recent detailed calculation made in a preceding period of the recoverable amount of a CGU (or group of CGUs) may be carried forward and used in the impairment test for that unit (or group of units) in the current period. When this is the case, the information for that unit (or group of units) that is incorporated into the disclosures required by IAS 36:134 and IAS 36:135 (set out above) relates to the carried forward calculation of recoverable amount. [IAS 36:136]

The comprehensive disclosures required by this section are illustrated in illustrative example 9 accompanying IAS 36.

12   Future developments

In September 2014, the IASB published ED/2014/4 *Measuring Quoted Investments in Subsidiaries, Joint Ventures, and Associates at Fair Value (Proposed amendments to IFRS 10, IFRS 12, IAS 27, IAS 28 and IAS 36 and Illustrative Examples for IFRS 13)*. The proposed amendments to IAS 36 in ED/2014/4 would apply when the recoverable amount of an investment in a subsidiary, joint venture or an associate which is quoted in an active market is assessed on the basis of fair value less cost of disposal. In such circumstances, the fair value of the investment would be determined on the basis of the quoted market prices without adjustment.

The comment period on the exposure draft closed on 16 January 2015. At the time of writing, the IASB is conducting further analysis and research on this issue and the amendments are not expected to be finalised until 2016.

A11 Inventories

Contents

1 Introduction

1.1 Overview of IAS 2

The accounting treatment for most types of inventory is prescribed in IAS 2 *Inventories*, which provides guidance for determining the cost of inventories and for subsequently recognising an expense, including any write-down to net realisable value. It also outlines acceptable methods of determining cost, including specific identification (in some cases), first-in first-out (FIFO) and weighted average cost.

1.2 Amendments to IAS 2 since the last edition of this manual

None. IAS 2 was most recently amended in May 2014.

2 Scope

2.1 Definition – inventories

IAS 2 is required to be applied when accounting for inventories (other than those specifically excluded – see **2.2**), which the Standard defines as assets:

[IAS 2:6]

- held for sale in the ordinary course of business;

- in the process of production for such sale; or

- in the form of materials or supplies to be consumed in the production process or in the rendering of services.

Inventories encompass:

[IAS 2:8]

- goods purchased and held for resale (e.g. merchandise purchased by a retailer and held for resale, or land and other property held for resale);

- finished goods produced, or work in progress being produced, by the entity; and

- materials and supplies awaiting use in the production process.

Example 2.1A

Classification of assets acquired for sale in the ordinary course of business

Entity X, a lessor, leases assets ordinarily under three-year agreements. At the end of the lease term, the lessee has the option either to return or to acquire the asset. Some of the leases contain an extension option, which allows

---

the lessee an additional three months to return or to acquire the asset. The extension option must be exercised prior to the end of the main lease term.

Entity X enters into 'residual value guarantee' contracts with Entity A, a third party. Under these contracts, Entity A will purchase the assets from Entity X at the end of each lease term at a predetermined price. Entity A receives a fee in return for providing the residual value guarantee.

When an extension option is exercised by the lessee, ownership of the asset is transferred to Entity A at the end of the main lease term for the predetermined price. During the extension period, Entity X passes the rental income to Entity A. At the end of the extension period, Entity A sells the asset either in the market or to the lessee. Rental income received by Entity A during the extension period is considered incidental to Entity A's principal activities, which are the provision of residual value guarantee contracts and selling the assets acquired.

In order to determine how to recognise the assets in the period from acquisition at the end of the main lease term to the point of sale, Entity A must establish how the assets are used in the business, i.e. whether they represent inventories or property, plant and equipment.

In the circumstances described, Entity A acquires the assets at the end of the main lease term to profit from selling them in the market. In accordance with IAS 2:6, the assets are classified as inventories because they are assets "held for sale in the ordinary course of business".

The assets acquired do not represent property, plant and equipment, in accordance with IAS 16 *Property, Plant and Equipment*, because they are not held primarily for rental by Entity A to others and are not expected to be used during more than one period.

Example 2.1B

Classification and measurement of pipeline fill

Company A operates a pipeline to transport crude oil. Company A does not produce or distribute crude oil; it merely provides the use of its pipeline to the buyer and seller in a contract for a usage fee. The seller and buyer independently negotiate the sales price, and either the buyer or the seller pays a fee to Company A for transporting the oil purchased/sold through its pipeline.

The pipeline needs to be full of oil at all times to be operational. Therefore, during initial construction of the pipeline, Company A purchases oil to fill the pipeline. Once the pipeline is operational, Company A charges a fixed fee for its transportation services and, in effect, swaps crude oil pushed into the pipeline by a seller for crude oil of the same grade and quality delivered to the customer at the exit point of the pipeline. Company A bears the risk of loss due to theft or line loss in excess of the maximums allowed under the contract. Such losses are rare and normally arise as the result of a pipeline spill that is covered by insurance.

> The pipeline fill meets the definition of an asset and should be recognised at cost when acquired. The pipeline fill does not meet the definition of property, plant and equipment under paragraph 6 of IAS 16. Rather, it should be classified as inventories in accordance with IAS 2:6 because it is held "in the form of materials or supplies to be consumed in the production process or in the rendering of services".
>
> Because an accounting transaction does not take place at the time of each swap of crude oil, no step-up in the value of inventories is recognised. The pipeline fill is measured at the lower of cost and net realisable value throughout the term of the pipeline's operations in accordance with IAS 2:9.

See **example 9.4.1** in **chapter A14** (or, for entities that have not yet adopted IFRS 15 *Revenue from Contracts with Customers*, **example 6.2.1E** in **appendix A1**) for a discussion of retention of title clauses.

The classification of spare parts, stand-by equipment and servicing equipment as inventories or property, plant and equipment is addressed at **3.2** in **chapter A7**.

IFRIC 20 *Stripping Costs in the Production Phase of a Surface Mine* addresses the classification of costs relating to production stripping activity in a surface mine as inventories or as a non-current asset – see **section 10** of **chapter A7**.

Supplies purchased during the research phase of a project, for example in the pharmaceutical industry, will not meet the definition of inventories prior to a decision to proceed with commercial production. Nevertheless, such supplies may qualify for recognition as an asset (see **example 4.8.4** in **chapter A9** for further dicussion).

2.2   Inventories excluded from the scope of IAS 2

IAS 2 applies to all inventories, except:

[IAS 2:2]

- financial instruments (addressed by IAS 32 *Financial Instruments: Presentation* and either IFRS 9 *Financial Instruments* or, for entities that have not yet adopted IFRS 9, IAS 39 *Financial Instruments: Recognition and Measurement* – see **Volume B** and **Volume C**, respectively); and

- biological assets related to agricultural activity and agricultural produce at the point of harvest (addressed by IAS 41 *Agriculture* – see **chapter A38**).

For entities that have not yet adopted IFRS 15 *Revenue from Contracts with Customers*, IAS 2:2 also refers to the exclusion from the scope of IAS 2 of work in progress arising under construction contracts, including directly related service contracts (which, for entities that have not yet adopted IFRS 15, are accounted for under IAS 11 *Construction Contracts* – see **appendix A2**).

IAS 2 does not apply to the measurement of inventories held by:

[IAS 2:3]

- producers of agricultural and forest products, agricultural produce after harvest, and minerals and mineral products, to the extent that they are measured at net realisable value in accordance with well-established practices in those industries; or

- commodity broker-traders who measure their inventories at fair value less costs to sell.

Although inventories held by the types of entities referred to in IAS 2:3 are excluded from the measurement requirements of IAS 2, the Standard requires that when such inventories are measured at net realisable value/ fair value less costs to sell, changes in those values are to be recognised in profit or loss in the period of change. [IAS 2:3] The other requirements of IAS 2 (e.g. regarding presentation and disclosure) apply in the normal way to such inventories.

For the avoidance of doubt, note that the requirements of IAS 2 apply in their entirety to:

- property intended for sale in the ordinary course of business or in the process of construction or development for such sale (e.g. property acquired exclusively with a view to subsequent disposal in the near future or for development and resale); and

- inventories held by producers of agricultural and forest products, agricultural produce after harvest, and minerals and mineral products, when they are not measured at net realisable value in accordance with well-established practices in those industries.

2.3   Costs incurred to fulfil contracts with customers

Costs incurred to fulfil a contract with a customer that do not give rise to inventories (or assets within the scope of another Standard – for example, IAS 16 *Property, Plant and Equipment* or IAS 38 *Intangible Assets*) are accounted for in accordance with IFRS 15 *Revenue from Contracts with Customers*. [IAS 2:8]

This cross reference to the requirements of IFRS 15 was added in May 2014 as a consequential amendment arising from that Standard. At the same time, the reference in IAS 2:8 to the nature of inventories recognised by a service provider was removed.

2.4   Inventories on consignment

In some industries it is common for a manufacturer to supply goods to a distributor 'on consignment'; the manufacturer retains the substantial risks and rewards of ownership and legal title to the goods until some future predetermined event occurs (e.g. sale to a third-party customer) which triggers transfer of the legal title to the distributor.

In such circumstances, the distributor (i.e. the buyer) will need to determine when it is appropriate to recognise inventories on consignment as an asset in its statement of financial position. IFRSs do not provide any guidance on accounting for consignment arrangements from the point of view of the buyer and, therefore, in accordance with IAS 8 *Accounting Policies, Changes in Accounting Estimates and Errors*, the distributor should determine an accounting treatment for inventories on consignment that results in information that is relevant and reliable. Until it is established that the transfer to the distributor is substantive, the goods should be treated as the manufacturer's inventories and excluded from the distributor's statement of financial position.

Paragraphs B77 and B78 of IFRS 15 *Revenue from Contracts with Customers* provides specific guidance on determining whether an arrangement is a consignment arrangement (see **9.4.4** in **chapter A14**) and require that revenue is not recognised (and, therefore, the inventory is not derecognised) by the manufacturer upon delivery of the goods if the delivered product is held on consignment.

For entities that have not yet adopted IFRS 15, IAS 18 *Revenue* provides specific guidance on consignment sales under which the recipient of the goods (the buyer) undertakes to sell goods on behalf of the shipper (the seller) and requires that revenue be "recognised by the shipper when the goods are sold by the recipient to a third party" [IAS 18:IE2(c)]. Equally, the risks and rewards of consignment inventories may not pass to the distributor until it has sold the inventories to a third-party customer and the manufacturer (the seller) would therefore not derecognise the inventories until that stage in the arrangement.

3   Measurement of inventories

3.1   Inventories to be measured at the lower of cost and net realisable value

Inventories are measured at the lower of cost and net realisable value. [IAS 2:9] The comparison of cost with net realisable value should, in principle, be carried out on an item-by-item basis but, if this is impracticable, groups of similar items may be considered together. It is unacceptable to compare the total net realisable value of all inventories with their total purchase price or production cost.

> The introduction to IAS 2 makes clear that, with the limited exception of the classes of inventory listed in **section 2** (i.e. those outside the scope of the Standard and those exempt from its measurement rules), it is not acceptable to adopt an accounting policy of carrying inventories at a current value.

3.2   Measurement of cost

3.2.1   Components of cost

IAS 2:10 specifies that the cost of inventories comprises:

- all costs of purchase (see **3.2.2**);
- costs of conversion (see **3.2.3**); and
- other costs incurred in bringing the inventories to their present location and condition (see **3.2.4**).

3.2.2   Costs of purchase

3.2.2.1   Items included in the cost of purchase

The costs of purchase of inventories include:

[IAS 2:11]

- purchase price;
- import duties and other taxes that are not recoverable by the entity (e.g. associated VAT paid to the extent that an entity cannot reclaim it);
- transport and handling costs; and
- other costs directly attributable to the acquisition of finished goods, materials and services.

Any trade discounts or rebates received are deducted in determining the costs of purchase of inventory.

3.2.2.2   Discounts and rebates

> **Example 3.2.2.2A**
>
> **Discounts and rebates**
>
> Entity A is a retailer that acquires products from manufacturers, which are sold to end users. The manufacturers grant incentives to Entity A on one of two bases:

- a 10 per cent prompt settlement discount on all purchases of inventories settled within 30 days of purchase; or
- rebates based on the volume of merchandise purchased or sold.

How should these discounts and rebates be accounted for by Entity A in each of the following circumstances:

- *Entity A acts as principal in the purchase of products from manufacturers and the sale of products to end users?*
- *Entity A acts as an agent of the manufacturers in making sales to end users?*

Entity A acts as principal

If Entity A acts as principal in the sale and purchase of products then, in accordance with IAS 2:11, rebates and discounts that have been received as a reduction in the purchase price of inventories should be taken into consideration in the measurement of the cost of those inventories.

Prompt settlement (cash) discount

Entity A should deduct prompt settlement discounts from the cost of the inventories. When measuring the cost of the inventories, Entity A should estimate the expected settlement discount to be received from the supplier.

Volume rebates

Similarly, volume rebates should be deducted from the cost of inventories. See **example 3.2.2.2B** for more detailed considerations regarding when the rebate should be recognised.

Entity A acts as agent

If Entity A is *not* purchasing the products as principal, and is instead acting as an agent, any rebate received will form part of the net commission revenue earned.

The distinction between an entity acting as a principal and as an agent is addressed at **3.6** in **chapter A14** (or, for entities that have not yet adopted IFRS 15, at **3.2** in **appendix A1**).

Example 3.2.2.2B

Cash refund based on volume of purchases

On 1 July 20X1, in a binding arrangement, a vendor offers a cash refund of CU1,000 to a customer if during the 12 months to 30 June 20X2 the customer purchases 1,000 units of a particular product. Historically, on average, the customer has purchased 1,700 units each year and there have been no significant changes in the trading relationship in the current period.

How should the customer account for the refund to be received from the vendor in its financial statements for the year ending 31 December 20X1 if the 1,000 unit threshold has not yet been reached?

The cash refund constitutes a volume rebate, to be accounted for as a reduction in the cost of inventories (see IAS 2:11, as discussed above). IAS 2:11 does not, however, specify the treatment of refunds or rebates that are anticipated but have not yet been 'earned' or the allocation of refunds or rebates to items of inventory.

Anticipation of refunds not yet earned

The question regarding refunds or rebates that are anticipated but that have not yet been earned in full is addressed in IAS 34 *Interim Financial Reporting* in the context of the preparation of interim financial statements, and it is appropriate to apply the principle established in IAS 34 to the preparation of annual financial statements in the circumstances described.

IAS 34:B23 states as follows.

"Volume rebates or discounts and other contractual changes in the prices of raw materials, labour, or other purchased goods and services are anticipated in interim periods, by both the payer and the recipient, if it is probable that they have been earned or will take effect. Thus, contractual rebates and discounts are anticipated but discretionary rebates and discounts are not anticipated because the resulting asset or liability would not satisfy the conditions in the *Conceptual Framework* that an asset must be a resource controlled by the entity as a result of a past event and that a liability must be a present obligation whose settlement is expected to result in an outflow of resources."

Therefore, in the circumstances described, if it is probable that the customer will purchase at least 1,000 units in the specified period (e.g. forecast purchase levels are in line with historical volumes), the refund (which is contractual) should be accrued as the units are purchased.

Units to which the refund should be allocated

The refund should be allocated to the units of inventory purchased on a systematic and rational basis. If the vendor's offer of a cash refund is a one-off incentive, and not expected to be repeated, it may be appropriate to account for the refund as a reduction in the cost of the first 1,000 units purchased, because the customer's entitlement to the refund is based only on the purchase of 1,000 units of inventory. Conversely, if the vendor routinely offers such a refund on an annual basis but on the condition that the customer purchases all inventories of this type from the vendor (i.e. an exclusive supply arrangement), it may be more appropriate to regard the refund as relating to all purchases in the year and account for it as a reduction in the cost of all units purchased. This assessment should be made on the basis of the specific facts and circumstances, including all relevant contractual terms.

3.2.2.3   Direct materials and wastage

When raw material is unavoidably subject to wastage and spoilage during production, it is generally appropriate to include the cost of such normal scrapping and wastage as part of the direct material cost of the product. Alternatively, if more practicable, the cost of direct materials unavoidably wasted or spoiled may be included in overheads as part of the costs of conversion. It is not appropriate, however, to include abnormal wastage in the carrying amount of inventories (see IAS 2:16(a)).

3.2.3   Costs of conversion

3.2.3.1   Items included in the cost of purchase

The costs of conversion of inventories include costs directly related to the units of production such as:

[IAS 2:12]

- direct labour, including all related employment taxes, and benefits and any share-based payment costs; and

- a systematic allocation of the fixed and variable production overheads incurred in converting materials into finished goods.

It is sometimes argued that overheads should be excluded from the cost of inventories on the grounds of prudence. Such an approach (sometimes called 'direct costing') is not acceptable under IAS 2, which requires a systematic allocation of production overheads.

Similarly, 'marginal costing' approaches, under which only costs that vary directly with volume of output are included in the measurement of inventories and costs that accrue on a time basis (such as some overheads) are excluded, are not acceptable under IAS 2 because they do not result in the allocation of fixed production overheads.

3.2.3.2   Direct labour

The cost of wages of employees directly engaged in production should be allocated to production activities on the basis of normal operating conditions. Labour costs that are the result of operating inefficiencies, such as abnormal idle capacity or abnormal rectification work, should not be included in inventory valuation. [IAS 2:13]

3.2.3.3   Overhead costs

The allocation of fixed production overheads to inventories should be based on the normal capacity of the production facilities, which is the production expected to be achieved on average over a number of periods under normal circumstances, taking into account the loss of capacity resulting from planned maintenance. The actual level of production may be used if it approximates to normal capacity. [IAS 2:13]

> Fixed production overheads are those indirect costs of production that remain relatively constant regardless of the volume of production. They may include:
>
> • depreciation;
>
> • rent of the factory building;
>
> • maintenance of the factory building and equipment; and
>
> • factory management and administration.
>
> When an entity adopts the revaluation model for items of property, plant and equipment (see **section 6** of **chapter A7**), it should consider, for the purpose of inventory valuation, depreciation based on the revalued amounts of those items.

When production levels are abnormally low, unallocated fixed overheads are recognised in profit or loss in the period in which they are incurred. In periods of abnormally high production, the amount of fixed overhead allocated to each unit of production is decreased so that inventories are not measured at above cost.

Variable production overheads are those indirect costs of production that vary directly, or nearly directly, with the volume of production. [IAS 2:12] Variable overheads may include indirect materials and indirect labour. They are allocated to each unit of production on the basis of the actual use of the production facilities.

> Overheads that are properly classified as selling costs should not be included in the cost of inventories
>
> Other non-production overheads should only be included when this is justified by exceptional circumstances. When firm sales contracts have been entered into for the provision of goods or services to customer specification, overheads (other than selling costs) relating to design, incurred before manufacture, may be included in arriving at cost.
>
> The process for determining the amount of overheads to be carried forward in inventories can be considered under two headings: (1) identifying the overheads to be included, and (2) allocating those overheads to production in a logical manner. It is necessary first to analyse overheads by function between production, marketing and distribution, and administration. There are practical problems in performing this analysis. For example, management salaries may include an element of supervision of production as well as of administration, and pension

costs are likely to cover employees in the production function as well as those in sales and general administration departments. Central services departments, such as accounts, may provide identifiable services for production. Costs should be allocated over the functions on a reasonable basis, which should be applied consistently and reviewed regularly.

The method for allocating overheads to production should be one that is appropriate to the nature of the product and the method of production. The most popular methods for allocating overheads are:

- by way of a labour-hour or machine-hour rate;
- in proportion to direct labour costs;
- in proportion to material costs;
- in proportion to prime costs; and
- equally to each unit of production. (This is only appropriate when a single product is being produced in a given cost centre.)

Whichever method for allocating overheads is adopted, the overheads should be allocated on the basis of the entity's normal level of activity. Overhead costs that are the result of operating inefficiencies, such as abnormal idle capacity or abnormal rectification work, should not be included in the inventory carrying amount.

Example 3.2.3.3

Lease costs included in the cost of inventories

An entity enters into a 99-year lease of land with the intention of constructing a building. The building will be sold together with any remaining lease interest over the land and is, therefore, classified as inventories when construction commences. Because of various required legal permits, construction begins in Year 6 of the lease and is completed in Year 10.

The operating lease expense incurred for the land (as determined in accordance with paragraph 33 of IAS 17 *Leases*) should be included in the cost of inventories. IAS 2:10 states that the cost of inventories should include all costs of "bringing the inventories to their present location and condition". The operating lease expense incurred for the land is required to construct the building and is, therefore, a cost of bringing the building to a condition in which it can be sold. However, only the operating lease expense incurred during the period of construction (i.e. Years 6 to 10 – the period during which the entity undertakes activities that are necessary to prepare the asset for intended sale) should be capitalised. All operating lease expense incurred outside of this period must be recognised in profit or loss.

3.2.3.4 Allocation of cost to joint products and by-products

Sometimes two products may result from the production process when joint products are produced or when a product and a by-product are produced. In such cases, when it is difficult to allocate costs between the two, a rational and consistent allocation method is chosen. For example, the cost of joint products may be allocated on the basis of relative sales values either at the stage in production when each product becomes identifiable or when production is complete. If an immaterial by-product results from production of the main product, the net realisable value of the by-product is often deducted from the cost of the main product. Because the value of the by-product is immaterial, this deduction does not result in the cost of the main product being understated. [IAS 2:14]

3.2.4 Other costs

3.2.4.1 Other costs to be included in the cost of inventories

Other costs are included in the cost of inventories only to the extent that they are incurred in bringing the inventories to their present location and condition.

3.2.4.2 Costs to be excluded from the cost of inventories

IAS 2:16 gives the following as examples of costs that should be excluded from the cost of inventories and recognised as expenses in the period in which they are incurred:

- abnormal amounts of wasted materials, labour, or other production costs;

- storage costs, unless those costs are necessary in the production process before a further production stage;

- administrative overheads that do not contribute to bringing inventories to their present location and condition; and

- selling costs.

Example 3.2.4.2

Other costs incurred in bringing inventories to their present location and condition

Company A, which redevelops and then sells real estate, purchases a disused petrol station and obtains planning permission from the local authority to redevelop the site for residential purposes. Planning permission is granted subject to the condition that Company A will also develop a recreation amenity on an adjacent site owned by the local authority.

Company A should include the costs incurred in developing the adjacent recreation amenity in the cost of its development property inventories. These

---

costs meet the definition of "costs incurred in bringing inventories to their present location and condition" because they were a necessary cost of redeveloping the disused petrol station into a residential site.

Specific attention should be paid to costs of distribution and transportation associated with moving inventories to their present location and condition for sale, which may include the following:

- transportation of goods from the supplier;

- transportation or distribution at an intermediate stage in the production process;

- transportation or distribution of inventories to a temporary storage location (e.g. warehouse), including costs incurred for receiving, marking, processing, picking and repackaging; and

- transportation or distribution of inventories from a warehouse or distribution centre to the initial point of sale.

Costs incurred in transporting an item from a warehouse to its initial point of sale should be capitalised to inventories. However, costs associated with moving inventories from one point of sale to another (e.g. transport of goods between stores) should not be included in the cost of inventories because the goods were already in a condition and location for sale before the move.

3.2.4.3   Borrowing costs

The extent to which borrowing costs should be included in the cost of inventories is determined on the basis of the requirements of IAS 23 *Borrowing Costs*.

IAS 23 expressly states that "inventories that are manufactured, or otherwise produced, over a short period of time, are not qualifying assets". Only inventories that take a 'substantial' period of time to get ready for their intended sale or use can meet the definition of a qualifying asset (see **section 3.2** of **chapter A18** for a discussion of what should be considered a 'substantial' period of time).

An example of circumstances when it would be appropriate to include borrowing costs in the cost of inventories is when the reporting entity holds maturing inventories (such as whisky). The maturing period is a necessary part of the period of production and borrowing costs incurred during that period are attributable to bringing the product to its existing condition. Such borrowing costs may therefore appropriately be included in the cost of inventories under IAS 2. See **3.5.3** in **chapter A18** for a discussion of the appropriate timing for cessation of capitalisation of borrowing costs incurred in respect of such inventories.

IAS 23 includes an optional scope exemption which allows an entity not to apply that Standard to inventories that are manufactured, or otherwise produced, in large quantities on a repetitive basis. The exemption is optional; therefore, an entity can choose, as a matter of accounting policy, whether to apply the requirements of IAS 23 to borrowing costs that relate to inventories produced in large quantities on a repetitive basis.

3.2.4.4   Inventories acquired on deferred settlement terms

When an entity acquires inventories on deferred settlement terms, the transaction may involve a financing element (e.g. when there is a difference between the amount paid and the amount that would have been paid if the inventories had been acquired on normal credit terms). In such circumstances, the financing element is not included in the cost of the inventories, but is recognised as an interest expense over the period of the financing. [IAS 2:18]

3.2.4.5   Inventories invoiced in a foreign currency

When inventories are invoiced in a foreign currency, the cost of those inventories should not include exchange differences.

Although this matter is not addressed directly in the body of IAS 2, the introduction to the Standard states that the capitalisation of such exchange differences is not permitted (see IAS 2:IN10). Prior to the revision of IAS 21 *The Effects of Changes in Foreign Exchange Rates* in 2003, that Standard had permitted the capitalisation of exchange differences in very limited circumstances. That exception to the general rule has been removed from IAS 21.

However, when the purchase of inventories in a foreign currency has been cash flow hedged under IFRS 9, the effective portion of hedging gains and losses previously accumulated in equity is included in the amount initially recognised for the inventories as a 'basis adjustment'(see **6.5.2** in **chapter B9**). For those entities that have not yet adopted IFRS 9, applying a basis adjustment under IAS 39 is optional (see **2.2.3** in **chapter C9**).

3.2.4.6   Transfer pricing

When the manufacturing process involves the transfer of work from one department to another, the transfer may be made at a price different from the cost incurred by the transferring department, either for reasons of convenience in accounting or as part of the system of management control. When this occurs, it is necessary for the purpose of determining the cost of closing inventories to adjust the carrying amount to actual cost, by eliminating any profits or losses arising at the separate department levels.

3.2.5 Costs of service providers

The paragraphs below refer to requirements under IAS 2:19, which have been deleted as a consequential amendment arising from IFRS 15 *Revenue from Contracts with Customers*. For entities that have adopted IFRS 15, costs incurred to fulfil a contract with a customer that do not give rise to inventories (or assets within the scope of another Standard – for example, IAS 16 *Property, Plant and Equipment* or IAS 38 *Intangible Assets*) are accounted for in accordance with that Standard (see **2.3**).

To the extent that service providers have inventories, they measure them at the costs of their production. These costs consist mainly of labour and overhead costs related to any parts of service projects for which revenue has not yet been recognised. The bulk of such costs would relate to the labour costs attributable to the personnel performing the work, with other overheads such as costs associated with photocopying and telephoning allocated to each assignment as appropriate. [IAS 2:19]

Prices charged by service providers will generally reflect a profit margin and an allocation for non-attributable overheads. These items will often be allocated to specific service projects in the internal costing system of the service provider. However, IAS 2 specifically prohibits their inclusion in the cost of inventories of service providers for reporting purposes. [IAS 2:19]

3.2.6 Cost of agricultural produce harvested from biological assets

Consistent with IAS 41 *Agriculture*, agricultural produce that an entity has harvested from its biological assets is measured on initial recognition at its fair value less costs to sell at the point of harvest. This is considered the cost of those inventories at that date for application of IAS 2. [IAS 2:20]

3.2.7 Techniques for the measurement of cost

Techniques for the measurement of cost, such as the standard cost method or the retail method, may be used provided that the results approximate to actual cost. [IAS 2:21]

The standard cost method is a method often used by manufacturing entities to allocate fixed and variable production overheads to each item of inventory produced. The standard cost of a unit of production is based on the budgeted amount of fixed production overheads and the normal capacity of the production facilities. Standard costs are revised to take account of variances that arise when actual performance varies from the budgeted figures on which the standard cost was based.

Standard costs should only be used for year-end inventory valuation purposes if they relate to actual costs incurred during the period. This can be achieved by frequent updating of standards or adjusting for the recorded variances.

The retail method may often be used by retailers who sell a large number of relatively homogeneous items with similar gross profit margins. The cost of inventories is determined by deducting the average margin from the selling price of the inventories. Such average margins take into account any reductions from the original selling price of items due to sales or other promotions. When the retail method is used, average margins are often determined on a departmental basis.

Example 3.2.7

Retail method

	Cost CU'000	Retail price CU'000
Opening inventories	300	400
Purchases	1,000	1,600
Total	1,300	2,000
Sales		(1,500)
Closing inventories at retail value		500

To convert closing inventories at retail value to closing inventories at cost, multiply by the ratio of cost:retail price for the year as follows.

CU1,300,000 / CU2,000,000 = 65%

65% × CU500,000 = CU325,000 = closing value of inventories

This method results in a valuation of inventories that approximates to average price and is, therefore, acceptable subject to certain constraints. The method only works satisfactorily for an entire department or shop if all of the lines held are expected to generate similar profit margins. For example, the inventories of a newsagent and confectioner normally include lines of widely differing profit margins; therefore, to arrive at an acceptable inventory valuation using the retail method, it is necessary to divide the inventories into categories according to the profit margin achieved. A further problem with the retail method arises if the selling price on slow-moving items has been marked down. If the normal gross profit percentage is then deducted from such items, this will result in them being valued below cost, giving a result that may well be excessively prudent and, accordingly, unacceptable. It is, therefore, necessary to ensure that the volume of marked-down items is insignificant or, alternatively, they should be segregated and valued separately.

3.2.8   Cost formulas

3.2.8.1   Use of cost formulas – general

Cost may be assigned to individual items of inventory, depending on their nature, either by the specific identification method or by the use of a cost formula. When the use of the specific identification method is inappropriate, IAS 2 allows a choice between two cost formulas: the weighted average formula and the first-in, first out (FIFO) formula. The use of the last-in, first out (LIFO) formula is prohibited under IAS 2. [IAS 2:IN13]

3.2.8.2   Cost formula to be consistent for inventories that are similar

Although IAS 2 permits a choice between the weighted average formula and FIFO for those inventories not measured by specific identification, it requires that the same cost formula is used for all inventories having a similar nature and use to the entity. For inventories with a different nature or use, a different cost formula may be justified. [IAS 2:25] Differences of geographical location or of tax rules will not, by themselves, justify the use of different cost formulas. [IAS 2:26]

3.2.8.3   Specific identification

IAS 2:23 requires that the cost of inventories of items that are not ordinarily interchangeable, and of goods or services produced and segregated for specific projects, should be assigned by using specific identification of their individual costs. The specific identification method entails assigning specific costs to identified items of inventory. Thus, this method is appropriate when items of inventory are produced for specific projects or when other items of inventory held could not be substituted for those items (e.g. antique cars or works of art).

The specific identification method is not appropriate for the routine production of inventories that are ordinarily interchangeable, because it would allow an entity to influence its reported profits by choosing which specific units to sell – and, hence, which otherwise identical products remain in inventory at the end of the reporting period – based on those products having higher or lower specific costs. Some entities may nevertheless have set up computer systems that allocate specific costs to inventories that are ordinarily interchangeable. Whether the valuations produced by such systems will be acceptable will depend on whether they reasonably approximate those that would have resulted from the use of cost formulas.

3.2.8.4   Weighted average cost

The weighted average cost formula assigns a value to each item of inventory based on the weighted average of items in inventories at the beginning of the period and the weighted average of items of inventories purchased or produced during the period. Depending on the inventory system of the reporting entity, the weighted average cost is calculated either on a periodic basis or on a perpetual basis as the inventories are received.

Example 3.2.8.4

Weighted average cost

An entity had opening inventories of 15,000 units at a weighted average cost of CU4 per unit, and made the following purchases during the year.

Date of purchases	Number of units	Cost per unit	Total cost
		CU	CU
1 January	15,000	4.20	63,000
1 April	20,000	4.50	90,000
1 May	25,000	4.10	102,500
1 July	10,000	4.40	44,000
1 October	5,000	4.50	22,500
Total	75,000		322,000

Closing inventories are 20,000 units.

Under the weighted average formula, the number of units in closing inventories is multiplied by the weighted average cost per unit for the year.

	Number of units	Cost per unit	Total cost
		CU	CU
Opening inventories	15,000	4.00	60,000
Date of purchase:			
1 January	15,000	4.20	63,000
1 April	20,000	4.50	90,000
1 May	25,000	4.10	102,500
1 July	10,000	4.40	44,000
1 October	5,000	4.50	22,500
Total	90,000		382,000

The weighted average cost per unit for the year is calculated as follows.

CU382,000 / 90,000 = CU4.24

The value of closing inventories is CU4.24 × 20,000 = CU84,800.

3.2.8.5   FIFO

The FIFO cost formula assumes that the items of inventory that were purchased or produced first are sold first. Therefore, at the end of the period, the items in inventory are valued using the prices for the most recent purchases.

Example 3.2.8.5

FIFO

The facts are the same as in **example 3.2.8.4**.

Under the FIFO formula, the first units held are the first units sold. Therefore, closing inventories are valued at the cost per unit of the latest purchases.

If 20,000 units are on hand at year end, the value of closing inventories is calculated as follows.

Date of purchases	Number of units	Cost per unit	Total cost
		CU	CU
October	5,000	4.50	22,500
July	10,000	4.40	44,000
May	5,000	4.10	20,500
Total	20,000		87,000

Thus, closing inventories are valued at CU87,000.

3.2.8.6 Changing from one cost formula to another

A reporting entity may decide to change from one cost formula to another (e.g. from the weighted average formula to FIFO) on the basis that the latter is more widely used in its particular industry and will, therefore, enhance comparability. A common question is whether such a change constitutes a change in accounting policy or a change in estimate. It is sometimes argued that it merely represents a change in estimate, in that it is a revision of the method of estimating cost. On balance, however, it seems appropriate to treat this as a change of accounting policy, for the following reasons.

- For inventories that are ordinarily interchangeable, IAS 2:24 states that a specific identification approach is inappropriate. Accordingly, the use of cost formulas is not merely a method of estimating the aggregate actual cost of individual items, because otherwise a specific identification approach would not be inappropriate, but would instead give the best possible estimate. Rather, cost formulas are used to arrive at a different figure that avoids the unacceptable distortions that would occur if a specific identification approach were adopted.

- IAS 2:36(a) requires disclosure of the accounting policies used for measuring inventories "including the cost formula used", which reinforces the view that the cost formula selected is a matter of accounting policy.

Requirements and disclosures relating to changes in accounting policies are discussed in **chapter A5**.

Other changes to the way in which inventories are measured (e.g. any changes to the basis for allocation of overheads or other costs of conversion to inventories) are likely to be changes of estimate rather than matters of accounting policy. Under IAS 8:39, the effect of a change in estimate should be separately disclosed, when material.

3.3 Determination of net realisable value

3.3.1 Measurement of net realisable value

IAS 2:6 defines net realisable value as "the estimated selling price in the ordinary course of business less the estimated costs of completion and the estimated costs necessary to make the sale". The net realisable value of an item of inventory may fall below its cost for many reasons, including damage, obsolescence, a decline in selling prices, or an increase in the estimate of costs to complete and market the inventories.

The Standard highlights the distinction between net realisable value (as defined in the previous paragraph) and the fair value of inventory. It explains that fair value reflects "the price at which an orderly transaction to sell the same inventory in the principal (or most advantageous) market for that inventory would take place between market participants at the measurement date". [IAS 2:7]

Net realisable value is the net amount that an entity expects to realise from the sale of inventories in the ordinary course of business and is, therefore, an entity-specific value. Fair value is not an entity-specific value. The net realisable value of inventories may not equal their fair value less costs to sell. [IAS 2:7] This will occur, for example, when the reporting entity has secured favourable binding sales contracts that have not been affected by more recent adverse market conditions.

Generally, estimates of net realisable value are made on an item-by-item basis. In some circumstances, however, it may be appropriate to group items of similar or related inventories. This may be the case when items of inventory:

[IAS 2:29]

- relate to the same product line and have similar purposes or end uses;
- are produced and marketed in the same geographical area; and

- cannot be practicably evaluated separately from other items in that product line.

> For entities that have not yet adopted IFRS 15, IAS 2 notes that service providers generally accumulate costs for each service for which a separate selling price is charged. Thus, when determining net realisable value, it is appropriate to consider each service separately. This requirement has been deleted as a consequential amendment arising from IFRS 15 *Revenue from Contracts with Customers*.

Example 3.3.1A

Determination of the net realisable value of an item of inventory with a long operating cycle

An entity is engaged in the production of an item of inventory with a long operating cycle. Production of the item normally takes six years to complete. Costs are accumulated over time and recognised as inventory. At the end of the second year of production, a further four years of work is required for the inventory item to be completed. No relevant market exists for the inventory in its current state.

IAS 2:30 states that estimates of net realisable value should be based on the most reliable evidence available at the time the estimates are made of the amounts the inventories are expected to realise.

At the end of the second year of production, how should the net realisable value of the inventory item be determined under IAS 2?

When estimating the net realisable value of inventories, management should consider all of the facts relating to the type of inventory and the operating environment at the time the estimates are made.

In the circumstances described, because no relevant market exists for the two-year work in progress, it may be the case that, in order to determine the net realisable value of the inventory at the end of the reporting period, the entity uses as its starting point the current selling price for the inventory in its completed state, deducting expected holding costs (including finance costs), outstanding costs of conversion and costs to sell.

An entity might alternatively use the forward price for sales of the completed inventory in four years' time. When this approach is adopted, the cash flows associated with the net realisable value should be discounted at an appropriate rate to determine an estimate of the net realisable value of the inventory in its present location and condition, consistent with IAS 2:30 and paragraph BCZ4 of IAS 36 *Impairment of Assets*. Consequently, it will be necessary to adjust the forward price for the effect of the time value of money and also for outstanding costs of conversion and costs to sell.

When estimating the net realisable value of inventories, management should consider all of the facts relating to the inventories and the operating environment at the time the estimates are made. Estimates are based on the most reliable evidence available at that time as to the amount that the inventories are likely to realise. These estimates take into consideration fluctuations in price or cost directly relating to events occurring after the reporting period to the extent that such events confirm conditions existing at the end of the reporting period. [IAS 2:30]

Example 3.3.1B

Sales after the reporting period

An item of inventory which cost CU100 is sold after the reporting period for CU80. A sale after the reporting period at a lower price generally provides evidence of the net realisable value of the inventories at the end of the reporting period and the closing inventories should therefore be carried at CU80 less any costs to sell.

However, this will not always be the case. If, for example, further investigation shows that the decrease in sales price arose because of damage to the inventories that occurred after the reporting period, this would indicate that the CU80 sales price did not reflect conditions existing at the end of the reporting period and that the loss in value should not be accounted for until the next period. In these circumstances, it would be necessary to assess whether the item could have been sold undamaged for an amount at or in excess of its cost (CU100) plus any costs to sell. If so, no write-down would be required at the end of the reporting period.

Example 3.3.1C

Decrease in net realisable value after the end of the reporting period for inventories under development

Entity P is a property developer. It is preparing its financial statements for the year ended 31 December 20X0, which will be authorised for issue on 31 March 20X1.

At 31 December 20X0, Entity P holds a property as development work in progress. Costs incurred to date are CU20 million. Estimated costs to complete are CU10 million (therefore, total costs will be CU30 million). Completion and sale of the development are expected within 18 to 24 months.

Entity P estimates net realisable value for development work in progress based on the projected sales price for the property when it is complete, discounted back to current value. Based on market information on sales prices for similar, finished properties at 31 December 20X0, net realisable value is estimated at CU32 million (implying a net development profit of CU2 million).

However, property prices in the relevant market are falling. At 31 March 20X1 (date of authorisation of financial statements), the observed sales prices for similar, finished properties have declined to CU27 million (implying a net development loss of CU3 million). Estimated costs to complete (and other applicable factors) are unchanged since year end.

> *Should Entity P recognise an inventory write-down in its 31 December 20X0 financial statements?*
>
> Yes. The development property is not available for sale at the year end. IAS 2:30 acknowledges that "fluctuations of price or cost directly relating to events occurring after the end of the period" are relevant to estimates of net realisable value "to the extent that such events confirm conditions existing at the end of the period". Because Entity P estimates net realisable value based on projected sales prices of completed property, discounted back to current value, information received after the end of the reporting period (including revised sales price estimates) provides further evidence as to conditions that existed at the end of the reporting period, unless the changes in sales prices clearly relate to a separate event subsequent to the period end.

When estimating the net realisable value of inventories, the purpose for which the inventories are held is taken into consideration. For example, if the inventories are held to satisfy firm sales contracts, the sales prices agreed in those contracts form the basis of the estimation. If the sales contracts are for less than the inventory quantities held, the net realisable value of the excess is based on general selling prices. [IAS 2:31]

3.3.2 *Writing inventories down to net realisable value*

When the net realisable value of an item of inventory is less than its cost, the excess is written off immediately in profit or loss.

Items of inventory are generally written down on an item-by-item basis. IAS 2 indicates that it is generally inappropriate to write down entire classifications of inventories, such as finished goods, or all of the inventories in a particular operating segment. [IAS 2:29]

Materials and other supplies held for use in the production of inventories are not written down below cost if the finished products in which they will be incorporated are expected to be sold at or above cost. However, when a decline in the price of materials indicates that the cost of the finished products will exceed net realisable value, the materials are written down to net realisable value. In such circumstances, the replacement cost of the materials may be the best available measure of their net realisable value. [IAS 2:32]

The costs necessary to make the sale should be determined in a manner consistent with the definition of 'costs of disposal' in IAS 36 *Impairment of Assets*, which states that these are "incremental costs directly attributable to the disposal of an asset, excluding finance costs and income tax expense". An incremental cost is one that would not be incurred if the activity was not undertaken. General overheads, therefore, may not be allocated for the purposes of determining costs to sell. Direct transaction costs must be allocated for the purposes of determining costs to sell.

705

3.3.3 Reversals of write-downs

Net realisable value estimates are made at the end of each reporting period. When subsequent evaluations show that the circumstances that previously caused inventories to be written down below cost no longer exist, or when there is clear evidence of an increase in net realisable value because of changed economic circumstances, write-downs of inventories previously recognised are required to be reversed. [IAS 2:33] This occurs, for example, when an item of inventory that is carried at net realisable value because its selling price had declined is still on hand in a subsequent period and its selling price has increased (though it would still be necessary, if the item had been on hand for a long time, to consider whether there might be obsolescence issues).

The amount of the write-down should be reversed through profit or loss so that the new carrying amount is the lower of the cost and the revised net realisable value. Therefore, the amount of the reversal is limited to the amount of the original write-down.

3.4 Recognition as an expense

The amount of inventories recognised as an expense in the period will generally be:

[IAS 2:34]

- the carrying amount of inventories sold in the period; and

- the amount of any write-down of inventories to net realisable value and all losses of inventories in the period; less

- the amount of any reversal in the period of any write-down of inventories, arising from an increase in net realisable value.

If inventories are used by the entity rather than being sold, their cost may be capitalised as part of the cost of another asset (e.g. property, plant and equipment). Their cost is then recognised as an expense through depreciation of that asset.

4 Presentation and disclosure

4.1 Presentation

IAS 1:54 requires that, when material, the total carrying amount of inventories (other than those included in disposal groups that are classified as held for sale – see **chapter A20**) should be presented as a separate item in the statement of financial position. The analysis of items between current and non-current is discussed in **section 4.1** of **chapter A4**.

4.2 Disclosure

4.2.1 Accounting policies

IAS 2:36(a) requires that financial statements should disclose the accounting policies adopted in measuring inventories, including the cost formula used.

4.2.2 Analysis of carrying amount

IAS 2:36(b) requires the total carrying amount of inventories to be disclosed, together with an analysis of the carrying amount in a manner appropriate to the entity.

Common classifications of inventories are as follows:

- merchandise;
- production supplies;
- materials;
- work in progress; and
- finished goods.

Entities in specialist industries should use a classification that is meaningful in the context of their operations; for example, property development entities could analyse their development portfolio as:

- land held for development;
- properties under construction; and
- completed properties held for sale.

The inventories of a service provider may simply be described as work in progress. [IAS 2:37]

Note that the reference in IAS 2:37 to the description of the inventories of service providers has been deleted as a consequential amendment arising from IFRS 15 *Revenue from Contracts with Customers*.

4.2.3 Expected realisation

IAS 1:61 requires that an entity should disclose for each asset that combines amounts expected to be recovered both within twelve months of and after twelve months from the end of the reporting period, the amount expected to be recovered after more than twelve months. It is appropriate for an entity to disclose the amount of inventories expected to be recovered after more than one year from the end of the reporting period. [IAS 1:65]

4.2.4   Inventories carried at fair value less costs to sell

IAS 2:36(c) requires separate disclosure of the carrying amount of inventories carried at fair value less costs to sell.

> As discussed in **2.2**, this requirement should in practice apply only to certain inventories held by commodity broker-traders. (As explained in **chapter A20**, when inventories are classified as held for sale as part of a disposal group, they continue to be measured in accordance with IAS 2. The disposal group itself may then be written down to fair value less costs to sell, but not the inventories *per se*.)

4.2.5   Amounts recognised in profit or loss

IAS 2 requires separate disclosure of:

* the amount of inventories recognised as an expense during the period; [IAS 2:36(d)]

* the amount of any write-down of inventories to net realisable value recognised as an expense in the period; [IAS 2:36(e)] and

* the amount of any reversal of any write-down recognised as a reduction in the inventories expense for the period. [IAS 2:36(f)]

In addition, disclosure is required of the circumstances or events that led to any recognised reversal of a write-down of inventories. [IAS 2:36(g)]

IAS 2:38 specifies that the amount of inventories recognised as an expense during the period, which is commonly described as cost of sales, consists of:

* the costs that have previously been included in the measurement of inventories that have now been sold;

* unallocated production overheads; and

* abnormal amounts of production costs of inventories.

4.2.6   Inventories pledged as security

IAS 2:36(h) requires entities to disclose the carrying amount of inventories pledged as security for liabilities.

A12 Provisions, contingent liabilities and contingent assets

Contents

1 Introduction

1.1 Overview of IAS 37

IAS 37 *Provisions, Contingent Liabilities and Contingent Assets* outlines the accounting for provisions (liabilities of uncertain timing or amount), together with contingent assets (possible assets) and contingent liabilities (possible obligations and present obligations that are not probable or not reliably measurable). Provisions are measured at the best estimate (including risks and uncertainties) of the expenditure required to settle the present obligation, and reflect the present value of expenditures required to settle the obligation when the time value of money is material.

1.2 Amendments to IAS 37 since the last edition of this manual

None. IAS 37 was most recently amended in May 2014.

2 Scope

2.1 Scope – general

The requirements of IAS 37 apply to all provisions, contingent liabilities and contingent assets other than those:

[IAS 37:1]

- resulting from executory contracts, except when the contract is onerous (see **2.2**); and

- covered by another Standard (see **2.3**).

Unlike IAS 16 *Property, Plant and Equipment* (see **section 2** of **chapter A7**), IAS 37 does not include a scope exclusion for the extractive industries. Therefore, the requirements of IAS 37 should be applied and liabilities recognised for restoration costs, for example, when the recognition and measurement criteria are met. Refer to Examples 2A, 2B and 3 in Section C of the implementation guidance accompanying IAS 37 for illustrations of the application of IAS 37 to the extractive industries (see **section 8**).

When a provision meets the definition of a financial instrument in IAS 32 *Financial Instruments: Presentation*, but is accounted for under IAS 37 because it is not within the scope of IFRS 9 *Financial Instruments* (or, for entities that have not yet adopted IFRS 9, IAS 39 *Financial Instruments: Recognition and Measurement*), the disclosure requirements of IFRS 7 *Financial Instruments: Disclosures* apply in addition to those of IAS 37.

2.2   Executory contracts

Executory contracts are contracts under which neither party has performed any of its obligations, or both parties have partially performed their obligations to an equal extent. [IAS 37:3] Executory contracts do not fall within the scope of IAS 37 unless they are onerous (see **3.9.2**).

Examples of executory contracts include:

* employee contracts in respect of continuing employment;

* contracts for future delivery of services such as gas and electricity;

* obligations to pay local authority charges; and

* most purchase orders.

Example 2.2

Executory contract

On 1 January 20X0, Company A enters into a contract with Company B for the manufacture and delivery of 100 units of component Q at five different dates in the future, i.e. 500 units are to be delivered in total. Payment is due on delivery of the units.

On 1 January 20X0, the contract between Company A and Company B is executory because neither party has performed any of its obligations; Company B has not manufactured or delivered any of the units, nor has Company A paid for any of them.

By 1 March 20X0, Company B has produced and delivered 200 of the units and Company A has paid in full for those 200 units. At this date, the contract between Company A and Company B continues to be executory because both parties have partially performed their obligations to an equal extent.

By 1 June 20X0, Company B has produced and delivered the full 500 units, but Company A has only paid for 400 units in total. The contract between Company A and Company B no longer meets the definition of an executory contract because the two parties have not performed under the terms of the contract to an equal extent. Company A is required to recognise a liability for the final 100 units of component Q for which it has not yet paid.

2.3   Provisions, contingent liabilities and contingent assets covered by other Standards

When another Standard deals with a specific type of provision, contingent liability or contingent asset, the more specific Standard should be applied. For example:

[IAS 37:5]

(a) for entities that have not yet adopted IFRS 15 *Revenue from Contracts with Customers*, provisions relating to construction contracts are dealt with under IAS 11 *Construction Contracts* (see **appendix A2**);

(b) provisions relating to income taxes are dealt with under IAS 12 *Income Taxes* (see **chapter A13**);

(c) provisions relating to leases generally fall within the scope of IAS 17 *Leases* (see **chapter A17**). However, because IAS 17 contains no specific requirements to deal with operating leases that have become onerous, IAS 37 applies to such onerous contracts;

(d) provisions relating to employee benefits are dealt with under IAS 19 *Employee Benefits* (see **chapter A15**);

(e) provisions relating to insurance contracts are dealt with under IFRS 4 *Insurance Contracts* (see **chapter A39**). However, IAS 37 applies to provisions, contingent liabilities and contingent assets of an insurer other than those arising from its contractual obligations and rights under insurance contracts within the scope of IFRS 4;

(f) contingent consideration of an acquirer in a business combination is dealt with under IFRS 3 *Business Combinations* (see **section 8.2** of **chapter A25**); and

(g) for entities that have adopted IFRS 15, provisions relating to contracts with customers are dealt with in accordance with that Standard (see **chapter A14**). However, because IFRS 15 contains no specific requirements to deal with contracts with customers that are, or have become, onerous, IAS 37 deals with such onerous contracts.

In addition, the acquirer's treatment of contingent liabilities assumed in a business combination is addressed by IFRS 3 *Business Combinations* (see **chapter A25**).

IAS 37 *does* apply to provisions for restructurings (including discontinued operations). When a restructuring meets the definition of a discontinued operation, additional disclosures may be required by IFRS 5 *Non-current Assets Held for Sale and Discontinued Operations* (see **chapter A20**). [IAS 37:9]

IAS 37:5(f) was added in December 2013 by consequential amendments arising from *Annual Improvements to IFRSs:2010-2012 Cycle*. In May 2014, consequential amendments arising from IFRS 15 *Revenue from Contracts with Customers* deleted the reference to the superseded IAS 11 in IAS 37:5(a) and added IAS 37:5(g).

2.4 Financial instruments

IAS 37 does not apply to financial instruments (including guarantees) that fall within the scope of IFRS 9 *Financial Instruments* or, for entities that have not yet adopted IFRS 9, IAS 39 *Financial Instruments: Recognition and Measurement* (see **chapter B1** and **chapter C1**, respectively). [IAS 37:2]

Financial guarantee contracts are not within the scope of IAS 37. They are within the scope of IFRS 9 (IAS 39), except in certain limited circumstances when the issuer may instead elect to apply IFRS 4 *Insurance Contracts* (see the discussion in **2.3** of **chapter B1** (for entities applying IFRS 9) and **2.3** of **chapter C1** (for entities applying IAS 39)).

Example 2.4

Liability with payment linked to future sales

Entity A faces a claim for an alleged infringement of intellectual property (IP) rights. On 31 December 20X1, in settlement of the claim, Entity A agrees to pay the claimant a fixed sum plus a variable amount calculated as 1 per cent of any revenue generated by Entity A over the next five years from sales of a specified product.

At 31 December 20X1, Entity A must consider whether to recognise a liability for the obligation to pay a variable amount on the basis of future sales. This will depend on whether the variable amount to be paid based on future sales represents a settlement for use of the IP in the past or compensation for the future use by Entity A of the underlying IP:

- if the sales-linked feature is a mechanism for determining the amount due for past use by Entity A of the IP (plus any compensatory or punitive element), Entity A should recognise a liability under IFRS 9 or IAS 39 at 31 December 20X1; whereas

- if the sales-linked payments relate to future use by Entity A of the underlying IP, the obligation arises as new sales are realised and represents an executory contract under IAS 37. In such circumstances, Entity A should not recognise a liability for the variable amount to be paid based on future sales at 31 December 20X1, unless the executory contract is determined to be onerous.

In practice, situations in which entities would recognise immediately a liability for the variable amount to be paid on the basis of future sales are expected to be rare.

2.5 Use of the term 'provision'

The use of the term 'provision' is restricted to liabilities of uncertain timing or amount. It does not cover adjustments to the carrying amounts of assets (such as depreciation, impairment and allowances for doubtful debts) for which the term 'provision' is used in some jurisdictions. [IAS 37:7]

2.6 Related expenditure

IAS 37 does not specify whether expenditure should be capitalised as an asset or treated as an expense. These issues are addressed in other Standards. Therefore, IAS 37 itself neither prohibits nor requires capitalisation of the costs recognised when a provision is made. [IAS 37:8]

3 Definition and recognition of provisions, contingent liabilities and contingent assets

3.1 Provisions

IAS 37 defines a provision as a liability of uncertain timing or amount, i.e. a subset of liabilities. [IAS 37:10] The Standard repeats the definition of a liability found in the *Conceptual Framework for Financial Reporting*, i.e. a present obligation of the entity arising from past events, the settlement of which is expected to result in an outflow from the entity of resources embodying economic benefits. [IAS 37:10]

A provision should be recognised when and only when:

[IAS 37:14]

- an entity has a present obligation (legal or constructive) as a result of a past event;

- it is probable that an outflow of resources embodying economic benefits will be required to settle the obligation; and

- a reliable estimate can be made of the amount of the obligation.

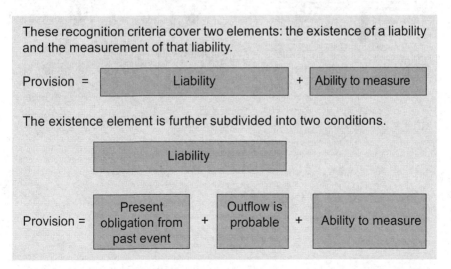

These recognition criteria cover two elements: the existence of a liability and the measurement of that liability.

Provision = | Liability | + | Ability to measure

The existence element is further subdivided into two conditions.

| Liability |

Provision = | Present obligation from past event | + | Outflow is probable | + | Ability to measure |

3.2   Contingent liabilities

A contingent liability is defined as:

[IAS 37:10]

- a possible obligation that arises from past events and whose existence will be confirmed only by the occurrence or non-occurrence of one or more uncertain future events not wholly within the control of the entity; or

- a present obligation that arises from past events that is not recognised because:

    - it is not probable that an outflow of resources embodying economic benefits will be required to settle the obligation; or

    - the amount of the obligation cannot be measured with sufficient reliability.

Under IAS 37, a reporting entity should not recognise a contingent liability in its statement of financial position. [IAS 37:27]

Therefore, a contingent liability, which is not recognised but is disclosed by way of note, results when one or more of the three recognition criteria for a provision, as outlined at **3.1**, is not met.

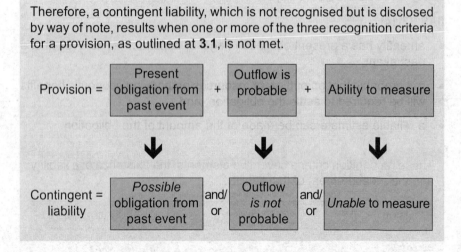

The table below illustrates the application of the recognition criteria.

Situation	Provision?	Action
Past event has occurred, resulting in a *possible* obligation for which a transfer of benefits is possible but not probable (see **3.6**).	✗	Unless the possibility of a transfer of benefits is remote, disclose a contingent liability.
Past event has occurred, resulting in a present obligation for which there may *possibly* be a transfer of benefits, but for which there probably will not.	✗	Unless the possibility of a transfer of benefits is remote, disclose a contingent liability.
Past event has occurred, resulting in a present obligation for which it is likely there will be a transfer of benefits, but a *reliable estimate cannot be made* of the amount of the obligation.	✗	Disclose a contingent liability. (N.B. This situation is likely to be very rare – see **3.8**).
Past event has occurred, resulting in a present obligation for which it is likely there will be a transfer of benefits; a reliable estimate can be made of the amount of the obligation.	✓	Recognise provision and make necessary disclosures.
An obligating event *has not taken place by the end of the reporting period*, but it takes place after the reporting period, resulting in an obligation for which it is likely there will be a transfer of benefits; a reliable estimate can be made of the amount of the obligation.	✗	Consider whether IAS 10 *Events after the Reporting Period* requires disclosure of the non-adjusting event (see **chapter A22**).

3.3 Contingent assets

A contingent asset is defined as a possible asset that arises from past events and whose existence will be confirmed only by the occurrence or non-occurrence of one or more uncertain future events not wholly within the control of the entity. [IAS 37:10]

Contingent assets are not recognised, but are disclosed by way of note when an inflow of economic benefits is probable. When the realisation of income is virtually certain, however, the related asset is not a contingent asset and its recognition is appropriate. [IAS 37:33]

3.4   Distinguishing provisions from other liabilities

Provisions can be distinguished from other types of liability, including those that involve uncertain amounts, by considering the events that give rise to the obligation and also the degree of uncertainty as to the amount of the liability. In each case, the definition of a liability will be met through the existence of a present obligation arising from a past event.

For example, trade payables are liabilities to pay for goods/services already received/supplied and which have been invoiced or otherwise agreed with the supplier. Accruals, on the other hand, are liabilities to pay for goods/ services already received/supplied but which have not been invoiced or otherwise agreed with the supplier. Although it is sometimes necessary to estimate the amount or timing of accruals, the uncertainty is generally much less than for provisions. Accruals are often reported as part of trade and other payables, whereas provisions are reported separately. [IAS 37:11]

Example	Classification	Degree of uncertainty
Goods or services received and invoiced	Trade payable	None
Goods or services received, but not invoiced	Accrual	Some
Legal claim from supplier for breach of exclusive supply agreement	Provision (if conditions met)	Significant

Amounts recognised as provisions will often relate to items such as legal claims, warranties given in respect of goods sold or services provided, restructurings and decommissioning obligations.

3.5   Present obligations and past events

3.5.1   Obligating event – definition

As will be clear from the table set out at **3.2**, the existence of a present obligation arising from a past obligating event is a key consideration when determining whether classification as a provision or as a contingent liability is appropriate.

As defined in IAS 37:10, an obligating event is an event that creates a legal or constructive obligation that results in an entity having no realistic alternative to settling that obligation. A legal obligation derives either from the terms of a contract (either explicit or implicit), or legislation or other operation of the law. A constructive obligation is an obligation deriving from an entity's actions when:

- by an established pattern of past practice, published policies or a sufficiently specific current statement, the entity has indicated to other parties that it will accept certain responsibilities; and

- as a result, the entity has created a valid expectation on the part of those other parties that it will discharge those responsibilities.

3.5.2 Provisions recognised for liabilities that exist at the end of the reporting period

Financial statements deal with the financial position of an entity at the end of its reporting period and not its possible position in the future. The only liabilities recognised in an entity's statement of financial position are those that exist at the end of the reporting period. Therefore, no provision is recognised for costs that need to be incurred to operate in the future, notwithstanding that such costs may be necessary to continue as a going concern. [IAS 37:18]

Accordingly, if an obligation exists at the end of the reporting period, that obligation will exist irrespective of whether the reporting entity continues to trade after the end of the reporting period. Conversely, any outflow that can be avoided by ceasing to trade will not be an obligation at the end of the reporting period.

A reporting entity may be aware of some future commitment to spend money, and may even feel less well off at the prospect of the expense. But future expenditure, however necessary, does not justify the recognition of a provision unless a liability exists at the end of the reporting period.

3.5.3 Provisions recognised for obligations that exist independently of future actions

It is only those obligations arising from past events that exist independently of the reporting entity's future actions that are recognised as provisions. [IAS 37:19] One example in which a provision is recognised might be for clean-up costs relating to environmental damage. Even if the entity changes its future business activities (at an extreme, by ceasing to trade), it will still incur the expenses relating to cleaning up, because of its past activities.

This can be contrasted with the circumstances in which ships and aircraft are required to undergo major work at regular intervals due to maritime and aviation law. No present obligation is created by the legal requirement to do the major work until the requisite number of hours or days have been completed. The cost of the major work is not recognised because, at the end of the reporting period, no obligation to undertake such major work exists independently of the entity's future actions – the entity could avoid the future expenditure by its future actions, for example by selling the ship or aircraft (see also summary of Examples 11A and 11B from IAS 37 in **8.1**).

3.5.4   Requirement for commitment to another party

An obligation always involves a commitment to another party. It is not necessary, however, to know the identity of the party to whom the obligation is owed – the obligation may be to the public at large. [IAS 37:20]

3.5.5   Requirement for management decisions to have been communicated to affected parties

It is because of the requirement for a clear commitment to another party, referred to in **3.5.4**, that a decision made by management before the end of the reporting period does not of itself give rise to a present obligation, unless it is communicated to those affected by it in a sufficiently specific manner to raise a valid expectation in them that the entity will discharge its responsibilities. [IAS 37:20]

3.5.6   Obligation arises as a result of changes in the law

It is possible that an event may not give rise to an obligation immediately, but may do so at a later date. This could be as a result of changes in the law or because an act (e.g. a sufficiently specific public statement) by the entity gives rise to a constructive obligation. For example, when an entity causes environmental damage, this may not give rise to an obligation for remedial costs if there is no applicable legislation. The causing of the damage will become an obligating event at a later date, however, if a new law requires the existing damage to be rectified or if the entity publicly accepts responsibility for rectification in a way that creates a constructive obligation. [IAS 37:21]

When details of new legislation have yet to be finalised, an obligation arises only when the legislation is virtually certain to be enacted as drafted (see **4.5.3**). Under IAS 37, such an obligation is treated as a legal obligation. In many cases, however, it will be impossible to be virtually certain of the enactment of a law until it is actually enacted. [IAS 37:22]

3.5.7   Smoothing of results

IAS 37 seeks to prevent artificial 'smoothing' of results. By basing the recognition of a provision on the existence of a present obligation, it rules out the recognition of any provision made simply to allocate expenses over more than one period or otherwise to smooth the results reported. For example, entities are not permitted to provide on an annual basis for items such as future repairs to assets, so as to produce a reasonably level charge each year. Unless dealt with through a component approach to depreciation (see **chapter A7**), such costs will instead generally be recognised in profit or loss when they are actually incurred, i.e. when the work is done. (Repairs and maintenance obligations under leases are discussed at **8.2**.)

3.6 Situations of uncertainty regarding present obligations

IAS 37:15 states that there will, on rare occasions, be circumstances when it is unclear whether a present obligation exists. In order to determine whether a present obligation exists under such circumstances (e.g. when the facts in a lawsuit are disputed), the Standard advises that account should be taken of all available evidence. Such evidence may include, for example, the opinion of experts. It will also include additional evidence contributed by events occurring after the reporting period. Preparers of financial statements should look at all of the available evidence and come to a reasoned judgement as to whether it is more likely than not that a present obligation exists. If it is more likely than not that a present obligation exists, a provision should be recognised. Otherwise, a contingent liability is disclosed, unless the possibility of any transfer of economic benefits in settlement is remote. [IAS 37:16]

3.7 Probable outflow of economic benefits

An essential element of the definition of a liability is the existence of an obligation to transfer economic benefits. Recognition of a provision is conditional on the transfer of economic benefits being 'probable'. For the purpose of IAS 37, probable is taken to mean more likely than not to occur. [IAS 37:23]

Thus, 'more likely than not' means that the probability that a transfer of economic benefits will occur is more than 50 per cent.

When a number of similar obligations exist (e.g. product warranties), the overall probability that a transfer of economic benefits will be made is determined by looking at the class of obligations as a whole. A typical situation will be that, despite the likelihood of an outflow of resources for any one item being small, it may well be probable that a transfer of some economic benefits will be needed to settle the class of obligations as a whole. When this is the case, assuming that the other recognition criteria are met, a provision is recognised (see **4.2**). [IAS 37:24]

3.8   Reliable estimate

The use of estimates is an inherent part of preparing financial statements. Provisions are clearly uncertain by nature, but IAS 37 emphasises that it should not be impossible to determine a range of possible outcomes and, from this range, to reach an appropriate conclusion that is sufficiently reliable for the provision to be recognised. IAS 37:26 concludes that the circumstances in which it will not be possible to reach a reliable estimate will be extremely rare. In those extremely rare circumstances, a liability exists that cannot be recognised. That liability will instead be disclosed as a contingent liability.

3.9   Specific applications of recognition criteria

3.9.1   Future operating losses

IAS 37 sets out two prohibitions on the recognition of provisions for future operating losses:

- a general prohibition, on the grounds that there is no present obligation and thus no liability (albeit that the expectation of future operating losses may indicate a need to test whether assets have been impaired); [IAS 37:63 - 65] and

- a specific prohibition in respect of future operating losses up to the date of a restructuring – again on grounds that there is no present obligation, unless the losses relate to an onerous contract (see **3.9.2**). [IAS 37:82]

In both circumstances, future operating losses relate to an activity that will continue, albeit in a restructured form, and are presumed to be avoidable (e.g. by an immediate closure of the loss-making activities). They are, therefore, appropriately recognised as the activity occurs.

3.9.2   Onerous contracts

A provision should be recognised for the present obligation arising under an onerous contract. [IAS 37:66] When assets dedicated to a contract are involved, however, a separate provision is recognised only after any impairment loss has been recognised in respect of those assets. [IAS 37:69]

An onerous contract is defined in IAS 37:10 as a contract in which the unavoidable costs of meeting the obligations under the contract exceed the economic benefits expected to be received under it. In other words, a provision should be recognised for any unavoidable net loss arising from the contract. The unavoidable costs under a contract reflect the least net cost of exiting from the contract, i.e. the lower of:

[IAS 37:68]

- the cost of fulfilling the contract; and
- any compensation or penalties arising from failure to fulfil the contract.

It is not appropriate to test for an onerous contract only by comparing the value of the goods or services to be received or provided with the amount to be paid or received. A mere fall in price does not necessarily mean that a contract is onerous. Instead, the test of whether a contract is onerous focuses on how the goods or services that are the subject of the contract will be used within the business.

Depending on the facts and circumstances, a contract may or may not relate to a cash-generating unit (CGU) and this will affect the determination as to whether the contract is onerous. For example, a vacant leasehold property is not part of any CGU of a lessee because it is not being used in the business. Accordingly, the assessment as to whether the lease contract is onerous will be carried out by comparing the cash flows to be generated through sub-letting with those to be paid out as rent. When the forecast cash outflows exceed the forecast cash inflows, a provision should be recognised at the lower of the net rent payable (i.e. rent payable net of forecast rental income) and any penalty payable for early termination of the lease.

In contrast, a contract to buy goods or services that will be used by a CGU is directly related to that CGU. Such a contract will be assessed as onerous if the cost of the items purchased causes the CGU to report a loss or increases the loss to be reported by the CGU.

It does not necessarily follow that a CGU reporting a loss has an onerous contract or contracts. Rather, it will always be necessary to consider individual contracts to assess whether the unavoidable costs of meeting the obligations under any contract exceed the economic benefits expected to be received under it. Onerous contracts may arise when an entity prepares financial statements on a basis other than that of a going concern. In those circumstances, contracts that would not normally be onerous (e.g. employee contracts) may become onerous (see **section 2.5** of **chapter A4** for further guidance).

Long-term contracts for the supply of goods or services when costs have risen or current market prices have fallen may be onerous and, if so, a provision is recognised to the extent that future supplies must be made at a loss. No provision is recognised under a contract for the supply of goods which is profitable but at a reduced margin compared to other contracts, because there is no probable net transfer of economic benefits by the reporting entity.

Example 3.9.2A

Recognition and measurement of onerous contracts

Entity A has entered into a contract with Entity B to supply goods for a fixed price of CU100. Because of price inflation, Entity A's expenditure to meet its obligations under the contract is expected to be CU120. No other benefits are expected under the contract. Therefore, the contract is considered to be onerous, and a provision should be recognised. Entity A estimates that any compensation or penalties arising from failure to fulfil the contract are equal to the cost of fulfilling the contract (i.e. CU120).

At the end of the reporting period, Entity A has commenced negotiations with Entity B with a view to increasing the price at which the goods are supplied under the contract. Entity A expects that Entity B will be willing to agree to such a price increase so as to avoid Entity A ceasing to trade as a result of the losses incurred under the contract (and, consequently, cutting off the source of supply of goods necessary for Entity B's own business).

Should the potential renegotiation of the supply contract between Entity A and Entity B be reflected in the amount of provision recognised for the onerous contract?

No. The onerous contract should be measured based on the contractual terms in existence at the end of the reporting period because that is Entity A's 'present obligation' required to be recognised and measured in accordance with IAS 37:66. Any future amendment to the terms of the contract would be a change in the obligation resulting in remeasurement of the provision when the amendment occurs.

As discussed in **4.5**, IAS 37:48 states that "future events that may affect the amount required to settle an obligation shall be reflected in the amount of a provision where there is sufficient objective evidence that they will occur". However, this reference to future events is not to changes in the underlying obligation, but to those future events that are factors in estimating the costs of meeting a present obligation (e.g. developments in the technology used to clean up a site – see **4.5.1**) or in assessing the extent to which a present contractual obligation is onerous (e.g. an expectation of subleasing a vacant property – see **example 3.9.2B**).

Should the provision recognised by Entity A be the entire cost of fulfilling the contract (CU120) or only the expected loss (CU20)?

Entity A should recognise a provision for the onerous contract equal to the expected loss of CU20.

IAS 37:10 defines an onerous contract as "a contract in which the unavoidable costs of meeting the obligations under the contract exceed the economic benefits expected to be received under it". IAS 37:68 further states that "[t]he unavoidable costs under a contract reflect the least net cost of exiting from the contract, which is the lower of the cost of fulfilling it and any compensation or penalties arising from failure to fulfil it".

Because IAS 37 refers to the net cost rather than the gross cost associated with the contract, the provision for the onerous contract should reflect the costs required to fulfil the contract net of any income that the entity will receive as a consequence of fulfilling the contract.

Example 3.9.2B

Vacant property

Company X has an operating lease over a property which it entered into several years ago. The property is now surplus to requirements and Company X has vacated it. The lease has three years to run with an associated expense of CU10,000 per year.

Company X believes it may be able to find a tenant to take a sublease of the property but that it might only receive CU8,000 per year from the sublease. Alternatively, the landlord is prepared to terminate the lease, and forgive the future rentals of CU30,000, if Company X makes a termination payment of CU5,500.

Because the property has been vacated, and the continuing rentals are not expected to be recoverable from subleasing the property, a provision should be recognised. The provision should represent the best estimate of the expenditure required to settle the obligation at the end of the reporting period. If Company X subleases the property, it expects to pay CU30,000 in lease rentals and receive CU24,000 in sublease rentals, which would leave a deficit of CU6,000 to be provided. However, in this case, the amount the landlord would accept to terminate the lease is CU5,500, which is lower. Accordingly, Company X should recognise an onerous lease provision of CU5,500, irrespective of whether it intends to terminate the lease or enter into a sublease.

(For simplicity, this example ignores the time value of money. If the effect of discounting is material, the future rental payments and receipts are discounted to their present value. If the net present value of future rental payments less receipts is less than CU5,500, provision is made for that lower amount. Present value calculations are discussed at **4.7**.)

Examples of contracts that do not meet the criteria for recognition of a provision are:

- those routine purchase orders, and similar contracts, which realistically could be cancelled by agreement with the vendor without paying compensation; and

- purchase orders when the future benefits from use of the asset exceed its cost, notwithstanding that compensation must be paid if the order is cancelled.

Executory contracts (i.e. contracts under which neither party has performed any of its obligations or both parties have performed their obligations to an equal extent) that are not onerous are excluded from the scope of IAS 37 (see **2.2**).

With the exception of onerous contracts, therefore, an entity will recognise no liability in respect of the purchase of goods or services until those goods or services are supplied, notwithstanding that the entity may become committed to paying for them at an earlier date.

3.9.3 Restructuring provisions

3.9.3.1 Definition of a restructuring

IAS 37 provides specific guidance on how the general recognition criteria for provisions should be applied to restructurings. A restructuring is defined as a programme that is planned and controlled by management, and materially changes either:

[IAS 37:10]

- the scope of a business undertaken by an entity; or
- the manner in which that business is conducted.

The term 'restructuring' therefore includes events such as:

[IAS 37:70]

- the sale or termination of a line of business;
- the closure of business locations in a country or region or the relocation of business activities from one country or region to another;
- changes in management structure (e.g. the elimination of a layer of management); and
- fundamental reorganisations that have a material effect on the nature and focus of the entity's operations.

3.9.3.2 Specific recognition criteria for restructuring provisions

The two principal requirements for the recognition of a provision for a restructuring are that the entity:

[IAS 37:72]

- has a detailed formal plan; and
- has raised a valid expectation in those affected that the plan will be carried out by starting to implement that plan or by announcing its main features to those affected by it.

The detailed formal plan must identify:

[IAS 37:72]

- the business or part of a business concerned;

- the principal locations affected;

- the location, function and approximate number of employees who will be compensated for terminating their services;

> Generally, it is not necessary for the plan to be so detailed that it identifies which individual employees will be leaving. However, it must be sufficiently detailed that those employees in the employee groups affected by the restructuring plan have a valid expectation that either they or their colleagues in the group will be affected.

- the expenditures that will be undertaken; and

- when the plan will be implemented.

Suitable evidence that an entity has started to implement a restructuring plan will, for example, be provided by:

[IAS 37:73]

- dismantling plant; or

- selling assets; or

- the public announcement of the main features of the plan.

Note, however, that a public announcement of a detailed plan to restructure constitutes a constructive obligation to restructure only if it is made in such a way and in sufficient detail (i.e. setting out the main features of the plan) that it gives rise to valid expectations in other parties such as customers, suppliers and employees (or their representatives) that the entity will carry out the restructuring. [IAS 37:73] Accordingly, for a plan to be sufficient to give rise to a constructive obligation when it is communicated to those affected by it, implementation of the plan should be planned to begin as soon as possible and to be completed within a timeframe that makes significant change to the plan unlikely. When either there is a long delay before commencement, or execution of the plan will take an unreasonably long time, the timeframe allows opportunities for the plan to be changed. Thus, it is unlikely that the reporting entity has raised a valid expectation that it is sufficiently committed to the restructuring. [IAS 37:74]

> When a restructuring plan will take quite a long time to be completed, it is possible that the entity may be demonstrably committed to earlier actions in the plan but not to later actions in the plan. In such circumstances, a provision should be recognised only for those actions to which the entity is committed (i.e. the earlier actions in the restructuring plan).
>
> The requirement for the existence of a valid expectation in those affected relates to the situation at the end of the reporting period. The fact that implementation has commenced by the date that the financial

statements are authorised for issue does not, by itself, provide evidence that a present obligation existed at the end of the reporting period.

A management or board decision to go ahead with its plan does not, by itself, give rise to a constructive obligation, unless it is accompanied by commencement of the plan, or by a suitable announcement. [IAS 37:75] An obligation may, however, result from earlier events taken together with such a decision. For example, negotiations with employee representatives for termination payments, or with purchasers for the sale of an operation, may have been concluded subject only to board approval. Once that approval has been obtained and communicated to the other parties, the entity has a constructive obligation to restructure if the general conditions set out above have been met. [IAS 37:76] In addition, a constructive obligation could arise if, as happens in some countries, a board includes non-management representatives such as employees, because a decision by such a board involves communication to those representatives. [IAS 37:77]

A valid expectation is unlikely to exist in either of the following circumstances:

* management has developed a detailed plan, but has not notified those affected by it, even though it can point to previous instances when it has proceeded with a plan; or

* management has developed a plan that involves the closure of one of two possible sites. It has made general indications to employees that one site will close, but has not communicated which of the two sites will close, in order to avoid alienation of employees at that site before implementation commences.

Example 3.9.3.2

Lease termination

An entity has developed a detailed formal plan for restructuring a business, and has announced the key features of the restructuring to all affected by it in a manner that meets the criteria of IAS 37. As part of the restructuring, the entity has entered into an oral agreement (i.e. a commitment has been established) with the landlord to terminate a lease and pay a settlement fee of CU1 million to the landlord. The settlement fee represents a direct cost resulting from the restructuring. The entity does not expect to be able to sublet the property; therefore, CU1 million represents the minimum expected obligation.

A provision should be recognised for the CU1 million settlement fee for the lease because a valid expectation has been created between the lessor and lessee that the lease will be terminated. The entity has a constructive restructuring obligation because it has publicly announced the plan to restructure. Such an announcement gives rise to valid expectations in other parties (e.g. the lessor) that the entity will carry out the restructuring, which includes the termination of the lease.

3.9.3.3   Sale of an operation as part of a restructuring

IAS 37:78 specifies that an obligation does not exist for the sale of an operation until the reporting entity is committed to the sale, i.e. there is a binding sale agreement. Until there is such an agreement, the reporting entity will be able to change its mind and, indeed, will be required to take another course of action if a purchaser cannot be found on acceptable terms. [IAS 37:79]

When a sale is only one element of a restructuring plan, a constructive obligation can arise for the other parts of the restructuring before a binding sale agreement exists. In such circumstances, the assets of the operation should be reviewed for impairment. [IAS 37:79]

3.9.3.4   Amounts to be included in a restructuring provision

The amounts to be included in a restructuring provision are restricted to the direct expenditures arising from the restructuring, i.e. those that are both:

[IAS 37:80]

- necessarily entailed by the restructuring; and

- not associated with the ongoing activities of the reporting entity.

3.9.3.5   Amounts to be excluded from a restructuring provision

Specific items that are excluded from restructuring provisions under IAS 37, on the basis that they relate to the ongoing activities of the business, are:

[IAS 37:81]

- retraining or relocating continuing staff;

- marketing; and

- investment in new systems and distribution networks.

Example 3.9.3.5

Relocation costs

An entity has decided to relocate one of its employees. The employee is aware of the impending move.

No provision should be recognised until the relocation occurs, because the relocation relates to the ongoing activities of the business.

3.9.3.6   Restructuring provision flowchart

The flowchart set out below details the steps necessary to determine whether a restructuring provision should be recognised.

Recognition of restructuring provisions

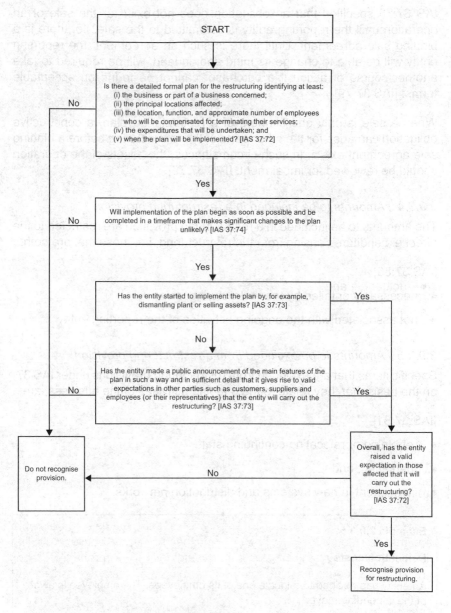

4   Measurement of provisions

4.1   Best estimate

The amount to be recognised as a provision under IAS 37 is the 'best estimate' of the expenditure required to settle the present obligation at the end of the reporting period. [IAS 37:36] The reference to the end of the reporting period does not preclude use of later additional evidence or better information, but indicates that the best estimate will be the amount that a reporting entity would rationally pay at the end of the reporting period to have the obligation taken away – by settlement or by transfer to a third party. [IAS 37:37]

> The addition of 'rationally' in IAS 37:37 suggests that, although it may be difficult to arrange settlement or transfer, there is nevertheless a point of balance, and thus a price, at which management, taking all possible outcomes into account, could be willing to settle.
>
> Ultimately, the best estimate will be determined based on the judgement of management and will reflect experience of similar transactions. In reaching that judgement, reports of independent experts may be required. Examples of relevant independent experts are:
>
> - solicitors and barristers;
>
> - surveyors and valuers;
>
> - loss adjusters;
>
> - actuaries; and
>
> - technical experts (e.g. regarding a decommissioning process).

4.2 Use of expected value

4.2.1 Large populations

When the provision relates to a large population of items, the use of an 'expected value' is appropriate to arrive at a best estimate of the obligation. This is the amount that takes account of all possible outcomes, using probabilities to weight the outcomes. [IAS 37:39] When there is a continuous range of possible outcomes, and each point in that range is as likely as any other, the mid-point of the range is used.

Expected value, as a method of estimation, has a number of desirable features. The method provides an estimate that reflects the entire probability distribution, i.e. all the possible outcomes weighted by their probabilities. For a given assessed distribution, the method has the advantage of objectivity in that different measurers would calculate the same estimate. Furthermore, expected value is additive (i.e. the expected value of a number of items is the sum of the expected values of the individual items).

Example 4.2.1

Best estimate: large populations

An entity faces 100 unrelated legal claims, each with an independent 40 per cent likelihood of success with no cost and a 60 per cent likelihood of failure with the cost of each claim to be CU1 million.

Using expected value, the statistical likelihood is that 60 per cent of the claims will result in a cost of CU1 million. Thus, the best estimate of the provision should be calculated as 60 per cent × 100 × CU1 million = CU60 million.

4.2.2 Single obligations

When a single obligation is being measured, IAS 37:40 indicates that the individual most likely outcome may be the best estimate of the liability. Even in such a case, however, it will be necessary to consider other possible outcomes. When the other possible outcomes are either mostly higher or mostly lower than the most likely outcome, the best estimate will be a higher or lower amount.

Thus, when the provision relates to a single event, or a small number of events, expected value as described in **4.2.1** is not a valid technique.

Example 4.2.2A

Best estimate: single obligation

An entity faces a single legal claim, with a 40 per cent likelihood of success with no cost and a 60 per cent likelihood of failure with a cost of CU1 million.

Expected value is not valid in this case because the outcome will never be a cost of CU600,000 (60 per cent × CU1 million); the outcome will either be nil or CU1 million. IAS 37:40 indicates that the provision may be estimated at the individual most likely outcome. In this example, it is more likely that a cost of CU1 million will result and, therefore, a provision for CU1 million should be recognised.

Generally, when the most likely outcome is close to the expected value, it will be appropriate to provide for the most likely outcome because expected value provides evidence of the probable outflow of benefits.

Example 4.2.2B

Best estimate: expected value (1)

An entity is required to replace a major component in an asset under warranty. Each replacement costs CU1 million. From experience, there is a 30 per cent chance of a single failure, a 50 per cent chance of two failures, and a 20 per cent chance of three failures.

The most likely outcome is two failures, costing CU2 million. The expected value is CU1.9 million ((30 per cent × CU1 million) + (50 per cent × CU2 million) + (20 per cent × CU3 million)). The expected value supports the provision for the most likely outcome of CU2 million.

When the most likely outcome and the expected value are not close together, it will often be appropriate to provide for whichever possible outcome is nearest to the expected value.

Example 4.2.2C

Best estimate: expected value (2)

An entity is required to replace a major component in an asset under a warranty. Each replacement costs CU1 million. From experience, there is a 40 per cent chance of a single failure, a 30 per cent chance of two failures, and a 30 per cent chance of three failures.

The most likely outcome is a single failure, costing CU1 million. The expected value is CU1.9 million ((40 per cent × CU1 million) + (30 per cent × CU2 million) + (30 per cent × CU3 million)). In this case, the most likely outcome of CU1 million has only a 40 per cent probability. There is a 60 per cent probability that the cost will be higher. The outcome closest to expected value is CU2 million (i.e. two failures) and, therefore, a provision for CU2 million should be recognised.

Irrespective of the method applied, in relation to very material items, entities may wish to consider whether it would be appropriate to provide any further information, e.g. the range of possible outcomes.

4.3 Tax

Under IAS 37, provisions are measured before tax. The tax consequences of the provision, and of changes in the provision, are considered separately under IAS 12 *Income Taxes* (see **chapter A13**). [IAS 37:41]

4.4 Risks and uncertainties

IAS 37 indicates that the "risks and uncertainties that inevitably surround many events and circumstances shall be taken into account in reaching the best estimate of a provision". [IAS 37:42] Caution is needed in making judgements under conditions of uncertainty, so that income or assets are not overstated and expenses or liabilities are not understated. However, uncertainty does not justify the creation of excessive provisions or a deliberate overstatement of liabilities. [IAS 37:43]

Also, adjustments for risk and uncertainty should not be double-counted. The most obvious situation in which this may happen is when risk is reflected both in estimated future cash flows and in the discount rate (see **4.7.2**). Disclosures regarding uncertainty required by the Standard should act as a safeguard against obvious error (see **10.2**).

4.5   Future events

4.5.1   Future events – general

In many cases, future events do not represent present obligations and, therefore, they are not provided for. Future events may, however, affect the measurement of a present obligation. IAS 37 requires that future events that may affect the amount required to settle an obligation should be reflected in the amount of a provision when there is sufficient objective evidence that they will occur. [IAS 37:48]

> The reference to future events in IAS 37:48 is to those future events that are factors in estimating the costs of meeting a present obligation (e.g. developments in technology used to clear up a site – see **4.5.2**) or in assessing the extent to which a present contractual obligation is onerous (e.g. an expectation of subleasing a property – see **example 3.9.2B**). However, it does not refer to possible future changes in the underlying obligation (e.g. to the potential for renegotiating the terms of an onerous contract – see **example 3.9.2A**).

4.5.2   Changes in technology

A common example of the anticipation of a future event in the measurement of a provision is the anticipation of the impact of future technology changes on site clean-up costs at the end of a site's life. The amount recognised as a provision for site clean-up costs should reflect the reasonable expectations of technically qualified, objective observers, taking account of all available evidence, as to the technology that will be available at the time of the clean-up. In this situation, IAS 37:49 requires the provision recognised to reflect the reduced costs arising from technology expected to be available at the time of the future clean-up. This allows cost reductions to be recognised for:

- increased experience in applying existing technology; and
- applying existing technology to a larger or more complex clean-up operation than has been carried out to date.

The development of a completely new technology should only be taken into account, however, when there is sufficient objective evidence that it will be available and that it will be effective for the required task. [IAS 37:49]

4.5.3   Changes in legislation

New legislation should be reflected in the measurement of a provision for an existing obligation when there is sufficient objective evidence that the legislation is virtually certain to be enacted. IAS 37 specifies that this will require evidence:

[IAS 37:50]

- of what the legislation will demand; and
- that the legislation will be enacted and implemented.

In practice, because of varying circumstances, there is no single event in the passage of new legislation prior to enactment that provides a general trigger point. In many cases, sufficient objective evidence will not exist until the new legislation is enacted.

4.6   Expected disposals of assets

Gains from expected disposals of assets should not be taken into account in measuring a provision, even if the expected disposal is closely linked to the event giving rise to the provision. [IAS 37:51 & 52]

Example 4.6

Expected disposals of assets

At the end of 20X1, an entity is demonstrably committed to the closure of some facilities, having drawn up a detailed plan and made appropriate announcements. The expected impact of the plan is as follows.

	20X2 CUm	20X3 CUm
Committed closure costs	−100	
Gain from sale of property		+20

The provision required at the end of 20X1 is CU100 million (ignoring discounting). The expected gain on the sale of the property is dealt with separately under the derecognition criteria in IAS 16 *Property, Plant and Equipment*.

4.7   Present value

4.7.1   Requirement to discount future cash flows – general

IAS 37 requires provisions to be discounted to present value when the effect of the time value of money is material. [IAS 37:45]

It will usually be appropriate to make an initial assessment as to whether the impact of discounting might be material before embarking on a potentially complex calculation. Quantifying materiality will depend on a range of factors, e.g. the size of the provision relative to other items in the statement of financial position and the impact of any adjustment on profit for the year. The following table summarises the impact of discounting a single future cash flow for a range of future dates and for a range of possible discount rates. Over a 40-year period, discounting typically reduces an amount to less than 15 per cent of its nominal amount (with the effect that most of the charge would be recognised through the unwinding of the discount).

Cash flow of 100 after:	Discount rate		
	5 per cent	7.5 per cent	10 per cent
1 year	95	93	91
2 years	91	87	83
3 years	86	80	75
4 years	82	75	68
5 years	78	70	62
10 years	61	49	39
15 years	48	34	24
20 years	38	24	15
40 years	14	6	2

4.7.2   Choice of discount rate

The discount rate (or rates) selected should:

[IAS 37:47]

- be pre-tax;
- reflect current market assessments of the time value of money; and
- reflect risks specific to the liability.

4.7.3   Adjusting for risk

4.7.3.1   Adjusting for risk – general

Under IAS 37, it is acceptable to reflect risk either in the estimation of cash flows or by adjusting the discount rate. The estimation of an adjusted discount rate is not a precise science. It may, therefore, be preferable, on grounds of simplicity, to deal with risk through a detailed estimation of cash flows to include the impact of risk, coupled with the use of a risk-free discount rate. Whichever method is used, care should be taken to avoid double-counting (or omitting) the effect of any risks.

It follows that, when risk is reflected in estimates of cash flows, the appropriate discount rate will be a pre-tax risk-free rate such as a current government bond rate.

Example 4.7.3.1A

Risk-free rate

An entity sells goods subject to a warranty. A provision is calculated for warranty claims based on detailed records of past faults in products. Because the estimation of cash flows takes account of risks specific to the warranty, the appropriate discount rate will be a risk-free rate (e.g. a government bond rate).

Example 4.7.3.1B

Risk-adjusting the discount rate

An entity's best estimate of the amount that it will have to pay to settle a liability in two years' time is CU1,000. The actual liability could be anything between CU500 and CU1,500. At the end of the reporting period, the entity knows that it could transfer the liability to a third party immediately if it agrees to pay that third party CU1,075 in two years' time. Accordingly, before taking the time value of money into account, the entity's best estimate of the outflow is CU1,000, excluding any risk adjustment, and the equivalent certain amount payable in two years' time is CU1,075, i.e. including an adjustment for risk of CU75. The amount of the provision recognised at the end of the reporting period should be the same whether the unadjusted best estimate or the risk-adjusted best estimate is used as the basis for the net present value calculation. The appropriate risk-free rate is 4 per cent per annum.

	Undiscounted amount	Net present value
	CU	CU
Risk-adjusted cash flow	1,075	994*
Expected cash flow (unadjusted for risk)	1,000	994#

* Using a risk-free rate of 4% on the risk-adjusted cash flow of CU1,075 gives a net present value of CU994.

\# To arrive at the same net present value (CU994), a risk-adjusted rate of 0.3% must be used to discount the expected cash flow of CU1,000.

As illustrated by this example, the risk-adjusted discount rate will generally be lower than the risk-free rate when discounting liabilities.

4.7.3.2 Effect of own credit risk

At its March 2011 meeting, the IFRS Interpretations Committee considered the question as to whether, if the discount rate is to be adjusted for risk, an entity's own credit risk (performance risk) should be considered a risk 'specific to the liability' as contemplated in IAS 37:47 (and, therefore, be taken into account in measuring the present value of the expenditures expected to be required to settle the obligation).

The Interpretations Committee noted that IAS 37 does not explicitly state whether an entity's own credit risk should be included as an adjustment to the discount rate used to measure non-financial liabilities.

Despite there being no explicit statement in IAS 37, the Committee did note its understanding that predominant practice is to exclude the effect of an entity's own credit risk, which is generally viewed in practice as a risk of the entity rather than a risk specific to the liability.

4.7.4 Pre-tax rates calculated from post-tax rates

Care should be taken in determining a pre-tax discount rate by adjusting a post-tax rate. Because the tax consequences of cash flows may occur in different periods, the pre-tax rate of return is not always the post-tax rate of return grossed up by the standard rate of tax. See **8.4.2** in **chapter A10** for further guidance on how to adjust a post-tax discount rate to arrive at a pre-tax discount rate.

4.7.5 Impact of inflation

When estimated cash flows are expressed in current prices, a real discount rate (i.e. reduced for the impact of future inflation) will be used. Alternatively, when cash flows are expressed in expected future prices (normally higher than current prices), a nominal discount rate will be used. The effects of inflation specific to the cash flows on the present value of those cash flows will be the same provided that one of the following methods is used:

- current (lower) prices discounted at a real (lower) rate; or

- future (higher) prices discounted at a nominal (higher) rate.

The real rate can be estimated by deducting the inflation rate from the nominal rate. Mathematically, the relationship between the nominal rate and the real rate is expressed by the following formula:

$$(1+ \text{real rate}) = (1+ \text{nominal rate})/(1+ \text{inflation rate}).$$

Example 4.7.5

Impact of inflation

Company A estimates that it will pay CU1,000 (in current prices) at the end of each of the next three years to settle a present obligation. If it takes into account inflation, assumed at 1.5 per cent per annum, these cash flows will increase to the amounts illustrated in the table below. Company A has established that the nominal discount rate (which includes inflation) is 4 per cent. By discounting the cash flows the net present value is CU2,858. By iteration, it is possible to calculate the real discount rate, i.e. the rate that would have to be applied to the cash flows excluding inflation to arrive at the same present value.

	Net present value	Year 1	Year 2	Year 3
	CU	CU	CU	CU
Cash flows adjusted for inflation of 1.5% per annum		1,015	1,030	1,046
NPV @ nominal discount rate of 4%	2,858			
Cash flows excluding inflation		1,000	1,000	1,000
NPV@ real discount rate of 2.46%	2,858			

The equivalent real rate is 2.46 per cent. It would be incorrect to discount the cash flows that exclude inflation (i.e. CU1,000 per year) using the nominal discount rate of 4 per cent because this would give an understated net present value of CU2,776.

Assuming no change in discount rate and no change in expected cash flows (i.e. inflation proves to be as assessed on initial recognition of the provision), the amount recognised each year to unwind the discount will be as follows:

	NPV @ 4% at start of the year	Cash flow	Year end carrying amount	Unwind of discount
	CU	CU	CU	CU
Year 1	2,858	(1,015)	1,957	114
Year 2	1,957	(1,030)	1,006	79
Year 3	1,006	(1,046)	–	40

The interest cost is made up of a discount factor being the real interest rate of 2.46 per cent and an inflation factor of 1.5 per cent. The interest cost should not be split between these elements for reporting purposes. Rather, the full nominal amount of the discount should be included as a borrowing cost consistent with other external borrowing costs.

5 Reimbursements

5.1 Recognition and presentation of reimbursements – general

An entity with a present obligation may be able to seek reimbursement of part or all of the expenditure from another party, for example via:

- an insurance contract arranged to cover a risk; or
- an indemnity clause in a contract; or
- a warranty provided by a supplier.

The basis underlying the recognition of a reimbursement is that any asset arising is separate from the related obligation. Consequently, such a reimbursement should be recognised only when it is virtually certain that it will be received if the entity settles the obligation. [IAS 37:53] This treatment is also consistent with the guidance on contingent assets.

When a provision has been recognised, the occurrence of the expenditure is taken to be certain for the purposes of assessing the probability of receiving reimbursement and judging whether it is virtually certain.

Note that it is the existence of the reimbursement asset that must be virtually certain, rather than its amount. An entity may be virtually certain that it has insurance to cover a particular provision, but it may not be certain of the precise amount that would be received from the insurer. Provided that the range of possible recoveries is such that the entity can arrive at a reliable estimate, it will be able to recognise this as an asset, even though the amount ultimately received may be different.

The appropriate presentation of a reimbursement is as follows:

* in the statement of financial position, a separate asset is recognised (which must not exceed the amount of the provision); [IAS 37:53] and

* in profit or loss, a net amount may be presented, being the anticipated cost of the obligation less the reimbursement. [IAS 37:54]

Example 5

Recognition of reimbursement due from insurance company

An entity has a high probability of losing a lawsuit in which it is the defendant. The entity's insurance company is expected to cover any loss incurred.

What amounts, if any, should the entity recognise in its statement of financial position in respect of the anticipated loss and reimbursement?

The outflow of resources expected on the loss of the lawsuit and the amounts expected to be recovered from the insurance company arise from the same past event. When the conditions of IAS 37:14 (see **3.1**) are met, the entity should recognise a liability for the expected outflow of resources, measured at the best estimate of the expenditure required to settle the obligation at the end of the reporting period as stated in IAS 37:36.

In respect of the expected recovery from the insurance company, the entity should assess the effectiveness of its insurance policy. Under IAS 37:53, it should recognise the amount expected to be reimbursed (as a separate asset) when, and only when, it is virtually certain that the claim will be received (i.e. unless there is doubt regarding the insurance claim).

> The amount recognised for the reimbursement should not exceed the amount of the provision.

Offset of a provision and the related reimbursement is never appropriate. If a reporting entity can avoid making payment in respect of an obligation in all circumstances (i.e. there can never be any recourse to the entity), then it has no liability and hence neither a provision nor a reimbursement asset should be recognised. In most cases, however, the entity will remain liable for the whole amount in question and will have to settle the full amount if the third party fails to pay for any reason. In these circumstances, no offset is permitted, irrespective of how unlikely it is that the entity will have to settle the obligation directly. [IAS 37:56 & 57]

If a reporting entity is jointly and severally liable for an obligation, it should provide for that part of the obligation which it is probable will be settled by the entity. The remainder, expected to be paid by other parties, is a contingent liability. [IAS 37:29 & 58]

If an entity has a provision and a matching reimbursement, and the time value of money is material to both, the question arises as to whether both should be discounted. In principle, both the asset and the liability should be discounted. If there will be a significant interval between the cash outflows and receiving the reimbursement, the reimbursement will be more heavily discounted; in such circumstances, if the gross inflows and outflows are the same, on initial recognition there will be a net cost. If (presumably rarely) the reimbursement will be received first, IAS 37:53 will restrict the discounted amount of the reimbursement so that it does not exceed the discounted amount of the provision. In profit or loss, the unwinding of the discount on the reimbursement may be offset against that on the provision.

When a reimbursement will not be received until some significant time after the outflows to which it relates, it is possible (though perhaps rare) that it may carry interest, or in some other way be increased, so as to reimburse the entity for the lost time value of money. The only restriction in IAS 37 is that the asset recognised (i.e. the discounted amount) must not exceed the provision recognised. It is, in principle, possible for the gross amount of reimbursement used in the discounting calculation to exceed the gross outflows expected (i.e. for the undiscounted asset to be greater than the undiscounted liability).

5.2   Collateralised or guaranteed loan commitments

Example 5.2

Collateralised or guaranteed loan commitments

Entity A has issued a non-cancellable loan commitment at market terms to Entity B. The loan commitment cannot be settled net, and Entity A has no past practice of selling the assets resulting from its loan commitments shortly after origination. Entity A did not designate this loan commitment at fair value through profit or loss; therefore, in accordance with paragraphs 2(g) and 2.3 of IFRS 9 *Financial Instruments* (or, for entities that have not yet adopted IFRS 9, paragraphs 2(h) and 4 of IAS 39 *Financial Instruments: Recognition and Measurement*), this loan commitment is scoped out of IFRS 9 (IAS 39) and should be accounted for under IAS 37.

Scenario 1

The loan subject to the loan commitment is guaranteed by another party (e.g. the parent of the borrowing entity or an insurer). That party will reimburse Entity A for any loss incurred if Entity B fails to make payments when due (i.e. if there is a breach of contract). The loan commitment has not been settled at the end of the reporting period; however, Entity A assesses that Entity B will not be able to repay the loan that it has committed to grant to Entity B.

Scenario 2

The loan subject to the loan commitment is a collateralised loan; that is, if Entity B fails to make payments when due, the legal ownership of the collateral (e.g. property) will be transferred to Entity A. The loan commitment has not been settled at the end of the reporting period; however, Entity A assesses that Entity B will not be able to repay the loan that it has committed to grant to Entity B.

How should Entity A account for the loan commitments under Scenarios 1 and 2 at the end of the reporting period?

General

In general, a provision should be recognised when the conditions set out in IAS 37:14 (see **3.1**) are met. That is, if Entity A has assessed at the end of the reporting period that Entity B will not be able to repay the loan that it has committed to grant to Entity B, a provision should be recognised.

Scenario 1

- The provision should be measured according to IAS 37:36 at "the best estimate of the expenditure required to settle the present obligation at the end of the reporting period". In accordance with IAS 37:53, Entity A should not take into account the guarantee provided by the parent or insurer when assessing the amount of the provision necessary at the end of the reporting period.

- The guarantee provided by the parent or insurer is a reimbursement right because Entity A "is able to look to another party to pay part or all of the expenditure required to settle a provision". [IAS 37:55] The guarantee, therefore, should be recognised as a separate asset. However, this should only be done when the criteria in IAS 37:53 are met, which requires that a reimbursement from another party is recognised only when it is virtually certain that reimbursement will be received if Entity B fails to make payment when due. The 'virtually certain' criteria may be met once Entity B's breach of contract has occurred (e.g. at the first interest payment date).

- If the guarantee was part of the same contractual arrangement (e.g. when the loan commitment issued to Entity B is guaranteed by the parent of Entity B, and the guarantee is part of the same contractual arrangement), then it would be bundled and an alternative treatment would be appropriate (see the answer for scenario 2 below).

Scenario 2

- Collateral held on the loan is not a reimbursement right because Entity A is not "able to look to another party to pay part or all of the expenditure required to settle a provision". [IAS 37:55] Accordingly, this collateral is not separate from the loan commitment and, when accounting for the provision, it should be treated as a net arrangement with a single counterparty (i.e. the collateral should be taken into account when measuring the provision amount).

- The provision is measured in accordance with IAS 37:36. Although the loan commitment is within the scope of IAS 37, in practice, a provision will be recognised at the amount equivalent to the impairment that would have been required under IAS 39:63, which states that "the amount of the loss is measured as the difference between the asset's carrying amount and the present value of estimated future cash flows". Additionally, IAS 39:AG84 indicates that "the calculation of the present value of the estimated future cash flows of a collateralised financial asset reflects the cash flows that may result from foreclosure, less costs for obtaining and selling the collateral, whether or not foreclosure is probable". Accordingly, the provision is recognised for the present value of the net non-recoverable amount (taking into account the value of the collateral, less the cost for obtaining and selling it).

6   Changes in provisions

Provisions should be reviewed at the end of each reporting period and adjusted to reflect current best estimates. [IAS 37:59]

Adjustments to provisions arise from three sources:

- revisions to estimated cash flows (both amount and likelihood);
- changes to present value due to the passage of time; and
- revisions of discount rates to reflect prevailing current market conditions.

In the years following the initial measurement of a provision at a present value, the present value will be restated to reflect estimated cash flows being closer to the measurement date. This unwinding of the discount relating to the passage of time should be recognised as a finance cost. [IAS 37:60] The effect of revising estimates of cash flows is not part of this unwinding and should be dealt with as part of any adjustment to the previous provision.

When a provision is no longer required (e.g. if it is no longer probable that a transfer of economic benefits will be required to settle the obligation), the provision should be reversed. [IAS 37:59]

The disclosure requirements in respect of changes in provisions are dealt with in **10.2.2**.

The degree of uncertainty associated with an obligation can change over time. In some cases, an obligation will be recognised initially as a provision due to the uncertainty surrounding the amount payable. Subsequently, after negotiation with the counterparty, an exact amount may be agreed. To the extent that the agreed amount is not settled immediately, it no longer meets the definition of a provision and, therefore, should be reclassified to another appropriate category within liabilities.

7   Use of provisions

One of the objectives of IAS 37 is to increase the transparency of accounting for provisions and, in particular, to prevent the use of an existing provision to meet a different undisclosed obligation. Accordingly, the Standard requires a provision to be used only for expenditures for which the provision was originally recognised. [IAS 37:61]

The disclosure requirements for provisions (see **10.2.2**), particularly the requirement to identify movements on each class of provision, are intended to reinforce this requirement.

8   Illustrative examples

8.1   Summary of illustrative examples from the implementation guidance accompanying IAS 37

The examples set out in Section C of the implementation guidance accompanying IAS 37 are summarised below, but in a tabular format, in order to identify reasons for particular items meeting, or not meeting, the definition of a provision. In all cases, it is assumed that a reliable estimate can be made.

Type of risk or cost	Present obligation as a result of a past event?	Probable transfer of benefits?	Conclusion
Warranty Example 1: Warranty given by a manufacturer under the terms of a contract for sale. Past experience shows that it is probable that claims will be received.	✓	✓	Provide at date of sale for legal obligation.
Contaminated land (1) Example 2A: Contaminated land – entity cleans up only to meet legal requirements, which are virtually certain to be enacted soon after the end of the reporting period.	✓	✓	Provide for expected legal obligation.
Contaminated land (2) Example 2B: Contaminated land – entity has no legal obligation, but meets widely publicised clean-up policy.	✓	✓	Provide for constructive obligation.
Decommissioning Example 3: Decommissioning – terms of a licence impose a legal obligation to remove an oil rig at the end of its life.	✓	✓	Provide on commissioning of asset and include in cost of oil rig.
Refunds policy Example 4: Refunds – retail store follows a published policy of providing refunds, even though there is no legal obligation.	✓	✓	Provide for constructive obligation.
Closure of a division (1) Example 5A: Closure of a division – board decision taken before the end of the reporting period, but not communicated to those affected and plan not commenced.	✗		No obligating event before the end of the reporting period.

Type of risk or cost	Present obligation as a result of a past event?	Probable transfer of benefits?	Conclusion
Closure of a division (2) Example 5B: Closure of a division – board decision, detailed plan completed, staff and customers notified before the end of the reporting period.	✓	✓	Provide for expected costs of closure.
Legal requirement to fit smoke filter Example 6: Introduction of legal requirement to fit smoke filters by 30 June 20X1.			
(a) At 31 December 20X0, the end of the reporting period.	✗		No obligating event at the end of the reporting period.
(b) At 31 December 20X1, the end of the reporting period (assuming filters not yet fitted).	✗		– no obligating event in respect of filters, but
	✓	✓	– provision may be required for any fines and penalties likely to be suffered.
Staff retraining Example 7: Staff retraining – need to retrain staff to meet new system requirements imposed by change in the law.	✗		No obligating event until training occurs.
Onerous contract Example 8: Onerous contract – operating lease rental payments on vacated property.	✓	✓	Provide for unavoidable lease payments.

Type of risk or cost	Present obligation as a result of a past event?	Probable transfer of benefits?	Conclusion
Guarantee Example 9: Guarantee – provided for another entity's borrowings. Although such guarantees were within the scope of IAS 37 when the Standard was originally issued, they are now within the scope of IFRS 9 *Financial Instruments* (or, for entities that have not yet adopted IFRS 9, IAS 39 *Financial Instruments: Recognition and Measurement*), except in limited circumstances in which IFRS 4 *Insurance Contracts* applies (see the discussion in **section 2.3** of **chapter B1** or in **section 2.3** of **chapter C1**). Example 9 provides an example of an accounting policy that IFRS 4 permits and that also complies with the requirements in IFRS 9 (or IAS 39) for financial guarantee contracts within the scope of IFRS 9 (or IAS 39).			
Court case Example 10: Unsettled court case			
(a) At 31 December 20X0, the end of the reporting period – lawyers advise that no liability will be proved.	✗		No obligation exists based on evidence.
(b) At 31 December 20X1, the end of the reporting period – lawyers advise that liability will be proved.	✓	✓	Provide for estimated settlement.

Type of risk or cost	Present obligation as a result of a past event?	Probable transfer of benefits?	Conclusion
Repairs and maintenance Example 11A: Repairs and maintenance – a furnace has a lining that needs to be replaced every five years for technical reasons. At the end of the reporting period, the lining has been in use for three years.	✗		No obligation exists independently of future actions. Expenditure capitalised when incurred and depreciated.
Refurbishment costs Example 11B: Refurbishment costs – legislative requirement – an airline is required by law to overhaul its aircraft once every three years.	✗		No obligation exists independently of future actions (the entity could sell the aircraft). Expenditure capitalised when incurred and depreciated.

8.2   Repairs and maintenance obligations under leases

Under some operating leases, the lessee is required to incur periodic charges for maintenance of the leased asset or to make good dilapidations or other damage occurring during the rental period. Because the lease is a legal contract, it may give rise to legal obligations. Accordingly, the principles of IAS 37, which generally preclude the recognition of provisions for repairs and maintenance, do not preclude the recognition of such liabilities in a lease once the event giving rise to the obligation under the lease has occurred.

Example 8.2

Lease of aircraft

An entity leases an aircraft under an operating lease. The aircraft has to undergo an expensive 'C check' after every 2,400 flying hours.

The requirement to perform a 'C check' does not give rise to a present obligation at the time the lease is signed because, until 2,400 hours have been flown, there is no obligation which exists independently of the entity's future actions. Even the intention to incur the cost of a 'C check' depends on the entity deciding to continue flying the aircraft. Therefore, no provision should be recognised for a future 'C check'. The cost of each successive 'C check' will instead be capitalised when it is incurred and amortised over the period to the next 'C check'.

This leaves the question of the condition in which the aircraft must be returned to the lessor at the end of the lease and of whether this creates a present obligation, and thus the requirement for a provision, at the time the lease is signed. The answer depends on what the lease terms state will happen when the aircraft is returned at the end of the lease. If no final 'C check' is required (i.e. in the final period, the client can use the aircraft for up to 2,399 flying hours and then return it without bearing any cost), no provision should be recognised because there is no legal obligation.

If a 'C check' is required at the end of the lease, irrespective of how many hours have been flown, full provision for the cost should be recognised at the start of the lease. The costs should be carried forward and written off over the shorter of the next 2,400 flying hours and the number of flying hours to the end of the lease – and similarly each time a 'C check' is carried out.

If, on returning the aircraft, the entity must make a payment towards the 'C check' which is in proportion to the number of hours flown (e.g. 75 per cent of the cost of a 'C check' for 1,800 hours flown), then an obligation is created as the aircraft is used. It will be appropriate to build up a provision based on the number of hours flown.

8.3   Obligations to restore leased property

Example 8.3

Obligations to restore leased property

Entity A is a lessee in a lease contract. As a condition of the lease and prior to return of the property to the lessor, Entity A is required to:

- remove any leasehold improvements, such as additional internal walls or partitioning fitted by the lessee; and

- repair the fabric of the building so that it is restored to its original condition at the date of inception of the lease, i.e. to make good any dilapidations.

When should Entity A recognise any provision in relation to restoration of the leased property?

If a lease agreement requires an item to be replaced if its standard falls below a specified level, no provision should be recognised until the point at which it is no longer possible for the entity to avoid replacing the item.

Generally, it will not be appropriate to build up a provision for restoring leased property gradually over the lease term, because typically that will not reflect how the obligation arises. For example, if a lease agreement requires carpets to be replaced or walls to be repainted at the end of the lease period, full provision for the associated cost will be required from the outset, because the outflow cannot be avoided.

Typically, a provision will be spread over the lease term when the associated costs are directly proportional to the length of time for which the associated asset has been used. This may be true for some elements of restoration relating to, for example, oil wells and landfill sites, but it is less common for property leases.

Accordingly, Entity A should provide for the cost of removing leasehold improvements when those leasehold improvements are first made (e.g. when additional internal walls and partitioning are fitted). Entity A should only provide for repairs to the fabric of the building once it is no longer possible for Entity A to avoid making those repairs.

8.4   Self-insurance – cost of accidents

When an entity self-insures (e.g. a retailer might decide not to insure itself in respect of the risk of minor accidents to its customers), it should recognise a provision each year for the costs of accidents that have occurred prior to the end of the reporting period. This provision should cover not only those claims that have been made prior to the end of the reporting period, but also claims potentially incurred but not reported (IBNR) at that date. It will be common that an accident has happened but the entity does not know of its occurrence. This in itself does not preclude the entity from recognising a provision – as long as a reliable estimate can be made of IBNR claims, probably based on past experience. Because the IBNR provision is, by definition, in respect of claims incurred before the end of the reporting period, the obligating event will have occurred by that date. IAS 37 does not, however, permit the recognition of a provision for the excess of the 'normal annual cost' over the cost of actual accidents in the year. In other words, a self-insuring entity is prevented from 'smoothing' the cost of accidents by making a buffer provision in a year when actual costs are low.

When a group self-insures by setting up a separate captive insurance subsidiary, any intragroup premiums charged or received will be eliminated on consolidation, reflecting the fact that, for the group, this is not external insurance cover.

Example 8.4

Adjustment of insurance premiums

Entity A has an insurance policy with premiums that are adjusted on the basis of actual losses incurred in that year. For example, if losses for a specific period exceed 100, Entity A will have to pay the insurer 80 per cent of the excessive losses in the form of additional premiums in that year.

Entity A should recognise a provision at the end of each reporting period for the additional premiums due as a result of losses in that year. In measuring that provision, Entity A should consider not only known losses but also losses incurred but not yet reported.

8.5 Vouchers issued for no consideration

A reporting entity may, for no consideration, distribute vouchers that can be used, sometimes within a set period, to obtain discounts on the entity's products and/or a third party's products. (Note that when such vouchers are issued as part of a sales transaction, it will be necessary to consider the unbundling implications of IFRS 15 *Revenue from Contracts with Customers* (see **section 6** of **chapter A14**) or, for entities that have not yet adopted IFRS 15, IFRIC 13 *Customer Loyalty Programmes* (see **section 5.6** of **appendix A1**).)

Applying IAS 37's recognition criteria, the questions to be considered are as follows.

- *Is there a present obligation?* Generally, the answer will be yes. But if the reporting entity reserves the right to terminate the scheme at any time, thus invalidating existing vouchers, there may or may not be a constructive obligation. In the absence of evidence that schemes have been terminated (and existing vouchers invalidated) in the past, however, it should be presumed that an obligation exists.

- *Is it probable that economic benefits will be transferred?* If, after vouchers are deducted, the entity's products are still being sold at a profit, the answer will be no – in which case no provision will be recognised. To the extent that products will be sold at a loss, however, or that a third party will be reimbursed for discounts, there will be a transfer of economic benefits.

- *Can a reliable estimate be made?* The answer here should be presumed to be yes, but in making the estimate the entity should consider how many vouchers are expected to be used.

In summary, if the criteria are met, provision should be recognised for the best estimate of the cost to the entity (which may not be the face value of the discounts). The entity will need to form a view as to how many vouchers are expected to be used and should also consider whether discounting is appropriate.

8.6 Costs of decommissioning an oil rig

Commissioning of a new oil rig creates an obligation to incur costs of decommissioning in the future, but also gives access to future economic benefits. A provision for the present value of costs of decommissioning should be recognised at the time of commissioning the oil rig and the amount recognised should be added to the cost of the rig. The provision should only include the costs that are an obligation resulting from commissioning the rig. The provision should not include any additional costs that will only be triggered by further drilling until that further drilling occurs.

IFRIC 1 *Changes in Existing Decommissioning, Restoration and Similar Liabilities* (see **4.4** in **chapter A7**) and IFRIC 5 *Rights to Interests arising from Decommissioning, Restoration and Environmental Rehabilitation Funds* (see **9.2**) address related issues.

8.7 Late delivery penalties

In some circumstances, a late delivery penalty may be incurred when goods are not supplied by a specified delivery date. At the end of its reporting period, an entity may know that it will not be able to meet the delivery date for goods to be supplied in the next year.

At its year end, before the original delivery date, should the entity recognise a provision for the penalty that will be payable when, as is expected, the goods are delivered late?

No. There is no past event because the late delivery of goods has not yet occurred. Consequently, there is neither a legal nor a constructive obligation to pay the penalty at the end of the current reporting period and no basis for recognising a provision for the penalty.

However, if the remaining part of the contract has, as a whole, become onerous as a result of the penalty clause, a provision should be recognised for any overall loss expected to result.

8.8 Repurchase agreements – trade-in right

Example 8.8

Repurchase agreements – trade-in right

In order to facilitate vehicle sales, a motor dealer offers specified-price trade-in arrangements on vehicles for sale that give a customer the right to trade in his or her vehicle toward the purchase of a new vehicle at some point in the future. The trade-in may be exercisable by the customer at a specified point in time or during a specified period of time.

Should the dealer recognise a provision for the cost of the guaranteed vehicle repurchases?

If the amount of credit that will be received upon exercise of a specified-price trade-in right is equal to or less than the estimated fair value of the vehicle at the trade-in date (determined on the date of the original sale of the vehicle subject to the specified-price trade-in right) and if the customer is required to pay a significant incremental amount in addition to the trade-in credit for the new vehicle at the trade-in date, then no revenue from the original sale of the vehicle should be allocated to the trade-in right and no provision should be recognised for the trade-in right at the time of the original sale. If the motor dealer subsequently determines, however, that the trade-in arrangement has become onerous, the motor dealer should recognise a provision for the onerous contract. In assessing whether, and to what extent, the trade-in arrangement has become onerous, the motor dealer should consider the net of:

- any loss that may be incurred upon the customer's exercise of the specified-price trade-in right (i.e. the difference between the trade-in price and the resale value at that date of the vehicle traded-in); and

- any profit that may be expected on the sale of the new vehicle to the customer at the trade-in date.

8.9 Employment disputes

Example 8.9

Employment disputes

An entity employs three professional seamen. Maritime law prescribes that registered professionals are paid a premium over unregistered professionals. The entity subsequently discovers that the professionals are not registered and, therefore, have been overpaid. The entity consequently reduces the salaries of these professionals who then take the matter to court. One employee wins the case and is awarded a CU70,000 retrenchment package. The other two lose on a technicality, but will appeal the decision. Lawyers are certain that the appeal will be successful.

A provision should be recognised for the best estimate of the costs to settle the appeal. The past event is the underpayment of the employees (after it was thought they were overpaid), and therefore occurred during the year. As a result of the court proceedings, a legal obligation to compensate one employee exists in the current year (for CU70,000). With regard to the other two seamen, the past event is the constructive dismissal (i.e. the reduction in salaries) that occurred during the year. Because it is probable (more likely than not) that the entity will be found liable, a present obligation exists. It is probable that economic benefits will flow from the entity.

9 IFRIC Interpretations

9.1 Emission Rights (IFRIC 3, since withdrawn)

9.1.1 IFRIC 3 – background

In December 2004, IFRIC 3 *Emission Rights* was issued to deal with the accounting by participants in a 'cap and trade' scheme. The Interpretation specified that a cap and trade scheme gives rise to an asset for allowances held, a government grant in respect of any allowances granted free of charge, and a liability for the obligation to deliver allowances, equal to the emissions made. However, the accounting required by IFRIC 3 led to a perceived mismatch: assets would either be recognised at historical amounts or revalued with changes recognised in other comprehensive income, whereas liabilities would be remeasured to fair value through profit or loss. Thus, an entity holding precisely the level of assets required to settle its liabilities would nevertheless report gains or losses if there were changes in fair value.

In 2005, as a result of these perceived problems with IFRIC 3, the Interpretation was withdrawn. The IASB has stated its intention to conduct a broader assessment of the nature of the various volatilities resulting from the application of IFRIC 3 and to consider whether and how it might be appropriate to amend existing Standards to reduce or eliminate some of those volatilities.

In the meantime, entities participating in cap and trade schemes will need to give careful thought to how they account for the assets and liabilities arising. One possible approach would be to follow the guidance set out in IFRIC 3 (see **9.1.2**). Two other possible approaches are outlined at **9.1.3** and **9.1.4**. The accounting policy adopted should be applied to all emission allowances and related liabilities on a consistent basis.

Although emission rights are typically regarded as intangible assets for most entities, if an entity is acting as a broker or trader, such that it acquires rights from one market participant and sells them on to another, the emission rights are likely to be inventories for that entity. In the event that an entity acquires emission rights far in excess of the emissions it is likely to make, with a view to selling those rights, those excess rights may qualify as inventories.

9.1.2 Approach 1: apply IFRIC 3

Emission rights are intangible assets that are accounted for in accordance with IAS 38 *Intangible Assets* and would be recognised initially at fair value. When allowances are issued for less than fair value, the difference between the amount paid (if any) and fair value would be accounted for as a government grant within the scope of IAS 20 *Accounting for Government Grants and Disclosure of Government Assistance*.

As emissions are made, a liability would be recognised for the obligation to deliver allowances equal to emissions that have been made. This liability would be a provision within the scope of IAS 37, and would be measured at the best estimate of the expenditure required to settle the present obligation at the end of the reporting period. This would usually be the present market price of the number of allowances required to cover emissions made up to the end of the reporting period.

Offset of the asset (emission credits held) and the liability (to deliver credits to the value of emissions made) would not be permitted.

9.1.3 Approach 2: government grant and an intangible asset initially at fair value, emission liability reflects carrying amounts

9.1.3.1 Intangible asset

Allowances allocated free of charge or for nominal consideration would be measured under the alternatives permitted in IAS 20 and IAS 38. It would seem preferable for allowances to be recognised as an asset only when issued. But an acceptable alternative would be for the entire period allocation to be recognised as an asset at the point at which the relevant authority finalises the allocation plan for the allowances.

Allowances allocated represent an intangible asset acquired by an entity free of charge or for nominal consideration. IAS 38:44 sets out two possible treatments. The entity could choose to recognise both the intangible asset and the government grant initially at fair value; alternatively, nominal value could be used (see **9.1.4**). The fair value approach might be considered as providing better accounting information, in that it results in a better representation of the economic resources and obligations of the entity.

Subsequent to initial recognition, the general requirements for intangible assets in IAS 38 would apply.

- IAS 38 permits an intangible asset to be remeasured at fair value when this can be measured by reference to an active market. Remeasurements are recognised in other comprehensive income. [IAS 38:75] The revalued amount is subject to amortisation and impairment testing between remeasurements. This accounting treatment precludes any reclassification to profit or loss of fair value increments accumulated in equity.

- IAS 38 also permits an intangible asset to be measured at cost less amortisation / impairment. [IAS 38:74] If an entity were to use this method, any difference between the carrying amount of the asset and the liability would be recognised in profit or loss upon settlement of the obligation (or sale of the allowances).

For most allowances traded in an active market, no amortisation will be required because the residual value will be the same as cost and, therefore, the depreciable amount will be zero. If the market value of the allowances falls below cost, or other indicators of impairment exist, then the guidance in IAS 36 *Impairment of Assets* should be followed to determine whether the assets are impaired.

9.1.3.2 Government grant

Allowances represent a non-monetary government grant and could be recognised at the fair value of the related asset or at a nominal amount.

[IAS 20:23] For the reasons noted above, it might be preferable for the government grant to be measured initially at fair value. The grant would be recognised as deferred income and recognised in profit or loss on a systematic basis over the compliance period, regardless of whether the allowances received continue to be held by the entity.

9.1.3.3 Emission liability

A liability for emissions would be recognised as incurred and measured at the best estimate of the expenditure required to settle the present obligation at the end of the reporting period, in accordance with IAS 37:36. Under cap and trade schemes, entities generally can settle the obligation created by the emission of pollutants only by surrendering allowances to the appropriate authority and cannot settle their obligations by making a cash payment or by transferring other assets.

When an entity measures allowances at fair value, the liability would be measured at the same amount, because this is the best estimate of the expenditure (economic resources) required to settle the obligation.

When an entity measures allowances at cost then, provided that it has sufficient allowances to satisfy the emission liability, the liability would be measured at the same amount (i.e. as the sum of the cost of the initial allowances received and the cost of any additional allowances purchased). If at the end of the reporting period the liability to deliver allowances exceeds the amount of allowances on hand, then the shortfall would be measured at the current fair (market) value of the short position. Consequently, if an entity chose to sell allowances during the year, and in doing so created a shortfall in the number of allowances held as compared to the total pollutants emitted at that date, it would remeasure the portion of the obligation related to the shortfall at the current market value of the allowances.

9.1.4 Approach 3: government grant and an intangible asset measured at nominal amounts (net liability approach)

Under this approach, when allowances are allocated free of charge or for nominal consideration, an intangible asset would be recognised and measured at a nominal amount when allowances are issued or allocated (i.e. the cost / nominal amount alternatives are adopted in IAS 20 and IAS 38). A credit entry for the government grant would be recognised in the statement of financial position at a nominal amount equal to the carrying amount of the allowances. [IAS 20:23]

No liability for emissions would be recognised provided that the entity has sufficient allowances to satisfy the emission liability, because the allowances granted (which are recognised only at a nominal amount) will be used to settle the liability. Therefore, no entries are required as long as the entity holds sufficient allowances to meet its emission obligations.

If at the end of the reporting period the liability to deliver allowances exceeds the amount of allowances on hand, then the shortfall should be measured at the current fair (market) value of the short position (as in **9.1.3**).

9.2 IFRIC 5 *Rights to Interests arising from Decommissioning, Restoration and Environmental Rehabilitation Funds*

9.2.1 IFRIC 5 – background

IFRIC 5 deals with the accounting, in the financial statements of the contributor, for interests in decommissioning, restoration and environmental rehabilitation funds established to fund some or all of the costs of decommissioning assets or to undertake environmental rehabilitation. Contributions to such funds may be voluntary or required by law. Funds may be established by a single contributor, or they may be established by multiple contributors. Such funds are generally separately administered by trustees. Entities make contributions that are invested on behalf of the fund by the trustees. The contributors retain the obligation to pay decommissioning costs, but they are able to obtain reimbursement from the fund up to the lower of the decommissioning costs incurred and the contributor's share of the assets of the fund. The contributors may have restricted access or no access to any surplus of assets of the fund over those used to meet eligible decommissioning costs.

The issues under consideration in IFRIC 5 are:

[IFRIC 5:6]

- how should a contributor account for its interest in a fund; and

- when a contributor has an obligation to make additional contributions (e.g. in the event of the bankruptcy of another contributor), how should that obligation be accounted for?

Note that the scope of IFRIC 5 is restricted to funds with separately-administered assets, when the contributor's right to access the assets is restricted. [IFRIC 5:4] A residual interest in a fund that extends beyond a right to reimbursement, such as a contractual right to distributions once all the decommissioning has been completed or on winding up the fund, may be an equity instrument within the scope of IFRS 9 *Financial Instruments* (or, for entities that have not yet adopted IFRS 9, IAS 39 *Financial Instruments: Recognition and Measurement*), and is not within the scope of IFRIC 5. [IFRIC 5:5]

9.2.2   Assessing the relationship between the contributor and the fund

The contributor is required to assess whether it has control or joint control of, or significant influence, over the fund, in accordance with relevant IFRSs, and to account for its interest by consolidation or the equity method, as appropriate under those Standards. [IFRIC 5:8]

9.2.3   Accounting for the obligation to pay decommissioning costs

The contributor's obligation to pay decommissioning costs should be recognised as a liability, separately from its interest in the fund, unless its contributions to the fund have extinguished its obligation to pay decommissioning costs (even in the event that the fund fails to pay). [IFRIC 5:7] Therefore, when an entity remains liable for expenditure, a provision should be recognised, even when reimbursement is available.

When a contributor has an obligation to make potential additional contributions (e.g. in the event of the bankruptcy of another contributor, or if the value of the investments held by the fund decreases to an extent that they are insufficient to fulfil the fund's reimbursement obligations), this obligation is a contingent liability that is accounted for under IAS 37. The contributor will recognise a liability only if it is probable that additional contributions will be made. [IFRIC 5:10]

9.2.4   Accounting for the contributor's interest in the fund

In the absence of control, joint control or significant influence, the contributor's right to reimbursement from the fund is accounted for in accordance with the rules set out in IAS 37 in respect of reimbursements. [IFRIC 5:9] Therefore, if the reimbursement is virtually certain to be received when the obligation is settled, it should be treated as a separate asset.

The reimbursement should be measured at the lower of the amount of the decommissioning obligation recognised, and the contributor's share of the fair value of the net assets of the fund attributable to contributors. [IFRIC 5:9] Therefore, recognition of an asset in excess of the recognised liability is prohibited. For example, rights to receive reimbursement to meet decommissioning liabilities that have yet to be recognised as a provision are not recognised.

Changes in the carrying amount of the right to receive reimbursement other than contributions to and payments from the fund should be recognised in profit or loss in the period in which those changes occur. [IFRIC 5:9]

9.2.5   Disclosure

Contributors are required to disclose the nature of interests in funds, and any restrictions on access to the assets in the funds. [IFRIC 5:11]

In addition, when the arrangements give rise to contingent liabilities or reimbursement rights that are accounted for under IAS 37, the relevant disclosure requirements of IAS 37 apply.

9.3 IFRIC 6 *Liabilities arising from Participating in a Specific Market – Waste Electrical and Electronic Equipment*

IFRIC 6 addresses the recognition of liabilities for waste management under the European Union's Directive on Waste Electrical and Electronic Equipment (the WE&EE Directive). Specifically, the Interpretation deals with waste from private households arising from products sold on or before 13 August 2005. It does not apply to waste from sources other than private households, nor to household waste arising from products sold after 13 August 2005.

The Interpretation is therefore quite narrow in scope. The general principles in IAS 37 should be applied to determine the appropriate recognition point for other remediation and recycling obligations. However IFRIC 6:7 states that "if, in national legislation, new waste from private households is treated in a similar manner to historical waste from private households, the principles of the Interpretation apply by reference to the hierarchy in paragraphs 10 – 12 of IAS 8". Therefore, before determining an accounting policy for 'new' household waste, entities will need to determine how the WE&EE Directive has been transposed into local law. The Interpretation will also be a source of authoritative guidance on the appropriate accounting for obligations that are imposed by similar cost attribution models.

Under the WE&EE Directive, the obligation to contribute to waste management costs is allocated proportionately to producers of the relevant type of equipment who participate in the market during a specified period (the measurement period). The IFRIC (now the IFRS Interpretations Committee) was asked to determine what constitutes the obligating event for the recognition of a provision for the waste management costs.

The IFRIC decided that the event that triggers liability recognition is participation in the market during a measurement period (and not the production of the equipment, nor the actual incurrence of waste management costs).

9.4 IFRIC 21 *Levies*

9.4.1 *IFRIC 21 – background*

IFRIC 21 *Levies* was issued in May 2013 and is effective for annual periods beginning on or after 1 January 2014, with earlier application permitted. IFRIC 21 provides guidance on when to recognise a liability for a levy imposed by a government; it applies both for levies that are accounted for in accordance with IAS 37 and those for which the timing and amount of the levy is certain.

The consensus in IFRIC 21 is consistent with the consensus in IFRIC 6 (see **9.3**). However, the Interpretations Committee decided not to withdraw IFRIC 6 because it provides useful information on the accounting for liabilities within its scope. [IFRIC 21:BC10]

IFRIC 21 was issued in response to a request to the IFRS Interpretations Committee to determine whether, under specified circumstances, IFRIC 6 (see **9.3**) should be applied by analogy to other levies charged for participation in a market on a specified date in order to identify the event that gives rise to a liability. The specific examples provided to the Committee in this regard included the United Kingdom bank levy, fees paid to the Federal Government by pharmaceutical manufacturers in the United States, a bank levy in Hungary, and the railway tax in France. The final Interpretation covers a broad range of levies, rather than focussing on levies charged to participate in a market.

9.4.2   Scope

IFRIC 21 addresses the accounting for a liability to pay a levy if either:

[IFRIC 21:2]

- the liability is within the scope of IAS 37 (i.e. the timing or amount of the levy is uncertain); or
- both the timing and the amount of the levy are certain.

IFRIC 21 does not address the appropriate accounting for the costs that arise from recognising a liability to pay a levy; the determination as to whether the recognition of a such a liability gives rise to an asset or an expense is made in accordance with other IFRSs. [IFRIC 21:3]

For the purposes of IFRIC 21, a levy is defined as "an outflow of resources embodying economic benefits that is imposed by governments on entities in accordance with legislation (ie laws and/or regulations), other than:

(a) those outflows of resources that are within the scope of other Standards(such as income taxes that are within the scope of IAS 12 *Income Taxes*); and

(b) fines or other penalties that are imposed for breaches of the legislation.

'Government' refers to government, government agencies and similar bodies whether local, national or international." [IFRIC 21:4]

Any 'levy' imposed by a government that meets the definition of an income tax (see **section 2** of **chapter A13**) is accounted for in accordance with IAS 12 rather than in accordance with IFRIC 21.

Amounts that are collected by entities on behalf of governments and remitted to governments (e.g. value added taxes) are not an 'outflow of resources' for the entity collecting and remitting those amounts. [IFRIC 21:BC6]. Consequently, they do not fall within the scope of IFRIC 21.

Note that:

[IFRIC 21:5, 6 & BC7]

- a payment made by an entity for the acquisition of an asset, or for the rendering of services, under a contractual agreement with a government, does not meet the definition of a levy because it is not 'imposed' by the government; and

- an entity is not required to apply IFRIC 21 to liabilities that arise from emissions trading schemes.

9.4.3 Obligating event that gives rise to the recognition of a liability to pay a levy

The obligating event that gives rise to a liability to pay a levy is the activity that triggers the payment of the levy, as identified by the legislation. [IFRIC 21:8]

If the activity that triggers the payment of the levy is the generation of revenue in the current period and the calculation of that levy is based on the revenue that was generated in a previous period, the obligating event for that levy is the generation of revenue in the current period. The generation of revenue in the previous period is necessary, but not sufficient, to create a present obligation. [IFRIC 21:8]

Example 9.4.3

A levy is triggered in full as soon as the entity generates revenue

[IFRIC 21:IE1, Example 2]

Entity B has an annual reporting period that ends on 31 December. In accordance with legislation, a levy is triggered in full as soon as an entity generates revenue in 20X1. The amount of the levy is calculated by reference to revenue generated by the entity in 20X0. Entity B generated revenue in 20X0 and in 20X1 starts to generate revenue on 3 January 20X1.

In this example, the liability is recognised in full on 3 January 20X1 because the obligating event, as identified by the legislation, is the first generation of revenue

---

in 20X1. The generation of revenue in 20X0 is necessary, but not sufficient, to create a present obligation to pay a levy. Before 3 January 20X1, Entity B has no present obligation to pay a levy. In other words, the activity that triggers the payment of the levy, as identified by the legislation, is the point at which Entity B first generates revenue in 20X1. The generation of revenue in 20X0 is not the activity that triggers the payment of the levy and the recognition of the liability. The amount of revenue generated in 20X0 only affects the measurement of the liability.

In the interim financial report (if any), the liability is recognised in full in the first interim period of 20X1 because the liability is recognised in full on 3 January 20X1.

The date on which the levy is paid does not affect the timing of recognition of the liability to pay a levy, because the obligating event is the activity that triggers the payment of the levy, and not the payment of the levy itself. [IFRIC 21:BC13]

9.4.4 Economic compulsion to continue to operate does not result in a constructive obligation

An entity does not have a constructive obligation to pay a levy that will be triggered by operating in a future period as a result of the entity being economically compelled to continue to operate in that future period. [IFRIC 21:8]

When drafting IFRIC 21, the Interpretations Committee considered an argument that, if it would be necessary for an entity to take unrealistic action in order to avoid an obligation to pay a levy that would otherwise be triggered by operating in the future, then a constructive obligation to pay the levy exists and a liability should be recognised (see IFRIC 21:15 for further discussion). However, the Committee rejected this argument, noting that if this rationale were applied, many types of future expenditure within the scope of IAS 37 would be recognised as liabilities. The Interpretations Committee noted that, in accordance with IAS 37:18 and 19:

[IFRIC 21:BC16]

- no provision is recognised for costs that need to be incurred to operate in the future; and

- it is only those obligations arising from past events existing independently of an entity's future conduct of its business that are recognised as provisions.

The Basis for Conclusions on IFRIC 21 further emphasises that there is no constructive obligation to pay a levy that relates to the future conduct of the business, even if:

[IFRIC 21:BC18]

- it is economically unrealistic for the entity to avoid the levy if it has the intention of continuing in business;

- there is a legal requirement to incur the levy if the entity does continue in business;

- it would be necessary for an entity to take unrealistic action to avoid paying the levy, such as to sell, or stop operating, property, plant and equipment;

- the entity made a statement of intent (and has the ability) to operate in the future period(s); or

- the entity has a legal, regulatory or contractual requirement to operate in the future period(s).

Example 9.4.4

A levy is triggered in full if the entity operates as a bank at a specified date

[IFRIC 21:IE1, Example 3]

Entity C is a bank and has an annual reporting period that ends on 31 December. In accordance with legislation, a levy is triggered in full only if an entity operates as a bank at the end of the annual reporting period. The amount of the levy is calculated by reference to the amounts in the statement of financial position of the entity at the end of the annual reporting period. The end of the annual reporting period of Entity C is 31 December 20X1.

In this example, the liability is recognised on 31 December 20X1 because the obligating event, as identified by the legislation, is Entity C operating as a bank at the end of the annual reporting period. Before that point, Entity C has no present obligation to pay a levy, even if it is economically compelled to continue to operate as a bank in the future. In other words, the activity that triggers the payment of the levy, as identified by the legislation, is the entity operating as a bank at the end of the annual reporting period, which does not occur until 31 December 20X1. The conclusion would not change even if the amount of the liability is based on the length of the reporting period, because the obligating event is the entity operating as a bank at the end of the annual reporting period.

In the interim financial report (if any), the liability is recognised in full in the interim period in which 31 December 20X1 falls because the liability is recognised in full on that date.

The preparation of financial statements under the going concern assumption does not imply that an entity has a present obligation to pay a levy that will be triggered by operating in a future period. [IFRIC 21:10]

9.4.5   *Obligating event that occurs over a period of time*

The liability to pay a levy is recognised progressively if the obligating event occurs over a period of time (i.e. if the activity that triggers the payment of the levy, as identified by the legislation, occurs over a period of time). For example, if the obligating event is the generation of revenue over a period of time, the corresponding liability is recognised as the entity generates that revenue. [IFRIC 21:11]

Example 9.4.5

A levy is triggered progressively as the entity generates revenue

[IFRIC 21:IE1, Example 1]

Entity A has an annual reporting period that ends on 31 December. In accordance with legislation, a levy is triggered progressively as an entity generates revenue in 20X1. The amount of the levy is calculated by reference to revenue generated by the entity in 20X1.

In this example, the liability is recognised progressively during 20X1 as Entity A generates revenue, because the obligating event, as identified by the legislation, is the generation of revenue during 20X1. At any point in 20X1, Entity A has a present obligation to pay a levy on revenue generated to date. Entity A has no present obligation to pay a levy that will arise from generating revenue in the future.

In the interim financial report (if any), the liability is recognised progressively as Entity A generates revenue. Entity A has a present obligation to pay the levy on revenue generated from 1 January 20X1 to the end of the interim period.

9.4.6   *Levy triggered when a minimum threshold is reached*

If an obligation to pay a levy is triggered when a minimum threshold is reached, the principles discussed in the previous sections should be applied. For example, if the obligating event is the reaching of a minimum activity threshold (such as a minimum amount of revenue or sales generated or outputs produced), the corresponding liability is recognised when that minimum activity threshold is reached. [IFRIC 21:12]

Example 9.4.6

A levy is triggered in full if the entity generates revenue above a minimum amount of revenue

[IFRIC 21:IE1, Example 4]

Entity D has an annual reporting period that ends on 31 December. In accordance with legislation, a levy is triggered if an entity generates revenue above CU50 million in 20X1.[a] The amount of the levy is calculated by reference to revenue generated above CU50 million, with the levy rate at 0 per cent for

---

the first CU50 million revenue generated (below the threshold) and 2 per cent above CU50 million revenue. Entity D's revenue reaches the revenue threshold of CU50 million on 17 July 20X1.

In this example, the liability is recognised between 17 July 20X1 and 31 December 20X1 as Entity D generates revenue above the threshold because the obligating event, as identified by the legislation, is the activity undertaken after the threshold is reached (ie the generation of revenue after the threshold is reached). The amount of the liability is based on the revenue generated to date that exceeds the threshold of CU50 million revenue.

In the interim financial report (if any), the liability is recognised between 17 July 20X1 and 31 December 20X1 as Entity D generates revenue above the threshold.

Variation:

Same fact pattern as above (ie a levy is triggered if Entity D generates revenue above CU50 million in 20X1), except that the amount of the levy is calculated by reference to all revenue generated by Entity D in 20X1 (ie including the first CU50 million revenue generated in 20X1).

In this example, the liability for the payment of the levy related to the first CU50 million revenue is recognised on 17 July 20X1 when the threshold is met, because the obligating event, as identified by the legislation, for the payment of that amount is the reaching of the threshold. The liability for the payment of the levy related to revenue generated above the threshold is recognised between 17 July 20X1 and 31 December 20X1 as the entity generates revenue above the threshold, because the obligating event, as identified by the legislation, is the activity undertaken after the threshold is reached (ie the generation of revenue after the threshold is reached). The amount of the liability is based on the revenue generated to date, including the first CU50 million revenue. The same recognition principles apply in the interim financial report (if any) as in the annual financial statements.

(a) In this Interpretation, currency amounts are denominated in 'currency units' (CU).

9.4.7 Levy subject to a pro rata activity threshold as well as an annual activity threshold

Example 9.4.7

Levy subject to a pro rata activity threshold as well as an annual activity threshold

Entity Q operates in a jurisdiction in which its activities are subject to a carbon tax. The tax becomes payable once emissions exceed a threshold of 25,000 tonnes of carbon dioxide equivalent greenhouse gases (carbon gases) in a calendar year.

> If an entity does not participate in the relevant activity for all of a calendar year, the annual threshold is reduced pro rata to the number of days in the year that the entity participated in the activity.
>
> Entity Q is preparing its annual financial statements for the year ended 31 March 20X1. Between 1 January 20X1 and 31 March 20X1, Entity Q emitted 10,000 tonnes of carbon gases. Entity Q did not exceed the annual threshold in the calendar year ended 31 December 20X0.
>
> The carbon tax meets the definition of a levy for the purposes of IFRIC 21.
>
> *At 31 March 20X1, is Entity Q required to accrue a liability for carbon tax?*
>
> No. In the circumstances described, Entity Q has not reached the annual threshold of 25,000 tonnes and consequently, in accordance with IFRIC 21:12 (see **9.4.6**), it should not recognise a liability for the carbon tax.
>
> No liability should be recognised even though Entity Q has exceeded the 'pro rata' threshold (i.e. it has exceeded the threshold that would have been applied had it ceased the relevant activity on 31 March 20X1).

This conclusion in **example 9.4.7** has been confirmed by the IFRS Interpretations Committee (see *IFRIC Update, March 2014*). The Interpretations Committee noted that in circumstances such as those described, the payment of the levy is triggered by the reaching of the annual threshold as identified by the legislation. The Interpretations Committee also noted that there is a distinction between a levy with an annual threshold that is reduced pro rata when a specified condition is met (such as described in **example 9.4.7**) and a levy for which an obligating event occurs progressively over a period of time as described in IFRIC 21:11 (see **9.4.5**); until the specified condition is met, the pro rata reduction in the threshold does not apply.

9.4.8   Levy prepaid in advance of present obligation

An entity should recognise an asset if it has prepaid a levy but does not yet have a present obligation to pay that levy. [IFRIC 21:14]

9.4.9   Recognising a liability to pay a levy in an interim financial report

An entity is required to apply the same recognition principles in the interim financial report that it applies in the annual financial statements. As a result, in the interim financial report, a liability to pay a levy:

[IFRIC 21:13]

- should not be recognised if there is no present obligation to pay the levy at the end of the interim reporting period; and

- should be recognised if a present obligation to pay the levy exists at the end of the interim reporting period.

9.4.10 *Effective date and transition*

IFRIC 21 is effective for annual periods beginning on or after 1 January 2014, with earlier application permitted. If an entity applies IFRIC 21 for an earlier period, it is required to disclose that fact. [IFRIC 21:A1]

Changes in accounting policies resulting from the initial application of IFRIC 21 are required to be accounted for retrospectively in accordance with IAS 8 *Accounting Policies, Changes in Accounting Estimates and Errors*. [IFRIC 21:A2]

10 Presentation and disclosure

10.1 Presentation

IAS 1 *Presentation of Financial Statements* requires that, when material, the aggregate carrying amount of the entity's provisions should be presented in the statement of financial position. [IAS 1:54(l)]

10.2 Disclosure

10.2.1 *Disclosures – general*

The objective of IAS 37 with respect to disclosure is to ensure that sufficient information is disclosed in the notes to the financial statements to enable users to understand the nature, timing and amount of provisions, contingent liabilities and contingent assets.

10.2.2 *Provisions*

For each class of provision, the following should be disclosed (comparative information is not required):

[IAS 37:84]

- the carrying amount at the beginning and end of the period;

- additional provisions recognised in the period, including increases to existing provisions;

- amounts used (i.e. incurred and charged against the provision) during the period;

- unused amounts reversed during the period; and

- the increase during the period in the discounted amount arising from the passage of time and the effect of any change in the discount rate.

The following should also be disclosed for each class of provision:

[IAS 37:85]

- a brief description of the nature of the obligation and the expected timing of any resulting outflows of economic benefits;

- an indication of the uncertainties about the amount or timing of those outflows. When necessary to provide adequate information, the entity should disclose the major assumptions made concerning future events (see **4.5**); and

- the amount of any expected reimbursement, stating the amount of any asset that has been recognised for that expected reimbursement.

In determining which provisions may be aggregated to form a class, it is necessary to consider whether the nature of the items is sufficiently similar for a single statement about them to fulfil the requirements outlined above with respect to disclosure of the nature of and uncertainties surrounding such liabilities. [IAS 37:87]

When a provision meets the definition of a financial instrument in IAS 32 *Financial Instruments: Presentation*, but is accounted for under IAS 37 because it is not within the scope of IFRS 9 *Financial Instruments* (or, for entities that have not yet adopted IFRS 9, IAS 39 *Financial Instruments: Recognition and Measurement*), the disclosure requirements of IFRS 7 *Financial Instruments: Disclosures* will apply in addition to those of IAS 37.

10.2.3 Contingent liabilities

For each class of contingent liability (unless the possibility of an outflow in settlement is remote), a brief description of the nature of the contingent liability should be provided. The following information should also be disclosed, if practicable:

[IAS 37:86]

- an estimate of its financial effect (based on the measurement requirements of IAS 37);

- an indication of the uncertainties relating to the amount or timing of any outflow; and

- the possibility of any reimbursement.

In determining which contingent liabilities may be aggregated to form a class, it is necessary to consider whether the nature of the items is sufficiently similar for a single statement about them to fulfil the requirements outlined above with respect to disclosure of the nature of and uncertainties surrounding such items. [IAS 37:87]

When a provision and a contingent liability arise from the same set of circumstances, the reporting entity should make the required disclosures in a way that clearly shows the link between the provision and the contingent liability. [IAS 37:88]

10.2.4   Contingent assets

When an inflow of economic benefits is probable, the entity should disclose a brief description of the nature of the contingent assets at the end of the reporting period and, if practicable, an estimate of their financial effect (based on the measurement requirements of IAS 37), taking care to avoid giving misleading indications of the likelihood of income arising. [IAS 37:89 & 90]

10.2.5   Exemptions from disclosure requirements

10.2.5.1   Exemption applying to disclosure of contingent liabilities and contingent assets

When any of the information required in respect of contingent liabilities and contingent assets, as set out in **10.2.3** and **10.2.4**, respectively, is not disclosed because it is not practicable to do so, that fact should be stated. [IAS 37:91]

10.2.5.2   Exemption applying to all disclosures

In extremely rare cases, it is conceivable that some or all of the disclosures required by IAS 37 can be expected to prejudice seriously the position of the entity in a dispute with other parties on the subject matter of the provision, contingent liability or contingent asset. In such cases, the reporting entity need not disclose the information, but it should disclose the general nature of the dispute, together with the fact that the information has not been disclosed and the reason why. [IAS 37:92]

A13 Income taxes

Contents

1   Introduction

1.1   Overview of IAS 12

IAS 12 *Income Taxes* follows a 'comprehensive balance sheet method' of accounting for income taxes, which recognises both the current tax consequences of transactions and events and the future tax consequences of the future recovery or settlement of the carrying amount of an entity's assets and liabilities. Differences between the carrying amount and tax base of assets and liabilities, and carried forward tax losses and credits, are recognised, with limited exceptions, as deferred tax liabilities or deferred tax assets, with the latter also being subject to a 'probable taxable profits' test.

1.2   Amendments to IAS 12 since the last edition of this manual

None. IAS 12 was most recently amended in May 2014.

2   Scope

2.1   Income taxes – definition

IAS 12 deals with accounting for income taxes. The Standard defines income taxes as including "all domestic and foreign taxes which are based on taxable profits. Income taxes also include taxes, such as withholding taxes, that are payable by a subsidiary, associate or joint arrangement on distributions to the reporting entity". [IAS 12:2]

The determination as to whether a tax is an 'income tax' is a matter requiring careful judgement based on the specific facts and circumstances. Factors to consider in making this determination include, but are not limited to, whether:

- the 'starting point' for determining the taxable amount is based on taxable profits rather than another metric (e.g. units of production);

- the tax is based on a 'taxable profit' notion, implying a net rather than a gross amount;

- the tax is based on actual income and expenses rather than a notional amount (e.g. on a tonnage capacity);

- the legal description or characteristics of the tax imply that the tax is calculated based on taxable profits; and

- there is any withholding related to the tax.

The IFRIC (now the IFRS Interpretations Committee) referred to this topic in the March 2006 *IFRIC Update*. The IFRIC noted that the definition of taxable profit implies that not all taxes are in the scope of IAS 12, and that the requirement to disclose an explanation of the relationship between the tax expense and the accounting profit implies that taxable profit need not be the same as accounting profit.

Taxes that are unlikely to meet the definition of an income tax include:

- sales taxes (because they are transactional taxes based on sales value rather than on taxable profits);
- production-based taxes (see **example 2.5A**); and
- 'tonnage' taxes (see **2.3**).

Care should be exercised in respect of taxes imposed in different jurisdictions that are referred to by common titles but for which the detailed application varies significantly between jurisdictions (such as 'petroleum revenue taxes' – see **example 2.5B**). The determination as to whether such taxes are income taxes should be made on a case-by-case basis.

2.2   Levies

IFRIC 21 *Levies* provides guidance on when to recognise a liability for a 'levy' imposed by a government; a levy is defined as "an outflow of resources embodying economic benefits that is imposed by governments on entities in accordance with legislation (ie laws and/or regulations), other than:

(a) those outflows of resources that are within the scope of other Standards (such as income taxes that are within the scope of IAS 12); and

(b) fines or other penalties that are imposed for breaches of the legislation".

Therefore, any levy imposed by a government should be assessed to determine if it meets the definition of an income tax (see **2.1**). If it does, it should be accounted for in accordance with IAS 12 rather than in accordance with IFRIC 21.

Section 9.4 of **chapter A12** provides a detailed description of the requirements of IFRIC 21.

2.3   Tonnage tax

In some jurisdictions, shipping entities can choose to be taxed by means of a 'tonnage tax' instead of under general corporate income tax regulations. Tonnage tax may be paid on the basis of tonnage transported, tonnage capacity or a notional profit.

The IFRIC (now the IFRS Interpretations Committee) have considered tonnage taxes, as reported in the May 2009 *IFRIC Update*. The IFRIC noted that taxes based on tonnage transported or tonnage capacity are based on a gross rather than a net amount, and taxes on notional income are not based on the entity's actual income and expenses. Such taxes should not be considered income taxes in accordance with IAS 12 and should not be presented as part of tax expense in the statement of comprehensive income. However, the IFRIC also noted that an entity subject to tonnage tax might present additional subtotals in the statement of comprehensive income if that presentation is relevant to an understanding of its financial performance.

2.4 Interest and penalties

In many jurisdictions, interest and penalties are assessed on underpayments or late payments of income tax. In some circumstances, interest and penalties arise because the tax amount payable could not be agreed with the tax authority until significantly after the due date. Alternatively, interest and penalties may arise because the entity has made a deliberate choice not to make the appropriate tax payments before the due date.

When there is no significant uncertainty with respect to the overall amount of income tax payable, and an entity deliberately delays payment of the amount, the resulting interest and penalties can be clearly distinguished from the assessed income tax. Accordingly, in such circumstances, the interest and penalties should not be presented as income tax in the financial statements, but should be separately presented on the basis of their nature (i.e. either as a finance cost (interest) or operating expense (penalties)).

However, in circumstances such as those described in **3.3.3.1**, when there is significant uncertainty regarding the amount of income tax to be paid, an entity may in the course of its discussions with the tax authorities delay making payment for the full amount of tax possibly payable (to avoid, for example, prejudicing a future appeal against the amount claimed as due by the tax authorities) and, by so doing, risk incurring interest and penalties. In such circumstances, possible interest and penalties can be seen as being part of the overall uncertain tax position and, as such, an accounting policy of presenting them as part of tax expense (income) is acceptable.

2.5 Hybrid taxes

Entities are sometimes subject to a tax that has different components. It is necessary to exercise careful judgement when determining whether each of the components meets the definition of an income tax under IAS 12.

Example 2.5A

Tax comprising both production- and profit-based components

Company A is subject to a tax made up of two discrete components – a production-based component and a profit-based component. The production-based component is a fixed minimum amount per tonne of product sold. The total tax, however, may exceed the fixed minimum per tonne depending on the entity's profitability.

The production-based component of the tax should not be considered an income tax because it is based on the weight of product sold rather than taxable profits; it is, therefore, outside the scope of IAS 12. On the other hand, any amounts due as a result of the profit-based component should be considered an income tax and within the scope of IAS 12.

The production-based component of the tax may be reported within either 'cost of goods sold' or 'operating expenses', though the former is preferable. In either case, the presentation should reflect the substance of the entity's operations and should be consistently applied.

Example 2.5B

Petroleum revenue tax

In many jurisdictions, taxes are imposed on 'petroleum revenue'; these taxes are generally designed to ensure that the tax authority benefits from 'super profits' generated by entities in certain resource sectors.

Petroleum revenue taxes vary from jurisdiction to jurisdiction, but they are generally determined based on revenue from extraction activities reduced by specified items of deductible expenditure. The deductions are often limited to items relating to the extraction activities, but may also include other amounts such as administration expenses and deductions based on assets held in the industry.

In addition, the amount of petroleum revenue tax paid will often itself be deductible when computing the entity's 'general' income tax liability.

The key characteristic that defines an income tax is that it is based on a measure of taxable profit. Whether a petroleum revenue tax in a particular jurisdiction is considered to be an income tax will depend on the rules in that specific jurisdiction and whether the basis for the tax is judged to be closer to a measure of revenue or a measure of net profit.

The fact that the 'taxable profit' for the purposes of the petroleum revenue tax differs from 'taxable profit' for the purpose of a jurisdiction's general income tax regime (e.g. because it relates to only part of the operations or because different deductions or allowances are available) is not in itself relevant because the basis for the petroleum revenue tax may still be considered to be a measure of net profit (albeit a different measure than that used as the basis for general income tax).

If the petroleum revenue tax is allowed as a deduction when computing the entity's general income tax liability, this does not preclude the petroleum revenue tax from being considered an income tax for the purposes of IAS 12. The reference in IAS 12:2 to 'all' domestic taxes indicates that there may be more than one form of income tax in a particular jurisdiction.

2.6 Investment tax credits

IAS 12:4 states that the Standard does not deal with methods of accounting for government grants or investment tax credits. IAS 12 does not provide a definition for investment tax credits, which is a term used in many tax jurisdictions to describe a wide range of tax arrangements. Accordingly, in practice, the first step in accounting for an investment tax credit is to determine whether it is within the scope of IAS 12. Even if a tax benefit is referred to by a tax authority as an investment tax credit, it is important to consider the substance to determine whether the tax benefit is outside the scope of IAS 12. A tax credit (outside the scope of IAS 12) provides a reduction to taxes payable and can be distinguished from a tax deduction (within the scope of IAS 12) which is factored into the determination of taxable income.

IAS 20 *Accounting for Government Grants and Disclosure of Government Assistance* (see **chapter A36**) has a broad scope exemption, not just for investment tax credits, but also for "government assistance that is provided for an entity in the form of benefits that are available in determining taxable income or are determined or limited on the basis of income tax liability".

When a tax credit is determined to be an investment tax credit (and, consequently, outside the scope of IAS 12 and IAS 20), it is a matter of judgement under IAS 8 *Accounting Policies, Changes in Accounting Estimates and Errors* to determine the most appropriate accounting treatment. It may be appropriate to analogise to IAS 12 or IAS 20. Generally, if an approach similar to IAS 12 is adopted, a credit will be recognised in profit or loss, and the related asset in the statement of financial position, when the entity satisfies the criteria to receive the credit. If the substance of the arrangement is considered to be closer to a government grant, and an IAS 20 approach is adopted, the credit will be recognised in profit or loss over the periods necessary to match the benefit of the credit with the costs for which it is intended to compensate.

2.7 Refundable tax credits

In some jurisdictions, tax credits may arise that have either or both of the following characteristics.

- The credit may be utilised to obtain a cash payment, rather than solely to reduce income tax payable in the year in which the credit is generated or to reduce income tax payable over a number of years. Therefore, the benefit is not dependent entirely on the entity having a future or past income tax liability against which the credit can be utilised (e.g. an entity may receive a full or partial cash payment despite being in a tax loss position).

- The credit may be utilised to receive a refund of a combination of income taxes and other non-income taxes paid during the year. For example, the tax credit may be offset first against income tax payable for the year, then against some other taxes (e.g. payroll taxes) incurred in the year, with any unused credit carried forward to subsequent years.

Such credits are often referred to as 'refundable' tax credits.

Whether refundable tax credits come within the scope of IAS 12 depends on the specific terms of the particular tax credits under consideration. The most appropriate accounting treatment for such refundable tax credits will be a matter of judgement to be determined under IAS 8. It will be necessary to look carefully at the substance of the particular credit, including the requirements that must be met in order to generate the credit and how the credit will be realised in practice. IAS 12 and IAS 20 are likely to provide the most appropriate references for the purpose of determining an appropriate accounting policy. For example, if the credit can be used to generate a cash payment and realisation is not dependent on any past or future income tax liability, then it may be reasonable to conclude that the credit is in the nature of a government grant and is not within the scope of IAS 12.

2.8 Additional tax deductions

Example 2.8

Additional tax deductions

Entity A will receive an additional tax deduction if it invests in more than 25 per cent of an investee abroad and it meets a number of specified conditions. The deduction is granted to encourage investment in foreign entities.

If the specified conditions are met, the additional tax deduction is 50 per cent of the cost of the investment. Entity A is permitted to use the deduction in the calculation of its current year's tax liability; alternatively, it can defer claiming the deduction, but only for a maximum of five years.

IAS 12:7 defines the tax base of an asset as "the amount that will be deductible for tax purposes against any taxable economic benefits that will flow to an entity when it recovers the carrying amount of the asset" (see also **4.2.1**).

In the circumstances described, the deduction is available independently of the recovery of the investment either through use or sale, and it is therefore not part of the tax base of the asset.

The incentive is not directly linked to any underlying asset. If deferred, it represents an unused tax deduction and, in accordance with IAS 12:34 (see **4.6.1**), a deferred tax asset should be recognised to the extent that it is probable that future taxable profit will be available against which the unused tax deduction can be used.

Note that arrangements of the type described in **example 2.8** are sometimes referred to as investment tax credits; however, use of the term 'investment tax credit' in local tax legislation is not necessarily consistent with the term's use in IAS 12 and it is necessary to review the detailed application of tax incentives referred to as investment tax credits in order to determine whether they are within the scope of IAS 12 (see **2.6**).

2.9 Classification of payments in a tax structuring transaction

When implementing tax planning strategies, entities will often incur costs payable to the designer of the strategy. In determining whether such costs meet the definition of income tax or should be treated as an operating expense, the entity will need to have regard to whether the payment is to the designer, or whether it is paid to the designer to be paid to the tax authorities on the entity's behalf.

Example 2.9

Classification of payments in a tax structuring transaction

Entity A has an effective domestic tax rate of 40 per cent. Entity A enters into a transaction with an investment bank which enables a portion of its activities (generating profit of CU1,000) to be taxed in a tax-haven jurisdiction rather than under Entity A's domestic tax regime.

The investment bank receives a 30 per cent fee based on total taxable profits before the transaction, of which it pays 10 per cent (CU30) over to the tax authorities in the tax-haven jurisdiction. The net result of the transaction on domestic tax is that tax is paid on 10 per cent of the original profit. The following table illustrates the effect of the transaction on taxable profits and tax payments.

	Before structuring	After structuring
	CU	CU
Taxable profit before structuring	1,000	1,000
Fee payable to investment bank	–	(300)
Domestic tax (40%)	(400)	(40)
Profit after fee payable to investment bank and domestic tax	600	660

Should the fee payable by Entity A to the investment bank be classified as income tax expense?

No, but consideration should be given to whether the tax paid by the investment bank was paid on Entity A's behalf.

Only amounts that are ultimately paid to tax authorities on Entity A's behalf should be considered as tax expenses. In the circumstances described, an evaluation needs to be performed as to whether, in substance, Entity A continues to bear the tax risk associated with the tax payment by the investment bank, or whether the bank makes the tax payment of CU30 on its own behalf. If Entity A retains substantially all of the tax risk associated with the tax payment by the investment bank, all direct and indirect payments to the tax authorities should be considered as a tax expense, resulting in the recognition of a tax expense of CU70 (CU40 domestic tax paid by Entity A and CU30 tax in the tax-haven jurisdiction paid on Entity A's behalf by the investment bank). If the investment bank takes over substantially all the tax risk, the entire fee paid to the investment bank will be an operating expense and the tax expense will be only the domestic tax of CU40.

In determining whether Entity A has retained the tax risk, the following factors should be considered:

- whether the tax authority has any power to demand payment from Entity A if the investment bank does not pay; and
- whether Entity A could be required to make further payments for the tax (or be entitled to refunds) if the onward payment proves to have been miscalculated.

2.10   Classification of payments to acquire tax losses

Example 2.10

Classification of payments to acquire tax losses

In some jurisdictions, the tax authority requires each entity to file its tax return as if it is a stand-alone tax payer which is taxed and pays income tax separately. However, within a tax group (e.g. a group of entities under common control), tax losses may be transferred between entities and used to offset the taxable income in the purchasing entity. The price to be paid for the tax losses is determined by agreement between the seller and the purchaser.

For example, Entity A and Entity B are both direct subsidiaries of Entity P. The tax rate in their jurisdiction is 30 per cent. Entity A acquires tax losses of CU100 from Entity B at an agreed price of CU50 and utilises the tax losses immediately.

In its separate financial statements, how should Entity A classify the payment made to Entity B to acquire the tax losses?

In this example, the payment of CU50 exceeds the tax benefit that Entity A has acquired (which is 30% × CU100 = CU30). The payment can only be considered a settlement of Entity A's income tax liability to the extent of that tax benefit. Therefore, only CU30 of the payment should be offset against Entity A's tax liability.

The accounting treatment for the excess payment of CU20 should reflect the substance of the transaction. In particular, it is necessary to consider whether Entity A has acquired anything else from Entity B that would correspond to the excess payment of CU20. If not, the substance of the transaction would seem to be that the excess payment of CU20 represents a distribution by Entity A which has been directed to Entity B in accordance with the wishes of their common parent, Entity P. Entity A should therefore recognise the CU20 as a distribution in equity.

In practice, the losses will be included in the tax return and Entity A will have recognised a lower tax expense and tax liability on the basis of the amounts in the tax return. The entries to reflect the cash payment of CU50 will therefore be as follows.

		CU	CU
Dr	Tax expense	30	
Dr	Distribution	20	
Cr	Cash		50

3 Current tax

3.1 Definitions

Current tax is defined as the amount of income taxes payable (recoverable) in respect of the taxable profit (tax loss) for a period. [IAS 12:5] It is the tax that the entity expects to pay (recover) in respect of a financial period.

Taxable profit (tax loss) is defined as the profit (loss) for a period, determined in accordance with the rules established by the tax authorities, upon which income taxes are payable (recoverable). [IAS 12:5]

3.2   Recognition of current tax assets and liabilities

3.2.1   *Recognition of current tax assets and liabilities – general*

IAS 12's basic requirement is that, to the extent that current tax for the current and prior reporting periods is unpaid, it should be recognised as a liability. Conversely, if the amount already paid in respect of current and prior periods exceeds the amount due for those periods, the excess should be recognised as an asset. [IAS 12:12]

Similarly, an asset is recognised if a tax loss can be carried back to recover the current tax paid in an earlier period. [IAS 12:13] Thus, if an entity has a tax loss in one year (e.g. 20X3), and this is carried back and used to recover tax paid in an earlier period (e.g. 20X2), the current tax benefit of the recovery is recognised in the year in which the loss arises (i.e. 20X3).

Generally, current tax is recognised in profit or loss. There are two exceptions:

[IAS 12:58]

- when the current tax arises as a result of a transaction or event that is recognised, in the same or a different period, outside profit or loss, either in other comprehensive income or directly in equity (see **3.2.2**); and

- when the current tax arises from a business combination (other than the acquisition by an investment entity of a subsidiary that is required to be measured at fair value through profit or loss – see **3.2.3**).

3.2.2   *Items recognised outside profit or loss*

3.2.2.1   *Items recognised outside profit or loss – general*
Current tax is recognised outside profit or loss if the tax relates to items that are recognised, in the same or a different period, outside profit or loss. When the current tax relates to items that are recognised in other comprehensive income, the tax is also recognised in other comprehensive income; when the tax relates to items that are recognised directly in equity, the tax is also recognised directly in equity. [IAS 12:61A]

3.2.2.2   *Items recognised in other comprehensive income*
Items required or permitted under IFRSs to be recognised in other comprehensive income include:

[IAS 12:62]

- revaluations of property, plant and equipment under IAS 16 *Property, Plant and Equipment*; and

- exchange differences on the translation of the financial statements of a foreign operation under IAS 21 *The Effects of Changes in Foreign Exchange Rates*.

Other items recognised in other comprehensive income that may affect current tax are movements in fair value of a financial asset measured at fair value through other comprehensive income under IFRS 9 *Financial Instruments* (or, for entities that have not yet adopted IFRS 9, movements in fair value on available-for-sale securities) when gains and losses are assessed for tax in the same period in which they are recognised in other comprehensive income.

3.2.2.3 *Items recognised directly in equity*

Items required or permitted under IFRSs to be credited or charged directly to equity include:

[IAS 12:62A]

- an adjustment to the opening balance of retained earnings resulting from a change in accounting policy that is accounted for retrospectively or the correction of an error under IAS 8 *Accounting Policies, Changes in Accounting Estimates and Errors*; and

- the initial recognition of the equity component of a compound financial instrument under IAS 32 *Financial Instruments: Presentation* (see **5.3.4**).

Another common situation when tax is charged directly to equity is when an entity is required to pay a portion of its dividends over to the tax authorities on behalf of the shareholders (often referred to as a 'withholding tax'). The amount paid or payable to the tax authorities is charged to equity as part of dividends (see also **4.7.3.5**). [IAS 12:65A]

The circumstances in which current tax is recognised directly in equity are quite limited. This treatment will be required when, under the tax rules in a particular jurisdiction, an item recognised directly in equity for accounting purposes affects the current tax expense or income for the period, for example:

- the transaction costs associated with the issue of an equity instrument are deductible for tax purposes in the period in which they are incurred;

- capital gains tax is charged relating to transactions in the entity's own equity instruments (see **example 3.2.2.3**); or

- the current tax deduction for an equity-settled share-based payment exceeds the cumulative profit or loss expense recognised in respect of that share-based payment (see **section 5.6**).

Example 3.2.2.3

Tax arising on sale of treasury shares held by a subsidiary

Company S (a subsidiary) holds 10 per cent of the ordinary shares of its parent (Company P). These shares are classified as treasury shares by the group. Company P buys back the shares from Company S. After the buy-back, the shares are cancelled, and the treasury shares in the consolidated financial statements are derecognised.

In accordance with the law in the tax jurisdiction in which the group operates, an entity is liable for capital gains tax (CGT) if it sells an asset for more than its base cost. In the circumstances under consideration, Company S sells the shares for more than their base cost and, therefore, incurs CGT on the sale. The group therefore incurs CGT on the sale.

In the consolidated financial statements, a transfer from one equity classification (the treasury share reserve) to another equity classification (share capital or another reserve as required by local law) is made to reflect the cancellation of shares. The CGT represents a transaction cost relating to the cancellation and should therefore be recognised directly in equity.

3.2.2.4   Uncertainty regarding amount to be recognised outside profit or loss

If an entity cannot determine the amount of current tax that relates to items recognised outside of profit or loss (either in other comprehensive income or directly in equity), the amount may be based on a reasonable pro rata allocation, or some other method achieving a more appropriate allocation. These circumstances are assumed to arise only rarely; such an uncertainty could arise, for example, when there are graduated rates of income tax and it is impossible to determine the rate at which a specific component of taxable profit (tax loss) has been taxed. [IAS 12:63]

Example 3.2.2.4

Pro rata allocation of tax between profit or loss and other comprehensive income

Entity A operates in a jurisdiction in which revaluations of property, plant and equipment are taxed when they are recognised for accounting purposes. In 20X1, Entity A recognises an accounting profit of CU1,000 and a revaluation gain in other comprehensive income of CU200. Total taxable profit is therefore CU1,200. Tax is charged at 20 per cent on the first CU600 of taxable profit and 30 per cent on any taxable profit above CU600.

Total tax for the year: CU600 × 20% + CU600 × 30% = CU300

In this graduated tax regime, it is not possible to make a determination as to which component of total taxable profit was taxed at each particular rate. Entity A therefore needs to allocate the current tax liability of CU300 between profit

---

or loss and other comprehensive income on a reasonable pro rata basis. Entity A's overall average tax rate is 25 per cent (CU300 tax payable on CU1,200 taxable profit), and the entity could use this average rate to make a reasonable allocation. The journal entry to recognise the current tax liability for the year would be as follows.

		CU	CU
Dr	Current income tax – profit or loss (CU1,000 × 25%)	250	
Dr	Current income tax – other comprehensive income (CU200 × 25%)	50	
Cr	Taxes payable – statement of financial position		300

To recognise the current tax liability for the year.

3.2.2.5 Reclassification from equity to profit or loss of current tax effects of gains and losses previously recognised in other comprehensive income

As discussed at **3.2.2.1**, IAS 12:61A requires that current tax or deferred tax relating to items that are recognised, in the same or a different period, outside of profit or loss should be recognised outside of profit or loss.

In some cases, IFRSs require that gains or losses initially recognised in other comprehensive income be subsequently reclassified to profit or loss. For example:

- specified gains and losses arising on cash flow hedges and net investment hedges previously recognised in other comprehensive income are reclassified from equity to profit or loss (subject to the conditions in IFRS 9 *Financial Instruments* or, for entities that have not yet adopted IFRS 9, IAS 39 *Financial Instruments: Recognition and Measurement*);

- for entities that have adopted IFRS 9, gains and losses arising on debt instruments measured at fair value through other comprehensive income previously recognised in other comprehensive income are reclassified from equity to profit and loss when the asset is disposed of;

- for entities that have not yet adopted IFRS 9, gains or losses arising on available-for-sale financial assets previously recognised in other comprehensive income are reclassified from equity to profit or loss when the asset is disposed of or is determined to be impaired; and

- on disposal or partial disposal of a foreign operation (other than a partial disposal of a subsidiary when control is retained), all or a portion of the foreign currency translation reserve is reclassified from equity to profit or loss as part of the gain or loss on disposal.

Whether such gains and losses are included in the determination of taxable profit in the period in which they are initially recognised in other comprehensive income depends on the rules in the particular tax jurisdiction.

If such gains and losses are subject to current tax when they are recognised in other comprehensive income, the question arises as to whether that current tax (initially recognised in other comprehensive income in accordance with IAS 12:61A) should be subsequently reclassified to profit or loss when the related gains and losses are reclassified.

The most appropriate treatment is that any current tax expense or benefit relating to the gains or losses reclassified should also be reclassified to profit or loss. Even though IAS 12 makes no reference to reclassification of the current tax effects previously recognised in other comprehensive income, the principle in IAS 12 is clear that the tax effects of a transaction (if any) should be reported in a consistent manner with the gains or losses to which they relate. This principle is applied when the gains and losses are initially recognised in other comprehensive income, and equally can be applied when the gains and losses are subsequently reclassified to profit or loss.

See **example 3.2.2.5** for an illustration of this approach. Note that, in the example, there is no impact on the effective tax rate of the entity, because both the realised loss and the related tax are recognised in profit or loss.

Example 3.2.2.5

Reclassification from equity to profit or loss of current tax effects of gains and losses previously recognised in other comprehensive income

Company Y has a portfolio of financial assets classified as available for sale in accordance with IAS 39. For financial reporting purposes, unrealised gains and losses on the assets are recognised in other comprehensive income. In accordance with IAS 12, any tax consequences are also recognised in other comprehensive income.

Under local tax laws, unrealised gains and losses on investment portfolios are included in the determination of taxable income or loss; consequently, the movement in the value of financial assets each year affects the current taxes payable.

In 20X1, the unrealised loss on the assets is CU5 million. There is no movement in the market value of the assets during 20X2. On the last day of 20X2, Company Y sells the assets, thereby crystallising the previously recognised pre-tax loss of CU5 million.

The tax rate for 20X1 and 20X2 is 30 per cent. Company Y has net taxable income in 20X1.

The journal entries for 20X1 are as follows.

		CU'000	CU'000
Dr	Unrealised loss on investments (other comprehensive income)	5,000	
Cr	Investment portfolio		5,000

To recognise the unrealised loss on the available-for-sale assets in other comprehensive income.

		CU'000	CU'000
Dr	Current tax liability	1,500	
Cr	Current tax benefit (other comprehensive income)		1,500

To recognise the tax consequences of the unrealised losses – computed based on mark-to-market accounting under local tax law (CU5 million × 30%).

The journal entries for 20X2 are as follows.

		CU'000	CU'000
Dr	Loss on sale (profit or loss)	5,000	
Cr	Unrealised loss on investments (other comprehensive income)		5,000

To recognise the reclassification from equity to profit or loss of the pre-tax loss on sale of the asset portfolio in 20X2.

		CU'000	CU'000
Dr	Current tax expense (other comprehensive income)	1,500	
Cr	Current tax benefit (profit or loss)		1,500

To recognise the reclassification from equity to profit or loss of the tax consequences of the realised loss on sale of the assets in 20X2.

3.2.2.6 Dividends

In some jurisdictions, income taxes are payable at a higher or lower rate if part or all of the net profit or retained earnings is paid out as a dividend to shareholders of the entity. In some other jurisdictions, income taxes may be refundable or payable if part or all of the net profit or retained earnings is paid out as a dividend to shareholders of the entity. In these circumstances, current and deferred tax assets and liabilities are measured at the tax rate applicable to undistributed profits. [IAS 12:52A]

In the circumstances described in the previous paragraph, the income tax consequences of dividends are recognised when a liability to pay the dividend is recognised. The income tax consequences of dividends are more directly linked to past transactions or events than to distributions to owners. Therefore, the income tax consequences of dividends are recognised in profit or loss for the period as required by IAS 12:58 except to the extent that the income tax consequences of dividends arise from the circumstances described in IAS 12:58(a) and (b) (see **3.2.1**). [IAS 12:52B]

3.2.3 *Current tax arising from business combinations*

Current tax arising from a business combination (other than the acquisition by an investment entity as defined in IFRS 10 *Consolidated Financial Statements* (see **section 13** of **chapter A24**) of a subsidiary that is required to be measured at fair value through profit or loss) should not be recognised in profit or loss. [IAS 12:58(b)]

IAS 12 does not specifically address the appropriate treatment in the consolidated financial statements of the acquirer for adjustments arising when a business combination has direct current tax consequences for the acquiree (paragraphs IAS 12:66 to 68, to which reference is made from IAS 12:58(b), only address the accounting for deferred tax). However, it can be assumed that adjustments to current tax should be treated consistently with adjustments to deferred tax; therefore, adjustments to current tax should also be accounted for as part of the initial accounting for the business combination.

For example, a change of ownership may result in a change in tax rate or loss of tax incentives. When those consequences result in an adjustment to current tax assets or liabilities, the remeasured current tax assets or liabilities should be included in the identifiable net assets recognised for the acquiree, and the adjustment will therefore affect the amount of the goodwill or the bargain purchase gain recognised in the consolidated financial statements.

The appropriate accounting in the financial statements of the acquiree will be determined in accordance with SIC-25 *Income Taxes – Changes in the Tax Status of an Entity or its Shareholders* (see **4.7.5**).

3.3 Measurement of current tax assets and liabilities

3.3.1 *Measurement of current tax assets and liabilities – general*

Current tax assets and liabilities for both the current and prior periods are measured at the amounts that are expected to be paid to (recovered from) the tax authorities, using the tax rates (and tax laws) that have been enacted or substantively enacted by the end of the reporting period. [IAS 12:46] See **section 4.5.2** for a discussion of the general issues that arise in respect of the appropriate tax rate to be used. **Section 4.5.2.3** discusses the meaning of 'substantively enacted'.

3.3.2   *Discounting current tax payable*

When current tax amounts fall due to be paid in future periods, the current tax should be recognised at a discounted amount if the effect of discounting is material. This may be contrasted with the accounting for deferred tax which, as required under IAS 12:53, is never discounted (see **4.5.3**).

Example 3.3.2

Discounting current tax payable

Entity A is a start-up entity. The local tax authority has granted a five-year partial deferral of tax payments to new businesses in the jurisdiction, for which Entity A is eligible. Under this arrangement, Entity A must pay 60 per cent of its current year tax bill at the end of the tax year, and 40 per cent is deferred until the end of the tax year five years later.

When measuring its liability for current tax, if the effect is material, Entity A should discount the amount deferred for five years. Entity A should recognise a current tax liability of 60 per cent of the total current tax bill, plus 40 per cent of the total current tax bill discounted for five years as a non-current tax liability.

The unwinding of the discount in subsequent periods should be presented as a finance cost, because it does not meet the definition of income tax expense in IAS 12.

3.3.3   *Uncertain tax positions*

3.3.3.1   *Uncertain tax positions – background*

Entities are required to calculate and pay income taxes in accordance with applicable tax law in each relevant tax jurisdiction. However, no tax legislation can clearly articulate the tax consequences of every possible transaction. Accordingly, the application of tax rules to complex transactions is sometimes open to interpretation, both by the preparers of financial statements (and the tax return) and by the tax authorities.

The tax authorities may challenge positions taken by an entity in determining its current income tax expense and either require further payments or disallow tax losses or other tax attributes. Tax positions taken by an entity when measuring its tax assets and liabilities for financial statement purposes (and when submitting its tax return) for which the interpretation of tax law is unclear are generally referred to as 'uncertain tax positions'.

Uncertain tax positions affect the amount recognised for current tax liabilities or assets, and are within the scope of IAS 12. IAS 12:46 provides that "[c]urrent tax liabilities (assets) for the current and prior periods shall be measured at the amount expected to be paid to (recovered from) the taxation authorities".

3.3.3.2   Recognition and measurement of uncertain tax positions

IAS 12 does not include explicit guidance regarding the recognition and measurement of uncertain tax positions. While income taxes are outside the scope of IAS 37 *Provisions, Contingent Liabilities and Contingent Assets*, the guidance in IAS 37:10 is considered relevant to uncertain tax positions because they may give rise to "a liability of uncertain timing or amount". Consequently, preparers may use the recognition and measurement criteria of IAS 37 by analogy when determining the appropriate recognition and measurement of uncertain tax positions. It would be inappropriate, however, to present the resulting liabilities with other provisions recognised under IAS 37, because IAS 37:5(b) specifically excludes from the scope of that Standard provisions that are addressed in IAS 12.

It should be presumed that any uncertain tax positions taken by an entity in determining its current tax liabilities (assets) will be examined by the appropriate tax authority having full knowledge of all relevant information.

Accordingly, an entity should follow a two-step process in accounting for its uncertain tax positions.

- Having already presumed 100 per cent detection risk by the relevant tax authority, the entity should determine whether, under IAS 37:14(b), it is *probable* that an outflow of economic resources will occur (i.e. the entity should consider whether it is probable that upon examination of the uncertain tax position by the tax authority, the entity would, for example, not be entitled to a particular tax credit or deduction or it would be assessed for tax on a particular income stream). Note that, under IAS 37, an outflow of economic resources is considered to be 'probable' if it is more likely than not to occur.

- If the probability threshold is met, the entity will need to measure the potential impact of the relevant tax authority's examination of the uncertain tax position; that is to say, the entity will need to make its best estimate of the amount of the tax benefit that will be lost. That amount may be determined in accordance with the guidance set out in IAS 37:39 and 40.

As stated in IAS 37:38, the best estimate of the amount to be provided is "determined by the judgement of the management of the entity, supplemented by experience of similar transactions and, in some cases, reports from independent experts".

3.3.3.3   Disclosures regarding uncertain tax positions

Disclosure requirements for uncertain tax positions are governed not only by IAS 12, but also by the requirement under IAS 1:125 to disclose key sources of estimation uncertainty when there is a significant risk of a material adjustment in carrying amounts of assets and liabilities within the next financial year.

When the uncertain tax position gives rise to a contingent tax liability for which no provision is recognised (e.g. because it is not probable that a payment will be made to the tax authority), an entity must still consider the requirements of IAS 12:88, which states that "[a]n entity discloses any tax-related contingent liabilities and contingent assets in accordance with IAS 37 ... contingent liabilities and contingent assets may arise, for example, from unresolved disputes with the taxation authorities".

> The recognition and measurement in a business combination of the potential liability arising from an uncertain tax position is addressed at **5.1.9**.

3.3.3.4   Recognition of an asset in relation to an uncertain tax position

Example 3.3.3.4

Recognition of an asset in relation to an uncertain tax position

Entity X is involved in a dispute with its local tax authority over a sum of CU100 and has, as required by local law, made a payment of that amount. This money will be held in escrow by the tax authority pending resolution of the dispute, at which point it will either be returned to Entity X or used to settle any tax liability arising from the dispute.

Entity X does not believe it to be probable that any tax liability will arise in relation to the disputed amount and, consequently, it has not recognised any obligation in this regard (see **3.3.3.2** for a discussion of the appropriate recognition criteria for such 'uncertain tax positions').

Should Entity X recognise the payment of CU100 as an asset?

Yes. This asset is not a contingent asset as defined in IAS 37 because, although the outcome of the uncertain future event (i.e. the resolution of the tax dispute) will confirm the means of recovery, there is no uncertainty regarding the 'existence' of the asset. The asset will either be recovered in the form of a cash refund from the tax authority or it will be used to settle the tax liability that may arise on resolution of the dispute.

Entity X should continue to monitor the underlying uncertain tax position, and should recognise an income tax expense if and when it is considered probable that the dispute will result in some or all of the CU100 being retained by the tax authority to settle any tax liability arising from the dispute.

3.4   Changes in the tax status of an entity or its shareholders

SIC-25 *Income Taxes – Changes in the Tax Status of an Entity or its Shareholders* deals with the appropriate accounting for the consequences of such changes. SIC-25, which applies equally to current and deferred taxes, is discussed in detail in **4.7.5**.

4   Deferred tax

4.1   Deferred tax – general approach

IAS 12 focuses on the statement of financial position by recognising the tax effects of temporary differences, i.e. differences between the carrying amount of an asset or a liability and its tax base.

Deferred tax liabilities are defined as the amounts of income taxes payable in future periods in respect of taxable temporary differences. [IAS 12:5]

Deferred tax assets are defined as the amounts of income taxes recoverable in future periods in respect of:

[IAS 12:5]

- deductible temporary differences;
- the carryforward of unused tax losses; and
- the carryforward of unused tax credits.

Deferred tax assets and liabilities are calculated using the following formulas.

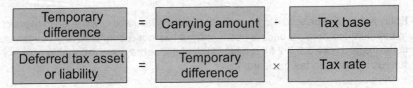

The recognition of deferred tax, therefore, relies on two central concepts:

- tax bases (as defined in **4.2.1**); and
- temporary differences (as defined in **4.3**).

The principal steps in arriving at deferred tax assets and liabilities under IAS 12 are as follows.

Step 1
Calculate the tax base of each asset and liability in the statement of financial position (see **section 4.2**). Note that temporary differences

can also arise when there is no associated asset or liability recognised for accounting purposes (see **4.2.4**).

Step 2

Calculate the temporary difference (if any) for each of the above items (see **section 4.3**).

Step 3

Identify those temporary differences that will give rise to deferred tax assets or liabilities taking into account the recognition criteria and initial exceptions laid down in the Standard (see **section 4.4**).

Step 4

Calculate the deferred tax attributable to those temporary differences by multiplying each temporary difference by the tax rate that is expected to apply when the temporary difference reverses based on enacted or substantively enacted tax rates (see **section 4.5**).

Step 5

Assess the recoverability of deferred tax assets arising from deductible temporary differences, carried forward unused tax losses and unused tax credits (see **section 4.6**).

Step 6

Recognise the movement between the deferred tax balances in the opening and closing statements of financial position in profit or loss, in other comprehensive income, in equity, or as part of the initial accounting for a business combination (thus affecting the goodwill or bargain purchase gain recognised) (see **section 4.7**).

4.2 Calculation of tax bases

4.2.1 Definition of tax base

The tax base of an asset or a liability is the amount attributed to that asset or liability for tax purposes. [IAS 12:5] IAS 12 describes separately the tax base of assets (see **4.2.2**), and of liabilities and revenue received in advance (see **4.2.3**).

The basic principle of IAS 12 is that, unless specifically exempted under IAS 12, entities should recognise deferred tax liabilities (assets) whenever settlement or recovery of the carrying amount of an asset or a liability would make future tax payments larger (smaller) than they would be if such recovery or settlement were to have no tax consequences. This may be helpful to remember when the tax base of an asset or a liability is not immediately apparent. [IAS 12:10]

4.2.2 Tax base of assets

The tax base of an asset is the amount that will be deductible for tax purposes against any taxable economic benefits that will flow to an entity when it recovers the carrying amount of the asset. [IAS 12:7] Taxable economic benefits could take the form of proceeds on disposal of an asset, or income earned through the use of an asset (e.g. manufacturing profits).

Future tax consequences are always calculated based on the realisation of the asset at its carrying amount. In reality, an entity will often generate economic benefits in excess of the carrying amount through use or sale. For example, a property may have a market value that is substantially greater than its carrying amount. IAS 12 does not require an estimate of the benefits that will be generated by the asset. Rather, deferred tax is calculated on the assumption that those benefits will be equal to the carrying amount of the asset.

When the economic benefits that flow from an asset are not taxable, the tax base of the asset is equal to its carrying amount. [IAS 12:7] Deferred taxes only arise when the tax base of an asset or a liability differs from its carrying amount. If the economic benefits that flow from an asset are not taxable (and the tax base of the asset is, therefore, equal to its carrying amount), the recovery of the asset will not have any deferred tax consequences.

Paragraph 7 of IAS 12 contains the following examples of the calculation of the tax base of an asset.

Example 4.2.2A

Tax base of an asset

[Examples following IAS 12:7]

(1) A machine cost 100. For tax purposes, depreciation of 30 has already been deducted in the current and prior periods and the remaining cost will be deductible in future periods, either as depreciation or through a deduction on disposal. Revenue generated by using the machine is taxable, any gain on disposal of the machine will be taxable and any loss on disposal will be deductible for tax purposes. *The tax base of the machine is 70.*

(2) Interest receivable has a carrying amount of 100. The related interest revenue will be taxed on a cash basis. *The tax base of the interest receivable is nil.*

(3) Trade receivables have a carrying amount of 100. The related revenue has already been included in taxable profit (tax loss). *The tax base of the trade receivables is 100.*

---

(4) Dividends receivable from a subsidiary have a carrying amount of 100. The dividends are not taxable. *In substance, the entire carrying amount of the asset is deductible against the economic benefits. Consequently, the tax base of the dividends receivable is 100.*[a]

(5) A loan receivable has a carrying amount of 100. The repayment of the loan will have no tax consequences. *The tax base of the loan is 100.*

[a] Under this analysis, there is no taxable temporary difference. An alternative analysis is that the accrued dividends receivable have a tax base of nil and that a tax rate of nil is applied to the resulting taxable temporary difference of 100. Under both analyses, there is no deferred tax liability.

Sometimes, the manner in which the carrying amount of an asset is recovered can affect the tax base of the asset. When this is the case, the tax base used should be consistent with the expected manner of recovery (see also **section 4.2.6**). [IAS 12:51A]

Example 4.2.2B

Expected manner of recovery of asset

[Based on IAS 12:51A, Example C]

An item of property, plant and equipment with a cost of 100 and a carrying amount of 80 is revalued to 150. No equivalent adjustment is made for tax purposes. Cumulative depreciation for tax purposes is 30. If the item is sold for more than cost, the cumulative tax depreciation of 30 will be included in taxable income and the sale proceeds in excess of an inflation-adjusted cost of 110 will also be taxed.

If the entity expects to recover the carrying amount by selling the item, the tax base is 80 (indexed cost of 110 less tax depreciation of 30).

If the entity expects to recover the carrying amount of the item by using the asset, its tax base is 70 (100 less tax depreciation of 30).

4.2.3 Tax base of liabilities

The tax base of a liability is its carrying amount, less any amount that will be deductible for tax purposes in respect of that liability in future periods. In the case of revenue received in advance, the tax base of the resulting liability is its carrying amount, less any amount of the revenue that will not be taxable in future periods. [IAS 12:8]

Future tax consequences are always calculated based on the settlement of the liability at its carrying amount. There may be occasions when the settlement of a liability is expected to exceed its current carrying amount (e.g. when a settlement premium is being accrued over the life of a debt instrument). IAS 12 does not require anticipation of the expected settlement amount. Instead, deferred tax is calculated on the assumption that the liability will be settled at its carrying amount.

When settlement of the liability at its carrying amount would have no tax consequences, the tax base of the liability is equal to its carrying amount. This will be the case when either the transaction has no tax implications (e.g. accrual of fines and penalties that are not tax deductible), or when the accounting and tax implications occur in the same period (e.g. accrued wages in respect of which a tax deduction is allowed at the same time as the expense is recognised).

Paragraph 8 of IAS 12 contains the following examples of the calculation of the tax base of a liability.

Example 4.2.3A

Tax base of a liability

[Examples following IAS 12:8]

(1)   Current liabilities include accrued expenses with a carrying amount of 100. The related expense will be deducted for tax purposes on a cash basis. *The tax base of the accrued expenses is nil.*

(2)   Current liabilities include interest revenue received in advance, with a carrying amount of 100. The related interest revenue was taxed on a cash basis. *The tax base of the interest received in advance is nil.*

(3)   Current liabilities include accrued expenses with a carrying amount of 100. The related expense has already been deducted for tax purposes. *The tax base of the accrued expenses is 100.*

(4)   Current liabilities include accrued fines and penalties with a carrying amount of 100. Fines and penalties are not deductible for tax purposes. *The tax base of the accrued fines and penalties is 100.*[b]

(5)   A loan payable has a carrying amount of 100. The repayment of the loan will have no tax consequences. *The tax base of the loan is 100.*

[b]   Under this analysis, there is no deductible temporary difference. An alternative analysis is that the accrued fines and penalties payable have a tax base of nil and that a tax rate of nil is applied to the resulting deductible temporary difference of 100. Under both analyses, there is no deferred tax asset.

In the case of revenue received in advance, the tax base of the liability is the carrying amount of the liability less the portion of the revenue received that has already been taxed (or is never taxable) and, consequently, will not be taxed in the future.

Tax base	=	Carrying amount	-	The amount of the revenue that will not be taxable in future periods

Example 4.2.3B

Revenue received in advance

On 31 December 20X1, Company A receives CU100 revenue in advance of performing services. The amount is recognised as deferred revenue in Company A's statement of financial position and it will be recognised in profit or loss as services are performed during the 20X2 reporting period. The revenue is taxed on receipt.

At 31 December 20X1, the carrying amount of the deferred revenue is CU100; the amount that will not be taxable in future periods is CU100 (because this has already been taxed). Therefore, the tax base of the deferred revenue is nil and a deductible temporary difference arises. A deferred tax asset is recognised in respect of this temporary difference subject to IAS 12's general recognition criteria; the 'initial recognition exception' (see **section 4.4.6**) does not apply because the recognition of the revenue affected taxable profit.

Example 4.2.3C

Government grant recognised as deferred income

Company B receives a government grant of CU150 to purchase a specified property. Company B recognises the government grant as deferred income in its statement of financial position, as permitted under paragraph 24 of IAS 20 *Accounting for Government Grants and Disclosure of Government Assistance.*

If the government grant is taxed on receipt, the same analysis as set out in **example 4.2.3B** applies, and a temporary difference equal to the carrying amount of the deferred income arises. A deferred tax asset is recognised in respect of this temporary difference subject to IAS 12's general recognition criteria; the 'initial recognition exception' (see **section 4.4.6**) does not apply because the receipt of the grant affected taxable profit.

If the government grant is taxed at the same time as it is recognised in profit or loss over the life of the related asset, all of the grant is taxable in future periods. Therefore, on initial recognition, the tax base will equal the carrying amount of the deferred income and no temporary difference arises.

If the government grant is not taxable, either on receipt or when it is recognised in profit or loss over the useful life of the related property, applying the formula above will give a tax base of nil. Consequently, a deductible temporary difference arises. However, because this difference arises on the initial recognition of the deferred income and the conditions in IAS 12:24 are met (see **4.4.3**), no deferred tax is recognised.

4.2.4 *Tax bases without an associated carrying amount*

Some items have a tax base but have no carrying amount (i.e. they are not recognised in the statement of financial position for accounting purposes). When a transaction does not give rise to, or affect the carrying amount of, an asset or a liability, but does affect the taxable income of future reporting periods, the tax base is calculated as the amount of the effect on taxable income in future reporting periods. In this case, the carrying amount of the asset or liability associated with the tax base is zero for the purposes of calculating temporary differences. [IAS 12:9]

Examples of such items include the following:

- research costs recognised as an expense in determining accounting profit in the period in which they are incurred but for which a tax deduction is allowed in a later period (see IAS 12:9);

- goodwill or other intangible assets recognised for local tax purposes, but not meeting the recognition criteria under IFRSs; and

- reserves in the local statutory books of the entity that will be taxable upon the occurrence of certain events (e.g. reclassification of the reserve, or upon liquidation of the entity). Such reserves are generally established upon receipt of a tax benefit.

A temporary difference may also arise when a transaction has given rise to an asset or a liability in previous reporting periods that is no longer included in the statement of financial position, but will affect taxable income in future reporting periods (e.g. an asset that is fully depreciated for accounting purposes but for which tax depreciation may still be claimed).

Example 4.2.4

Pre-operating costs expensed but not deductible in current period

An entity may incur pre-operating costs. Under IAS 38 *Intangible Assets*, these costs are required to be recognised as an expense when incurred. If local tax laws do not allow an immediate deduction, but do allow a future deduction, the difference between the tax base of the pre-operating costs (i.e. the amount that the tax authorities will permit as a deduction in future periods) and the carrying amount (nil) is a temporary difference.

4.2.5 Tax bases for the purpose of consolidated financial statements

For an entity preparing consolidated financial statements, temporary differences are calculated using:

[IAS 12:11]

- carrying amounts taken from the consolidated statement of financial position; and

- tax bases as determined by reference to the method of tax computation. If the tax authorities calculate tax by reference to each individual entity in the group, the tax bases will be taken from the individual entities' tax computations. If the tax authorities calculate tax using consolidated amounts, the tax bases will be taken from the consolidated tax amounts.

Example 4.2.5

Tax base generated as a result of intragroup transfer

A group undertakes an internal restructuring whereby Subsidiary A sells an item of intellectual property with no carrying amount to Subsidiary B for CU100. Subsidiary B is able to claim a tax deduction for the amortisation of the purchased intangible asset over 5 years.

IFRS 10 *Consolidated Financial Statements* requires that intragroup profits be eliminated in full. Therefore, from the group perspective, the intellectual property has a carrying amount of nil and a tax base of CU100. Accordingly, a deductible temporary difference has arisen in respect of which a deferred tax asset should be recognised provided that it is probable that taxable profit will be available against which the deductible temporary difference can be utilised. The corresponding gain should be recognised in profit or loss.

The deferred tax impact of eliminations of unrealised profits arising on intragroup transfers is discussed in detail at **5.2**.

4.2.6   *Alternative tax rates and tax bases according to management intent*

4.2.6.1   Tax rate and tax base to reflect the manner in which the entity expects to recover the asset or settle the liability

When the amount of tax payable or receivable is dependent upon how the entity recovers the asset or settles the liability, the rate and tax base used to calculate the deferred tax balances should reflect the manner in which the entity expects, at the end of the reporting period, to recover the asset or settle the liability. [IAS 12:51] IAS 12:51A indicates that the manner of recovery or settlement may affect either, or both, the applicable tax rate and the tax base of an asset or a liability.

Specific rules apply in relation to the recovery of non-depreciable assets (see **4.2.6.2**) and investment property (see **4.2.6.3**).

Example 4.2.6.1A

Alternative tax rates for use and disposal of an item of property, plant and equipment (1)

The carrying amount of an item of property, plant and equipment is CU400,000 (cost of CU500,000 less accumulated depreciation of CU100,000). The asset's tax base is CU300,000 (tax depreciation of CU200,000 having been claimed to date).

Income generated from the use of the asset is taxed at 25 per cent and, therefore, the tax depreciation will be recovered at 25 per cent. If the asset were sold, any excess of the disposal proceeds over the asset's tax base would be taxed at 30 per cent.

The taxable temporary difference is CU100,000. If the entity intends to continue to use the asset in its business, generating taxable income, the deferred tax liability is CU25,000 (CU100,000 at 25 per cent). If, instead, the entity intends to dispose of the asset, the deferred tax liability is CU30,000 (CU100,000 at 30 per cent).

Further examples are given in IAS 12:51A.

Example 4.2.6.1B

Alternative tax rates for use and disposal of an item of property, plant and equipment (2)

The facts are as in **example 4.2.6.1A**, except that the entity intends to use the asset until its carrying amount is CU300,000 and its tax base is CU100,000. At that point, the entity will sell the asset, and will be taxed on the difference between the amount recovered through sale and the tax base.

In accordance with the general principles of IAS 12, deferred tax is calculated on the assumption that the value of the asset will be recovered at its carrying amount. The entity will therefore recover another CU100,000 from the asset through its use, and receive CU200,000 of allowable deductions during that period. The entity will then recover CU300,000 from the sale of the asset, and receive CU100,000 of allowable deductions. In total, the entity expects to recover CU400,000 from the asset and receive CU300,000 of deductions.

The tax rate applicable at the time the temporary difference reverses is 25 per cent in respect of use and 30 per cent in respect of sale. The entity must therefore use both tax rates in determining the deferred tax balance to take account of the fact that the temporary difference will reverse at different rates. Accordingly, the entity's deferred tax liability in respect of the asset is calculated as follows.

$$[(CU100,000 - CU200,000)] \times 25\% + [(CU300,000 - CU100,000)] \times 30\%$$
$$= CU35,000$$

A more complicated situation arises when, in a particular tax jurisdiction, the recovery of an asset through use is subject to one type of income tax and recovery through sale is subject to another type of income tax (potentially at a different rate). In such circumstances, it is often necessary to consider separately the tax bases and temporary differences arising from recovery through use and recovery through sale, particularly when the tax regime is such that there are effectively two distinct tax systems applicable to the recovery of the asset. Any deductible temporary differences need to be assessed for recognition in accordance with the usual requirements, separately from any taxable temporary difference arising. This is illustrated in **example 4.2.6.1C**.

Example 4.2.6.1C

Recovery through sale and use under different income taxes

Company D acquires machinery in a business combination. The machinery is initially recognised in the consolidated financial statements at its fair value at the date of acquisition of CU150. Company D is not entitled to claim any tax deductions if the machinery is used in its operations and, therefore, the machinery's tax base for recovery through use is nil.

Company D expects to use the asset for a number of years and then sell it for its currently estimated residual value of CU50. The income on sale of the machinery is subject to a different type of income tax and, when the machinery is sold, a tax deduction of CU100 (the original cost of the asset when purchased by the acquiree) will be available. Therefore, the asset's tax base for recovery through sale is CU100.

The tax rates expected to apply when the temporary differences reverse are 10 per cent in respect of use and 30 per cent in respect of sale. In the tax jurisdiction in which Company D operates, losses on sale of this type of property, plant and equipment can only be recovered against gains on disposal of similar assets and not against general operating profits.

Company D should recognise deferred tax as follows.

	Carrying amount	Tax base	Taxable (deductible) temporary difference	Deferred tax liability (asset)
	CU	CU	CU	CU
Recovery through use	100	Nil	100	10
Recovery through sale	50	100	(50)	(15)*

* The possible deferred tax asset that is expected to arise from the sale of the machinery must be assessed for recoverability. If it is not probable that suitable future taxable profit will be available against which the deductible temporary difference can be utilised, the deferred tax asset should not be recognised.

4.2.6.2 Non-depreciable assets measured under the revaluation model in IAS 16

A specific issue arises in respect of non-depreciable assets. As discussed in **4.2.6.1**, the measurement of deferred tax should generally reflect the manner in which the entity intends to recover the carrying amount of the asset. However, when an asset has an unlimited life (i.e. it is non-depreciable), the question arises as to how the term 'recovery' should be interpreted.

The measurement of deferred tax liabilities or assets arising from non-depreciable assets measured at a revalued amount under IAS 16 should reflect the tax consequences of recovering the carrying amount of the non-depreciable asset through sale, regardless of the basis of measuring the carrying amount of that asset. [IAS 12:51B]

Accordingly, if the tax consequences that would arise from the sale of a revalued non-depreciable asset differ from the tax consequences of using the asset, the deferred tax asset or liability arising should be measured based on the assumption that the asset will be sold. [IAS 12:51B]

Generally, the future economic benefits will be derived from an asset (and, therefore, the carrying amount of the asset will be recovered) through sale, through use, or through use and subsequent sale. Recognition of depreciation implies that the carrying amount of a depreciable asset is expected to be recovered through use to the extent of its depreciable amount, and through sale at its residual value. Consistently with this, the carrying amount of a non-depreciable asset, such as land having an unlimited life, will be recovered only through sale. In other words, because the asset is not depreciated, no part of its carrying amount is expected to be recovered (i.e. consumed) through use. [IAS 12:BC6]

Example 4.2.6.2A

Non-depreciable asset – freehold land

Company E holds freehold land and accounts for it on a revaluation basis under IAS 16. The carrying amount of the land is CU900,000, which is its current market value. The tax base on sale of the land will be its original cost of CU500,000. The land is used for the storage of Company E's raw materials. The tax rate applicable to manufacturing income is 25 per cent but, on disposal of a capital asset, any proceeds in excess of cost are taxed at 30 per cent. There is currently no intention to sell the land.

The taxable temporary difference between the carrying amount and the tax base of the freehold land is CU400,000. Although the asset is being used by Company E to generate manufacturing income, the carrying amount of the land is not being recovered in that way; the value of the land does not diminish over time through use. All of the value of the land will be recovered through its eventual sale and, therefore, the applicable tax rate is 30 per cent, and the deferred tax liability arising is CU120,000.

If, for tax purposes, there was an indexation allowance on the land for the purposes of calculating the gain on disposal of the land, this indexed amount would be the tax base of the land.

IAS 12:BC6 points to land having an unlimited life and being non-depreciable. Land is the only asset that should be assumed to be non-depreciable (with some exceptions such as quarries and landfill sites –

see IAS 16:58). Assets such as some intangible assets that are simply not being depreciated because they have an indefinite life, or because their current residual value is at or above carrying amount, are not non-depreciable for the purposes of these requirements. IAS 12's general principles apply to such assets, namely that temporary differences should be recognised based on the expected manner of recovery.

Example 4.2.6.2B

Brand with an indefinite useful life

Company F has a brand that is considered to have an indefinite useful life and, in accordance with the requirements of paragraph 107 of IAS 38 *Intangible Assets*, is therefore not being amortised. The carrying amount of the brand is its original cost of CU900,000. Under local tax law, the brand is being amortised over 10 years. At 31 December 20X3, the tax base of the brand after three years' tax amortisation is CU630,000. This tax base is either deductible over the life of the asset or upon sale. The tax rate applicable to trading profits is 25 per cent but, if the intangible asset were to be disposed of, the capital gain arising would be taxed at 30 per cent. There is currently no intention to dispose of the brand.

In accordance with the general requirements of IAS 12:51, the measurement of deferred tax should reflect the tax consequences that would follow from the manner in which the entity expects to recover the asset. In the circumstances described, the brand is expected to be recovered through use in Company F's trading operations. The brand is not considered to be a non-depreciable asset for the purposes of IAS 12:51B (see discussion above).

On this basis, the taxable temporary difference between the carrying amount and the tax base of the brand is CU270,000. The applicable tax rate is 25 per cent and the deferred tax liability arising is CU67,500.

4.2.6.3   Investment property measured at fair value

If a deferred tax liability or asset arises from investment property that is measured using the fair value model in IAS 40, there is a rebuttable presumption that the carrying amount of the investment property will be recovered through sale. Accordingly, unless the presumption is rebutted, the measurement of the deferred tax liability or deferred tax asset is required to reflect the tax consequences of recovering the carrying amount of the investment property entirely through sale. [IAS 12:51C]

The rebuttable presumption established in IAS 12:51C is rebutted if the investment property is depreciable and the investment property is held within a business model whose objective is to consume substantially all of the economic benefits embodied in the investment property over time, rather than through sale. [IAS 12:51C]

Provided that sufficient evidence is available to support the rebuttal, the presumption can be rebutted in circumstances other than those explicitly described in IAS 12:51C.

This conclusion was confirmed by the IFRS Interpretations Committee in November 2011. The Committee noted that a presumption is a matter of consistently applying a principle (or an exception) in IFRSs in the absence of acceptable reasons to the contrary and that it is rebutted when there is sufficient evidence to overcome the presumption. Because IAS 12:51C is expressed as a rebuttable presumption, and because the sentence explaining the rebuttal of the presumption does not express the rebuttal as 'if and only if', the Committee considered that the presumption could be rebutted in other circumstances, provided that sufficient evidence is available to support that rebuttal.

If the presumption is rebutted, the general requirements of IAS 12:51 and IAS 12:51A apply (i.e. expected manner of recovery is based on management intent – see **4.2.6.1**).

The rebuttable presumption in IAS 12:51C also applies when a deferred tax liability or a deferred tax asset arises from measuring investment property in a business combination if the entity will use the fair value model when subsequently measuring that investment property. [IAS 12:51D]

For entities applying the specific requirements for investment properties measured at fair value in accordance with IAS 12:51B to 51D, the general principles regarding the recognition and measurement of deferred tax assets in IAS 12:24 to 36 still apply. [IAS 12:51E]

Example 4.2.6.3, which is reproduced from IAS 12, illustrates the application of IAS 12:51C.

The example illustrates the distinction, when the presumption in IAS 12:51C is rebutted, between the treatment of buildings, which are depreciable, and land, which is not depreciable.

Example 4.2.6.3

Investment property measured at fair value

[Example illustrating IAS 12:51C]

An investment property has a cost of 100 and fair value of 150. It is measured using the fair value model in IAS 40. It comprises land with a cost of 40 and fair value of 60 and a building with a cost of 60 and fair value of 90. The land has an unlimited useful life.

Cumulative depreciation of the building for tax purposes is 30. Unrealised changes in the fair value of the investment property do not affect taxable profit. If the investment property is sold for more than cost, the reversal of the cumulative tax depreciation of 30 will be included in taxable profit and taxed at an ordinary tax rate of 30%. For sales proceeds in excess of cost, tax law specifies tax rates of 25% for assets held for less than two years and 20% for assets held for two years or more.

Because the investment property is measured using the fair value model in IAS 40, there is a rebuttable presumption that the entity will recover the carrying amount of the investment property entirely through sale. If that presumption is not rebutted, the deferred tax reflects the tax consequences of recovering the carrying amount entirely through sale, even if the entity expects to earn rental income from the property before sale.

The tax base of the land if it is sold is 40 and there is a taxable temporary difference of 20 (60 – 40). The tax base of the building if it is sold is 30 (60 – 30) and there is a taxable temporary difference of 60 (90 – 30). As a result, the total taxable temporary difference relating to the investment property is 80 (20 + 60).

In accordance with [IAS 12:47], the tax rate is the rate expected to apply to the period when the investment property is realised. Thus, the resulting deferred tax liability is computed as follows, if the entity expects to sell the property after holding it for more than two years:

	Taxable Temporary Difference	Tax Rate	Deferred Tax Liability
Cumulative tax depreciation	30	30%	9
Proceeds in excess of cost	50	20%	10
Total	80		19

If the entity expects to sell the property after holding it for less than two years, the above computation would be amended to apply a tax rate of 25%, rather than 20%, to the proceeds in excess of cost.

If, instead, the entity holds the building within a business model whose objective is to consume substantially all of the economic benefits embodied in the building over time, rather than through sale, this presumption would be rebutted for the building. However, the land is not depreciable. Therefore the presumption of recovery through sale would not be rebutted for the land. It follows that the deferred tax liability would reflect the tax consequences of recovering the carrying amount of the building through use and the carrying amount of the land through sale.

The tax base of the building if it is used is 30 (60 – 30) and there is a taxable temporary difference of 60 (90 – 30), resulting in a deferred tax liability of 18 (60 at 30%).

The tax base of the land if it is sold is 40 and there is a taxable temporary difference of 20 (60 – 40), resulting in a deferred tax liability of 4 (20 at 20%).

> *As a result, if the presumption of recovery through sale is rebutted for the building, the deferred tax liability relating to the investment property is 22 (18 + 4).*

In many jurisdictions, it is common for an investment property to be held within a corporate structure that holds only one material asset, the investment property itself. When the parent disposes of the property, it will dispose of it within that corporate shell because, in many cases, this will shield the parent entity from adverse tax consequences.

IAS 12:11 requires temporary differences in the consolidated financial statements to be determined by comparing the carrying amounts of assets and liabilities in the consolidated financial statements with the appropriate tax base (see **4.2.5**). These amounts are sometimes referred to as 'inside basis differences'. In the case of an asset or a liability of a subsidiary that files separate tax returns, the tax base is the amount that will be taxable or deductible on the recovery (settlement) of the asset (liability) in the tax returns of the subsidiary.

In addition, IAS 12:38 requires the determination of the temporary difference related to the shares held by the parent in the subsidiary by comparing the parent's share of the net assets of the subsidiary in the consolidated financial statements, including the carrying amount of goodwill, with the tax base of the shares for the purposes of the parent's tax returns (see **section 4.4.7**). This amount is sometimes referred to as an 'outside basis difference'. IAS 12 includes no exception to these requirements for single asset subsidiaries and, consequently, both components of deferred tax are required to be recognised in consolidated financial statements (subject to the requirements of IAS 12:39 and 44 limiting the recognition of outside basis differences, and the general recognition criteria in IAS 12 for any deferred tax assets) even if the parent expects to sell an investment property within a corporate shell.

This conclusion was confirmed by the IFRS Interpretations Committee in July 2014.

4.2.6.4   Convertible instrument with different tax treatments on redemption and conversion

Under IAS 32 *Financial Instruments: Presentation*, the requirement to separate the equity and financial liability components of a compound instrument is consistent with the principle that a financial instrument should be classified in accordance with its substance, rather than its legal form. The expected manner of recovery is not taken into account in establishing this classification.

In some jurisdictions, the tax treatment for a convertible instrument may differ depending on whether the instrument is settled in cash or by the delivery of shares. Unlike IAS 32, IAS 12:51 and 51A require that the tax base and the rate used to determine the deferred tax assets and liabilities reflect the manner in which the entity expects to settle the instrument.

However, when settlement is outside the control of the issuer, the presumed settlement should be aligned with the IAS 32 classification (i.e. cash settlement should be presumed) unless there is strong evidence that the instrument will be settled by the delivery of shares.

4.2.6.5 Change in management's expectation as to the manner in which an asset will be recovered, or a liability settled

When there is a change in management's expectation as to the manner in which an asset will be recovered, or a liability settled, the change may affect the measurement of the related deferred tax balances.

The deferred tax impact should be remeasured based on management's revised intentions and the adjustment recognised in profit or loss or, to the extent that it relates to items previously recognised outside profit or loss, in other comprehensive income or directly in equity. Amounts reported in prior periods are not restated.

4.2.7 Rollover relief

In some jurisdictions, an entity may be entitled to 'rollover relief' when it disposes of a capital asset for a profit and replaces it with an equivalent asset. In such circumstances, the gain on disposal may not have any impact for tax purposes until the replacement asset is disposed of, when it is taken into account via the 'capital' (or sale) tax base of the replacement asset. When the entity disposes of the replacement asset, it is required to pay the tax on the gain on disposal of the replacement asset together with the tax on the gain on disposal of the original asset.

In many cases, the 'rollover' of the gain on the disposal of the original asset into the tax base of the replacement asset merely postpones, rather than eliminates, the payment of tax, and IAS 12:20(b) requires that a deferred tax liability be recognised.

In some jurisdictions, the manner of recovery of the replacement asset will determine whether the rollover relief gives rise to a postponement of tax or to permanent relief. However, until the replacement asset is acquired, deferred tax should be recognised on the basis that rollover relief will give rise only to postponement of tax, i.e. the potential permanent relief should not be anticipated. If the original asset is sold and there is a time delay before the replacement asset is acquired, the entity should continue to recognise the deferred tax.

If the replacement asset is recovered entirely through use, an entity should give careful consideration to the effect of rollover relief on the tax payments flowing from its recovery when determining the tax base of a replacement asset based on the expected manner of recovery.

4.2.8   Revaluation of the tax base

The tax base of an asset may change as a result of a revaluation of the asset for tax purposes. For example, local tax law may specify that the tax base of a particular type of asset is adjusted for inflation each year (see **4.4.7.9**). The effects of other revaluations for tax purposes are discussed at **4.7.3.9**.

See also **4.4.7.8** for the impact of foreign currency adjustments when the tax base of an asset or a liability is determined in a currency other than the entity's functional currency.

4.3   Calculation of temporary differences

4.3.1   Temporary differences – general

Under IAS 12, deferred tax balances are recognised in respect of temporary differences. A temporary difference arises when the carrying amount of an asset or a liability differs from its tax base. For many transactions, there is no difference between the accounting and the tax treatment; no temporary difference and, consequently, no deferred tax balance arises.

4.3.2   Definition of temporary difference

IAS 12 defines a temporary difference as the difference between the carrying amount of an asset or a liability in the statement of financial position and its tax base. [IAS 12:5]

Temporary differences can arise in a number of circumstances, for example:

- when income or expenses are included in accounting profit in one period but included in taxable profit in a different period (i.e. timing differences);

- in a business combination, when the carrying amounts of assets and liabilities are adjusted to their fair values at the date of acquisition, but the tax bases of those assets and liabilities are not affected by the business combination or are affected differently;

- when an asset or a liability is revalued, but the tax base of the asset or liability is not adjusted;

- when the tax authority permits indexation of, or other adjustments to, the cost of an asset for tax purposes, but the asset is not revalued for accounting purposes;

- in respect of non-tax deductible goodwill which arises in a business combination; and

- on the initial recognition of an asset or a liability, for example, if part or all of the cost of an asset will not be deductible for tax purposes.

Temporary differences are determined by reference to the carrying amount of an asset or a liability. [IAS 12:55]

> The carrying amounts used in the calculation of temporary differences are determined from the accounting records. If applicable, carrying amounts are calculated net of any allowances or deductions, such as allowances for doubtful debts or impairment losses.

There are two types of temporary differences – taxable temporary differences and deductible temporary differences. These are discussed in detail in the following sections.

4.3.3 Taxable temporary differences

Taxable temporary differences are temporary differences that will result in taxable amounts in determining the taxable profit (tax loss) of future periods when the carrying amount of the asset or liability is recovered or settled. [IAS 12:5]

Taxable temporary differences are, therefore, differences that will give rise to taxable income in the future; they increase future taxable profit, and so give rise to deferred tax liabilities.

In the context of an asset, a taxable temporary difference arises when the carrying amount of the asset exceeds its tax base (e.g. an asset is depreciated more quickly for tax purposes than for accounting purposes). As the carrying amount of the asset is recovered, the economic benefits subject to tax (i.e. the profits generated by the use of the asset equal to the carrying amount of the asset) will exceed the remaining future tax deductions available (the tax base). The tax effect of this taxable temporary difference gives rise to a deferred tax liability.

In the context of a liability, a taxable temporary difference arises when the tax base of the liability exceeds its carrying amount (e.g. a foreign currency loan payable which has been reduced for accounting purposes by an exchange gain that will be taxable when the loan is settled). If the loan is settled at its carrying amount, a taxable gain will arise; this is a taxable temporary difference.

4.3.4 Deductible temporary differences

Deductible temporary differences are temporary differences that will result in amounts that are deductible in determining the taxable profit (tax loss) of future periods when the carrying amount of the asset or liability is recovered or settled. [IAS 12:5]

Deductible temporary differences are, therefore, differences that decrease taxable income in the future, and so they give rise to deferred tax assets.

IAS 12:26 gives some examples of deductible temporary differences that result in deferred tax assets, as follows.

- Retirement benefit costs may be deducted in determining accounting profit as service is provided by the employee, but deducted in determining taxable profit either when contributions are paid to a fund by the entity or when retirement benefits are paid by the entity. A temporary difference exists between the carrying amount of the liability and its tax base – the tax base of the liability is usually nil. Such a deductible temporary difference results in a deferred tax asset because economic benefits will flow to the entity in the form of a deduction from taxable profits when contributions are made to the plan or retirement benefits are paid.

- Research costs are recognised as an expense in determining accounting profit in the period in which they are incurred but may not be permitted as a deduction in determining taxable profit (tax loss) until a later period. The difference between the tax base of the research costs (i.e. the amount the tax authorities will permit as a deduction in future periods) and the carrying amount of nil is a deductible temporary difference that results in a deferred tax asset.

- With limited exceptions, an entity recognises the identifiable assets acquired and liabilities assumed in a business combination at their fair values at the acquisition date. When a liability assumed is recognised at the acquisition date but the related costs are not deducted in determining taxable profits until a later period, a deductible temporary difference arises which results in a deferred tax asset. A deferred tax asset also arises when the fair value of an identifiable asset acquired is less than its tax base. In both cases, the resulting deferred tax asset affects the goodwill or bargain purchase gain recognised.

- Assets may be carried at fair value, or may be revalued, without an equivalent adjustment being made for tax purposes. A deductible temporary difference arises if the tax base of the asset exceeds its carrying amount.

In the context of an asset, a deductible temporary difference arises when the tax base of the asset exceeds its carrying amount (e.g. when the carrying amount of a financial asset has been reduced by an allowance for irrecoverable amounts, but the allowance is not deductible for tax purposes until settlement). If the asset is settled at its carrying amount, a net deduction will arise; this is a deductible temporary difference.

In the context of a liability, a deductible temporary difference arises when the carrying amount of the liability exceeds its tax base (e.g. when interest payable has been accrued, but no tax deduction is available until the interest is paid). If the liability is settled at its carrying amount, a net deduction will arise; this is a deductible temporary difference.

A useful guide for determining whether temporary differences are taxable or deductible is set out below.

	Carrying amount – tax base	Type of temporary difference	Gives rise to...
Asset	Positive	Taxable	Deferred tax liability
Asset	Negative	Deductible	Deferred tax asset
Liability	Positive	Deductible	Deferred tax asset
Liability	Negative	Taxable	Deferred tax liability

4.4 Recognition of deferred taxes on temporary differences identified

4.4.1 Recognition of temporary differences – general

Having identified all of the temporary differences that exist at the end of the reporting period (see **section 4.3**), the next step is to pinpoint those temporary differences that will give rise to deferred tax assets or liabilities in the statement of financial position, using the recognition criteria laid down in the Standard.

Sections 4.4.2 and **4.4.3** set out the requirements for recognition of taxable temporary differences and deductible temporary differences, respectively. **Sections 4.4.4** to **4.4.6** provide more detail regarding the circumstances in which identified temporary differences are not recognised.

4.4.2 Recognition of taxable temporary differences

A deferred tax liability should be recognised for all taxable temporary differences, unless the deferred tax liability arises from:

[IAS 12:15]

- the initial recognition of goodwill; or

- the initial recognition of an asset or a liability in a transaction which:

  - is not a business combination; and

  - at the time of the transaction affects neither accounting profit nor taxable profit (tax loss).

An entity should recognise a deferred tax liability for all taxable temporary differences associated with investments in subsidiaries, branches and associates, and interests in joint arrangements, except to the extent that both of the following conditions are satisfied:

[IAS 12:39]

- the parent, investor, joint venturer or joint operator is able to control the timing of the reversal of the temporary difference; and

- it is probable that the temporary difference will not reverse in the foreseeable future.

4.4.3   Recognition of deductible temporary differences

A deferred tax asset should be recognised for all deductible temporary differences to the extent that it is probable that taxable profit will be available against which the deductible temporary difference can be utilised, unless the deferred tax asset arises from the initial recognition of an asset or a liability in a transaction that:

[IAS 12:24]

- is not a business combination; and

- at the time of the transaction, affects neither accounting profit nor taxable profit (tax loss).

IAS 12 is silent with regard to the meaning of 'probable' in the context of IAS 12:24. IAS 37 *Provisions, Contingent Liabilities and Contingent Assets* defines the term 'probable' as 'more likely than not'. [IAS 37:23] The footnote to IAS 37:23 acknowledges that this definition is not necessarily applicable to other IFRSs. However, in the absence of any other guidance, the term 'probable' should be applied as 'more likely than not'.

In March 2009, the IASB issued an exposure draft (ED) containing proposals for an IFRS that would replace IAS 12. Although a replacement Standard was not finalised, the ED provides useful guidance on the meaning of 'probable' because it uses the term 'more likely than not' and notes in the Basis for Conclusions that this is consistent with the term 'probable' as used in IAS 37 and IFRS 3 *Business Combinations*.

See **section 4.6.2** for a discussion of factors to be considered when assessing the availability of future taxable profit.

An entity should recognise a deferred tax asset for all deductible temporary differences arising from investments in subsidiaries, branches and associates, and interests in joint arrangements, to the extent that, and only to the extent that, it is probable that:

[IAS 12:44]

- the temporary difference will reverse in the foreseeable future; and
- taxable profit will be available against which the temporary difference can be utilised.

The availability of future taxable profits is discussed in **section 4.6.2**.

4.4.4   Recognition exceptions – general

As detailed in **4.4.2** and **4.4.3**, deferred tax assets and liabilities should be recognised on all temporary differences except for those arising from:

- in relation to deferred tax liabilities only, the initial recognition of goodwill (see **section 4.4.5**); or
- the initial recognition of an asset or a liability in a transaction which (i) is not a business combination and (ii) at the time of the transaction affects neither accounting profit nor taxable profit (tax loss) (see **section 4.4.6**); or
- certain differences associated with investments in subsidiaries, branches and associates, and interests in joint arrangements (see **section 4.4.7**).

In addition to the exceptions noted, a further condition must be met before a deferred tax asset can be recognised in respect of deductible temporary differences – it must be probable that taxable profit will be available against which the deferred tax asset can be utilised. This probability criterion is discussed in detail in **4.6.1**.

> Deferred tax liabilities are recognised for all taxable temporary differences except for those meeting the exceptions described above. Tax planning opportunities, as referred to in IAS 12:30 and discussed at **4.6.5**, relate only to the determination of taxable profits available to support the recognition of deferred tax assets. Tax planning opportunities should not be used to justify non-recognition of a deferred tax liability on a taxable temporary difference that exists at the end of the reporting period.

4.4.5   Recognition exceptions – the initial recognition of goodwill

4.4.5.1   Taxable temporary differences arising on the initial recognition of goodwill

The tax deductibility of reductions or impairments in the carrying amount of goodwill varies among jurisdictions according to the tax laws. When a reduction of goodwill is not deductible against taxable income, the tax base of the goodwill is nil, and a taxable temporary difference arises equal to the carrying amount of the goodwill.

Although a taxable temporary difference exists at initial recognition, IAS 12 prohibits the recognition of the resulting deferred tax liability. The underlying rationale for this exception is that, if a deferred tax liability were set up in respect of the goodwill at the time of the business combination, this would decrease the total for the net assets recognised. Because goodwill is a residual, this would further increase goodwill and the increase would also need to be tax-effected. [IAS 12:21 & 21A]

Subsequent reductions in a deferred tax liability that is unrecognised because it arises from the initial recognition of goodwill are also regarded as arising from the initial recognition of goodwill and, therefore, they are not recognised. [IAS 12:21A]

In contrast, deferred tax liabilities associated with goodwill are recognised to the extent that they do not arise from the initial recognition of that goodwill. [IAS 12:21B] This is illustrated in **examples 4.4.5.1A** to **C**.

Example 4.4.5.1A

Taxable temporary difference arising on the initial recognition of non-tax deductible goodwill

Company A acquires Company B for consideration of CU500. The fair value of the identifiable net assets of Company B at the acquisition date is CU400, resulting in goodwill of CU100. The goodwill is not tax deductible and, therefore, has a tax base of nil, but IAS 12:15 prohibits the recognition of the resulting deferred tax liability on the temporary difference of CU100.

Subsequently, the goodwill is impaired by CU20 and, therefore, the amount of the taxable temporary difference relating to the goodwill is reduced from CU100 to CU80, with a resulting decrease in the value of the unrecognised deferred tax liability. The decrease in the value of the unrecognised deferred tax liability is also regarded as relating to the initial recognition of the goodwill and is not recognised.

Example 4.4.5.1B

Taxable temporary difference arising on goodwill that is wholly tax deductible

The facts are as for **example 4.4.5.1A**, except that the goodwill is deductible for tax purposes at 20 per cent per year starting in the year of acquisition. Thus, the tax base of the goodwill is CU100 on initial recognition and CU80 at the end of the year of acquisition. If the carrying amount of goodwill at the end of the year of acquisition remains unchanged at CU100 (i.e. it has not been impaired), a taxable temporary difference of CU20 arises in that year. That taxable temporary difference does not relate to the initial recognition of the goodwill and, therefore, the resulting deferred tax liability is recognised. The temporary difference will reverse when the acquired business (including the goodwill) is sold or the goodwill is impaired.

Example 4.4.5.1C

Taxable temporary difference arising on goodwill that is partially tax deductible

The facts are as for **example 4.4.5.1A**, except that CU80 of the goodwill is deductible for tax purposes at 25 per cent per year starting in the year of acquisition. The carrying amount of the goodwill that is non-tax deductible is CU20, but no deferred tax liability is initially recognised on this temporary difference of CU20. The tax rate is 30 per cent.

At the end of the year of acquisition, the carrying amount of the total goodwill remains CU100 (i.e. it has not been impaired). No deferred tax liability is recognised for the initial temporary difference of CU20 in relation to the non-tax deductible goodwill. A deferred tax liability of CU6 (30% × CU20) is recognised for the temporary difference between the carrying amount (CU80) and the tax base (CU60) of the tax deductible goodwill because that taxable temporary difference does not relate to the initial recognition of the goodwill. The temporary difference will reverse when the acquired business (including the goodwill) is sold or the goodwill is impaired.

4.4.5.2   Deductible temporary differences arising on the initial recognition of goodwill

As discussed above and illustrated in **examples 4.4.5.1A** and **4.4.5.1C**, IAS 12:15 prohibits the recognition of a deferred tax liability in relation to a taxable temporary difference arising on the initial recognition of goodwill. There is no equivalent prohibition on the recognition of deferred tax assets arising from deductible temporary differences in such circumstances.

IAS 12:32A specifically addresses the circumstances in which the carrying amount of goodwill arising in a business combination is less than its tax base and states that the difference gives rise to a deferred tax asset that should be recognised as part of the accounting for the business combination to the extent that it is probable that it will be recovered.

Example 4.4.5.2

Tax deductible goodwill exceeds the carrying amount of goodwill

Company A acquires Company B for consideration of CU500. The fair value of the identifiable net assets of Company B at the acquisition date is CU400, resulting in goodwill of CU100 (before any adjustment for a deferred tax asset arising on that goodwill). For tax purposes, a deduction of CU120 is available in respect of the goodwill. The tax rate is 30 per cent.

Following the requirements of IAS 12:32A, a deferred tax asset is recognised for the deductible temporary difference between the carrying amount and tax base of the goodwill, subject to the general recognition requirements of IAS 12. Because the carrying amount of goodwill is generally the residual purchase price over fair value of identifiable assets acquired and liabilities assumed

---

(including deferred tax balances), a simultaneous equation (as illustrated below) is used to determine the final carrying amount of goodwill to be recognised in the business combination.

Equation 1 – Calculation of goodwill

	CU
Consideration	500
Less: Fair value of identifiable net assets	(400)
Less: Deferred tax asset on goodwill	(DTA)
Goodwill (GW)	100 – DTA

Equation 2 – Calculation of deferred tax asset

	CU
Tax base of goodwill	120
Less: Carrying amount of goodwill	(GW)
Deductible temporary difference	120 – GW
Tax rate	30%
Deferred tax asset on goodwill (DTA)	$0.3 \times (120 - GW)$

Substituting Equation 2 into Equation 1

$GW = 100 - DTA = 100 - 0.3(120 - GW) = 100 - 36 + 0.3(GW) = 64 + 0.3(GW)$

Rearranged to

$0.7(GW) = 64 \rightarrow GW = CU91.43$

The calculated goodwill figure is then used to determine the deferred tax asset.

$DTA = 0.3(120 - GW) = 0.3(120 - 91.43) = CU8.57$

Therefore, the final goodwill calculation is as follows.

	CU
Consideration	500.00
Less: Fair value of identifiable net assets	(400.00)
Deferred tax asset	(8.57)
Goodwill (GW)	91.43

See **section 7.2.16** of **chapter A3** for a discussion of the accounting, on transition to IFRSs, for deferred tax relating to goodwill that has previously been written off directly to equity.

4.4.6   Recognition exceptions – initial recognition of an asset or a liability

4.4.6.1   Conditions for application of the initial recognition exception

IAS 12 requires the recognition of deferred tax in respect of temporary differences arising when an asset or a liability results from any one of the following:

- a transaction that affects accounting profit (e.g. anticipation of income receivable (asset), or accrual of costs payable (liability)); or

- a transaction that affects taxable profit (e.g. expenditure on assets such as computer equipment allowed for tax purposes when paid (asset), or deferral of income recognition in respect of funds that are taxable when received (liability)); or

- a business combination.

IAS 12 prohibits the recognition of deferred tax on the initial recognition of an asset or a liability in any other circumstances. [IAS 12:22] The following flowchart illustrates these rules.

Temporary difference arising on the initial recognition of an asset or a liability

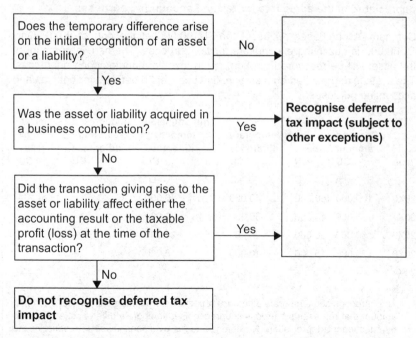

One example given in IAS 12 is that of an asset for which there is no deduction against taxable profits for depreciation. Assuming that the entity intends to recover the value of the asset through use, the tax base of the asset is nil. Therefore, a taxable temporary difference equal to the cost of the asset arises on initial recognition. However, the Standard does not permit a deferred tax liability to be recognised because the initial recognition of the asset is not part of a business combination and does not affect either accounting profit or taxable profit. Further, no deferred tax is recognised as a result of depreciating the asset.

The prohibition on recognition is based on the argument that, if a deferred tax liability were recognised, the equivalent amount would have to be added to the asset's carrying amount in the statement of financial position, or be recognised in profit or loss at the date of initial recognition, and this would make the financial statements 'less transparent'. [IAS 12:22(c)] This exception is based on pragmatism and the desire to avoid the particular financial statement effects discussed, rather than any particular conceptual basis. The exception has a particular effect in jurisdictions where some or all of the initial expenditure on assets is disallowed for tax purposes.

4.4.6.2   Application of the initial recognition exception

The following examples illustrate the application of the initial recognition exception.

Example 4.4.6.2A

Deferred tax liability arising on the recognition of an asset – asset depreciated at the same rate for tax and accounting purposes

Company A purchases an asset for CU100,000 at the end of 20X0. Only CU60,000 is qualifying expenditure for tax purposes. The carrying amount of the asset will be recovered through use in taxable manufacturing operations. The asset is depreciated on a straight-line basis at 25 per cent for both tax and accounting purposes.

Year	Carrying amount CU	Tax base CU	Temporary difference CU	Unrecognised temporary difference CU	Recognised temporary difference CU	Deferred tax liability CU
	A	B	A – B = C	D*		
20X0	100,000	60,000	40,000	40,000	–	–
20X1	75,000	45,000	30,000	30,000	–	–
20X2	50,000	30,000	20,000	20,000	–	–
20X3	25,000	15,000	10,000	10,000	–	–
20X4	–	–	–	–	–	–

*   The unrecognised temporary difference reflects the proportion of the asset's carrying amount that represents the original unrecognised temporary difference, as reduced by subsequent depreciation. No deferred tax is ever recognised in respect of the original temporary difference.

Subsequent to initial recognition, additional temporary differences may arise in respect of the same asset or liability (e.g. due to different depreciation rates for accounting and tax purposes). In such circumstances, the deferred tax effect of those additional temporary differences is recognised in accordance with the usual requirements.

Effectively what is required, as illustrated in **example 4.4.6.2B**, is to deduct from the temporary difference at each period end the proportion of the asset's (or the liability's) carrying amount that represents the unrecognised temporary difference at the date of acquisition, as reduced by subsequent depreciation or amortisation. Deferred tax is provided in respect of the remainder of the temporary difference (the recognised temporary difference) in accordance with the usual requirements.

Example 4.4.6.2B

Deferred tax liability arising on the recognition of an asset – different deprecation rates for tax and accounting purposes

The facts are as per **example 4.4.6.2A**, but the asset is depreciated on a straight-line basis at 25 per cent for accounting purposes and 331/3 per cent for tax purposes. The tax rate is 30 per cent.

Year	Carrying amount CU	Tax base CU	Temporary difference CU	Unrecognised temporary difference CU	Recognised temporary difference CU	Deferred tax liability CU
	A	B	A – B = C	D*	C – D = E**	E × 30%
20X0	100,000	60,000	40,000	40,000	–	–
20X1	75,000	40,000	35,000	30,000	5,000	1,500
20X2	50,000	20,000	30,000	20,000	10,000	3,000
20X3	25,000	–	25,000	10,000	15,000	4,500
20X4	–	–	–	–	–	–

*   As per **example 4.4.6.2A**

**   The recognised temporary difference reflects the difference between cumulative tax and cumulative accounting depreciation on the original tax base of the asset.

Additional temporary differences will also arise when the asset is subsequently revalued, as illustrated below.

Example 4.4.6.2C

Deferred tax liability arising on the recognition of an asset – asset subsequently revalued

The facts are as per **example 4.4.6.2A** (i.e. depreciation on a straight-line basis at 25 per cent for both tax and accounting purposes), but the asset is revalued for accounting purposes to CU120,000 at the end of 20X1. The tax rate is 30 per cent.

Year	Carrying amount CU	Tax base CU	Temporary difference CU	Unrecognised temporary difference CU	Recognised temporary difference CU	Deferred tax liability CU
	A	B	A − B = C	D*	C − D = E**	E × 30%
20X0	100,000	60,000	40,000	40,000	–	–
20X1	120,000	45,000	75,000	30,000	45,000	13,500
20X2	80,000	30,000	50,000	20,000	30,000	9,000
20X3	40,000	15,000	25,000	10,000	15,000	4,500
20X4	–	–	–	–	–	–

*   As per **example 4.4.6.2A**

** The recognised temporary difference is the amount by which the asset has been revalued upwards in comparison with the depreciated original cost (i.e. the difference between CU120,000 and CU75,000, being the carrying amount of the asset at the time of the revaluation), less depreciation of the revaluation uplift.

4.4.6.3   Available tax deductions exceed the cost of the asset ('super deductions')

Example 4.4.6.3A

Additional tax deduction available when assets are brought into use

On 31 December 20X0, Manufacturing Entity A enters into a capital expansion project that qualifies for tax deductions based on 150 per cent of the cost of new manufacturing assets (CU80,000). The deduction in excess of the cost of the assets (the additional tax deduction) is deductible in the determination of taxable income in the period when the assets are brought into use (20X1).

The carrying amount of the assets will be recovered through use in taxable manufacturing operations. The cost of the assets is depreciated on a straight-line basis at 25 per cent for accounting purposes and 331/3 per cent for tax purposes.

The tax rate is 30 per cent.

Note that the tax deduction in excess of the cost of the assets (available when the assets are brought into use in 20X1) satisfies the conditions for the initial recognition exception under IAS 12:24 because the transaction (i.e. the incurrence of capital expenditure) (1) is not a business combination, and (2) affects neither accounting nor taxable profit on initial recognition.

Year	Carrying amount CU	Tax base CU	Temporary difference CU	Unrecognised temporary difference CU	Recognised temporary difference CU	Deferred tax liability CU
	A	B	A − B = C	D*	C − D = E	E × 30%
20X0	80,000	120,000	-40,000	-40,000	−	−
20X1	60,000	53,333	6,667	−	6,667	2,000
20X2	40,000	26,667	13,334	−	13,334	4,000
20X3	20,000	−	20,000	−	20,000	6,000
20X4	−	−	−	−	−	−

* The unrecognised temporary difference represents the proportion of the additional tax deduction not yet claimed.

The accounting treatment described results in a lower effective tax rate in 20X1 when the assets are brought into use (and the additional tax deduction of CU40,000 is claimed) and a constant effective tax rate from 20X2 to 20X4.

Example 4.4.6.3B

Additional tax deduction available over several periods

The facts are as per **example 4.4.6.3A**, except the additional tax deduction is claimed evenly over three years, commencing when the assets are brought into use in 20X1.

Year	Carrying amount CU	Tax base CU	Temporary difference CU	Unrecognised temporary difference CU	Recognised temporary difference CU	Deferred tax liability CU
	A	B	A − B = C	D*	C − D = E	E × 30%
20X0	80,000	120,000	-40,000	-40,000	−	−
20X1	60,000	80,000	-20,000	-26,667	6,667	2,000
20X2	40,000	40,000	−	-13,333	13,334	4,000
20X3	20,000	−	-20,000	−	20,000	6,000
20X4	−	−	−	−	−	−

* The unrecognised temporary difference reflects the proportion of the additional tax deduction not yet claimed.

The additional tax deduction is allowed over several periods, resulting in the reversal of the temporary difference that is subject to the initial recognition exception over time. This reduces the effective tax rate evenly throughout the period over which the tax deductions are realised.

4.4.6.4   Acquisition of investment property

At the time of acquisition of an investment property, an entity should determine whether the acquisition is considered to be the acquisition of a single asset, or whether it is considered to be a business combination as defined in accordance with IFRS 3. The acquisition of a single asset is a transaction to which the initial recognition exception would generally apply and, if so, no deferred tax would be recognised for any taxable temporary difference at the date of acquisition. Conversely, the acquisition of assets in a business combination does not attract the initial recognition exception and, therefore, deferred tax would be recognised on any taxable temporary differences arising at the date of acquisition.

In determining whether the acquisition of an investment property is a business combination, an entity should refer to the guidance in IAS 40:14A (see **3.2** in **chapter A8**).

The deferred tax accounting for the acquisition will automatically follow the accounting determination as to whether the acquisition meets the definition of a business combination under IFRS 3; it is not an independent decision for the purposes of applying IAS 12.

4.4.6.5   Government grants

Deferred tax assets can arise on the initial recognition of an asset, although more rarely than deferred tax liabilities. The example cited in IAS 12 for a deferred tax asset arising on initial recognition is when a non-taxable government grant related to an asset is deducted in arriving at the carrying amount of the asset but, for tax purposes, is not deducted from the asset's depreciable amount (i.e. its tax base). The carrying amount of the asset is less than its tax base, giving rise to a deductible temporary difference. Under IAS 20 *Accounting for Government Grants and Disclosure of Government Assistance*, the government grant may also be set up as deferred income, in which case the difference between the deferred income and its tax base of nil is a deductible temporary difference. Whichever method of presentation is adopted, the entity does not recognise the resulting deferred tax asset. [IAS 12:33]

4.4.6.6   Recognition exceptions applied by an acquiree prior to a business combination

An entity acquired in a business combination may not have recognised deferred taxes on temporary differences related to some assets or liabilities in its individual financial statements because, when the asset or liability was first recognised, the initial recognition exception applied.

Although the acquired entity does not recognise deferred tax on these items in its individual financial statements, the recognition exception does not apply when the assets and liabilities of the acquired entity are initially recognised in the new consolidated group. Deferred tax will be recognised on any temporary differences at the date of acquisition because, from the group's perspective, the assets and liabilities are initially recognised as part of a business combination and, therefore, the conditions for the initial recognition exception are not met.

4.4.6.7 *Transfers of assets between group entities*

In some circumstances, an entity within a group will acquire assets and liabilities in a business combination and subsequently transfer one or more of the acquired assets to another entity within the group. In the consolidated financial statements of the group, because the assets were acquired in a business combination, the initial recognition exception does not apply and deferred tax should be recognised on any taxable temporary difference arising at the date of acquisition and subsequently (including any difference arising on the subsequent transfer of the assets between entities within the group).

However, from the perspective of the individual entity within the group to which assets have been subsequently transferred, often the transfer will not constitute a business combination, but rather the acquisition of individual assets. In such circumstances, in the individual financial statements of the entity to which the assets have been transferred, any taxable temporary difference arising on the initial recognition of the assets is subject to the initial recognition exception and no deferred tax liability should be recognised at the point of transfer. In the consolidated financial statements of the group, the unrecognised deferred tax liability would then be reinstated as a consolidation adjustment.

A similar analysis applies when an intragroup transfer results in a deductible temporary difference, with the recognition of any deferred tax asset in the consolidated financial statements being subject to IAS 12's general recognition criteria (see **4.6.1**).

4.4.6.8 *Temporary differences arising as a result of changes in tax legislation*

Temporary differences may arise as a result of changes in tax legislation in a variety of ways, for example:

- when a new income tax is introduced to replace or complement the existing income tax regime; or

- when an allowance for depreciation of specified assets is amended or withdrawn.

The initial recognition exception in IAS 12:15(b) does not apply in respect of temporary differences that arise as a result of changes in tax legislation. IAS 12:15(b) provides an exception from the general requirement to recognise a deferred tax liability for all taxable temporary differences that arise on the initial recognition of an asset or a liability in a transaction which (1) is not a business combination, and (2) at the time of the transaction affects neither accounting profit nor taxable profit (tax loss). Therefore, it can only be applied when an asset or a liability is first recognised.

Accordingly, when additional temporary differences arise as a result of the introduction of a new tax, and not when an asset or a liability is first recognised, the deferred tax effect of the additional temporary differences should be recognised. The deferred tax effect of any additional temporary difference arising in such circumstances will be recognised (subject to the general recognition criteria in IAS 12 for deferred tax assets) and presented as required by IAS 12:58.

The fact that the initial recognition exception can only be applied when an asset or a liability is first recognised results in inconsistent accounting under IAS 12 for assets owned by an entity when a change in tax legislation is introduced as compared to assets acquired after that date.

4.4.7 Recognition exceptions – investments in subsidiaries, branches and associates, and interests in joint arrangements

4.4.7.1 Temporary differences associated with investments in subsidiaries, branches and associates, and interests in joint arrangements

Temporary differences arise when the carrying amount of an investment differs from its tax base (which is often cost). Examples of circumstances in which temporary differences may arise include:

[IAS 12:38]

- the existence of undistributed profits in the subsidiary, branch, associate or joint arrangement (when profits have been consolidated or accounted for using the equity method);

- movements in the carrying amount of a foreign operation due to changes in foreign exchange rates when a parent and its subsidiary have different functional currencies; or

- a reduction in the carrying amount of an investment in an associate to its recoverable amount without a corresponding change in its tax base.

Additionally, temporary differences can arise due to adjustments made to the tax base of the investment as a result of local tax law. These may include adjustments as a result of controlled foreign company laws, deemed taxable distributions of dividends, or tax elections.

A temporary difference arising in consolidated financial statements may be different from that in the parent's separate financial statements if the parent carries the investment at cost or revalued amount. [IAS 12:38]

Differences associated with investments in subsidiaries, associates and joint arrangements generally arise in consolidated financial statements because the profits of the investee have been recognised (whether by consolidation or the equity method) but the tax base of the investment remains unchanged. The tax effects that would arise if those profits were distributed (e.g. withholding tax) should be considered. Unlike the 'general' recognition exceptions (see **4.4.4**), IAS 12 does not prohibit the recognition of deferred tax assets and liabilities in respect of these differences. Instead, it imposes particular conditions for such recognition.

4.4.7.2 *Recognition of taxable temporary differences associated with investments in subsidiaries, branches and associates, and interests in joint arrangements*

An entity should recognise a deferred tax liability for all taxable temporary differences associated with investments in subsidiaries, branches and associates, and interests in joint arrangements, except to the extent that both of the following conditions are satisfied:

[IAS 12:39]

- the parent, investor, joint venturer or joint operator is able to control the timing of the reversal of the temporary difference; and

- it is probable that the temporary difference will not reverse in the foreseeable future.

4.4.7.3 *Recognition of deductible temporary differences associated with investments in subsidiaries, branches and associates, and interests in joint arrangements*

An entity should recognise a deferred tax asset for all deductible temporary differences arising from investments in subsidiaries, branches and associates, and interests in joint arrangements, to the extent that, and only to the extent that, it is probable both:

[IAS 12:44]

- that the temporary difference will reverse in the foreseeable future; and

- that taxable profit will be available against which the temporary difference can be utilised.

IAS 12 does not define 'foreseeable future'. However, it is reasonable to analogise to the guidance in IAS 1 *Presentation of Financial Statements* regarding the going concern assumption underlying the preparation of financial statements. IAS 1:26 refers to a period that "is at least, but not limited to, twelve months from the end of the reporting period". Therefore, for the purposes of applying IAS 12, it is reasonable to expect that the 'foreseeable future' would be at least twelve months from the end of the reporting period. However, depending on the facts and circumstances (including management intent), it may be a longer period.

4.4.7.4   Recognition of temporary differences associated with investments in subsidiaries

For investments in subsidiaries, the temporary difference generally represents the difference between the net investment accounted for in the consolidated financial statements (effectively the parent's share of the subsidiary's net assets including any associated goodwill) and the tax base of the investment.

A parent/subsidiary relationship involves the parent controlling its subsidiary, including the subsidiary's dividend policy. Accordingly, IAS 12 provides that when a parent has determined that it is probable that undistributed profits in a subsidiary will not be distributed in the foreseeable future, the parent does not recognise deferred tax on those undistributed profits. The same considerations apply to investments in branches. [IAS 12:40]

The Standard provides no specific guidance regarding the factors to be considered by the parent in order to determine whether distribution of the subsidiary's profits (and, therefore, reversal of a taxable temporary difference) is probable. Factors that might be considered in making the assessment include, but are not limited to:

- any plans for reinvestment to grow the business of the subsidiary;

- the past pattern of dividend payments;

- whether the parent needs the funds that would be generated by a dividend from its subsidiary to enable it to make a dividend payment or satisfy any other cash requirement;

- whether cash and distributable profits are available to pay dividends;

- whether a binding agreement exists regarding the amount of dividends to be paid out;

- whether there is a policy of paying out a certain percentage of profits each year;

- whether there is intent to dispose of the subsidiary before any distribution is made; and

- whether any legal or taxation requirements effectively create an economic compulsion to pay distributions.

When a parent requires its subsidiary to remit only a portion of undistributed earnings, the parent should recognise a deferred tax liability only for the portion of the undistributed earnings expected to be remitted in the foreseeable future.

If circumstances change, and it becomes probable that some or all of the undistributed earnings of the subsidiary in respect of which deferred tax has not been recognised will be remitted in the foreseeable future, the parent should recognise the additional deferred tax liability as an expense of the current period; prior year amounts are not restated.

If a subsidiary is classified as a discontinued operation under IFRS 5 *Non-current Assets Held for Sale and Discontinued Operations* (see **chapter A20**), this does not affect the requirements regarding the recognition of deferred tax assets. Therefore, a deferred tax asset should be recognised to the extent that it is probable that a temporary difference will reverse in the foreseeable future, and that taxable profit will be available against which the temporary difference can be utilised.

If a parent has recognised deferred tax in relation to its investment in a subsidiary classified as a discontinued operation, that deferred tax should be included in the accounting for the disposal of the subsidiary through sale or otherwise. Particular considerations apply when the parent retains an interest such that the investee is accounted for subsequently as an associate (see **4.4.7.7**).

Example 4.4.7.4A

Profits in a subsidiary not expected to be distributed in the foreseeable future

Company A has a subsidiary with a carrying amount of CU200 and a tax base of CU100. Company A controls the distribution of dividends by the subsidiary. Company A does not have any need for the subsidiary to make a distribution, and in fact has active plans for the undistributed profits to be reinvested to grow the business of the subsidiary. In these circumstances, Company A should not recognise a deferred tax liability in respect of the temporary difference of CU100, because Company A can control the timing of the reversal and the temporary difference is not expected to reverse in the foreseeable future.

Example 4.4.7.4B

Profits in a subsidiary expected to be distributed in the foreseeable future

The facts are as per **example 4.4.7.4A**, except that Company A has encountered a cash flow problem. In order to resolve this problem, Company A needs to extract the increased value in the subsidiary in the form of cash dividends. In these circumstances, Company A should recognise the deferred tax liability for the portion of the earnings to be remitted because, although it can control the timing of the reversal, it is probable that the temporary difference will reverse in the foreseeable future.

Example 4.4.7.4C

Parent does not control timing of payment of dividends

The facts are as per **example 4.4.7.4A**, except that the subsidiary operates in a foreign jurisdiction. In that jurisdiction, the determination as to whether profits are returned to foreign investors or are reinvested in the business is made through regulatory channels. While Company A can express a preference, it is the local regulator who determines when profits are paid out as dividends. In these circumstances, Company A should recognise the deferred tax liability for all unremitted earnings of the subsidiary because it does not control the timing of the reversal of the temporary difference.

Example 4.4.7.4D

Temporary difference arising in relation to a loan forming part of net investment

Company B has a functional currency of US dollars. It makes a loan in Euro to its wholly-owned subsidiary, Company D, which has a functional currency of Euro. The loan is assessed under IAS 21 *The Effects of Changes in Foreign Exchange Rates* to be part of Company B's net investment in Company D.

In Company B's separate financial statements, in accordance with IAS 21:32, the loan is retranslated at the end of the reporting period, with exchange differences recognised in profit or loss. The exchange differences arising from the loan will only be assessed for tax purposes when the loan is repaid.

Because the loan forms part of Company B's net investment in Company D, the requirements of IAS 12:39 (see **4.4.2**) should be applied in relation to the loan.

Company B can control the repayment of the loan which forms part of its net investment in the subsidiary. Therefore, Company B is able to control when tax will be incurred on the exchange differences, and is able to control the timing of the reversal of the temporary difference. Because settlement is neither planned nor likely to occur in the foreseeable future (a condition for the loan to qualify as part of Company B's net investment under IAS 21:15), it is probable that the temporary difference arising from the exchange differences will not reverse in the foreseeable future.

Consequently, Company B should not recognise deferred tax on the exchange differences arising on the foreign currency loan to Company D. In addition, Company B should comply with the disclosure requirements of IAS 12:81(f).

Example 4.4.7.4E

Deferred tax on overseas income derived from a subsidiary that is only taxed on repatriation

Company A has a subsidiary, Company C, which operates in a foreign tax jurisdiction. During the year, Company A made an interest earning loan of CU100,000 to Company C that is not considered to be part of its net investment in Company C for the purposes of IAS 21:15. The interest income from the loan is not taxable while held in the foreign tax jurisdiction and is only taxed on repatriation. Company A has no current intention to repatriate the interest income.

At the end of the current financial year, the total interest earned is CU10,000 and the carrying amount of the loan is CU110,000. The tax base of the interest earned is nil.

Company A should recognise a deferred tax liability in respect of the interest earned on the loan; Company A is required to recognise a tax liability on the difference between the carrying amount of CU10,000 and the tax base of nil.

The exception in IAS 12:38 to 45 relates to differences between the carrying amount and the tax base of investments in subsidiaries, branches, associates, and interests in joint arrangements; the exception does not apply to temporary differences that exist between the carrying amount of amounts receivable from or payable to the investee and their tax bases.

4.4.7.5 Recognition of temporary differences associated with investments in associates

In consolidated financial statements, investments in associates are generally accounted for using the equity method of accounting. Under the equity method, the investment is initially recognised at cost and the carrying amount is then increased or decreased by the investor's share of the profit or loss and other comprehensive income of the investee, less any distributions received from the associate. The tax arising in respect of the investee's profit or loss and other comprehensive income is recognised in the financial statements of the investee, and is therefore reflected in the amounts accounted for by the investor using the equity method of accounting, which are reported net of tax. Any additional tax arising on any dividends received by the investor from the associate will also be reflected in the investor's own financial statements.

It may be that additional tax implications would arise if the investor were to realise its investment in the associate – whether through distribution of the retained profits of the associate or through disposal. For example, dividend income might be taxable or partially taxable in the hands of the investor; withholding taxes might be applied in the associate's country of operation; capital gains tax might be payable on disposal of the investment. In any of these circumstances, a temporary difference may exist.

Under IAS 12's recognition rules (see **4.4.2**), taxable temporary differences associated with investments in associates should be accounted for except when:

- the investor controls the timing of the reversal of the temporary difference; and

- it is probable that the temporary difference will not reverse in the foreseeable future.

Because an investor/associate relationship does not involve control, an investor in an associate should normally recognise deferred tax arising in relation to the undistributed profits of an associate, unless there is strong evidence of an agreement that profits will not be distributed in the foreseeable future.

Example 4.4.7.5A

Undistributed profits in an associate

Company B has an associate, Company A, which operates in Country Z. In its consolidated financial statements for the year ended 31 December 20X3, Company B recognised its CU20,000 share of the profits of Company A for that period using the equity method of accounting.

During the period, Company A paid interim dividends of CU5,000 to Company B out of its current year profits. No tax arises in Company B's country of operation on receipt of the dividends. However, under the laws of Country Z, additional tax is payable on distributed profits at 25 per cent and is not recoverable.

Because Company B is not able to control the timing of the reversal of the taxable temporary difference, in its consolidated financial statements it must also recognise the tax consequences that would arise if the remainder of its share of Company A's current year profits (i.e. CU15,000) were distributed. A deferred tax liability of CU3,750 (CU15,000 × 25%) should therefore be recognised in the consolidated financial statements to 31 December 20X3, in addition to the recognition of the tax consequences arising from the remittance of CU5,000.

Example 4.4.7.5B

Investment in associate – determination of the expected manner of recovery

Company A has a 20 per cent interest in Company B and exercises significant influence over Company B. The investment in Company B is accounted for in the consolidated financial statements of Company A using the equity method of accounting. Dividends received from Company B are not taxable; however, any capital gain on disposal of the investment in Company B would be taxed at a rate of 15 per cent.

IAS 12.51A requires that an entity should measure deferred tax liabilities and deferred tax assets using the tax rate and the tax base that are consistent with the expected manner of recovery of an asset. Accordingly, the tax rate should reflect the expected manner of recovery of the asset.

How should the 'expected manner of recovery' of Company A's investment in Company B (and, consequently, the appropriate rate for measurement of the deferred tax liability) be determined?

The carrying amount of an investment in an associate can be recovered in a variety of ways, for example by:

- receiving dividends (or other distribution of profit);
- sale to a third party; or
- receiving residual assets upon liquidation of the associate.

The determination of the expected manner of recovery of an investment in an associate will often require careful judgement. In the circumstances described, factors to consider in making this judgement include, but are not limited to:

- whether Company A intends to sell its interest in Company B;
- the dividend yield on the investment; and
- the reason for acquiring and holding the investment.

When, for example, there has been a regular flow of dividends from the investment in the past, and there is no evidence of an intention to dispose of the associate (even though a disposal may be a possibility at some future point), this may lead to a determination that the investment will be recovered through remittance of earnings by dividend.

If the investment is expected to be recovered partly through dividends and partly upon sale or liquidation (e.g. if Company A has a plan to sell its investment in Company B at a later date and expects to receive dividends until the sale of the investment), the temporary difference should be disaggregated and different tax rates applied to each part in order to be consistent with the expected manner of recovery. See example **4.2.6.1B** for an illustration of the calculation of a deferred tax liability when an asset is expected to be recovered partly through use and partly through sale.

The conclusions above were confirmed by the IFRS Interpretations Committee in the March 2015 *IFRIC Update*.

For deductible temporary differences arising in relation to investments, it is not necessary to consider the investor's ability to control distributions from the investee. Recognition of the deferred tax asset is only required if it is probable that the temporary difference will reverse in the foreseeable future and that taxable profit will be available against which the temporary difference can be utilised.

4.4.7.6   Recognition of temporary differences associated with interests in joint arrangements

Under IFRS 11 *Joint Arrangements*, the accounting for a joint arrangement is determined by whether the arrangement is classified as a joint venture or a joint operation (as defined in that Standard).

Irrespective of the method of accounting for joint arrangements, the same general considerations apply in respect of deferred tax.

The arrangement between the parties to a joint arrangement usually deals with the distribution of the profits and identifies whether decisions on such matters require the consent of all of the parties or a group of the parties. When the joint venturer or joint operator can control the timing of the distribution of its share of profits of the joint arrangement, and it is probable that its share of the profits will not be distributed in the foreseeable future, a deferred tax liability is not recognised. [IAS 12:43]

Interests in joint ventures

The determination as to who controls the timing of the reversal of the temporary difference in the case of joint ventures is not as clear-cut as it is for associates (see **4.4.7.5**). Investments in joint ventures involve joint control, i.e. there is a contractual agreement to share control and no joint venturer exercises unilateral control.

The arrangements for distributions or disposals of shareholdings are generally dealt with in the joint venture agreement. In most cases, although each joint venturer cannot unilaterally declare a dividend, neither can such dividend be declared without each joint venturer's agreement. Therefore, each joint venturer has the ability to prevent distributions and, accordingly, prevent the reversal of the temporary difference. If this is the case, no deferred tax liability should be recognised if the joint venturer does not anticipate that it will authorise such distributions in the foreseeable future.

Interests in joint operations

Under IFRS 11, the determination of the tax implications for joint operations will depend on whether the joint operation is structured through a legal entity.

For joint arrangements that are structured through a legal entity but are determined to be joint operations because of other facts and circumstances (see **chapter A27**), the same considerations apply as above for joint ventures.

For joint operations that are not structured through a legal entity, the absence of a legal entity would mean that the joint operator does not generally have the ability to control the reversal of the temporary difference. Accordingly, deferred tax should normally be recognised.

4.4.7.7   Change in investment from subsidiary to associate

A parent may cease to have control over a subsidiary (e.g. because the parent sells a portion of the investment or because the subsidiary issues additional shares to a third party) but may retain some of its ownership interest such that the investment is subsequently classified as an associate and is, therefore, accounted for using the equity method. This change from subsidiary to associate may have deferred tax consequences.

When the parent did not previously recognise deferred tax in respect of temporary differences associated with the investment in the subsidiary (on the basis that it could control the timing of the reversal of such differences and it was not considered probable that the temporary differences would reverse in the foreseeable future), the change in status will generally require this determination to be revisited. Because an investor/associate relationship does not involve control, it will be determined in the majority of cases that the investor no longer has control over the timing of the reversal of the temporary differences associated with the investment, and deferred tax will need to be recognised in respect of the difference between the carrying amount of the investment in the associate and its tax base.

Under IFRS 10 *Consolidated Financial Statements*, when a transaction results in a parent losing control of a subsidiary, any investment retained in the former subsidiary is recognised at its fair value at the date when control is lost. In such circumstances, there is a change in the temporary differences associated with the investment; after the transaction, the temporary differences will include not only the investor's share of the undistributed profits of the associate and foreign exchange differences etc., but also the fair value uplift of the investment.

4.4.7.8   Foreign currency adjustments

The non-monetary assets and liabilities of an entity are measured in its functional currency (see **chapter A19**). If an entity's taxable profit or tax loss (and, consequently, the tax base of its non-monetary assets and liabilities) is determined in a different currency, changes in the exchange rate give rise to temporary differences that result in a recognised deferred tax liability or asset (subject to the general recognition criteria). The resulting deferred tax is recognised in profit or loss. [IAS 12:41]

IAS 12 is clear that when the tax base of a non-monetary asset is determined in a different currency from the functional currency of the entity, temporary differences will arise and deferred tax should be calculated. However, there is no guidance on how the deferred tax should be calculated.

In general, the most appropriate methodology will be to convert the tax base into the functional currency using the closing rate. This should be compared with the asset's carrying amount in the financial statements, which will have been converted at the rate ruling on the date of recognition. The deferred tax is then calculated at the tax rate expected to apply when the temporary difference reverses.

Example 4.4.7.8A

Tax base of asset denominated in a foreign currency

Company B, a Sterling functional currency entity, owns an asset in the United States. At 1 January 20X1, the tax base of the asset is US$120 and the carrying amount is £50. The exchange rate is £0.5 = US$1, resulting in a temporary difference of £10 (US$120 × 0.5 = £60 less £50).

At 31 December 20X1, the carrying amount and the US$ tax base of the asset have not changed, but the exchange rate is now £0.52 = US$1, resulting in a temporary difference of £12 (US$120 × 0.52 = £62 less £50). The movement of £2 represents an increase in the temporary difference as a result of the movement in the exchange rate.

Company B's tax rate will be applied to the movement of £2 and the resulting value recognised as part of deferred tax expense for the year, even though the movement is attributable to an exchange rate movement.

The asset may be subject to depreciation; if so, part of the movement in the temporary difference would arise from the depreciation of the carrying amount.

When an entity owns a subsidiary that is taxed in a currency other than that subsidiary's functional currency, a translation difference will arise on the calculated deferred tax balance in that subsidiary's financial statements. On consolidation, that exchange difference is recognised in profit or loss; it is not transferred to the foreign currency translation reserve because the translation difference does not result from the accounting for the reporting entity's net investment in a foreign operation.

Example 4.4.7.8B

Tax base of subsidiary's assets and liabilities denominated in a foreign currency

Group A prepares consolidated financial statements which are presented in Sterling, and include a subsidiary with a functional currency of US dollars. However, that subsidiary pays taxes that are calculated and denominated in

Sterling (the local currency of the subsidiary). Accordingly, the tax bases of the assets and liabilities in the subsidiary's financial statements are denominated in Sterling. Therefore, changes in exchange rates give rise to temporary differences. The resulting deferred tax is recognised in profit or loss in the financial statements of the subsidiary.

The amount is also recognised as part of the tax expense (income) in profit or loss in Group A's consolidated financial statements (rather than being recognised in other comprehensive income) because it reflects the genuine foreign currency exposure between the functional currency of the subsidiary and the tax cash flows of that subsidiary.

In some jurisdictions, tax returns and tax bases are permitted to be calculated in an entity's functional currency, even if that currency is not the local currency. The current tax liability is then translated into local currency for payment to the tax authorities. In such circumstances, foreign exchange gains and losses will not generally arise on the entity's temporary differences (which are computed in the functional currency), but a foreign exchange gain or loss can arise on differences between the accrual of the income tax provision in the functional currency and the payment of the liability in local currency. This is a genuine foreign currency exposure between the functional currency and the tax cash flows and is recognised in profit or loss.

4.4.7.9 Inflation adjustments

The tax law for a particular foreign jurisdiction may permit or require the taxpayer to adjust the tax base of an asset or a liability to take into account the effects of inflation. The inflation-adjusted tax base of an asset or a liability would be used to determine the future taxable or deductible amounts. If a foreign subsidiary has such inflation-indexed assets or liabilities, it cannot use the exceptions from recognition of deferred tax associated with investments in subsidiaries under IAS 12:39 and IAS 12:44 (see **4.4.2** and **4.4.3**) to avoid recognising the related deferred tax liabilities or assets.

The temporary differences relate to the foreign operation's own assets and liabilities, rather than to the reporting entity's investment in that foreign operation. Consequently, the foreign subsidiary recognises the resulting deferred tax liability or asset as appropriate in its domestic financial statements. The resulting deferred tax is recognised in profit or loss.

Example 4.4.7.9

Tax base of assets adjusted for inflation

Company X (with Sterling as its functional currency) has an overseas subsidiary (in a country where the inflation rate is not considered hyperinflationary) whose functional currency is the Euro.

At the beginning of 20X2, the foreign jurisdiction enacted tax legislation that increased the tax base of depreciable assets by 10 per cent. That increase will permit the overseas subsidiary to deduct additional depreciation in the current and future years. Immediately prior to the change in tax legislation, the base of the overseas subsidiary's depreciable assets is €1,000 for both tax and financial reporting purposes; the foreign tax rate is 50 per cent, and the current exchange rate between Sterling and the Euro is £1 = €2.

Therefore, at the beginning of 20X2, the overseas subsidiary should recognise a deferred tax asset resulting from the temporary difference between the carrying amount of the depreciable asset and the indexed tax base of €50 ([€1,000 × 10 per cent] × 50%) (subject to IAS 12's general recognition criteria for deferred tax assets).

In the consolidated financial statements, the deferred tax asset of the subsidiary should be translated to £25 (€50 × 0.5) based on the current exchange rate.

In certain jurisdictions, the indexation allowance is only available upon sale, and does not affect the tax base available for tax depreciation. Therefore, if the expected manner of recovery of the asset (and, consequently, the deferred tax associated with the asset) is based on use, the indexation allowance should not be considered.

4.5   Measurement of deferred tax assets and liabilities

4.5.1   Computation of deferred tax assets and liabilities

To calculate the amount of a deferred tax asset or liability, the following formula may be useful.

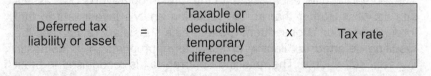

$$\text{Deferred tax liability or asset} = \text{Taxable or deductible temporary difference} \times \text{Tax rate}$$

A deferred tax asset can also arise from unused tax losses and tax credits that have been carried forward. These deferred tax assets are calculated as follows.

Deferred tax asset	=	Unused tax losses and / or tax credits	x	Tax rate

Thus, an important consideration is what tax rate should be used. This is considered in **section 4.5.2**.

4.5.2 Tax rates and laws

4.5.2.1 Tax rates and laws – general

Deferred tax balances are calculated using the tax rates that are expected to apply to the reporting period or periods when the temporary differences reverse, based on tax rates and tax laws enacted or substantively enacted at the end of the reporting period. [IAS 12:47]

When the tax rates that will apply to the entity are expected to vary in coming years (e.g. in start-up situations when tax concessions are granted in the early years), it is necessary to anticipate the year in which the temporary difference will reverse so that the deferred tax asset or liability can be calculated at the appropriate rate.

4.5.2.2 Progressive or graduated tax rates

In some jurisdictions, the tax rate varies according to the amount of taxable profit earned in a period. This creates a potential issue when it is necessary to predict the tax rate that will apply when a temporary difference reverses. IAS 12 addresses this situation and requires that, in such circumstances, deferred tax assets and liabilities should be measured using the average rates that are expected to apply in the periods in which the temporary differences are expected to reverse. [IAS 12:49]

For entities that expect graduated tax rates to be a significant factor, careful judgement should be exercised in determining the appropriate average tax rate to be used when measuring deferred tax assets and liabilities.

The determination of the appropriate tax rate may require an estimate of future taxable income for the year(s) in which existing temporary differences or carryforwards will enter into the determination of income tax. That estimate of future income includes:

- income or loss excluding reversals of temporary differences; and

- reversals of existing taxable and deductible temporary differences.

The following example illustrates the measurement of deferred tax assets and liabilities when graduated tax rates are a significant factor.

Example 4.5.2.2

Graduated tax rates

At the end of 20X1, Company X has CU30,000 of deductible temporary differences that are expected to result in tax deductions of CU10,000 for each of the next three years – 20X2, 20X3 and 20X4.

Company X operates in a jurisdiction that has a graduated tax rate structure. The graduated tax rates are as follows.

Income > CU	Income ≤ CU	Tax rate
–	50,000	15%
50,000	75,000	25%
75,000	100,000	34%
100,000	335,000	39%
335,000	10,000,000	34%
10,000,000	15,000,000	35%
15,000,000	18,333,333	38%
18,333,333	–	34%

Company X's estimates for pre-tax income for the three years 20X2, 20X3 and 20X4 are CU410,000, CU110,000 and CU60,000, respectively, exclusive of reversing temporary differences. The estimated taxable income and income taxes payable for those years is computed as follows.

	Future years		
	20X2 CU	20X3 CU	20X4 CU
Estimated pre-tax income	410,000	110,000	60,000
Reversing deductible temporary differences	(10,000)	(10,000)	(10,000)
Estimated taxable income (A)	400,000	100,000	50,000
Tax based on graduated tax rates:			
(CU50,000 × 15%)	7,500	7,500	7,500
(CU25,000 × 25%)	6,250	6,250	–
(CU25,000 × 34%)	8,500	8,500	–
(CU235,000 × 39%)	91,650	–	–
(over CU335,000 × 34%)	22,100	–	–
Estimated tax (B)	136,000	22,250	7,500
Applicable tax rate (C = B/A)	34 %	22.25 %	15 %
Deferred tax credit (CU10,000 × C), CU	3,400	2,225	1,500

Provided that the probable realisation criterion established under IAS 12 is met, Company A should recognise a deferred tax asset at the end of 20X1 of CU7,125 (CU3,400 + CU2,225 + CU1,500).

4.5.2.3   Substantively enacted tax rates

IAS 12 requires that deferred tax assets and liabilities be measured based on rates and laws that have been 'enacted or substantively enacted' by the end of the reporting period. It is not appropriate to anticipate changes to tax rates or laws that have not been substantively enacted.

Whether or not a law has actually been enacted by the end of the reporting period is a fact that will be immediately clear. However, when a new rate or law is announced at or before the end of the reporting period, but the formalities of the enactment process have not been finalised, it will be necessary to determine whether such announcement and any procedures or processes that have occurred prior to the end of the reporting period constitute substantive enactment.

The determination as to whether new tax rates are considered to be 'substantively enacted' is a matter requiring careful judgement, based on the specific facts and circumstances. Factors to consider in assessing that determination include, but are not limited to, the following:

- the legal system and related procedures or processes necessary for enactment of the tax law change;

- the nature and extent of the remaining procedures or processes;

- the extent to which the remaining procedures or processes are perfunctory; and

- the timing of the remaining procedures or processes.

IAS 12 acknowledges that, in some jurisdictions, the announcement of new tax rates and tax laws by the government may have the substantive effect of enactment, even if formal enactment takes place some months later. In these circumstances, tax assets and liabilities are measured using the announced rates. [IAS 12:48] In other countries, it may be necessary for virtually all of the legal stages towards enactment to have been completed before the rates can be considered to be substantively enacted.

The IASB decided as part of the US/IFRS convergence project to clarify that 'substantively enacted' means that any expected change in the tax rate is virtually certain. This proposed clarification was included in the exposure draft for the replacement Standard for IAS 12 (which, although a replacement Standard was not finalised, provides useful guidance on the meaning of 'substantive enactment'). The IASB noted that in some jurisdictions (e.g. the US) enactment may not be virtually certain until the change is signed into law. The Board discussed whether 'substantively enacted' should be based on the probability of enactment or on the process of enactment. The Board decided that reaching a specified stage in the process should be required. It further decided that the specified stage should be that the process of enactment is complete, which is when the remaining steps will not change the outcome.

4.5.2.4 Changes in tax rates after the reporting period

When there is a change in tax rates or laws after the reporting period, no adjustment is made to the carrying amounts of deferred tax assets and liabilities. However, when the effect of the change is such that "non-disclosure could influence the economic decisions of users taken on the basis of the financial statements", disclosure will be required in accordance with IAS 10 *Events after the Reporting Period*. [IAS 10:21]

Example 4.5.2.4

Change in tax rate after the reporting period

Company D has recognised interest receivable of CU1,000 in its statement of financial position as at 31 March 20X3. The interest will be taxed when it is received, which will be during the year ending 31 March 20X4. At 31 March 20X3, the tax rate is 16 per cent. On 5 April 20X3, it is announced that the tax rate for the year ending 31 March 20X4 will be increased to 17.5 per cent; the change is enacted on 25 April 20X3. The financial statements for the year ended 31 March 20X3 are authorised for issue on 30 June 20X3.

The taxable temporary difference in respect of the interest receivable is CU1,000. A deferred tax liability of CU160 will be included in Company D's financial statements for the year ended 31 March 20X3. Although it is known at the time that the financial statements are authorised for issue that the interest income will be taxed at 17.5 per cent when it is received, IAS 12 precludes using the 17.5 per cent rate to calculate the deferred tax liability because this rate was neither enacted nor substantively enacted by 31 March 20X3. If the effect of the change is sufficiently significant, disclosure will be required in accordance with IAS 10.

4.5.2.5 Phased-in tax rates

A phased-in change in tax rates occurs when the tax law specifies that in future periods the tax rate applied to taxable income will change (e.g. the tax law provides that the corporate tax rate will be 43 per cent in 20X1, 38 per cent in 20X2 and 35 per cent for 20X3 and later years).

IAS 12:47 requires deferred tax assets and liabilities to be measured using the enacted (or substantively enacted) tax rates expected to apply to taxable income in the years in which the temporary differences are expected to reverse. Consequently, enacted or substantively enacted changes in tax laws or rates that become effective for particular future years must be considered when determining the tax rate to apply when measuring the tax consequences of temporary differences that are expected to reverse in those years. This exercise may require assumptions to be made regarding tax elections that will be made in future years (based on management expectations), and estimates to be made for the amounts of profit or loss anticipated in the future years when those temporary differences are expected to reverse.

4.5.2.6   Tax rate varies according to whether profits are distributed

In some jurisdictions, income taxes are payable at a higher or lower rate if part or all of the net profit or retained earnings are paid out as a dividend to shareholders. Equally, income taxes may be refundable or payable if part or all of the net profit or retained earnings is paid out as a dividend to shareholders of the entity. In such circumstances, IAS 12 stipulates that the rate to be used for the purposes of measurement of both current and deferred tax assets and liabilities is the tax rate applicable to undistributed profits. [IAS 12:52A]

The income tax consequences of a dividend should only be accounted for when the dividend is recognised as a liability in the financial statements. [IAS 12:52B]

Example 4.5.2.6A

Higher income tax rate on undistributed profits

Company G has undistributed profits of CU1,000 in its statement of financial position at 31 December 20X3. Under local tax regulations, income taxes are payable at a higher rate on undistributed profits (50 per cent) than on distributed profits (35 per cent). Company G has traditionally paid dividends to shareholders equivalent to 25 per cent of the taxable profit for the year. It continues that dividend policy by paying an interim dividend in March 20X4, before the 31 December 20X3 financial statements are authorised for issue.

A current tax liability of CU500 (CU1,000 × 50 per cent) will be included in the financial statements for the year ended 31 December 20X3, even though Company G knows that a portion of the taxable profit will be taxed at a lower rate due to the interim dividend payment.

In accordance with IAS 10, the liability for the 20X4 interim dividend is not recognised in the financial statements for the year ended 31 December 20X3 and, therefore, the tax consequences of that dividend are not taken into account at 31 December 20X3. The impact of the reduction in tax rates will be recognised at the time the dividend is recognised, which will be when the criteria for recognition of a liability are met.

Although the current and deferred tax assets and liabilities of an entity are always measured at the undistributed rate in its individual financial statements, future distributions are anticipated to some extent when those financial statements are subsequently incorporated into consolidated financial statements of a group or are incorporated into the financial statements of an investor using the equity method. If, for example, Entity A is an associate of Investor I and Entity A's financial statements are incorporated into the financial statements of Investor I using the equity method, the application of IAS 12:39 and IAS 12:44 (see **4.4.2** and **4.4.3**) may require deferred tax to be recognised presuming the distribution of earnings from Entity A. To the extent that such distribution is assumed, Investor I should use the 'distributed tax rate' to measure the resulting deferred tax assets or liabilities.

IAS 12:52B clarifies that the income tax consequences of dividends are more directly related to the past events and transactions that gave rise to the tax liability or asset than to the distributions to owners. If additional income taxes are payable or refundable when profits are distributed, although the timing of the recognition of the rate change is related to the recognition of the dividend in the financial statements, the incremental tax effect should not be dealt with in equity. Rather, it should generally be dealt with in profit or loss for the period, unless it arose as a result of an underlying transaction or event recognised outside profit or loss, or a business combination, in line with the general rules set out in IAS 12:58 (see **section 4.7**).

Example 4.5.2.6B

Recognition of incremental tax effect of dividend payment

Company A has undistributed profits of CU1,500 in its statement of financial position at 31 December 20X3, all distributable under local law. CU500 of those profits were recognised in other comprehensive income because they arose from the revaluation of an item of property, plant and equipment that was subsequently sold (the revaluation uplift of CU500 was transferred from revaluation surplus to retained earnings when the asset was disposed of and was not recognised in profit or loss). Under local tax regulations, income taxes are payable at a higher rate on undistributed profits (50 per cent) than on distributed profits (35 per cent).

Prior to any dividend being declared, at 31 December 20X3, a current tax liability of CU750 was recognised on these earnings. Of this amount, CU250 (CU500 × 50%) was recognised in other comprehensive income and CU500 (CU1,000 × 50%) was recognised in profit or loss.

The distribution of all available profits in March 20X4 results in a reduction of the tax liability of CU225 [CU1,500 × 15%]. The reduction should be allocated between profit or loss and other comprehensive income based on the original recognition of the tax liability, resulting in the following journal entry.

	CU	CU
Dr Current tax liability	225	
Cr Income tax (profit or loss)		150
Cr Income tax (other comprehensive income)		75
To recognise the reduction in the tax liability.		

4.5.2.7   Tax holidays

When a tax jurisdiction grants an exemption from an income tax for a specified period, the event is sometimes referred to as a 'tax holiday'. For example, the jurisdiction may, for economic reasons, provide the exemption from income taxes for a specified period if an entity constructs a manufacturing facility located within the jurisdiction.

IAS 12 does not specifically address the subject of tax holidays; consequently, the general principles of IAS 12 should be applied.

An entity that is entitled to a tax holiday should calculate temporary differences in the usual manner if temporary differences originating during the tax holiday period will affect future taxable income. However, assuming that the conditions for exemption from taxation continue to be met, deferred tax should not be recognised in respect of temporary differences that are scheduled to reverse during the tax holiday period, because no net expense or benefit will result (e.g. because a zero per cent tax rate will apply to taxable income or deduction upon reversal).

See **example 4.5.2.7A** for two illustrative examples of tax holiday regimes.

Example 4.5.2.7A

Tax holidays – examples

Example 1

In Jurisdiction X, under the terms of its tax holiday programme, an entity meeting the required criteria will be exempt from income taxes for the first 5 years of operation in Jurisdiction X.

During the tax holiday period, an entity is required to compute its tax liability in the usual manner, but a zero per cent tax rate is applied to the taxable profit. If an entity incurs tax losses during the tax holiday period, the losses will be available for carryforward and use after the tax holiday without restriction.

Under this system, temporary differences may arise during the tax holiday and reverse after the tax holiday, with tax consequences. To the extent that temporary differences are expected to reverse after the tax holiday, deferred tax assets and liabilities should be recognised for any temporary differences. Similarly, tax losses generated during the tax holiday period that are expected to be utilised after the tax holiday should be recognised as deferred tax assets (subject to the general recognition criteria for deferred tax assets).

Example 2

In Jurisdiction Y, under the terms of its tax holiday programme, an entity meeting the required criteria will be exempt from income taxes for the first 5 years of operation in Jurisdiction Y.

During the tax holiday period, an entity is not required to compute an income tax liability (e.g. it may file no income tax return or simply file an income tax return reporting its statutory profit and with a copy of the tax holiday agreement). If an entity incurs losses during the tax holiday period, the losses are not available for carryforward after the tax holiday. Tax depreciation (capital allowances) on the entity's assets commences following the tax holiday. Once the tax holiday expires, the entity computes its tax liabilities in the usual manner.

Under this system, no deferred tax assets will be recognised for losses arising during the tax holiday. The tax base of assets and liabilities may not change during the tax holiday, but the carrying amounts of the entity's assets and liabilities will still change, and temporary differences may arise. Deferred taxes should be recognised for any temporary differences arising during the tax holiday period that will reverse after the tax holiday.

Example 4.5.2.7B

Tax holiday period not yet commenced

Entity A is a start-up entity. The tax laws in the relevant jurisdiction state that start-up entities are exempt from taxation for five years, commencing from the year in which the entity begins to generate taxable income.

Entity A is currently generating losses and it expects to continue to do so for three years. Therefore, it expects that it will not be required to pay tax for the next eight years.

When determining to what extent deferred tax should be recognised, when should Entity A assume that the tax holiday period begins?

As discussed above, deferred tax should not be recognised in respect of temporary differences that are scheduled to reverse during a tax holiday period, assuming that the conditions for exemption from taxation continue to be met.

In the circumstances described, when considering which temporary differences will reverse during the tax holiday period, Entity A should assume that the holiday period begins immediately and lasts for five years. To extend the assumed holiday period to take account of future periods in which losses are anticipated (i.e. in this example, to extend the holiday period to eight years) would be equivalent to anticipating future tax losses, which is not permitted.

In the circumstances described, at each reporting date until the entity produces taxable profit, the applicable tax holiday period should be assumed to be five years from that date.

4.5.3 Discounting

IAS 12 prohibits the use of discounting for the measurement of deferred tax assets and liabilities. [IAS 12:53]

This prohibition is not based on any conceptual argument. Rather, it reflects the practical issues involved in arriving at a reliable determination of deferred tax assets and liabilities on a discounted basis, which would require detailed scheduling of the expected timing of the reversal of every temporary difference. Having concluded that such detailed scheduling would be impracticable or highly complex in many circumstances (and, therefore, that it would be inappropriate to require discounting), the Standard removes the option to discount deferred tax balances because that would reduce comparability of deferred tax balances between entities.

4.6 Recognition of deferred tax assets

4.6.1 Recognition of deferred tax assets – general

Deferred tax assets can arise from deductible temporary differences (e.g. when the carrying amount of an asset is less than its tax base), or from the ability to carry forward unused tax losses and unused tax credits.

Under IAS 12, subject to the exceptions listed at **4.4.3**, deferred tax assets are recognised for all deductible temporary differences and all unused tax losses and tax credits, to the extent that it is probable that future taxable profit will be available against which they can be utilised. [IAS 12:24 & 34]

When an entity has a deferred tax asset that has not been recognised because it failed this recoverability test, the entity is required to reassess the position at the end of each subsequent reporting period. When the test is subsequently met, the asset is recognised at that later date; this may occur, for example, if there is an improvement in trading conditions such that it becomes more likely that sufficient taxable profits will be generated in the future. [IAS 12:37]

Conversely, when a deferred tax asset has been recognised in the statement of financial position, its carrying amount should be reviewed at the end of each subsequent reporting period and reduced to the extent that it is no longer probable that sufficient taxable profit will be available to enable its recovery. [IAS 12:56]

4.6.2   *Availability of future taxable profits*

A deferred tax asset represents a future tax deduction. It is, therefore, only valuable if the entity will have sufficient future taxable profits against which the deduction can be offset. Therefore, an important question to answer is when it can be considered probable that an entity will have sufficient taxable profits available in the future to enable the deferred tax asset to be recovered.

> The term 'probable' is not defined in IAS 12. As noted at **4.4.3**, the term is subject to varying interpretations, but is generally agreed to mean at least more likely than not (i.e. a probability of greater than 50 per cent).

IAS 12 states that it is probable that an entity will have sufficient taxable profit available in the future to enable a deferred tax asset to be recovered when:

- there are sufficient taxable temporary differences relating to the same tax authority and the same taxable entity that are expected to reverse either in the same period as the expected reversal of the deductible temporary difference or in periods into which a tax loss arising from the deferred tax asset can be carried back or forward; [IAS 12:28] or

- it is probable that the entity will have sufficient taxable profit, relating to the same tax authority and the same taxable entity, in the same period as the reversal of the deductible temporary difference (or in the periods into which a tax loss arising from the deferred tax asset can be carried back or forward). In making this evaluation, taxable amounts arising from deductible temporary differences that are expected to originate in future periods should be ignored (because these will need further future taxable profits in order to be utilised); [IAS 12:29(a)] or

- tax planning opportunities are available to the entity that will create taxable profit in appropriate periods. [IAS 12:29(b)]

Thus, when looking for future taxable income to justify the recognition of a deferred tax asset, entities can look to:

- future reversals of existing taxable temporary differences (see **4.6.3**);

- future taxable profit (see **4.6.4**); and

- tax planning opportunities, i.e. actions that the entity could take to create or increase taxable profits in future periods so as to utilise the available tax deductions before they expire (see **4.6.5**).

4.6.3 *Future reversals of existing taxable temporary differences*

As noted above, in order to justify the anticipated recovery of a deductible temporary difference against existing taxable differences, the following conditions must be met:

[IAS 12:28]

- the taxable differences must relate to the same tax authority and the same taxable entity; and

- the taxable differences must be expected to reverse either in the same period as the deferred tax asset reverses, or in a period into which any tax loss arising from the reversal of the deferred tax asset can be carried forward or back.

IAS 12 does not specifically address how an entity should schedule the reversal pattern for existing temporary differences. It is generally only necessary to schedule the reversal of taxable temporary differences when deferred tax assets have limited lives (i.e. they are subject to expiry). Because of cost benefit considerations, there may be more than one approach to scheduling reversal patterns. However, it is apparent from the discussion in IAS 12:35 and 36 that two concepts underlie the determination of the reversal patterns for existing temporary differences:

- the year(s) in which temporary differences result in taxable or deductible amounts generally are determined by the timing of the recovery of the related asset or the settlement of the related liability; and

- the tax law determines whether future reversals of temporary differences will result in taxable and deductible amounts that offset each other in future years.

Note that an entity may not take account of future originating temporary differences (e.g. planned future capital expenditure) when assessing future reversals of temporary differences, because those differences will only arise as a result of future events or transactions.

Example 4.6.3A

Forecasting future reversals of existing taxable temporary differences

Company C has made a tax loss for the year and has identified the following temporary differences at 31 December 20X3:

- taxable temporary differences related to accelerated tax depreciation, expected to reverse in 20X4 and 20X5 – CU4,000; and

- deductible temporary differences in respect of pre-operating costs expensed for accounting purposes in 20X3 but allowed for tax purposes over five years – CU2,800.

Company C is expected to make losses for the foreseeable future. Tax is payable at 20 per cent. Tax losses may be carried forward, but not back.

Anticipated reversals of Company C's existing temporary differences are as follows.

	20X4	20X5	20X6	20X7
	CU	CU	CU	CU
Accelerated tax depreciation	(2,000)	(2,000)	–	–
Pre-operating costs	700	700	700	700

At 31 December 20X3, a deferred tax liability is recognised in respect of the accelerated tax depreciation, amounting to CU800 (CU4,000 × 20%). The deferred tax asset recognised in respect of the pre-operating costs is limited to CU280 (CU1,400 × 20%). Future tax deductions are available for the remainder of the pre-operating costs. However, because the reversals occur in periods when they cannot be used against existing taxable temporary differences, their recognition cannot be justified on the basis of those temporary differences. Other expected sources of taxable income or tax planning opportunities would need to be identified in order to support the recognition of the remainder of the deferred tax asset. In the above example this seems unlikely because Company C is, and is forecast to continue to be, a loss-making entity (see **4.6.4.4**).

Example 4.6.3B

Impact of expected future tax losses on the recognition of deferred tax assets when there are reversing taxable temporary differences

During the year ending 31 December 20X1, Entity A incurs tax losses of CU100. At 31 December 20X1, Entity A has tax losses carried forward of CU100 and accumulated taxable temporary differences of CU150. Entity A estimates that the accumulated taxable temporary differences will reverse over the following three years. Entity A also expects to incur further tax losses of CU200 over the same period. The tax rate is 30 per cent.

Assume that, in the jurisdiction in which Entity A operates, tax losses are permitted to be carried forward for a maximum of five years to be offset, without restriction, against future taxable profits. At 31 December 20X1, is Entity A required to recognise a deferred tax asset in respect of the tax losses carried forward?

Yes. Given that suitable reversing taxable temporary differences are available, Entity A is required to recognise a deferred tax asset of CU30 (CU100 × 30 per cent) in respect of the losses carried forward at 31 December 20X1, regardless of its expectations of future losses.

In accordance with IAS 12:28 and 35, a deferred tax asset is recognised to the extent that taxable temporary differences of an appropriate type are available and expected to reverse in the relevant period. The reversing taxable temporary differences enable the utilisation of the accumulated tax losses and are sufficient to justify the recognition of a deferred tax asset. Consequently, future tax losses are not taken into consideration.

However if, at a reporting date, unused tax losses exceed the amount of suitable available taxable temporary differences, a deferred tax asset is only recognised in respect of losses to the value of the taxable temporary differences, unless it is probable that the entity will have appropriate future taxable profit or tax planning opportunities are available to the entity that will create appropriate taxable profit.

Assume the same facts, except that the applicable tax law restricts the recovery of tax losses to 60 per cent of taxable profit in each year. Is the deferred tax asset to be recognised by Entity A restricted to 60 per cent of the taxable temporary differences?

Yes. When tax laws limit the extent to which unused tax losses can be recovered against future taxable profits in each year, the amount of the deferred tax asset recognised is similarly restricted. This is because when the taxable temporary differences reverse, the amount of tax losses that can be utilised by that reversal is reduced as specified by the tax law.

Therefore, in the circumstances under consideration, the deferred tax asset required to be recognised in respect of the available taxable temporary differences is CU27 (CU150 × 60% × 30%). Entity A should consider future taxable profits and tax planning opportunities before the tax losses expire to determine whether recognition of an additional deferred tax asset in respect of the remaining CU10 (CU100 ☐ (CU150 × 60%)) of tax losses carried forward is appropriate.

The conclusions above were confirmed by the IFRS Interpretations Committee in the May 2014 *IFRIC Update*.

4.6.4   Future taxable profits

4.6.4.1   Assessment of future taxable profits – consideration of future events

In general, entities should consider all currently available information about the availability of future taxable profits. However, certain future events should not be anticipated or considered in determining the realisability of deferred tax assets. These items include, but are not limited to, the following:

- changes in tax laws or rates (except those that are substantively enacted);

- expected business combinations;

- anticipated future income from events beyond the entity's control and that are non-recurring or unusual in nature (e.g. forgiveness of indebtedness for purposes of avoiding derecognition of a deferred tax asset); and

- events dependent on future market conditions or otherwise not within the entity's control.

4.6.4.2 Indicators of future taxable profits

In evaluating whether it is probable that taxable profit will be available, the nature and timing of such profit should be considered.

The following are some examples of factors that may support the assertion that it is probable that taxable profit will be available.

Contracts or firm sales backlog that will produce sufficient taxable income to realise the deferred tax asset based on existing sales prices and cost structures:

- an entity enters into a long-term contract that will generate sufficient future taxable income to enable it to utilise all existing operating loss carryforwards; or

- during the current year, an entity acquired another entity that operates in a different industry that is characterised by stable profit margins. Assuming that the group is taxed on a consolidated basis or that group relief is available, the acquiree's existing contracts will produce sufficient taxable income to enable utilisation of the loss carryforwards.

An excess of appreciated asset value over the tax bases of an entity's net assets in an amount sufficient to realise the deferred tax asset:

- an entity has invested in land that has appreciated in value. If the land were sold at its current market value, the sale would generate sufficient taxable income to utilise all tax loss carryforwards. The entity will sell the land and realise the gain if the operating loss carryforward would otherwise expire unused.

A strong earnings history exclusive of the loss that created the future deductible amount coupled with evidence indicating that the loss is not a continuing condition:

- an entity incurs operating losses that result in a carryforward for tax purposes. The loss resulted from the disposal of a subsidiary whose operations are not critical to the continuing entity and the entity's historical earnings, exclusive of the subsidiary losses, have been strong.

Conversely, there may be indicators that future taxable profits will not be available. The following are some examples of factors that may rebut the assertion that it is probable that taxable profit will be available.

History of losses in recent years (see also **4.6.4.4**):

- an entity has incurred operating losses for financial reporting and tax purposes during recent years. The losses for financial reporting purposes exceed operating income for financial reporting purposes as measured on a cumulative basis from the most recent preceding years; or

- a currently profitable entity has a majority ownership interest in a newly formed subsidiary that has incurred operating and tax losses since its inception. The subsidiary is consolidated for financial reporting purposes. The tax jurisdiction in which the subsidiary operates prohibits it from filing a consolidated tax return (or otherwise obtaining group relief) from its parent or other group entities; or

- the entity is a start-up business or development stage enterprise or is emerging from a financial reorganisation or bankruptcy. In the early years of operation, these types of entities will frequently have a history of losses coupled with limited evidence of ability to meet budgets.

A history of operating loss or tax credit carryforwards expiring unused:

- an entity has generated tax credit carryforwards during the current year. During the past several years, tax credits that originated in prior years expired unused. There are no available tax planning strategies that would enable the entity to utilise the tax benefit of the carryforwards.

Unsettled circumstances that if unfavourably resolved would adversely affect profit levels on a continuing basis:

- during the past several years, an entity has manufactured and sold devices to the general public. The entity has discovered, through its own product testing, that the devices may malfunction under certain conditions. No malfunctions have been reported. However, management is concerned about the appropriateness of continuing to sell the product and that product generates significant revenue.

4.6.4.3   Non-recurring items

Frequently, entities will extrapolate from current profit levels to forecast future taxable profits (having due regard to anticipated growth levels etc.). When assessing the sustainability of current profit levels, it is important to make appropriate adjustments for past non-recurring items, which generally are not indicative of an entity's ability to generate taxable income in future years.

Non-recurring items that will affect the level of profitability in future accounting periods should also be considered (however, as discussed in **4.6.4.1**, this does not extend to anticipating future events).

Examples of non-recurring items that should be excluded include, but are not limited to, the following:

- one-time restructuring charges;

- large litigation settlements or awards that are not expected to recur in future years;

- historical interest expense on debt that has been restructured or refinanced;

- historical fixed costs that have been reduced or eliminated; and

- severance payments relating to management changes.

Examples of items that may have an impact on the determination of future profit or loss for a number of years include, but are not limited to, the following:

- poor operating results caused by an economic downturn, government intervention or changes in regulation; and

- operating losses attributable to a change in the focus of a subsidiary or business unit.

4.6.4.4   History of recent losses

When an entity has incurred losses in recent years, additional caution should be exercised before a deferred tax asset is recognised. IAS 12 points out that "the existence of unused tax losses is strong evidence that future taxable profit may not be available". It goes on to say that, if there are insufficient deferred tax liabilities reversing in appropriate periods and entities, there must be "convincing other evidence" that there will be sufficient taxable profit. [IAS 12:35]

In assessing the probability that taxable profits will be available, the following should be considered:

[IAS 12:36]

- whether the entity has sufficient taxable temporary differences relating to the same tax authority and the same taxable entity, which will result in taxable amounts against which the unused tax losses or unused tax credits can be utilised before they expire;

- whether it is probable that the entity will have taxable profits before the unused tax losses or unused tax credits expire;

- whether the unused tax losses result from identifiable causes that are unlikely to recur; and

- whether tax planning opportunities are available to the entity that will create taxable profit in the period in which the unused tax losses or unused tax credits can be utilised.

The assessment as to whether an entity will have sufficient taxable profits in the future to realise a deferred tax asset is a matter requiring careful judgement based on the facts and circumstances available.

The very existence of losses calls future profitability into question and IAS 12:36(c) notes that preparers need to consider whether unused tax losses result from identifiable causes that are unlikely to recur. When the losses are expected to recur, it is unlikely that a deferred tax asset can be recognised. However, the source of the losses may have been addressed, for example, through disposal of loss-making operations, restructurings, or reductions of ongoing costs.

A history of recent losses is objectively verifiable evidence and, as a result, carries more weight than other evidence that embodies some degree of subjectivity. For this reason, whenever an entity has suffered cumulative losses in recent years, it is difficult to support the recognition of a deferred tax asset based on forecasts of future profits without a demonstrated turnaround to operating profitability. In other words, an entity that has cumulative losses will not generally be able to use forecast future profits to support a conclusion that realisation of an existing deferred tax asset is probable, unless that forecast is supported by strong evidence (which will need to be disclosed in accordance with IAS 12:82 – see **6.2.2**). Examples of such evidence may include significant new contracts, an increase in the level of orders, or the disposal of an unprofitable segment.

In addition to these considerations, particular attention needs to be paid to restrictions on:

- the number of years for which the losses can be carried forward; and
- the types of profit against which the losses can be offset.

There is no specific time restriction in IAS 12 regarding the length of the 'look-forward' period which is used to determine whether taxable profits will be available. The length of the period used will depend on a number of entity-specific factors, including the entity's historical profitability, accuracy of budgetary controls and expected future activities.

The entity assesses whether any portion of the total available unused tax losses or tax credits is likely to be utilised before they expire. To the extent that it is not probable that taxable profit will be available against which the unused tax losses or unused tax credits can be utilised, the deferred tax asset is not recognised. [IAS 12:36]

4.6.5   Tax planning opportunities

Tax planning opportunities are actions that the entity can take to create or increase taxable income in a particular period before the expiry of a tax loss or tax credit carryforward. [IAS 12:30] Although such opportunities are future actions, the entity is entitled to consider them in justifying the recognition of a deferred tax asset.

Examples of tax planning opportunities include:

[IAS 12:30]

- being able to elect to have an income source taxed at an earlier point (e.g. electing to have interest income taxed on a receivable, rather than a receipts, basis);

- being able to defer to a future period the claim for certain tax deductible items (e.g. waiving a claim to first year allowances on an item of equipment, and instead taking annual allowances on the full amount in future periods);

- selling and leasing back assets that have appreciated in value, but for which the tax base has not been adjusted to reflect the appreciation; and

- selling an asset that generates non-taxable income in order to purchase another investment that generates taxable income.

In order to use a tax planning opportunity as support for the recognition of a deferred tax asset, the entity must have the ability to implement the chosen tax planning strategy. For example, a plan to take a pension holiday in order to boost taxable profit in a particular period so as to utilise tax losses that are about to expire can only be taken into account if the strategy can be controlled by the entity (e.g. it cannot be prevented by pension regulations, and is likely to be accepted by the pension fund trustees and the workforce).

The amount of the future taxable profits expected to be generated by such proposed strategies must be reduced by the cost of the strategies. The actions must be commercially viable and without significant adverse consequences – otherwise, it is unlikely that management would proceed.

4.6.6   Acquisition of tax losses at less than fair value

Example 4.6.6

Acquisition of tax losses at less than fair value

Company A acquires Company B, which is a shell entity with valuable unused tax losses. Company B does not meet the definition of a business under

IFRS 3 *Business Combinations* and, therefore, the transaction is not a business combination for the purposes of that Standard.

Company A acquires Company B (and, therefore, the tax losses) for CU100,000. This is significantly lower than the tax asset that would be recognised in respect of the tax losses under IAS 12 (CU1 million). Company A expects to be able to utilise all of the available losses.

On the date of acquisition, Company A should recognise the deferred tax asset acquired at the amount paid (i.e. at CU100,000).

Subsequently, the unused tax losses in Company B are available for use against Company A's taxable profits. Accordingly, the deferred tax asset recognised at the date of acquisition should be assessed and measured in accordance with IAS 12:34 which requires that "[a] deferred tax asset shall be recognised for the carryforward of unused tax losses and unused tax credits to the extent that it is probable that future taxable profit will be available against which the unused tax losses and tax credits can be utilised".

Therefore, Company A should determine the extent to which it is probable that future taxable profits will be available against which the unused tax losses can be utilised and the deferred tax asset should be remeasured to reflect this amount. Any remeasurement should be recognised in profit or loss for the period.

In the circumstances described, if it is probable that Company A will be able to utilise all of the tax losses, the deferred tax asset should be remeasured to CU1 million with the resulting gain of CU900,000 recognised in profit or loss.

The assessment as to whether it is probable that the tax losses will be utilised should be based on the guidance provided in IAS 12:35 and IAS 12:36 (see **4.6.4.4**).

4.7 Recognition of movement in deferred tax balances

4.7.1 Recognition of movement in deferred tax balances – general principle

In determining how the deferred tax effects of a transaction or other event should be recognised, the underlying principle is that the accounting for such deferred tax effects should follow the accounting for the transaction or event itself. [IAS 12:57]

4.7.2 Recognition of deferred tax in profit or loss

Deferred tax should be recognised as income or an expense and included in profit or loss for the period, except to the extent that the tax arises from:

[IAS 12:58]

- a transaction or event which is recognised, in the same or a different period, outside profit or loss, either in other comprehensive income or directly in equity (see **section 4.7.3**); or

- a business combination (other than the acquisition by an investment entity of a subsidiary that is required to be measured at fair value through profit or loss – see **5.1**).

Most deferred tax liabilities and deferred tax assets arise when income or expense is included in accounting profit in one period, but is included in taxable profit (tax loss) in a different period. The resulting deferred tax is recognised in profit or loss. Examples are when:

[IAS 12:58]

- interest, royalty or dividend revenue is received in arrears and is included in accounting profit in accordance with IFRS 15 *Revenue from Contracts with Customers* or IFRS 9 *Financial Instruments* (or, for entities that have not yet adopted IFRS 9, IAS 39 *Financial Instruments: Recognition and Measurement*), but is included in taxable profit (tax loss) on a cash basis; and

- costs of intangible assets have been capitalised in accordance with IAS 38 and are being amortised in profit or loss, but were deducted for tax purposes when they were incurred.

> For entities that have not yet adopted IFRS 15 *Revenue from Contracts with Customers*, the accounting for interest, royalty and dividend revenue is dealt with in IAS 18 *Revenue*.

4.7.3 Recognition of deferred tax outside profit or loss

4.7.3.1 Deferred tax recognised outside profit or loss – general

Deferred tax is recognised outside profit or loss if the tax relates to items that are recognised, in the same or a different period, outside profit or loss. When the deferred tax relates to items that are recognised in other comprehensive income, the tax is also recognised in other comprehensive income (see **4.7.3.2**). When the deferred tax relates to items that are recognised directly in equity, the tax is also recognised in equity (see **4.7.3.3**). [IAS 12:61A]

4.7.3.2 Items recognised in other comprehensive income

Items required or permitted under IFRSs to be recognised in other comprehensive income include:

- exchange differences on the translation of the financial statements of a foreign operation under IAS 21 *The Effects of Changes in Foreign Exchange Rates*;

- the recognition of fair value movements on some financial assets (see **5.3.3**);

- the revaluation of property, plant and equipment under IAS 16 *Property, Plant and Equipment* (see **4.7.3.3**); and

- actuarial gains and losses relating to defined benefit pension obligations (see **section 5.8**).

Exchange differences arising on the translation of financial statements only give rise to deferred tax when the criteria in IAS 12:39 and IAS 12:44 are met, and an entity has accrued for the reversal of the temporary difference between the carrying amount of its investment (including foreign exchange gains and losses) and its tax base (see **section 4.4.7**).

4.7.3.3   Revaluations of property, plant and equipment

The most common example of deferred tax recognised in other comprehensive income is when an item of property, plant and equipment is revalued (see also **section 5.4**).

When an entity accounts for a class of assets on a revaluation basis under IAS 16, fair value movements are generally recognised in other comprehensive income and accumulated in a revaluation reserve. While the carrying amount of the asset changes, the associated tax base may not, resulting in the creation of a, or a change in an existing, temporary difference. Under IAS 12:61A, deferred tax arising on a revaluation that is recognised in other comprehensive income is also recognised in other comprehensive income. This deferred tax is generally offset against the revaluation reserve (although such offset is not required, and the entity may choose to offset the deferred tax against another equity reserve).

While the original deferred tax arising on the revaluation is recognised in other comprehensive income, the subsequent release of that deferred tax liability due to the depreciation of the increased carrying amount is not credited in other comprehensive income, but in profit or loss, along with the depreciation expense.

This is an important principle. The deferred tax liability is initially recognised in other comprehensive income. However, because the effects of recovering the asset through use (the recognition of a depreciation expense and the generation of taxable profits) are dealt with in profit or loss, the release of the deferred tax liability (against the current tax liability arising) is also dealt with in profit or loss.

These principles are illustrated in **example 4.7.3.3**.

Example 4.7.3.3

Asset revaluation and subsequent recovery of asset – recognition of deferred tax

Company I revalues an item of property, plant and equipment from a carrying amount of CU95,000 to CU150,000. The tax base of the asset, which is not affected by the revaluation, is CU90,000. The carrying amount of the property is expected to be recovered through use. The applicable tax rate is 30 per cent. A deferred tax liability of CU1,500 (CU5,000 × 30%) has been recognised in respect of the taxable temporary difference of CU5,000 prior to the revaluation.

An additional taxable temporary difference of CU55,000 (CU150,000 – CU95,000) arises on revaluation, giving rise to an additional deferred tax liability of CU16,500 (CU55,000 × 30%). The following entries recognise the revaluation and the additional deferred tax liability.

		CU	CU
Dr	Property, plant and equipment	55,000	
Cr	Revaluation gain (other comprehensive income)		55,000
Dr	Income tax (other comprehensive income)	16,500	
Cr	Deferred tax liability		16,500

To recognise the revaluation and the deferred tax liability.

In subsequent periods, the property will be depreciated for both accounting and tax purposes, changing the temporary difference. Any movements in the deferred tax liability are recognised in profit or loss. For example, if the carrying amount of the property at the end of the next reporting period is CU130,000 and the tax base is CU85,000, there is a taxable temporary difference of CU45,000 and a deferred tax liability of CU13,500 (CU45,000 × 30%). The movement for the year is recognised as follows.

		CU	CU
Dr	Deferred tax liability (CU1,500 + CU16,500 – CU13,500)	4,500	
Cr	Income tax (profit or loss)		4,500

To recognise the movement for the year.

IAS 16 does not specify whether an entity should transfer each year from revaluation surplus to retained earnings an amount equal to the difference between the depreciation or amortisation on a revalued asset and the depreciation or amortisation based on the historical cost of that asset. If an entity makes such a transfer, the amount transferred is net of any related deferred tax. Similar considerations apply to transfers made on the disposal of an item of property, plant or equipment. [IAS 12:64]

4.7.3.4   Items recognised directly in equity

Items required or permitted under IFRSs to be credited or charged directly to equity include:

- an adjustment to the opening balance of retained earnings resulting from a change in accounting policy that is accounted for retrospectively under IAS 8 or the correction of an error (see **chapter A5**);

- the initial recognition of the equity component of a compound financial instrument under IAS 32 *Financial Instruments: Presentation* (see **5.3.4**);

- when the expected tax deduction for an equity-settled share-based payment exceeds the cumulative profit or loss expense recognised in respect of that share based payment (see **section 5.6**); and

- when a withholding tax is charged on dividend distributions (see **4.7.3.5**).

4.7.3.5   Withholding tax

A tax jurisdiction may assess an entity with a 'withholding tax', which is paid to the tax authorities on behalf of the shareholders when the entity makes a dividend distribution. Such withholding tax is charged to equity as part of the dividends. [IAS 12:65A]

When a 'withholding tax' is neither paid on behalf of the shareholders nor gives rise to a future benefit for the entity, it should be dealt with as a higher rate of tax applied to distributed profits – see **4.5.2.6**.

If an entity obtains a future benefit as a result of withholding the tax from amounts distributed (e.g. if the tax withheld is deductible against future dividend receipts), the initial payment to the tax authorities is not a withholding tax as contemplated in IAS 12; in such circumstances, the initial payment to the tax authorities should be recognised as an increase in income tax expense (rather than being accounted for as part of the dividend distribution), with the future tax benefit likewise recognised as a component of tax in profit or loss. The resulting tax asset will be considered for recoverability – see **4.6.1**.

Example 4.7.3.5 illustrates the appropriate treatment for two types of withholding tax.

Example 4.7.3.5

Withholding tax

Scenario 1 – withholding tax as contemplated in IAS 12:65A

Company Y decides to pay dividends of CU100 to its shareholders. Local tax law requires Company Y to withhold 35 per cent of the dividends and to pay the amount withheld over to the tax authorities. The tax is paid to the tax authorities

---

on behalf of the shareholders and does not give rise to a future benefit for Company Y.

Company Y should record the following journal entries.

		CU	CU
Dr	Retained earnings – distribution	100	
Cr	Cash		65
Cr	Payable		35

To recognise the dividend payment and related liability to pay tax on shareholders' behalf.

		CU	CU
Dr	Payable	35	
Cr	Cash		35

To recognise payment of the taxes withheld.

Scenario 2 – withholding tax with future benefit for entity paying dividends

Company Z decides to pay dividends of CU100 to its shareholders. Local tax law requires Company Z to withhold 35 per cent of the dividends and to pay the amount withheld over to the tax authorities. Company Z obtains a future tax credit equal to the amount paid to the tax authorities in connection with the dividends; the tax credit can be used to offset tax liabilities arising over the following three years.

Company Z should record the following journal entries.

		CU	CU
Dr	Current tax expense	35	
Dr	Retained earnings – distribution	65	
Cr	Cash		65
Cr	Taxes payable		35

To recognise the dividend payment and the liability to pay tax on the distribution.

		CU	CU
Dr	Deferred tax asset	35	
Cr	Deferred tax income		35

To recognise the future tax benefit.

		CU	CU
Dr	Taxes payable	35	
Cr	Cash		35

To recognise payment of the taxes withheld.

As with any other deferred tax asset, the recognition of the deferred tax is dependent on meeting the recognition criteria in IAS 12:24. If those criteria are not met, Company Z would not recognise the deferred tax asset upon payment of the tax, but rather if and when the recognition criteria are met.

IAS 12:65A addresses the treatment of withholding tax by the entity paying the withholding tax; the Standard does not address how the recipient of the dividend should account for the withholding tax. However, to the extent that withholding tax is paid entirely on behalf of the recipient, the recipient should recognise the dividend income at its gross amount (i.e. before deduction of withholding tax); the tax suffered on the dividend income should be recognised by the recipient in profit or loss as part of its tax expense.

4.7.3.6 Uncertainty regarding the amount to be recognised outside profit or loss

When, in exceptional circumstances, an entity is unable to determine the amount of deferred tax that relates to items recognised outside profit or loss, IAS 12 allows the entity to base the amount on a reasonable pro rata allocation or some other method achieving a more appropriate allocation.

Such uncertainty can arise, for example, when:

[IAS 12:63]

- there are graduated rates of income tax, and it is impossible to determine the rate at which a specific component of taxable profit (tax loss) has been taxed; or

- a change in the tax rate or other tax rules affects a deferred tax asset or liability relating (in whole or in part) to an item that was previously recognised outside profit or loss; or

- an entity determines that a deferred tax asset should be recognised, or should no longer be recognised in full, and the deferred tax asset relates (in whole or in part) to an item that was previously recognised outside profit or loss.

An example of how such an allocation might be made is set out in **3.2.2.4**.

4.7.3.7 Reversal of deferred tax expense on reclassification from equity to profit or loss of gains and losses previously recognised in other comprehensive income

IAS 12:61A requires that current or deferred tax relating to items that are recognised, in the same or a different period, outside of profit or loss should be recognised outside of profit or loss.

In some cases, IFRSs require that gains or losses initially recognised in other comprehensive income be subsequently reclassified to profit or loss. For example:

- specified gains and losses arising on cash flow hedges and net investment hedges previously recognised in other comprehensive income are reclassified from equity to profit or loss (subject to the conditions in IFRS 9 *Financial Instruments* or, for entities that have not yet adopted IFRS 9, IAS 39 *Financial Instruments: Recognition and Measurement*);

- for entities that have adopted IFRS 9, gains and losses arising on debt instruments measured at fair value through other comprehensive income previously recognised in other comprehensive income are reclassified from equity to profit and loss when the asset is disposed of;

- for entities that have not yet adopted IFRS 9, gains or losses arising on available-for-sale financial assets previously recognised in other comprehensive income are reclassified from equity to profit or loss when the asset is disposed of; and

- on disposal or partial disposal of a foreign operation (other than a partial disposal of a subsidiary when control is retained), all or a portion of the foreign currency translation reserve is reclassified from equity to profit or loss as part of the gain or loss on disposal.

Whether such gains and losses are included in the determination of taxable profit in the period in which they are initially recognised in other comprehensive income depends on the rules in the particular tax jurisdiction.

If such gains and losses give rise to temporary differences (and, consequently, deferred tax balances) when they are recognised in other comprehensive income, when the gains and losses are subsequently reclassified to profit or loss and any current tax arising at that point is recognised in profit or loss, the deferred tax balance will be reversed. The question arises as to whether the reversal of the deferred tax balance should be recognised in other comprehensive income or in profit or loss.

The most appropriate treatment is that the reversal should be recognised in other comprehensive income because that is where the deferred tax was initially recognised.

See **example 4.7.3.7** for an illustration of this approach. Note that in the example there is no impact on the effective tax rate of the entity.

Example 4.7.3.7

Reversal of deferred tax expense on reclassification from equity to profit or loss of gains and losses previously recognised in other comprehensive income

Company Y has a portfolio of financial assets classified as available for sale in accordance with IAS 39. For financial reporting purposes, unrealised gains and losses on the assets are recognised in other comprehensive income. In accordance with IAS 12, any tax consequences are also recognised in other comprehensive income.

Under local tax laws, unrealised gains and losses on investment portfolios are not included in the determination of taxable income or loss; rather, taxable gains or losses arise only when a financial asset is disposed of. Because the movement in the value of financial assets does not affect current tax, deferred taxes should be computed in respect of the resulting temporary differences between the carrying amount of the financial assets (fair value) and their tax base.

In 20X1, there is unrealised loss on the assets of CU10 million. There is no movement in the market value of the assets during 20X2. On the last day of 20X2, Company Y sells the assets, thereby crystallising the previously recognised pre-tax loss of CU10 million.

The tax rate for 20X1 and 20X2 is 30 per cent. Company Y has net taxable income in 20X1.

The journal entries for 20X1 are as follows.

		CU'000	CU'000
Dr	Unrealised loss on investments (other comprehensive income)	10,000	
Cr	Investment portfolio		10,000

To recognise the unrealised loss on the available-for-sale assets in other comprehensive income.

		CU'000	CU'000
Dr	Deferred tax asset	3,000	
Cr	Deferred tax benefit (other comprehensive income)		3,000

To recognise the tax consequences of the temporary difference resulting from the unrealised losses on the assets (CU10 million × 30 per cent – IAS 12's general recognition criteria assumed to be met).

Note – there is no impact on the effective tax rate of the entity, because both the unrealised loss and the related deferred tax are recognised outside profit or loss.

The journal entries for 20X2 are as follows.

		CU'000	CU'000
Dr	Loss on sale (profit or loss)	10,000	
Cr	Unrealised loss on investments (other comprehensive income)		10,000

To recognise the reclassification from equity to profit or loss of the pre-tax loss on sale of the asset portfolio in 20X2.

		CU'000	CU'000
Dr	Deferred tax benefit (other comprehensive income)	3,000	
Cr	Deferred tax asset		3,000
Dr	Current tax liability	3,000	
Cr	Current tax benefit (profit or loss)		3,000

To recognise the current tax benefit on realisation of the loss on the asset portfolio, and deferred tax expense representing utilisation of the deferred tax asset previously recognised.

4.7.3.8   Recognition of deferred tax arising from a business combination

When a business combination occurs, deferred tax balances can arise from a number of sources. These are described in detail in **section 5.1**.

The amount of deferred tax arising from each of these sources is recognised and included as part of the identifiable net assets at the date of acquisition. The combined effect, therefore, affects the amount of the goodwill or bargain purchase gain arising on acquisition.

4.7.3.9   Revaluations for tax purposes

When an asset is revalued for tax purposes and that revaluation is related to an accounting revaluation of an earlier period, or to one that is expected to be carried out in a future period, the tax effects of both the asset revaluation and the adjustment of the tax base are recognised in other comprehensive income in the periods in which they occur. [IAS 12:65]

When an asset is revalued for tax purposes but there has not been, and is not to be, an accounting revaluation, the tax effects of the adjustment of the tax base are recognised in profit or loss. [IAS 12:65]

The most common examples of revaluations for tax, but not accounting, purposes are as follows:

- when tax authorities calculate the taxable gain on disposal of a capital asset by reference to a base cost that represents the original cost of the asset uplifted by an allowance to reflect inflation over the period of ownership or the market value of value of the asset at a specified date (see **examples 4.7.3.9A** and **4.7.3.9B**); and

- when a group undertakes a transaction between two group entities which is internal to the group (and hence does not change group carrying amounts) but gives rise to a new tax base (see **example 4.2.5** for an illustration).

Example 4.7.3.9A

Tax base increased by inflation index in each period

Company J purchases an investment property for CU10,000 and accounts for it using the fair value model under IAS 40 *Investment Property* (i.e. recognising changes in the property's fair value in profit or loss and not depreciating it). The carrying amount of the property will be recovered through sale. The allowable cost for tax purposes is increased by an agreed inflation index in each period.

The tax rate for capital profits is 30 per cent and the agreed inflation increment in each period under consideration is 5 per cent and there are no changes in the fair value of the property (i.e. its carrying amount remains at CU10,000). The deferred tax consequences for the first three years are calculated as follows.

Year	Carrying amount CU	Tax base CU	Deductible temporary difference CU	Deferred tax asset CU
20X0	10,000	10,000	–	–
20X1	10,000	10,500	500	150
20X2	10,000	11,025	1,025	308

The recognition of the resultant deferred tax asset is dependent on the availability of future profits against which the capital loss can be offset.

If the deferred tax asset is recognised, the resulting credit is to profit or loss. Therefore, at the end of 20X1, the required journal entry is as follows.

		CU	CU
Dr	Deferred tax asset	150	
Cr	Income tax (profit or loss)		150

To recognise the deferred tax asset.

Example 4.7.3.9B

Accounting for increased allowances based on market value uplifts

Entity B operates in the extractives industry. At the beginning of 20X1, Entity B's local tax authority introduces new legislation that permits Entity B to calculate tax depreciation for certain mining assets using the market value of the assets at a specified date, rather than the cost or carrying amount of the assets. The tax depreciation calculated on the basis of the market value at the specified date is referred to as the 'starting base allowance'. The carrying amount of the assets in the financial statements of Entity B is not adjusted.

If there is insufficient profit against which the annual tax depreciation allowance can be used in any taxable period, the excess is carried forward and is available for use as a deduction against taxable profit in future periods.

How should Entity B recognise the market value uplift (i.e. the adjustment to the available tax depreciation as a result of applying the market value approach)?

Entity B should recognise the market value uplift as part of the tax base of the related mining assets so that, at the specified date, the tax base of the assets is increased to the starting base allowance.

The amount of the starting base allowance, including the market value uplift, is attributed to the related assets under the tax regime and becomes the basis for tax depreciation allowances in future periods. Therefore, the market value uplift forms part of the tax base of the related assets as defined in IAS 12:7 (i.e. "the amount that will be deductible for tax purposes against any taxable economic benefits that will flow to an entity when it recovers the carrying amount of the asset").

Because the carrying amount of the assets in the financial statements is not adjusted, a deductible temporary difference arises because the tax base of the assets is higher than their carrying amount. A deferred tax asset should be recognised to the extent that the recognition criteria in IAS 12:24 are met (see **4.4.3**), and the corresponding credit is recognised in profit or loss in accordance with IAS 12:65.

Because the temporary difference arises when the new tax legislation is introduced, rather than on initial recognition of the mining assets, the initial recognition exception does not apply (see also **4.4.6.8**).

The conclusions above were confirmed by the IFRS Interpretations Committee in the July 2012 *IFRIC Update*.

4.7.4 Changes in the carrying amount of a deferred tax asset or liability

The carrying amount of a deferred tax asset or liability may change for reasons other than a change in the temporary difference itself. Such changes might arise as a result of:

- a change in tax rates or laws; or

- reassessment of the recoverability of a deferred tax asset; or

- a change in the expected manner of recovery of an asset or the expected manner of settlement of a liability.

In such circumstances, IAS 12 requires that the change in deferred tax balances be recognised in profit or loss, except to the extent that it relates to items previously recognised outside profit or loss. [IAS 12:60]

For example, when a deferred tax amount has previously been recognised in other comprehensive income at the time of the revaluation of an asset, and the deferred tax liability subsequently changes because of a change in tax rates, the adjustment to the deferred tax liability to reflect the revised tax rates is also recognised in other comprehensive income.

The same principle applies to a change of intention. For example, when an entity has previously estimated the deferred tax liability arising on the revaluation of an owner-occupied property on the basis that it would continue to be used to generate taxable manufacturing profits, and a decision is subsequently made to dispose of the property, thus reducing the deferred tax liability, the adjustment to the deferred tax liability is also reflected in other comprehensive income.

4.7.5 Changes in the tax status of an entity or its shareholders

A change in the tax status of an entity or its shareholders may have consequences for the entity by increasing or decreasing its tax assets or liabilities. This may occur, for example, when an entity's equity shares are publicly listed for the first time, or when a controlling shareholder moves to a foreign country. As a result of such an event, the entity may be taxed differently, which may have an immediate effect on its current and deferred tax assets and liabilities. SIC-25 *Income Taxes – Changes in the Tax Status of an Entity or its Shareholders* prescribes the accounting treatment for such changes.

SIC-25 requires that the current and deferred tax consequences of a change in tax status be included in profit or loss for the period, unless those consequences relate to transactions or events that result, in the same or a different period, in a direct credit or charge to the recognised amount of equity or in amounts recognised in other comprehensive income. Those tax consequences that relate to changes in the recognised amount of equity, in the same or a different period (not included in profit or loss), should be charged or credited directly to equity. Those tax consequences that relate to amounts recognised in other comprehensive income should be recognised in other comprehensive income. [SIC-25:4]

Effectively, this means that an analysis is required of the original accounting for the transactions or events that gave rise to the current and deferred tax balances. To the extent that those transactions or events were charged or credited directly in equity (e.g. withholding tax on dividend payments), any incremental tax effects should also be charged or credited directly to equity. To the extent that those transactions or events were recognised in other comprehensive income (e.g. certain asset revaluations), any incremental tax effects should also be recognised in other comprehensive income. Thus, the aggregate amount of tax recognised outside profit or loss will be the amount that would have been recognised outside profit or loss if the new tax status had applied previously.

Example 4.7.5

Change in the tax status of an entity

Entity P has a deferred tax liability of CU1,000 arising in respect of total temporary differences of CU4,000. A CU800 temporary difference exists in respect of a previous revaluation of property, plant and equipment. All other temporary differences relate to items recognised in profit or loss.

Entity P is sold into foreign ownership and, as a consequence, the tax rate increases from 25 per cent to 30 per cent. To recognise the resulting increase in the deferred tax liability, the following journal entry is recorded.

		CU	CU
Dr	Income tax (profit or loss) [(30% − 25%) × (CU4,000 − CU800)]	160	
Dr	Income tax (other comprehensive income) [(30% − 25%) × CU800]	40	
Cr	Deferred tax liability		200

To recognise the increase in the deferred tax liability resulting from the change in tax status.

When there is uncertainty as to the amount that was previously dealt with outside profit or loss, it may be necessary to make an allocation on a reasonable basis (see **3.2.2.4** and **4.7.3.6**).

> Note that SIC-25 does not permit the effect on deferred tax balances that arose at the time of a previous business combination to be dealt with as an adjustment to goodwill. The change in tax status is a post-acquisition event, and so is accounted for post-acquisition. Because the original deferred tax was not dealt with in equity or in other comprehensive income, the incremental effect is required to be dealt with in profit or loss.

If the change in tax rate is a result of an entity being acquired in a business combination, in the individual financial statements of the entity (the acquiree), the adjustments to current and deferred tax assets and liabilities will be accounted for in accordance with SIC-25, as discussed in the previous paragraphs. However, in the consolidated financial statements of the new parent (the acquirer), the accounting for the acquisition will reflect the current and deferred tax assets and liabilities measured using the revised tax rates – and, consequently, the incremental effect of the acquisition will be reflected as an adjustment to goodwill or the bargain purchase gain arising on acquisition. [IAS 12:58(b)]

The effect of a voluntary change in the tax status of an entity should be recognised when the change is approved or, if no approval is necessary, when the election is formally notified (e.g. if approval of the change is perfunctory). A change in tax status that results from a change in tax law will be recognised on the enactment date or the substantively enacted date if applicable. Substantively enacted tax rates are discussed further at **4.5.2.3**.

5   Specific applications

5.1   Business combinations

5.1.1   Deferred tax arising from business combinations – general

When a business combination occurs, new or adjusted deferred tax balances can arise from the following sources:

- fair value adjustments on consolidation resulting in carrying amounts of assets or liabilities in the consolidated financial statements that differ from the carrying amounts in the acquiree's financial statements and, consequently, from their tax bases when equivalent adjustments are not recognised for tax purposes (see **5.1.2**);

- additional assets or liabilities recognised on acquisition that are not recognised in the financial statements of the acquiree (see **5.1.3**);

- additional deferred tax balances recognised on acquisition that are not recognised by the acquiree, because of the initial recognition exception (see **5.1.4**); and

- deferred tax assets not previously recognised by the acquiree because the recoverability criteria could not be met at the entity level but can be met at a group level, e.g. potential for offsetting taxable profits and losses between group entities (see **5.1.5**).

When deferred tax arises at the time of a business combination, and it has not been recognised by the acquiree prior to the acquisition, it must be recognised and taken into account in the initial accounting for the business combination. It will, therefore, affect the measurement of the goodwill or the bargain purchase gain arising on acquisition.

Reverse acquisitions (see **section 12** of **chapter A25**) occur when a business combination results in the legal subsidiary obtaining control.

Under IFRS 3 *Business Combinations*, a reverse acquisition is accounted for as a business combination in which the entity that issues securities (the legal acquirer) is identified as the acquiree for accounting purposes on the basis of the guidance in paragraphs B13 to B18 of that Standard. In such circumstances, the requirements of IFRS 3 to recognise assets and liabilities of the acquiree at fair value are applied to the assets and liabilities of the legal parent.

When accounting for a reverse acquisition, deferred tax should be recognised in the consolidated financial statements in the same way as for other business combinations. In some jurisdictions, tax law may permit the legal parent to adjust the tax values of its assets and liabilities and these amounts should be used to determine the tax base of each item for the business combination accounting. If the tax law permits an adjustment to the carrying amount of the legal subsidiary's tax values, in IFRS 3 terms these changes relate to the acquirer's assets and liabilities rather than to those of the acquiree (i.e. because the legal subsidiary is the accounting acquirer); consequently, the deferred tax impact of adjustments to the legal subsidiary's tax values should be recognised outside of the accounting for the business combination (i.e. in profit or loss or other comprehensive income, as appropriate).

In the separate financial statements of the legal parent (if prepared), deferred tax should be measured on the basis of the carrying amounts of the assets and liabilities in those financial statements.

5.1.2   Fair value adjustments

With limited exceptions, the identifiable assets, liabilities and contingent liabilities of the acquiree are recognised in the consolidated financial statements at their fair values at the acquisition date. This will often result in different carrying amounts from those recognised in the acquiree's individual financial statements. However, the tax bases of the assets and liabilities may remain unchanged.

For example, when the fair value of an asset at the date of acquisition is higher than its carrying amount in the acquiree's financial statements, and the asset is recognised at the higher amount for consolidation purposes, the tax base of the asset is unlikely to be affected. In these circumstances, a taxable temporary difference arises as a result of the acquisition. The deferred tax liability arising from the taxable temporary difference is recognised in the consolidated financial statements to reflect the future tax consequences of recovering the recognised fair value of the asset. This is illustrated in **example 5.1.5**.

5.1.3   Additional assets or liabilities recognised on acquisition

On acquisition, additional assets and liabilities may be identified that are not recognised in the financial statements of the acquiree. This will commonly be the case, for example, in respect of intangible assets. When such additional assets or liabilities are recognised, the deferred tax implications should also be recognised. The newly recognised assets or liabilities reflect economic benefits and outflows of the acquiree; therefore, any deferred tax should be measured at the acquiree's tax rate. These additional assets and liabilities recognised, and any related deferred tax, will be included as part of the identifiable net assets acquired. This is illustrated in **example 5.1.5**.

The recognition of goodwill may also have deferred tax implications – see **section 4.4.5** for discussion and illustrative examples.

5.1.4 *Additional deferred tax balances recognised on acquisition*

In some circumstances, the deferred tax impact of temporary differences may not have been recognised in the acquiree's financial statements because those differences fell within one of IAS 12's recognition exceptions. For example, the differences may have arisen on the initial recognition of an asset or a liability (see **section 4.4.6**) and, consequently, may not have been recognised. In these circumstances, the deferred tax impact of such temporary differences should be recognised in the consolidated financial statements even though it is not recognised in the individual financial statements of the acquiree.

These additional deferred tax balances are recognised on acquisition because, from the group's perspective, the initial recognition of the asset or liability results from a business combination and, therefore, under the rules set out at **section 4.4.6**, the deferred tax impact should be recognised. This is illustrated in **example 5.1.5**.

5.1.5 *Deferred tax assets not previously recognised by the acquiree*

In some circumstances, deferred tax assets (e.g. in respect of tax losses) may not have been recognised by the acquiree due to concerns about the recoverability of the assets in the light of anticipated levels of profitability. However, following the acquisition, in some tax jurisdictions, the losses may become available for use by other group entities, and therefore be considered recoverable. Because the asset is now recoverable from a group perspective, the deferred tax asset is recognised at the time of acquisition.

Conversely, as a result of the acquisition, some deferred tax assets previously recognised by the acquiree may no longer be available due to restrictions imposed by tax law following a change of ownership. In such cases, the deferred tax asset should not be recognised in the acquiree's statement of financial position and would, therefore, result in increased goodwill.

The example below illustrates the deferred tax effects discussed at **5.1.2** to **5.1.5**.

Example 5.1.5

Deferred tax arising on a business combination

Company K acquires 100 per cent of Company L, which holds two properties and sundry other assets. Property A (carrying amount CU100 in Company L's financial statements) and property B (carrying amount CU150 in Company L's financial statements) are, for tax and accounting purposes, depreciated over 10 years and will be recovered through use in taxable manufacturing activities. The tax rate is 30 per cent.

The following information is relevant at the date of acquisition.

- Company K pays cash consideration of CU380 for the acquisition.
- The fair values of properties A and B are measured at CU130 and CU140, respectively.
- An additional intangible asset is identified for recognition in respect of patents held by Company L; the fair value of the intangible asset is CU50 and its tax base is nil.
- Company L has other net assets with a carrying amount of CU30; the fair value of the other net assets is also CU30 and the tax base is also CU30.
- The tax bases of properties A and B are CU50 and CU150, respectively. A temporary difference arose on the acquisition of property A by Company L and, therefore, no deferred tax liability was recognised due to the initial recognition exception.
- Company L has tax losses available for offset against the future profits of any group entity amounting to CU20. It is probable that future taxable profit will be available within the group to absorb these losses. No deferred tax asset has previously been recognised by Company L in respect of these tax losses.

The goodwill arising on the acquisition of Company L is calculated as follows.

Net assets of Company L	Carrying amount in Company L's financial statements	Fair value	Tax base	Temporary difference	Tax rate	Deferred tax liability (asset)
	CU	CU	CU	CU	CU	CU
Property A	100	130	50	80	30%	24
Property B	150	140	150	(10)	30%	(3)
Intangible asset	–	50	–	50	30%	15
Other net assets	30	30	30	–	–	–
Tax loss c/f	–	–	–	(20)	30%	(6)
Total	280	350	230	100		30
Deferred tax arising on acquisition		(30)				
Identifiable net assets acquired		320				
Consideration		380				
Goodwill		60				

5.1.6 Deferred tax assets not previously recognised by the acquirer

Circumstances may also arise when, as a result of an acquisition, the probability of realising a pre-acquisition deferred tax asset *of the acquirer* changes so that the acquirer considers it probable that it will recover its own deferred tax asset that was not recognised prior to the business combination. For example, the acquirer may be able to utilise the benefit of its unused tax losses against the future taxable profits of the acquiree. In such circumstances, the acquirer recognises a deferred tax asset, but does not include it as part of the accounting for the business combination, and it is not taken into account in measuring the goodwill or bargain purchase gain arising in the business combination. [IAS 12:67]

5.1.7 Intangible assets recognised for accounting but not tax purposes

Depending on the tax jurisdiction and on how a business combination is structured, the carrying amounts of goodwill and intangible assets recognised under IFRS 3 may be greater than, less than, or equal to their tax bases. For example, due to differences between accounting rules and tax legislation, the amounts recognised in a business combination as separately identifiable intangible assets under IFRSs may not be separately recognised for tax reporting purposes, and may instead be included within goodwill.

In a business combination, IFRS 3 requires the recognition, separately from goodwill, of identifiable intangible assets. The local tax laws may not permit the recognition of intangible assets for tax purposes in determining the amount of tax deductible goodwill.

In such circumstances, when comparing the carrying amounts of the assets acquired to their respective tax bases in order to identify temporary differences, the intangible assets and goodwill should not be aggregated; they should be analysed separately for IAS 12 purposes. This is so even if it would otherwise appear that the tax base for goodwill corresponds to amounts recognised as intangible assets under IFRSs. This is illustrated in the following example.

Example 5.1.7

Deferred tax on intangible assets and goodwill arising on a business combination

Entity A acquires the net assets of Entity B on 15 September 20X9 in a transaction accounted for as a business combination under IFRS 3. As part of the recognition and measurement of identifiable assets and liabilities, intangible assets (customer lists) of CU15 million are identified and recognised; goodwill of CU5 million is also recognised.

For local tax reporting purposes, however, no intangible assets are recognised; instead tax deductible goodwill of CU20 million is recognised.

When comparing the carrying amounts of the assets acquired to their individual tax bases for the purpose of computing temporary differences at the date of acquisition, should the carrying amount of the customer lists and the goodwill as recognised in the consolidated financial statements be aggregated and compared with the tax base of the goodwill?

No. While it would appear that the CU15 million of additional tax deductions available for goodwill equates to the tax base of the customer lists recognised, the intangible assets and goodwill should not be aggregated, but analysed separately under IAS 12.

The result is a taxable temporary difference of CU15 million on the intangible assets for which a deferred tax liability is recognised. In addition, a deferred tax asset is recognised for the excess tax deductible goodwill (CU20 million) over the recognised goodwill (CU5 million) to the extent that it is probable that taxable profit will be available against which the deductible temporary difference can be utilised.

The deferred tax asset and liability will continue to be analysed separately over their respective lives.

5.1.8 Post-acquisition recognition of acquiree's deferred tax assets

At the date of acquisition, there may be tax losses in the acquiree available for carryforward or deductible temporary differences that do not qualify for recognition as deferred tax assets when the business combination is initially accounted for. These items may subsequently meet the criteria for recognition, and IAS 12 requires that the entity should recognise such acquired deferred tax benefits that it realises after the business combination as follows:

[IAS 12:68]

- acquired deferred tax benefits recognised within the 'measurement period' (i.e. within one year after the acquisition date) that result from new information about facts and circumstances that existed at the acquisition date reduce the amount of any goodwill related to that acquisition. If the carrying amount of that goodwill is zero, any remaining deferred tax benefits are recognised in profit or loss; and

- all other acquired deferred tax benefits realised are recognised in profit or loss (or outside profit or loss if otherwise required by IAS 12).

Example 5.1.8

Realisation of tax loss carryforward after a business combination

Company Q, with a December year end, acquires a new subsidiary, Company R, on 31 March 20X1. Company R has tax losses accumulated in previous periods giving rise to a potential deferred tax asset of CU50 million. In the initial accounting for the business combination, Company Q takes the preliminary view that these losses are not available for offset against the profits of other group entities, and does not recognise a deferred tax asset. The goodwill arising on the acquisition amounts to CU20 million.

In February 20X2 (i.e. within the 'measurement period'), upon request from Company Q, the tax authority provides its opinion that Company R's losses can be offset against certain of the profits of other group entities – the relevant profits amounting to a deferred tax asset of CU30 million at the date of acquisition. This opinion reflects the tax authority's view on how the existing tax legislation at the date of acquisition should be applied to the circumstances of Company Q and Company R at that date; accordingly, it is judged to be new information about facts and circumstances that existed at the acquisition date.

In the circumstances described, had Company Q sought advice from the tax authority at the time of the acquisition, a deferred tax asset of CU30 million could potentially have been recognised in the initial accounting for the business combination. Under IAS 12:68, because the additional information was obtained during the measurement period and it reflects facts and circumstances at the acquisition date, goodwill should be adjusted for the subsequent recognition of the deferred tax asset. However, the retrospective adjustment of goodwill is limited to the amount of the goodwill; therefore, only CU20 million is adjusted directly against goodwill in the 20X2 financial statements and the balance of CU10 million is recognised in profit or loss.

> If the other group entities earn profits subsequent to the date of acquisition against which more of Company R's losses can be utilised, the effect is recognised in profit or loss.

The discussion in **example 5.1.8** reflects the requirements of IAS 12 following consequential amendments arising from IFRS 3 (as revised in 2008). Prior to those amendments, the subsequent realisation of all deferred tax assets acquired in a business combination was recognised in profit or loss with a consequential reduction in the carrying amount of goodwill to the amount that would have been recognised if the deferred tax asset had been recognised as an identifiable asset from the acquisition date, regardless of the date of realisation.

IAS 12:93 and 94 set out the transition provisions regarding the application of the revised requirements. Under those provisions, the revised IAS 12:68 applies to changes in recognised deferred tax assets occurring after the date of adoption of IFRS 3 (as revised in 2008), arising from business combinations that occurred before or after the date of adoption of IFRS 3 (as revised in 2008). This means that an acquirer does not adjust the accounting for prior business combinations for changes in previously recognised deferred tax assets outside the relevant 'measurement period'. Instead, from the date when IFRS 3 (as revised in 2008) is applied, the acquirer recognises changes in recognised deferred tax assets as an adjustment to profit or loss (or, if IAS 12 requires, outside profit or loss). Goodwill is no longer adjusted.

5.1.9   Recognition and measurement in a business combination of the potential liability arising from an uncertain tax position

> **Example 5.1.9**
>
> **Recognition and measurement in a business combination of the potential liability arising from an uncertain tax position**
>
> Entity A acquires Entity B in a business combination. Entity B has an uncertain tax position at the acquisition date which could result in a cash outflow of CU100. Entity B estimates that at the date of acquisition the probability that an outflow will result from the uncertain tax position is 30 per cent.
>
> *For the purposes of its consolidated financial statements, at the date of acquisition of Entity B, how should Entity A account for the potential liability arising from Entity B's uncertain tax position?*
>
> Neither IAS 12 nor IFRS 3 addresses this issue specifically. In the absence of definitive guidance, Entity A should select one of the following alternatives:
>
> • Option 1 – the potential tax liability could be recognised when the economic outflow is probable (an 'IAS 12 approach') (see **section 3.3.3**); or

- Option 2 – the potential tax liability could be recognised at its fair value at the acquisition date (an 'IFRS 3 approach').

Entity A should select one of these approaches as an accounting policy choice and apply it consistently in all business combinations. The alternatives are discussed in more detail below.

Option 1 – IAS 12 approach

This option is based on the view that the uncertain tax position is outside the scope of the recognition and measurement requirements of IFRS 3 and that the potential tax liability should be accounted for in accordance with IAS 12. This view is supported by IFRS 3:IN9 which states that assets and liabilities falling within the scope of IAS 12 should be accounted for at acquisition in accordance with the recognition and measurement requirements of that Standard rather than in accordance with IFRS 3.

If Entity A selects this approach, it applies the method described at **section 3.3.3** both initially and for subsequent measurement.

Consequently, if Entity A selects this option as its accounting policy, it should not recognise a liability in respect of the uncertain tax position at the date of acquisition because, at that date, it is not probable (i.e. less than 50 per cent probability) that an outflow of economic resources will occur. If, subsequent to the acquisition date, it becomes probable that an outflow of resources will occur, Entity A will recognise the tax liability at its best estimate of that outflow, with the resulting charge recognised in profit or loss.

Option 2 – IFRS 3 approach

This option is based on the view that the general principles of IFRS 3 should be applied because IFRS 3 does not explicitly exclude current tax assets and liabilities from the scope of its recognition and measurement requirements. Although, as discussed under Option 1, the introduction to IFRS 3 appears to scope out all tax balances, within the body of the Standard there is no reference to excluding current tax balances – only deferred tax balances in accordance with IFRS 3:24 and 25.

IFRS 3 requires the recognition of contingent liabilities at fair value if they can be measured reliably. Under Option 2, Entity A recognises and measures the uncertain tax liability in the business combination by analogy to the treatment of contingent liabilities acquired in a business combination. The tax liability is therefore measured at its fair value at the acquisition date, which takes into account the likelihood that the tax will become payable. Thereafter, in line with the treatment of contingent liabilities under IFRS 3:56, the liability arising from the uncertain tax position should be recognised at the higher of (1) the amount initially recognised, and (2) the amount that would be recognised by analogy to IAS 37 *Provisions, Contingent Liabilities and Contingent Assets* (see **section 3.3.3**).

5.1.10 Tax deductible goodwill of the acquiree in a business combination

---

Example 5.1.10

Tax deductible goodwill of the acquiree in a business combination

Entity A acquires 100 per cent of Entity B for consideration of CU100. At the acquisition date, Entity B has:

- goodwill from a previous business combination with a tax base of CU40 in a jurisdiction with a tax rate of 20 per cent; and
- other identifiable assets and liabilities with a total fair value of CU50.

Following its acquisition by Entity A, Entity B will be entitled to continue to claim tax deductions on the previously recognised goodwill and expects to have sufficient taxable profits available to utilise those deductions as they arise. The relevant tax rate is 20 per cent.

How should the effect of the tax deductions available on the goodwill previously recognised by Entity B be treated in the consolidated financial statements of Entity A at the acquisition date?

It depends. Because goodwill represents the economic benefits arising from intangible assets that are not individually identified and separately recognised in a business combination, it may not be apparent whether the goodwill recognised on the acquisition of Entity B by Entity A arises from the same factors that gave rise to the goodwill previously recognised by Entity B. There may be circumstances when it is clear that there is no link between the previously recognised goodwill and the goodwill arising on the current business combination. There may be less common circumstances when it is clear that the goodwill recognised by Entity A is the 'same' goodwill as that previously recognised by Entity B. However, in most cases, it will not be obvious whether there is a link between the goodwill previously recognised by Entity B and the goodwill arising when Entity A acquires Entity B. In such circumstances, if the pre-existing goodwill tax deductions are to be treated as relating to the goodwill arising on the current acquisition, it must be demonstrated that the factors that gave rise to the pre-existing goodwill continue to exist and contribute to goodwill on the current acquisition.

Scenarios 1 and 2 below illustrate contrasting circumstances.

Scenario 1 – no link identified

Entity B is a holding company with two subsidiaries – one an active manufacturing entity and the other a financial services entity in 'run-off' (i.e. no longer operating other than to hold existing financial assets to their maturity). The tax deductible goodwill recognised by Entity B arose on the acquisition of the financial services entity.

In this scenario, it is evident that any goodwill arising on the acquisition of Entity B by Entity A relates to the manufacturing subsidiary. Because there is no link between the goodwill recognised by Entity A and the tax deductible goodwill previously recognised by Entity B, for the purposes of Entity A's consolidated

---

financial statements, the tax base of CU40 does not have an associated carrying amount.

The goodwill of CU50 recognised by Entity A (i.e. consideration of CU100 less net fair value of identifiable assets and liabilities of CU50) has a tax base of CUnil, giving rise to a taxable temporary difference of CU50. No deferred tax is recognised in respect of this taxable temporary difference because it arises on the initial recognition of goodwill (see **4.4.5.1**). In addition, the goodwill previously recognised by Entity B has a tax base of CU40 and a carrying amount of CUnil, giving rise to a deductible temporary difference of CU40 which is not subject to the initial recognition exception. Consequently, subject to IAS 12's general recognition criteria, a deferred tax asset of CU8 (CU40 × 20%) is recognised in respect of Entity B's original goodwill.

At acquisition, therefore, Entity A recognises a deferred tax asset of CU8, Entity B's other identifiable assets and liabilities at their net fair value of CU50 and goodwill of CU42.

After the acquisition date, as tax deductions are claimed by Entity B in respect of the goodwill, the deferred tax asset reduces and the deferred tax expense in profit and loss offsets the current tax deduction claimed. When all available deductions have been claimed (or have expired unclaimed), no deferred tax asset will remain.

Scenario 2 – link identified

Entity B is a shell entity which acquired another entity in a transaction giving rise to tax deductible goodwill immediately before, and in anticipation of, its own acquisition by Entity A.

In this scenario, it is clear that the goodwill recognised by Entity A is substantially the same as the tax deductible goodwill previously recognised by Entity B. Consequently, the tax deductible goodwill previously recognised by Entity B gives rise to a tax base considered to relate to the goodwill recognised by Entity A.

The goodwill of CU50 recognised by Entity A therefore has a tax base of CU40, giving rise to a taxable temporary difference of CU10. No deferred tax is recognised in respect of this taxable temporary difference because it arises on the initial recognition of goodwill (see **4.4.5.1**).

At acquisition, therefore, Entity A recognises Entity B's identifiable assets and liabilities at their net fair value of CU50 and goodwill of CU50.

After the acquisition date, as tax deductions are claimed by Entity B in respect of the goodwill, a deferred tax expense will be recognised in profit or loss and a deferred tax liability will be recognised in Entity A's consolidated financial statements. The deferred tax expense offsets the current tax deductions claimed. When all available deductions have been claimed (or have expired unclaimed), a deferred tax liability of CU8 (i.e. temporary difference of CU40 not covered by the initial recognition exception at 20 per cent) will remain in place until the goodwill recognised by Entity A is either impaired or disposed of.

5.2 Eliminations of unrealised intragroup profits

When a group entity sells goods to another group entity, the seller recognises profits made on those sales in its individual financial statements. If those goods are still held in inventories by the purchaser at the end of the reporting period, the profit recognised by the seller, when viewed from the standpoint of the group as a whole, has not yet been earned, and will not be earned until the goods are eventually sold outside the group. On consolidation, the unrealised profit on closing inventories is eliminated from the group's profit, and the closing inventories of the group are recognised at cost to the group. The tax consequences to the seller (both current and deferred, if any), however, are not eliminated. If tax is charged on the results of individual entities, and not on the group, the seller will pay tax on any profits generated from the intragroup sales, even though some of those profits may be unrealised from the group's perspective.

Such consolidation adjustments may have a deferred tax impact in the consolidated financial statements. The intragroup elimination is made as a consolidation adjustment and not in the financial statements of any individual reporting entity. Therefore, the elimination will result in the creation of a temporary difference as far as the group is concerned between the carrying amount of the inventories in the consolidated financial statements and the tax base (assumed to be the carrying amount in the purchaser's individual financial statements). The deferred tax effects arising in respect of this temporary difference should be recognised in accordance with the usual principles.

The tax rate to be used when recognising the deferred tax balance arising from the elimination of unrealised profits on intragroup transactions is determined by reference to the tax jurisdiction where the temporary difference will reverse. This will generally be the tax rate in the purchaser's jurisdiction, because the deduction is available at that rate when the unrealised profit is realised from the sale to an unrelated third party. If the tax rate in the purchaser's jurisdiction differs from that in the seller's, the deferred tax recognised may not equal the tax currently payable by the seller.

Example 5.2

Elimination of intragroup profits in inventories

Company P sells inventories costing CU200 to its overseas subsidiary, Company S, for CU300. Company P's tax rate is 40 per cent, Company S's is 50 per cent. At the end of the reporting period, Company S still holds the inventories.

Company P recognises a current tax liability of CU40 (CU100 × 40%) relating to the profit on sale of the inventories but does not recognise any deferred tax balances because there are no future tax consequences from Company P's point of view.

Company S is entitled to a future deduction for the CU300 paid for the inventories and this is therefore the asset's tax base from Company S's perspective. Consequently, in Company S's individual financial statements, the tax base is equal to the carrying amount and no temporary difference arises.

Company P prepares consolidated financial statements and, for financial reporting purposes, gains and losses on intragroup transactions are eliminated on consolidation. Therefore, on consolidation, the carrying amount of the inventories is reduced from CU300 to CU200 (to eliminate the unrealised profit). A CU100 deductible temporary difference arises, representing the difference between the carrying amount (CU200) and the tax base (CU300). A deferred tax asset is calculated by multiplying the temporary difference of CU100 by 50 per cent, because the deduction is available to Company S at that rate when the unrealised profit is realised outside the group on sale of the inventories by Company S. Available evidence supports a conclusion that realisation of the deferred tax asset representing the tax benefit of Company S's deductible temporary differences is probable. The deferred tax asset arising of CU50 is therefore recognised on consolidation.

The impact of this intragroup transaction on Company P's consolidated financial statements is shown below in the following journal entries.

		CU	CU
Dr	Current tax expense (CU100 × 40%)	40	
Dr	Deferred tax asset (CU100 × 50%)	50	
Cr	Current tax payable		40
Cr	Deferred tax benefit		50

To recognise the impact of the intragroup transaction.

In a subsequent period, Company S sells the inventories that it acquired from Company P to an unrelated third party for the same amount that it had previously paid Company P, i.e. CU300. The journal entry to reflect the sales and related tax consequences to be reflected in the consolidated financial statements of Company P is as follows.

		CU	CU
Dr	Cash	300	
Dr	Cost of goods sold	200	
Dr	Income tax expense	50	
Cr	Sales		300
Cr	Inventories		200
Cr	Deferred tax asset		50

To recognise the sales and related tax consequences.

5.3   Financial instruments

5.3.1   *Investments in securities – general*

Investments in securities can often give rise to significant temporary differences. In order to determine the deferred tax implications for various types of investments, it is necessary to understand the tax rules relating to those investments. Particularly, an entity should take care to understand the tax implications that arise from the recovery of the investment through dividends ('use'), sale, or a combination of the two. It is then necessary to determine how the carrying amount of the investments will be recovered.

When an entity has an investment in an equity instrument it may be appropriate to presume that the carrying amount will be recovered through sale. This will be the case if the dividends anticipated from the investment are not expected to represent a realisation of part of the carrying amount of the investment.

Sometimes it will be necessary to consider how a financial asset has been classified under IFRS 9 *Financial Instruments* (or, for entities that have not yet adopted IFRS 9, IAS 39 *Financial Instruments: Recognition and Measurement*). For example, financial assets measured at amortised cost under IFRS 9 are so classified based on the premise that the entity's business model objective is to hold those assets to collect contractual cash flows. Similarly, financial assets classified as held-to-maturity under IAS 39 are so classified based on the premise that they will not be sold prior to their maturity. When considering any tax implications, the same assumptions should be used.

5.3.2   *Financial instruments at fair value through profit or loss or classified as held for trading*

For financial instruments that are measured at fair value through profit or loss in accordance with IFRS 9 (see **chapters B2** and **B3**) or, for entities that have not yet adopted IFRS 9, that are classified as held for trading or at fair value through profit or loss in accordance with IAS 39 (see **chapters C2** and **C3**), fair value gains and losses are recognised in profit or loss. If these gains and losses are taxable, they may be taxed when they are recognised in the financial statements, or it may be that they are not reflected in tax computations until the instrument is sold or settled. When tax is assessed based on fair value movements recognised in profit or loss, there are no deferred tax implications because the gains and losses are assessed for tax in the same period in which they are recognised in profit or loss. In contrast, when gains and losses are not reflected in tax computations until the instrument is sold or settled, deferred tax consequences may arise.

5.3.3 Financial assets measured at fair value through other comprehensive income and available-for-sale financial assets

Similar issues will arise in relation to financial assets measured at fair value through other comprehensive income under IFRS 9 (see **chapters B2** and **B3**) or, for entities that have not yet adopted IFRS 9, that are classified as available for sale (AFS) under IAS 39 (see **chapters C2** and **C3**). The main difference is that the change in fair value on these assets is reported in other comprehensive income (apart from dividend income that does not clearly represent a recovery of part of the cost of the investment under IFRS 9; under IAS 39, changes in fair value recognised in other comprehensive income exclude impairment losses, exchange gains and losses, and interest and dividend income). Thus, if a deferred tax balance arises on an asset measured at fair value through other comprehensive income, or an available-for-sale asset, the deferred tax impact may also be dealt with in other comprehensive income (rather than in profit or loss) in the same manner as the deferred tax effects of revaluations of other assets.

See **4.7.3.7** for a more detailed consideration of the deferred tax implications when fair value movements on financial assets measured through other comprehensive income (under IFRS 9) and available-for-sale financial assets (under IAS 39) are subsequently reclassified to profit or loss.

The assessment regarding the realisation of tax benefits from unrealised losses on available-for-sale financial assets often depends on the inherent assumptions used for financial reporting purposes concerning the ultimate recovery of the carrying amount of the securities.

IAS 12:16 concludes that it is inherent in the recognition of an asset that its carrying amount will be recovered in the form of economic benefits that flow to the entity in future periods. Therefore, ordinarily, an entity should assume recovery of the carrying amount of its investments in equity instruments measured at fair value through other comprehensive income (or, under IAS 39, its available-for-sale debt securities) at their fair values at the end of each reporting period. Generally, whenever there is an unrealised holding loss, recovery at fair value would result in a capital loss deduction.

In some jurisdictions, the tax law may allow utilisation of capital losses only through offset against capital gains. In such circumstances, entities need to assess whether realisation of the loss is probable based on available evidence. For example, evidence considered might include (1) available capital loss carryback recovery of taxes paid in prior years, and (2) tax planning strategies to sell appreciated capital assets that would generate capital gain income. In these situations, available evidence should be evaluated to determine if it is probable that the entity would have sufficient capital gain income during the carryback and carryforward periods prescribed under tax law. However, in making such an assessment, the carryback and carryforward periods do not commence until the loss is realised.

5.3.4   Compound financial instruments

IAS 12 contains guidance on calculating deferred tax in relation to compound financial instruments that are accounted for under IAS 32 *Financial Instruments: Presentation*. Compound financial instruments are instruments that an entity has issued that contain both a liability and an equity component (e.g. issued convertible debt). In the case of convertible debt, the separate components are a liability component (representing borrowing with an obligation to repay), and an equity component (representing the embedded option to convert the liability into equity of the entity).

Under IAS 32, the equity and liability components of a compound instrument are accounted for separately – the proceeds of issue are allocated between the separate elements. The amount initially recognised as a liability is the present value of the cash flows discounted at a market rate for equivalent debt without the equity feature. Because the holders of the compound instrument are effectively purchasing an equity interest, the coupon on the compound instrument is almost always lower than it would be for the equivalent debt without the equity feature. Therefore, the value assigned to the debt portion of the compound instrument will be lower than the total proceeds received. For example, CU100 proceeds from the issue of a convertible bond could be allocated CU90 to debt and CU10 to equity – the carrying amount of the liability component (CU90) is less than the face value of the instrument (CU100). The detailed requirements for accounting for compound instruments are considered in **chapter B3** (or, for entities that have not yet adopted IFRS 9, in **chapter C3**).

In some jurisdictions, the tax base of the liability component on initial recognition is equal to the initial carrying amount of the sum of the liability and equity components (i.e. CU100 in the above example). If the instrument were settled at an amount equal to the carrying amount of its liability component (which is generally less than the face value and, therefore, less than the tax base), a taxable gain arises, and so a deferred tax liability arising from this taxable temporary difference is recognised. In the example cited above, if the bond were settled for CU90 (its carrying amount), a gain of CU10 would arise which could be taxable.

IAS 12's 'initial recognition exception' (see **section 4.4.6**) does not apply in this situation – a deferred tax liability should be recognised. This is because the temporary difference arises not from the initial recognition of the instrument, but rather from the separate recognition of the equity component. [IAS 12:23]

Because the equity component of the compound financial instrument is recognised directly in equity, the deferred tax liability arising is also recognised directly in equity. The deferred tax should be charged directly to the carrying amount of the equity component.

However, as the discount associated with the liability component of the compound financial instrument unwinds, the reduction of the associated deferred tax liability is recognised in profit or loss and not directly in equity. The recognition of the deferred tax credit in profit or loss is consistent with the recognition of the associated expense in profit or loss related to unwinding the discount on the liability component. [IAS 12:23]

In jurisdictions where any gain on settlement of the liability would not be taxable, the tax base of the liability is always equal to its carrying amount, and no temporary difference arises.

Example 5.3.4

Convertible note accounted for as a compound instrument

On 31 December 20X0, Company R issues a convertible note with a face value of CU10,000 that matures in three years. There is no interest payable during the period, but the holder has the option to convert the note into a fixed number of shares at the end of the three-year period. Had Company R issued debt with no conversion rights that matured in three years, the interest rate on the bonds would have been 9 per cent.

Under IAS 32, the note is split into its liability and equity components. Using a discount rate of 9 per cent (i.e. the rate at which Company R could have issued equivalent debt with no conversion rights), the present value of the instrument is CU7,722. This is taken to be the value of the liability component, giving rise to an amount recognised directly in equity of CU2,278.

There are no tax consequences if the note is repaid at its face value, and a taxable gain arises if the note is settled for less than its face value. Therefore, the tax base of the instrument is CU10,000. The tax rate is 17.5 per cent.

If the liability were settled at its carrying amount (CU7,722), a taxable profit would arise. Thus, on the initial separation of the liability and equity components, a taxable temporary difference of CU2,278 arises. This gives rise to a deferred tax liability of CU399 (CU2,278 × 17.5%). This amount is netted against the amount recognised in respect of the equity component of the note.

The following entries are recognised at the date of issue of the convertible note.

		CU	CU
Dr	Cash	10,000	
Cr	Convertible note payable		7,722
Cr	Equity		2,278
Dr	Equity	399	
Cr	Deferred tax liability		399

To recognise the issue of the convertible note.

Each year, imputed interest on the liability will be recognised, increasing the carrying amount of the liability component and reducing the associated deferred tax liability. The reduction in the deferred tax liability is recognised in profit or loss.

The movements over the life of the convertible note can be summarised as follows.

	20X0 CU	20X1 CU	20X2 CU	20X3 CU
Liability and interest				
Opening liability		7,722	8,417	9,174
Imputed interest (9%)		695	757	826
Closing liability	7,722	8,417	9,174	10,000
Deferred tax liability				
Convertible note carrying amount	7,722	8,417	9,174	10,000
Tax base	10,000	10,000	10,000	10,000
Taxable temporary difference	2,278	1,583	826	–
Deferred tax liability (at 17.5%)	399	277	145	–
Deferred tax income (profit or loss)	–	122	132	145

5.3.5   Impact of IFRS 9 or IAS 39 hedging requirements on non-financial items

The recognition of a 'basis adjustment' for a non-financial asset or liability in accordance with IFRS 9:6.5.11(d)(i) (or, for entities that have not yet adopted IFRS 9, IAS 39:98(b)) may cause the carrying amount of the asset or liability to be different from its tax base. This may occur when the tax value ascribed to the asset or liability under the relevant tax jurisdiction is determined other than by reference to the carrying amount in the financial statements (e.g. the basis adjustment is not recognised for tax purposes at the same time as the carrying amount of the asset is adjusted for accounting purposes). Deferred tax should generally be recognised for the temporary difference arising from the difference between the carrying amount in the financial statements and the tax base.

When the different accounting and tax treatments are due to a basis adjustment, the temporary difference arises after the initial recognition of the asset or liability. Accordingly, the initial recognition exceptions in IAS 12:15 (taxable temporary differences – see **4.4.1**) and IAS 12:24 (deductible temporary differences – see **4.4.2**) do not apply and deferred tax should be recognised (subject to IAS 12's general recognition criteria).

For further information regarding deferral of hedging gains and losses into non-financial assets see **2.2.3** in **chapter B9** (or, for entities that have not yet adopted IFRS 9, see **2.2.3** in **chapter C9**).

Example 5.3.5

Cash flow hedge of forecast purchases

On 4 January 20X2, Company D has forecast purchases of 100,000 kg of cocoa on or about 31 December 20X2 from a Brazilian supplier, Company B, for a price of US$180,000. Company D's functional currency is Sterling, and Company B has a US$ functional currency. On 4 January 20X2, Company D designates the cash flow of the forecast purchase as a hedged item and enters into a currency forward contract to buy US$180,000 based on the forecast payment (100,000 kg at US$1.8 per kg). The forward contract locks in the value of the US$ amount to be paid at a rate of US$1.8:£1. At inception of the hedge, the derivative is on-market (i.e. fair value is zero). The terms of the currency forward contract and the forecast purchase match each other, and the entity designates the forward foreign exchange risk as the hedged risk.

On 31 December 20X2, the transaction occurs as expected. The fair value of the forward contract is positive £12,500 because the US dollar has continued to strengthen against Sterling. The forward contract has been fully effective in hedging the forward rate of the forecast transaction and, accordingly, all of the gain of £12,500 has been recognised in other comprehensive income.

Company D is required to reclassify such gains and losses and include them in the initial cost of the non-financial asset in accordance with IFRS 9:6.5.11(d)(i). (For entities that have not yet adopted IFRS 9, the treatment is available as an accounting policy choice in accordance with IAS 39:98(b).)

The inventories are recognised in Company D's financial statements at £100,000, being the cash payment of £112,500 (US$180,000 translated at the spot rate on 31 December 20X2), net of the gain on the forward contract of £12,500. The applicable tax rate is 30 per cent and the local tax law does not permit a reduction of the inventories for the gain on the hedging instrument. Accordingly, the tax base of the inventories is £112,500. Company D should, subject to the normal recoverability criteria, recognise a deferred tax asset of £3,750 (£12,500 × 30%) in respect of the temporary difference arising from the inclusion of the hedging gains in the initial cost of the inventories. Because the £3,750 arises on the reclassification of the hedging instrument (rather than on initial recognition of the inventories), the initial recognition exception does not apply. Under local tax law, fair value gains and losses on the hedging instrument result in taxable gains and losses when they are realised. The journal entries to be recorded as at 31 December 20X2 are as follows.

		£	£
Dr	Forward contract	12,500	
Cr	Other comprehensive income		12,500

To recognise the unrealised gain on the forward contract in other comprehensive income.

		£	£
Dr	Other comprehensive income	3,750	
Cr	Deferred tax liability		3,750

To recognise the tax consequences arising from the unrealised gain on the forward contract.

		£	£
Dr	Inventories	112,500	
Cr	Cash		112,500

To recognise the purchase of cocoa as inventory.

		£	£
Dr	Cash	12,500	
Cr	Forward contract		12,500

To recognise the settlement of the forward contract.

		£	£
Dr	Deferred tax liability	3,750	
Cr	Other comprehensive income		3,750
Dr	Income tax expense	3,750	
Cr	Current tax payable		3,750

To recognise the current tax payable on settlement of the forward contract.

		£	£
Dr	Other comprehensive income	12,500	
Cr	Inventories		12,500

To recognise the gain on the forward contract as a 'basis adjustment' for the inventories.

		£	£
Dr	Deferred tax asset	3,750	
Cr	Income tax expense		3,750

To recognise the deferred tax asset arising from the temporary difference on the inventories.

5.4 Properties carried at a revalued amount under IAS 16

5.4.1 Revaluation of properties

When a property is revalued under IAS 16 *Property, Plant and Equipment*, its carrying amount is increased or decreased, but there is generally no effect on the tax base of the property. As a result, deferred tax balances arise. Generally, the recognition of deferred tax arising on a revaluation is consistent with the treatment of the revaluation itself.

5.4.2 Upward revaluations

The upward revaluation of a property accounted for under IAS 16 generally gives rise to a deferred tax liability. By increasing the carrying amount of the property, the entity is acknowledging that it expects to generate returns in excess of the original carrying amount, which will lead to future taxable profits, and so tax payable.

When an upward revaluation is recognised, the deferred tax liability arising is calculated by reference to the expected manner of recovery of the property. The upward revaluation is recognised in other comprehensive income (unless it represents the reversal of a downward revaluation previously recognised in profit or loss). The deferred tax expense should, therefore, also be recognised in other comprehensive income.

Over the period of use when the temporary difference reverses, the release of the deferred tax liability will be credited to profit or loss (see **4.7.3.3**). The deferred tax liability recognised at the date of revaluation represents a provision for the tax expected to arise on those benefits. The release of the deferred tax liability to profit or loss over the period in which those future economic benefits (i.e. taxable profits) are earned offsets the current tax expense in those years to the extent that it was anticipated at the date of the revaluation. This is illustrated in **example 5.4.2**.

Example 5.4.2

Deferred tax impact of property revaluation

An item of property, plant and equipment is acquired for CU1,000. It is depreciated for tax and accounting purposes over five years. At the end of the third year, it is revalued to CU1,200. The value of the property is expected to be recovered through use in a taxable manufacturing activity. The tax rate is 30 per cent.

	Carrying amount	Tax base	Temporary difference	Deferred tax liability	Movement for the year
	CU	CU	CU	CU	CU
01/01/20X1	1,000	1,000	–	–	–
31/12/20X1	800	800	–	–	–
31/12/20X2	600	600	–	–	–
31/12/20X3	1,200	400	800	240	240
31/12/20X4	600	200	400	120	(120)
31/12/20X5	–	–	–	–	(120)

The required journal entries at the end of 20X3 are as follows.

		CU	CU
Dr	Property, plant and equipment	200	
Dr	Property, plant and equipment – accumulated depreciation	600	
Cr	Gain on revaluation (other comprehensive income)		800
Dr	Income tax (other comprehensive income)	240	
Cr	Deferred tax liability		240

To recognise the required entries at the end of 20X3.

In both 20X4 and 20X5, the following entry will be recorded, to reflect the reversal of the temporary difference arising on revaluation.

		CU	CU
Dr	Deferred tax liability	120	
Cr	Income tax (profit or loss)		120

To recognise the tax effect of the reversal of the temporary difference arising on revaluation.

5.4.3   Downward revaluations and impairment losses

Recognition of downward revaluations and impairments of properties accounted for under IAS 16 is either in profit or loss or other comprehensive income, depending on where previous gains and losses recognised on the property have been presented. The accounting for properties under IAS 16 is discussed in further detail in **chapter A7**.

The write-down of a property for accounting purposes can give rise to a deferred tax asset, or a reduction in a deferred tax liability, depending on the tax base of the property. Any deferred tax asset arising is recognised to the extent that it is probable that sufficient taxable profit will be available in the future to allow the benefit of that deferred tax asset to be recovered.

When a property accounted for in accordance with IAS 16 has previously been revalued, and a downward valuation subsequently occurs that is recognised in other comprehensive income (i.e. to the extent that the subsequent downward valuation does not exceed the amount held in the revaluation surplus in respect of that same asset), the deferred tax effects previously recognised in other comprehensive income are reversed through other comprehensive income. If the downward revaluation exceeds the amount of revaluation surplus, the excess is recognised in profit or loss. In such circumstances, the deferred tax movement should also be split between amounts recognised in other comprehensive income and profit or loss.

Impairments are treated in the same manner as downward revaluations.

These principles are illustrated in **example 5.4.3**.

Example 5.4.3

Downward revaluation

An item of property, plant and equipment is acquired for CU1,000. It is depreciated for tax and accounting purposes over 10 years on a straight-line basis. The value of the property is expected to be recovered through use in a taxable manufacturing activity. The entity is a profitable manufacturing entity with its deferred tax assets fully recognised.

At the end of the third year (when the carrying amount is CU700), the asset is revalued to CU1,050 but no adjustment is made to its tax base. At the end of the sixth year, when the carrying amount of the asset is CU600 (i.e. CU1,050 − (3 × CU150)), it is revalued downward to CU200. The tax rate is 30 per cent.

The impact of these events is summarised as follows.

Initially, the revaluation uplift and the related deferred tax are recognised in other comprehensive income and accumulated in the revaluation reserve. Each year a transfer is made from the revaluation reserve to retained earnings equal to the depreciation of the revaluation surplus net of tax.

At the time of the downward revaluation, the balance in the revaluation reserve is CU140. This is calculated as follows.

	CU
	CU
Original revaluation uplift	350
Deferred tax thereon (CU350 × 30%)	(105)
	245
Three years' depreciation on net uplift (CU245 × 3/7)	(105)
	140

Therefore, the first CU200 of the downward revaluation is recognised as a loss in other comprehensive income, net of CU60 related tax. The remaining downward revaluation of CU200 is recognised in profit or loss (along with CU60 related tax).

The downward revaluation reduces the carrying amount below the tax base, resulting in a deferred tax asset which is recognised because the entity has forecast taxable profits.

	Carrying amount				Deferred tax liability (asset)	Movement for the year	Recognised in	
	Historical cost	Revaluation uplift	Tax base	Temporary difference			Other comp. income	Profit or loss
	CU	CU	CU	CU	CU	CU	CU	CU
20X0	1,000	–	1,000	–	–	–	–	–
20X1	900	–	900	–	–	–	–	–
20X2	800	–	800	–	–	–	–	–
20X3	700	350	700	350	105	105	105	–
20X4	600	300	600	300	90	(15)	–	(15)
20X5	500	250	500	250	75	(15)	–	(15)
20X6	200	–	400	(200)	(60)	(135)	(60)	(75)
20X7	150	–	300	(150)	(45)	15	–	15
20X8	100	–	200	(100)	(30)	15	–	15
20X9	50	–	100	(50)	(15)	15	–	15
20Y0	–	–	–	–	–	15	–	15

If a decision is subsequently taken to dispose of the property, then the deferred tax implications will need to be re-examined. Because the temporary difference is calculated on the basis of management expectations as to the manner of recovery of the property, when those expectations change the deferred tax position may also change.

5.4.4   Properties to be recovered through disposal – 'clawback' of tax depreciation

It may be anticipated that the carrying amount of a revalued property will be recovered through sale (whether based on management intent or on the presumptions established in IAS 12 for non-depreciable properties and investment properties – see **section 4.2.6**). In such cases, the deferred tax implications are determined on the basis of the tax consequences of disposal of the property. It may be that the profit on disposal will be fully taxable, in which case the deferred tax liability arising on any revaluation of the property will be equal to the revaluation uplift multiplied by the tax rate. However, frequently, the taxation of capital gains is on a different basis (e.g. the taxable gain arising may be limited to the amount of tax depreciation previously claimed). This is often referred to as a 'claw-back'.

In such circumstances (i.e. when the disposal is not itself subject to income tax, but any deduction for tax depreciation previously claimed is taxable as a 'claw-back'), the tax base is the carrying amount less future taxable amounts. This may or may not be equal to the cost less tax depreciation to date. This point is illustrated in **example 5.4.4**.

Example 5.4.4

Property to be recovered through disposal

A building (classified as property, plant and equipment) is acquired for CU1,000 on 1 January 20X1. No deferred tax arises on initial recognition of the property, which is to be depreciated (both for tax and accounting purposes) over five years. At the end of 20X1, when its carrying amount and tax written down value is CU800, the property is remeasured to its fair value of CU1,200. At that date, it is expected that the carrying amount of the property will be recovered through disposal.

If the property were disposed of, the taxable gain arising would be limited to the amount of the tax depreciation previously claimed. The tax rate is 30 per cent.

At 31 December 20X1   Carrying amount (fair value) = CU1,200

Tax base = CU1,000*

Temporary difference = CU1,200 – CU1,000 = CU200

Deferred tax liability = CU200 × 30% = CU60

---

*   The tax base is the carrying amount of CU1,200 less future taxable amounts (i.e. the allowances that would be clawed back on disposal) of CU200. In these circumstances, the tax base for IAS 12 is not equal to the tax written down value of CU800 (cost less accumulated tax depreciation to date).

Therefore, at the end of 20X1, a deferred tax liability of CU60 is recognised; because it relates to the revaluation of the property, the debit of CU60 is recognised in other comprehensive income.

5.5   Foreign currency translation

5.5.1   *Assets or liabilities held directly*

When an entity holds a foreign-currency denominated monetary asset or liability directly, retranslation at each period end results in a change in the carrying amount for accounting purposes, and a foreign exchange gain or loss that is generally recognised in profit or loss. When applicable tax law does not allow for an equivalent change in tax base, and recovery of an increased carrying amount would be taxable, a temporary difference arises on retranslation which is required to be recognised. In most circumstances, the related deferred tax is recognised in profit or loss. However, when the exchange gain or loss is itself recognised in other comprehensive income, the deferred tax is also recognised in other comprehensive income.

When the entity holds a non-monetary asset that is located overseas, the asset is recognised at its historical cost, being the original foreign currency purchase price translated at the rate on the date of purchase. When the realisation of that asset will give rise to tax consequences in the foreign country, the tax base of the asset will change as the exchange rate changes. This will give rise to a temporary difference because the recognised carrying amount of the asset does not change (see also **4.4.7.8**).

5.5.2   Consolidated financial statements

When a reporting entity incorporates the financial statements of foreign operations in its consolidated financial statements (whether by the equity method or consolidation), the deferred tax consequences will need to be evaluated. A foreign operation is defined as an entity that is a subsidiary, associate, joint arrangement or branch of a reporting entity, the activities of which are based or conducted in a country or currency other than those of the reporting entity. [IAS 21:8]

Once a foreign operation's own financial statements have been prepared in its functional currency, they must then be translated into the presentation currency of the investing entity or group, before they can be incorporated into the group's consolidated financial statements. This is dealt with in IAS 21 *The Effects of Changes in Foreign Exchange Rates* and discussed further in **chapter A19**.

The basic approach is to translate the statement of financial position using the closing rate of exchange, and income and expenses at the rates ruling on the date of transaction (or an average rate can often be used as an approximation). Exchange differences arising are recognised in other comprehensive income.

From a deferred tax perspective, this approach should not give rise to any additional temporary differences on the assets and liabilities of the foreign operation itself. This is because the carrying amounts and the tax bases of the assets and liabilities of the foreign operation are all translated using the same year-end exchange rate, and any deferred taxes will have already been recognised by the foreign operation.

Although temporary differences do not result directly from the translation of the financial statements of these foreign operations, temporary differences can still arise on their consolidation due to differences between the net investment accounted for in the consolidated financial statements (effectively the parent's share of the net assets of the operation), and the tax base of the investment itself held by the parent (see **section 4.4.7**).

When a parent has a loan to a foreign subsidiary that is considered to be part of the net investment in the foreign operation, the parent will assess the likelihood of reversal of the temporary difference relating to the loan in the same manner as the temporary differences relating to the subsidiary's equity are considered. Therefore, if the parent is able to control the timing of the reversal of those temporary differences and the reversal is not expected to occur in the foreseeable future, the deferred tax would not be recognised. Conversely, if the parent has an interest-earning deposit in the subsidiary, the deferred tax arising from temporary differences would be recognised, as the exception relates to investments in subsidiaries and not to individual assets within those subsidiaries (see examples **4.4.7.4D** and **4.4.7.4E**).

5.6   Share-based payments

5.6.1   Deferred tax arising from share-based payment transactions – general

In some jurisdictions, entities receive tax deductions for share-based payments, although the deduction may not always equal the accounting expense, nor be in the same period as the accounting expense is recognised. For example, an entity may operate a share option scheme whereby the tax deduction occurs when the share options are exercised, and the amount is based on the entity's share price on the exercise date. [IAS 12:68A]

The difference between the tax base of the employee services received to date (being the amount accrued to date that the tax authorities will permit as a deduction in future periods), and the carrying amount for accounting purposes (i.e. nil), is a deductible temporary difference that results in a deferred tax asset. If the amount of the future tax deduction is not known at the end of the period, it should be estimated, based on information available at the end of the period. For example, if the deduction is based on the entity's share price on the exercise date (or some other future date), the measurement of the deductible temporary difference should be based on the entity's share price at the end of the period. [IAS 12:68B]

Example 5.6.1A

Calculation of deductible temporary difference arising from share-based payment transactions

On 1 January 20X1, Entity A grants share options to its employees that vest after three years of service. Under the tax law of the jurisdiction in which

---

Entity A operates, a tax deduction will arise when the options are exercised and will be based on the intrinsic value of the options at that time.

At 31 December 20X2 (i.e. two years into the three-year vesting period), 100 options remain outstanding but Entity A expects that only 50 of these will be exercised; the remainder are expected either not to vest (due to employees leaving service before the end of the vesting period) or to expire unexercised (due to employees choosing not to exercise their rights under the options). The intrinsic value of each option, which is based on Entity A's share price at 31 December 20X2, is CU10 and the tax rate is 30 per cent.

Consistent with IAS 12:68B and Example 5 in the Illustrative Examples accompanying IAS 12, Entity A is required to calculate a deductible temporary difference that is based on the intrinsic value of the options at the end of the reporting period and the proportion of the service period which has elapsed.

When Entity A applies the requirements of IAS 12:68B, should the deductible temporary difference be calculated based on the total number of options outstanding at the end of the reporting period, or on the number of options expected to be exercised?

The deductible temporary difference should be calculated based on the number of options expected to be exercised. This is consistent with the requirements of IAS 12:68B, which states that "the amount the taxation authorities will permit as a deduction in future periods . . . shall be estimated, based on information available at the end of the period".

In the circumstances described, Entity A should therefore calculate a deductible temporary difference of CU333 (50 options expected to be exercised × CU10 × 2/3) and should recognise a deferred tax asset of CU100 (CU333 × 30 per cent), subject to the general recognition criteria in IAS 12 for deferred tax assets.

Note that, in applying these requirements, it will generally be the case that the number of options expected to be exercised will be the same as the number expected to vest because the options will only give rise to a deductible temporary difference if they are 'in the money' and, logically, an employee would be expected to exercise an option to purchase a share for less than its market value. In addition, assumptions made about vesting of instruments for the purpose of these calculations should be consistent with expectations used when calculating the IFRS 2 expense.

If the amount of the accrued tax deduction exceeds the amount of the related cumulative remuneration expense, this indicates that the deduction relates not only to the remuneration expense but also to an equity item. Hence, in accordance with IAS 12:58, the excess of the associated current or deferred tax should be recognised directly in equity. [IAS 12:68C]

Example 5.6.1B

Current and deferred tax arising from cash-settled share-based payments

Company A grants its employees cash-settled share appreciation rights (SARs) that vest after three years of service. The relevant tax authority of the country in which Company A is established allows a tax deduction not equal to the cash paid, but based on a different formula. To calculate the corresponding deferred tax under IAS 12:68B, Company A must estimate the amount of the tax deduction to be received in future periods by using information available at the end of the reporting period. Sometimes the amount of the estimated tax deduction measured in accordance with IAS 12:68B or ultimately received may exceed the cumulative remuneration expense recognised under IFRS 2 *Share-based Payment*.

In a cash-settled scheme of this nature, would recognition of the amount of the tax deduction in excess of the cumulative remuneration expense result in recognition, directly in equity, of the current or deferred tax arising from this excess in accordance with IAS 12:68C?

No. Although IAS 12:68C does not explicitly state that it relates only to equity-settled share-based payments, the justification given for the accounting treatment is that the excess deduction indicates that the deduction relates to an equity item as well as to the remuneration expense. In the case of cash-settled share-based payments, such awards are classified as liabilities. Therefore, there is no equity item recognised to which the deduction could relate and, accordingly, it is appropriate to recognise the entire deduction in profit or loss.

IAS 12 Appendix B contains an example of how to calculate the deferred tax asset associated with an employee share remuneration scheme.

In some cases tax deductions may be expected upon the exercise by the holder of vested share options. Because a tax deduction is expected, a deferred tax asset may have been recognised. If the holder fails to exercise the option (i.e. the share options lapse), the tax deductions cease to be expected, although the IFRS 2 expense will remain. Accordingly, there ceases to be a deductible temporary difference and the deferred tax asset should be written off to profit or loss, or to equity, consistent with the manner in which the asset was recognised (e.g. profit or loss to the extent of compensation expense, equity for any excess).

Sometimes employee share schemes are modified (e.g. from equity-settled to cash-settled). These modifications can change the accounting for the scheme (e.g. by requiring that a liability be recognised). The accounting implications of employee share schemes are considered in **chapter A16**. However, it is important to note that the modification may also affect any deferred tax balances recognised.

5.6.2   Changes in deferred tax on share awards replaced in a business combination

Often, as part of a business combination, the acquirer will issue equity-settled share-based payment awards to replace share options held by the employees of the acquiree. A portion of the market-based measure of the replacement awards is attributed to pre-combination services and, therefore, forms part of the consideration transferred in the business combination.

If the replacement awards are tax deductible, a deferred tax asset is recognised at the acquisition date based on the estimated tax deduction that will be received. Subsequent to the acquisition date, the acquirer's share price may change, in which case the deferred tax asset should be remeasured to reflect the anticipated tax deduction.

There are two acceptable methods of accounting for the subsequent remeasurement of the deferred tax asset related to pre-combination services. An entity should select one as an accounting policy choice to be applied consistently to all similar transactions.

Alternative 1: apply the principle established in IAS 12:68A - 68C

IAS 12:68C states that, in the context of share-based payments, "[i]f the amount of the tax deduction (or estimated future tax deduction) exceeds the amount of the related cumulative remuneration expense, this indicates that the tax deduction relates not only to remuneration expense but also to an equity item. In this situation, the excess of the associated current or deferred tax should be recognised directly in equity".

In the context of replacement awards granted as part of a business combination, the cumulative remuneration expense is comprised of the amount attributed to pre-combination services at the acquisition date (as determined in accordance with paragraph B58 of IFRS 3 *Business Combinations*) and the amount of compensation expense recognised for the replacement awards since the date of the business combination, if any. Therefore, the tax deduction related to the excess over the acquisition-date market-based value would be recognised in equity under the principle in IAS 12:68C.

Alternative 2: recognise all changes to the deferred tax assets related to pre-combination services in profit or loss

This alternative is based on the fact that Example 6 of IAS 12 does not appear to apply the principle in IAS 12:68C to distinguish whether a portion of the increase in the deferred tax asset should be recognised in equity rather than in profit or loss. The example indicates that, subsequent to the business combination, the intrinsic value of the options has increased above the market-based value of the replacement awards measured on the acquisition date. In the example, the entire change in the deferred tax asset appears to be recognised as "deferred tax income". Accordingly, based on Example 6 of IAS 12, it appears acceptable to recognise all movements in deferred tax assets related to pre-combination services in profit or loss.

Example 5.6.2 provides a numerical illustration of both of these approaches.

Example 5.6.2

Changes in tax deductions for share awards replaced in a business combination

On 1 January 20X1, Company A acquires Company B in a business combination. On the acquisition date, the employees of Company B hold fully vested share options with a market-based value of CU120. As part of the business combination, the share options held by employees of Company B are replaced by fully vested share options of Company A with a market-based value of CU120. In accordance with paragraphs B56 to B62 of IFRS 3, the market-based value of the replacement awards is determined to relate to pre-combination services and forms part of the consideration transferred to acquire Company B.

A tax deduction is available when the share options are exercised, based on the intrinsic value of the awards on the date of exercise. The tax rate applicable to Company A is 40 per cent. On the acquisition date, the intrinsic value of the awards is CU100 and, accordingly, a deferred tax asset of CU40 is recognised on that date.

On 31 December 20X1, the intrinsic value of the replacement awards has increased to CU150 such that the deferred tax asset related to the replacement awards is CU60. The increase in the deferred tax asset is recognised using either of the following two alternatives.

Alternative 1: apply the principle established in IAS 12:68A - 68C

The estimated future tax deduction of CU150 exceeds the amount of the cumulative remuneration expense of CU120 (the cumulative remuneration expense being equal to the acquisition-date market-based value because no compensation expense in respect of the replacement awards relates to the post-combination period).

Accordingly, the deferred tax asset related to the excess of CU30 is recognised in equity. Therefore, the increase of CU20 in the deferred tax asset is recognised as follows.

Increase in deferred tax asset for the year	CU20	(CU60 – CU40)
Excess recognised in equity	CU12	(CU30 × 40%)
Deferred tax income recognised in profit or loss	CU8	

> *Alternative 2: recognise all changes in the deferred tax assets related to pre-combination services in profit or loss*
>
> Under this alternative, the increase of CU20 in the deferred tax asset is recognised in profit or loss.
>
> Either of the above treatments is acceptable as an accounting policy choice to be applied consistently to all similar transactions.

5.6.3 Changes in deferred tax on share awards recognised on first-time adoption

Paragraph D2 of IFRS 1 *First-time Adoption of International Financial Reporting Standards* provides an exemption that allows entities not to apply IFRS 2 retrospectively to specified share-based payment awards on transition to IFRSs (see **7.3** of **chapter A3**).

Therefore, for a share option scheme awarded prior to the date of transition to IFRSs that meets the specific requirements of the exemption, an entity that recognised a remuneration expense under its previous GAAP is permitted not to restate that expense, but recognises no further expense.

The entity may be entitled to receive a tax deduction when the options are exercised based on the intrinsic value of the options at the date of exercise. IAS 12:68A to 68C require that a deferred tax asset should be recognised on all deductible temporary differences relating to share options. On the date of transition to IFRSs, the entity recognises a deferred tax asset based on the difference between the fair value of the underlying shares and the exercise price of the options. Because this is an adjustment on transition to IFRSs, it is recognised in equity.

Subsequent changes in the amount of the deferred tax asset (based on the difference between the fair value of the underlying shares on the valuation date and the exercise price of the options) should be recognised in profit or loss or in equity, depending on the expense actually recognised for the awards.

The entity should determine the 'cumulative remuneration expense' related to the estimated future tax deduction, as referred to in IAS 12:68C, by reference to the original remuneration expense recognised under previous GAAP. If the amount of the estimated future tax deduction on a subsequent reporting date is higher than the remuneration expense recognised under previous GAAP, this implies that the tax deduction relates not only to the remuneration expense but also to an equity item. In such circumstances, the changes in the deferred tax asset should be recognised partially in profit or loss (to the extent that the deferred tax asset relates to the cumulative remuneration expense recognised), with the residual recognised in equity. Similarly, if the amount of the estimated future tax deductions on a subsequent reporting date falls below the remuneration expense recognised under previous GAAP, the resulting reduction in the deferred tax asset should be recognised in equity to the extent of any amounts previously recognised in equity, with any excess recognised in profit or loss.

If no remuneration expense was recognised prior to transition to IFRSs, the 'cumulative remuneration expense' under IFRSs would be considered to be nil and all subsequent changes in the deferred tax asset would be recognised in equity. This is illustrated in **example 5.6.3**.

Example 5.6.3

Changes in deferred tax assets for share awards recognised on first-time adoption of IFRSs

Entity A granted 100 share options with an exercise price of CU1 per share option to employees on 1 January 2001 (i.e. before the mandatory application of IFRS 2 *Share-based Payment* on 7 November 2002). The arrangement involved a five-year vesting period, following which employees have the right to exercise the options for 10 years. Entity A adopted IFRSs in 2008, with a transition date of 1 January 2007. A tax deduction is available when the share options are exercised, based on the intrinsic value of the awards at the date of exercise.

Entity A recognised a remuneration expense of CU400 for this arrangement under its previous GAAP. As permitted by IFRS 1:D2, Entity A did not apply IFRS 2 retrospectively to these share options at the date of transition to IFRSs.

On 1 January 2007, the date of transition, the fair value of Entity A's shares is CU3 per share, and all of the share options have vested and remain outstanding. Accordingly, the share options have an intrinsic value of CU2 per share (i.e. fair value of CU3 – exercise price of CU1). Assuming a tax rate of 30 per cent, on transition to IFRSs Entity A recognises a deferred tax asset of CU60 (CU2 × 100 share options × 30 per cent), with an offsetting adjustment to equity.

On 31 December 2007, Entity A's share price has increased to CU8 per share such that the share options have an intrinsic value of CU7 per share option. The deferred tax asset relating to the share-based payment arrangement is now calculated as CU210 (i.e. CU7 × 100 share options × 30 per cent), resulting in a deferred tax credit of CU150 (i.e. deferred tax asset of CU210 at the end of the period less CU60 at the date of transition). The deferred tax credit is recognised partly in profit or loss and partly in equity as follows.

Estimated future tax deductions (CU7 × 100 share options)	CU700
Cumulative remuneration expense (previous GAAP)	CU400
Excess deduction	CU300
Deferred tax income for the period	CU150
Amount recognised directly in equity (CU300 × 30%)	CU90
Recognised in profit or loss	CU60

If, however, the cumulative remuneration expense recognised under previous GAAP had been reversed on transition to IFRSs, then the entire CU150 of tax benefit would be recognised in equity.

On 31 December 2008, Entity A's share price has decreased to CU4 per share, resulting in an intrinsic value of the options of CU3 (CU4 – CU1). Accordingly, the estimated future tax deductions are now CU300 (CU3 intrinsic value × 100 share options) and the deferred tax asset is measured at CU90 (CU300 × 30 per cent). The resulting deferred tax debit of CU120 (CU210 deferred tax asset at 31 December 2007 less deferred tax asset of CU90 at 31 December 2008) is recognised partly in profit or loss and partly in equity as follows.

Deferred tax expense for the period	CU120
Amount in excess of cumulative remuneration expense previously recognised directly in equity (CU300 × 30%)	CU90
Recognised in profit or loss	CU30

If no remuneration expense was recognised prior to transition to IFRSs, then the entire CU120 of tax expense would be recognised in equity.

5.7 Finance leases

5.7.1 Deferred tax arising from finance leases – general

Leasing transactions frequently give rise to deferred tax effects, but IAS 12 does not provide any specific guidance on how to account for those effects.

The appropriate accounting treatment for leases is established in IAS 17 *Leases* and is discussed in detail in **chapter A17**.

If a lease is classified as a finance lease, the lessee recognises the leased asset and a corresponding lease liability in its statement of financial position; it also recognises the asset's depreciation and finance costs related to the lease liability in profit or loss.

In some jurisdictions, the tax treatment of finance leases is consistent with the accounting treatment. In other jurisdictions, however, a finance lease may be classified as an operating lease for tax purposes and tax deductions may be available only for the lease payments as they are paid (i.e. no deduction for asset depreciation or finance costs).

Sections 5.7.2 and **5.7.3** discuss the appropriate accounting for the two most common tax treatments for finance leases.

5.7.2 Finance lease treatment for tax and financial reporting purposes

When the entity receives tax deductions in respect of the leased asset (depreciation allowance) and the lease liability (deduction for finance costs) in the same way as if the asset had been purchased using a loan, no special tax considerations arise. The requirements of IAS 12 are applied separately to the leased asset and the lease liability.

When the leased asset is recognised initially, if the tax base of the asset is the same as the carrying amount under IFRSs, no temporary difference arises. If the tax base ascribed to the asset is different from the carrying amount, a temporary difference arises, but no deferred tax is recognised due to the application of the initial recognition exception under IAS 12:22(c) (see **section 4.4.6**). As the asset is depreciated, accounting and tax depreciation rates may differ, resulting in new deductible or taxable temporary differences for which deferred tax may be recognised in accordance with the general principles of IAS 12.

The lease liability is likely to have a tax base equal to its carrying amount because deductions are given in future for the finance cost portion of the lease payment, which is not reflected in the carrying amount of the lease liability at inception.

5.7.3 Finance lease under IAS 17 but tax deductions based on rental payments

When the lease is treated as an operating lease for tax purposes and tax deductions are received for the lease payments as they are paid (and not for depreciation or finance costs), the appropriate accounting is more complex. Given the lack of guidance in the existing literature, alternative approaches may be acceptable.

Two acceptable approaches to accounting for the deferred tax consequences in such circumstances are explained below.

Approach 1 – apply the IAS 12 requirements to the leased asset and the lease liability separately

The leased asset has a tax base of zero; the lease liability also has a tax base of zero because the lease payments are deductible in future (as lease rental payments). This gives rise to a temporary difference on initial recognition of both the leased asset and the lease liability that is not recognised due to the application of the initial recognition exception in IAS 12:22(c).

Subsequently, the temporary differences decrease as the asset is depreciated and the liability is repaid. No deferred tax is recognised on either the leased asset or the lease liability due to continued application of the initial recognition exception (assuming no new temporary differences arise).

Therefore, this approach may result in no deferred tax being recognised either initially or over the term of the lease. The impact of this may be that while the profit on the lease generally increases over time, as the interest expense decreases, the tax deductions are timed more evenly.

Approach 2 – apply the IAS 12 requirements to the leasing transaction as a whole

An alternative approach that results in the recognition of deferred tax is also seen in practice. This approach seeks to reflect the linkage between the leased asset and the lease liability and recognise deferred tax on an aggregate temporary difference basis. This method yields an effective tax rate that more closely reflects the economics of the overall lease transaction.

At inception of the lease, there is no net lease asset or liability, no tax base and, therefore, no temporary difference.

Subsequently, as depreciation on the asset (generally straight-line) initially exceeds the rate at which the debt reduces (due to lease payments made less interest recognised under the effective interest method), a net liability arises resulting in a deductible temporary difference on which a deferred tax asset should be recognised if recoverable. Assuming that the lease liability is not repaid in advance, the total discounted cash outflows should equal the total rental payments deductible for income tax purposes.

5.8   Post-retirement benefits

5.8.1   Temporary differences arising from post-retirement benefits – general

The accounting for defined benefit retirement benefit plans and other post-retirement benefits often gives rise to temporary differences.

Tax deductions for payments into defined benefit retirement benefit plans are often allowed on a different measurement basis and in a different time period compared to the expense recognised in the financial statements under IAS 19 *Employee Benefits*. For example, the tax deduction may be available:

- when cash contributions are paid (in some jurisdictions, the deduction is spread over a period of time); or

- when the actual benefits are paid to individuals (this usually applies for unfunded schemes).

As a result temporary differences are likely to arise.

5.8.2 Deferred tax asset

A net defined benefit liability can be considered to represent the future funding the entity will be required to provide for the defined benefit scheme. If the entity will be able to claim future tax deductions for such funding, the tax base of the net defined benefit liability will be zero.

This will give rise to a deductible temporary difference. In addition, a deductible temporary difference will arise if tax deductions for contributions to a retirement benefit plan are not given in the year the contribution is paid but in later years (e.g. when the benefits are paid). In accordance with IAS 12, the entity should recognise a deferred tax asset for this temporary difference to the extent it is recoverable (see **section 4.6**).

5.8.3 Deferred tax liability

When an entity has a net defined benefit asset in respect of a surplus in its retirement benefit plan, this represents over-funding for which tax deductions may have been received; consequently, a taxable temporary difference arises and a deferred tax liability should be recognised.

The manner of recovery of a surplus may affect the tax consequences; for example, in some jurisdictions, refunds from a retirement benefit plan may be subject to tax at a rate different from the normal income tax rate.

IFRIC 14 *IAS 19 – The Limit on a Defined Benefit Asset, Minimum Funding Requirements and their Interaction* provides guidance on how to assess the recoverability of a net defined benefit asset (see **section 7.4** of **chapter A15**). Application of this guidance may result in the recognition of an asset because there is legally an unconditional right to a refund. Such a refund may be taxable at a rate other than the normal income tax rate.

A net defined benefit asset may be recovered through the receipt of a taxable refund or through reduced contributions. IAS 12 requires deferred taxes to be assessed based on the expected method of recovery of the underlying asset.

IFRIC 14 states that "the economic benefit available does not depend on how the entity intends to use the surplus". Accordingly, recognition of an asset under IFRIC 14 because there is legally an unconditional right to a refund does not necessarily imply that the entity expects to recover the asset through a refund.

If it is expected that the asset will be recovered through reduced contributions, the normal income tax rate may be the most appropriate rate to be applied to the temporary difference. However, if a refund is expected, the rate applicable to refunds should be applied.

Note, however, that it would not be appropriate (in the absence of other negative factors) to argue that no deferred tax should be recognised in relation to the net defined benefit asset on the basis it may be eliminated by future market movements or other measurement factors. This is because deferred taxes are measured by reference to the carrying amount at the reporting date, not a theoretical, possible or even probable future carrying amount.

5.8.4   Allocation of tax between profit or loss and other comprehensive income

IAS 12 requires that current and deferred tax should be recognised outside profit or loss if the tax relates to items that are recognised outside profit or loss (see **3.2.2.1**). To the extent that gains or losses are recognised in other comprehensive income under IAS 19, it is necessary to consider what amount of the current or deferred tax relates to those gains and losses. In addition, it is often not possible to determine whether contributions paid (generally the basis for tax deductions) relate to items recognised in profit or loss or items recognised in other comprehensive income. When there is no clear relationship between the expense recognised in profit or loss and the tax deductions received in the period, the current and deferred tax expense will need to be allocated between profit or loss and other comprehensive income on a reasonable basis. [IAS 12:63]

One acceptable methodology is to allocate tax deductions arising during the period first to items recognised in profit or loss, and then to allocate the remainder, if any, to the items in other comprehensive income. However, if the total tax exceeds all retirement benefit items recognised multiplied by the tax rate, that excess may be taken to profit or loss because it does not clearly relate to items reported in other comprehensive income.

Example 5.8.4

Defined benefit liability with an actuarial loss

	Defined benefit liability CU	Current tax deduction (30%) CU	Deferred tax asset (30%) CU
Brought forward	(200)		60
Profit or loss – net pension cost	(50)	15	–
Other comprehensive income – actuarial loss	(30)	6[a]	3[b]
Contribution paid / deduction received	70	21	
Carried forward	(210)		63

[a] This amount represents the remainder of the total tax deduction of CU21 in the current period after the maximum possible amount of CU15 has been allocated to amounts recognised in profit or loss.

[b] The movement between the amounts of deferred tax asset brought forward and carried forward in this case is deemed to arise on the actuarial loss because the total tax recognised in other comprehensive income is not in excess of tax on the actuarial loss (CU30 × 30% = CU9).

5.9 Decommissioning obligations

Under IAS 16 *Property, Plant and Equipment*, the cost of an item of property, plant and equipment includes the initial estimate of the costs of any decommissioning, restoration or similar obligation established under IAS 37 *Provisions, Contingent Liabilities and Contingent Assets*. The total cost of the asset is depreciated over its useful economic life unless the asset is measured under a revaluation model.

At the time of initial recognition of the asset, the carrying amount of the asset includes the estimated decommissioning cost capitalised on acquisition; however, the tax authorities may only permit tax deductions for the purchase price of the asset, with tax deductions for decommissioning costs allowed only as the decommissioning costs are paid.

IAS 12 contains no specific guidance on decommissioning obligations and there are two acceptable approaches. One approach is to apply the requirements of the Standard in the normal way to the separate asset and liability. The alternative approach views the asset and its related decommissioning liability together. Both of these methods are seen in practice.

Approach 1: view asset and liability separately

Under this approach, at initial recognition the tax base of the asset is generally its purchase price and excludes the capitalised decommissioning costs, thereby creating a taxable temporary difference. Because the temporary difference arises on the initial recognition of the asset, no deferred tax liability is recognised on acquisition in accordance with IAS 12:15. Assuming the asset is not being remeasured, if there are subsequent increases in the estimate of the decommissioning obligation, this will result in an increase in the carrying amount of the asset in accordance with IFRIC 1 *Changes in Existing Decommissioning, Restoration and Similar Liabilities*. This increases the temporary difference associated with the asset and a deferred tax liability is recognised in accordance with the general principles of IAS 12. Changes in the temporary difference giving rise to deferred tax may also arise in subsequent periods if the depreciation period differs from the period over which tax deductions are received.

Any subsequent decreases in the estimate of the decommissioning obligation would lead to a corresponding reduction in the carrying amount of the asset. If this reduces the temporary difference that existed at initial recognition, there are no deferred tax consequences.

The tax base of the decommissioning liability is the carrying amount less deductions to be received as the costs are incurred. Assuming deductions will be received when the costs are paid, the tax base of the liability is nil. Therefore, at initial recognition a deductible temporary difference exists but, similar to the asset above, no deferred tax asset is recognised because the temporary difference arises on initial recognition of the decommissioning liability.

The carrying amount of the decommissioning obligation will subsequently be increased by the unwinding of the discount, and will also be adjusted for any change in estimate of the ultimate cash outflows. An increase in the temporary difference associated with the liability will give rise to the recognition of a deferred tax asset in accordance with the general principles of IAS 12.

An increase in estimate of the decommissioning obligation will, therefore, lead to the recognition of a deferred tax liability in respect of the related asset and a deferred tax asset in respect of the decommissioning liability.

Approach 2: view asset and liability together

The other acceptable approach seen in practice is to view the asset and its related decommissioning liability in aggregate. This approach seeks to reflect the linkage between the asset and the related decommissioning liability and recognises deferred taxes on the aggregate temporary difference, rather than the two individual temporary differences. This method yields an effective tax rate that more closely reflects the economics of the asset ownership over its life.

This approach is based on the view that the decommissioning asset and the obligation are related and, therefore, should be viewed as a whole. The temporary differences related to the asset and the liability are aggregated and deferred taxes are recognised only on an overall temporary difference.

Subsequently, as the asset is depreciated and the decommissioning liability increases with the unwind of interest (using the effective interest method), a temporary difference will arise in respect of which deferred taxes should be recognised.

5.10 Hedge of net investment in a foreign operation

Entities sometimes enter into transactions to hedge their net investment in a foreign subsidiary (e.g. through the use of a foreign currency loan, or a forward contract). Under IFRS 9 *Financial Instruments* (or, for entities that have not yet adopted IFRS 9, IAS 39 *Financial Instruments: Recognition and Measurement*), such a transaction may be designated as a hedge of the foreign currency exposure of a net investment in a foreign operation (see **chapter B9** or, for entities that have not yet adopted IFRS 9, see **chapter C9**). Gains and losses on the effective portion of such hedging transactions are recognised in other comprehensive income in the entity's consolidated financial statements.

If the tax base of the hedging instrument is different from its carrying amount, this creates a temporary difference and deferred tax should be recognised. This is the case regardless of whether deferred tax has been provided in respect of the parent's investment in a foreign subsidiary. To the extent that the hedge is effective, the tax consequences of establishing a deferred tax asset or liability for the hedging transaction are reported in other comprehensive income in accordance with IAS 12:61A. Recognition of amounts outside profit or loss is discussed further at **section 4.7.3**.

Example 5.10

Hedge of a net investment in a foreign subsidiary

Company A (functional currency Sterling) has a wholly-owned US subsidiary, Company B (functional currency US$), which has net assets of US$120,000. Company A hedges its net investment in Company B using a US$100,000 loan. Assuming that the hedge is perfectly effective and that all the other hedge accounting requirements of IFRS 9 (or, for entities that have not yet adopted IFRS 9, IAS 39) are met, the exchange gain or loss on retranslating the loan

---

will be recognised in other comprehensive income in Company A's consolidated financial statements. When the retranslation of the loan changes its carrying amount, but not its tax base, deferred tax on the resulting temporary difference is also recognised in other comprehensive income.

5.11 Deferred tax resulting from impairment of assets

As discussed in **chapter A10**, IAS 36 *Impairment of Assets* requires that a review for impairment be carried out if events or changes in circumstances indicate that the carrying amount of certain assets within the scope of IAS 36 may not be recoverable. An asset is considered to be impaired when its recoverable amount declines below its carrying amount. The recoverable amount of an asset is the higher of its fair value less costs of disposal and its value in use.

The calculation of the impairment loss is based on an assumption that the entity will choose to recover the carrying amount of the asset in the most beneficial way. Therefore, if the entity could earn more by selling the asset rather than by continuing to use it, it would choose to sell the asset, and vice versa.

Although an impairment loss may be measured under IAS 36 by reference to fair value less costs of disposal, rather than value in use, this does not necessarily mean that, for the purposes of measuring the related deferred tax asset or liability, management must change its expected manner of recovery in accordance with IAS 12:51A, and now use the tax base applicable to recovery through sale rather than use.

Impairment losses recognised in respect of assets carried on a historical cost basis are recognised in profit or loss; for assets carried at a revalued amount, impairment losses are treated as revaluation decreases (which may or may not lead to an expense being recognised in profit or loss).

Because an impairment loss affects the carrying amount of an asset, it affects the relationship between the asset's carrying amount and its tax base. Therefore, any deferred tax asset or liability is determined by comparing the revised carrying amount of the asset with its tax base. [IAS 36:64]

In many jurisdictions, tax deductions for assets are received at a faster rate than expense is recognised for financial reporting purposes, either because of differing depreciation methods or because different useful lives are ascribed under tax law. While this generally results in a deferred tax liability position, the recognition of an impairment loss in a reporting period may cause the carrying amount of the asset to fall below its tax base (see **example 9.1** in **chapter A10**).

In accordance with IAS 12, an entity recognises a deferred tax asset to the extent that it is probable that taxable profit will be available against which the deductible temporary difference can be utilised (see **section 4.6** for recognition of deferred tax assets).

5.12   Group relief

The deferred tax position of each group entity should be determined separately and the results aggregated (with some adjustments) to determine the group position. Adjustments may need to be made to reflect the deferred tax consequences of the availability of group relief altering the view of recoverability of deferred tax assets.

When losses are expected to be surrendered to another group entity that is expected to pay for the group relief then the 'deferred tax asset' may well be assessed as recoverable and recognised even though the 'asset' is actually a receipt from another group entity that recovers it from the tax authority. When losses are expected to be surrendered to another group entity but no payment is likely to be received, the entity surrendering the losses would not normally be able to assess the asset as recoverable. However, the deferred tax asset would be recognised on consolidation to the extent that the other entity is expected to utilise the losses.

When a payment is made between group entities in consideration for the transfer of tax losses, it is necessary to exercise judgement to determine the substance of the transaction (see **2.10**).

6   Presentation and disclosure

6.1   Presentation

6.1.1   Tax expense

The tax expense or income related to profit or loss from ordinary activities should be presented as part of profit or loss in the statement(s) of profit or loss and other comprehensive income. [IAS 12:77]

IAS 12 notes that, although IAS 21 *The Effects of Changes in Foreign Exchange Rates* requires certain exchange differences to be recognised as income or expense, that Standard does not specify where such differences should be presented in the statement of comprehensive income. Therefore, IAS 12 states that when exchange differences on deferred foreign tax liabilities or assets are recognised in the statement of comprehensive income, such differences may be classified as deferred tax expense (income) if that presentation is considered to be the most useful to financial statement users. [IAS 12:78]

An entity may incur expenses that are linked to the income tax expense, for example, fees payable to tax consultants for their tax advice (see also **2.9**) and to accountants who assist the entity in preparing its tax returns.

Amounts paid other than to the tax authority in connection with an entity's tax expense do not represent income taxes. Therefore, such amounts should be treated as either an administrative or other expense in the entity's statement of comprehensive income depending on the format adopted, i.e. classification of expenses either by function or by nature.

When a payment is made between group entities in consideration for the transfer of tax losses, it is necessary to exercise judgement to determine the substance of the transaction (see **2.10**).

Example 6.1.1

Presentation of payments of non-income taxes that can be claimed as an allowance against taxable profit

Entity A is required to make production-based royalty payments to Taxing Authority 1. These payments can be claimed as an allowance against taxable profit for the computation of income taxes payable to Taxing Authority 2. The production-based royalty payments do not, in themselves, meet the definition of income tax and, therefore, are outside the scope of IAS 12 (see **2.1**), whereas the income tax payable to Taxing Authority 2 is within the scope of IAS 12.

Should the production-based royalty payments to Taxing Authority 1 be presented as a tax expense in Entity A's statement of comprehensive income?

No. The 'tax expense' line item required to be presented under paragraph 82(d) of IAS 1 is intended to require an entity to present taxes that meet the definition of income taxes under IAS 12. Because the production-based royalty payments are not income taxes, they should not be presented within that line item.

The conclusions above were confirmed by the IFRS Interpretations Committee in the July 2012 *IFRIC Update*.

It is possible for an entity to designate a derivative as a cash flow hedge of the cash flow variability of a tax liability arising on the foreign exchange gain or loss on a foreign currency borrowing. Provided that such a hedge has been appropriately designated and documented, the hedge is a qualifying cash flow hedge of a non-financial liability (the tax liability) under IFRS 9 *Financial Instruments* (or, for entities that have not yet adopted IFRS 9, IAS 39 *Financial Instruments: Recognition and Measurement*).

Both IFRS 9 and IAS 39, the Standards which prescribe the hedge accounting rules in terms of recognition and measurement, are silent on where the gains and losses on derivatives designated as hedging derivatives should be presented within profit or loss. It has become customary, and is useful to the users of the financial statements, for the hedging effects of derivatives to be presented in the statement of comprehensive income in the same line as the item that they hedge. Therefore, although the hedging gain or loss is clearly not an income tax as defined by IAS 12, an argument can be made for including the effects of the derivatives, which an entity has entered into as hedges of its tax liability, in the tax line in the statement of comprehensive income.

When an entity chooses to present derivative gains/losses relating to designated tax hedging derivatives within the tax line, this accounting policy choice should be applied consistently from period to period. Furthermore, appropriate separate disclosure in the notes of the amount attributable to hedging gains/losses should be made.

6.1.2   Presentation of the release of a deferred tax liability on disposal of an asset

---

Example 6.1.2

Presentation of the release of a deferred tax liability on disposal of an asset

Entity X owns an asset and has recognised a deferred tax liability resulting from accelerated tax depreciation on that asset.

Entity Y purchases the asset from Entity X and, as permitted by local tax law, elects to retain the tax base of the asset as it was when held by Entity X. As a result of this election, Entity X pays no tax on the disposal of the asset, but the proceeds of disposal received from Entity Y are lower than would otherwise be expected to reflect the reduced tax allowance available to Entity Y.

When Entity X derecognises the related deferred tax liability on disposal of the asset, should this reversal be presented as part of the gain or loss on disposal of the asset or as part of tax expense (tax income)?

The reversal of the deferred tax liability should be presented as part of Entity X's tax expense (tax income) because it falls within the definition of tax expense (tax income) in IAS 12:5 ("the aggregate amount included in the determination of profit or loss for the period in respect of current tax and deferred tax").

The deferred tax expense previously recognised reflected the expected tax consequences with regards to the recovery of the asset. Actual recovery of the value of the asset has been achieved with no tax payable. Therefore, from Entity X's perspective, the temporary difference has reversed and the effect of that reversal should be reflected as part of tax expense (tax income).

6.1.3   Statement of financial position

The presentation of both current and deferred tax in the statement of financial position is addressed in IAS 1 (and not in IAS 12) as follows:

- liabilities and assets for current tax should be presented in the statement of financial position; [IAS 1:54]

- deferred tax liabilities and deferred tax assets should be presented in the statement of financial position; [IAS 1:54] and

- when an entity presents current and non-current assets, and current and non-current liabilities, as separate classifications in its statement of financial position, it should not classify deferred tax assets (liabilities) as current assets (liabilities). [IAS 1:56]

Liabilities or assets arising from uncertain tax positions should be included in the statement of financial position within the amounts for current tax liabilities (or assets) and presented as current or non-current based on the general principles of IAS 1. The effect of uncertain tax positions on profit or loss or other comprehensive income (depending on the nature of the uncertain tax position) should be included in the same line item as tax expense (income).

Although uncertain tax positions are similar in nature to provisions as defined in IAS 37 *Provisions, Contingent Liabilities and Contingent Assets* (see **3.3.3.3**), it would be inappropriate to present the resulting liabilities with other provisions recognised under IAS 37, because they are explicitly excluded from the scope of IAS 37.

6.1.4   Offset of tax assets and liabilities

6.1.4.1   Offset of tax assets and liabilities – general

In a similar approach to that taken in IAS 1, IAS 12 takes a strong line on the extent to which tax assets and liabilities can be offset against one another to present only a net figure in the statement of financial position.

6.1.4.2   Offset of current tax assets and liabilities

An entity should offset current tax assets and current tax liabilities if, and only if, the entity:

[IAS 12:71]

- has a legally enforceable right to set off the recognised amounts; and

- intends either to settle on a net basis, or to realise the asset and settle the liability simultaneously.

IAS 12 explains that an entity normally has a legally enforceable right to set off current tax assets against current tax liabilities when they relate to income taxes levied by the same tax authority, and that authority permits the entity to make or receive a single net payment. [IAS 12:72]

When an entity is preparing consolidated financial statements, current tax assets and liabilities arising from different group entities should not be offset unless:

[IAS 12:73]

- the entities concerned have a legally enforceable right to make or receive a single net payment; and

- the entities intend to make or receive such a net payment or to recover the asset and settle the liability simultaneously.

6.1.4.3   Offset of deferred tax assets and liabilities

An entity should offset deferred tax assets and deferred tax liabilities if, and only if:

[IAS 12:74]

- the entity has a legally enforceable right to set off current tax assets against current tax liabilities; and

- the deferred tax assets and the deferred tax liabilities relate to income taxes levied by the same tax authority on either:

  - the same taxable entity; or

  - different taxable entities which intend either to settle current tax liabilities and assets on a net basis, or to realise the assets and settle the liabilities simultaneously, in each future period in which significant amounts of deferred tax liabilities or assets are expected to be settled or recovered.

Under the above rules, deferred tax assets and liabilities arising in the same legal entity (which is also a single taxable entity) can generally be offset. However, when, for example, the taxable entity has capital losses carried forward that can only be used to reduce future capital gains, those losses can only be offset against deferred tax liabilities to the extent that recognised deferred tax liabilities arise from unrealised capital gains.

In a consolidation situation, the first condition to overcome is the requirement for the balances to be levied by the same tax authority. This effectively prohibits the offset of deferred tax assets and liabilities arising in different jurisdictions.

Even for entities operating within the same jurisdiction, except when there are formal group relief or consolidated taxation arrangements, it will be unusual for the tax authority to permit net settlement between different taxable entities.

Therefore, in preparing consolidated financial statements, the deferred tax balances of the separate entities will generally be aggregated without further setting off the deferred tax balances of one entity against those of another.

The above rules mean that, for disclosure purposes, there is no need for detailed scheduling of the timing of reversals of each temporary difference. In rare circumstances, an entity may have a legally enforceable right of set-off, and an intention to settle net, for some periods but not for others. In such situations, detailed scheduling may be required to establish reliably whether the deferred tax liability of one taxable entity will result in increased tax payments in the same period in which a deferred tax asset of another taxable entity will result in decreased payments by that second taxable entity. [IAS 12:75 & 76]

When an entity is required to offset deferred tax assets and deferred tax liabilities in its statement of financial position because it meets the conditions in IAS 12:74 (see above), the entity is not necessarily entitled to offset the related deferred tax income and deferred tax expense. IAS 12:58 requires the individual components of tax expense or tax benefit to be allocated to profit or loss for the period except to the extent that the tax arises from a transaction or event which is recognised in the same or a different period outside of profit and loss, either in other comprehensive income or directly in equity. The ability to offset the amounts in the statement of financial position does not override the requirement for the income and expense to be appropriately classified.

Example 6.1.4.3

Offsetting deferred tax income and expense

During the year, Company A revalues an item of property, plant and equipment upward by CU1,000 to CU21,000, recognising the increase in other comprehensive income. The tax base of the property, plant and equipment is CU20,000.

At the same time, Company A incurs an operating tax loss of CU800 during the period which, under the relevant tax legislation, can be carried forward indefinitely. The requirements for recognition of the deferred tax asset arising from the tax loss carried forward are satisfied. In addition, the requirements for offsetting deferred tax assets and liabilities in IAS 12:74 are met. The tax rate is 30 per cent.

Company A recognises a deferred tax liability of CU300 (CU1,000 temporary difference × 30%) and a deferred tax asset of CU240 (CU800 loss × 30%). The two amounts are set off in the statement of financial position so that a net deferred tax liability of CU60 (CU300 – CU240) is recognised. However, the deferred tax arising on the revaluation is recognised in other comprehensive income and the effect of the current year's loss is recognised in profit or loss.

6.2 Disclosure

6.2.1 Statement of comprehensive income

6.2.1.1 Major components of tax expense (income)

The major components of tax expense (income) should be disclosed separately, including:

[IAS 12:79 & 80]

- current tax expense (income);

- any adjustments recognised in the period for current tax of prior periods;

- the amount of deferred tax expense (income) relating to the origination and reversal of temporary differences;

- the amount of deferred tax expense (income) relating to changes in tax rates or the imposition of new taxes;

- the amount of the benefit arising from a previously unrecognised tax loss, tax credit or temporary difference of a prior period that is used to reduce current tax expense;

- the amount of the benefit from a previously unrecognised tax loss, tax credit or temporary difference of a prior period that is used to reduce deferred tax expense;

- deferred tax expense arising from the write-down, or reversal of a previous write-down, of a deferred tax asset in accordance with IAS 12:56; and

- the amount of tax expense (income) relating to those changes in accounting policies and errors that are included in profit or loss in accordance with IAS 8 *Accounting Policies, Changes in Accounting Estimates and Errors*, because they cannot be accounted for retrospectively.

In respect of discontinued operations, the financial statements should disclose separately the tax expense relating to:

[IAS 12:81(h)]

- the gain or loss on discontinuance; and

- the profit or loss from the ordinary activities of the discontinued operation for the period, together with the corresponding amounts for each prior period presented.

For each type of temporary difference, and each type of unused tax losses and unused tax credits, the financial statements should disclose the amount of the deferred tax income or expense recognised in profit or loss, if this is not apparent from the changes in the amounts recognised in the statement of financial position. [IAS 12:81(g)(ii)]

6.2.1.2   Reconciliation of tax expense or income

IAS 12 requires the presentation of an explanation of the relationship between the tax expense (income) and accounting profit in either or both of the following forms:

[IAS 12:81(c) & 86]

- a numerical reconciliation between tax expense (income) and the product of accounting profit multiplied by the applicable tax rate(s), disclosing also the basis on which the applicable tax rate(s) is (are) computed; or

- a numerical reconciliation between the average effective tax rate (being the tax expense (income) divided by the accounting profit) and the applicable tax rate, disclosing also the basis on which the applicable tax rate is computed.

An explanation is required of changes in the applicable tax rate(s) compared to the previous accounting period. [IAS 12:81(d)]

6.2.2   Statement of financial position

For each type of temporary difference, and each type of unused tax losses and unused tax credits, the financial statements should disclose the amount of the deferred tax assets and liabilities recognised in the statement of financial position for each period presented. The amount of deferred tax income or expense recognised in profit or loss in respect of each temporary difference must also be disclosed where it is not apparent from the changes in the amounts recognised in the statement of financial position. [IAS 12:81(g)(i)]

The following should also be disclosed:

[IAS 12:81(e) & (f)]

- the amount (and expiry date, if any) of deductible temporary differences, unused tax losses and unused tax credits for which no deferred tax asset is recognised in the statement of financial position; and

- the aggregate amount of temporary differences associated with investments in subsidiaries, branches and associates and interests in joint arrangements, for which deferred tax liabilities have not been recognised.

It would often be impracticable to compute the amount of unrecognised deferred tax liabilities arising from investments in subsidiaries, branches and associates and interests in joint arrangements, so IAS 12 requires an entity to disclose the aggregate amount of the underlying temporary differences but does not require disclosure of the deferred tax liabilities.

Nevertheless, when practicable, entities are encouraged to disclose the amounts of the unrecognised deferred tax liabilities because financial statement users may find such information useful. [IAS 12:87]

An entity should disclose the amount of a deferred tax asset and the nature of the evidence supporting its recognition, when:

[IAS 12:82]

- the utilisation of the deferred tax asset is dependent on future taxable profits in excess of the profits arising from the reversal of existing taxable temporary differences; and

- the entity has suffered a loss in either the current or preceding period in the tax jurisdiction to which the deferred tax asset relates.

When current and deferred tax assets and liabilities are measured at the tax rate applicable to undistributed profits, but the net income taxes payable will be affected if part of the retained earnings is paid out as a dividend to shareholders, the entity should disclose:

[IAS 12:82A & 87A]

- the nature of the potential income tax consequences that would result from the payment of dividends to its shareholders. This includes the important features of the income tax systems and the factors that will affect the amount of the potential income tax consequences of dividends;

- the amounts of the potential income tax consequences that are practicably determinable; and

- whether there are any potential income tax consequences that are not practicably determinable.

It is not always practicable to compute the total amount of the potential income tax consequences that would result from the payment of dividends to shareholders (e.g. when an entity has a lot of overseas subsidiaries). However, even in such circumstances, usually some consequences may be easily determinable, and these should be disclosed. IAS 12 cites the example of a consolidated group, when the parent and some of its subsidiaries may have paid income taxes at a higher rate on undistributed profits and are aware of the amount that would be refunded on the payment of future dividends to shareholders from consolidated retained earnings. In this case, the refundable amount is disclosed.

When some or all potential income tax consequences cannot be determined, the entity should disclose that there are additional potential income tax consequences not practicably determinable. In the parent's separate financial statements, the disclosure of the potential income tax consequences relates to the parent's retained earnings. [IAS 12:87B]

When current and deferred tax assets and liabilities are measured at the tax rate applicable to undistributed profits, but the net income taxes payable will be affected if part of the retained earnings is paid out as a dividend to shareholders, an entity required to provide the disclosures listed above may also be required to provide disclosures related to temporary differences associated with investments in subsidiaries, branches and associates or interests in joint arrangements. For example, an entity may be required to disclose the aggregate amount of temporary differences associated with investments in subsidiaries for which no deferred tax liabilities have been recognised. [IAS 12:81(f)] If it is impracticable to compute the amounts of unrecognised deferred tax liabilities there may be amounts of potential income tax consequences of dividends not practicably determinable related to these subsidiaries. [IAS 12:87C]

6.2.3   Other disclosure requirements

Other disclosure requirements include:

- the aggregate current and deferred tax relating to items that are charged or credited directly to equity; [IAS 12:81(a)]

- the amount of income tax relating to each component of other comprehensive income (revaluation surplus, foreign exchange reserve etc.); [IAS 12:81(ab)]

- the amount of income tax consequences of dividends to shareholders of the entity that were proposed or declared before the financial statements were authorised for issue, but are not recognised as a liability in the financial statements; [IAS 12:81(i)]

- if a business combination in which the entity is the acquirer causes a change in the amount recognised for its pre-acquisition deferred tax asset (under IAS 12:67 – see **5.1.6**), the amount of that change; [IAS 12:81(j)]

- if the deferred tax benefits acquired in a business combination are not recognised at the acquisition date but are recognised after the acquisition date (under IAS 12:68 – see **5.1.8**), a description of the event or change in circumstances that caused the deferred tax benefits to be recognised; [IAS 12:81(k)]

- any tax-related contingent liabilities and contingent assets in accordance with IAS 37 (e.g. from unresolved disputes with the tax authorities); [IAS 12:88] and

- when changes in tax rates or tax laws are enacted or announced after the reporting period, any significant impact on the entity's current and deferred tax assets and liabilities. [IAS 10:22(h) & IAS 12:88]

The disclosure for uncertain tax positions is governed not only by the requirements of IAS 12 but also by the requirement under IAS 1:116 to disclose key sources of estimation uncertainty when there is a significant risk of a material adjustment in carrying amounts of assets and liabilities within the next financial year (see **7.3** in **chapter A4**).

When the uncertain tax position gives rise to a contingent tax liability for which no provision is recognised (e.g. because it is not probable that a payment will be made to the tax authority), an entity must still consider the requirements of IAS 12:88, which states that "[a]n entity discloses any tax-related contingent liabilities and contingent assets in accordance with IAS 37 ... contingent liabilities and contingent assets may arise, for example, from unresolved disputes with the taxation authorities".

7 Future developments

In August 2014, the IASB issued exposure draft ED/2014/3 *Recognition of Deferred Tax Assets for Unrealised Losses (Proposed amendments to IAS 12)*. The exposure draft proposes amendments to IAS 12 to clarify the recognition of deferred tax assets for unrealised losses related to debt instruments measured at fair value.

The proposed amendments would clarify the following:

- that unrealised losses on debt instruments measured at fair value and measured at cost for tax purposes can give rise to deductible temporary differences; and

- that the carrying amount of an asset does not limit the estimation of probable future taxable profits. The amended Standard would specify that, when comparing deductible temporary differences with future taxable profits, the future taxable profits would exclude tax deductions resulting from the reversal of those deductible temporary differences.

The comment period on this exposure draft ended on 18 December 2014. At the time of writing, final amendments are expected late in 2015 or early in 2016.

A14 Revenue from contracts with customers

Contents

1   Introduction

1.1   Overview of IFRS 15

IFRS 15 *Revenue from Contracts with Customers* outlines a single comprehensive model for entities to use in accounting for revenue arising from contracts with customers. The core principle is that an entity recognises revenue to depict the transfer of goods or services to customers in an amount that reflects the consideration to which the entity expects to be entitled in exchange for those goods or services.

IFRS 15 was issued in May 2014 and is required to be applied for annual periods beginning on or after 1 January 2018 (see **15.1**). For annual periods beginning before 1 January 2018, entities may continue to apply the predecessor Standards and related Interpretations (see below). Alternatively, entities may choose to apply IFRS 15 in advance of the effective date, provided that they disclose that fact (see **section 15** for detailed transition provisions).

IFRS 15 supersedes the following:

- IAS 18 *Revenue* (see **appendix A1**);

- IAS 11 *Construction Contracts* (see **appendix A2**);

- IFRIC 13 *Customer Loyalty Programmes* (see **5.6** in **appendix A1**);

- IFRIC 15 *Agreements for the Construction of Real Estate* (see **2.2** in **appendix A1**);

- IFRIC 18 *Transfers of Assets from Customers* (see **2.4** in **appendix A1**); and

- SIC-31 *Revenue-Barter Transactions Involving Advertising Services* (see **4.5** in **appendix A1**).

1.2   Comparison of IFRS 15 with predecessor IFRSs

IFRS 15 is a complex Standard, introducing far more prescriptive requirements than were previously included in IFRSs, and it may result in substantial changes to revenue recognition policies for some entities. It requires the application of significant judgement in some areas, but in other areas it is relatively prescriptive, allowing little room for judgement.

Whereas IAS 18 provides separate revenue recognition criteria for goods and services, this distinction is removed under IFRS 15. The new Standard focuses instead on the identification of performance obligations and distinguishes between performance obligations that are satisfied 'at a point in time' and those that are satisfied 'over time', which is determined by the manner in which control of goods or services passes to the customer. The new model means that revenue may be recognised over time for some deliverables previously accounted for as goods (e.g. some contract manufacturing); it also means that revenue may be recognised at a point in time for some deliverables previously accounted for as services (e.g. some construction contracts).

Specific topics on which more prescriptive requirements have been introduced include:

* the identification of a contract with a customer;
* the identification of distinct performance obligations and the allocation of the transaction price between those obligations;
* accounting for variable consideration and significant financing components;
* recognition of revenue arising from licences; and
* presentation and disclosure of revenue from contracts with customers, and other balances related to revenue.

Other changes include:

* the scope of IFRS 15 has been expanded to cover costs relating to contracts, distinguishing between costs of obtaining a contract and costs of fulfilling a contract, and providing detailed guidance on when it is appropriate to capitalise such costs;
* whereas IAS 11 provides specific requirements for accounting for construction contracts, such contracts are accounted for in accordance with the general principles of IFRS 15;
* the recognition of interest revenue and dividend revenue are not within the scope of IFRS 15. These matters are now dealt with under IFRS 9 *Financial Instruments* (or, for entities that have not yet adopted IFRS 9, IAS 39 *Financial Instruments: Recognition and Measurement*); and
* specifically excluded from the scope of IFRS 15 are non-monetary exchanges between entities in the same line of business to facilitate sales to customers or potential customers. This scope exclusion is different from the related guidance under IAS 18:12 which refers to exchange transactions that are not regarded as transactions that generate revenue – these are transactions in which goods or services are "exchanged or swapped for goods or services which are of a similar nature and value".

The disclosures required by IFRS 15 are likely to be much more extensive than those previously provided in accordance with IAS 11 and IAS 18, and additional disclosures are also required in interim financial reports prepared in accordance with IAS 34 *Interim Financial Reporting*. In some cases, entities may need to consider changes to existing systems and processes in order to capture the information to be disclosed.

1.3   Amendments to IFRS 15 since the last edition of this manual

None. IFRS 15 has not been amended since it was issued in May 2014.

1.4   Application of the IFRS 15 framework

The overview below is intended to provide a guide for users to navigate the key concepts of IFRS 15. The overview does not summarise all of the requirements of the Standard – users should refer to the more detailed discussions later in this chapter and to the text of the Standard for a complete understanding.

In order to meet the core principle of recognising revenue to depict the transfer of promised goods or services to customers in an amount that reflects the amount of consideration to which an entity expects to be entitled in exchange for those goods or services, IFRS 15 adopts a five-step model (see **section 4** for background).

Requirement of the Standard	Detailed discussion
Step 1 requires an entity to **identify the contract** with the customer. A contract does not have to be written in order for it to meet the criteria for revenue recognition; however, it does need to create enforceable rights and obligations. IFRS 15 provides detailed guidance on how to identify a contract. This step also considers when it is appropriate to combine contracts (see **5.5**) and the implications for revenue recognition of modifying a contract (see **section 10**).	Section 5
Step 2 requires an entity to **identify the distinct goods or services** promised within the contract. Distinct goods and services should be accounted for as separate deliverables (this process is sometimes known as 'unbundling'). These distinct goods and services are referred to as 'performance obligations'. Specific guidance should be considered to determine whether a good or service is distinct. Further guidance is also provided in IFRS 15 to identify distinct performance obligations in particular scenarios: • warranties (see **6.3.4**); • customer options to purchase additional goods and services at a discount (or for free) (see **6.3.5**); and • non-refundable upfront fees (see **6.3.6**).	Section 6
Step 3 requires an entity to **determine the transaction price** for the contract. This will be affected by a number of factors including: • variable consideration (see **section 7.2**); • the extent to which the recognition of variable consideration should be constrained (see **7.3**);	Section 7

• significant financing components within a contract, which will require an adjustment for the time value of money (see **section 7.4**);	
• if non-cash consideration is received in exchange for transferring promised goods or services (see **7.5**); and	
• if any consideration is payable to the customer as part of the transaction (see **7.6**).	
Step 4 requires an entity to **allocate the transaction price** determined in Step 3 to the performance obligations identified in Step 2. IFRS 15 requires this allocation to be based on the stand-alone selling price of each performance obligation and includes detailed requirements on how any discounts or variable consideration should be treated in the allocation (see **8.3** and **8.5**, respectively). Further guidance is included within IFRS 15 regarding how entities should account for: • 'breakage' (customers' unexercised rights) (see **section 7.7**); and • changes in the transaction price (see **8.6**). In principle, allocation on a stand-alone selling price basis requires a calculation to be performed for each contract containing more than one performance obligation. This may prove a significant logistical challenge for entities with a very large number of different contracts, and in some cases changes to existing systems may be needed.	**Section 8**
Step 5 specifies how an entity should **determine when to recognise revenue** in relation to a performance obligation, and whether that revenue should be recognised at a point in time or over a period of time. IFRS 15 focuses on when control of the good or service passes to the customer, which may be over time or at a point in time.	**Section 9**
IFRS 15 includes specific guidance on licences. It distinguishes between two different types of licence (right of use and right to access), with the timing of revenue recognition being different for each.	**Section 11**
IFRS 15 includes guidance on how to account for **costs relating to a contract**, distinguishing between costs of obtaining a contract and costs of fulfilling a contract. When this results in costs being capitalised, additional guidance is provided on determining an appropriate amortisation period and on impairment considerations.	**Section 12**
Detailed guidance is provided in IFRS 15 on both the **presentation and disclosure** of the revenue balance, and other balances related to revenue in the financial statements.	**Sections 13 and 14**

On adoption of IFRS 15, entities are able to **transition** using either: • a fully retrospective approach (with some elective practical expedients); or • a modified approach to retrospective application, which requires a cumulative catch-up adjustment to be made to equity at the start of the year in which the Standard is first applied (i.e. prior years presented are not restated).	**Section 15**

1.5 Convergence project with FASB

IFRS 15 is the result of a convergence project between the IASB and the US Financial Accounting Standards Board (FASB). IFRS 15 and the equivalent US standard are nearly fully converged, the main differences relating to:

[IFRS 15: Appendix A to Basis for Conclusions]

• the collectability threshold for contracts;

• interim disclosures;

• timing of adoption;

• reversal of impairment losses; and

• requirements for non-public entities.

1.6 Transition Resource Group for Revenue Recognition

Following the publication of IFRS 15, and the equivalent US GAAP standard, the IASB and the FASB formed the IASB/FASB Joint Transition Resource Group for Revenue Recognition (TRG) to help the boards identify and consider any diversity in practice in applying the standards and to address implementation issues as they arise. See **16.1** for further details.

2 Definitions

Appendix A to IFRS 15 provides the following definitions for terms used in the Standard.

• A **contract** is defined as "[a]n agreement between two or more parties that creates enforceable rights and obligations".

• A **contract asset** is defined as "[a]n entity's right to consideration in exchange for goods or services that the entity has transferred to a customer when that right is conditioned on something other than the passage of time (for example, the entity's future performance)".

- A **contract liability** is defined as "[a]n entity's obligation to transfer goods or services to a customer for which the entity has received consideration (or the amount is due) from the customer".

- A **customer** is defined as "[a] party that has contracted with an entity to obtain goods or services that are an output of the entity's ordinary activities in exchange for consideration".

- **Income** is defined as "[i]ncreases in economic benefits during the accounting period in the form of inflows or enhancements of assets or decreases of liabilities that result in an increase in equity, other than those relating to contributions from equity participants".

- A **performance obligation** is defined as "[a] promise in a contract with a customer to transfer to the customer either:

  (a) a good or service (or a bundle of goods or services) that is distinct; or

  (b) a series of distinct goods or services that are substantially the same and that have the same pattern of transfer to the customer".

- **Revenue** is defined as "[i]ncome arising in the course of an entity's ordinary activities".

- The **stand-alone selling price** of a good or service is defined as "[t]he price at which an entity would sell a promised good or service separately to a customer".

- The **transaction price** for a contract with a customer is defined as "[t]he amount of consideration to which an entity expects to be entitled in exchange for transferring promised goods or services to a customer, excluding amounts collected on behalf of third parties".

3   General principles and scope

3.1   Objective of IFRS 15

The objective of IFRS 15 is to establish the principles that should be applied by an entity in order to report useful information to users of financial statements about the nature, amount, timing and uncertainty of revenue and cash flows arising from a contract with a customer. [IFRS 15:1]

3.2   Core principle of IFRS 15

The core principle of IFRS 15 is that an entity recognises revenue to depict the transfer of promised goods or services to customers, reflecting the amount of consideration to which the entity expects to be entitled in exchange for those goods or services. [IFRS 15:2]

When applying IFRS 15, it is important to evaluate the terms of the contract and all relevant facts and circumstances. [IFRS 15:3]

3.3 Consistent application of IFRS 15

IFRS 15 should be applied consistently to contracts with similar characteristics and in similar circumstances. This requirement for consistent application is specifically extended to the use of any practical expedients. [IFRS 15:3]

3.4 Practical expedient – application to a portfolio of contracts (or performance obligations)

Although IFRS 15 specifies the accounting for an individual contract with a customer, the Standard allows as a practical expedient that it can be applied to a portfolio of contracts (or performance obligations) with similar characteristics provided that it is reasonably expected that the effects on the financial statements of applying a portfolio approach will not differ materially from applying IFRS 15 to the individual contracts (or performance obligations) within that portfolio. When accounting for a portfolio, estimates and assumptions that reflect the size and composition of the portfolio should be used. [IFRS 15:4]

Some entities manage a very large number of customer contracts and offer a wide array of product combination options (e.g. entities in the telecommunications industry may offer a wide selection of handsets and wireless usage plan options). For these entities, it would take significant effort to apply some of the requirements of IFRS 15 (e.g. the requirement to allocate the stand-alone selling price to the identified performance obligations as described in **section 8**) on an individual contract basis. In addition, the capability of information technology systems to capture the relevant information may be limited.

Entities will need to evaluate whether they are eligible to use a portfolio approach under IFRS 15:4. IFRS 15 does not provide explicit guidance on how to (1) evaluate 'similar characteristics', and (2) establish a reasonable expectation that the effects of applying a portfolio approach would not differ materially from those of applying the Standard at a contract or performance obligation level. Accordingly, entities will need to exercise significant judgement in determining that the contracts or performance obligations that they have segregated into portfolios have similar characteristics at a sufficiently granular level to ensure that the outcome of using a particular portfolio approach can reasonably be expected not to differ materially from the results of applying the Standard to each contract or performance obligation in the portfolio individually.

In segregating contracts (or performance obligations) with similar characteristics into portfolios, entities should apply objective criteria associated with the particular contracts or performance obligations and their accounting consequences. When determining whether particular contracts have similar characteristics, entities may find it helpful to focus particularly on those characteristics that have the most significant accounting consequences under IFRS 15 in terms of their effect on the timing of revenue recognition or the amount of revenue recognised. Accordingly, the assessment of which characteristics are most important for determining similarity will depend on an entity's specific circumstances. However, there may also be practical constraints on the entity's ability to use existing systems to analyse a portfolio of contracts, and these constraints could affect its determination of how the portfolio should be segregated.

The table below lists objective criteria that entities might consider when assessing whether particular contracts or performance obligations have similar characteristics in accordance with IFRS 15:4. Because any of the requirements in IFRS 15 could have significant consequences for a particular portfolio of contracts, the list provided is not exhaustive.

Objective criteria	Example
Contract deliverables	Mix of products and services, options to acquire additional goods and services, warranties, promotional programmes
Contract duration	Short-term, long-term, committed or expected term of contract
Terms and conditions of the contract	Rights of return, shipping terms, bill and hold, consignment, cancellation privileges and other similar clauses
Amount, form and timing of consideration	Fixed, time and material, variable, upfront fees, non-cash, significant financing component
Characteristics of the customers	Size, type, creditworthiness, geographical location, sales channel
Characteristics of the entity	Volume of contracts that include the different characteristics, historical information available
Timing of transfer of goods or services	Over time or at a point in time

Example 3.4A

Application of the portfolio approach

Entity A offers various combinations of handsets and usage plans to its customers under two-year contracts. It offers two handset models: an older model that it offers free of charge (stand-alone selling price is CU250); and the most recent model, which offers additional features and functionalities and for which the entity charges CU200 (stand-alone selling price is CU500). The entity also offers two usage plans: a 400-minute plan and an 800-minute plan. The 400-minute plan sells for CU40 per month, and the 800-minute plan sells for CU60 per month (which also corresponds to the stand-alone selling price for each plan).

The table below illustrates the possible product combinations and the allocation of consideration for each under IFRS 15.

Product combination	Total transaction price	Revenue on handset		Revenue on usage	
			% of total contract		% of total contract
	CU	CU*	revenue	CU	revenue
Customer A Old handset, 400 minutes	960	198	21	762	79
Customer B Old handset, 800 minutes	1,440	213	15	1,227	85
Customer C New handset, 400 minutes	1,160	397	34	763	66
Customer D New handset, 800 minutes	1,640	423	26	1,217	74

* In this example, the proportion of the total transaction price allocated to handset revenue is determined by comparing the stand-alone selling price for the phone to the total of the stand-alone selling prices of the components of the contract.

  Customer A: (CU250/(CU250+CU960) × CU960) = CU198

  Customer B: (CU250/(CU250+CU1,440) × CU1,440) = CU213

  Customer C: (CU500/(CU500+CU960) × CU1,160) = CU397

  Customer D: (CU500/(CU500+CU1,440) × CU1,640) = CU423

As the table indicates, the effects of each product combination on the financial statements differ from those of the other product combinations. The four customer contracts have different characteristics, and it may be difficult to demonstrate that Entity A 'reasonably expects' that the financial statement effects of applying the guidance to the portfolio (the four contracts together) 'would not differ materially' from those of applying the guidance to each individual contract. The percentage of contract consideration allocated to the handset under the various product combinations ranges from 15 per cent to 34 per cent. Entity A may consider that this range is too wide to apply a portfolio approach; if so, some level of segregation would be required. Alternatively, Entity A might determine that there are two portfolios – one for old handsets and the other for new handsets. Under this alternative approach, Entity A would need to perform additional analysis to assess whether the accounting consequences of using two rather than four portfolios would result in financial statement effects that differ materially.

The circumstances described in **example 3.4A** are relatively straightforward. In practice, however, the contracts illustrated could involve additional layers of complexity, such as (1) different contract durations; (2) different call and text messaging plans; (3) different pricing schemes (e.g. fixed or variable pricing based on usage); (4) different promotional programmes, options, and incentives; and (5) contract modifications. Accounting for such contracts could be further complicated by the rapid pace of change in product offerings.

In general, the more specific the criteria an entity uses to segregate its contracts or performance obligations into portfolios (i.e. the 'greater' the extent of disaggregation), the easier it should be for the entity to conclude that the results of applying the guidance to a particular portfolio are not expected to differ materially from the results of applying the guidance to each individual contract (or performance obligation) in the portfolio. However, further disaggregation into separate sub-portfolios is likely to improve the overall accuracy of estimates only if those sub-portfolios have some characteristics that are different. For example, segregating on the basis of geographical location may not be beneficial if similar combinations of products and services that have similar terms and conditions are sold to a similar group of customers in different geographical areas. Likewise, segregating on the basis of whether contract terms allow a right of return may not be necessary if the returns are not expected to be significant.

While there is no requirement in IFRS 15 to quantitatively evaluate whether using a portfolio approach would produce an outcome materially different from that of applying the guidance at the contract or performance obligation level, an entity should be able to demonstrate why it reasonably expects the two outcomes not to differ materially. The entity may do so by various means depending on its specific circumstances (subject to the constraints of a cost-benefit analysis). Such means include, but are not limited, to the following:

- data analytics based on reliable assumptions and underlying data (internally- or externally-generated) related to the portfolio;

- a sensitivity analysis that evaluates the characteristics of the contracts or performance obligations in the portfolio and the assumptions used to determine a range of potential differences in applying the different approaches; and

- a limited quantitative analysis, supplemented by a more extensive qualitative assessment that may be performed when the portfolios are disaggregated.

Typically, some level of objective and verifiable information would be necessary to demonstrate that using a portfolio approach would not result in a materially different outcome. An entity may also wish to (1) consider whether the costs of performing this type of analysis potentially outweigh the benefits of accounting on a portfolio basis, and (2) assess whether it is preferable to invest in systems solutions that would allow accounting on an individual contract basis.

Example 3.4B

Application of a portfolio approach to part of a customer base

Entity A is a telecommunications company that has a large number of contracts with customers with similar characteristics. Entity A does not elect to use a portfolio approach as specified in IFRS 15:4 when accounting for revenue from those contracts; instead, it has developed specialised computer systems that enable it to recognise revenue on a contract-by-contract basis.

At a later date, Entity A acquires Entity B, which operates in the same jurisdiction as Entity A and also has a large number of contracts with customers with characteristics that are similar to those of Entity A. Entity B, which does not have computer systems that would enable it to recognise revenue on a contract-by-contract basis, has previously elected to use a portfolio approach under IFRS 15:4 when accounting for revenue from those contracts.

In its consolidated financial statements, is Entity A permitted to use a portfolio approach only for contracts with Entity B's customers?

Yes. Entity A is permitted to use a portfolio approach to account for Entity B's contracts with customers provided that Entity A reasonably expects that the effects of using that approach would not differ materially from applying IFRS 15 on a contract-by-contract basis.

The requirement in IFRS 15:3 to apply IFRS 15 consistently, including the use of any practical expedients, to contracts with similar characteristics and in similar circumstances does not override the overall concept of materiality. The practical expedient in IFRS 15:4 is only available if it is reasonably expected that the financial statement effects of applying a portfolio approach would not differ materially from the effects of applying IFRS 15 to the individual contracts within that portfolio. Accordingly, it is possible for entities to prepare consolidated financial statements using a mixture of approaches because the resulting accounting effects are not reasonably expected to differ materially.

3.5 Scope of IFRS 15

3.5.1 Scope – general

IFRS 15 should be applied to all contracts with customers, except the following:

[IFRS 15:5]

(a) lease contracts within the scope of IAS 17 *Leases* (see **chapter A17**);

(b) insurance contracts within the scope of IFRS 4 *Insurance Contracts* (see **chapter A39**);

(c) financial instruments and other contractual rights or obligations within the scope of IFRS 9 *Financial Instruments* (see **volume B**) (or, for entities that have not yet adopted IFRS 9, IAS 39 *Financial Instruments: Recognition and Measurement* – see **volume C**), IFRS 10 *Consolidated Financial Statements* (see **chapter A24**), IFRS 11 *Joint Arrangements* (see **chapter A27**), IAS 27 *Separate Financial Statements* (see **chapter A29**) and IAS 28 *Investments in Associates and Joint Ventures* (see **chapter A26**); and

(d) non-monetary exchanges between entities in the same line of business to facilitate sales to customers or potential customers. For example, IFRS 15 would not apply to a contract between two oil companies that agree to an exchange of oil to fulfil demand from their customers in different specified locations on a timely basis.

Note that the wording in (d) above is different from the equivalent requirement in IAS 18. IAS 18 instead refers to goods or services that are "exchanged or swapped for goods or services which are of a similar nature and value". [IAS 18:12]

Entities are not permitted to recognise revenue arising from a non-monetary transaction that is scoped out of the Standard in accordance with IFRS 15:5(d). As explained in IFRS 15:BC58, the IASB noted that, in an exchange transaction of this nature, the party exchanging inventory with the entity meets the definition of a customer and that, in the absence of this specific scope exclusion, entities might recognise revenue once for the exchange of inventory and then again for the sale of inventory to the end customer. The IASB concluded that this outcome would be inappropriate because it would have grossed up revenues and expenses, making it difficult for financial statement users to assess the entity's performance and gross margins. In addition, the counterparty in such an exchange transaction could be viewed as acting as a supplier rather than as a customer.

Example 3.5.1

Accounting for the lapse of warrants

An entity has issued warrants (options issued on the entity's own shares) for cash. These warrants meet the definition of equity instruments under IAS 32 *Financial Instruments: Presentation* and, accordingly, the amount received for issuing them was credited to equity. The warrants lapse unexercised.

No revenue should be recognised when the warrants lapse unexercised. The definition of income (which encompasses both revenue and gains in accordance with the *Conceptual Framework for Financial Reporting* – see **7.4.1** in **chapter A2**) excludes contributions from equity participants. The issuance of warrants is a transaction with owners (equity participants). The fact that an equity participant no longer has an equity claim on the assets of the entity does not convert the equity contribution into income. Amounts for warrants classified as equity instruments may be transferred to another account within equity (e.g. contributed surplus) as of the date the warrants expire.

3.5.2 Scope limited to contracts with 'customers'

IFRS 15 applies to a contract (other than a contract listed in IFRS 15:5) only if the counterparty to the contract is a customer; a customer is defined as "[a] party that has contracted with an entity to obtain goods or services that are an output of the entity's ordinary activities in exchange for consideration". [IFRS 15:6 & Appendix A]

As an example of a counterparty to a contract that is *not* a customer, the Standard cites a counterparty that has contracted with the entity to participate in an activity or process in which the parties to the contract share in the risks and benefits that result from the activity or process (such as developing an asset in a collaborative arrangement) rather than to obtain the output of the entity's ordinary activities. [IFRS 15:6]

3.5.3 Contracts partially within the scope of IFRS 15

A contract with a customer may be partially within the scope of IFRS 15 and partially within the scope of the other Standards listed in **3.5.1**.

[IFRS 15:7]

(a) If the other Standards specify how to separate and/or initially measure one or more parts of the contract, then an entity first applies the separation and/or measurement requirements of those Standards. The amounts of the parts of the contract that are initially measured in accordance with other Standards are excluded from the transaction price. The requirements of IFRS 15:73 to 86 (see **section 8**) are then applied to allocate the amount of the transaction price that remains (if any) to each performance obligation within the scope of IFRS 15 and to any other parts of the contract identified by IFRS 15:7(b).

(b) If the other Standards do not specify how to separate and/or initially measure one or more parts of the contract, then IFRS 15 is applied to separate and/or initially measure the part (or parts) of the contract.

3.5.4 Scope – contract costs

IFRS 15 specifies the accounting for the incremental costs of obtaining a contract with a customer and for the costs incurred to fulfil a contract with a customer if those costs are not within the scope of another Standard (see **section 12**). These requirements only apply to the costs incurred that relate to a contract with a customer (or part of that contract) that is within the scope of IFRS 15. [IFRS 15:8]

3.6   Principal versus agent considerations

When another party is involved in providing goods or services to a customer, the entity should determine whether the nature of its promise is a performance obligation to provide the specified goods or services itself (i.e. it is acting as a principal) or to arrange for the other party to provide those goods or services (i.e. it is acting as an agent). [IFRS 15:B34]

Assessing whether an entity is acting as a principal or as an agent requires judgement in some circumstances, and different conclusions can significantly affect the amount and timing of revenue recognised.

An entity is a principal if the entity controls a promised good or service before the entity transfers the good or service to a customer. However, if the entity obtains legal title to a product only momentarily before legal title is transferred to a customer, that does not necessarily mean the entity is a principal in the transaction. It is possible for a principal in a contract to satisfy a performance obligation by itself or engage another party (e.g. a subcontractor) to satisfy some or all of a performance obligation on its behalf. When a principal satisfies a performance obligation, the entity recognises revenue in the gross amount of consideration to which it expects to be entitled in exchange for those goods or services transferred. [IFRS 15:B35]

An entity is an agent if the performance obligation is to arrange for the provision of goods or services by another party. When an agent satisfies a performance obligation, the entity recognises revenue in the amount of any fee or commission to which it expects to be entitled in exchange for arranging for the other party to provide its goods or services. An entity's fee or commission might be the net amount of consideration that the entity retains after paying the other party the consideration received in exchange for the goods or services to be provided by that party. [IFRS 15:B36]

Indicators that an entity is an agent (and, therefore, does not control the good or service before it is provided to a customer) include the following:

[IFRS 15:B37]

(a)   another party is primarily responsible for fulfilling the contract;

(b)   the entity does not have inventory risk at any point during the contract (i.e. before or after the goods have been ordered by a customer, during shipping or on return);

(c)   the entity does not have discretion in establishing prices for the other party's goods or services and, therefore, the benefit that the entity can receive from those goods or services is limited;

(d)   the entity's consideration is in the form of a commission; and

(e)   the entity is not exposed to credit risk for the amount receivable from a customer in exchange for the other party's goods or services.

Example 3.6A

Arranging for the provision of goods or services (entity is an agent) (website operation)

[IFRS 15:IE231 - IE233, Example 45]

An entity operates a website that enables customers to purchase goods from a range of suppliers who deliver the goods directly to the customers. When a good is purchased via the website, the entity is entitled to a commission that is equal to 10 per cent of the sales price. The entity's website facilitates payment between the supplier and the customer at prices that are set by the supplier. The entity requires payment from customers before orders are processed and all orders are non-refundable. The entity has no further obligations to the customer after arranging for the products to be provided to the customer.

To determine whether the entity's performance obligation is to provide the specified goods itself (ie the entity is a principal) or to arrange for the supplier to provide those goods (ie the entity is an agent), the entity considers the nature of its promise. Specifically, the entity observes that the supplier of the goods delivers its goods directly to the customer and thus the entity does not obtain control of the goods. Instead, the entity's promise is to arrange for the supplier to provide those goods to the customer. In reaching that conclusion, the entity considers the following indicators from [IFRS 15:B37] as follows:

(a) the supplier is primarily responsible for fulfilling the contract – ie by shipping the goods to the customer;

(b) the entity does not take inventory risk at any time during the transaction because the goods are shipped directly by the supplier to the customer;

(c) the entity's consideration is in the form of a commission (10 per cent of the sales price);

(d) the entity does not have discretion in establishing prices for the supplier's goods and, therefore, the benefit the entity can receive from those goods is limited; and

(e) neither the entity, nor the supplier, has credit risk because payments from customers are made in advance.

Consequently, the entity concludes that it is an agent and its performance obligation is to arrange for the provision of goods by the supplier. When the entity satisfies its promise to arrange for the goods to be provided by the supplier to the customer (which, in this example, is when goods are purchased by the customer), the entity recognises revenue in the amount of the commission to which it is entitled.

In **example 3.6A**, an important feature of the fact pattern is that the entity has no further obligations to the customer after arranging for the products to be provided to the customer. If this is not the case (e.g. because the entity would be responsible to the customer if the products were faulty), then the analysis could be different.

Example 3.6B

Promise to provide goods or services (entity is a principal) (equipment with unique specifications)

[IFRS 15:IE234 - IE238, Example 46]

An entity enters into a contract with a customer for equipment with unique specifications. The entity and the customer develop the specifications for the equipment, which the entity communicates to a supplier that the entity contracts with to manufacture the equipment. The entity also arranges to have the supplier deliver the equipment directly to the customer. Upon delivery of the equipment to the customer, the terms of the contract require the entity to pay the supplier the price agreed to by the entity and the supplier for manufacturing the equipment.

The entity and the customer negotiate the selling price and the entity invoices the customer for the agreed-upon price with 30-day payment terms. The entity's profit is based on the difference between the sales price negotiated with the customer and the price charged by the supplier.

The contract between the entity and the customer requires the customer to seek remedies for defects in the equipment from the supplier under the supplier's warranty. However, the entity is responsible for any corrections to the equipment required resulting from errors in specifications.

To determine whether the entity's performance obligation is to provide the specified goods or services itself (ie the entity is a principal) or to arrange for another party to provide those goods or services (ie the entity is an agent), the entity considers the nature of its promise. The entity has promised to provide the customer with specialised equipment; however, the entity has subcontracted the manufacturing of the equipment to the supplier. In determining whether the entity obtains control of the equipment before control transfers to the customer and whether the entity is a principal, the entity considers the indicators in [IFRS 15:B37] as follows:

(a)   the entity is primarily responsible for fulfilling the contract. Although the entity subcontracted the manufacturing, the entity is ultimately responsible for ensuring that the equipment meets the specifications for which the customer has contracted.

(b)   the entity has inventory risk because of its responsibility for corrections to the equipment resulting from errors in specifications, even though the supplier has inventory risk during production and before shipment.

(c)   the entity has discretion in establishing the selling price with the customer, and the profit earned by the entity is an amount that is equal to the difference between the selling price negotiated with the customer and the amount to be paid to the supplier.

(d)   the entity's consideration is not in the form of a commission.

(e)   the entity has credit risk for the amount receivable from the customer in exchange for the equipment.

The entity concludes that its promise is to provide the equipment to the customer. On the basis of the indicators in [IFRS 15:B37], the entity concludes that it controls the equipment before it is transferred to the customer. Thus, the entity is a principal in the transaction and recognises revenue in the gross amount of consideration to which it is entitled from the customer in exchange for the equipment.

Example 3.6C

Promise to provide goods or services (entity is a principal) (airlines)

[IFRS 15:IE239 - IE243, Example 47]

An entity negotiates with major airlines to purchase tickets at reduced rates compared with the price of tickets sold directly by the airlines to the public. The entity agrees to buy a specific number of tickets and must pay for those tickets regardless of whether it is able to resell them. The reduced rate paid by the entity for each ticket purchased is negotiated and agreed in advance.

The entity determines the prices at which the airline tickets will be sold to its customers. The entity sells the tickets and collects the consideration from customers when the tickets are purchased; therefore there is no credit risk.

The entity also assists the customers in resolving complaints with the service provided by airlines. However, each airline is responsible for fulfilling obligations associated with the ticket, including remedies to a customer for dissatisfaction with the service.

To determine whether the entity's performance obligation is to provide the specified goods or services itself (ie the entity is a principal) or to arrange for another party to provide those goods or services (ie the entity is an agent), the entity considers the nature of its promise. The entity determines that its promise is to provide the customer with a ticket, which provides the right to fly on the specified flight or another flight if the specified flight is changed or cancelled. In determining whether the entity obtains control of the right to fly before control transfers to the customer and whether the entity is a principal, the entity considers the indicators in [IFRS 15:B37] as follows:

(a) the entity is primarily responsible for fulfilling the contract, which is providing the right to fly. However, the entity is not responsible for providing the flight itself, which will be provided by the airline.

(b) the entity has inventory risk for the tickets because they are purchased before they are sold to the entity's customers and the entity is exposed to any loss as a result of not being able to sell the tickets for more than the entity's cost.

(c) the entity has discretion in setting the sales prices for tickets to its customers.

(d) as a result of the entity's ability to set the sales prices, the amount that the entity earns is not in the form of a commission, but instead depends on the sales price it sets and the costs of the tickets that were negotiated with the airline.

The entity concludes that its promise is to provide a ticket (ie a right to fly) to the customer. On the basis of the indicators in [IFRS 15:B37], the entity concludes that it controls the ticket before it is transferred to the customer. Thus, the entity concludes that it is a principal in the transaction and recognises revenue in the gross amount of consideration to which it is entitled in exchange for the tickets transferred.

Example 3.6D

Arranging for the provision of goods or services (entity is an agent)

[IFRS 15:IE244 - IE248, Example 48]

An entity sells vouchers that entitle customers to future meals at specified restaurants. These vouchers are sold by the entity and the sales price of the voucher provides the customer with a significant discount when compared with the normal selling prices of the meals (for example, a customer pays CU100 for a voucher that entitles the customer to a meal at a restaurant that would otherwise cost CU200). The entity does not purchase vouchers in advance; instead, it purchases vouchers only as they are requested by the customers. The entity sells the vouchers through its website and the vouchers are non-refundable.

The entity and the restaurants jointly determine the prices at which the vouchers will be sold to customers. The entity is entitled to 30 per cent of the voucher price when it sells the voucher. The entity has no credit risk because the customers pay for the vouchers when purchased.

The entity also assists the customers in resolving complaints about the meals and has a buyer satisfaction programme. However, the restaurant is responsible for fulfilling obligations associated with the voucher, including remedies to a customer for dissatisfaction with the service.

To determine whether the entity is a principal or an agent, the entity considers the nature of its promise and whether it takes control of the voucher (ie a right) before control transfers to the customer. In making this determination, the entity considers the indicators in [IFRS 15:B37] as follows:

(a)   the entity is not responsible for providing the meals itself, which will be provided by the restaurants;

(b)   the entity does not have inventory risk for the vouchers because they are not purchased before being sold to customers and the vouchers are non-refundable;

(c)   the entity has some discretion in setting the sales prices for vouchers to customers, but the sales prices are jointly determined with the restaurants; and

(d)   the entity's consideration is in the form of a commission, because it is entitled to a stipulated percentage (30 per cent) of the voucher price.

The entity concludes that its promise is to arrange for goods or services to be provided to customers (the purchasers of the vouchers) in exchange for a commission. On the basis of the indicators in [IFRS 15:B37], the entity concludes that it does not control the vouchers that provide a right to meals before they are transferred to the customers. Thus, the entity concludes that it is an agent in the arrangement and recognises revenue in the net amount of consideration to which the entity will be entitled in exchange for the service, which is the 30 per cent commission it is entitled to upon the sale of each voucher.

If an entity is no longer acting as a principal, because another entity has assumed the performance obligations and contractual rights in a contract so that the entity is no longer obliged to satisfy the performance obligation, the entity should not recognise revenue for that performance obligation. Instead, the entity should evaluate whether it is now acting as an agent. [IFRS 15:B38]

When, having considered the requirements of IFRS 15:B34 to B38, an entity determines that it acts as a principal in the sale of goods or services, or both, it should recognise revenue for the gross amount to which it is entitled. This is the case even when the entity sells some goods or services to third parties at an amount equal to the cost of the goods or services. The practice of selling goods or providing services at an amount equal to cost does not mean that the proceeds should be presented as a cost reimbursement; revenue and expenses should be presented gross.

3.7 Recognition of revenue as principal or agent – additional examples

3.7.1 Royalty payments

Example 3.7.1

Royalty payments

Entity A has agreed to pay a royalty to Entity B for the use of intellectual property rights that Entity A requires to make sales to its customers. The royalty is specified as a percentage of gross proceeds from Entity A's sales to its customers less contractually defined costs. Entity A is the principal in the sales transactions with its customers (i.e. it must provide the goods and services itself and does not act as an agent for Entity B).

In Entity A's financial statements, should the royalty payments be netted against revenue or recognised as a cost of fulfilling the contract?

Because Entity A is the principal in respect of the sales to its customers, it should recognise its revenue on a gross basis and the royalty as a cost of fulfilling the contract. Guidance on the appropriate accounting for the costs of fulfilling a contract, including whether such costs should be capitalised or expensed, is provided in IFRS 15:95 to 104 (see **section 12**).

3.7.2 Offsetting revenue and expenses for shared commissions

Example 3.7.2

Offsetting revenue and expenses for shared commissions

Company A has signed a contract with an insurance company under which it receives a commission for every policy it sells on behalf of the insurance company. Company A contracts with individual financial advisers to sell these insurance policies and agrees to split the commission evenly with the financial advisers. Company A provides administrative facilities and office space to the financial advisers. The insurance company is aware of the arrangements between Company A and the financial advisers, but its contractual relationship is with Company A and Company A is responsible for providing the service to the insurance company. The insurance company pays the full commission to Company A, which then pays half of the commission to the financial adviser who sold the policy.

Company A has determined that it is acting as a principal in this arrangement, in accordance with IFRS 15:B34 to B38.

Is Company A permitted to offset the amount it pays to the financial advisers against the commission revenue it receives from the insurance company?

No. Company A is acting as a principal in providing services to the insurance company and not as an agent for the financial advisers. Accordingly, it is required to present the revenue it receives for those services as a gross amount.

3.7.3 Income tax withheld in a different country

Example 3.7.3

Income tax withheld in a different country

Company X performs consulting services for Company C, which is located in a different country from Company X. Company C withholds 20 per cent of Company X's fee as a local income tax withholding and transmits this amount to its local government on behalf of Company X (Company X retains the primary responsibility to pay the tax in Company C's tax jurisdiction). Company C pays the remaining 80 per cent to Company X. The countries do not have a tax treaty, and Company X is not required to file a tax return in Company C's country. Company X was fully aware that the 20 per cent income tax would be withheld in Company C's country when it agreed to perform the consulting services for Company C.

If Company X's fee is CU100 and Company C remits CU80 to Company X and CU20 to the local government, does Company X have revenue of CU100 and tax expense of CU20 or net revenue of CU80?

Company X is the principal in providing the consulting services to Company C. Company X also has the primary responsibility to pay the tax in Company C's tax jurisdiction, and Company C is simply paying the tax on Company X's behalf (acting as a collection agent). Consequently, Company X should recognise revenue in the gross amount of consideration to which it expects to be entitled in exchange for those services and should therefore report revenue of CU100 and income tax expense of CU20.

3.7.4 *Shipping and handling costs charged to customers*

Many vendors charge customers for shipping and handling of goods. Shipping costs include costs incurred to move the product from the seller's place of business to the buyer's designated location and include payments to third-party shippers. But they may also include costs incurred directly by the seller (e.g. salaries and overheads related to the activities to prepare the goods for shipment).

Handling costs include costs incurred to store, move and prepare the products for shipment. Generally, handling costs are incurred from when the product is removed from finished goods inventories to when the product is provided to the shipper and may include an allocation of internal overheads.

Shipping and handling costs may be included in the price of the product. Alternatively, the vendor may charge its customers a separate fee for shipping and handling costs. In some cases, the separate fee may be a standard amount that does not necessarily correlate directly with the costs incurred for the specific shipment. In other cases, the separate fee may be a direct reimbursement for shipping and any direct incremental handling costs incurred or may include a margin on top of those costs.

For example, Company S sells goods to a customer and bills the customer for shipping and handling costs. Company S needs to consider how to present the amounts billed for shipping and handling in profit or loss.

The appropriate presentation of amounts billed to a customer for shipping and handling will depend on an analysis of the principal versus agent considerations in IFRS 15 related to shipping and handling services (see **3.6**). If control of the goods transfers on receipt by the customer (e.g. FOB destination – see **9.4.6**), the vendor will generally be considered to be the principal in the shipping and handling service. If, however, control of the goods transfers when the goods are shipped, the vendor will need to determine whether it is principal or agent with respect to the shipping service.

If, after consideration of the requirements of IFRS 15:B34 to B38 (see **3.6**), Company S determines that it is responsible for shipping and handling as a principal, then all amounts related to shipping and handling billed to a customer in a sale transaction represent revenues earned for the goods provided (and the shipping services rendered, if the shipping service represents a distinct performance obligation) and should be presented as revenue.

However, if Company S considers the requirements of IFRS 15:B34 to B38 and determines that it is not responsible to the customer for shipping but is instead acting merely as the buyer's agent in arranging for a third party to provide shipping services to the buyer, then Company S should not report the amount charged by that third party for shipping as its own revenue. Instead, Company S should report as revenue only the commission it receives (if any) for arranging shipping, which is the excess of any amounts charged to the customer for shipping by Company S over any amounts paid to the third party for those services.

Example 3.7.4

Classification of shipping costs incurred on products sold

Company A sells and ships goods to a customer and has concluded that it is the principal on the sale of goods and associated shipping. Company A analyses expenses by function in its statement of comprehensive income.

How should Company A classify costs incurred for shipping goods to customers?

Company A may adopt a policy of including shipping and handling costs in cost of sales. This treatment is permitted by paragraph 38 of IAS 2 *Inventories*, which states that the circumstances of the entity may warrant the inclusion of distribution costs in cost of sales.

Alternatively, shipping and handling costs may be included in a separate 'distribution costs' classification or, if insignificant, in 'other operating expenses'. Company A should ensure that:

- the classification is appropriate to the entity's circumstances;
- the classification is consistent from year to year; and
- material items are separately identified, as required by paragraph 97 of IAS 1 *Presentation of Financial Statements* (see **5.4.1** in **chapter A4**).

3.7.5 Value added tax rebate

Example 3.7.5

Value added tax rebate

In Country C, when software is sold to distributors or end users, software developers are required to collect 17 per cent value added tax (VAT) as agents for the government (this rate is consistent with VAT on other similar items). As a measure to subsidise the software development industry, 14 per cent is rebated by the government to the developer almost immediately.

Assume software is sold by Entity S for CU117 inclusive of VAT. The sales invoice indicates a sales price of CU100 before VAT, with VAT of CU17 corresponding to the 17 per cent VAT rate. As a result of the sale, Entity S receives a rebate of CU14 from the government.

How much revenue should Entity S recognise?

In accordance with IFRS 15:47 (see **7.1**), CU17 is excluded from revenue because it is being collected on behalf of a third party. Therefore, Entity S should recognise a total of CU100 as revenue. Paragraph 3 of IAS 20 *Accounting for Government Grants and Disclosure of Government Assistance* defines a government grant as "assistance by government in the form of transfers of resources to an entity in return for past or future compliance with certain conditions relating to the operating activities of the entity" (see **3.3** in **chapter A36**). The 14 per cent VAT rebate is regarded as a government grant to encourage the software development industry. Therefore, Entity S should recognise revenue of CU100 and government grant income of CU14. In accordance with IAS 20:29, the CU14 may be presented separately or as 'other income' (see **6.2** in **chapter A36**).

3.8   Repurchase agreements

3.8.1   Repurchase agreements – general

A repurchase agreement is a contract in which an entity sells an asset and also promises or has the option (either in the same contract or in another contract) to repurchase the asset. The repurchased asset may be the asset that was originally sold to the customer, an asset that is substantially the same as that asset, or another asset of which the asset that was originally sold is a component. [IFRS 15:B64]

Repurchase agreements generally come in three forms:

[IFRS 15:B65]

- an entity's obligation to repurchase the asset (a forward contract – see **3.8.2**);
- an entity's right to repurchase the asset (a call option – see **3.8.2**); and
- an entity's obligation to repurchase the asset at the customer's request (a put option – see **3.8.3**).

3.8.2   A forward contract or call option

If an entity has an obligation or a right to repurchase the asset (a forward contract or a call option), a customer does not obtain control of the asset because the customer is limited in its ability to direct the use of, and obtain substantially all of the remaining benefits from, the asset even though the customer may have physical possession of the asset. Therefore, the contract is accounted for as either:

[IFRS 15:B66]

- a lease in accordance with IAS 17 *Leases* (see **chapter A17**) if the entity has an obligation or a right to repurchase the asset for an amount that is less than its original selling price; or

- a financing arrangement (as discussed below) if the entity has an obligation or a right to repurchase the asset for an amount that is equal to or more than its original selling price.

The time value of money should be considered when comparing the repurchase price with the selling price. [IFRS 15:B67]

If the repurchase agreement is a financing arrangement, the entity should continue to recognise the asset and it should recognise a liability for any consideration received from the customer. The difference between the amount of consideration received from the customer and the amount of consideration to be paid to the customer should be recognised as interest and, if applicable, as processing or holding costs (e.g. insurance). [IFRS 15:B68]

If the option lapses unexercised, the liability is derecognised and a corresponding amount of revenue is recognised. [IFRS 15:69]

Example 3.8.2

Repurchase agreements (1)

[IFRS 15:IE315 - IE318, Example 62 (extract)]

An entity enters into a contract with a customer for the sale of a tangible asset on 1 January 20X7 for CU1 million.

Case A – Call option: financing

The contract includes a call option that gives the entity the right to repurchase the asset for CU1.1 million on or before 31 December 20X7.

Control of the asset does not transfer to the customer on 1 January 20X7 because the entity has a right to repurchase the asset and therefore the customer is limited in its ability to direct the use of, and obtain substantially all of the remaining benefits from, the asset. Consequently, in accordance with [IFRS 15:B66(b)], the entity accounts for the transaction as a financing arrangement, because the exercise price is more than the original selling price. In accordance with [IFRS 15:B68], the entity does not derecognise the asset and instead recognises the cash received as a financial liability. The entity also recognises interest expense for the difference between the exercise price (CU1.1 million) and the cash received (CU1 million), which increases the liability.

On 31 December 20X7, the option lapses unexercised; therefore, the entity derecognises the liability and recognises revenue of CU1.1 million.

3.8.3 A put option

If an entity has an obligation to repurchase the asset at the customer's request (a put option) at a price that is lower than the original selling price of the asset, the entity should consider at inception of the contract whether the customer has a significant economic incentive to exercise that right. If the customer exercises the put option, it has in effect paid consideration to the entity for the right to use a specified asset for a period of time. Therefore, if the customer has a significant economic incentive to exercise the put option, the agreement is accounted for as a lease in accordance with IAS 17. [IFRS 15:B70]

Various factors should be considered to determine whether a customer has a significant economic incentive to exercise a put option, including the relationship of the repurchase price to the expected market value of the asset at the date of the repurchase and the amount of time until the option expires. For example, if it is expected that the repurchase price will significantly exceed the market value of the asset, this indicates that the customer may have a significant economic incentive to exercise the put option. [IFRS 15:B71]

If the repurchase price of the asset is equal to or greater than the original selling price and is more than the expected market value of the asset, the contract is in effect a financing arrangement and is accounted for as described in **3.8.2**. [IFRS 15:B73]

The agreement will be accounted for as if it were a sale of a product with a right of return (see **7.2.2**) if either:

- the customer does not have a significant economic incentive to exercise the option at a price that is lower than the original selling price of the asset; [IFRS 15:B72] or

- the repurchase price of the asset is equal to or greater than the original selling price and is less than or equal to the expected market value of the asset, and the customer does not have a significant economic incentive to exercise its option. [IFRS 15:B74]

When comparing the repurchase price with the selling price, an entity should consider the time value of money. [IFRS 15:B75]

If the option lapses unexercised, the entity should derecognise the liability and recognise revenue. [IFRS 15:B76]

Example 3.8.3

Repurchase agreements (2)

[IFRS 15:IE315 & IE319 - IE321, Example 62 (extract)]

An entity enters into a contract with a customer for the sale of a tangible asset on 1 January 20X7 for CU1 million.

Case B – Put option: lease

Instead of having a call option, the contract includes a put option that obliges the entity to repurchase the asset at the customer's request for CU900,000 on or before 31 December 20X7. The market value is expected to be CU750,000 on 31 December 20X7.

At the inception of the contract, the entity assesses whether the customer has a significant economic incentive to exercise the put option, to determine the accounting for the transfer of the asset (see [IFRS 15:B70 to B76]). The entity concludes that the customer has a significant economic incentive to exercise the put option because the repurchase price significantly exceeds the expected market value of the asset at the date of repurchase. The entity determines there are no other relevant factors to consider when assessing whether the customer has a significant economic incentive to exercise the put option. Consequently, the entity concludes that control of the asset does not transfer to the customer, because the customer is limited in its ability to direct the use of, and obtain substantially all of the remaining benefits from, the asset.

In accordance with [IFRS 15:B70 to B71], the entity accounts for the transaction as a lease in accordance with IAS 17 *Leases*.

3.9 Application of IFRS 15 guidance under other Standards

The requirements of IFRS 15 used to (1) assess when control of an asset passes from an entity (see **section 9**), and (2) measure any consideration (see **section 7**) for the purposes of calculating the profit or loss on the disposal of an asset, should be applied when any of the following types of asset are disposed of:

- property, plant and equipment in the scope of IAS 16 *Property, Plant and Equipment* (see **chapter A7**);

- intangible assets in the scope of IAS 38 *Intangible Assets* (see **chapter A9**); and

- investment properties in the scope of IAS 40 *Investment Property* (see **chapter A8**).

When the amount of consideration to be included in calculating the gain or loss subsequently changes, this is accounted for in accordance with the requirements for changes in the transaction price in IFRS 15 (see **7.1** and **7.2**).

4 The five-step model for recognising revenue from contracts with customers

The introduction to IFRS 15 explains that an entity recognises revenue by applying a model consisting of five steps in order to meet the Standard's core principle (see **3.2**). The five steps are as follows.

[IFRS 15:IN7]

Step 1: Identify the contract(s) with a customer (see **section 5**).

Step 2: Identify the performance obligations in the contract (see **section 6**).

Step 3: Determine the transaction price (see **section 7**).

Step 4: Allocate the transaction price to the performance obligations in the contract (see **section 8**).

Step 5: Recognise revenue when (or as) the entity satisfies a performance obligation (see **section 9**).

While these five steps are stated sequentially in the introduction to IFRS 15, they are neither labelled as such nor dealt with in this order in either the body of the Standard or in Appendix B – Application Guidance. In a manner consistent with other IFRSs, the requirements of IFRS 15 adhere to the framework of recognition, measurement, presentation and disclosure. As a result, the steps are not presented sequentially in IFRS 15 but rather as follows:

- recognition – this deals with the requirements of Step 1 (identification of a contract), Step 2 (identifying separate performance obligations) and Step 5 (recognition of revenue when (or as) the entity satisfies a performance obligation); and

- measurement – this deals with the requirements of Step 3 (determination of the transaction price) and Step 4 (allocation of the transaction price to the performance obligations in the contract).

Application of all five steps

Generally, an entity should consider all five steps for every contract. However, the entity may find that, after considering the specific facts and circumstances of a particular contract, one of the steps is not relevant. This may occur, for example, in a contract for which the entity has determined in Step 2 that it has only a single performance obligation. In such circumstances, Step 4 (allocation of the transaction price) will often not be applicable and the entity can, in effect, jump from Step 3 to Step 5.

Order of the steps

An entity would generally be expected to apply the five steps in sequential order. However, the entity may sometimes need to consider a later step before applying an earlier one.

Consider the following examples:

- In applying Step 1 to determine whether a contract exists and reviewing the collectability threshold as required in IFRS 15:9(e) (see **5.1**), an entity will need to consider the "amount of consideration to which it will be entitled in exchange for the promised goods or services". The amount of consideration "may be less than the price stated in the contract if the consideration is variable because the entity may offer the customer a price concession". As a result, the entity would need to apply Step 3 (determination of the transaction price) and estimate the expected discounts or price concessions before being able to conclude that a valid contract exists under Step 1.

- In Step 2 (identification of the performance obligations), IFRS 15:22(b) requires entities to identify as a performance obligation "a series of distinct goods or services that are substantially the same and that have the same pattern of transfer to the customer" (see **6.1**). In accordance with IFRS 15:23, that series is a performance obligation only when the two criteria are met: (1) the performance obligation satisfies the criteria in Step 5 to be recognised over time, and (2) the same method to measure progress is used. Therefore, the determination in Step 2 as to whether a series of distinct goods or services is a performance obligation relies on the requirements in Step 5. As a result, an entity would need to understand and make a determination about Step 5 before being able to apply Step 2 (the identification of its performance obligations).

5   Step 1: Identify the contract(s) with a customer

5.1   Identification of the contract(s) with a customer – general

The first step in the five-step model is to identify whether a contract exists and meets specified criteria. Entities are required to account for a contract with a customer that is within the scope of IFRS 15 only when the all of the following criteria are met:

[IFRS 15:9]

(a) the contract has been approved (either in writing, orally, or in accordance with other customary business practices) by the parties to the contract, and the parties are committed to perform their respective obligations;

(b) the entity can identify each party's rights regarding the goods or services to be transferred;

(c) the entity can identify the payment terms for the goods or services to be transferred;

(d) the contract has commercial substance (i.e. the risk, timing or amount of the entity's future cash flows is expected to change as a result of the contract); and

(e) it is probable that the entity will collect the consideration to which it will be entitled in exchange for the goods or services to be transferred to the customer.

> In contrast, IAS 18 does not include explicit requirements for a contract to exist.

A contract is an agreement between two or more parties that creates enforceable rights and obligations. Enforceability of the rights and obligations in a contract is a matter of law. As noted at IFRS 15:9(a), contracts can be written, oral or implied by an entity's customary business practices. Practices and processes for establishing contracts with customers vary across legal jurisdictions, industries and entities. They may also vary within an entity (e.g. they may depend on the class of customer or the nature of the promised goods or services). Such practices and processes will need to be considered to determine whether and when an agreement with a customer creates enforceable rights and obligations. [IFRS 15:10]

> A question arises as to whether it is appropriate for an entity to apply the revenue recognition model in IFRS 15 when it does not yet have a written sales agreement, but a written sales agreement is being prepared.
>
> An entity applies the revenue recognition model in IFRS 15 when there is an agreement between two or more parties that creates enforceable rights and obligations. Whether the agreed terms are written, oral or evidenced otherwise (e.g. by the entity's customary business practices), a contract exists if the agreement creates rights and obligations that are enforceable against the parties. Determining whether a contractual right or obligation is enforceable is a question of law and the factors that determine enforceability may differ between jurisdictions. The best evidence of an enforceable agreement is a written contract, especially if the seller's standard practice is to use written contracts.
>
> Although IFRS 15 does not require a written contract as evidence of an agreement, a contract that is being prepared but has not yet been signed may be evidence that agreement has not yet been reached. Entities should use caution before recognising revenue in such circumstances, because the apparent absence of a contractual understanding between the parties may make it unlikely that the conditions in IFRS 15:9 have been met.

IFRS 15:9(e) requires an evaluation as to whether it is probable that the consideration to which the entity will be entitled will be collected. In order to make this assessment, the entity should only consider the customer's ability and intention to pay the consideration when it is due. It may be the case that the consideration to which an entity is ultimately entitled will be less than the price stated in the contract, because the customer may be offered a price concession. In such cases, the entity will need to apply IFRS 15's guidance on variable consideration (see **sections 7.1** and **7.2**). [IFRS 15:9(e)]

Example 5.1A

Consideration is not the stated price – implicit price concession

[IFRS 15:IE7 - IE9, Example 2]

An entity sells 1,000 units of a prescription drug to a customer for promised consideration of CU1 million. This is the entity's first sale to a customer in a new region, which is experiencing significant economic difficulty. Thus, the entity expects that it will not be able to collect from the customer the full amount of the promised consideration. Despite the possibility of not collecting the full amount, the entity expects the region's economy to recover over the next two to three years and determines that a relationship with the customer could help it to forge relationships with other potential customers in the region.

When assessing whether the criterion in [IFRS 15:9(e)] is met, the entity also considers [IFRS 15:47 and IFRS 15:52(b) (see **section 7**)]. Based on the assessment of the facts and circumstances, the entity determines that it expects to provide a price concession and accept a lower amount of consideration from the customer. Accordingly, the entity concludes that the transaction price is not CU1 million and, therefore, the promised consideration is variable. The entity estimates the variable consideration and determines that it expects to be entitled to CU400,000.

The entity considers the customer's ability and intention to pay the consideration and concludes that even though the region is experiencing economic difficulty, it is probable that it will collect CU400,000 from the customer. Consequently, the entity concludes that the criterion in [IFRS 15:9(e)] is met based on an estimate of variable consideration of CU400,000. In addition, on the basis of an evaluation of the contract terms and other facts and circumstances, the entity concludes that the other criteria in [IFRS 15:9] are also met. Consequently, the entity accounts for the contract with the customer in accordance with the requirements in IFRS 15.

Example 5.1B

Implicit price concession

[IFRS 15:IE10 - IE13, Example 3]

An entity, a hospital, provides medical services to an uninsured patient in the emergency room. The entity has not previously provided medical services to this patient but is required by law to provide medical services to all emergency room patients. Because of the patient's condition upon arrival at the hospital, the entity provides the services immediately and, therefore, before the entity can determine whether the patient is committed to perform its obligations under the contract in exchange for the medical services provided. Consequently, the contract does not meet the criteria in [IFRS 15:9] and, in accordance with [IFRS 15:14], the entity will continue to assess its conclusion based on updated facts and circumstances.

After providing services, the entity obtains additional information about the patient including a review of the services provided, standard rates for such services and the patient's ability and intention to pay the entity for the services provided. During the review, the entity notes its standard rate for the services provided in the emergency room is CU10,000. The entity also reviews the patient's information and to be consistent with its policies designates the patient to a customer class based on the entity's assessment of the patient's ability and intention to pay.

Before reassessing whether the criteria in [IFRS 15:9] have been met, the entity considers [IFRS 15:47 and IFRS 15:52(b) (see **section 7**)]. Although the standard rate for the services is CU10,000 (which may be the amount invoiced to the patient), the entity expects to accept a lower amount of consideration in exchange for the services. Accordingly, the entity concludes that the transaction price is not CU10,000 and, therefore, the promised consideration is variable. The entity reviews its historical cash collections from this customer class and other relevant information about the patient. The entity estimates the variable consideration and determines that it expects to be entitled to CU1,000.

In accordance with [IFRS 15:9(e)], the entity evaluates the patient's ability and intention to pay (ie the credit risk of the patient). On the basis of its collection history from patients in this customer class, the entity concludes it is probable that the entity will collect CU1,000 (which is the estimate of variable consideration). In addition, on the basis of an assessment of the contract terms and other facts and circumstances, the entity concludes that the other criteria in [IFRS 15:9] are also met. Consequently, the entity accounts for the contract with the patient in accordance with the requirements in IFRS 15.

In some cases, contracts with customers may have no fixed duration and may be capable of being terminated or modified by either party at any time. Alternatively, contracts may automatically renew on a periodic basis that is specified in the contract. IFRS 15 should be applied for the duration of the contract (i.e. the contractual period) in which the parties to the contract have present enforceable rights and obligations. [IFRS 15:11]

A contract does not exist if each party to the contract has a unilateral enforceable right to terminate a wholly unperformed contract without compensating the other party (or parties). A contract is wholly unperformed if both of the following criteria are met:

[IFRS 15:12]

- any promised goods or services have not yet been transferred to the customer; and

- the entity has not yet received, and is not yet entitled to receive, any consideration in exchange for promised goods or services.

5.2   Reassessing the criteria for identifying a contract

If, at the inception of a contract, the criteria to qualify for revenue recognition set out in IFRS 15:9 (see **5.1**) are met, an entity should not reassess those criteria unless there is an indication of a significant change in facts and circumstances. For example, if a customer's ability to pay the consideration deteriorates significantly, an entity would reassess whether it is probable that the entity will collect the consideration to which the entity will be entitled in exchange for the remaining goods or services that will be transferred to the customer. [IFRS 15:13]

Example 5.2

Reassessing the criteria for identifying a contract

[IFRS 15:IE14 - IE17, Example 4]

An entity licences a patent to a customer in exchange for a usage-based royalty. At contract inception, the contract meets all the criteria in [IFRS 15:9] and the entity accounts for the contract with the customer in accordance with the requirements in IFRS 15. The entity recognises revenue when the customer's subsequent usage occurs in accordance with [IFRS 15:B63 (see **11.3**)].

Throughout the first year of the contract, the customer provides quarterly reports of usage and pays within the agreed-upon period.

During the second year of the contract, the customer continues to use the entity's patent, but the customer's financial condition declines. The customer's current access to credit and available cash on hand are limited. The entity continues to recognise revenue on the basis of the customer's usage throughout the second year. The customer pays the first quarter's royalties but makes nominal payments for the usage of the patent in Quarters 2 - 4. The entity accounts for any impairment of the existing receivable in accordance with IFRS 9 *Financial Instruments*.

During the third year of the contract, the customer continues to use the entity's patent. However, the entity learns that the customer has lost access to credit and its major customers and thus the customer's ability to pay significantly

---

deteriorates. The entity therefore concludes that it is unlikely that the customer will be able to make any further royalty payments for ongoing usage of the entity's patent. As a result of this significant change in facts and circumstances, in accordance with [IFRS 15:13], the entity reassesses the criteria in [IFRS 15:9] and determines that they are not met because it is no longer probable that the entity will collect the consideration to which it will be entitled. Accordingly, the entity does not recognise any further revenue associated with the customer's future usage of its patent. The entity accounts for any impairment of the existing receivable in accordance with IFRS 9 *Financial Instruments*.

For entities that have not yet adopted IFRS 9, the references in **example 5.2** would instead be to IAS 39 *Financial Instruments: Recognition and Measurement*.

If a contract with a customer does not meet the criteria in IFRS 15:9 (see **5.1**), the entity should continue to assess the contract to determine whether those criteria are subsequently met. [IFRS 15:14]

5.3 Consideration received when the criteria for a contract are not met

If the criteria for revenue recognition in IFRS 15:9 (see **5.1**) are not met, but consideration is received from the customer, that consideration should be recognised as revenue only when either of the following events has occurred:

[IFRS 15:15]

- the entity has no remaining obligations to transfer goods or services to the customer and all, or substantially all, of the consideration promised by the customer has been received by the entity and is non-refundable; or

- the contract has been terminated and the consideration received from the customer is non-refundable.

When the entity has received consideration from a customer, but is unable to recognise revenue until either (1) one of the events in IFRS 15:15 occurs (see above), or (2) the criteria in IFRS 5:9 are subsequently met (see **5.2**), the consideration should be presented as a liability until such point that the entity is entitled to recognise the balance as revenue (see **section 13**). Depending on the specific facts and circumstances, the liability recognised represents an obligation of the entity to either transfer goods or services in the future or refund the consideration received. In both cases, the liability should be measured at the amount of consideration received from the customer. [IFRS 15:16]

Example 5.3

Collectability of the consideration

[IFRS 15:IE3 - IE9, Example 1]

An entity, a real estate developer, enters into a contract with a customer for the sale of a building for CU1 million. The customer intends to open a restaurant in the building. The building is located in an area where new restaurants face high levels of competition and the customer has little experience in the restaurant industry.

The customer pays a non-refundable deposit of CU50,000 at inception of the contract and enters into a long-term financing agreement with the entity for the remaining 95 per cent of the promised consideration. The financing arrangement is provided on a non-recourse basis, which means that if the customer defaults, the entity can repossess the building, but cannot seek further compensation from the customer, even if the collateral does not cover the full value of the amount owed. The entity's cost of the building is CU600,000. The customer obtains control of the building at contract inception.

In assessing whether the contract meets the criteria in [IFRS 15:9], the entity concludes that the criterion in [IFRS 15:9(e)] is not met because it is not probable that the entity will collect the consideration to which it is entitled in exchange for the transfer of the building. In reaching this conclusion, the entity observes that the customer's ability and intention to pay may be in doubt because of the following factors:

(a) the customer intends to repay the loan (which has a significant balance) primarily from income derived from its restaurant business (which is a business facing significant risks because of high competition in the industry and the customer's limited experience);

(b) the customer lacks other income or assets that could be used to repay the loan; and

(c) the customer's liability under the loan is limited because the loan is non-recourse.

Because the criteria in [IFRS 15:9] are not met, the entity applies [IFRS 15:15 to 16] to determine the accounting for the non-refundable deposit of CU50,000. The entity observes that none of the events described in [IFRS 15:15] have occurred – that is, the entity has not received substantially all of the consideration and it has not terminated the contract. Consequently, in accordance with [IFRS 15:16], the entity accounts for the non-refundable CU50,000 payment as a deposit liability. The entity continues to account for the initial deposit, as well as any future payments of principal and interest, as a deposit liability, until such time that the entity concludes that the criteria in [IFRS 15:9] are met (ie the entity is able to conclude that it is probable that the entity will collect the consideration) or one of the events in [IFRS 15:15] has occurred. The entity continues to assess the contract in accordance with [IFRS 15:14] to determine whether the criteria in [IFRS 15:9] are subsequently met or whether the events in [IFRS 15:15] have occurred.

5.4 Partial satisfaction of a performance obligation prior to identifying a contract

Guidance on the appropriate accounting when an entity commences activities on a specified contract prior to agreeing all of the contract terms with the customer or prior to the contract satisfying the identification criteria in IFRS 15:9 is set out at **9.3.4**.

5.5 Combining contracts

Two or more contracts entered into at or near the same time with the same customer (or related parties of the customer) should be combined and accounted for as a single contract if one or more of the following criteria are met:

[IFRS 15:17]

(a) the contracts are negotiated as a package with a single commercial objective;

(b) the amount of consideration to be paid in one contract is dependent on the price or performance of the other contract; or

(c) the goods or services promised in the contracts (or some of the goods or services promised in each of the contracts) are a single performance obligation (see **section 6**).

5.6 Modifying contracts

A contract may be modified after an entity has already accounted for some or all of the revenue relating to that contract. The impact on revenue recognition will depend on how that contract has been modified. This is discussed in **section 10**.

6 Step 2: Identify the performance obligations

6.1 Identification of performance obligations – general

Once an entity has established that it has a contract to which the five-step model can be applied, the next step is to assess whether there are goods or services promised in the contract that represent separate performance obligations. A separate performance obligation can be either:

[IFRS 15:22]

(a) a good or service (or a bundle of goods or services) that is 'distinct' (see **section 6.3**); or

(b) a series of distinct goods or services that are substantially the same and that have the same pattern of transfer to the customer.

> Illustrative Example 25 accompanying IFRS 15 provides an example of scenario (b) above (see **example 7.3C**).

In respect of IFRS 15:22(b) above, a series of distinct goods or services has the same pattern of transfer to the customer if both of the following criteria are met:

[IFRS 15:23]

(a) each distinct good or service in the series that the entity promises to transfer to the customer meets the criteria in IFRS 15:35 to be a performance obligation satisfied over time (see **9.2**); and

(b) in accordance with IFRS 15:39 and 40 (see **section 9.3**), the same method would be used to measure the entity's progress towards complete satisfaction of the performance obligation to transfer each distinct good or service in the series to the customer.

> The notion of a performance obligation is similar to the notions of deliverables, components or elements of a contract in the Standards superseded by IFRS 15. Although the notion of a performance obligation is implicit in those Standards, the term 'performance obligation' has not been defined previously. [IFRS 15:BC84]
>
> Moreover, although IAS 18:13 refers to 'separately identifiable components' of a transaction, IAS 18 includes almost no guidance on how to identify such components.
>
> The process of identifying the performance obligations in a contract is sometimes referred to as 'unbundling', and is not optional.
>
> Proper identification of the performance obligations in a contract is critical to achieving the core principle in IFRS 15 (see **3.2**). Failure to identify and account for the separate performance obligations in a contract could result in the incorrect timing of revenue recognition.
>
> As a practical matter, it may not be necessary to apply the Standard's detailed requirements on unbundling if the amounts recognised and disclosed in the financial statements will be the same irrespective of whether unbundling is applied. For example, when control of two or more goods or two or more services is transferred at exactly the same time, or on the same basis over the same period of time, and if those items do not need to be segregated for disclosure purposes, then it will not be necessary to unbundle each of those concurrently delivered items, because the amount and timing of revenue recognised and disclosed would not differ if the items were unbundled.

If an entity concludes that a series of distinct goods or services meets the requirements of IFRS 15:22(b), it is required to treat that series as a single performance obligation and may not choose to regard the distinct goods or services in the series as individual performance obligations.

IFRS 15:BC113 clarifies the IASB's intent to mandate the use of this simplification, stating that they "decided to specify that a promise to transfer a series of distinct goods or services that are substantially the same and that have the same pattern of transfer to the customer *would be a single performance obligation* if two criteria are met" (emphasis added).

The issue was discussed by the IASB/FASB Joint Transition Resource Group for Revenue Recognition (see **16.1**) in March 2015.

When identifying the performance obligations in a contract, IFRS 15:22(b) requires a "series of distinct goods or services that are substantially the same and have the same pattern of transfer to the customer" to be identified as a single performance obligation.

A series of goods or services will often be transferred consecutively (e.g. a contract to provide the same package of cleaning services each week for 52 weeks) but in some cases it may not (e.g. a cleaning contract under which no services are provided in some weeks and, in other weeks, cleaning begins before the previous week's work has been completed).

In referring to the 'same pattern of transfer to the customer', IFRS 15:22(b) does not require that the goods or services are transferred consecutively in order to be identified as a single performance obligation. Neither of the criteria in IFRS 15:23 refer to the consecutive transfer of goods or services to the customer and both could be met in, for example, the cleaning contract described above.

This issue was discussed by the IASB/FASB Joint Transition Resources Group for Revenue Recognition (see **16.1**) in March 2015.

6.2   Promises in contracts with customers

The goods or services that will be transferred to the customer are usually explicitly stated in the contract. However, the performance obligations identified in a contract with a customer may not be limited to the goods or services that are explicitly stated in that contract. This is because a contract with a customer may also include promises that are implied by an entity's customary business practices, published policies or specific statements when, at the time of entering into the contract, those promises create a valid expectation of the customer that the entity will transfer a good or service to the customer. [IFRS 15:24]

Example 6.2

Explicit and implicit promises in a contract

[IFRS 15:IE59 - IE65, Example 12]

An entity, a manufacturer, sells a product to a distributor (ie its customer) who will then resell it to an end customer.

Case A – Explicit promise of service

In the contract with the distributor, the entity promises to provide maintenance services for no additional consideration (ie 'free') to any party (ie the end customer) that purchases the product from the distributor. The entity outsources the performance of the maintenance services to the distributor and pays the distributor an agreed-upon amount for providing those services on the entity's behalf. If the end customer does not use the maintenance services, the entity is not obliged to pay the distributor.

Because the promise of maintenance services is a promise to transfer goods or services in the future and is part of the negotiated exchange between the entity and the distributor, the entity determines that the promise to provide maintenance services is a performance obligation (see [IFRS 15:26(g)]). The entity concludes that the promise would represent a performance obligation regardless of whether the entity, the distributor, or a third party provides the service. Consequently, the entity allocates a portion of the transaction price to the promise to provide maintenance services.

Case B – Implicit promise of service

The entity has historically provided maintenance services for no additional consideration (ie 'free') to end customers that purchase the entity's product from the distributor. The entity does not explicitly promise maintenance services during negotiations with the distributor and the final contract between the entity and the distributor does not specify terms or conditions for those services.

However, on the basis of its customary business practice, the entity determines at contract inception that it has made an implicit promise to provide maintenance services as part of the negotiated exchange with the distributor. That is, the entity's past practices of providing these services create valid expectations of the entity's customers (ie the distributor and end customers) in accordance with [IFRS 15:24]. Consequently, the entity identifies the promise of maintenance services as a performance obligation to which it allocates a portion of the transaction price.

Case C – Services are not a performance obligation

In the contract with the distributor, the entity does not promise to provide any maintenance services. In addition, the entity typically does not provide maintenance services and, therefore, the entity's customary business practices, published policies and specific statements at the time of entering into the contract have not created an implicit promise to provide goods or services to its customers. The entity transfers control of the product to the distributor and, therefore, the contract is completed. However, before the sale to the end customer, the entity makes an offer to provide maintenance services to any party that purchases the product from the distributor for no additional promised consideration.

The promise of maintenance is not included in the contract between the entity and the distributor at contract inception. That is, in accordance with [IFRS 15:24], the entity does not explicitly or implicitly promise to provide maintenance services to the distributor or the end customers. Consequently, the entity does not identify the promise to provide maintenance services as a performance obligation. Instead, the obligation to provide maintenance services is accounted for in accordance with IAS 37 *Provisions, Contingent Liabilities and Contingent Assets*.

An activity that is undertaken to fulfil a contract is not a performance obligation unless it transfers a good or service to a customer. For example, a services provider may need to perform various administrative tasks to set up a contract. The performance of those tasks does not transfer a service to the customer as the tasks are performed. Therefore, those set-up activities are not a performance obligation. [IFRS 15:25]

6.3 Distinct goods or services

6.3.1 Determining whether goods or services are 'distinct'

Promised goods or services may include, among other items:

[IFRS 15:26]

(a) sale of goods produced by an entity (e.g. inventory of a manufacturer);

(b) resale of goods purchased by an entity (e.g. merchandise of a retailer);

(c) resale of rights to goods or services purchased by an entity (e.g. a ticket resold by an entity acting as a principal – see **3.6**);

(d) performing a contractually agreed-upon task (or tasks) for a customer;

(e) providing a service of standing ready to provide goods or services (e.g. unspecified updates to software that are provided on a when-and-if-available basis) or of making goods or services available for a customer to use as and when the customer decides;

(f) providing a service of arranging for another party to transfer goods or services to a customer (e.g. acting as an agent of another party – see **3.6**);

(g) granting rights to goods or services to be provided in the future that a customer can resell or provide to its customer (for example, an entity selling a product to a retailer promises to transfer an additional good or service to an individual who purchases the product from the retailer);

(h) constructing, manufacturing or developing an asset on behalf of a customer;

(i)   granting licences (see **section 11**); and

(j)   granting options to purchase additional goods or services that provide the customer with a material right (see **6.3.5**).

Both of the following criteria must be met in order for a good or service to be classified as distinct:

[IFRS 15:27]

(a)   the customer can benefit from the good or service either on its own or together with other resources that are readily available to the customer (i.e. the good or service is capable of being distinct); and

(b)   the entity's promise to transfer the good or service to the customer is separately identifiable from other promises in the contract (i.e. the good or service is distinct within the context of the contract).

For some goods or services, a customer may be able to benefit from a good or service on its own, i.e. if the good or service can be used, consumed, sold for an amount greater than scrap value or otherwise held in a way that generates economic benefits. For other goods or services, a customer may be able to benefit from the good or service only in conjunction with other readily available resources. A readily available resource is a good or service that is sold separately (by the entity or another entity) or a resource that the customer has already obtained from the entity (including goods or services that the entity will have already transferred to the customer under the contract) or from other transactions or events.

Various factors may provide evidence that the customer can benefit from a good or service either on its own or in conjunction with other readily available resources. If an entity regularly sells a good or service separately, this indicates that a customer can benefit from the good or service on its own or with other readily available resources. [IFRS 15:28]

When considering the criterion in IFRS 15:27(b) (see above), factors which indicate that an entity's promise to transfer a good or service to a customer is separately identifiable include:

[IFRS 15:29]

(a)   the entity does not provide a significant service of integrating the good or service with other goods or services promised in the contract into a bundle of goods or services that represent the combined output for which the customer has contracted. In other words, the entity is not using the good or service as an input to produce or deliver the combined output specified by the customer;

(b)   the good or service does not significantly modify or customise another good or service promised in the contract; and

(c)   the good or service is not highly dependent on, or highly interrelated with, other goods or services promised in the contract. For example, the fact that a customer could decide to not purchase the good or service without significantly affecting the other promised goods or services in the contract might indicate that the good or service is not highly dependent on, or highly interrelated with, those other promised goods or services.

Example 6.3.1

Determining whether goods or services are distinct

[IFRS 15:IE49 - 58, Example 11]

Case A – Distinct goods or services

An entity, a software developer, enters into a contract with a customer to transfer a software licence, perform an installation service and provide unspecified software updates and technical support (online and telephone) for a two-year period. The entity sells the licence, installation service and technical support separately. The installation service includes changing the web screen for each type of user (for example, marketing, inventory management and information technology). The installation service is routinely performed by other entities and does not significantly modify the software. The software remains functional without the updates and the technical support.

The entity assesses the goods and services promised to the customer to determine which goods and services are distinct in accordance with [IFRS 15:27]. The entity observes that the software is delivered before the other goods and services and remains functional without the updates and the technical support. Thus, the entity concludes that the customer can benefit from each of the goods and services either on their own or together with the other goods and services that are readily available and the criterion in [IFRS 15:27(a)] is met.

The entity also considers the factors in [IFRS 15:29] and determines that the promise to transfer each good and service to the customer is separately identifiable from each of the other promises (thus the criterion in [IFRS 15:27(b)] is met). In particular, the entity observes that the installation service does not significantly modify or customise the software itself and, as such, the software and the installation service are separate outputs promised by the entity instead of inputs used to produce a combined output.

On the basis of this assessment, the entity identifies four performance obligations in the contract for the following goods or services:

(a) the software licence;

(b) an installation service;

(c) software updates; and

(d) technical support.

The entity applies [IFRS 15:31 to 38] to determine whether each of the performance obligations for the installation service, software updates and technical support are satisfied at a point in time or over time. The entity also assesses the nature of the entity's promise to transfer the software licence in accordance with [IFRS 15:B58 (see **11.2**)].

Case B – Significant customisation

The promised goods and services are the same as in Case A, except that the contract specifies that, as part of the installation service, the software is to be substantially customised to add significant new functionality to enable the software to interface with other customised software applications used by the customer. The customised installation service can be provided by other entities.

The entity assesses the goods and services promised to the customer to determine which goods and services are distinct in accordance with [IFRS 15:27]. The entity observes that the terms of the contract result in a promise to provide a significant service of integrating the licenced software into the existing software system by performing a customised installation service as specified in the contract. In other words, the entity is using the licence and the customised installation service as inputs to produce the combined output (ie a functional and integrated software system) specified in the contract (see [IFRS 15:29(a)]). In addition, the software is significantly modified and customised by the service (see [IFRS 15:29(b)]). Although the customised installation service can be provided by other entities, the entity determines that within the context of the contract, the promise to transfer the licence is not separately identifiable from the customised installation service and, therefore, the criterion in [IFRS 15:27(b)] (on the basis of the factors in [IFRS 15:29] is not met. Thus, the software licence and the customised installation service are not distinct.

As in Case A, the entity concludes that the software updates and technical support are distinct from the other promises in the contract. This is because the customer can benefit from the updates and technical support either on their own or together with the other goods and services that are readily available and because the promise to transfer the software updates and the technical support to the customer are separately identifiable from each of the other promises.

On the basis of this assessment, the entity identifies three performance obligations in the contract for the following goods or services:

(a)   customised installation service (that includes the software licence);

(b)   software updates; and

(c)   technical support.

The entity applies [IFRS 15:31 to 38 (see **section 9**)] to determine whether each performance obligation is satisfied at a point in time or over time.

6.3.2   No exemption from accounting for goods or services considered to be perfunctory or inconsequential

An entity may enter into a contract in which it promises to transfer Product A and Item B to a customer. Product A and Item B meet the criteria in IFRS 15:27 to be considered distinct and do not meet the criteria in IFRS 15:22(b) (i.e. they do not constitute a series of distinct goods or services that are substantially the same and have the same pattern of transfer to the customer (see **6.1**)). Item B may be either a substantive promise in the arrangement (e.g. free maintenance on Product A for two years) or inconsequential (e.g. a promise to participate in a joint committee, delivery of an installation or training manual, a simple installation process that only requires unpacking and plugging in, a simple inspection service).

IFRS 15:BC89 and BC90 clarify that *all* goods or services promised to a customer as a result of a contract give rise to performance obligations because those promises were made as part of the negotiated exchange between the entity and its customer.

Although the entity may consider some of those goods or services to be marketing incentives or incidental goods or services, they are goods or services for which the customer pays and to which the entity should allocate consideration for revenue recognition purposes if they meet the definition of a performance obligation. Although Item B may be considered to be perfunctory or inconsequential, it cannot be ignored. Instead, an entity would assess whether the performance obligation is immaterial to its financial statements as described in IAS 8 *Accounting Policies, Changes in Accounting Estimates and Errors* (see **2.4** in **chapter A5**).

6.3.3 Goods and services that are not distinct

If a promised good or service is not distinct, an entity combines that good or service with other promised goods or services until it identifies a bundle of goods or services that is distinct. In some cases, that will result in all the goods or services promised in a contract being accounted for as a single performance obligation. [IFRS 15:30]

Example 6.3.3

Goods and services are not distinct

[IFRS 15:IE45 - IE48, Example 10]

An entity, a contractor, enters into a contract to build a hospital for a customer. The entity is responsible for the overall management of the project and identifies various goods and services to be provided, including engineering, site clearance, foundation, procurement, construction of the structure, piping and wiring, installation of equipment and finishing.

The promised goods and services are capable of being distinct in accordance with [IFRS 15:27(a)]. That is, the customer can benefit from the goods and services either on their own or together with other readily available resources. This is evidenced by the fact that the entity, or competitors of the entity, regularly sells many of these goods and services separately to other customers. In addition, the customer could generate economic benefit from the individual goods and services by using, consuming, selling or holding those goods or services.

> However, the goods and services are not distinct within the context of the contract in accordance with [IFRS 15:27(b)] (on the basis of the factors in [IFRS 15:29]). That is, the entity's promise to transfer individual goods and services in the contract are not separately identifiable from other promises in the contract. This is evidenced by the fact that the entity provides a significant service of integrating the goods and services (the inputs) into the hospital (the combined output) for which the customer has contracted.
>
> Because both criteria in [IFRS 15:27] are not met, the goods and services are not distinct. The entity accounts for all of the goods and services in the contract as a single performance obligation.

6.3.4   Warranties

Entities often provide a warranty in connection with the sale of a product (whether a good or service). The nature of that warranty can vary significantly across industries and contracts. Some warranties provide the customer with assurance that the related product will function as the parties intended because it complies with agreed-upon specifications (an 'assurance-type' warranty). Other warranties provide the customer with a service in addition to the assurance that the product complies with agreed-upon specifications (a 'service-type' warranty). [IFRS 15:B28]

When the customer can purchase a warranty separately (e.g. because the warranty is priced or negotiated separately), the warranty is a distinct service because the entity has promised to provide that service in addition to the product that has the functionality described in the contract. In such circumstances, the promised warranty is accounted for as a separate performance obligation. This will require a portion of the transaction price to be allocated to the warranty service provided (see **section 8**). [IFRS 15:B29]

When the customer cannot purchase a warranty separately, it should be accounted for in accordance with IAS 37 *Provisions, Contingent Liabilities and Contingent Assets* (see **chapter A12**) unless the promised warranty, or a part of the promised warranty, is a service-type warranty. [IFRS 15:B30]

When considering whether a service-type warranty is being provided, an entity considers factors such as:

[IFRS 15:B31]

(a) whether the warranty is required by law – if the entity is required by law to provide a warranty, the existence of that law indicates that the promised warranty is not a performance obligation because such requirements typically exist to protect customers from the risk of purchasing defective products;

(b) the length of the warranty coverage period – the longer the coverage period, the more likely it is that a service-type warranty exists because it is more likely to provide a service in addition to the assurance that the product complies with the agreed-upon specifications; and

(c) the nature of the tasks that the entity promises to perform – if it is necessary for an entity to perform specified tasks to provide an assurance-type warranty (e.g. a return shipping service for a defective product), then those tasks are likely not to give rise to a performance obligation.

If a warranty, or a part of a warranty, is a service-type warranty, it is accounted for as a separate performance obligation and a portion of the transaction price is allocated to the warranty. If an entity promises both an assurance-type warranty and a service-type warranty but cannot reasonably account for them separately, both warranties should be accounted for together as a single performance obligation. [IFRS 15:B32]

A law that requires an entity to pay compensation if its products cause harm or damage does not give rise to a performance obligation. For example, a manufacturer might sell products in a jurisdiction in which the law holds the manufacturer liable for any damages (e.g. to personal property) that might be caused by a consumer using a product for its intended purpose. Similarly, an entity's promise to indemnify the customer for liabilities and damages arising from claims of patent, copyright, trademark or other infringement by the entity's products does not give rise to a performance obligation. Such obligations should be accounted for in accordance with IAS 37. [IFRS 15:B33]

Example 6.3.4

Warranties

[IFRS 15:IE223 - IE229, Example 44]

An entity, a manufacturer, provides its customer with a warranty with the purchase of a product. The warranty provides assurance that the product complies with agreed-upon specifications and will operate as promised for one year from the date of purchase. The contract also provides the customer with the right to receive up to 20 hours of training services on how to operate the product at no additional cost.

The entity assesses the goods and services in the contract to determine whether they are distinct and therefore give rise to separate performance obligations.

The product is distinct because it meets both criteria in [IFRS 15:27]. The product is capable of being distinct in accordance with [IFRS 15:27(a) & 28], because the customer can benefit from the product on its own without the training services. The entity regularly sells the product separately without the training services. In addition, the product is distinct within the context of the contract in accordance with [IFRS 15:27(b) & 29], because the entity's promise to transfer the product is separately identifiable from other promises in the contract.

In addition, the training services are distinct because they meet both criteria in [IFRS 15:27]. The training services are capable of being distinct in accordance with [IFRS 15:27(a) and 28], because the customer can benefit from the training services together with the product that has already been provided by the entity. In addition, the training services are distinct within the context of the contract in accordance with [IFRS 15:27(b) and 29], because the entity's promise to transfer the training services is separately identifiable from other promises in the contract. The entity does not provide a significant service of integrating the training services with the product (see [IFRS 15:29(a)]). The training services are not significantly modified or customised by the product (see [IFRS 15:29(b)]). The training services are not highly dependent on, or highly interrelated with, the product (see [IFRS 15:29(c)]).

The product and training services are each distinct and therefore give rise to two separate performance obligations.

Finally, the entity assesses the promise to provide a warranty and observes that the warranty provides the customer with the assurance that the product will function as intended for one year. The entity concludes, in accordance with [IFRS 15:B28 to B33], that the warranty does not provide the customer with a good or service in addition to that assurance and, therefore, the entity does not account for it as a performance obligation. The entity accounts for the assurance-type warranty in accordance with the requirements in IAS 37.

As a result, the entity allocates the transaction price to the two performance obligations (the product and the training services) and recognises revenue when (or as) those performance obligations are satisfied.

6.3.5   Customer options for additional goods or services

Customer options to acquire additional goods or services for free or at a discount come in many forms, including sales incentives, customer award credits (or points), contract renewal options or other discounts on future goods or services. [IFRS 15:B39]

When a contract grants the customer an option to acquire additional goods or services, that option gives rise to a performance obligation in the contract only when it provides a material right to the customer that the customer would not have received without entering into that contract (e.g. a discount is incremental to the range of discounts typically given for those goods or services to that class of customer in that geographical area or market). If the option provides a material right to the customer, the customer is, in effect, paying the entity in advance for future goods or services. Therefore the entity should defer the recognition of revenue allocated to that option until those future goods or services are transferred, or when the option expires. [IFRS 15:B40]

If the amount that the customer would pay for the additional good or service reflects the stand-alone selling price for that good or service, the option does not provide the customer with a material right even if the option can only be exercised by entering into a previous contract. In these circumstances, the entity has merely made a marketing offer, and it will account in accordance with IFRS 15 only when the customer exercises the option to purchase the additional goods or services. [IFRS 15:B41]

IFRS 15:74 requires an entity to allocate the transaction price to performance obligations on a relative stand-alone selling price basis (see **section 8**). If the stand-alone selling price for a customer's option to acquire additional goods or services is not directly observable, an entity is required to estimate it. The estimate should reflect the discount that the customer would obtain when exercising the option, adjusted for both:

[IFRS 15:B42]

(a) any discount that the customer could receive without exercising the option; and

(b) the likelihood that the option will be exercised.

IFRS 15 provides a practical alternative to estimating the stand-alone selling price of an option when the customer has a material right to acquire future goods or services and those goods or services are similar to the original goods or services in the contract and are provided in accordance with the terms of the original contract. In this scenario, the transaction price can be allocated to the optional goods or services by reference to the goods or services expected to be provided and the corresponding expected consideration. This simplified approach is illustrated in IFRS 15 Illustrative Example 51, which is reproduced as **example 6.3.5C**. These options are typically for contract renewals. [IFRS 15:B43]

Example 6.3.5A

Option that provides the customer with a material right (discount voucher)

[IFRS 15:IE250 - IE253, Example 49]

An entity enters into a contract for the sale of Product A for CU100. As part of the contract, the entity gives the customer a 40 per cent discount voucher for any future purchases up to CU100 in the next 30 days. The entity intends to offer a 10 per cent discount on all sales during the next 30 days as part of a seasonal promotion. The 10 per cent discount cannot be used in addition to the 40 per cent discount voucher.

Because all customers will receive a 10 per cent discount on purchases during the next 30 days, the only discount that provides the customer with a material right is the discount that is incremental to that 10 per cent (ie the additional 30 per cent discount). The entity accounts for the promise to provide the incremental discount as a performance obligation in the contract for the sale of Product A.

To estimate the stand-alone selling price of the discount voucher in accordance with [IFRS 15:B42], the entity estimates an 80 per cent likelihood that a customer

---

will redeem the voucher and that a customer will, on average, purchase CU50 of additional products. Consequently, the entity's estimated stand-alone selling price of the discount voucher is CU12 (CU50 average purchase price of additional products × 30 per cent incremental discount × 80 per cent likelihood of exercising the option). The stand-alone selling prices of Product A and the discount voucher and the resulting allocation of the CU100 transaction price are as follows:

Performance obligation	Stand-alone selling price
	CU
Product A	100
Discount voucher	12
Total	112

	Allocated transaction price	
Product A	89	(CU100 ÷ CU112 x CU100)
Discount voucher	11	(CU12 ÷ CU112 x CU100)
Total	100	

The entity allocates CU89 to Product A and recognises revenue for Product A when control transfers. The entity allocates CU11 to the discount voucher and recognises revenue for the voucher when the customer redeems it for goods or services or when it expires.

Example 6.3.5B

Option that does not provide the customer with a material right (additional goods or services)

[IFRS 15:IE254 - IE256, Example 50]

An entity in the telecommunications industry enters into a contract with a customer to provide a handset and monthly network service for two years. The network service includes up to 1,000 call minutes and 1,500 text messages each month for a fixed monthly fee. The contract specifies the price for any additional call minutes or texts that the customer may choose to purchase in any month. The prices for those services are equal to their stand-alone selling prices.

The entity determines that the promises to provide the handset and network service are each separate performance obligations. This is because the customer can benefit from the handset and network service either on their own or together with other resources that are readily available to the customer in accordance with the criterion in [IFRS 15:27(a)]. In addition, the handset and network service are separately identifiable in accordance with the criterion in [IFRS 15:27(b)] (on the basis of the factors in [IFRS 15:29]).

The entity determines that the option to purchase the additional call minutes and texts does not provide a material right that the customer would not receive without entering into the contract (see [IFRS 15:B41]). This is because the prices of the additional call minutes and texts reflect the stand-alone selling prices for those services. Because the option for additional call minutes and texts does not grant the customer a material right, the entity concludes it is not a performance obligation in the contract. Consequently, the entity does not allocate any of the transaction price to the option for additional call minutes or texts. The entity will recognise revenue for the additional call minutes or texts if and when the entity provides those services.

Example 6.3.5C

Option that provides the customer with a material right (renewal option)

[IFRS 15:IE257 - IE266, Example 51]

An entity enters into 100 separate contracts with customers to provide one year of maintenance services for CU1,000 per contract. The terms of the contracts specify that at the end of the year, each customer has the option to renew the maintenance contract for a second year by paying an additional CU1,000. Customers who renew for a second year are also granted the option to renew for a third year for CU1,000. The entity charges significantly higher prices for maintenance services to customers that do not sign up for the maintenance services initially (ie when the products are new). That is, the entity charges CU3,000 in Year 2 and CU5,000 in Year 3 for annual maintenance services if a customer does not initially purchase the service or allows the service to lapse.

The entity concludes that the renewal option provides a material right to the customer that it would not receive without entering into the contract, because the price for maintenance services are significantly higher if the customer elects to purchase the services only in Year 2 or 3. Part of each customer's payment of CU1,000 in the first year is, in effect, a non-refundable prepayment of the services to be provided in a subsequent year. Consequently, the entity concludes that the promise to provide the option is a performance obligation.

The renewal option is for a continuation of maintenance services and those services are provided in accordance with the terms of the existing contract. Instead of determining the stand-alone selling prices for the renewal options directly, the entity allocates the transaction price by determining the consideration that it expects to receive in exchange for all the services that it expects to provide, in accordance with [IFRS 15:B43].

The entity expects 90 customers to renew at the end of Year 1 (90 per cent of contracts sold) and 81 customers to renew at the end of Year 2 (90 per cent of the 90 customers that renewed at the end of Year 1 will also renew at the end of Year 2, that is 81 per cent of contracts sold).

At contract inception, the entity determines the expected consideration for each contract is CU2,710 [CU1,000 + (90 per cent × CU1,000) + (81 per cent × CU1,000)]. The entity also determines that recognising revenue on the basis of costs incurred relative to the total expected costs depicts the transfer of services to the customer. Estimated costs for a three-year contract are as follows:

	CU
Year 1	600
Year 2	750
Year 3	1,000

Accordingly, the pattern of revenue recognition expected at contract inception for each contract is as follows:

	Expected costs adjusted for likelihood of contract renewal	Allocation of consideration expected
	CU	CU
Year 1	600 (CU600 × 100%)	780 (CU600 / CU2,085 × CU2,710)
Year 2	675 (CU750 × 90%)	877 (CU675 / CU2,085 × CU2,710)
Year 3	810 (CU1,000 × 81%)	1,053 (CU810 / CU2,085 × CU2,710)
Total	2,085	2,710

Consequently, at contract inception, the entity allocates to the option to renew at the end of Year 1 CU22,000 of the consideration received to date [cash of CU100,000 – revenue to be recognised in Year 1 of CU78,000 (CU780 × 100)].

Assuming there is no change in the entity's expectations and the 90 customers renew as expected, at the end of the first year, the entity has collected cash of CU190,000 [(100 × CU1,000) + (90 × CU1,000)], has recognised revenue of CU78,000 (CU780 × 100) and has recognised a contract liability of CU112,000.

Consequently, upon renewal at the end of the first year, the entity allocates CU24,300 to the option to renew at the end of Year 2 [cumulative cash of CU190,000 less cumulative revenue recognised in Year 1 and to be recognised in Year 2 of CU165,700 (CU78,000 + CU877 × 100)].

If the actual number of contract renewals was different than what the entity expected, the entity would update the transaction price and the revenue recognised accordingly.

Example 6.3.5D

Customer loyalty programme

[IFRS 15:IE267 - IE270, Example 52]

An entity has a customer loyalty programme that rewards a customer with one customer loyalty point for every CU10 of purchases. Each point is redeemable for a CU1 discount on any future purchases of the entity's products. During a reporting period, customers purchase products for CU100,000 and earn 10,000 points that are redeemable for future purchases. The consideration is fixed and the stand-alone selling price of the purchased products is CU100,000. The entity expects 9,500 points to be redeemed. The entity estimates a stand-alone selling price of CU0.95 per point (totalling CU9,500) on the basis of the likelihood of redemption in accordance with [IFRS 15:B42].

The points provide a material right to customers that they would not receive without entering into a contract. Consequently, the entity concludes that the promise to provide points to the customer is a performance obligation. The entity allocates the transaction price (CU100,000) to the product and the points on a relative stand-alone selling price basis as follows:

	CU	
Product	91,324	[CU100,000 x (CU100,000 stand-alone selling price / CU109,500)]
Points	8,676	[CU100,000 x (CU9,500 stand-alone selling price / CU109,500)]

At the end of the first reporting period, 4,500 points have been redeemed and the entity continues to expect 9,500 points to be redeemed in total. The entity recognises revenue for the loyalty points of CU4,110 [(4,500 points ÷ 9,500 points) × CU8,676] and recognises a contract liability of CU4,566 (CU8,676 − CU4,110) for the unredeemed points at the end of the first reporting period.

At the end of the second reporting period, 8,500 points have been redeemed cumulatively. The entity updates its estimate of the points that will be redeemed and now expects that 9,700 points will be redeemed. The entity recognises revenue for the loyalty points of CU3,493 {[(8,500 total points redeemed ÷ 9,700 total points expected to be redeemed) × CU8,676 initial allocation] − CU4,110 recognised in the first reporting period}. The contract liability balance is CU1,073 (CU8,676 initial allocation − CU7,603 of cumulative revenue recognised).

6.3.6 Non-refundable upfront fees

A customer may be charged a non-refundable upfront fee at or near contract inception (e.g. joining fees in health club membership contracts, activation fees in telecommunication contracts, setup fees in some services contracts and initial fees in some supply contracts). [IFRS 15:B48]

An entity should assess whether the fee relates to the transfer of a promised good or service which represents a separate performance obligation. Even though a non-refundable upfront fee can relate to an activity that the entity is required to undertake at or near contract inception to fulfil the contract, in many cases that activity does not result in the transfer of a promised good or service to the customer (see **6.2**). Instead, the upfront fee is an advance payment for future goods or services and is recognised as revenue when those future goods or services are provided. If the entity grants the customer the option to renew the contract and that option provides the customer with a material right (see **6.3.5**), the revenue recognition period is extended beyond the initial contractual period. [IFRS 15:B49]

If the non-refundable upfront fee relates to a good or service, the entity should evaluate whether to account for the good or service as a separate performance obligations. [IFRS 15:B50]

An entity may charge a non-refundable fee, some of which is to compensate for costs incurred in setting up a contract or other administrative costs. If those setup activities do not satisfy a performance obligation, the entity should disregard those activities (and related costs) when measuring progress to assess when to recognise revenue (see **9.3.2**). This is because those costs do not depict the transfer of services to the customer. It will also be necessary to consider whether the costs incurred in setting up a contract should be capitalised (see **12.3**). [IFRS 15:B51]

> Under IFRS 15, the timing of recognition of revenue is not based on cash receipt or payment schedules. Instead, an entity recognises revenue when (or as) it satisfies a performance obligation by transferring control of a promised good or service to a customer.
>
> When consideration is received by an entity before the related performance obligation is satisfied, the advance payment should not be recognised as revenue until that obligation is satisfied. Instead, the entity should recognise the consideration received as a contract liability (i.e. deferred revenue) in its statement of financial position.

Example 6.3.6A

Non-refundable upfront fee

[IFRS 15:IE272 - IE274, Example 53]

An entity enters into a contract with a customer for one year of transaction processing services. The entity's contracts have standard terms that are the same for all customers. The contract requires the customer to pay an upfront fee to set up the customer on the entity's systems and processes. The fee is a nominal amount and is non-refundable. The customer can renew the contract each year without paying an additional fee.

The entity's setup activities do not transfer a good or service to the customer and, therefore, do not give rise to a performance obligation.

The entity concludes that the renewal option does not provide a material right to the customer that it would not receive without entering into that contract (see [IFRS 15:B40]). The upfront fee is, in effect, an advance payment for the future transaction processing services. Consequently, the entity determines the transaction price, which includes the non-refundable upfront fee, and recognises revenue for the transaction.

Example 6.3.6B

Upfront fees received upon entering into a contract – club membership fees

An entity operates a fitness club. The key terms of its contractual arrangements with customers are as follows.

- Customers are required to pay a joining fee of CU100 upon entering into the contract.

- Each contract has a term of one year. During the contractual period, customers are required to pay a monthly fee of CU100 (irrespective of their usage of the club during that month).

- The joining fee is not refundable, even if the customer never uses the club during the one-year contract period.

Should the entity recognise the joining fee as revenue when it is received, on the basis that it is non-refundable?

No. Under IFRS 15, an entity should recognise revenue when (or as) it satisfies a performance obligation by transferring a promised good or service to a customer.

In the circumstances under consideration, customers pay the joining fee and monthly fees to use the facilities provided by the fitness club. The performance obligation is therefore to provide fitness club facilities for customers' use and the joining fee is part of the consideration paid by customers to use the facilities in the future. No performance obligation has been satisfied when the fee is received and, therefore, no revenue should be recognised at that time.

Instead, the joining fee should be recognised as a liability. Such consideration would be included in the transaction price and recognised as revenue when (or as) the associated performance obligation(s) are satisfied.

---

7 Step 3: Determine the transaction price

7.1 Determination of the transaction price – general

The transaction price is the amount of consideration to which an entity expects to be entitled in exchange for transferring promised goods or services to a customer, excluding those amounts collected on behalf of third parties (e.g. some sales taxes). It may include fixed amounts, variable amounts, or both. Both the terms of the contract and the entity's customary business practices need to be considered in order to determine the transaction price. [IFRS 15:47]

The estimate of the transaction price will be affected by the nature, timing and amount of consideration promised by a customer. In determining the transaction price, the effects of all of the following should be considered:

[IFRS 15:48]

(a) variable consideration (see **7.2**);

(b) constraining estimates of variable consideration (see **7.3**);

(c) the existence of a significant financing component in the contract (see **7.4**);

(d) non-cash consideration (see **7.5**); and

(e) consideration payable to a customer (see **7.6**)

For the purpose of determining the transaction price, it should be assumed that the goods or services will be transferred to the customer as promised in accordance with the existing contract and that there will be no cancellation, renewal or modification. [IFRS 15:49]

IAS 18 includes little guidance on variable consideration and the other topics listed above. In addition, IAS 18 is silent on whether the time value of money should be taken into account when a customer pays in advance.

An entity should only take a customer's credit risk into account when determining the discount rate used to adjust the promised consideration for a significant financing component, if any.

IFRS 15:47 specifies that the transaction price is the amount to which an entity expects to be *entitled*, rather than the amount it expects to *collect*. The determination of the amount to which an entity expects to be entitled is not affected by the risk of whether it expects the customer to default (i.e. the customer's credit risk). IFRS 15:BC260 to 261 explain that this approach was adopted to enable users of the financial statements to analyse 'gross' revenue (i.e. the amount to which the entity is entitled) separately from the effect of receivables management (or bad debts).

However, when the timing of payments due under the contract provides the customer with a significant benefit of financing, the transaction price is adjusted to reflect the time value of money. IFRS 15:BC239 indicates that, in such circumstances, an entity will take a customer's credit risk into account in determining the appropriate discount rate to apply. As illustrated in **example 7.4.6D**, this rate will affect the amount of revenue recognised for the transfer of goods or services under the contract.

It should also be noted that a customer's credit risk is a factor in the determination of whether a contract exists, because one of the criteria for identification of a contract in IFRS 15:9 is that collection of consideration to which the entity is entitled is probable.

7.2 Estimating variable consideration

7.2.1 Variable consideration

If the consideration includes a variable amount, the entity is required to estimate the amount of consideration to which it will be entitled in exchange for transferring the promised goods or services to the customer. [IFRS 15:50]

Examples of variable consideration include discounts, rebates, refunds, credits, price concessions (see **example 7.3A**), incentives (see **example 7.3B**), performance bonuses and penalties (see **example 7.2.1A**). Consideration can also vary if entitlement to the consideration is contingent on the occurrence or non-occurrence of a future event. Examples include a product sold with a right of return or a fixed amount promised as a performance bonus on achievement of a specified milestone. [IFRS 15:51]

Example 7.2.1A

Penalty gives rise to variable consideration

[IFRS 15:IE102 - IE104, Example 20]

An entity enters into a contract with a customer to build an asset for CU1 million. In addition, the terms of the contract include a penalty of CU100,000 if the construction is not completed within three months of a date specified in the contract.

The entity concludes that the consideration promised in the contract includes a fixed amount of CU900,000 and a variable amount of CU100,000 (arising from the penalty).

The entity estimates the variable consideration in accordance with [IFRS 15:50 to 54] and considers the requirements in [IFRS 15:56 to 58 (see **7.3**)] on constraining estimates of variable consideration.

The fact that consideration may vary may be explicitly set out in the contract. However, a contract also includes variable consideration if either of the following circumstances exists:

[IFRS 15:52]

(a) the customer has a valid expectation arising from the entity's customary business practices, published policies or specific statements that the entity will accept an amount of consideration less than that stated in the contract (i.e. it is expected that the entity will offer a price concession). This offer may be referred to as a discount, rebate, refund or credit in certain jurisdictions or industries; or

(b) other facts and circumstances indicate that it is the entity's intention to offer a price concession to the customer when entering into the contract with the customer.

One of the following methods should be used to estimate the amount of variable consideration, depending on which method better predicts the amount of consideration to which the entity will be entitled:

[IFRS 15:53]

(a) the expected value method – this may be appropriate when the entity has a large number of contracts with similar characteristics and is calculated as the sum of probability-weighted amounts in a range of possible consideration amounts; and

(b) the most likely amount – this may be appropriate when a contract has only two possible outcomes (e.g. the amount received is based on whether a performance bonus is achieved, or not). It is the single most likely amount in a range of possible consideration amounts (i.e. the single most likely outcome of the contract).

The method an entity uses to estimate variable consideration is not a free choice; the entity should use whichever method will better predict the amount of consideration to which it will become entitled.

When a contract has only two possible outcomes, it will often be appropriate to estimate variable consideration by using a method based on the most likely amount.

When the entity has a large number of contracts with similar characteristics, and the outcome for each contract is independent of the others, the expected value method may better predict the overall outcome for the contracts in aggregate. This will be true even when each individual contract has only two possible outcomes (e.g. a sale with a right of return). This is because an entity will often have better information about the probabilities of various outcomes when there are a large number of similar transactions.

It is important, however, to consider carefully whether the outcome for each contract is truly independent of the others. For example, if the outcome is binary but is determined by the occurrence or non-occurrence of the same event for all contracts (i.e. the variable amount will be received either for all of the contracts or for none of them), the expected value is unlikely to be a good predictor of the overall outcome and the entity may need to use the most likely amount method to estimate the variable consideration in the contracts.

Example 7.2.1B

Selection of method for estimating variable consideration

Each year, Entity A's performance is ranked against that of its competitors in a particular jurisdiction. All of Entity A's customer contracts specify that a fixed bonus of CU500 will be due to Entity A if it is ranked in the top quartile. Entity A has approximately 1,000 customer contracts.

Should Entity A estimate the variable consideration (i.e. the bonus) on the basis of the expected value or the most likely amount?

Entity A should estimate the variable consideration on the basis of the most likely amount. Although Entity A has a large number of contracts, the outcomes are not independent because they all depend on the same criterion (i.e. the ranking of Entity A against its competitors). The bonus will be payable under either all the contracts or none of them. Consequently, the overall outcome for the contracts in aggregate will be binary, and the expected value will not be a good predictor of that overall outcome.

Example 7.2.1C

Estimating variable consideration

[IFRS 15:IE105 - IE108, Example 21]

An entity enters into a contract with a customer to build a customised asset. The promise to transfer the asset is a performance obligation that is satisfied over time. The promised consideration is CU2.5 million, but that amount will be reduced or increased depending on the timing of completion of the asset. Specifically, for each day after 31 March 20X7 that the asset is incomplete, the promised consideration is reduced by CU10,000. For each day before 31 March 20X7 that the asset is complete, the promised consideration increases by CU10,000.

In addition, upon completion of the asset, a third party will inspect the asset and assign a rating based on metrics that are defined in the contract. If the asset receives a specified rating, the entity will be entitled to an incentive bonus of CU150,000.

In determining the transaction price, the entity prepares a separate estimate for each element of variable consideration to which the entity will be entitled using the estimation methods described in [IFRS 15:53]:

(a) the entity decides to use the expected value method to estimate the variable consideration associated with the daily penalty or incentive (ie CU2.5 million, plus or minus CU10,000 per day). This is because it is the method that the entity expects to better predict the amount of consideration to which it will be entitled.

(b) the entity decides to use the most likely amount to estimate the variable consideration associated with the incentive bonus. This is because there are only two possible outcomes (CU150,000 or CU0) and it is the method that the entity expects to better predict the amount of consideration to which it will be entitled.

The entity considers the requirements in [IFRS 15:56 to 58 (see **7.3**)] on constraining estimates of variable consideration to determine whether the entity should include some or all of its estimate of variable consideration in the transaction price.

The method applied should be used consistently throughout the contract when estimating the effect of an uncertainty on an amount of variable consideration to which the entity will be entitled. All the information (historical, current and forecast) that is reasonably available to the entity should be considered in assessing the amount of variable consideration, and a reasonable number of possible consideration amounts should be identified. This information would typically be similar to the information that management uses during the bid-and-proposal process and in establishing prices for promised goods or services. [IFRS 15:54]

Under IFRS 15:53, when the consideration promised in a contract with a customer includes a variable amount that is accounted for in accordance with IFRS 15, an entity should estimate the amount of consideration to which it will be entitled by using either of the following methods: (1) expected value, or (2) most likely amount. IFRS 15:54 requires that an entity apply one method consistently throughout the contract and consider all reasonably available information when estimating the amount of variable consideration to which it will be entitled.

When a contract contains multiple elements of variability, an entity can use more than one method (i.e. the expected value method and the most likely amount method) to estimate the amount of variable consideration to be included in the transaction price. Example 21 of the Illustrative Examples accompanying IFRS 15 (**example 7.2.1C**) shows that an entity should prepare a separate estimate for each element of variable consideration in a contract (i.e. for each uncertainty) by using either the expected value method or the most likely amount, whichever method better predicts the amount of consideration to which it will be entitled.

Because IFRS 15:54 requires entities to apply one method consistently to each variable element throughout the contract, it would not be appropriate to switch between the expected value method and the most likely amount for a particular variable element during the life of a contract.

An entity should also consider the guidance in IFRS 15:56 to 58 on constraining estimates of variable consideration to determine whether it should include some or all of the variable consideration in the transaction price.

Example 7.2.1D

Using more than one method to estimate variable consideration within one contract

Entity A, an information technology service provider, enters into a contract with a customer to develop the customer's website. To induce Entity A to complete the project on a timely basis, and to provide a solution that drives business growth for the customer, the fee receivable by Entity A under the contract includes variable consideration which is determined as follows.

- One element of the fee is based on the performance of the website and is determined by using a sliding scale from CU500,000 to CU1 million. The amount earned is based on a formula that uses a number of metrics (e.g. the number of pages viewed and the number of unique visitors) measured over the two-year period after the website is completed and fully functional.

- The other element of the fee is based on the timely completion of the website and is determined as follows:

  - CU1 million if the website is completed and fully functional within 90 days of signing the contract; or

  - CU500,000 if the website is completed and fully functional more than 90 days after the contract is signed.

Having considered the guidance in IFRS 15:53 on selecting an appropriate method for estimating the amount of variable consideration, Entity A applies the following methods to each element of variability in the contract:

- the amount of consideration related to the performance of the customer's website is estimated by using the expected value method because Entity A estimates that it could be entitled to a wide range of possible consideration amounts (any amount between CU500,000 and CU1 million); and

- the amount of consideration related to the timely completion of the website is estimated by using the most likely amount method because this element of variable consideration has only two possible outcomes (CU1 million if the website is completed and fully functional within 90 days or CU500,000 if the website is completed and fully functional after more than 90 days).

Entity A should continue to use the selected method for each element consistently for the entire duration of the contract.

7.2.2 Sale with a right of return

In some contracts, an entity transfers control of a product to a customer and also grants the customer the right to return the product for various reasons (e.g. dissatisfaction with the product) and receive a combination of the following:

[IFRS 15:B20]

(a) a full or partial refund of any consideration paid;

(b) a credit that can be applied against amounts owed, or that will be owed, to the entity; or

(c) another product in exchange.

To account for the transfer of products with a right of return (and for some services that are provided subject to a refund), the entity should recognise all of the following:

[IFRS 15:B21]

(a) an amount of revenue for the products transferred based on the consideration to which the entity expects to be entitled (therefore, revenue should not be recognised for the products expected to be returned);

(b) a refund liability for the amounts expected to be refunded (see **7.2.3** and **section 13**); and

(c) an asset, with a corresponding adjustment to cost of sales, for the entity's right to recover products from customers on settling the refund liability.

An entity's promise to stand ready to accept a returned product during the return period is not accounted for as a performance obligation in addition to the obligation to provide a refund. [IFRS 15:B22]

Entities frequently offer customers the right to return a product within a specified period after its initial sale, provided that the customer has not used or damaged the product. As noted in IFRS 15:B22, a right of return is not a separate performance obligation. However, a customer's right to return a product may affect the amount of revenue recognised (the transaction price) because revenue may only be recognised for goods that are not expected to be returned. In accordance with IFRS 15:56, the transaction price should only include amounts for sales subject to return to the extent that it is highly probable that there will not be a significant reversal of cumulative revenue after the uncertainty associated with expected returns is resolved.

The transaction price should be estimated in the same way as any other variable consideration (see **example 7.2.2**) and should reflect the amount to which the entity expects to be entitled, which should be adjusted to exclude amounts expected to be reimbursed or credited to customers, by using either the expected value method or the most likely amount (as discussed in **7.2.1**).

For example, when a retail store has a policy that allows a customer to return a product within 30 days for any reason, no amount of the transaction price is allocated to the 'service' of standing ready to accept the returned product. Instead, the transaction price is estimated and constrained to the amount for which the entity expects it is highly probable that significant reversal will not occur when the uncertainty associated with expected returns is resolved. An adjustment to revenue will then be recognised when the level of returns is known after 30 days or by updating the estimated transaction price as of any reporting date falling within that period.

The requirements of IFRS 15 in respect of determining the transaction price, including the guidance on constraining estimates of variable consideration (see **7.3**), should be applied to determine the amount of consideration to which the entity expects to be entitled (i.e. excluding the products expected to be returned). When amounts are received (or become receivable) to which an entity does not expect to be entitled, revenue is not recognised when the products are transferred to the customers, but instead a refund liability is recognised. The amount to which the entity expects to be entitled should then be reassessed at the end of each reporting period, and a corresponding change made to the transaction price and, therefore, to the amount of revenue recognised. [IFRS 15:B23]

The refund liability should be updated at the end of each reporting period for changes in expectations about the amount of refunds. Any corresponding adjustments are recognised as revenue (or as reductions of revenue). [IFRS 15:B24]

An asset recognised for an entity's right to recover products from a customer on settling a refund liability should initially be measured by reference to the former carrying amount of the product (e.g. inventory) less any expected costs to recover those products (including potential decreases in the value to the entity of returned products). At the end of each reporting period, the measurement of the asset should be updated for changes in expectations about products to be returned. The asset should be presented separately from the refund liability. [IFRS 15:B25]

Example 7.2.2

Right of return

[IFRS 15:IE110 - IE115, Example 22]

An entity enters into 100 contracts with customers. Each contract includes the sale of one product for CU100 (100 total products × CU100 = CU10,000 total consideration). Cash is received when control of a product transfers. The entity's customary business practice is to allow a customer to return any unused product within 30 days and receive a full refund. The entity's cost of each product is CU60.

The entity applies the requirements in IFRS 15 to the portfolio of 100 contracts because it reasonably expects that, in accordance with [IFRS 15:4], the effects on the financial statements from applying these requirements to the portfolio would not differ materially from applying the requirements to the individual contracts within the portfolio.

Because the contract allows a customer to return the products, the consideration received from the customer is variable. To estimate the variable consideration to which the entity will be entitled, the entity decides to use the expected value method (see [IFRS 15:53(a)]) because it is the method that the entity expects to better predict the amount of consideration to which it will be entitled. Using the expected value method, the entity estimates that 97 products will not be returned.

The entity also considers the requirements in [IFRS 15:56 to 58] on constraining estimates of variable consideration to determine whether the estimated amount of variable consideration of CU9,700 (CU100 × 97 products not expected to be returned) can be included in the transaction price. The entity considers the factors in [IFRS 15:57] and determines that although the returns are outside the entity's influence, it has significant experience in estimating returns for this product and customer class. In addition, the uncertainty will be resolved within a short time frame (ie the 30-day return period). Thus, the entity concludes that it is highly probable that a significant reversal in the cumulative amount of revenue recognised (ie CU9,700) will not occur as the uncertainty is resolved (ie over the return period).

The entity estimates that the costs of recovering the products will be immaterial and expects that the returned products can be resold at a profit.

Upon transfer of control of the 100 products, the entity does not recognise revenue for the three products that it expects to be returned. Consequently, in accordance with [IFRS 15:55] and [IFRS 15:B21], the entity recognises the following:

(a)   revenue of CU9,700 (CU100 × 97 products not expected to be returned);

(b)   a refund liability of CU300 (CU100 refund × 3 products expected to be returned); and

(c)   an asset of CU180 (CU60 × 3 products for its right to recover products from customers on settling the refund liability).

The requirements of IFRS 15:56 to 58 on constraining estimates of variable consideration are discussed at **7.3**.

When a customer exchanges one product for another of the same type, quality, condition and price (e.g. one colour or size for another), this is not considered a return transaction for the purposes of applying IFRS 15. [IFRS 15:B26]

The right of a customer to return a defective product in exchange for a functioning product should be accounted for by applying the guidance on warranties (see **6.3.4**). [IFRS 15:B27]

7.2.3   Refund liabilities

If an entity receives consideration from a customer and expects to refund some or all of that consideration to the customer, a refund liability is recognised. The refund liability is measured at the amount of consideration received (or receivable) to which the entity does *not* expect to be entitled (i.e. amounts not included in the transaction price). The refund liability is updated at the end of each reporting period for changes in circumstances and corresponding changes made to the transaction price and, therefore, the contract liability. IFRS 15 includes specific guidance when the refund liability relates to a sale with a right of return (see **7.2.2**). [IFRS 15:55]

7.2.4 Cash discounts

Example 7.2.4

Cash discounts

A seller offers a cash discount for immediate or prompt payment (i.e. earlier than required under the normal credit terms). A sale is made for CU100 with the balance due within 90 days. If the customer pays within 30 days, the customer will receive a 10 per cent discount on the total invoice. The seller sells a large volume of similar items on these credit terms (i.e. this transaction is part of a portfolio of similar items). The seller has elected to apply the practical expedient set out in IFRS 15:63 (see **7.4.2**) and, therefore, will not adjust the promised amount of consideration for the effects of a significant financing component.

How should the seller account for this early payment incentive?

IFRS 15 defines 'transaction price' as "the amount of consideration to which an entity expects to be entitled in exchange for transferring promised goods or services to a customer". This amount can vary because of discounts, rebates, refunds, credits, incentives, performance bonuses, penalties, price concessions or other similar items.

In the circumstances described, revenue is CU100 if the discount is not taken and CU90 if the discount is taken. As a result, the amount of consideration to which the entity will be entitled is variable.

Under IFRS 15, if the consideration promised in a contract includes a variable amount, an entity should estimate the amount of variable consideration to which it will be entitled by (1) using either the 'expected value' or the 'most likely amount' method (whichever method the entity expects would better predict the amount of consideration to which it will be entitled), and then (2) considering the effect of the constraint in accordance with IFRS 15:56 to 58 (see **7.3**).

Therefore, the seller should recognise revenue when or as the performance obligation is satisfied, net of the amount of cash discount expected to be taken, measured as described in the previous paragraph.

For example, if the discount is taken in 40 per cent of transactions, the expected value will be calculated as follows.

(CU100 x 60%) + (CU90 x 40%) = CU96

If the proportion of transactions for which the discount is taken is always close to 40 per cent (i.e. it is within a narrow range around 40 per cent), then it is likely that the estimate of variable consideration will not need to be constrained, and revenue of CU96 will be recognised.

If, however, the proportion of transactions for which the discount is taken varies significantly, it may be necessary to apply the constraint, which will result in the recognition of less revenue. For example, historical records might show that, although the long-term average is 40 per cent, there is great variability from month to month and that the proportion of transactions for which the discount is taken is frequently as high as 70 per cent (but has never been higher than that). In such a scenario, the seller might conclude that only 30 per cent of the variable consideration should be included, because inclusion of a higher amount might result in a significant revenue reversal. In that case, the amount of revenue recognised would be restricted to the following.

(CU100 × 30%) + (CU90 × 70%) = CU93

7.2.5 Reassessment of variable consideration

The estimated transaction price is updated at the end of each reporting period (including updating the assessment of whether an estimate of variable consideration should be constrained – see **7.3**) to represent the circumstances present at the end of the reporting period and any changes in circumstances during the reporting period. IFRS 15 specifies how changes in the estimated transaction price should be recognised (see **8.5**). [IFRS 15:59]

7.3 Constraining estimates of variable consideration

IFRS 15 includes separate requirements in relation to the recognition of revenue for a sales-based or usage-based royalty promised in exchange for a licence of intellectual property. These are discussed at **11.2**.

For all other types of variable consideration, variable consideration should only be included in the transaction price to the extent that it is highly probable that a significant reversal in the amount of cumulative revenue recognised will not occur when the uncertainty associated with the variable consideration is subsequently resolved. [IFRS 15:56]

The term 'highly probable' is intended here to mean that 'the future event or events are likely to occur'. [IFRS 15:BC211]

An entity should consider both the likelihood and the magnitude of the revenue reversal when assessing whether it is highly probable that a significant reversal in the amount of cumulative revenue recognised will not occur once the uncertainty related to the variable consideration is subsequently resolved. Factors that may increase the likelihood or the magnitude of a revenue reversal include the following:

[IFRS 15:57]

(a) the amount of consideration is highly susceptible to factors outside the entity's influence. For example volatility in a market, the judgement or actions of third parties, weather conditions or a high risk of obsolescence of the promised good or service;

(b) the uncertainty about the amount of consideration is not expected to be resolved for a long period of time;

(c) the experience (or other evidence) that the entity has with similar types of contracts is limited, or that experience (or other evidence) has limited predictive value;

(d) the entity has a practice of either offering a broad range of price concessions or changing the payment terms and conditions of similar contracts in similar circumstances; and

(e) there are a large number and broad range of possible consideration amounts within the contract.

Example 7.3A

Price concessions

[IFRS 15:IE116 - IE123, Example 23]

An entity enters into a contract with a customer, a distributor, on 1 December 20X7. The entity transfers 1,000 products at contract inception for a price stated in the contract of CU100 per product (total consideration is CU100,000). Payment from the customer is due when the customer sells the products to the end customers. The entity's customer generally sells the products within 90 days of obtaining them. Control of the products transfers to the customer on 1 December 20X7.

On the basis of its past practices and to maintain its relationship with the customer, the entity anticipates granting a price concession to its customer because this will enable the customer to discount the product and thereby move the product through the distribution chain. Consequently, the consideration in the contract is variable.

Case A – Estimate of variable consideration is not constrained

The entity has significant experience selling this and similar products. The observable data indicate that historically the entity grants a price concession of approximately 20 per cent of the sales price for these products. Current market information suggests that a 20 per cent reduction in price will be sufficient to move the products through the distribution chain. The entity has not granted a price concession significantly greater than 20 per cent in many years.

To estimate the variable consideration to which the entity will be entitled, the entity decides to use the expected value method (see [IFRS 15:53(a)]) because it is the method that the entity expects to better predict the amount of consideration to which it will be entitled. Using the expected value method, the entity estimates the transaction price to be CU80,000 (CU80 × 1,000 products).

The entity also considers the requirements in [IFRS 15:56 to 58] on constraining estimates of variable consideration to determine whether the estimated amount of variable consideration of CU80,000 can be included in the transaction price. The entity considers the factors in [IFRS 15:57] and determines that it has significant previous experience with this product and current market information that supports its estimate. In addition, despite some uncertainty resulting from factors outside its influence, based on its current market estimates, the entity expects the price to be resolved within a short time frame. Thus, the entity concludes that it is highly probable that a significant reversal in the cumulative

---

amount of revenue recognised (ie CU80,000) will not occur when the uncertainty is resolved (ie when the total amount of price concessions is determined). Consequently, the entity recognises CU80,000 as revenue when the products are transferred on 1 December 20X7.

Case B – Estimate of variable consideration is constrained

The entity has experience selling similar products. However, the entity's products have a high risk of obsolescence and the entity is experiencing high volatility in the pricing of its products. The observable data indicate that historically the entity grants a broad range of price concessions ranging from 20–60 per cent of the sales price for similar products. Current market information also suggests that a 15–50 per cent reduction in price may be necessary to move the products through the distribution chain.

To estimate the variable consideration to which the entity will be entitled, the entity decides to use the expected value method (see [IFRS 15:53(a)]) because it is the method that the entity expects to better predict the amount of consideration to which it will be entitled. Using the expected value method, the entity estimates that a discount of 40 per cent will be provided and, therefore, the estimate of the variable consideration is CU60,000 (CU60 × 1,000 products).

The entity also considers the requirements in [IFRS 15:56 to 58] on constraining estimates of variable consideration to determine whether some or all of the estimated amount of variable consideration of CU60,000 can be included in the transaction price. The entity considers the factors in [IFRS 15:57] and observes that the amount of consideration is highly susceptible to factors outside the entity's influence (ie risk of obsolescence) and it is likely that the entity may be required to provide a broad range of price concessions to move the products through the distribution chain. Consequently, the entity cannot include its estimate of CU60,000 (ie a discount of 40 per cent) in the transaction price because it cannot conclude that it is highly probable that a significant reversal in the amount of cumulative revenue recognised will not occur. Although the entity's historical price concessions have ranged from 20–60 per cent, market information currently suggests that a price concession of 15–50 per cent will be necessary. The entity's actual results have been consistent with then-current market information in previous, similar transactions. Consequently, the entity concludes that it is highly probable that a significant reversal in the cumulative amount of revenue recognised will not occur if the entity includes CU50,000 in the transaction price (CU100 sales price and a 50 per cent price concession) and therefore, recognises revenue at that amount. Therefore, the entity recognises revenue of CU50,000 when the products are transferred and reassesses the estimates of the transaction price at each reporting date until the uncertainty is resolved in accordance with [IFRS 15:59].

Note that in **example 7.3A**, it is assumed as part of the fact pattern that control of the products transfers to the distributor at contract inception. However, the fact that the distributor only becomes obliged to pay for the products when it sells them to end customers is an indication that this might be a consignment arrangement. Consignment arrangements are discussed at **9.4.4**.

Example 7.3B

Volume discount incentive

[IFRS 15:IE124 - IE128, Example 24]

An entity enters into a contract with a customer on 1 January 20X8 to sell Product A for CU100 per unit. If the customer purchases more than 1,000 units of Product A in a calendar year, the contract specifies that the price per unit is retrospectively reduced to CU90 per unit. Consequently, the consideration in the contract is variable.

For the first quarter ended 31 March 20X8, the entity sells 75 units of Product A to the customer. The entity estimates that the customer's purchases will not exceed the 1,000-unit threshold required for the volume discount in the calendar year.

The entity considers the requirements in [IFRS 15:56 to 58] on constraining estimates of variable consideration, including the factors in [IFRS 15:57]. The entity determines that it has significant experience with this product and with the purchasing pattern of the entity. Thus, the entity concludes that it is highly probable that a significant reversal in the cumulative amount of revenue recognised (ie CU100 per unit) will not occur when the uncertainty is resolved (ie when the total amount of purchases is known). Consequently, the entity recognises revenue of CU7,500 (75 units × CU100 per unit) for the quarter ended 31 March 20X8.

In May 20X8, the entity's customer acquires another company and in the second quarter ended 30 June 20X8 the entity sells an additional 500 units of Product A to the customer. In the light of the new fact, the entity estimates that the customer's purchases will exceed the 1,000-unit threshold for the calendar year and therefore it will be required to retrospectively reduce the price per unit to CU90.

Consequently, the entity recognises revenue of CU44,250 for the quarter ended 30 June 20X8. That amount is calculated from CU45,000 for the sale of 500 units (500 units × CU90 per unit) less the change in transaction price of CU750 (75 units × CU10 price reduction) for the reduction of revenue relating to units sold for the quarter ended 31 March 20X8 (see [IFRS 15:87 and 88]).

Example 7.3C

Management fees subject to the constraint

[IFRS 15:IE129 - IE133, Example 25]

On 1 January 20X8, an entity enters into a contract with a client to provide asset management services for five years. The entity receives a two per cent quarterly management fee based on the client's assets under management at the end of each quarter. In addition, the entity receives a performance-based incentive fee of 20 per cent of the fund's return in excess of the return of an observable market index over the five-year period. Consequently, both the management fee and the performance fee in the contract are variable consideration.

The entity accounts for the services as a single performance obligation in accordance with [IFRS 15:22(b)], because it is providing a series of distinct services that are substantially the same and have the same pattern of transfer (the services transfer to the customer over time and use the same method to measure progress – that is, a time-based measure of progress).

At contract inception, the entity considers the requirements in [IFRS 15:50 to 54] on estimating variable consideration and the requirements in [IFRS 15:56 to 58] on constraining estimates of variable consideration, including the factors in [IFRS 15:57]. The entity observes that the promised consideration is dependent on the market and thus is highly susceptible to factors outside the entity's influence. In addition, the incentive fee has a large number and a broad range of possible consideration amounts. The entity also observes that although it has experience with similar contracts, that experience is of little predictive value in determining the future performance of the market. Therefore, at contract inception, the entity cannot conclude that it is highly probable that a significant reversal in the cumulative amount of revenue recognised would not occur if the entity included its estimate of the management fee or the incentive fee in the transaction price.

At each reporting date, the entity updates its estimate of the transaction price. Consequently, at the end of each quarter, the entity concludes that it can include in the transaction price the actual amount of the quarterly management fee because the uncertainty is resolved. However, the entity concludes that it cannot include its estimate of the incentive fee in the transaction price at those dates. This is because there has not been a change in its assessment from contract inception – the variability of the fee based on the market index indicates that the entity cannot conclude that it is highly probable that a significant reversal in the cumulative amount of revenue recognised would not occur if the entity included its estimate of the incentive fee in the transaction price. At 31 March 20X8, the client's assets under management are CU100 million. Therefore, the resulting quarterly management fee and the transaction price is CU2 million.

At the end of each quarter, the entity allocates the quarterly management fee to the distinct services provided during the quarter in accordance with [IFRS 15:84(b) and 85 (see **8.5**)]. This is because the fee relates specifically to the entity's efforts to transfer the services for that quarter, which are distinct from the services provided in other quarters, and the resulting allocation will be consistent with the allocation objective in [IFRS 15:73]. Consequently, the entity recognises CU2 million as revenue for the quarter ended 31 March 20X8.

7.4 Significant financing component

7.4.1 Significant financing component – meaning

In determining the transaction price, a promised amount of consideration is adjusted for the effects of the time value of money if the timing of payments agreed to by the parties to the contract provides the customer or the entity with a significant benefit of financing the transfer of goods or services to the customer. In such circumstances, the contract contains a significant financing component which may exist irrespective of whether the promise of financing is stated explicitly in the contract or implied by the payment terms agreed to by the parties to the contract. [IFRS 15:60]

7.4.2 Practical expedient – no adjustment required for financing component for contracts of one year or less

When the entity expects, at contract inception, that the period between the entity transferring a good or service and the customer paying for it will be one year or less, IFRS 15 does not require adjustment of the consideration for the effects of a significant financing component. [IFRS 15:63] If this practical expedient is taken, it should be applied consistently to contracts with similar characteristics and in similar circumstances. [IFRS 15:3]

Example 7.4.2

Requirement to discount trade receivables

Entity A, a retailer, offers interest-free financing to its customers. Depending on the type of product purchased, the financing arrangement gives the customer interest-free financing for a period of 12, 15 or 18 months. The customer pays equal monthly instalments from the date of purchase over the financing period. This is common industry practice in the country where Entity A is located, and other retailers offer similar financing arrangements. No recent cash transactions are available from which Entity A can make a reliable estimate of the cash sales price. On the basis of prevailing interest rates in the relevant market, Entity A estimates that the customer would be able to borrow from other sources at an interest rate of 18 per cent.

In accordance with IFRS 15:61(b) (see **7.4.3**), Entity A believes that as a result of the combination of (1) the length of time between the transfer of goods and payment, and (2) the high interest rates at which the customer can obtain financing, the arrangement contains a significant financing component.

Is Entity A required to adjust the transaction prices in all its interest-free financing sale arrangements to reflect the effects of the time value of money?

In accordance with IFRS 15:60, entities are required to adjust the promised amount of consideration even when a significant financing component is not explicitly identified in the contract. However, IFRS 15:63 provides a practical expedient for contracts with a significant financing component when the period between the transfer of goods and the customer's payment is, at contract inception, expected to be one year or less.

Consequently, in the circumstances described, Entity A is required to adjust the sales price for all of arrangements other than those with a contractual period of 12 months or less. For arrangements with a contractual period of 12 months or less, Entity A is permitted to adjust the sales price when it identifies a significant financing component, which it may wish to do to align with its other contracts; however, it is not required to do so.

> If Entity A takes advantage of the practical expedient under IFRS 15:63, it is required to do so consistently in similar circumstances for all contracts with similar characteristics.

7.4.3   Identification of a significant financing component

7.4.3.1   Relevant factors for the identification of a significant financing component

The objective of the requirement in IFRS 15:60 is for an entity to recognise revenue at an amount that reflects the price that a customer would have paid if the customer had paid cash for the goods or services when (or as) they transfer to the customer (i.e. the cash selling price). All relevant facts and circumstances should be considered in assessing (1) whether a contract contains a financing component, and (2) whether that financing component is significant to the contract. Relevant considerations include the following:

[IFRS 15:61]

(a)   the difference, if any, between the amount of promised consideration and the cash selling price of the promised goods or services; and

(b)   the combined effect of:

   (i)   the expected length of time between when the entity transfers the promised goods or services to the customer and when the customer pays for those goods or services; and

   (ii)   the prevailing interest rates in the relevant market.

7.4.3.2   Determining at what level the 'significance' of a financing component should be assessed

IFRS 15:61 specifically requires an entity to consider all relevant facts and circumstances in assessing whether a contract contains a financing component and whether that financing component is *significant to the contract*. Consequently, the significance of a financing component should be assessed in the context of the individual contract rather than, for example, for a portfolio of similar contracts or at a performance obligation level.

The basis of this requirement is explained in IFRS 15:BC234, which states as follows.

"During their redeliberations, the boards clarified that an entity should consider only the *significance* of a financing component at a contract level rather than consider whether the financing is *material* at a portfolio level. The boards decided that it would have been unduly burdensome to require an entity to account for a financing component if the effects of the financing component were not material to the individual contract, but the combined effects for a portfolio of similar contracts were material to the entity as a whole."

As a consequence, some financing components will not be identified as significant – and, therefore, the promised amount of consideration will not be adjusted – even though they might be material in aggregate for a portfolio of similar contracts.

Although a financing component can only be *quantified* by considering individual performance obligations, the *significance* of a financing component is not assessed at the performance obligation level. To illustrate, an entity may typically sell Product X, for which revenue is recognised at a point in time, on extended credit terms such that, when Product X is sold by itself, the contract contains a significant financing component. The entity may also sell Product X and Product Y together in a bundled contract, requiring the customer to pay for Product Y in full at the time control is transferred but granting the same extended credit terms for Product X. If the value of Product Y is much greater than the value of Product X, any financing component in respect of Product X may be too small to be assessed as significant in the context of the larger bundled contract. Therefore, in such circumstances, the entity would:

- adjust the promised consideration for a significant financing component when Product X is sold by itself; but

- not adjust the promised consideration for a significant financing component when Product X is sold together with Product Y in a single contract.

7.4.4 Circumstances that do not give rise to a significant financing component

A contract with a customer does not include a significant financing component if any of the following factors exist:

[IFRS 15:62]

(a) the customer paid for the goods or services in advance and the timing of the transfer of those goods or services is at the discretion of the customer;

(b) a substantial amount of the consideration promised by the customer is variable and the amount or timing of that consideration varies on the basis of the occurrence or non-occurrence of a future event that is not substantially within the control of the customer or the entity (e.g. if the consideration is a sales-based royalty); or

(c) the difference between the promised consideration and the cash selling price of the good or service (as described in IFRS 15:61 – see **7.4.3.1**) arises for reasons other than the provision of finance to either the customer or the entity, and the difference between those amounts is proportional to the reason for the difference (see **examples 7.4.4A** and **7.4.4B**). For example, the payment terms might provide the entity or the customer with protection from the other party failing adequately to complete some or all of its obligations under the contract.

There is no presumption in the Standard as to whether a significant financing component exists when there is a difference in timing between when goods or services are transferred and when the promised consideration is paid. An entity should apply judgement to determine whether payment terms are providing financing or are for another valid reason, and whether or not the difference in amounts is proportional to that reason.

This issue was discussed by the IASB/FASB Joint Transition Resources Group for Revenue Recognition (see **16.1**) in March 2015.

If the implied interest rate in an arrangement is zero (i.e. interest free-financing) such that the consideration to be received is equal to the cash selling price (i.e. the amount that would be received from a customer choosing to pay for the goods or services in cash when (or as) they are delivered), it should not automatically be assumed that there is no significant financing component. A difference between the amount of promised consideration and the cash selling price is only one of the indicators that should be considered in determining whether a significant financing component exists. The fact that an entity provides what appears to be zero interest financing does not necessarily mean that the cash selling price is the same as the cash selling price that would have been paid by another customer who has opted to pay over time. Accordingly, determining a 'cash selling price' for a customer paying over time may require judgement.

This issue was discussed by the IASB/FASB Joint Transition Resources Group for Revenue Recognition (see **16.1**) in March 2015.

Example 7.4.4A

Withheld payments on a long-term contract

[IFRS 15:IE141 & IE142, Example 27]

An entity enters into a contract for the construction of a building that includes scheduled milestone payments for the performance by the entity throughout the contract term of three years. The performance obligation will be satisfied over time and the milestone payments are scheduled to coincide with the entity's expected performance. The contract provides that a specified percentage of each milestone payment is to be withheld (ie retained) by the customer throughout the arrangement and paid to the entity only when the building is complete.

The entity concludes that the contract does not include a significant financing component. The milestone payments coincide with the entity's performance and the contract requires amounts to be retained for reasons other than the provision of finance in accordance with [IFRS 15:62(c)]. The withholding of a specified percentage of each milestone payment is intended to protect the customer from the contractor failing to adequately complete its obligations under the contract.

Example 7.4.4B

Advance payment

[IFRS 15:IE152 - IE154, Example 30]

An entity, a technology product manufacturer, enters into a contract with a customer to provide global telephone technology support and repair coverage for three years along with its technology product. The customer purchases this support service at the time of buying the product. Consideration for the service is an additional CU300. Customers electing to buy this service must pay for it upfront (ie a monthly payment option is not available).

To determine whether there is a significant financing component in the contract, the entity considers the nature of the service being offered and the purpose of the payment terms. The entity charges a single upfront amount, not with the primary purpose of obtaining financing from the customer but, instead, to maximise profitability, taking into consideration the risks associated with providing the service. Specifically, if customers could pay monthly, they would be less likely to renew and the population of customers that continue to use the support service in the later years may become smaller and less diverse over time (ie customers that choose to renew historically are those that make greater use of the service, thereby increasing the entity's costs). In addition, customers tend to use services more if they pay monthly rather than making an upfront payment. Finally, the entity would incur higher administration costs such as the costs related to administering renewals and collection of monthly payments.

In assessing the requirements in [IFRS 15:62(c)], the entity determines that the payment terms were structured primarily for reasons other than the provision of finance to the entity. The entity charges a single upfront amount for the services because other payment terms (such as a monthly payment plan) would affect the nature of the risks assumed by the entity to provide the service and may make it uneconomical to provide the service. As a result of its analysis, the entity concludes that there is not a significant financing component.

7.4.5   Measuring the amount of revenue when a transaction includes a significant financing component

When a significant financing component is identified, IFRS 15:60 requires "an entity to adjust the promised amount of consideration for the effects of the time value of money".

IFRS 15:61 states as follows.

"The objective when adjusting the promised amount of consideration for a significant financing component is for an entity to recognise revenue at an amount that reflects the price that a customer would have paid for the promised goods or services if the customer had paid cash for those goods or services when (or as) they transfer to the customer (ie the cash selling price)."

However, IFRS 15:64 (see **7.4.6**) states, in part, as follows.

"To meet the objective in [IFRS 15:61] when adjusting the promised amount of consideration for a significant financing component, an entity shall use the discount rate that would be reflected in a separate financing transaction between the entity and its customer at contract inception. That rate would reflect the credit characteristics of the party receiving financing in the contract, as well as any collateral or security provided by the customer or the entity, including assets transferred in the contract."

IFRS 15:64 also states that "[a]n entity *may* be able to determine that rate by identifying the rate that discounts the nominal amount of the promised consideration to the price that the customer would pay in cash for the goods or services when (or as) they transfer to the customer" (emphasis added).

Accordingly, although the objective described in IFRS 15:61 is to determine the 'cash selling price', IFRS 15:64 makes clear that such price is required to be consistent with the price that would be determined by using an appropriate discount rate to discount the promised consideration.

Therefore, in practice, the entity may make an initial estimate of the amount of revenue either:

(1) by determining the appropriate discount rate (see **7.4.6**) and using that rate to discount the promised amount of consideration; or

(2) by estimating the cash selling price directly – but only if the discount rate thereby implied is consistent with a rate that would be reflected in a separate financing transaction between the entity and its customer.

Irrespective of the approach it adopts, the entity may need to perform further analysis if the amounts estimated appear unreasonable or inconsistent with other evidence relating to the transaction.

- If the entity estimates revenue by discounting the promised consideration, it may be required to perform further analysis if that estimate appears unreasonable and inconsistent with other evidence of the cash selling price. For example, if the amount of revenue estimated appears significantly higher than the normal cash selling price, this may indicate that the discount rate has not been determined on an appropriate basis.

- If the entity estimates revenue by estimating the cash selling price directly, it may be required to perform further analysis if the resulting discount rate appears unreasonable and inconsistent with other evidence of the rate that would be reflected in a separate financing transaction between the entity and its customer. If the rate is clearly significantly lower or higher than would be reflected in a separate financing transaction, it will not be appropriate to measure revenue by reference to the cash selling price; instead, the entity should estimate revenue by discounting the promised consideration at an appropriately estimated discount rate.

7.4.6 Determining the discount rate

To meet the objective in IFRS 15:61 (see **7.4.3.1**), the discount rate used should reflect that which would be used in a separate financing transaction between the entity and its customer at contract inception. That rate would reflect the credit characteristics of the party receiving financing in the contract, as well as any collateral or security provided by the customer or the entity, including assets transferred in the contract. This may be determined by identifying the rate that discounts the nominal amount of the promised consideration to the price that the customer would pay in cash for the goods or services when (or as) they transfer to the customer. After contract inception, the discount rate is not updated for changes in interest rates or other circumstances (such as a change in the assessment of the customer's credit risk). [IFRS 15:64]

Example 7.4.6A

Determining the discount rate

[IFRS 15:IE143 - IE147, Example 28]

An entity enters into a contract with a customer to sell equipment. Control of the equipment transfers to the customer when the contract is signed. The price stated in the contract is CU1 million plus a five per cent contractual rate of interest, payable in 60 monthly instalments of CU18,871.

Case A – Contractual discount rate reflects the rate in a separate financing transaction

In evaluating the discount rate in the contract that contains a significant financing component, the entity observes that the five per cent contractual rate of interest

---

reflects the rate that would be used in a separate financing transaction between the entity and its customer at contract inception (ie the contractual rate of interest of five per cent reflects the credit characteristics of the customer).

The market terms of the financing mean that the cash selling price of the equipment is CU1 million. This amount is recognised as revenue and as a loan receivable when control of the equipment transfers to the customer. The entity accounts for the receivable in accordance with IFRS 9.

Case B – Contractual discount rate does not reflect the rate in a separate financing transaction

In evaluating the discount rate in the contract that contains a significant financing component, the entity observes that the five per cent contractual rate of interest is significantly lower than the 12 per cent interest rate that would be used in a separate financing transaction between the entity and its customer at contract inception (ie the contractual rate of interest of five per cent does not reflect the credit characteristics of the customer). This suggests that the cash selling price is less than CU1 million.

In accordance with [IFRS 15:64], the entity determines the transaction price by adjusting the promised amount of consideration to reflect the contractual payments using the 12 per cent interest rate that reflects the credit characteristics of the customer. Consequently, the entity determines that the transaction price is CU848,357 (60 monthly payments of CU18,871 discounted at 12 per cent). The entity recognises revenue and a loan receivable for that amount. The entity accounts for the loan receivable in accordance with IFRS 9.

For entities that have not yet adopted IFRS 9, the reference in **example 7.4.6A** would instead be to IAS 39 *Financial Instruments: Recognition and Measurement*.

Example 7.4.6B

Determining the appropriate discount rate when accounting for a significant financing component in an individual contract

Entity A sells industrial products to customers under contracts for which payment is due 24 months after delivery.

Entity A determines that the contract terms give customers a significant benefit of financing the purchase of the industrial products. In accordance with IFRS 15:60, it adjusts the transaction price and corresponding amount of revenue recognised for the sale of the goods to take into account the effect of the time value of money.

Entity A does not intend to apply a portfolio approach in determining the effects of this financing benefit.

How might Entity A determine the appropriate discount rate to apply to the payments to be received from its customers?

Under IFRS 15:64, Entity A should use the discount rate that would be reflected in a separate financing transaction between itself and its customer at contract inception. The manner in which Entity A identifies this rate will depend on the type of information to which it has access for individual customers.

In determining this discount rate, Entity A may find it useful to consider the following:

- the normal rate at which Entity A would provide secured or unsecured lending (whichever is appropriate) to this customer (e.g. any interest rate that would be normal for the entity to offer to this customer);

- the normal rate at which other entities would provide secured or unsecured lending (whichever is appropriate) to this customer (e.g. the rate charged to the customer for bank loans). Note, however, that IFRS 15:64 requires a rate specific to a financing transaction between the entity and its customer;

- the cash sales price offered for this product to customers with similar demographic characteristics;

- any interest rate explicitly stated in the contract with the customer. However, this will not always be an appropriate rate (e.g. when a customer is offered interest-free credit or when a low interest rate is used to incentivise the customer);

- the level of certainty regarding the customer's credit characteristics that Entity A obtains as a result of its due diligence processes (e.g. obtaining credit ratings); and

- historical evidence of any defaults or slow payment by this customer.

Appropriate adjustments should be made to rates associated with any of these factors when they are not directly comparable to those of the transaction being considered.

Example 7.4.6C

Determining the appropriate discount rate when accounting for a significant financing component in a contract using a portfolio approach

Entity A is a retail business that enters into a large number of similar contracts in which it sells products to individual customers and payment is due 24 months after delivery.

Entity A determines that the contract terms give customers a significant benefit of financing the purchase of the products. Accordingly, under IFRS 15:60, Entity A adjusts the transaction price and corresponding amount of revenue recognised for the sale of the goods to take into account the effect of the time value of money.

Entity A reasonably expects that the financial statement effects of calculating a discount rate that applies to the portfolio of contracts would not differ materially from the discount rates that would apply to individual contracts. Therefore, in accordance with IFRS 15:4, it intends to apply such a portfolio approach (see **3.4**).

> How might Entity A determine the appropriate discount rate to apply to a portfolio of contracts?
>
> Under IFRS 15:64, Entity A should use the discount rate that would be reflected in a separate financing transaction between itself and its customers at contract inception.
>
> Factors that may be relevant to determining such a rate are discussed in **example 7.4.6B**. However, in applying a portfolio approach, Entity A will need to consider the demographic characteristics of the customers as a group to estimate the discount rate on a portfolio basis. If the demographic characteristics of customers within this group vary significantly, it may not be appropriate to treat them as a single portfolio and it may be necessary to further sub-divide the customer group when making this determination.

Example 7.4.6D

Advance payment and assessment of discount rate

[IFRS 15:IE148 - IE151, Example 29]

An entity enters into a contract with a customer to sell an asset. Control of the asset will transfer to the customer in two years (ie the performance obligation will be satisfied at a point in time). The contract includes two alternative payment options: payment of CU5,000 in two years when the customer obtains control of the asset or payment of CU4,000 when the contract is signed. The customer elects to pay CU4,000 when the contract is signed.

The entity concludes that the contract contains a significant financing component because of the length of time between when the customer pays for the asset and when the entity transfers the asset to the customer, as well as the prevailing interest rates in the market.

The interest rate implicit in the transaction is 11.8 per cent, which is the interest rate necessary to make the two alternative payment options economically equivalent. However, the entity determines that, in accordance with [IFRS 15:64], the rate that should be used in adjusting the promised consideration is six per cent, which is the entity's incremental borrowing rate.

The following journal entries illustrate how the entity would account for the significant financing component:

(a) recognise a contract liability for the CU4,000 payment received at contract inception:

Cash	CU4,000	
Contract liability		CU4,000

(b) during the two years from contract inception until the transfer of the asset, the entity adjusts the promised amount of consideration (in accordance with [IFRS 15:65]) and accretes the contract liability by recognising interest on CU4,000 at six per cent for two years:

| Interest expense | CU494[a] | |
| Contract liability | | CU494 |

[a] CU494 = CU4,000 contract liability × (6 per cent interest per year for two years).

(c)   recognise revenue for the transfer of the asset:

| Contract liability | CU4,494 | |
| Revenue | | CU4,494 |

Example 7.4.6E

Advance payment and time value of money

Entity A, a homebuilder, is selling apartment units in a new building for which construction has not yet commenced. The estimated time to complete construction is 18 months. Entity A has concluded that its performance obligation (i.e. delivery of the apartment) will be satisfied upon completion of construction, which is also when title and possession are passed to the customer. The cash sales price upon completion of construction is CU500,000. Customers are offered a discount of CU75,000 on the cash sales price if they pay in full in advance; therefore, the price for customers paying in advance is CU425,000.

Entity A has concluded after analysis of the contract that the advance payment represents a significant financing component (i.e. its customers are providing finance to pay for construction costs). On the basis of interest rates in the market, Entity A has concluded that an annual rate of approximately 10 per cent reflects the rate at which Entity A and its customer would have entered into a separate financing transaction. Consequently, Entity A imputes a discount rate of approximately 10 per cent to discount the cash sales price (i.e. CU500,000) to the 'advance' sales price (i.e. CU425,000).

When an advance cash payment is received from a customer, Entity A recognises a contract liability of CU425,000. Subsequently, Entity A accrues interest on the liability balance to accrete the balance to CU500,000 over the 18-month period until it expects its performance obligation to be satisfied. Entity A capitalises the interest in accordance with IAS 23 *Borrowing Costs*. When control of the apartment transfers to the customer, Entity A recognises CU500,000 as revenue.

The following journal entries illustrate how Entity A should account for the significant financing component.

		CU	CU
Dr	Cash	425,000	
Cr	Contract liability		425,000

To record a contract liability for the CU425,000 received at contract inception.

	CU	CU
Dr Inventories	75,000	
Cr Contract liability		75,000

To record the interest accrued on the contract liability from contract inception to the transfer of the asset.

Over the 18 months from contract inception to transfer of the asset.

	CU	CU
Dr Contract liability	500,000	
Cr Revenue		500,000

To record the revenue arising on the sale of the apartment when control passes to the customer.

Example 7.4.6F

Deferred consideration: discounting on the basis of interest rate

On 1 January 20X1, Entity B sells an item of equipment for CU100,000 under a financing agreement that has no stated interest rate. On the date of sale, Entity B transfers control of the equipment to the customer, and Entity B concludes that the contract meets the criteria in IFRS 15:9 (see **5.1**), including the collectability criterion. The first annual instalment of CU20,000 is due on 31 December 20X1, one year from the date of sale, and each subsequent year for five years. The policy of not charging interest is consistent with normal industry practice.

Entity B has separately determined that the transaction includes a significant financing component (see **7.4.3**). To estimate the transaction price by discounting the future receipts, Entity B uses a "rate that would be reflected in a separate financing transaction between [Entity B] and its customer at contract inception". Entity B determines that the appropriate annual rate is 10 per cent. Assume that the receivable arising from the transaction is measured at amortised cost subsequent to initial recognition.

Calculation of the net present value of the stream of payments

If there is no down payment and there are five annual instalments of CU20,000, with an interest rate of 10 per cent, the net present value of the stream of payments forming the consideration is CU75,816. Therefore, upon transfer of control of the equipment, CU75,816 is recognised as revenue from the sale of goods and the related receivable is recognised.

Calculation of the amount of interest earned in each period

The difference between CU100,000 and CU75,816 (i.e. CU24,184) will be recognised as interest revenue as it becomes due each year, as calculated below.

	Receivable at 1 January	Interest revenue	Payment received	Receivable at 31 December
	CU	CU	CU	CU
	A	B=(Ax10%)	C	A+B–C
20X1	75,816	7,581	20,000	63,397
20X2	63,397	6,340	20,000	49,737
20X3	49,737	4,974	20,000	34,711
20X4	34,711	3,471	20,000	18,182
20X5	18,182	1,818	20,000	–
		24,184	100,000	

Journal entries

		CU	CU
Dr	Accounts receivable	75,816	
Cr	Revenue		75,816

To record the revenue arising on the sale when control of the equipment transfers to the customer.

		CU	CU
Dr	Cash	20,000	
Cr	Accounts receivable		12,419
Cr	Interest revenue		7,581

To record the first annual payment due one year from the date of purchase.

At each subsequent year end, Entity B should record the same journal entry using the amounts from the table above.

Note that this example does not take into account any impairment assessment that would be required in accordance with IFRS 9 (or, for entities that have not yet adopted IFRS 9, IAS 39).

Example 7.4.6G

Deferred consideration: discounting to current cash sales price

The facts are the same as in **example 7.4.6F**.

If the buyer had paid in full for the equipment at the point of transfer, Entity B estimates that the cash selling price would have been CU76,000.

Assume that the receivable arising from the transaction is measured at amortised cost after initial recognition.

Determination of the discount rate for the customer

IFRS 15:64 indicates that a selling entity may be able to determine the discount rate to be used to adjust the transaction price "by identifying the rate that discounts the nominal amount of the promised consideration to the price that the customer would pay in cash for the goods or services when (or as) they transfer to the customer". Therefore, Entity B determines the interest rate that discounts CU100,000 to CU76,000 (i.e. the cash selling price) over a 5-year period, given no down-payment and five annual instalments of CU20,000. This interest rate is approximately 9.91 per cent, which is judged to be consistent with a rate that would be reflected in a separate financing transaction between Entity B and its customer. Upon transfer of the equipment, CU76,000 is recognised as revenue from the sale of goods and the related receivable is recognised.

Calculation of the amount of interest earned in each period

The difference between CU100,000 and CU76,000 (i.e. CU24,000) will be recognised as interest revenue as it becomes due each year, as calculated below.

	Receivable at 1 January	Interest revenue	Payment received	Receivable at 31 December
	CU	CU	CU	CU
	A	B=(Ax9.91%)	C	A+B–C
20X1	76,000	7,528	20,000	63,528
20X2	63,528	6,292	20,000	49,820
20X3	49,820	4,935	20,000	34,755
20X4	34,755	3,443	20,000	18,198
20X5	18,198	1,802	20,000	–
		24,000	100,000	

Journal entries

		CU	CU
Dr	Accounts receivable	76,000	
Cr	Revenue		76,000

To record the revenue arising on the sale when control of the equipment transfers to the customer.

		CU	CU
Dr	Cash	20,000	
Cr	Accounts receivable		12,472
Cr	Interest revenue		7,528

To record the first annual payment due one year from the date of purchase.

At each subsequent year end, Entity B should record the same journal entry by using the amounts from the table above.

Note that this example does not take into account any impairment assessment that would be required in accordance with IFRS 9 (or, for entities that have not yet adopted IFRS 9, IAS 39).

7.4.7 *Presentation of the effects of financing*

The effects of financing (interest revenue or interest expense) are presented separately from revenue from contracts with customers in the statement of comprehensive income. Interest revenue or interest expense is recognised only to the extent that a contract asset (or receivable) or a contract liability is recognised in accounting for a contract with a customer. [IFRS 15:65]

Example 7.4.7

Significant financing component and right of return

[IFRS 15:IE135 - IE140, Example 26]

An entity sells a product to a customer for CU121 that is payable 24 months after delivery. The customer obtains control of the product at contract inception. The contract permits the customer to return the product within 90 days. The product is new and the entity has no relevant historical evidence of product returns or other available market evidence.

The cash selling price of the product is CU100, which represents the amount that the customer would pay upon delivery for the same product sold under otherwise identical terms and conditions as at contract inception. The entity's cost of the product is CU80.

The entity does not recognise revenue when control of the product transfers to the customer. This is because the existence of the right of return and the lack of relevant historical evidence means that the entity cannot conclude that it is highly probable that a significant reversal in the amount of cumulative revenue recognised will not occur in accordance with [IFRS 15:56 to 58]. Consequently, revenue is recognised after three months when the right of return lapses.

The contract includes a significant financing component, in accordance with [IFRS 15:60 to 62]. This is evident from the difference between the amount of promised consideration of CU121 and the cash selling price of CU100 at the date that the goods are transferred to the customer.

The contract includes an implicit interest rate of 10 per cent (ie the interest rate that over 24 months discounts the promised consideration of CU121 to the cash selling price of CU100). The entity evaluates the rate and concludes that it is commensurate with the rate that would be reflected in a separate financing transaction between the entity and its customer at contract inception. The following journal entries illustrate how the entity accounts for this contract in accordance with [IFRS 15:B20 to B27].

(a) When the product is transferred to the customer, in accordance with [IFRS 15:B21]:

Asset for right to recover product to be returned   CU80(a)

Inventory   CU80

(a) This example does not consider expected costs to recover the asset.

(b) During the three-month right of return period, no interest is recognised in accordance with [IFRS 15:65] because no contract asset or receivable has been recognised.

(c) When the right of return lapses (the product is not returned):

Receivable   CU100(a)

Revenue   CU100

Cost of sales   CU80

Asset for product to be returned   CU80

(a) The receivable recognised would be measured in accordance with IFRS 9. This example assumes there is no material difference between the fair value of the receivable at contract inception and the fair value of the receivable when it is recognised at the time the right of return lapses. In addition, this example does not consider the impairment accounting for the receivable.

Until the entity receives the cash payment from the customer, interest revenue would be recognised in accordance with IFRS 9. In determining the effective interest rate in accordance with IFRS 9, the entity would consider the remaining contractual term.

For entities that have not yet adopted IFRS 9, the references in **example 7.4.7** would instead be to IAS 39 *Financial Instruments: Recognition and Measurement*.

7.5   Non-cash consideration

When a customer promises consideration in a form other than cash, an entity measures the non-cash consideration (or promise of non-cash consideration) at fair value. [IFRS 15:66]

When the fair value of the non-cash consideration cannot be reasonably estimated, the consideration is measured indirectly by reference to the stand-alone selling price of the goods or services promised to the customer (or class of customer) in exchange for the consideration. [IFRS 15:67]

The fair value of the non-cash consideration may vary because of the form of the consideration (e.g. a change in the price of a share that an entity is entitled to receive from a customer). If the fair value of the non-cash consideration promised by a customer varies for reasons other than only the form of the consideration (e.g. the fair value could vary because of the entity's performance), the requirements in respect of constraining variable consideration are applied (see **7.3**). [IFRS 15:68]

If a customer contributes goods or services (e.g. materials, equipment or labour) to facilitate the entity's fulfilment of the contract, the entity should assess whether it has obtained control of those contributed goods or services. If so, the contributed goods or services are accounted for as non-cash consideration received from the customer. [IFRS 15:69]

Example 7.5

Entitlement to non-cash consideration

[IFRS 15, IE156 - IE158, Example 31]

An entity enters into a contract with a customer to provide a weekly service for one year. The contract is signed on 1 January 20X1 and work begins immediately. The entity concludes that the service is a single performance obligation in accordance with [IFRS 15:22(b)]. This is because the entity is providing a series of distinct services that are substantially the same and have the same pattern of transfer (the services transfer to the customer over time and use the same method to measure progress – that is, a time-based measure of progress).

In exchange for the service, the customer promises 100 shares of its common stock per week of service (a total of 5,200 shares for the contract). The terms in the contract require that the shares must be paid upon the successful completion of each week of service.

The entity measures its progress towards complete satisfaction of the performance obligation as each week of service is complete. To determine the transaction price (and the amount of revenue to be recognised), the entity measures the fair value of 100 shares that are received upon completion of each weekly service. The entity does not reflect any subsequent changes in the fair value of the shares received (or receivable) in revenue.

7.6 Consideration payable to a customer

Consideration payable to a customer includes cash amounts that an entity pays, or expects to pay, to the customer (or to other parties that purchase the entity's goods or services from the customer). Consideration payable to a customer also includes credit or other items (e.g. a coupon or voucher) that can be applied against amounts owed to the entity (or to other parties that purchase the entity's goods or services from the customer). An entity should account for consideration payable to a customer as a reduction of the transaction price and, therefore, of revenue unless the payment to the customer is in exchange for a distinct good or service (as described in IFRS 15:26 to 30 – see **section 6.3**) that the customer transfers to the entity. If the consideration payable to a customer includes a variable amount, the transaction price is estimated (including assessing whether the estimate of variable consideration is constrained) in accordance with IFRS 15:50 to 58 (see **section 7.2**). [IFRS 15:70]

If consideration payable to a customer is a payment for a distinct good or service from the customer, then an entity should account for the purchase of the good or service in the same way that it accounts for other purchases from suppliers. If the amount of consideration payable to the customer exceeds the fair value of the distinct good or service that the entity receives from the customer, then the excess is accounted for as a reduction of the transaction price. If the entity cannot reasonably estimate the fair value of the good or service received from the customer, it should account for all of the consideration payable to the customer as a reduction of the transaction price. [IFRS 15:71]

Accordingly, if consideration payable to a customer is accounted for as a reduction of the transaction price, it is recognised when (or as) the later of either of the following events occurs:

[IFRS 15:72]

(a) the entity recognises revenue for the transfer of the related goods or services to the customer; and

(b) the entity pays or promises to pay the consideration (even if the payment is conditional on a future event). That promise might be implied by the entity's customary business practices.

Example 7.6

Consideration payable to a customer

[IFRS 15:IE160 - IE162, Example 32]

An entity that manufactures consumer goods enters into a one-year contract to sell goods to a customer that is a large global chain of retail stores. The customer commits to buy at least CU15 million of products during the year. The contract also requires the entity to make a non-refundable payment of CU1.5 million to the customer at the inception of the contract. The CU1.5 million payment will compensate the customer for the changes it needs to make to its shelving to accommodate the entity's products.

The entity considers the requirements in [IFRS 15:70 to 72] and concludes that the payment to the customer is not in exchange for a distinct good or service that transfers to the entity. This is because the entity does not obtain control of any rights to the customer's shelves. Consequently, the entity determines that, in accordance with [IFRS 15:70], the CU1.5 million payment is a reduction of the transaction price.

The entity applies the requirements in [IFRS 15:72] and concludes that the consideration payable is accounted for as a reduction in the transaction price when the entity recognises revenue for the transfer of the goods. Consequently, as the entity transfers goods to the customer, the entity reduces the transaction price for each good by 10 per cent (CU1.5 million ÷ CU15 million). Therefore, in the first month in which the entity transfers goods to the customer, the entity recognises revenue of CU1.8 million (CU2.0 million invoiced amount less CU0.2 million of consideration payable to the customer).

7.7 Customers' unexercised rights – 'breakage'

7.7.1 Customers' unexercised rights – general

IFRS 15:106 requires that, when an entity receives a prepayment from a customer, the entity should recognise a contract liability (in the amount of the prepayment) for its performance obligation to transfer, or to be ready to transfer, goods or services in the future (see **section 13**). The contract liability is derecognised, and revenue is recognised, when those goods or services are transferred (i.e. when the performance obligation is satisfied). [IFRS 15:B44]

When a customer makes a non-refundable prepayment to an entity, the customer has a right to receive a good or service in the future and, therefore, the entity is obliged to be ready to transfer a good or service in the future. However, customers may not always exercise all of their contractual rights; those unexercised rights are often referred to as 'breakage'. [IFRS 15:B45]

If an entity expects to be entitled to a breakage amount in a contract liability, that amount is recognised as revenue in proportion to the pattern of rights exercised by the customer. If an entity does not expect to be entitled to a breakage amount, revenue for the expected breakage amount should be recognised when the likelihood of the customer exercising its remaining rights becomes remote. The guidance on constraining variable consideration in IFRS 15:56 to 58 (see **7.3**) should be considered to determine whether an entity expects to be entitled to a breakage amount. [IFRS 15:B46]

An entity should recognise a liability (and not revenue) for any consideration received that is attributable to a customer's unexercised rights which the entity is required to remit to another party (e.g. a government entity in accordance with applicable unclaimed property laws). [IFRS 15:B47]

7.7.2 Gift certificates that may not be redeemed

Gift certificates sold by a retailer can be used by the holder to purchase goods up to the amount indicated on the gift certificate. The retailer should assess when to recognise revenue in respect of those gift certificates.

Gift certificates typically represent a non-refundable prepayment to an entity that gives the customer a right to receive goods or services in the future (and obliges the entity to stand ready to transfer the goods or services). Under IFRS 15, revenue should be recognised when (or as) an entity satisfies a performance obligation by transferring a promised good or service to a customer (see **9.1**). In this case, the retailer satisfies its performance obligation when the customer redeems the gift certificate and the retailer supplies the associated goods or services to the customer. Accordingly, upon receipt of a prepayment from a customer, the retailer should recognise a contract liability for its performance obligation to transfer, or to stand ready to transfer, the goods or services in the future. The entity should derecognise that contract liability (and recognise revenue) when it transfers those goods or services and, therefore, satisfies its performance obligation.

Customers may not exercise all of their contractual rights for various reasons. IFRS 15 states that such unexercised rights are often referred to as 'breakage'. Under IFRS 15:B44 to B47, revenue arising from the breakage can be recognised before the vendor is legally released from its obligation in some circumstances. The following circumstances are specifically discussed in the Standard:

*   IFRS 15:B46 states that "[i]f an entity *expects to be entitled* to a breakage amount in a contract liability, the entity shall recognise the expected breakage amount as revenue in proportion to the pattern of rights exercised by the customer" (emphasis added). Under this approach, the estimated value of gift certificates that an entity expects will not be redeemed would be recognised as revenue proportionately as the remaining gift certificates are redeemed. For example, assume that a retailer issues CU1,000 of gift certificates and, in accordance with IFRS 15:56 to 58 (see **7.3**), expects that CU200 of breakage will result on the basis of a portfolio assessment indicating that 20 per cent of the value of all gift certificates sold will not be redeemed. Therefore, the proportion of the value of gift certificates not expected to be redeemed compared to the proportion expected to be redeemed is 20:80. Each time part of a gift certificate is redeemed, a breakage amount equal to 25 per cent (20 ÷ 80) of the face value of the redeemed amount will be recognised as additional revenue (e.g. if a gift certificate for CU40 is redeemed, the breakage amount released will be CU10, such that the total revenue recognised is CU50).

    Entities should not recognise breakage as revenue immediately upon the receipt of payment, even if there is historical evidence to suggest that performance will not be required for a certain percentage of transactions. In IFRS 15:BC400, the IASB notes that it rejected an approach that would have required an entity to recognise estimated breakage as revenue immediately upon the receipt of prepayment from a customer. The IASB decided that, because the entity has not performed under the contract, recognising revenue would not be a faithful depiction of the entity's performance and could also have understated its obligation to stand ready to provide future goods or services.

    To determine whether an entity expects to be entitled to a breakage amount, an entity should consider the requirements in IFRS 15:56 to 58 on constraining estimates of variable consideration. The entity should use judgement and consider all facts and circumstances when applying this guidance.

- IFRS 15:B46 also states that "[i]f an entity *does not expect to be entitled* to a breakage amount, the entity shall recognise the expected breakage amount as revenue when the likelihood of the customer exercising its remaining rights becomes remote" (emphasis added). For example, assume that a retailer issues CU1,000 of gift certificates and applies the guidance in IFRS 15:56 to 58, but concludes that it does not expect to be entitled to a breakage amount. Each time part of a gift certificate is redeemed, revenue will be recognised equal to the face value of the redeemed amount. Later, after CU800 has been redeemed, the entity may determine that there is only a remote possibility that any of the outstanding gift certificate balances will in due course be redeemed. If so, the entity should release the remaining contract liability of CU200 and recognise revenue of CU200 at that time.

8 Step 4: Allocate the transaction price to the performance obligations in the contract

8.1 Allocation of the transaction price to the performance obligations – general

When allocating the transaction price to each performance obligation, the objective is to allocate amounts that depict the consideration to which the entity expects to be entitled in exchange for transferring each of the performance obligations to the customer. [IFRS 15:73]

IFRS 15 requires the transaction price to be allocated to each performance obligation identified in the contract on a relative stand-alone selling price basis (see **8.2**), subject to exceptions that may be applicable when allocating discounts (see **8.3**) and when allocating consideration that includes variable amounts (see **8.5**). [IFRS 15:74]

The requirements to allocate the transaction price do not apply if a contract has only one performance obligation. However, the requirements for allocating consideration that includes variable amounts (see **8.5**) may apply if an entity promises to transfer a series of distinct goods or services identified as a single performance obligation in accordance with IFRS 15:22(b) (see **section 6**) and the promised consideration includes variable amounts. [IFRS 15:75]

IAS 18 does not include any guidance on how to allocate revenue between the separately identifiable components of a transaction.

In principle, allocation on a stand-alone selling price basis requires a calculation to be performed for each contract containing more than one performance obligation. This may prove a significant logistical challenge for entities with a very large number of different contracts, and in some cases changes to existing systems may be needed.

8.2 Allocation based on stand-alone selling price

8.2.1 Determining the stand-alone selling price of distinct goods and services

The stand-alone selling price of the distinct good or service underlying each performance obligation in the contract is determined at contract inception and the transaction price is allocated in proportion to those stand-alone selling prices. [IFRS 15:76]

The stand-alone selling price is the price at which an entity would sell a promised good or service separately to a customer. The best evidence of the stand-alone selling price is the observable price of a good or service when it is sold separately in similar circumstances and to similar customers. A contractually stated price or a list price for a good or service may be (but is not be presumed to be) the stand-alone selling price. [IFRS 15:77]

8.2.2 Estimation of the stand-alone selling price when not directly observable

If a stand-alone selling price is not directly observable, it is estimated at an amount that would result in the allocation of the transaction price meeting the objective in IFRS 15:73 (see **8.1**). All information (including market conditions, entity-specific factors and information about the customer or class of customer) that is reasonably available to the entity should be considered when estimating the stand-alone selling price. The use of observable inputs should be maximised for this estimation, and the methods used should be applied consistently in similar circumstances. [IFRS 15:78]

If the stand-alone selling price of a good or service is not directly observable, suitable methods for estimating the price include, but are not limited to:

[IFRS 15:79]

(a) an adjusted market assessment approach – by evaluating the market in which it sells goods or services, the entity estimates the price that a customer in that market would be willing to pay for those goods or services. This approach may also include referring to prices from competitors for similar goods or services and adjusting those prices as necessary to reflect the entity's costs and margins;

(b) an expected cost plus a margin approach – by forecasting the expected costs of satisfying a performance obligation and then adding an appropriate margin for that good or service; and

(c) a residual approach – estimating the stand-alone selling price by reference to the total transaction price less the sum of the observable stand-alone selling prices of other goods or services promised in the contract. However, this approach can only be used if one of the following criteria is met:

  (i) the entity sells the same good or service to different customers (at or near the same time) for a broad range of amounts (i.e. the selling price is highly variable because a representative stand-alone selling price is not discernible from past transactions or other observable evidence); or

  (ii) the entity has not yet established a price for that good or service and the good or service has not previously been sold on a stand-alone basis (i.e. the selling price is uncertain).

8.2.3 Estimation of the stand-alone selling price using a combination of methods

A combination of methods may need to be used to estimate the stand-alone selling prices of the goods or services promised in the contract if two or more of those goods or services have highly variable or uncertain stand-alone selling prices. For example, the residual approach may be used to estimate the aggregate stand-alone selling price for those promised goods or services with highly variable or uncertain stand-alone selling prices, but then another method may be used to further analyse that residual amount so as to estimate the stand-alone selling prices of the individual goods or services within it. [IFRS 15:80]

For example, consider a contract which includes two separate software licences (each of which meets the criteria for using the residual approach to estimate the stand-alone selling price) along with other goods and services for which stand-alone selling prices are directly observable. Each software licence and the other goods and services would be considered distinct performance obligations for the purposes of recognising revenue in accordance with IFRS 15.

In such circumstances, a residual approach may be used to estimate the stand-alone selling price for the two software licences in aggregate, and another method (such as an adjusted market assessment approach) may be used to allocate that single residual amount between the two licences.

When estimating the amount to be allocated to each distinct performance obligation in this way, an entity should consider the guidance in IFRS 15:73 and 78.

When an entity uses a combination of methods, the entity should evaluate whether allocating the transaction price at those estimated stand-alone selling prices is consistent with the allocation objective in IFRS 15:73 (see **8.1**) and the requirements for estimating stand-alone selling prices in IFRS 15:78. [IFRS 15:80]

As discussed above, IFRS 15:78 requires the entity to maximise the use of observable inputs.

Example 8.2.3

Allocation methodology

[IFRS 15:IE164 - IE166, Example 33]

An entity enters into a contract with a customer to sell Products A, B and C in exchange for CU100. The entity will satisfy the performance obligations for each of the products at different points in time. The entity regularly sells Product A separately and therefore the stand-alone selling price is directly observable. The stand-alone selling prices of Products B and C are not directly observable.

Because the stand-alone selling price for Products B and C are not directly observable, the entity must estimate them. To estimate the stand-alone selling prices, the entity uses the adjusted market assessment approach for Product B and the expected cost plus a margin approach for Product C. In making those estimates, the entity maximises the use of observable inputs (in accordance with [IFRS 15:78]). The entity estimates the stand-alone selling prices as follows:

Product	Stand-alone selling price	Method
	CU	
Product A	50	Directly observable (see [IFRS 15:77])
Product B	25	Adjusted market assessment approach (see [IFRS 15:79(a)])
Product C	75	Expected cost plus a margin approach (see [IFRS 15:79(b)])
Total	150	

The customer receives a discount for purchasing the bundle of goods because the sum of the stand-alone selling prices (CU150) exceeds the promised consideration (CU100). The entity considers whether it has observable evidence about the performance obligation to which the entire discount belongs (in accordance with [IFRS 15:82]) and concludes that it does not. Consequently, in accordance with [IFRS 15:76 and 81], the discount is allocated proportionately across Products A, B and C. The discount, and therefore the transaction price, is allocated as follows:

Product	Allocated transaction price	
	CU	
Product A	33	(CU50 / CU150 x CU100)
Product B	17	(CU25 / CU150 x CU100)
Product C	50	(CU75 / CU150 x CU100)
Total	100	

8.3 Allocation of a discount

When the sum of the stand-alone selling prices of the goods or services promised in the contract exceeds the promised consideration in a contract, the customer has received a discount for purchasing a bundle of goods or services. The discount should be allocated proportionately to all performance obligations in the contract unless there is observable evidence that the entire discount does not relate to all performance obligations in the contract. [IFRS 15:81]

A discount is allocated entirely to one or more, but not all, performance obligations in the contract if all of the following criteria are met:

[IFRS 15:82]

(a) the entity regularly sells each distinct good or service (or each bundle of distinct goods or services) in the contract on a stand-alone basis;

(b) the entity also regularly sells on a stand-alone basis a bundle (or bundles) of some of those distinct goods or services on a stand-alone basis at a discount to the stand-alone selling prices; and

(c) the discount attributable to each bundle of goods or services described in (b) is substantially the same as the discount in the contract and an analysis of the goods or services in each bundle provides observable evidence of the performance obligation (or performance obligations) to which the entire discount in the contract belongs.

When the discount is allocated entirely to one or more performance obligations in the contract in accordance with IFRS 15:82, the allocation is made before using the residual approach to estimate the stand-alone selling price of a good or service in accordance with IFRS 15:79(c) (see **8.2**). [IFRS 15:83]

IFRS 15:82 will typically apply only to contracts for which there are at least three performance obligations. This is because an entity could demonstrate that a discount relates to two or more performance obligations when it has observable information supporting the stand-alone selling price of a group of those promised goods or services when they are sold together. The Basis for Conclusions on IFRS 15 notes that it may be possible for an entity to have sufficient evidence to be able to allocate a discount to only one performance obligation in accordance with the criteria in IFRS 15:82, but the IASB expected that this could only occur in rare cases. [IFRS 15:BC283]

Example 8.3

Allocating a discount

[IFRS 15:IE167 - IE177, Example 34]

An entity regularly sells Products A, B and C individually, thereby establishing the following stand-alone selling prices:

Product	Stand-alone selling price CU
Product A	40
Product B	55
Product C	45
Total	140

In addition, the entity regularly sells Products B and C together for CU60.

Case A – Allocating a discount to one or more performance obligations

The entity enters into a contract with a customer to sell Products A, B and C in exchange for CU100. The entity will satisfy the performance obligations for each of the products at different points in time.

The contract includes a discount of CU40 on the overall transaction, which would be allocated proportionately to all three performance obligations when allocating the transaction price using the relative stand-alone selling price method (in accordance with [IFRS 15:81]). However, because the entity regularly sells Products B and C together for CU60 and Product A for CU40, it has evidence that the entire discount should be allocated to the promises to transfer Products B and C in accordance with [IFRS 15:82].

If the entity transfers control of Products B and C at the same point in time, then the entity could, as a practical matter, account for the transfer of those products as a single performance obligation. That is, the entity could allocate CU60 of the transaction price to the single performance obligation and recognise revenue of CU60 when Products B and C simultaneously transfer to the customer.

If the contract requires the entity to transfer control of Products B and C at different points in time, then the allocated amount of CU60 is individually allocated to the promises to transfer Product B (stand-alone selling price of CU55) and Product C (stand-alone selling price of CU45) as follows:

Product	Allocated transaction price	
	CU	
Product B	33	(CU55 / CU100 total stand-alone selling price x CU60)
Product C	27	(CU45 / CU100 total stand-alone selling price x CU60)
Total	100	

Case B – Residual approach is appropriate

The entity enters into a contract with a customer to sell Products A, B and C as described in Case A. The contract also includes a promise to transfer Product D. Total consideration in the contract is CU130. The stand-alone selling price for Product D is highly variable (see [IFRS 15:79(c)]) because the entity sells Product D to different customers for a broad range of amounts (CU15–CU45). Consequently, the entity decides to estimate the stand-alone selling price of Product D using the residual approach.

Before estimating the stand-alone selling price of Product D using the residual approach, the entity determines whether any discount should be allocated to the other performance obligations in the contract in accordance with [IFRS 15:82 and 83].

As in Case A, because the entity regularly sells Products B and C together for CU60 and Product A for CU40, it has observable evidence that CU100 should be allocated to those three products and a CU40 discount should be allocated to the promises to transfer Products B and C in accordance with [IFRS 15:82]. Using the residual approach, the entity estimates the stand-alone selling price of Product D to be CU30 as follows:

Product	Stand-alone selling price	Method
	CU	
Product A	40	Directly observable (see [IFRS 15:77])
Products B and C	60	Directly observable with discount (see [IFRS 15:82])
Product D	30	Residual approach (see [IFRS 15:79(c)])
Total	100	

The entity observes that the resulting CU30 allocated to Product D is within the range of its observable selling prices (CU15 – CU45). Therefore, the resulting allocation (see above table) is consistent with the allocation objective in [IFRS 15:73] and the requirements in [IFRS 15:78].

Case C – Residual approach is inappropriate

The same facts as in Case B apply to Case C except the transaction price is CU105 instead of CU130. Consequently, the application of the residual approach would result in a stand-alone selling price of CU5 for Product D (CU105 transaction price less CU100 allocated to Products A, B and C). The entity concludes that CU5 would not faithfully depict the amount of consideration to which the entity expects to be entitled in exchange for satisfying its performance obligation to transfer Product D, because CU5 does not approximate the stand-alone selling price of Product D, which ranges from CU15–CU45. Consequently, the entity reviews its observable data, including sales and margin reports, to estimate the stand-alone selling price of Product D using another suitable method. The entity allocates the transaction price of CU105 to Products A, B, C and D using the relative stand-alone selling prices of those products in accordance with [IFRS 15:73 to 80].

8.4   Allocation of a premium

As noted in **8.3**, when the sum of the stand-alone selling prices of the individual performance obligations in a multiple-element arrangement exceeds the promised consideration, IFRS 15:81 requires any discount under the contract to be allocated proportionately to all performance obligations unless an entity has observable evidence that the entire discount is related only to one or more, but not all, of the performance obligations in the contract. IFRS 15:82 specifies the criteria an entity is required to meet to conclude that the discount does not need to be allocated proportionately to all performance obligations.

IFRS 15 does not, however, explicitly discuss situations in which the promised consideration in a contract exceeds the sum of the stand-alone selling prices of the individual performance obligations, which would suggest that a customer is paying a premium for purchasing the goods or services. Although such situations may not be common, they can arise when, for example, an entity sells its goods or services for a broad range of amounts. In such circumstances, an entity may apply the adjusted market assessment approach described in IFRS 15:79 (see **8.2**) to each performance obligation in the contract, which could result in a determination that the total transaction price of the contract exceeds the aggregate value of stand-alone selling prices of those goods or services.

This scenario is expected to be relatively uncommon and, before assessing how to allocate an apparent premium, an entity should consider the potential that an error, such as one of the following, has been made in the analysis:

- a significant financing component in the contract has not been identified;

- the contract includes an incentive (i.e. performance bonus) that has not been identified;

- additional performance obligations have not been identified; or

- the stand-alone selling prices of performance obligations have not been correctly identified.

If, after further assessment, it is determined that a premium exists, the entity should allocate that premium in a manner consistent with the requirements of IFRS 15 for allocation of a discount (i.e. on a relative stand-alone selling price basis in accordance with IFRS 15:74 (see **8.1**), subject to the exception in IFRS 15:81 to 83).

8.5   Allocation of variable consideration

Variable consideration may be attributable either to the entire contract or to a specific part of the contract, such as either of the following:

[IFRS 15:84]

(a) one or more, but not all, performance obligations in the contract (e.g. a bonus may be contingent on the transfer of a particular good or service within a specified period of time); or

(b) one or more, but not all, distinct goods or services promised in a series of distinct goods or services that forms part of a single performance obligation in accordance with IFRS 15:22(b) (see **section 6**) (e.g. the consideration promised for the second year of a two-year cleaning service contract will increase based on a specified inflation index).

The variable amount (and subsequent changes to that amount) is allocated entirely to a performance obligation or to a distinct good or service that forms part of a single performance obligation in accordance with IFRS 15:22(b) if both of the following criteria are met:

[IFRS 15:85]

(a) the terms of a variable payment relate specifically to efforts to satisfy the performance obligation or transfer the distinct good or service (or to a specific outcome from satisfying the performance obligation or transferring the distinct good or service); and

(b) the allocation of the variable amount of consideration entirely to the performance obligation or the distinct good or service is consistent with the objective set out in IFRS 15:73 (see **8.1**) when considering all of the performance obligations and payment terms in the contract.

The allocation requirements in IFRS 15:73 to 83 are applied to allocate the remaining amount of the transaction price that does not meet the criteria in IFRS 15:85. [IFRS 15:86]

Example 8.5

Allocation of variable consideration

[IFRS 15:IE178 - IE187, Example 35]

An entity enters into a contract with a customer for two intellectual property licences (Licences X and Y), which the entity determines to represent two performance obligations each satisfied at a point in time. The stand-alone selling prices of Licences X and Y are CU800 and CU1,000, respectively.

Case A – Variable consideration allocated entirely to one performance obligation

The price stated in the contract for Licence X is a fixed amount of CU800 and for Licence Y the consideration is three per cent of the customer's future sales of products that use Licence Y. For purposes of allocation, the entity estimates its sales-based royalties (ie the variable consideration) to be CU1,000, in accordance with [IFRS 15:53].

To allocate the transaction price, the entity considers the criteria in [IFRS 15:85] and concludes that the variable consideration (ie the sales-based royalties) should be allocated entirely to Licence Y. The entity concludes that the criteria in [IFRS 15:85] are met for the following reasons:

(a) the variable payment relates specifically to an outcome from the performance obligation to transfer Licence Y (ie the customer's subsequent sales of products that use Licence Y).

(b) allocating the expected royalty amounts of CU1,000 entirely to Licence Y is consistent with the allocation objective in [IFRS 15:73]. This is because the entity's estimate of the amount of sales-based royalties (CU1,000) approximates the stand-alone selling price of Licence Y and the fixed amount of CU800 approximates the stand-alone selling price of Licence X. The entity allocates CU800 to Licence X in accordance with [IFRS 15:86]. This is because, based on an assessment of the facts and circumstances relating to both licences, allocating to Licence Y some of the fixed consideration in addition to all of the variable consideration would not meet the allocation objective in [IFRS 15:73].

The entity transfers Licence Y at inception of the contract and transfers Licence X one month later. Upon the transfer of Licence Y, the entity does not recognise revenue because the consideration allocated to Licence Y is in the form of a sales-based royalty. Therefore, in accordance with [IFRS 15:B63 (see **11.3**)], the entity recognises revenue for the sales-based royalty when those subsequent sales occur.

When Licence X is transferred, the entity recognises as revenue the CU800 allocated to Licence X.

Case B – Variable consideration allocated on the basis of stand-alone selling prices

The price stated in the contract for Licence X is a fixed amount of CU300 and for Licence Y the consideration is five per cent of the customer's future sales of products that use Licence Y. The entity's estimate of the sales-based royalties (ie the variable consideration) is CU1,500 in accordance with [IFRS 15:53].

To allocate the transaction price, the entity applies the criteria in [IFRS 15:85] to determine whether to allocate the variable consideration (ie the sales-based royalties) entirely to Licence Y. In applying the criteria, the entity concludes that even though the variable payments relate specifically to an outcome from the performance obligation to transfer Licence Y (ie the customer's subsequent sales of products that use Licence Y), allocating the variable consideration entirely to Licence Y would be inconsistent with the principle for allocating the transaction price. Allocating CU300 to Licence X and CU1,500 to Licence Y does not reflect a reasonable allocation of the transaction price on the basis of the stand-alone selling prices of Licences X and Y of CU800 and CU1,000, respectively. Consequently, the entity applies the general allocation requirements in [IFRS 15:76 to 80].

The entity allocates the transaction price of CU300 to Licences X and Y on the basis of relative stand-alone selling prices of CU800 and CU1,000, respectively. The entity also allocates the consideration related to the sales-based royalty on a relative stand-alone selling price basis. However, in accordance with [IFRS 15:B63], when an entity licenses intellectual property in which the consideration is in the form of a sales-based royalty, the entity cannot recognise revenue until the later of the following events: the subsequent sales occur or the performance obligation is satisfied (or partially satisfied).

Licence Y is transferred to the customer at the inception of the contract and Licence X is transferred three months later. When Licence Y is transferred, the entity recognises as revenue the CU167 (CU1,000 ÷ CU1,800 × CU300) allocated to Licence Y. When Licence X is transferred, the entity recognises as revenue the CU133 (CU800 ÷ CU1,800 × CU300) allocated to Licence X.

In the first month, the royalty due from the customer's first month of sales is CU200. Consequently, in accordance with [IFRS 15:B63], the entity recognises as revenue the CU111 (CU1,000 ÷ CU1,800 × CU200) allocated to Licence Y (which has been transferred to the customer and is therefore a satisfied performance obligation). The entity recognises a contract liability for the CU89 (CU800 ÷ CU1,800 × CU200) allocated to Licence X. This is because although the subsequent sale by the entity's customer has occurred, the performance obligation to which the royalty has been allocated has not been satisfied.

8.6 Changes in the transaction price

After the inception of the contract, the transaction price can change for various reasons, including the resolution of uncertain events or other changes in circumstances. [IFRS 15:87]

Other than for a contract modification (see **section 10**), any subsequent changes to the transaction price are allocated to the performance obligations on the same basis as at contract inception. Consequently, the transaction price is not reallocated to reflect changes in stand-alone selling prices after contract inception. Amounts allocated to a satisfied performance obligation are recognised as revenue, or as a reduction of revenue, in the period in which the transaction price changes. [IFRS 15:88]

A change in the transaction price is allocated entirely to one or more, but not all, performance obligations or distinct goods or services promised in a series that forms part of a single performance obligation in accordance with IFRS 15:22(b) only if the criteria in IFRS 15:85 (see **8.5**) on allocating variable consideration are met. [IFRS 15:89]

A change in the transaction price that arises as a result of a contract modification is accounted for in accordance with IFRS 15:18 to 21 (see **section 10**). When a change in transaction price occurs after a contract modification, IFRS 15 includes additional guidance on how to apply the requirements of IFRS 15:87 to 89, and that additional guidance is described in **10.4**.

9   Step 5: Determine when to recognise revenue

9.1   Satisfaction of performance obligations

9.1.1   Revenue recognised when (or as) performance obligations are satisfied

Revenue is recognised when (or as) the entity satisfies a performance obligation by transferring a promised good or service (i.e. an asset) to the customer. An asset is transferred when (or as) the customer obtains control of that asset. [IFRS 15:31]

An entity determines at the inception of the contract whether it satisfies each performance obligation over time (see **section 9.2**) or at a point in time (see **section 9.4**). If an entity does not satisfy a performance obligation over time, the performance obligation is satisfied at a point in time. [IFRS 15:32]

IFRS 15 requires entities to determine whether a performance obligation is satisfied (and revenue is recognised) over time, or whether a performance obligation is satisfied (and revenue is recognised) at a point in time for all contracts. No practical expedients are available that would permit, for example for contracts with a short duration (e.g. less than a year), simply defaulting to point-in-time recognition.

Entities should carefully analyse the contractual arrangement in accordance with the requirements of IFRS 15:35 to determine whether the performance obligation is satisfied over time or at a point in time, even for short-duration contracts.

9.1.2 Meaning of control

Goods and services are assets, even if only momentarily, when they are received and used (as in the case of many services). Control of an asset refers to the ability to direct the use of, and obtain substantially all of the remaining benefits from, the asset. Control includes the ability to prevent other entities from directing the use of, and obtaining the benefits from, an asset. The benefits of an asset are the potential cash flows (inflows or savings in outflows) that can be obtained directly or indirectly in many ways, such as:

[IFRS 15:33]

- using the asset to produce goods or provide services (including public services);
- using the asset to enhance the value of other assets;
- using the asset to settle liabilities or reduce expenses;
- selling or exchanging the asset;
- pledging the asset to secure a loan; and
- holding the asset.

When evaluating whether a customer obtains control of an asset, an entity should consider any agreement to repurchase the asset (see **section 3.8**). [IFRS 15:34]

9.1.3 Application of IFRS 15's model for revenue recognition

Unlike IAS 18, which has separate requirements for goods and for services, IFRS 15 applies a single model (based on control) to all revenue transactions in order to determine when revenue should be recognised. Under the IFRS 15 model, revenue may be recognised over time for some deliverables previously accounted for as goods (e.g. some contract manufacturing). Equally, revenue may be recognised at a point in time for some deliverables previously accounted for as services (e.g. some construction contracts).

For example, it may not necessarily be appropriate for entities that are delivering goods (e.g. contract manufacturers and other customer manufacturing arrangements) to recognise revenue at a particular point in time. Entities should carefully analyse the contractual arrangement in accordance with the three criteria in IFRS 15:35 (see **9.2.1**) to determine whether the promise in the contract to construct and transfer goods to the customer is a performance obligation that will be satisfied over time or at a point in time.

If an entity's obligation to produce a customised product meets one of the criteria in IFRS 15:35 for revenue recognition over time (e.g. the entity's performance does not create an asset with an alternative use, and the entity has an enforceable right to payment for performance completed to date), revenue related to that product would be recognised as the product is *produced*, not when the product is *delivered* to the customer.

For example, an entity that has a contract with an original equipment manufacturer (OEM) to produce a customised part for the OEM's product would meet the criteria for revenue recognition over time if the customised part has no alternative use other than as a part for the OEM's product and the entity has an enforceable right to payment for performance completed to date "at all times throughout the duration of the contract". IFRS 15:36 and 37 as well as IFRS 15:B6 to B13 provide detailed guidance on whether an asset has an alternative use to the entity and whether an entity has an enforceable right to payment for performance completed to date (see **section 9.2.4**). An entity would need to carefully analyse the contractual arrangements and the specific facts and circumstances to determine whether those criteria are met.

If it concludes that revenue should be recognised over time, the entity would then be required to select a method of recognising revenue over time that most faithfully depicts the entity's performance to date for producing the product (see **section 9.3**). Therefore, contract revenue and related contract costs should be recognised as revenue and cost of sales when the entity performs (i.e. the products are produced) rather than when the products are delivered to the customer.

Conversely, it is not always appropriate for entities that are providing a service (e.g. a construction contract) to assume that they meet the criteria and recognise revenue over time. Rather, they need to assess whether the criteria outlined in IFRS 15:35 are met (see **9.2.1**).

The assessment should be made at contract inception. If a contract does not meet any of the criteria set out in IFRS 15:35, the entity should recognise revenue at a point in time rather than over time.

The entity should carefully analyse the terms of the contractual arrangement(s) in accordance with the requirements set out in IFRS 15:35 to determine whether the performance obligation is satisfied over time or at a particular point in time.

Accordingly, entities that had recognised revenue over time under IAS 11 or IAS 18 should not assume that they will continue to be able to do so under IFRS 15.

9.2 Revenue recognised over time

9.2.1 Criteria for recognition of revenue over time

When any of the following criteria are met, this demonstrates that the entity is transferring control of a good or service over time (i.e. satisfying a performance obligation over time) and, consequently, should recognise revenue over time:

[IFRS 15:35]

(a) the customer simultaneously receives and consumes the benefits provided by the entity's performance as the entity performs (see **9.2.2**);

(b) the performance of the entity creates or enhances an asset (e.g. work in progress) that the customer controls as the asset is created or enhanced (see **9.2.3**); or

(c) the entity's performance does not create an asset with an alternative use to the entity and the entity has an enforceable right to payment for performance completed to date (see **section 9.2.4**).

It is possible for an entity to satisfy more than one of the criteria in IFRS 15:35 – they are not intended to be mutually exclusive. For example, in some cases it may be determined that both criterion (b) and criterion (c) are met.

9.2.2 Simultaneous receipt and consumption of benefits of the entity's performance

In some cases, it will be straightforward to assess whether a customer receives and simultaneously consumes the benefits of an entity's performance as the entity performs. For example, there are certain routine or recurring services (such as a cleaning service) where the receipt and simultaneous consumption by the customer of the benefits of the performance can be easily identified. [IFRS 15:B3]

In circumstances in which the assessment is not straightforward, a performance obligation is considered to be satisfied over time if the entity can determine that another entity, hypothetically contracted to fulfil the remaining performance obligation, would not need to substantially re-perform the work completed to date. In determining whether this is the case, the entity should make both of the following assumptions:

[IFRS 15:B4]

(a) disregard potential contractual restrictions or practical limitations that otherwise would prevent the entity from transferring the remaining performance obligation to another entity; and

(b)   presume that another entity fulfilling the remainder of the performance obligation would not have the benefit of any asset that is presently controlled by the entity and that would remain controlled by the entity if the performance obligation were to transfer to another entity.

Example 9.2.2

Customer simultaneously receives and consumes the benefits

[IFRS 15:IE67 & IE68, Example 13]

An entity enters into a contract to provide monthly payroll processing services to a customer for one year.

The promised payroll processing services are accounted for as a single performance obligation in accordance with [IFRS 15:22(b)]. The performance obligation is satisfied over time in accordance with [IFRS 15:35(a)] because the customer simultaneously receives and consumes the benefits of the entity's performance in processing each payroll transaction as and when each transaction is processed. The fact that another entity would not need to re-perform payroll processing services for the service that the entity has provided to date also demonstrates that the customer simultaneously receives and consumes the benefits of the entity's performance as the entity performs. (The entity disregards any practical limitations on transferring the remaining performance obligation, including setup activities that would need to be undertaken by another entity.) The entity recognises revenue over time by measuring its progress towards complete satisfaction of that performance obligation in accordance with [IFRS 15:39 to 45] and [IFRS 15:B14 to B19].

The requirements of IFRS 15:22 on identifying performance obligations are discussed in **section 6**. The requirements of IFRS 15:39 to 45 and B14 to B19 on measuring progress are discussed in **section 9.3**.

9.2.3   Customer controls the asset as it is created or enhanced

To determine whether a customer controls an asset as it is created or enhanced in accordance with IFRS 15:35(b), an entity should apply the requirements for control (see **9.1** and **9.4**). The asset that is being created or enhanced (e.g. a work-in-progress asset) could be either tangible or intangible. [IFRS 15:B5]

9.2.4   Entity's performance does not create an asset with an alternative use to the entity and the entity has an enforceable right to payment for performance completed to date

9.2.4.1   Third criterion for recognition of revenue over time – general

The third criterion for recognition of revenue over time is that the entity's performance does not create an asset with an alternative use to the entity and the entity has an enforceable right to payment for performance completed to date. [IFRS 15:35(c)]

> This third criterion was developed because the IASB observed that, in some cases, applying the criteria in IFRS 15:35(a) and (b) could be challenging. Criterion (c) may be necessary for services that may be specific to a customer (e.g. consulting services that ultimately result in a professional opinion for the customer) but also for the creation of tangible (or intangible) goods. [IFRS 15:BC132]

9.2.4.2 *Entity's performance does not create an asset with an alternative use*

An asset is considered to have no alternative use to an entity if either:

[IFRS 15:36]

- the entity is restricted by contract from readily directing the asset for another use during the creation or enhancement of that asset; or

- the entity is limited in practice from readily directing the asset in its completed state for another use.

This assessment is made at the inception of the contract, after which an entity does not update the assessment of the alternative use of an asset unless the parties to the contract approve a contract modification that substantively changes the performance obligation (see **section 10**). [IFRS 15:36]

In order to assess whether an asset has an alternative use to an entity in accordance with IFRS 15:36, the entity should consider the effects of contractual restrictions and practical limitations on its ability to readily direct that asset for another use (e.g. selling it to a different customer). The possibility of the contract with the customer being terminated is not relevant to this assessment. [IFRS 15:B6]

A contractual restriction must be substantive in order for the asset not to have an alternative use to the entity, meaning that a customer could enforce its rights to the promised asset if the entity tried to direct the asset for another use. In contrast, a contractual restriction is not substantive if, for example, an asset is largely interchangeable with other assets that the entity could transfer to another customer without breaching the contract and without incurring significant costs that it would otherwise not have incurred in relation to that contract. [IFRS 15:B7]

A practical limitation exists if an entity would incur significant economic losses to direct the asset for another use. This could arise because the entity would incur significant costs to rework the asset, or would only be able to sell the asset at a significant loss. For example, an entity may be practically limited from redirecting assets that either have design specifications that are unique to a customer or are located in remote areas. [IFRS 15:B8]

Example 9.2.4.2

Asset has no alternative use to the entity

[IFRS 15:IE73 - IE76, Example 15]

An entity enters into a contract with a customer, a government agency, to build a specialised satellite. The entity builds satellites for various customers, such as governments and commercial entities. The design and construction of each satellite differ substantially, on the basis of each customer's needs and the type of technology that is incorporated into the satellite.

At contract inception, the entity assesses whether its performance obligation to build the satellite is a performance obligation satisfied over time in accordance with [IFRS 15:35].

As part of that assessment, the entity considers whether the satellite in its completed state will have an alternative use to the entity. Although the contract does not preclude the entity from directing the completed satellite to another customer, the entity would incur significant costs to rework the design and function of the satellite to direct that asset to another customer. Consequently, the asset has no alternative use to the entity (see [IFRS 15:35(c), 36 and B6 to B8]) because the customer-specific design of the satellite limits the entity's practical ability to readily direct the satellite to another customer.

For the entity's performance obligation to be satisfied over time when building the satellite, [IFRS 15:35(c)] also requires the entity to have an enforceable right to payment for performance completed to date. This condition is not illustrated in this example.

9.2.4.3 Enforceable right to payment for performance completed to date

To evaluate whether an enforceable right to payment for performance completed to date exists, the terms of the contract should be considered, as well as any laws that apply to the contract. The right to payment for performance completed to date does not need to be for a fixed amount. However, at all times throughout the contract, the entity must be entitled to an amount that at least compensates it for performance completed to date if the contract is terminated by either the customer, or another party, for reasons other than the entity's failure to perform as promised. [IFRS 15:37]

An entity has a right to payment for performance completed to date if there would be entitlement to an amount that at least compensates the entity for its performance completed to date in the event that the customer or another party terminates the contract for reasons other than the entity's failure to perform as promised. Such an amount would need to approximate or exceed the selling price of the goods or services transferred to date (for example, recovery of the costs incurred by an entity in satisfying the performance obligation plus a reasonable profit margin); entitlement only to compensation for the entity's potential loss of profit if the contract were to be terminated is not sufficient. Compensation for a reasonable profit margin need not equal the profit margin expected if the contract was fulfilled as promised, but an entity should at least be entitled to either of the following amounts:

[IFRS 15:B9]

(a) a proportion of the expected profit margin in the contract that reasonably reflects the extent of the entity's performance under the contract before termination by the customer (or another party); or

(b) a reasonable return on the entity's cost of capital for similar contracts (or the entity's typical operating margin for similar contracts) if the contract-specific margin is higher than the return the entity usually generates from similar contracts.

Example 9.2.4.3A

Assessing alternative use and right to payment

[IFRS 15:IE69 - IE72, Example 14]

An entity enters into a contract with a customer to provide a consulting service that results in the entity providing a professional opinion to the customer. The professional opinion relates to facts and circumstances that are specific to the customer. If the customer were to terminate the consulting contract for reasons other than the entity's failure to perform as promised, the contract requires the customer to compensate the entity for its costs incurred plus a 15 per cent margin. The 15 per cent margin approximates the profit margin that the entity earns from similar contracts.

The entity considers the criterion in [IFRS 15:35(a)] and the requirements in [IFRS 15:B3 and B4] to determine whether the customer simultaneously receives and consumes the benefits of the entity's performance. If the entity were to be unable to satisfy its obligation and the customer hired another consulting firm to provide the opinion, the other consulting firm would need to substantially re-perform the work that the entity had completed to date, because the other consulting firm would not have the benefit of any work in progress performed by the entity. The nature of the professional opinion is such that the customer will receive the benefits of the entity's performance only when the customer receives the professional opinion. Consequently, the entity concludes that the criterion in [IFRS 15:35(a)] is not met.

However, the entity's performance obligation meets the criterion in [IFRS 15:35(c)] and is a performance obligation satisfied over time because of both of the following factors:

(a) in accordance with [IFRS 15:36 and B6 to B8], the development of the professional opinion does not create an asset with alternative use to the entity because the professional opinion relates to facts and circumstances that are specific to the customer. Therefore, there is a practical limitation on the entity's ability to readily direct the asset to another customer.

(b)   in accordance with [IFRS 15:37 and B9 to B13], the entity has an enforceable right to payment for its performance completed to date for its costs plus a reasonable margin, which approximates the profit margin in other contracts.

Consequently, the entity recognises revenue over time by measuring the progress towards complete satisfaction of the performance obligation in accordance with [IFRS 15:39 to 45 and B14 to B19 (see **section 9.3**)].

Example 9.2.4.3B

Enforceable right to payment for performance completed to date

[IFRS 15:IE77 - IE80, Example 16]

An entity enters into a contract with a customer to build an item of equipment. The payment schedule in the contract specifies that the customer must make an advance payment at contract inception of 10 per cent of the contract price, regular payments throughout the construction period (amounting to 50 per cent of the contract price) and a final payment of 40 per cent of the contract price after construction is completed and the equipment has passed the prescribed performance tests. The payments are non-refundable unless the entity fails to perform as promised. If the customer terminates the contract, the entity is entitled only to retain any progress payments received from the customer. The entity has no further rights to compensation from the customer.

At contract inception, the entity assesses whether its performance obligation to build the equipment is a performance obligation satisfied over time in accordance with [IFRS 15:35].

As part of that assessment, the entity considers whether it has an enforceable right to payment for performance completed to date in accordance with [IFRS 15:35(c), 37 and B9 to B13] if the customer were to terminate the contract for reasons other than the entity's failure to perform as promised. Even though the payments made by the customer are non-refundable, the cumulative amount of those payments is not expected, at all times throughout the contract, to at least correspond to the amount that would be necessary to compensate the entity for performance completed to date. This is because at various times during construction the cumulative amount of consideration paid by the customer might be less than the selling price of the partially completed item of equipment at that time. Consequently, the entity does not have a right to payment for performance completed to date.

Because the entity does not have a right to payment for performance completed to date, the entity's performance obligation is not satisfied over time in accordance with [IFRS 15:35(c)]. Accordingly, the entity does not need to assess whether the equipment would have an alternative use to the entity. The entity also concludes that it does not meet the criteria in [IFRS 15:35(a) or (b)] and thus, the entity accounts for the construction of the equipment as a performance obligation satisfied at a point in time in accordance with [IFRS 15:38 (see **section 9.4**)].

An entity's right to payment for performance completed to date does not need to be a present unconditional right to payment. In many cases, an unconditional right to payment only exists at an agreed-upon milestone or upon complete satisfaction of the performance obligation. In assessing whether it has a right to payment for performance completed to date, an entity should consider whether it would have an enforceable right to demand or retain payment for performance completed to date if the contract were to be terminated before completion for reasons other than the entity's failure to perform as promised. [IFRS 15:B10]

In some contracts, a customer does not have the right to terminate the contract, or can only do so at specified times during the life of the contract. If a customer terminates a contract without having the right to do so at that time (including when a customer fails to perform its obligations as promised), the contract (or other laws) might entitle the entity to continue to transfer to the customer the goods or services promised in the contract and require the customer to pay the consideration promised in exchange for those goods or services. In those circumstances, an entity has a right to payment for performance completed to date because it has a right to continue to perform its obligations in accordance with the contract and to require the customer to perform its obligations (which include paying the promised consideration). [IFRS 15:B11]

An enforceable right to payment would exist if the contract or other laws in the jurisdiction require the entity and the customer to complete their respective obligations. The Basis for Conclusions on IFRS 15 notes that this is often referred to as 'specific performance'. [IFRS 15:BC147]

As part of this assessment, the contractual terms as well as any legislation or legal precedent that could supplement or override those contractual terms should be considered, including whether:

[IFRS 15:B12]

(a) legislation, administrative practice or legal precedent gives the entity a right to payment for performance to date even though it is not specified in the contract with the customer;

(b) relevant legal precedent indicates that similar rights to payment for performance completed to date in similar contracts have no binding legal effect; or

(c) the customary business practices of the entity of choosing not to enforce a right to payment has resulted in the right being rendered unenforceable in that legal environment. However, notwithstanding that an entity may choose to waive its right to payment in similar contracts, an entity would continue to have a right to payment to date if, in the contract with the customer, its right to payment for performance to date remains enforceable.

Although it specifies the timing and amount of consideration that is payable by a customer, the payment schedule specified in a contract does not necessarily indicate whether an entity has an enforceable right to payment for performance completed to date. This is because, for example, the contract could specify that the consideration received from the customer is refundable for reasons other than the entity failing to perform as promised in the contract. [IFRS 15:B13]

Example 9.2.4.3C

Assessing whether a performance obligation is satisfied at a point in time or over time

[IFRS 15:IE81 - IE90, Example 17]

An entity is developing a multi-unit residential complex. A customer enters into a binding sales contract with the entity for a specified unit that is under construction. Each unit has a similar floor plan and is of a similar size, but other attributes of the units are different (for example, the location of the unit within the complex).

Case A – Entity does not have an enforceable right to payment for performance completed to date

The customer pays a deposit upon entering into the contract and the deposit is refundable only if the entity fails to complete construction of the unit in accordance with the contract. The remainder of the contract price is payable on completion of the contract when the customer obtains physical possession of the unit. If the customer defaults on the contract before completion of the unit, the entity only has the right to retain the deposit.

At contract inception, the entity applies [IFRS 15:35(c)] to determine whether its promise to construct and transfer the unit to the customer is a performance obligation satisfied over time. The entity determines that it does not have an enforceable right to payment for performance completed to date because, until construction of the unit is complete, the entity only has a right to the deposit paid by the customer. Because the entity does not have a right to payment for work completed to date, the entity's performance obligation is not a performance obligation satisfied over time in accordance with [IFRS 15:35(c)]. Instead, the entity accounts for the sale of the unit as a performance obligation satisfied at a point in time in accordance with [IFRS 15:38 (see **section 9.4**)].

Case B – Entity has an enforceable right to payment for performance completed to date

The customer pays a non-refundable deposit upon entering into the contract and will make progress payments during construction of the unit. The contract has substantive terms that preclude the entity from being able to direct the unit to another customer. In addition, the customer does not have the right to terminate the contract unless the entity fails to perform as promised. If the customer defaults on its obligations by failing to make the promised progress payments as and when they are due, the entity would have a right to all of the consideration promised in the contract if it completes the construction of the

---

unit. The courts have previously upheld similar rights that entitle developers to require the customer to perform, subject to the entity meeting its obligations under the contract.

At contract inception, the entity applies [IFRS 15:35(c)] to determine whether its promise to construct and transfer the unit to the customer is a performance obligation satisfied over time. The entity determines that the asset (unit) created by the entity's performance does not have an alternative use to the entity because the contract precludes the entity from transferring the specified unit to another customer. The entity does not consider the possibility of a contract termination in assessing whether the entity is able to direct the asset to another customer.

The entity also has a right to payment for performance completed to date in accordance with [IFRS 15:37 and B9 to B13]. This is because if the customer were to default on its obligations, the entity would have an enforceable right to all of the consideration promised under the contract if it continues to perform as promised.

Therefore, the terms of the contract and the practices in the legal jurisdiction indicate that there is a right to payment for performance completed to date. Consequently, the criteria in [IFRS 15:35(c)] are met and the entity has a performance obligation that it satisfies over time. To recognise revenue for that performance obligation satisfied over time, the entity measures its progress towards complete satisfaction of its performance obligation in accordance with [IFRS 15:39 to 45 and B14 to B19 (see **section 9.3**)].

In the construction of a multi-unit residential complex, the entity may have many contracts with individual customers for the construction of individual units within the complex. The entity would account for each contract separately. However, depending on the nature of the construction, the entity's performance in undertaking the initial construction works (ie the foundation and the basic structure), as well as the construction of common areas, may need to be reflected when measuring its progress towards complete satisfaction of its performance obligations in each contract.

Case C – Entity has an enforceable right to payment for performance completed to date

The same facts as in Case B apply to Case C, except that in the event of a default by the customer, either the entity can require the customer to perform as required under the contract or the entity can cancel the contract in exchange for the asset under construction and an entitlement to a penalty of a proportion of the contract price.

Notwithstanding that the entity could cancel the contract (in which case the customer's obligation to the entity would be limited to transferring control of the partially completed asset to the entity and paying the penalty prescribed), the entity has a right to payment for performance completed to date because the entity could also choose to enforce its rights to full payment under the contract. The fact that the entity may choose to cancel the contract in the event the customer defaults on its obligations would not affect that assessment (see [IFRS 15:B11]), provided that the entity's rights to require the customer to continue to perform as required under the contract (ie pay the promised consideration) are enforceable.

9.2.4.4   Real estate sales – example

Example 9.2.4.4

Real estate sales before completion by a property developer

Entity A, a real estate developer, entered into sales and purchase agreements with various buyers before the completion of a property project. The properties are located in Country B. The sales and purchase agreements include the following key terms:

- a specific unit is identified in the contract;
- Entity A is required to complete the property in all respects in compliance with the conditions set out in the sales agreement and the related building plans within two years from the time when the sales contracts are entered into;
- the property remains at Entity A's risk until delivery;
- the buyer is not permitted at any time before delivery to sub-sell the property or transfer the benefit of the agreement. However, the buyer can at any time before the date of assignment mortgage the property in order to finance the acquisition of the property;
- the sales agreement can be cancelled only when both the buyer and Entity A agree to do so – in effect, the buyer does not have the right to cancel the sales agreement. If both the buyer and Entity A agree to cancel the contract, Entity A has the right to retain 10 per cent of the total purchase price, and the buyer is required to pay for all necessary legal and transaction costs incurred by Entity A in relation to the cancellation;
- if Entity A fails to complete the development of the property within the specified two-year period, the buyer has the right to rescind the sales contract and Entity A is required to repay to the buyer all amounts paid by the buyer together with interest. Otherwise, the buyer does not have a right to cancel the contract; and
- the purchase consideration is payable as follows:
  - 5 per cent of the purchase consideration upon entering into the sales agreement;
  - 5 per cent of the purchase consideration within one month from the date when the sales agreement is entered into;
  - 5 per cent of the purchase consideration within three months from the date when the sales agreement is entered into; and
  - the remaining 85 per cent of the purchase consideration upon delivery of the property.

Note that, for simplicity, this example does not consider whether there is a significant financing element.

Should Entity A recognise revenue over time or at a point in time?

Under IFRS 15, an entity satisfies a performance obligation over time when it transfers control of the promised good or service over time. IFRS 15:35 states that an entity transfers control of a good or service over time and, consequently, satisfies a performance obligation and recognises revenue over time if one of the following criteria is met:

(a) the customer simultaneously receives and consumes the benefits provided by the entity's performance as the entity performs;

(b) the entity's performance creates or enhances an asset (e.g. work in progress) that the customer controls as the asset is created or enhanced; or

(c) the entity's performance does not create an asset with an alternative use to the entity and the entity has an enforceable right to payment for performance completed to date.

Criterion IFRS 15:35(a) is not relevant in determining whether revenue from real estate sales (before completion) should be recognised over time or at a point in time. This is because buyers generally do not consume all of the benefits of the property as the real estate developers construct the property; rather, those benefits are consumed in the future.

Criterion IFRS 15:35(b) is not directly relevant in the circumstances under consideration because, without further consideration of criterion 15:35(c), a conclusion cannot be reached about whether the buyers have control of the property as Entity A develops the property.

Entity A should focus on criterion IFRS 15:35(c), and in particular:

• whether an asset has been created with an alternative use to the real estate developer; and

• whether the real estate developer has an enforceable right to payment for performance completed to date.

Has an asset been created with an alternative use to Entity A?

In accordance with IFRS 15:36, an asset does not have an alternative use to an entity if the entity is either restricted contractually from readily directing the asset for another use during the creation or enhancement of that asset, or is limited practically from readily directing the asset in its completed state for another use.

With regard to contract restriction, IFRS 15:B6 states that the entity does not consider the possibility of a contract termination in assessing whether the entity is able to direct the asset to another customer.

Because, in the circumstances under consideration, each sales contract specifies the unit to be delivered, the property unit does not have an alternative use to Entity A. The contract precludes Entity A from transferring the specified unit to another buyer.

> *Does Entity A have an enforceable right to payment for performance completed to date?*
>
> The payment schedule specified in the sales and purchase agreement does not correspond to the performance completed to date. However, in assessing whether it has the right to payment for performance completed to date, Entity A should not only consider the payment schedule, but should also consider the requirements of IFRS 15:B11 (see **9.2.4.3**).
>
> In the circumstances under consideration, the sales agreement can be cancelled only if both the property developer and the buyer agree to do so. In effect, the buyer does not have the discretion to terminate the contract as it wishes.
>
> IFRS 15:37 requires an entity to consider the terms of the contract, as well as any laws that apply to the contract, when evaluating whether it has an enforceable right to payment for performance completed to date. If, taking into account practice and legal precedent in Country B, Entity A has the right to continue to perform the contract and be entitled to all of the consideration as promised, even if the buyer acts to terminate the contract (as articulated in IFRS 15:B11 and IFRS 15:B86), Entity A has the enforceable right to payment for performance completed to date.
>
> The same response (i.e. recognition of revenue over time) applies irrespective of whether Entity A allows buyers to choose to pay the consideration on the basis of the agreed-upon payment schedule or to pay all of the consideration upfront (with a specified percentage of discount given to the buyer).
>
> *Should Entity A recognise revenue over time or at a point in time?*
>
> Because the asset does not have an alternative use to Entity A, and provided that Entity A has an enforceable right to payment for performance completed to date, it should recognise revenue over time. However, if Entity A does not have an enforceable right to payment for the performance completed to date, the criterion in IFRS 15:35(c) is not met and Entity A should recognise revenue at a point in time (i.e. at the point when the control of the property unit is transferred to the buyer, which would normally be at the time of delivery).

9.3   Measuring progress for revenue recognised over time

9.3.1   Measuring progress for revenue recognised over time – general

9.3.1.1   Recognition of revenue over time when reasonable measure of progress available

For each performance obligation satisfied over time (see **section 9.2**), revenue is recognised over time by measuring the progress towards complete satisfaction of that performance obligation. The objective is to depict the performance in transferring control of goods or services promised to a customer (i.e. the satisfaction of an entity's performance obligation). [IFRS 15:39]

A single method of measuring progress for each performance obligation satisfied over time is applied, and should be applied consistently to similar performance obligations and in similar circumstances. At the end of each reporting period, progress towards complete satisfaction of a performance obligation satisfied over time should be remeasured. [IFRS 15:40]

There are a number of possible methods of measuring progress, including output methods and input methods (see **9.3.2** and **section 9.3.3**). When determining the appropriate method for measuring progress, the nature of the good or service that the entity promised to transfer to the customer should be considered. [IFRS 15:41]

Example 9.3.1.1

Measuring progress when making goods or services available

[IFRS 15:IE92 - IE94, Example 18]

An entity, an owner and manager of health clubs, enters into a contract with a customer for one year of access to any of its health clubs. The customer has unlimited use of the health clubs and promises to pay CU100 per month.

The entity determines that its promise to the customer is to provide a service of making the health clubs available for the customer to use as and when the customer wishes. This is because the extent to which the customer uses the health clubs does not affect the amount of the remaining goods and services to which the customer is entitled. The entity concludes that the customer simultaneously receives and consumes the benefits of the entity's performance as it performs by making the health clubs available. Consequently, the entity's performance obligation is satisfied over time in accordance with [IFRS 15:35(a)].

The entity also determines that the customer benefits from the entity's service of making the health clubs available evenly throughout the year. (That is, the customer benefits from having the health clubs available, regardless of whether the customer uses it or not.) Consequently, the entity concludes that the best measure of progress towards complete satisfaction of the performance obligation over time is a time-based measure and it recognises revenue on a straight-line basis throughout the year at CU100 per month.

Any goods or services for which the entity has not transferred control to the customer should be excluded from the measurement of progress. [IFRS 15:42]

As circumstances change over time, an entity should update the measure of progress to reflect any changes in the outcome of the performance obligation. These changes are accounted for as a change in accounting estimate in accordance with IAS 8 *Accounting Policies, Changes in Accounting Estimates and Errors* (see **chapter A5**). [IFRS 15:43]

9.3.1.2 Recognition of revenue over time when no reasonable measure of progress available

Revenue is only recognised for a performance obligation satisfied over time if the entity can reasonably measure its progress. This is not possible if the entity lacks reliable information that would be required to apply an appropriate method to measure the progress. [IFRS 15:44]

In some circumstances (e.g. in the early stages of a contract), it may not be possible to reasonably measure the outcome of a performance obligation, but there may be an expectation that the entity will be able to recover the costs incurred in satisfying the performance obligation. In such circumstances, revenue is recognised only to the extent of the costs incurred until such time that the entity can reasonably measure the outcome of the performance obligation. [IFRS 15:45]

Example 9.3.1.2

Progress towards complete satisfaction of a performance obligation cannot be reasonably measured

A contractor enters into a building contract with fixed consideration of CU1,000 (i.e. revenue is fixed). The contract is expected to take three years to complete and satisfies one of the criteria in IFRS 15:35 for revenue to be recognised over time. At the end of Year 1, management is unable to reasonably measure its progress towards complete satisfaction of the performance obligation (e.g. because it cannot reasonably measure total costs under the contract). Taking into account the progress to date, management expects that total contract costs will not exceed total contract revenues. Costs of CU100 have been incurred in Year 1.

In these circumstances, because the contractor is not able to reasonably measure the progress towards complete satisfaction of the performance obligation, but expects that costs are recoverable, only revenue of CU100 should be recognised in Year 1. Therefore, in Year 1, revenue and costs of services of CU100 are recognised, resulting in no profit margin.

9.3.2 Output methods for measuring progress toward complete satisfaction of a performance obligation

Output methods recognise revenue on the basis of direct measurements of the value to the customer of the goods or services transferred to date relative to the remaining goods or services promised under the contract. Examples of output methods include surveys of performance completed to date, appraisals of results achieved, milestones reached, time elapsed and units produced or units delivered. When an entity evaluates whether to apply an output method to measure its progress, it should consider whether the output selected would faithfully depict the entity's performance towards complete satisfaction of the performance obligation. This would not be the case if the output selected fails to measure some of the goods or services for which control has transferred to the customer. For example, output methods based on units produced or units delivered would not be appropriate if, at the end of the reporting period, the entity's performance has produced work in progress or finished goods controlled by the customer that are not included in the measurement of the output. [IFRS 15:B15]

If an entity has a right to consideration from a customer in an amount that corresponds directly with the value to the customer of the entity's performance completed to date (e.g. a service contract in which an entity bills a fixed amount for each hour of service provided), IFRS 15 provides a practical expedient whereby the entity may recognise revenue based on the amount it has a right to invoice. [IFRS 15:B16]

Output methods sometimes have disadvantages. The outputs used to measure progress may not be directly observable and the information required to apply them may not be available to an entity without undue cost. Therefore, it may be necessary to apply an input method (see **9.3.3**). [IFRS 15:B17]

9.3.3 Input methods for measuring progress toward complete satisfaction of a performance obligation

9.3.3.1 Input methods – general

Input methods recognise revenue on the basis of the entity's efforts or inputs to the satisfaction of a performance obligation (e.g. resources consumed, labour hours expended, costs incurred, time elapsed or machine hours used) relative to the total expected inputs required in order to satisfy the performance obligation. If the entity's efforts or inputs are expended evenly throughout the performance period, it may be appropriate for the entity to recognise revenue on a straight-line basis. [IFRS 15:B18]

However, there may not be a direct relationship between an entity's inputs and the transfer of control of goods or services to a customer. Therefore, an entity should exclude the effects of any inputs that, in accordance with the objective of measuring progress in IFRS 15:39 (see **9.3.1**), do not depict the performance of the entity in transferring control of goods or services to the customer. For instance, when using a cost-based input method, an adjustment to the measure of progress may be required in the following circumstances:

[IFRS 15:B19]

(a) when a cost incurred does not contribute to an entity's progress in satisfying the performance obligation. For example, an entity would not recognise revenue on the basis of costs incurred that are attributable to significant inefficiencies in the entity's performance which were not reflected in the price of the contract (e.g. the costs of unexpected amounts of wasted materials, labour or other resources); or

(b) when a cost incurred is not proportionate to the entity's progress in satisfying the performance obligation. When this is the case, the best depiction of the entity's performance may be to adjust the input method to recognise revenue only to the extent of that cost incurred. For example, a faithful depiction of an entity's performance may be to recognise revenue at an amount equal to the cost of a good used to satisfy the performance obligation if the entity expects at inception of the contract that all of the following conditions would be met:

(i)   the good is not distinct;

(ii) the customer is expected to obtain control of the good significantly before receiving services related to the good;

(iii) the cost of the transferred good is significant relative to the total expected costs to completely satisfy the performance obligation; and

(iv) the entity procures the good from a third party and is not significantly involved in designing and manufacturing the good (but the entity is acting as a principal – see **3.6**).

When an entity uses an input method to measure progress towards complete satisfaction of a performance obligation satisfied over time, it is not appropriate for the entity to include costs incurred to obtain a contract in the measurement of contract costs.

Under cost-based input methods, costs of obtaining a contract should not be included in the measurement of progress to completion because they do not depict the transfer of control of goods or services to the customer. IFRS 15:39 states that an entity's objective, when measuring progress, is to depict its performance in transferring control of goods or services promised to a customer. IFRS 15:B19 also specifies that inputs that do not depict such performance are excluded from the measurement of progress under an input method.

Costs of obtaining a contract are not a measure of fulfilling it and, accordingly, are excluded in the measurement of progress (both from the measure of progress to date and the estimate of total costs to satisfy the performance obligation) irrespective of whether they are recognised as an asset in accordance with IFRS 15:91 (see **12.1**). Such assets are amortised on a systematic basis that is consistent with the transfer to the customer of the goods or services to which the asset relates. Accordingly, rather than being used to determine the pattern of revenue recognition, capitalised costs of obtaining a contract are amortised in accordance with the expected pattern of transfer of goods or services.

Example 9.3.3.1A

Uninstalled materials

[IFRS 15:IE95 - IE100, Example 19]

In November 20X2, an entity contracts with a customer to refurbish a 3-storey building and install new elevators for total consideration of CU5 million. The promised refurbishment service, including the installation of elevators, is a single performance obligation satisfied over time. Total expected costs are CU4 million, including CU1.5 million for the elevators. The entity determines that it acts as a principal in accordance with [IFRS 15:B34 to B38], because it obtains control of the elevators before they are transferred to the customer.

A summary of the transaction price and expected costs is as follows:

	CU
Transaction price	5,000,000
Expected costs:	
Elevators	1,500,000
Other costs	2,500,000
Total expected costs	4,000,000

The entity uses an input method based on costs incurred to measure its progress towards complete satisfaction of the performance obligation. The entity assesses whether the costs incurred to procure the elevators are proportionate to the entity's progress in satisfying the performance obligation, in accordance with [IFRS 15:B19]. The customer obtains control of the elevators when they are delivered to the site in December 20X2, although the elevators will not be installed until June 20X3. The costs to procure the elevators (CU1.5 million) are significant relative to the total expected costs to completely satisfy the performance obligation (CU4 million). The entity is not involved in designing or manufacturing the elevators.

The entity concludes that including the costs to procure the elevators in the measure of progress would overstate the extent of the entity's performance. Consequently, in accordance with [IFRS 15:B19], the entity adjusts its measure of progress to exclude the costs to procure the elevators from the measure of costs incurred and from the transaction price. The entity recognises revenue for the transfer of the elevators in an amount equal to the costs to procure the elevators (ie at a zero margin).

As of 31 December 20X2 the entity observes that:

(a)   other costs incurred (excluding elevators) are CU500,000; and

(b)   performance is 20 per cent complete (ie CU500,000 ÷ CU2,500,000).

Consequently, at 31 December 20X2, the entity recognises the following:

	CU
Revenue	2,200,000[a]
Costs of goods sold	2,000,000[b]
Profit	200,000

[a] Revenue recognised is calculated as (20 per cent x CU3,500,000) + CU1,500,000. (CU3,500,000 is CU5,000,000 transaction price – CU1,500,000 cost of elevators.)

[b] Cost of goods sold is CU500,000 of costs incurred + CU1,500,000 costs of elevators.

Example 9.3.3.1B

Treatment of prepaid costs for work to be performed in the future

A contractor undertakes a three-year contract. At the end of Year 1, management estimates that the total revenue on the contract will be CU1,000 and that total costs will be CU900, of which CU300 has been incurred to date. Of the CU300 incurred to date, CU50 is related to materials purchased in Year 1 that will be used in Year 2. The materials purchased in advance are generic in nature and were not specifically produced for the contract. The contractor has determined that the contract is a single performance obligation that will be satisfied over time. The contractor calculates progress on a contract using an input method based on the proportion of costs incurred to date compared to total anticipated contract costs.

IFRS 15:B19 states that "an entity shall exclude from an input method the effects of any inputs that ... do not depict the entity's performance in transferring control of goods or services to the customer".

Materials purchased that are yet to be used do not form part of the costs that contribute to the transfer of control of goods or services to the customer. For example, if materials have been purchased that the contractor is merely holding at the job site, and these materials were not specifically produced or fabricated for any projects, transfer of control of such materials will generally not have passed to the customer.

Accordingly, in the circumstances under consideration, an adjustment is required for the purchased materials not yet used as illustrated in the following table.

	CU
Costs incurred to date	300
Less: materials purchased for later years	(50)
Costs incurred for work performed to date	250
Total estimated costs	900
Percentage completion at end of year 1	28%

> Therefore, in Year 1, contract revenue of CU280 (28 per cent of CU1,000) and contract costs of CU250 are recognised in profit or loss. Contract costs of CU50 corresponding to the purchased materials not yet used are recognised as inventories.

9.3.3.2   Abnormal or unexpected wastage

In many construction and manufacturing contracts, some level of wastage is normal and unavoidable as part of the construction or manufacturing process. Expected levels of wastage will be forecast in an entity's budgets and estimates, and included in contract costs. However, there may be circumstances when an entity experiences significant unexpected levels of wasted materials, labour or other resources. Entities will need to consider how to account for such abnormal wastage.

IFRS 15 contains specific guidance on accounting for costs to fulfil a contract (see **12.3**). IFRS 15:98(b) specifies that costs of wasted materials, labour or other resources that are not reflected in the price of the contract should be recognised as expenses when incurred.

Abnormal waste costs do not represent additional progress towards satisfaction of an entity's performance obligation and, if revenue is being recognised over time, should be excluded from the measurement of such progress. If the entity is using costs incurred to date as an input method to measure progress towards complete satisfaction of its performance obligation, it should be careful to ensure that revenue attributed to work carried out is not increased to offset additional costs incurred when abnormal or excessive costs arise as a result of inefficiency or error. In particular, IFRS 15:B19(a) states that, when using a cost-based input method, entities may be required to adjust the measure of progress when costs are incurred that are "attributable to significant inefficiencies in the entity's performance that were not reflected in the price of the contract".

9.3.4   Partial satisfaction of a performance obligation prior to identifying a contract

Entities sometimes commence activities on a specific anticipated contract (e.g. construction of an asset) prior to agreeing all of the contract terms with the customer or prior to the contract satisfying the criteria for identification in IFRS 15:9 (see **5.1**).

In some cases, these activities result in the transfer of a good or service to the customer at the date the contract meets those criteria (e.g. when, at that point, the partly completed asset becomes under the customer's control) such that a performance obligation meeting the criteria in

IFRS 15:35 for recognition of revenue over time is partially satisfied. In such circumstances, when the performance obligation is satisfied over time (see **9.3**), the entity should recognise revenue on a cumulative catch-up basis at that date, reflecting its progress towards complete satisfaction of the performance obligation.

In calculating the required cumulative catch-up adjustment, the entity should consider the requirements in IFRS 15:31 to 45 in respect of determining when a performance obligation is satisfied to determine the goods or services that the customer controls as at the date the criteria in IFRS 15:9 are met.

An entity will also need to consider how to account for fulfilment-type costs incurred in the period prior to identifying the contract. If other IFRSs are applicable to those costs, the entity should apply the guidance in those other IFRSs. If it is determined that other IFRSs are not applicable, an entity should capitalise such costs as costs to fulfil an anticipated contract, subject to the criteria in IFRS 15:95 (see **12.3**). On the date the criteria in IFRS 15:9 are met, such costs would immediately be expensed if they relate to progress made to date or to services already transferred to the customer.

Costs that do not satisfy the criteria in other IFRSs nor in IFRS 15:95 for recognition as an asset (e.g. general and administrative costs that are not explicitly chargeable to the customer under the contract) should be expensed as incurred in accordance with IFRS 15:98.

This issue was discussed by the IASB/FASB Joint Transition Resource Group for Revenue Recognition (see **16.1**) in March 2015.

Example 9.3.4A

Partial satisfaction of performance obligation prior to identifying the contract (1)

In this example, it is assumed that the criteria for recognising revenue over time are met. In practice, whether those criteria are met will depend on a careful evaluation of facts and circumstances.

An entity is constructing an apartment block consisting of ten apartments. In the period prior to commencing construction, the entity has signed contracts (meeting the criteria in IFRS 15:9) with customers for six of the apartments in the apartment block but not for the remaining four. The entity uses standard contract terms for each apartment, such that the entity is contractually restricted from readily directing the apartment for another use during its construction, and also has an enforceable right to payment for performance completed to date.

For the six apartments for which contracts have been signed with customers, the construction of each apartment represents the transfer of a performance obligation over time, because the criteria in IFRS 15:35(c) are met. Accordingly, revenue is recognised as those six apartments are constructed, reflecting progress made to date, and the costs incurred in relation to those six apartments are expensed to the extent that they relate to progress made to date.

For the four apartments for which contracts have not yet been signed with customers, costs are initially capitalised. Subsequently, on the date that a contract is signed with a customer and the criteria in IFRS 15:9 are met, a cumulative catch-up of revenue (and expensing of related capitalised costs) should be recognised for that apartment.

Example 9.3.4B

Partial satisfaction of performance obligation prior to identifying the contract (2)

In this example, it is assumed that the criteria for recognising revenue over time are met. In practice, whether those criteria are met will depend on a careful evaluation of facts and circumstances.

An entity is constructing a piece of specialised equipment to an individual customer's specifications. Due to a delay in obtaining the customer's approval for the contract, the entity commences work on constructing the equipment prior to the contract being signed. Consequently, the costs incurred in performing this work are initially capitalised. Subsequently, the contract is approved, and the terms of the contract are such that the criteria for recognition of revenue over time are met. On the date that the contract is signed and the criteria in IFRS 15:9 are met, a cumulative catch-up of revenue (and expensing of capitalised costs), reflecting progress made to date, should be recognised for the partially-constructed equipment.

9.4 Revenue recognised at a point in time

9.4.1 Revenue recognised at a point in time – general

If a performance obligation is not satisfied over time (see **section 9.2**), it is satisfied at a point in time. To determine the point in time at which a customer obtains control of a promised asset (and, therefore, the performance obligation is satisfied), the requirements of IFRS 15:31 to 34 are considered (see **section 9.1**). Indicators of the transfer of control should also be considered; these include, but are not limited to, the following.

[IFRS 15:38]

(a) The entity has a present right to payment for the asset: if a customer is presently obliged to pay for an asset, this may indicate that the customer has obtained the ability to direct the use of, and obtain substantially all of the remaining benefits from, the asset in exchange.

(b) The customer has legal title to the asset: legal title may indicate which party to a contract has the ability to direct the use of, and obtain substantially all of the remaining benefits from, an asset or to restrict the access of other entities to those benefits. Therefore, the transfer of legal title of an asset may indicate that the customer has obtained control of the asset. However, if an entity retains legal title solely as protection against the customer's failure to pay, those rights of the entity would not preclude the customer from obtaining control of an asset (see **example 9.4.1**).

(c)   The entity has transferred physical possession of the asset: the customer's physical possession of an asset may indicate that the customer has the ability to direct the use of, and obtain substantially all of the remaining benefits from, the asset or to restrict the access of other entities to those benefits. However, physical possession may not always coincide with control of an asset. For example, in some repurchase agreements and in some consignment arrangements, a customer or consignee may have physical possession of an asset that the entity controls. Conversely, in some bill-and-hold arrangements, the entity may have physical possession of an asset that the customer controls. Further guidance on such arrangements is set out in **section 3.8**, and at **9.4.4** and **9.4.5**.

(d)   The customer has the significant risks and rewards of ownership of the asset: the transfer of the significant risks and rewards of ownership of an asset to the customer may indicate that the customer has obtained the ability to direct the use of, and obtain substantially all of the remaining benefits from, the asset. However, when evaluating the risks and rewards of ownership of a promised asset, an entity excludes any risks that give rise to a separate performance obligation in addition to the performance obligation to transfer the asset. For example, an entity may have transferred control of an asset to a customer but not yet satisfied an additional performance obligation to provide maintenance services related to the transferred asset.

(e)   The customer has accepted the asset: the customer's acceptance of an asset may indicate that it has obtained the ability to direct the use of, and obtain substantially all of the remaining benefits from, the asset. Further guidance on how to evaluate the effect of a contractual customer acceptance clause on when control of an asset is transferred is considered at **9.4.3**.

The indicators in IFRS 15:38 are not criteria that must be met before an entity can conclude that control of a good or service has transferred to a customer. Rather, these indicators are factors that are often present if a customer has control of an asset and they are provided to help entities apply the principle of control. [IFRS 15:BC155] However, each indicator may not in isolation be sufficient to demonstrate the transfer of control (as noted in, for example, IFRS 15:38(c) with respect to physical possession of an asset). An entity may therefore need to perform a careful analysis when one or more indicators are not present and the entity believes that control has been transferred.

Appendix B to IFRS 15 includes additional guidance on assessing the transfer of control in circumstances such as repurchase agreements, consignment arrangements, bill-and-hold arrangements, customer acceptance and trial and evaluation arrangements. When it is appropriate to do so, an entity should apply this guidance in addition to considering the indicators in IFRS 15:38.

Example 9.4.1

Retention of title to enforce payment

As a matter of policy, a seller writes its sales contracts so that legal title passes when consideration for the goods is received rather than when the goods are delivered. A transaction is entered into at an agreed, fixed price and the related goods are delivered to a customer who is not a particular credit risk. At the point of delivery, the customer accepts and takes physical possession of the goods, and incurs an obligation to pay for the goods. Assume that the criteria for recognising revenue over time are not met.

In these circumstances, is it appropriate for the seller to recognise revenue when the goods are delivered?

Yes. A core principle in IFRS 15 is that revenue is recognised when (or as) an entity satisfies a performance obligation by transferring a promised good or service (i.e. an asset) to a customer. An asset is transferred when (or as) the customer obtains control of that asset. As stated in IFRS 15:33 (see **9.1.2**), control of an asset refers to the ability to direct the use of, and obtain substantially all of the remaining benefits from, the asset. Control includes the ability to prevent other entities from directing the use of and obtaining the benefits from an asset.

IFRS 15:38 lists indicators for entities to consider when determining whether control has been transferred (see above). The list is not intended to be exhaustive.

In the circumstances described, control of the goods has transferred from the seller to the customer even though title has not. Transfer of title may be an indicator that control of the asset has transferred to the customer, but it is not determinative. IFRS 15:38(b) specifically states that "[i]f an entity retains legal title solely as protection against the customer's failure to pay, those rights of the entity [are protective rights and] would not preclude a customer from obtaining control of an asset". Consequently, if other indicators demonstrate that control of the asset has transferred to the customer, revenue should be recognised.

9.4.2 Impact of governing laws

When an entity sells the same item in a number of jurisdictions on exactly the same written contract terms, the timing of revenue recognition may differ between the jurisdictions.

It is not sufficient only to consider written contract terms in determining when control of an asset has been transferred to a customer. IFRS 15 acknowledges that the timing of transfer of control can also be affected by governing laws.

- As indicated in IFRS 15:37 and B12 (see **9.2.4.3**), laws that apply to a contract may affect whether an entity has an enforceable right to payment for performance to date and, consequently, whether revenue should be recognised over time.

- In some jurisdictions, title does not legally transfer until the customer obtains physical possession of the goods.

- In some jurisdictions, property transactions (often residential property transactions) and distance sale transactions (such as sales via internet, phone, mail order or television) are required to include a period during which the customer has an absolute legal right to rescind the transaction (sometimes referred to as a 'cooling off' period). For such transactions, it may be appropriate for entities to consider the guidance on whether a contract has been identified under IFRS 15 and when customer acceptance occurs in determining the timing of revenue recognition.

9.4.3 Customer acceptance

IFRS 15:38(e) notes that the customer's acceptance of an asset may indicate that the customer has obtained control of the asset. Customer acceptance clauses allow a customer to cancel a contract or require an entity to take remedial action if a good or service does not meet agreed-upon specifications, and should be considered when evaluating when a customer obtains control of a good or service. [IFRS 15:B83]

When an entity can objectively determine that control of a good or service has been transferred to the customer in accordance with the agreed-upon specifications in the contract, then the customer acceptance is a formality and does not affect the entity's determination of when the customer has obtained control of the good or service. For example, if the customer acceptance clause is based on meeting specified size and weight characteristics, an entity would be able to determine whether those criteria have been met before receiving confirmation of the customer's acceptance. Experience with contracts for similar goods or services may provide evidence that a good or service provided to the customer is in accordance with the agreed-upon specifications in the contract. If revenue is recognised before customer acceptance, consideration should still be given as to whether there are any remaining performance obligations (e.g. installation of equipment) that should be accounted for separately. [IFRS 15:B84]

However, if an entity cannot objectively determine that the good or service provided to the customer is in accordance with the agreed-upon specifications in the contract, then it cannot conclude that the customer has obtained control until the entity receives the customer's acceptance. In this circumstance, the entity cannot determine that the customer has the ability to direct the use of, and obtain substantially all of the remaining benefits from, the good or service. [IFRS 15:B85]

When a product is delivered to a customer for trial or evaluation purposes and the customer is not committed to pay any consideration until the trial period lapses, control of the product is not transferred to the customer until either the customer accepts the product or the trial period lapses. [IFRS 15:B86]

9.4.4 Consignment arrangements

When an entity delivers a product to another party (such as a dealer or a distributor) for sale to end customers, it should evaluate whether that other party has obtained control of the product at that point in time. A product that has been delivered to another party may be held in a consignment arrangement if that other party has not obtained control of the product. Accordingly, revenue is not recognised upon delivery of a product to another party if the delivered product is held on consignment. [IFRS 15:B77]

Indicators that an arrangement is a consignment arrangement include the following:

[IFRS 15:B78]

(a) the product is controlled by the entity until a specified event occurs, such as the sale of the product to a customer of the dealer or until a specified period expires;

(b) the entity is able to require the return of the product or transfer the product to a third party (such as another dealer); and

(c) the dealer does not have an unconditional obligation to pay for the product (although it might be required to pay a deposit).

9.4.5 Bill-and-hold arrangements

A bill-and-hold arrangement is a contract under which an entity bills a customer for a product but the entity retains physical possession of the product until it is transferred to the customer at a point in time in the future. For example, a customer may request an entity to enter into such a contract because of a lack of available space for the product or because of delays in the customer's production schedules. [IFRS 15:B79]

For some contracts, control is transferred either when the product is delivered to the customer's site or when the product is shipped, depending on the terms of the contract (including delivery and shipping terms – see **9.4.6**). However, for other contracts, a customer may obtain control of a product even though the physical possession of the product remains with the entity. In that case, the customer has the ability to direct the use of, and obtain substantially all of the remaining benefits from, the product even though it has decided not to exercise its right to take physical possession of that product and the entity, therefore, does not control the product. Instead, the entity is providing custodial services to the customer over the customer's asset. [IFRS 15:B80]

In addition to applying the requirements in IFRS 15:38 (see **9.4.1**), all of the following criteria are required to be met for a customer to have obtained control of a product in a bill-and-hold arrangement:

[IFRS 15:B81]

(a)   the reason for the bill-and-hold arrangement must be substantive (e.g. the customer has requested the arrangement);

(b)   the product must be identified separately as belonging to the customer;

(c)   the product currently must be ready for physical transfer to the customer; and

(d)   the entity cannot have the ability to use the product or to direct it to another customer.

If an entity recognises revenue for the sale of a product on a bill-and-hold basis, it should consider whether it has remaining performance obligations (e.g. for custodial services) to which a portion of the transaction price should be allocated (see **section 8**). [IFRS 15:B82]

9.4.6   Shipping terms

Under IFRS 15, revenue is recognised when (or as) an entity satisfies a performance obligation by transferring a promised good or service (i.e. an asset) to a customer. An asset is transferred when (or as) the customer obtains control of that asset. Therefore, in determining when to recognise revenue, an entity should evaluate when the customer obtains control of the asset, by considering how the guidance in IFRS 15 would be applied to the specific fact pattern.

If it is determined that revenue should be recognised at a point in time, an analysis of the shipping terms will form part of the assessment of when control passes. This is because shipping terms will typically specify when title passes and will also affect when the risks and rewards of ownership transfer to the customer; accordingly, they will be relevant in the assessment of two of the five indicators of transfer of control set out in IFRS 15:38 (see **9.4.1**).

If a written sales contract does not explicitly set out shipping terms, the following should be taken into account in determining when control of the goods has transferred to the customer:

- the standard shipping terms in the jurisdiction and in the industry;

- the legal environment of whichever jurisdiction governs the sale transaction; and

- the entity's customary business practices, to the extent that they would be relevant to the contractual terms.

Example 9.4.6

Goods shipped FOB destination but shipping company assumes risk of loss

Company A, which sells goods 'free on board (FOB) destination' (i.e. title does not pass to the buyer until the goods reach the agreed destination), is responsible for any loss in transit. To protect itself from loss, Company A contracts with the shipping company for the shipping company to assume total risk of loss while the goods are in transit.

Is it appropriate for Company A to recognise revenue when the goods are shipped?

No. Under IFRS 15, Company A can only recognise revenue when it has satisfied its performance obligation by transferring control of the promised goods to the customer. As stated in IFRS 15:33 (see **9.1.2**), control of an asset refers to the ability to direct the use of, and obtain substantially all the remaining benefits from, the asset. Control includes the ability to prevent other entities from directing the use of, and obtaining the benefits from, an asset. IFRS 15:38 includes a list of five indicators to determine whether control has been transferred (see **9.4.1**).

Company A has not satisfied the performance obligation when the goods are shipped; the performance obligation is to provide the customer with the goods, whose title and physical possession will only be passed to the customer when the goods reach the agreed destination. Further, the fact that Company A has managed its risk while the goods are in transit by contracting with the shipping company does not mean that it has transferred control of the goods to the customer at the time when the goods are shipped.

After performing the above analysis, Company A determines that control does not pass to the customer until the goods reach the agreed destination.

Generally, when goods are shipped with standard FOB destination shipping terms, control of the goods will be transferred to the customer when the goods arrive at the point of the agreed destination. However, entities should carefully consider both the terms of the contract and other relevant facts and circumstances to determine when control of the goods is transferred to the customer, especially when a contract contains other than standard shipping terms.

When goods are shipped 'free on board (FOB) shipping point', title passes to the buyer when the goods are shipped, and the buyer is responsible for any loss in transit. On the other hand, when goods are shipped FOB destination, title does not pass to the buyer until delivery, and the seller is responsible for any loss in transit.

Some sellers use FOB shipping point terms but have practices or arrangements with their customers which result in the seller's continuing to bear risk of loss or damage while the goods are in transit. If there is damage or loss, the seller is obliged to provide (or has a practice of providing) the buyer with replacement products at no additional cost. The seller may insure this risk with a third party or 'self-insure' the risk (however, the seller is not acting solely as the buyer's agent in arranging shipping and insurance in the arrangements). These types of shipping terms are commonly referred to as 'synthetic FOB destination' shipping terms because the seller has retained the risk of loss or damage during transit so that all of the risks and rewards of ownership have not been substantively transferred to the buyer.

The seller will need to evaluate when control of a good transfers to a customer under FOB shipping point terms if the seller has a practice (or an arrangement with the customer) that results in the seller's continuing to bear the risk of loss or damage while the goods are in transit.

When control of a good (that represents a separate performance obligation) is deemed to transfer at a point in time, an entity should use judgment in applying the guidance and indicators provided in IFRS 15 to evaluate the impact of shipping terms and practices in determining when control of the good is transferred to the customer.

Under typical, unmodified FOB shipping point terms, the seller usually has a legal right to payment upon shipment of the goods; title and risk of loss of/damage to the shipped goods are transferred to the buyer, and the seller transfers physical possession of the shipped goods (assuming that the buyer, not the seller, has the ability to re-direct or otherwise control the shipment through the shipping company). Typically, any customer acceptance term would need to be evaluated separately to determine its impact on when control of a good is transferred to the buyer. However, if the seller can objectively determine that the shipped goods meet the agreed-upon specifications in the contract with the buyer, customer acceptance would be deemed a formality as noted in IFRS 15:B84 (see **9.4.3**). Therefore, under typical unmodified FOB shipping point terms, the buyer would obtain control of the shipped goods, and revenue (subject to the other requirements of IFRS 15) would be recognised upon shipment.

The typical FOB shipping point terms as described above may be modified such that a seller is either (1) obliged to the buyer to replace goods lost or damaged in transit (a legal obligation), or (2) not obliged but has a history of replacing any damaged or lost goods at no additional cost (a constructive obligation). Such an obligation is an indicator that the seller would need to consider in determining when the buyer has obtained control of the shipped goods. In these situations, the seller should evaluate whether the buyer has obtained the 'significant' risks and rewards of ownership of the shipped goods even though the seller maintains the risk of loss of/damage to the goods during shipping. Such evaluation would include (1) a determination of how the obligation assumed by the seller affects the buyer's ability to sell, exchange, pledge, or otherwise use the asset (as noted in IFRS 15:33), and (2) a consideration of the likelihood and potential materiality of lost or damaged goods during shipping. This determination of whether the significant risks and rewards have been transferred would constitute only one indicator (not in itself determinative) of whether the buyer has obtained control of the shipped goods and should be considered along with the other four indicators in IFRS 15:38 (see **9.4.1**). Recognition of revenue upon shipment (subject to the other requirements of IFRS 15) would be appropriate if the seller concludes that the buyer has obtained 'control' of the goods upon shipment (on the basis of an overall evaluation of the indicators in IFRS 15:38 and other guidance in the Standard).

If control is considered to be transferred upon shipment, the seller would be required under IFRS 15:38(d) to consider whether the risk of loss or damage it assumed during shipping gives rise to another performance obligation (a distinct service-type obligation in accordance with IFRS 15:27) and, if so, to account for such obligation separately in accordance with the Standard. For example, such risks may represent another performance obligation if goods are frequently lost or damaged during shipping.

10 Contract modifications

10.1 Contract modifications – general

A contract modification is a change in the scope or price (or both) of a contract that is approved by the parties to the contract. In some industries and jurisdictions, it may be described as a 'change order', a 'variation' or an 'amendment'. A contract modification occurs when the parties to a contract approve a modification that either creates new or changes existing enforceable rights and obligations of the parties to the contract. As with the original contract, a contract modification can be approved in writing, by oral agreement or implied by customary business practices. If the contract modification has not yet been approved, IFRS 15 should continue to be applied to the existing contract until the contract modification is approved. [IFRS 15:18]

When the parties to a contract are in dispute about the scope or price (or both) of a modification, or the scope of the contract modification has been approved but the corresponding change in price has not been finalised, it is still possible that a contract modification has occurred. In determining whether the rights and obligations that are created or changed by a modification are enforceable, all relevant facts and circumstances should be considered, including the terms of the contract and other evidence. If the parties to a contract have approved a change in the scope of the contract but have not yet determined the corresponding change in price, the new transaction price arising from the modification should be estimated (see **sections 7.2** and **7.3**). [IFRS 15:19]

> Previous revenue recognition requirements did not include a general framework for accounting for contract modifications. [IFRS 15:BC76] The approach required by IFRS 15 may be different from that previously applied by an entity.

10.2   Contract modification accounted for as a separate contract

An entity should account for a contract modification as a separate contract if both of the following conditions are met:

[IFRS 15:20]

(a)   the scope of the contract increases because of the addition of promised goods or services that are distinct (see **section 6.3**); and

(b)   the price of the contract increases by an amount that reflects the stand-alone selling price of the additional promised goods or services, considering any appropriate adjustments to that price to reflect the circumstances of the particular contract. For example, an entity may adjust the stand-alone selling price of an additional good or service for a discount that the customer receives, because the entity does not need to incur the selling-related costs that it would have incurred when selling a similar good or service to a new customer.

> If the modification is accounted for as a separate contract, it follows that the original contract is treated as unmodified for the purposes of IFRS 15.

Example 10.2

Modification of a contract for goods (1)

[IFRS 15:IE19 - IE21, Example 5 (extract)]

An entity promises to sell 120 products to a customer for CU12,000 (CU100 per product). The products are transferred to the customer over a six-month period. The entity transfers control of each product at a point in time. After the entity

---

has transferred control of 60 products to the customer, the contract is modified to require the delivery of an additional 30 products (a total of 150 identical products) to the customer. The additional 30 products were not included in the initial contract.

Case A – Additional products for a price that reflects the stand-alone selling price

When the contract is modified, the price of the contract modification for the additional 30 products is an additional CU2,850 or CU95 per product. The pricing for the additional products reflects the stand-alone selling price of the products at the time of the contract modification and the additional products are distinct (in accordance with [IFRS 15:27]) from the original products.

In accordance with [IFRS 15:20], the contract modification for the additional 30 products is, in effect, a new and separate contract for future products that does not affect the accounting for the existing contract. The entity recognises revenue of CU100 per product for the 120 products in the original contract and CU95 per product for the 30 products in the new contract.

10.3 Contract modification not accounted for as a separate contract

If a contract modification is not accounted for as a separate contract in accordance with IFRS 15:20 (see **10.2**), the promised goods or services not yet transferred at the date of the contract modification (i.e. the remaining promised goods or services) should be accounted for as follows.

[IFRS 15:21]

(a) If the remaining goods or services are distinct from the goods or services transferred on or before the date of the contract modification, the contract modification should be accounted for as if it were a termination of the existing contract and the creation of a new contract (see **examples 10.3A** and **10.3B**). The amount of consideration to be allocated to the remaining performance obligations (or to the remaining distinct goods or services in a single performance obligation) is the sum of:

   (i) the consideration promised by the customer (including amounts already received from the customer) that was included in the estimate of the transaction price and that had not been recognised as revenue; and

   (ii) the consideration promised as part of the contract modification.

(b) If the remaining goods or services are not distinct and, therefore, form part of a single performance obligation that is partially satisfied at the date of the contract modification, the contract modification should be accounted for as if it were a part of the existing contract. The effect that the contract modification has on the transaction price, and on the measure of progress towards complete satisfaction of the performance obligation, is recognised as an adjustment to revenue (either as an increase in or a reduction of revenue) at the date of the contract modification (i.e. on a cumulative catch-up basis) (see **example 10.3C**).

(c) When the remaining goods or services are a combination of items (a) and (b), the unsatisfied (or partially unsatisfied) performance obligations in the modified contract are accounted for in a manner that is consistent with the objectives above.

Example 10.3A

Modification of a contract for goods (2)

[IFRS 15:IE19 & IE22 - IE24, Example 5 (extract)]

An entity promises to sell 120 products to a customer for CU12,000 (CU100 per product). The products are transferred to the customer over a six-month period. The entity transfers control of each product at a point in time. After the entity has transferred control of 60 products to the customer, the contract is modified to require the delivery of an additional 30 products (a total of 150 identical products) to the customer. The additional 30 products were not included in the initial contract.

Case B – Additional products for a price that does not reflect the stand-alone selling price

During the process of negotiating the purchase of an additional 30 products, the parties initially agree on a price of CU80 per product. However, the customer discovers that the initial 60 products transferred to the customer contained minor defects that were unique to those delivered products. The entity promises a partial credit of CU15 per product to compensate the customer for the poor quality of those products. The entity and the customer agree to incorporate the credit of CU900 (CU15 credit × 60 products) into the price that the entity charges for the additional 30 products. Consequently, the contract modification specifies that the price of the additional 30 products is CU1,500 or CU50 per product. That price comprises the agreed-upon price for the additional 30 products of CU2,400, or CU80 per product, less the credit of CU900.

At the time of modification, the entity recognises the CU900 as a reduction of the transaction price and, therefore, as a reduction of revenue for the initial 60 products transferred. In accounting for the sale of the additional 30 products, the entity determines that the negotiated price of CU80 per product does not reflect the stand-alone selling price of the additional products. Consequently, the contract modification does not meet the conditions in [IFRS 15:20] to be accounted for as a separate contract. Because the remaining products to be delivered are distinct from those already transferred, the entity applies the requirements in [IFRS 15:21(a)] and accounts for the modification as a termination of the original contract and the creation of a new contract.

Consequently, the amount recognised as revenue for each of the remaining products is a blended price of CU93.33 {[(CU100 × 60 products not yet transferred under the original contract) + (CU80 × 30 products to be transferred under the contract modification)] ÷ 90 remaining products}.

Example 10.3B

Modification of a services contract

[IFRS 15:IE33 - IE36, Example 7]

An entity enters into a three-year contract to clean a customer's offices on a weekly basis. The customer promises to pay CU100,000 per year. The stand-alone selling price of the services at contract inception is CU100,000 per year. The entity recognises revenue of CU100,000 per year during the first two years of providing services. At the end of the second year, the contract is modified and the fee for the third year is reduced to CU80,000. In addition, the customer agrees to extend the contract for three additional years for consideration of CU200,000 payable in three equal annual instalments of CU66,667 at the beginning of years 4, 5 and 6. After the modification, the contract has four years remaining in exchange for total consideration of CU280,000. The stand-alone selling price of the services at the beginning of the third year is CU80,000 per year. The entity's stand-alone selling price at the beginning of the third year, multiplied by the remaining number of years to provide services, is deemed to be an appropriate estimate of the stand-alone selling price of the multi-year contract (ie the stand-alone selling price is 4 years × CU80,000 per year = CU320,000).

At contract inception, the entity assesses that each week of cleaning service is distinct in accordance with [IFRS 15:27]. Notwithstanding that each week of cleaning service is distinct, the entity accounts for the cleaning contract as a single performance obligation in accordance with [IFRS 15:22(b)]. This is because the weekly cleaning services are a series of distinct services that are substantially the same and have the same pattern of transfer to the customer (the services transfer to the customer over time and use the same method to measure progress – that is, a time-based measure of progress).

At the date of the modification, the entity assesses the remaining services to be provided and concludes that they are distinct. However, the amount of remaining consideration to be paid (CU280,000) does not reflect the stand-alone selling price of the services to be provided (CU320,000).

Consequently, the entity accounts for the modification in accordance with [IFRS 15:21(a)] as a termination of the original contract and the creation of a new contract with consideration of CU280,000 for four years of cleaning service. The entity recognises revenue of CU70,000 per year (CU280,000 ÷ 4 years) as the services are provided over the remaining four years.

Example 10.3C

Unapproved change in scope and price

[IFRS 15:IE42 & IE43, Example 9]

An entity enters into a contract with a customer to construct a building on customer-owned land. The contract states that the customer will provide the entity with access to the land within 30 days of contract inception. However, the entity was not provided access until 120 days after contract inception because of storm damage to the site that occurred after contract inception. The contract specifically identifies any delay (including force majeure) in the entity's access to customer-owned land as an event that entitles the entity to compensation that is equal to actual costs incurred as a direct result of the delay. The entity is able to demonstrate that the specific direct costs were incurred as a result of the delay in accordance with the terms of the contract and prepares a claim. The customer initially disagreed with the entity's claim.

The entity assesses the legal basis of the claim and determines, on the basis of the underlying contractual terms, that it has enforceable rights. Consequently, it accounts for the claim as a contract modification in accordance with [IFRS 15:18 to 21]. The modification does not result in any additional goods and services being provided to the customer. In addition, all of the remaining goods and services after the modification are not distinct and form part of a single performance obligation. Consequently, the entity accounts for the modification in accordance with [IFRS 15:21(b)] by updating the transaction price and the measure of progress towards complete satisfaction of the performance obligation. The entity considers the constraint on estimates of variable consideration in [IFRS 15:56 to 58] when estimating the transaction price.

10.4   Change in transaction price after a contract modification

When a change in transaction price occurs after a contract modification, the requirements of IFRS 15:87 to 89 (see **8.6**) are applied to allocate the change in the transaction price in one of the following ways.

[IFRS 15:90]

(a) When the change in the transaction price is attributable to an amount of variable consideration promised before the modification and the modification is accounted for in accordance with IFRS 15:21(a) (i.e. prospectively – see **10.3**), it is allocated to the performance obligations identified in the contract before the modification.

(b) In all other cases where the modification was not accounted for as a separate contract in accordance with IFRS 15:20, the change in the transaction price is allocated to the performance obligations in the modified contract (i.e. the performance obligations that were unsatisfied or partially unsatisfied immediately after the modification).

Example 10.4A

Change in the transaction price after a contract modification

[IFRS 15:IE25 - IE32, Example 6]

On 1 July 20X0, an entity promises to transfer two distinct products to a customer. Product X transfers to the customer at contract inception and Product Y transfers on 31 March 20X1. The consideration promised by the customer includes fixed consideration of CU1,000 and variable consideration that is estimated to be CU200. The entity includes its estimate of variable consideration in the transaction price because it concludes that it is highly probable that a significant reversal in cumulative revenue recognised will not occur when the uncertainty is resolved.

The transaction price of CU1,200 is allocated equally to the performance obligation for Product X and the performance obligation for Product Y. This is because both products have the same stand-alone selling prices and the variable consideration does not meet the criteria in [IFRS 15:85] that requires allocation of the variable consideration to one but not both of the performance obligations.

When Product X transfers to the customer at contract inception, the entity recognises revenue of CU600.

On 30 November 20X0, the scope of the contract is modified to include the promise to transfer Product Z (in addition to the undelivered Product Y) to the customer on 30 June 20X1 and the price of the contract is increased by CU300 (fixed consideration), which does not represent the stand-alone selling price of Product Z. The stand-alone selling price of Product Z is the same as the stand-alone selling prices of Products X and Y.

The entity accounts for the modification as if it were the termination of the existing contract and the creation of a new contract. This is because the remaining Products Y and Z are distinct from Product X, which had transferred to the customer before the modification, and the promised consideration for the additional Product Z does not represent its stand-alone selling price. Consequently, in accordance with [IFRS 15:21(a)], the consideration to be allocated to the remaining performance obligations comprises the consideration that had been allocated to the performance obligation for Product Y (which is measured at an allocated transaction price amount of CU600) and the consideration promised in the modification (fixed consideration of CU300). The transaction price for the modified contract is CU900 and that amount is allocated equally to the performance obligation for Product Y and the performance obligation for Product Z (ie CU450 is allocated to each performance obligation).

After the modification but before the delivery of Products Y and Z, the entity revises its estimate of the amount of variable consideration to which it expects to be entitled to CU240 (rather than the previous estimate of CU200). The entity concludes that the change in estimate of the variable consideration can be included in the transaction price, because it is highly probable that a significant reversal in cumulative revenue recognised will not occur when the uncertainty is resolved. Even though the modification was accounted for as if it were the termination of the existing contract and the creation of a new contract in accordance with [IFRS 15:21(a)], the increase in the transaction price of CU40 is attributable to variable consideration promised before the modification. Therefore, in accordance with [IFRS 15:90], the change in the transaction price is allocated to the performance obligations for Product X and Product Y on the same basis as at contract inception. Consequently, the entity recognises revenue of CU20 for Product X in the period in which the change in the transaction price occurs. Because Product Y had not transferred to the customer before the contract modification, the change in the transaction price that is attributable to Product Y is allocated to the remaining performance obligations at the time of the contract modification. This is consistent with the accounting that would have been required by [IFRS 15:21(a)] if that amount of variable consideration had been estimated and included in the transaction price at the time of the contract modification.

The entity also allocates the CU20 increase in the transaction price for the modified contract equally to the performance obligations for Product Y and Product Z. This is because the products have the same stand-alone selling prices and the variable consideration does not meet the criteria in [IFRS 15:85] that require allocation of the variable consideration to one but not both of the performance obligations. Consequently, the amount of the transaction price allocated to the performance obligations for Product Y and Product Z increases by CU10 to CU460 each.

On 31 March 20X1, Product Y is transferred to the customer and the entity recognises revenue of CU460. On 30 June 20X1, Product Z is transferred to the customer and the entity recognises revenue of CU460.

Example 10.4B

Modification resulting in a cumulative catch-up adjustment to revenue

[IFRS 15:IE37 - IE41, Example 8]

An entity, a construction company, enters into a contract to construct a commercial building for a customer on customer-owned land for promised consideration of CU1 million and a bonus of CU200,000 if the building is completed within 24 months. The entity accounts for the promised bundle of goods and services as a single performance obligation satisfied over time in accordance with [IFRS 15:35(b)] because the customer controls the building during construction. At the inception of the contract, the entity expects the following:

	CU
Transaction price	1,000,000
Expected costs	700,000
Expected profit (30%)	300,000

At contract inception, the entity excludes the CU200,000 bonus from the transaction price because it cannot conclude that it is highly probable that a significant reversal in the amount of cumulative revenue recognised will not occur. Completion of the building is highly susceptible to factors outside the entity's influence, including weather and regulatory approvals. In addition, the entity has limited experience with similar types of contracts.

The entity determines that the input measure, on the basis of costs incurred, provides an appropriate measure of progress towards complete satisfaction of the performance obligation. By the end of the first year, the entity has satisfied 60 per cent of its performance obligation on the basis of costs incurred to date (CU420,000) relative to total expected costs (CU700,000). The entity reassesses the variable consideration and concludes that the amount is still constrained in accordance with [IFRS 15:56 to 58]. Consequently, the cumulative revenue and costs recognised for the first year are as follows:

	CU
Revenue	600,000
Costs	420,000
Gross profit	180,000

In the first quarter of the second year, the parties to the contract agree to modify the contract by changing the floor plan of the building. As a result, the fixed consideration and expected costs increase by CU150,000 and CU120,000, respectively. Total potential consideration after the modification is CU1,350,000 (CU1,150,000 fixed consideration + CU200,000 completion bonus). In addition, the allowable time for achieving the CU200,000 bonus is extended by 6 months to 30 months from the original contract inception date. At the date of the modification, on the basis of its experience and the remaining work to be performed, which is primarily inside the building and not subject to weather conditions, the entity concludes that it is highly probable that including the bonus in the transaction price will not result in a significant reversal in the amount of cumulative revenue recognised in accordance with [IFRS 15:56] and includes the CU200,000 in the transaction price. In assessing the contract modification, the entity evaluates [IFRS 15:27(b)] and concludes (on the basis of the factors in [IFRS 15:29]) that the remaining goods and services to be provided using the modified contract are not distinct from the goods and services transferred on or before the date of contract modification; that is, the contract remains a single performance obligation.

Consequently, the entity accounts for the contract modification as if it were part of the original contract (in accordance with [IFRS 15:21(b)]). The entity updates its measure of progress and estimates that it has satisfied 51.2 per cent of its performance obligation (CU420,000 actual costs incurred ÷ CU820,000 total expected costs). The entity recognises additional revenue of CU91,200 [(51.2 per cent complete × CU1,350,000 modified transaction price) – CU600,000 revenue recognised to date] at the date of the modification as a cumulative catch-up adjustment.

10.5 Contract modification resulting in a reduction in scope of a contract

IFRS 15 provides specific guidance on how to account for a contract modification, defined as "a change in the scope or price (or both) of a contract that is approved by the parties to the contract".

Specifically, IFRS 15:20 sets out the requirements when there is an increase in the scope of a contract and a commensurate increase in the price (see **10.2**). All other contract modifications are accounted for in accordance with IFRS 15:21 (see **10.3**). Specifically:

- if the remaining goods or services (i.e. those not yet transferred at the date of the modification) are distinct from the goods or services transferred on or before the date of the contract modification, the contract modification is accounted for as if it were a termination of the existing contract and creation of a new contract; or

- if the remaining goods or services are not distinct from the goods or services transferred on or before the date of the contract modification, the contract modification is accounted for as if it were a part of the existing contract, and an adjustment (on a cumulative catch-up basis) is recognised to revenue.

Therefore, a contract modification resulting in a decrease in scope (i.e. the removal from the contract of promised goods or services) should be accounted for as either (1) termination of the existing contract and the creation of a new contract or (2) a cumulative catch-up adjustment to the existing contract, depending on whether the remaining goods or services in the contract are distinct from those transferred prior to the modification.

The modification cannot be accounted for as a separate contract as the criterion in IFRS 15:20(a) specifying an increase in scope of the contract is not met.

Examples 10.5A and **Examples 10.5B** illustrate the appropriate accounting for modifications resulting in a reduction in the scope of a contract.

Example 10.5A

Reduction in scope of a contract when remaining goods or services are distinct

Entity A enters into a contract with a customer to provide Product X and 12 months of services to be used in conjunction with Product X, in return for consideration of CU140; the services portion of the contract qualifies as a series in accordance with IFRS 15:22(b). Product X and the services are each determined to be distinct, with consideration of CU40 allocated to Product X (recognised on delivery of Product X) and CU100 allocated to the services portion of the contract (recognised over the 12-month service period).

Six months after the start of the contract (by which time, Entity A has recognised revenue of CU40 for delivery of Product X, revenue of CU50 for services provided to date and received payment from the customer of CU110), the customer decides to reduce the level of service required and Entity A agrees to a reduction in price in return for this such that the customer will pay only another CU10 in addition to the payments already made.

Given that the remaining six months of service are distinct from both the delivery of Product X and those services provided in the first six months of the contract, this decrease in scope (and price) should be accounted for as a termination of the existing contract and the creation of a new contract as required by IFRS 15:21(a), with revenue for the services still to be provided measured at

---

CU30 (CU50 remaining consideration under the existing contract that had not been recognised as revenue less the CU20 reduction in total consideration agreed as part of the contract modification).

Example 10.5B

Reduction in scope of a contract when remaining goods or services are not distinct

Entity A enters into a contract to produce a single large item of specialised machinery for a customer. Multiple components are used in the production of the specialised machinery, but they are significantly integrated such that Entity A is using the goods as inputs to produce the combined output of the specialised machinery. Four months into the contract term, the customer decides to source a component of the project from an alternative source and Entity A agrees to this contract modification which reduces the contract scope. Given that the remaining goods or services to be provided are not distinct from those already provided, this contract modification is accounted for as part of the existing contract, and a cumulative catch-up adjustment is recognised in revenue at the time the modification occurs as required by IFRS 15:21(b).

Example 10.4B illustrates the calculation of a cumulative catch-up adjustment under IFRS 15:21(b).

---

11 Licensing

11.1 Licensing – general

A licence establishes a customer's rights to the intellectual property of an entity. Licences of intellectual property may include:

[IFRS 15:B52]

- software and technology;
- motion pictures, music and other forms of media and entertainment;
- franchises; and
- patents, trademarks and copyrights.

In addition to a promise to grant a licence to a customer, an entity may also promise to transfer other goods or services to the customer. Such promises may be explicitly stated in the contract or implied by customary business practices, published policies or specific statements (see **6.2**). When a contract with a customer includes a promise to grant a licence in addition to other promised goods or services, an entity is required to identify each of the performance obligations in the contract (see **section 6**). [IFRS 15:B53]

If the promise to grant a licence is not distinct from other promised goods or services in the contract (see **section 6.3**), the promise to grant a licence and the other promised goods or services are accounted for together as a single performance obligation. Examples of licences that are not distinct from other goods or services include:

[IFRS 15:B54]

- a licence that forms a component of a tangible good and that is integral to the functionality of the good; and

- a licence that the customer can benefit from only in conjunction with a related service (such as an online service provided by the entity that enables, by granting a licence, the customer to access content).

When the licence is not distinct, an entity should determine whether the performance obligation (which includes the promised licence) is a performance obligation that is satisfied over time or at a point in time (see **section 9**). [IFRS 15:B55]

> IFRS 15:BC407 explains that "[t]he boards noted that in some cases the combined good or service transferred to the customer may have a licence as its primary or dominant component. When the output that is transferred is a licence or when the licence is distinct, the entity would apply the criteria in [IFRS 15:B58 (see **11.2.2**)] to determine whether the promised licence provides the customer with access to the entity's intellectual property or a right to use the entity's intellectual property".

11.2   Determining the nature of the entity's promise to grant a licence

11.2.1   Requirement to determine the nature of the entity's promise to grant a licence

When an entity's promise to grant a licence is distinct from the other promised goods or services in the contract, and is therefore accounted for as a separate performance obligation, an entity is required to determine whether the licence transfers to a customer either at a point in time or over time. In order to assess the appropriate timing of revenue recognition in this case, an entity should consider whether the nature of the entity's promise in granting the licence to a customer is to provide the customer with:

[IFRS 15:B56]

- a right to access the entity's intellectual property as it exists throughout the licence period (see **11.2.2**); or

- a right to use the entity's intellectual property as it exists at the point in time at which the licence is granted (see **11.2.3**).

When determining whether the promise to grant a licence provides a customer with (1) a right to access an entity's intellectual property, or (2) a right to use an entity's intellectual property, the entity should consider whether the customer can direct the use of, and obtain substantially all of the remaining benefits from, the licence at the point in time at which it is granted. A customer cannot direct the use of, and obtain substantially all of the remaining benefits from, a licence at the point in time at which the licence is granted if the intellectual property to which the customer has rights changes throughout the licence period. The intellectual property will change (and, therefore, affect the entity's assessment of when the customer controls the licence) when the entity continues to be involved with its intellectual property and the entity undertakes activities that significantly affect the intellectual property to which the customer has rights. In such circumstances, the licence provides the customer with a right to access the entity's intellectual property. In contrast, if the intellectual property to which the customer has rights will not change after the point in time at which the licence is granted, any activities undertaken by the entity merely change its own asset (i.e. the underlying intellectual property), which may affect the entity's ability to provide future licences; however, those activities would not affect the determination of what the licence provides or what the customer controls. [IFRS 15:B57]

The following factors should be disregarded when determining whether a licence provides a right to access the entity's intellectual property or a right to use the entity's intellectual property:

[IFRS 15:B62]

- restrictions of time, geographical region or use – these restrictions define the attributes of the promised licence, rather than defining whether the entity satisfies its performance obligation at a point in time or over time; and

- guarantees provided by the entity that it has a valid patent to intellectual property and that it will defend that patent from unauthorised use – a promise to defend a patent right is not a performance obligation because the act of defending a patent protects the value of the entity's intellectual property assets and provides assurance to the customer that the licence transferred meets the specifications of the licence promised in the contract.

11.2.2 Entity grants the customer a right to access the entity's intellectual property

The nature of an entity's promise in granting a licence is a promise to provide a right to access the entity's intellectual property if all of the following criteria are met:

[IFRS 15:B58]

(a) the contract requires, or the customer reasonably expects, that the entity will undertake activities that significantly affect the intellectual property to which the customer has rights;

(b)   the rights granted by the licence directly expose the customer to any positive or negative effects of the entity's activities identified in IFRS 15:B58(a); and

(c)   those activities do not result in the transfer of a good or a service to the customer as those activities occur.

Customary business practices, published policies and specific statements are some of the factors that may indicate whether a customer could reasonably expect that an entity will undertake activities that significantly affect the intellectual property. The existence of a shared economic interest (e.g. a sales-based royalty) between the entity and the customer related to the intellectual property to which the customer has rights may also indicate that the customer could reasonably expect that the entity will undertake such activities. [IFRS 15:B59]

If the criteria in IFRS 15:B58 are met, the promise to grant a licence is accounted for as a performance obligation satisfied over time because the customer will simultaneously receive and consume the benefit from the entity's performance of providing access to its intellectual property as the performance occurs (see **section 9.2**). It will be necessary to select an appropriate method to measure its progress towards complete satisfaction of that performance obligation to provide access (see **section 9.3**). [IFRS 15:B60]

11.2.3   Entity grants the customer a right to use the entity's intellectual property

If the criteria in IFRS 15:B58 (see **11.2.2**) are not met, the entity has in effect provided a right to use the intellectual property as that intellectual property exists (in terms of form and functionality) at the point in time at which the licence is granted to the customer. This means that the customer can direct the use of, and obtain substantially all of the remaining benefits from, the licence at the point in time at which the licence transfers and the revenue is recognised at a point in time (see **section 9.4**). However, revenue cannot be recognised for a licence that provides a right to use the entity's intellectual property before the beginning of the period during which the customer is able to use and benefit from the licence. For example, if a software licence period begins before an entity provides (or otherwise makes available) a code to the customer that enables them to immediately use the software, revenue cannot be recognised until that code has been provided (or otherwise made available). [IFRS 15:B61]

Example 11.2.3A

Electronic delivery of software – assessing when control transfers to the customer when the licence requires an access code or product key

Entity A sells right-to-use software licences to customers that give customers access to the software via Entity A's web site. Customers need either an access

---

code to download the software or a product key to activate the software once downloaded. The software cannot be used on the customer's hardware without the access code or the product key.

IFRS 15:B61 states, in part, as follows.

> "An entity should apply [15:38] to determine the point in time at which the licence transfers to the customer. However, revenue cannot be recognised for a licence that provides a right to use the entity's intellectual property before the beginning of the period during which the customer is able to use and benefit from the licence. For example, if a software licence period begins before an entity provides (or *otherwise makes available*) to the customer a code that enables the customer to immediately use the software, the entity would not recognise revenue before that code has been provided (or *otherwise made available*)." (emphasis added)

Entity A should consider the guidance on control in paragraphs IFRS 15:31 to 34 and the indicators in IFRS 15:38 related to determining when a customer obtains control of the software licence.

In some circumstances, control of the software licence may be transferred to the customer before the access code or product key is delivered. In particular, there may be situations in which the access code or product key has not been delivered but is nonetheless made available to the customer at any time on demand. In such circumstances, it will be necessary to consider whether control has passed to the customer by focusing on the indicators in IFRS 15:38. For example, if the customer has accepted the software, the entity is entitled to a non-refundable payment and the licence term has begun, an entity may conclude that control of the software licence has been transferred even though the access code or product key has not been provided to the customer. These situations may be viewed as analogous to bill-and-hold arrangements as discussed at IFRS 15:B79 to B82 (see **9.4.5**).

If payment terms or acceptance depend on delivery of the software access code or product key, or if Entity A is not yet in a position to make the code or key available, it would be unlikely that the entity could conclude that control of a software licence has been transferred until the access code or product key has been provided to the customer.

Example 11.2.3B

Electronic delivery of software – assessing when control transfers to the customer in a hosting agreement

Entity Y enters into a licence and hosting software arrangement with Customer X that allows Customer X to access via the internet and use software that Entity Y physically hosts on its servers. Customer X is required to pay a non-refundable licence fee of CU1,000 at the inception of the arrangement. Customer X accepts the software, and the licence term begins once the hosting service commences. As part of the arrangement, Customer X has the right to take possession of the software at any time during the contract period without incurring additional costs or diminution of the software's utility or value (i.e. there are no contractual or practical barriers to Customer X exercising its right to take possession of the software and Customer X is able to benefit from the software on its own or with readily available resources).

Entity Y concludes that the software licence and hosting service are each distinct and that the software licence gives Customer X a right to use Entity Y's intellectual property. If Customer X exercises its right to take possession of the software, Entity Y will immediately provide an access code that will enable Customer X to download the software.

When is control of the software licence transferred to Customer X?

In this scenario, Customer X is required to pay the non-refundable licence fee at the inception of the arrangement; Customer X has accepted the software and the licence term begins once the hosting service commences; and Entity Y has made the access code available to Customer X at any time on demand. Therefore, it seems reasonable for Entity Y to conclude that control of the software licence is transferred to Customer X when the licence term and hosting service begin.

Example 11.2.3C

Electronic delivery of software – assessing when control transfers to the customer for suite of software licences

Entity A enters into a five-year licence agreement with Customer B under which Customer B purchases licences to a suite of software products consisting of five modules. At the inception of the arrangement, Customer B is required to make a non-refundable payment of CU5 million to Entity A for the licences to all five modules, and the licence term for the suite of licences begins on 1 January 20X5. Customer B has previewed all five modules and accepted the software as of 1 January 20X5, but has only obtained the access codes for, and downloaded, four of the five modules. Customer B installs the modules itself and expects that it will take three months to install the four modules. Customer B does not download the fifth module immediately because of system limitations but plans to obtain the access code and install the fifth module once installation of the first four modules is complete. The access code for the fifth module is available to Customer B on demand.

In this scenario, Customer B is required to pay the non-refundable licence fee at the inception of the arrangement; Customer B has accepted the software; the licence terms have begun; and the access code for the fifth module is available to Customer B at any time on demand. Therefore, it seems reasonable for Entity A to conclude that control of the licences for all five modules is transferred to Customer B on 1 January 20X5.

11.2.4 Determining the nature of the entity's promise to grant a licence – examples

---

Example 11.2.4A

Right to use intellectual property

[IFRS 15:IE276 & IE277, Example 54]

Using the same facts as in Case A in Example 11 (see [**example 6.3.1**]), the entity identifies four performance obligations in a contract:

(a)   the software licence;

(b)   installation services;

(c)   software updates; and

(d)   technical support.

The entity assesses the nature of its promise to transfer the software licence in accordance with [IFRS 15:B58]. The entity observes that the software is functional at the time that the licence transfers to the customer, and the customer can direct the use of, and obtain substantially all of the remaining benefits from, the software when the licence transfers to the customer. Furthermore, the entity concludes that because the software is functional when it transfers to the customer, the customer does not reasonably expect the entity to undertake activities that significantly affect the intellectual property to which the licence relates. This is because at the point in time that the licence is transferred to the customer, the intellectual property will not change throughout the licence period. The entity does not consider in its assessment of the criteria in [IFRS 15:B58 (see **11.2.2**)] the promise to provide software updates, because they represent a separate performance obligation. Therefore, the entity concludes that none of the criteria in [IFRS 15:B58] are met and that the nature of the entity's promise in transferring the licence is to provide a right to use the entity's intellectual property as it exists at a point in time – ie the intellectual property to which the customer has rights is static. Consequently, the entity accounts for the licence as a performance obligation satisfied at a point in time.

Example 11.2.4B

Licence of intellectual property

[IFRS 15:IE278 - IE280, Example 55]

An entity enters into a contract with a customer to licence (for a period of three years) intellectual property related to the design and production processes for a good. The contract also specifies that the customer will obtain any updates to that intellectual property for new designs or production processes that may be developed by the entity. The updates are essential to the customer's ability to use the licence, because the customer operates in an industry in which technologies change rapidly. The entity does not sell the updates separately and the customer does not have the option to purchase the licence without the updates.

The entity assesses the goods and services promised to the customer to determine which goods and services are distinct in accordance with [IFRS 15:27 (see **6.3.1**)]. The entity determines that although the entity can conclude that the customer can obtain benefit from the licence on its own without the updates (see [IFRS 15:27(a)]), that benefit would be limited because the updates are critical to the customer's ability to continue to make use of the licence in the rapidly changing technological environment in which the customer operates.

In assessing whether the criterion in [IFRS 15:27(b)] is met, the entity observes that the customer does not have the option to purchase the licence without the updates and the customer obtains limited benefit from the licence without the updates. Therefore, the entity concludes that the licence and the updates are highly interrelated and the promise to grant the licence is not distinct within the context of the contract, because the licence is not separately identifiable from the promise to provide the updates (in accordance with the criterion in [IFRS 15:27(b)] and the factors in [IFRS 15:29 (see **6.2**)]).

The entity applies [IFRS 15:31 to 38 (see **section 9**)] to determine whether the performance obligation (which includes the licence and the updates) is satisfied at a point in time or over time. The entity concludes that because the customer simultaneously receives and consumes the benefits of the entity's performance as it occurs, the performance obligation is satisfied over time in accordance with [IFRS 15:35(a)].

Example 11.2.4C

Identifying a distinct licence

[IFRS 15:IE281 - IE288, Example 56]

An entity, a pharmaceutical company, licenses to a customer its patent rights to an approved drug compound for 10 years and also promises to manufacture the drug for the customer. The drug is a mature product; therefore the entity will not undertake any activities to support the drug, which is consistent with its customary business practices.

Case A – Licence is not distinct

In this case, no other entity can manufacture this drug because of the highly specialised nature of the manufacturing process. As a result, the licence cannot be purchased separately from the manufacturing services.

The entity assesses the goods and services promised to the customer to determine which goods and services are distinct in accordance with [IFRS 15:27 (see **6.3.1**)]. The entity determines that the customer cannot benefit from the licence without the manufacturing service; therefore, the criterion in [IFRS 15:27(a)] is not met. Consequently, the licence and the manufacturing service are not distinct and the entity accounts for the licence and the manufacturing service as a single performance obligation.

The entity applies [IFRS 15:31 to 38 (see **section 9**)] to determine whether the performance obligation (ie the bundle of the licence and the manufacturing services) is a performance obligation satisfied at a point in time or over time.

Case B – Licence is distinct

In this case, the manufacturing process used to produce the drug is not unique or specialised and several other entities can also manufacture the drug for the customer.

The entity assesses the goods and services promised to the customer to determine which goods and services are distinct in accordance with [IFRS 15:27 (see **section 6.3**)]. Because the manufacturing process can be provided by other entities, the entity concludes that the customer can benefit from the licence on its own (ie without the manufacturing service) and that the licence is separately identifiable from the manufacturing process (ie the criteria in [IFRS 15:27] are met). Consequently, the entity concludes that the licence and the manufacturing service are distinct and the entity has two performance obligations:

(a) licence of patent rights; and

(b) manufacturing service.

The entity assesses, in accordance with [IFRS 15:B58], the nature of the entity's promise to grant the licence. The drug is a mature product (ie it has been approved, is currently being manufactured and has been sold commercially for the last several years). For these types of mature products, the entity's customary business practices are not to undertake any activities to support the drug. Consequently, the entity concludes that the criteria in [IFRS 15:B58] are not met because the contract does not require, and the customer does not reasonably expect, the entity to undertake activities that significantly affect the intellectual property to which the customer has rights. In its assessment of the criteria in [IFRS 15:B58], the entity does not take into consideration the separate performance obligation of promising to provide a manufacturing service. Consequently, the nature of the entity's promise in transferring the licence is to provide a right to use the entity's intellectual property in the form and the functionality with which it exists at the point in time that it is granted to the customer. Consequently, the entity accounts for the licence as a performance obligation satisfied at a point in time.

The entity applies [IFRS 15:31 to 38 (see **section 9**)] to determine whether the manufacturing service is a performance obligation satisfied at a point in time or over time.

11.3 Sales-based or usage-based royalties

11.3.1 Sales-based or usage-based royalties – general

Although IFRS 15 includes general guidance on constraining estimates of variable consideration (see **7.3**), that guidance does not apply to a sales-based or usage-based royalty promised in exchange for a licence of intellectual property.

Instead, revenue for a sales-based or usage-based royalty promised in exchange for a licence of intellectual property is recognised only when (or as) the later of the following events occurs:

[IFRS 15:B63]

- the subsequent sale or usage occurs; and
- the performance obligation to which some or all of the sales-based or usage-based royalty has been allocated has been satisfied (or partially satisfied).

11.3.2   Scope of sales-based or usage-based royalties exception

The sales-based or usage-based royalty exception in IFRS 15:B63 should be applied by the licensor when accounting for the transfer of a licence of intellectual property promised in exchange for a sales-based or usage-based royalty; a sale of intellectual property does not qualify for the exception and should be accounted for under the general revenue measurement and recognition guidance in IFRS 15.

The IASB decided against applying the exception for sales-based or usage-based royalties to intellectual property more broadly. Although this exception might not be consistent with the principle of recognising some or all of the estimate of variable consideration, the IASB has specified that, in these limited circumstances, this disadvantage was outweighed by the simplicity of these requirements, as well as by the relevance of the resulting information for this type of transaction. This exception should not be applied by analogy to other types of promised goods or services or other types of variable consideration. The board's full rationale for this decision is set out in paragraphs BC415 to BC421 of IFRS 15.

Example 11.3.2A

Licence of intellectual property

Entity A provides its customer with a licence to broadcast one of Entity A's movies on the customer's networks in exchange for a royalty of CU10,000, payable each time the movie is broadcast over the five-year licence period. Entity A considers the guidance in IFRS 15:B57 to B62 and concludes that Entity A has promised to its customer a right to use Entity A's intellectual property (i.e. Entity A has satisfied its performance obligation at the point in time that the customer is able to use and benefit from the licence). Entity A applies the requirements of IFRS 15:B63 and does not recognise any revenue when the licence is transferred to the customer. Instead, Entity A recognises revenue of CU10,000 each time the customer uses the licensed intellectual property and broadcasts Entity A's movie.

Example 11.3.2B

Sale of intellectual property

Entity B sells the copyright to one of its music albums (i.e. all rights related to the intellectual property) to a customer in exchange for a promise of future payments equal to CU1 for each album sold by the customer in the future and CU0.01 for each time a song on the album is played on the radio. Entity B considers the guidance in IFRS 15:31 to 38 and determines that its performance obligation is satisfied at the point in time that it transfers the copyright to the customer.

In accordance with IFRS 15:47 to 48, upon transferring control of the intellectual property to the customer, Entity B recognises revenue equal to its estimate of the amount to which it will be entitled, subject to the constraint on variable consideration specified by IFRS 15:56 to 57. Entity B then updates its estimate and records a cumulative catch-up adjustment at each subsequent reporting period as required by IFRS 15:59.

11.3.3 Examples of sales-based or usage-based royalties

Example 11.3.3A

Franchise rights

[IFRS 15:IE289 - IE296, Example 57]

An entity enters into a contract with a customer and promises to grant a franchise licence that provides the customer with the right to use the entity's trade name and sell the entity's products for 10 years. In addition to the licence, the entity also promises to provide the equipment necessary to operate a franchise store. In exchange for granting the licence, the entity receives a sales-based royalty of five per cent of the customer's monthly sales. The fixed consideration for the equipment is CU150,000 payable when the equipment is delivered.

Identifying performance obligations

The entity assesses the goods and services promised to the customer to determine which goods and services are distinct in accordance with [IFRS 15:27 (see **6.3.1**)]. The entity observes that the entity, as a franchisor, has developed a customary business practice to undertake activities such as analysing the customer's changing preferences and implementing product improvements, pricing strategies, marketing campaigns and operational efficiencies to support the franchise name. However, the entity concludes that these activities do not directly transfer goods or services to the customer because they are part of the entity's promise to grant a licence and, in effect, change the intellectual property to which the customer has rights.

The entity determines that it has two promises to transfer goods or services: a promise to grant a licence and a promise to transfer equipment. In addition, the entity concludes that the promise to grant the licence and the promise to transfer the equipment are distinct. This is because the customer can

---

benefit from each promise (ie the promise of the licence and the promise of the equipment) on their own or together with other resources that are readily available (see [IFRS 15:27(a)]). (That is, the customer can benefit from the licence together with the equipment that is delivered before the opening of the franchise and the equipment can be used in the franchise or sold for an amount other than scrap value.) The entity also determines that the franchise licence and equipment are separately identifiable, in accordance with the criterion in [IFRS 15:27(b)], because none of the factors in [IFRS 15:29 (see **6.3.1**)] are present. Consequently, the entity has two performance obligations:

(a)   the franchise licence; and

(b)   the equipment.

Allocating the transaction price

The entity determines that the transaction price includes fixed consideration of CU150,000 and variable consideration (five per cent of customer sales).

The entity applies [IFRS 15:85 (see **8.5**)] to determine whether the variable consideration should be allocated entirely to the performance obligation to transfer the franchise licence. The entity concludes that the variable consideration (ie the sales-based royalty) should be allocated entirely to the franchise licence because the variable consideration relates entirely to the entity's promise to grant the franchise licence. In addition, the entity observes that allocating CU150,000 to the equipment and the sales-based royalty to the franchise licence would be consistent with an allocation based on the entity's relative stand-alone selling prices in similar contracts. That is, the stand-alone selling price of the equipment is CU150,000 and the entity regularly licences franchises in exchange for five per cent of customer sales. Consequently, the entity concludes that the variable consideration (ie the sales-based royalty) should be allocated entirely to the performance obligation to grant the franchise licence.

Application guidance: licensing

The entity assesses, in accordance with [IFRS 15:B58], the nature of the entity's promise to grant the franchise licence. The entity concludes that the criteria in [IFRS 15:B58 (see **11.2.2**)] are met and the nature of the entity's promise is to provide access to the entity's intellectual property in its current form throughout the licence period. This is because:

(a)   the entity concludes that the customer would reasonably expect that the entity will undertake activities that will affect the intellectual property to which the customer has rights. This is on the basis of the entity's customary business practice to undertake activities such as analysing the customer's changing preferences and implementing product improvements, pricing strategies, marketing campaigns and operational efficiencies. In addition, the entity observes that because part of its compensation is dependent on the success of the franchisee (as evidenced through the sales-based royalty), the entity has a shared economic interest with the customer that indicates that the customer will expect the entity to undertake those activities to maximise earnings.

(b) the entity also observes that the franchise licence requires the customer to implement any changes that result from those activities and thus exposes the customer to any positive or negative effects of those activities.

(c) the entity also observes that even though the customer may benefit from the activities through the rights granted by the licence, they do not transfer a good or service to the customer as those activities occur.

Because the criteria in [IFRS 15:B58] are met, the entity concludes that the promise to transfer the licence is a performance obligation satisfied over time in accordance with [IFRS 15:35(a) (see **9.2.1**)].

The entity also concludes that because the consideration is in the form of a sales-based royalty, the entity applies [IFRS 15:B63] and, after the transfer of the franchise licence, the entity recognises revenue as and when those sales occur.

Example 11.3.3B

Access to intellectual property (comic strips)

[IFRS 15:IE297 - IE302, Example 58]

An entity, a creator of comic strips, licenses the use of the images and names of its comic strip characters in three of its comic strips to a customer for a four-year term. There are main characters involved in each of the comic strips. However, newly created characters appear regularly and the images of the characters evolve over time. The customer, an operator of cruise ships, can use the entity's characters in various ways, such as in shows or parades, within reasonable guidelines. The contract requires the customer to use the latest images of the characters.

In exchange for granting the licence, the entity receives a fixed payment of CU1 million in each year of the four-year term.

In accordance with [IFRS 15:27 (see **6.3.1**)], the entity assesses the goods and services promised to the customer to determine which goods and services are distinct. The entity concludes that it has no other performance obligations other than the promise to grant a licence. That is, the additional activities associated with the licence do not directly transfer a good or service to the customer because they are part of the entity's promise to grant a licence and, in effect, change the intellectual property to which the customer has rights.

The entity assesses the nature of the entity's promise to transfer the licence in accordance with [IFRS 15:B58 (see **11.2.2**)]. In assessing the criteria the entity considers the following:

(a) the customer reasonably expects (arising from the entity's customary business practices) that the entity will undertake activities that will affect the intellectual property to which the customer has rights (ie the characters). Those activities include development of the characters and the publishing of a weekly comic strip that includes the characters.

(b) the rights granted by the licence directly expose the customer to any positive or negative effects of the entity's activities because the contract requires the customer to use the latest characters.

(c) even though the customer may benefit from those activities through the rights granted by the licence, they do not transfer a good or service to the customer as those activities occur.

Consequently, the entity concludes that the criteria in [IFRS 15:B58] are met and that the nature of the entity's promise to transfer the licence is to provide the customer with access to the entity's intellectual property as it exists throughout the licence period. Consequently, the entity accounts for the promised licence as a performance obligation satisfied over time (ie the criterion in [IFRS 15:35(a) (see **9.2.1**)] is met).

The entity applies [IFRS 15:39 to 45 (see **9.3.1**)] to identify the method that best depicts its performance in the licence. Because the contract provides the customer with unlimited use of the licensed characters for a fixed term, the entity determines that a time-based method would be the most appropriate measure of progress towards complete satisfaction of the performance obligation.

Example 11.3.3C

Right to use intellectual property

[IFRS 15:IE303 - IE306, Example 59]

An entity, a music record label, licenses to a customer a 1975 recording of a classical symphony by a noted orchestra. The customer, a consumer products company, has the right to use the recorded symphony in all commercials, including television, radio and online advertisements for two years in Country A. In exchange for providing the licence, the entity receives fixed consideration of CU10,000 per month. The contract does not include any other goods or services to be provided by the entity. The contract is non-cancellable.

The entity assesses the goods and services promised to the customer to determine which goods and services are distinct in accordance with [IFRS 15:27 (see **6.2.1**)]. The entity concludes that its only performance obligation is to grant the licence.

In accordance with [IFRS 15:B58 (see **11.2.2**)], the entity assesses the nature of the entity's promise to grant the licence. The entity does not have any contractual or implied obligations to change the licensed recording. Thus, the intellectual property to which the customer has rights is static. Consequently, the entity concludes that the nature of its promise in transferring the licence is to provide the customer with a right to use the entity's intellectual property as it exists at the point in time that it is granted. Therefore, the promise to grant the licence is a performance obligation satisfied at a point in time. The entity recognises all of the revenue at the point in time when the customer can direct the use of, and obtain substantially all of the remaining benefits from, the licensed intellectual property.

Because of the length of time between the entity's performance (at the beginning of the period) and the customer's monthly payments over two years (which are non-cancellable), the entity considers the requirements in [IFRS 15:60 to 65 (see **section 7.4**)] to determine whether a significant financing component exists.

Example 11.3.3D

Sales-based royalty for a licence of intellectual property (movie distribution company)

[IFRS 15:IE307 & IE308, Example 60]

An entity, a movie distribution company, licenses Movie XYZ to a customer. The customer, an operator of cinemas, has the right to show the movie in its cinemas for six weeks. In exchange for providing the licence, the entity will receive a portion of the operator's ticket sales for Movie XYZ (ie variable consideration in the form of a sales-based royalty). The entity concludes that its only performance obligation is the promise to grant the licence.

The entity observes that regardless of whether the promise to grant the licence represents a right to access the entity's intellectual property, or a right to use the entity's intellectual property, the entity applies [IFRS 15:B63] and recognises revenue as and when the ticket sales occur. This is because the consideration for its licence of intellectual property is a sales-based royalty and the entity has already transferred the licence to the movie to which the sales-based royalty relates.

Example 11.3.3E

Access to intellectual property (sports team logo)

[IFRS 15:IE309 - IE313, Example 61]

An entity, a well-known sports team, licenses the use of its name and logo to a customer. The customer, an apparel designer, has the right to use the sports team's name and logo on items including t-shirts, caps, mugs and towels for one year. In exchange for providing the licence, the entity will receive fixed consideration of CU2 million and a royalty of five per cent of the sales price of any items using the team name or logo. The customer expects that the entity will continue to play games and provide a competitive team.

The entity assesses the goods and services promised to the customer to determine which goods and services are distinct in accordance with [IFRS 15:27 (see **6.2.1**)]. The entity concludes that its only performance obligation is to transfer the licence. That is, the additional activities associated with the licence do not directly transfer a good or service to the customer because they are part of the entity's promise to grant the licence and, in effect, change the intellectual property to which the customer has rights.

The entity assesses the nature of the entity's promise to transfer the licence in accordance with [IFRS 15:B58 (see **11.2.2**)]. In assessing the criteria the entity considers the following:

(a)   the entity concludes that the customer would reasonably expect that the entity will undertake activities that will affect the intellectual property (ie the team name and logo) to which the customer has rights. This is on the basis of the entity's customary business practice to undertake activities such as continuing to play and providing a competitive team. In addition, the entity observes that because some of its consideration is dependent on the success of the customer (through the sales-based royalty), the entity has a shared economic interest with the customer, which indicates that the customer will expect the entity to undertake those activities to maximise earnings.

(b)   the entity observes that the rights granted by the licence (ie the use of the team's name and logo) directly expose the customer to any positive or negative effects of the entity's activities.

(c)   the entity also observes that even though the customer may benefit from the activities through the rights granted by the licence, they do not transfer a good or service to the customer as those activities occur.

The entity concludes that the criteria in [IFRS 15:B58] are met and the nature of the entity's promise to grant the licence is to provide the customer with access to the entity's intellectual property as it exists throughout the licence period. Consequently, the entity accounts for the promised licence as a performance obligation satisfied over time (ie the criterion in [IFRS 15:35(a) (see **9.2.1**)] is met).

The entity then applies [IFRS 15:39 to 45 (see **9.3.1**)] to determine a measure of progress that will depict the entity's performance for the fixed consideration. For the consideration that is in the form of a sales-based royalty, [IFRS 15:B63] applies; therefore, the entity recognises revenue as and when the sales of items using the team name or logo occur.

Example 11.3.3F

Recognition of sales-based royalties – information received from the licensee after the end of the reporting period

Entity A enters into a software licence with Entity B that allows inclusion of the software in computers sold by Entity B to third parties. Under the terms of the licence, Entity A receives royalties on the basis of the number of computers sold that include the licensed software.

Upon delivery of the software to Entity B, Entity A satisfied the performance obligation to which the sales-based royalty was allocated. Thereafter, Entity A receives quarterly sales data in arrears, which allows it to calculate the royalty payments due under the licence.

Should Entity A recognise revenue (royalty payments) for computer sales made by Entity B up to the end of its reporting period even though sales data had not been received at the end of that reporting period?

Yes. Provided that the related performance obligation has been satisfied (as is the case in the circumstances under consideration), IFRS 15:B63 requires that sales-based royalties received for a licence of intellectual property be recognised when the subsequent sale by the licensee occurs, not when information on that sale is received.

In this scenario, royalties should be recognised for sales made by Entity B up to the end of Entity A's reporting period on the basis of sales data received before Entity A's financial statements are authorised for issue (the receipt of such data constitutes an adjusting event in accordance with IAS 10 *Events After the Reporting Period*) and, if necessary, an estimate of sales made in any period not covered by such data. It would not be appropriate for entities to omit sales-based royalties from financial statements merely because the associated sales data were received after the end of the reporting period.

11.3.4 Fixed royalty payments for a licence of intellectual property receivable on reaching sales-based or usage-based milestones

In many industries it is common for contracts relating to a licence of intellectual property to include payment terms that are tied to milestones. These milestone payments are frequently structured such that entitlement to or payment of an amount specified in the contract is triggered once a sales target (i.e. specified level of sales) has been reached (e.g. a CU10 million milestone payment is triggered once cumulative sales by the licensee exceed CU100 million).

Revenue in respect of such milestone payments should be recognised when the sales-based or usage-based milestone is reached (or later if the related performance obligation has not been satisfied), as required by the exception for sales-based or usage-based royalties set out in IFRS 15:B63 (see **11.3.1**). This requirement applies to milestone payments that are triggered by reference to sales- or usage-based thresholds even when the milestone amount to be paid is fixed.

However, this exception should not be applied to milestone payments that relate to the occurrence of any other event or indicator (e.g. regulatory approval or proceeding into a beta phase of testing).

IFRS 15:BC415 states that "[t]he boards decided that for a licence of intellectual property for which the consideration is based on the customer's subsequent sales or usage, an entity should not recognise any revenue for the variable amounts until the uncertainty is resolved (ie when a customer's subsequent sales or usage occurs)". This paragraph illustrates the boards' intent that the exception should apply to consideration only when it is (1) related to licences of intellectual property, and (2) based on the customer's subsequent sales or usage.

12 Contract costs

12.1 Contract costs – general

IFRS 15 introduces guidance on how to account for costs associated with a contract with a customer when they do not fall within the scope of another Standard. It distinguishes between:

- costs of obtaining a contract (see **12.2**); and
- costs of fulfilling a contract (see **12.3**).

When considering how to account for costs that are incurred before a contract exists (i.e. pre-contract costs), it is important to keep in mind that they may include both costs of obtaining a contract and costs of fulfilling a contract, and that the requirements in respect of each are different. In particular, IFRS 15:95 (see **12.3**) makes clear that, in some circumstances, it may be appropriate to recognise an asset for costs incurred to fulfil a contract that does not yet exist (i.e. a specific anticipated contract).

12.2 Costs of obtaining a contract

Costs to obtain a contract that would have been incurred irrespective of whether the contract was obtained are recognised as an expense when incurred, unless those costs are explicitly chargeable to the customer irrespective of whether the contract is obtained. [IFRS 15:93]

The incremental costs of obtaining a contract with a customer are recognised as an asset if the entity expects to recover those costs. [IFRS 15:91] Those incremental costs are costs incurred to obtain a contract with a customer that would not have been incurred if the contract had not been obtained. [IFRS 15:92]

Therefore, costs incurred in the effort to obtain a contract (e.g. the costs of preparing a proposal) that are payable irrespective of whether the effort is successful cannot be capitalised – they do not qualify as 'incremental costs' for the purposes of IFRS 15. Only costs that would not have been incurred if the effort was not successful (e.g. a sales commission) can be recognised as an asset.

If the amortisation period (see **12.4.1**) of the asset resulting from the incremental costs would be one year or less, IFRS 15 provides a practical expedient whereby those costs can be expensed when incurred. [IFRS 15:94]

Example 12.2

Incremental costs of obtaining a contract

[IFRS 15:IE189 - IE191, Example 36]

An entity, a provider of consulting services, wins a competitive bid to provide consulting services to a new customer. The entity incurred the following costs to obtain the contract:

	CU
External legal fees for due diligence	15,000
Travel costs to deliver proposal	25,000
Commissions to sales employees	10,000
Total costs incurred	50,000

In accordance with [IFRS 15:91], the entity recognises an asset for the CU10,000 incremental costs of obtaining the contract arising from the commissions to sales employees because the entity expects to recover those costs through future fees for the consulting services. The entity also pays discretionary annual bonuses to sales supervisors based on annual sales targets, overall profitability of the entity and individual performance evaluations. In accordance with [IFRS 15:91], the entity does not recognise an asset for the bonuses paid to sales supervisors because the bonuses are not incremental to obtaining a contract. The amounts are discretionary and are based on other factors, including the profitability of the entity and the individuals' performance. The bonuses are not directly attributable to identifiable contracts.

The entity observes that the external legal fees and travel costs would have been incurred regardless of whether the contract was obtained. Therefore, in accordance with [IFRS 15:93], those costs are recognised as expenses when incurred, unless they are within the scope of another Standard, in which case, the relevant provisions of that Standard apply.

12.3 Costs of fulfilling a contract

If the costs incurred in fulfilling a contract with a customer are not within the scope of another Standard (e.g. IAS 2 *Inventories*, IAS 16 *Property, Plant and Equipment* or IAS 38 *Intangible Assets*), an asset is recognised for the costs incurred to fulfil a contract only if those costs meet all of the following criteria:

[IFRS 15:95]

(a) the costs relate directly to a contract or to an anticipated contract that the entity can specifically identify (e.g. costs relating to services to be provided under renewal of an existing contract or costs of designing an asset to be transferred under a specific contract that has not yet been approved);

(b) the costs generate or enhance resources of the entity that will be used in satisfying (or in continuing to satisfy) performance obligations in the future; and

(c) the costs are expected to be recovered.

When costs incurred in fulfilling a contract with a customer are within the scope of other Standards, they are accounted for in accordance with those other Standards. [IFRS 15:96]

> Accordingly, if costs are within the scope of another Standard, and that Standard requires them to be expensed, it is not appropriate to argue that they should be capitalised in accordance with IFRS 15.

Costs that relate directly to a contract (or a specific anticipated contract) include any of the following:

[IFRS 15:97]

(a) direct labour (e.g. salaries and wages of employees who provide the promised services directly to the customer);

(b) direct materials (e.g. supplies used in providing the promised services to a customer);

(c) allocations of costs that relate directly to the contract or to contract activities (e.g. costs of contract management and supervision, insurance and depreciation of tools and equipment used in fulfilling the contract);

(d) costs that are explicitly chargeable to the customer under the contract; and

(e) other costs that are incurred only because an entity entered into the contract (e.g. payments to subcontractors).

An entity recognises the following costs as expenses when incurred:

[IFRS 15:98]

(a) general and administrative costs (unless those costs are explicitly chargeable to the customer under the contract, as per IFRS 15:97(d));

(b) costs of wasted materials, labour or other resources to fulfil the contract that were not reflected in the price of the contract;

(c) costs that relate to satisfied performance obligations (or partially satisfied performance obligations) in the contract (i.e. costs that relate to past performance); and

(d) costs for which an entity cannot distinguish whether the costs relate to unsatisfied performance obligations or to satisfied performance obligations (or partially satisfied performance obligations).

Example 12.3

Costs that give rise to an asset

[IFRS 15:IE192 - IE196, Example 37]

An entity enters into a service contract to manage a customer's information technology data centre for five years. The contract is renewable for subsequent one-year periods. The average customer term is seven years. The entity pays an employee a CU10,000 sales commission upon the customer signing the contract. Before providing the services, the entity designs and builds a technology platform for the entity's internal use that interfaces with the customer's systems. That platform is not transferred to the customer, but will be used to deliver services to the customer.

Incremental costs of obtaining a contract

In accordance with [IFRS 15:91], the entity recognises an asset for the CU10,000 incremental costs of obtaining the contract for the sales commission because the entity expects to recover those costs through future fees for the services to be provided. The entity amortises the asset over seven years in accordance with [IFRS 15:99], because the asset relates to the services transferred to the customer during the contract term of five years and the entity anticipates that the contract will be renewed for two subsequent one-year periods.

Costs to fulfil a contract

The initial costs incurred to set up the technology platform are as follows:

	CU
Design services	40,000
Hardware	120,000
Software	90,000
Migration and testing of data centre	100,000
Total costs	350,000

The initial setup costs relate primarily to activities to fulfil the contract but do not transfer goods or services to the customer. The entity accounts for the initial setup costs as follows:

(a) hardware costs – accounted for in accordance with IAS 16 *Property, Plant and Equipment*.

(b) software costs – accounted for in accordance with IAS 38 *Intangible Assets*.

(c) costs of the design, migration and testing of the data centre – assessed in accordance with [IFRS 15:95] to determine whether an asset can be recognised for the costs to fulfil the contract. Any resulting asset would be amortised on a systematic basis over the seven-year period (ie the five-year contract term and two anticipated one-year renewal periods) that the entity expects to provide services related to the data centre.

> In addition to the initial costs to set up the technology platform, the entity also assigns two employees who are primarily responsible for providing the service to the customer. Although the costs for these two employees are incurred as part of providing the service to the customer, the entity concludes that the costs do not generate or enhance resources of the entity (see [IFRS 15:95(b)]). Therefore, the costs do not meet the criteria in [IFRS 15:95] and cannot be recognised as an asset using IFRS 15. In accordance with [IFRS 15:98], the entity recognises the payroll expense for these two employees when incurred.

12.4 Amortisation and impairment of contract costs

12.4.1 Amortisation of capitalised contract costs

An asset recognised in respect of a cost of obtaining or fulfilling a contract should be amortised on a systematic basis that is consistent with the transfer to the customer of the goods or services to which the asset relates. The asset may relate to goods or services to be transferred under a specific anticipated contract (as described in IFRS 15:95(a) – see **12.3**). [IFRS 15:99]

IFRS 15 does not provide specific guidance on the method an entity should use to amortise these assets. Amortisation of capitalised costs on a 'systematic basis' should take into account the expected timing of transfer of the goods and services related to the asset (which typically corresponds to the period and pattern in which revenue will be recognised in the financial statements). The pattern in which the related revenue is recognised could be significantly front-loaded, back-loaded or seasonal, and costs should be amortised accordingly.

To determine the pattern of transfer, entities may need to analyse the specific terms of each arrangement. In determining the appropriate amortisation method, they should consider all relevant factors including:

- experience with, and ability to reasonably estimate, the pattern of transfer; and

- the timing of the transfer of control of the goods or services to the customer.

In some situations, more than one amortisation method may be acceptable if this reasonably approximates the expected period and pattern of transfer of goods and services. However, an amortisation method is unacceptable if it is not expected to reflect the period and pattern of such transfer. When entities select a method, they should apply it consistently to similar contracts. If there is no evidence to suggest that a specific pattern of transfer can be expected, a straight-line amortisation method may be appropriate.

If the pattern in which contractual goods or services are transferred over the contract term varies significantly each period, it may be appropriate to use an amortisation model that more closely aligns with the variations in the transfer pattern. For example, amortisation could be allocated to the periods on the basis of the proportion of the total goods or services transferred each period. If the cost is related to goods or services transferred at a point in time, it follows that the amortised cost should be recognised at the same point in time.

When the contractual goods or services are transferred over an uncertain duration, entities should consider whether the relationship with the customer is expected to extend beyond the initial term of "a specific anticipated contract" (as referred to in IFRS 15:99 and described in IFRS 15:95(a)). For example, if an entity enters into a four-year contract with a customer but the customer relationship is expected to continue for six years, the appropriate amortisation period may be six years (i.e. the expected duration of the relationship).

When an entity's customer has been granted a material right to acquire future goods or services, and revenue related to the material right is being deferred, an entity should consider whether it would be appropriate to allocate to that right a portion of the costs that are capitalised in accordance with IFRS 15:91 or IFRS 15:95.

In situations in which the customer has been granted a material right to acquire future goods or services, and some revenue is being deferred in respect of that right, it would typically be reasonable also to regard a proportion of the costs capitalised in accordance with IFRS 15:91 or 95 as relating to that right. The amortisation is updated to reflect a significant change in the entity's expected timing of transfer to the customer of the goods or services to which the asset relates. Any change is accounted for as a change in accounting estimate in accordance with IAS 8 (see **chapter A5**). [IFRS 15:100]

12.4.2 *Impairment of contract costs*

An impairment loss is recognised in profit or loss to the extent that the carrying amount of an asset recognised in respect of a cost of obtaining or fulfilling a contract exceeds:

[IFRS 15:101]

(a)   the remaining amount of consideration that the entity expects to receive in exchange for the goods or services to which the asset relates; less

(b)   the costs that relate directly to providing those goods or services (see **12.3**) and that have not been recognised as expenses.

When applying IFRS 15:101 to determine the amount of consideration that an entity expects to receive, the principles for determining the transaction price (except for the requirements for constraining estimates of variable consideration – see **7.3**) should be considered and adjusted to reflect the effects of the customer's credit risk. [IFRS 15:102]

Any impairment losses for assets related to the contract recognised in accordance with another Standard (e.g. IAS 2, IAS 16 and IAS 38) should be recognised before an entity recognises an impairment loss for an asset recognised in respect of a cost of obtaining or fulfilling a contract. After applying the impairment test in IFRS 15:101, an entity should include the resulting carrying amount of the asset recognised in respect of a cost of obtaining or fulfilling a contract in the carrying amount of the cash-generating unit to which the asset belongs for the purpose of applying IAS 36 *Impairment of Assets* to that cash-generating unit. [IFRS 15:103]

A reversal of some or all of an impairment loss previously recognised in accordance with IFRS 15:101 is recognised in profit or loss when the impairment conditions no longer exist or have improved. The increased carrying amount of the asset cannot exceed the amount that would have been determined (net of amortisation) if no impairment loss had been recognised previously. [IFRS 15:104]

13   Presentation of contract assets and contract liabilities

When either party to a contract has performed, an entity is required to present the contract in the statement of financial position as a contract asset or a contract liability, depending on the relationship between the entity's performance and the customer's payment. Any unconditional rights to consideration are presented separately as a receivable. [IFRS 15:105]

A contract liability arises if a customer pays consideration, or if the entity has a right to consideration that is unconditional (i.e. a receivable), before the good or service is transferred to the customer. The liability should be recognised either when the payment is made or when the payment is due (whichever is earlier). The contract liability represents the obligation to transfer goods or services to a customer for which consideration has been received (or an amount of consideration is due) from the customer. [IFRS 15:106]

A contract asset arises if an entity performs by transferring goods or services to a customer before the consideration is paid or before payment is due. The balance excludes any amounts presented as a receivable. The contract asset represents the right to consideration in exchange for goods or services that have been transferred to a customer. The asset should be assessed for impairment in accordance with IFRS 9 *Financial Instruments* (or, for entities that have not yet adopted IFRS 9, IAS 39

Financial Instruments: Recognition and Measurement) and, when relevant, the impairment is measured, presented and disclosed on the same basis as a financial asset that is within the scope of IFRS 9 (or IAS 39) (see also **14.2**). [IFRS 15:107]

A receivable is a right to consideration that is unconditional, i.e. only the passage of time is required before payment of that consideration is due. For example, a receivable will be recognised if the entity has a present right to payment even though that amount may be subject to refund in the future. The receivable should be accounted for in accordance with IFRS 9 (or IAS 39). At initial recognition of the receivable, any difference between the measurement of the receivable in accordance with IFRS 9 (or IAS 39) and the corresponding amount of revenue recognised should be presented as an expense (e.g. as an impairment loss). [IFRS 15:108]

IFRS 15 uses the terms 'contract asset' and 'contract liability' but does not prohibit an entity from using alternative descriptions in the statement of financial position for those items. If an alternative description is used for a contract asset, sufficient information should be provided to enable a user of the financial statements to distinguish between receivables and contract assets. [IFRS 15:109]

IFRS 15 provides the following examples, which illustrate how contract assets, contract liabilities and receivables should be considered in relation to each other.

Example 13A

Contract liability and receivable

[IFRS 15:IE198 - IE200, Example 38]

Case A – Cancellable contract

On 1 January 20X9, an entity enters into a cancellable contract to transfer a product to a customer on 31 March 20X9. The contract requires the customer to pay consideration of CU1,000 in advance on 31 January 20X9. The customer pays the consideration on 1 March 20X9. The entity transfers the product on 31 March 20X9. The following journal entries illustrate how the entity accounts for the contract:

(a) the entity receives cash of CU1,000 on 1 March 20X9 (cash is received in advance of performance):

Cash	CU1,000	
Contract liability		CU1,000

(b) the entity satisfies the performance obligation on 31 March 20X9:

Contract liability	CU1,000	
Revenue		CU1,000

Case B – Non-cancellable contract

The same facts as in Case A apply to Case B except that the contract is non-cancellable. The following journal entries illustrate how the entity accounts for the contract:

(a)   the amount of consideration is due on 31 January 20X9 (which is when the entity recognises a receivable because it has an unconditional right to consideration):

Receivable	CU1,000	
Contract liability		CU1,000

(b)   the entity receives the cash on 1 March 20X9:

Cash	CU1,000	
Receivable		CU1,000

(c)   the entity satisfies the performance obligation on 31 March 20X9:

Contract liability	CU1,000	
Revenue		CU1,000

If the entity issued the invoice before 31 January 20X9 (the due date of the consideration), the entity would not present the receivable and the contract liability on a gross basis in the statement of financial position because the entity does not yet have a right to consideration that is unconditional.

Example 13B

Contract asset recognised for the entity's performance

[IFRS 15:IE201 - IE204, Example 39]

On 1 January 20X8, an entity enters into a contract to transfer Products A and B to a customer in exchange for CU1,000. The contract requires Product A to be delivered first and states that payment for the delivery of Product A is conditional on the delivery of Product B. In other words, the consideration of CU1,000 is due only after the entity has transferred both Products A and B to the customer. Consequently, the entity does not have a right to consideration that is unconditional (a receivable) until both Products A and B are transferred to the customer.

The entity identifies the promises to transfer Products A and B as performance obligations and allocates CU400 to the performance obligation to transfer Product A and CU600 to the performance obligation to transfer Product B on the basis of their relative stand-alone selling prices. The entity recognises revenue for each respective performance obligation when control of the product transfers to the customer.

The entity satisfies the performance obligation to transfer Product A:

Contract asset	CU400	
Revenue		CU400

The entity satisfies the performance obligation to transfer Product B and recognises the unconditional right to consideration:

Receivable	CU1,000	
Contract asset		CU400
Revenue		CU600

Example 13C

Receivable recognised for the entity's performance

[IFRS 15:IE205 - IE208, Example 40]

An entity enters into a contract with a customer on 1 January 20X9 to transfer products to the customer for CU150 per product. If the customer purchases more than 1 million products in a calendar year, the contract indicates that the price per unit is retrospectively reduced to CU125 per product.

Consideration is due when control of the products transfers to the customer. Therefore, the entity has an unconditional right to consideration (ie a receivable) for CU150 per product until the retrospective price reduction applies (ie after 1 million products are shipped).

In determining the transaction price, the entity concludes at contract inception that the customer will meet the 1 million products threshold and therefore estimates that the transaction price is CU125 per product. Consequently, upon the first shipment to the customer of 100 products the entity recognises the following:

Receivable	CU15,000[a]	
Revenue		CU12,500[b]
Refund liability (contract liability)		CU2,500

[a] CU150 per product × 100 products
[b] CU125 transaction price per product × 100 products

The refund liability (see [IFRS 15:55]) represents a refund of CU25 per product, which is expected to be provided to the customer for the volume-based rebate (ie the difference between the CU150 price stated in the contract that the entity has an unconditional right to receive and the CU125 estimated transaction price).

14   Disclosure

14.1   Disclosure – general

The objective of the disclosure requirements in IFRS 15 is that sufficient information is disclosed to enable users of financial statements to understand the nature, amount, timing and uncertainty of revenue and cash flows arising from contracts with customers. To achieve the objective, disclosure should be included of both qualitative and quantitative information about all of the following:

[IFRS 15:110]

(a)   its contracts with customers (see **14.2**);

(b)   the significant judgements, and changes in the judgements, made in applying IFRS 15 to those contracts (see **14.3**); and

(c)   any assets recognised from the costs to obtain or fulfil a contract with a customer in accordance with IFRS 15:91 or IFRS 15:95 (see **14.4**).

The level of detail necessary to satisfy the disclosure objective, and how much emphasis to place on each of the various requirements, will need to be considered. The disclosures presented should be aggregated or disaggregated in order that useful information is not obscured by either the inclusion of a large amount of insignificant detail or the aggregation of items that have substantially different characteristics. [IFRS 15:111]

Information need not be disclosed in accordance with IFRS 15 if it has already been provided in accordance with another Standard. [IFRS 15:112]

IAS 8:8 states that accounting policies in IFRSs do not need to be applied when the effect of their application is not material (see **3.1** in **chapter A5**). IAS 1:31 states that an entity need not provide a specific disclosure required by an IFRS if the information is not material (see **2.7** in **chapter A4**). Entities should assess both quantitative and qualitative factors to determine the materiality of information about revenue from contracts with customers. This applies not only to recognition and measurement but also to disclosures in the financial statements.

This concept is reiterated by the requirement in paragraph IFRS 15:111 to "consider the level of detail necessary to satisfy the disclosure objective and how much emphasis to place on each of the various requirements" and by IFRS 15:BC331, which states as follows.

"The boards also decided to include disclosure requirements to help an entity meet the disclosure objective. However, those disclosures should not be viewed as a checklist of minimum disclosures, because some disclosures may be relevant for some entities or industries but may be irrelevant for others. The boards also observed that it is important for an entity to consider the disclosures together with the disclosure objective and materiality. Consequently, [IFRS 15:111] clarifies that an entity need not disclose information that is immaterial."

This assessment should be made for each reporting period because a disclosure deemed to be irrelevant or immaterial in previous periods may subsequently become material as a result of increases in the monetary values to be disclosed or changes in other qualitative factors.

Entities should also consider the views of local regulators on the appropriate approach to assessing materiality in the context of disclosures.

14.2 Contracts with customers

14.2.1 Disclosure of revenue and impairment losses

Disclosure is required of all of the following amounts for the reporting period unless those amounts are presented separately in the statement of comprehensive income in accordance with other Standards:

[IFRS 15:113]

• revenue recognised from contracts with customers, which should be disclosed separately from other sources of revenue; and

• any impairment losses recognised (in accordance with IFRS 9 *Financial Instruments* or, for entities that have not yet adopted IFRS 9, IAS 39 *Financial Instruments: Recognition and Measurement*) on any receivables or contract assets arising from an entity's contracts with customers, which should be disclosed separately from impairment losses from other contracts.

14.2.2 Disaggregation of revenue

Revenue recognised from contracts with customers should be disaggregated into categories that depict how the nature, amount, timing and uncertainty of revenue and cash flows are affected by economic factors. [IFRS 15:114]

Consequently, the extent to which an entity's revenue is disaggregated for the purposes of this disclosure will depend on the facts and circumstances that pertain to the entity's contracts with customers. Some entities may need to use more than one type of category to meet the objective for disaggregating revenue. Other entities may meet the objective by using only one type of category to disaggregate revenue. [IFRS 15:B87]

When selecting the type of category (or categories) to use to disaggregate revenue, an entity should consider how information about the entity's revenue has been presented for other purposes, including:

[IFRS 15:B88]

(a) disclosures presented outside the financial statements (e.g. in earnings releases, annual reports or investor presentations);

(b) information regularly reviewed by the chief operating decision maker for evaluating the financial performance of operating segments; and

(c) other information that is similar to the types of information identified in (a) and (b) above which is used by the entity or users of the entity's financial statements to evaluate the entity's financial performance or make resource allocation decisions.

Examples of categories that might be appropriate include:

[IFRS 15:B89]

- type of good or service (e.g. major product lines);

- geographical region (e.g. country or region);

- market or type of customer (e.g. government and non-government customers);

- type of contract (e.g. fixed-price and time-and-materials contracts);

- contract duration (e.g. short-term and long-term contracts);

- timing of transfer of goods or services (e.g. revenue from goods or services transferred to customers at a point in time and revenue from goods or services transferred over time); and

- sales channels (e.g. goods sold directly to consumers and goods sold through intermediaries).

In addition, sufficient information should be disclosed to enable users of financial statements to understand the relationship between the disclosure of disaggregated revenue and revenue information that is disclosed for each reportable segment, if the entity applies IFRS 8 *Operating Segments* (see **chapter A30**). [IFRS 15:115]

Example 14.2.2

Disaggregation of revenue – quantitative disclosures

[IFRS 15:IE210 & IE211, Example 41]

An entity reports the following segments: consumer products, transportation and energy, in accordance with IFRS 8 *Operating Segments*. When the entity prepares its investor presentations, it disaggregates revenue into primary geographical markets, major product lines and timing of revenue recognition (ie goods transferred at a point in time or services transferred over time).

The entity determines that the categories used in the investor presentations can be used to meet the objective of the disaggregation disclosure requirement in

---

[IFRS 15:114], which is to disaggregate revenue from contracts with customers into categories that depict how the nature, amount, timing and uncertainty of revenue and cash flows are affected by economic factors. The following table illustrates the disaggregation disclosure by primary geographical market, major product line and timing of revenue recognition, including a reconciliation of how the disaggregated revenue ties in with the consumer products, transportation and energy segments, in accordance with [IFRS 15:115].

Segments	Consumer products CU	Transport CU	Energy CU	Total CU
Primary geographical markets				
North America	990	2,250	5,250	8,490
Europe	300	750	1,000	2,050
Asia	700	260	–	960
	1,990	3,260	6,250	11,500
Major goods/service lines				
Office supplies	600	–	–	600
Appliances	990	–	–	990
Clothing	400	–	–	400
Motorcycles	–	500	–	500
Automobiles	–	2,760	–	2,760
Solar panels	–	–	1,000	1,000
Power plant	–	–	5,250	5,250
	1,990	3,260	6,250	11,500
Timing of revenue recognition				
Goods transferred at a point in time	1,990	3,260	1,000	6,250
Services transferred over time	–	–	5,250	5,250
	1,990	3,260	6,250	11,500

14.2.3 Contract balances

An entity should disclose:

[IFRS 15:116]

- the opening and closing balances of receivables, contract assets and contract liabilities from contracts with customers, if not otherwise separately presented or disclosed;
- revenue recognised in the reporting period that was included in the contract liability balance at the beginning of the period; and
- revenue recognised in the reporting period from performance obligations satisfied (or partially satisfied) in previous periods (e.g. changes in transaction price).

An entity should explain how the timing of satisfaction of its performance obligations relates to the typical timing of payment (see **14.2.4**) and the effect that those factors have on the contract asset and the contract liability balances. The explanation provided may use qualitative information. [IFRS 15:117]

An explanation should be provided of the significant changes in the contract asset and the contract liability balances during the reporting period, including both qualitative and quantitative information. Examples of changes in the entity's balances of contract assets and contract liabilities may include:

[IFRS 15:118]

- changes due to business combinations;
- cumulative catch-up adjustments to revenue which affect the corresponding contract asset or contract liability, including adjustments arising from a change in the measure of progress, a change in an estimate of the transaction price (including any changes in the assessment of whether an estimate of variable consideration is constrained) or a contract modification;
- impairment of a contract asset;
- a change in the time frame for a right to consideration to become unconditional (i.e. for a contract asset to be reclassified to a receivable); and
- a change in the time frame for a performance obligation to be satisfied (i.e. for the recognition of revenue arising from a contract liability).

14.2.4   Performance obligations

Information should be disclosed about an entity's performance obligations in contracts with customers, including a description of all of the following:

[IFRS 15:119]

- when the entity typically satisfies its performance obligations (e.g. upon shipment, upon delivery, as services are rendered or upon completion of service), including when performance obligations are satisfied in a bill-and-hold arrangement;
- the significant payment terms (e.g. when payment is typically due, whether the contract has a significant financing component, whether the consideration amount is variable and whether the estimate of variable consideration is typically constrained – see **7.3**);
- the nature of the goods or services that the entity has promised to transfer, highlighting any performance obligations to arrange for another party to transfer goods or services (i.e. if the entity is acting as an agent);
- obligations for returns, refunds and other similar obligations; and
- types of warranties and related obligations.

14.2.5 Transaction price allocated to the remaining performance obligations

When an entity has performance obligations that it has not yet satisfied, it should disclose:

[IFRS 15:120]

- the aggregate amount of the transaction price allocated to the performance obligations that are unsatisfied (or partially unsatisfied) as at the end of the reporting period; and

- in relation to that amount, an explanation of when it expects to recognise the revenue, which it can disclose either:

  - on a quantitative basis using the time bands that would be most appropriate for the duration of the remaining performance obligations; or

  - by using qualitative information.

IFRS 15 provides a practical expedient whereby this information does not need to be disclosed for a performance obligation where either:

[IFRS 15:121]

(a) the performance obligation is part of a contract that originally was expected to have a duration of one year or less; or

(b) the entity has a right to consideration from a customer in an amount that corresponds directly with the value to the customer of the entity's performance completed to date (e.g. a service contract in which an entity bills a fixed amount for each hour of service provided) (see **9.3.1**).

An entity should explain qualitatively if it has applied this practical expedient, and whether any consideration from contracts with customers is not included in the transaction price and, therefore, not included in the information disclosed in accordance with IFRS 15:120. For example, an estimate of the transaction price would not include any estimated amounts of variable consideration that are constrained (see **7.2**). [IFRS 15:122]

Example 14.2.5A

Disclosure of the transaction price allocated to the remaining performance obligations

[IFRS 15:IE212 - IE219, Example 42]

On 30 June 20X7, an entity enters into three contracts (Contracts A, B and C) with separate customers to provide services. Each contract has a two-year non-cancellable term. The entity considers the requirements in [IFRS 15:120 to 122] in determining the information in each contract to be included in the disclosure

---

of the transaction price allocated to the remaining performance obligations at 31 December 20X7.

Contract A

Cleaning services are to be provided over the next two years typically at least once per month. For services provided, the customer pays an hourly rate of CU25.

Because the entity bills a fixed amount for each hour of service provided, the entity has a right to invoice the customer in the amount that corresponds directly with the value of the entity's performance completed to date in accordance with [IFRS 15:B16]. Consequently, no disclosure is necessary if the entity elects to apply the practical expedient in [IFRS 15:121(b)].

Contract B

Cleaning services and lawn maintenance services are to be provided as and when needed with a maximum of four visits per month over the next two years. The customer pays a fixed price of CU400 per month for both services. The entity measures its progress towards complete satisfaction of the performance obligation using a time-based measure.

The entity discloses the amount of the transaction price that has not yet been recognised as revenue in a table with quantitative time bands that illustrates when the entity expects to recognise the amount as revenue. The information for Contract B included in the overall disclosure is as follows:

	20X8	20X9	Total
	CU	CU	CU
Revenue expected to be recognised on this contract as of 31 December 20X7	4,800[(a)]	2,400[(b)]	7,200

[(a)] CU4,800 = CU400 × 12 months.
[(b)] CU2,400 = CU400 × 6 months.

Contract C

Cleaning services are to be provided as and when needed over the next two years. The customer pays fixed consideration of CU100 per month plus a one-time variable consideration payment ranging from CU0–CU1,000 corresponding to a one-time regulatory review and certification of the customer's facility (ie a performance bonus). The entity estimates that it will be entitled to CU750 of the variable consideration. On the basis of the entity's assessment of the factors in [IFRS 15:57], the entity includes its estimate of CU750 of variable consideration in the transaction price because it is highly probable that a significant reversal in the amount of cumulative revenue recognised will not occur. The entity measures its progress towards complete satisfaction of the performance obligation using a time-based measure.

The entity discloses the amount of the transaction price that has not yet been recognised as revenue in a table with quantitative time bands that illustrates when the entity expects to recognise the amount as revenue. The entity also includes a qualitative discussion about any significant variable consideration that is not included in the disclosure. The information for Contract C included in the overall disclosure is as follows:

	20X8	20X9	Total
	CU	CU	CU
Revenue expected to be recognised on this contract as of 31 December 20X7	1,575[a]	788[b]	2,363

[a] Transaction price = CU3,150 (CU100 × 24 months + CU750 variable consideration) recognised evenly over 24 months at CU1,575 per year.

[b] CU1,575 / 2 = CU788 (ie for 6 months of the year).

In addition, in accordance with [IFRS 15:122], the entity discloses qualitatively that part of the performance bonus has been excluded from the disclosure because it was not included in the transaction price. That part of the performance bonus was excluded from the transaction price in accordance with the requirements for constraining estimates of variable consideration.

Example 14.2.5B

Disclosure of the transaction price allocated to the remaining performance obligations – qualitative disclosure

[IFRS 15:IE220 & IE221, Example 43]

On 1 January 20X2, an entity enters into a contract with a customer to construct a commercial building for fixed consideration of CU10 million. The construction of the building is a single performance obligation that the entity satisfies over time. As of 31 December 20X2, the entity has recognised CU3.2 million of revenue. The entity estimates that construction will be completed in 20X3, but it is possible that the project will be completed in the first half of 20X4.

At 31 December 20X2, the entity discloses the amount of the transaction price that has not yet been recognised as revenue in its disclosure of the transaction price allocated to the remaining performance obligations. The entity also discloses an explanation of when the entity expects to recognise that amount as revenue. The explanation can be disclosed either on a quantitative basis using time bands that are most appropriate for the duration of the remaining performance obligation or by providing a qualitative explanation. Because the entity is uncertain about the timing of revenue recognition, the entity discloses this information qualitatively as follows:

"As of 31 December 20X2, the aggregate amount of the transaction price allocated to the remaining performance obligation is CU6.8 million and the entity will recognise this revenue as the building is completed, which is expected to occur over the next 12–18 months."

14.3 Significant judgements in the application of IFRS 15

14.3.1 Requirement to disclose significant judgements – general

Disclosure should be made of the judgements, and changes in the judgements, made in applying IFRS 15 that have significantly affected the determination of the amount and timing of revenue from contracts with customers. In particular, an entity should provide an explanation of the judgements, and changes in the judgements, used in determining both of the following:

[IFRS 15:123]

- the timing of satisfaction of performance obligations (see **14.3.2**); and
- the transaction price and the amounts allocated to performance obligations (see **14.3.3**).

14.3.2 Determining the timing of revenue recognition

When performance obligations are satisfied over time, the following should be disclosed:

[IFRS 15:124]

- the methods used to recognise revenue (e.g. a description of the output methods or input methods used and how those methods are applied); and
- an explanation of why the methods used provide a faithful depiction of the transfer of goods or services.

When performance obligations are satisfied at a point in time, the entity should disclose significant judgements made in evaluating when a customer obtains control of promised goods or services. [IFRS 15:125]

14.3.3 Determining the transaction price and how it is allocated

Disclosure is required regarding the methods, inputs and assumptions used for all of the following:

[IFRS 15:26]

- determining the transaction price (which includes, but is not limited to, estimating variable consideration, adjusting the consideration for the effects of the time value of money and measuring non-cash consideration);
- assessing whether an estimate of variable consideration is constrained (see **7.3**);
- allocating the transaction price, including estimating stand-alone selling prices of promised goods or services and allocating discounts and

variable consideration to a specific part of the contract (if applicable); and

- measuring obligations for returns, refunds and other similar obligations.

14.4 Capitalised costs

An entity is required to provide descriptions of both of the following:

[IFRS 15:127]

- the judgements made in determining the amount of the costs incurred to obtain or fulfil a contract with a customer (in accordance with IFRS 15:91 (see **12.2**) or IFRS 15:95 (see **12.3**)); and

- the method used to determine the amortisation for each reporting period.

The following should also be disclosed:

[IFRS 15:128]

- the closing balances of assets recognised from the costs incurred to obtain or fulfil a contract with a customer (in accordance with IFRS 15:91 or IFRS 15:95), by main category of asset (e.g. costs to obtain contracts with customers, pre-contract costs and setup costs); and

- the amount of amortisation and any impairment losses recognised in the reporting period.

14.5 Disclosure regarding the use of practical expedients

If an entity has elected to use the practical expedient in either IFRS 15:63 (about the existence of a significant financing component – see **7.4.2**) or IFRS 15:94 (about the incremental costs of obtaining a contract – see **12.2**), it should disclose that fact. [IFRS 15:129]

15 Effective date and transition

15.1 Effective date

IFRS 15 is required to be adopted for annual reporting periods beginning on or after 1 January 2018, with earlier application permitted. If an entity chooses to apply IFRS 15 for an annual period beginning before 1 January 2018, it is required to disclose that fact. [IFRS 15:C1]

When IFRS 15 was issued in May 2014, the effective date of the Standard was annual periods beginning on or after 1 January 2017. In July 2015, the IASB confirmed a one-year deferral of the effective date of the Standard. The exceptional circumstances which give rise to the deferral are as follows:

- the IASB's tentative decision to propose amendments to IFRS 15 (see **16.2**);

- the delay in the publication of the Standard in 2014 which, in turn, reduced the amount of time for entities to implement the Standard; and

- the benefits of retaining an effective date that is generally aligned with the FASB (who have deferred the adoption date of the equivalent US standard by one year).

15.2   Transition

15.2.1   Transition to IFRS 15 – general

IFRS 15 provides detailed guidance for entities transitioning to the Standard for the first time. Entities should apply one of the following methods for this purpose:

[IFRS 15:C3]

- a fully retrospective approach – applying IFRS 15 retrospectively to each prior reporting period presented in accordance with IAS 8 *Accounting Policies, Changes in Accounting Estimates and Errors* (see **chapter A5**), subject to the expedients in IFRS 15:C5 (see **15.2.2**); or

- a modified approach – applying IFRS 15 retrospectively with the cumulative effect of initially applying IFRS 15 recognised at the date of initial application in accordance with IFRS 15:C7 to C8 (see **15.2.3**).

For the purposes of these transition provisions:

[IFRS 15:C2]

- the date of initial application is the start of the reporting period in which an entity first applies IFRS 15 (e.g. for an entity adopting IFRS 15 for the first time in the year beginning 1 January 2017, the date of initial application is 1 January 2017); and

- a completed contract is one for which the entity has transferred all of the goods or services identified in accordance with IAS 11 *Construction Contracts*, IAS 18 *Revenue* and related Interpretations.

15.2.2   Fully retrospective approach

When an entity opts to use the fully retrospective approach, it is permitted to use one or more of the following practical expedients:

[IFRS 15:C5]

- for completed contracts (see **15.2.1**), the entity is not required to restate contracts that begin and end within the same annual reporting period;

- for completed contracts that have variable consideration, the entity may use the transaction price at the date the contract was completed rather than estimating variable consideration amounts for the comparative reporting periods; and

- the disclosure requirements of IFRS 15:120 (see **14.2.5**) need not be applied for reporting periods presented before the date of initial application (see **15.2.1**).

An entity should apply any of the practical expedients described above consistently to all contracts within all reporting periods presented. The entity should also disclose the following information:

[IFRS 15:C6]

- the expedients that have been used; and

- to the extent reasonably possible, a qualitative assessment of the estimated effect of applying each of those expedients.

Notwithstanding the requirements of IAS 8:28 (see **3.4.1** in **chapter A5**), when IFRS 15 is first applied, an entity need only present the quantitative information required by IAS 8:28(f) for the annual period immediately preceding the first annual period for which IFRS 15 is applied (the 'immediately preceding period') and only if the entity applies IFRS 15 retrospectively in accordance with IFRS 15:C3(a). An entity may choose to present this information for the current period or for earlier comparative periods, but is not required to do so. [IFRS 15:C4]

15.2.3   Modified approach

When the entity opts to use the modified approach, it should recognise the cumulative effect of initially applying IFRS 15 as an adjustment to the opening balance of retained earnings (or other component of equity, as appropriate) of the annual reporting period that includes the date of initial application (see **15.2.1**) (i.e. the adjustment is made to the statement of financial position at the start of the current reporting period). IFRS 15 is then applied retrospectively only to contracts that are not completed contracts (see **15.2.1**) at the date of initial application (e.g. 1 January 2017 for an entity adopting IFRS 15 for the first time in the year beginning 1 January 2017). [IFRS 15:C7]

If this method is used, the following should be disclosed for reporting periods that include the date of initial application:

[IFRS 15:C8]

(a) the amount by which each financial statement line item is affected in the current reporting period by the application of IFRS 15 as compared to IAS 11, IAS 18 and related Interpretations that were in effect before the change; and

(b) an explanation of the reasons for significant changes identified in (a) above.

If an entity elects the modified retrospective method when IFRS 15 is first adopted (see **15.2.3**), the cumulative effect of initially applying IFRS 15 is recognised as of the date of initial application, and comparative periods are not restated. Accordingly, an entity would not be required to provide the disclosures under IFRS 15:110 to 129 for the comparative periods presented.

However, IFRS 15:C8 specifies that, in the year of initial application of IFRS 15, entities electing to use the modified retrospective method are required to disclose the impact of changes to financial statement line items as a result of applying IFRS 15 (rather than previous IFRSs) and to include an explanation of the reasons for significant changes.

16   Future developments

16.1   Transition Resource Group for Revenue Recognition

Following the publication of IFRS 15, and the equivalent US GAAP standard, the IASB and the FASB formed the IASB/FASB Joint Transition Resource Group for Revenue Recognition (TRG). This group, which comprises both IFRS and US GAAP constituents, is intended to help the boards identify and consider any diversity in practice in applying the standards and to address implementation issues as they arise. The TRG does not issue guidance but discusses issues in public. In circumstances when the TRG concludes that further guidance may be helpful to users of the standards, it refers the issue to the IASB and the FASB for consideration (see **16.3**).

Further information about the TRG and summaries of its discussions can be found at:

www.ifrs.org/About-us/IASB/Advisory-bodies/Joint-Revenue-Transition-Resource-Group/Pages/Home.aspx

16.2   Clarifications to IFRS 15

The IASB issued the exposure draft ED/2015/6 *Clarifications to IFRS 15* in July 2015 in response to a number of issues brought to the attention of the IASB and the FASB by the TRG (see **16.1**). The TRG identified five topics for further consideration (identifying performance obligations, principal versus agent considerations, licensing, collectability, and measuring non-cash consideration). In addition, some stakeholders requested additional practical expedients. The exposure draft proposes targeted amendments in three of these areas, as well as some further transition reliefs.

- **Identifying performance obligations** IFRS 15 requires an entity to identify performance obligations on the basis of distinct promised goods or services. To clarify the concept of 'distinct', the IASB is proposing to amend the illustrative examples in IFRS 15.

- **Principal versus agent considerations** When another party is involved in providing goods or services to a customer, IFRS 15 requires an entity to determine whether it is the principal in the transaction, or an agent, on the basis of whether it controls the goods or services before they are transferred to the customer. To clarify how to assess control, the IASB is proposing to amend and extend the application guidance on this issue, to amend some of the existing examples, and to add two more examples.

- **Licensing** When an entity grants a licence to a customer that is distinct from other promised goods or services, the entity is required to determine whether the licence is transferred at a point in time or over time on the basis of whether the contract requires the entity to undertake activities that significantly affect the intellectual property to which the customer has rights. To clarify when an entity's activities significantly affect the intellectual property, the IASB is proposing to amend and extend the application guidance on this issue and some examples. In addition, the IASB is proposing to extend the application guidance with respect to the royalties constraint.

- **Transition relief** The IASB is proposing two additional practical expedients on transition to IFRS 15.

  - An entity may use hindsight in identifying the satisfied and unsatisfied performance obligations in a contract that has been modified before the beginning of the earliest period presented and in determining the transaction price.

  - An entity electing to use the full retrospective method is not required to apply IFRS 15 retrospectively to completed contracts at the beginning of the earliest period presented.

- **Other topics** In the exposure draft, the IASB expressly asks whether constituents agree with the assessment that amendments to IFRS 15 with respect to collectability, measuring non-cash consideration, and a practical expedient with respect to the presentation of sales taxes, are not required.

The comment period for the exposure draft closes on 28 October 2015.

Notably, the FASB has decided to propose more extensive amendments to its revenue standard.

A15 Employee benefits

Contents

1 Introduction

1.1 Overview of IAS 19

IAS 19 *Employee Benefits* outlines the accounting requirements for employee benefits, including short-term benefits (e.g. wages and salaries, annual leave), post-employment benefits such as retirement benefits, other long-term benefits (e.g. long service leave) and termination benefits. The Standard establishes the principle that the cost of providing employee benefits should be recognised in the period in which the benefit is earned by the employee, rather than when it is paid or payable, and outlines how each category of employee benefits should be measured, providing detailed guidance in particular about post-employment benefits.

1.2 Amendments to IAS 19 since the last edition of this manual

IAS 19 was most recently amended in September 2014 by *Annual Improvements to IFRSs: 2012–2014 Cycle*. The amendments clarify that the high quality bonds used to estimate the discount rate for post-employment benefit obligations should be denominated in the same currency as the benefits to be paid and that, consequently, the depth of the market for high quality bonds should be assessed at the currency level. The September 2014 amendments are effective for annual periods beginning on or after 1 January 2016, with earlier application permitted (see **7.3.6.1**).

2 Objective and scope

2.1 Objective of IAS 19

The objective of IAS 19 is to prescribe the accounting and disclosure for employee benefits. The Standard requires an entity to recognise:

[IAS 19:1]

- a liability when an employee has provided service in exchange for employee benefits to be paid in the future; and

- an expense when the entity consumes the economic benefit arising from service provided by an employee in exchange for employee benefits.

2.2 Scope of IAS 19

2.2.1 Scope of IAS 19 – general

IAS 19 is required to be applied by an employer in accounting for all employee benefits, except those to which IFRS 2 *Share-based Payment* applies (see **chapter A16**). [IAS 19:2] The employee benefits to which IAS 19 applies include those provided:

[IAS 19:4]

- under formal plans or other formal agreements between an entity and individual employees, groups of employees or their representatives;

- under legislative requirements, or through industry arrangements, whereby entities are required to contribute to national, state, industry or other multi-employer plans; or

- by those informal practices that give rise to a constructive obligation. Informal practices give rise to a constructive obligation when the entity has no realistic alternative but to pay employee benefits. An example of a constructive obligation is when a change in the entity's informal practices would cause unacceptable damage to its relationship with employees.

2.2.2 Employee benefits – definition

IAS 19 defines employee benefits as all forms of consideration given by an entity in exchange for service rendered by employees or for the termination of employment. [IAS 19:8] This includes:

[IAS 19:6]

- benefits provided either to employees or to their dependents or beneficiaries; and

- benefits settled by payments (or the provision of goods or services) either directly to employees or to others (e.g. spouses, children or dependants, or to insurance companies).

For the purposes of IAS 19, 'employees' are considered to include directors and other management personnel, and to encompass those providing service on a full-time, part-time, permanent, casual or temporary basis. [IAS 19:7]

The Standard divides the employee benefits within its scope into four categories, which are discussed in the following sections of this chapter:

- **section 3** – short-term employee benefits;

- **sections 4 to 8** – post-employment benefits;

- **section 9** – other long-term employee benefits; and

- **section 10** – termination benefits.

2.2.3 Statutory employee profit-sharing schemes

The following example considers whether profit-sharing benefit plans under which employees are entitled to receive a share of the 'taxable profits' of an entity should be accounted for in accordance with IAS 12 *Income Taxes* or IAS 19.

Example 2.2.3

Statutory employee profit-sharing scheme

Entity A operates in a jurisdiction where statutory employee profit-sharing arrangements require employers to share 10 per cent of profit, calculated in accordance with applicable tax laws (subject to specific exceptions), with employees.

This statutory profit-sharing scheme falls within the scope of IAS 19. Although the arrangement calculates amounts payable to employees in accordance with applicable tax laws, it meets the definition of an employee benefit in IAS 19:8 because the amounts are paid to the employees in exchange for services rendered. Therefore, the employee profit-sharing arrangement described should be accounted for in accordance with IAS 19 and not by analogy to IAS 12 *Income Taxes* or IAS 37 *Provisions, Contingent Liabilities and Contingent Assets*.

The objective of IAS 19 is to recognise compensation expense only when the employee has provided the related service. Consequently, Entity A should not recognise an asset or a liability related to future expected reversals of differences between taxable profit and accounting profit in connection with such an employee profit-sharing arrangement.

The features of statutory profit-sharing arrangements vary between jurisdictions. Features may include the following:

- the annual payment to individual employees may be limited to a specified amount, with any excess paid to the government to fund public programmes (e.g. worker education, investments);

- an entity may be permitted to apply tax losses carried forward from earlier accounting periods to reduce its profit-sharing obligation; and

- if the tax authorities adjust an entity's taxable income, the entity may be required to recalculate the profit-sharing amount for the period. If the entity made an overpayment to the employees in the previous year(s), the entity may have a right to claim a refund from the employees (even if they are no longer employed with the entity).

Even when the plans include additional features such as those described above, the substance of the arrangement remains that of a profit-sharing employee benefit to which IAS 19 applies.

This conclusion has been confirmed by the IFRS Interpretations Committee (see *IFRIC Update*, November 2010).

2.2.4 Costs of employees placed on temporary suspension

Example 2.2.4

Costs of employees placed on temporary suspension

Company A temporarily suspends employees during difficult economic periods when there is a downturn in production activity. Company A and the employees enter into a temporary suspension agreement, under which:

- employees remain employed during periods of suspension on the same terms as their current employment contracts;

- during the suspension period, employees collect unemployment benefits from the State as well as a reduced salary from Company A so that the amount of cash they receive each month equates to a percentage of their current salary (i.e. Company A commits to pay employees the difference between the unemployment insurance they receive and an agreed percentage (e.g. 75 per cent) of their current salaries);

- employees are not required to physically be at work during the suspension period;

- Company A has the right to call the employees back to work as necessary during the suspension period (e.g. as production activity fluctuates); and

- employees cannot take up work elsewhere during the suspension period (i.e. they are required to stay at home unless they resign, in which case a fixed notice period is required).

The suspension of employees is expected to last for a period of between six months and two years depending on Company A's needs and the economic environment. Schemes such as these have been developed in countries where the State is reluctant to change redundancy laws in favour of employers but is willing to offer a form of subsidy by paying unemployment benefits to employees during suspension periods.

Should Company A recognise a liability for the expected cost of the suspended employees when the temporary suspension agreement is first enforced?

When the employer uses a temporary suspension arrangement of this nature in order to reduce its employment costs during periods of reduced activity, the costs of the temporary suspension should be classified as a short-term benefit similar to a paid absence (e.g. holiday or leave pay). Short-term paid absences only give rise to a liability when they are accumulating, as discussed in IAS 19:13 and IAS 19:18. This is not the case in the circumstances described because the employees only have a right to receive payments as suspension occurs and for as long as suspension lasts. Company A has the discretion to ask some or all of its employees to return to work at any time and revert to normal working arrangements and remuneration. Therefore, in these circumstances, the costs of suspension should be recognised over the suspension period and should not be accrued at the outset.

Note that, in the circumstances described, the payments should not be classified as termination benefits; they are paid in exchange for *suspension* of the employees' employment rather than in exchange for *termination* of

> the employees' employment (as would be required under the definition of termination benefits in IAS 19:8 – see **section 10**).

3   Short-term employee benefits

3.1   Short-term employee benefits – definition

Short-term employee benefits are defined as employee benefits (other than termination benefits) that are expected to be settled wholly before 12 months after the end of the annual reporting period in which the employees render the related service. [IAS 19:8] They include items such as the following, if expected to be settled wholly before 12 months after the end of the annual reporting period in which the employees render the related services:

[IAS 19:9]

- wages, salaries and social security contributions;

- paid annual leave and paid sick leave;

- profit-sharing and bonuses; and

- non-monetary benefits (e.g. access to medical care, housing, cars, free or subsidised goods or services) for current employees.

Note that the distinction between benefits classified as short-term and 'other' long-term benefits under IAS 19 is important for recognition and measurement but does not affect the decision on presentation of any associated liability as current or non-current in the statement of financial position (see **4.1.7.2** in **chapter A4**).

3.2   Classification of employee benefits as short- or long-term

3.2.1   Focus on timing of expected settlement

The focus in the definition of short-term benefits is on the timing of the *expected* settlement rather than when the employee is entitled to the benefit. The simplified measurement approach permitted for short-term benefits is intended to apply only to those benefits in respect of which measurement on an undiscounted basis is not materially different from the present value of the benefit. When benefits are classified on the basis of the employee's entitlement, rather than on when the benefits are expected to be settled, this is not necessarily so (see IAS 19:BC18 and BC19 for further discussion).

The basis for classifying benefits as short- and 'other' long-term benefits under IAS 19 and the basis for presenting liabilities as current and non-current under IAS 1 are not consistent; the former focuses on expectations regarding the timing of settlement, whereas the latter focuses on when amounts are due to be settled. Consequently, a benefit may be classified as an other long-term benefit under IAS 19 (because employees are not expected to take all of their benefits within 12 months of the period in which the benefits are earned) but may be presented entirely as a current liability (because the employees are entitled to receive the benefits 'on demand', for example if they were to leave the entity's employment). See **4.1.7.2** in **chapter A4** for further discussion.

Example 3.2.1

Classification of employee benefits as short- or long-term

Employees of Company A accumulate annual leave on a pro rata basis over each calendar year. Unused annual leave can be carried forward indefinitely and must be paid up in cash when an employee leaves Company A's employment. Experience demonstrates that employees use their accumulated annual leave over a period longer than two years.

Under IAS 19, the unused annual leave would not meet the definition of a short-term benefit because it is not *expected* to be settled wholly within 12 months after the end of the annual period in which the employee renders service. Consequently, it would be classified as an other long-term benefit (the residual classification) and accounted for accordingly (see **section 9**).

3.2.2   Short-term benefits expected to be settled wholly within 12 months

The definition in IAS 19 refers to classification on the basis of whether the benefit is expected to be settled 'wholly' within 12 months after the end of the annual reporting period in which the related service is rendered. Therefore, benefits that are expected to be settled over a period of time can only be classified as short-term if all of the settlements are expected to occur within that 12-month period.

3.2.3   Assessment for individual employee or for the workforce as a whole?

While IAS 19 does not provide any specific guidance on the unit of account to be used in evaluating the period over which the benefit is expected to be settled (e.g. whether the assessment should be performed at the individual employee level or for the workforce as a whole), IAS 19:BC20 indicates that the IASB concluded that the classification of the benefits should reflect the characteristics of the benefits, rather than the demographic or financial assumptions at a point in time. In addition, IAS 19:BC21 states that the Board considered requiring an entity to classify benefits on an employee-by-employee basis, but concluded that this would not be practical and would not meet the objectives of the classification.

To illustrate, in **example 3.2.1**, some employees of Company A may always use their annual leave in full within 12 months after the end of the annual reporting period, but others may receive benefit later (e.g. in cash when they cease employment). The fact that some employees will receive benefit more than 12 months after the end of the annual reporting period means that all annual leave is classified as an other long-term benefit; it is not appropriate to classify the same benefit differently for individual employees or groups of employees merely because of different expectations regarding when they will claim it.

3.2.4 Change in classification of short-term benefits

An entity is required to consider whether a benefit still meets the definition of a short-term benefit if either of the following events occurs:

[IAS 19:10]

- the characteristics of the benefit change (e.g. a change from a non-accumulating benefit to an accumulating benefit); or

- there is a change in expectation regarding the timing of settlement that is not temporary.

An entity need not reclassify a short-term employee benefit if the entity's expectations of the timing of settlement change temporarily. [IAS 19:10]

The IASB believes that the classification of a short-term employee benefit should be revisited if it no longer meets the definition (e.g. if the expected settlement date of a benefit classified initially as a short-term employee benefit changes subsequently to a date more than 12 months after the end of the reporting period) because the undiscounted amount of that benefit could differ materially from its present value. However, the Board also concluded that a temporary change in expectation should not trigger reclassification because such a change would not be indicative of a change in the underlying characteristics of the benefit. [IAS 19:BC20(c)]

Similar concerns do not arise when a benefit previously classified as long-term subsequently meets the definition of a short-term benefit (e.g. if expectations regarding the timing of settlement change so that the benefit is now expected to be settled wholly within 12 months of the end of the period in which service is rendered). In such circumstances, the only effect of reclassification would be that the benefit would be subsequently measured at an undiscounted amount - but that would not be expected to result in a measurement that differs materially from its present value. [IAS 19:BC20(c)]

3.3 Recognition and measurement – short-term employee benefits

3.3.1 Recognition and measurement of short-term employee benefits – general

An entity should recognise the undiscounted amount of short-term employee benefits earned by an employee in exchange for services rendered during the accounting period:

[IAS 19:11]

- in the statement of financial position, as a liability (accrued expense), after deducting any amounts already paid, or as an asset (prepaid expense), if the amount already paid exceeds the undiscounted amount of the benefits, to the extent that the prepayment is recoverable (e.g. by means of a reduction in future payments or a cash refund); and

- in profit or loss, as an expense, unless another Standard requires or permits inclusion of the benefits in the cost of an asset (e.g. as part of staff costs capitalised in a self-constructed property – see **chapter A7**).

The cost of all short-term employee benefits is recognised as noted above. No actuarial assumptions are required (therefore, there are no actuarial gains or losses to address) and, due to their short-term nature, obligations are dealt with on an undiscounted basis.

3.3.2 Non-monetary short-term benefits

When non-monetary short-term benefits are provided, the cost of providing such benefits is measured at the cost to the employer of providing the benefit and is recognised using the same principles as are applied to monetary employee benefits.

3.3.3 Short-term paid absences

An entity may pay employees for absence for various reasons (e.g. holidays, sickness and short-term disability, maternity or paternity leave, jury service and military service). Short-term paid absences may be classified as accumulating or non-accumulating. [IAS 19:14]

Accumulating paid absences are those that can be carried forward and used in future accounting periods if the current accounting period's entitlement is not used in full. Accumulating paid absences may be further sub-divided as vesting (when employees are entitled to a cash payment for unused entitlement on leaving the entity) or non-vesting (when no such entitlement arises). [IAS 19:15]

Non-accumulating paid absences cannot be carried forward, i.e. any unused entitlement is lost at the end of the current period and the employee is not entitled to a cash payment for unused entitlement on leaving the entity. This is commonly the case for sick pay (to the extent that unused past entitlement does not increase future entitlement), maternity or paternity leave, and paid absences for jury service or military service. [IAS 19:18]

In applying the general requirements set out at **3.3.1** to the expected cost of short-term paid absences:

[IAS 19:13 & 16]

- for accumulating paid absences, the expense should be recognised when the employees render service that increases their entitlement to future paid absences, based on the additional amount that the entity expects to pay as a result of the unused entitlement accumulated at the end of the reporting period; and

- for non-accumulating paid absences, the expense should be recognised only when the absences occur. This is because employee service does not increase the amount of the benefit.

For accumulating absences, the difference between vesting and non-vesting does not affect whether an obligation exists and should be recognised, but does affect the measurement of that obligation, because there is a possibility that employees may leave before they use an accumulating non-vesting entitlement. Therefore, the expense is measured as the additional amount that the entity expects to pay, rather than the maximum amount that it could be obliged to pay. [IAS 19:15]

Example 3.3.3

Measurement of obligation for short-term paid absences

Company A has 200 employees, who are each entitled to 20 working days of paid leave each year. Paid leave is first taken out of the current year's entitlement and then out of the balance brought forward from the previous year (a LIFO basis). Unused leave cannot be carried forward more than one year. Employees are not entitled to a cash payment for unused leave if they leave Company A's employment.

At 31 December 20X1, the average unused entitlement is 3 days per employee (i.e. 600 days in total). Based on past experience, Entity A expects that 175 employees will take no more than their annual entitlement in 20X2 and that the remaining 25 employees will, in total, use 70 days of the entitlement brought forward from 20X1.

The benefit described can be carried forward if the current period's entitlement is not used in full, but only for 12 months; it is therefore an 'accumulating' short-term paid absence. The accumulating paid leave is non-vesting, because employees are not entitled to a cash payment for unused leave when they leave Company A's employment (see IAS 19:15).

IAS 19:16 requires Company A to recognise an obligation at 31 December 20X1 for the amount it expects to pay as a result of the unused entitlement that has accumulated at the end of the period. IAS 19:15 clarifies that, for non-vesting entitlements, the possibility that some employees will not take their entitlement should be reflected in that measurement.

Therefore, at 31 December 20X1, Company A recognises a liability and an expense equal to the undiscounted amount of 70 days of paid leave (i.e. the number of days of the entitlement that are expected to be taken).

IAS 19:17 acknowledges that, in many cases, an entity may not need to make detailed computations to estimate that there is no material obligation for unused paid absences. For example, a sick leave obligation is likely to be material only if there is a formal or informal understanding that unused paid sick leave may be taken as paid annual leave.

3.3.4   Profit-sharing and bonus plans

3.3.4.1   Profit-sharing and bonus plans – general

In applying the general requirements set out at **3.3.1** to the expected cost of profit-sharing and bonus plans, an entity should recognise the expected cost when, and only when:

[IAS 19:19]

- it has a present legal or constructive obligation to make such payments as a result of past events; and

- a reliable estimate of the obligation can be made.

In this context, a present obligation exists when, and only when, the entity has no realistic alternative but to make the payments. [IAS 19:19] The requirements therefore follow closely the general recognition criteria for provisions under IAS 37 *Provisions, Contingent Liabilities and Contingent Assets* (see **chapter A12**). Even when an entity has no legal obligation to pay a bonus, past practice of paying bonuses may give rise to a constructive obligation, if the entity has no realistic alternative but to pay the bonus. [IAS 19:21]

The costs of profit-sharing and bonus plans are recognised as an expense (and not as a distribution of profit) because they result from employee service and not from a transaction with the entity's owners. [IAS 19:23]

3.3.4.2 Employee's entitlement to bonus or profit-share depends on the employee remaining in employment

An employee's entitlement to a profit-share may depend on the employee remaining with the entity for a specified period. In such circumstances, the plan creates a constructive obligation as employees render service that increases the amount to be paid if they remain in service until the end of that specified period. [IAS 19:20]

The fact that some employees may leave without receiving payments offered under profit-sharing and bonus plans is reflected in the measurement of the obligation. It is not appropriate to defer recognition of the obligation until the employee completes the entitlement period. [IAS 19:20 & 21]

Example 3.3.4.2

Profit-sharing plan

A profit-sharing plan requires Company B to pay a specified proportion of its profit before tax for the financial year to 30 June 20X1 to employees who serve throughout the calendar year 20X1. If no employees leave during the year, the total profit-sharing payments for the year will be 3 per cent of profit before tax. Company B estimates that staff turnover will reduce the payments to 2.5 per cent of profit before tax.

Although the payment is measured as a proportion of the profits for the financial year to 30 June 20X1, performance is based on an employee's service during the calendar year 20X1. Accordingly, Company B recognises a liability and an expense of 50 per cent of 2.5 per cent of the profit before tax at 30 June 20X1. A further expense of 50 per cent of 2.5 per cent should be recognised in the next period, together with a true up for any difference between the estimated amounts and the actual amounts paid.

3.3.4.3 Bonus or profit-share payable based on continued employment for additional period

It is common practice for employees to be entitled to a bonus that is determined by reference to performance in a specific period but payable at a future date when that performance condition has been measured. Often there is a requirement for continued employment until that payment date, but the bonus is otherwise unconditional. For example, an entity with a 30 June reporting date pays a bonus in respect of each financial year to employees who have provided services during the financial year (the 'earning' period) and remain on the payroll until 30 September. The bonus pool is determined as a percentage of the entity's profits during the earning period; the additional period from 1 July to 30 September is necessary to determine the entity's profits and the bonus payable to individual employees.

The question arises as to whether the additional service condition (i.e. the requirement to remain in employment during the three-month administrative period up to 30 September) should be taken into account when considering the period over which the bonus expense is recognised.

IAS 19 is not explicit in this regard. IAS 19:20 requires the obligation to be measured and recognised as an expense "as employees render service that increases the amount to be paid if they remain in service until the end of the specified period", reflecting the possibility that some employees may leave without receiving bonus payments.

In the circumstances described, one interpretation of this requirement could be that the expense should be recognised as the employees render the service that increases the amount to be paid. Because the amount of the bonus does not increase after the earning period, the obligation should be measured at 30 June for the full amount expected to be paid, taking into consideration the expected forfeitures.

Another interpretation could be that an obligation arises as employees render services when they remain in service until 30 September, thereby suggesting that the period over which the bonus expense is recognised should include the three-month administrative period. This interpretation is consistent with the recognition of an expense relating to share-based payments over the vesting period in accordance with IFRS 2 *Share-based Payment*.

Because the wording of IAS 19 is not sufficiently clear, a case can be made for both interpretations and entities should adopt one of these approaches as an accounting policy choice.

Note that this conclusion (i.e. that the entity can select one of two approaches as an accounting policy choice) only applies when the additional period is administrative in nature, which will only be the case if the additional period is relatively short.

If profit-sharing and bonus payments are not expected to be settled wholly before 12 months after the end of the annual reporting period in which the employees render the related service, those payments are classified as other long-term employee benefits (see **section 9**). [IAS 19:24]

3.3.4.4   When can a reliable estimate be made of the obligation under a bonus or profit-sharing plan?

As noted at **3.3.4.1**, one of the necessary conditions for recognition of the expected cost of a bonus or profit-sharing plan is that a reliable estimate of the obligation can be made. An entity can make a reliable estimate of its legal or constructive obligation under a profit-sharing or bonus plan when, and only when:

[IAS 19:22]

- the formal terms of the plan contain a formula for determining the amount of the benefit; or

- the amounts to be paid are determined before the financial statements are authorised for issue; or

- past practice gives clear evidence of the amount of the constructive obligation.

3.4 Disclosure – short-term employee benefits

IAS 19 does not specify any particular disclosure requirements for short-term employee benefits, but other Standards may require disclosures. For example:

[IAS 19:25]

- IAS 24 *Related Party Disclosures* requires disclosures about employee benefits for key management personnel; and

- IAS 1 *Presentation of Financial Statements* requires disclosure of the employee benefits expense.

4 Post-employment benefits

4.1 Post-employment benefits – definition

Post-employment benefits are defined as employee benefits (other than termination benefits and short-term employee benefits) that are payable after the completion of employment. [IAS 19:8]

This definition captures retirement benefits (e.g. pensions and lump sum payments on retirement) and other post-employment benefits (e.g. post-employment life insurance and access to medical care). If an entity provides such benefits, the requirements of IAS 19 apply irrespective of whether a separate entity is established to receive contributions and to pay benefits. [IAS 19:26]

4.2 Post-employment benefit plans – definition

Post-employment benefit plans are formal or informal arrangements under which an entity provides post-employment benefits for one or more employees. [IAS 19:8]

The accounting treatment and required disclosures for a post-employment benefit plan depend upon whether it is classified as a defined contribution or a defined benefit plan (see **4.3**). In addition to addressing defined contribution and defined benefit plans generally, IAS 19 also sets out requirements for insured benefits (see **4.5**), and multi-employer plans, group plans and state plans (see **section 5**).

4.3 Distinguishing between defined contribution and defined benefit post-employment benefit plans

4.3.1 Classification of post-employment benefit plans

There are two main types of post-employment benefit plans:

[IAS 19:8]

- **defined contribution plans** are post-employment benefit plans under which an entity pays fixed contributions into a separate entity (a fund) and will have no legal or constructive obligation to pay further contributions if the fund does not hold sufficient assets to pay all employee benefits relating to employee service in the current and prior periods; and

- **defined benefit plans** are post-employment benefit plans other than defined contribution plans.

4.3.2 Classification of a post-employment benefit plan to be determined based on the substance of the arrangement

The classification as either a defined contribution plan or a defined benefit plan (see **4.3.1**) depends on the economic substance of the plan as derived from its principal terms and conditions. [IAS 19:27]

4.3.3 Nature of obligations under a defined contribution plan

IAS 19 explains that, under a defined contribution plan, the amount of post-employment benefits received by an employee is determined by the amount of contributions paid to a post-employment benefit plan or to an insurance company, together with any investment returns arising from the contributions, so that actuarial risk (that benefits will be less than expected) and investment risk (that assets invested will be insufficient to meet expected benefits) fall, in substance, on the employee. [IAS 19:28]

4.3.4 Nature of obligations under a defined benefit plan

Under a defined benefit plan:

[IAS 19:30]

- the entity's obligation is to provide the agreed benefits to current and former employees; and

- actuarial risk and investment risk fall, in substance, on the entity so that if actuarial or investment experience are worse than expected, the entity's obligation may be increased.

Examples of circumstances in which an entity's obligation is not limited to the amount that it agrees to contribute to a fund (and, hence, the plan is a defined benefit plan) are when the entity has a legal or constructive obligation through:

[IAS 19:29]

- a plan benefit formula that is not linked solely to the amount of contributions and requires the entity to provide further contributions if assets are insufficient to meet the benefits in the plan benefit formula;

- a guarantee, either indirectly through a plan or directly, of a specified return on contributions; or

- informal practices that give rise to a constructive obligation. For example, a constructive obligation may arise when an entity has a history of increasing benefits for former employees to keep pace with inflation even where there is no legal obligation to do so.

As can be seen from the first bullet above, the existence of a benefit formula does not, by itself, create a defined benefit plan, but rather that there needs to be a link between the benefit formula and contributions that creates a legal or constructive obligation to contribute further amounts to meet the benefits specified by the benefit formula. This is an important factor to consider in the classification of a plan that has a benefit formula for the benefits to be paid if there are sufficient plan assets, but not requiring the employer to pay additional contributions if there are insufficient plan assets to pay those benefits. In such circumstances, in effect, the benefit payments are based on the lower of the benefit formula and the plan assets available. A plan of this nature is a defined contribution plan. [IAS 19:BC30] The following example illustrates this principle.

Example 4.3.4

Defined contribution plan with target benefits

An employer has a target benefit plan, the contributions to which are determined on the basis of each employee's age on joining the plan, projected average salary at retirement, projected mortality, and retirement age. When an employee joins the plan, a contribution percentage is computed for that employee based on relevant demographic information. Thereafter, the employer contributes that specific percentage of the employee's salary to the plan. If the employee's salary or other factors change, the employer's contribution rate will not change.

The plan is structured so that the employer's contributions accumulate in each individual employee's account. Investment gains or losses on assets in the plan accrue to the employees on a pro rata basis and are not considered in computing the employer's future contributions. If an employee's account balance at retirement or termination either exceeds or falls short of the target amount, the account balance will not be adjusted by the employer. Employees receive only the funds credited to their accounts.

This plan meets the definition of a defined contribution plan. The target benefit plan has a complex formula to compute the employer's pension contributions. However, the benefit computation is not adjusted for investment gains, losses or forfeitures on the assets contributed to the employee's individual account. As a result, the actuarial and investment risks associated with the plan effectively fall to the employee and, therefore, the plan is a defined contribution plan.

4.4   Funded and unfunded post-employment benefit plans

4.4.1   Funded and unfunded post-employment benefit plans – general

IAS 19 notes that post-employment benefit plans can be either funded or unfunded, but it does not formally define these terms. Funded plans are taken to be those under which plan assets (see **4.4.2**) are held in a separate entity, usually under the supervision of an administrator. The administrator typically manages the investment of contributions and the payment of benefit entitlements to employees in accordance with the plan rules.

4.4.2   Plan assets – definition

Although IAS 19 does not define funded and unfunded plans, it does define 'plan assets', which the Standard takes into account in measuring the surplus or deficit associated with a post-employment benefit plan. Plan assets comprise:

[IAS 19:8]

- assets held by a long-term employee benefit fund; and
- qualifying insurance policies.

Assets held by a long-term employee benefit fund are assets (other than non-transferable financial instruments issued by the reporting entity) that:

[IAS 19:8]

(a) are held by an entity (a fund) that is legally separate from the reporting entity and exists solely to pay or fund employee benefits; and

(b) are available to be used only to pay or fund employee benefits, are not available to the reporting entity's own creditors (even in bankruptcy), and cannot be returned to the reporting entity, unless either:

   (i)   the remaining assets of the fund are sufficient to meet all the related employee benefit obligations of the plan or the reporting entity; or

   (ii) the assets are returned to the reporting entity to reimburse it for employee benefits already paid.

If these criteria are not met, it appears that the plan should be regarded as unfunded for the purposes of IAS 19. The entity should consider whether any assets underlying employee benefit plans which do not qualify as plan assets should instead appear in its own statement of financial position, because they are either held directly by the entity or, for example, by a structured entity controlled by it, which would be consolidated in accordance with IFRS 10 *Consolidated Financial Statements* (see **chapter A24**).

4.5 Insured benefits

A post-employment benefit plan that is funded by insurance premiums is treated as a defined benefit plan if the entity (either directly or indirectly through the plan) has a legal or constructive obligation either:

[IAS 19:46]

- to pay the employee benefits directly when they fall due; or

- to pay further amounts if the insurer does not pay all future employee benefits relating to employee service in the current or prior periods.

In the absence of such a legal or constructive obligation, the plan is treated as a defined contribution plan. [IAS 19:46]

Therefore, insured plans are subject to the same distinction between accounting and funding as other plans. It should not be assumed, merely because an entity insures benefits arising under a defined benefit plan, that the plan assets are necessarily equal to the plan liabilities. IAS 19:47 notes that the benefits insured by an insurance policy need not have a direct or automatic relationship with the entity's obligation for employee benefits.

If the entity retains a legal or constructive obligation, payment of the insurance premium is, in substance, an investment to meet the obligation. In such circumstances, the entity should account for its 'qualifying' insurance policies as plan assets (see **7.3.7.4**) and for other insurance policies as reimbursement rights (if the policies meet the criterion established in IAS 19:116 – see **7.3.7.6**). [IAS 19:48]

When an insurance policy is in the name of a specified plan participant or a group of plan participants, and the entity does not have any legal or constructive obligation to cover any loss on the policy, the entity has no obligation to pay benefits to the employees and the insurer has sole responsibility for paying the benefits. The payment of fixed premiums under such contracts is, in substance, the settlement of the employee benefit obligation, rather than an investment to meet the obligation. Consequently, the entity no longer has an asset or a liability and the entity should treat such payments as contributions to a defined contribution plan. [IAS 19:49]

5 Multi-employer plans, group plans and state plans

5.1 Multi-employer plans

5.1.1 Multi-employer plans – definition

Multi-employer plans are defined contribution plans (other than state plans) or defined benefit plans (other than state plans) that:

[IAS 19:8]

- pool the assets contributed by various entities that are not under common control; and
- use those assets to provide benefits to employees of more than one entity, on the basis that contribution and benefit levels are determined without regard to the identity of the entity that employs the employees concerned.

5.1.2 Requirement to distinguish between defined contribution and defined benefit multi-employer plans

Multi-employer plans should be classified as defined contribution or defined benefit plans based on the criteria discussed in **section 4**, and accounted for accordingly. [IAS 19:32]

The Standard cites as one example of a multi-employer defined benefit plan a plan under which:

[IAS 19:35]

- the plan is financed on a pay-as-you-go basis: contributions are set at a level that is expected to be sufficient to pay the benefits falling due in the same period and future benefits earned during the current period will be paid out of future contributions; and
- employees' benefits are determined by the length of their service and the participating entities have no realistic means of withdrawing from the plan without paying a contribution for the benefits earned by employees up to the date of withdrawal. Such a plan creates actuarial risk for the entity: if the ultimate cost of benefits already earned at the end of the reporting period is more than expected, the entity will have either to increase its contributions or to persuade employees to accept a reduction in benefits. Therefore, such a plan is a defined benefit plan.

5.1.3 Accounting for participation in a defined benefit multi-employer plan

If an entity participates in a defined benefit multi-employer plan, the entity should account for its proportionate share of the defined benefit obligation, plan assets and cost associated with the plan, and provide disclosures, in the same way as for any other defined benefit plan, unless the exemption discussed at **5.1.4** is available. [IAS 19:33 & 36]

In determining when to recognise and how to measure a liability relating to the wind-up of a multi-employer defined benefit plan, or the entity's withdrawal from a multi-employer defined benefit plan, an entity should apply the requirements of IAS 37 *Provisions, Contingent Liabilities and Contingent Assets* (see **chapter A12**). [IAS 19:39]

5.1.4 Exemption for insufficient information

IAS 19 acknowledges that an entity may not be able to identify its share of the underlying financial position and performance of the plan with sufficient reliability for accounting purposes. This may occur if:

[IAS 19:36]

- the plan exposes the participating entities to actuarial risks associated with the current and former employees of other entities, with the result that there is no consistent and reliable basis for allocating the obligations, plan assets and cost to individual entities participating in the plan; or

- the entity does not have access to sufficient information about the plan to satisfy the requirements of IAS 19.

In such circumstances (i.e. the entity participates in a multi-employer plan that is a defined benefit plan, but there is not sufficient information available to use defined-benefit accounting), the entity should:

[IAS 19:34]

- account for the plan as if it were a defined contribution plan; and

- make appropriate disclosures (see **5.1.7**).

IAS 19 emphasises that, if a participant in a defined benefit multi-employer plan:

- accounts on a defined contribution basis because it has insufficient information to apply defined-benefit accounting, but

- is party to a contractual agreement that determines how a surplus would be distributed or a deficit funded,

it should recognise the asset or liability arising from that contractual agreement, and the resulting income or expense in profit or loss. [IAS 19:37] This requirement is illustrated in **example 5.1.4**, which is reproduced from the Standard.

Example 5.1.4

Multi-employer plans

[Example illustrating IAS 19:37]

An entity participates in a multi-employer defined benefit plan that does not prepare plan valuations on an IAS 19 basis. It therefore accounts for the plan as if it were a defined contribution plan. A non-IAS 19 funding valuation shows a deficit of CU100 million in the plan. The plan has agreed under contract a schedule of contributions with the participating employers in the plan that will eliminate the deficit over the next five years. The entity's total contributions under the contract are CU8 million.

The entity recognises a liability for the contributions adjusted for the time value of money, and an equal expense in profit or loss.

5.1.5   Distinguishing between multi-employer plans and group administration plans

Multi-employer plans may be differentiated from group administration plans (also known as common investment funds). Group administration plans allow participating employers to pool their assets for investment purposes, thus reducing administration and investment management costs. The claims of the different participating employers on the assets are segregated for the sole benefit of their employees and other beneficiaries of their plans, so that there is no particular accounting problem in obtaining the information relating to a particular employer. Participating employers are not exposed to the actuarial risks attaching to the obligations of the other participating employers. [IAS 19:38]

Plans of this nature should be classified as either defined contribution or defined benefit in the usual manner. [IAS 19:38]

5.1.6   Change from defined-contribution to defined-benefit accounting for a multi-employer plan

Example 5.1.6

Change from defined-contribution to defined-benefit accounting for a multi-employer plan

Company A contributes to a multi-employer defined benefit plan. However, because the plan has never been able to provide its participants with sufficient information for them to apply the accounting requirements in IAS 19:33, Company A has always accounted for the plan as if it were a defined contribution plan in accordance with the exemption in IAS 19:34 (see **5.1.4**).

At 31 December 20X1, the plan is, for the first time, able to provide the participants with sufficient information for them to apply the accounting requirements in IAS 19:33.

The effect of the change from defined-contribution accounting to defined-benefit accounting should be treated as a change in estimate in accordance with IAS 8 *Accounting Policies, Changes in Accounting Estimates and Errors*, and not as a change in accounting policy.

Although Company A's accounting policy has always been to recognise its defined benefit liability (or asset), prior to being provided with the necessary information at 31 December 20X1, Company A was not in a position to do so. Company A was required to account for the plan as a defined contribution plan, with the cost of the plan measured at an amount equal to the contributions made. From 31 December 20X1, Company A has sufficient information to enable it to measure reliably the defined benefit liability (or asset) at that date, and the cost going forward. The best estimate of the liability, and not the basis of accounting for the plan, has changed and the adjustment to the carrying amount is, therefore, a change in estimate. The effect of the change in estimate should be recognised in profit or loss in the year in which the new information is obtained.

5.1.7 Disclosure – multi-employer plans

If an entity participates in a multi-employer defined benefit plan (whether accounted for as a defined benefit plan or as a defined contribution plan under the exemption discussed in **5.1.4**), the entity is required to disclose:

[IAS 19:148(a) - (c)]

- a description of the funding arrangements, including the method used to determine the entity's rate of contributions and any minimum funding requirements;

- a description of the extent to which the entity can be liable to the plan for other entities' obligations under the terms and conditions of the multi-employer plan; and

- a description of any agreed allocation of a deficit or surplus on:

  - wind-up of the plan; or

  - the entity's withdrawal from the plan.

If an entity participates in a multi-employer defined benefit plan, and sufficient information is available for defined-benefit accounting, the entity is also required to disclose all of the information required under IAS 19:135 to 147 (see **8.2**). [IAS 19:33]

If an entity participates in a multi-employer plan that is a defined benefit plan, but there is not sufficient information available to use defined-benefit accounting, the following additional disclosures are required instead of the information required under IAS 19:139 to 147:

[IAS 19:148(d)]

- the fact that the plan is a defined benefit plan;
- the reason why sufficient information is not available to enable the entity to account for the plan as a defined benefit plan;
- the expected contributions to the plan for the next annual reporting period;
- information about any deficit or surplus in the plan that may affect the amount of future contributions, including the basis used to determine that deficit or surplus and the implications, if any, for the entity; and
- an indication of the level of participation of the entity in the plan compared with other participating entities. Examples of measures that might provide such an indication include the entity's proportion of the total contributions to the plan or the entity's proportion of the total number of active members, retired members, and former members entitled to benefits, if that information is available.

5.2   Group plans

5.2.1   Group plans – general

A defined benefit plan that shares risks between various entities under common control (e.g. various subsidiaries within a group) is not a multi-employer plan for the purposes of IAS 19. [IAS 19:40] IAS 19:41 specifies the accounting requirements for such plans (referred to below as 'group plans').

5.2.2   Recognition of cost by individual group entities

Information is obtained about the group plan as a whole measured in accordance with IAS 19 on the basis of assumptions that apply to the group plan. The amounts recognised in individual entities will vary, however, depending on the arrangements that exist for charging the net IAS 19 cost to individual group entities:

[IAS 19:41]

- if there is a contractual agreement or stated policy for charging to individual group entities the net defined benefit cost for the group plan as a whole measured in accordance with IAS 19, each group entity should recognise in its separate or individual financial statements the net defined benefit cost so charged; or
- if there is no such agreement or policy, the net defined benefit cost should be recognised in the separate or individual financial statements of the group entity that is legally the sponsoring employer for the plan. Each of the other group entities should recognise, in its separate or individual financial statements, a cost equal to its contribution payable for the period.

As stated above, IAS 19:41 requires that if there is a contractual agreement or stated policy for charging the IAS 19 net defined benefit cost for a group plan to individual group entities, each entity should, in its separate or individual financial statements, account for its share as a defined benefit plan (i.e. recognise a defined benefit asset or liability). The contractual agreement or stated policy must apply in respect of "the net defined benefit cost for the plan as a whole measured in accordance with [IAS 19]". The net defined benefit cost is a number calculated for financial reporting purposes that may not have a direct relationship with the payment of cash contributions.

A contractual agreement or stated policy relating to the payment of cash contributions that are based on the actuarial assumptions and methods applied to funding valuations is not sufficient because these are usually different from those used for IAS 19 purposes.

Therefore, for a group entity to meet the requirement for a contractual agreement or stated policy (i.e. in order to account for its share of the defined benefit plan), the group should establish a policy for a reasonable allocation of the IAS 19 net defined benefit cost. The allocation could be based, for example, on the proportion of contributions paid to the scheme or the proportion of pensionable payroll of each entity.

5.2.3 Identification of the sponsoring entity

IAS 19 does not provide any guidance on how to identify the entity legally sponsoring the plan, although IAS 19:BC48 clarifies that, in the absence of a contractual agreement or a stated policy, by default, the sponsoring entity will be the entity that bears the risks relating to the plan. The identity of the sponsoring employer could also be established from the plan's legal documentation, such as the plan rules. In some cases, this may not give a fair presentation; for example, the legal sponsor may be a dormant subsidiary with no substance. Such cases would be unusual but would require careful consideration.

5.2.4 Disclosure – group plans

IAS 19 emphasises that participation in a group plan is a related party transaction. [IAS 19:42] Accordingly, each group entity participating in such a plan is required to disclose in its separate or individual financial statements:

[IAS 19:149]

(a) the contractual agreement or stated policy for charging the net defined benefit cost or the fact that there is no such policy;

(b) the policy for determining the contribution to be paid by the entity;

(c) if the entity accounts for an allocation of the net defined benefit cost in accordance with IAS 19:41 (see **5.2.2**), all the information about the plan as a whole required by IAS 19:135 to 147 (see **8.2**); and

(d) if the entity accounts for the contribution payable for the period rather than an allocation of the net defined benefit cost, as is permitted in some circumstances under IAS 19:41 (see **5.2.2**), the information about the plan as a whole required by IAS 19:135 to 137, 139, 142 to 144, 147(a) and 147(b) (see **8.2**).

Entities are permitted to disclose the information about the plan as a whole required under IAS 19149:(c) and (d) by cross-reference to disclosures in another group entity's financial statements if the following conditions are met:

[IAS 19:150]

- that group entity's financial statements separately identify and disclose the information required about the plan; and

- that group entity's financial statements are available to users of the financial statements on the same terms as the financial statements of the entity and at the same time as, or earlier than, the financial statements of the entity.

5.3 State plans

5.3.1 State plans – general

IAS 19:44 explains that state plans "are established by legislation to cover all entities (or all entities in a particular category, for example, a specific industry) and are operated by national or local government or by another body (for example, an autonomous agency created specifically for this purpose) that is not subject to control or influence by the reporting entity".

The Standard notes that some plans established by an entity provide both compulsory benefits, as a substitute for benefits that would otherwise be covered under a state plan, and additional voluntary benefits. Such plans are not state plans. [IAS 19:44]

5.3.2 Requirement to distinguish between defined contribution and defined benefit state plans

State plans should be classified as defined contribution or defined benefit plans based on the criteria discussed in **section 4**. State plans are required to be accounted for in the same way as multi-employer plans (see **5.1**). [IAS 19:43]

Most commonly, state plans are defined contribution plans. For these plans, a participating employer's liability is restricted to contributions payable in a period, with the plan being funded on a pay-as-you-go basis. If the entity ceases to employ members of the state plan, it is no longer liable for further payments even if the benefits of employees for prior periods under the state plan require additional funding. In rare cases, a state plan may be considered a defined benefit plan. [IAS 19:45]

6 Defined contribution plans

6.1 Recognition and measurement – defined contribution plans

6.1.1 Recognition and measurement for a defined contribution plan – general

The definition of a defined contribution plan is set out at **4.3**.

Accounting for defined contribution plans is straightforward because the reporting entity's obligation for each period is determined by the amounts to be contributed for that period. Consequently, no actuarial assumptions are required to measure the obligation or the expense and there is no possibility of any actuarial gain or loss. [IAS 19:50]

An entity should recognise the contribution payable to a defined contribution plan in exchange for services rendered by an employee in an accounting period:

[IAS 19:51]

- in the statement of financial position, as:

  - a liability (accrued expense), after deducting any contribution already paid, to the extent that not all of the contributions due for service before the end of the reporting period have been paid at that date; or

  - an asset (prepaid expense), if the amount already paid exceeds the contributions due for service before the end of the reporting period, to the extent that the prepayment is recoverable (e.g. by means of a reduction in future payments or a cash refund); and

- as an expense, unless another Standard requires or permits inclusion of the contribution in the cost of an asset.

6.1.2 Contributions to a defined contribution plan not expected to be settled within 12 months

If outstanding contributions to a defined contribution plan are not expected to be settled wholly within 12 months after the end of the annual reporting period in which the employees render the related service, they should be discounted using the discount rate specified by IAS 19 for post-employment benefit obligations (see **7.3.6**). [IAS 19:52] All other defined contribution liabilities are measured on an undiscounted basis. [IAS 19:50]

6.1.3   Defined contribution plans with vesting conditions

Under the terms of some defined contribution post-employment benefit plans, employees' entitlements to benefits are subject to their remaining in the sponsoring entity's employment for a minimum period (a vesting condition). Contributions made in respect of an employee who subsequently fails to meet this requirement revert to the entity upon the employee leaving service.

In these circumstances, the entity should recognise its contributions to the plan as an expense in the period for which they are paid because IAS 19:51 (see **6.1.1**) requires that contributions to a defined contribution scheme should be recognised as an expense over the period of service that results in an obligation to pay those contributions to the separate entity that runs the plan, rather than over the period of service that entitles an employee to receive benefits (i.e. the vesting period).

Refunds due to the entity from the defined contribution plan should be recognised as an asset and as income when the entity becomes entitled to the refund (i.e. when the employee leaves service before meeting the vesting condition).

This conclusion, which is illustrated in **example 6.1.3**, is consistent with the view expressed previously by the IFRS Interpretations Committee (see the July 2011 edition of *IFRIC Update*).

Example 6.1.3

Defined contribution plans with vesting conditions

Entity E sponsors a defined contribution post-employment benefit plan for its 10 employees. It pays contributions of CU100 per year (CU10 per employee) to the plan.

Under the terms of the plan, employees only become entitled to post-employment benefits if they remain in Entity E's employment for a minimum of three years. Contributions made in respect of an employee who leaves before the three-year period is completed are refunded to Entity E.

Two employees leave at the start of Year 3, so that Entity E becomes entitled to a refund of CU40 (2 employees × CU10 × 2 years) in Year 3.

Entity E is obliged to pay contributions of CU10 per employee per year. It recognises an expense that is based on this obligation, without reference to the period over which the employees become entitled to the benefits. Therefore, Entity E recognises an expense in respect of contributions payable of CU100 in each of Years 1 and 2 and CU80 in Year 3. The refund of CU40 is recognised as an asset and as income in Year 3 – resulting in a net expense of CU40 in Year 3.

6.2 Disclosure – defined contribution plans

The amount recognised as an expense for defined contribution plans should be disclosed. [IAS 19:53]

Additional disclosures regarding contributions to defined contribution plans for key management personnel may be required in accordance with IAS 24 *Related Party Disclosures* (see **section 5.2** of **chapter A23**). [IAS 19:54]

7 Defined benefit plans

7.1 Defined benefit plans – general

The definition of a defined benefit plan is set out at **4.3**.

Defined benefit plans may be unfunded, or they may be wholly or partly funded by contributions by an entity, and sometimes its employees, into an entity, or fund, that is legally separate from the reporting entity and from which the employee benefits are paid. The payment of funded benefits when they fall due depends not only on the financial position and the investment performance of the fund but also on an entity's ability, and willingness, to make good any shortfall in the fund's assets. Therefore, the entity is, in substance, underwriting the actuarial and investment risks associated with the plan. Consequently, the expense recognised for a defined benefit plan is not necessarily the amount of the contribution due for the period. [IAS 19:56]

7.2 Recognition and measurement – defined benefit plans

7.2.1 Recognition and measurement for defined benefit plans – general

Accounting for defined benefit plans is much more complex than accounting for defined contribution plans. It requires the use of actuarial techniques and assumptions to measure the obligation and expense, with the obligation being measured on a discounted basis. The possibility of actuarial gains and losses also arises because assumptions used very often differ from actual outcomes. [IAS 19:55]

7.2.2 Requirement to account for both legal and constructive obligations in relation to defined benefit plans

An entity should account for both its legal and its constructive obligations in relation to a defined benefit plan. A constructive obligation arises from an entity's informal practices when the entity has no realistic alternative but to pay employee benefits (e.g. when a change in the entity's informal practices would cause unacceptable damage to its relationship with employees). [IAS 19:61] An example cited by IAS 19 is when the formal terms of a plan permit the employer to terminate its obligations under the plan. In practice, it would generally be very difficult for an employer to take such a course of action (without payment) so that, unless there is evidence to the contrary, it should be assumed that the employer will continue to provide benefits over the remaining working lives of employees. [IAS 19:62]

Example 7.2.2

Employer with history of improving pension benefits retrospectively

Company O is a manufacturer with a work force whose compensation and other employee benefits are governed by a union contract established through a collective bargaining process. Company O has a history of granting improvements in pension benefits, to both retirees and active employees, during the collective bargaining process. The improvements have sometimes taken the form of fixed monetary increases in monthly benefits, lump sum payments made outside the pension plans, or formula-based cost-of-living adjustment (COLA) increases in the monthly benefit. There is no evidence of a present commitment to increase plan benefits other than Company O's history of retrospective plan amendments.

Careful judgement should be exercised in assessing whether a constructive obligation has arisen.

In the circumstances described, the employer's practice is to provide improvements only during the collective bargaining process, not during any informal process. The increases in benefits historically have been awarded in several different forms. Therefore, it does not appear that the employer has set a pattern of increases in pension benefits that can be projected reliably to give rise to a constructive obligation. However, if the practice established by an employer were that of a consistent pension-benefit enhancement as part of union negotiations that clearly established a pattern (always a COLA increase, or always fixed monetary increases), it could be concluded that a constructive obligation exists and that those additional benefits should be included in the measurement of the projected benefit obligation.

7.2.3 Four-step approach to accounting for defined benefit plans

Accounting for defined benefit plans involves four steps, as summarised in the following table. When an entity has more than one defined benefit plan, these steps should be followed separately for each material plan. [IAS 19:57]

Step 1	Determining the surplus or deficit	This involves: [IAS 19:57(a)] • using an actuarial technique (the projected unit credit method) to make a reliable estimate of the ultimate cost to the entity of the benefit that employees have earned in return for their service in the current and prior periods (see **7.3.2** to **7.3.5**); • discounting that benefit using an appropriate discount rate in order to determine the present value of the defined benefit obligation and the current service cost (see **7.3.6**); and • deducting the fair value of any plan assets (see **7.3.7**) from the present value of the defined benefit obligation.
Step 2	Determining the amount of the net defined benefit liability (asset)	The amount of the net defined benefit liability (asset) is the amount of the deficit or surplus determined at Step 1 adjusted for any effect of limiting a net defined benefit asset to the asset ceiling (see **section 7.4**).
Step 3	Determining amounts to be recognised in profit or loss	The amounts to be recognised in profit or loss are: • current service cost (see **7.5.2**); • any past service cost and gain or loss on settlement (see **section 7.5.3**); and • net interest on the net defined benefit liability (asset) (see **7.5.4**).
Step 4	Determining the remeasurements of the net defined benefit liability (asset) to be recognised in other comprehensive income	The remeasurements of the net defined benefit liability (asset) comprise (see **7.6**): • actuarial gains and losses; • return on plan assets, excluding amounts included in net interest on the net defined benefit liability (asset); and • any change in the effect of the asset ceiling, excluding amounts included in net interest on the net defined benefit liability (asset).

7.2.4 *Actuarial valuations*

7.2.4.1   *Frequency of valuations*

IAS 19 does not specify the frequency of valuations, either for the measurement of plan assets or the determination of the present value of the defined benefit obligation. The Standard requires that an entity should determine the net defined benefit liability (asset) (see **section 7.3**) for a defined benefit plan with sufficient regularity that the amounts recognised in the financial statements do not differ materially from the amounts that would be determined at the end of the reporting period. [IAS 19:58]

> Although many entities carry out actuarial valuations annually, at the end of the reporting period, some carry out full actuarial valuations less frequently (e.g. every three years) and update approximately to the end of each annual reporting period. Relevant factors to consider in determining the frequency of actuarial valuations may include the volatility of the economic environment and the impact of the defined benefit obligation and costs on the financial statements.
>
> Although local legislation may not require a full plan valuation every year, in order to meet the requirement of IAS 19:58, it may be necessary for some aspects of the valuation to be revisited at the end of each reporting period (e.g. the fair value of plan assets and financial assumptions such as the discount rate and the rate of salary increase). Demographic assumptions, such as mortality rates and rate of employee turnover, may not require revision annually.

7.2.4.2 Involvement of an actuary

IAS 19 encourages, but does not require, an entity to involve a qualified actuary in the measurement of all material post-employment benefit obligations. [IAS 19:59]

> Although IAS 19 does not require the involvement of a qualified actuary, in practice it will usually be difficult to value material defined benefit obligations without actuarial involvement.

7.2.4.3 Timing of valuations

IAS 19 does not require that an actuarial valuation be carried out at the reporting date. It acknowledges that, for practical reasons, an entity may request a qualified actuary to carry out a detailed valuation of the obligation before the end of the reporting period. In such circumstances, the results of that valuation are required to be updated for any material transactions and other material changes in circumstances (including changes in market prices and interest rates) up to the end of the reporting period. [IAS 19:59]

7.2.4.4 Requirements for valuations at interim reporting dates

IAS 19 does not set out any requirements as to what is expected in terms of an actuarial valuation for an interim reporting period under IAS 34 *Interim Financial Reporting*. IAS 34:B9 states that "[p]ension cost for an interim period is calculated on a year-to-date basis by using the actuarially determined pension cost rate at the end of the prior financial year, adjusted for significant market fluctuations since that time and for significant curtailments, settlements, or other significant one-time events". The application of this requirement is discussed at **5.6.7** in **chapter A32**.

7.3 Step 1 – determining the deficit or surplus

7.3.1 Calculation of the deficit or surplus

The deficit or surplus is calculated as the difference between:

[IAS 19:8]

- the present value of the defined benefit obligation (see **7.3.2**); and
- the fair value of plan assets (if any) (see **7.3.7**).

Therefore, the first step involves measuring separately the defined benefit obligation and the plan assets, if any.

7.3.2 Present value of the defined benefit obligation

The present value of a defined benefit obligation is the present value, without deducting any plan assets, of expected future payments required to settle the obligation resulting from employee service in the current and prior periods. [IAS 19:8]

The final cost of a defined benefit plan is influenced by many variables (e.g. final salaries, employee turnover and mortality, employee contributions and medical cost trends). [IAS 19:66] The use of actuarial techniques to value an obligation and allocate it to accounting periods allows an entity to measure an obligation with sufficient reliability to justify recognition of a liability. The whole of the obligation is discounted, even if part of it is expected to be settled before 12 months after the reporting period. [IAS 19:69]

Several steps are required to measure the present value of a defined benefit obligation and the associated current service cost. These steps, which are considered in the following sections, are:

[IAS 19:66]

- to apply an actuarial valuation method (see **7.3.3**);
- to attribute benefit to the employees' periods of service (see **7.3.4**); and
- to make actuarial assumptions (see **7.3.5**).

The determination of an appropriate discount rate to arrive at the present value is considered at **7.3.6**.

7.3.3 Actuarial valuation method

Under IAS 19, an entity is required to use the projected unit credit method to determine the present value of its defined benefit obligation, the related current service cost and, when applicable, past service cost. [IAS 19:67]

The projected unit credit method treats each period of service as giving rise to an additional unit of benefit entitlement and measures each unit separately to build up the final obligation. It requires an entity to attribute benefit to the current period (in order to determine current service cost) and the current and prior periods (in order to determine the present value of defined benefit obligations). An entity should attribute benefit to periods in which the obligation to provide post-employment benefits arises. That obligation arises as employees render services in return for post-employment benefits that the entity expects to pay in future reporting periods. Actuarial techniques allow an entity to measure that obligation with sufficient reliability to justify recognition of a liability. [IAS 19:68 & 71]

No other valuation method is permitted under IAS 19.

The projected unit credit method referred to by IAS 19 is sometimes also called the 'accrued benefit method pro-rated on service' or the 'benefit/ years of service' method. [IAS 19:68]

The measurement of the liability should reflect the expected date of employees leaving service and should be discounted to a present value using the projected unit credit method (as illustrated in the examples below). It is not acceptable to measure the liability for vested benefits at an undiscounted amount (i.e. at the amount that would be payable if all employees left the entity at the end of the reporting period).

This conclusion has been confirmed by the IFRIC (now the IFRS Interpretations Committee) (see *IFRIC Update*, April 2002).

Example 7.3.3, which is reproduced from the Standard, provides a simple illustration of the application of the projected unit credit method.

Example 7.3.3

Projected Unit Credit Method

[Example illustrating IAS 19:68]

A lump sum benefit is payable on termination of service and equal to 1 per cent of final salary for each year of service. The salary in year 1 is CU10,000 and is assumed to increase at 7 per cent (compound) each year. The discount rate used is 10 per cent per year. The following table shows how the obligation builds up for an employee who is expected to leave at the end of year 5, assuming that there are no changes in actuarial assumptions. For simplicity, this example ignores the additional adjustment needed to reflect the probability that the employee may leave the entity at an earlier or later date.

Year	1	2	3	4	5
	CU	CU	CU	CU	CU
Benefit attributed to					
– *prior years*	0	131	262	393	524
– *current year (1% of final salary)*	131	131	131	131	131
– *current and prior years*	131	262	393	524	655
Opening obligation	0	89	196	324	476
Interest at 10%	0	9	20	33	48
Current service cost	89	98	108	119	131
Closing obligation	89	196	324	476	655

Note:

1. *The opening obligation is the present value of benefit attributed to prior years.*
2. *The current service cost is the present value of benefit attributed to the current year.*
3. *The closing obligation is the present value of benefit attributed to current and prior years.*

7.3.4 Attributing benefit to periods of service

7.3.4.1 Attributing benefit to periods of service – general

When determining the present value of the defined benefit obligation, current service cost and (when applicable) past service cost, an entity should attribute benefit to periods of service using the plan's benefit formula. [IAS 19:70]

An exception to the foregoing is made when an employee's service in later years will lead to a materially higher level of benefit than in earlier years, as discussed in **7.3.4.3**. [IAS 19:70]

The obligation increases until the date when further service by the employee will lead to no material amount of further benefits. Therefore, all benefit is attributed to periods ending on or before that date. [IAS 19:73]

The following examples are included in IAS 19 to illustrate the attribution of benefit to periods of service.

Example 7.3.4.1

Attributing benefit to periods of service (1)

[Examples illustrating IAS 19:71]

1. A defined benefit plan provides a lump sum benefit of CU100 payable on retirement for each year of service.

> *A benefit of CU100 is attributed to each year. The current service cost is the present value of CU100. The present value of the defined benefit obligation is the present value of CU100, multiplied by the number of years of service up to the end of the reporting period.*
>
> *If the benefit is payable immediately when the employee leaves the entity, the current service cost and the present value of the defined benefit obligation reflect the date at which the employee is expected to leave. Thus, because of the effect of discounting, they are less than the amounts that would be determined if the employee left at the end of the reporting period.*
>
> 2. A plan provides a monthly pension of 0.2 per cent of final salary for each year of service. The pension is payable from the age of 65.
>
> *Benefit equal to the present value, at the expected retirement date, of a monthly pension of 0.2 per cent of the estimated final salary payable from the expected retirement date until the expected date of death is attributed to each year of service. The current service cost is the present value of that benefit. The present value of the defined benefit obligation is the present value of monthly pension payments of 0.2 per cent of final salary, multiplied by the number of years of service up to the end of the reporting period. The current service cost and the present value of the defined benefit obligation are discounted because pension payments begin at the age of 65.*

7.3.4.2   Unvested benefits and benefits payable only if a specified event occurs

Employee service gives rise to an obligation under a defined benefit plan even if the benefits are not vested (e.g. if they are conditional on future employment). Employee service before the vesting date gives rise to a constructive obligation because, at the end of each successive reporting period, the amount of future service that an employee will have to render before becoming entitled to the benefit is reduced. The probability that some employees may not ultimately satisfy any vesting conditions is reflected in the measurement of the defined benefit obligation. [IAS 19:72]

Similarly, although some post-employment benefits (e.g. post-employment medical benefits) become payable only if a specified event occurs when an employee is no longer employed, an obligation is created when the employee renders service that will provide entitlement to the benefit if the specified event occurs. The probability that the specified event will occur affects the measurement of the obligation, but does not determine whether the obligation exists. [IAS 19:72]

The following examples, which are reproduced from the Standard, illustrate the application of IAS 19:72.

Example 7.3.4.2

Attributing benefit to periods of service (2)

[Examples illustrating IAS 19:72]

1. A plan pays a benefit of CU100 for each year of service. The benefits vest after ten years of service.

    A benefit of CU100 is attributed to each year. In each of the first ten years, the current service cost and the present value of the obligation reflect the probability that the employee may not complete ten years of service.

2. A plan pays a benefit of CU100 for each year of service, excluding service before the age of 25. The benefits vest immediately.

    No benefit is attributed to service before the age of 25 because service before that date does not lead to benefits (conditional or unconditional). A benefit of CU100 is attributed to each subsequent year.

7.3.4.3   Circumstances in which benefit is attributed on a straight-line basis

Benefit is generally attributed to individual accounting periods under the plan's benefit formula (see **7.3.4.1**). However, if an employee's service in later years will lead to a materially higher level of benefit than in earlier years, an entity attributes benefit on a straight-line basis from:

[IAS 19:70 & 73]

*   the date when service by the employee first leads to benefits under the plan (whether or not the benefits are conditional on further service), until

*   the date when further service by the employee will lead to no material amount of further benefits under the plan, other than from further salary increases.

That is because the employee's service throughout the entire period will ultimately lead to benefit at that higher level. [IAS 19:73]

Example 7.3.4.3

Attributing benefit to periods of service (3)

[Examples illustrating IAS 19:73]

1. A plan pays a lump sum benefit of CU1,000 that vests after ten years of service. The plan provides no further benefit for subsequent service.

    A benefit of CU100 (CU1,000 divided by ten) is attributed to each of the first ten years.

    The current service cost in each of the first ten years reflects the probability that the employee may not complete ten years of service. No benefit is attributed to subsequent years.

2. A plan pays a lump sum retirement benefit of CU2,000 to all employees who are still employed at the age of 55 after twenty years of service, or who are still employed at the age of 65, regardless of their length of service.

   For employees who join before the age of 35, service first leads to benefits under the plan at the age of 35 (an employee could leave at the age of 30 and return at the age of 33, with no effect on the amount or timing of benefits). Those benefits are conditional on further service. Also, service beyond the age of 55 will lead to no material amount of further benefits. For these employees, the entity attributes benefit of 100 (2,000 divided by 20) to each year from the age of 35 to the age of 55.

   For employees who join between the ages of 35 and 45, service beyond twenty years will lead to no material amount of further benefits. For these employees, the entity attributes benefit of CU100 (CU2,000 divided by twenty) to each of the first twenty years.

   For an employee who joins at the age of 55, service beyond ten years will lead to no material amount of further benefits. For this employee, the entity attributes benefit of CU200 (CU2,000 divided by ten) to each of the first ten years.

   For all employees, the current service cost and the present value of the obligation reflect the probability that the employee may not complete the necessary period of service.

3. A post-employment medical plan reimburses 40 per cent of an employee's post-employment medical costs if the employee leaves after more than ten and less than twenty years of service and 50 per cent of those costs if the employee leaves after twenty or more years of service.

   Under the plan's benefit formula, the entity attributes 4 per cent of the present value of the expected medical costs (40 per cent divided by ten) to each of the first ten years and 1 per cent (10 per cent divided by ten) to each of the second ten years. The current service cost in each year reflects the probability that the employee may not complete the necessary period of service to earn part or all of the benefits. For employees expected to leave within ten years, no benefit is attributed.

4. A post-employment medical plan reimburses 10 per cent of an employee's post-employment medical costs if the employee leaves after more than ten and less than twenty years of service and 50 per cent of those costs if the employee leaves after twenty or more years of service.

   Service in later years will lead to a materially higher level of benefit than in earlier years. Therefore, for employees expected to leave after twenty or more years, the entity attributes benefit on a straight-line basis under [IAS 19:71]. Service beyond twenty years will lead to no material amount of further benefits. Therefore, the benefit attributed to each of the first twenty years is 2.5 per cent of the present value of the expected medical costs (50 per cent divided by twenty).

   For employees expected to leave between ten and twenty years, the benefit attributed to each of the first ten years is 1 per cent of the present value of the expected medical costs. For these employees, no benefit is attributed to service between the end of the tenth year and the estimated date of leaving.

   For employees expected to leave within ten years, no benefit is attributed.

7.3.4.4   Amount of benefit is a constant proportion of final salary

When the amount of a benefit is a constant proportion of final salary for each year of service, future salary increases will affect the amount required to settle the obligation that exists for service before the end of the reporting period, but do not create an additional obligation. Therefore:

[IAS 19:74]

- for the purpose of IAS 19:70 (see **7.3.4.3**), salary increases do not lead to further benefits, even though the amount of the benefits is dependent on final salary; and

- the amount of benefit attributed to each period is a constant proportion of the salary to which the benefit is linked.

Example 7.3.4.4

Attributing benefit to periods of service (4)

[Example illustrating IAS 19:74]

Employees are entitled to a benefit of 3 per cent of final salary for each year of service before the age of 55.

Benefit of 3 per cent of estimated final salary is attributed to each year up to the age of 55. This is the date when further service by the employee will lead to no material amount of further benefits under the plan. No benefit is attributed to service after that age.

By completing the allocation of current service cost at the time that no further benefit accrues, this cost is allocated over a period that is shorter than the period over which an employee is expected to provide service to the employer. The reason for this, as explained in IAS 19:70, is that the subsequent period of employment yields no material amount of further benefits.

7.3.4.5   Death-in-service benefits

IAS 19 does not specifically address the question of accounting for death-in-service benefits. See **section 9.4** for a discussion of the considerations regarding the appropriate accounting treatment for such benefits.

7.3.4.6   Career Average Revalued Earnings plans

In some jurisdictions, entities may offer to employees 'Career Average Revalued Earnings' (CARE) pension plans, also referred to as 'Pension Builder Plans'. Such plans generally provide a defined benefit pension that is determined by the employee's years of service and the average salary earned over the period of service. The plan formula is typically stated as follows:

"A member shall accrue for each year of service: accrual rate x current (or average) salary*"

Such plans should be measured using the projected unit credit method, taking into account estimated future salary increases as required by IAS 19:87(b) and IAS 19:90 (see **7.3.5.4**). IAS 19:70 states, in part, that:

"[i]n determining the present value of its defined benefit obligations ... an entity shall attribute benefit to periods of service under the plan's benefit formula. However, if an employee's service in later years will lead to a materially higher level of benefit than in earlier years, an entity shall attribute benefit on a straight-line basis ...."

The CARE pension plan formula described above does attribute a higher level of benefit to later years and, therefore, an entity should assess whether this is likely to be materially higher, in which case the benefits should be attributed on a straight-line basis.

* To maintain a pension plan's purchasing power, the salary in each year is typically revalued (either to give an adjusted current salary or to determine the adjusted average salary) in line with a specified index (e.g. price inflation) between the date of accrual and the date of retirement. The index used to revalue salaries earned in past years is typically lower than the wage increase over the period of service.

7.3.5 Actuarial assumptions

7.3.5.1 Actuarial assumptions – general

The actuarial assumptions used for the purposes of measuring a defined benefit obligation should be unbiased and mutually compatible. [IAS 19:75] Actuarial assumptions are an entity's best estimates of the variables that will determine the ultimate cost of providing post-employment benefits. [IAS 19:76] They should be neither imprudent nor excessively conservative, and should reflect the economic relationships between factors such as inflation, rates of salary increase and discount rates. For example, all assumptions that depend on a particular inflation level (such as assumptions about interest rates and salary and benefit increases) in any given future period should assume the same inflation level in that period. [IAS 19:77 & 78]

IAS 19:76 explains that actuarial assumptions comprise:

(a) demographic assumptions about the future characteristics of current and former employees (and their dependants) who are eligible for benefits. Demographic assumptions deal with matters such as:

(i) mortality (see **7.3.5.2**);

(ii) rates of employee turnover, disability and early retirement;

    (iii) the proportion of plan members with dependants who will be eligible for benefits;

    (iv) the proportion of plan members who will select each form of payment option under the plan terms; and

    (v) claim rates under medical plans; and

(b) financial assumptions, dealing with items such as:

    (i) the discount rate (see **7.3.6**);

    (ii) benefit levels (excluding any cost of the benefits to be met by employees), and future salary (see **7.3.5.4**);

    (iii) in the case of medical benefits, future medical costs, including claim handling costs (i.e. the costs that will be incurred in processing and resolving claims, including legal and adjuster's fees) (see **7.3.5.5**); and

    (iv) taxes payable by the plan on contributions relating to service before the reporting date or on benefits resulting from that service (see **7.3.5.6**).

7.3.5.2 Mortality assumptions

Mortality assumptions should be determined by reference to the entity's best estimate of the mortality of plan members both during and after employment. In order to estimate the ultimate cost of the benefit, the entity should take into consideration expected changes in mortality (e.g. by modifying standard mortality tables with estimates of mortality improvements). [IAS 19:81 & 82]

IAS 19 therefore explicitly requires that the mortality assumptions used to determine the defined benefit obligation should be current estimates of the expected mortality rates of plan members, both during and after employment. In the IASB's view, current mortality tables might need to be adjusted for expected changes in mortality (such as expected mortality improvement) to provide the best estimate of the amount that reflects the ultimate cost of settling the defined benefit obligation. [IAS 19:BC142]

7.3.5.3 Financial assumptions

Financial assumptions should be based on market expectations, at the end of the reporting period, for the period over which the obligations will be settled. [IAS 19:80] Discount rates and other financial assumptions should not be inflation-adjusted (i.e. 'nominal' rates should be used) unless inflation-adjusted measures (i.e. 'real' rates) are more reliable (e.g. in a hyperinflationary economy, or when benefits are index-linked and there is a deep market in index-linked bonds of the same currency and term). [IAS 19:79]

7.3.5.4   Salaries and benefit levels

The measurement of the defined benefit obligation should reflect:

[IAS 19:87]

- the terms of the plan regarding benefit levels, and any constructive obligation that extends those terms, at the end of the reporting period;
- any estimated future salary increases that affect the benefits payable;
- the effect of any limit on the employer's share of the cost of the future benefits;
- contributions from employees or third parties that reduce the ultimate cost to the entity of those benefits; and
- estimated future changes in the level of any state benefits that affect the benefits payable under a defined benefit plan, if, and only if, either:
  - those changes were enacted before the end of the reporting period; or
  - historical data, or other reliable evidence, indicate that those state benefits will change in some predictable manner (e.g. in line with future changes in general price levels or general salary levels).

Accordingly, actuarial assumptions should reflect only those future benefit changes that are set out in the formal terms of the plan (and any constructive obligation that extends those terms) at the end of the reporting period. This would include the effect of any obligations arising from, for example:

[IAS 19:88]

- the entity's past history of increasing benefits (e.g. to mitigate the effects of inflation) when there is no indication that this practice will change in the future;
- the entity's obligation (either as required by the terms of the plan or under a constructive obligation that extends those terms) to use any surplus in the plan for the benefit of plan participants (see **7.5.3.2**); or
- benefits that vary in response to a performance target or other criteria. For example, the terms of the plan may state that it will pay reduced benefits or require additional contributions from employees if the plan assets are insufficient. The measurement of the obligation reflects the best estimate of the effect of the performance target or other criteria.

In contrast, actuarial assumptions should not reflect future benefit changes that are not set out in the formal terms of the plan (and for which there is no constructive obligation) at the end of the reporting period. Instead, when such changes to the terms of the plan are introduced, they should be reflected either (1) in past service cost (to the extent that they have a retrospective impact), or (2) in current service cost for the periods after the change (to the extent that they change benefits for service after the change). [IAS 19:89]

When estimating future salary increases, account should be taken of inflation, seniority, promotion and any other relevant factors (both internal and external), such as the scarcity or surplus of potential employees with the required skills. [IAS 19:90]

Some defined benefit plans limit the contributions that an entity is required to pay. The ultimate cost of the benefits takes account of the effect of a limit on contributions. The effect of a limit on the entity's contributions is determined over the shorter of (1) the estimated life of the entity, and (2) the estimated life of the plan. [IAS 19:91]

Some post-employment benefits are linked to variables such as the level of state-provided retirement benefits or medical care. In such cases, the measurement of the benefits should reflect the best estimate of such variables, based on past history and other reliable evidence. [IAS 19:95]

> Such changes should be reflected if they were enacted before the end of the reporting period, or if past history and other reliable evidence indicate that the state benefits will change in a predictable manner (e.g. in line with general salary or price levels).

7.3.5.5   *Post-employment medical benefits*

When measuring post-employment medical benefits, additional assumptions are required in order to account for estimated future changes in the cost of medical services. They include general inflation and specific changes in future medical costs, level and frequency of claims, technological advances, changes in the health status of participants in the plan, and changes in the utilisation and delivery of health care. In making these assumptions, reference should be made to historical data from the entity's own records and, when necessary, external data from other entities, insurers, medical providers and other sources. It is important that such assumptions are adjusted when the population providing the historical data differs from that for which the obligation arises. For example, the level and frequency of claims may be sensitive to age, sex and current health status of those benefiting under the plan. They should also be adjusted where there is reliable evidence that historical trends will not continue. [IAS 19:96 - 98]

7.3.5.6   *Taxes paid by a defined benefit plan*

> Taxes paid by a defined benefit plan should be treated differently based on the nature of the amounts to which they relate. Estimates of taxes payable by the plan on contributions relating to service before the reporting date and on benefits resulting from that service should be included in the measurement of the defined benefit obligation; all

other taxes paid by the plan are required to be deducted from the actual return on plan assets (see **7.6**). [IAS 19:BC121]

The inclusion of taxes payable in the list of actuarial assumptions at IAS 19:76 (see **7.3.5.1**) means that entities will need to develop actuarial assumptions about the timing and amount of taxes payable by the plan on contributions and benefits arising from services received before the reporting date.

7.3.5.7   Pension promises based on performance targets

Defined benefit plans may include pension promises that are based on achieving specific performance targets, such as additional pensionable earnings in the form of bonuses for achieving specified performance targets, arrangements relating to additional sponsor contributions, or additional years of deemed service. IAS 19:88(c) clearly indicates that the measurement of the obligation should reflect the best estimate of the effect of the performance target or other criteria.

7.3.5.8   Subsequent introduction of new state cost

When a state introduces, in an unpredictable manner, a new significant state cost (e.g. a tax related to contributions or benefits) associated with an existing employer's defined benefit obligation, and there is no impact on the ultimate benefit to be received by employees, the change should be treated as a change in actuarial assumptions (and not as a plan amendment).

IAS 19:57(a)(i), IAS 19:66 and IAS 19:76 clearly indicate that the entity should take into account all elements that will influence the ultimate cost of providing the defined benefit. In addition, IAS 19:76(b)(iv) states that actuarial assumptions include financial assumptions about "taxes payable by the plan on contributions relating to service before the reporting date or on benefits resulting from that service".

More generally, IAS 19:76 states that actuarial assumptions are an entity's best estimates of the variables that will determine the ultimate cost of providing post-employment benefits. When an entity does not explicitly state an assumption about such a variable, it is effectively making an assumption of zero value for that element. Any resulting differences from actual numbers are experience adjustments.

When there is a change in a post-employment benefit cost without a change in the benefits to be paid to employees, this change should be accounted for as a change in actuarial assumptions.

7.3.5.9 *Changes resulting from action by government*

The accounting for changes caused by government actions should be the same as the accounting for changes made by an employer.

In some circumstances, it may be difficult to determine whether the change affects actuarial assumptions (resulting in an actuarial gain or loss) or benefits payable (resulting in past service cost), and judgement will be required. **Example 7.3.5.9** illustrates the impact of a change in legislation affecting actuarial assumptions.

Example 7.3.5.9

Change in legislation affecting actuarial assumptions

Entity X operates a defined benefit pension plan. Under the plan rules, members can choose, on retirement, to receive an annual pension or to exchange part of the pension for a tax-free lump sum payment. The plan rules specify a commutation rate of 9:1, which means that a member can exchange one unit of annual pension for a tax-free lump sum payment of nine units. The lump sum amount is subject to a maximum set by the tax authority.

Changes in tax legislation increase the maximum lump sum amount that a member can receive tax-free.

In the past, members generally preferred to take the immediate lump sum payment rather than the ongoing pension, either from a liquidity perspective or because they underestimated the effective value of the pension.

The increased lump sum maximum might allow Entity X to mitigate the adverse effects of increasing longevity and falling interest rates. For example, when the applicable commutation rate no longer reflects a cost-neutral exchange rate of pension versus lump sum, an increase in the maximum lump sum amount (with the same commutation rate) will lead to a reduction in the defined benefit obligation on the basis of the assumption that members will choose the maximum lump sum payment on retirement.

Because of the change in tax legislation, Entity X amends the scheme rules to permit members to opt for the 'increased' lump sum amount on retirement. No other amendments are made to the scheme rules, and the commutation rate remains the same.

The legislative change alters how members can choose to receive the benefits, not the overall benefits that members are entitled to. The amount available to members on retirement, which can be taken as an annual pension or a lump sum, does not change. Because members are no better or worse off, amending the defined benefit plan solely to reflect this legislative change does not substantively alter the plan and, therefore, should not be treated as a plan amendment. IAS 19:76(a)(iv) states that actuarial assumptions include demographic assumptions about "the proportion of plan members who will select each form of payment option available under the plan terms".

The pension fund retains the long-term risk for any amounts taken as a pension (i.e. amounts the employee chooses not to receive as a lump sum). As part of the actuarial valuation, the employer assesses (1) how many employees are expected to take part of their overall benefits as a lump sum, and (2) how much each employee is expected to take. If the legislation changes to allow more to be taken as a lump sum, it is likely that the actuarial assumptions regarding the amounts taken as a lump sum will change, resulting in an actuarial gain or loss.

7.3.5.10   Contributions from employees or third parties

The requirements of IAS 19 for contributions from employees and third parties were amended by *Defined Benefit Plans: Employee Contributions (Amendments to IAS 19)* issued in November 2013. The November 2013 amendments, which are reflected in the requirements described in this section, simplified the treatment of non-discretionary contributions to defined benefit plans linked to service so that, following the November 2013 amendments:

- contributions from employees or third parties that are linked solely to the employee's service rendered in the same period in which they are paid may be treated as a reduction in the service cost and accounted for in that same period; and

- other contributions should be attributed to periods of service in the same way as gross benefits under the scheme.

The November 2013 amendments are effective for annual periods beginning on or after 1 July 2014, with earlier application permitted. The amendments are required to be applied retrospectively. If an entity applies the November 2013 amendments for an annual period beginning before 1 July 2014, it is required to disclose that fact. [IAS 19:175]

Some defined benefit plans require or permit employees or third parties to contribute to the cost of the plan. Contributions by employees or third parties may be set out in the terms of the plan, or arise from a constructive obligation, or be payable at the employee's or third party's discretion. [IAS 19:92]

When contributions by employees or third parties are discretionary, they reduce service cost when they are paid to the plan. [IAS 19:92]

When contributions from employees or third parties are set out in the formal terms of the plan (or arise from a constructive obligation that goes beyond those terms), the appropriate treatment depends on whether the contributions are linked to service. [IAS 19:93]

Contributions from employees or third parties that are not linked to service affect remeasurements of the net defined benefit liability (asset). An example of contributions that are not linked to service is when the contributions are required to reduce a deficit arising from losses on plan assets or from actuarial losses. [IAS 19:93]

Contributions from employees or third parties that are linked to service reduce the service cost, as follows:

[IAS 19:93]

(a) if the amount of the contribution is dependent on the number of years of service (e.g. if the employee is required to contribute a higher percentage of salary in later years of service), the contributions should be attributed to periods of service using the same attribution method required by IAS 19:70 for the gross benefit (i.e. generally using the plan's contribution formula, but on a straight-line basis in specified circumstances – see **7.3.4.3**); and

(b) if the amount of the contributions is independent of the number of years of service, the contributions may be recognised as a reduction of the service cost in the period in which the related service is rendered. Examples of contributions that are independent of the number of years of service include those that are a fixed percentage of the employee's salary, a fixed amount throughout the service period or dependent on the employee's age.

The treatment in IAS 19:93(b) is a practical expedient to simplify the attribution requirements for some simple types of contributory plans. Although the IASB believes that all contributions from employees or third parties that are required by the terms of a defined benefit plan should form part of the post-employment benefit rather than the short-term employee benefit, they acknowledge that in some circumstances the costs of applying complex attribution requirements exceed the benefits. [IAS 19:BC150C]

The requirements outlined in IAS 19:93 are summarised in the following diagram, which is reproduced from the Standard.

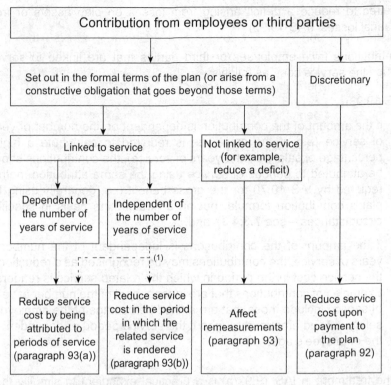

(1) This dotted arrow means that an entity is permitted to choose either accounting

An entity is also required to consider whether third party contributions reduce the cost of the benefits to the entity or are in fact a reimbursement right as described in IAS 19:116 (see **7.3.7.6**). [IAS 19:92]

For contributions from employees or third parties that are attributed to periods of service in accordance with IAS 19:93(a) (see above), changes in the contributions result in:

[IAS 19:94]

- current and past service cost (if those changes are not set out in the formal terms of a plan and do not arise from a constructive obligation); and

- actuarial gains and losses (if those changes are set out in the formal terms of a plan or arise from a constructive obligation).

7.3.5.11   Pension benefits grossed-up to compensate for tax payable by employee

Some entities meet their defined benefit obligation by purchasing non-participating annuity contracts that are distributed to the employees. These contracts do not require any contribution ('participation') from employees. The receipt of the non-participating annuity contracts by the employee may trigger a taxable event for the employee upon distribution. Some entities compensate their employees so that the after-tax benefit to the employee is the same as if the annuity contracts were not taxable, although this is commonly not a formal feature of the retirement benefit plan.

If the tax compensation payments are a formal feature of the retirement benefit plan, or the employer has established a pattern of making such payments such that a constructive obligation has arisen (see IAS 19:61), the payments should be considered part of the benefits payable under the plan and should be included in the measurement of the defined benefit obligation.

In contrast, if the tax compensation payments are made as a 'one-off' event (e.g. if the tax is a one-off tax imposed by the tax authority for one or two years only, or the employer voluntarily makes the payments for one or two years only without creating any obligation to continue to do so), the tax compensation payments should be regarded as additional compensation expense and recognised in the current period.

7.3.5.12 Social security contributions by employer

Example 7.3.5.12

Social security contributions by employer

An entity operates a defined benefit plan with the following features.

- The benefit to be paid out at the age of 60 amounts to CU1,000.
- The entity, at the time the benefit is paid, will pay employer social security tax of CU200.
- The entity is also required to withhold the employee's social security tax of CU150.
- The net benefit received by the employee is CU850 (CU1,000 □ CU150).
- Cash paid out by the entity is CU1,200 (CU1,000 + CU200).
- The amount of social security tax contributed by the employer is calculated as a percentage of the employee benefits granted.

IAS 19:76(b)(iv) states that actuarial assumptions include financial assumptions about "taxes payable by the plan on contributions relating to service before the reporting date or on benefits resulting from that service". Employer social security tax levied on the benefits paid out to employees is a directly related inherent cost of receiving services from employees and, consequently, is an example of a tax payable by the plan on benefits resulting from those services.

In the circumstances described, the social security tax contributed by the employer represents part of a defined benefit of CU1,200 under which the employee will have to pay 100 per cent of the employer and employee social security contributions that would reduce the net pay-out to CU850. Therefore, by assuming a percentage of that contribution, either voluntarily or by legislation,

> the entity should recognise the cost of the social security payment in the same manner as the underlying benefit, by including its cost in the calculation of the present value of the defined benefit obligation.

7.3.5.13   Administration costs

Costs relating to the management of the plan assets should be deducted in determining the return on plan assets (see **7.6**). Other administration costs should be recognised in profit or loss when the administration services are provided. [IAS 19:BC125]

Although administration costs other than those deducted in determining the return on plan assets should theoretically be taken into account in measuring the defined benefit obligation, the IASB has opted for immediate recognition in profit or loss as a practical expedient to avoid the need to attribute costs between current and past service cost and future service. [IAS 19:BC127]

The IASB noted that, in some cases, a total fee is charged for both managing plan assets and other administration services. However, the Board did not consider the cost of managing plan assets would be excessively costly or difficult to estimate under these circumstances. An entity could estimate such costs by estimating the administration costs if there were no plan assets, or by observing the prices for such services in the market. [IAS 19:BC125 - BC128]

7.3.6   Determination of an appropriate discount rate

7.3.6.1   Determination of an appropriate discount rate – general

The topic of the determination of an appropriate discount rate for the purpose of measuring defined benefit obligations has been the subject of much debate in recent years. It is currently being considered as part of the IASB's wider research project on discount rates (see **11.2**).

The discount rate is one of the most important assumptions utilised in measuring defined benefit obligations. The rate used should reflect the time value of money, but not credit risk specific to an entity, nor the risk that future experience may differ from assumptions, nor the actuarial or investment risk. [IAS 19:84]

IAS 19 specifies that:

[IAS 19:83]

- the rate used to discount post-employment benefit obligations (both funded and unfunded) should be determined by reference to market yields at the end of the reporting period on high quality corporate bonds;

- for currencies for which there is no deep market in such high quality corporate bonds, the market yields (at the end of the reporting period) on government bonds denominated in that currency should be used; and

- the currency and term of the corporate bonds or government bonds should be consistent with the currency and estimated term of the post-employment benefit obligations.

IAS 19:83 was amended in September 2014 by *Annual Improvements to IFRSs: 2012–2014 Cycle* to clarify that the high quality bonds used to estimate the discount rate for post-employment benefit obligations should be denominated in the same currency as the benefits to be paid. Consequently, the depth of the market for high quality corporate bonds is required to be assessed at the currency level.

These amendments are particularly designed to provide clarification in the context of a regional market sharing the same currency (e.g. the Eurozone). Prior to amendment, the wording of IAS 19:83 could have been read to imply that the basket of high quality corporate bonds used for the purpose of estimating an appropriate discount rate should be determined at a country level, and not at a currency level.

The IASB was also asked to clarify whether these amendments prohibit an entity that operates in a country/regional market in which there is a deep market for high quality corporate bonds from using only the high quality corporate bonds issued in its own country/regional market. The Board noted that the amendments only clarify that the depth of the market for high quality corporate bonds should be assessed at a currency level and not a country/regional market level; the Standard does not require that the basket of high quality corporate bonds used to determine the discount rate for post-employment obligations must include all the high quality corporate bonds issued in a currency. [IAS 19:BC150E]

The September 2014 amendments are effective for annual periods beginning on or after 1 January 2016, with earlier application permitted. If an entity applies the September 2014 amendments for a period beginning before 1 January 2016, it is required to disclose that fact. [IAS19:176]

The effect of the September 2014 amendments is required to be recognised from the beginning of the earliest comparative period presented in the first financial statements in which the amendments are applied. Any initial adjustment arising from the application of the amendments is required to be recognised in retained earnings at the beginning of that period. [IAS 19:177]

IAS 19 does not provide any further guidance on the meaning of the term 'high quality corporate bonds'. In practice, the term is generally taken to refer to corporate bonds with one of the two highest ratings from a recognised rating agency in jurisdictions in which such an agency exists.

7.3.6.2   Term of bonds and obligations

The requirement for the term of the bonds to be consistent with the term of the obligations means that the discount rate should reflect the estimated timing of the benefit payments. The Standard notes that, in practice, this may be achieved by applying a single weighted average discount rate that reflects the estimated timing and amount of benefit payments and the currency in which the benefits are to be paid. [IAS 19:85]

If there is no deep market for bonds of a sufficiently long maturity date to match that of all of the obligation payments, the entity may extrapolate current market rates for a shorter period along the yield curve. [IAS 19:86]

7.3.7   Plan assets

7.3.7.1   Components of plan assets

Plan assets comprise:

[IAS 19:8]

- assets held by a long-term employee benefit fund (see **7.3.7.3**); and

- qualifying insurance policies (see **7.3.7.4**).

Plan assets are reduced by any liabilities of the fund that do not relate to employee benefits (e.g. trade and other payables, and liabilities resulting from derivative financial instruments). [IAS 19:114]

7.3.7.2   Items excluded from plan assets

Plan assets exclude:

[IAS 19:114]

- unpaid contributions due from the reporting entity to the fund; and

- any non-transferable financial instruments issued by the entity and held by the fund.

7.3.7.3   Assets held by a long-term employee benefit fund

These are assets (other than non-transferable financial instruments issued by the reporting entity) that:

[IAS 19:8]

- are held by an entity (a fund) that is legally separate from the reporting entity and exists solely to pay or fund employee benefits; and

- are available to be used only to pay or fund employee benefits, are not available to the reporting entity's own creditors (even in bankruptcy) and cannot be returned to the reporting entity, unless either:

  - the remaining assets of the fund are sufficient to meet all of the related employee benefit obligations of the plan or the reporting entity; or

  - the assets are returned to the reporting entity to reimburse it for employee benefits already paid.

IAS 19 does not define the term 'non-transferable financial instruments'. In practice, financial instruments excluded under IAS 19:114 are financial instruments that are issued by the reporting entity and held by a fund that cannot be transferred, sold, pledged or otherwise assigned by the fund to another party without the reporting entity's permission (i.e. the only possibility open to the fund is to hold the financial instrument to maturity).

Any funding arrangements that do not meet the criteria in IAS 19:8 should not be recognised as plan assets. The entity should consider whether the assets intended to fund its pension obligations should instead be recognised as its own assets in its statement of financial position, either because they are held directly by the entity or by a structured entity that is consolidated under IFRS 10 *Consolidated Financial Statements*.

7.3.7.4 Qualifying insurance policies

A qualifying insurance policy is an insurance policy issued by an insurer that is not a related party of the reporting entity (as defined in IAS 24 *Related Party Disclosures*), if the proceeds of the policy:

[IAS 19:8]

- can be used only to pay or fund employee benefits under a defined benefit plan; and

- are not available to the reporting entity's own creditors (even in bankruptcy) and cannot be paid to the reporting entity, unless either:

  - the proceeds represent surplus assets that are not needed for the policy to meet all of the related employee benefit obligations; or

  - the proceeds are returned to the reporting entity to reimburse it for employee benefits already paid.

Example 7.3.7.4

Insurance policy issued by a related party

Company A offers its employees defined pension benefits through a pension fund. The pension fund acquires an insurance policy from Company A's subsidiary, Company B.

The insurance policy should be included as part of plan assets in Company A's financial statements (consolidated or separate) only if it meets the definition of either:

- an asset held by a long-term employee benefit fund; or
- a qualifying insurance policy.

The policy does not meet the definition of a qualifying insurance policy (see above) because it is issued by a related party. Therefore, to qualify as a plan asset, the insurance policy must meet the definition of an asset held by a long-term employee benefit fund. That definition sets out certain criteria that must be met (see **7.3.7.3**), but it automatically excludes non-transferable financial instruments issued by the reporting entity.

Consequently, in Company A's consolidated financial statements, the insurance policy cannot qualify as a plan asset unless it is a 'transferable financial instrument' (because the policy is issued by an entity within the consolidated group). An insurance policy issued by a group entity that covers the employees in a fund is often non-transferable and, consequently, will not meet the definition of a plan asset. For Company A's separate financial statements, the insurance policy is not considered to be issued by the 'reporting entity'. Accordingly, in those financial statements, the insurance policy will qualify as a plan asset if the criteria in **7.3.7.3** are met, *even if* the policy is a non-transferable financial instrument.

This conclusion has been confirmed by the IFRIC (now the IFRS Interpretations Committee) (see *IFRIC Update*, January 2008).

See **chapter A23** for guidance on whether an entity is a related party.

7.3.7.5 *Measurement of plan assets*

The fair value of any plan assets is deducted from the present value of the defined benefit obligation in determining the deficit or surplus. [IAS 19:113]

Fair value is defined as "the price that would be received to sell an asset or paid to transfer a liability in an orderly transaction between market participants at the measurement date. (See IFRS 13 *Fair Value Measurement*.)" [IAS 19:8]

When plan assets include qualifying insurance policies that exactly match the amount and timing of part or all of the benefits payable under the plan, the fair value of those insurance policies is deemed to be the present value of the related obligations (subject to any reduction required if the amounts receivable under the insurance policies are not recoverable in full). [IAS 19:115]

Example 7.3.7.5

Measurement of qualifying insurance policies that match the benefits payable

Company A sponsors a defined benefit pension plan. Its defined benefit obligation under IAS 19 is measured at CU100. Company A buys an insurance policy from an insurance company, Company B, which will cover the entire obligation and exactly match the payments due to the employees in accordance with the benefit formula in the plan (both in amount and timing). Company B is not a related party as defined in IAS 24 *Related Party Disclosures*. It is determined that the policy represents a 'qualifying' insurance policy as defined in IAS 19:8. Company B charges CU120 for the insurance policy.

What value should be attributed to the insurance policy for the purposes of measuring plan assets and, if that value is not cost, how should Company A account for the difference?

In accordance with IAS 19:115, qualifying insurance policies should be reflected in plan assets at their fair value, which is defined to be the present value of the related defined benefit obligation, i.e. CU100.

In respect of the difference between this amount and the cost of the policy (CU120), either of the following treatments would generally be acceptable:

(a)   the excess of CU20 is considered a cost of the obligation being effectively assumed by Company B and is immediately recognised as an expense in profit or loss; or

(b)   Company A initially recognises the insurance policy at CU120. The policy is then immediately remeasured in line with IAS 19:115. The difference of CU20 is treated as an actuarial loss and is recognised as part of remeasurements in OCI.

In some circumstances, it may be possible to determine that the difference (or a part of it) clearly relates to transaction costs. In those circumstances, the amount determined to represent transaction costs is immediately recognised as an expense in profit or loss. Any remaining difference is recognised using either treatment (a) or (b) above, based on the entity's accounting policy.

7.3.7.6   Reimbursements

When an entity is able to look to another party (e.g. an insurer) to pay part or all of the expenditure required to settle a defined benefit obligation, but the arrangement does not meet the definition of a qualifying insurance policy (see **7.3.7.4**), the reimbursement right is not a plan asset and, therefore, should not be presented as a deduction in determining the deficit or surplus. The appropriate accounting for such reimbursement rights is set out in IAS 19:116. [IAS 19:117 & 118]

When, and only when, it is virtually certain that another party will reimburse some or all of the expenditure required to settle a defined benefit obligation, an entity should recognise its right to reimbursement as a separate asset. The entity should measure the asset at fair value. The entity should disaggregate and recognise changes in the fair value of its right to reimbursement in the same way as for changes in the fair value of plan assets (see **7.5.4**). The components of defined benefit cost recognised in accordance with IAS 19:120 may be recognised net of amounts relating to changes in the carrying amount of the right to reimbursement. [IAS 19:116]

If the right to reimbursement arises under an insurance policy that exactly matches the amount and timing of part or all of the benefits payable under the plan, the fair value of the reimbursement is deemed to be the present value of the related obligations (subject to any reduction required if reimbursement is not recoverable in full). [IAS 19:119]

IAS 19:140(b) (see **8.2.3**) requires the entity to disclose a brief description of the link between the reimbursement right and the related obligation.

The guidance above on reimbursements does not apply to qualifying insurance policies – they are accounted for as plan assets, as discussed at **7.3.7.4**. [IAS 19:117]

7.3.7.8   Transfer of a non-cash asset to an employee benefit fund

---

Example 7.3.7.8

Transfer of a non-cash asset to an employee benefit fund

Entity A provides various defined benefit post-employment benefit plans to its employees. In lieu of a cash contribution, Entity A funds one of its plans by transferring to the employee benefit fund an investment property. After the transfer, the fund is entitled to all rewards and assumes all risks related to the property.

Entity A accounts for investment properties using the cost model in accordance with IAS 40 *Investment Property*. At the date of the transfer, the fair value of the investment property exceeds its depreciated cost in the financial statements of Entity A.

How should Entity A account for the contribution of the investment property to the pension fund?

The appropriate accounting treatment for the contribution depends on whether, following the transfer, the investment property meets the definition of a plan asset in IAS 19:8. In considering whether this is the case, it is important to bear in mind that the following are excluded from the definition of plan assets:

- assets that are available to the entity's creditors (whether on bankruptcy or otherwise); and
- non-transferable financial assets issued by the entity.

If the investment property meets the definition of a plan asset upon transfer, at that date Entity A should:

- derecognise the investment property;
- recognise an increase in plan assets corresponding to the fair value of the investment property transferred; and
- as required by IAS 40:69, recognise the gain on disposal of the investment property (representing the increase in value that occurred while the property was held by Entity A) in profit or loss.

Subsequent to the transfer, changes in the fair value of the investment property (excluding amounts included in net interest on the net defined benefit liability (asset)) would be recognised in other comprehensive income as remeasurements because they represent a return on plan assets.

If the investment property does not meet the definition of a plan asset upon transfer, Entity A should continue to account for it as an investment property using IAS 40's cost model, with any returns due to the plan (e.g. rental income) recognised as a contribution when paid.

7.3.7.9 Measurement of longevity swaps

An entity may enter into a number of arrangements to manage the risks arising from obligations under a defined benefit plan. One example of such an arrangement is a 'longevity swap' under which the risk of plan members living longer (or shorter) than expected is transferred from the plan to an external party (usually an insurance company or a bank). If a defined benefit plan enters into such an arrangement, it pays fixed amounts and receives variable amounts, which are settled on a net basis. The amounts under the variable leg are calculated at the amounts actually paid to beneficiaries.

IAS 19 does not contain any specific guidance on the appropriate treatment for longevity swaps. This fact pattern was considered by the IFRS Interpretations Committee, as reported in the March 2015 *IFRIC Update*. The Committee did not publish a consensus on the appropriate treatment for a longevity swap. However, it did note its understanding that, when such transactions take place, the predominant practice is to account for a longevity swap as a single instrument, measured at fair value as part of plan assets, with changes in fair value being recognised in other comprehensive income in accordance with IAS 19:120(c), rather than to split the contract into two components and apply the requirements of IAS 19:115 for qualifying insurance policies to the receive leg.

7.4 Step 2 – determining the amount of the net defined benefit liability (asset)

7.4.1 Determining the amount of the net defined benefit liability (asset) – general

The entity is required to recognise the net defined benefit liability (asset) in the statement of financial position. [IAS 19:63] The net defined benefit liability or asset is the deficit or surplus, adjusted for any effect of limiting a net defined benefit asset to the asset ceiling (see section **7.4.2**). [IAS 19:8]

When an entity has a surplus in a defined benefit plan, the net defined benefit asset should be measured at the lower of:

[IAS 19:64]

• the surplus in the defined benefit plan; and

• the asset ceiling, determined using the discount rate specified in IAS 19:83 (see **7.3.6**).

A net defined benefit asset may arise when a defined benefit plan has been overfunded or when actuarial gains have arisen. It is appropriate for an entity to recognise a net defined benefit asset in such cases because:

[IAS 19:65]

• the entity controls a resource, which is the ability to use the surplus to generate future benefits;

• that control is a result of past events (contributions paid by the entity and service rendered by the employee); and

• future economic benefits are available to the entity in the form of a reduction in future contributions or a cash refund, either directly to the entity or indirectly to another plan in deficit. The asset ceiling is the present value of those future benefits.

7.4.2 IFRIC 14 **The Limit on a Defined Benefit Asset, Minimum Funding Requirements and their Interaction**

7.4.2.1 The 'asset ceiling' – general

As noted in **7.4.1**, IAS 19:64 limits the measurement of a net defined benefit asset to the lower of the surplus in the defined benefit plan and the asset ceiling. The asset ceiling is defined as the present value of any economic benefits available in the form of refunds from the plan or reductions in future contributions to the plan. [IAS 19:8]

IFRIC 14 addresses three specific questions:

- when refunds or reductions in future contributions should be regarded as available in accordance with the definition of the asset ceiling in IAS 19:8;

- how a minimum funding requirement might affect the availability of reductions in future contributions; and

- when a minimum funding requirement might give rise to a liability.

These points are discussed in **7.4.2.2** to **7.4.2.5**.

The Interpretation applies to all post-employment defined benefits and other long-term employee defined benefits.

In June 2015, the IASB issued an exposure draft proposing a number of amendments to IFRIC 14 (see **11.1**).

7.4.2.2 When are refunds 'available'?

IFRIC 14 requires that the availability of a refund or reduction in future contributions should be determined on the basis of the terms and conditions of the plan, and any relevant statutory requirements. [IFRIC 14:7] As a general principle, an economic benefit in the form of a refund or reduction in future contributions is available if the entity can realise that benefit at some point during the life of the plan or when the plan liabilities are settled, even if the benefit is not realisable immediately at the end of the reporting period. [IFRIC 14:8]

The economic benefit available does not depend on how the entity intends to use the surplus – it is the maximum economic benefit that is available from refunds, reductions in future contributions, or a combination of both. In making such estimates, the assumptions made regarding refunds and reductions in future contributions should not be mutually exclusive. [IFRIC 14:9]

In the absence of statutory or contractual minimum funding requirements (see **7.4.2.4**), *a refund* is generally available to an entity only when the entity has an unconditional right to the refund:

[IFRIC 14:11]

(a) during the life of the plan, without assuming that the plan liabilities must be settled in order to obtain the refund (e.g. in some jurisdictions, the entity may have a right to a refund during the life of the plan, irrespective of whether the plan liabilities are settled); or

(b) assuming the gradual settlement of the plan liabilities over time until all members have left the plan; or

(c) assuming the full settlement of the plan liabilities in a single event (i.e. as a plan wind-up).

An unconditional right to a refund can exist whatever the funding level of a plan at the end of the reporting period. [IFRIC 14:11]

If the entity's right to a refund of a surplus depends on the occurrence or non-occurrence of one or more uncertain future events not wholly within its control, the entity does not have an unconditional right and should not recognise an asset. [IFRIC 14:12]

Whether a pension surplus is 'available' will depend on a careful assessment of the legal requirements and the rules of the particular plan, often codified in a trust deed. In some jurisdictions, trustees have the ability or right to protect the interests of members, and to prevent entities from acting 'unreasonably'. Trustees or other third parties may have rights such as the ability to prevent or restrict the payment of a refund.

The circumstances in which the trustees have the ability to prevent any or all of a surplus being refunded to an entity would clearly fall within the guidance of IFRIC 14:12 as a contingent event beyond the entity's control that would prevent it from having an unconditional right to the refund and, consequently, from recognising an asset. In such circumstances, the determination of the extent to which the trustees' right of approval restricts the availability of the surplus is a matter requiring careful judgement; this would include, for example, consideration as to whether an entity could successfully challenge in court a decision by the trustees that the entity regards as unreasonable, such as refusal by the trustees to allow a refund.

IFRIC 14:BC10 clarifies that the entity's ability to improve benefits should not be taken into consideration in measuring the defined benefit obligation unless (1) the future benefit changes are set out in the formal terms of the plan, or (2) there is a constructive obligation at the end of the accounting period. However, a unilateral unlimited right of the trustees to enhance benefits would prevent an entity from having an unconditional right to a surplus even if the trustees have not yet committed to those improvements.

IFRIC 14:11(b) requires consideration of whether a refund would be available assuming the gradual settlement of pension liabilities. When considering gradual settlement, it is necessary to consider what happens at final settlement and, perhaps more importantly, when the plan is closed and members are reducing. For example, once only a limited number of employees are left in the plan, trustees may be required to wind up the plan and secure employees' benefits by purchasing matching insurance policies. IFRIC 14:14 requires an entity to "include the costs to the plan of settling the plan liabilities" and to deduct "costs of any insurance premiums that may be required to secure the liability" (see **7.4.2.3**).

7.4.2.3 Measurement of the economic benefit

The entity should measure the economic benefit available *as a refund* as the amount of the surplus at the end of the reporting period (i.e. the fair value of the plan assets less the present value of the defined benefit obligation) that the entity has a right to receive as a refund, less any associated costs (e.g. taxes other than income tax). [IFRIC 14:13]

IFRIC 14:13 refers specifically to the fair value of plan assets at the end of the reporting period. Consequently, a change of investment strategy (e.g. a move into bonds), whether determined by the entity or by the trustees, represents a potential future change in the fair value of plan assets that should not be taken into account until the investment decision is actually made and the fair value of the plan assets changes.

In measuring the amount of a refund available when the plan is wound up (under IFRIC 14:11(c) – see **7.4.2.2**), the entity should include the costs of settling the liabilities and making the refund (e.g. professional fees and insurance costs should be deducted to the extent that they would be paid by the plan). [IFRIC 14:14]

If the refund is determined as the full amount or a proportion of the surplus, rather than a fixed amount, the amount is calculated without further adjustment for the time value of money, even if the refund is realisable only at a future date, because both the defined benefit obligation and the fair value of the plan assets are already measured on a present value basis. [IFRIC 14:15]

If there is no minimum funding requirement for contributions relating to future service, the economic benefit available as *a reduction in future contributions* is the future service cost to the entity for each period over the shorter of the expected life of the plan and the expected life of the entity. The future service cost to the entity excludes amounts that will be borne by employees. [IFRIC 14:16]

The benefit should be determined using assumptions consistent with those used to determine the defined benefit obligation and based on conditions that exist at the end of the reporting period. This means, an entity should assume:

[IFRIC 14:17]

- no change to the benefits provided by a plan in the future until the plan is amended; and

- a stable workforce, unless the entity makes a reduction in the number of employees covered by the plan. When such a reduction has been made, the assumption about the future workforce should include the reduction.

Example 7.4.2.3

Stable workforce assumption

Entity A operates a defined benefit plan with a minimum funding requirement. Under the terms of the plan, Entity A has an unconditional right to a reduction in future contributions for any excess contributions above the minimum funding requirement.

Over the next five years, Entity A expects that its workforce will decrease by approximately 20 per cent due to declining demand for its products. However, at the end of the reporting period, Entity A is not yet committed to reducing the number of employees covered by the plan.

Is it appropriate for Entity A to consider the expected decrease in its workforce when calculating the economic benefit available as a reduction in the future contributions to the defined benefit plan?

No. IFRIC 14:22 requires an entity to determine the economic benefit available as a reduction in future contributions as the present value of the future service costs to the entity for each year less the estimated minimum funding contributions required in respect of the future accrual of benefits in that year (see **7.4.2.4**).

In determining the estimated future service costs, IFRIC 14:17 requires the assumption of a stable workforce in the future unless the entity has reduced the number of employees covered by the plan by the end of the reporting period.

Contributions made to the defined benefit plan that do not provide available economic benefits are recognised as an expense in the period they are incurred.

This conclusion was confirmed by the IFRIC (now the IFRS Interpretations Committee) in the context of IAS 19(1998) (see *IFRIC Update*, November 2008) and is not affected by the 2011 revision of IAS 19.

7.4.2.4   *The impact of minimum funding requirements*

In many jurisdictions, entities are required, either by law or by agreement with plan managers/trustees, to provide a minimum amount or level of contributions to post-employment benefit plans over a given period, so as to improve the security of the post-employment benefit promise made to the members of such plans. Such commitments are generally referred to as minimum funding requirements.

For the purposes of IFRIC 14, minimum funding requirements are defined as any requirements to fund a post-employment or other long-term defined benefit plan. [IFRIC 14:5] Therefore, both statutory and contractual requirements are covered by the Interpretation.

If a minimum funding requirement is in place for a particular plan, IFRIC 14 distinguishes between contributions that are required to cover:

[IFRIC 14:18]

(a) any existing shortfall for past service on the minimum funding basis; and

(b) future service.

Under (a), the minimum funding requirement relates to services already received by an entity and does not affect future contributions for future service. [IFRIC 14:19] To the extent that the contributions payable to cover an existing shortfall on a funding basis will not be available after they have been paid into the plan for a refund or reduction in future contributions, the entity should recognise a liability when the obligation to make such contributions arises. [IFRIC 14:24] In other words, if paying the contribution would give rise to an IAS 19 surplus or an increased surplus that would be irrecoverable, this is akin to an onerous contract and a liability should be recognised.

The liability recognised should reduce the net defined benefit asset or increase the net defined benefit liability so that no gain or loss is expected to result from applying IAS 19:64 when the contributions are paid. [IFRIC 14:24]

For contributions that are required to cover the future accrual of benefits, if there is a minimum funding requirement for contributions relating to future service, the economic benefit available as a reduction in future contributions (and, therefore, the surplus that should be recognised as an asset) is the sum of:

[IFRIC 14:20]

(a) any amount that reduces future minimum funding requirement contributions for future services because the entity made a prepayment (i.e. any such amount that the entity has paid before being required to do so); and

(b) the estimated future service cost in each period less the estimated minimum funding requirement contributions that would be required for future service in those periods if there were no prepayment of those contributions as described in (a).

The estimate of the future minimum funding requirement contributions for future service should:

[IFRIC 14:21]

• take into account the effect of any existing surplus determined using the minimum funding basis (but excluding the prepayment described in paragraph 20(a));

• be based on assumptions consistent with the minimum funding basis and, for any factors not specified by that basis, on assumptions consistent with those used to determine the defined benefit obligation and with the situation that exists at the end of the reporting period as determined by IAS 19; and

- include any changes in the future minimum funding contributions expected as a result of the entity paying the minimum contributions when they are due; but

- exclude the effect of expected changes in the terms and conditions of the minimum funding basis that are not substantively enacted or contractually agreed at the end of the reporting period.

If the minimum funding requirement contributions for future service exceed the future IAS 19 service cost in any given period, that excess reduces the amount of the economic benefit available as a reduction in future contributions. [IFRIC 14:22]

IFRIC 14:22 clarifies that while the amount calculated under IFRIC 14:20(b) may be negative for a given period (i.e. the estimated minimum funding requirement contribution for that period exceeds the estimated future service cost for that same period), the total amount calculated under IFRIC 14:20(b) can never be less than zero. Accordingly, the economic benefit available as a reduction in future contributions will never be less than the amount of the minimum funding prepayment, if any.

In some jurisdictions, contribution rates are determined by law, while in others individual entities and the plan managers/trustees negotiate the appropriate level of funding. When the latter is the case, the assumptions to be used for determining the minimum funding requirement may not be clearly defined. It may be necessary to consider the overall funding objective and the basis on which the current contribution schedule was agreed to assess how contributions may be determined in the future. Contribution schedules tend to be more flexible for immature plans (i.e. plans with a high proportion of active employees) than for mature or closed plans. If future contribution levels will be revised to reflect changes in the economic circumstances of the plan (i.e. if contributions may be adjusted downwards or if entities may even take 'contribution holidays' in the event that the scheme is in surplus, an 'economic benefit in the form of reductions in future contributions' will generally be available. On the other hand, if contributions will always be higher than the IAS 19 cost, an analysis of the rules on refunds (see **7.4.2.2**) would be required.

The following illustrative examples accompany, but are not part of, IFRIC 14.

Example 7.4.2.4A

Effect of the minimum funding requirement when there is an IAS 19 surplus and the minimum funding contributions payable are fully refundable to the entity

[IFRIC 14:IE1 & IE2, Example 1]

An entity has a funding level on the minimum funding requirement basis (which is measured on a different basis from that required under IAS 19) of 82 per cent in Plan A. Under the minimum funding requirements, the entity is required to increase the funding level to 95 per cent immediately. As a result, the entity has a statutory obligation at the end of the reporting period to contribute 200 to Plan A immediately. The plan rules permit a full refund of any surplus to the entity at the end of the life of the plan. The year-end valuations for Plan A are set out below.

Fair value of assets	1,200
Present value of defined benefit obligation under IAS 19	(1,100)
Surplus	100

Application of requirements

IFRIC 14:24 requires the entity to recognise a liability to the extent that the contributions payable are not fully available. Payment of the contributions of 200 will increase the IAS 19 surplus from 100 to 300. Under the rules of the plan this amount will be fully refundable to the entity with no associated costs. Therefore, no liability is recognised for the obligation to pay the contributions and the net defined benefit asset is 100.

Example 7.4.2.4B

Effect of a minimum funding requirement when there is an IAS 19 deficit and the minimum funding contributions payable would not be fully available

[IFRIC 14:IE3 - IE8, Example 2]

An entity has a funding level on the minimum funding requirement basis (which is measured on a different basis from that required under IAS 19) of 77 per cent in Plan B. Under the minimum funding requirements, the entity is required to increase the funding level to 100 per cent immediately. As a result, the entity has a statutory obligation at the end of the reporting period to pay additional contributions of 300 to Plan B. The plan rules permit a maximum refund of 60 per cent of the IAS 19 surplus to the entity and the entity is not permitted to reduce its contributions below a specified level which happens to equal the IAS 19 service cost. The year-end valuations for Plan B are set out below.

Fair value of assets	1,000
Present value of defined benefit obligation under IAS 19	(1,100)
Deficit	(100)

Application of requirements

The payment of 300 would change the IAS 19 deficit of 100 to a surplus of 200. Of this 200, 60 per cent (120) is refundable.

Therefore, of the contributions of 300, 100 eliminates the IAS 19 deficit and 120 (60 per cent of 200) is available as an economic benefit. The remaining 80 (40 per cent of 200) of the contributions paid is not available to the entity.

IFRIC 14:24 requires the entity to recognise a liability to the extent that the additional contributions payable are not available to it.

Therefore, the net defined benefit liability is 180, comprising the deficit of 100 plus the additional liability of 80 resulting from the requirements in paragraph 24 of IFRIC 14. No other liability is recognised in respect of the statutory obligation to pay contributions of 300.

Summary

Fair value of assets	1,000
Present value of defined benefit obligation under IAS 19	(1,100)
Deficit	(100)
Effect of the asset ceiling	(80)
Net defined benefit liability	(180)

When the contributions of 300 are paid, the net defined benefit asset will be 120.

Example 7.4.2.4C

Effect of a minimum funding requirement when the contributions payable would not be fully available and the effect on the economic benefit available as a future contribution reduction

[IFRIC 14:IE9 - IE21, Example 3]

An entity has a funding level on the minimum funding basis (which it measures on a different basis from that required by IAS 19) of 95 per cent in Plan C. The minimum funding requirements require the entity to pay contributions to increase the funding level to 100 per cent over the next three years. The contributions are required to make good the deficit on the minimum funding basis (shortfall) and to cover future service.

Plan C also has an IAS 19 surplus at the end of the reporting period of 50, which cannot be refunded to the entity under any circumstances.

The nominal amounts of contributions required to satisfy the minimum funding requirements in respect of the shortfall and the future service for the next three years are set out below.

Year	Total contributions for minimum funding requirement	Contributions required to make good the shortfall	Contributions required to cover future service
1	135	120	15
2	125	112	13
3	115	104	11

Application of requirements

The entity's present obligation in respect of services already received includes the contributions required to make good the shortfall but does not include the contributions required to cover future service.

The present value of the entity's obligation, assuming a discount rate of 6 per cent per year, is approximately 300, calculated as follows:

$$[120/(1.06) + 112/(1.06)^2 + 104/(1.06)^3]$$

When these contributions are paid into the plan, the IAS 19 surplus (ie the fair value of assets less the present value of the defined benefit obligation) would, other things being equal, increase from 50 to 350 (300 + 50).

However, the surplus is not refundable although an asset may be available as a future contribution reduction.

In accordance with IFRIC 14:20, the economic benefit available as a reduction in future contributions is the sum of:

(a) any amount that reduces future minimum funding requirement contributions for future service because the entity made a prepayment (ie paid the amount before being required to do so); and

(b) the estimated future service cost in each period in accordance with IFRIC 14:16 & 17, less the estimated minimum funding requirement contributions that would be required for future service in those periods if there were no prepayment as described in (a).

In this example there is no prepayment as described in IFRIC 14:20(a). The amounts available as a reduction in future contributions when applying IFRIC 14:20(b) are set out below.

Year	IAS 19 service cost	Minimum contributions required to cover future service	Amount available as contribution reduction
1	13	15	(2)
2	13	13	0
3	13	11	2
4+	13	9	4

Assuming a discount rate of 6 per cent, the present value of the economic benefit available as a future contribution reduction is therefore equal to:

$(2)/(1.06) + 0/(1.06)^2 + 2/(1.06)^3 + 4/(1.06)^4 \ldots = 56$

Thus in accordance with IAS 19:58(b), the present value of the economic benefit available from future contribution reductions is limited to 56.

IFRIC 14:24 requires the entity to recognise a liability to the extent that the additional contributions payable will not be fully available. Therefore, the effect of the asset ceiling is 294 (50 + 300 − 56).

The entity recognises a net defined benefit liability of 244 in the statement of financial position. No other liability is recognised in respect of the obligation to make contributions to fund the minimum funding shortfall.

Summary

Surplus	50
Net defined benefit asset (before consideration of the minimum funding requirement)	50
Effect of the asset ceiling	(294)
Net defined benefit liability	(244)

When the contributions of 300 are paid into the plan, the net defined benefit asset will become 56 (300 − 244).

Example 7.4.2.4D

Effect of a prepayment when a minimum funding requirement exceeds the expected future service charge

[IFRIC 14:IE22 - IE27, Example 4]

An entity is required to fund Plan D so that no deficit arises on the minimum funding basis. The entity is required to pay minimum funding requirement contributions to cover the service cost in each period determined on the minimum funding basis.

Plan D has an IAS 19 surplus of 35 at the beginning of 20X1. This example assumes that the discount rate and expected return on assets are 0 per cent, and that the plan cannot refund the surplus to the entity under any circumstances but can use the surplus for reductions of future contributions.

The minimum contributions required to cover future service are 15 for each of the next five years. The expected IAS 19 service cost is 10 in each year.

The entity makes a prepayment of 30 at the beginning of 20X1 in respect of years 20X1 and 20X2, increasing its surplus at the beginning of 20X1 to 65. That prepayment reduces the future contributions it expects to make in the following two years, as follows:

Year	IAS 19 service cost	Minimum funding requirement contribution before prepayment	Minimum funding requirement contribution after prepayment
20X1	10	15	0
20X2	10	15	0
20X3	10	15	15
20X4	10	15	15
20X5	10	15	15
Total	50	75	45

In accordance with paragraphs 20 and 22 of IFRIC 14, at the beginning of 20X1, the economic benefit available as a reduction in future contributions is the sum of:

(a) 30, being the prepayment of the minimum funding requirement contributions; and

(b) nil. The estimated minimum funding requirement contributions required for future service would be 75 if there was no prepayment. Those contributions exceed the estimated future service cost (50); therefore the entity cannot use any part of the surplus of 35 noted in [the second paragraph of this example].

Assuming a discount rate of 0 per cent, the present value of the economic benefit available as a reduction in future contributions is equal to 30. Thus in accordance with paragraph 64 of IAS 19 the entity recognises a net defined benefit asset of 30 (because this is lower than the IAS 19 surplus of 65).

7.4.2.5   IFRIC 14 – disclosure

IFRIC 14 does not specify any additional disclosure requirements, but notes that, under paragraph 125 of IAS 1 *Presentation of Financial Statements*, entities are required to disclose information about the key sources of estimation uncertainty that have a significant risk of causing an adjustment to the carrying amount of assets and liabilities within the next financial year. Therefore, the entity should disclose information about the key sources of estimation uncertainty at the end of the reporting period that have a significant risk of causing a material adjustment to the carrying amount of the net asset or liability in the statement of financial position. This might include disclosure of any restrictions on the realisability of the surplus or disclosure of the basis used to determine the amount of the economic benefit available. [IFRIC 14:10]

7.5   Step 3 – determining amounts to be recognised in profit or loss

7.5.1   Determining amounts to be recognised in profit or loss – general

The amounts to be recognised in profit or loss in respect of a defined benefit plan are as follows:

[IAS 19:8 & 120(a) & (b)]

- current service cost (see **7.5.2**);
- any past service cost and gain or loss on settlement (see section **7.5.3**); and
- net interest on the net defined benefit liability (asset) (see **7.5.4**).

When employee costs are capitalised as part of the cost of an asset (e.g. inventories under IAS 2 *Inventories* or self-constructed property in accordance with IAS 16 *Property, Plant and Equipment*), the appropriate proportion of the components listed above is included in the employee costs capitalised. [IAS 19:121]

IAS 19 uses the term 'service cost' to mean the aggregate of current service cost, past service cost and any gain or loss on settlement. [IAS 19:8]

7.5.2   Current service cost

Current service cost is the increase in the present value of the defined benefit obligation resulting from employee service in the current period. [IAS 19:8]

7.5.3   Past service cost and gain or loss on settlement

7.5.3.1   Past service cost and gain or loss on settlement – general

Past service cost is the change in the present value of the defined benefit obligation for employee service in prior periods, resulting from a plan amendment (the introduction or withdrawal of, or changes to, a defined benefit plan) or a curtailment (a significant reduction by the entity in the number of employees covered by a plan). [IAS 19:8 & 102]

> While the definition of past service cost distinguishes between past service cost arising from plan amendments and those arising from curtailments, this distinction has little impact on the financial statements because all past service costs are recognised in profit or loss in the period in which they occur.

Before determining past service cost, or a gain or loss on settlement, an entity should remeasure the net defined benefit liability (asset) using the current fair value of plan assets and current actuarial assumptions (including current market interest rates and other current market prices) reflecting the benefits offered under the plan before the plan amendment, curtailment or settlement. [IAS 19:99]

The entity is then required to identify changes in the present value of the defined benefit obligation arising from the plan amendment, curtailment or settlement. It is not always necessary to identify each of these components separately; an entity need not distinguish between past service cost resulting from a plan amendment, past service cost resulting from a curtailment and a gain or loss on settlement if these transactions occur together. [IAS 19:100] This would arise, for example, when a plan is terminated with the result that the obligation is settled and the plan ceases to exist. However, the termination of a plan is not a settlement if the plan is replaced by a new plan that offers benefits that are, in substance, the same. [IAS 19:101]

In some cases, a plan amendment occurs before a settlement, such as when an entity changes the benefits under the plan and settles the amended benefits later. In such circumstances, the entity should recognise past service cost before any gain or loss on settlement. [IAS 19:100]

7.5.3.2 Recognition of past service cost

An entity is required to recognise past service cost as an expense at the earlier of the following dates:

[IAS 19:103]

- when the plan amendment or curtailment occurs (see below); and

- when the entity recognises related restructuring costs (see **3.9.3** in **chapter A12**) or termination benefits (see **section 10**).

A plan amendment occurs when an entity introduces, or withdraws, a defined benefit plan or changes the benefits payable under an existing defined benefit plan. [IAS 19:104]

A curtailment occurs when an entity significantly reduces the number of employees covered by a plan. A curtailment may arise from an isolated event, such as the closing of a plant, discontinuance of an operation or termination or suspension of a plan. [IAS 19:105]

IAS 19 requires an entity to recognise a curtailment when it 'occurs'. In the Basis for Conclusions on IAS 19, the IASB states as follows.

"If a plan amendment or curtailment occurs in isolation (ie it is not triggered by a settlement, termination benefit or restructuring), determining when the plan amendment occurs requires the exercise of judgement. The timing of recognition would depend on the individual facts and circumstances and how they interact with the constructive obligation requirements in [IAS 19:61 and 62]." [IAS 19:BC158] (See **7.2.2**.)

Past service cost may be either positive (when benefits are introduced or changed so that the present value of the defined benefit obligation increases) or negative (when benefits are withdrawn or changed so that the present value of the defined benefit obligation decreases). [IAS 19:106]

When an entity reduces benefits payable under an existing defined benefit plan and, at the same time, increases other benefits payable under the plan for the same employees, the entity treats the change as a single net change. [IAS 19:107]

Past service cost excludes:

[IAS 19:108]

- the effect of differences between actual and previously assumed salary increases on the obligation to pay benefits for service in prior years (there is no past service cost because actuarial assumptions allow for projected salaries);

- underestimates and overestimates of discretionary pension increases when an entity has a constructive obligation to grant such increases (there is no past service cost because actuarial assumptions allow for such increases);

- estimates of benefit improvements that result from actuarial gains or from the return on plan assets that have been recognised in the financial statements if the entity is obliged, by either the formal terms of a plan (or a constructive obligation that goes beyond those terms) or legislation, to use any surplus in the plan for the benefit of plan participants, even if the benefit increase has not yet been formally awarded (there is no past service cost because the resulting increase in the obligation is an actuarial loss – see **7.3.5.4**); and

- the increase in vested benefits (i.e. benefits that are not conditional on future employment) when, in the absence of new or improved benefits, employees complete vesting requirements (there is no past service cost because the entity recognised the estimated cost of benefits as current service cost as the service was rendered).

7.5.3.3   Gains and losses on settlement

The gain or loss on a settlement is the difference between:

[IAS 19:109]

- the present value of the defined benefit obligation being settled, as determined on the date of settlement; and

- the settlement price, including any plan assets transferred and any payments made directly by the entity in connection with the settlement.

An entity is required to recognise a gain or loss on the settlement of a defined benefit plan when the settlement occurs. [IAS 19:110] A settlement is a transaction that eliminates all further legal or constructive obligations for part or all of the benefits provided under a defined benefit plan (other than a payment of benefits to, or on behalf of, employees that is set out in the terms of the plan and included in the actuarial assumptions). [IAS 19:8] For example:

[IAS 19:111]

- a one-off transfer of significant employer obligations under the plan to an insurance company through the purchase of an insurance policy is a settlement; but

- a lump sum cash payment, under the terms of the plan, to plan participants in exchange for their rights to receive specified post-employment benefits is not.

> Consistent with the view expressed previously by the IFRIC (now the IFRS Interpretations Committee) (see *IFRIC Update*, May 2008), IAS 19 clarifies that a settlement (for which a gain or loss is recognised in profit or loss) is a payment of benefits that is not set out in the terms of the plan (and which, therefore, could not have been considered in developing actuarial assumptions). The payment of benefits that are set out in the terms of the plan (including where there are options on the nature of the benefit payments) would be included in the actuarial assumptions and if a gain or loss arose upon payment of those benefits it would be an actuarial gain or loss, to be recognised in OCI as part of remeasurements. [IAS 19:BC163]

An entity may acquire an insurance policy to fund some or all of the employee benefits relating to employee service in the current and prior periods. The acquisition of such a policy is not a settlement if the entity retains a legal or constructive obligation to pay further amounts if the insurer does not pay the employee benefits specified in the insurance policy. IAS 19's requirements regarding the recognition and measurement of reimbursement rights under insurance policies that are not plan assets are discussed at **7.3.7.6**. [IAS 19:112]

Example 7.5.3.3

Settlement of defined benefit plan with an unrecognised surplus

In its statement of financial position, Entity X recognises the following amounts in respect of its defined benefit plan.

	CU
Fair value of plan assets	40
Present value of defined benefit obligation	(35)
Effect of asset ceiling	(5)
	–

No net defined benefit asset has been recognised in accordance with IAS 19:64 because it was determined that no economic benefits were available in the form of refunds from the plan or reductions in future contributions to the plan.

In full settlement of its defined benefit obligation, Entity X transfers all of the plan assets to a third party and pays an additional CU10 to that third party. Entity X does not retain any legal or constructive obligation to the members of the plan.

IAS 19:110 requires Entity X to recognise a gain or loss on settlement of its defined benefit plan immediately in profit or loss. The gain or loss is calculated in accordance with IAS 19:109 (see above), and after remeasuring the obligation and plan assets using current actuarial assumptions and market prices. The values above include the effect of that remeasurement.

When Entity X calculates the gain or loss on settlement of its defined benefit plan to be recognised in profit or loss, what is the impact of the previously unrecognised surplus?

IAS 19 does not specifically address this issue and it appears that two alternative treatments (as described below) are acceptable. Whichever of these alternatives is selected as an accounting policy by Entity X, it should be applied consistently and disclosed when the effect is material.

Alternative 1

In applying IAS 19:109, the reference to 'plan assets transferred' could be read as referring to the *full* value of those assets (i.e. before the limitation imposed by the asset ceiling). If this approach is adopted, at the date of settlement Entity X should recognise the previously unrecognised surplus of CU5 as a gain in other comprehensive income (OCI).

Consequently, Entity X would recognise a settlement loss of CU15 in profit or loss (i.e. the defined benefit obligation settled of CU35 less plan assets transferred of CU40 less settlement payment of CU10).

Alternative 2

In applying IAS 19:109, the reference to the 'plan assets transferred' could be read as referring to the *recognised* value of those assets (i.e. after the limitation imposed by the asset ceiling). If this approach is adopted, the asset ceiling remains in place on settlement and no gain or loss is required to be recognised in OCI.

Consequently, Entity X would recognise a settlement loss of CU10 (i.e. the defined benefit obligation settled of CU35 less recognised plan assets transferred of CU35 less settlement payment of CU10).

7.5.4 Net interest on the net defined benefit liability (asset)

Net interest on the net defined benefit liability (asset) is the change during the period in the net defined benefit liability (asset) that arises from the passage of time. [IAS 19:8]

Net interest on the net defined benefit liability (asset) is determined by multiplying the net defined benefit liability (asset) by the discount rate specified in IAS 19:83 (see **7.3.6**), both as determined at the start of the annual reporting period, taking account of any changes in the net defined benefit liability (asset) during the period as a result of contribution and benefit payments. [IAS 19:123]

> The net interest calculation takes account of changes in the net defined benefit liability (asset) during the period as a result of contribution and benefit payments. It does not take account of any other movements in the net defined benefit liability (asset) during the period, such as actuarial gains and losses.

IAS 19 explains that net interest on the net defined benefit liability (asset) can be viewed as comprising interest income on plan assets, interest cost on the defined benefit obligation and interest on the effect of the asset ceiling. [IAS 19:124]

Interest income on plan assets is a component of the return on plan assets, and is determined by multiplying the fair value of the plan assets by the discount rate specified in IAS 19:83 (see **7.3.6**), both as determined at the start of the annual reporting period, taking account of any changes in the plan assets held during the period as a result of contributions and benefit payments. The difference between the interest income on plan assets and the return on plan assets is included in the remeasurement of the net defined benefit liability (asset). [IAS 19:125]

Interest on the effect of the asset ceiling is part of the total change in the effect of the asset ceiling, and is determined by multiplying the effect of the asset ceiling by the discount rate specified in IAS 19:83 (see **7.3.6**), both as determined at the start of the annual reporting period. The difference between that amount and the total change in the effect of the asset ceiling is included in the remeasurement of the net defined benefit liability (asset). [IAS 19:126]

7.6 Step 4 – determining the remeasurements of the net defined benefit liability (asset) to be recognised in other comprehensive income

Remeasurements of the net defined benefit liability (asset) are required to be recognised in other comprehensive income. [IAS 19:120(c)] Such remeasurements are not reclassified to profit or loss in a subsequent period. However, an entity may transfer those amounts recognised in other comprehensive income within equity. [IAS 19:122]

Remeasurements of the net defined benefit liability (asset) comprise:

[IAS 19:8 & 127]

- actuarial gains and losses;
- the return on plan assets, excluding amounts included in net interest on the net defined benefit liability (asset) (see **7.5.4**); and
- any change in the effect of the asset ceiling, excluding amounts included in net interest on the net defined benefit liability (asset) (see **7.5.4**).

Actuarial gains and losses are decreases or increases in the present value of the defined benefit obligation because of experience adjustments (the effects of differences between the previous actuarial assumptions and what has actually occurred) and changes in actuarial assumptions. [IAS 19:8] Causes of actuarial gains and losses include, for example:

[IAS 19:128]

- unexpectedly high or low rates of employee turnover, early retirement or mortality or of increases in salaries, benefits (if the formal or constructive terms of a plan provide for inflationary benefit increases) or medical costs;
- the effect of changes to assumptions concerning benefit payment options;
- the effect of changes in estimates of future employee turnover, early retirement or mortality or of increases in salaries, benefits (if the formal or constructive terms of a plan provide for inflationary benefit increases) or medical costs; and
- the effect of changes in the discount rate.

Actuarial gains and losses do not include changes in the present value of the defined benefit obligation because of the introduction, amendment, curtailment or settlement of the defined benefit plan, or changes to the benefits payable under the defined benefit plan. Such changes result in past service cost or gains or losses on settlement. [IAS 19:129]

The return on plan assets is interest, dividends and other income derived from the plan assets, together with realised and unrealised gains or losses on the plan assets, less:

[IAS 19:8 & 130]

- any costs of managing the plan assets; and
- any tax payable by the plan itself, other than tax included in the actuarial assumptions used to measure the defined benefit obligation.

Other administration costs are not deducted from the return on plan assets. [IAS 19:130]

For further discussion of administration costs, see **7.3.5.13**.

8 Presentation and disclosure for defined benefit plans

8.1 Presentation – defined benefit plans

8.1.1 Offset

An asset relating to one plan should be offset against a liability relating to another plan when, and only when, an entity:

[IAS 19:131]

- has a legally enforceable right to use a surplus in one plan to settle obligations under the other plan; and

- intends either to settle the obligations on a net basis, or to realise the surplus in one plan and settle its obligation under the other plan simultaneously.

IAS 19:132 notes that these offsetting criteria are similar to those established for financial instruments in IAS 32 *Financial Instruments: Presentation*.

In practice, such offset will be available only rarely.

8.1.2 Current/non-current distinction

IAS 19 does not specify whether an entity should distinguish current and non-current portions of assets and liabilities arising from post-employment benefits. [IAS 19:133] The implications of this are considered at **4.1.7.1** in **chapter A4**.

8.1.3 Components of defined benefit cost

Under IAS 19:120, an entity is required to recognise service cost and net interest on the net defined benefit liability (asset) in profit or loss. The Standard does not specify how an entity should present service cost and net interest on the net defined benefit liability (asset). The entity should determine an appropriate presentation under IAS 1 *Presentation of Financial Statements*. [IAS 19:134]

Accordingly, entities have a choice as to whether to present service cost and net interest on the net defined benefit liability (asset) separately or as a single net figure. Such a decision is an accounting policy choice, and should therefore be disclosed appropriately and applied consistently for all plans.

8.2   Disclosure – defined benefit plans

8.2.1   General

IAS 19 requires extensive disclosures in respect of defined benefit plans.

An entity should disclose information that:

[IAS 19:135]

- explains the characteristics of its defined benefit plans and risks associated with them (see **8.2.2**);

- identifies and explains the amounts in its financial statements arising from its defined benefit plans (see **8.2.3**); and

- describes how its defined benefit plans may affect the amount, timing and uncertainty of the entity's future cash flows (see **8.2.4**).

To meet these objectives, an entity should have regard to all the following:

[IAS 19:136]

- the level of detail necessary to satisfy the disclosure requirements;

- how much emphasis to place on each of the various requirements;

- how much aggregation or disaggregation to undertake; and

- whether users of financial statements need additional information to evaluate the quantitative information disclosed.

If the disclosures provided in accordance with IAS 19 and other IFRSs are insufficient to meet the objectives above, additional information necessary to meet those objectives should be disclosed. For example, an entity might present an analysis of the present value of the defined benefit obligation that distinguishes the nature, characteristics and risks of the obligation. Such a disclosure could distinguish:

[IAS 19:137]

- between amounts owing to active members, deferred members, and pensioners;

- between vested benefits and accrued but not vested benefits; and/or

- between conditional benefits, amounts attributable to future salary increases and other benefits.

An entity is required to assess whether all or some disclosures should be disaggregated to distinguish plans or groups of plans with materially different risks. For example, an entity might disaggregate disclosure about plans showing one or more of the following features:

[IAS 19:138]

- different geographical locations;
- different characteristics such as flat salary pension plans, final salary pension plans or post-employment medical plans;
- different regulatory environments;
- different reporting segments; and/or
- different funding arrangements (e.g. wholly unfunded, wholly or partly funded).

8.2.2 Characteristics of defined benefit plans and risks associated with them

An entity should disclose:

[IAS 19:139]

- information about the characteristics of its defined benefit plans, including:
  - the nature of the benefits provided by the plan (e.g. final salary defined benefit plan or contribution-based plan with guarantee);
  - a description of the regulatory framework in which the plan operates (e.g. the level of any minimum funding requirements), and any effect of the regulatory framework on the plan, such as the asset ceiling (see **7.4.2**); and
  - a description of any other entity's responsibilities for the governance of the plan, e.g. responsibilities of trustees or of board members of the plan;
- a description of the risks to which the plan exposes the entity, focused on any unusual, entity-specific or plan-specific risks, and of any significant concentrations of risk. For example, if plan assets are invested primarily in one class of investments (e.g. property), the plan may expose the entity to a concentration of property market risk; and
- a description of any plan amendments, curtailments and settlements.

8.2.3 Explanation of amounts in the financial statements

An entity should provide a reconciliation from the opening balance to the closing balance for each of the following, if applicable:

[IAS 19:140]

- the net defined benefit liability (asset), showing separate reconciliations for:
  - plan assets;
  - the present value of the defined benefit obligation; and

- the effect of the asset ceiling; and

- any reimbursement rights. An entity should also describe the relationship between any reimbursement right and the related obligation.

Each reconciliation listed above should show each of the following, if applicable:

[IAS 19:141]

- current service cost;

- interest income or expense;

- remeasurements of the net defined benefit liability (asset), showing separately:

  - the return on plan assets, excluding amounts included in interest income or expense;

  - actuarial gains and losses arising from changes in demographic assumptions (see **7.3.5.1**);

  - actuarial gains and losses arising from changes in financial assumptions (see **7.3.5.1**); and

  - changes in the effect of limiting a net defined benefit asset to the asset ceiling, excluding amounts included in interest income or expense. An entity should also disclose how it determined the maximum economic benefit available (i.e. whether those benefits would be in the form of refunds, reductions in future contributions or a combination of both);

- past service cost and gains and losses arising from settlements. As permitted by IAS 19:100 (see **section 7.5.3**), past service cost and gains and losses arising from settlements need not be distinguished if they occur together;

- the effect of changes in foreign exchange rates;

- contributions to the plan, showing separately those by the employer and by plan participants;

- payments from the plan, showing separately the amount paid in respect of any settlements; and

- the effects of business combinations and disposals.

The fair value of the plan assets should be disaggregated into classes that distinguish the nature and risks of those assets, subdividing each class of plan asset into those that have a quoted market price in an active market as defined in IFRS 13 *Fair Value Measurement* and those that do not. For example, and considering the level of disclosure discussed in IAS 19:136 (see **8.2.1**), an entity might distinguish between:

[IAS 19:142]

- cash and cash equivalents;

- equity instruments (segregated by industry type, company size, geography etc.);

- debt instruments (segregated by type of issuer, credit quality, geography etc.);

- real estate (segregated by geography etc.);

- derivatives (segregated by type of underlying risk in the contract, e.g. interest rate contracts, foreign exchange contracts, equity contracts, credit contracts, longevity swaps etc.);

- investment funds (segregated by type of fund);

- asset-backed securities; and

- structured debt.

An entity should disclose:

[IAS 19:143]

- the fair value of the entity's own transferable financial instruments held as plan assets; and

- the fair value of plan assets that are property occupied by, or other assets used by, the entity.

An entity should disclose the significant actuarial assumptions used to determine the present value of the defined benefit obligation (see **7.3.5.1**). Such disclosure should be in absolute terms (e.g. as an absolute percentage, and not just as a margin between different percentages and other variables). When an entity provides disclosures in total for a grouping of plans, it should provide such disclosures in the form of weighted averages or relatively narrow ranges. [IAS 19:144]

8.2.4   Amount, timing and uncertainty of future cash flows

An entity should disclose:

[IAS 19:145]

- a sensitivity analysis for each significant actuarial assumption (as disclosed under IAS 19:144 – see **8.2.3**) as of the end of the reporting period, showing how the defined benefit obligation would have been affected by changes in the relevant actuarial assumption that were reasonably possible at that date;

- the methods and assumptions used in preparing these sensitivity analyses and the limitations of those methods; and

- changes from the previous period in the methods and assumptions used in preparing the sensitivity analyses, and the reasons for such changes.

An entity should disclose a description of any asset-liability matching strategies used by the plan or the entity, including the use of annuities and other techniques, such as longevity swaps, to manage risk. [IAS 19:146]

To provide an indication of the effect of the defined benefit plan on the entity's future cash flows, an entity should disclose:

[IAS 19:147]

- a description of any funding arrangements and funding policy that affect future contributions;

- the expected contributions to the plan for the next annual reporting period; and

- information about the maturity profile of the defined benefit obligation. This will include the weighted average duration of the defined benefit obligation and may include other information about the distribution of the timing of benefit payments, such as a maturity analysis of the benefit payments.

8.2.5 *Multi-employer plans and group plans*

Disclosure requirements for multi-employer plans and group plans are listed at **5.1.7** and **5.2.4**, respectively.

8.2.6 *Disclosure requirements in other IFRSs*

When required by IAS 24 *Related Party Disclosures* (see **chapter A23**), an entity should disclose information about:

[IAS 19:151]

- related party transactions with post-employment benefit plans; and

- post-employment benefits for key management personnel.

When required by IAS 37 *Provisions, Contingent Liabilities and Contingent Assets* (see **chapter A12**), an entity should disclose information about contingent liabilities arising from post-employment benefit obligations. [IAS 19:152]

9 Other long-term employee benefits

9.1 Other long-term employee benefits – definition

'Other' long-term employee benefits are all employee benefits other than short-term employee benefits, post-employment benefits and termination benefits. [IAS 19:8]

Other long-term employee benefits include items such as the following, if not expected to be settled wholly before 12 months after the end of the annual reporting period in which the employees render the related service:

[IAS 19:153]

- long-term paid absences such as long-service or sabbatical leave;

- jubilee or other long-service benefits;

- long-term disability benefits;

- profit-sharing and bonuses; and

- deferred remuneration.

9.2 Recognition and measurement – other long-term benefits

9.2.1 Recognition and measurement of other long-term benefits – general

The measurement of other long-term employee benefits is a simplified version of the requirements for post-employment benefits discussed in **sections 4** to **7**. In particular, remeasurements are not recognised in other comprehensive income. [IAS 19:154]

9.2.2 Measurement of surplus or deficit

In recognising and measuring the surplus or deficit in an other long-term employee benefit plan, an entity is required to follow the requirements described in IAS 19:56 to 98 and IAS 19:113 to 115. An entity is required to follow the requirements described in IAS 19:116 to 119 for the purpose of recognising and measuring any reimbursement right. In aggregate, these requirements are discussed in **sections 7.3** and **7.4** (i.e. Steps 1 and 2 described for the measurement of the deficit or surplus in a defined benefit post-employment benefit plan). [IAS 19:155]

As discussed at **4.1.7.2** in **chapter A4**, some obligations for other long-term employee benefits may be presented as current liabilities (based on the employees' entitlement to take their benefits within 12 months of the reporting period rather than on the expected timing of payment). In measuring such obligations, the question arises as to whether amounts should be discounted to reflect the expected timing of payment.

IAS 19:155 requires that other long-term benefit obligations be measured using the same valuation methodology as defined benefit post-employment benefit obligations (except that remeasurements are required to be recognised in profit or loss). In particular, IAS 19:69 specifies that "[a]n entity discounts the whole of [an other long-term] benefit obligation, even if part of the obligation is expected to be settled before twelve months after the reporting period".

Therefore, a current liability arising from other long-term employee benefits should be measured as a discounted amount.

9.2.3   Amount recognised in profit or loss

The expense recognised in profit or loss (or in the cost of an asset, when capitalisation is permitted or required) for other long-term employee benefits is the net total of:

[IAS 19:156]

* service cost;
* net interest on the net defined benefit liability (asset); and
* remeasurements of the net defined benefit liability (asset).

9.2.4   Long-term disability benefit

An example of a long-term employee benefit discussed in IAS 19 is long-term disability benefit. If the amount of such a benefit is independent of years of service (i.e. the level of benefit is the same for any disabled employee regardless of years of service), no cost is recognised until an event occurs that causes a long-term disability. If the level of benefit is dependent on years of service, an obligation should be recognised as the service is rendered, based upon the probability and timing of payments expected to be made. [IAS 19:157]

9.3   Disclosure – other long term employee benefits

IAS 19 has no specific disclosure requirements for other long-term employment benefits, but notes that disclosures may be required under IAS 1 *Presentation of Financial Statements* (when the expense is material) or under IAS 24 *Related Party Disclosures* (if in relation to key management personnel).

In particular, the extensive disclosure requirements for post-employment benefits (discussed in **section 8.2**) do not apply to other long-term employment benefits.

9.4 Death-in-service benefits

9.4.1 Death-in-service benefits – general

Death-in-service benefits are employee benefits payable if an employee dies while employed by the entity. These arrangements may take various forms, including lump sum payments and widows' pensions.

Accounting for death-in-service benefits raises several issues that are not addressed in IAS 19.

The subject has been discussed by the IFRIC (now the IFRS Interpretations Committee) – see *IFRIC Update*, January 2008. The IFRIC discussions concerning death-in-service benefits focused on the appropriate manner for attributing those benefits to periods of service. The IFRIC noted the requirement in paragraph 67(b) of IAS 19 (as issued in 1998) (now IAS 19:70(b)) to attribute the cost of benefits until the date when future service by the employee will lead to no material amount of future benefits under the plan, other than from salary increases.

In the case of death-in-service benefits, the IFRIC noted that:

- the expected date of death would be the date at which no material amount of further benefit would arise from the plan;

- using different mortality assumptions for a defined benefit pension plan and an associated death-in-service benefit would not comply with the requirement in paragraph 72 of IAS 19 (as issued in 1998) (now IAS 19:75) to use actuarial assumptions that are mutually compatible; and

- if the conditions in paragraph 39 of IAS 19 as issued in 1998 (now IAS 19:46) were met, then accounting for death-in-service benefits on a defined contribution basis would be appropriate.

The appropriate accounting for death-in-service benefits depends on the nature of the arrangements, including:

- whether the benefits depend on the length of service or are the same irrespective of the length of service; and

- whether the benefits are provided through a post-employment benefit plan or through a stand-alone arrangement.

Although the IFRIC only considered the issue under IAS 19 as issued in 1998, the paragraphs in question have not been modified since 2008. Consequently, the discussion above remains valid.

9.4.2   Benefits related to length of service

Although IAS 19 does not specifically mention death-in-service benefits, it refers to long-term disability benefits (which may have similar features to death-in-service benefits) as an example of 'other' long-term benefits. IAS 19:157 states that if the level of benefit depends on the length of service, an obligation arises when the service is rendered. Measurement of that obligation reflects the probability that payment will be required and the length of time for which payment is expected to be made. Therefore, when the level of death-in-service benefits is related to the length of service, the benefits should be attributed over the service life of the employee until the expected date of death of the employee.

If death-in-service benefits are provided as part of a defined benefit plan, an entity would recognise actuarial gains and losses arising on the death-in-service benefits as part of remeasurements of the defined benefit plan in other comprehensive income.

If death-in-service benefits related to the period of service are provided through a stand-alone plan, they would represent an other long-term employee benefit. Applying IAS 19:157 by analogy, such benefits would be attributed over the service period until the expected date of death of the employee, and actuarial gains and losses arising on such plans would be recognised in profit or loss in accordance with IAS 19:156.

9.4.3   Benefits unrelated to length of service – stand-alone plans

IAS 19:157 states that if the level of benefits is the same regardless of years of service (e.g. a lump sum fixed amount), the expected cost of those benefits is recognised when an event occurs that causes long-term disability. Applying IAS 19:157 by analogy for death-in-service benefits that are fixed irrespective of any period of service, it would be appropriate to recognise an expense only when an employee dies.

9.4.4   Benefits unrelated to length of service – benefits provided under a defined benefit plan

The calculation of the liabilities of a defined benefit retirement benefit plan will include an assumption about employees dying before reaching normal retirement age. Such an assumption will generally result in a reduction of the liability recognised. It might, therefore, be thought imprudent to recognise that reduction without recognising the additional liabilities that will arise under the death-in-service benefit arrangements if an employee dies before normal retirement age.

The basic approach for defined benefit plans under IAS 19 is to calculate the expected obligation and attribute that benefit to periods of service. When the death-in-service benefit is a lump sum amount regardless of length of service, there is no plan benefit formula that can be used to attribute the benefit to periods of service. In the absence of such a formula, it would seem appropriate to attribute the benefit on a straight-line basis until the expected date of death of the employee, although it appears that the alternative (i.e. recognition of an expense only when an employee dies) may be justified by reference to IAS 19:157.

Example 9.4.4

Measurement of incapacity benefit or death-in-service benefit based on service life

An entity operates a defined benefit post-employment benefit plan. Under the terms of the plan, the employee is entitled to a pension of 1/60th of final earnings for each year of service until retirement. If an employee becomes incapacitated or dies prior to the normal retirement date, the benefit paid (to the employee or the employee's dependant) is based on the years of employment until the date of incapacity or death, and credit is given for 50 per cent of the years from that date until the normal retirement date.

For example, an employee works for 20 years and then becomes incapacitated 10 years prior to the normal retirement date. The benefit paid is 25/60ths based on 25 years of service (the 20 years actually worked plus 50 per cent of the remaining years until the normal retirement date).

In the circumstances described, the assumptions used for attributing benefits to service periods should reflect that, for employees expected to become incapacitated or to die prior to their normal retirement date, the service period would only encompass the period until the expected incapacity or death. A consistent benefit formula should be used over the years of service to reflect the value of the benefit. The expense should be attributed to the periods of service under the benefit formula because the employee's service does not result in a materially higher level of benefit in later years than in earlier years.

In determining costs, actuaries will make assumptions about the number of employees who are expected to become incapacitated or to die prior to normal retirement date. Therefore, for the employees not expected to reach retirement age, the total expected benefit payable, including that related to credited years not actually worked (in this example, 50 per cent of the years between the date of expected incapacity or death and the normal retirement date) will be attributed to the years of expected service up to the date of expected incapacity or death.

10 Termination benefits

10.1 Termination benefits – definition

Termination benefits are defined as employee benefits provided in exchange for the termination of an employee's employment as a result of either:

[IAS 19:8]

- an entity's decision to terminate an employee's employment before the normal retirement date; or

- an employee's decision to accept an offer of benefits in exchange for the termination of employment.

Termination benefits are considered a separate category of employment benefits because the event that gives rise to an obligation is the termination of employment rather than employee service. [IAS 19:159]

The form of the employee benefit does not determine whether it is provided in exchange for service or in exchange for termination of the employee's employment. Termination benefits are typically lump sum payments, but sometimes also include:

[IAS 19:161]

- enhancement of post-employment benefits, either indirectly through an employee benefit plan or directly; and/or

- salary until the end of a specified notice period if the employee renders no further service that provides economic benefits to the entity.

Indicators that an employee benefit is provided in exchange for services (i.e. that it is not a termination benefit) include the following:

[IAS 19:162]

- the benefit is conditional on future service being provided (including benefits that increase if further service is provided); and

- the benefit is provided in accordance with the terms of an employee benefit plan.

Termination benefits differ from post-employment benefits in that an entity can avoid paying them if it does not offer them and does not terminate an employee's contract of employment. Thus, termination benefits (or redundancy payments) arise not from the rendering of service by an employee, but from the termination of that service. Consequently, they do not relate to future benefits and should be recognised as an expense immediately when the entity can no longer withdraw its offer (see **10.3**).

Example 10.1A

Payments for early retirement accounted for as termination benefits

Company A is an entity that encourages employees to retire at the age of 58 years instead of the national retirement age of 65 years. The post-retirement programme in Company A's country is a state pension plan. The state sets out the conditions for an employee to receive retirement benefits before the age of 65 years. This benefit does not form part of an employee's contractual terms and conditions of employment and, each year, Company A can decide whether or not to offer early retirement to its employees. Company A is not, therefore, obligated to make such an offer. Although the retirement benefit for persons between the ages of 58 and 65 years is paid for by the government, Company A is required to fund a portion of those payments.

An employee who is offered an early retirement plan can either accept or reject the offer. The offer is normally made prior to the employee's early retirement date (this period may vary from a few months to a couple of years). If the employee does not accept the offer, he or she will continue service until normal retirement age. Early retirement plans are normally implemented to reduce the work force by a means other than compulsory redundancy. An entity may propose early retirement plans to a selected category of employees.

Under IAS 19:8, termination benefits are those payable as a result of an employee's decision to accept an offer of benefits in exchange for the termination of employment. Accordingly, the arrangements described above should be accounted for as termination benefits.

Example 10.1B

Distinguishing between benefits provided in exchange for services and termination benefits

Entity A is an entity that encourages employees within a specified age group to reduce levels of service in advance of the national retirement age. Entity A offers bonus payments to eligible employees in exchange for a 50 per cent reduction in working hours. Employment is terminated at the end of a required service period. The bonus payments are wholly conditional on the completion of the required service period (typically one to six years).

The bonus payments described above should not be accounted for as termination benefits under IAS 19. The definition of termination benefits (see above) requires that the benefits have been provided in exchange for the termination of an employee's employment, rather than in exchange for services. In distinguishing between benefits provided in exchange for services and termination benefits, it is necessary to consider:

- all the relevant facts and circumstances for each individual entity's offer of benefits;
- the indicators set out in IAS 19:162 that an employee benefit is provided in exchange for services (the list is not exhaustive), i.e. if:

> - the benefit is conditional on future service being provided (including benefits that increase if further service is provided); or
>
> - the benefit is provided in accordance with the terms of an employee benefit plan; and
>
> - the definitions of the employee benefit categories in IAS 19.
>
> In the circumstances described, Entity A's arrangement has attributes of both required service and termination benefits. However, Entity A's arrangement would not meet the definition of a termination benefit because, consistent with IAS 19:162(a), the fact that the bonus payments are wholly conditional upon completion of employee service over a period indicates that the benefits are in exchange for that service.
>
> This conclusion was confirmed by the IFRS Interpretations Committee (see *IFRIC Update*, January 2012).

Termination benefits do not include employee benefits resulting from termination of employment at the request of the employee without an entity's offer, or as a result of mandatory retirement requirements; those benefits are post-employment benefits. [IAS 19:160]

Some termination benefits are provided in accordance with the terms of an existing employee benefit plan (e.g. by statute, employment contract or union agreement), or they may be implied as a result of the employer's past practice of providing similar benefits. Employee benefits provided in accordance with the terms of an employee benefit plan are termination benefits if they both result from an entity's decision to terminate an employee's employment and are not conditional on future service being provided. [IAS 19:163]

If an entity makes an offer of benefits available for more than a short period, or there is more than a short period between the offer and the expected date of actual termination, the entity should consider whether it has established a new employee benefit plan and, therefore, whether the benefits offered under that plan are termination benefits or post-employment benefits. [IAS 19:163]

10.2   Employee benefits payable irrespective of reason for employee departure

Certain employee benefits are payable irrespective of the reason for an employee's departure (subject to any vesting or minimum service requirements) but the timing of their payment is uncertain. Therefore, although such benefits may be described in some jurisdictions as termination indemnities or termination gratuities, they are post-employment benefits rather than termination benefits and should be accounted for as post-employment benefits. [IAS 19:164]

Some entities provide a lower level of benefit for termination of employment at the request of the employee (in substance, a post-employment benefit) than for termination of employment at the request of the entity. In such circumstances, the difference between the benefit provided for termination of employment at the request of the employee and a higher benefit provided at the request of the entity is a termination benefit. [IAS 19:160]

10.3 Recognition of termination benefits

A liability and an expense should be recognised for termination benefits at the earlier of the following dates:

[IAS 19:165]

- when the entity can no longer withdraw the offer of those benefits; and

- when the entity recognises costs for a restructuring that is within the scope of IAS 37 *Provisions, Contingent Liabilities and Contingent Assets* and involves the payment of termination benefits.

In considering the issue of the timing of recognition of termination benefits, the Board decided that the factor determining the timing of recognition is the entity's inability to withdraw the offer of termination benefit. The Board also determined that the inability to withdraw an offer is triggered by different events based on whether the termination is subject to acceptance by the employee or is imposed upon the employee.

In the first scenario (termination benefits payable as a result of an employee's decision to accept an offer of benefits in exchange for the termination of employment), the time when an entity can no longer withdraw the offer of termination benefits is the earlier of:

[IAS 19:166]

- when the employee accepts the offer; and

- when a restriction (e.g. a legal, regulatory or contractual requirement or other restriction) on the entity's ability to withdraw the offer takes effect. This would be when the offer is made, if the restriction existed at the time of the offer.

In the second scenario (for termination benefits payable as a result of an entity's decision to terminate an employee's employment), the entity can no longer withdraw the offer when the entity has communicated to the affected employees a plan of termination meeting all of the following criteria:

[IAS 19:167]

- actions required to complete the plan indicate that it is unlikely that significant changes to the plan will be made;

- the plan identifies the number of employees whose employment is to be terminated, their job classifications or functions and their locations (but the plan need not identify each individual employee) and the expected completion date; and

- the plan establishes the termination benefits that employees will receive in sufficient detail that employees can determine the type and amount of benefits they will receive when their employment is terminated.

Example 10.3

Termination benefits requiring regulatory approval

Entity D has offered voluntary non-statutory termination benefits to specific union employees. The identified employees have accepted the termination benefits; approval has also been obtained from the employees' union. No further acceptance procedures are required from the employees' perspective.

All non-statutory termination benefits in the jurisdiction are required to be approved by the National Employment Agency. In the circumstances under consideration, the offer of benefits was made by Entity D subject to that approval, which has not yet been obtained. At the reporting date, Entity D is not entitled to withdraw the offer, although it may be rejected by the National Employment Agency.

Should Entity D recognise the termination benefits prior to receiving regulatory approval?

Yes. In accordance with IAS 19:165(a), the entity should recognise a liability and an expense for the termination benefits when it can no longer withdraw the offer of those benefits.

IAS 19:166 clarifies that, for termination benefits payable as a result of an employee's decision to accept an offer of benefits in exchange for the termination of employment, the time when an entity can no longer withdraw the offer of termination benefits is the earlier of:

- when the employee accepts the offer; and
- when a restriction (e.g. a legal, regulatory or contractual requirement or other restriction) on the entity's ability to withdraw the offer takes effect. This would be when the offer is made, if the restriction existed at the time of the offer.

In the circumstances described, the entity is committed to making the termination payments once the employees have accepted the offer. The fact that regulatory approval may not be received is not relevant in determining when the liability and expense should be recognised.

When an entity recognises termination benefits, the entity may also have to account for a plan amendment or a curtailment of other employee benefits (see **section 7.5.3**). [IAS 19:168]

10.4   Measurement of termination benefits

The measurement requirements for termination benefits are determined in accordance with their nature. Accordingly, an entity should measure termination benefits as follows:

[IAS 19:169]

- if the termination benefits are an enhancement to post-employment benefits, IAS 19's requirements for post-employment benefits should be applied; otherwise

- if the termination benefits are expected to be settled wholly before 12 months after the end of the annual reporting period in which the termination benefit is recognised, IAS 19's requirements for short-term employee benefits should be applied; and

- if the termination benefits are not expected to be settled wholly before 12 months after the end of the annual reporting period, IAS 19's requirements for other long-term employee benefits should be applied.

Because termination benefits are not provided in exchange for service, the requirements of IAS 19:70 to 74 (see **section 7.3.4**) relating to the attribution of the benefit to periods of service are not relevant. [IAS 19:170]

The following example is reproduced from the Standard.

Example 10.4

Recognition and measurement of termination benefits

[Example illustrating IAS 19:159 - 170]

Background

As a result of a recent acquisition, an entity plans to close a factory in ten months and, at that time, terminate the employment of all of the remaining employees at the factory. Because the entity needs the expertise of the employees at the factory to complete some contracts, it announces a plan of termination as follows.

Each employee who stays and renders service until the closure of the factory will receive on the termination date a cash payment of CU30,000. Employees leaving before closure of the factory will receive CU10,000.

There are 120 employees at the factory. At the time of announcing the plan, the entity expects 20 of them to leave before closure. Therefore, the total expected cash outflows under the plan are CU3,200,000 (ie 20 × CU10,000 + 100 × CU30,000). As required by IAS 19:160, the entity accounts for benefits provided in exchange for termination of employment as termination benefits and accounts for benefits provided in exchange for services as short-term employee benefits.

Termination benefits

The benefit provided in exchange for termination of employment is CU10,000. This is the amount that an entity would have to pay for terminating the employment regardless of whether the employees stay and render service until closure of the factory or they leave before closure. Even though the employees can leave before closure, the termination of all employees' employment is a result of the entity's decision to close the factory and terminate their employment (ie all employees will leave employment when the factory closes). Therefore the entity recognises a liability of CU1,200,000 (ie 120 × CU10,000) for the termination benefits provided in accordance with the employee benefit plan at the earlier of when the plan of termination is announced and when the entity recognises the restructuring costs associated with the closure of the factory.

Benefits provided in exchange for service

The incremental benefits that employees will receive if they provide services for the full ten-month period are in exchange for services provided over that period. The entity accounts for them as short-term employee benefits because the entity expects to settle them before twelve months after the end of the annual reporting period. In this example, discounting is not required, so an expense of CU200,000 (ie CU2,000,000 ÷ 10) is recognised in each month during the service period of ten months, with a corresponding increase in the carrying amount of the liability.

When termination benefits are offered as part of a restructuring and are not expected to be settled wholly before 12 months after the end of the reporting period, they will be measured differently from other non-current provisions recognised as a result of the restructuring in accordance with IAS 37. This is due to the fact that IAS 37 requires the present value of expenditures to be determined using a pre-tax discount rate that reflects current market assessments and risks specific to the liability.

In contrast, IAS 19 requires all termination benefits that are not expected to be settled wholly before 12 months after the end of the reporting period to be measured as an other long-term employee benefit and, therefore, to be discounted using a discount rate determined with reference to market yields on high quality corporate bonds. If there is no deep market in such high quality corporate bonds, the market yields on government bonds should be used instead.

10.5 Disclosure – termination benefits

There are no specific disclosure requirements for termination benefits in IAS 19, but disclosures may be required by other Standards, for example:

[IAS 19:171]

- IAS 24 *Related Party Disclosures*, when termination benefits relate to key management personnel; and

- IAS 1 *Presentation of Financial Statements*, which requires disclosure of employee benefits expense.

11 Future developments

11.1 Proposed amendments to IAS 19 and IFRIC 14

In June 2015, the IASB issued ED/2015/5 *Remeasurement on a Plan Amendment, Curtailment or Settlement/Availability of a Refund from a Defined Benefit Plan*. The proposed amendments include clarification that:

- when determining the availability of a refund from a defined benefit plan:

  - the amount of the surplus an entity recognises as an asset on the basis of a future refund should not include amounts that other parties (e.g. the plan trustees) can use for other purposes (e.g. to enhance pension benefits) without the entity's consent; and

  - if other parties can wind up the plan without the entity's consent, the entity should not assume a right to a refund on the basis of gradual settlement of the plan;

- when a significant event occurs (e.g. a plan amendment, curtailment or settlement), the current service cost and net interest for the period following the significant event should be determined using the assumptions used when remeasuring the net defined benefit asset or liability; and

- any current service cost or net interest in the current reporting period prior to a plan amendment, curtailment or settlement should not be included in the past service cost or the gain or loss on settlement.

The comment deadline for these proposals is 19 October 2015.

11.2 Determination of an appropriate discount rate

The issue of the determination of an appropriate discount rate for the purpose of measuring defined benefit obligations has been the subject of much debate in recent years. This subject is being addressed by the IASB's research project on discount rates, which will:

- examine differences in the discount rate requirements in IFRSs;

- explain why those differences exist; and

- assess whether there are inconsistencies that should be addressed by the IASB.

At the time of writing, Board discussions on this subject had not yet commenced.

A16 Share-based payment

Contents

1   Introduction

1.1   Overview of IFRS 2

IFRS 2 *Share-based Payment* requires an entity to recognise share-based payment transactions (such as granted shares, share options or share appreciation rights) in its financial statements, including transactions with employees or other parties to be settled in cash, other assets or equity instruments of the entity. Specific requirements are included for equity-settled and cash-settled share-based payment transactions, as well as those for which the entity or the supplier has a choice of settlement by cash or equity instruments.

It is important to appreciate that IFRS 2 may be applicable even when the counterparty receives cash from the entity. This is because the scope of the Standard includes cash-settled share-based payment transactions, as explained in **section 2**.

The expense recognised under IFRS 2 is unaffected by whether the award is satisfied by an issue of new shares or by shares being purchased in the market. When shares are purchased in the market, an employee share trust may be involved (see **section 9**).

1.2   Amendments to IFRS 2 since the last edition of this manual

None. IFRS 2 was most recently amended in December 2013.

2   Scope

2.1   Scope – general

IFRS 2 should be applied to each 'share-based payment transaction' as defined in IFRS 2:Appendix A (see **2.2**) subject to the exceptions in IFRS 2:3A to 6 (see **2.4** to **2.7**).

2.2   Scope – definitions

Appendix A of IFRS 2 provides the following definitions for terms relating to the scope of the Standard.

- A **share-based payment transaction** is "[a] transaction in which the entity
  - (a) receives goods or services from the supplier of those goods or services (including an employee) in a share-based payment arrangement, or
  - (b) incurs an obligation to settle the transaction with the supplier in a share-based payment arrangement when another group entity receives those goods or services".

IFRS 2 does not include a formal definition of either goods or services, although IFRS 2:5 specifies that goods would include inventories, consumables, property, plant and equipment, intangible assets and other non-financial assets, and that equity instruments granted to employees are within the scope of the Standard. As discussed at **2.8**, IFRS 2:2 confirms that goods or services do not have to be identifiable to be within the scope of IFRS 2.

IFRS 2 does not apply to transactions in which an entity acquires goods as part of the net assets acquired in a business combination as defined in IFRS 3 *Business Combinations* or to the contribution of a business on formation of a joint venture as defined in IFRS 11 *Joint Arrangements* (see **section 2.6**).

- A **share-based payment arrangement** is "[a]n agreement between the entity (or another group entity or any shareholder of any group entity) and another party (including an employee) that entitles the other party to receive
  - (a) cash or other assets of the entity for amounts that are based on the price (or value) of equity instruments (including shares or share options) of the entity or another group entity, or
  - (b) equity instruments (including shares or share options) of the entity or another group entity,

  provided that the specified vesting conditions, if any, are met".

  A footnote to IFRS 2 notes that, for this purpose, a 'group' is defined in Appendix A of IFRS 10 *Consolidated Financial Statements* as "a parent and its subsidiaries" from the perspective of the reporting entity's ultimate parent.

Cash-settled Share Appreciation Rights (SARs) are the most common example of an arrangement under which the entity acquires goods or services by incurring a liability to transfer cash or other assets for amounts based on the price (or value) of the entity's shares or other equity instruments; such arrangements are sometimes referred to as 'phantom option schemes'. Typically, these schemes put the employees in the same position as if they had been granted options, but they involve a cash payment to the employees equal to the gain that would have been made by exercising the notional options and immediately selling the shares in the market.

- An **equity instrument** is defined as "[a] contract that evidences a residual interest in the assets of an entity after deducting all of its liabilities".

  This definition is consistent with paragraph 11 of IAS 32 *Financial Instruments: Presentation*.

- **Equity instrument granted** is defined as "[t]he right (conditional or unconditional) to an equity instrument of the entity conferred by the entity on another party under a share-based payment arrangement".

2.3 Identifying share-based payment transactions – examples

2.3.1 Cash payment based on earnings multiple

Example 2.3.1

Cash payment based on earnings multiple

Company N, an unlisted entity, issued instruments to its employees that entitle them to a cash payment equal to the increase in Company N's 'share price' (as defined) between the grant date and the vesting date. The terms and conditions of the instrument define the 'share price' as a specified multiple of EBITDA divided by the number of shares in issue.

Arrangements of this nature will not usually be in the scope of IFRS 2 because a specified multiple of EBITDA will not necessarily reflect the fair value of the shares; historical earnings is only one of the inputs used to determine the fair value of shares in an entity. Such arrangements will more likely fall within the scope of IAS 19 *Employee Benefits*.

2.3.2 Remuneration scheme based on a profit formula

Example 2.3.2

Remuneration scheme based on a profit formula

Company A has a deferred bonus incentive scheme. The value of the entitlements is based on a formula derived from Company A's net profit (adjusted for specified items) and then divided by a fixed number. This entitlement vests over 3 years. The payment to the employee on vesting date, or the date that the employee chooses to receive settlement after the entitlement has vested, is funded by the cash resources of Company A.

For example: entitlement value = (operating profit × 10) ÷ CU100 million

	Year 1	Year 2	Year 3
	CUm	CUm	CUm
Operating profit	3,000	3,500	4,100
	CU	CU	CU
Entitlement value	300	350	410

A participant who exercises his or her right to receive settlement for a vested entitlement will receive the difference between the current entitlement value and the grant date entitlement value in cash.

In the example, if a participant received 100 entitlements at an entitlement value of CU250, the participant would receive CU16,000 (100 × (CU410 – CU250)) at the end of Year 3.

This remuneration scheme does not fall within the scope of IFRS 2. The entitlements issued by Company A represent a bonus scheme that does not result in the issue of equity instruments or in a liability that is linked to the price of Company A's shares or other equity instruments of Company A; the scheme is an employee benefits scheme within the scope of IAS 19. The benefits payable under the scheme do not meet the definition of 'short-term employee benefits' under IAS 19 because they are not expected to be settled wholly within twelve months after the end of the annual reporting period in which the related service is rendered. Therefore, the recognition and measurement requirements of IAS 19 for other long-term employee benefits should be applied.

2.3.3   Employee share loan plans

In November 2005, the IFRIC (now the IFRS Interpretations Committee) was asked to consider the accounting treatment of employee share loan plans. Under many such plans, employee share purchases are facilitated by means of a loan from the grantor with recourse only to the shares. The IFRIC was asked whether the loan should be considered as part of a potential share-based payment, with the entire arrangement treated as an option under IFRS 2, or whether the loan should be accounted for separately as a financial asset. The IFRIC noted that when the loan is with recourse only to the shares (sometimes referred to as 'limited recourse' or 'non-recourse'), the issue of shares using the proceeds of the loan would be treated as a grant of options that are exercised when the loan is repaid. The IFRIC determined that it would not expect diversity in practice and, therefore, did not take this item onto its agenda.

Example 2.3.3A and **example 2.3.3B** illustrate the application of this principle to a non-recourse loan. **Example 2.3.3C** examines the contrasting position of a full recourse loan.

Example 2.3.3A

Employee share loan plans

Company R grants loans to its employees that subsequently are to be used by the employees to buy shares in Company R. For the purpose of obtaining settlement of the loans, Company R only has recourse to the shares bought by the employees.

Should these loans be considered part of a share-based payment arrangement accounted for under IFRS 2 (with the entire arrangement treated as an option), or should they be accounted for as financial assets in accordance with IFRS 9

Financial Instruments *(or, for entities that have not yet adopted IFRS 9, IAS 39 Financial Instruments: Recognition and Measurement)?*

The employee share loan plan should be accounted for in accordance with IFRS 2 because it falls within the scope of IFRS 2:2(c) – i.e. it results in "transactions in which the entity receives ... services and the terms of the arrangement provide ... the supplier of those ... services with a choice of whether the entity settles the transaction in cash ... or by issuing equity instruments".

Because, for the purpose of obtaining settlement of the loans, Company R only has recourse to the shares bought by the employees, Company R effectively issues share options to its employees who use the loans granted to pay for the shares. Exercise of the options would be on the date or dates when the loan is repaid by the employee.

Example 2.3.3B

Non-recourse loan to purchase shares

Company L provides an interest-free loan in the amount of CU100 to one of its executives to purchase shares with a fair value of CU100 in the open market. The shares are used as collateral for the loan balance and, therefore, cannot be sold by the executive during the four-year vesting period. If the executive remains employed with Company L at the end of four years, the entire amount of the loan is forgiven and the shares are released from all restrictions. If the executive leaves Company L's employment during the vesting period, the shares are transferred to Company L and, regardless of value, are considered full payment of the loan.

Because the executive has no risk of owing more than the shares are worth, the substance of the transaction is the issue of restricted shares that vest at the end of four years and, therefore, the transaction is within the scope of IFRS 2. As a result, the fair value of the restricted shares at the grant date should be expensed over the vesting period.

Example 2.3.3C

Full recourse loan to purchase shares

Company L provides an interest-free loan in the amount of CU100 to one of its executives to purchase shares with a fair value of CU100 in the open market under the following terms:

- the shares are used as collateral for the loan balance and, therefore, cannot be sold by the executive during the four-year vesting period;
- if the executive remains employed with Company L at the end of the four years, the entire amount of the loan is forgiven and the shares are released from all restrictions;
- if the executive leaves Company L's employment during the vesting period, the shares are returned to Company L; and

- if the market price of the shares at the date the executive leaves Company L is less than the amount repayable under the loan, Company L has recourse to the personal assets of the executive.

To conclude whether the substance of this arrangement represents the granting of share options under IFRS 2, all facts and circumstances should be assessed carefully. In particular, the following factors should be considered:

- whether the employer intends to seek repayment beyond the shares issued; and

- whether the employer has a history of demanding repayment of loan amounts in excess of the fair value of shares.

If it is concluded that the loan represents a full recourse lending arrangement, Company L should account for the loan in accordance with IFRS 9 (or, for entities that have not yet adopted IFRS 9, IAS 39), including the recognition of any interest-free component as an expense. If the loan is subsequently forgiven, the resulting expense is recognised under IAS 19 as an employee benefit.

2.3.4 Bonus to be settled either in cash or in shares 'to the value of'

Example 2.3.4

Bonus to be settled either in cash or in shares 'to the value of'

Entity P agrees to pay its employees a bonus based on performance criteria unrelated to its share price. The bonus is determined as a monetary sum. The terms of the arrangement permit Entity P the choice of settlement in cash (e.g. CU5,000) or shares to the value of that cash (CU5,000/market value of shares at date of settlement); Entity P has a practice of settling in shares.

The arrangement meets the definition of a share-based payment arrangement under IFRS 2. An equity-settled share-based payment transaction is defined in IFRS 2:Appendix A as a share-based payment transaction "in which the entity receives goods or services as consideration for equity instruments of the entity". Because Entity P has a practice of settling in shares and has not created a constructive obligation to settle in cash, the award is not a cash-settled share-based payment and, accordingly, is classified as an equity-settled share-based payment.

IFRS 2:BC266 specifically notes that classification as equity-settled or cash-settled on this basis is not consistent with the requirements of IAS 32 for other circumstances when the entity has a choice regarding the manner of settlement. IAS 32 requires arrangements under which the entity has a choice of settlement to be classified either wholly as a liability (if the contract is a derivative contract) or as a compound instrument (if the contract is a non-derivative contract).

Refer to **example 5.2.3.4** for guidance on the measurement of an award of shares to a monetary value.

2.3.5   *Employees' taxes on share-based payments paid by employer*

Example 2.3.5

Employees' taxes on share-based payments paid by employer

Entity A grants share options to senior employees under a share-based payment arrangement within the scope of IFRS 2. Options granted under the arrangement vest after four years if the employees remain in Entity A's employment at that date.

Under the tax regime in which Entity A operates, the employee is taxed at the grant date based on the market value of the shares at that date. The tax paid at grant date cannot be recovered in the event that the share options do not vest.

Under the terms of the share-based payment arrangement, Entity A has agreed to pay the employees' taxes on behalf of the employees. The employees have no obligation to refund the taxes paid on their behalf.

The employees' tax should be expensed in the period in which it is due.

The employees' tax is paid at grant date and it is not reimbursable. Payment of the employees' tax by Entity A on behalf of its employees is a separate benefit from the grant of share options. In substance, it is a cash-settled share-based payment award with no vesting period because it cannot be recovered by Entity A if the employees leave before the end of the four-year vesting period.

2.3.6   *Preference shares with conversion option issued as consideration for purchase of goods*

Example 2.3.6

Preference shares with conversion option issued as consideration for purchase of goods

Company A acquires an intellectual property intangible asset from Company X. Consideration is in the form of preference shares issued at the time of the transaction.

The issued preference shares have the following characteristics:

- entitlement to an annual non-discretionary 8 per cent dividend to perpetuity;
- the holder of the shares has the right to convert the preference shares to ordinary shares of Company A (adjusted only for capital reorganisations or capitalisation issues that affect all holders of the ordinary shares). The holder can exercise this option at any time from the date of issue of the instruments;
- entitlement to a share of net assets on liquidation after distribution to another class of preference shareholders; and
- no maturity date (i.e. will remain in existence unless converted).

Should the arrangement be accounted for in accordance with the requirements of IFRS 2, or in accordance with IAS 32 and IFRS 9 (or, for entities that have not yet adopted IFRS 9, IAS 39)?

The arrangement should be accounted for as a share-based payment transaction under IFRS 2. Company A has received goods from Company X and has, in return, provided Company X with a choice of settlement in cash (perpetual dividend stream) or equity (ordinary shares). Consequently, the transaction falls within the scope of IFRS 2:2(c).

IFRS 2:35 clarifies that if an entity has granted the counterparty the right to choose whether a share-based payment transaction is settled in cash or by the issue of equity instruments, the entity has granted a compound instrument. The instrument has:

- a liability component – Company X's right to receive a perpetual stream of 8 per cent dividends; and
- an equity component – Company X's right to convert to ordinary shares.

Each component is accounted for separately as required by IFRS 2:35:

- the liability component is measured at fair value; and
- the equity component is measured as the difference between the fair value of the intangible asset received and the fair value of the liability component, at the date when the goods or services are received.

The liability component should, in accordance with IFRS 2:30, be recognised in the statement of financial position at fair value and remeasured at the end of each accounting period, with all movements in fair value being recognised in profit or loss. The fair value of the equity component is recognised in equity, with no further remeasurement.

If Company X chooses to exercise the conversion option, at the date of conversion, the liability component is remeasured to its fair value and is transferred directly to equity as the consideration for the equity instruments issued (see IFRS 2:39).

The recognition of liability and equity components at the date of issue of the preference shares is similar to the equivalent requirements of IAS 32; however, the treatment of the liability component subsequent to the issue of the preference shares differs from the equivalent requirements of IFRS 9 (or, for entities that have not yet adopted IFRS 9, IAS 39), which would not require the liability component to be remeasured to fair value on an ongoing basis.

The application of these requirements is illustrated in **example 7.2.3**.

2.3.7 Share options purchased by employees at fair value but including a service condition

---

Example 2.3.7

Share options purchased by employees at fair value but including a service condition

Entity A grants one share option to each of its 100 employees. The share options will vest at the end of two years provided that (1) the employee remains in Entity A's employment at that date, and (2) the EBITDA of Entity A for the second year achieves a specified target.

At the grant date, each recipient is required to make a cash payment of CU100 to Entity A based on an estimated fair value of the share option which reflects the probability that the target EBITDA will be achieved in the second year. Excluding the effect of the EBITDA condition, the fair value of each option would be CU300.

Cash paid by the employees is not refundable in any circumstances. If an employee leaves the employment of Entity A, or if Entity A does not achieve the target EBITDA, no shares will be issued and the employee will not be entitled to a repayment. Accordingly, both the service and the non-market vesting condition are deemed to be substantive.

The transaction should be accounted for as a share-based payment arrangement, with the EBITDA target treated as a non-market vesting condition.

Notwithstanding that the employee is required to pay 'fair value' for the share option, the terms of the arrangement are such that the entity receives additional consideration for the share option in the form of the employee's service for two years. Therefore, the transaction meets IFRS 2's definition of an equity-settled share-based payment transaction and falls within the scope of IFRS 2. The value of the employee's service is measured at CU200, which is the difference between the value assigned to the option in accordance with IFRS 2 (i.e. CU300 – excluding the effect of non-market vesting conditions) and the price paid by the employee (CU100).

Payments by employees are accounted for as equity transactions when the cash is received, with no subsequent adjustment made other than a possible transfer between components of equity when shares are issued or options lapse unexercised.

2.3.8 Awards made by shareholders

IFRS 2:3A states that a share-based payment transaction may be settled by a shareholder (of any group entity) and still be within the scope of IFRS 2 (see also **2.4.1**).

When a shareholder provides shares for the purposes of an employee share scheme, it will generally be clear that these benefits form part of the remuneration of the employees for their services to the entity. A charge to profit or loss will, therefore, be required in accordance with IFRS 2 for the services received.

On the other hand, a shareholder may make a gift of shares to a close relative who is coincidentally an employee of the entity. Such a gift might not form part of the remuneration of the employee but it will be necessary to look carefully at the facts of each case. For example, it would be necessary to consider whether similar benefits were given to other employees and whether the gift of shares was in any way conditional on continuing employment with the entity.

The most common instance when equity instruments are provided by a shareholder rather than the entity that has received the goods or services is within groups.

2.4   Groups

2.4.1   Parent and subsidiaries

It is often the case that employees of a subsidiary will receive part of their remuneration in the form of shares in the parent, or less commonly in shares of some other group entity. In such circumstances, IFRS 2 requires the entity that has received the benefit of the services to recognise an expense. This is so even if the equity instruments issued are those of another group entity.

The scope of the Standard includes an entity that:

[IFRS 2:3A]

* receives goods or services when another entity in the same group (or a shareholder of any group entity) has the obligation to settle the share-based payment transaction; or

* has an obligation to settle a share-based payment transaction when another entity in the same group receives the goods or services;

unless the transaction is clearly for a purpose other than payment for goods or services supplied to the entity receiving them.

Example 2.4.1

Services received in equity-settled share-based payment transaction

Company P is a publicly listed entity that applies US GAAP. Company P has a majority-owned subsidiary, Company S, which applies IFRSs. Company P issues share options in Company P's ordinary shares to certain employees of Company S.

Company S receives the benefit of the services provided by its employees. As a result, Company S should recognise the expense related to the share-based payment, regardless of whether Company S, or another group entity, issues the share options and regardless of any accounting applied by Company P under US GAAP. When Company P issues the share options, it may also be appropriate to recognise a capital contribution from Company P to Company S (see **section 8**).

2.4.2 Meaning of 'entity' in the context of groups

The definition of a share-based payment arrangement (see **2.2**) refers when appropriate to an 'entity or another group entity'.

IFRS 2 is clear that an expense must be recognised by the entity that has received the benefit of the goods or services. When the parent provides the shares, the other side of this accounting entry is a credit to equity which is in the nature of a capital contribution. IFRS 2 addresses the accounting for group cash-settled share-based payment transactions in the separate or individual financial statements of the entity receiving the goods or services when the entity has no obligation to settle the share-based payment transactions. The Standard also provides guidance on the circumstances in which an arrangement is equity-settled from the perspective of the group but cash-settled from the perspective of the subsidiary (and vice versa). However, IFRS 2 does not address the effect of charges made between group entities in connection with share-based payment arrangements. The requirements of IFRS 2 for group share-based payment arrangements and some related issues not addressed by the Standard are considered in detail in **section 8**.

2.5 Transactions with owners in their capacity as owners

The requirements of IFRS 2 should not be applied to transactions with parties (e.g. employees) in their capacity as holders of equity instruments of the entity (referred to as 'owners' in IAS 1 *Presentation of Financial Statements*). For example, a rights issue may be offered to all holders of a particular class of equity (e.g. a right to acquire additional shares at a price that is less than the fair value of those instruments). If an employee is offered the chance to participate purely because he/she is a holder of that class of equity, IFRS 2 is not applied. The requirements of IFRS 2 are only relevant for transactions in which goods or services are acquired. [IFRS 2:4]

Example 2.5

Shares purchased from employee shareholders at fair value

Company D purchases its own shares from employees (in their capacity as shareholders) for an amount that equals the fair value of those shares. This

> transaction would be considered a purchase of treasury shares and is not within the scope of IFRS 2. However, if Company D pays an amount in excess of fair value only to its employees, that excess would be considered a remuneration expense (see **example 5.5.2D**).

2.6   Business combinations and formations of joint ventures

2.6.1   Goods acquired in a business combination or on formation of a joint venture generally excluded from the scope of IFRS 2

IFRS 2 applies to share-based payment transactions in which an entity acquires or receives goods or services. Goods include inventories, consumables, property, plant and equipment, intangible assets and other non-financial assets. However, IFRS 2 is not applied to transactions in which an entity acquires goods as part of the net assets acquired in a business combination (as defined by IFRS 3 *Business Combinations*), in a combination of entities or businesses under common control (as described in IFRS 3:B1 to B4), or the contribution of a business on formation of a joint venture (as defined by IFRS 11 *Joint Arrangements*). [IFRS 2:5]

2.6.2   Equity instruments granted to employees of the acquiree in their capacity as employees

Equity instruments issued in a business combination in exchange for control of the acquiree are not within the scope of IFRS 2. But equity instruments granted to employees of the acquiree in their capacity as employees (e.g. in return for continued services in the post-combination period) are within the scope of IFRS 2. Similarly, the cancellation, replacement or other modification of share-based payment arrangements because of a business combination or other equity restructuring are accounted for in accordance with IFRS 2. [IFRS 2:5]

2.6.3   Equity instruments granted to previous owners of the acquiree who are also employees

When shares are issued in a business combination to previous owners of the acquiree who are also employees of the acquiree, it is necessary to determine to what extent they are purchase consideration and to what extent they are share-based payments. IFRS 3 provides guidance for determining whether equity instruments issued in a business combination are part of the consideration transferred in exchange for control of the acquiree (and, therefore, within the scope of IFRS 3) or are in return for continued service to be recognised in the post-combination period (and, therefore, within the scope of IFRS 2). This guidance is considered in **section 8.3.3** of **chapter A25**.

IFRS 3 also provides guidance on the appropriate accounting for pre-existing acquiree share-based payment awards, both vested and unvested, by an acquirer, including those that lapse, are replaced or are un-replaced (see **section 8.3.4** of **chapter A25**).

2.6.4 Shares issued by joint ventures in exchange for contributions received

When joint ventures are formed, they frequently issue shares in exchange for contributions from venturers. These contributions can be received in various forms (e.g. cash, assets or businesses).

When the contribution is in the form of cash and the shares are not issued as consideration for goods or services, the cash contribution is received from the venturers in their capacity as owners. It is, therefore, outside the scope of IFRS 2 for the joint venture and should be accounted for in accordance with IAS 32.

However, when a venturer contributes assets that do not comprise a business (e.g. property, plant and equipment or an intangible asset) on the formation of a joint venture, these transactions are within the scope of IFRS 2 for the joint venture because the joint venture issues shares as consideration for goods. Such transactions should be accounted for as equity-settled share-based payment transactions with non-employees.

Transactions in which a venturer contributes a business in exchange for shares in the joint venture are outside the scope of IFRS 2 and IFRS 3 for the joint venture. The selection of appropriate accounting policies for such transactions involves similar considerations to those for combinations of entities or businesses under common control which are also outside the scope of IFRS 3 (see **2.3.2** in **chapter A25**).

2.7 Financial instruments

IFRS 2 does not apply to share-based payment transactions in which the entity receives or acquires goods or services under a contract within the scope of paragraphs 8 to 10 of IAS 32 or paragraphs 2.4 to 2.7 of IFRS 9 (or, for entities that have not yet adopted IFRS 9, paragraphs 5 to 7 of IAS 39). [IFRS 2:6]

IAS 32 and IFRS 9 (IAS 39) both state that they should be applied to contracts to buy or sell a non-financial item that can be settled net in cash or by another financial instrument, or by exchanging financial instruments, as if the contracts were financial instruments (apart from contracts entered into and continuing to be held for the purpose of the receipt or delivery of a non-financial item in accordance with the entity's expected purchase, sale or usage requirements (the 'own-use' exemption)). Such contracts are considered in **chapter B1** (or, for entities that have not yet adopted IFRS 9, **chapter C1**). IFRS 2:BC28 explains that the IASB concluded that such contracts should remain within the scope of IAS 32 and IFRS 9 (IAS 39) and, consequently, they are excluded from the scope of IFRS 2.

Example 2.7

Interaction with IAS 32 and IFRS 9

Company C enters into a forward contract to buy 1,000 units of a commodity for consideration of 2,000 of Company C's ordinary shares. Company C can settle the contract net in cash or another financial instrument, but does not intend to do so because the commodity is being purchased for the purpose of receipt in accordance with Company C's expected usage requirements; Company C does not have a past practice of settling similar contracts net in cash. Accordingly, the transaction is within the scope of IFRS 2 because it involves the issue of shares in exchange for goods.

However, if Company C had a practice of settling these contracts net, or Company C did not intend to take physical delivery of the commodity, the forward contract would be within the scope of IAS 32 and IFRS 9 (or, for entities that have not yet adopted IFRS 9, IAS 39) and, therefore, IFRS 2 would not apply.

Example 2.3.6 addresses the accounting for preference shares with a conversion option that are issued as consideration for the purchase of goods.

2.8   Goods or services cannot be specifically identified

IFRS 2 applies to share-based payment transactions, whether or not the entity can identify specifically some or all of the goods or services received. [IFRS 2:2] Accordingly, the Standard applies to transactions when the identifiable consideration received (or to be received) by the entity, including cash and the fair value of identifiable non-cash consideration, appears to be less than the fair value of the equity instruments granted or the liability incurred.

In the absence of specifically identifiable goods or services, other circumstances may indicate that goods or services have been, or will be, received. In this case IFRS 2 applies. [IFRS 2:2]

If the identifiable consideration received appears to be less than the fair value of the equity instruments granted, or the liability incurred, typically this circumstance indicates that other consideration (i.e. unidentifiable goods or services) has been, or will be, received. [IFRS 2:13A]

The entity measures any identifiable goods and services in accordance with IFRS 2. Any unidentifiable goods or services received are then measured as the difference between the fair value of the share-based payment and the fair value of any identifiable goods or services received.

The unidentifiable goods or services are measured at grant date although, for cash-settled arrangements, the liability is remeasured at the end of each reporting period until it is settled. [IFRS 2:13A]

IFRS 2 gives the example of a grant of shares to a charitable organisation for nil consideration as an instance when it may be difficult to demonstrate that goods or services have been, or will be, received. It notes that a similar situation might arise in transactions with other parties. [IFRS 2:IG5A]

An illustrative example accompanying IFRS 2 deals with a situation in which an entity grants shares for no consideration to parties who form a particular section of community, as a means of enhancing its corporate image. The example notes that the economic benefits might take a variety of forms such as increasing the entity's customer base, attracting and retaining employees, and improving its chances of being awarded contracts.

There may be no obvious benefits of this kind in circumstances when shares are required by law to be issued at below their market value. However, IFRS 2 should still be applied and an expense recognised. This might be viewed as 'the price of staying in business' or akin to a form of taxation.

For transactions with parties other than employees, IFRS 2 establishes a rebuttable presumption that the fair value of the goods or services received can be estimated reliably. The IASB concluded that goods or services that are unidentifiable cannot be reliably measured and so the rebuttable presumption is relevant only for identifiable goods or services. Therefore, in this case, it is necessary to derive the value of the unidentifiable goods or services received from the value of the equity instruments. [IFRS 2:BC128D]

This approach might be seen to imply that it is always necessary to consider the fair value of the equity instruments granted to see if this is greater than the fair value of the goods or services received. This is not so. IFRS 2:BC128C states that "[t]he Board noted that it is neither necessary nor appropriate to measure the fair value of goods or services as well as the fair value of the share-based payment for every transaction in which the entity receives goods or non-employee services".

In practice, it will be necessary to consider this issue only in those circumstances when the value of the goods or services received 'appears to be' less than the fair value of the equity instruments granted. For example, it would not be necessary to obtain a valuation of unquoted shares that had been issued as consideration for non-employee services unless there were indications that some other non-identifiable goods or services had also been obtained.

When the value of the shares is known because they are quoted in a market and this produces a materially different value from the value attributed to the services in accordance with IFRS 2, an additional expense may need to be recognised for unidentified goods and services. In such situations, all evidence needs to be considered carefully to understand the substance of the transaction and the reason for the apparent discrepancy. This may, in some cases, indicate that additional services were received. In other cases, the services may have been difficult to value and the conflicting evidence may prompt a reconsideration of that value. In rare cases, the arrangements may indeed relate to unidentified goods or services (e.g. because the difference represents a charitable donation).

The phrase 'the fair value of the share-based payment' refers to the value of the particular share-based payment concerned. For example, an entity might be required by legislation to issue some portion of its shares to nationals of a particular country, which may be transferred only to other nationals of that country. Such transfer restrictions may affect the fair value of the shares concerned. They may have a fair value that is less than the fair value of otherwise identical shares that do not carry the transfer restrictions. In such circumstances, if it is the restricted shares that are granted, the phrase 'the fair value of the share-based payment' in IFRS 2 refers to the fair value of the restricted shares and not to the fair value of the unrestricted shares. [IFRS 2:IG5C]

2.9   Employment taxes on share-based payments

In some jurisdictions, employment taxes may be payable which are determined by reference to the gain made by the employee on the exercise of share options.

When the amount of tax is based on the gain made by the employee (i.e. intrinsic value at exercise date), the following questions arise:

- *does the entity have a liability before the employee exercises the options?*

- *if so, how should that liability be measured at the end of each reporting period?*

Such payments of tax are outside the scope of IFRS 2 because they are not payments to the suppliers of goods or services. However, these are similar to the questions addressed in IFRS 2 for cash-settled share-based payments. A liability should, therefore, be recognised at the end of each reporting period for such tax. This is consistent with the requirements of IAS 37 *Provisions, Contingent Liabilities and Contingent Assets* as well as those of IFRS 2 because the 'obligating event' is the granting of the options by the entity rather than the exercise of the options by the employees. The liability could be measured on the same basis as required by IFRS 2, although it is acceptable to use intrinsic value at the end of the reporting period rather than fair value determined using an option pricing model, given that the liability is outside the scope of IFRS 2. Measuring the liability at fair value in accordance with IFRS 2 is nevertheless to be preferred.

Under IFRSs, staff costs generally are within the scope of IAS 19 *Employee Benefits*, which requires staff costs to be recognised over the period in which services are provided. Therefore, in the absence of any conflicting interpretation by the IFRS Interpretations Committee, the liability could be built up over the vesting period.

3 Classification of share-based payment transactions

3.1 Classification of share-based payment transactions – general

Under IFRS 2, different accounting is required for different types of share-based payment transactions. Three types of transactions are identified in IFRS 2:

[IFRS 2:2]

- equity-settled share-based payment transactions (see **section 3.2**);
- cash-settled share-based payment transactions (see **section 3.3**); and
- transactions in which the entity receives or acquires goods or services and the terms of the arrangement provide either the entity or the supplier of those goods or services with a choice as to whether the entity settles the transaction in cash (or other assets) or by issuing equity instruments (see **3.4**).

3.2 Equity-settled share-based payment transactions

3.2.1 Equity-settled share-based payment transaction – definition

Appendix A of IFRS 2 defines an **equity-settled share-based payment transaction** as "[a] share-based payment transaction in which the entity

(a) receives goods or services as consideration for its own equity instruments (including shares or share options), or

(b) receives goods or services but has no obligation to settle the transaction with the supplier".

Accordingly, if a subsidiary receives goods or services but has no obligation to settle the transaction because its parent, or another group entity, is instead obliged to do so, that transaction meets the definition of an equity-settled share-based payment transaction.

3.2.2   Cash payments to employees made by acquirer in a business combination

Some equity-settled share-based payment arrangements include a clause that, in the event of a change in control of the entity, the employees will be required (or may be permitted) to sell their shares or share options to the acquirer on the same terms as are available to other vendors (i.e. at the same price, adjusted, if appropriate, for the option exercise price).

Such a clause does not alter the classification of the arrangement as equity-settled under IFRS 2. The entity does not have any obligation to pay cash if it is acquired. An acquirer may incur such an obligation in the future as a consequence of the acquisition of the entity. However, that obligation would be outside of the scope of IFRS 2 from the acquired entity's perspective because it does not have the obligation to make the payment.

Therefore, the fact that a potential acquirer may pay cash to the employees at some point in the future does not affect the entity's assessment that this is an equity-settled arrangement.

3.2.3   Entity agrees to sell shares on behalf of employees

Sometimes employees may not want to become long-term investors in an entity. As a result, they may wish to realise equity-settled awards in cash as soon as possible after the awards vest. To facilitate this realisation process, the entity may agree either to sell the shares in the market on the employee's behalf or to engage a broker to do so.

If it is clear that the entity does not have an obligation to pay cash until the shares are sold in the market (and, therefore, the entity is not exposed to share price movements), then this agreement may not make an equity-settled share-based payment a cash-settled one if in selling the shares the entity is acting as an agent of the employee. This will also be the case when the entity merely facilitates the sale through a broker and the broker acts as an agent of the employee. Any brokerage costs incurred by the entity represent an employee benefit under IAS 19 and, therefore, should be included within employee expenses.

However, if the entity has created a valid expectation that it will repurchase the shares from the employee on its own account, this will normally make the arrangement cash-settled.

3.3 Cash-settled share-based payment transactions

3.3.1 Cash-settled share-based payment transaction – definition

Appendix A of IFRS 2 defines a **cash-settled share-based payment transaction** as "[a] share-based payment transaction in which the entity acquires goods or services by incurring a liability to transfer cash or other assets to the supplier of those goods or services for amounts that are based on the price (or value) of equity instruments (including shares or share options) of the entity or another group entity".

Therefore, the definition includes transactions when the transfer of cash or other assets is based on the price (or value) of the equity instruments of another group entity (e.g. a parent).

IFRS 2 includes separate measurement requirements for equity-settled and cash-settled share-based payment transactions, which are discussed in the remainder of this chapter. Business combinations, the contribution of a business on formation of a joint venture, and certain arrangements within the scope of IAS 32 are excluded from the scope of IFRS 2 as discussed at **2.6** and **2.7**.

3.3.2 Conflict between IFRS 2 and IAS 32

The liability/equity distinction in IFRS 2 is drawn along different lines from the general requirements of IAS 32 (see **chapter B3** or, for entities that have not yet adopted IFRS 9, **chapter C3**). This is explained in the following example.

Example 3.3.2

Equity-settled or cash-settled?

Company A issues 1,000 share options to an employee with an exercise price of CU15 per share. After completion of the vesting period, the employee will receive shares with a total value equal to the intrinsic value of the options (referred to below as equity-settled SARs).

The share options should be accounted for as equity-settled because settlement will be by delivery of equity instruments.

The number of shares that could be issued under the equity-settled SARs and the value of each share issued are variable. IFRS 2:BC106 and BC108 note that, if the debt/equity requirements of IAS 32 were applied to share-based payment transactions, instruments when the number of shares issued is variable would be considered a liability. They would, therefore, be treated similarly to a cash-settled share-based payment. As a result, IFRS 2:BC110 explains that the debt/equity requirements in IAS 32, whereby some obligations to issue equity instruments are classified as liabilities, should not be applied in the IFRS on share-based payments. IFRS 2:BC107 gives a SAR settled in

---

> shares as an example of an instrument that would be accounted for differently between IAS 32 and IFRS 2.

3.4   Transactions with settlement alternatives

A share-based payment transaction may provide either the entity or the counterparty with a choice as to whether settlement occurs in equity instruments or cash. The basic principles to be applied in such circumstances are as set out below.

For share-based payment transactions in which the terms of the arrangement provide either the entity or the counterparty with the choice of whether the entity settles the transaction in cash (or other assets) or by issuing equity instruments, the transaction is, or the components of that transaction are, accounted for:

[IFRS 2:34]

- as a cash-settled share-based payment transaction if, and to the extent that, the entity has incurred a liability to settle in cash or other assets; or

- as an equity-settled share-based payment transaction if, and to the extent that, no such liability has been incurred.

IFRS 2 contains more detailed requirements concerning how to apply these principles to share-based payment transactions in which the terms of the arrangement:

- provide the counterparty with a choice of settlement (see **section 7.2**); or

- provide the entity with a choice of settlement (see **7.3**).

Contingent cash settlement provisions are considered at **7.4**. Circumstances when the terms of settlement are modified are considered at **section 5.5.3** (for modification of an arrangement that has been accounted for as an equity-settled share-based payment transaction) and **6.4.2** (for modification of an arrangement that has been accounted for as a cash-settled share-based payment transaction).

3.5   Equity awards settled net of tax

The settlement of employees' equity-settled awards sometimes results in the employee receiving a reduced number of shares and a payment being made to the tax authority to settle the related tax liability. The value of the shares received is the total value of the award earned reduced by the amount of tax paid by the employer based on the employee's tax liability on the transaction. The question arises as to whether this type of settlement arrangement results in the award being considered partly cash-settled.

Whether this type of settlement arrangement should be treated as partly cash-settled or entirely equity-settled depends on whether the employer is acting as an agent for the employee in settling the employee's tax liability. The arrangement should be treated as entirely equity-settled if the employer is considered to be acting as an agent for the employee.

The assessment as to whether the entity is acting as an agent for the employee should be made on the basis of the facts and circumstances of each case. There will be circumstances when it is clear that the entity is acting as an agent (e.g. when the entity offers a broker's service to sell employees' shares and passes the cash to the tax authorities, but accepts no liability itself).

In some tax jurisdictions, the tax authority specifies situations in which the entity has a statutory duty to act as agent for its employees and remit tax on behalf of the employees.

This topic has been considered by the IFRS Interpretations Committee but no consensus emerged. The Committee identified a number of issues arising in this context for which the application of the requirements of IFRS 2 caused concern, such as separately classifying components of a single award. The Interpretations Committee has recommended to the IASB that this topic should be included in a future agenda proposal for IFRS 2.

4 Vesting and non-vesting conditions

4.1 Vesting – general

The approach to be adopted in relation to the timing of recognition of share-based payments depends largely on the concept of vesting. Appendix A of IFRS 2 defines **vest** as "[t]o become an entitlement. Under a share-based payment arrangement, a counterparty's right to receive cash, or other assets, or equity instruments of the entity vests when the counterparty's entitlement is no longer conditional on the satisfaction of vesting conditions".

If equity instruments vest immediately, it is generally assumed that the consideration for those equity instruments has been received (see **5.1.1**). If equity instruments do not vest immediately, the terms 'vesting conditions' and 'vesting period', as defined by IFRS 2, are important because they will determine the timing of recognition of share-based payments and will also affect measurement. These, and related, terms are considered in detail in **4.3** to **4.8**.

4.2   December 2013 amendments to clarify the definition of a vesting condition

Significant amendments were made to IFRS 2 in December 2013 by *Annual Improvements to IFRSs: 2010-2012 Cycle*. The amendments were made to clarify the definition of 'vesting condition' so as to ensure the consistent classification of conditions attached to share-based payments. Separate definitions for 'performance condition' and 'service condition' (which were previously part of the definition of vesting condition) were added to the Standard to make the description of each condition clearer and reduce diversity in the application of the guidance. The majority of the clarifications surround the definition of a performance condition (see **4.5**). The overall effect of the amendments is likely to be that conditions may be treated as non-vesting conditions that were previously determined to be vesting conditions.

The revised definitions are required to be applied prospectively to share-based payment transactions for which the grant date is on or after 1 July 2014, with earlier application permitted. If the revised definitions are applied for an award made before 1 July 2014, that fact is required to be disclosed. [IFRS 2:63B]

The IASB decided that the December 2013 amendments should be applied prospectively to avoid the use of hindsight in determining the grant date fair value of awards made in previous periods. [IFRS 2:BC370]

Sections 4.3 to **4.8** reflect the revised definitions of 'vesting condition' and related terms, and describe the principal effects of the December 2013 amendments. Entities that have not yet adopted the December 2013 amendments should refer to previous editions of this manual for the definitions that apply prior to the amendments.

4.3   Vesting condition – definition

Appendix A of IFRS 2 defines a **vesting condition** as "[a] condition that determines whether the entity receives the services that entitle the counterparty to receive cash, other assets or equity instruments of the entity, under a share-based payment arrangement. A vesting condition is either a service condition or a performance condition".

This definition is clear that vesting conditions are restricted to only service conditions (see **4.4**) and performance conditions (see **4.5**). A market condition (see **4.6**) is a type of performance condition.

A share-based payment vests when the counterparty's entitlement to it is no longer conditional on future service or performance conditions. Therefore, restrictive conditions such as non-compete provisions and transfer restrictions, which apply after the counterparty has become entitled to the share-based payment, are not vesting conditions. [IFRS 2:BC171B]

4.4 Service condition – definition

Appendix A of IFRS 2 defines a **service condition** as "[a] vesting condition that requires the counterparty to complete a specified period of service during which services are provided to the entity. If the counterparty, regardless of the reason, ceases to provide service during the vesting period, it has failed to satisfy the condition. A service condition does not require a performance target to be met".

The **vesting period** is "[t]he period during which all the specified vesting conditions of a share-based payment arrangement are to be satisfied".

Prior to the December 2013 amendments, IFRS 2 provided no specific guidance on how to account for a share-based payment award when the entity terminates an employee's employment. The December 2013 amendments have expanded the definition of a service condition to clarify that an employee's failure to complete a required service period for any reason (which would include termination of employment) is considered to be a failure to satisfy a service condition. The accounting consequence in such circumstances is that the compensation expense should be reversed. [IFRS 2:BC365 & BC366]

4.5 Performance condition – definition

Appendix A of IFRS 2 defines a performance condition as follows.

"A vesting condition that requires:

(a)   the counterparty to complete a specified period of service (ie a service condition); the service requirement can be explicit or implicit; and

(b)   specified performance target(s) to be met while the counterparty is rendering the service required in (a).

The period of achieving the performance target(s):

(a)   shall not extend beyond the end of the service period; and

(b)   may start before the service period on the condition that the commencement date of the performance target is not substantially before the commencement of the service period.

A performance target is defined by reference to:

(a)   the entity's own operations (or activities) or the operations or activities of another entity in the same group (ie a non-market condition); or

(b) the price (or value) of the entity's equity instruments or the equity instruments of another entity in the same group (including shares and share options) (ie a market condition).

A performance target might relate either to the performance of the entity as a whole or to some part of the entity (or part of the group), such as a division or an individual employee."

Therefore, a performance condition (which is a vesting condition) must involve both a service condition and a performance target. A performance target with no related service condition is a non-vesting condition (see **4.7**).

Examples of performance conditions include the vesting of options based upon:

- the total shareholder return (TSR) of the entity, either in absolute terms or relative to a comparator group or index (market-based);

- meeting a specific target share price (market-based); or

- levels of revenues (non-market-based).

The December 2013 amendments have expanded the definition of a performance condition (previously part of the definition of a vesting condition) considerably. The effect has been to provide clarification on a number of issues, including the following.

- For share-based payment transactions involving entities in the same group, a performance target can be set by reference to the price (or value) of another entity (or entities) within the same group (see IFRS 2:BC337).

- Regarding the duration of the performance target relative to the duration of the related service condition, the IASB has clarified that:

  [IFRS 2:BC339 - BC345]

  - the start of the period of achieving the performance target may be before the beginning of the service period, provided that the gap is not significant. The Board decided to allow some flexibility regarding the relative start dates following assertions by respondents to the exposure draft preceding the amendments that it is common for a performance target to start before the service period. For example, a performance target could be set as a measure of growth in earnings per share between the most recently published financial statements on the grant date and the most recently published financial statements before the vesting date. If some flexibility regarding the relative start dates were not allowed, then a relatively minor difference in the way that awards are structured could lead to a different classification of the performance target (i.e. as either a non-vesting condition or a performance (vesting condition), which could lead to difference in accounting; and

- the period over which the performance target is achieved should not extend beyond the service period. Consequently, the counterparty is required to complete the required period of service and to meet the performance target(s) while the counterparty is rendering the service required. A performance target that extends beyond the service period is a non-vesting condition (see **5.3.15**).

- The specified period of service that the counterparty is required to complete may be either implicit or explicit. [IFRS 2:BC346]

- It is not necessary for there to be a demonstrable correlation between an employee's responsibility and a performance target in order for that target to be a performance condition. The revised definition states explicitly that a performance target may relate to the performance of the entity as a whole or to some part of it, such as a division or an individual employee. [IFRS 2:BC347 - BC352]

- A target based on the performance of a share market index (e.g. a stock exchange index required to reach a specified target) is not a performance condition; it is a non-vesting condition. This is the case even if the entity's shares form part of the share market index. This conclusion is based on the fact that a share market index not only reflects the performance of the entity but also the performance of other entities outside the group. [IFRS 2:BC353 - BC358]

4.6 Market condition – definition

Appendix A of IFRS 2 defines a **market condition** as "[a] performance condition upon which the exercise price, vesting or exercisability of an equity instrument depends that is related to the market price (or value) of the entity's equity instruments (or the equity instruments of another entity in the same group), such as:

(a) attaining a specified share price or a specified amount of intrinsic value of a share option; or

(b) achieving a specified target that is based on the market price (or value) of the entity's equity instruments (or the equity instruments of another entity in the same group) relative to an index of market prices or equity instruments of other entities.

A market condition requires the counterparty to complete a specified period of service (ie a service condition); the service requirement can be explicit or implicit".

Similar to the definition of a performance condition (see **4.5**), the December 2013 amendments have clarified that, for share-based payment transactions involving entities in the same group, a market condition can be based on the market price of another entity in the same group.

Vesting and non-vesting conditions and their impact on the treatment of equity-settled share-based payment transactions are considered further at **section 5.3**.

4.7   Non-vesting conditions

IFRS 2 contains no formal definition for a 'non-vesting condition' (although implementation guidance on the split between vesting and non-vesting conditions is provided in the flowchart set out in IFRS 2:IG24 – see **5.3.1**). In the Basis for Conclusions on IFRS 2, the IASB observes that it can be inferred that a non-vesting condition is any condition that is not a vesting condition. [IFRS 2:BC363 - BC364]

IFRS 2:BC171A notes that "the feature that distinguishes a performance condition from a non-vesting condition is that the former has an explicit or implicit service requirement and the latter does not".

The following are examples of non-vesting conditions:

- a requirement to subscribe for shares to become entitled to be granted free 'matching shares' in certain types of share schemes;

- the payment of contributions to an SAYE scheme; and

- meeting a specific commodity index target.

Under SAYE share option schemes, employees save a regular amount, usually through deduction from salary, which is applied to cover the exercise price of the options when they are exercised. Employees are free to stop contributing to the scheme and obtain a refund of contributions at any time, but forfeit their entitlement to exercise the options if they do so. IFRS 2 makes clear that the payment of contributions into an SAYE scheme is not a vesting condition; it does not meet the definition of a performance condition because it has no link to service.

Non-vesting conditions are taken into account when estimating the fair value of the equity instruments at grant date. This is the same as the treatment of a market-based vesting condition. For example, on a grant of SAYE options, an estimate should be made of the number of employees who will cease to contribute to the scheme, otherwise than through termination of their employment, before the options vest. The grant date fair value should be reduced accordingly. Failure to meet a non-vesting condition (e.g. by ceasing to contribute to an SAYE scheme) should be accounted for as a cancellation of the options so that the expense will be accelerated.

4.8 Summary of the classification of conditions

IFRS 2:IG4A provides the following flowchart to illustrate the evaluation as to whether a condition is a service or performance condition or a non-vesting condition.

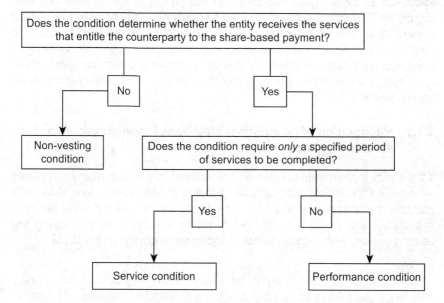

5 Recognition and measurement: equity-settled transactions

5.1 Recognition of equity-settled transactions

5.1.1 Recognition of equity-settled transactions – general

The goods or services received or acquired in an equity-settled share-based payment transaction are recognised as the goods are obtained or the services are received, with a corresponding increase in equity. [IFRS 2:7]

The goods or services received in a share-based payment transaction may qualify for recognition as an asset. If not, they are recognised as an expense. [IFRS 2:8]

Services are typically consumed immediately, in which case an expense is recognised as the counterparty renders service. Goods might be consumed over a period of time or, in the case of inventories, sold at a later date, in which case an expense is recognised when the goods are consumed or sold. However, sometimes it is necessary to recognise an expense before the goods or services are consumed or sold, because they do not qualify for recognition as assets. For example, an entity might acquire goods as part of the research phase of a project to develop a new product. Although those goods have not been consumed, they might not qualify for recognition as assets under the applicable IFRS. [IFRS 2:9]

It will normally be relatively straightforward to ascertain when goods are received, but this is not necessarily so when services are involved. The approach to be adopted in relation to the timing of recognition depends largely on the concept of vesting (see **section 4**). If equity instruments vest immediately then, in the absence of evidence to the contrary, it is presumed that the consideration for the instruments (e.g. employee services) has been received. The consideration (i.e. an expense or asset, as appropriate) should, therefore, be recognised in full, with a corresponding increase in equity. [IFRS 2:14]

5.1.2 Recognition of an equity-settled transaction subject to a service condition

If the equity instruments granted do not vest until the counterparty completes a specified period of service (i.e. a service condition – see **4.4**), it is presumed that the service period equals the vesting period. The services are accounted for as they are rendered by the counterparty during the vesting period, with a corresponding increase in equity. [IFRS 2:15]

> For example, an entity may grant share options which vest only once its employees have completed a specified period of employment – say, three years. In this scenario, the entity will recognise an expense over the three-year vesting period because the consideration for the share options (i.e. the employee service) is received over that period.

5.1.3 Recognition of an equity-settled transaction subject to a performance condition

If an employee is granted share options conditional upon the achievement of a performance condition and remaining in the entity's employ until that performance condition is satisfied (i.e. a performance condition – see **4.5**), and the length of the vesting period varies depending on when that performance condition is satisfied, the entity presumes that the services to be rendered by the employee as consideration for the share options will be received in the future, over the expected vesting period. The entity estimates the length of the expected vesting period at grant date, based on the most likely outcome of the performance condition. If the performance condition is a market condition (see **4.6**), the estimate of the length of the expected vesting period should be consistent with the assumptions used in estimating the fair value of the options granted, and should not be subsequently revised. If the performance condition is not a market condition, the entity revises its estimate of the length of the vesting period, if necessary, if subsequent information indicates that the length of the vesting period differs from previous estimates. [IFRS 2:15(b)]

5.1.4 Adjustments after vesting date

Having recognised the goods or services received in accordance with the requirements of IFRS 2 (and a corresponding increase in equity), no subsequent adjustment should be made to equity after vesting date. For example, the amount recognised for services received from an employee is not subsequently reversed if the vested equity instruments are later forfeited or, in the case of share options, are not exercised. This requirement does not, however, preclude a transfer from one component of equity to another. [IFRS 2:23]

For example, the expense recognised in accordance with IFRS 2 is not reversed if options vest but are not exercised because they are 'out of the money' or simply because the employee elects not to do so.

5.1.5 Presentation of increases in equity arising from equity-settled share-based payment transactions

For equity-settled share-based payment transactions, IFRS 2:7 (see **5.1.1**) requires the recognition of a 'corresponding increase in equity' for goods or services received and recognised. There is nothing in IFRSs to require or prohibit the presentation of the credit entry in a separate component of equity. This is true whether the credit entry is in relation to the entity's own equity instruments or those of its parent, in which case the credit entry is in the nature of a capital contribution by the parent (as described in **example 8.3.2**).

There is also nothing in IFRSs to prohibit the credit entry being recognised in retained earnings. However, local legal and regulatory requirements may need to be taken into account when determining the most appropriate treatment. In some jurisdictions, these requirements may require the credit entry to be regarded as capital and, consequently, prohibit its inclusion in retained earnings.

The position becomes more complicated when an employee share trust is involved, which is the case with some employee share schemes. For example, it may seem most appropriate to take the IFRS 2 credit entry to the 'employee share trust reserve' which represents the deduction within equity for own shares held. However, the IFRS 2 credit entry based on grant date fair value is unlikely to equal the purchase price of the shares in the trust less any exercise price, so a difference will build up. These issues are addressed at **9.5**.

5.2   Measurement of equity-settled transactions

5.2.1   Measurement of equity-settled transactions – general

For equity-settled share-based payment transactions, the goods or services received and the corresponding increase in equity are measured directly at the fair value of the goods or services received, unless that fair value cannot be estimated reliably. If it is not possible to estimate reliably the fair value of the goods or services received, the fair value of the equity instruments granted is used as a proxy. [IFRS 2:10] A limited exception to this requirement applies in rare circumstances when the entity is unable to estimate reliably the fair value of the equity instruments granted at the measurement date (see **5.4.8**).

Appendix 2 of IFRS 2 defines fair value as "[t]he amount for which an asset could be exchanged, a liability settled, or an equity instrument granted could be exchanged, between knowledgeable, willing parties in an arm's length transaction".

IFRS 2 uses the term 'fair value' in a way that differs in some respects from the definition of fair value in IFRS 13 *Fair Value Measurement*. When applying IFRS 2, an entity should measure fair value in accordance with the guidance in IFRS 2, not IFRS 13. [IFRS 2:6A]

Market conditions (see **4.6**) are taken into account when estimating the fair value of the equity instruments granted. All non-vesting conditions (see **4.7**) are similarly taken into account. However, non-market vesting conditions are not taken into account for this purpose. This is explained further at **section 5.3**.

5.2.2   Measurement of transactions with parties other than employees

5.2.2.1   Transactions with parties other than employees – measurement at the fair value of goods or services received

For transactions with parties other than employees, there is a rebuttable presumption that the fair value of the goods or services received can be estimated reliably. This fair value should be measured at the date the entity receives the relevant goods or services. This presumption should be rebutted only in those 'rare cases' in which the fair value of the goods or services received cannot be estimated reliably. In such circumstances, the fair value is measured indirectly by reference to the fair value of the equity instrument granted, measured at the date the entity receives the relevant goods or services. [IFRS 2:13]

> **Example 5.2.2.1**
>
> **Issue of shares for goods or services from non-employees**
>
> Company P issues shares to its external lawyers for services related to a recent lawsuit that Company P defended. The lawyers spent 100 hours working on the case. From other recent invoices from the lawyers, Company P determines that the fair value of the services received is CU300 per hour.
>
> The services received, and the corresponding increase in equity, should be measured directly at the fair value of the services received, i.e. CU30,000 (100 × CU300). Under IFRS 2:13, which introduces a rebuttable presumption that the fair value of goods or services received from parties other than employees can be reliably measured, Company P should not measure the transaction based on the fair value of the shares granted to the lawyers.

5.2.2.2 *Transactions with parties other than employees – measurement at the fair value of equity instrument granted*

For transactions with parties other than employees, in the exceptional circumstances when the presumption that the fair value of the goods or services received can be estimated reliably is rebutted (e.g. if the entity cannot identify the specific goods or services received – see **2.8**), the fair value of the equity instruments granted is used as a proxy.

If the goods or services are received on more than one date, the entity should measure the fair value of the equity instruments granted on each date when goods or services are received. The entity should apply that fair value when measuring the goods or services received on that date. [IFRS 2:IG6]

It is possible to use an approximation in some cases. If an entity received services continuously during a three-month period, and its share price did not change significantly during that period, the entity could use the average share price during the three-month period when estimating the fair value of the equity instruments granted. [IFRS 2:IG7]

5.2.3 **Measurement of transactions with employees and others providing similar services**

5.2.3.1 *Employees and others providing similar services – definition*

Appendix A of IFRS 2 defines **employees and others providing similar services** as "[i]ndividuals who render personal services to the entity and either (a) the individuals are regarded as employees for legal or tax purposes, (b) the individuals work for the entity under its direction in the same way as individuals who are regarded as employees for legal or tax purposes, or (c) the services rendered are similar to those rendered by employees. For example, the term encompasses all management personnel, ie those persons having authority and responsibility for planning, directing and controlling the activities of the entity, including non-executive directors".

Further references to employees in this chapter will include others providing similar services.

The determination as to whether an individual is 'similar to an employee' is a matter requiring careful judgement.

The following factors may indicate that the counterparty in a share-based payment transaction is an employee or is providing services similar to an employee.

- The purchasing entity is paying for the right to use certain individuals and not the actual output from the individuals (i.e. the purchasing entity has the risk of downtime).

- The individuals are under the direct supervision of the purchasing entity.

- The contract depends on the services from a specified individual.

- The purchasing entity receives substantially all of the output from the individual for a specified period of time.

- The individuals perform services that are similar to services currently provided by employees.

Factors to indicate that an individual is not an employee or providing services similar to an employee include the following.

- The individual performs services that cannot legally be provided by employees.

- The individual uses technology that is not legally available to the purchasing entity to perform the services.

5.2.3.2 Transactions with employees generally to be measured at the fair value of the equity instruments granted

The IASB has taken the view that the fair value of the equity instruments granted should be used for measuring transactions with employees and others providing similar services. This is because, in such transactions, "typically it is not possible to estimate reliably the fair value of the services received". The fair value of those equity instruments is measured at grant date. [IFRS 2:11 & 12]

5.2.3.3 Cash received from employees entering a share purchase plan

---

Example 5.2.3.3

Cash received from employees entering a share purchase plan

Entity R offers all its employees the opportunity to participate in an employee share purchase plan. The employees have a limited time to decide whether to accept the offer. The plan entitles the employees to purchase a maximum of 100 shares each at a purchase price of CU0.10 per share (the nominal value of a share). The purchase price is lower than the fair value of the shares at the grant date.

The employees are required to pay the purchase price on accepting the offer and receive the shares immediately. However, they must remain employed with Entity R for five years before being permitted to sell the shares. If an employee leaves before the vesting period ends, Entity R will automatically repurchase the shares from the employee at CU0.10 per share. The employees are not entitled to dividends on the shares during the vesting period.

This is an equity-settled share-based payment arrangement because the employees are ultimately only entitled to receive shares. However, the distinctive feature of this share purchase plan is that the shares are delivered immediately on receipt of the cash payment even though they do not vest for five years. In substance, the employees do not receive the shares until they vest unconditionally.

To reflect the prepaid purchase price and the potential that the shares will be repurchased, Entity R should recognise the cash received as a financial liability until the end of the vesting period, at which time it will be reclassified to equity provided that the employee is still employed by Entity R. If the employee leaves Entity R before the end of the vesting period, Entity R repays the original purchase price to the employee and derecognises the financial liability.

Because the financial liability could be repaid at any time within the vesting period, it will be measured at CU0.10 per share. The 'prepayment' of the exercise price will be factored into the grant date fair value of the share option.

Entitlement to dividends during the vesting period would be factored into the fair value determination (see **5.4.5.6**), but would otherwise not affect the accounting treatment described above. (The appropriate treatment of any dividends paid during the vesting period is discussed in **example 5.4.5.6**.)

5.2.3.4 Shares to a monetary value

Example 5.2.3.4

Shares to a monetary value

On 1 January 20X5 (the grant date), an entity grants share awards to each of its employees to the value of CU1,500. If an employee remains employed with the entity until 31 December 20X7, the shares will vest and the employee will receive as many shares as are (on 31 December 20X7) worth CU1,500.

> **How should the entity account for this share-based payment?**
>
> The grant is an equity-settled share-based payment because the employees will receive shares. The fair value of the awards should be determined at the grant date (i.e. 1 January 20X5). Therefore, the grant date fair value of the awards is CU1,500. Although the time value of money is ignored for simplicity in this example, it should be considered in the determination of the fair value of the award. Vesting conditions are either service conditions or performance conditions. In this case, employment is a service condition because the condition relates to the provision of services only and does not require a performance target to be met. This is reflected by adjusting the expense for changes in the number of awards that are expected to vest based on meeting this service condition.
>
> The actual number of shares issued in settlement of the awards will vary according to the share price on the vesting date, but the total value of the awards will not change. Therefore, the expense should not be adjusted for changes in the number of shares that will be issued as a result of changes in the market value of the shares.
>
> Therefore, the entity will recognise CU1,500 as an expense over the vesting period, subject to the service condition (i.e. employment), regardless of how many shares are actually issued on the vesting date.
>
> This approach is illustrated below.
>
> At 1 January 20X5, the market price per share is CU5. At 31 December 20X7, it is CU10. At 31 December 20X5 and 20X6, the entity expects that 95 per cent of the employees will remain employed until 31 December 20X7. Ultimately, 96 per cent of the employees remain in service at 31 December 20X7.
>
> At the grant date, the fair value of the awards issued per employee is CU1,500.
>
> | Year | Calculation of expense: grant date fair value of awards issued × proportion expected to vest | Remuneration expense for period | Cumulative remuneration expense |
> |---|---|---|---|
> | | | CU | CU |
> | 1 | (CU1,500 × 100 employees) × 95% expected to vest × 1/3 years | 47,500 | 47,500 |
> | 2 | (CU1,500 × 100 employees) × 95% expected to vest × 2/3 years | 47,500 | 95,000 |
> | 3 | (CU1,500 × 100 employees) × 96% actually vested × 3/3 years | 49,000 | 144,000 |

5.2.3.5 Reload features

Some share options have a 'reload feature'. This entitles the employee to automatic grants of additional share options whenever he/she exercises previously granted share options and pays the exercise price in the entity's shares rather than in cash. Typically, the employee is granted a new share option, called a reload option, for each share surrendered when exercising the previous share option. The exercise price of the reload option is usually set at the market price of the shares on the date the reload option is granted. [IFRS 2:BC188]

Appendix A of IFRS 2 defines a **reload feature** as "[a] feature that provides for an automatic grant of additional share options whenever the option holder exercises previously granted options using the entity's shares, rather than cash, to satisfy the exercise price".

Appendix A of IFRS 2 defines a **reload option** as "[a] new share option granted when a share is used to satisfy the exercise price of a previous share option".

IFRS 2 requires that for options with a reload feature, the feature should not be taken into account when estimating the fair value of options granted at the measurement date. Instead, a reload option should be accounted for as a new option grant, if and when a reload option is subsequently granted. [IFRS 2:22]

As discussed in IFRS 2:BC189 to BC192, it may theoretically be preferable to take account of reload features when measuring the fair value of options granted. The exposure draft that preceded IFRS 2 proposed this treatment 'when practicable'. However, in the light of comments received, the IASB decided to require the treatment set out above in all cases.

Example 5.2.3.5

Award with reload feature

Company M issues 100 share options to one of its directors. The total exercise price for the options is CU100. However, there is a reload feature under which the director can surrender shares to the total value of CU100 instead of paying the exercise price in cash and become entitled to a number of new share options. In this example, that number is equal to the number of shares surrendered.

If the market value of the shares on exercise is CU10, the director will surrender 10 shares worth CU100 in total to cover the exercise price on 100 options. He

---

will then be granted 10 new options. These new options represent a new grant and are accounted for in the usual way in accordance with IFRS 2 (i.e. an expense is recognised over the applicable vesting period based on the grant date fair value of the new options).

5.2.3.6   Share price denominated in a foreign currency

IFRS 2 does not make reference to share-based payment transactions in which the share price is denominated in a foreign currency. An appropriate treatment for such transactions can, however, be derived from the general principles of IAS 21 *The Effects of Changes in Foreign Exchange Rates* as discussed in **example 5.2.3.6**.

Example 5.2.3.6

Share-based payment arrangements with share and option exercise price denominated in a foreign currency

Company E is a UK entity with Sterling as its functional currency. Company E is registered on the New York Stock Exchange with a current market price of US$15 per share. Company E issues 100 options to its employees with an exercise price of US$15 per share and a vesting period of three years. The share options can only be equity-settled.

At the date of issue of the options, the fair value of each option is determined to be US$15 and the exchange rate is US$1.5/£1.

Given that the share price is quoted in a currency other than the functional currency of the entity, how should these arrangements be accounted for?

As discussed in **example 3.3.2**, the debt/equity requirements of IAS 32 (which would require a contract to issue shares for a fixed amount of foreign currency cash to be classified as a liability) do not apply to share-based payments.

Because the options will be settled in Company E's shares, they should be accounted for as equity-settled share-based payments by expensing the grant date fair value in functional currency terms (£10 per option, £1,000 in total in this example) over the vesting period. Changes in the exchange rate over the life of the options will not change the amount expensed.

This issue is considered at **6.2.2** in relation to cash-settled share-based payment transactions.

5.2.3.7 *Number of shares to be issued determined by reference to the relative fair value of shares of another group entity*

Example 5.2.3.7

Number of shares to be issued determined by reference to the relative fair value of shares of another group entity

Entity A owns 100 per cent of Entity B.

On 1 January 20X5 (the grant date), Entity B grants share options to each of its employees, conditional on them remaining in employment until 31 December 20X7.

The share-based payment arrangement specifies that each employee of Entity B will receive as many of Entity A's shares as are, on 31 December 20X7, of the same value as 1,000 shares of Entity B.

The fair value of both Entity A's and Entity B's shares can be reliably obtained on 1 January 20X5 and 31 December 20X7.

The grant is an equity-settled share-based payment because the employees will receive shares. The fair value of the awards should be determined as of the grant date (i.e. 1 January 20X5).

The actual number of Entity A's shares issued in settlement of the awards will vary according to the relative fair values of Entity A's and Entity B's shares on the vesting date, but there is no target that the fair value of Entity B's shares needs to meet for vesting to occur. The fair values are only used as a converter to define the number of Entity A's shares to be issued; they do not constitute a vesting condition.

The expense measured at the grant date will not be adjusted for changes in the number of shares of Entity A that will be issued as a result of changes in the fair value of the shares in Entity B.

Employment is a service condition that is reflected by adjusting the expense for changes in the number of awards that are expected to vest based on meeting this service condition.

5.3 Impact of vesting and non-vesting conditions on equity-settled transactions

5.3.1 *Impact of vesting and non-vesting conditions – general*

As discussed in **section 4**, the concepts of vesting and non-vesting conditions are significant both for recognising and for measuring equity-settled share-based payment transactions.

IFRS 2:IG24 provides the following table which categorises, with examples, the various conditions that determine whether a counterparty receives an equity instrument granted and the accounting treatment of share-based payments with those conditions under IFRS 2.

Summary of conditions that determine whether a counterparty receives an equity instrument granted					
VESTING CONDITIONS			**NON-VESTING CONDITIONS**		
Service conditions	Performance conditions		Neither the entity nor the counterparty can choose whether the condition is met	Counterparty can choose whether to meet the condition	Entity can choose whether to meet the condition
	Performance conditions that are market conditions	Other performance conditions			
Example conditions Requirement to remain in service for three years	Target based on the market price of the entity's equity instruments	Target based on a successful initial public offering with a specified service requirement	Target based on a commodity index	Paying contributions towards the exercise price of a share-based payment	Continuation of the plan by the entity
Include in grant date fair value? No	Yes	No	Yes	Yes	Yes[a]
Accounting treatment if the condition is not met after the grant date and during the vesting period Forfeiture. The entity revises the expense to reflect the best available estimate of the number of equity instruments expected to vest.	No change to accounting. The entity continues to recognise the expense over the remainder of the vesting period.	Forfeiture. The entity revises the expense to reflect the best available estimate of the number of equity instruments expected to vest.	No change to accounting. The entity continues to recognise the expense over the remainder of the vesting period.	Cancellation. The entity recognises immediately the amount of the expense that would otherwise have been recognised over the remainder of the vesting period.	Cancellation. The entity recognises immediately the amount of the expense that would otherwise have been recognised over the remainder of the vesting period.
(paragraph 19)	(paragraph 21)	(paragraph 19)	(paragraph 21A)	(paragraph 28A)	(paragraph 28A)

[a]   In the calculation of the fair value of the share-based payment, the probability of continuation of the plan by the entity is assumed to be 100 per cent.

The treatment of vesting, non-vesting and performance conditions is summarised in the following diagram and is more fully described below.

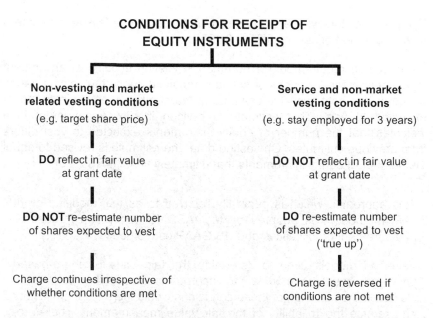

**CONDITIONS FOR RECEIPT OF
EQUITY INSTRUMENTS**

Non-vesting and market related vesting conditions (e.g. target share price)	**Service and non-market vesting conditions** (e.g. stay employed for 3 years)
DO reflect in fair value at grant date	**DO NOT** reflect in fair value at grant date
DO NOT re-estimate number of shares expected to vest	**DO** re-estimate number of shares expected to vest ('true up')
Charge continues irrespective of whether conditions are met	Charge is reversed if conditions are not met

IFRS 2 distinguishes between market conditions (see **4.6**) and conditions other than market conditions (referred to generally as 'non-market conditions').

Market conditions, such as a target share price upon which vesting is conditional, are taken into account when estimating the fair value of the equity instruments granted. Therefore, for grants of equity instruments with market conditions, the entity recognises the goods or services received from a counterparty who satisfies all other vesting conditions (e.g. service conditions) irrespective of whether that market condition is satisfied. [IFRS 2:21]

Similarly, all non-vesting conditions are taken into account when estimating the fair value of the equity instruments granted. Therefore, for grants of equity instruments with non-vesting conditions, the goods or services received from a counterparty that satisfies all vesting conditions that are not market conditions (e.g. services received from an employee who remains in service for the specified period of service) are recognised, irrespective of whether those non-vesting conditions are satisfied. [IFRS 2:21A]

Vesting conditions other than market conditions are not taken into account when estimating the fair value of the shares or share options at the measurement date. Instead, those non-market vesting conditions are taken into account by adjusting the number of equity instruments included in the measurement of the transaction so that, ultimately, the amount recognised for goods or services received is based on the number of equity instruments that eventually vest. Therefore, on a cumulative basis, no amount is recognised for goods or services received if the equity instruments granted do not vest because of a failure to satisfy non-market vesting conditions.

For example, this will be the case when an employee fails to complete a specified period of service. [IFRS 2:19]

To apply this requirement for non-market vesting conditions, an amount is recognised for the goods or services received during the vesting period based on the best available estimate of the number of equity instruments expected to vest. That estimate is revised if subsequent information indicates that the number of equity instruments expected to vest differs from previous estimates. On vesting date, the estimate is revised to equal the number of equity instruments that ultimately vest. [IFRS 2:20]

This approach, which is generally referred to as the 'modified grant date method', was adopted by the IASB for two primary reasons: measurement practicalities and US GAAP convergence.

Valuation models used to determine the fair value of share-based payments could be modified to incorporate non-market conditions. However, the inclusion of these conditions would increase the difficulty and reduce the reliability of the fair value measurement. Therefore, non-market conditions are not included in the grant date fair value calculation due to the practical difficulties of measuring these conditions as noted in IFRS 2:BC184.

The operation of these requirements in practice is illustrated by the examples set out in the following sections.

5.3.2 Non-market vesting condition

The following example, which is taken from the implementation guidance accompanying IFRS 2, illustrates the basic approach to be adopted in relation to a non-market vesting condition.

Example 5.3.2A

Non-market vesting condition

[IFRS 2:IG, Example 1A]

Background

An entity grants 100 share options to each of its 500 employees. Each grant is conditional upon the employee working for the entity over the next three years. The entity estimates that the fair value of each share option is CU15.

On the basis of a weighted average probability, the entity estimates that 20 per cent of employees will leave during the three-year period and therefore forfeit their rights to the share options.

Application of requirements

Scenario 1

If everything turns out exactly as expected, the entity recognises the following amounts during the vesting period, for services received as consideration for the share options.

Year	Calculation	Remuneration expense for period CU	Cumulative remuneration expense CU
1	50,000 options × 80% × CU15 × 1/3 years	200,000	200,000
2	(50,000 options × 80% × CU15 × 2/3 years) – CU200,000	200,000	400,000
3	(50,000 options × 80% × CU15 × 3/3 years) – CU400,000	200,000	600,000

Scenario 2

During year 1, 20 employees leave. The entity revises its estimate of total employee departures over the three-year period from 20 per cent (100 employees) to 15 per cent (75 employees). During year 2, a further 22 employees leave. The entity revises its estimate of total employee departures over the three-year period from 15 per cent to 12 per cent (60 employees). During year 3, a further 15 employees leave. Hence, a total of 57 employees forfeited their rights to the share options during the three-year period, and a total of 44,300 share options (443 employees × 100 options per employee) vested at the end of year 3.

Year	Calculation	Remuneration expense for period CU	Cumulative remuneration expense CU
1	50,000 options × 85% × CU15 × 1/3 years	212,500	212,500
2	(50,000 options × 88% × CU15 × 2/3 years) – CU212,500	227,500	440,000
3	(44,300 options × CU15) – CU440,000	224,500	664,500

The following example illustrates the use of probabilities when assessing non-market vesting conditions.

Example 5.3.2B

Use of probabilities to assess non-market vesting conditions

Background

Company A has issued 10 options to 10 employees (i.e. 100 options in total). The options will vest at the end of Year 2 of an employee's continued employment (i.e. the 'service condition') and after Company A has met a specified level of earnings-per-share (EPS) growth compared with the EPS for Year 0. However, the number of options that will vest depends on the extent of the EPS growth. Provided that an employee remains in employment, the options will vest according to the following EPS growth percentages at the end of Year 2:

- less than 4 per cent – none of the options will vest;
- between 4 per cent and 10 per cent – 50 per cent of the options will vest; and
- more than 10 per cent – all options will vest.

Therefore, if all employees remain in employment, the number of options expected eventually to vest can only be 0, 50 or 100.

Application of requirements

Scenario 1

All employees are expected to remain in employment until the end of Year 2.

The target EPS growth vesting condition is a non-market performance condition. During the vesting period, an entity is required to recognise an expense (or asset, if applicable) by determining the total number of equity instruments that are expected to vest eventually as a result of the fulfilment of non-market-based conditions (IFRS 2:19). An entity should only use probabilities when determining whether a non-market-based condition will be met – the amount recognised in accordance with IFRS 2 reflects the most likely outcome, not a weighted average of outcomes.

For example, if an entity believes that there is a 90 per cent chance that a performance target will be met, the accounting for this transaction during the vesting period should reflect the target being met. The entity would recognise 100 per cent of the total expense for the reporting period (as long as all other vesting conditions are met), not 90 per cent of the total expense for the reporting period.

At the end of Year 1, Company A should estimate the most probable EPS growth figure for the end of Year 2 (using, for example, budget information or historical EPS growth) and should use this estimate to determine the number of options that will vest.

At each future reporting date, Company A should reassess expected EPS growth and 'true up' the expense accordingly. This requirement may result in greater volatility in the amount of expense recognised from year to year.

Scenario 2

Only eight employees are expected to remain until the end of Year 2.

If only 80 per cent of the employees are expected to remain employed by the entity at the end of two years, the number of options expected to vest would need to be adjusted to incorporate the impact of the service condition (e.g. staff turnover rate should be analysed). Therefore, the actual number of options expected to vest, after the impact of the service condition and the number of employees expected to remain with the entity are taken into account, can only be one of the following:

- 0 (i.e. no options are expected to vest);
- 40 (50 per cent of 80 per cent of 100 – i.e. 50 per cent of the options are expected to vest); or
- 80 (100 per cent of 80 per cent of 100 – i.e. all options are expected to vest).

Many of the examples in the implementation guidance accompanying IFRS 2 employ percentages for determining the number of employees expected to meet a service condition. These percentages are used to estimate the number of equity instruments that will actually vest, not the probability that the employee will meet the service condition. That is, an entity expects that 80 per cent of its employees will meet the service condition, not that there is an 80 per cent chance of the service condition being met.

5.3.3 *Vesting period varies with a non-market condition*

The length of the vesting period might vary depending on when a performance condition is met. If an employee is granted share options that are conditional on the achievement of a performance condition and on remaining in employment until that performance condition is satisfied, it is presumed that the services to be rendered by the employee will be received in the future, over the expected vesting period. When this is the case, the length of the estimated vesting period at grant date is estimated based on the most likely outcome of the performance condition. [IFRS 2:15]

If the performance condition is a market condition, the estimated length of the vesting period should be consistent with the assumptions used in estimating the fair value of the options granted and should not subsequently be revised. If the performance condition is a non-market condition, the initial estimate of the length of the vesting period should be revised if subsequent information indicates that the length of the vesting period differs from the previous estimate.

The following example, taken from the implementation guidance accompanying IFRS 2, illustrates the circumstances when the vesting period varies according to the achievement of a non-market condition (a specified increase in earnings).

Example 5.3.3

Grant with a performance condition, in which the length of the vesting period varies

[IFRS 2:IG, Example 2]

Background

At the beginning of year 1, the entity grants 100 shares each to 500 employees, conditional upon the employees' remaining in the entity's employ during the vesting period. The shares will vest at the end of year 1 if the entity's earnings increase by more than 18 per cent; at the end of year 2 if the entity's earnings increase by more than an average of 13 per cent per year over the two-year period; and at the end of year 3 if the entity's earnings increase by more than an average of 10 per cent per year over the three-year period. The shares have a fair value of CU30 per share at the start of year 1, which equals the share price at grant date. No dividends are expected to be paid over the three-year period.

By the end of year 1, the entity's earnings have increased by 14 per cent, and 30 employees have left. The entity expects that earnings will continue to increase at a similar rate in year 2, and therefore expects that the shares will vest at the end of year 2. The entity expects, on the basis of a weighted average probability, that a further 30 employees will leave during year 2, and therefore expects that 440 employees will vest in 100 shares each at the end of year 2.

By the end of year 2, the entity's earnings have increased by only 10 per cent and therefore the shares do not vest at the end of year 2. 28 employees have left during the year. The entity expects that a further 25 employees will leave during year 3, and that the entity's earnings will increase by at least 6 per cent, thereby achieving the average of 10 per cent per year.

By the end of year 3, 23 employees have left and the entity's earnings had increased by 8 per cent, resulting in an average increase of 10.67 per cent per year. Therefore, 419 employees received 100 shares at the end of year 3.

Application of requirements

Year	Calculation	Remuneration expense for period CU	Cumulative remuneration expense CU
1	440 employees × 100 shares × CU30 × 1/2	660,000	660,000
2	(417 employees × 100 shares × CU30 × 2/3) – CU660,000	174,000	834,000
3	(419 employees × 100 shares × CU30 × 3/3) – CU834,000	423,000	1,257,000

Granting share options contingent on an initial public offering (IPO) of an entity is another example of an award with a variable vesting period depending on a non-market vesting condition. However, no expense will be recognised unless and until the IPO is probable. This may not be the case on grant date. Therefore, in practice, the expense may sometimes be recognised over a relatively short period between the IPO becoming probable and taking place. As explained at **5.3.15**, an IPO may be a non-vesting condition if the exercise of the options is not linked to service continuing until the IPO.

5.3.4 Number of options vesting is dependent on a non-market performance condition

A similar approach will be adopted when the number of equity instruments that might vest with each employee varies. This is illustrated in the following example which is taken from the implementation guidance accompanying IFRS 2.

Example 5.3.4

Grant with a performance condition, in which the number of equity instruments varies

[IFRS 2:IG, Example 3]

Background

At the beginning of year 1, Entity A grants share options to each of its 100 employees working in the sales department. The share options will vest at the end of year 3, provided that the employees remain in the entity's employ, and provided that the volume of sales of a particular product increases by at least an average of 5 per cent per year. If the volume of sales of the product increases by an average of between 5 per cent and 10 per cent per year, each employee will receive 100 share options. If the volume of sales increases by an average of between 10 per cent and 15 per cent each year, each employee will receive 200 share options. If the volume of sales increases by an average of 15 per cent or more, each employee will receive 300 share options.

On grant date, Entity A estimates that the share options have a fair value of CU20 per option. Entity A also estimates that the volume of sales of the product will increase by an average of between 10 per cent and 15 per cent per year, and therefore expects that, for each employee who remains in service until the end of year 3, 200 share options will vest. The entity also estimates, on the basis of a weighted average probability, that 20 per cent of employees will leave before the end of year 3.

By the end of year 1, seven employees have left and the entity still expects that a total of 20 employees will leave by the end of year 3. Hence, the entity expects that 80 employees will remain in service for the three-year period. Product sales have increased by 12 per cent and the entity expects this rate of increase to continue over the next 2 years.

By the end of year 2, a further five employees have left, bringing the total to 12 to date. The entity now expects only three more employees will leave during year 3, and therefore expects a total of 15 employees will have left during the three-year period, and hence 85 employees are expected to remain. Product sales have increased by 18 per cent, resulting in an average of 15 per cent over the two years to date. The entity now expects that sales will average 15 per cent or more over the three-year period, and hence expects each sales employee to receive 300 share options at the end of year 3.

By the end of year 3, a further two employees have left. Hence, 14 employees have left during the three-year period, and 86 employees remain. The entity's sales have increased by an average of 16 per cent over the three years. Therefore, each of the 86 employees receives 300 share options.

Application of requirements

Year	Calculation	Remuneration expense for period CU	Cumulative remuneration expense CU
1	80 employees × 200 options × CU20 × 1/3	106,667	106,667
2	(85 employees × 300 options × CU20 × 2/3) − CU106,667	233,333	340,000
3	(86 employees × 300 options × CU20 × 3/3) − CU340,000	176,000	516,000

5.3.5   *Exercise price dependent on a non-market condition*

The exercise price might vary depending on whether non-market vesting conditions are satisfied. This is illustrated in the following example taken from the implementation guidance accompanying IFRS 2.

Example 5.3.5

Grant with a performance condition, in which the exercise price varies

[IFRS 2:IG, Example 4]

Background

At the beginning of year 1, an entity grants to a senior executive 10,000 share options, conditional upon the executive's remaining in the entity's employ until the end of year 3. The exercise price is CU40. However, the exercise price drops to CU30 if the entity's earnings increase by at least an average of 10 per cent per year over the three-year period.

On grant date, the entity estimates that the fair value of the share options, with an exercise price of CU30, is CU16 per option. If the exercise price is CU40, the entity estimates that the share options have a fair value of CU12 per option.

During year 1, the entity's earnings increased by 12 per cent, and the entity expects that earnings will continue to increase at this rate over the next two years. The entity therefore expects that the earnings target will be achieved, and hence the share options will have an exercise price of CU30.

During year 2, the entity's earnings increased by 13 per cent, and the entity continues to expect that the earnings target will be achieved.

During year 3, the entity's earnings increased by only 3 per cent, and therefore the earnings target was not achieved. The executive completes three years' service, and therefore satisfies the service condition. Because the earnings target was not achieved, the 10,000 vested share options have an exercise price of CU40.

Application of requirements

Because the exercise price varies depending on the outcome of a performance condition that is not a market condition, the effect of that performance condition (i.e. the possibility that the exercise price might be CU40 and the possibility that the exercise price might be CU30) is not taken into account when estimating the fair value of the share options at grant date. Instead, the entity estimates the fair value of the share options at grant date under each scenario (i.e. exercise price of CU40 and exercise price of CU30) and ultimately revises the transaction amount to reflect the outcome of that performance condition, as illustrated below.

Year	Calculation	Remuneration expense for period	Cumulative remuneration expense
		CU	CU
1	10,000 options × CU16 × 1/3	53,333	53,333
2	(10,000 options × CU16 × 2/3) – CU53,333	53,334	106,667
3	(10,000 options × CU12 × 3/3) – CU106,667	13,333	120,000

5.3.6   A market condition and a non-market condition

The following example, taken from the implementation guidance accompanying IFRS 2, illustrates the operation of the requirements of IFRS 2 for a grant of options with a market condition (a specified increase in share price) and a non-market service condition (continuing employment).

Example 5.3.6A

Grant with a market condition

[IFRS 2:IG, Example 5]

Background

At the beginning of year 1, an entity grants to a senior executive 10,000 share options, conditional upon the executive remaining in the entity's employ until the end of year 3. However, the share options cannot be exercised unless the share price has increased from CU50 at the beginning of year 1 to above CU65 at the end of year 3. If the share price is above CU65 at the end of year 3, the share options can be exercised at any time during the next seven years, i.e. by the end of year 10.

The entity applies a binomial option pricing model, which takes into account the possibility that the share price will exceed CU65 at the end of year 3 (and hence the share options become exercisable) and the possibility that the share price will not exceed CU65 at the end of year 3 (and hence the options will be forfeited). It estimates the fair value of the share options with this market condition to be CU24 per option.

Application of requirements

Because paragraph 21 of IFRS 2 requires the entity to recognise the services received from a counterparty who satisfies all other vesting conditions (e.g. services received from an employee who remains in service for the specified service period), irrespective of whether that market condition is satisfied, it makes no difference whether the share price target is achieved. The possibility that the share price target might not be achieved has already been taken into account when estimating the fair value of the share options at grant date. Therefore, if the entity expects the executive to complete the three-year service period, and the executive does so, the entity recognises the following amounts in years 1, 2 and 3:

Year	Calculation	Remuneration expense for period	Cumulative remuneration expense
		CU	CU
1	10,000 options × CU24 × 1/3	80,000	80,000
2	(10,000 options × CU24 × 2/3) – CU80,000	80,000	160,000
3	(10,000 options × CU24) – CU160,000	80,000	240,000

As noted above, these amounts are recognised irrespective of the outcome of the market condition. However, if the executive left during year 2 (or year 3), the amount recognised during year 1 (and year 2) would be reversed in year 2 (or year 3). This is because the service condition, in contrast to the market condition, was not taken into account when estimating the fair value of the share options at grant date. Instead, the service condition is taken into account by adjusting the transaction amount to be based on the number of equity instruments that ultimately vest, in accordance with paragraphs 19 and 20 of the IFRS.

Another example in which share options are granted with both market conditions and non-market conditions is set out below.

Example 5.3.6B

Share option grant with both market and non-market performance conditions

Company H issued 100 share options to certain of its employees that will vest if accumulated revenues for five years reach CU1 billion and its share price exceeds CU50 on the fifth anniversary of the grant date. The employees will have to be employed with Company H at the end of the five-year vesting period to receive the options. The share options will expire if any of these conditions has not been met at the end of the five-year vesting period.

IFRS 2:21 states that the grant date fair value of a share-based payment with market-based performance conditions that has met all its other vesting conditions should be recognised, irrespective of whether that market condition is achieved. Company H determines the grant date fair value of the share-based payment excluding the non-market-based performance factor (accumulated revenues), but including the market-based performance factor (share price).

Assuming Company H determines that the fair value of the share-based payment (after taking into consideration the probability that the share price target of CU50 will be met) at the date of grant is CU20 per option, the cumulative expense recognised over the expected vesting period in the following scenarios would be:

- if all vesting conditions are met, CU2,000 [100 options × CU20];
- if all vesting conditions are met, except that the market-based performance condition of share price exceeding CU50 is not achieved, CU2,000 [100 options × CU20];
- if all vesting conditions are met, except that the non-market-based performance condition of accumulated revenues reaching CU1billion is not achieved, nil expense; and
- if all vesting conditions are met, except that employees who received half of the options leave Company H's employment prior to the vesting date, CU1,000 [50 options × CU20].

> Therefore, when there are both market and non-market conditions that have to be met, an entity will still need to estimate whether non-market conditions will be satisfied even if ultimately no share options vest due to market conditions.

5.3.7   A market condition when the vesting period varies

The effect of a vesting condition may be to change the length of the vesting period. In this case, IFRS 2:15 requires the entity to presume that the services to be rendered by the employees as consideration for the equity instruments granted will be received in the future, over the expected vesting period. Hence, the entity will have to estimate the length of the expected vesting period at grant date, based on the most likely outcome of the performance condition. If the performance condition is a market condition, the estimate of the length of the expected vesting period must be consistent with the assumptions used in estimating the fair value of the share options granted and is not subsequently revised.

The following example, taken from the implementation guidance accompanying IFRS 2, illustrates the application of IFRS 2 when the vesting period varies with a market condition (a specified increase in the share price).

Example 5.3.7

Grant with a market condition, in which the length of the vesting period varies

[IFRS 2:IG, Example 6]

Background

At the beginning of year 1, an entity grants 10,000 share options with a ten-year life to each of ten senior executives. The share options will vest and become exercisable immediately if and when the entity's share price increases from CU50 to CU70, provided that the executive remains in service until the share price target is achieved.

The entity applies a binomial option pricing model, which takes into account the possibility that the share price target will be achieved during the ten-year life of the options, and the possibility that the target will not be achieved. The entity estimates that the fair value of the share options at grant date is CU25 per option. From the option pricing model, the entity determines that the mode of the distribution of possible vesting dates is five years. In other words, of all the possible outcomes, the most likely outcome of the market condition is that the share price target will be achieved at the end of year 5. Therefore, the entity estimates that the expected vesting period is five years. The entity also estimates that two executives will have left by the end of year 5, and therefore expects that 80,000 share options (10,000 share options × 8 executives) will vest at the end of year 5.

Throughout years 1 - 4, the entity continues to estimate that a total of two executives will leave by the end of year 5. However, in total three executives leave, one in each of years 3, 4 and 5. The share price target is achieved at the end of year 6. Another executive leaves during year 6, before the share price target is achieved.

Application of requirements

Paragraph 15 of the IFRS requires the entity to recognise the services received over the expected vesting period, as estimated at grant date, and also requires the entity not to revise that estimate. Therefore, the entity recognises the services received from the executives over years 1 - 5. Hence, the transaction amount is ultimately based on 70,000 share options (10,000 share options × 7 executives who remain in service at the end of year 5). Although another executive left during year 6, no adjustment is made, because the executive had already completed the expected vesting period of 5 years. Therefore, the entity recognises the following amounts in years 1 - 5:

Year	Calculation	Remuneration expense for period CU	Cumulative remuneration expense CU
1	80,000 options × CU25 × 1/5	400,000	400,000
2	(80,000 options × CU25 × 2/5) – CU400,000	400,000	800,000
3	(80,000 options × CU25 × 3/5) – CU800,000	400,000	1,200,000
4	(80,000 options × CU25 × 4/5) – CU1,200,000	400,000	1,600,000
5	(70,000 options × CU25) – CU1,600,000	150,000	1,750,000

5.3.8 Contingent issue of shares for goods or services from non-employees

Example 5.3.8

Contingent issue of shares for goods or services from non-employees

Company G enters into an agreement with lawyers currently assisting in its defence of a lawsuit. If Company G is successful in winning the case, it will issue 100 of its own shares to the lawyers. If Company G is not successful, it will issue 20 of its own shares to the lawyers.

Company G expenses the amount it expects to pay to the lawyers over the service period (being the variable period to settlement of the law suit). At the end of each reporting period, Company G should make its best estimate as to whether it will win the case, as well as the most likely outcome of the period over which the case will be settled. This estimate should be revised at the end of each reporting period as long as the case is not settled.

The total expense recognised up to the date of settlement should equal the fair value of services received. This value should be calculated directly (taking into account the differential between the value of services received in winning and in losing the case – one being five times the other in this example based upon the number of shares to be delivered), unless a reliable estimate cannot be made on this basis, in which case the value should be determined indirectly by reference to the fair value of the equity instruments granted, measured at the date the entity receives the services.

5.3.9   Equity instruments vesting in instalments

Example 5.3.9

Equity instruments vesting in instalments (graded vesting)

Company A grants its employees 1,000 share options each with a fair value of CU10. The options vest pro rata over the service period (one-fourth each year). Under IFRS 2:IG11, entities are required to treat each instalment as a separate share option grant because each instalment has a different vesting period and, therefore, the grant date fair value of each instalment is likely to be different. This is because the length of the vesting period will affect, for example, the likely timing of cash flows arising from the exercise of the options.

The following table summarises how the total fair value of CU10,000 [1,000 × CU10] should be allocated to each of the four years in the vesting period. (Note that, for simplicity, it is assumed that the grant date fair value is CU10 for each tranche. In practice, as explained above, the grant date fair value might be slightly different for each tranche.)

Award	Year 1	Year 2	Year 3	Year 4
	CU	CU	CU	CU
Tranche 1 [(10,000/4) × 1/1]	2,500			
Tranche 2 [(10,000/4) × 1/2]	1,250	1,250		
Tranche 3 [(10,000/4) × 1/3]	833	833	834	
Tranche 4 [(10,000)/4) × 1/4]	625	625	625	625
Total expense	5,208	2,708	1,459	625

5.3.10   Distinguishing market and non-market vesting conditions

For the majority of vesting conditions, it is straightforward to determine whether they should be viewed as market or non-market conditions. However, it is not always so straightforward to make this distinction as illustrated in the following examples.

Example 5.3.10A

Market and non-market vesting conditions (index)

Company A issues share options to certain of its employees that vest if, and when, Company A's share price growth (as a percentage) exceeds the average share price growth of Company A's 10 most significant competitors. Share price growth is calculated based on share prices only and does not factor in dividends or other factors.

IFRS 2:Appendix A defines one form of a market condition as a "condition upon which the exercise price, vesting, or exercisability of an equity instrument depends that is related to ... achieving a specified target that is based on the market price of the entity's equity instruments ... relative to an index of market prices of equity instruments of other entities". IFRS 2 does not provide guidance on what constitutes an index.

While the term 'index' would appear to require a comparison of more than one entity, there clearly is no requirement that the index be a published, standard index such as the S&P 500 or FTSE 100. The following criteria should be considered in determining whether an index exists:

- the fair value at the date of grant can be reliably determined by reference to the index;

- the share prices of the entities in the index are readily available in an active market such that accurate and reliable measurements of fair value can be determined at a specific point in time; and

- a consistent and reasonable formula is used to determine the effects of the entities' performance on the performance of the index.

If these criteria are met, Company A would have a strong case for demonstrating that the vesting condition is a market condition.

This example refers to circumstances in which the performance of an entity's shares is judged by reference to a market index. Note that, as discussed at **4.5**, a condition based solely on the performance of a share index is not a performance condition.

Example 5.3.10B

Ranking of share price within a population

Company A issues share options to certain employees that vest if Company A's share price growth (as a percentage) ranks in the top quartile of the largest 100 entities in its market. Share price growth is calculated based on share price only and does not take account of dividends or other factors.

Should this vesting condition be considered a market condition?

It depends. The ranking within an index or group of entities may be representative of an index if it meets the criteria described in **example 5.3.10A** – notably that the vesting condition be measured via a consistent formula based on the prices of shares in an active market. In such cases, a vesting condition based on a ranking should be considered a market condition.

Example 5.3.10C

Total shareholders' return as a market condition

Company A issues share options to certain employees, the vesting of which is subject to a Total Shareholders' Return (TSR) condition. TSR is the internal rate of return on the entity's shares calculated by assuming that:

- someone bought the share at the start of the performance period;

- any dividends received on the share had been used to buy more shares ('dividend shares') when received; and

- the shares (plus dividend shares) were sold at the end of the performance period.

For example, if no dividends were paid and the share price increased from CU100 to CU107 after one year, the TSR would be 7 per cent.

Company A's TSR condition works by comparing the entity's TSR with that of an index of the 100 largest entities in its market. For example, if Company A's TSR were to be placed in the top 30th percentile, then 90 per cent of the award would vest.

The criteria for an index described in **example 5.3.10A** are met.

A TSR calculation includes not only changes in the entity's share price, but the effects of dividends. Nevertheless, a TSR condition should be considered a market condition because movements in the share price are the predominant factor in its calculation.

5.3.11   Good leavers and bad leavers

Vesting conditions may distinguish between 'good leavers' and 'bad leavers'. In practice, a good leaver is often defined in the terms of a share-based arrangement as an employee who leaves the entity due to injury, disability, death, redundancy or on reaching normal retirement age (see **example 5.3.11**). A bad leaver is usually defined as any other leaver (e.g. due to resignation).

For example, an entity may grant options with a specified period of service as a vesting condition. A good leaver will be entitled to exercise all or some of the options when leaving the entity during the specified period of service. A bad leaver loses any entitlement to the award when he/she leaves during the vesting period.

Such arrangements represent share-based payment arrangements with a variable vesting period for good leavers (see **5.3.3**). When calculating the IFRS 2 expense, the entity estimates how many good and bad leavers it expects to have. If the estimate of good leavers is material, a separate estimate should be made of the vesting period(s) for good leavers and that vesting period should be reassessed at the end of each reporting period. When accounting for all other employees (i.e. non-leavers and bad leavers), the estimate of bad leavers is used to true up the IFRS 2 expense for those failing to meet the service condition. Once the shares have vested, there is no further true up for leavers, regardless of whether they are good leavers or bad leavers. **Example 5.3.16** illustrates the accounting for pro rata vesting of shares for good leavers.

However, this guidance applies only if good and bad leavers are defined in the terms and conditions of the award. In other cases (i.e. when management or a remuneration committee determines whether an employee is a good or a bad leaver only at the time when the employee leaves employment), the particular arrangements should be considered carefully. The exercise of discretion by management may be a modification of the award and should be accounted for as such or it may affect the determination of grant date (see **example 5.4.1.3**).

Example 5.3.11

Awards exercisable on retirement

Company A grants an award that vests in five years if the employees stay in employment until the end of that period. If an employee leaves earlier because of reaching the retirement age of 60, that employee will still be entitled to receive the full award at his or her retirement date.

Under this arrangement, the vesting period for those employees who, at the grant date, are more than 55 years old is shorter than the general vesting period of five years. Company A will need to determine how many employees have shorter vesting periods and recognise the grant date fair value of these awards over the applicable vesting periods. If the award is granted to an employee aged 60 or over, the award would in effect vest immediately and should be recognised as an expense in full at the grant date.

The grant date fair value of these awards may also be affected because a shorter vesting period affects the life of the options as an input to the option pricing model.

This applies even when some of the employees decide to stay and work beyond their retirement age because the employees could leave at any time after reaching the age of 60 without forfeiting the right to the award.

5.3.12 Matching share awards

Matching share awards take various forms but generally involve an arrangement under which an employee is given shares in the entity to 'match' those for which he/she subscribes. Often this is linked to a bonus payment. For example, if an employee elects to take the bonus in the form of shares to the value of the bonus, the entity makes a matching share award. The award typically has a vesting condition relating to continuing employment and/or a non-vesting condition relating to holding the purchased shares for a prescribed period.

The determination of the vesting period for a matching share award is not always straightforward. Arrangements vary with regard to whether the employee has discretion to take the bonus in cash or shares and whether the entity has discretion to provide the matching shares. When there is no discretion, the start of the vesting period for the matching share award will generally be the date when the bonus arrangements are established. However, in other cases it may be a later date. The facts and circumstances of each case should be considered carefully.

Accounting for a bonus which will be settled in a variable number of shares to the value of the bonus is considered at **5.2.3.4**.

The appropriate measurement date for matching share awards is considered at **5.4.1.5**.

5.3.13   *Allocation of expense when there are multiple vesting conditions*

Example 5.3.13

Allocation of expense when there are multiple vesting conditions

Entity A enters into a share-based payment arrangement with certain of its employees, which contains a three-year service condition beginning on 1 January 20X1 and ending on 31 December 20X3. In addition, there is a one-year non-market performance condition assessed during the period 1 January 20X1 to 31 December 20X1.

How should Entity A recognise the share-based payment expense given that there are multiple vesting conditions with different reference periods?

Entity A should allocate the expense using a straight-line method over the service period of three years, unless there is compelling evidence that a different expense recognition pattern is appropriate.

IFRS 2:15 requires that if the equity instruments do not vest until the counterparty completes a specified period of service, an entity should presume that the services to be rendered by the counterparty will be received in the future, during the vesting period. However, the Standard is silent regarding which pattern of expense allocation should be used if there are multiple vesting conditions with different reference periods.

In the circumstances described, there is no evidence that employee services provided in the different periods are explicitly different. Therefore, allocation of the share-based payment expense on a straight-line basis is the most appropriate method.

5.3.14 Effect of planned restructuring event in estimating the number of awards expected to vest

Example 5.3.14

Effect of planned restructuring event in estimating the number of awards expected to vest

An entity intends to restructure some of its operations. At the end of the reporting period, the costs associated with the restructuring plan do not meet the criteria for recognition of a provision under IAS 37 *Provisions, Contingent Liabilities and Contingent Assets*. However, the restructuring plan has been approved by the entity's board of directors and will be announced shortly after the end of the reporting period. The entity considers that it is probable that the restructuring will take place. As part of the restructuring plan, the entity expects to terminate the employment of some employees who hold unvested share-based payment awards accounted for under IFRS 2. The terminations are expected to occur before the vesting date of the share-based payment awards and would result in forfeiture based on the existing terms of the share-based payment arrangement. However, the entity intends to change the terms of the arrangement to accelerate vesting of the awards held by employees terminated as a result of the restructuring plan.

At the end of the reporting period, how should the entity estimate the number of awards expected to vest?

Under IFRS 2:20, an entity recognises an expense based on the best available estimate of the number of awards expected to vest. The entity should revise this estimate if the number of instruments expected to vest changes. In the circumstances described, it is considered probable that the restructuring will take place. Therefore, at the end of the reporting period, the entity should reduce the number of awards expected to vest to reflect the forfeiture that will result when the employment of the employees is terminated under the planned restructuring. That is, the entity should reverse the expense previously recognised for the effect of awards that are no longer expected to vest because of the planned restructuring, under the terms of the arrangement in effect at the end of the reporting period.

Separately, the impact of changes to the terms of the share-based payment arrangement should only be reflected in the determination of the IFRS 2 expense on modification of the awards. Therefore, only when the terms of the arrangement have been modified (i.e. in the next reporting period) will the entity apply the requirements of IFRS 2:27 and consider these revised terms in assessing the number of awards expected to vest in accordance with IFRS 2:B43(c).

5.3.15   Conditions relating to completion of an initial public offering (IPO)

When determining the appropriate treatment of a condition related to the successful completion of an IPO, it is necessary to consider whether there is a related service condition.

One of the examples of a vesting condition in the table below IFRS 2:IG24 (see **5.3.1**) is the successful completion of an IPO *together with* a specified service requirement (i.e. an employee is required to be employed at the time an IPO is successfully completed). It is also clear that the successful completion of an IPO *without* any related service condition is a non-vesting condition.

If the service period is shorter than the period to the IPO, the IPO should be treated as a non-vesting condition (as clarified by the IASB in the December 2013 amendments to IFRS 2 – see **4.5**). This would be the case if there is a service condition for a limited period (e.g. two years) and the employees are then free to leave while retaining their right to exercise the options at a later date if the IPO is achieved. In this case, any expense recognised for the options granted to employees who leave before meeting the two-year service condition will be reversed. There will be no reversal, if the IPO does not occur, in relation to the employees who are still employed at the end of the two-year service period. However, as noted above, the grant date fair value will have been adjusted to take account of the probability that the IPO will not occur.

Examples 5.3.15A to **15C** illustrate the appropriate accounting for share-based payment conditions involving the completion of an IPO.

Example 5.3.15A

IPO and a service condition when IPO determines vesting period

An entity grants 100 share options each to 10 of its employees. The grant is conditional on a successful IPO within the next four years, and employees working for the entity over the period until the IPO. Therefore, the vesting period is dependent on the timing of the IPO. The fair value of each share option at grant date is CU60.

At the end of Year 1, no employees have left, but the entity expects two to leave by the end of the service period. The entity believes that it is not probable that there will be a successful IPO within the next three years.

At the end of Year 2, one employee has left, and the entity expects one more employee to leave during the next year. The entity now believes that it is probable that there will be a successful IPO before the end of Year 3.

The IPO is completed successfully six months after the beginning of Year 3. Prior to the completion of the IPO, one further employee has left and the entity expects another two to leave in the final year.

During Year 4, another two employees leave as expected.

The IPO condition is a non-market performance condition because it is not related to the entity's share price and it must be met within a specified period during which the employees must remain in employment with the entity.

IFRS 2:19 requires that vesting conditions, other than market conditions, are not taken into account when estimating the fair value of the share options at the measurement date. Instead, vesting conditions are taken into account by adjusting the number of equity instruments included in the measurement of the transaction amount.

Therefore, the determination of grant date fair value excludes the probability of a successful IPO within the service period.

Year 1

The entity believes that it is not probable that there will be a successful IPO within the service period; therefore, the number of equity instruments expected to vest is zero. As a result, no accounting entries are recognised.

Year 2

Because the entity believes that it is probable that there will be a successful IPO before the end of Year 3 and eight employees are expected to be employed until the completion of the IPO, a share-based payment expense is years. Because no amounts were recognised in Year 1, the expense in Year 2 is recognised as follows.

		CU	CU
Dr	Share-based payment expense		
	[(CU60 × 100 × 8)/3) × 2]	32,000	
Cr	Equity		32,000

To recognise the share-based payment expense.

Year 3

Because the IPO is completed successfully six months after the beginning of Year 3 and eight employees remained employed at the time of the IPO, the final vesting period is two and a half years. Therefore, the remainder of the share-based payment expense is recognised as follows.

		CU	CU
Dr	Share-based payment expense		
	[(CU60 × 100 × 8) – CU32,000]	16,000	
Cr	Equity		16,000

To recognise the share-based payment expense.

Year 4

Because the IPO is completed successfully six months after the beginning of Year 3 and the share options are vested in full at that point, no further share-based payment expense is recognised in Year 4, regardless of whether any more employees leave.

In practice, the determination as to whether it is probable that an IPO will occur is difficult because it is dependent on factors outside the entity's control. Often it will not be possible to conclude that an IPO is probable until plans are well advanced.

Note that, in the circumstances described above, the completion of the IPO determines the required service period and so the vesting period over which the expense is spread is changed as the expectation of occurrence and timing of the IPO changes. **Example 5.3.15B** addresses the accounting if the timing of the IPO does not alter the vesting period of the share-based payments.

Example 5.3.15B

IPO and a service condition when vesting period is fixed

An entity grants 100 share options each to 10 of its employees. The grant is conditional on employees working for the entity over the next four years, and a successful IPO within that service period. Therefore, the vesting period is four years. The fair value of each share option at grant date is CU60.

At the end of Year 1, no employees have left, but the entity expects two to leave by the end of the service period. The entity believes that it is not probable that there will be a successful IPO within the next three years.

At the end of Year 2, one employee has left, and the entity expects one more employee to leave during the next year. The entity now believes that it is probable that there will be a successful IPO before the end of Year 3.

The IPO is completed successfully six months after the beginning of Year 3. Prior to completion of the IPO, another employee has left and the entity expects another two to leave in the final year.

During Year 4 another two employees leave as expected.

The IPO condition is a non-market performance condition because it is not related to the entity's share price and it must be met within a specified period during which the employees must remain in employment with the entity.

IFRS 2:19 requires that vesting conditions, other than market conditions, are not taken into account when estimating the fair value of the share options at the measurement date. Instead, vesting conditions are taken into account by adjusting the number of equity instruments included in the measurement of the transaction amount.

Therefore, the determination of grant date fair value excludes the probability of a successful IPO within the service period.

Year 1

The entity believes that it is not probable that there will be a successful IPO within the service period; therefore, the number of equity instruments expected to vest is zero. As a result, no accounting entries are recognised.

Year 2

Because the entity believes that it is probable that there will be a successful IPO before the end of Year 3 (and eight employees are expected to remain in employment to the end of Year 4), a share-based payment expense is recognised. Because no amounts were recognised in Year 1, the expense in Year 2 is recognised as follows.

		CU	CU
Dr	Share-based payment expense		
	[(CU60 × 100 × 8)/4) × 2]	24,000	
Cr	Equity		24,000

To recognise the share-based payment expense.

Year 3

Because the IPO has been completed successfully six months after the beginning of Year 3 (and six employees are expected to remain in employment to the end of Year 4), a share-based payment expense is recognised as follows.

		CU	CU
Dr	Share-based payment expense		
	[(CU60 × 100 × 6)/4) × 3] – CU24,000	3,000	
Cr	Equity		3,000

To recognise the share-based payment expense.

Year 4

As expected, another two employees have left; therefore, the remainder of the share-based payment expense is recognised as follows.

		CU	CU
Dr	Share-based payment expense		
	[(CU60 × 100 × 6) – CU27,000]	9,000	
Cr	Equity		9,000

To recognise the share-based payment expense.

In practice, the determination as to whether it is probable that an IPO will occur is difficult because it is dependent on factors outside the entity's control. Often it will not be possible to conclude that an IPO is probable until plans are well advanced.

Note that, in the circumstances described above, the completion of the IPO did not alter the required service period of four years and so the vesting period over which the expense is spread was not changed. **Example 5.3.15A** addresses the accounting if the timing of the IPO determines the vesting period of the share-based payments.

Example 5.3.15C

Share-based payment conditions – IPO with no service period

An entity grants 100 share options each to 10 of its employees. The grant is conditional on the completion of a successful IPO within five years. There is no service condition attached to the awards and employees that leave the employment of the entity prior to the successful completion of the IPO will continue to be entitled to the reward if the IPO occurs within five years.

The successful IPO is a non-vesting condition because the vesting of the share options is not dependent on the entity receiving the services that entitle the employees to the reward. IFRS 2:21A requires all non-vesting conditions to be taken into account when determining the grant date fair value of the equity instruments granted. The grant date fair value of the options should, therefore, reflect the probability of a successful IPO.

Assume that on grant date the entity estimates that the share options have a fair value of CU30 per option.

Because there is no service period attached to the awards, the expense should be recognised immediately:

		CU	CU
Dr	Share-based payment expense		
	[CU30 × 10 × 100]	30,000	
Cr	Equity		30,000

To recognise the share-based payment expense.

The above entries are not reversed if the IPO is unsuccessful.

5.3.16 Pro rata vesting for good leavers

Example 5.3.16

Pro rata vesting for good leavers

Entity A grants each of its employees 100 shares conditional solely on the employee remaining in employment with Entity A for three years. However, if an employee leaves Entity A's employment at any time during the three-year period for one of a number of reasons specified in the scheme (including, for example, termination by Entity A without cause, and invalidity), he/she will be entitled to a pro rata allocation of the 100 shares based on the number of days of service completed. (Employees entitled to such allocations are defined in the scheme as 'good leavers'.)

How should Entity A recognise the share-based payment expense for the arrangement described?

In the circumstances described, the most appropriate reflection of the service charge is achieved by allocating the share-based payment expense on a straight-line basis up to the date of vesting (i.e. the end of the three-year period).

As discussed at **5.3.11**, arrangements of this nature represent share-based payment arrangements with a variable vesting period for good leavers (i.e. the general vesting period is three years but it will be less if the employee is a good leaver within three years). A good leaver's entitlement to receive a pro rata number of shares when he or she leaves Entity A's employment within the three-year period means that the number of shares receivable upon vesting is also variable.

IFRS 2:15 requires that an entity should account for services as they are rendered by the counterparty during the vesting period. The application of this principle to grants with a variable vesting period and a variable number of equity instruments receivable is illustrated in **example 5.3.3** and **example 5.3.4**, respectively. In both examples, the variability is addressed by making an estimate of the vesting period or number of equity instruments and revising that estimate at the end of each reporting period until vesting occurs.

In the circumstances described, the interaction between the vesting period and the number of equity instruments receivable means that a straight-line allocation of the expense for 100 shares over three years will reflect both of the sources of variability for good leavers. This is because after, say, 18 months, the cumulative expense for 100 shares and a vesting period of three years will be the same as for 50 shares and a vesting period of 18 months. As discussed at **5.3.11**, the entity's total cumulative expense will be reduced due to the estimated number of bad leavers.

This example may be distinguished from a graded vesting scheme (see **example 5.3.9**) under which awards vest in separate tranches. In contrast, here, the award vests at only one date (the earlier of three years from the grant date and the date of leaving as a good leaver).

5.4 Determining the fair value of equity instruments granted

5.4.1 Measurement date and grant date

5.4.1.1 Measurement date and grant date – definitions

When transactions are measured by reference to the fair value of the equity instruments granted, that fair value should be determined at the 'measurement date'. Appendix A of IFRS 2 provides the following definitions.

- The **measurement date** is "[t]he date at which the fair value of the equity instruments granted is measured for the purposes of this IFRS.

For transactions with employees and others providing similar services, the measurement date is grant date [see below]. For transaction with parties other than employees (and those providing similar services), the measurement date is the date the entity obtains the goods or the counterparty renders service".

- The **grant date** is "[t]he date at which the entity and another party (including an employee) agree to a share-based payment arrangement, being when the entity and the counterparty have a shared understanding of the terms and conditions of the arrangement. At grant date the entity confers on the counterparty the right to cash, other assets, or equity instruments of the entity, provided the specified vesting conditions, if any, are met. If that arrangement is subject to an approval process (for example, by shareholders), grant date is the date when that approval is obtained".

5.4.1.2 Determination of the grant date for a share-based bonus plan

---

Example 5.4.1.2

Determination of the grant date for a share-based bonus plan

On 1 January 20X1, Company A enters into an agreement with each of its executives whereby Company A will issue shares to each executive. The number of shares to be issued will vary in line with growth in revenue and profits for the year ended 31 December 20X1. Depending on audited revenue and profit growth for that year (which will be known at 31 March 20X2), Company A will issue between nil and 100 restricted shares to each employee.

The restricted shares will vest if the executive remains in Company A's employment at the end of a further three years. Therefore, the earliest an executive will be able to sell his or her restricted shares is at the end of 20X4. The board of directors has already approved the formula and no further approvals are needed.

At what date should the fair value of the shares issued be measured – 1 January 20X1 or 31 March 20X2?

IFRS 2:11 requires that the fair value of the equity instruments should be measured at the grant date, which is defined in IFRS 2:Appendix A as "the date at which the entity and another party … agree to a share-based payment arrangement, being when the entity and the counterparty have a shared understanding of the terms and conditions of the arrangement". In the circumstances described, at 1 January 20X1 all parties understand the terms and, therefore, this should be viewed as the grant date.

An estimate of the number of shares that will vest is made at 1 January 20X1. A fair value is assigned to each share. Because the formula used to determine the number of shares that will finally be issued is considered a non-market vesting condition that should be accounted for using the 'true up' method in IFRS 2, the number of shares is adjusted at 31 March 20X2 based on the number of restricted shares actually issued to the executives. The fair value of each share should be based on its value at 1 January 20X1.

5.4.1.3 Grant date – requirement for agreement to a shared understanding of the terms and conditions

Two key factors that need to be considered when deciding on the grant date are:

- both parties need to 'agree' to a share-based payment; and

- both parties must have a shared understanding of the terms and conditions.

The word 'agree' is used in its usual sense and means that there must be both an offer and acceptance of that offer. The date of grant is when the other party accepts an offer and not when the offer is made. In some instances the agreement might be implicit (i.e. not by signing a formal contract) and this is the case for many share-based payment arrangements with employees. In these cases, the employees' agreement is evidenced by their commencing to render services. [IFRS 2:IG2]

For both parties to have agreed to the share-based payment arrangement, they must have a shared understanding of the terms and conditions of the arrangement. If some of the terms and conditions of the arrangement are agreed on one date, with the remainder of the terms and conditions agreed on a later date, then grant date is on that later date, when all of the terms and conditions have been agreed. For example, consider the situation when an entity agrees to issue share options to an employee, but the exercise price of the options will be set by a remuneration committee that meets in three months' time. The grant date is when the exercise price is set by the remuneration committee. [IFRS 2:IG3]

The scenario described in the previous paragraph differs from that described in **example 5.4.1.2**. In **example 5.4.1.2**, the number of restricted shares to be issued, although not known, is the subject of an agreed formula which considers revenue and profit growth. In the circumstances described in the previous paragraph, the exercise price is not agreed until it is set by the remuneration committee because until then it remains subject to the committee's discretion.

Example 5.4.1.3

Performance target at the discretion of the remuneration committee

Company P granted share options to its employees. The share options vest over a three-year period assuming that a specified performance target is achieved. However, under the terms of the grant, the remuneration committee has the power to vary the performance target at any time until vesting.

The terms of the agreement should be reviewed carefully to understand the limits of the remuneration committee's power. When the committee has wide discretion to vary the performance condition and is expected to use this discretion in practice, it is likely that the grant date of the options will be when they vest (i.e. when the committee exercises its discretion and the performance target is fixed). This is because there is no shared understanding of the terms of the award until that date (see below for further consideration).

However, in other cases, it will be apparent that the power to vary the performance target is intended to be used only in very rare and unusual circumstances. In such cases, it may be reasonable to assume that this term has little substance and should be ignored when accounting for the arrangement. In the event that the power is used at a later date, the amendment to the performance target should be accounted for as a modification (see **section 5.5**).

When the committee's discretion is substantive, so that the grant date is not considered to occur until the options vest, this means that the grant date occurs after the employees to whom the equity instruments are granted have begun rendering services. However, IFRS 2:13 requires the entity to recognise the services when received. The guidance in IFRS 2:IG4 states that "the entity should estimate the grant date fair value of the equity instruments (e.g. by estimating the fair value of the equity instruments at the end of the reporting period)" for the purpose of recognising the services received during the period between the date of commencement of service and the grant date. Once the grant date occurs (in the example above, assuming the committee's discretion is substantive, when the options vest), the entity revises the earlier estimate so that the amounts recognised for services received in respect of the grant are ultimately based on the grant date fair value of the equity instruments.

5.4.1.4   Grant date – requirement for employee acceptance

Share-based payment arrangements take various forms. Some arrangements require explicit employee acceptance (often for legal or tax reasons). Others permit implicit acceptance evidenced by the employee rendering service.

Entities must carefully consider all the details of a share-based payment arrangement in assessing whether a requirement for explicit employee acceptance affects the determination of the grant date. Relevant considerations include, but are not limited to, whether the terms of the arrangement:

- require an employee's explicit agreement (e.g. by requiring the employee to sign the arrangement), in which case the grant date would normally be the date the employee accepts the offer by signing. However, if the offer requires shareholders' approval, the grant date would be the later of the date the shareholders approve the arrangement and the date the employee agrees to the arrangement in accordance with IFRS 2:IG4; or

- do not require an employee's explicit agreement, in which case the grant date would normally be the date the employee starts rendering services. However, if shareholders' approval is required, the grant date cannot be before the shareholders approve the arrangement.

Sometimes there is a time lapse between the date when the shareholders approve the plan and when the approval of the plan is communicated to the employee. Normally the communication process is an administrative process and, consequently, the communication process does not defer the grant date.

The entity should also consider whether the requirement for explicit acceptance by the employee is a substantive feature of the arrangement. In making this assessment, the entity should consider whether, for example:

- the employee is required to accept the offer explicitly because acceptance of the awards triggers another event (e.g. the employee's liability to tax arising from the award), or whether acceptance is implicit by virtue of the employee providing services; or

- the employee has a choice between accepting the share-based payment award or taking the compensation in an alternative form (e.g. free membership of insurance scheme offered by the employer).

If explicit acceptance by the employee is judged not to be a substantive feature, the grant date should not be delayed until the acceptance documents have been received.

The following example illustrates the application of these principles.

Example 5.4.1.4

Effect of employee acceptance conditions on grant date

In Country B, an individual is taxed in the period that share-based payments are received. As a result, prior to issuing share-based payments to its employees, Company X first issues an offer letter to each employee detailing the amount of shares or share options and the exercise price. Each employee has 30 days in which to return the offer letter to accept the options.

What is the grant date – the date of offer or the date of acceptance?

In many cases, the determination as to whether the requirement for rejection or acceptance is explicit or implicit requires careful analysis of the facts and circumstances. In the circumstances described, the requirement to accept is explicit and has substance, given that the employee will be taxed immediately on the options received. While the employee understands all of the terms and conditions, the employer does not (until acceptance) have a full understanding of how many share options will be issued. Therefore, due to the explicit acceptance requirement, grant date would be the date of acceptance.

The date of grant determines the date the options should be measured, but does not affect the recognition period of the expense; that is, the option should be recognised as an expense over the service period. If the service period begins prior to the grant date (e.g. from the offer date), Company X should begin expensing the share-based payment at the date of offer at an amount that will approximate to the fair value of the share-based payment to be determined at grant date. If the period between the offer date and the grant date crosses the reporting date, the fair value should be remeasured at the reporting date. Once an employee accepts, that date would be the grant date and the fair value would be determined at that date.

5.4.1.5   Measurement date – matching share awards

Matching share awards take various forms but generally involve an arrangement under which an employee is given shares in the entity to 'match' those for which the employee subscribes. Often this is linked to a bonus payment. For example, if an employee elects to take the bonus in the form of shares to the value of the bonus, the entity makes a matching share award. The award typically has a vesting condition relating to continuing employment and/or a non-vesting condition relating to holding the purchased shares for a prescribed period.

The determination of the measurement date for a matching share award is not always straightforward. Arrangements vary with regard to whether the employee has discretion to take the bonus in cash or shares and whether the entity has discretion to provide the matching shares. The measurement date is the grant date, which is when the entity and the employee have a shared understanding of the terms and conditions of the arrangement. When there is no discretion, the measurement date for the matching share award will generally be the date when the bonus arrangements are established. However, in other cases it may be a later date. The facts and circumstances of each case should be considered carefully.

Accounting for a bonus which will be settled in a variable number of shares to the value of the bonus is considered at **5.2.3.4**.

The appropriate vesting period for matching share awards is considered at **5.3.12**.

5.4.2 Measuring fair value by reference to the fair value of goods or services – volume rebates

---

Example 5.4.2

Measuring fair value by reference to the fair value of goods or services – volume rebates

Company A purchases 1,000 computers in return for 5,000 of Company A's ordinary shares, trading at CU100 each. The seller generally sells the same computers individually for CU700 each. Company A currently trades several thousand shares a day, such that 5,000 shares would be readily convertible to cash by the seller.

How should the fair value of the computers received be determined?

When determining fair value by reference to the value of the goods or services, care should be taken to ensure that volume rebates or other discounts are considered. When the value of the goods or services received does not appear to be commensurate with the value of the equity instruments issued, the difference may be due to volume rebates. If this is the case, the amount recognised should be the fair value net of any volume rebates.

In the circumstances described, the difference between CU500,000 [5,000 × CU100] (the market value of the shares issued by Company A) and CU700,000 [1,000 × CU700] (the fair value of 1,000 computers purchased individually) may relate to a volume rebate that should be considered in the valuation. If this is the case, CU500,000 is the appropriate measure for the computers.

5.4.3 Measuring fair value by reference to the fair value of equity instruments

When share-based payment transactions are measured by reference to the fair value of the equity instruments granted, ideally that fair value should be determined by reference to market prices. For example, in the case of an issuance of shares that must be forfeited if the employee leaves service during a three-year period, the share-based payment will be measured at the fair value of the shares at the date of grant. A share price or valuation of the entity at the date of grant would be sufficient to determine the fair value of those shares and it would not be necessary to recalculate this value unless the grant was modified.

When market prices do not exist for share options, the fair value should be determined by applying a valuation technique, usually in the form of an option pricing model. [IFRS 2:B4]

IFRS 2 does not prescribe the use of a specific valuation methodology. The overriding principle implicit in the guidance in IFRS 2:B5 is that, in the selection of the appropriate option pricing model, an entity considers factors that knowledgeable and willing market participants would consider.

Generally, this will be an issue requiring careful consideration by preparers, possibly requiring the involvement of valuation experts.

> It may be acceptable, and even necessary, to use different models for different schemes to reflect their particular features. It may also sometimes be appropriate to use different models for different grants under the same scheme (e.g. to change to a more complex model as amounts become more material). However, other than in the case of material error, the grant date fair value should not be adjusted, once it has been determined using a particular model, even if that model is no longer used for new grants.

Appendix B to IFRS 2 discusses measurement of the fair value of shares and share options granted, focusing on specific terms and conditions that are common features of a grant of shares or share options to employees. Examples of the types of decisions related to measurement that entities are required to make include the following.

Items to determine	Accounting decisions
Pricing model	Black-Scholes, binomial, Monte Carlo etc.
Expected life assumption/employee behaviour	For variable exercise dates, assumptions are needed as to when employees are likely to exercise their options (e.g. in a financially optimal manner; when the option is in the money at a certain time, e.g. vesting date; when the share price hits a specified share price ('barrier'); or based on historical behaviour).
Current share price	Share price can be determined on the basis of closing price on grant date or the average price on grant date.
Expected volatility	There are various methods to calculate this amount (e.g. based on historical experience, implied volatility of traded options, volatility of comparator entities, or industry index).
Expected dividends	This should be the expected future dividends over the expected life of the award. This should be in line with the entity's policy, although this may be derived from historical experience or experience of competitors.
Risk-free interest rate	This should generally be the implied yield available at the date of grant on zero-coupon government issues of the country in whose currency the exercise price is expressed and of duration that is similar to the expected life of the award.

These items are addressed in more detail in **section 5.4.4**.

The fair value of cash-settled share-based payments, such as share appreciation rights (SARs), should be measured by using a model similar to one used for share options. That is, future share price increases and other variables have a similar effect on the fair value of many forms of cash-settled share-based payment transactions.

5.4.4 Valuation models

5.4.4.1 Widely accepted valuation models

Three widely accepted valuation models are generally used to value equity options: the Black-Scholes model, the binomial model and Monte Carlo model.

These three models are compared and contrasted in **5.4.4.2** to **5.4.4.4**.

5.4.4.2 Black-Scholes

Application of the Black-Scholes model (sometimes referred to as the Black-Scholes-Merton formula) is a straightforward calculation, which requires only the six minimum inputs noted in **5.4.5**.

The Black-Scholes approach requires a single expected life assumption as to when the option is likely to be exercised, does not allow for variable exercise dates and is not able to factor in any market conditions.

On the issue of expected early exercise, IFRS 2:B5 states that "many employee options have long lives, are usually exercisable during the period between vesting date and the end of the options' life, and are often exercised early. These factors should be considered when estimating the grant date fair value of the options. For many entities, this might preclude the use of the Black-Scholes-Merton formula, which does not allow for the possibility of exercise before the end of the option's life and may not adequately reflect the effects of expected early exercise".

IFRS 2:B17, however, notes that this will not always be the case, stating that "the means by which the effects of expected early exercise are taken into account depends upon the type of option pricing model applied. For example, expected early exercise could be taken into account by using an estimate of the option's expected life ... as an input into an option pricing model (e.g. the Black-Scholes-Merton formula). Alternatively, expected early exercise could be modelled in a binomial or similar option pricing model that uses contractual life as an input".

5.4.4.3   Binomial model

The binomial model is more complex to apply than the Black-Scholes model, but allows more factors to be taken into account (i.e. variable exercise dates and some market-based vesting conditions).

The binomial model breaks down the time to expiration into potentially a large number of time intervals or steps. A tree of share prices is initially produced working forward from the present time to expiration of the option. At each step it is assumed that the share price will move up or down by an amount calculated using the volatility assumption and the length of each time interval. The probabilities of upward and downward movements are calculated using risk-neutral probabilities derived from the size of the upward and downward steps and the risk-free rate of return. This produces a binomial distribution, or tree, of underlying share prices. The tree represents all possible paths that the share price could take during the life of the option. The effect of dividends on the share price is adjusted for in the binomial tree as they are expected to be paid during the contractual life. At the end of the tree – that is, the expiration of the option – all the terminal option payoffs for each of the final possible share prices are known as they simply equal their intrinsic values.

Next, the 'option values' at each step of the tree are calculated working back from expiration to the present. The option values at each step are used to derive the option values at the preceding step of the tree using a risk-neutral valuation. This risk-neutral valuation uses the risk-free rate of interest as a discount factor and risk-neutral probabilities of the share price moving up or down. At any point during the option's life at which exercise would be permitted, the higher of the intrinsic value (i.e. the value of the option if it were to be exercised) and the 'option value' (i.e. the value of the option if it were to be held) is taken (because a rational investor would exercise when exercising an option would give a higher value than holding on to it). In this way, the binomial model takes into account variable exercise dates. Certain adjustments to option values as a result of market-based vesting features can also be worked into the calculations at the required point in time. At the start of the tree, the option's fair value is obtained.

5.4.4.4   Monte Carlo model

A Monte Carlo model works by simulating a large number of projected random outcomes for how the share price may move in future. The relevant share price may be that of the entity and, if applicable, those of comparator entities, e.g. when there are market-based performance conditions based on relative total shareholder return.

On the basis of each simulated share price (or set of comparator entity share prices), the proportion of awards that would vest and the resultant pay-off is determined. This is then discounted back to the valuation date at the risk-free interest rate. The procedure is then repeated a large number of times to determine the expected (average) value of the award at the valuation date.

5.4.5 Basic factors affecting the valuation of share-based payments

5.4.5.1 Basic inputs required to be considered by valuation models

Most employee share-based payments granted will not have an equivalent instrument traded in an active market and, therefore, when the determination of their fair values is required by IFRS 2, valuation models will need to be applied. IFRS 2 requires, at a minimum, that all valuation models consider the following six basic inputs:

[IFRS 2:B6]

- the exercise price of the option (see **5.4.5.2**);
- the current price of the underlying shares (see **5.4.5.3**);
- the expected life of the option (see **5.4.5.4**);
- the expected volatility of the share price (see **5.4.5.5**);
- the dividends expected on the shares (see **5.4.5.6**); and
- the risk-free interest rate for the life of the option (see **5.4.5.7**).

These variables have been widely accepted as required inputs into valuations. Therefore, it is useful first to review these basic inputs. Other factors affecting the valuation of share-based payments are addressed in **section 5.4.6**.

For some of the inputs listed above, it is likely that there will be a range of reasonable expectations, e.g. for exercise behaviour of employees. If this is the case, the fair value should be calculated by weighting each amount within the range of probabilities of occurrence. [IFRS 2:B12]

5.4.5.2 Exercise price

IFRS 2 does not provide guidance on the determination of the exercise price. The exercise price should be determined from the agreement.

It is possible for the exercise price to be variable. For example, an exercise price dependent on a non-market vesting condition is considered at **5.3.5**.

5.4.5.3 Current share price

IFRS 2 does not provide guidance on the determination of the current share price.

The current share price should be determined in accordance with an entity's accounting policy. That policy may dictate the use of closing price or average price at the grant date. Whichever method is chosen, it should be used consistently between periods and among plans.

5.4.5.4   Expected life

There are several factors that affect the expected life of a typical non-traded share option given to employees, such as vesting features and various behavioural considerations. These factors and others are discussed in greater detail in **section 5.4.6**.

> Some ways that the expected life of a share option may be determined are:
>
> - by creating a binomial lattice that includes all the appropriate factors – the lattice outcomes will determine when the exercise date is most likely to occur; or
>
> - by taking factors, such as those listed below, employee risk aversion and behaviour into consideration and estimating an expected life that is then used in, for example, a Black-Scholes model.

Factors to consider in estimating the expected exercise date of a share option include:

[IFRS 2:B18]

- the length of the vesting period, because share options typically cannot be exercised before they vest;

- historical experience related to actual lives of share options;

- the price of underlying shares (employees may tend to exercise options when the share price reaches a specified level above the exercise price);

- the expected volatility of the underlying shares (employees tend to exercise options earlier on highly volatile shares); and

- the employee's level within the organisation.

IFRS 2 suggests that different groups of employees may have homogeneous exercise behaviours and, therefore, determining the expected life for each homogeneous group may be more accurate than an expected life for all recipients of an option grant. [IFRS 2:B20] That is, one share option granted to the Chief Executive Officer may have a different value from one share option granted to a factory worker at the same time with the same term. For example, the Chief Executive Officer might have a greater understanding of when it is optimal to exercise the award and might have less restrictive cash flow constraints compared to the average worker. If the Black-Scholes model is used, IFRS 2 requires the use of the expected life of the option.

Alternatively, exercise behaviours can be modelled into a binomial or similar option pricing model that uses contractual life.

5.4.5.5 Expected volatility

Volatility is a measure of the amount by which a share price is expected to fluctuate during a period. [IFRS 2:B22] Many of the concerns about determining the fair value of non-traded employee share options relate to determining the estimate of expected volatility over the term of the option.

Volatility may be measured by reference to the implied volatility in traded options. However, the trading of such options is quite thin and the terms tend to be much shorter than the terms of most employee share options. There is also empirical evidence that options with the same term but different strike prices have different implied volatility. This is a factor that cannot be included in the Black-Scholes model, which assumes a constant volatility.

Historical volatility is often used as a rebuttable presumption for long-term options because there is evidence that volatilities are mean-reverting. Therefore, using the long-term average historical volatility for long-term options would be sufficient if there were no reasons to assume that historical volatility would not generally be representative of future volatility. Some have suggested a blended approach utilising both implied volatility and historical volatility.

The historical volatility may be problematic for newly listed and unlisted entities. If a newly listed entity does not have sufficient historical information, it should nevertheless compute historical volatility for the longest period for which trading activity is available. It can also consider the historical volatility of similar entities following a comparable period in their lives. [IFRS 2:B26]

The unlisted entity will not have historical information to consider when estimating expected volatility. Instead, it should consider other factors, including historical or implied volatility of similar listed entities. [IFRS 2:B27 & B29]

Many factors should be considered when estimating expected volatility. For example, the estimate of volatility might first focus on implied volatilities for the terms that were available in the market and compare the implied volatility to the long-term average historical volatility for reasonableness.

In addition to implied and historical volatility, IFRS 2 suggests the following factors to be considered in estimating expected volatility:

[IFRS 2:B25]

- the length of time an entity's shares have been publicly traded;
- appropriate and regular intervals for price observations; and

- other factors indicating that expected future volatility might differ from past volatility (e.g. extraordinary volatility in historical share prices).

5.4.5.6   Expected dividends

Whether expected dividends should be included in the measurement of share-based payments depends on whether the holder is entitled to dividends or dividend equivalents. For example, if employees are granted options and are entitled to dividends on the underlying shares or dividend equivalents (which might be paid in cash or applied to reduce the exercise price) between grant date and exercise date, the options granted should be valued as if no dividends will be paid on the underlying shares. That is to say, the input to the option pricing model for expected dividends should be zero. [IFRS 2:B31 & B32] If the holder of the option or share is entitled to dividends between the grant date and the exercise date, expected dividends should not be included in the fair value measurement. [IFRS 2:B33]

If the employees are not entitled to dividends or dividend equivalents during the vesting period (or, in the case of options, before exercise), the grant date valuation of the rights to shares or options should take expected dividends into account. That is to say, when the fair value of an option is estimated, expected dividends should be included in the application of the option pricing model. When the fair value of a share grant is estimated, that valuation should be reduced by the present value of dividends expected to be paid during the vesting period. [IFRS 2:B34]

IFRS 2 notes that assumptions about expected dividends should generally be based on publicly available information. An entity that does not pay dividends and has no plans to do so should assume an expected dividend yield of zero. However, a newly formed entity with no history of paying dividends might expect to begin paying dividends during the expected lives of its employee share options. Those entities could use an average of their past dividend yield (zero) and the mean dividend yield of an appropriately comparable peer group. [IFRS 2:B36]

Option pricing models usually require expected dividend yield, as input into the models. However, the models can be modified to use an expected dividend amount rather than a yield. If an entity uses the amount, it should consider its historical patterns of increases in dividends. For example, if an entity's policy has generally been to increase dividends by 3 per cent per year, its estimated option value should not assume a fixed dividend amount throughout the option's life unless there is evidence to support this. [IFRS 2:B35]

Example 5.4.5.6

Accounting for dividends paid on share options

Company B purchases its own shares in the market and holds them in an employee share trust (over which Company B has control) for use in settlement

---

of an award of options to its employees. Under the terms of the award, if an employee leaves Company B within three years of the grant, the employee forfeits the share options. After three years of service, the options vest and an employee is eligible to receive shares on payment of a predetermined exercise price.

Consider the following three scenarios.

Scenario A: employees are not entitled to dividends on the shares declared prior to vesting.

Scenario B: employees are entitled to dividends in cash on the shares and any dividends declared are paid to the employees. The exercise price is unaffected by these dividends and, if the shares are forfeited, the employees retain the dividends declared and paid up to that date.

Scenario C: employees are notionally entitled to dividends, but the dividends are automatically applied to reduce the exercise price. If the shares are forfeited, the employee loses the right to dividends accrued and applied to reduce the exercise price.

- *How should dividends declared and paid on the shares be treated in measuring the share options?*
- *How should dividends be accounted for in Company B's financial statements when declared?*

IFRS 2:B32 and B34 clarify that when dividends are paid to the option holders before the exercise of the options, the value of those options is greater than the value of options for which there is no dividend entitlement prior to exercise.

Scenario A: employees not entitled to dividends declared prior to vesting

When no dividend accrues to employees, the fair value of the share options at grant date should be reduced by the present value of dividends expected to be paid during the vesting period (for example, by including the expected dividend yield in a Black-Scholes calculation).

When the share-based payment related to these options is recognised, provided that they are classified as equity-settled share-based payments, the appropriate journal entry for the shares expected to vest is as follows.

Dr	Share-based payment expense	XXX
Cr	Equity	XXX

To recognise the share-based payment expense.

Dividends accrued on the shares held by the employee share trust are eliminated from the aggregate of dividends paid and proposed by Company B (see **section 9.2**).

Scenario B: dividends declared are paid to employees

When dividends are paid to the option holders before the exercise date of the options, the share options should be valued as if no dividends will be paid on the underlying shares during the vesting period (for example, by including an expected dividend yield of zero per cent in a Black-Scholes calculation). As a result, the grant date valuation is not reduced by the present value of the dividends expected to be paid during the vesting period.

The accounting for any dividends paid on the underlying shares will depend on whether the underlying shares are expected to vest. Provided that the share-based payment is equity-settled:

- for awards that are expected to vest, IFRS 2 treats the employees as holders of equity share options. Therefore, any dividends paid on these share options are recognised directly in equity. This is consistent with the principles of paragraph 35 of IAS 32 which states that "[d]istributions to holders of an equity instrument shall be debited by the entity directly to equity, net of any related income tax benefit". In addition, expensing the dividends through profit or loss as additional compensation when paid would result in double counting of an expense that has already been reflected in the grant date fair value of the award recognised under IFRS 2; and

- for awards that are not expected to vest (due to employees expected to leave during the three-year service period), employees are not treated as holders of equity share options. Any cash paid as 'dividends' on those share options represents employee remuneration in accordance with IAS 19 *Employee Benefits* and should, therefore, be recognised as an expense. The expense is measured at the amount of cash paid on these shares. Expensing these dividends through profit or loss does not result in double counting because no cumulative expense will be recognised under IFRS 2 for awards not expected to vest due to non-fulfilment of a service condition.

The appropriate journal entries are as follows.

Share-based payment expense related to the share options that are expected to vest (provided that they are considered to be an equity-settled share-based payment).

Dr	Share-based payment expense	XXX	
Cr	Equity		XXX

To recognise the share-based payment expense.

Dividends paid on share options that are expected to vest.

Dr	Equity/retained earnings	XXX	
Cr	Cash		XXX

To recognise the dividends paid on share options that are expected to vest.

Dividends paid on share options that are NOT expected to vest.

Dr	Employee expense	XXX
Cr	Cash	XXX

To recognise the dividends paid on share options that are not expected to vest.

If the assessment of the number of shares expected to vest changes, there will need to be an adjustment to reverse or increase the share-based payment expense as appropriate, together with an adjustment to increase or decrease the amount of dividend considered an additional employee expense.

Scenario C: dividends reduce exercise price, lost if shares forfeited

When dividends are automatically applied to reduce the exercise price, the input for dividends into the valuation of the option is the same as in Scenario B, as indicated in IFRS 2:B32.

When the share-based payment expense related to these options is recognised, provided that they are considered to be an equity-settled share-based payment, the appropriate journal entry is as follows.

Dr	Share-based payment expense	XXX
Cr	Equity	XXX

To recognise the share-based payment expense.

When the dividends are declared, the entity may make a transfer from retained earnings to another component of equity for the amount of the dividends because this represents a part of the exercise price 'paid' by the employee. This is relevant only if the credit to equity under IFRS 2 is made to a separate reserve (see **5.1.5**).

5.4.5.7 Risk-free interest rate

The risk-free interest rate affects the price of an option in a less intuitive way than expected volatility or expected dividends. As interest rates increase, the value of a call option also increases. This is because the present value of the exercise price will decrease.

IFRS 2 states that the risk-free interest rate should be the implied yield available at the date of grant on zero-coupon government issues in whose currency the exercise price is expressed, with a remaining term equal to the expected life of the option being valued. It may be necessary to use an appropriate substitute in some circumstances. [IFRS 2:B37]

5.4.6   Other factors affecting the valuation of share-based payments

5.4.6.1   Impact of variables that are not factored into the Black-Scholes model

There are certain variables that affect the value of many employee share options that are not factored into the standardised Black-Scholes model. The inability to incorporate these factors directly into the Black-Scholes model limits its usefulness in estimating the fair value of the options. While the approach in IFRS 2 attempts to 'fix' this fault through adjustments to the inputs to the Black-Scholes calculation (e.g. expected life versus contractual life), many believe these adjustments are not enough. **Sections 5.4.6.2** to **5.4.6.8** discuss in more detail some of these additional assumptions. However, depending upon materiality levels, the additional benefits derived from a model that involves these assumptions may not be worth the costs of preparing that model.

5.4.6.2   Performance conditions

As further explained in **section 5.3**, IFRS 2 requires that market-based performance related vesting features be included in the determination of the fair value at the date of grant. Additionally, IFRS 2 requires the entity to estimate the vesting period at the date of grant and recognise the related expense over that period. There is no subsequent adjustment to the vesting period when the vesting period depends on a performance condition that is market-based.

Under IFRS 2, a non-market-based performance condition should not be included in the determination of the fair value at the grant date. For grants with such vesting conditions, at the end of each reporting period, the cumulative expense should equal that proportion of the charge that would have been expensed based on the multiple of the latest estimate of the number of awards that will meet that condition and the fair value of each award, i.e. it should be trued up at the end of each reporting period.

5.4.6.3   Non-vesting conditions

As further explained in **section 5.3**, non-vesting conditions are factored into the fair value calculation.

5.4.6.4   Non-transferability

Many believe non-transferability after the vesting period does not have a material impact on the valuation of an option from the perspective of the issuer. However, because the shareholding is typically a disproportionate part of an employee's wealth, it may have a significant impact on their behaviour and, therefore, the expected life of the option. Several valuation experts have stated that the inability to transfer an employee share option does not violate option pricing model assumptions because there is no assumption about the transferability of the option in the calculation.

When estimating the fair value of an employee share option at the grant date, IFRS 2 requires the use of expected life to exercise instead of the option's contractual life to expiration to take into account the option's non-transferability. However, valuation experts agree that the use of an average expected life to exercise is not a theoretically accurate way to capture the option's non-transferability. They argue that looking only at the average expected life of the share option distribution could not capture information about that distribution. Therefore, some believe employee behaviours that result in early exercise should be explicitly modelled using a more dynamic option pricing model – such as the binomial model.

Furthermore, many valuation experts now believe that no discount is warranted for non-transferability during the vesting period. If the premise of fair value, as discussed above, is to estimate the amount that a hypothetical market participant would pay for such an option, then the estimate should incorporate employee characteristics only to the extent that they would affect the amount and timing of cash flows of the option. The only alternatives facing the employee during the vesting period are to vest or not to vest – and those two alternatives are addressed under the modified grant date approach in IFRS 2.

IFRS 2:B3 indicates that post-vesting transfer restrictions should be taken into account when estimating the fair value of the shares granted, but only to the extent that the post-vesting transfer restrictions affect the price that a knowledgeable willing market participant would pay for those shares. If the shares are actively traded in a deep and liquid market, post-vesting transfer restrictions may have little, if any, effect on the price that a knowledgeable, willing market participant would pay for those shares.

Example 5.4.6.4

Effect of post-vesting transfer restrictions when measuring fair value of equity instruments

Company A operates a share purchase plan for its employees. Company A's shares are listed and are actively traded. There are no vesting conditions; therefore, the shares vest immediately on grant date.

The plan stipulates post-vesting transfer restrictions such that employees cannot sell their shares until the end of a five-year period beginning on the grant date. The sale of those shares is legally prohibited before the end of the five-year

---

period. Consequently, employees are required to pay the subscription price on the grant date, but they are unable to take advantage of market fluctuations during the following five years. The shares are held in a trust until the transfer restrictions expire. Dividends distributed during the restriction period are held by the trust.

In order to measure the effect of the post-vesting transfer restrictions, Company A considers a methodology that combines bank borrowings as if to acquire unrestricted shares on the market (the same number as granted in the plan) at the beginning of the five-year period and a forward to sell shares kept in the trust at the end of the five-year period. The fair value determined by such a methodology depends mainly on the interest rate applied to the borrowings. Typically, a financial markets participant (such as a bank) would be able to borrow money at a low rate such that the fair value would be less than the fair value determined on the basis of an interest rate applicable to an individual employee who does not have ready access to financial markets.

IFRS 2:Appendix A defines fair value as the "amount for which an asset could be exchanged, a liability settled, or an equity instrument granted could be exchanged, between knowledgeable, willing parties in an arm's length transaction". Based on this definition, under Company A's valuation methodology, the interest rate applied to the borrowings should be the rate applicable to the instrument. Therefore, an employee's ability to source such borrowings is not considered.

5.4.6.5   Stated exercise restrictions

Stated exercise restrictions (e.g. restrictions on exercise or sale of shares by employees) will affect the value both directly and through their impact on the behaviour of holders. The easiest way to see this is to note that employees may find themselves holding a large proportion of their wealth in the form of shares whereas, in the absence of such restrictions, they would hold a more diversified portfolio. This, in turn, will affect their behaviour and, generally (but not invariably) will cause them to exercise as early as possible so as to be out of the restricted period as fast as possible. A history of exercising options as early as possible demonstrates that the value given by the employer is less than the amount attributable to the full term of the option.

The effects of exercise restrictions will be similar to the effects of non-transferability features as discussed above. Therefore, stated exercise restrictions should be evaluated when estimating the fair value of employee share options based on their effect on the expected future cash flows from the options.

5.4.6.6   Behavioural considerations

There are many factors that affect the value of share options through their impact on employee behaviour. Behavioural considerations are critical and should be included in the valuation of share options. This is a familiar consideration in the financial markets. The entire mortgage market, for example, revolves around estimation of the behavioural influences on prepayments.

IFRS 2 requires behavioural considerations to be included in the model through an adjustment to the expected life of the option. Many believe, however, that this will generally be inadequate since the life of the option will depend on the returns for both the entity and for the market and the mechanism for this dependency will be determined by the group characteristics noted, such as risk aversion, diversification, and tax considerations. For example, as individuals grow wealthier in a rising market, the costs of poor diversification may decline and that will reduce occurrences of early exercise of the share options.

5.4.6.7 Long-term nature of employee share options

The long-term nature of employee share option grants is significant and will clearly affect valuation. The Black-Scholes model uses one set of assumptions at grant date that do not change during the expected life of the options, while a binomial model can use varying assumptions at grant date depending on expected changes to the inputs during the expected life. A typical employee share option can have a contractual life of 10 years. Therefore, the use of static model inputs is not grounded in reality. Because changes in those factors over time can have a significant impact on option value, failure to model such changes over the term of the option can result in overstating or understating the fair value of an option.

Based on the results of research and discussions with valuation experts, fair value for an employee share option should incorporate at the measurement date volatility factors for discrete time periods over the term of the option, interest and dividend rates and exercise patterns over the term of the option, to correspond with historical evidence and/ or current expectations, to the extent material. It is to be expected that applying a more dynamic option pricing model with changing inputs will be more difficult and, therefore, a cost benefit analysis (taking into consideration materiality) should be completed.

5.4.6.8 Effects of options granted on the capital structure of an entity

Typically, the shares underlying traded options are acquired from existing shareholders and, therefore, have no dilutive effect. [IFRS 2:B38]

Capital structure effects of non-traded options, such as dilution, can be significant and are generally anticipated by the market at the date of grant. Nevertheless, except in most unusual cases, they should have no impact on the individual employee's decision. The market's anticipation will depend, among other matters, on whether the process of share returns is the same or is altered by the dilution and the cash infusion. In many situations, the number of employee share options issued relative to the number of shares outstanding is not significant and, therefore, the effect of dilution on share price can be ignored.

IFRS 2 suggests that the issuer should consider whether the possible dilutive effect of the future exercise of options granted has an effect on the fair value of those options at grant date by an adjustment to option pricing models and factor it into the valuation. [IFRS 2:B41]

5.4.7   Example of employee share purchase plan

The following example is taken from the implementation guidance accompanying IFRS 2 and illustrates some issues about the valuation of equity instruments.

Example 5.4.7

[IFRS 2:IG, Example 11]

Employee share purchase plan

Background

An entity offers all its 1,000 employees the opportunity to participate in an employee share purchase plan. The employees have two weeks to decide whether to accept the offer. Under the terms of the plan, the employees are entitled to purchase a maximum of 100 shares each. The purchase price will be 20 per cent less than the market price of the entity's shares at the date the offer is accepted and the purchase price must be paid immediately upon acceptance of the offer. All shares purchased must be held in trust for the employees, and cannot be sold for five years. The employee is not permitted to withdraw from the plan during that period. For example, if the employee ceases employment during the five-year period, the shares must nevertheless remain in the plan until the end of the five-year period. Any dividends paid during the five-year period will be held in trust for the employees until the end of the five-year period.

In total, 800 employees accept the offer and each employee purchases, on average, 80 shares, i.e. the employees purchase a total of 64,000 shares. The weighted-average market price of the shares at the purchase date is CU30 per share, and the weighted-average purchase price is CU24 per share.

Application of requirements

For transactions with employees, IFRS 2 requires the transaction amount to be measured by reference to the fair value of the equity instruments granted (IFRS 2:11). To apply this requirement, it is necessary first to determine the type of equity instrument granted to the employees. Although the plan is described as an employee share purchase plan (ESPP), some ESPPs include option features and are therefore, in effect, share option plans. For example, an ESPP might include a 'lookback feature', whereby the employee is able to purchase shares

---

at a discount, and choose whether the discount is applied to the entity's share price at the date of grant or its share price at the date of purchase. Or an ESPP might specify the purchase price, and then allow the employees a significant period of time to decide whether to participate in the plan. Another example of an option feature is an ESPP that permits the participating employees to cancel their participation before or at the end of a specified period and obtain a refund of amounts previously paid into the plan.

However, in this example, the plan includes no option features. The discount is applied to the share price at the purchase date, and the employees are not permitted to withdraw from the plan.

Another factor to consider is the effect of post-vesting transfer restrictions, if any. Paragraph B3 of IFRS 2 states that, if shares are subject to restrictions on transfer after vesting date, that factor should be taken into account when estimating the fair value of those shares, but only to the extent that the post-vesting restrictions affect the price that a knowledgeable, willing market participant would pay for that share. For example, if the shares are actively traded in a deep and liquid market, post-vesting transfer restrictions may have little, if any, effect on the price that a knowledgeable, willing market participant would pay for those shares.

In this example, the shares are vested when purchased, but cannot be sold for five years after the date of purchase. Therefore, the entity should consider the valuation effect of the five-year post-vesting transfer restriction. This entails using a valuation technique to estimate what the price of the restricted share would have been on the purchase date in an arm's length transaction between knowledgeable, willing parties. Suppose that, in this example, the entity estimates that the fair value of each restricted share is CU28. In this case, the fair value of the equity instruments granted is CU4 per share (being the fair value of the restricted share of CU28 less the purchase price of CU24). Because 64,000 shares were purchased, the total fair value of the equity instruments granted is CU256,000.

In this example, there is no vesting period. Therefore, in accordance with paragraph 14 of IFRS 2, the entity should recognise an expense of CU256,000 immediately.

However, in some cases, the expense relating to an ESPP might not be material. IAS 8 *Accounting Policies, Changes in Accounting Estimates and Errors* states that the accounting policies in IFRSs need not be applied when the effect of applying them is immaterial (IAS 8, paragraph 8). IAS 8 also states that an omission or misstatement of an item is material if it could, individually or collectively, influence the economic decisions that users make on the basis of the financial statements. Materiality depends on the size and nature of the omission or misstatement judged in the surrounding circumstances. The size or nature of the item, or a combination of both, could be the determining factor (IAS 8:5). Therefore, in this example, the entity should consider whether the expense of CU256,000 is material.

It is unusual that the example in the implementation guidance accompanying IFRS 2 explicitly refers to the possibility that the charge might not be material. This might equally be true of most other requirements of this or other Standards. Caution should be exercised in deciding that a charge otherwise required by IFRS 2 is not material. IAS 8 provides guidance on the meaning of 'material' in the context of errors.

5.4.8   Measurement of equity instruments when fair value is not reliably measurable

IFRS 2 provides an exemption from fair value when the fair value of the equity instruments issued cannot be reliably measured. In these rare cases, the grant is initially measured at its intrinsic value and adjusted at the end of each reporting period for any change in intrinsic value until the options are either exercised, forfeited or lapse.

Appendix A of IFRS 2 defines **intrinsic value** as "[t]he difference between the fair value of the shares to which the counterparty has the (conditional or unconditional) right to subscribe or which it has the right to receive, and the price (if any) the counterparty is (or will be) required to pay for those shares. For example, a share option with an exercise price of CU15, on a share with a fair value of CU20, has an intrinsic value of CU5".

The IASB concluded that 'in rare cases only' in which it is not possible to estimate the grant date fair value of the equity instrument granted, the alternative treatment of using intrinsic values should be permitted. [IFRS 2:BC199] No further guidance is provided in IFRS 2 regarding the nature of the rare circumstances which would justify the use of this approach. Although unlisted entities may find it particularly difficult to apply IFRS 2, it should be remembered that even when the intrinsic value approach is used, it will still be necessary to have an estimate of the fair value of the shares at the end of each reporting period. Also, entities may be discouraged from following this route because the expense recognised using the intrinsic value approach will, in most circumstances, be higher (and more volatile) than that which would be recognised on the basis of fair value at grant date.

In the rare cases in which fair value is not reliably measurable, the equity instruments granted are measured at their intrinsic value, initially at the date when the entity obtains the goods or the counterparty renders the services. The instrument is subsequently remeasured at intrinsic value at the end of each reporting period and at the date of final settlement, with any change in intrinsic value recognised in profit or loss. For a grant of share options, the share-based payment arrangement is finally settled when the options are exercised, are forfeited (e.g. upon cessation of employment) or lapse (e.g. at the end of the option's life). [IFRS 2:24(a)]

When this approach is used, the goods or services received should be recognised based on the number of equity instruments that ultimately vest or, when applicable, are ultimately exercised. This means that in the case of share options, the goods or services received are recognised during the vesting period in accordance IFRS 2:14 and 15 (see **section 5.1**) except that the requirements of IFRS 2:15(b) concerning market conditions do not apply. The amount recognised for goods or services received during the vesting period is based on the number of share options expected to vest. That estimate is revised if subsequent information indicates that the number of options expected to vest differs from previous estimates. On vesting date, the estimate is revised to equal the number of equity instruments that ultimately vested. After vesting date, the amount recognised for goods or services received is reversed if the options are later forfeited, or lapse at the end of the option's life. [IFRS 2:24(b)]

If the intrinsic value approach is used, it is not necessary to apply IFRS 2:26 to 29, which deal with modifications to the terms and conditions on which equity instruments were granted, including cancellation and settlement (see **section 5.5**). This is because any modifications to the terms and conditions on which the equity instruments were granted will be taken into account when applying the intrinsic value method described above. [IFRS 2:25]

However, if an equity instrument to which the intrinsic value method has been applied is settled and the settlement occurs during the vesting period, the settlement is accounted for as an acceleration of vesting. The amount that would otherwise have been recognised for services received over the remainder of the vesting period is, therefore, recognised immediately. In this case, any payment made on settlement is accounted for as the repurchase of equity instruments (i.e. as a deduction from equity) except to the extent that the payment exceeds the intrinsic value of the equity instruments measured at the repurchase date. Any such excess is recognised as an expense. [IFRS 2:25]

The application of the intrinsic value method is illustrated in the following example which is taken from the implementation guidance accompanying IFRS 2.

Example 5.4.8

Grant of share options that is accounted for by applying the intrinsic value method

[IFRS 2:IG, Example 10]

Background

At the beginning of year 1, an entity grants 1,000 share options to 50 employees. The share options will vest at the end of year 3, provided the employees remain in service until then. The share options have a life of 10 years. The exercise price is CU60 and the entity's share price is also CU60 at the date of grant.

At the date of grant, the entity concludes that it cannot estimate reliably the fair value of the share options granted.

At the end of year 1, three employees have ceased employment and the entity estimates that a further seven employees will leave during years 2 and 3. Hence, the entity estimates that 80 per cent of the share options will vest.

Two employees leave during year 2, and the entity revises its estimate of the number of share options that it expects will vest to 86 per cent.

Two employees leave during year 3. Hence, 43,000 share options vested at the end of year 3.

The entity's share price during years 1 - 10, and the number of share options exercised during years 4 - 10, are set out below. Share options that were exercised during a particular year were all exercised at the end of that year.

Year	Share price at year-end	Number of share options exercised at year-end
1	63	0
2	65	0
3	75	0
4	88	6,000
5	100	8,000
6	90	5,000
7	96	9,000
8	105	8,000
9	108	5,000
10	115	2,000

Application of requirements

In accordance with paragraph 24 of the IFRS, the entity recognises the following amounts in years 1 - 10.

Year	Calculation	Expense for period CU	Cumulative expense CU
1	50,000 options × 80% × (CU63 – CU60) × 1/3 years	40,000	40,000
2	50,000 options × 86% × (CU65 – CU60) × 2/3 years – CU40,000	103,333	143,333
3	43,000 options × (CU75 – CU60) – CU143,333	501,667	645,000

Year	Calculation	Expense for period	Cumulative expense
		CU	CU
4	37,000 outstanding options × (CU88 – CU75) + 6,000 exercised options × (CU88 – CU75)	559,000	1,204,000
5	29,000 outstanding options × (CU100 – CU88) + 8,000 exercised options × (CU100 – CU88)	444,000	1,648,000
6	24,000 outstanding options × (CU90 – CU100) + 5,000 exercised options × (CU90 – CU100)	(290,000)	1,358,000
7	15,000 outstanding options × (CU96 – CU90) + 9,000 exercised options × (CU96 – CU90)	144,000	1,502,000
8	7,000 outstanding options × (CU105 – CU96) + 8,000 exercised options × (CU105 – CU96)	135,000	1,637,000
9	2,000 outstanding options × (CU108 – CU105) + 5,000 exercised options × (CU108 – CU105)	21,000	1,658,000
10	2,000 exercised options × (CU115 – CU108)	14,000	1,672,000

5.5 Modifications to equity-settled transactions (including cancellations and settlements)

5.5.1 Modifications

5.5.1.1 Modifications – general

An entity may decide to modify the terms of an existing equity instrument granted in a share-based payment transaction. For example, if there is a decline in the entity's share price an employer may decide to reduce the exercise price of options previously issued to employees, thus increasing their fair value. IFRS 2's requirements in this area are expressed in the context of transactions with employees. However, the requirements also apply to share-based payment transactions with parties other than employees that are measured by reference to the fair value of the equity instruments granted. In this case, any references to grant date are instead used to refer to the date the entity obtains the goods or the counterparty renders service. [IFRS 2:26]

As a minimum, the services received are measured at the grant date fair value, unless the instruments do not vest because of a failure to satisfy a non-market vesting condition that was specified at grant date. This applies irrespective of any modifications to the terms and conditions on which the instruments were granted (including cancellation or settlement). In addition, the effects of modifications that increase the total fair value of the share-based payment arrangement, or are otherwise beneficial to the employee, are recognised. [IFRS 2:27]

Therefore, a modification that results in a decrease in the fair value of equity instruments does not result in a reduction in the expense recognised in future periods. However, the effects of modifications that increase fair value are recognised. Appendix B of IFRS 2 provides guidance on how this requirement should be implemented. This guidance, which forms an integral part of the Standard, is summarised in the following sections.

The transition provisions of IFRS 2 (and, for first-time adopters, the provisions of IFRS 1) do not require the Standard to be applied to awards granted before 7 November 2002. IFRS 2 does not address the modification of such awards. For such modifications, it will be necessary to recognise any incremental fair value as a result of the modification. However, this should not require the recognition of an expense for the original grant date fair value because this is not required under the transition provisions of IFRS 2 or IFRS 1.

5.5.1.2   Modification increases the fair value of the equity instruments granted

The fair value of the equity instruments granted may be increased, for example by reducing the exercise price of share options. When this happens, the incremental fair value is measured by comparing the fair value of the instrument immediately before and immediately after the modification. This incremental fair value is then included in the measurement of the amount recognised for services received.

If the modification occurs during the vesting period, the incremental fair value granted is included in the measurement of the amount recognised for services received over the period from the modification date until the date when the modified equity instruments vest. The amount based on the grant date fair value of the original equity instruments continues to be recognised over the remainder of the original vesting period.

If the modification occurs after vesting date, the incremental fair value granted is recognised immediately. If the employee is required to complete an additional period of service before becoming unconditionally entitled to the modified equity instruments, the incremental fair value granted will be recognised over the vesting period. [IFRS 2:B43(a)]

The following example, which is taken from the implementation guidance accompanying IFRS 2, illustrates the approach that should be adopted for a simple option repricing.

Example 5.5.1.2

Grant of share options that are subsequently repriced

[IFRS 2:IG, Example 7]

Background

At the beginning of year 1, an entity grants 100 share options to each of its 500 employees. Each grant is conditional upon the employee remaining in service over the next three years. The entity estimates that the fair value of each option is CU15. On the basis of a weighted average probability, the entity estimates that 100 employees will leave during the three-year period and therefore forfeit their rights to the share options.

Suppose that 40 employees leave during year 1. Also suppose that by the end of year 1, the entity's share price has dropped, and the entity reprices its share options, and that the repriced share options vest at the end of year 3. The entity estimates that a further 70 employees will leave during years 2 and 3, and hence the total expected employee departures over the three-year vesting period is 110 employees. During year 2, a further 35 employees leave, and the entity estimates that a further 30 employees will leave during year 3, to bring the total expected employee departures over the three-year vesting period to 105 employees. During year 3, a total of 28 employees leave, and hence a total of 103 employees ceased employment during the vesting period. For the remaining 397 employees, the share options vested at the end of year 3.

The entity estimates that, at the date of repricing, the fair value of each of the original share options granted (ie before taking into account the repricing) is CU5 and that the fair value of each repriced share option is CU8.

Application of requirements

Paragraph 27 of the IFRS requires the entity to recognise the effects of modifications that increase the total fair value of the share-based payment arrangement or are otherwise beneficial to the employee. If the modification increases the fair value of the equity instruments granted (eg by reducing the exercise price), measured immediately before and after the modification, paragraph B43(a) of Appendix B requires the entity to include the incremental fair value granted (ie the difference between the fair value of the modified equity instrument and that of the original equity instrument, both estimated as at the date of the modification) in the measurement of the amount recognised for services received as consideration for the equity instruments granted. If the modification occurs during the vesting period, the incremental fair value granted is included in the measurement of the amount recognised for services received over the period from the modification date until the date when the modified equity instruments vest, in addition to the amount based on the grant date fair value of the original equity instruments, which is recognised over the remainder of the original vesting period.

The incremental value is CU3 per share option (CU8 – CU5). This amount is recognised over the remaining two years of the vesting period, along with remuneration expense based on the original option value of CU15.

The amounts recognised in years 1 - 3 are as follows:

Year	Calculation	Remuneration expense for period	Cumulative remuneration expense
		CU	CU
1	(500 – 110) employees × 100 options × CU15 × 1/3	195,000	195,000
2	(500 – 105) employees × 100 options × (CU15 × 2/3 + CU3 × 1/2) – CU195,000	259,250	454,250
3	(500 – 103) employees × 100 options × (CU15 + CU3) – CU454,250	260,350	714,600

5.5.1.3   Modification increases the number of equity instruments granted

If the modification increases the number of equity instruments granted, the fair value of the additional equity instruments granted, measured at the date of the modification, is included in the measurement of the amount recognised for services received, consistent with the requirements in **5.5.1.2**.

For example, if the modification occurs during the vesting period, the fair value of the additional equity instruments granted is included in the amount recognised for services received over the period from the modification date until the date when the additional equity instruments vest. This is in addition to the amount based on the grant date fair value of the equity instruments originally granted which is recognised over the remainder of the original vesting period. [IFRS 2:B43(b)]

The additional equity instruments granted as a result of the modification are, therefore, accounted for in the same way as a new grant of equity instruments on the date of the modification. The related expense is recognised over the remainder of the vesting period, in addition to the expense on the original grant.

Example 5.5.1.3

Modification increases the number of equity instruments granted

On 1 January 20X1, Company A puts in place a share-based payment arrangement under which employees will receive 10,000 shares in Company A free of charge if they stay in employment for three years. At 1 January 20X1 (the grant date), Company A's share price is CU6.

During the first half of 20X1, Company A's share price falls significantly. On 1 July 20X1, Company A modifies the scheme so that participating employees who are still employed at 31 December 20X3 will receive twice as many shares (i.e. 20,000 shares rather than 10,000 shares). On 1 July 20X1, Company A's share price is CU2.50.

At 31 December 20X1, Company A expects that shares will vest for 90 per cent of the employees (i.e. 18,000 shares are expected to vest).

Company A does not anticipate paying any dividends before 31 December 20X3 and, accordingly, the fair value of each equity instrument is determined to be Company A's share price at the grant date.

At the end of 20X1, Company A is 1/3 (12 out of 36 months) of the way through the vesting period for the original grant, and 1/5 (6 out of 30 months) of the way through the vesting period for the additional grant. Therefore, the expense for 20X1 is calculated as follows.

$(10,000 \times CU6 \times 1/3 \times 90\%) + (10,000 \times CU2.50 \times 1/5 \times 90\%) = CU22,500.$

5.5.1.4 Vesting conditions modified in a manner that is beneficial to the employee

The vesting conditions may be modified in a way that is beneficial to the employee. For example, the vesting period may be reduced or a performance condition might be eliminated or made less demanding. When the modification affects a market condition it is accounted for as described at **5.5.1.2**. In all other cases, the modified vesting conditions are taken into account when applying the requirements of IFRS 2:19 to 21 (see **section 5.3.1**). [IFRS 2:B43(c)]

The following example illustrates a modification that is beneficial to the employee as a result of the removal of a market condition.

Example 5.5.1.4A

Removal of a market condition (1)

Company A issues 100 options each to 100 employees. The options vest if:

(a) the employees remain in employment for three years; and

(b) the share price increases to CU9 by the end of the three-year vesting period.

The share price at grant date is CU5 and the fair value of each option is CU3. It is expected that 90 of the employees will remain in Company A's employment for the three years.

In Year 1, the expense recognised is as follows.

		CU	CU
Dr	Profit or loss		
	[100 options × CU3 × 90 employees × 1/3]	9,000	
Cr	Equity		9,000

To recognise the share-based payment expense.

At the beginning of Year 2, the market-based vesting condition (share price target) is removed. At this date, the fair value of each option with the share price target is CU2 and the fair value of each option without the share price target is CU3.50. Thus, an incremental fair value of CU1.50 per option is given to the employees. It is now expected that 92 employees will remain in Company A's employment until the end of Year 3.

In Year 2, the expense recognised is as follows.

In respect of the original scheme

		CU	CU
Dr	Profit or loss		
	[(100 options × CU3 × 92 employees × 2/3) – CU9,000]	9,400	
Cr	Equity		9,400

To recognise the share-based payment expense relating to original scheme.

In respect of the modification

		CU	CU
Dr	Profit or loss		
	[100 options × CU1.50 × 92 employees × 1/2]	6,900	
Cr	Equity		6,900

To recognise the share-based payment expense relating to modification.

At the end of Year 3, 88 employees are still in employment. The expense recognised is as follows.

In respect of the original scheme

		CU	CU
Dr	Profit or loss		
	[(100 options × CU3 × 88 employees) – CU9,000 – CU9,400]	8,000	
Cr	Equity		8,000

To recognise the share-based payment expense relating to original scheme.

In respect of the modification

		CU	CU
Dr	Profit or loss		
	[(100 options × CU1.50 × 88 employees) – CU6,900]	6,300	
Cr	Equity		6,300

To recognise the share-based payment expense relating to modification.

The following example illustrates a modification that is beneficial to the employee as a result of the removal of a non-market condition. The removal of a non-market performance condition will increase the likelihood of the instruments vesting. Overall, this will only be reflected by an increased expense in profit or loss if, and to the extent that, more instruments ultimately vest as a result of the modification.

Example 5.5.1.4B

Removal of a non-market condition (1)

Company A issues 100 options each to 100 employees. The options vest if:

(a) the employees remain in employment for three years; and

(b) earnings per share (EPS) for Year 3 is at least CU1.

The fair value of each option is CU3. It is expected that 90 of the employees will remain in Company A's employment for the three years. At the beginning of Year 1, it is expected that the EPS condition will be met.

In Year 1, the expense recognised is as follows.

		CU	CU
Dr	Profit or loss		
	[100 options × CU3 × 90 employees × 1/3]	9,000	
Cr	Equity		9,000

To recognise the share-based payment expense.

In Year 2, because it is no longer expected that the EPS condition will be met, the expense previously recognised is reversed.

		CU	CU
Dr	Equity	9,000	
Cr	Profit or loss		9,000

To recognise the reversal of the share-based payment expense.

In Year 3, the EPS condition is removed. At the end of Year 3, 88 employees are still in employment. The expense recognised is as follows (reflecting the options vesting in the absence of the now removed EPS condition).

		CU	CU
Dr	Profit or loss		
	[(100 options × CU3 × 88 employees) – nil]	26,400	
Cr	Equity		26,400

To recognise the share-based payment expense.

The effect of modifications which replace a market condition with a non-market condition is considered at **5.5.1.7**. The effect of a modification which replaces a non-market condition with a market condition is considered at **5.5.1.8**.

5.5.1.5 Terms or conditions modified in a manner that is not beneficial to the employee

The terms and conditions of the equity instruments granted may be varied in a manner that reduces the total fair value of the share-based payment arrangement, or is otherwise not beneficial to the employee. In this case, the entity continues to account for the services received as if the modification had not occurred (other than for a cancellation of some or all of the equity instruments granted which is considered at **5.5.2**). [IFRS 2:B44]

This situation is unlikely to be common in practice because it is difficult to see why employees would consent to their agreed benefits being made less attractive. However, if this requirement did not exist it would be possible for management to reduce or eliminate the expense for 'out of the money' options because the employees might accept that they would receive no benefit anyway.

If the modification reduces the fair value of the equity instruments granted, measured immediately before and after the modification, the decrease in fair value is not taken into account. The amount recognised for services received continues to be measured based on the grant date fair value of the instrument originally granted. [IFRS 2:B44(a)]

If the modification reduces the number of equity instruments granted to an employee, the reduction is accounted for as a cancellation of that portion of the grant (see **5.5.2**). [IFRS 2:B44(b)]

If the vesting conditions are modified in a manner that is not beneficial to the employee (e.g. by increasing the vesting period), the modified vesting conditions are not taken into account when applying the requirements of IFRS 2:19 to 21 (see **5.3**). [IFRS 2:B44(c)]

The following example, taken from the implementation guidance accompanying IFRS 2, illustrates the application of this requirement.

Example 5.5.1.5

Grant of share options with a vesting condition that is subsequently modified

[IFRS 2:IG, Example 8]

Background

At the beginning of year 1, the entity grants 1,000 share options to each member of its sales team, conditional upon the employee's remaining in the entity's employ for three years, and the team selling more than 50,000 units of a particular product over the three-year period. The fair value of the share options is CU15 per option at the date of grant.

During year 2, the entity increases the sales target to 100,000 units. By the end of year 3, the entity has sold 55,000 units, and the share options are forfeited. Twelve members of the sales team have remained in service for the three-year period.

Application of requirements

Paragraph 20 of the IFRS requires, for a performance condition that is not a market condition, the entity to recognise the services received during the vesting period based on the best available estimate of the number of equity instruments expected to vest and to revise that estimate, if necessary, if subsequent information indicates that the number of equity instruments expected to vest differs from previous estimates. On vesting date, the entity revises the estimate to equal the number of equity instruments that ultimately vested. However, paragraph 27 of the IFRS requires, irrespective of any modifications to the terms and conditions on which the equity instruments were granted, or a cancellation or settlement of that grant of equity instruments, the entity to recognise, as a minimum, the services received, measured at the grant date fair value of the equity instruments granted, unless those equity instruments do not vest because of failure to satisfy a vesting condition (other than a market condition) that was specified at grant date. Furthermore, paragraph B44(c) of Appendix B specifies that, if the entity modifies the vesting conditions in a manner that is not beneficial to the employee, the entity does not take the modified vesting conditions into account when applying the requirements of paragraphs 19–21 of the IFRS.

Therefore, because the modification to the performance condition made it less likely that the share options will vest, which was not beneficial to the employee, the entity takes no account of the modified performance condition when recognising the services received. Instead, it continues to recognise the services received over the three-year period based on the original vesting conditions. Hence, the entity ultimately recognises cumulative remuneration expense of CU180,000 over the three-year period (12 employees × 1,000 options × CU15).

The same result would have occurred if, instead of modifying the performance target, the entity had increased the number of years of service required for the share options to vest from three years to ten years. Because such a modification would make it less likely that the options will vest, which would not be beneficial to the employees, the entity would take no account of the modified service condition when recognising the services received. Instead, it would recognise the services received from the twelve employees who remained in service over the original three-year vesting period.

5.5.1.6   Adjustments to preserve the rights of holders

Share options or other share-based payment arrangements may change in the case of capital changes such as bonus issues, rights issues and demergers in order to preserve the rights of the holders. For example, in the event of a one-for-one bonus issue, the number of shares in issue will double and the share price will fall by half. Therefore, to avoid the option holders being disadvantaged, it would be usual for the exercise price to be halved and the number of options to be doubled.

Such an adjustment would not result in an additional expense due to modification under IFRS 2 in the following circumstances.

- Preservation of rights in the case of a capital change is part of the scheme rules at inception. If this is the case, the adjustment is made in accordance with the original terms of the grant and there has, therefore, been no modification to the terms and conditions of the grant. This may be the case even if there is no explicit requirement in the written rules of the scheme to make the adjustment. It is important to consider whether such a requirement was implicit in the agreement and, therefore, the entity has merely acted in accordance with the original grant. For example, in some jurisdictions it may be the norm for such adjustments to be made, in which case a court might conclude that there was an implicit contract term in the absence of any evidence to the contrary.

- The option holders are treated in their capacity as equity holders, not as providers of goods or services. This is the case if an equivalent adjustment is made to all other equity or compound instruments (e.g. any convertible bonds) that would otherwise be affected at the time of the capital change and, as stated in IFRS 2:4, means that the adjustment is not subject to the requirements of IFRS 2.

If neither of these circumstances applies, or if other amendments to the terms are made that confer any additional benefit on the employees, the adjustment will be a modification and it will be necessary to compare the fair value of the rights immediately before and after the adjustment.

5.5.1.7 Replacement of a market condition with a non-market condition

The following example is similar to **example 5.5.1.4A** in that a market condition has been removed, but in this case it has been replaced with a non-market condition. There will usually be an incremental fair value because an equity instrument with no market conditions attached will be more valuable than the same equity instrument with a market condition attached. However, whether that incremental fair value is charged as an expense will depend on whether the replacement non-market condition is met.

Example 5.5.1.7

Replacement of a market condition with a non-market condition

Company A issues 100 options each to 100 employees. The options vest if:

(a) the employees remain in employment for three years; and

(b) the share price increases to CU9 by the end of the three-year vesting period.

The share price at grant date is CU5 and the fair value of each option is CU3. It is expected that 90 of the employees will remain in Company A's employment for the three years.

At the beginning of Year 2, the market-based vesting condition (share price target) is removed and replaced with an earnings per share (EPS) condition such that, for the options to vest, EPS for Year 3 must be at least CU1.

At this date, the fair value of each option with the share price target is CU2 and the fair value of each option without the share price target is CU3.50. Therefore, an incremental fair value of CU1.50 per option is being given to the employees. It is now expected that 92 employees will remain in Company A's employment until the end of Year 3, and that the EPS target will be met.

At the end of Year 3, 88 employees are still in employment.

Scenario A: the EPS target is met

In Year 1, the expense recognised is as follows.

		CU	CU
Dr	Profit or loss		
	[100 options × CU3 × 90 employees × 1/3]	9,000	
Cr	Equity		9,000

To recognise the share-based payment expense.

In Year 2, the expense recognised is as follows.

In respect of the original scheme

		CU	CU
Dr	Profit or loss		
	[(100 options × CU3 × 92 employees × 2/3) – CU9,000]	9,400	
Cr	Equity		9,400

To recognise the share-based payment expense in respect of original scheme.

In respect of the modification

		CU	CU
Dr	Profit or loss		
	[100 options × CU1.50 × 92 employees × 1/2]	6,900	
Cr	Equity		6,900

To recognise the share-based payment expense in respect of modification.

In Year 3, the expense recognised is as follows.

In respect of the original scheme

		CU	CU
Dr	Profit or loss		
	[(100 options × CU3 × 88) – CU9,000 – CU9,400]	8,000	
Cr	Equity		8,000

To recognise the share-based payment expense in respect of original scheme.

In respect of the modification

		CU	CU
Dr	Profit or loss		
	[(100 options × CU1.50 × 88) – CU6,900]	6,300	
Cr	Equity		6,300

To recognise the share-based payment expense in respect of modification.

Scenario B: the EPS target is not met

In the event that the EPS target is not met, the incremental expense in respect of the modification is reversed because the non-market condition has not been met. However, in accordance with IFRS 2:B42, Company A continues to recognise the expense in respect of the original scheme because, although the options have failed to vest, this was not because of failure to satisfy a vesting condition specified at the grant date.

Therefore, the expense recognised in Year 3 would be as follows.

In respect of the original scheme

		CU	CU
Dr	Profit or loss		
	[(100 options × CU3 × 88) – CU9,000 – CU9,400]	8,000	
Cr	Equity		8,000

To recognise the share-based payment expense in respect of original scheme.

In respect of the modification (reversal of expense previously recognised)

		CU	CU
Dr	Equity	6,900	
Cr	Profit or loss		6,900

To reverse the share-based payment expense in respect of modification.

It is possible that the modification might be structured with the intention that the fair value to the employee is the same before and after the modification. For example, this might be the case if the probability of the replacement non-market condition being met is the same as the probability of the original market condition being met. However, as illustrated in **example 5.5.1.7**, such a modification may result in an additional expense in accordance with the requirements of IFRS 2. This is a consequence of the different manner in which IFRS 2 treats market and non-market conditions.

5.5.1.8 Replacement of a non-market condition with a market condition

The following example is similar to **example 5.5.1.4B** in that a non-market condition has been removed but in this case it has been replaced with a market condition.

Example 5.5.1.8

Replacement of a non-market condition with a market condition

Company A issues 100 options each to 100 employees. The options vest if:

(a)   the employees remain in employment for three years; and

(b)   earnings per share (EPS) for Year 3 is at least CU1.

The fair value of each option at grant date is CU3. It is expected that 90 of the employees will remain in Company A's employment for the three years. At the start of Year 1, it is expected that the EPS condition will be met.

In Year 1, the expense recognised is as follows.

		CU	CU
Dr	Profit or loss		
	[100 options × CU3 × 90 employees × 1/3]	9,000	
Cr	Equity		9,000

To recognise the share-based payment expense.

At the beginning of Year 2, the EPS condition is removed and replaced with a market-based performance condition such that the share price must reach CU9 by the end of the vesting period. It is expected that 92 employees will remain in Company A's employment for the three years.

At the date of the modification, the fair value of the option with the share price target is CU2 and the fair value of the option without the share price target is CU3.50. Value to the employees is decreased but, under IFRS 2:B44, this decrease is not accounted for.

The original grant date fair value must continue to be recognised as an expense except to the extent that the shares do not vest because a service or non-market performance condition that was present at grant date is not met. The only such condition that continues to exist once the EPS condition is removed is the employment condition.

In Year 2, the expense recognised is as follows.

		CU	CU
Dr	Profit or loss		
	[100 options × CU3 × 92 employees × 2/3 – CU9,000]	9,400	
Cr	Equity		9,400

To recognise the share-based payment expense.

At the end of Year 3, 88 employees are still in employment and the share price target is not met, so the expense recognised is as follows.

		CU	CU
Dr	Profit or loss		
	[(100 options × CU3 × 88 employees) – CU9,000 – CU9,400]	8,000	
Cr	Equity		8,000

To recognise the share-based payment expense.

The share-based payment expense is not reversed even though the options do not vest as a result of the market-based performance condition (the share price target). This is the case even though the effect of the market-based performance condition (i.e. reduction in fair value of the options) was not reflected in the measurement of the compensation expense as a result of IFRS 2:B44.

Replacement of a non-market performance condition with a market-based performance condition will, therefore, result in the need to recognise an expense equal to the original grant date fair value irrespective of whether the replacement market-based performance condition is met. In particular, replacement of a non-market performance condition that is not ultimately met with a market condition that is also not ultimately met will result in the need to recognise an expense that would not otherwise have been recognised. This is a consequence of the different manner in which market and non-market performance conditions are treated under IFRS 2.

5.5.1.9 Several modifications in one

IFRS 2:27 requires an entity to recognise the effects of modifications that increase the total fair value of the share-based payment arrangement or are otherwise beneficial to the employee in addition to the amount recognised for service received measured at the grant date fair value.

In determining the fair value of modifications, IFRS 2:B42 to B44 provide the following guidance.

Modifications beneficial to employees:

- for those that increase the fair value of the equity instruments granted or modify a market condition, the incremental fair value granted (difference between fair value measured immediately before and after the modification) is included in the amount recognised for services received over the period from the modification date until the date when the modified equity instruments vest; and

- for those that modify the vesting conditions (other than market conditions), an adjustment is made for the number of awards expected to vest.

Modifications not beneficial to employees:

- for those that reduce the fair value of the equity instruments granted or modify a market condition, an entity continues to recognise the amount for services received based on the grant date fair value; and

- for those that modify the vesting conditions (other than market conditions), the modified vesting conditions are not taken into account and the grant date fair value is recognised over the original vesting period.

IFRS 2 does not explicitly address when several modifications to a share-based payment arrangement are made at one time. However, the application of the principles set out in IFRS 2:B42 to B44 in such cases is illustrated in **example 5.5.1.9A** to **5.5.1.9C**.

Example 5.5.1.9A

Modification by reducing both the exercise price and the vesting period

Company A awards share options to its 10 employees, which vest if the employee remains in employment for four years. The fair value of the award is CU100 (i.e. CU10 per employee). It is expected that eight employees will remain in employment until the end of Year 4.

In Year 1, the following entry is recorded.

		CU	CU
Dr	Profit or loss [CU10 × 8 employees × 1/4]	20	
Cr	Equity		20

To recognise the share-based payment expense.

At the beginning of the second year, Company A modifies share options by (1) reducing the exercise price, and (2) reducing the vesting period to three years.

The reduction of the exercise price increases the fair value of the award. Assume that, as a result of this modification, the fair value of the awards at the date of the modification has been increased by CU16 (i.e. CU1.6 per employee). This additional value is recognised over the period to the revised vesting date (i.e. in Years 2 and 3).

As required by IFRS 2:B43(c), a reduction in the vesting period is beneficial to the employees. The reduction in service period may affect the number of share options expected to vest and, therefore, the cumulative expense that will be recognised over the revised vesting period.

Assume that, after the modifications, it is expected that all 10 employees will complete the vesting period and the total expense recognised over three years will be CU116 (i.e. value of CU11.6 for 10 employees). At the end of Year 3, all 10 employees remain in employment.

In Year 2, the following entry is recorded.

		CU	CU
Dr	Profit or loss [(CU10 × 10 employees) × 2/3 − CU20 + (CU1.6 × 10 employees) × 1/2]	55	
Cr	Equity		55

To recognise the share-based payment expense.

In Year 3, the following entry is recorded.

		CU	CU
Dr	Profit or loss [(CU10 × 10 employees) + (CU1.6 × 10 employees) – CU20 – CU55]	41	
Cr	Equity		41

To recognise the share-based payment expense.

Example 5.5.1.9B

Modification by reducing the exercise price and increasing the vesting period

Company A awards share options to its 10 employees, which vest if the employee remains in employment for four years. The fair value of the award is CU100 (i.e. CU10 per employee). It is expected that eight employees will remain in employment until the end of year 4.

In each of Years 1 and 2, the following entry is recorded.

		CU	CU
Dr	Profit or loss [CU10 × 8 employees × 1/4]	20	
Cr	Equity		20

To recognise the share-based payment expense.

After two years, Company A modifies share options by (1) reducing the exercise price, and (2) increasing the vesting period to five years.

The reduction of the exercise price increases the fair value of the award. Assume that, as a result of this modification, the fair value of the awards has been increased by CU16 (i.e. CU1.6 per employee). This additional value is recognised over the period to the revised vesting date.

As confirmed by IFRS 2:B44(c), an increase in the vesting period is not beneficial to the employees. Accordingly, the grant date fair value (i.e. the fair value measured based on the original terms of the award) is recognised over the original vesting period of four years.

At the date of modification, it is estimated that eight employees will remain in employment until the end of Year 4 and that only five employees will stay until the end of Year 5.

- The grant date fair value is recognised over the original vesting period of four years [IFRS 2:B44(c)] for eight employees [IFRS 2:B42].
- The modification relating to the reduction of the exercise price vests over the remaining three years of the new vesting period of five years [IFRS 2:B43(a)] for five employees.

In Year 3, the following entry is recorded.

		CU	CU
Dr	Profit or loss [(CU10 × 8 employees × 3/4 – CU40) + (CU1.60 × 5 employees × 1/3)]	22.67	
Cr	Equity		22.67

To recognise the share-based payment expense.

By the end of Year 4, only seven employees remain (instead of the expected eight employees). It is still expected that five employees will stay until the end of Year 5.

In Year 4, the following entry is recorded.

		CU	CU
Dr	Profit or loss [(CU10 × 7 employees × 4/4 – CU60) + (CU1.60 × 5 employees × 1/3)]	12.67	
Cr	Equity		12.67

To recognise the share-based payment expense.

By the end of Year 5, as expected, only five employees remain.

In Year 5, the following entry is recorded.

		CU	CU
Dr	Profit or loss [CU1.60 × 5 employees × 1/3]	2.66	
Cr	Equity		2.66

To recognise the share-based payment expense.

The total expense over five years is CU78 (i.e. the grant date fair value of CU10 for seven employees and additional CU1.6 for five employees).

Example 5.5.1.9C

Modification by reducing the exercise price and decreasing the number of shares granted (without modification affecting the vesting period)

Company A awards 1,000 share options to one employee, which vest if the employee remains in employment for two years. The fair value of the award is CU10,000 (i.e. CU10 per share option).

In Year 1, the following entry is recorded.

		CU	CU
Dr	Profit or loss [CU10 × 1,000 share options × 1/2]	5,000	
Cr	Equity		5,000

To recognise the share-based payment expense.

At the beginning of the second year, Company A modifies the share option award by (1) reducing the number of granted share options from 1,000 to 800, and (2) reducing the exercise price of the share option.

The appropriate accounting depends on whether the effects of the modifications increase the total fair value of the award.

IFRS 2:B42 requires an entity to "recognise the effects of modifications that increase the total fair value of the share-based payment arrangement or are otherwise beneficial to the employee". Because, in this example, the modifications are linked, they will be considered as one modification to determine this impact (i.e. the modification in total is either beneficial or not beneficial to the counterparty). The incremental value is calculated as the change in the 'total fair value' before and after the modification.

Assume that the fair value of a share option before and after the reduction in exercise price is CU7 and CU11.

The total change in the fair value of the grant is, therefore, CU1,800 [(800 × CU11) − (1,000 × CU7)].

In Year 2, the following entry is recorded.

		CU	CU
Dr	Profit or loss [(CU10 × 1,000 share options × 1/2) − CU5,000 + (800 × CU11) − (1,000 × CU7)]	6,800	
Cr	Equity		6,800

To recognise the share-based payment expense.

The total expense over two years is CU11,800 [CU10,000 + CU1,800].

5.5.2 Cancellations and settlements

An entity may cancel or settle a grant of equity instruments during the vesting period. IFRS 2 includes requirements that deal with such situations. This does not cover those cases when a grant is forfeited when the vesting conditions are not satisfied which are dealt with in accordance with IFRS 2's requirements for vesting conditions (see **section 5.3**).

IFRS 2:28 refers to circumstances when "a grant of equity instruments is cancelled or settled during the vesting period". Therefore, all cancellations must be dealt with in accordance with IFRS 2:28 irrespective of whether it is the entity or the counterparty that cancels the arrangements.

Similarly, if an entity or counterparty can choose whether to meet a non-vesting condition, the entity treats the failure to meet that non-vesting condition during the vesting period as a cancellation, irrespective of whether the entity or the counterparty fails to meet the non-vesting condition. [IFRS 2:28A]

A practical example of this is when an employee stops making payments into an SAYE option scheme and, therefore, forfeits his or her entitlement under the scheme. The failure to make contributions is a failure to meet a non-vesting condition and is, therefore, accounted for as a cancellation.

The cancellation or settlement of an equity instrument is accounted for as an acceleration of vesting. The amount that would otherwise have been recognised for services received over the remainder of the vesting period is, therefore, recognised immediately. [IFRS 2:28(a)]

Any payment made to the employee on cancellation or settlement is accounted for as a repurchase of an equity interest (i.e. as a deduction from equity) except to the extent that the payment exceeds the fair value of the equity instrument granted, measured at the repurchase date. Any such excess is recognised as an expense. [IFRS 2:28(b)]

If the share-based payment arrangement included liability components, the fair value of the liability at the date of cancellation or settlement should be remeasured. Any payment made to settle the liability component is accounted for as an extinguishment of the liability.

IFRS 2:28(a) requires that an "entity shall account for the cancellation or settlement as an acceleration of vesting, and shall therefore recognise immediately the amount that otherwise *would have been* recognised for services received over the remainder of the vesting period" (emphasis added). The Standard does not specify whether the amount that 'would have been' recognised refers to the compensation expense that would have been recognised if all of the awards outstanding at the settlement date had vested, or whether it should take into account the entity's estimate of the number of awards that would have vested if the settlement had not occurred.

In the absence of clear guidance on the issue, an entity may adopt either alternative as an accounting policy choice. The accounting policy adopted should be disclosed and applied consistently.

Regardless of the treatment adopted as an accounting policy, entities will need to consider whether additional compensation expense should be recognised under IFRS 2:28(b) by comparing the settlement payment to the fair value of the awards measured at the settlement date. Although not explicitly stated in IFRS 2:28(b), the settlement payment should be compared to the settlement date fair value of the number of awards used to determine 'the amount that would have been recognised over the remaining vesting period' (i.e. in a manner consistent with the choice of accounting policy described above). **Example 5.5.2A** illustrates the alternative accounting policies.

Example 5.5.2A

Meaning of 'would have been' as used in IFRS 2:28

At the beginning of 20X0, Entity A granted 100 equity-settled share-based awards to each of 120 employees. The number of awards depends on whether specified profit thresholds are met at the end of the second year. The awards vest if the employees remain in Entity A's employment for two years. At the grant date, Entity A estimates that 80 employees will complete the required two-year service period and that 90 per cent of the awards held by those employees will vest (based on the profits estimated for Years 1 and 2 at the grant date); therefore, 7,200 awards (i.e. 90 awards for 80 employees) are expected to vest.

At the beginning of 20X1, Entity A settles all 12,000 awards in cash (all employees remained in Entity A's employment at that date).

At the date of settlement, consistent with estimates made at the grant date, Entity A estimates that if the awards had remained in place until the contractual vesting date, 80 employees would have completed the required two-year service period and 90 per cent of the awards held by those employees would have vested.

The fair value of each award on the grant date was CU10 and on the settlement date was CU6.

How should Entity A determine the amount that 'would have been' recognised over the remaining vesting period as required by IFRS 2:28(a)?

The various alternatives for Entity A as explained above are illustrated below.

Scenario 1: settlement amount for each award outstanding is lower than the fair value of the award at the settlement date

Assume that Entity A settles each award for cash of CU5.

Accounting policy to recognise expense that would have been recognised if all of the awards outstanding at the settlement date had vested

- Compensation expense recognised in 20X0 is CU36,000 [(7,200 × CU10)/2].

- Compensation expense recognised upon settlement under IFRS 2:28(a) is CU84,000 [(12,000 × CU10) – CU36,000 compensation expense recognised in prior period].

- Additional compensation expense recognised upon settlement under IFRS 2:28(b) is nil because the payment made on settlement (CU5 × 12,000) is lower than the fair value of the awards measured at the settlement date (CU6 × 12,000).

- Total compensation expense is CU120,000.

Accounting policy to recognise expense taking into account the estimate of the number of awards that would have vested had settlement not occurred

- Compensation expense recognised in 20X0 is CU36,000 [(7,200 × CU10)/2].

- Compensation expense recognised upon settlement under IFRS 2:28(a) is CU36,000 [(7,200 × CU10) – CU36,000 compensation expense recognised in prior period].

- Additional compensation expense recognised upon settlement under IFRS 2:28(b) is CU16,800, representing the excess of the payment made on settlement (CU5 × 12,000) over the fair value of the awards measured at the settlement date (CU6 × 7,200).

- Total compensation expense is CU88,800.

Scenario 2: settlement amount for each award outstanding is greater than the fair value of the awards at the settlement date

Assume that Entity A settles each award for cash of CU7.

Accounting policy to recognise expense that would have been recognised if all of the awards outstanding at the settlement date had vested

- Compensation expense recognised in 20X0 is CU36,000 [(7,200 × CU10)/2].

- Compensation expense recognised upon settlement under IFRS 2:28(a) is CU84,000 [(12,000 × CU10) – CU36,000 compensation expense recognised in prior period].

- Additional compensation expense recognised upon settlement under IFRS 2:28(b) is CU12,000, representing the excess of the payment made on settlement (CU7 × 12,000) over the fair value of the awards measured at the settlement date (CU6 × 12,000).

- Total compensation expense is CU132,000.

Accounting policy to recognise expense taking into account the estimate of the number of awards that would have vested had settlement not occurred

- Compensation expense recognised in 20X0 is CU36,000 [(7,200 × CU10)/2].

- Compensation expense recognised upon settlement under IFRS 2:28(a) is CU36,000 [(7,200 × CU10) – CU36,000 compensation expense recognised in prior period].

- Additional compensation expense recognised upon settlement under IFRS 2:28(b) is CU40,800, representing the excess of the payment made on settlement (CU7 × 12,000) over the fair value of the awards measured at the settlement date (CU6 × 7,200).

- Total compensation expense is CU112,800.

IFRS 2 also deals with the situation when new equity instruments may be granted to an employee in connection with the cancellation of existing equity instruments. If new equity instruments are granted and they are identified, on the date when they are granted, as replacement equity instruments for the cancelled equity instruments, this is accounted for as a modification of the original equity instruments (see **5.5.1**). The incremental fair value granted is the difference between the fair value of the replacement equity instruments and the net fair value of the cancelled equity instruments at the date the replacement equity instruments are granted. The net fair value of the cancelled equity instruments is their fair value, immediately before the cancellation, less the amount of any payment made to the employee that is accounted for as deduction from equity in accordance with IFRS 2:28(b). [IFRS 2:28(c)]

If the entity does not identify new equity instruments granted as replacement equity instruments for those cancelled, the new equity instruments are accounted for as a new grant.

IFRS 2 appears to imply a free choice as to whether an entity decides to identify replacement instruments. As illustrated in **example 5.5.2B**, it will often be attractive to identify the new options as replacements because this will avoid accelerating the expense recognised for the original options. However, it would not give a fair presentation to characterise equity instruments as replacements when they were clearly unrelated to the cancelled instruments.

The determination as to whether the issue of new options is a replacement of cancelled options requires careful assessment of the facts and circumstances surrounding such transactions. IFRS 2 does not provide specific guidance in this area. Factors that may indicate that a new issue of options is a replacement of cancelled options include:

- the new share options are with the same participants as the cancelled options;

- the new share options are issued at a fair value that is broadly consistent with the fair value of the cancelled options determined either at their original grant date (indicating a repricing) or the cancellation date (indicating a replacement);

- the transactions to issue and cancel the options are part of the same arrangement;

- the cancellation of the options would not have occurred unless the new options were issued; and

- the cancellation of the options does not make commercial sense without the issue of the new options (and *vice versa*).

If vested equity instruments are repurchased from employees, the payment made is accounted for as a deduction from equity, except to the extent that the payment exceeds the fair value of the repurchased instruments, measured at the repurchase date. Any such excess is recognised as an expense. [IFRS 2:29]

These requirements are illustrated by the following example.

Example 5.5.2B

Replacement of share options

Company O issued options with a four-year vesting period to employees in 20X3. The options had an exercise price of CU10 per share and the aggregate fair value of the options determined at the grant date was CU100,000. In 20X5, Company O cancelled those options and issued new options with an exercise price of CU3 per share.

The aggregate fair value of the new share options at the grant date is CU75,000, while the aggregate fair value of the cancelled options at that date is CU20,000.

If the new issue of options is considered a replacement of the cancelled options

Company O accounts for the transaction in the same way as for a modification. Therefore, Company O will continue to expense the portion of the CU100,000 not yet recognised over the original vesting period. Additionally, Company O will expense the incremental fair value of the new instruments over the old instruments determined at the date of modification (in this example, CU55,000 [CU75,000 – CU20,000]) over the remaining vesting period. Therefore, a total of CU155,000 is expensed related to these options.

If the new issue of options is not considered a replacement of the cancelled share options

The remaining portion of the original fair value of CU100,000 is expensed immediately and the fair value of the new issue is recognised over its vesting period. Therefore, a total of CU175,000 is expensed related to these options, much of the expense in earlier periods.

The following example considers the situation when the replacement options are issued by a different entity in a group.

Example 5.5.2C

Issue of new options as a replacement of cancelled options

Company S is a publicly listed subsidiary of Company P which is also publicly listed. Company P decides to de-list Company S by purchasing all of its outstanding shares from existing shareholders at an amount determined to be fair value. As part of the transaction, all outstanding share options in Company S are cancelled. In return, Company P issues share options in Company P to the same employees of Company S whose share options in Company S were cancelled. The fair value of the new share options determined at the grant date approximates the fair value of the replaced options determined at the cancellation date. In addition, the vesting terms and option lives of the new share options are adjusted to ensure consistency with the cancelled options.

In the circumstances described, even though the share options are in a different entity that has a different risk profile from Company S, the intention is to replace

> value held by the employees. Therefore, the transaction should be considered a replacement of equity instruments and accounted for in accordance with IFRS 2:28(c).

The following example considers the settlement in cash of a fully vested equity-settled share-based payment.

Example 5.5.2D

Settlement in cash of a fully vested equity-settled share-based payment

On 1 January 20X5, Company A issued 100 share options with an exercise price of CU15 per option to certain of its employees. The options vest if the employees remain employed by Company A for four years. The share options can only be settled by delivery of Company A's equity instruments and, therefore, they are classified as equity-settled share-based payments. At the grant date, the fair value of the instruments was determined to be CU5 per option.

As at 31 December 20X8, Company A had recognised a cumulative expense of CU500 [(CU5 × 100) × 4/4 years] because all options had vested. On that date, Company A decided to settle the fully vested equity-settled share-based payments in cash to the value of the share options (rather than settling by delivery of equity instruments). The fair value of the share options as at 31 December 20X8 is CU2,400. Therefore, Company A will pay the employees CU2,400 in cash.

In accordance with IFRS 2:29, a cash payment made to settle a fully vested equity-settled share-based payment should be accounted for as a repurchase of equity instruments. Accordingly, the payment made to the employees is accounted for as a deduction from equity, except to the extent that the payment exceeds the fair value of the instruments repurchased, measured at the repurchase date. Any such excess should be recognised as an additional remuneration expense.

Therefore, the cash settlement of CU2,400 is accounted for as a reduction in equity. If the payment made to the employees had been greater than CU2,400 (the fair value of the original awards at settlement date), Company A would have recognised the excess in profit or loss as an additional remuneration expense.

5.5.3 Changes to method of settlement of equity-settled transactions

5.5.3.1 Addition of a cash alternative

An entity may decide, during the vesting period for an equity-settled transaction, to add an employee option to choose a cash alternative. From the date of such a modification, the transaction should be accounted for as a compound instrument as outlined at **section 7.2**. This approach is illustrated in the **example 5.5.3.1A** which is taken from the implementation guidance accompanying IFRS 2.

Example 5.5.3.1A

Grant of shares, with a cash alternative subsequently added

[IFRS 2:IG, Example 9]

Background

At the beginning of year 1, the entity grants 10,000 shares with a fair value of CU33 per share to a senior executive, conditional upon the completion of three years' service. By the end of year 2, the share price has dropped to CU25 per share. At that date, the entity adds a cash alternative to the grant, whereby the executive can choose whether to receive 10,000 shares or cash equal to the value of 10,000 shares on vesting date. The share price is CU22 on vesting date.

Application of requirements

Paragraph 27 of the IFRS requires, irrespective of any modifications to the terms and conditions on which the equity instruments were granted, or a cancellation or settlement of that grant of equity instruments, the entity to recognise, as a minimum, the services received measured at the grant date fair value of the equity instruments granted, unless those equity instruments do not vest because of failure to satisfy a vesting condition (other than a market condition) that was specified at grant date. Therefore, the entity recognises the services received over the three-year period, based on the grant date fair value of the shares.

Furthermore, the addition of the cash alternative at the end of year 2 creates an obligation to settle in cash. In accordance with the requirements for cash-settled share-based payment transactions (paragraphs 30 - 33 of the IFRS), the entity recognises the liability to settle in cash at the modification date, based on the fair value of the shares at the modification date and the extent to which the specified services have been received. Furthermore, the entity remeasures the fair value of the liability at the end of each reporting period and at the date of settlement, with any changes in fair value recognised in profit or loss for the period. Therefore, the entity recognises the following amounts:

Year	Calculation	Expense CU	Equity CU	Liability CU
1	Remuneration expense for year:			
	10,000 shares × CU33 × 1/3	110,000	110,000	
2	Remuneration expense for year:			
	(10,000 shares × CU33 × 2/3) – CU110,000	110,000	110,000	
	Reclassify equity to liabilities:			
	10,000 shares × CU25 × 2/3		(166,667)	166,667
3	Remuneration expense for year:			
	(10,000 shares × CU33 × 3/3) – CU220,000	110,000*	26,667	83,333

Year	Calculation	Expense CU	Equity CU	Liability CU
	Adjust liability to closing fair value:			
	(CU166,667 + CU83,333) –			
	(CU22 × 10,000 shares)	(30,000)		(30,000)
	Total	300,000	80,000	220,000

* Allocated between liabilities and equity, to bring in the final third of the liability based on the fair value of the shares as at the date of the modification.

Example 5.5.3.1B is based on similar facts to **example 5.5.3.1A** but assumes that the share price has increased rather than decreased by the end of Year 2.

Example 5.5.3.1B

Equity-settled share-based payment when a cash alternative is subsequently offered

At the beginning of Year 1, an entity grants 10,000 shares with a fair value of CU33 per share to a senior executive, conditional on the completion of three years of service. By the end of Year 2, the share price has increased to CU50 per share. At that date, the entity adds a cash alternative to the grant, whereby the executive can choose whether to receive 10,000 shares, or take the cash equivalent to the value of the 10,000 shares on the vesting date. This cash alternative has the same value as the shares. The share price decreased to CU45 at the end of Year 3.

IFRS 2:27 requires an entity to "recognise, as a minimum, services received measured at the grant date fair value of the equity instruments granted, unless those equity instruments do not vest because of failure to satisfy a vesting condition (other than a market condition) that was specified at grant date". In addition, the entity must recognise in profit or loss the effects of modifications that increase the total fair value of the share-based payment arrangement.

Because the modification to the share-based payment to add a cash alternative does not increase the total fair value of the share-based payment arrangement at the date of the modification, the entity continues to recognise an IFRS 2 expense for the services received during the three-year period, based on the grant date fair value of the shares.

However, the addition of the cash alternative at the end of Year 2 creates an obligation to settle in cash. In accordance with the requirements for cash-settled share-based payment transactions (IFRS 2:30 to 33), the entity recognises the liability to settle in cash at the modification date. In a manner consistent with **example 5.5.3.1A**, the liability is measured at the value of the shares on the date of modification, pro-rated for the effect of the service condition. This effect of the modification is recognised in equity and not in profit or loss. Thereafter, the cost of the original equity grant is recognised in profit or loss. The increase in the liability for the remaining service period, which is based on the modification-date value, is recognised in equity. Subsequent remeasurement of the liability to fair value at each reporting date and at the date of settlement is recognised in profit or loss.

Year	Calculation	Expense CU	Equity CU	Liability CU
1	Remuneration expense for year:			
	10,000 shares × CU33 × 1/3	110,000	110,000	
2	Remuneration expense for year:			
	(10,000 shares × CU33 × 2/3) – CU110,000	110,000	110,000	
	Reclassify equity to liabilities:			
	10,000 shares × CU50 × 2/3		(333,333)	333,333
3	Remuneration expense for year:			
	(10,000 shares × CU33 × 3/3) – CU220,000	110,000	110,000	
	Final third of liability at modification value:			
	(10,000 shares × CU50 × 3/3) – CU333,333		(166,667)	166,667
	Remeasurement of liability:			
	(10,000 shares × CU45 ×3/3) – CU500,000	(50,000)		(50,000)
	Total	280,000	(170,000)	450,000

In the entry in Year 2, therefore, the value of the cash modification is recognised in equity and not in profit or loss. In Year 3, the cost of the original equity grant is recognised in profit or loss, along with the remeasurement in the liability value to CU450,000 at the end of the year. The remaining unvested portion of the fair value of the liability at the modification date, which is CU166,667 [(10,000 shares × CU50 × 3/3) – CU333,333], is recognised in equity.

5.5.3.2   Change from equity-settled to cash-settled

The following example considers a change in the terms whereby options that were originally to be equity-settled will be cash-settled.

Example 5.5.3.2

Modification from an equity-settled to a cash-settled share-based payment arrangement during the vesting period

On 1 January 20X3, Company A issued 100 share options to certain employees, with a strike price of CU15 per option. The options vest if the employees remain in Company A's employment after four years. The share options can only be settled by delivery of Company A's equity instruments and, therefore, they are classified as equity-settled share-based payments. Company A determined the fair value of the instruments to be CU5 per option.

At 31 December 20X4, Company A had recognised a cumulative expense of CU250 [(CU5 × 100) × 2/4 years], because it expected all of the options to vest. On 1 January 20X5, Company A modified the options so that they could only be settled in cash. Therefore, upon settlement, Company A will pay the employees in cash the amount equal to the intrinsic value on the settlement date. On the date of modification, the fair value of each share option is determined to be CU8.

IFRS 2:B43, which contains guidance on the application of IFRS 2:27, states, in part, that "if the modification increases the fair value of the equity instruments granted ..., measured immediately before and after the modification, the entity shall include the incremental fair value granted in the measurement of the amount recognised for services received as consideration for the equity instruments granted". IFRS 2:B43 further clarifies that the "incremental fair value granted is the difference between the fair value of the modified equity instrument and that of the original equity instrument, both estimated as at the date of the modification".

Therefore, the fair value of the share options is reclassified from equity to liability to the extent to which specified services have been received, i.e. CU400 (CU800 × 2/4) as follows.

		CU	CU
Dr	Equity	400	
Cr	Liability		400

To recognise the reclassification from equity to liability.

This results in a cumulative debit within equity of CU150, comprising the debit of CU400 arising on the modification less the credit of CU250 which arose under the equity-settled arrangements prior to the modification date (IFRS 2:BC267 and BC268).

6 Recognition and measurement: cash-settled transactions

6.1 Recognition of cash-settled transactions

6.1.1 Recognition of cash-settled transactions – general

As indicated in **2.2**, IFRS 2 applies to transactions in which the entity acquires goods or services by incurring a liability to transfer cash or other assets for amounts based on the price (or value) of the shares or other equity instruments of the entity or of another group entity.

The most common examples of such arrangements are cash-settled Share Appreciation Rights (SARs) which are also sometimes referred to as 'phantom option schemes' (see **2.2**).

For cash-settled share-based payment transactions, the goods or services acquired and the liability incurred are measured at the fair value of the liability. Until the liability is settled, the liability is remeasured at fair value at the end of each reporting period (and the settlement date). Any changes in fair value are recognised in profit or loss for the period. [IFRS 2:30]

IFRS 2 uses the term 'fair value' in a way that differs in some respects from the definition of fair value in IFRS 13 *Fair Value Measurement*. When applying IFRS 2, an entity should measure fair value in accordance with the guidance in IFRS 2, not IFRS 13. [IFRS 2:6A]

The effect of vesting conditions on the fair value measurement is discussed at **6.3**.

For cash-settled share-based payment transactions, under IFRS 2:30, the goods or services acquired and the liability incurred are measured at the fair value of the liability. Until the liability is settled, the liability is remeasured at fair value at the end of each reporting period (and at the settlement date) and any changes in fair value are recognised in profit or loss for the period.

However, if the amount recognised for the goods or services received was capitalised as part of the carrying amount of an asset recognised in the entity's statement of financial position, the carrying amount of that asset can be adjusted for the effects of the liability remeasurement during the period that is the shorter of:

- the period during which costs are eligible for capitalisation in accordance with whichever Standard is applicable to the asset in question (e.g. IAS 2 for inventories, IAS 16 for property, plant and equipment etc.); and

- the vesting period.

Subsequent to the capitalisation period, the carrying amount of that asset is not adjusted for any further remeasurement of the liability and any subsequent changes in the fair value of the liability are recognised in profit or loss.

The services received and the liability to pay for those services are recognised as the employees render service. For example, some SARs vest immediately and the employees are not, therefore, required to complete a specified period of service to become entitled to the cash payment. In the absence of evidence to the contrary, it should be presumed that the services rendered by the employees in exchange for the SARs have been received. In this case, the expense for the services received and the liability to pay for them should be recognised immediately. But if the rights do not vest until the employees have completed a specified period of service, the services received and the liability to pay for them should be recognised as the employees render service during the period. [IFRS 2:32]

6.1.2 Presentation of liability

The following example considers the presentation and disclosure of the liability for cash-settled SARs.

Example 6.1.2

Presentation of SARs in the statement of financial position

Company C issues 12 cash-settled share appreciation rights (SARs) to certain of its employees. The SARs vest over a three-year period. At the end of the vesting period, Company C expects that three of the SARs will be exercised within one year and the remaining nine SARs will be exercised after one year.

Company C should consider whether the liability should be presented separately in the statement of financial position, and whether it should be presented as current or non-current.

IFRS 2 does not require separate presentation of the carrying amount of liabilities relating to share-based payments in the statement of financial position, but requires this information to be disclosed in the financial statements. Liabilities arising from share-based payments are financial liabilities, although they are excluded from the scope of IAS 32 and IFRS 9 (or, for entities that have not yet adopted IFRS 9, IAS 39).

Therefore, an entity should consider whether share-based payment liabilities should be grouped with other financial liabilities in the statement of financial position. Paragraph 29 of IAS 1 *Presentation of Financial Statements* requires each material class of similar items to be presented separately in the financial statements. Items of a dissimilar nature or function are presented separately unless they are immaterial. IAS 1:30 explains that if a line item is not individually material, it is aggregated with other items either on the face of the financial statements or in the notes. Share-based payment liabilities are likely to be different from other financial liabilities in nature and function.

IAS 1:60 requires separate presentation in the statement of financial position for current and non-current liabilities. In the circumstances described, because all of the SARs can be exercised within the next year, these liabilities should be presented as current liabilities in Year 3. If Company C determines that presentation on a liquidity basis is more relevant, the current portion of the liability should be disclosed in accordance with IAS 1:61.

6.2 Measurement of cash-settled transactions

6.2.1 Measurement of cash-settled transactions – general

The liability is measured, initially and at the end of each reporting period until settled, at the fair value of the SARs by applying an option pricing model, taking into account the terms and conditions upon which the rights were granted and the extent to which the employees have rendered service to date. The use of option pricing models is considered in **section 5.4.4**.

A simpler approach would have been to base the liability on the intrinsic value of the SARs at the end of the reporting period (i.e. the difference between the fair value of the shares and the exercise price, if any). It can be argued that the additional cost and effort of using an option pricing model is not justified given that the cumulative expense is always trued up to the actual cash payment. However, the IASB rejected this approach and concluded that measuring SARs at intrinsic value would be inconsistent with the fair value measurement basis applied in the rest of IFRS 2.

The following example, which is taken from the implementation guidance accompanying IFRS 2, illustrates the application of these requirements.

Example 6.2.1

Cash-settled share appreciation rights

[IFRS 2:IG, Example 12]

Background

An entity grants 100 cash share appreciation rights (SARs) to each of its 500 employees, on condition that the employees remain in its employ for the next three years.

During year 1, 35 employees leave. The entity estimates that a further 60 will leave during years 2 and 3. During year 2, 40 employees leave and the entity estimates that a further 25 will leave during year 3. During year 3, 22 employees leave. At the end of year 3, 150 employees exercise their SARs, another 140 employees exercise their SARs at the end of year 4 and the remaining 113 employees exercise their SARs at the end of year 5.

The entity estimates the fair value of the SARs at the end of each year in which a liability exists as shown below. At the end of year 3, all SARs held by the remaining employees vest. The intrinsic values of the SARs at the date of

---

exercise (which equal the cash paid out) at the end of years 3, 4 and 5 are also shown below.

Year	Fair value	Intrinsic value
1	CU14.40	
2	CU15.50	
3	CU18.20	CU15.00
4	CU21.40	CU20.00
5		CU25.00

Application of requirements

Year	Calculation	Expense CU	Liability CU
1	(500 – 95) employees × 100 SARs × CU14.40 × 1/3	194,400	194,400
2	(500 – 100) employees × 100 SARs × CU15.50 × 2/3 – CU194,400	218,933	413,333
3	(500 – 97 – 150) employees × 100 SARs × CU18.20 – CU413,333	47,127	460,460
	+ 150 employees × 100 SARs × CU15.00	225,000	
	Total	272,127	
4	(253 – 140) employees × 100 SARs × CU21.40 – CU460,460	(218,640)	241,820
	+ 140 employees × 100 SARs × CU20.00	280,000	
	Total	61,360	
5	CU0 – CU241,820	(241,820)	0
	+ 113 employees × 100 SARs × CU25.00	282,500	
	Total	40,680	
	Total	787,500	

Note that remeasurement of the liability is not recognised as one amount immediately. Instead this amount is spread over the remaining vesting period of the liability.

6.2.2   Share price denominated in a foreign currency

Example 6.2.2

Cash-settled share-based payment arrangement with share price and option exercise price denominated in a foreign currency

Company E is a UK entity with Sterling as its functional currency. Company E is registered on the New York Stock Exchange with a current market price of US$15 per share. Company E issues 100 options to its employees with an exercise price of US$15 per share and a vesting period of three years. The share options can only be cash settled.

For cash-settled share options, the liability recognised would be considered a US dollar denominated liability and would need to be remeasured at the end of each reporting period (the remeasurement would include the effect of changes in the exchange rate).

This issue is considered at **5.2.3.6** in relation to equity-settled share-based payments.

6.3   Vesting conditions

An issue that arises is whether vesting conditions should be considered in determining the fair value of cash-settled share-based payments. The requirements of IFRS 2 are not clear in this regard.

IFRS 2:30 requires that the liability incurred from a cash-settled share-based payment transaction should be measured at the fair value of the liability. There is no discussion in IFRS 2 regarding whether the fair value of the liability for a cash-settled share-based payment should include the effects of vesting conditions.

The definition of fair value is "[t]he amount for which an asset could be exchanged, a liability settled, or an equity instrument granted could be exchanged, between knowledgeable, willing parties in an arm's length transaction". [IFRS 2:Appendix A] From this perspective, the fair value measurement should include all terms and conditions, including all vesting conditions.

However, non-market vesting conditions are excluded from the grant date fair value of equity-settled share-based payments because the 'true up' model is applied to those transactions. As noted in IFRS 2:19, the exclusion of non-market vesting conditions from the measurement of equity-settled share-based payments has the effect of creating a measurement that is not a true fair value measurement. Similar statements are not made regarding the measurement of cash-settled share-based payments.

Example 6.2.1 (which is taken from the implementation guidance accompanying IFRS 2) provides an illustration of the accounting for one form of cash-settled share-based payments (share appreciate rights, or SARs). In this illustration, employees must remain in the entity's employment for the next three years for their SARs to vest. The illustration does not include the effects of this vesting condition in determining the fair value of the SARs at the end of each reporting period, but bases the total liability on the best estimate of the number of SARs that will vest.

While **example 6.2.1** excludes one type of non-market vesting condition (remaining in the employment of an entity for a specified period of time), it is not clear whether the implication of this exclusion should extend to other non-market vesting conditions, such as achieving a target revenue.

Given the lack of clarity regarding how vesting conditions should be reflected in the fair value measurement, it appears that there are two acceptable approaches; an entity should measure the liability arising from a cash-settled share-based payment on one of the following bases:

- at true fair value (i.e. the fair value measurement of the liability reflects all vesting and non-vesting conditions, including service and non-market performance conditions); or

- by analogy to the measurement of equity-settled share-based payments (i.e. the fair value measurement of the liability reflects market and non-vesting conditions only. Service and non-market performance conditions are taken into account by adjusting the number of rights to receive cash that are expected to vest).

An entity should choose one of the two approaches as an accounting policy and apply this policy consistently. Whichever approach is adopted, until the liability is settled, an entity should remeasure the fair value of the liability at the end of each reporting period and at the date of settlement with any changes in fair value recognised in profit or loss for that period.

6.4 Modifications to cash-settled transactions

6.4.1 Modifications, cancellations and settlements

IFRS 2 does not make specific reference to the treatment of modifications to cash-settled share-based payment arrangements.

A modification of a cash-settled share-based payment arrangement such as a share appreciation right (SAR) is accounted for as the exchange of the original award for a new award. However, because cash-settled share-based payment transactions are remeasured based on their fair value at each reporting date, no special guidance is necessary in accounting for a modification of a cash-settled award that remains a cash-settled award after the modification. The requirements of IFRS 2:33 apply to the measurement of cash-settled share-based payment transactions (i.e. the liability is measured at the fair value of the SARs multiplied by the proportion of the vesting period which has been completed). Any increase or decrease in the value of the liability would be recognised immediately in profit or loss or, when the relevant criteria are met, included in the cost of an asset (e.g. when a payment to employees relates to the construction of property, plant and equipment). The application of this treatment to two possible modifications of SARs is illustrated in **examples 6.4.1A** and **6.4.1B**.

Example 6.4.1A

Reduction of the vesting period of a cash-settled share-based payment transaction

100 cash-settled SARs are granted on 1 January 20X0 with a fair value of CU10 each. The terms of the award require the employee to provide service for four years in order to earn the award. At the end of the second year of service (20X1), the employer modifies the terms of the award to require only three years of service from the employee to earn the award. The fair value of each SAR at each reporting date is as follows:

31 December 20X0	CU12
31 December 20X1	CU20
31 December 20X2	CU15

The following journal entries reflect the accounting for the award at each period end (assuming there are no expected forfeitures).

At 31 December 20X0

		CU	CU
Dr	Profit or loss [CU12 × 100 awards × 1 year/4 years of service required]	300	
Cr	Liability		300

To recognise the share-based payment expense and associated liability.

At 31 December 20X1

		CU	CU
Dr	Profit or loss [(CU20 × 100 awards × 2 years/3 years of service required) = CU1,333 – CU300 previously recognised]	1,033	
Cr	Liability		1,033

To recognise the share-based payment expense and remeasurement of associated liability.

At 31 December 20X2

		CU	CU
Dr	Profit or loss [(CU15 × 100 awards × 3 years/3 years of service required) = CU1,500 – CU1,333 previously recognised]	167	
Cr	Liability		167

To recognise the share-based payment expense and remeasurement of associated liability.

Example 6.4.1B

Cancellation of a cash-settled share-based payment transaction

100 cash-settled SARs are granted on 1 January 20X0 with a fair value of CU10 each. The terms of the award require the employee to provide service for four years in order to earn the award. At the end of the second year of service (20X1), the employer cancels the award without issuing any replacement award or cash. The fair value of each SAR at each reporting date is as follows.

31 December 20X0	CU12
31 December 20X1	CU5

The following journal entries reflect the accounting for the award at each period end (assuming there are no expected forfeitures).

At 31 December 20X0

		CU	CU
Dr	Profit or loss [CU12 × 100 awards × 1 year/4 years of service required]	300	
Cr	Liability		300

To recognise the share-based payment expense and associated liability.

At 31 December 20X1		
	CU	CU
Dr Liability	300	
Cr Profit or loss		300

To recognise the reversal of the share-based payment expense and associated liability.

Because, in this example, the award is cancelled without issuing anything in return, the value of the liability at 31 December 20X1 should be adjusted to CUnil. Therefore, all prior share-based payment expense recognised should be reversed.

6.4.2   Changes to methods of settlement of cash-settled transactions

IFRS 2 does not specify how to account for a modification of a share-based payment arrangement from cash-settled to equity-settled; the guidance in IFRS 2 deals only with modifications to the terms and conditions of equity-settlement arrangements.

The principles of IFRS 2 are generally consistent with those of US GAAP, namely FASB Accounting Standards Codification (ASC) Topic 718, *Stock Compensation*. In particular, modifications to the terms and conditions of equity-settled share-based payments are generally treated consistently under IFRS 2 and ASC 718. ASC 718 also specifies how to account for a modification to a share-based payment arrangement that results in a change in its classification from being cash-settled to equity-settled, and it is appropriate for such modifications to be accounted for in the same way under IFRS 2.

The guidance in ASC 718 requires the existing cash-settled liability to be reclassified to equity at the date of modification. The cash-settled share-based payment expense recognised up to the date of modification is not adjusted and the expense recognised from the date of modification over the remainder of the vesting period is determined based on the fair value of the reclassified equity award at the date of the modification. In other words, the modification is accounted for as if the liability existing at the date of modification is effectively settled with an equity award with the same fair value.

Example 6.4.2

Modification from cash-settled to equity-settled

On 1 January 20X3, Company A issues 100 share options to some of its employees with a strike price of CU15 per option. The share options vest if the employee remains in Company A's employment after four years. The share options can only be cash-settled. Company A has determined that the fair value of the instruments at the date of grant is CU5 per option.

At 31 December 20X4, the fair value of the cash-settled share-based payment is CU6 per option. To date, Company A has recognised a cumulative share-based payment expense of CU300 [(CU6 × 100) × 2/4 years] because Company A expects all of the options to vest. On 1 January 20X5, Company A modifies the options such that they can only be settled by delivery of Company A's equity instruments (one share option entitles the employee to one ordinary share of Company A, and there is no change to the strike price of CU15). No other terms or vesting conditions of the share-based payment arrangement are amended.

Applying the requirements of ASC 718, at the date of modification (1 January 20X5), Company A is required to derecognise the existing cash-settled liability because the liability has effectively been settled by the issue of an equity instrument. The existing cash-settled liability is, therefore, reclassified to equity. The cash-settled compensation cost recognised to date is not adjusted, except for subsequent 'true up' if vesting conditions are not met. The compensation cost to be recognised over the remaining vesting period is based on the fair value of the equity instrument at the time of the modification. Therefore, the cumulative compensation cost recognised for the share-based payment arrangement will reflect fair value for the equity award at 1 January 20X5.

In this example, the fair value at modification is CU6 per option. The cost to be recognised in each of 20X5 and 20X6 (Years 3 and 4 of the award), provided that all awards vest, will be CU150:

20X5: [(CU6 × 100) × 3/4 years] – CU300	CU150
20X6: [(CU6 × 100) × 4/4 years] – CU450	CU150

6.4.3 Repricing of cash-settled transactions

Example 6.4.3

Repricing of cash-settled transactions

Company T issues cash-settled share appreciation rights (SARs) to employees with a fair value of CU100 on 1 January 20X6. The SARs vest over a period of four years. At 31 December 20X6, the fair value of the SARs is CU120 and, therefore, Company T has a liability of CU30 [CU120 × 1/4]. On 1 January 20X7, Company T reprices the SARs so that the fair value of the award is now CU280. The modification affects no other terms or conditions of the SARs, and does not change the number of SARs expected to vest.

The repricing increases the value of the SARs and, therefore, the incremental value should be recognised over the vesting period. Because one quarter of the vesting period is complete, the liability should be increased to CU70 – requiring the immediate recognition of CU40 [(CU280 × 1/4) – CU30] of remuneration expense. Therefore, if the fair value did not change in the remaining three years, CU70 [(CU280 – CU70) × 1/3)] would be recognised in profit or loss in each of the remaining three years.

7 Recognition and measurement: transactions with settlement alternatives

7.1 Transactions with settlement alternatives – general

For share-based payment transactions in which the terms of the arrangement provide either the entity or the counterparty with the choice of whether the entity settles the transaction in cash (or other assets) or by issuing equity instruments, the transaction, or the components of that transaction, are accounted for:

[IFRS 2:34]

- as a cash-settled share-based payment transaction if, and to the extent that, the entity has incurred a liability to settle in cash or other assets; or

- as an equity-settled share-based payment transaction if, and to the extent that, no such liability has been incurred.

IFRS 2 contains more detailed requirements concerning how to apply this principle to share-based payment transactions in which the terms of the arrangement:

- provide the counterparty with a choice of settlement (see **7.2**); and

- provide the entity with a choice of settlement (see **7.3**).

Contingent cash settlement provisions are considered at **7.4**. Circumstances when there is a modification to the terms of settlement are considered at **5.5.3** (for modification of an arrangement that has been accounted for as an equity-settled share-based payment transaction) and **6.4.2** (for modification of an arrangement that has been accounted for as a cash-settled share-based payment transaction).

References to cash, in the remainder of this section, also include other assets.

7.2 Counterparty's choice as to the manner of settlement

7.2.1 Recognition of a compound instrument

If the counterparty has the choice as to whether an entity settles a share-based payment transaction in cash or with equity instruments, the entity has granted a compound financial instrument, similar to convertible debt. The instrument has:

- a debt component – the counterparty's right to demand cash; and

- an equity component – the counterparty's option to receive equity instruments rather than cash.

Each component is accounted for separately, in a manner similar to the equivalent requirements of IAS 32, as described below.

Example 7.2.1 illustrates the need to consider the substance of the arrangement when the cash alternative is provided through a separate agreement.

Example 7.2.1

Counterparty choice in settlement of a share-based payment

Company A grants share options to its employees that vest over a three-year period. These share options can only be settled by the issue of Company A's shares at the end of the vesting period. In a separate legal agreement entered into at the same time as the grant of the share options, Company A issues a put option to its employees that can (at the option of the employee) require Company A to settle the share options in cash, based on the intrinsic value of the options at the settlement date. The put option is only exercisable between the vesting date and the expiration of the options.

The two contracts (share options and written put option) should be linked and the transaction accounted for as a share-based payment with a cash alternative.

The substance of this arrangement is the issue of an equity instrument to employees with a cash alternative. Therefore, the accounting should be the same whether the transaction is consummated through one or more contracts. As a result, Company A should measure the liability component at fair value first, and then measure the equity component at fair value, taking into account the fact that the employee must forfeit the right to receive cash in order to receive the equity instrument (see IFRS 2:37). Because the fair value of the equity component in this example would be nil (see **7.2.2**), the transaction is accounted for in the same way as a cash-settled share-based payment up to the date of exercise.

7.2.2 Initial measurement of the debt and equity components

For transactions with parties other than employees, the fair value of goods or services is measured directly (if that is possible with sufficient reliability – see **5.2.2.1** and **5.4.8**). For such transactions, the equity component is measured as the difference between the fair value of the goods or services received and the fair value of the debt component, at the date when goods or services are received. [IFRS 2:35] This is the basic approach that is adopted for compound instruments that are accounted for under IAS 32 (see **section 3** of **chapter B3** or, for entities that have not yet adopted IFRS 9, **section 3** of **chapter C3**).

For other transactions, including those with employees, the fair value of the compound financial instrument is measured at the measurement date, taking into account the terms and conditions on which the rights to cash or equity instruments were granted. [IFRS 2:36] To do this, the debt component is measured first and then the equity component is measured. The fact that the counterparty must forfeit the right to receive cash to receive the equity instrument should be taken into account. The fair value of the compound financial instrument is the sum of the fair values of the two components. [IFRS 2:37]

Under IAS 32:32, the carrying amount of the equity instruments is determined by deducting the fair value of the financial liability from the fair value of the compound financial instrument as a whole. This is straightforward when the fair value of the combined instrument is reliably known (e.g. when it is the proceeds of an issue for cash). However, IFRS 2:BC260 explains that, when this is not the case, it will be necessary to estimate the fair value of the compound instrument itself. The IASB therefore concluded, as stated above, that the compound instrument should be measured first by valuing the liability component (i.e. the cash alternative) and then valuing the equity component and adding the two components together.

Entities will often structure share-based payment transactions in which the counterparty has the choice of settlement in such a way that the fair value of one settlement alternative is the same as the other. For example, the counterparty might have the choice of receiving share options or cash-settled share appreciation rights. In such cases, the fair value of the equity component is zero and, consequently, the fair value of the compound financial instrument is the same as the fair value of the debt component. [IFRS 2:37]

IFRS 2 notes that, conversely, if the fair values of the settlement alternatives differ, the fair value of the equity component will usually be greater than zero. In such circumstances, the fair value of the compound financial instrument will be greater than the fair value of the debt component.

IFRS 2:BC259 explains that the fair value of the compound financial instrument will usually exceed both:

- the individual fair value of the cash alternative – because of the possibility that the shares or share options may be more valuable than the cash alternative; and

- that of the shares or options – because of the possibility that the cash alternative may be more valuable than the shares or options.

But, as explained above, in many practical situations the fair value of the settlement alternatives will be the same and there will be no equity component.

Example 7.2.2

Share-based payment with settlement alternatives – measurement and recognition

On 1 January 20X1, an entity enters into an agreement with 10 employees whereby the employees receive a bonus payment of CU300 if they complete a 3-year service period.

On completion of the 3-year service period, the employees can choose between the following settlement alternatives:

- Alternative A – receive the full amount of CU300 in cash; or
- Alternative B – receive CU150 in cash and the remaining 50 per cent of the reward in the form of shares that are, on 31 December 20X3, worth CU150 (say 500 shares).

Employees that opt for settlement Alternative B will, in addition to the original 500 shares, receive a further 500 shares (i.e. 'matching shares') upon completion of an additional 2-year service period (i.e. they have to be employed until 31 December 20X5). Employees that leave employment during the additional 2-year service period forfeit the matching shares and the original 500 shares awarded (i.e. they lose the first award even if the initial 3-year service period was completed).

The award can be summarised as follows:

- cash of CU300 at the end of Year 3; or
- cash of CU150 at the end of Year 3, plus shares worth CU300 as at 31 December 20X3 (original award of shares worth CU150 plus the matching shares worth CU150) with all shares subject to remaining in employment until the end of Year 5.

In accordance with IFRS 2:35, an entity that has granted a counterparty the right to choose whether a share-based payment transaction is settled in cash or by issuing equity instruments has granted a compound financial instrument which includes a debt component (the right to demand settlement in cash) and an equity component (the right to demand settlement in equity instruments).

The fair value of the compound financial instrument is measured at the grant date (1 January 20X1) taking into account the terms and conditions under which the rights to cash or equity instruments are granted. To arrive at this measurement, the fair value of the debt component should be measured first and then the fair value of the equity component should be measured, adjusting for the fact that the counterparty must forfeit the right to receive cash to receive the equity instrument. The fair value of the compound instrument is the sum of the fair values of the two components. [IFRS 2:37]

In this example, it is assumed for simplicity that the fair value of the debt component is CU300 and the fair value of the equity component is CU150.

In the three years to 31 December 20X3, expenses of CU300 and CU90 (CU150 × 3/5) are recognised on the debt and equity components, respectively.

If the employees choose Alternative B (i.e. they take settlement of part of the share-based arrangement in shares at 31 December 20X3), the portion of the liability settled in shares at that date (CU150) will be reclassified to equity.

If the employees opt for Alternative A (i.e. cash settlement at 31 December 20X3), the scheme has vested and the total grant date fair value of the compound financial instrument should, therefore, be recognised. As a result, the unrecognised portion of the equity component (CU150 × 2/5 = CU60) will be recognised as a share-based payment expense at 31 December 20X3.

7.2.3   Subsequent accounting for the debt and equity components

Once the debt and equity components have been separately identified and measured, the goods or services received in respect of each component are accounted for separately. For the debt component, the goods or services received, and a corresponding liability, are recognised in accordance with the requirements applying to cash-settled transactions (see **section 6**). For the equity component, if any, the goods or services received are recognised as the counterparty supplies goods or renders services in accordance with the requirements for equity-settled transactions (see **section 5**). [IFRS 2:38]

At the date of settlement, the liability is remeasured at its fair value. If equity instruments are issued in settlement rather than cash, the liability is transferred direct to equity as the consideration for the equity instruments issued. [IFRS 2:39]

If settlement is in cash rather than equity instruments, the payment made is applied to settle the liability in full. Any equity component previously recognised remains in equity. By electing to receive cash settlement, the counterparty forfeited the right to receive equity instruments. But this does not preclude a transfer from one component of equity to another. [IFRS 2:40]

The application of these requirements is illustrated by the following example which is taken from the implementation guidance accompanying IFRS 2. It illustrates the circumstances in which the cash alternative is less favourable than the equity-settled alternative and so the equity component is not zero.

Example 7.2.3

Subsequent accounting when counterparty has choice of settlement

[IFRS 2:IG, Example 13]

Background

An entity grants to an employee the right to choose either 1,000 phantom shares (i.e. a right to a cash payment equal to the value of 1,000 shares) or 1,200 shares. The grant is conditional upon the completion of three years' service. If the employee chooses the share alternative, the shares must be held for three years after vesting date.

At grant date, the entity's share price is CU50 per share. At the end of years 1, 2 and 3, the share price is CU52, CU55 and CU60, respectively. The entity does not expect to pay dividends in the next three years. After taking into account the effects of the post-vesting transfer restrictions, the entity estimates that the grant date fair value of the share alternative is CU48 per share.

At the end of year 3, the employee chooses:

Scenario 1: The cash alternative

Scenario 2: The equity alternative

Application of requirements

The fair value of the equity alternative is CU57,600 (1,200 shares × CU48). The fair value of the cash alternative is CU50,000 (1,000 phantom shares × CU50). Therefore, the fair value of the equity component of the compound instrument is CU7,600 (CU57,600 – CU50,000).

The entity recognises the following amounts:

Year		Expense CU	Equity CU	Liability CU
1	Liability component:			
	(1,000 × CU52 × 1/3)	17,333		**17,333**
	Equity component:			
	(CU7,600 × 1/3)	2,533	2,533	
2	Liability component:			
	(1,000 × CU55 × 2/3) – CU17,333	19,333		19,333
	Equity component:			
	(CU7,600 × 1/3)	2,533	2,533	
3	Liability component:			
	(1,000 × CU60) – CU36,666	23,334		23,334
	Equity component:			
	(CU7,600 × 1/3)	2,534	2,534	
End Year 3	Scenario 1: cash of CU60,000 paid			(60,000)
	Scenario 1 totals	67,600	7,600	0
	Scenario 2: 1,200 shares issued		60,000	(60,000)
	Scenario 2 totals	67,600	67,600	0

7.3 Entity's choice as to the manner of settlement

The terms of a share-based payment transaction may provide an entity with the choice as to whether to settle in cash or by issuing equity instruments.

In this case, it is necessary to determine whether the entity has a present obligation to settle in cash and to account for the transaction accordingly. IFRS 2 states that the entity has a present obligation to settle in cash if:

[IFRS 2:41]

- the choice of settlement in equity instruments has no commercial substance, for example because the entity is legally prohibited from issuing shares; or

- the entity has a past practice or stated policy of settling in cash; or

- the entity generally settles in cash whenever the counterparty asks for cash settlement.

When the entity has a present obligation to settle in cash, the transaction is accounted for as a cash-settled transaction (see **section 6**). [IFRS 2:42]

If no such obligation exists, the transaction is accounted for in accordance with IFRS 2's requirements for equity-settled transactions (see **section 5**).

The application of these classification requirements is illustrated in **example 7.3**.

Example 7.3

Classification of an employee share option plan in which the entity has the choice of settlement

Company A, a listed entity, grants its employees options to acquire ordinary shares in Company A. Company A's shares trade in an active market. The exercise of the options is conditional upon the achievement of certain performance conditions during the vesting period. In addition, the holders of the options have to be employed within the group headed by Company A or can be retired, if they retire at the normal retirement age.

Employees can exercise the options over a period of 5 years. Following the exercise of an option, the employee is required to sell the shares obtained immediately. Company A has first right to purchase these shares at a price equal to the market price at the moment employees exercise the underlying options. If Company A chooses not to purchase the shares, there are no constraints on how the employees dispose of the shares, or to whom. There is no enforcement mechanism by Company A.

Company A has the legal right to buy its own shares in the market, and has sufficient authorised capital to issue new shares to deliver the required number of shares to the employees upon exercise.

The share option scheme is a new arrangement, and there have been no other arrangements in the past when the entity has had a choice of cash or equity settlement; therefore, there is no evidence regarding past practice of settlement in cash. The share option scheme has been approved by the shareholders without objection, and no indication was provided as to what course of action

---

Company A would take when the exercise date is reached (i.e. whether Company A would seek to acquire the shares based on its pre-emptive right or choose not to do so).

Company A represents that it will act in its own interest every time it has the right to buy back shares, and that it does not believe any situation exists which would force it to buy back the shares given to the employees under the scheme.

Under applicable regulatory rules, employees cannot exercise their rights during a 'closed period'. Therefore, employees will not be able to sell shares in a closed period.

When employees exercise the options granted by Company A, they are obliged to sell the shares on the date of exercise. Company A has first right to purchase these shares. In substance, this right to repurchase shares immediately gives Company A an option to settle the share-based payment transaction in cash. Therefore, IFRS 2:41 to 43 apply.

IFRS 2:41 requires an entity that has a choice of settlement to determine whether it has a present obligation to settle the share-based payment transaction in cash. The entity has a present obligation to settle in cash if the choice of settlement in equity instruments has no commercial substance (e.g. because the entity is legally prohibited from issuing shares), or the entity has a past practice or a stated policy of settling in cash, or generally settles in cash whenever the counterparty asks for cash settlement.

If an entity with a choice of settlement has no present obligation to settle the transaction in cash, IFRS 2:43 requires that "the entity shall account for the transaction in accordance with the requirements applying to equity-settled share-based payment transactions, in paragraphs 10 – 29".

The management of Company A considers all relevant facts and circumstances to determine whether there are any factors that could create an obligation to deliver cash and concludes that there are no situations in which the entity would have a legal obligation, or has created a constructive obligation, to repurchase the shares and thereby deliver cash.

In particular:

- there is an active market in which the shares could be sold;
- from a legal perspective, Company A has sufficient authorised share capital in order to be able to issue new shares;
- current shareholders raised no objection to the scheme in the general shareholders' meeting and the entity did not raise an expectation of a particular action;
- no restrictions on trading in a closed period apply as exercise is prohibited in this period; and
- there is no stated policy or constructive obligation created by past practice.

Therefore, this scheme should be accounted for as an equity-settled share-based payment arrangement.

> However, it remains the responsibility of management to consider all facts and circumstances affecting the entity to determine whether there are any other circumstances in which the entity would have an obligation to repurchase the shares, resulting in a different conclusion.

On settlement of an arrangement that is accounted for as equity-settled (i.e. because there is no obligation to settle in cash):

[IFRS 2:43]

- if the entity elects to settle in cash, the cash payment is accounted for as the repurchase of an equity interest. It is, therefore, treated as a deduction from equity except as described below; and

- if the entity elects to settle by issuing equity instruments, no further accounting is required except as noted below and except for a transfer from one component of equity to another component of equity, if necessary.

> These requirements are not consistent with the requirements of IAS 32 for other circumstances in which the entity has a choice of settlement. IAS 32 requires such arrangements to be classified wholly as a liability (if the contract is a derivative contract) or as a compound instrument (if the contract is a non-derivative contract). The IASB decided to retain this difference pending the outcome of its longer-term project on the distinction between liabilities and equity. [IFRS 2:BC266]

If the entity elects for the settlement alternative with the higher fair value, as at the date of settlement, the entity should recognise an additional expense for the excess value given. That is:

[IFRS 2:43]

- the difference between the cash paid and the fair value of the equity instruments that would have been issued; or

- the difference between the fair value of the equity instruments issued and the amount of cash that would otherwise have been paid.

> Thus, an additional expense is recognised when an entity elects to use the settlement alternative with the higher fair value. But this does not mean that the expense recognised will be the same as it would have been if the method of settlement assumed at the outset was the same as the actual method of settlement. For example, consider the case of share appreciation rights when the cash-settled and equity-settled alternatives have the same fair value because the cash payment is equal to the gain that would arise on exercise of the options. If these were assumed to be cash-settled from the outset, the cumulative expense recognised would be based on the actual cash payment made

(i.e. intrinsic value on exercise). If these were assumed to be equity-settled from the outset, the cumulative expense recognised would be based on fair value at grant date (which would usually be lower).

If the entity concluded, at the outset, that there was no obligation to settle in cash but it subsequently did so, the expense recognised would be based on fair value at grant date and would not be adjusted to the amount of the cash payment made. The IASB considered and rejected the argument that an additional expense should be recognised in these circumstances as described in IFRS 2:BC267.

If the entity has the choice of settlement, it may, therefore, appear advantageous to conclude that there is no obligation to settle in cash and to account for the arrangements as equity-settled. When the entity has no past practice or stated policy of settling in cash, there is nothing in the Standard to prevent this. But an entity that tried to exploit this could do so only for a limited time because it might, in due course, establish a practice of settling in cash.

7.4 Contingently cash-settled share-based payments

IFRS 2 does not address specifically the treatment of share-based payment transactions that may be settled in cash on the occurrence of a contingent event which is in the control of neither the entity nor the counterparty.

For example, an entity might grant share-based payment rights to its employees that will be settled in shares if the entity has successfully completed an initial public offering (IPO) at the end of the service period, but in cash if it has not.

An IPO (or other change of control) normally requires shareholder approval. The shareholders of an entity are generally not considered to be a part of the entity because they act as investors and not on behalf of the entity. When a shareholder is faced with a decision to sell his or her shares, he or she makes that decision as an investor and not as part of the entity even if he or she is also a director or employee of the entity.

Consequently, in such circumstances, the outcome as to whether the award is settled by delivery of equity or cash is not within the control of either the entity or the counterparty to the transaction (the employees) and the transaction is not a share-based payment with a cash alternative for either the employer or the employee.

Unlike transactions in which either the counterparty or the entity has the choice of settlement in cash or in equity shares (see **sections 7.1** to **7.3**), IFRS 2 provides no specific guidance on the accounting for contingently cash-settled share-based payments.

This issue was considered by the IASB, which did not conclude on a single appropriate treatment and decided in April 2014 not to amend IFRS 2 to address such arrangements specifically.

As a result, more than one treatment may be acceptable, including the two approaches set out below. Whichever treatment is selected, it should be applied consistently as an accounting policy choice.

The 'probable' approach

Under this approach, by analogy to the criteria for recognition of a liability under IAS 37 *Provisions, Contingent Liabilities and Contingent Assets*, the share-based payment is classified as either cash-settled or equity-settled in its entirety depending on which outcome is probable at each reporting date. Any change in the probable method of settlement is treated as a change in accounting estimate, with the cumulative expense 'trued-up' to reflect the appropriate charge for the method of settlement now considered probable.

The 'compound instrument' approach

Under this approach, by analogy to the requirements of IFRS 2 when the counterparty has a choice of settlement method, both a debt component (reflecting the entity's possible obligation to settle in cash) and an equity component (reflecting the possible obligation to settle in equity shares) are recognised.

IFRS 2 provides no specific guidance on how to treat the contingent settlement condition under such an approach, but an acceptable method would be to classify it as a vesting or non-vesting condition at the level of each of the debt and equity components (so, to treat the two components as if they had been granted in isolation of the other).

The application of these two approaches is illustrated in **example 7.4**.

Example 7.4

Contingently cash-settled share-based payments

On 1 January 20X0, Entity A grants share-based payment rights to 100 employees. The options vest if the employee remains in employment until 31 December 20X2, at which point he or she will receive:

- 100 equity shares if Entity A has successfully completed an IPO by that date; or
- cash equal to the value of 100 equity shares if it has not.

Further relevant details are as follows.

- Entity A's accounting policy is to treat vesting and non-vesting conditions on cash-settled share-based payments in a manner consistent with the requirements for equity-settled share-based payments (see **6.3** for further explanation).

- Throughout the vesting period, it is expected that 80 of the 100 employees will remain in service until 31 December 20X2.

On 1 January 20X0:

- successful completion of an IPO is considered to have a 20 per cent probability; and
- the fair value (in isolation) of the equity-settled element of the grant is determined to be CU90 (excluding the effect of the contingency).

On 31 December 20X0:

- successful completion of an IPO is still considered to have a 20 per cent probability; and
- the fair value (in isolation) of the cash-settled element of the grant is determined to be CU150 (excluding the effect of the contingency).

On 31 December 20X1:

- successful completion of an IPO is now considered to have an 80 per cent probability; and
- the fair value (in isolation) of the cash-settled element of the grant is determined to be CU150 (excluding the effect of the contingency).

On 31 December 20X2:

- the fair value of 100 shares is CU200; and
- a successful IPO has been completed – the 80 employees still in service receive 100 shares each.

In these circumstances, the two approaches described in **7.4** would be applied as follows.

The probable approach

At 31 December 20X0

The most probable method of settlement is considered to be in cash. Accordingly, the share-based payment is accounted for as cash-settled in its entirety.

	CU	CU
Dr Share-based payment expense [CU150 × 100 shares × 80 employees × 1/3]	400,000	
Cr Liability		400,000

Being recognition of cash-settled share-based payment expense.

At 31 December 20X1

The most probable method of settlement is now considered to be in equity shares. Accordingly, the share-based payment is accounted for on a cumulative basis as equity-settled in its entirety using its grant-date fair value of CU90.

		CU	CU
Dr	Share-based payment expense [CU90 × 100 × 80 × 2/3 – CU400,000]	80,000	
Dr	Liability	400,000	
Cr	Equity		480,000

Being recognition of equity-settled share-based payment expense and derecognition of cash-settled share-based payment liability.

At 31 December 20X2

The share-based payment transaction finally results in delivery of equity shares. Accordingly, the share-based payment is accounted for as equity-settled in its entirety.

		CU	CU
Dr	Share-based payment expense [CU90 × 100 × 80 – CU480,000]	240,000	
Cr	Equity		240,000

Being recognition of equity-settled share-based payment expense.

The compound instrument approach

As described in **5.3.15** and **example 5.3.15B**, a condition requiring an IPO to occur while the employee remains in service is treated as a non-market performance condition.

At 31 December 20X0

In respect of the liability component of the arrangement, the non-market performance condition (non-occurrence of an IPO) is expected to be met. Accordingly, an expense and a liability are recognised in respect of this component.

In respect of the equity component of the arrangement, the non-market performance condition (occurrence of an IPO) is not expected to be met. Accordingly, no expense is recognised in respect of this component.

		CU	CU
Dr	Share-based payment expense [CU150 × 100 × 80 employees × 1/3]	400,000	
Cr	Liability		400,000

Being recognition of cash-settled share-based payment expense.

At 31 December 20X1

In respect of the liability component of the arrangement, the non-market performance condition (non-occurrence of an IPO) is not now expected to be met. Accordingly, on a cumulative basis no expense and no liability are recognised in respect of this component.

In respect of the equity component of the arrangement, the non-market performance condition (occurrence of an IPO) is expected to be met. Accordingly, on a cumulative basis an expense is recognised in respect of this component.

	CU	CU
Dr Liability	400,000	
Cr Cash-settled share-based payment expense		400,000
Dr Share-based payment expense [CU90 × 100 × 80 employees × 2/3]	480,000	
Cr Equity		480,000

Being recognition of equity-settled share-based payment expense and derecognition of cash-settled share-based payment liability.

At 31 December 20X2

In respect of the liability component of the arrangement, the non-market performance condition (non-occurrence of an IPO) is not met. Accordingly, on a cumulative basis no expense and no liability are recognised in respect of this component.

In respect of the equity component of the arrangement, the non-market performance condition (occurrence of an IPO) is met. Accordingly, on a cumulative basis an expense is recognised in respect of this component.

	CU	CU
Dr Share-based payment expense [CU90 × 100 × 80 employees − CU480,000]	240,000	
Cr Equity		240,000

Being recognition of equity-settled share-based payment expense.

In this example, the accounting resulting from the two approaches is consistent. The accounting under the compound instrument approach would differ, however, if the contingency were classified as a market condition or non-vesting condition or if the entity adopted a different accounting policy to conditions applied to cash-settled share-based payments.

8 Accounting by entities within groups

8.1 Accounting by entities within groups – general

As explained at **section 2.4**, it is often the case that employees of a subsidiary will receive part of their remuneration in the form of shares in the parent, or less commonly in some other group entity. When this is the case, IFRS 2 requires the entity that has received the benefit of the services to recognise the expense. This is so even if the equity instruments issued are those of another entity within the group.

IFRS 2 also specifies the accounting for group cash-settled share-based payment transactions in the separate or individual financial statements of the entity receiving the goods or services when the entity has no obligation to settle the share-based payment transactions (see **8.4.5**).

This section also deals with some related issues, such as intragroup recharges, which are not addressed in IFRSs.

The requirements of IFRS 2 concerning share-based payment transactions among group entities focus on transactions with employees. They also apply to similar transactions with suppliers of goods or services other than employees. [IFRS 2:B46]

For share-based payment transactions among group entities, in its separate or individual financial statements, the entity receiving the goods or services measures the goods or services received as either an equity-settled or a cash-settled share-based payment transaction by assessing:

- the nature of the awards granted; and
- its own rights and obligations.

The amount recognised by the entity receiving the goods or services may differ from the amount recognised by the consolidated group or by another group entity settling the share-based payment transaction. [IFRS 2:43A]

The entity receiving the goods or services measures them as equity-settled share-based payment transactions when:

- the awards granted are its own equity instruments; or
- the entity has no obligation to settle the share-based payment transaction.

The entity subsequently remeasures such an equity-settled share-based payment transaction only for changes in non-market vesting conditions. In all other circumstances, the entity receiving the goods or services measures them as a cash-settled share-based payment transaction. [IFRS 2:43B]

The entity settling a share-based payment transaction, when another entity in the group receives the goods or services, recognises the transaction as an equity-settled share-based payment transaction only if it is settled in the entity's own equity instruments. Otherwise, the transaction is recognised as a cash-settled share-based payment transaction. [IFRS 2:43C]

Some group transactions involve repayment arrangements that require one group entity to pay another group entity for the provision of the share-based payments to the suppliers of goods or services. In such cases, the entity that receives the goods or services accounts for the share-based payment transaction in accordance with IFRS 2:43B regardless of any intragroup repayment arrangements.

The classification of common forms of share-based payment arrangement in consolidated, parent and subsidiary financial statements is summarised below.

Entity receiving goods or services	Entity with obligation to settle	Settled in	Classification		
			Parent's separate financial statements	Subsidiary's individual financial statements	Consolidated financial statements
Subsidiary	Subsidiary	Subsidiary's equity	N/A (see **8.2**)	Equity (see **8.2**)	Equity
Subsidiary	Subsidiary	Cash	N/A (see **8.4.3**)	Cash (see **8.4.3**)	Cash
Subsidiary	Subsidiary	Parent's equity	N/A (see **8.4.4**)	Cash (see **8.3.3**)	Equity
Subsidiary	Parent	Subsidiary's equity	Cash (see **8.2**)	Equity (see **8.2**)	Equity
Subsidiary	Parent	Parent's equity	Equity (see **8.4.2**)	Equity (see **8.3.2**)	Equity
Subsidiary	Parent	Cash	Cash (see **8.4.5**)	Equity (see **8.4.5**)	Cash

8.2 Share-based payment arrangements involving an entity's own equity instruments

IFRS 2 addresses whether the following transactions involving an entity's own equity instruments should be accounted for as equity-settled or cash-settled under the requirements of IFRS 2:

[IFRS 2:B48]

- an entity grants to its employees rights to equity instruments of the entity (e.g. share options) and either chooses or is required (either by contract or necessity) to buy equity instruments (i.e. treasury shares) from another party, to satisfy its obligation to its employees; and

- an entity's employees are granted rights to equity instruments of the entity (e.g. share options), either by the entity itself or by its shareholders, and the shareholders of the entity provide the equity instruments needed.

Share-based payment transactions in which an entity receives services as consideration for its own equity instruments are accounted for as equity-settled. IFRS 2 confirms that this applies regardless of whether the entity chooses or is required to buy those equity instruments from another party to satisfy its obligations to its employees. This also applies regardless of whether:

[IFRS 2:B49]

- the employee's rights to the entity's equity instruments were granted by the entity itself or by its shareholders; or

- the share-based payment arrangement was settled by the entity or by its shareholders.

> These requirements are straightforward and simply remove any doubt that such transactions should be accounted for as equity-settled even though the entity may not itself issue or transfer any equity instruments as part of the transaction.

If the shareholder has an obligation to settle the transaction with its investee's employees, it provides equity instruments of its investee rather than its own. Therefore, if the investee is in the same group as the shareholder, the shareholder measures its obligation in accordance with the requirements applicable to cash-settled share-based payment transactions in the shareholder's separate financial statements and those applicable to equity-settled share-based payment transactions in the shareholder's consolidated financial statements. [IFRS 2:B50]

> If the shareholder has no such obligation, it has no accounting entries to make because it is not party to the transaction.

8.3   Share-based payment arrangements involving equity instruments of the parent – accounting in the subsidiary's financial statements

8.3.1   Share-based payment arrangements involving equity instruments of the parent – general requirements for the subsidiary's financial statements

IFRS 2 also addresses share-based payment arrangements that involve two or more entities within the same group and relate to an equity instrument of another group entity. For example, the employees of a subsidiary may be granted rights to equity instruments of its parent as consideration for the services they provide to the subsidiary. [IFRS 2:B51]

IFRS 2 addresses the following share-based payment arrangements:

[IFRS 2:B52]

- a parent grants rights to its equity instruments direct to the employees of its subsidiary so that the parent (and not the subsidiary) has the obligation to provide the employees of the subsidiary with the equity instruments needed (addressed at **8.3.2**); and

- a subsidiary grants rights to equity instruments of its parent to its employees so that the subsidiary (and not the parent) has the obligation to provide its employees with the equity instruments needed (addressed at **8.3.3**).

IFRS 2 assumes that it is clear whether the parent or the subsidiary granted the rights to equity instruments and prescribes a different accounting treatment in each case. It may not, in practice, be clear which entity in a group granted the rights to the employees. Often this is done by mutual agreement between the subsidiary and the parent. The application of IFRS 2 in these circumstances is considered at **8.3.4**.

IFRS 2 does not address the appropriate accounting for any intragroup payments that may be made in the scenarios described (which is considered at **8.5**). However, the Standard does state that classification of the share-based arrangement is not affected by the existence (or otherwise) of payment arrangements between a subsidiary and parent.

8.3.2 Parent grants rights to its equity instruments to employees of its subsidiary

When a parent grants rights to its equity instruments to employees of its subsidiary, the subsidiary does not have an obligation to provide its parent's equity instruments to its employees. The arrangement is accounted for as equity-settled in the consolidated financial statements. The subsidiary should, in its own separate financial statements, measure the services received from its employees in accordance with the requirements of IFRS 2 applicable to equity-settled share-based payment transactions. There will be a corresponding increase recognised in equity as a capital contribution from the parent. [IFRS 2:B53]

This requirement is straightforward to apply. The expense recognised in the consolidated financial statements is 'pushed down' into the accounts of the relevant subsidiaries that receive the services of the employees.

Example 8.3.2

Parent grants rights to its equity instruments to employees of its subsidiary

Parent P grants each of Subsidiary S's 100 employees 30 shares in Parent P, subject to the conditions that they remain in employment for three years and that Subsidiary S meets a specified profit target. The fair value on grant date is CU5 per share. Assume that at the outset, and at the end of Years 1 and 2, it is expected that the profit target will be met and that no employees leave. Subsidiary S is not required to reimburse Parent P for the shares granted to its employees.

At the end of Year 3, the profit target is met.

Accounting by Subsidiary S

In each of Years 1 to 3, Subsidiary S will recognise an IFRS 2 expense in profit or loss, and a corresponding entry in equity, which reflects the capital contribution it receives from Parent P.

		CU	CU
Dr	Profit or loss [CU5 × 30 × 100 / 3 years]	5,000	
Cr	Equity (capital contribution)		5,000

To recognise the share-based payment expense.

Because Subsidiary S has no obligation to reimburse Parent P for the share-based payment, no further accounting entries are required when the shares are transferred to the employees by Parent P.

There is no requirement in IFRSs to credit the capital contribution to a separate component of equity. Therefore, it may be credited to retained earnings if this is permitted in the legal jurisdiction in which Subsidiary S operates (see general discussion of this issue at **5.1.5**).

The accounting in the separate financial statements of the parent is addressed in **example 8.4.2A**.

8.3.3   Subsidiary grants rights to equity instruments of its parent to its employees

When the subsidiary grants rights to equity instruments of its parent to employees, the subsidiary accounts for the transaction with its employees as cash-settled. This requirement applies irrespective of how the subsidiary obtains the equity instruments to satisfy the obligations to its employees. [IFRS 2:B55]

The practical implications of accounting for arrangements as cash-settled in the subsidiary while they are equity-settled from the perspective of the group are considered further at **8.8**.

IFRS 2 does not address the accounting required in the subsidiary when it has recognised a liability for a cash-settled share-based payment arrangement but subsequently makes no cash payment because the parent provides the shares without any right to reimbursement. IFRS 2 addresses transactions with settlement alternatives (see **3.4**) but this guidance does not apply to the circumstances under consideration because the guidance envisages only the grantor of the rights or the counterparty having the choice whereas, in this case, the choice lies with a third party (i.e. the parent). If the parent satisfies the subsidiary's obligation, the liability will be removed from the statement of financial position of the subsidiary with the credit recognised in equity as a capital contribution from the parent. The expense recognised in respect of the services received is not reversed (see **example 8.4.4**).

8.3.4 Determining which entity has granted the rights

To apply the requirements of IFRS 2 set out at **8.3.2** and **8.3.3**, it will be necessary to determine which entity in the group granted the rights to the employees and thereby assumed the obligation to settle the transaction with the employees. This will require a careful assessment of the particular facts and circumstances. The factors to be considered include, but are not limited to:

- the contractual terms of the share scheme;

- any formal documentation provided to the employees that are granted the rights;

- any other communications provided to employees;

- whether the scheme is specific to one subsidiary or covers a number of subsidiaries within a group; and

- any other aspects of the arrangements, whether formally documented or not.

8.4 Share-based payment arrangements involving equity instruments of the parent – accounting in the parent's separate financial statements

8.4.1 Share-based payment arrangements involving equity instruments of the parent – general requirements for the parent's financial statements

IFRS 2 states that when a parent grants rights to its equity instruments to the employees of its subsidiary, the parent does have an obligation to settle the transaction with the subsidiary's employees by providing the parent's own equity instruments. Therefore, the parent measures its obligation in accordance with the requirements applicable to equity-settled share-based payment transactions. [IFRS 2:B54]

IFRS 2 offers no further guidance on application of the requirement to account for such transactions in the parent's separate financial statements.

The illustrative example accompanying IFRIC D17 (the exposure draft upon which IFRIC 11 *IFRS 2 – Group and Treasury Share Transactions* was based) did, however, include entries in the separate financial statements of the parent. The illustrative example accompanying D17 dealt with the case when the parent has granted the rights so that the arrangement is equity-settled for both the group and the subsidiary but it is possible to apply the same principles in other cases (see **8.4.2** to **8.4.4**).

8.4.2   Equity-settled for the group and the subsidiary

The illustrative example accompanying IFRIC D17 suggested that the parent should recognise an entry each year to debit the cost of investment in subsidiary and credit equity with an amount equal to the expense recognised in the subsidiary in accordance with IFRS 2. This was not explained in the Basis for Conclusions which accompanied IFRIC D17 but the rationale was that the parent had made a capital contribution to the subsidiary (assuming the subsidiary had not paid fair value as reimbursement to the parent) by taking on the cost of remunerating the subsidiary's employees that the subsidiary would otherwise have had to bear, and had also granted an equity instrument in accepting the obligation to those employees. This is consistent with the credit to equity recognised in the subsidiary.

Increasing the cost of investment in a subsidiary may, in rare cases, give rise to impairment issues and this should be considered when appropriate.

Example 8.4.2A

Equity-settled for the group and the subsidiary (1)

The facts are the same as in **example 8.3.2**.

Accounting by Parent P

In each of Years 1 to 3, Parent P would recognise the enhancement to its investment in Subsidiary S, and a corresponding entry in equity which reflects the capital contribution being made to Subsidiary S and the equity instruments being granted to Subsidiary S's employees.

		CU	CU
Dr	Cost of investment	5,000	
Cr	Equity		5,000

To recognise the grant of equity instruments to employees of subsidiary.

Additional entries will be required when Parent P transfers the shares to the employees. These entries will depend on whether Parent P issues new shares or utilises shares purchased in the market and held as treasury shares. The entries may also be affected by the involvement of an employee share trust (see **8.7**).

In the same way that the subsidiary will 'true up' the IFRS 2 expense to reflect changes in non-market vesting conditions, so will the parent 'true up' its contributions to the subsidiary. This will usually result in symmetrical accounting for the capital contribution between the parent and subsidiary.

Example 8.4.2B

Equity-settled for the group and the subsidiary (2)

The facts are the same as in **example 8.3.2** except that at the end of Year 3 the profit target is not met.

Accounting by Parent P

In each of Years 1 and 2, Parent P will recognise an enhancement to its investment in Subsidiary S, and a corresponding entry in equity, which reflect the capital contribution being made to Subsidiary S and the equity instruments being granted to Subsidiary S's employees.

		CU	CU
Dr	Cost of investment	5,000	
Cr	Equity		5,000

To recognise the grant of equity instruments to employees of subsidiary.

At the end of Year 3, the profit target is not met, so Parent P must 'true up' the amounts recognised to reflect the non-market vesting condition not being met.

		CU	CU
Dr	Equity	10,000	
Cr	Cost of investment		10,000

To recognise the true up in respect of equity instruments granted to employees of subsidiary.

This true up in Parent P mirrors the accounting entries in Subsidiary S.

8.4.3 Cash-settled for the group and the subsidiary

A scheme will only be accounted for as cash-settled both by the group and by the subsidiary when the subsidiary itself has the obligation to transfer cash or other assets (other than equity instruments of the group) to its employees. (Historically, this approach might also have been applied by a subsidiary that was not yet applying IFRS 2 as amended in July 2009 whose parent had the obligation to transfer cash or other assets (other than equity instruments of the group) to that subsidiary's employees. IFRS 2 now makes clear that such a subsidiary should regard the arrangement as equity-settled – see **8.4.5**.)

No accounting is required by the parent when the subsidiary has the obligation to its employees and makes a cash payment to satisfy the obligation. When the subsidiary has the obligation to make a cash payment to its employees but the parent settles the obligation on behalf of the subsidiary, the amount of the cash payment is accounted for as a capital contribution, increasing the cost of investment in the subsidiary in the parent's separate financial statements and increasing equity in the subsidiary's financial statements.

When the parent has the obligation to make a cash payment to the employees of its subsidiary, the parent recognises the amount of the cash payment as a capital contribution, increasing the cost of investment in its subsidiary. The subsidiary accounts for such a scheme as equity-settled. Such arrangements are considered further at **8.4.5**.

8.4.4   Equity-settled for the group but cash-settled for the subsidiary

Example 8.4.4

Equity-settled for the group but cash-settled for the subsidiary

Subsidiary S has entered into a share-based payment arrangement with its employees under which Subsidiary S has the obligation to deliver shares of Parent P to its employees. Subsequently, Parent P provides the shares to the employees to satisfy Subsidiary S's obligation. Parent P has no right to reimbursement from Subsidiary S.

How should Subsidiary S and Parent P account for the original share-based payment arrangement and its subsequent settlement by Parent P?

Accounting by Subsidiary S

IFRS 2:B55 requires that arrangements should be accounted for as cash-settled by the subsidiary if it is the subsidiary that has granted rights to employees over its parent's equity instruments, irrespective of how the subsidiary obtains the equity instruments to satisfy its obligation to its employees. Therefore, in the circumstances described, Subsidiary S initially recognises a liability for its obligation, which is measured in accordance with the requirements of IFRS 2 regarding cash-settled transactions.

When the parent subsequently provides shares to the subsidiary's employees for no consideration, the subsidiary should recognise the credit arising from the derecognition of the liability directly in equity as a capital contribution received from the parent. The expense recognised in respect of the services received is not reversed.

Accounting by Parent P

Parent P does not account for the share-based payment arrangement prior to settling the subsidiary's obligation because it is not party to the share-based payment arrangement.

When Parent P provides the shares to the subsidiary's employees for no consideration, it should recognise a capital contribution to Subsidiary S in its separate financial statements. There are two acceptable views regarding the value at which that capital contribution should be recognised:

- the equity-settled amount recognised in the consolidated financial statements; or
- the cash-settled amount recognised in the subsidiary's financial statements.

Recognition at the equity-settled amount recognised in the consolidated financial statements is based on the argument that when the parent has not made a cash payment to settle the share-based payment award but has issued its own equity instruments to satisfy the obligation, the credit to equity in the parent's separate financial statements should be the same as the equivalent credit in the consolidated financial statements because they relate to the same equity instrument.

However, recognition of a capital contribution for the same amount as the cash-settled amount recognised in the subsidiary's financial statements is more logical and consistent with the fact that, under IFRS 2, the parent has no obligation. Although the group has an obligation that will be settled by the issuance of equity instruments, the parent creates an equity instrument of its own at the entity level only when it provides the shares to the subsidiary's employees. From the parent's perspective, the equity instruments are issued to settle the cash-settled liability of the subsidiary on its behalf and, therefore, measurement of that capital contribution for the same amount is reasonable.

The parent should select one of the approaches as its accounting policy and apply it consistently.

Practical application of these principles is considered further at **8.8**.

8.4.5 Cash-settled for the group but equity-settled for the subsidiary

An entity may receive goods or services from its suppliers (including employees) under share-based payment arrangements that are cash-settled when the entity itself does not have any obligation to make the required payments to its suppliers. For example, a parent (not the entity itself) may have an obligation to make the required cash payments to the employees of the entity and:

[IFRS 2:B56]

- the employees of the entity will receive cash payments that are linked to the price of its own equity instruments; or

- the employees of the entity will receive cash payments that are linked to the price of its parent's equity instruments.

In this case, the subsidiary does not have an obligation to settle the transaction with its employees. Therefore, the subsidiary accounts for the transaction as equity-settled and recognises a corresponding increase in equity as a contribution from its parent. The subsidiary remeasures the cost of the transaction subsequently for any changes resulting from non-market vesting conditions not being met. This differs from the measurement of the transaction as cash-settled in the consolidated financial statements of the group. [IFRS 2:B57]

The parent has an obligation to settle the transaction with the employees and the consideration is cash. The parent and the consolidated group measure the obligation in accordance with the requirements of IFRS 2 applicable to cash-settled share-based payment transactions. [IFRS 2:B58]

IFRS 2 does not address the treatment of the debit entry arising from recognition and remeasurement of the obligation in the parent's separate financial statements. However, it will be debited to the cost of investment in the subsidiary as a capital contribution. The amount of this contribution will be a different amount from the capital contribution recognised in the subsidiary in accordance with IFRS 2:B57. In some cases, it may be necessary to consider whether the investment in the subsidiary is impaired.

8.5   Intragroup recharges

IFRS 2 does not address the appropriate accounting for intragroup recharges, except to say that intragroup payment arrangements should not affect the accounting for the underlying share-based payment arrangement.

Although the appropriate accounting for intragroup recharges is not addressed in IFRS 2, an illustrative example accompanying IFRIC D17 (the exposure draft upon which the now superseded IFRIC 11 and requirements of IFRS 2:43A to 43D were based) indicated that if the parent levies an intragroup recharge on the subsidiary, the amount of that recharge is offset against the capital contribution arising for the share-based payment in the individual and separate financial statements of the subsidiary and in any separate financial statements of the parent. The example also indicated that if the amount of the recharge exceeds the capital contribution, that excess is accounted for as a distribution from the subsidiary to the parent. Thus, in effect, IFRIC D17 proposed to account for any difference between share-based payment expense and reimbursement as a transaction with shareholders (i.e. a capital contribution or distribution).

The same logic applies irrespective of whether an arrangement is an equity-settled or cash-settled share-based payment arrangement in the parent's separate financial statements and the consolidated financial statements.

Some complexities may arise if the timing of the intragroup recharges is different from the recognition of the expense under IFRS 2. For example, it is possible that the recharge might be levied only when the options are exercised by the employees. Some of these issues are considered in detail in **examples 8.5A** to **8.5D**.

These examples distinguish between circumstances in which a right to reimbursement exists at the inception of the share-based payment arrangement and circumstances in which there is no such right. A right to reimbursement may exist in the absence of a written contract. For example, it may exist if it is the clear intention of the parties, when the share-based payment arrangement is established, that reimbursement will occur and the basis for calculating the amount of that reimbursement is also agreed at that time.

When the recharge made exceeds the expense recognised in accordance with IFRS 2, as will typically be the case if the recharge is based on the intrinsic value on exercise of the options, the excess will be accounted for as a distribution by the subsidiary. Consequently, it will not be recognised as an expense in the subsidiary's financial statements, but it will be recognised as a distribution received (dividend income) in the parent's separate financial statements. This is illustrated in **example 8.5D**.

The fact that the excess recharge will be accounted for as a distribution does not necessarily mean that it will be a distribution as a matter of law. The position may vary according to the legal jurisdiction. Legal advice should be sought when necessary.

There is no specific requirement in IFRSs to present intragroup recharges for share-based payments in this way, but the net approach illustrated in IFRIC D17 appears reasonable and has been used as the basis for **examples 8.5A** and **8.5C** when the parent has a right to reimbursement. Nevertheless, other approaches may also be acceptable, provided that the share-based payment expense recognised remains the amount determined in accordance with IFRS 2.

For example, an entity may elect to account separately for services received (as a capital contribution) and for payments made (as a distribution), without offsetting the two. Moreover, when the amount payable to the parent is conditional on share awards vesting, a reimbursement obligation might be measured at fair value. Whatever the approach adopted, careful judgement should be applied to ensure that the accounting properly reflects the substance of the arrangement.

The potential for differing analyses of intragroup recharge arrangements was acknowledged by the IFRS Interpretations Committee in May 2013 when it discussed the recognition of a subsidiary's liability to pay its parent an intragroup recharge in circumstances similar to those described in **example 8.5C** (i.e. a requirement to reimburse the parent upon settlement of the share-based payment awards by the parent). The Committee did not reach a conclusion but did note that its outreach activities suggested diversity in practice, with some viewing the recharge and the share-based payments as linked and recognising both from the date of grant over the vesting period (the approach illustrated in **example 8.5C**) and others treating the recharge as a separate transaction recognised by analogy with liabilities, the distribution of equity or as an executory contract.

Example 8.5A

Reimbursement over the term of the arrangement

A parent, Company P, grants 30 of its shares to each of 100 employees of its subsidiary, Company S, on condition that the employees remain employed by Company S for three years. Assume that at the outset, and at the end of Years 1 and 2, it is expected that all of the employees will remain employed for all three years. At the end of Year 3, none of the employees has left. The fair value of the shares on grant date is CU5 per share.

Company S agrees to reimburse Company P over the term of the arrangement for 75 per cent of the final expense recognised by Company S. Over that period, Company S expects to recognise an expense totalling CU15,000 and, therefore, expects the total reimbursement to be CU11,250 (CU15,000 × 75 per cent). Company S therefore reimburses Company P CU3,750 (CU11,250 × 1/3) each year.

The following illustrates one of several acceptable approaches (as discussed above) to accounting for recharges of share-based payment costs.

Accounting by Company S

In each of Years 1 to 3, Company S recognises an IFRS 2 expense in profit or loss, the cash paid to Company P, and the balance of the capital contribution it has received from Company P.

	CU	CU
Dr Profit or loss	5,000	
Cr Cash		3,750
Cr Equity (capital contribution)		1,250

To recognise the share-based payment expense and partial reimbursement to parent.

Accounting by Company P

In each of Years 1 to 3, Company P recognises an increase in equity for the instruments being granted, the cash reimbursed by Company S, and the balance of the capital contribution it has made to Company S.

	CU	CU
Dr Cost of investment	1,250	
Dr Cash	3,750	
Cr Equity		5,000

To recognise the grant of equity instruments to employees of subsidiary less partial reimbursement from subsidiary.

Example 8.5B

Reimbursement (if any) at the end of the arrangement when initially there exists no right to reimbursement

The facts are as in **example 8.5A**, except that, before vesting, there exists no right to reimbursement. At the end of the arrangement (i.e. when the shares vest), Company S agrees to pay Company P 75 per cent of the final expense recognised by Company S.

The following illustrates one of several acceptable approaches to accounting for recharges of share-based payment costs.

Accounting by Company S

In each of Years 1 to 3, Company S recognises the IFRS 2 expense in profit or loss and a capital contribution from Company P.

	CU	CU
Dr Profit or loss	5,000	
Cr Equity (capital contribution)		5,000

To recognise the share-based payment expense.

At the end of Year 3, all the shares vest and Company S pays Company P CU11,250. The payment is treated as a distribution to Company P.

		CU	CU
Dr	Equity (distribution)	11,250	
Cr	Cash		11,250

To recognise the distribution to parent.

Accounting by Company P

In each of Years 1 to 3, Company P recognises an increase in equity for the instruments being granted and the capital contribution made to Company S.

		CU	CU
Dr	Cost of investment	5,000	
Cr	Equity		5,000

To recognise the grant of equity instruments to employees of subsidiary.

At the end of Year 3, all the shares vest and Company S pays Company P CU11,250. The payment is recognised as dividend income in profit or loss by Company P.

		CU	CU
Dr	Cash	11,250	
Cr	Dividend income (profit or loss)		11,250

To recognise the distribution from subsidiary.

If the increased cost of investment and reduction in the value of Company S from the payment of a dividend result in the carrying amount of Company P's investment in Company S no longer being supportable, Company P should also recognise an impairment loss in respect of the cost of its investment in Company S.

Example 8.5C

Reimbursement at the end of the arrangement when there is a right to reimbursement

The facts are as in **example 8.5A**, except that, on grant date, Company S and Company P enter into a binding agreement under which Company S will reimburse Company P 75 per cent of the final expense recognised by Company S. The payment is made at the end of the arrangement (i.e. when the shares vest).

The following illustrates one of several acceptable approaches for accounting for recharges of share-based payment costs.

Accounting by Company S

In each of Years 1 to 3, Company S recognises the IFRS 2 expense in profit or loss, a payable due to Company P for 75 per cent of this amount, and a capital contribution from Company P for the balance.

		CU	CU
Dr	Profit or loss	5,000	
Cr	Intragroup payables		3,750
Cr	Equity (capital contribution)		1,250

To recognise the share-based payment expense and accrual of partial reimbursement to parent.

At the end of Year 3, all the shares vest and Company S pays Company P CU11,250, settling the liability previously recognised.

		CU	CU
Dr	Intragroup payables	11,250	
Cr	Cash		11,250

To recognise the settlement of reimbursement to parent.

Accounting by Company P

In each of Years 1 to 3, Company P recognises an increase in equity for the instruments being granted and a receivable from Company S and the balance of the capital contribution it has made to Company S.

		CU	CU
Dr	Intragroup receivables	3,750	
Dr	Cost of investment	1,250	
Cr	Equity		5,000

To recognise the grant of equity instruments to employees of subsidiary less accrual of partial reimbursement from subsidiary.

At the end of Year 3, all the shares vest and Company S pays Company P CU11,250.

		CU	CU
Dr	Cash	11,250	
Cr	Intragroup receivables		11,250

To recognise the settlement of reimbursement by subsidiary.

For simplicity, this example assumes that any effect of discounting would not be material. When reimbursement balances are very large, consideration should be given to whether discounting is necessary.

A common situation is that reimbursement is based on the intrinsic value on vesting (or on actual exercise in the case of options). This will often result in a reimbursement that exceeds the grant date fair value recognised under IFRS 2. The excess of the amount of the reimbursement over the IFRS 2 expense will be accounted for as a distribution by the subsidiary. This is illustrated in the following example.

Example 8.5D

Reimbursement at the end of the arrangement equal to the intrinsic value at that date when initially there is no right to reimbursement

The facts are as in **example 8.5A**, except that Company S pays Company P at the end of the arrangement an amount equal to the intrinsic value of the shares at that date. This amount is CU25,000.

For simplicity, it has been assumed that there is no entitlement to the reimbursement and that it is, therefore, accounted for only when made. Otherwise it would be necessary for Company S to estimate the amount of the accrued reimbursement to be recognised at the end of each reporting period.

The following illustrates one of several acceptable approaches for accounting for recharges of share-based payment costs.

Accounting by Company S

In each of Years 1 to 3, Company S recognises the IFRS 2 expense in profit or loss and a capital contribution from Company P.

		CU	CU
Dr	Profit or loss	5,000	
Cr	Equity (capital contribution)		5,000

To recognise the share-based payment expense.

At the end of Year 3, all the shares vest and Company S pays Company P CU25,000. The payment is treated as a distribution by Company P.

		CU	CU
Dr	Equity (distribution)	25,000	
Cr	Cash		25,000

To recognise the distribution to parent.

Accounting by Company P

In each of Years 1 to 3, Company P recognises an increase in equity for the instruments being granted and the capital contribution made to Company S.

	CU	CU
Dr Cost of investment	5,000	
Cr Equity		5,000

To recognise the grant of equity instruments to employees of subsidiary.

At the end of Year 3, all the shares vest and Company S pays Company P CU25,000. The payment is treated as dividend income by Company P.

	CU	CU
Dr Cash	25,000	
Cr Profit or loss (dividend income)		25,000

To recognise the distribution from subsidiary.

If the increased cost of investment and reduction in the value of Company S from the payment of a dividend result in the carrying amount of Company P's investment in Company S no longer being supportable, Company P should also recognise an impairment loss in respect of the cost of its investment in Company S.

8.6 Transfers of employees between group entities

8.6.1 Transfers of employees between group entities: parent has obligation

A parent may grant rights to its equity instruments to the employees of its subsidiaries that are conditional upon the completion of continuing service with the group (rather than a specified subsidiary) for a specified period. An employee may, therefore, transfer employment from one subsidiary to another during the specified vesting period without the employee's rights under the arrangements being affected. If the subsidiaries have no obligation to settle the share-based payment transaction with their employees, they account for it as an equity-settled transaction. When this is the case, each subsidiary measures the services received from its employee by reference to the fair value of the equity instruments at the date when the rights were originally granted by the parent and the proportion of the vesting period served by the employee with that subsidiary. [IFRS 2:B59]

Such an employee, after transferring between group entities, may fail to satisfy a vesting condition (e.g. the employee may leave the group before completing the required period of service) other than a market condition. In this case, because the vesting condition is service to the group, each subsidiary adjusts the amount previously recognised in respect of the services received from the employee in accordance with IFRS 2:19. Consequently, if the rights to equity instruments do not vest because of a failure to meet a vesting condition (other than a market condition), no amount is recognised on a cumulative basis for the services received from that employee in the financial statements of both subsidiaries. [IFRS 2:B61]

This requirement for all affected entities to 'true up' at vesting date means that a subsidiary may need to make adjustments to its share-based payment expense several years after an employee has transferred elsewhere within the group.

8.6.2 Transfers of employees between group entities: subsidiary has obligation

If the subsidiary has an obligation to settle the transaction with its employees in its parent's equity instruments, it accounts for the transaction as cash-settled. IFRS 2 requires that each subsidiary measures the services received on the basis of grant date fair value of the equity instruments for the proportion of the vesting period the employee served with each subsidiary. In addition, each subsidiary recognises any change in the fair value of the equity instruments during the employee's service period with each subsidiary. [IFRS 2:B60]

IFRS 2:B61 deals with failure to meet vesting conditions and appears to refer back to IFRS 2:B60 because it begins with the words 'such employees'. However, the requirements of IFRS 2:19 regarding the treatment of vesting conditions may not be relevant to cash-settled arrangements (see **5.3**). In practice, any failure to meet a non-market vesting condition will be reflected in the remeasurement of the liability and accounted for in accordance with IFRS 2:B60 so there is no need to apply IFRS 2:B61.

In each case it will be necessary to consider which entity or entities in the group have the obligation to settle with the employee and recognise their liabilities accordingly. This will depend on the particular terms of the scheme. Each subsidiary will recognise an expense in relation to the period of service with that subsidiary in accordance with IFRS 2:B60. When one subsidiary assumes the cumulative liability for past service provided to other subsidiaries, the assumption of this liability at the date of transfer will be debited to equity as it is a form of distribution. The other subsidiaries should credit the release of their liability to equity as a capital contribution (i.e. the expense previously recognised for the service previously provided by the employee is not reversed merely because the liability will be settled by another party).

8.7 Effect of the use of employee share trusts

Employee share trusts may potentially be accounted for in two different ways depending on the circumstances. When the assets and liabilities of the trust are recognised as those of the sponsoring entity (see **5.12** in **chapter A29**), any obligations of the trust will be regarded as obligations of the sponsoring entity.

The analysis will be different when the trust is regarded as a subsidiary (see **section 9**). In such circumstances, the rights and obligations of the trust will be reflected in its own individual financial statements, rather than those of the sponsoring entity.

It will be necessary to apply the requirements of IFRS 2:B46 to B61 and the other guidance in this section to the particular facts of each case. In particular, the guidance at **8.3.4** will be relevant to determining which entity has granted the rights and, therefore, has the obligation to employees.

The analysis might be further complicated when in practice three entities are involved in the arrangement. The third entity might be a fellow subsidiary or intermediate parent which grants the options and delivers the shares to the employees (either directly or via an employee share trust).

8.8 Subsidiary purchases parent's shares

8.8.1 Subsidiary purchases parent's shares to settle cash-settled obligation to employees

To settle its obligation to employees, the subsidiary will often need to acquire its parent's shares either in the market or directly from the parent.

Example 8.8.1

Subsidiary purchases parent's shares to settle cash-settled obligation to employees

A subsidiary has an obligation under a share-based payment arrangement to deliver its parent's shares to its employees. To settle its obligation to its employees, the subsidiary will need to acquire its parent's shares either in the market or directly from the parent.

In accordance with IFRS 2:43B, the subsidiary accounts for this as a cash-settled share-based payment arrangement.

The accounting by the subsidiary depends upon (1) whether it purchases the shares at the vesting date or at an earlier date, and (2) if it purchases the shares before the vesting date, whether the subsidiary applies IFRS 9 or IAS 39 in accounting for its financial instruments.

Subsidiary purchases shares at the vesting date

When the subsidiary purchases the required shares in the market at the vesting date, the price paid for the shares (less any exercise price paid by the employees) is usually the same as the liability already recognised, so that no gain or loss arises on settlement. The subsidiary is not required to recognise any movements in equity arising from the arrangements because it has not

---

issued any equity instruments and it has not received any capital contribution from its parent.

When the parent issues the required shares to the subsidiary at the vesting date at market price, from the subsidiary's perspective this is no different from purchasing shares in the market, and the treatment described in the previous paragraph is appropriate. The parent should recognise an issue of shares for full consideration in the usual manner.

When the parent issues the required shares to the subsidiary at the vesting date for no consideration, or for consideration lower than market price, the difference between the consideration paid and market value represents a capital contribution from the parent to the subsidiary and does not result in any change to the expense recognised under IFRS 2.

Subsidiary purchases shares prior to the vesting date and applies IFRS 9

If a subsidiary purchases and holds shares in its parent, they are recognised and measured as financial assets in the individual financial statements of the subsidiary even though they are treated as treasury shares in the consolidated financial statements of the parent. Under IFRS 9, the shares will either be classified as at fair value through profit or loss (FVTPL) (which is the default category) or designated as at fair value through other comprehensive income (FVTOCI).

Under either classification, the carrying amount of the shares at the vesting date (less any exercise price paid by the employees) is usually the same as the liability already recognised, so that no gain or loss will arise on settlement (when assets are designated as at FVTOCI under IFRS 9, the cumulative gains or losses accumulated in other comprehensive income are not reclassified to profit or loss on disposal).

Subsidiary purchases shares prior to the vesting date and applies IAS 39

Under IAS 39 (for entities that have not yet adopted IFRS 9), in the subsidiary's financial statements, the shares are either classified as available for sale (AFS) (which is the default category) or designated as at FVTPL if the relevant requirements of IAS 39 are met.

Under IAS 39, one of the circumstances in which an asset may be designated as at FVTPL is when the designation results in more relevant information because it eliminates or significantly reduces a measurement or recognition inconsistency (sometimes referred to as 'an accounting mismatch') that would otherwise arise from measuring the assets or liabilities, or recognising the gains and losses on them, on different bases. The determination as to whether designation as at FVTPL eliminates or significantly reduces an accounting mismatch should be based on a careful analysis of the specific facts and circumstances in each case.

When shares are classified as at FVTPL, the carrying amount of the shares at the vesting date (less any exercise price paid by the employees) is usually the same as the liability already recognised, so that no gain or loss arises on settlement.

When the shares are classified as AFS, although the carrying amount of the shares at the vesting date (less any exercise price paid by the employees) is usually the same as the liability already recognised, a gain or loss may arise on settlement because the cumulative gains or losses previously recognised in other comprehensive income are reclassified to profit or loss on disposal (i.e. when the shares are delivered to employees). The shares cannot be designated as a hedging instrument in a hedge of the share-based payment obligation.

8.8.2 Hedge accounting

Although 'economic hedges' can be achieved for some share-based arrangements, as described at **8.8.1**, IFRS 9 (or, for entities that have not yet adopted IFRS 9, IAS 39) sets out detailed rules on hedge accounting, including which items can be hedged and which instruments can qualify as hedging instruments.

Under IFRS 9 (or IAS 39), it is not possible to apply hedge accounting to an equity-settled share-based payment arrangement because that Standard prohibits own equity as a hedged item.

Although a liability recognised under a cash-settled share-based payment arrangement can qualify as a hedged item, it is important to note that under IAS 39 the subsidiary cannot designate shares in its parent (whether held directly or via an employee share trust) as a hedging instrument. IFRS 9 permits a non-derivative financial asset measured at FVTPL, which would include a holding of an equity instrument, to be designated as a hedging instrument. Instead of purchasing the shares of the parent before the vesting date, a subsidiary might consider purchasing options over its parent's shares and designating them as a hedging instrument in hedging the forecast employee expense. However, it will still need to meet the detailed requirements of IFRS 9 (or IAS 39) in order to achieve hedge accounting.

9 Employee share trusts

9.1 Background

Employee share trusts (sometimes established in conjunction with employee share ownership plans (ESOPs) or employee share plans), created by a sponsoring entity for employees, are designed to facilitate employee shareholding and are often used as vehicles for distributing shares to employees under remuneration schemes. The detailed structures of individual trusts are many and varied, as are the reasons for establishing them.

Reasons for establishing employee share trusts include the following (although it should be noted that some of these are not permitted in all jurisdictions):

- to fund a matching programme for a sponsor's defined contribution plan or other employee benefits;

- to raise new capital or to create a marketplace for existing shares;

- to replace lost benefits from the termination of other employee benefit plans or to provide benefits under post-retirement plans (particularly medical benefits);

- to be part of the financing package in leveraged buy-outs;

- to provide tax-advantaged means for owners to terminate ownership;

- to be part of a long-term programme to restructure the equity section of a sponsor's statement of financial position; and

- to defend the entity against a hostile takeover.

Employee share trusts can be leveraged or non-leveraged. In a leveraged employee share trust, the plan borrows money to purchase shares, usually guaranteed by the sponsor.

The detailed structure of an employee share trust often includes the following:

- the trust holds shares in the sponsoring entity (or another group entity) to be sold or transferred to employees under the terms of a share-based payment plan;

- the trust acquires shares either directly from the sponsoring entity or by purchasing them in the market. These acquisitions may be financed by a cash contribution or loan from the sponsoring entity or by a third-party loan (often guaranteed by the sponsoring entity); and

- the activities of the trust are narrowly defined, typically in a trust deed.

9.2   Determining whether an entity controls an employee share trust

9.2.1   Determining whether an entity controls an employee share trust – general

IFRS 10 *Consolidated Financial Statements* includes no scope exemption for employee share trusts. Accordingly, an entity applying IFRS 10 will need to consider whether it controls an employee share trust; if so, a number of accounting implications follow (see **9.3**).

In accordance with the general definition of control in IFRS 10 (see **section 5** of **chapter A24**), an employee share trust should be consolidated if the sponsoring entity has:

- power over the relevant activities of the trust (see **9.2.2**);

- exposure, or rights, to variable returns from its involvement with the trust (see **9.2.3**); and

- the ability to use its power over the trust to affect the amount of its returns (see **9.2.4**).

9.2.2 *Power over the relevant activities of the trust*

The relevant activities of an employee share trust will typically be the acquisition and disposal of shares (either to employees under the terms of a remuneration scheme or, in the case of excess shares held, returned to the sponsoring entity or sold in the market) and the financing of these activities.

A trust's activities will typically be defined by a deed and managed by appointed trustees, meaning that it will generally not be controlled by means of voting rights. The sponsoring entity may retain power over these activities in a number of ways, for example:

- by including in the deed governing the activities of the trust or in another contractual arrangement (e.g. a loan agreement or loan guarantee) a requirement that the sponsoring entity's shares be acquired and disposed of at the direction of the sponsoring entity;

- by appointing as trustees employees of the sponsoring entity who will make decisions as *de facto* agents of the sponsoring entity (see **8.3** in **chapter A24**); or

- by limiting the scope of activities permitted by the trust deed to acquiring and distributing shares in accordance with remuneration schemes determined by the sponsoring entity.

9.2.3 *Exposure, or rights, to variable returns from involvement with the trust*

As discussed in IFRS 10:B56 (see **7.1** in **chapter A24**), 'variable returns' are broadly defined. In the context of an employee share trust, it should be noted that generally the trust's purpose and design is to hold assets that will be used to settle the sponsoring entity's obligations under a remuneration scheme. Should the trust fail to do so (e.g. if there are not sufficient shares in the trust to settle the obligation), the sponsoring entity is likely to remain liable to its employees under the terms of the remuneration scheme (i.e. the sponsoring entity has, in effect, guaranteed that the trust will be in a position to provide sufficient assets to employees).

Variable returns from the trust may also include:

- default risk on a loan due from the trust;

- payments due as a result of the sponsoring entity's guarantee of the trust's loan from a third party;

- the return of surplus assets to the sponsoring entity if the shares do not vest or any profit made by the trust is required to be paid to the sponsoring entity;

- the sponsoring entity guarantees a minimum value of the shares; and

- the assets of the trust can be recaptured by the sponsoring entity or its creditors (e.g. in a bankruptcy situation).

9.2.4 Ability to use power over the trust to affect the amount of returns

The entity will need to consider whether its power over the trust can be used to influence its variable returns. For example, default risk on a loan from the trust could be affected by a decision regarding whether to use shares held by the trust to satisfy employee share plans or to sell them and use the proceeds to repay the loan. Alternatively, an entity's ability to determine when shares are transferred to the trust could expose it to variability in its requirement to transfer additional shares sufficient to fulfil its obligations under remuneration schemes.

In addition, it should be noted that the trust's primary purpose (settlement of the sponsoring entity's obligations under remuneration schemes) suggests that the sponsoring entity will act on its own account (i.e. as principal) in making decisions related to the trust. IFRS 10:B58 makes clear that a decision maker is not acting as an agent simply because other parties (in this case, the employees) can benefit from the decisions that it makes.

9.3 Accounting implications when a sponsoring entity controls an employee share trust

When a sponsoring entity has control over an employee share trust, the assets and liabilities of the trust (including the shares it holds in the sponsoring entity) should be recognised in the consolidated financial statements. Shares in the sponsoring entity held by a consolidated employee share trust should, in accordance with paragraph 33 of IAS 32, be treated as treasury shares. Accordingly:

- consideration paid or received for the trust's purchase or sale of the sponsoring entity's own shares should be shown as separate amounts in the statement of changes in equity;

- no gain or loss should be recognised in profit or loss on the purchase, sale, issue or cancellation of the sponsoring entity's own shares;

- any dividend income on the sponsoring entity's own shares should be excluded in determining profit before tax and deducted from the aggregate of dividends paid and proposed; and

- the sponsoring entity's own shares held should be excluded from the denominator for the purpose of calculating both basic and diluted earnings per share.

In addition, finance costs and any administration expenses of the trust should be recognised as they accrue and not as funding payments are made to the trust.

Sufficient information should be disclosed in the financial statements of the sponsoring entity to enable readers to understand the significance of the trust in the context of the sponsoring entity. Specifically, an employee share trust will typically be considered a structured entity for the purposes of applying the disclosure requirements of IFRS 12 *Disclosure of Interests in Other Entities* (see **chapter A28**) and any shares held by a consolidated trust will be disclosed in accordance with paragraph 79 of IAS 1 *Presentation of Financial Statements* (see **4.5.2.4** in **chapter A4**).

9.4 Identification of sponsoring entity

As explained at **5.12** in **chapter A29**, in some cases it will be appropriate to account for the assets and liabilities of an employee share trust in the separate financial statement of the sponsoring entity. However, it is not always straightforward to determine which entity within a group is the sponsoring entity.

If an employee share trust is set up to hold shares that will be used to settle share awards granted by a particular entity, it is likely that the entity that has the obligation to the employees will be the sponsoring entity of the trust because that is the entity that needs to acquire the shares to meet its obligations. **Section 8.3.4** provides guidance on the factors to consider in determining which entity has this obligation.

When a parent makes a share award to the employees of its subsidiary, the parent has the obligation to settle the share award. When this is the case, it is unlikely to be appropriate to treat the subsidiary as the sponsoring employer of a trust set up to hold shares to settle the share awards because, as discussed at **5.12** in **chapter A29**, this would result in recognition of the shares as an asset on the statement of financial position but there would be no corresponding obligation to settle the share awards. However, each situation will require judgement based on the particular facts.

9.5   Presentation of movements in equity relating to an employee share trust

This section considers the accounting entries that may be required within equity in the consolidated financial statements when an entity's own shares are held by an employee share trust that is consolidated by the entity. From the perspective of the consolidated financial statements (and entity-only financial statements when a 'look-through' approach is applied (see **5.12** in **chapter A29**)), such shares are 'treasury shares' and are deducted from equity in accordance with IAS 32:33. IAS 32:34 states that the amount of treasury shares held should be disclosed separately either in the statement of financial position or in the notes. This can be done either by presenting treasury shares as a separate component of equity or by including the deduction from equity within another component of equity, for example within retained earnings (disclosed by way of note). It may be clearer to present a separate component of equity when the amount is material.

Example 9.5

Presentation of movements in equity relating to employee share trusts

For the purposes of the following illustration, it is assumed that a separate employee share (or ESOP) reserve is maintained.

When shares are purchased in the market by an employee share trust, they will initially be recognised as a debit to the employee share trust reserve for the price paid. For example, suppose that the price paid is CU1,000.

		CU	CU
Dr	Employee share reserve	1,000	
Cr	Cash		1,000

To recognise the acquisition of shares for cash.

Exercise price is lower than price paid by the employee share trust

If options are subsequently granted over those shares with an exercise price of CU800, the following entry will generally be required when the share options are exercised.

		CU	CU
Dr	Cash	800	
Dr	Equity	200	
Cr	Employee share reserve		1,000

To remove balance from the employee share reserve when options are exercised.

This is because it is illogical to leave a balance on the employee share reserve which relates to shares that are no longer held. The difference between the price paid by the employee share trust to purchase the shares initially and the amount received when the shares are reissued upon exercise of the options must be recognised in equity and retained earnings may be an appropriate caption.

Exercise price is higher than price paid by the employee share trust

If options are subsequently granted over those shares with an exercise price of CU1,300, the following entry will generally be required when the share options are exercised.

		CU	CU
Dr	Cash	1,300	
Cr	Employee share reserve		1,000
Cr	Equity		300

To remove balance from the employee share trust reserve when options are exercised.

Any excess of the amount received upon exercise of the options over the price paid by the employee share trust to purchase the shares initially is accounted for directly in equity, for example in retained earnings or another part of equity specified by local law and regulations.

Note that this example does not deal with the accounting entries in equity that may be required by IFRS 2. These are discussed at **5.1.5**. They will generally involve a credit to equity equal to the expense recognised. Whether this credit is recognised in retained earnings or as a separate reserve will depend on the entity's accounting policy.

When recognising the IFRS 2 expense, it may be tempting to recognise the credit entry in the employee share reserve when one exists and the options are to be satisfied by using the shares held by the trust. However, in practice, this does not generally make sense. The credit entry is based on the fair value at grant date and is unlikely to coincide with the difference between the purchase price of the shares by the trust and the option exercise price (if any). Therefore, recognising the credit entry in the employee share reserve would likely result in an employee share reserve balance that is not meaningful because it represents neither the cost of treasury shares held by the trust nor the value of the IFRS 2 expense. In an employee share arrangement, it is, therefore, generally preferable for the credit entry arising from IFRS 2 and the effects of any purchase of own shares through the employee share trust to be considered separately.

9.6   Accounting for share awards settled via an employee share trust

Example 9.6

Accounting for share awards settled via an employee share trust

A trust is created by a sponsoring entity, Company P, which is a listed entity. The trust is designed to facilitate shareholding by employees and is used to distribute shares in Company P to its employees under its share-based payment arrangements.

The trust may be funded in a number of ways and may also obtain shares in Company P in a number of ways. For example, the trust may receive a loan from Company P with which it may either subscribe for new shares in Company P or purchase shares in Company P in the market. Alternatively, the trust may finance subscription for, or purchase of, shares in Company P by raising a third-party loan guaranteed by Company P.

The trust purchases 100 shares in Company P for CU10,000. At the same time, Company P grants 100 shares to 10 of its employees under a share-based payment arrangement; the principal terms of the arrangement are that each employee will be granted 10 shares conditional on completing three years of service. At the end of the three-year vesting period, the employees can elect to either receive the shares or to receive cash equal to the fair value of the shares at that time. When an employee exercises the option to receive cash, the trust may either sell the shares in Company P or it may obtain funding in order to settle Company P's share-based payment arrangement with the employees on Company P's behalf.

How should Company P and the trust account for this arrangement in their separate financial statements?

(This example does not consider the accounting for the transaction to finance the purchase of the shares.)

Company P

In Company P's separate financial statements, the substance is a share-based payment arrangement for employees with a cash alternative (i.e. the entity has granted a compound financial instrument).

IFRS 2 will be applied in the usual way to determine the expense to be recognised in Company P's profit or loss; the fact that a trust has been established to facilitate settlement of Company P's commitment does not alter the accounting under IFRS 2.

The fair value of the liability component of the compound instrument should be determined first, and then the equity component should be measured at fair value, taking into account the fact that the employee must forfeit the right to receive cash in order to receive the equity instrument (see IFRS 2:37). In this scenario, the value of the equity component would be nil and, as a consequence, the transaction would be accounted for in the same way as a cash-settled share-based payment up to the date of exercise (see also **example 7.2.1**).

Depending on the nature of the trust, it may be appropriate for Company P to account for its investment in the trust as a subsidiary or to adopt a 'look-through' approach (i.e. accounting for the trust as, in substance, an extension of itself). For further guidance, see the discussion at **5.12** in **chapter A29**.

Trust

The shares in Company P are recognised as an asset (as noted above, financing of this acquisition is ignored in this example).

The trust does not recognise a liability in respect of the share-based payment arrangement because it is not the employing entity and does not receive the benefit of the employee services and it does not have the obligation to the employees (i.e. the trust settles the award on Company P's behalf).

10   Disclosure

10.1   Disclosure requirements – general

Paragraphs 44 to 52 of IFRS 2 set out detailed disclosure requirements for share-based payments. The main requirements are summarised below. Additional information should be disclosed if the detailed information required to be disclosed by the IFRS does not satisfy the principles in IFRS 2:44, 46 and 50 (see **10.2**, **10.3** and **10.4**). [IFRS 2:52]

When separate financial statements are presented for a parent, these disclosures will be required for both the parent's separate financial statements and for the consolidated financial statements of the group. Some of the disclosures (e.g. regarding the nature of the schemes and the option pricing models used) will be common to both and need not be repeated. However, some details (e.g. regarding the numerical details of the number of options outstanding) will have to be disclosed separately for the parent as well as for the group.

Paragraph 8 of IAS 8 *Accounting Policies, Changes in Accounting Estimates and Errors* states that accounting policies set out in IFRSs do not need to be applied when the effect is not material. IAS 1:31 states that an entity need not provide a specific disclosure required by an IFRS if the information is not material. Both quantitative and qualitative factors should be assessed to determine materiality of share-based payment transactions. This applies not only to recognition and measurement but also to disclosures in the financial statements.

In addition to the IFRS 2 disclosure requirements, however, there may be local legal or regulatory requirements (e.g. in company law or listing rules). Such local requirements may apply irrespective of materiality, or different materiality considerations may be relevant (e.g. whether the arrangements are material to an individual director).

When no IFRS 2 disclosures are provided on the basis of materiality, but the existence of share-based payment arrangements is disclosed in other parts of the annual report, the potential implications should be considered. Users of the financial statements may interpret the inconsistency as an error. To avoid such a misunderstanding, it may be useful to include an explanation that the IFRS 2 disclosures have been omitted because the amounts involved are not material.

10.2   Nature and extent of share-based payments

An entity should disclose information that enables users of the financial statements to understand the nature and extent of share-based payment arrangements that existed during the period. [IFRS 2:44] To give effect to this principle, IFRS 2 specifies that at least the following should be disclosed:

[IFRS 2:45]

- a description of each type of share-based payment arrangement that existed at any time during the period, including the general terms and conditions of each arrangement such as:
  - the vesting requirements;
  - the maximum term of options granted; and
  - the method of settlement (e.g. whether in cash or equity).

  An entity with substantially similar types of share-based payment arrangements may aggregate this information, unless separate disclosure of each arrangement is necessary to satisfy the principle in IFRS 2:44;

- the number and weighted average exercise prices of share options for each of the following groups of options:
  - outstanding at the beginning of the period;
  - granted during the period;
  - forfeited during the period;

- exercised during the period;

- expired during the period;

- outstanding at the end of the period; and

- exercisable at the end of the period;

- for share options exercised during the period, the weighted average share price at the date of exercise. If options were exercised on a regular basis throughout the period, the weighted average share price during the period may instead be disclosed; and

- for share options outstanding at the end of the period, the range of exercise prices and weighted average contractual life. If the range of exercise prices is wide, the outstanding options should be divided into ranges that are meaningful for assessing the number and timing of additional shares that may be issued and the cash that may be received upon exercise of those options.

As explained at **8.6.1**, a parent may grant rights to its equity instruments to the employees of its subsidiaries which are conditional upon the completion of continuing service with the group, rather than a specified subsidiary, for a specified period. In accordance with IFRS 2:B59 and B61, each subsidiary will recognise an expense for the period of service of the employee with that subsidiary and may also need to 'true up' for the outcome of any non-market vesting conditions. The question arises as to whether the disclosure requirements described above apply only in relation to the current employees of a subsidiary or extend to former employees who are now employed elsewhere in the group.

When deciding on the appropriate disclosures, regard should be had to the principle in IFRS 2:44 that the information should enable users of the financial statements to understand the nature and extent of share-based payment arrangements that existed during the period. Therefore, disclosures should, at a minimum, deal with options held by employees of the entity during the financial year. The table of options required by IFRS 2:45(b) should include a line or column to adjust for the numbers for employees transferring in or out of the entity. On this basis, the number of options outstanding at the end of the period will include only current employees; employees who have transferred to another subsidiary will be included in that subsidiary's disclosures.

A subsidiary may remain exposed to adjustments to the expense recognised for former employees when there are non-market vesting conditions. This may require disclosure, in some cases, if the effect is, or is expected to be, material.

10.3   How fair value is determined

An entity should disclose information that enables users of the financial statements to understand how the fair value of the goods or services received, or the fair value of the equity instruments granted, during the period was determined. [IFRS 2:46]

To give effect to this principle, IFRS 2 specifies that at least the following should be disclosed if the entity has measured the fair value of goods and services received indirectly, by reference to the fair value of the equity instruments granted:

[IFRS 2:47]

- for share options granted during the period, the weighted average fair value of those options at the measurement date and information on how the fair value was measured, including:

  - the option pricing model used and the inputs to that model, including the weighted average share price, exercise price, expected volatility, option life, expected dividends, the risk-free interest rate and any other inputs to the model, including the method used and the assumptions made to incorporate the effects of expected early exercise;

  - how expected volatility was determined, including an explanation of the extent to which it was based on historical volatility; and

  - whether and how any other features of the option grant were incorporated into the measurement of fair value, such as a market condition;

- for other equity instruments granted during the period (i.e. other than share options) the number and weighted average fair value of those equity instruments at the measurement date, and information on how that fair value was determined, including:

  - if the fair value was not measured on the basis of observable market price, how it was determined;

  - whether and how expected dividends were incorporated into the measurement of fair value; and

  - whether and how any other features of the equity instruments granted were incorporated into the measurement of fair value; and

- for share-based payment arrangements that were modified during the period:

  - an explanation of those modifications;

  - the incremental fair value granted as a result of those modifications; and

  - information on how the incremental fair value was measured.

If the entity has measured directly the fair value of goods or services received during the period, disclosure is required of how that fair value was determined (e.g. whether fair value was measured at a market price for those goods or services). [IFRS 2:48]

The presumption in IFRS 2:13 is that, in the case of transactions with parties other than employees, the fair value of the goods or services received can be estimated reliably (see **5.2.2**). If that presumption has been rebutted, that fact should be disclosed together with an explanation of why the presumption was rebutted. [IFRS 2:49]

10.4 Effect of share-based payment transactions on profit or loss and financial position

An entity should disclose information that enables users of the financial statements to understand the effect of share-based payment transactions on its profit or loss for the period and on its financial position. [IFRS 2:50] To give effect to this principle, IFRS 2 specifies that at least the following should be disclosed:

[IFRS 2:51]

- the total expense recognised for the period arising from share-based payment transactions in which the goods or services received did not qualify for recognition as assets and hence were recognised immediately as an expense, including separate disclosure of that portion of the total expense that arises from transactions accounted for as equity-settled share-based payment transactions; and

- for liabilities arising from share-based payment transactions:

  - the total carrying amount at the end of the period; and

  - the total intrinsic value at the end of the period of liabilities for which the counterparty's right to cash or other assets had vested by the end of the period (e.g. vested share appreciation rights).

10.5 Illustrative disclosures

Illustrative disclosures for share-based payment transactions are included in the implementation guidance accompanying IFRS 2 (IFRS 2:IG23) and in Deloitte's IFRS model financial statements, available on *www.iasplus. com/en*.

11 Future developments

In November 2014, the IASB published ED/2014/5 *Classification and Measurement of Share-based Payment Transactions* which proposes a number of amendments to IFRS 2. The proposed amendments would, if issued, clarify the Standard in three areas.

- The accounting for the effect of vesting and non-vesting conditions for cash-settled share-based payments should follow the same approach as already required in IFRS 2 for equity-settled share-based payments.

- When a share-based payment transaction with employees is settled net, it should be classified as equity-settled in its entirety, provided that the share-based payment would have been classified as equity-settled had it not included the net settlement feature.

- When a share-based payment transaction is modified, such that a cash-settled arrangement becomes equity-settled, the original liability recognised in respect of the cash-settled share-based payment is derecognised and the equity-settled share-based payment is recognised at the modification date fair value to the extent services have been rendered up to the modification date. Any difference between the carrying amount of the liability as at the modification date and the amount recognised in equity at the same date would be recognised in profit or loss immediately.

The comment period closed on 25 March 2015. At the time of writing, the IASB is analysing responses to the exposure draft with a view to determining the next step in the project.